Tudor England

An Encyclopedia

Advisory Editors

Tudor England
An Encyclopedia

Arthur F. Kinney and David W. Swain
General Editors

Eugene D. Hill and William B. Long
Co-Editors

Editorial Assistants
Francisco J. Borge and R. Morgan Griffin

Garland Publishing, Inc.
New York and London   2001

Published in 2001 by
Garland Publishing, Inc.
29 West 35th Street
New York, NY 10001

Garland is an imprint of the Taylor & Francis Group

Production Editor:	Andrea Johnson
Copyeditor:	Carl Buehler
Photo Researchers:	David Evett
	Martin Levick
Composition/Project Management:	A Good Thing, Inc.
Production Director:	Laura-Ann Robb
Development Manager:	Richard Steins
Publishing Director, Reference:	Sylvia K. Miller

10 9 8 7 6 5 4 3 2 1

Library of Congress Cataloging-in-Publication Data is available from the Library of Congress.

Tudor England : an encyclopedia / editors, Arthur F. Kinney, David W. Swain
    Includes bibliographical references and index.
    ISBN 0-8153-0793-4 (alk. paper)

Printed on acid-free, 150-year-life paper
Manufactured in the United States of America

For our parents:

Arthur Frederick and Gladys Mudge Kinney

in memoriam

and

Arlene Denise and Robert Alfred Swain

Contents

Preface

The explosive growth of archival and interpretive study concerning early modern England catches the excitement and bewilderment of discovery and change during the Tudors' century of English rule. England at the accession of Henry VII in 1485 was struggling to put into place a stable monarchy following the bloody Wars of the Roses. The nation that began to emerge from a century of plague and war was agrarian, rural, and largely uneducated. Although England remained a country of towns, London began to thrive as the center of commerce and power. The features of medieval scholastic learning were slowly being challenged by Continental humanism, driven by the revival of classical texts and their rapid dissemination through printing. Like all of Europe, England was Catholic, with a Latin Bible accessible only to priests and scholars. Music and art were primarily liturgical, and literary works were heavily religious. Except for a body of church plays that helped to popularize religious beliefs, other forms of literature were undergoing revival and new forms were emerging.

Naming just a few of those who defined their age suggests the profound changes of the sixteenth century: Machiavelli, More, Erasmus, Holbein, Luther, Calvin, Copernicus, Vesalius, Galileo, Montaigne, Marlowe, Spenser, Shakespeare—not to mention the troubled life of Henry VIII and his wives, or of the boy-king Edward VI, or "bloody" Mary Tudor, or of Elizabeth I and her mythic "golden years." England under the Tudors moved from a monarchy threatened by pretenders through the strong (even tyrannical) rule of Henry VIII to a time when her advisors implored Elizabeth I to marry to protect the Tudor succession. And this was also an age of courtiers and churchmen, poets and soldiers, explorers and pirates, vagabonds and players, religious exiles and martyrs, anonymous women and powerful widows; the vitality of their lives forms a rich backdrop for this century of rulers, thinkers, and writers.

During this great century of changes the Protestant Reformation (and the subsequent Catholic Counter Reformation) tried the souls of men and women and led to popular uprisings and religious wars, with Henry VIII's separation from Rome during the 1530s changing the direction of the English church. Monasteries and nunneries were dissolved and their lands possessed by the crown. Village priests who had intoned Latin behind an exclusive altar now ministered to their parishes in the vernacular; the Bible, now in English, entered many homes, often along with John Foxe's "Book of Martyrs." Protestants fled persecution under Mary's Catholic revival, and many returned with Elizabeth's accession to call for a more radical, "puritan" reformation.

The rapid growth of grammar schools and universities swiftly spread literacy, and literary culture blossomed during the 1590s in the rich climate of patronage and popular demand for print. Humanist learning mingled rhetorical sophistication with the revival of classical and Italian forms. An active and profitable stage fostered the enduring achievements of Elizabethan playwrights, while an energetic culture of "cheap print" gave rise to pamphlet wars and a popular literature of great variety. Historians, diarists, and critics recorded everything from histories of the world to outbreaks of plague and riot, to play performances, to unnatural births and strange occurrences in nature. On a more sophisticated level, courtiers circulated poetry in manuscript, vying for preferment. Pirate printers quickly capitalized on commercial successes in all genres.

Population recovered, aided by innovations in agriculture, and life expectancy slowly increased. The enclosures throughout the Midlands and elsewhere altered the very face of the countryside and the structure of local life, as tenant farming gave way to the pasturage of sheep, driven by an expanding market for cloth. Professions beckoned children of poor farmers and tradespeople to apprenticeships in England's commercial cities, and the new "middling" classes went up to the universities on the stipends of new patrons of education. Many never returned home. Instead, they joined the men-about-town at the Inns of Court in London, seeking patronage or position; they jostled in the streets among the homeless and vagabonds who could no longer rely on church poor relief; or they competed with foreign professionals over monopolies weakened by the new economic displacements of centralized trade. Overseas, merchants and explorers competed for resources and territory; an insular England built, by century's end, Europe's largest navy, and through trade and exploration of Russia, Africa, and the New World mapped trade routes and new lands onto the globe.

Such change is now difficult to imagine and perhaps more difficult to understand, yet we can recover much of the Tudor world from its records. The purpose of this book is not merely to imagine such change but to record it by drawing on new work in every field. A renewed interest in archival research has resulted in the fundamental change of some perceptions of the Tudor age and added detail and justification for other interpretations. Every field of Tudor study—history, religion, art, music, politics, science, society, literature—has been affected, so that poetry or sermons can now seem just as politically engaged as speeches in Parliament (or in the theater), dramatizing and persuading through humanist rhetoric. Archeologists have recently contributed materially to theater history through excavations of Elizabethan playhouses. Fields of study such as economic and natural history are now in exciting dialogue with the traditional studies of history and literature. The early Tudor period is now receiving renewed attention, and political and social historians are reexamining the roles played by religious change and a powerful nobility.

Although no single volume can attempt to capture entirely the current state of scholarship in Tudor studies, we have sought the advice of specialists in each major field of research, and, in turn, they have called on some of our best and most active scholars to record as succinctly as possible many of the facts as we now know them. This encyclopedia aims to be a thorough survey that will serve specialists and teachers as a quick reference in which to find information or check details, and also serve as a point of departure for students who want general overviews and further direction from selective bibliographies. For general readers this volume will illuminate the complexities that underlie "the Age of Shakespeare."

Arthur F. Kinney and David W. Swain

Using This Book

Matters of selecting, defining, and proportioning entries are always difficult, and we have attempted to do so by thinking of the possible needs of our readers and the intended uses of this book. To be of use to both students and specialists in a wide range of fields, this volume first attempts to provide essential information about the people who defined the Tudor age: the circumstances of their birth and education (if known), the primary importance of their work or careers, their social or intellectual connections and influences, and the ideas, events, or works for which they are principally remembered. Second, events that shaped political, religious, social, or economic life are narrated in detail and placed in their historical context. Finally, terms, philosophies, and genres are given definitions and related to exemplary thinkers or writers and their works. Throughout this volume we have attempted to demonstrate how ill-suited the Tudor age is to the academic partitions we impose on it, and how easily important figures defy categorization. We find a playwright who is also a spy, a king who is also a composer; a mathematician who also explored the New World, a travel writer who never traveled, and a devout queen whose zeal made her a byword for martyrdom.

To draw readers from general information to specific detail, we have commissioned long survey articles for all major fields and topics such as music, Ireland, language, drama, historiography, the English Reformation, and medicine. Each of these entries (and all others) will point readers to specific entries on individual writers, events, ideas, or artistic forms using "see also" references. We have chosen to treat generally some large subjects in such entries as **Foreign Relations and Diplomacy** because they resist easy subdivision, while others such as literary influences on English writers justify individual treatments such as **French Literature, Influence of.** The former choice has the advantage of a unified view by a major scholar; the latter allows specialists to separate the strands of England's literary fabric. In general, we have designated entries by familiar or self-explanatory terms such as **Government, Central** or **Government, Local,** but in ambiguous cases such as the many ecclesiastical and judicial courts, we have listed them by separate names such as **Star Chamber, Court of.** Biographical entries present special problems. Following modern usage, we alphabetize by surname, not by title. However, Tudor history is replete with sequentially titled members of important families, often identically named, so we have treated them in family entries for the Hamiltons, Stanleys, Talbots, and others. Where a title is frequently used, as in the cases of **Burghley** or **Essex,** we have cross-referenced their titles to entries on **William Cecil** and **Robert Devereux.** Cross-references are also provided for names and terms for which we could not justify separate entries but to which many entries refer. For example, **Montaigne** is cross-referenced to his translator, **John Florio,** his genre, the **Essay,** and the philosophy associated with him, **Pyrrhonism. Warfare** will draw readers to **Military History, Ordnance,** and important battles such as the **Armada.** Finally, without standardized spellings such popular names as **John Davies** and **John Davis** make it easy to confuse several figures, but we hope the curious reader will investigate them all, for even in such things as names the Tudor age can delight and surprise. Our hope is that this volume will spark the curiosity of the generalist and renew the related interests of the specialist. It has certainly done so for us.

Dates, Quotations, and Bibliographies

Establishing firm dates during the Early Modern period is difficult; we have used the most widely accepted dates for births, deaths, and events, although in some cases recent research has corrected dates found in the *Dictionary of National Biography* (now under revision) and other standard references. Where possible, entry authors have noted the basis for new conjectures. Approximate or conjectural dates are all indicated by "c." Because the Gregorian calendar was not adopted in Tudor England and in other Protestant states, we have retained Old Style/New Style dating where records are ambiguous or specific dates are unknown. For example, Pope Gregory XIII introduced the reformed calendar on February 24, 1582, but in Tudor England this date would still be 1581; 1581/1582 would indicate that the date fell between the Gregorian New Year of January 1 and March 25, the New Year observed in England.

We have followed the wishes of entry authors in either modernizing or retaining old spelling. Where a modern edition does not exist, we have generally not modernized quotations or titles. Because spelling was fluid, there were often variations in titles between different printings (*Myrrour, Mirour, Mirror,* for example), and we have not attempted to standardize them. Rather, they represent the vitality of evolving Tudor English and the realities of the printing trade.

Finally, every entry author has provided a basic bibliography of primary and secondary sources. These are by no means exhaustive, and although every attempt has been made to represent the most recent work, readers are encouraged to research work done after 1997 and to consult the topical bibliographical essays at the end of the volume. We have chosen not to list, except in rare instances, entries in the now-dated *Dictionary of National Biography,* but we are pleased to include here work by some of the researchers on the new *DNB*.

Acknowledgments

Our debts are many. This project would have been impossible without the passion for the Tudor period and dedication to their work of more than 250 contributing scholars. For their capacity to distill their scholarship with care and clarity, often under tight deadlines, we are amazed and grateful. Our advisory editors have guided us through the difficulties and pitfalls of editing work outside our specialties, and their contribution to the focus and coverage of this volume is on every page. Particular thanks go to those advisory editors who contributed bibliographical essays to our Appendix. And for their remarkable contributions we want to thank especially Ian Archer for his unstinting generosity; Gerald Bray, whose tireless work fills many of these pages; and Susan Cerasano, John Currin, Brian Dietz, Moti Feingold, Donald Woodward, and Laura Youens for their assiduous labors. Few issues were more debated than that of illustration, and for their work in overseeing and securing these illustrations we are particularly indebted to our advisory editors Ruth Luborsky and David Evett, and for his aid as we neared production, Martin Levick.

During the daily management of this long project, David Swain benefited from the support, help, and patient ears of many friends and colleagues, among them Lynne Bodon, Walter Chmielewski, James Dutcher, Barclay Greene, Kirby Farrell, Parmita Kapadia, Robert Keefe, C. Kay Smith, Barbara Timblin, Philip White, and especially Joanna Feltham. Special thanks go to the former and present staff of the Massachusetts Center for Renaissance Studies, under whose auspices this volume was prepared. In particular, this project would not have been completed without the generous contributions of advice, expertise, and production work by R. Morgan Griffin and Francisco J. Borge. For their help in converting disks, particular gratitude goes to Rachel Kuzmeskus, Lydia Peterson, Earl Roy, and Peter Woodsum, without whom we would have foundered. For their unflagging support and guidance we wish to thank our patient editors at Garland Publishing: Gary Kuris, who commissioned the project, Marianne Lown, who saw it grow, and Joanne Daniels, Richard Steins, and Andrea Johnson, who saw it to print. And we are especially thankful to the Department of English at University of Massachusetts Amherst, which hosted this project during its formative years and nourished it with moral and financial support.

Arthur F. Kinney, David W. Swain,
Eugene D. Hill, and William B. Long

A Tudor Chronology

This chronology outlines the Tudor period by selecting important events, developments, and publications that significantly marked individual years. As the focus of this volume is broadly cultural, the editors have juxtaposed political or ecclesiastical developments with events and publications that shaped popular culture and economy. Because establishing firm dates often proves difficult, the editors have chosen to arrange events in approximate chronological sequence followed by publications that certainly or probably appeared in that year. Conjectural dating is indicated by (?). Our hope is that nonspecialist readers will be drawn by individual subjects in this chronology to specialized entries contained in this volume. As an outline, this chronology can only provide a sketch of the complex picture of England under the Tudors.

1485
Victorious at Bosworth Field, Henry Tudor is crowned as Henry VII.
William Caxton publishes Sir Thomas Malory's *Morte d'Arthur.*

1486
Yorkist risings against Henry VII are suppressed.

1487
Lambert Simnel is crowned Edward VI in Dublin by Yorkists.
Simnel's forces defeated at battle of Stoke, last of the Wars of the Roses.

1488
Duke Humphrey's Library opens at Oxford.

1489
Popular unrest in north over taxation to support French war in Brittany.

1491
Perkin Warbeck claims right to the throne.
Birth of the future Henry VIII.

1492
Henry leads army against Boulogne.
Peace of Etaples signed.

1493
Embassy to Low Countries protests favorable treatment of pretender Perkin Warbeck.

1494
Poynings' Law makes Ireland directly subject to England.

1495
Trial and execution of Sir William Stanley for complicity in Warbeck conspiracy.
Everyman performed in England for the first time.

1496
John Cabot sails to the Americas on voyage of exploration and colonization.
James IV of Scotland invades Northumberland in support of Warbeck.

1497
Capture of Perkin Warbeck.
Cabot returns after discovery of Nova Scotia and Newfoundland.

1498
Desiderius Erasmus visits Oxford.

1499

Perkin Warbeck and earl of Warwick are executed.

Wynkyn de Worde prints Sir John Mandeville's *Travels*.

1500

Henry VII confers at St. Omer with Philip the Handsome of Burgundy.

1501

Arthur, Prince of Wales, marries Katherine of Aragon.

1502

Death of Arthur, Prince of Wales.

James IV of Scotland marries Margaret Tudor.

1503

Henry, Prince of Wales, is betrothed to Katherine of Aragon.

Appointment of master of the wards.

1504

Parliament enacts legislation to prevent price fixing by merchant companies.

William Warham is appointed archbishop of Canterbury.

John Colet is named dean of St. Paul's.

1505

Lady Margaret Beaufort founds Christ's College, Cambridge.

Polydore Vergil commissioned by king to write history of the kingdom.

1506

Yorkist pretender, Edmund de la Pole, lodged in Tower.

1507

Royal printing press founded in Edinburgh.

1508

William Dunbar's poems printed at Edinburgh.

1509

Henry VII dies.

Succession of Henry VIII, who marries Katherine of Aragon.

Erasmus returns to England.

John Colet founds St. Paul's School.

Alexander Barclay translates Sebastian Brant's *Ship of Fools*.

1510

Parliament enacts sumptuary legislation.

1511

Erasmus is appointed professor of Greek and divinity at Cambridge.

Henry VIII joins the Holy League.

1512

College of Physicians is founded.

Chapel of Henry VII at Westminster completed.

1513

Henry invades France.

James IV of Scotland invades England, is defeated at Flodden Field, and killed.

Tournai surrenders to Holy League.

William Lyly publishes his Latin grammar.

1514

Louis XII of France marries Mary Tudor, the king's sister.

Anglo-French Treaty signed.

1515

Widowed Mary Tudor marries Charles Brandon, duke of Suffolk.

Thomas Wolsey is appointed cardinal and lord chancellor.

Parliament regulates work hours and wages; enacts conversion of land to arable use.

1516

Henry VIII's daughter Mary is born.

Thomas Wolsey's Hampton Court Palace completed.

Thomas More publishes *Utopia* in Latin in Louvain.

John Skelton's *Magnyficence* performed at court (?).

1517

London apprentices attack alien workers.

Commission of Inquiry into Enclosures is established.

Printing press established in Oxford.

1518

Wolsey negotiates Treaty of London; dauphin is betrothed to Princess Mary.

Thomas More becomes a privy councilor.

1519

Henry VIII intervenes as candidate in imperial election.

Charles, nephew of Katherine of Aragon, elected Emperor Charles V.

1520

Henry VIII and Francis I meet at the Field of Cloth of Gold; Henry also meets Charles V.

Cambridge Protestants meet secretly at the White Horse Inn.

1521

Edward Stafford, duke of Buckingham, executed for treason.

Luther's works are burned at St. Paul's churchyard before Wolsey.

Henry VIII publishes in Latin his *Defense of the Seven Sacraments* against Martin Luther.

Pope Leo X titles Henry "Defender of the Faith."

1522
Wolsey unsuccessfully attempts to become pope.

Wolsey prepares for war against France and Scotland.

1523
England at war with France and Scottish nobles.

Sir Thomas More is elected speaker of the House of Commons.

1524
Wolsey appointed papal legate for life.

Wynkyn de Worde prints anonymous English translation of *Gesta Romanorum*.

1525
Wolsey gives Hampton Court to the king.

William Tyndale's English New Testament is printed on the Continent.

1526
Tyndale's translation sharply attacked by More and others; 6,000 copies seized and burned.

Hans Holbein welcomed at court.

1527
Treaty of Westminster between England and France against Charles V.

Henry VIII takes first steps toward divorcing Katherine of Aragon.

Holbein paints "The Family of Thomas More."

Hector Boece writes *Scotorum Historia*.

1528
Pope Clement VII moves slowly on proposed divorce.

William Tyndale publishes *Obedience of a Christian Man*.

1529
Wolsey falls from power.

Sir Thomas More is appointed lord chancellor.

Reformation Parliament meets.

1530
Universities of Oxford and Cambridge judge in favor of Henry's divorce.

Wolsey is arrested and dies before imprisonment.

Council of the North is reformed.

1531
Henry VIII is recognized as supreme head of the church in England.

Sir Thomas Elyot brings out *The Boke Named the Governour*.

1532
The Submission of the Clergy is made to Henry VIII.

Sir Thomas More resigns as lord chancellor.

Robert Dudley, earl of Leicester, is born.

Erasmus's *The Institution of Christian Marriage* (1526) translated.

1533
Henry VIII marries Anne Boleyn in secret.

Anne Boleyn is crowned queen.

Pope Clement VII excommunicates Henry.

Princess Elizabeth is born to Anne Boleyn.

John Heywood publishes several comic dramatic interludes.

1534
Act of Succession declares Mary illegitimate and Elizabeth heir to the crown.

Sir Thomas More and John Fisher are imprisoned.

Acts of Submission, Supremacy, and First Fruits and Tenths.

John Bourchier translates Antonio de Guevara's *Golden Booke of Marcus Aurelius*.

1535
Thomas Cromwell begins visitation of religious houses and commissions *Valor Ecclesiasticus*.

More and Fisher are executed.

Thomas Starkey publishes *Dialogue between Reginald Pole and Thomas Lupset*.

1536
Dissolution of the Lesser Monasteries enacted; Court of Augmentations formed to transfer land to crown.

Anne Boleyn is executed.

Henry VIII marries Jane Seymour.

Tyndale executed.

Uprising against religious innovation (the Pilgrimage of Grace) in north.

Cromwell gives Council in the Marches jurisdiction over Wales.

1537
Pilgrimage of Grace is put down.

Miles Coverdale puts out first complete Bible printed in English.

Queen Jane Seymour dies after giving birth to Edward.

1538
Henry commissions Hans Holbein to paint prospective brides for his fourth marriage, among them Anne of Cleves.

Sir Thomas Elyot issues his Latin-English dictionary.

Cromwell orders English Bible placed in every church.
Pope Paul III decisively excommunicates Henry VIII.
Members of Pole family are executed for treason.
Work begins on Nonsuch Palace.

1539
Great Bible published.
Dissolution of Greater Monasteries enacted.
The Six Articles of Religion enacted to restore conservative beliefs.

1540
Henry VIII marries Anne of Cleves; marriage is annulled.
Henry VIII marries Catherine Howard.
Cromwell is executed.

1541
Queen Catherine Howard is accused of adultery and sent to Tower of London.
Parliament declares Henry VIII king of Ireland.

1542
Queen Catherine Howard is executed.
Cardinal Robert Bellarmine and Mary Queen of Scots are born.
Debasement of coinage begins.
Edward Hall publishes *The Union of the Two Noble and Illustre Families of Lancaster and York.*

1543
Henry marries Catherine Parr.
William Byrd is born.

1544
Henry VIII captures Boulogne.
Anglo-Scottish conflicts along Borders.

1545
Roger Ascham publishes elegant treatise on archery, *Toxophilus.*
Scottish and French conflicts continue.

1546
Anne Askew is burned at Smithfield for denying transsubstantiation.
Anglo-French Treaty gives English control of Boulogne.

1547
Henry Howard, earl of Surrey, is executed for treason.
Henry VIII dies.
Nine-year-old Edward VI succeeds his father.
Thomas Cranmer's *Book of Homilies* is published.
Nonsuch Palace completed.
Vagabonds (or Sturdy Beggars) Act.
Dissolution of the Chantries enacted.

1548
Hugh Latimer preaches his celebrated Sermon on the Plough.

1549
Act of Uniformity establishes use of the Book of Common Prayer.
Prayer Book rebellion suppressed.
Kett's Rebellion suppressed.

1550
Peace of Boulogne ends war with France.
Sir William Cecil is appointed Secretary of State and Privy Councilor.

1551
Ralph Robinson translates More's *Utopia* into English.
Corn shortages throughout the land.

1552
Walter Ralegh and Edmund Spenser are born.
Royal commission recommends reforming courts of revenue.

1553
Cranmer promulgates the Forty-two Articles of Religion.
Edward VI dies.
Jane Grey is proclaimed queen.
Mary Tudor defeats Jane Grey and becomes queen.
Act of Repeal revives Mass, ritual worship, and clerical celibacy.
Thomas Wilson's *Art of Rhetoric* is published.

1554
Protestants go into exile in Germany and Switzerland.
Sir Thomas Wyatt leads Protestant revolt against Spanish marriage, which is suppressed.
Jane Grey is executed and Elizabeth is sent to the Tower.
Queen Mary marries Philip of Spain.
Parliament relaxes apprenticeship regulation to stimulate urban weaving industry.
Exchequer absorbs most courts of revenue to centralize government finance.

1555
Protestants are burned, notably Nicholas Ridley and Hugh Latimer.
Cardinal Pole succeeds Cranmer as archbishop of Canterbury.

1556
Thomas Cranmer is burned at stake.
A Short Treatise of Politike Power published by Marian exile, John Ponet.

1557

Parliament restricts cloth manufacture to towns with established industry.

Tottel's Miscellany is published.

The Stationer's Company is incorporated.

1558

Mary dies and is succeeded by Elizabeth I.

Richard Mulcaster publishes account of the queen's progress through London.

Protestant exiles return from Continent.

1559

Parliament passes Acts of Supremacy and Uniformity; Marian Act of Repeal is repealed.

Matthew Parker becomes archbishop of Canterbury.

England helps Scottish lords expel French from Scotland.

First edition of *Mirror for Magistrates* is published.

1560

Treaty of Edinburgh ends French rule of Scotland.

The Geneva Bible is published.

Shane O'Neill, earl of Tyrone, opposes English rule in Ireland.

1561

Francis Bacon is born.

Sir Thomas Hoby brings out his translation of Castiglione's *The Courtier.*

Mary Queen of Scots returns to Scotland from France.

1562

Elizabeth nearly dies of smallpox.

John Jewel publishes his *Apology for the Church of England.*

O'Neill submits to Elizabeth.

John Hawkins begins slaving expeditions to Africa.

1563

Parliament presses Elizabeth to marry.

Thirty-nine Articles are approved, but not enacted.

John Foxe brings to press his *Acts and Monuments.*

Statute of Artificers establishes uniform apprenticeship system.

John Shute publishes *The First and Chief Grounds of Architecture.*

Barnabe Googe publishes *Eclogues, Epitaphs, and Sonnets.*

1564

William Shakespeare, Christopher Marlowe, and Henry Chettle are born.

1565

Mary Queen of Scots marries Henry, Lord Darnley.

Royal College of Physicians is authorized to perform human dissections.

Gorboduc, by Sackville and Norton, becomes the first printed tragedy.

1566

Thomas Gresham founds the Royal Exchange.

Ralph Royster Doister, by Nicholas Udall, becomes the first printed comedy.

1567

Darnley is murdered.

Mary Queen of Scots is deposed and imprisoned in Scotland.

Arthur Golding completes his translation of Ovid's *Metamorphoses.*

1568

Mary Queen of Scots escapes and flees to England.

William Allen founds college at Douai for English Catholics.

1569

Northern Rebellion led by Catholic earls is put down.

1570

Pope excommunicates Elizabeth and absolves her subjects from allegiance.

Roger Ascham publishes *The Scholemaster.*

Euclid's *Elements of Geometry* is translated, with an important preface by John Dee.

1571

Subscription to Thirty-nine Articles is enforced upon clergy by Parliament

The Ridolfi Conspiracy is discovered.

1572

John Donne is born.

Thomas Cartwright denounces Anglican ceremonies in *The Admonition to Parliament.*

1573

Francis Drake sights the Pacific.

Inigo Jones and William Laud are born.

1574

The Earl of Leicester's theatrical company is formed.

1575

Dutch Anabaptists are burned at Smithfield.

Elizabeth visits Robert Dudley, earl of Leicester, at Kenilworth; George Gascoigne publishes an account.

1576

Peter Wentworth is imprisoned for attacking queen's interference with Parliament.

James Burbage builds the first permanent theater in
London.
David Rowland translates the Spanish picaresque novel
Lazarillo de Tormes.

1577
Archbishop Edmund Grindal is suspended for refusal to
suppress Puritan "prophesyings."
Raphael Holinshed publishes his *Chronicles of England,
Scotland, and Ireland.*
Francis Drake begins his circumnavigation of the
globe.

1578
John Lyly breaks stylistic ground with *Euphues, the
Anatomy of Wit.*

1579
Stephen Gosson attacks the immorality of stage plays in
The Schoole of Abuse.
The duke of Alençon visits to court Elizabeth.
Earl of Desmond leads revolt in Ireland, aided by Spanish
troops.
Edmund Spenser's *Shepherd's Calendar* is published
anonymously.

1580
Robert Parsons and Edmund Campion lead a Jesuit mis-
sion to England.
Francis Drake completes his circumnavigation of the globe.
John Stowe publishes his *Chronicles of England.*
Sir Philip Sidney writes his *Defense of Poesy.*

1581
Recusancy laws enacted by Parliament against Roman
Catholics.
Negotiations are held regarding a marriage between Eliz-
abeth and the duke of Alençon.
Edmund Campion is executed for treason.

1582
George Buchanan's *Scottish History* is published.
University of Edinburgh is founded.

1583
John Whitgift is chosen archbishop of Canterbury.
The Throckmorton Plot to replace Elizabeth with Mary
of Scotland is uncovered.
Philip Stubbes publishes *The Anatomy of Abuses.*

1584
The Spanish ambassador Mendoza is expelled for com-
plicity in Throckmorton Plot.
Reginald Scott publishes *The Discoverie of Witchcraft.*

1585
The acting company the Lord Chamberlain's Men is formed.
Leicester leads English army to help Protestants in the
Netherlands.

1586
The Babington Plot to kill Elizabeth is uncovered.
Severe famine follows harvest failures.
Mary Queen of Scots is convicted of treason.
Sir Philip Sidney dies of wounds incurred at Zutphen in
the Low Countries.
William Camden publishes *Brittania* in Latin.

1587
Elizabeth at last signs death warrant for Mary Queen of
Scots, who is then beheaded.
Sir Christopher Hatton is named Lord Chancellor.
Sir Walter Ralegh sails to found a New World colony.
Sir Francis Drake weakens Spanish fleet in several battles.

1588
The Spanish Armada is defeated.
The Martin Marprelate controversy rages.
Robert Dudley, Earl of Leicester, dies.
Richard Hakluyt publishes *The Principall Navigations.*

1589
Marprelate press is discovered.
George Puttenham publishes *The Arte of English Poesie.*

1590
The Countess of Pembroke's *Arcadia* by Philip Sidney is
published.
Edmund Spenser publishes Books 1–3 of *The Faerie Queene.*

1591
Army led by Robert Earl of Essex goes to France to aid
Henry IV at Rouen.
Philip Sidney's *Astrophel and Stella* is published.

1592
Riots in London against apprentices and masterless men.
Plague returns to London.

1593
London theaters are closed most of the year because of
plague.
Puritan Henry Barrow and Brownist John Penry are
executed.
Christopher Marlowe is killed in a tavern.

1594
Richard Hooker publishes Books 1–4 of his *Laws of
Ecclesiastical Polity.*
Thomas Nashe publishes *The Unfortunate Traveler.*

1595

The Jesuit Robert Southwell is executed.

Earl of Tyrone leads Ulster revolt and appeals for Spanish aid.

Sir Walter Ralegh visits Guiana in search of El Dorado.

The Swan Theater opens.

1596

An English expedition under the Earl of Essex sacks Cadiz.

Wreck of Spanish fleet bound for invasion of Ireland.

Harvest failure leads to food riots in Kent.

Spenser completes *The Faerie Queene.*

1597

More food riots in Kent, Sussex, and Norfolk.

Continuing threat of Spanish invasion through Ireland.

Sir Francis Bacon publishes a volume of ten *Essays.*

1598

John Florio brings out his Italian-English Dictionary.

William Cecil, Lord Burghley, dies.

Earl of Tyrone defeats English at Battle of the Yellow Ford in Ulster.

Parliament enacts Relief of the Poor and Punishment of Rogues.

John Stowe publishes *A Survey of London.*

1599

The Earl of Essex fails in his mission to Ireland and is imprisoned.

James VI of Scotland publishes his *Basilikon Doron* on kingship.

The Globe Theatre opens on Bankside, Southwark.

1600

The English East India Company is founded.

James VI survives the Gowrie Plot.

William Gilbert publishes *De Magnete.*

1601

Revolt led by Earl of Essex fails, and he is executed for treason.

At last Elizabethan Parliament, queen is obliged to promise relief from burdensome monopolies.

Spanish fleet arrives to aid in Tyrone's rebellion.

1602

The Bodleian Library opens at Oxford.

Spanish surrender, and Tyrone submits to Elizabeth.

Jesuit and secular priests are enjoined.

1603

Queen Elizabeth dies and is succeeded by James VI of Scotland.

Puritan clergy present James with Millenary Petition.

Sir Walter Ralegh is found guilty of high treason and imprisoned.

John Florio translates Montaigne's *Essays.*

1604

Hampton Court conference.

Anglo-Spanish Peace Treaty ends war.

James adopts title "King of Great Britain, France and Ireland."

Contributors

*Independent scholar
~Emeritus faculty
‡Affiliation at time of writing
†Deceased

Simon Adams
University of Strathclyde
Alençon and Anjou, Duke of
Dudley, Robert, Earl of Leicester
Kenilworth
Robsart, Amy

Michael V. C. Alexander
Virginia Polytechnic Institute
Education, History of
Grammar Schools
Mulcaster, Richard
Universities

Iska Alter
Hofstra University
Stubbes, Philip

Christy Anderson
Yale University
Architecture

John C. Appleby
Liverpool Hope University College
Cabot, John
Cabot, Sebastian
Colonial Development
Discovery and Exploration
Drake, Francis
Frobisher, Martin
Grenville, Richard
Hawkins, John
Hawkins, Richard
Piracy
Privateering

Adam Apt *
Astrology
Astronomy

Ian W. Archer
Keble College, Oxford
Apprentices
Audley, Thomas
Barton, Elizabeth
Bromley, Sir Thomas
Childbirth
Clothing and Costume
Funerary practices
Guilds
London
Margaret of York, Dutchess of Burgundy
Mary Tudor, Dutchess of Suffolk
Merchant Taylors
Pole, Edmund de la, Earl of Suffolk
Stafford, Edward, Duke of Buckingham
Talbot Family

John Michael Archer
University of New Hampshire, Durham
Espionage
Walsingham, Sir Francis

Frank Ardolino
University of Hawaii, Honolulu
Kyd, Thomas

Dana Aspinall
Assumption College
Breton, Nicholas
Chettle, Henry

John Astington
Erindale College, University of Toronto
Alabaster, William
Tarlton, Richard

Peter Barber
British Library
Mapmaking
Norden, John
Saxton, Christopher

Reid Barbour
University of North Carolina, Chapel Hill
Deloney, Thomas
Riche, Barnaby

William Barker
Memorial University of Newfoundland
Harvey, Gabriel

Michael Bath
University of Strathclyde
Emblem Books

N. W. Bawcutt
University of Liverpool
Buc, George

Peter Beal
Sotheby's, London
Manuscripts

Dan Beaver
Penn State University
Games and Sports

Barrett Beer
Kent State University
Dudley, John, Duke of Northumberland
Seymour, Edward
Seymour, Thomas

A. L. Beier
Illinois State University
Pedlars

Elaine Beilin
Framingham State College
Askew, Anne

David Bergeron
University of Kansas
Homosexuality
Processions, Lord Mayor's
Progresses, Royal

Steven Berkowitz
Fu Jen University, Taipei
Buchanan, George
Daniel, Samuel
Elegy
Elyot, Thomas
Rogers, Daniel

Normand Berlin
~University of Massachusetts, Amherst
Sackville, Thomas

Herbert Berry
University of Saskatchewan ✓
Theaters

Norman Blake
University of Sheffield
Caxton, William

Elizabethanne Boran
Trinity College, Dublin
Ramism

Francisco J. Borge
‡University of Oviedo, Spain
Boorde, Andrew
Hariot, Thomas,
Lane, Ralph
Mendoza, Bernardino de

Jeremy Boulton
University of Newcastle
Southwark

Glen Bowman
‡University of Minnesota, Twin Cities
Audley, Thomas
Ponet, John

Stephen Brachlow
Baptist Theological Seminary, Richmond
Anabaptists
Barrow, Henry
Browne, Robert
Greenwood, John

Michael Braddick
University of Sheffield
Taxation

Ciaran Brady
Trinity College, Dublin
Ireland, History of

Gerald Bray
Beeson Divinity School, Samford University
Adiaphora
Admonition Controversy
Advertisements, Book of
Anglicanism
Annates
Atheism
Aylmer, John, Bishop of London
Baro, Peter
Bible Commentary

Manners, Roger, Fifth Earl of Rutland
Percy Family
Yelverton, Christopher

Lothar Cerny
Fachhochschule, Köln
Literary Criticism
Peele, George

Walter Chmielewski
‡University of Massachusetts, Amherst
Gowrie Conspiracy
Whetstone, George

Sandra Clark
Birbeck College, University of London
Popular Literature

Kathleen Conway
Wheaton College
Fenton, Geoffrey
Grafton, Richard

Harold Cook
University of Wisconsin, Madison
Medicine and Health

John P. D. Cooper
St. Hugh's College, Oxford
Paget, William
Russell, John, Earl of Bedford
Sadler, Sir Ralph
Wriothesley, Thomas

Edward Cotrill
‡University of Massachusetts, Amherst
Babington, Gervase

A. D. Cousins
MacQuarie University
Lyric

Hugh D. Craig
University of Newcastle
Harington, Sir John

Mary Thomas Crane
Boston College
Commonplace Books
Epigrams

Claire M. Cross
University of York
Hastings, Henry, Third Earl of Huntingdon

Charles Crupi
Albion College
Greene, Robert

John Curley
‡New York University
Edwardes, Richard
Mayne, Cuthbert

John M. Currin*
Allen, William
Archpriest Controversy
Aske, Robert
Bosworth Field
Campion, Edmund
Clitherow, Margaret
English College of Rome
Henry VII
Jesuits
Monastic Orders
Parsons, Robert
Recusancy
Roses, Wars of the
Simnel, Lambert
Stanley Family
Stapleton, Thomas
Warham, William
Wolsey, Thomas

Eric Daigre
‡University of Minnesota, Twin Cities
Pettie, George

J. F. R. Day
Troy State University
Heraldry

David Dean
Carleton University
Hatton, Christopher
Parliament History
Wentworth, Paul
Wentworth, Peter

Thomas Deans
Kansas State University
Davis, John
Davys, John
O'Donnell, Hugh Roe, Lord of Connell
Sidney, Henry

Wayne DeYoung
‡Ohio State University
Marian Martyrs

Brian Dietz
University of Glasgow
Agrarian Uprisings
Cloth Industries
Cloth Trade

East India Company
Fish and Fishing
Industry and Manufacture
Joint Stock Companies
Merchant Adventurers
Monopolies
Regulated Companies
Shipbuilding
Sumptuary Laws
Trade, Inland
Trade, Overseas
Transportation

Catherine Maria Don Diego
Central Michigan University
Googe, Barnabe

Elizabeth Story Donno
The Huntington Library
Fleming, Abraham

Susan Doran
St. Mary's University College
Accession Day
Foreign Relations and Diplomacy
Radcliffe, Sir Thomas

Jason W. R. Dorsett
Oriel College, Oxford
Patronage

Jason Drake
‡New York University
Hall, Joseph

Ralph Drayton
‡University of Wisconsin, Madison
Plague

Louise Durning
Oxford Brookes University
Sculpture

James Dutcher
Holyoke Community College
Babington, Anthony
Babington Plot
Barclay, Alexander

Richard Dutton
University of Lancaster
Censorship
Revels Office

Alan D. Dyer
University of Wales, Bangor
Towns

Peter Edwards
Roehampton Institute, Surrey
Horses and Horsemanship
Hunting

Philip Edwards*
Gilbert, Humphrey
Hakluyt, Richard
Horses and Horsemanship
Travel Literature

David Eltis
Eton College
Archery
Military History

Melinda Emmons
‡New York University
Brant, Sebastian
Stubbs, John

William Engel*
Florio, John
Meres, Francis

Robert C. Evans
Auburn University
Paradox

David Evett
Cleveland State Unversity
Engraving and Illustration
Hardwick, Elizabeth

David Farley-Hills
University College of Swansea
Barnes, Barnabe

Alan Farmer
‡New York University
Poynings, Edward

Mordechai Feingold
Virginia Polytechnic Institute
Bales, Peter
Bright, Timothy
Coxe, Leonard
Creighton, James
Gerard, John
Humphrey, Lawrence
Turner, William
Twyne, John
Vives, Juan Luis

Margaret Ferguson
University of California, Davis
Cary, Elizabeth

Anne Ferry* —
Language, History of English

Michael Flachmann
California State University, Bakersfield
Baldwin, William

Peter Fleming
University of the West of England
Bristol

David Frantz
Ohio State University
Pornography

David Freeman
Sir Wilfred Grenfell College, Memorial University of
    Newfoundland
Broughton, Hugh
Heath, Nicholas
Popham, John

Alice T. Friedman
Wellesley College
Woolaton Hall

Barry Gaines
University of New Mexico
Arthurian Legend

Gayle Gaskill
College of St. Catherine
Flodden Field, Battle of
Grey, Lady Jane

Malcolm Gaskill
Anglia Polytechnic University
Witchcraft

Hillary Gatti
University of Rome "La Sapienza"
Bruno, Giordano

Lee W. Gibbs
Cleveland State University
Alesius, Alexander
Articles of Religion
Becon, Thomas
Calvinism
Church Calendar
Church of Scotland
Church Polity
Hamilton, Patrick
Hooker, Richard
Knox, John
Leslie, John, Bishop of Ross
Melville, Andrew
Perkins, William

Smith, Henry
Whitaker, William
Wishart, George

Ernest Gilman
New York University
Holbein, Hans

Darryl J. Gless
University of North Carolina, Chapel Hill
Fraunce, Abraham
Spenser, Edmund

William L. Godshalk
University of Cincinnati
Churchyard, Thomas

Mark Goldblatt
Fashion Institute of Technology
Adamson, Patrick, Archbishop of St. Andrews
Antichrist
Bainbridge, Christopher, Cardinal Archbishop of York
Barlow, William, Bishop of Chichester
Beaton, David, Cardinal Archbishop of St. Andrews
Bilson, Thomas, Bishop of Winchester
Browne, George, Archbishop of Dublin
Chantry
Christopher, John, Bishop of Chichester
Cox, Richard
Field, Richard, Dean of Glouchester
Grindal, Edmund, Archbishop of Canterbury
Longland, John, Bishop of Lincoln
Morton, John Cardinal
Overall John, Bishop of Norwich
Ridley, Nicholas, Bishop of London
Sandys, Edwin, Archbishop of York
Sternhold, Thomas
Travers, Walter
Whitgift, John, Archbishop of Canterbury

Barclay Green
Fort Lewis College
Leland, John
Warner, William

Larry Green
University of South California, Los Angeles
Ciceronianism
Logic
Rainolde, Richard
Rhetoric

R. Morgan Griffin
‡University of Massachusetts, Amherst
Devereux, Walter
Hayward, John
O'Neill, Hugh, Second Earl of Tyrone

Steven Gunn
Merton College, Oxford
Brandon, Charles, Duke of Suffolk

Richard Haber
Western New England College
Euphuism

Jay Halio
University of Delaware, Newark
Drama, Performance and Staging

Donna Hamilton
University of Maryland
Munday, Anthony

Paul Hammer
University of New England, Australia
Devereux, Robert, Earl of Essex

Margaret P. Hannay
Siena College
Sidney, Mary, Countess of Pembroke

Peter Happé*
Bale, John
Fulwell, Ulpian
Heywood, John
Vice, The

Andrea Harkness
‡University of New Hampshire, Durham
Hoby, Margaret

Nancy Lenz Harvey
University of Cincinnati
Elizabeth of York

Chris R. Hassel
Vanderbilt University
Calendar, Secular

William P. Haugaard
Seabury-Western Theological Seminary
Reformation, English

Edmund Hayes
Worcester Polytechnic Institute
Rastell, John

Theo van Heijnsbergen
University of Glasgow
Douglas, Gavin
Dunbar, William
Erskine, John, Earl of Mar
Maitland, John
Stuart, Francis

Richard Helgerson
University of California, Santa Barbara
Drayton, Michael

Morison, Fynes
Stow, John

Richard A. Helmholz
University of Chicago
Canon Law

Steven Hindle
University of Warwick
Poor Laws
Social Classes and Social Order
Vagrants

Barbara Hodgdon
Drake University
Nashe, Thomas

Michael Holahan
Southern Methodist University
Jonson, Ben

Heidi Holder
Central Michigan University
Gosson, Stephen

Joan Ozark Holmer
Georgetown University
Fairy Lore

Victor Houliston
University of Witwatersrand, South Africa
Moffet, Thomas

R. A. Houston
University of St. Andrews
Literacy
Population and Demographics

Maurice Howard
University of Sussex
Interior Decoration

Richard Hoyle
University of Central Lancashire
Pilgrimage of Grace

Clifford Huffman
State University of New York, Stony Brook
Wolfe, John

Suzanne Hull
The Henry E. Huntington Library
Household Books
Marriage Manuals

Sarah Hutton
University of Hertfordshire, Watford
Digby, Everard
Neoplatonism
Pyrrhonism
Skepticism

Sybil Jack
University of Sydney
Court of Wards
Exchequer
Mildmay, Walter
Paulet, William

Sears Jayne*
Chester, Robert
Parry, Robert

Robert C. Johnson
Miami University of Ohio
Preston, Thomas

Stephen Johnston
Museum of the History of Science, Oxford
Digges, Leonard
Digges, Thomas
Ordnance
Recorde, Robert

J. Gwynfor Jones
University of Cardiff
Wales, History of

Elise Jorgens
Western Michigan University, Kalamazoo
Song

Parmita Kapadia
Fort Lewis College
Hawes, Stephen

Carol V. Kaske
Cornell University
Romance

Lauren Kassell
Edinburgh University
Alchemy
Forman, Simon

N. H. Keeble
University of Stirling
Latimer, Hugh, Bishop of Worcester

Robert Kellerman
‡Central Michigan University
Broadsides
Pastoral

Roy Kendall*
Baines, Richard

Harry Keyshian
Farleigh-Dickinson University
Dekker, Thomas

Dean Kernan*
Aristotelianism
Humanism

John King
Ohio State University
Bilney, Thomas
Bradford, John
Frith, John
Foxe, John
Hooper, John, Bishop of Glouchester and Worcester
Philpot, John
Rogers, John
Whitchurch, Edward

Louis Knafla
University of Calgary
Chancery
Common Law
Courts, Ecclesiastical
Court of Common Pleas
Court of King's and Queen's Bench
Egerton, Thomas
Law, Civil
Star Chamber

Roslyn L. Knutson
University of Arkansas
Davies, John, of Hereford
Theater Companies, Adult

Elizabeth Kunz*
Bastard Feudalism

Douglas Lanier
University of New Hampshire, Durham
Porter, Henry
Roydon, Matthew
Udall, Nicholas

Charles S. Larkowski
Wright State University
Anglican Church Music
Anthem
Motet

Stanford Lehmberg
University of Minnesota, Twin Cities
Government, Central Administration of
Royal Family

Charles Leiby
‡New York University
Bryskett, Lodowick
Lok, Henry

Michael Leslie
Rhodes College
Gardens

Zachary Lesser
‡Columbia University
Machyn, Henry

Ronald L. Levao
Rutgers University
Marlowe, Christopher

Jill L. Levenson
Trinity College, University of Toronto
Brooke, Arthur

Carol Levin
University of Nebraska, Lincoln
Elizabeth I

Richard A. Levin
University of California, Davis
Wriothesley, Henry, Earl of Southampton

F. J. Levy
University of Washington
Antiquarianism
Camden, William
Fabyan, Robert
Hall, Edward
Hooker, John (alias Vowell)
Stanyhurst, Richard

Naomi Liebler
Montclair State University
Folklore and Folk Rituals

Chih-hsin Lin
‡New York University
Willobie, William

Candace Lines
‡University of Minnesota, Twin Cities
Northern Rebellion

Nigel Llewellyn
Unversity of Sussex
Painting

David Loades
University of Wales, Bangor
Philip II

Daniel T. Lochman
Southwest Texas State
Colet, John

Joseph Loewenstein
Washington University, St. Louis
Puttenham, George

Pamela O. Long*
Technology

William B. Long*
Printing, Publishing, and Bookbinding, History of

Scott Lucas
The Citadel
Holinshed, Raphael
James IV
Margaret Tudor, Queen of James IV
Throckmorton, Sir Nicholas

Bridget Gellert Lyons
Rutgers University
Coke, Edward

Catherine Macleod
National Portrait Gallery, London
Hilliard, Nicholas
Miniature Painting

Peter Marshall
University of Warwick
Clergy

Christopher Martin
Boston University
Carew, Richard
Chaloner, Thomas
Hoby, Thomas
North, Thomas
Sidney, Philip

Steven May
Georgetown College
Ralegh, Sir Walter
Verse Anthologies

Thomas Mayer
Augustana College
Catholicism
Pole, Reginald, Archbishop of Canterbury
Political Theory
Starkey, Thomas
Trent, Council of

Richard McCoy
Queen's College, City University of New York
Court
Knighthood

Adrianna McCrea*
Senecanism

Elizabeth McCutcheon
University of Hawaii, Manoa
More, Thomas
Roper, Margaret
Utopia

John McDiarmid
New College of University of South Florida
Cheke, John
Lily, William
Linacre, Thomas
Wilson, Thomas

James E. McGoldrick
Cedarville College
Lutheranism

Paula McQuade
University of Chicago
Ridolfi Plot
Treason

Peter Medine
University of Arizona
Satire

Stephen Merriam
Brown University
Wyatt, Thomas

Robert Miola
Loyola College, Baltimore
Classical Literature, Influence of
Classical Literature, English Translations

Leonel L. Mitchell
Notre Dame University
Baptism
Eucharist
Liturgy
Marriage and Marriage Law
Matrimony
Ordinal

David K. Money
Wolfson College, Cambridge
Neo-Latin Literature

Peter R. Moore*
Royal Household (with William A. Sessions)
Privy Chamber (with William A. Sessions)

Victor Morgan
University of East Anglia
Government, Local
Justice of the Peace
Sheriff

Joseph C. Morin
University of Maryland, Baltimore
Air
Byrd, William
Consort Music
Keyboard Music

Robert Mueller
Utah State University
Bacon, Nicholas
Cavendish, Thomas
Knollys, Francis
Knollys, Lettice
Puckering, John
Wray, Christopher

Craig Muldrew
European University, Florence
Gresham, Thomas
Money, Inflation and Moneylending
Royal Exchange
Price Revolution

John J. Mulryan
St. Bonaventure University
Dictionaries

Barry Nash
Hofstra University
Lambarde, William

Alan H. Nelson
University of California, Berkeley
De Vere, Edward
Rastell, William

Hillary Nunn
‡Michigan State University
Marston, John

Anne M. O'Donnell
Catholic University of America
Erasmus, Desiderius
Fisher, John, Bishop of Rochester
Tyndale, William

Lena Cowen Orlin
University of Maryland, Baltimore County
Harrison, William

Geoffrey Parker
Ohio State University
Armada, Spanish

Paul G. Stanwood
~University of British Columbia
Andrewes, Lancelot

Ted-Larry Pebworth
University of Michigan, Dearborn
Donne, John

G. W. Pigman III
California Institute of Technology
Gascoigne, George

Anne Lake Prescott
Barnard College
French Literature, Influence of
Grimald, Nicholas

Wilfrid Prest
University of Adelaide
Inns of Court

Stephen Pumfrey
University of Lancaster
Gilbert, William

Jon Quitslund
George Washington University
Didactic Poetry

Ronald Rebholz
Stanford University
Greville, Fulke

Constance Relihan
Auburn University
Lodge, Thomas

Lawrence Rhu
University of South Carolina
Italian Literature, Influence of

Glenn Richardson
St. Mary's University College
Field of the Cloth of Gold

Todd R. Ridder
University of Dayton
Sarum, Use of

Gregory Ripple
‡Fordham University
Rich, Lord Richard
Rizzio, David
Throckmorton Plot

Thomas P. Roche, Jr.
Princeton University
Petrarchanism
Sonnet Sequences

Philip Rollinson
University of South Carolina
Hymns

Nicola Royan
University of St. Andrews
Boece, Hector
Douglas Family

Martha Tuck Rozett
University at Albany
Cornwallis, William
Essay

Gerald Rubio
†University of Guelph
Arcadia

Paul Salzman
La Trobe University
Prose Fiction

Diana Scarisbrick*
Jewelry

R. J. Schoeck
~University of Colorado
Foxe, Richard, Bishop of Winchester

John Schofield
Museum of London
St. Paul's Cathedral

Liam Semler
MacQuairie University
Bateman, Stephen

William A. Sessions
Georgia State University
Howard, Henry, Earl of Surrey
Privy Chamber (with Peter R. Moore)
Royal Household (with Peter R. Moore)
Tottel, Richard

James Shapiro
Columbia University
Jews

Michael Shapiro
University of Illinois
Theater Companies, Boys

James A. Sharpe
University of York
Capital Punishment
Crime
Criminal Law
Magic

William H. Sherman
University of Maryland, College Park
Dee, John
Reading Practices

Frederick H. Shriver
General Theological Seminary
Arminianism
Bancroft, Richard, Bishop of London
Lambeth Articles
Saravia, Hadrian

Timothy Shroder
Partridge Fine Arts, London
Goldsmith's Work

Thurley Simon
Museum of London
Royal Palaces

A. J. Slavin
University of Louisville
Cromwell, Thomas

Charlotte Spivack
University of Massachusetts, Amherst
Davies, Sir John
Norton, Sir Thomas

John Staines
Yale University
Davison, William
Hepburn, James, Earl of Bothwell
Parry, William

John Steadman
The Huntingdon Library
Epic

William Streitberger
University of Washington
Tilney, Edmund

Andrea Sununu
DePauw University
Turberville, George
Tusser, Thomas

David W. Swain
‡University of Massachusetts, Amherst
Agas, Ralph
Arthur Tudor
Dudley, Edmund
Empson, Richard
Howard, Thomas, Fourth Duke of Norfolk
Scot, Reginald
Spanish Literature, Influence of
Warbeck, Perkin

David G. Sylvester*
Cinque Ports

Juan E. Tazón
University of Oviedo, Spain
Stukeley, Thomas

Joan Thirsk*
Agriculture
Enclosures
Food and Diet

Kerri Thomsen
Concordia University, Irvine
Adlington, William
Berners, John Bourchier, Lord

Robert Tittler
Concordia University, Montreal
Chapuys, Eustace
Edward VI
Kett's Rebellion
Mary I
Wyatt's Rebellion

Rebecca Totaro
Florida Gulf Coast University
Hunnis, William

David Vaisey
Bodleian Library, Oxford
Bodley, Thomas

Alvin P. Vos
State University of New York, Binghampton
Ascham, Roger

Paul Voss
Georgia State University
News Quartos

Susan Wabuda
Fordham University
Blount, Charles, Lord Mountjoy
Fiztroy, Henry, Duke of Richmond

Raymond Waddington
University of California, Davis
Chapman, George

Greg Walker
University of Leicester
Henry VIII

John Wall
North Carolina State University
Sermons

Retha Warnicke
Arizona State University
Anne of Cleves
Beaufort, Margaret, Countess of Richmond
Boleyn, Anne
Howard, Catherine
Parr, Catherine

John A. Watkins
University of Minnesota, Twin Cities
Drama, History of

Tom Webster
University of Edinburgh
Land and Landscape

Stanley Wells
The Shakespeare Birthplace Trust, Stratford-on-Avon
Shakespeare, William

Philip White
Centre College
Tichborn, Chidiock

Charles Whitney
University of Nevada
Bacon, Francis

David Wiles
Royal Holloway and Bedford New College, University of
    London
Armin, Robert

William P. Williams
Northern Illinois University
Handwriting

Neal Wood
York University, Ontario
Fortescue, John
Smith, Thomas

Linda Woodbridge
Penn State University
Jest Books

Donald Woodward
University of Hull
Coal Industry
Economy
Fairs and Markets
Inns, Taverns, and Alehouses

Daniel Woolf
McMaster University
History, Writing of
Vergil, Polydore

Jenny Wormald
St. Hilda's College, Oxford
Hamilton Family
James V
James VI
Mary Queen of Scots
Scotland, History of

H. R. Woudhuysen
University College London
Book Ownership

George T. Wright
University of Arizona
Versification

Jonathan Wright
‡Auburn University
Cavendish, George
Day, John

Laura S. Youens
George Washington University
Ballad
Bull, John
Campion, Thomas
Carol
Carols
Cornysh, William
Dance Music
Dowland, John
Eton Choirbook
Fayrfax, Robert
Henry VIII, Composer
Madrigals
Morley, Thomas
Music, History of
Sheppard, John
Tallis, Thomas
Taverner, John
Tomkins, Thomas
Weelkes, Thomas
Wilbye, John

Laura Hunt Yungblut
University of Dayton
Aliens
Immigration

A

Accession Day

During the later sixteenth century, the anniversary of the monarch's accession became a national day of celebration. Under Henry VIII, the festivities at court associated with his accession on April 22 were subsumed in the celebrations of St. George's Day (April 23) held either at Windsor or Greenwich. Elizabeth's accession day, November 17, however, developed into an annual festival, which acted as a vehicle to express adoration for the queen. At court, the festivities centered on the accession day tilts, which, under the imaginative eye of Sir Henry Lee, the master of the armoury and queen's champion, became elaborate neo-chivalric entertainments full of sophisticated allegories and symbolism. At the local level, the day was never a public holiday but was celebrated as a festival of thanksgiving marked by bell ringing, bonfires, and church services with special prayers.

BIBLIOGRAPHY

Cressy, David. *Bonfires and Bells: National Memory and the Protestant Calendar in Elizabethan and Stuart England.* 1989.

Strong, Roy. *The Cult of Elizabeth: Elizabethan Portraiture and Pageantry.* 1977.

———. "The population of the accession day of Queen Elizabeth I." *Journal of the Warburg and Courtauld Institutes,* vol. 21. 1959.

Yates, Frances. Astraea: *The Imperial Theme in the Sixteenth Century.* 1975.

Susan Doran

SEE ALSO

Calendar, Secular; Elizabeth I

Actors

A combination of public support and the construction of purpose-built playhouses fueled the development of the acting profession. The earliest players were liveried servants, connected with aristocratic households or the court interludes. They performed periodically, at the prerogative of their lords, and otherwise earned an uncertain living. The construction of public playhouses turned the occasional nature of performing into a more consistent, professional setting, establishing the companies on a more permanent footing, and creating opportunities for players to earn a more regular wage. Thus, by the 1590s, the itinerant player had turned into a shareholder, capable of earning a sizeable income. Throughout the heyday of the theater, between two and four adult companies dominated the theatrical scene, principally the Lord Admiral's Prince Henry's Elector Palatine's Men, and the Lord Chamberlain's King's Men.

There seems not to have been a "typical actor" in terms of origins, education, or talent. Actors came from a variety of backgrounds. Some, like Edward Alleyn, were armigerous by birth while others were orphans apprenticed into companies by parish officials eager to avoid the stringent requirements of contemporary poor laws. Most actors seem to have been moderately well educated (though not university educated). A significant number were freemen of the London guilds, and those who left acting frequently returned to their trades. Actors could be classified as masters, hirelings, or apprentices. Masters (often coterminous with shareholders) invested heavily in the company and/or playhouse and bore the brunt of the responsibility for commissioning playbooks, purchasing costumes and props, and maintaining the playhouse.

Hirelings were paid for each performance, or on a weekly or monthly basis, but they were not extended the opportunity to make a long-term investment. Apprentices were essentially the boy players (some of whom were paid a small annual wage in return for room, board, and training). Most adult companies consisted of roughly twelve men (the shareholders) and three or four boys, few of whom continued into adulthood as actors. (The boy companies—most of them attached to schools such as the Merchant Taylors School or St. Paul's—functioned as separate entities from the adult companies. Their popularity vacillated, and they tended to perform either at the private playhouses or at court.)

Scholarly debate has not yet determined whether acting styles were naturalistic or highly stylized, although dramatic fashions clearly changed. What is clear, however, is that talent was as individualistic as the players themselves. Popular historical culture has privileged the actors of Shakespeare's company, especially his principal tragedian (Richard Burbage), the loyal friends who constituted the First Folio of his plays (John Heminges and Henry Condell), and his clowns (Will Kemp, Richard Tarlton, and Robert Armin). However, accounts of players from other companies—such as Edward Alleyn, William Bird, and Edward Juby—indicate that English audiences enjoyed the talents of many competent (perhaps even charismatic) actors, a surprising number of whom devoted an entire lifetime to performing with a particular company.

BIBLIOGRAPHY

Baldwin, T.W. *The Organization and Personnel of the Shakespearean Company.* 1927.

Bentley, Gerald E. *The Jacobean and Caroline Stage.* 1941.

———. *The Profession of Player in Shakespeare's Time, 1590–1642.* 1984.

Chambers, E.K. *The Elizabethan Stage.* 1923.

Davies, W.R. *Shakespeare's Boy Actors.* 1939.

Gair, Reavley. *The Children of Paul's.* 1982.

Gurr, Andrew. *The Shakespearian Playing Companies.* 1996.

Hillebrand, H.N. *The Child Actors.* 1926.

Joseph, Bertram. *Elizabethan Acting.* 1964.

King, T.J. *Casting Shakespeare's Plays: London Actors and Their Roles, 1590–1642.* 1992.

Mann, David. *The Elizabethan Player.* 1991.

Nungezer, Edwin. *A Dictionary of Actors.* 1929.

Shapiro, Michael. *Children of the Revels.* 1977.

Streitberger, W.R. "Personnel and Professionalization." In *A New History of the Early English Drama.* John D. Cox and David Scott Kastan, eds., pp. 337–335. 1997.

S.P. Cerasano

SEE ALSO

Alleyn, Edward; Armin, Robert; Burbage, Richard; Kemp, Will; Tarlton, Richard; Theaters; Theater Companies, Adult; Theater Companies, Boys

Acts of Religion

See Submission of the Clergy, Supremacy, Acts of; Uniformity, Acts of

Adamson, Patrick (1537–1592)

Born in Perth, Scotland, and educated at St. Andrews, Patrick Adamson, archbishop of St. Andrews, was appointed minister at Ceres in Fife in 1563. He came to feel intellectually stifled and, in 1566, renounced the position, spending the next five years abroad. He was briefly imprisoned in Paris for an impolitic poem exalting the newborn son of Mary Queen of Scots as "serenissimus princeps" of Scotland, England, France, and Ireland; later, in Geneva, he studied Calvinism with Theodore Beza. Adamson returned to Scotland, and the ministry, around 1572, and published a catechism and a Latin translation of the Scottish Confession of Faith. Raised to archbishop in 1576, he skirmished with Presbyterian factions—in one incident a woman who cured him of an illness was accused of witchcraft and burned at the stake. He served as ambassador to Elizabeth I's court in England in 1583, and, on his return, wrote his *Declaration of the King's Majesty's Intention in the late Acts of Parliament* (1585). His Presbyterian foes, led by Andrew and James Melville, launched a new series of attacks on his character and beliefs, culminating in his excommunication by the Synod of Fife in 1586. Adamson summarily excommunicated the Melvilles, and James VI (the "serenissimus princeps," later James I of England) interceded on Adamson's behalf. The next year, though, he was excommunicated again, by the General Assembly, and now without the king's support, Adamson was reduced to seeking the aid of Andrew Melville, who coerced him into a dubious recantation of his *Declaration.* Adamson's other writings include Latin versions of several biblical books. He died in 1592.

BIBLIOGRAPHY
Calderwood, David. *True History of the Church of Scotland.* 1678.
Wilson, Thomas. Memorial in Adamson's complete works, *De Sacro Pastoris Munere.* 1619.

Mark Goldblatt

SEE ALSO
James VI and I; Melville, Andrew

Adiaphora

The translation of the Greek word *adiaphora* is "things indifferent." The concept goes back to the earliest days of Christianity, when local churches developed customs peculiar to themselves that were not always readily understood or accepted elsewhere. The wider church was forced to distinguish between the essentials of the faith and the nonessentials. Before the Reformation, a pattern had been worked out whereby each autonomous branch of the church could determine its own rites and ceremonies, as long as these did not affect matters of doctrine. A good example of this is the way in which the Roman Catholic Church has accepted a married priesthood in the Eastern (Greek) rite, but forbidden it in the Western (Latin) rite. At the same time, each church was entitled, even expected, to enforce its discipline within its own sphere.

At the Reformation, Archbishop Thomas Cranmer used this principle to justify the changes he wanted to make to the rites and ceremonies of the Church of England, explaining this in the essay "On Ceremonies" in the Book of Common Prayer. In Elizabethan England, both the supporters of the establishment and the Puritans agreed that "things indifferent" could be decided by the local church, but they disagreed about how this should be done in practice.

Unfortunately, the establishment contained a large number of traditionalists who wanted to retain as much of the pre-Reformation ceremonial as possible. It also contained a number of inflexible disciplinarians not prepared to tolerate even minor divergences from the official norm. The Puritans did not usually object to the idea of order in worship, but they were disturbed that so much of what they saw reminded them of the Roman ways they had rejected. They also thought that a greater degree of flexibility was possible, and that severe disciplinary measures should not be taken against clergy merely because of a difference of opinion or practice concerning *adiaphora*.

The weakness of the establishment position was theological. It could not provide a biblical or spiritual rationale for its insistence on matters of indifference. On the other hand, the weakness of the Puritans was practical. They rejected the status quo, but could not agree about what to put in its place.

It was the tragedy of Elizabethan England that, as time went on, opinions on both sides hardened and moderates in both camps were silenced or ejected. In the end the Puritans were driven out of the church, leaving an Anglicanism in which the *adiaphora* were both compulsory and a mark of distinction from other Protestants.

BIBLIOGRAPHY
Collinson, Patrick. *The Elizabethan Puritan Movement.* 1990.

Gerald L. Bray

SEE ALSO
Book of Common Prayer; Church of England; Cranmer, Thomas; Puritanism; Reformation, English

Adlington, William (c. 1541–?)

Best known for his translation of Lucius Apuleius's *The Golden Asse* (1566), William Adlington completed his translation while at University College, Oxford; little else is known about him. The story of Lucius's transformation into an ass, and his subsequent adventures and eventual return to human form through the divine intervention of Isis, also contains the myth of Cupid and Psyche. Both this myth and Lucius's adventures were extremely popular, and *The Golden Asse* was reprinted in 1571, 1582, 1596, and 1600(?). In 1582, Stephen Gosson complained, *"The Golden Ass . . .* ha[s] been thoroughly ransacked to furnish the Playe houses in London"; after 1582, *The Golden Asse* was "ransacked" by Chapman, Heywood, Jonson, and Marston, and in 1600, Henslowe commissioned Dekker, Chettle, and Day to write a play (now lost) by the same name. Adlington's translation was also an important source for Shakespeare's asinine transformations in *The Comedy of Errors* and *A Midsummer Night's Dream*, and Psyche's trials in *All's Well That Ends Well* and in *Cymbeline*.

Adlington may also be the author of a 1579 tract, *A Speciall Remedie against the Furious Force of lawless Love*, and of an unpublished Latin poem, *The annotami of the Masse* (1561).

A

BIBLIOGRAPHY

Adlington, William, trans. *The Golden Ass.* Revised by Stephen Gaselee Loeb Classical Library. 1915; repr. 1974.

Benedikz, B.S. "A Note on Two Protestant Verse Polemics." *Cahiers Elisabethains,* vol. 21, pp. 49–53.

Starnes, D.T. "Shakespeare and Apuleius." *PMLA,* vol. 60, pp. 1021–1050.

Tobin, J.J.M. *Shakespeare's Favorite Novel: A Study of* The Golden Asse *As Prime Source.* 1984.

Kerri Lynne Thomsen

SEE ALSO

Classical Literature, English Translations

Admonition Controversy

The admonition controversy is the name given to a doctrinal debate that developed as a result of two petitions, or *Admonitions,* composed in 1572. Puritans had been accused of opposing practices in the church thought to be nonessential, such as clerical vestments, and their protests had been dismissed accordingly, but the authors of the *Admonitions* took matters much further than this. They claimed that the very nature of the ministry, and thus of the church, was at stake in the controversies between them and the church authorities. What they wanted was a Presbyterianism modeled after the polity at Geneva, in which all ministers would be thoroughly trained and examined before being ordained. They also wanted ministers to be equal and given collective responsibility for church government. The *Admonitions* emphasized the preaching of the pure Word of God, what they deemed the correct administration of the sacraments, and above all the need to discipline ministers who failed to perform their duties adequately.

The first *Admonition* was presented to Parliament in June of 1572, too late to have any real effect on deliberations. But its clear and determined prose caused a flurry of excitement and led to various attempts to counter its effect. Before the end of the year, a second (and less impressive) *Admonition* had appeared, in answer to these critics. Authorship of the first *Admonition* is generally ascribed to Thomas Wilcox, but the second *Admonition* remains anonymous, in spite of attempts to assign it to Thomas Cartwright or one of his associates. Men of the persuasion that agreed with the beliefs in these documents were coming to be called Puritans, and one purpose of the *Admonitions* was to clarify what for many was still an unclear doctrinal position.

Clearly, the *Admonitions* touched a raw nerve in the church, since many of the criticisms opponents voiced touched on abuses. The church authorities were already trying to correct the more flagrant ones, and in a series of measures taken in 1571, they had legislated for a more learned and more clearly Protestant ministry. The authors of the *Admonitions* no doubt felt that time was on their side; but the speed at which they wished to push ahead was unacceptable to the government, and the queen was hostile to any change in her settlement. Nor did defenders of this settlement neglect to make a case against the *Admonitions.* John Whitgift did that with his *Answer to the Admonition* late in 1572; if his reply makes much duller reading than the original tract, the criticisms he leveled against it were devastating. Thomas Cartwright felt obliged to reply to Whitgift (1573), and this in turn produced an even longer work from the former in *Defence of the Answer* (1574). The controversy continued for many years, and was not ended until Cartwright finally accepted the Elizabethan Settlement in 1585.

Agitation began almost immediately to have the *Admonitions* confiscated. A proclamation to this effect was issued on June 11, 1573, but results proved disappointing. In London, for example, not a single copy was recovered. The *Admonitions* became and remained a basic statement of Puritan demands, and they circulated unofficially for many years. They were still sufficiently known in the 1590s for Richard Hooker to have used them as a basic statement for the Puritanism he set out to refute in his *Laws of Ecclesiastical Polity.*

BIBLIOGRAPHY

Frere, W.H., and C.E. Douglas. *Puritan Manifestoes.* 1907.

Lake, Peter. *Anglicans and Puritans? Presbyterianism and English Conformist Thought from Whitgift to Hooker.* 1988

McGinn, D. *The Admonition Controversy.* 1949.

Whitgift, John. *Works.* 3 vols. John Ayre, ed. Parker Society. 1851–1853.

Gerald L. Bray

SEE ALSO

Cartwright, Thomas; Hooker, Richard; Puritanism; Whitgift, John

Advertisements, The Book of

A title given to the articles of Archbishop Matthew Parker, which he drew up in 1564 in response to Puritan demands for further reformation of the church. They are a defense of the Elizabethan Settlement of 1559, and make special provision for public worship and the administration of the sacraments in the church. Among other things, they enjoin kneeling at Holy Communion (already provided for in the Royal Injunctions of 1559), and provide for the examination of candidates for the ministry.

Their most famous section concerns the wearing of vestments, which is set out in great detail as a response to the contemporary controversy concerning their use. Parker sent them to Queen Elizabeth I for her signature (March 3, 1565), but this was refused. He tried again on March 12, 1566, but met with another refusal. At that point, he published them on his own authority. This action has been the subject of enormous controversy, even though it is clear that Parker could not have acted as he did without the Queen's tacit approval.

Many of the Advertisements were incorporated in the Canons of 1604, and thus remained part of the church's law until the canons were revised in 1969.

BIBLIOGRAPHY
Gee, H., and W.J. Hardy. *Documents Illustrative of English Church History.* 5th edition, pp. 467–475. 1910.
Gerald L. Bray

SEE ALSO
Elizabeth I; Injunctions, Royal; Parker, Matthew; Reformation, English

Agas, Ralph (c. 1540–1621)

Surveyor and mapmaker Ralph (or Radulph) Agas was born in Suffolk and worked there for more than forty years. Agas is known for a bird's-eye-view map of Oxford (drawn 1578; engraved 1588), and a famous overview of London, Westminster, and Southwark (c. 1590), of which only three later reproductions survive. Measuring six feet three inches by two feet four inches, this map of London is more detailed than those in John Norden's *Speculum Britanniae* (1593), but is similar to Georg Braun and Frans Hogenberg's map in *Civitates Orbis Terrarum* (1572 and after), with which it shared a common source from the late 1550s; thus, both its dating and its attribution have proven controversial.

The scholarly reputation of Agas as a cartographer rests instead on his work as an estate surveyor during the 1580s and 1590s. While maps drawn to scale were being made as early as the 1540s, they were primarily of fortifications drawn by military engineers; but by the 1580s there existed a market for scaled, detailed civil maps commissioned by landowners willing to pay more to supplement traditional written surveys. Agas was part of an emerging profession of estate surveyors who developed local cartography in the late Elizabethan period. In a pamphlet promoting his work, *A Preparative to Platting of Landes and Tenements for Surveigh* (1596), he claimed that accurate surveying and mapping ("platting") would prevent "an exceeding losse to the common weale, a dangerous harming of peace between Lord and his tennants, between neighbor and neighbor &c. which otherwise by such Serveighs might be kept sound and inviolate." Agas applied to surveying his knowledge of customary tenures and old titles, Latin and paleography, and he advertised the value of his work to wealthy lords (among them Lord Burghley) and to the crown in a printed circular, claiming "that more abuse in concealments, incroachments, &c. hath beene offered in these last 100 yeares than in 500 before and that many doe now refuse (as more hereafter will) to pay their rents and duties." Most highly regarded by scholars is his estate map of Toddington in Bedfordshire (1581), which shows such details as villages and individual homes, streams and bridges, hedgerows and lanes, scaled forty inches to the mile on a map measuring more than eleven by eight feet. This extraordinary map is among the best records of the landscape of Tudor towns. Ralph Agas died in 1621 in his hometown of Stoke-by-Nyland in Suffolk.

BIBLIOGRAPHY
Beresford, Maurice. *History on the Ground.* 1957.
Harvey, P.D.A. *Maps in Tudor England.* 1993.
———. "Estate Surveyors and the Spread of the Scale-map in England, 1550–80." *Landscape History,* vol. 15, pp. 37–49.
Overall, Henry James, ed. *Civitas Londinum.* Facsimile. 1874.
Tyacke, Sarah. *English Map-making, 1500–1650: Historical Essays.* 1983.
———, and John Huddy. *Christopher Saxton and Tudor Mapmaking.* 1980.
David W. Swain

SEE ALSO
Land and Landscape; Mapmaking; Norden, John; Saxton, Christopher

Agrarian Uprisings

The Tudors were ever watchful for signs of unrest among the common people, anxious that discontent

A

might not find expression in "tumults" and "mutinies." As poverty, unemployment, and vagrancy became more widespread and crime rates rose, such fears were well founded. Major popular revolts, when localized riots spread by contagion, as in the southwest in 1497, or the Pilgrimage of Grace in 1536, were rare, and there were none after Kett's Rebellion in 1549. But most years witnessed minor disturbances in the countryside. Agrarian uprisings fell into two main categories: food riots, which took the form of the staying [withholding] or seizing of food, were a normal occurrence when the harvest was bad; and enclosure riots, when hedges and fences restricting access to former common pasture land or dividing it into consolidated farms were torn down. Both elements were frequently combined in the more serious protests, though resentment at enclosures may have festered over a long period. Hostility toward tax collectors was a further source of discontent, particularly in the early Tudor period, while industrial unemployment became a factor as more of the rural poor became dependent on by-employment, or part-time work in the industry and manufacture of metal or cloth.

Nonetheless, Tudor England was not a country prone to serious popular disturbance. While fear of unrest was constant, the scale, distribution, and nature of the uprisings mitigated the danger they posed. Rioters were counted in their tens, not hundreds, and only in times of extreme hardship, as in the 1590s, was there high incidence of food and enclosure riots. Even in times of crisis agrarian uprisings tended to be localized. Protests at the scarcity and price of food were most common in counties surrounding the capital, which drew on their supplies at the expense of the local consumer, and areas adjacent to ports that exported grain. Enclosure riots were most common in the mixed farming regions in the east, the Midland plain and in the south, where the survival of open fields and high population levels created a greater potential for conflict between the encloser and the small peasant farmer. Enclosure had considerable significance in those regions, and riots in Kent, for example, in Elizabeth I's reign were endemic. What is striking, however, is the restraint and conservatism of the rioters, there and elsewhere, even in extreme circumstances.

In the Oxfordshire revolt in 1596 there were undertones of class hostility. But only ten or twenty were involved and talk of offering violence to members of the gentry was far from representative of the mood, manner, and motivation of the great majority of uprisings. Objectives were typically limited: not too much was demanded,

and the manner was restrained and deferential. Authority was defied but not rejected, while violence toward people was rarely shown. For the small number of rioters, their action was the last resort in defense of the legitimate rights that, while not necessarily enforceable in law, were nevertheless validated, or seen to be, by usage and tradition. Food riots asserted the basic right to buy essential foodstuffs at a reasonable price when local magistrates had failed to ensure that this should be done. Middlemen who manipulated the market were more normally the rioters' target than the authorities themselves, particularly if the traders were outsiders. Similarly, crowds taking the law into their own hands justified their action by appealing to custom and usage in the absence or failure of legal protection. The growing inability of the manorial courts in particular to resolve local disputes was an important factor in pushing complainants into alternative action; and the tearing down of fences and hedges, like the preventing of food from leaving the locality, was one option open to them.

The crown and the ruling elite were, in turn, not unsympathetic to those who demanded food at a "just price," or who reacted strongly to the enclosure of common land that was vital to subsistence. In the early Tudor period the government tried to fix food prices, and when failure to do so was eventually conceded, it continued to intervene frequently in the grain trade, controlling exports even in times of good harvests. Enclosures also attracted much attention. Legislation in 1488 and 1489 was the forerunner of numerous measures designed to limit enclosure and conversion to pasture, although there was a marked lack of interest shown in Elizabeth's reign before the Great Dearth prompted legislation in 1597 reasserting traditional policy. This was reversed four years later by a Parliament that represented the interests of commercialized agriculture. But for the period as a whole the landlord, like the crown, had been conscious of his obligations to his tenants, often protecting them in times of hardship by deferring rents and extending credit even to the poorer folk. Although their lot deteriorated, the rural poor were spared famine, if not dearth, and the nature of their protests was in marked contrast to the peasant revolts in neighboring countries.

BIBLIOGRAPHY

Fletcher, Anthony. *Tudor Rebellions.* 1968.
Manning, R.B. *Village Revolts: Social Protest and Popular Disturbance in England, 1509–1640.* 1988.
Wrightson, Keith. *English Society, 1580–1680.* 1982.

Brian Dietz

SEE ALSO
Enclosure; Food and Diet; Kett's Rebellion; Pilgrimage of Grace; Poor Laws; Vagrants

Agriculture

Agriculture is sometimes defined narrowly as the management of land that is plowed to grow arable crops, principally cereals; defined more broadly, it describes the management of all land, and here it is used in the second, wider sense. The Tudor period yields for the first time enough documents to reveal more clearly than ever before the farming specialities of England's varied farming regions and the fortunes of the different farming classes, including the average peasant farmer.

A sharp rise in population, starting in the early decades of the sixteenth century, greatly augmented the demand for the basic foods after a long period of stability in the fifteenth century. Rising prices now spurred farmers to respond vigorously, as profit motivated gentry to resume farming their own home farms. As a consequence, they enlarged their own acreages, and pushed to the limits their right to improve commons for their own benefit, claiming that they still left enough for their tenants' use, even though their actions plainly caused hardship. Sometimes they chose farming specialities that reduced the demand for labor (notably by turning arable land into grazing pastures for animals), and they raised the rents demanded of their tenants. Inflation justified, or at least explained, these actions; but at worst, tenants were dispossessed by the semilegal and illegal strategies of their landlords. The increasing number of unemployed inevitably pushed wages down, and both government policy and the remarks of critical observers showed deep concern for the distress of landless people and the shortage of farms to sustain peasant families. Sturdy plowmen were valued to defend the realm in time of war, and their numbers could not be allowed to fall. Yet agricultural conditions stimulated the enterprise of the better-off yeomen while it depressed the conditions of subsistence farmers and laborers.

Since a sufficient supply of grain was the first necessity to feed a rising population, and many pastures had replaced arable land following the Black Death, much grassland was plowed up again. On the best lands, mostly in the eastern half of England, cereal production was intensified, using animal dung, and urban and industrial waste like soap ashes and rags, to far better effect than ever before. Where possible, the years of fallow were reduced from one in every two years to one in three. Large areas of arable land in central England were traditionally farmed in common fields by villagers, who accepted common field regulations and grazed their animals in common after harvest and in the fallow year. This deference to the will, and the agreed rules, of a whole village community irked individualists at this time, for prices gave farmers a strong incentive to strive for higher food production. Their moves to enclose their own land, and put an end to all common grazing over it, mounted strongly in the Midland counties, and set up severe tensions in rural communities. However, in the best cases, enclosure raised the productivity of arable land, for efficient farmers could now plan their own strategies independently of their neighbors. This and other measures, like the use of grass leys, which were introduced for several years into the arable rotation to improve fertility, help to explain how an increasing population was fed. But common-field farmers also adapted their practices to accommodate improvements, and they should not always be seen as obstacles to change.

Estimating the contribution of different factors to greater agricultural production in the sixteenth century is a tempting exercise, but it relies on much guesswork. The more intensive methods that were used have to be set alongside an increasing acreage under the plow, and neither of these can be precisely measured. Nor should the role of livestock and many new crops be ignored. Famine was not brought to an end in Tudor England, but a long period without serious food shortages lasted between the mid-1560s and early 1580s, and by the middle of the next century the results showed clearly, when grain became so plentiful that prices fell and continued low for another hundred years.

Keeping the land in good health from one generation to the next was a fundamental article of faith among Tudor countrymen, and its fertility depended on keeping livestock. A mixed farming system was therefore universal, but the balance between arable and pasture varied greatly between regions. On the western side of the country, climate, altitude, and rainfall generally encouraged pasture farming, although farmers always tried to grow enough cereals to feed their households. In the poorer climatic and soil conditions of northern England, oats were the main crop for bread and oatcakes. Elsewhere, barley was the staple grain, furnishing the ordinary man's bread and drink, and even feeding livestock in places like Leicestershire, where the lack of river transport made grain markets inaccessible. The most profitable cereal was wheat, grown best in eastern England, and wheaten bread was increasingly eaten by the prosperous in towns.

In the most specialized pastoral areas, the breeding and feeding of cattle and sheep were the prime interest, and more meat eating and a growing demand for wool by the cloth industry stimulated this branch of farming. Stories about the slaughter of nearly all cattle and sheep at Michaelmas are a myth, for breeding animals could be overwintered successfully. Butchers received in autumn only those that had been led by drovers in season from the west and north to the south and east for final fattening. Horse breeding was another expanding activity, especially in the west and north, for increasing numbers were needed for war in Henry VIII's reign, and in Elizabeth I's reign for riding, for coaches, and for racing by the gentry. Packhorses and workhorses became essential with the growth of industries and commerce. A more vigorous market in dairy produce began to develop in certain regions, such as Cheshire and North Shropshire, though the most noticeable expansion of this activity was delayed until the seventeenth century.

During the Tudor period the stimulus to farm enriched many gentry, as well as merchants who then bought landed estates and farmed energetically. Their personal interest in farming developed under continental influence, and agrarian experiments began that would in the next century considerably diversify agriculture. Industrial crops like rapeseed, woad, saffron, hemp, and flax were grown, either for the first time or more intensively than before, while the well-to-do tasted new and better fruits and vegetables made possible by new horticultural methods. In the 1520s, making use of Flemish, Dutch, and French expertise, ale brewers introduced hops to flavor and preserve beer, thereby creating a new cash crop in the southeast. Henry VIII also established a cherry orchard in Kent, and rapeseed made an appearance on trial in the 1560s near King's Lynn in Norfolk.

Implements of husbandry underwent little change. Different parts of the country already had their own favored designs of plows, hand tools, and carts; but some refinements in shape were doubtless adopted by Englishmen who had working contact with religious refugees from Flanders, Holland, and France who settled as farmers. In place of two-wheeled carts, four-wheeled vehicles became more common on the farm toward the end of the sixteenth century.

Improvements in livestock breeds and management, as opposed to a simple increase in their numbers, are difficult to identify. The country already had many different breeds of sheep and cattle, exploited regionally according to local terrain and local farming systems. Almost certainly milk cows and ewes were imported from Europe to diversify the existing stock, but such efforts by individuals are rarely documented. Riding horses, on the other hand, were regularly imported by the king, nobility, and gentry from Flanders, Spain, France, Italy, and the Arab world. Draft horses from Flanders were deemed urgent in Henry VIII's reign, when English breeds were found too weak to draw heavy loads of army provisions in wartime. Meanwhile, a steady flow of cattle and sheep arrived in England from Scotland and Wales.

The spread of information on alternative farming systems available in 1500 relied on travel, which gentlemen, but not peasants, could afford; on gossip in inns and alehouses; and on observing one's neighbors. Methods greatly improved by 1600 because gentlemen began to write books of husbandry, beginning with Fitzherbert in 1523, on farming in his native Derbyshire. Thomas Tusser wrote on eastern England, ensuring that his words fixed themselves in men's memories by using rhymed verse, and Reynolde Scot wrote an illustrated book on how to grow hops. Others with experience abroad described livestock management, while Gervase Markham wrote books on general farming in southern England. He published an anonymous work about making more arable land on the Wealden clays of the Medway valley in Kent, vividly illustrating the careful observation and many experiments needed to make more plowland.

One notable innovation at the end of the century improved the supply of early spring grass by floating water meadows, first practiced and publicized in the Golden valley in Herefordshire by Rowland Vaughan, but practiced thereafter in Wiltshire, Hampshire, and further east. River water enriched with silt was allowed to flow over the grassland in winter, keeping the soil warm through months of frost and ice, and then was drained off in spring to permit the growth of a lush crop of early grass. This fed lambs and calves that sold—for high prices—before most cattle were ready.

With the same zest for improving land and growing arable crops, fenland drainage began to be discussed around 1560, motivated by Italian and Dutch examples. It made no real headway until after 1600, when it stirred up long disputes because it damaged existing pasture land, which had relied on luxuriant grass for livestock in the summer. But it exemplified the general desire to grow more grain wherever possible. Reclaiming marshland from the sea met fewer objections, and made large differences to the total land resources of coastal parishes. At first, salt marsh was used for sheep grazing until the salt had drained away, when the land grew good arable crops. Yet even here disputes began on whether such gains belonged legally to the local inhabitants or the crown. Forests also underwent piecemeal clearances to provide fuel for iron founding, glassmaking, and for firing small manufacturing furnaces. Since woodlands were not usually replanted, grassland was opened up that might later serve as arable land.

The optimistic, expansive, and more commercial mood of Tudor farming enterprise is clearly reflected in the varied directions of change. These involved enclosure of land, more specialization between farming regions, and more attention to the profit and loss of different farming practices. With respect to particular crops and animals, cautious historians are reluctant to estimate the resulting increase of productivity in any precise figures, since the measurements never exactly compare like with like. But all agree on the general observations that farmers managed to feed a much larger population in 1600 than in 1500; that variety was introduced into the diets of the well-to-do that would spread to more people in the next century; and that the attention given to industrial crops created much new work and decreased reliance on costly imports.

BIBLIOGRAPHY

Campbell, Bruce M., and Mark Overton. "A New Perspective on Medieval and Early Modern Agriculture: Six Centuries of Norfolk Farming, c. 1250–c. 1850." *Past and Present*, vol. 141. 1993.

Kerridge, E. *The Agricultural Revolution.* 1967.

Thirsk, Joan, ed. *The Agrarian History of England and Wales, IV, 1500–1640.* 1967.

———. *England's Agricultural Regions and Agrarian History, 1500–1750.* 1987.

Joan Thirsk

SEE ALSO

Cloth Industry; Enclosure; Food and Diet; Horses and Horsemanship; Industry and Manufacture; Immigration; Population and Demography; Tusser, Thomas

Air

Coming into use in England and France during the sixteenth century, the term "air" or "ayre" is loosely synonymous with "song" or "tune." Its usage became so prevalent

in Tudor England that by 1597, Thomas Morley, in his *A Plaine and Easie Introduction to Practicall Musicke,* used it for nearly every secular vocal form, save the madrigal, which was considered the most serious of musical compositions.

The term acquires a more precise meaning as it becomes connected with the emerging English lute-song tradition that flourished in courtly society from the late sixteenth through the mid-seventeenth centuries. Of exquisite refinement and beauty, it came into vogue with *First Booke of Songes or Ayres* (1597), by John Dowland, a collection of some twenty songs set principally for solo voice accompanied by lute. The success of this songbook encouraged many composers, most notably Thomas Campion, John Danyel, Alfonso Ferrabosco (the second), Robert Jones, Francis Pilkington, and Philip Rosseter, to compose and publish similar editions. The last significant collection, *Songs of 3.4.5. & 6. parts* by Thomas Tomkins, was published in 1622.

As with Dowland's first book of lute songs, composers published their ayres with supplemental musical parts—usually an optional part for bass viol and additional vocal parts—typically allowing for a performance of the piece either as a solo song with instrumental accompaniment or as a part-song for several voices and/or instruments. In addition to the flexibility in performance, the genre of English lute ayres also spans a remarkable stylistic variety of songs ranging from flowing contrapuntal works to short harmonic settings of simple tunes.

Some of the finest examples of the extended contrapuntal ayre are found in John Dowland's *A Pilgrimes Solace* (1612), in which a continuous polyphonic accompanimental texture supports an expressive vocal line whose dramatic effect is heightened by splashes of chromaticism. The other extreme is found in the songs of Thomas Campion, whose concern for the intelligibility of a song's poetic text led him to compose short, simple, and homophonic "light" ayres.

Still further, one finds the dance ayre, i.e., a song composed in the form and style of a courtly dance. *Flow my teares,* a vocal pavan composed by John Dowland, who specialized in this type of song, is perhaps the most famous of dance ayres; its popularity is confirmed by the many instrumental versions of it that have survived with the title *Lachrimae,* which give rise to the notion that it first took form as an instrumental piece and only later was set with its poetic text.

The term "ayre" was also used to describe the aesthetic quality of a musical work rather than the work itself. In this usage, the term refers to an "inherent correctness" brought

A

forth when the work's fundamental components—principally melody and harmony—amplify and heighten the effect of the whole. In this sense it is clearly related to the more general, nonmusical, meaning of this word, which refers to the overall outward appearance of an object.

BIBLIOGRAPHY

Doughtie, Edward. *Lyrics from English Airs, 1596–1632.* 1970.

Pattison, Bruce. *Music and Poetry of the English Renaissance.* 2nd edition. 1962.

Spink, Ian. *English Song: Dowland to Purcell.* 1974.

Warlock, Peter. *The English Air.* 1926.

————, and Philip Wilson, eds. *English Ayres, Elizabethan and Jacobean.* 6 vols. 1927–1931.

Joseph C. Morin

SEE ALSO

Campion, Thomas; Dowland, John; Morley, Thomas; Song

Alabaster, William (1568–1640)

A poet and clergyman, William Alabaster was educated at Westminster School and at Cambridge, where he studied between 1584 and 1592. He converted to Catholicism in his late twenties, subsequently spending several years in continental Europe before returning permanently to England and the Anglican Church after 1610. He wrote in Latin, Greek, Hebrew, and English in a variety of genres and styles, but before 1603 he appears not to have published any of his works, which circulated in manuscript. His Latin epic in praise of Queen Elizabeth I, *Elisaeis,* written while at Cambridge, was commended by Spenser in *Colin Clout's Come Home Again* (ll. 400–15); also at Cambridge, Alabaster wrote a Latin tragedy, *Roxana,* which survives in several manuscripts and two published versions, both from 1632. In 1597, he wrote a prose tract giving his "Seven Motives" for conversion to the Roman Church; it appears to have remained in manuscript and is not extant, but it elicited two published replies in 1598 (John Racster), and 1599 (Roger Fenton). Alabaster's sonnets in English, on religious themes, also date from this period; surviving in a variety of manuscript anthologies, they were first published in a modern edition in 1959.

BIBLIOGRAPHY

Binns, J.W. *Seneca and Neo-Latin Tragedy in England.* 1974.

Caro, Robert Vincent. "Rhetoric and Meditation in the Sonnets of William Alabaster." Dissertation, University of Michigan, Ann Arbor. 1977.

Coldewey, John C. *William Alabaster's* Roxana: *Some Textual Considerations.* Medieval and Renaissance Texts and Studies. 1985.

O'Connell, Michael. "*The Elisaeis* of William Alabaster." *Studies in Philology,* vol. 76, no. 5.

Story, G.M., and Helen Gardner. *The Sonnets of William Alabaster.* 1959.

John Astington

SEE ALSO

Neo-Latin Literature; Spenser, Edmund; Verse Anthologies

Alchemy

Alchemy is the pursuit of a substance that is sometimes called gold, sometimes the philosophers' stone, and sometimes the elixir of life. This substance is produced by combining certain minerals and subjecting them to a series of procedures. Which minerals are used and how they are combined is a secret that is conveyed from master to pupil orally, and in texts encoded with tropes and symbols. In general, some combination of mercury, lead, sulfur, and salt was subjected to complex processes of heating and cooling, and was transformed in stages into silver and gold. This process might take hours, weeks, or years.

There was a strong tradition of the alchemical pursuit of the elixir of life in medieval England. This had lapsed in the fifteenth century, and the few who practiced alchemy did so in pursuit of riches. This changed in the second half of the sixteenth century. Alchemy was revived and transformed following the ideas of Paracelsus. A Swiss-German physician who opposed established medicine, Paracelsus advocated the merits of traditional, or folk, medicine, stressed the analogy between the microcosm (the body) and the macrocosm (the universe), and challenged the humoral model of the body with the principle that all things were composed of salt, sulfur, and mercury. Following Paracelsus, alchemists increasingly defined their pursuits as spiritual: the creation of the philosophers' stone was analogous to the creation of the world, the knowledge of which was imparted through divine revelation. At the same time, alchemical theories of disease and chemical therapies were becoming increasingly popular.

The interest in alchemy in the 1570s is marked by the publication of a few books and pamphlets on distillation with alchemical and Paracelsian components. The earliest of these was Francis Coxe's *Treatise of the Making and Use of Diverse Oils, Unguents, Emplasters, and Distilled Waters* (1575). The same year John Hester compiled *The True and Perfect Order to Distill Oils out of all manner of Spices, Seeds, Roots and Gums.* Hester was to publish numerous alchemical texts, including the *Key to Philosophy* (1580), which has a section attributed to Paracelsus. The first true text by Paracelsus printed in English was *Joyful News out of Helvetia* (1579). Like Hester, Thomas Hill was also involved in the publication of alchemical texts.

With a couple of exceptions, the printed alchemical treatises were largely compendia of alchemical recipes, occasionally with an introduction of the principles of alchemy. More rigorous alchemical and Paracelsian ideas were found in the numerous printed Latin books that were imported from the Continent, as well as in hundreds of manuscripts, in Latin and in English, which were in circulation. These texts were transcribed by those ranging from Edward Barlow, a London apothecary, to John Dee. Dee set up an alchemical laboratory at his house at Mortlake, where he, like the group of alchemists who were patronized by Mary Herbert, countess of Pembroke, conducted alchemical experiments.

An Alchemist and his Apparatus. From Conrad Gesner, *The Practise of . . . Phisicke* (1599). Reproduced from the original by permission of the Henry E. Huntington Library and Art Gallery.

At the same time Dee was engaging in experimental and textual pursuits of the secrets of the alchemists, he outlined projects for utilizing scientific innovations for chemical substances. Under Elizabeth I, initiatives were taken to support innovations in the methods for exploiting England's mineral resources, and in 1568, those undertaking these projects were incorporated into the Society for Mineral and Battery Works. The same year those pursuing chemical innovations were incorporated into the Commonalty for the Mines Royal. Various projects, many of which succeeded, and which ranged from improved techniques for mining base metals to the production of saltpeter, were begun in the 1570s, relying on the expertise of continental practitioners.

Many medical practitioners incorporated chemical remedies, such as the use of mercury to treat syphilis, within the traditional Galenic principles of medicine. The London College of Physicians officially objected to chemical remedies, made clear in their dispute with Francis Anthony over his *aurum potable* in the early years of the seventeenth century. Although the college as an institution deprecated alchemical medicine, individual members, such as Thomas Moffett, patronized by Mary Herbert, actively supported alchemical endeavors. Despite the college, chemical remedies were widely available, and Paracelsian recipes were incorporated into general, vernacular medical works. Chemical theories of disease, as articulated by Paracelsus and his followers, were expounded by several English physicians. In 1585, Robert Bostocke published *The Difference Between the Ancient Physic and the Latter Physic.* This treatise argues that Galenism had become corrupt and that Paracelsus had rediscovered the tenets of the ancient and true medicine that had been practiced by Adam after the Fall.

By the end of the sixteenth century, alchemy was established as a subject with which anyone interested in medicine or hermetic philosophy would have to reckon.

BIBLIOGRAPHY

Debus, Allen. *The English Paracelsians.* 1965.

Webster, Charles. "Alchemical and Paracelsian Medicine." In *Health, Medicine and Mortality in the Sixteenth Century.* Charles Webster, ed. 1979.

Schuler, Robert M., ed. *Alchemical Poetry, 1575–1700: from previously unpublished manuscripts.* 1995.

Lauren Kassell

SEE ALSO

Dee, John; Herbert, Mary; Medicine and Health; Moffett, Thomas

A

Alehouses
See Inns, Taverns, and Alehouses

Alençon and Anjou, Duke of (1555–1584)

The youngest son of Henri II and Catherine de Medici, Hercule-François de Valois was created duke of Alençon in 1566. As heir to his brother, Henri III, and leader of the *politiques,* he came to play a prominent role in French politics in the mid-1570s. In 1576, he mediated the settlement of the Fifth War of Religion, for which he was created duke of Anjou, a title previously held by Henri III. The Dutch rebels were impressed by his apparent ability to transcend the religious divide, and he became a candidate for the governorship of the Netherlands. In 1578, his negotiations with the Dutch revived proposals of marriage to Elizabeth I, which had been initiated by his mother in 1572. The marriage offered a means of uniting England and France behind the rebels, but it encountered the old objections to a foreign Catholic consort, reinforced by doubts about Anjou's motives and concerns whether Elizabeth ought to marry at forty-five.

In October 1578, Anjou sent his *valet de chambre,* Jehan de Simier, to sound English opinion. Simier was persuaded by a group of English Catholics that Robert Dudley, earl of Leicester, led the opposition to the marriage and attempted to overthrow him. When Anjou himself visited England in August 1579, he triggered a wave of public opposition, epitomized by John Stubbs's tract *The Gaping Gulf.* He made major efforts to repair the damage, for his acceptance of the lordship of the Netherlands in September 1580 made English support vital. A marriage treaty was negotiated in May 1581, but it was contingent on Henri III subsidizing him, which the king refused to do. In a final attempt to win over Elizabeth, Anjou paid a second visit in November 1581, but she agreed only to provide moral support for his *Joyeuse Entré* in February 1582. Quickly frustrated in the Netherlands, Anjou attempted a coup d'etat in January 1583 ("the French fury"). After its failure he retired to France, where he died of tuberculosis in June 1584.

If transitory, Anjou's significance lay in the possibility that he might create an Anglo-French alliance in support of the Dutch. Although there are still questions about the extent of Elizabeth's encouragement and the possible orchestration of the English opposition, his schemes ultimately foundered on suspicions about his ambitions and his failure to win over his brother. The "Anjou Match" did have the unexpected consequence of initiating the cult of the Virgin Queen, which was created essentially to dissuade Elizabeth from marriage.

BIBLIOGRAPHY

Berry, Lloyd E., ed. *John Stubbs's Gaping Gulf.* 1968.

Bossy, John. "English Catholics and the French Marriage." *Recusant History,* vol. 5. 1959.

Doran, Susan. *Monarchy and Matrimony: The Courtships of Elizabeth I.* 1996.

Holt, Mack P. *The Duke of Anjou and the Politique Struggle during the Wars of Religion.* 1986.

MacCaffrey, Wallace T. "The Anjou Match and the Making of Elizabethan Foreign Policy." In *The English Commonwealth, 1547–1640.* Peter Clark, et al., eds. 1979.

Yates, Frances A. *The Valois Tapestries.* 1959.

Simon Adams

SEE ALSO

Elizabeth I; Dudley, Robert; Foreign Relations and Diplomacy; Stubbs, John

Alesius, Alexander (1500–1565)

Scottish Protestant divine born in Edinburgh on April 23, 1500. Alexander Alesius studied at St. Andrews, where he became a canon. He was converted to Protestantism by Patrick Hamilton's persuasive defense of Lutheran teachings and his heroic death at the stake in 1528. Shortly thereafter, Alesius was imprisoned for delivering a Latin oration condemning clerical incontinence. He fled to Germany in 1532, and the following year met Martin Luther and Philipp Melanchthon in Wittenberg and signed the Augsburg Confession. While there, he wrote a treatise against a decree of the Scottish bishops that forbade the laity to read the Bible in the vernacular. He was excommunicated in 1534 by the bishop of Ross. Arriving the following year in England, Alesius was appointed lecturer in divinity at Cambridge. Opposition to his Protestant views soon forced his departure for London, where he studied and practiced medicine. Alesius again found it prudent to leave for Germany in 1539, and in 1540, he was appointed professor of theology at Frankfurt-on-the-Oder. In 1543, he moved to Leipzig, where he held several academic offices and wrote numerous exegetical and theological works. He revisited England during the reign of Edward VI, when he made a Latin translation of the 1549 *Book of Common Prayer.* He died in Leipzig on March 17, 1565.

BIBLIOGRAPHY
Donaldson, Gordon. *The Scottish Reformation.* 1960.
Oxford Dictionary of the Christian Church, p. 32. 1958.
Lee W. Gibbs

SEE ALSO
Book of Common Prayer; Hamilton, Patrick

Aliens

Nonnatives had been a relatively minor but familiar part of the English urban landscape throughout the later Middle Ages, but the changing nature of their presence and perceptions about it in the sixteenth century created virtually new circumstances with which the crown had to deal as it sought to balance the potentially beneficial and potentially dangerous aspects of the situation. As the civil, religious, and economic upheavals in Europe escalated through the century, changes in the immigration stream into England followed suit. By the reign of Elizabeth I, the volume of immigration had increased dramatically, alien occupational and residential settlement patterns had changed, and a dichotomy had developed in native perceptions about the aliens' presence.

The steady trickle of continental immigration into England grew into a virtual flood in the Tudor era, beginning after the break with Rome in the 1530s and peaking in the 1560s and 1570s, as indicated by a number of surveys of aliens conducted by the central government after mid-century. The foreign population in London essentially doubled in the period, and unlike the case in earlier centuries, the overwhelming majority were permanent rather than transitory or semipermanent residents. Also, the immigrants of the later Tudor period were predominantly of Dutch or Flemish origin, whereas earlier populations had been mostly Italian or German. Many of these changes can be attributed to the fact that while most earlier aliens had been merchants and those associated with them, the disturbances of the sixteenth century made refugees of thousands of skilled and unskilled workers, many of whom sought refuge in England for reasons of conscience, economic opportunity, and geographic proximity. As the new arrivals crowded first into the capital and then dispersed— whether on their own initiative or by crown directive— to the towns of the southeast, they tended to settle in ever-greater concentrations where other aliens had settled before them. These areas were usually liberties or poor wards, chosen because of certain legal protections in the case of the former, and in that of the latter, because many of the immigrants were refugees who had left home with few or no portable resources other than their own skills.

The rising numbers of aliens and their increasing concentration in limited areas of London and other towns, such as Norwich and Colchester, brought to the surface in some natives open hostility against them, while others supported and defended the concept of asylum for confessional brethren. An argument can be made for a strain of xenophobia permeating English attitudes toward the foreigners, as illustrated in a number of outbursts of greater or lesser magnitude against them over the course of the period and in examples of the portrayal of aliens in contemporary literature. This argument is given added support by evidence that many natives continued to view both immigrants of many years' residence and English-born children of immigrants as aliens. Xenophobia was mitigated by evidence that many aliens assimilated over time, particularly in the second and third generations. The principal issue, however, in this split in perceptions was one of economic consideration. Native workers felt threatened by the new resident aliens whom they viewed as economic competitors, and resented the privileges and protections granted to them by the crown. Elizabeth I and her councilors viewed the immigrants as bringing badly needed new skills and technologies into the English economy, and instituted privileges and protections to encourage economic development through the opportunity provided by the aliens' fortuitous arrival.

BIBLIOGRAPHY
Greengrass, Mark. "Protestant exiles and their assimilation into early modern England." *Immigrants and Minorities,* vol. 4, no. 3, pp. 68–81.
Grell, Ole Peter. *Calvinist Exiles in Tudor and Stuart England.* 1996.
Gwynn, Robin. *The Huguenot Heritage: the History and Contributions of Huguenots in Britain.* 1985.
Yungblut, Laura Hunt. *Strangers Settled Here Amongst Us: Policies, Perceptions and the Presence of Aliens in Elizabethan England.* 1996.
Laura Hunt Yungblut

SEE ALSO
Immigration; Jews; London; Population and Demography

A

Allen, William (1532–1594)

William Cardinal Allen, humanist, theologian, and polemicist, was the founder of the Catholic English College at Douai, and the spiritual and political leader of the exiled English Catholic community and of the Catholic mission to Elizabethan England. Born in Rossall, Lancashire, into a minor gentry family, Allen entered Oriel College, Oxford, in 1547. Three years later, he earned the B.A. and election as fellow, and, the following years, the M.A. His talent for rhetoric and logic were honed by his mentor, Morgan Philipps, who later joined him in the founding of Douai.

Allen had a promising career ahead of him in the restored Catholic Church of Mary I. He was appointed principal of St. Mary's Hall, Oxford, in 1556, and, the following year, a proctor of the university. In 1558, he was made a canon of York, even though he had not been ordained to holy orders. Allen was one of more than a hundred Oxbridge dons who emigrated to the University of Louvain following the enactment of the Elizabethan Settlement. In 1561–1562, he earned his living tutoring Christopher Blount, who later was executed for his part in the earl of Essex's rebellion of 1600. Illness forced Allen to return in 1562 to his native Lancashire, where he recovered his health. With his firm belief that there could be no salvation outside the Catholic Church, he set himself to preaching against the occasional conformity practiced by some Catholics in England, and his abilities as a preacher won back many lapsed Catholics. While in the household of the duke of Norfolk, he wrote his *Certain Brief Reasons Concerning Catholic Faith,* which was published at Douai in 1564.

Notoriety forced him into exile again in 1565. Two years later, Allen, now ordained a priest, traveled to Rome with Phillips and with Jean Vendeville, a law professor from the university at Douai, where they won the approval of Pope Pius V for the founding of an English college at Douai. At first, Allen may have conceived the college as purely academic. In any event, he and Vendeville soon came to envision it as a training ground for missionaries to England. Despite financial difficulties, the college became a success. It ordained its first priest in 1573, and sent its first missionaries into England the following year. The college relocated to Rheims in 1578, after it was expelled by the Calvinists who had come to power in Douai, but it returned in 1593.

Allen received authority to license English priests: his strategy for the mission was to educate them well and have them focus on the gentry. Allen completed his own formal studies in theology, earning the B.D. in 1569 and the D.D. in 1571. In 1575–1576, he helped with the conversion of the English hospice in Rome into a second English college. He visited Rome again in 1579 to involve the Jesuits directly in the English mission, and he approved of their supervision of the English College in Rome. Illness forced Allen to resign as president of the college at Rheims in 1585. After recovering his health at Spa, he settled permanently in Rome. In 1587, Philip II of Spain and the Jesuit Robert Parsons urged Pope Sixtus V to create Allen a cardinal, hoping that he might preside over a restored Catholic Church in England should the Armada succeed. These hopes, however, sank with King Philip's fleet, and in 1589, Allen had to content himself with the post of apostolic librarian.

Although Allen instructed his missionary priests to concern themselves with the spiritual needs of English Catholics and to avoid involving themselves with Protestants and with English politics, he believed that intervention by the Catholic powers was necessary if the Catholic faith in England were to be preserved and restored. He thus supported the schemes of the Guise to replace Elizabeth, first with Mary Queen of Scots, and then with her son, James VI. After James formally embraced Protestantism, Allen turned to Philip II as the champion of English Catholics, and he became associated with Parsons's pro-Spanish activities. Elizabeth and her ministers regarded the English missionaries as traitors. Allen, in his *Defence of the English Catholics* (1584), denied that the missionaries were seeking the overthrow of the queen; yet in his *Defence of Sir William Stanley's Surrender of Deventer* (1587), and in his *Admonition to the Nobility and People of England and Ireland* (1588), he defended the pope's authority to depose princes and denied that Elizabeth exercised legitimate rule of England, thus confirming in the minds of the queen's ministers their view of the missionaries' treasonable intentions. Allen, who had grown out of touch with the English Catholics, was mistaken in his belief that they would rise in support of King Philip.

Apart from his ten theological and polemical writings, Allen helped revise the Vulgate, texts of the works of St. Augustine of Hippo, and Gregory Martin's English translation of the Bible, which came to be known as the Douai-Rheims Bible. Allen lived to see publication of the New Testament in 1582; the Old Testament appeared in 1609, fifteen years after his death on October 16, 1594.

BIBLIOGRAPHY

Bossy, John. *English Catholic Community, 1570–1850.* 1975.

Camm, Bede. *William Cardinal Allen*. 1914.

Clancy, Thomas J. *Papist Pamphleteers: The Allen-Persons Party and the Political Thought of the Counter-Reformation in England, 1572–1615*. 1964.

Duffy, Eamon. "William Cardinal Allen, 1532–1594," *Recusant History*, vol. 22, pp. 265–290.

Hicks, Leo. "Cardinal Allen and the Society." *The Month*, no. 160 (1932), pp. 342–353, 434–443; 428–436.

———. "Allen and Deventer." *The Month*, no. 163 (1934), pp. 507–517.

———. "Cardinal Allen's Admonition." *The Month*, no. 186 (1949), pp. 30–39.

Haile, Martin. *An Elizabethan Cardinal: William Allen*. 1914.

Holmes, Peter. *Resistance and Compromise: The Political Thought of English Catholics*. 1982.

Knox, Thomas F. *The First and Second Diaries of the English College, Douay*. 1878.

———. *Letters and Memorials of William Allen*. 1882.

Mattingly, Garrett. "William Allen and Catholic Propaganda in England." *Travaux d' Humanisme et Renaissance*, vol. 27, pp. 325–339.

McGrath, Patrick. *Papists and Puritans under Elizabeth I*. 1967.

Meyer, Arnold O. *England and the Catholic Church under Queen Elizabeth*. J.R. Mckee, Trans. 1915.

Pollen, John H. *The English Catholics in the Reign of Queen Elizabeth*. 1920.

Prichard, Arnold. *Catholic Loyalism in Elizabethan England*. 1979.

Renold, P. *Letters of William Allen and Richard Barret, 1572–1598*. Catholic Record Society, vol. 58.

John M. Currin

SEE ALSO

English College of Rome; Jesuits; Mary I; Parsons, Robert; Reformation, English

Alleyn, Edward (1566–1626)

Actor, entrepreneur, benefactor, founder of Dulwich College, Alleyn was the son of Edward Alleyn, Sr., innholder of St. Botolph's Bishopsgate and gentleman porter to Queen Elizabeth I. When Alleyn was four his father died, bequeathing to his wife and sons a fair amount of property and a coat of arms that Edward later traced back as far as his grandfather. Alleyn's older brother, John, was servant to Lord Sheffield. By 1586, Edward was listed as a player to the earl of Worcester, and two years later, Edward and John were joint owners of playbooks and other theatrical properties. In 1592, Alleyn was acknowledged as one of the greatest English players, having established this reputation, in large measure, by performing the lead roles in Christopher Marlowe's plays, including Tamburlaine the Great, Doctor Faustus, and perhaps Barabas in *The Jew of Malta*. Alleyn was distinguished for his powerful voice and a unique, charismatic style, described by one contemporary as "strutting and bellowing."

In 1592, Alleyn married the stepdaughter of Philip Henslowe, owner of the Rose playhouse. He continued to perform on stage with his company (the Lord Admiral's Men) throughout the next five years, during which time he also served as manager of the company and liaison between the players and Henslowe. Alleyn returned to playing during the autumn of 1600 to launch the opening of the Fortune playhouse—which he built earlier that year in partnership with Henslowe. However, before long he had again "retired" to the duties of theater ownership and property management, returning occasionally to playing for special performances. Most notably, Alleyn appeared as the Genius of the City in the magnificent entertainment presented to King James I on his triumphant passage through London (March, 1604); and he was described concurrently as one of the players to James's son, Prince Henry, even though he seems never to have acted regularly during this period.

Alleyn's investments included the Bear Garden, in which he had an interest as early as 1594; and in 1604, he and Henslowe received a patent as masters of the royal game of bears, bulls, and mastiff dogs. Alleyn shared other investments with Henslowe as well, including the conversion of the Bear Garden into the Hope (a playhouse/baiting arena) in 1613; and on Henslowe's death, Alleyn took over his father-in-law's investments. By 1606, Alleyn had purchased much of the manor of Dulwich at great cost, and in 1613, he had moved there permanently. Having no children, he built a joint school and pensioners' home that he named the college of God's Gift at Dulwich. The formal foundation ceremony occurred in the college chapel in September, 1619, attended by Francis Bacon and the archbishop of Canterbury, among others.

Alleyn's wife, Joan, died in June, 1623. Six months later he married Constance, daughter of the poet John Donne, then dean of St. Paul's Cathedral. By this time, Alleyn was unquestionably the most socially prominent actor-entrepreneur of his age, with contacts including many leaders of the church and government, among them Bacon, Sir Julius Caesar (master of the rolls), Lancelot

A

Andrewes (dean of Winchester), and the earl of Arundel. In his later years Alleyn seems to have coveted a knighthood, an aspiration that never came to pass. He died at Dulwich in November, 1626, almost two months after his sixtieth birthday, and was buried in the college chapel. Although he had no issue, he did manage to amass a small fortune. Alleyn's foundation, continuing today as Dulwich College, was endowed by real estate in London and the freehold of the Fortune playhouse. His nephew served as executor and first warden of the college. Most of his contemporaries remembered him as the master of the bears, and as a social benefactor and literary patron of writers such as Thomas Dekker and John Taylor, the writer-poet.

BIBLIOGRAPHY

Cerasano, S.P. "Competition for the King's Men?: Alleyn's Blackfriars Venture." *Medieval & Renaissance Drama in England,* vol. 4, pp. 173–186.

———. "Edward Alleyn's Early Years: His Life and Family." *Notes and Queries,* vol. 34, no. 2, pp. 237–243.

———. "Tamburlaine and Edward Alleyn's Ring." *Shakespeare Survey,* vol. 47, pp. 171–179.

———. "The Master of the Bears in Art and Enterprise." *Medieval & Renaissance Drama in England,* vol. 5, pp. 195–209.

S.P. Cerasano

SEE ALSO

Actors; Henslowe, Philip; Marlowe, Christopher; Theaters

America
See Colonial Development; Discovery and Exploration

Anabaptists

"Anabaptist" is derived from the Greek word meaning "rebaptizer." While Anabaptists never used the term themselves, their rejection of infant baptism was one distinguishing feature of their theology. They believed that baptism applied only to believers who first made a profession of personal faith; the rite signified the external witness of an inner covenant of faith with God through Christ. Other fundamental beliefs generally included a commitment to pacifism, separation of church and state, nonparticipation in government, refusal to swear oaths, holding a community of goods, and espousing free will

against original sin. In addition, Melchiorite Anabaptists embraced a millenarian eschatology and a "celestial flesh" Christology in which Jesus did not share the human flesh of Mary.

Although evidence of Anabaptism in Tudor England exists, its extent is difficult to assess. Efforts are hampered by the problem of defining normative Anabaptism with any precision given the polygenetic origins of the movement, the plurality of influences at work in its formation, and the confessional diversity of various Anabaptist sects across Europe. In England what was often labeled "Anabaptist" by the authorities could as credibly be attributed to Lollardy, which continued to flourish in the sixteenth-century religious underworld. There is no evidence, for example, that any of the accused English "Anabaptists" in Tudor England had undergone a second baptism. The problem of identifying Anabaptism is exacerbated by the tendency of contemporaries to apply the term indiscriminately and pejoratively to nonconformity of any kind, producing a fear of dissent among propertied classes.

While precise information is lacking, there are indications of something like Anabaptist activity among native English radicals, as well as Dutch and Flemish immigrants, under Henry VIII. For example, three English subjects were arrested in London in 1532, along with one Scotsman, for smuggling and distributing Anabaptist literature, and for holding "strange opinions" concerning the humanity of Christ, a likely reference to Melchiorite Christology. Following the defeat of militant Anabaptism at Münster in 1535, persecution drove some Dutch Anabaptists to seek refuge in England, where they encountered severe treatment: between 1535 and 1540 some twenty Dutch Anabaptists and one English citizen were executed.

Alarmed by reports that Dutch Anabaptists were making converts in England, the Privy Council had several suspected English Anabaptists arrested in 1549. Among them was the well-known Joan Bouchard, a woman of social standing with Lollard connections and a Melchiorite Christology, who was burned at Smithfield. In 1550, Robert Cooche engaged William Turner, dean of Wells, in a theological debate over issues of original sin and infant baptism. Crooche's heretical opinions prompted a published response from John Knox. Meanwhile, John Hooper noted a "frenzy" of Anabaptist activity in the counties of Kent and Sussex. Two years later, Archbishop Thomas Cranmer made a concerted effort to suppress Anabaptism in the same region.

The Marian persecution effectively silenced Anabaptist activity in England. Under Elizabeth, Anabaptism resurfaced. On Easter, 1575, a group of Flemish Anabaptists was arrested in London. They had successfully proselytized one Englishman, a carpenter known only as "S.B." He appears to have embraced various Anabaptist convictions, including pacifism, noncompliance with the judicial system, and refusal to swear an oath.

The impact of Anabaptism on radical religion in Tudor England is difficult to establish. There is, for example, no demonstrable evidence of direct influence on Puritan Separatism, even if several members of Francis Johnson's Separatist congregation in Amsterdam were excommunicated in the 1590s for having fallen "into the heresies of the Anabaptists." While fresh research continues to uncover the complexities of the movement, Anabaptism in Tudor England appears to have remained a highly diverse and generally insular sectarian phenomenon.

BIBLIOGRAPHY
Heriot, Duncan B. "Anabaptism in England during the 16th and 17th Century." *Transactions,* Congregational Historical Society, vol. 12 (1935), pp. 256–271.
Horst, Irvin Buckwalter. *The Radical Brethren.* 1972.
Williams, George Hunstan. *The Radical Reformation.* 1962.

Stephen Brachlow

SEE ALSO
Aliens; Cranmer, Thomas; Hooper, John; Knox, John; Marian Martyrs

Andrewes, Lancelot (1555–1626)

The life of Lancelot Andrewes extends through the reigns of four different sovereigns. Born during the reign of Mary I, within a year of Richard Hooker, Andrewes was to become one of Elizabeth's favorite chaplains, and a brilliantly successful court preacher, theologian, and divine to James I and his son, Charles. Born into a prosperous merchant family, the eldest of thirteen children, Andrewes's precocity destined him for an academic career. After leaving the Merchant Taylors' School, he matriculated at Pembroke Hall, Cambridge, at the age of sixteen, in 1571, having obtained a newly endowed Greek scholarship there. Andrewes was to remain centered at Cambridge for the next thirty-four years, his concerns being principally academic; his later years, from 1605 until his death, are concerned with ever more responsible and demanding ecclesiastical administration. He was successively bishop of Chichester (1605–1609), Ely (1609–1619), and Winchester (1619–1626); a translator of the famous "Authorized Version" of the Bible (1611); and always a much favored polemicist and preacher.

During the earlier part of his life, Andrewes collected numerous preferments and offices, which he seems to have occupied conscientiously. He held the benefice of St. Giles, Cripplegate, in London, two prebendaries, one at St. Paul's, the other at Southwark. Besides a chaplaincy to the queen, he held also the same position to Archbishop Whitgift; and in 1601, he was made dean of Westminster Abbey. Meanwhile, in 1578, he had been elected master of his college, which, through administrative skill, he was able to turn from debt to prosperity. Throughout the years of the sixteenth century, Andrewes continued his diligent study of numerous ancient and modern languages and of systematic theology. In this last discipline, he was especially remarkable for bringing patristic teaching, both of the Greek and Latin fathers, into the English church.

Most of Andrewes's sermons and controversial writings belong to the period after 1603, but there are extant a number of earlier sermons that he preached at his parish of St. Giles, Cripplegate, or else at court. In these works he displays his characteristic learning, "witty" style, and "high church" beliefs. In his "Sermon of Imaginations" of 1592, preached at St. Giles (on Acts 2:42), Andrewes carefully defines his commitment to ritual ceremonies, the episcopacy, frequent communion, and regular prayer. In another sermon, preached at Whitehall, on John 20:23, in 1600, "Of the Power of Absolution," Andrewes argues strongly for the necessity of repentance and sacramental confession. But perhaps Andrewes is best remembered now for *Preces Privatae,* or Private Prayers, gathered over many years out of many ancient sources, and organized according to seasons and times. These prayers show Andrewes's deep devotion to the fathers, from whom he gleans many phrases and ideas, which in turn he adapted into his own compositions, evidently using them regularly in his private meditations. John Henry Newman translated them in his *Tracts for the Times* (no. 88, 1840), and they have ever since remained popular.

BIBLIOGRAPHY
Andrewes, Lancelot. *Works.* 11 vols. J.P. Wilson and James Bliss, eds. Library of Anglo-Catholic Theology. 1841–1854.

A

Lossky, Nicholas. *Lancelot Andrewes The Preacher (1555–1626): The Origins of the Mystical Theology of the Church of England.* 1991.

Story, G.M., ed. *Lancelot Andrewes: Sermons.* 1967.

Welsby, Paul A. *Lancelot Andrewes 1555–1626.* 1958.

P.G. Stanwood

SEE ALSO
Bible Translations; Sermons

Anglican Church Music

The history of Anglican Church music officially begins in 1549, when the first Act of Uniformity went into effect, mandating the English language rites of the Book of Common Prayer. Experiments with vernacular worship that preceded the official change are not well documented, but an English litany was printed in 1544, and there were various English-language services sung by the Chapel Royal in 1547 and 1548. A second prayer book appeared in 1552, and in it were several significant liturgical changes, but the liturgy hereafter was subjected to only minor alterations. The first two prayer books made scant mention of music, and the same is true of the first Elizabethan prayer book (1559); musical usage seems not to have settled into traditional forms until the earlier 1600s, but the Tudor composers nonetheless established a foundation on which the later development of Anglican Church music rests.

Most of the music of the Anglican rite falls under the two broad headings of "service" and "anthem." A service is a setting of any or all of the ordinary items of the three principal observances of the Church of England: matins (or morning prayer), evensong, and Holy Communion. For matins (a conflation of the Roman matins and lauds) the ordinary items are *Venite, Te Deum,* and *Benedictus;* for evensong (combining essential parts of Roman vespers and compline), *Magnificat and Nunc dimittis;* for communion, *Kyrie, Gloria, Creed, Sanctus, Benedictus,* and *Agnus Dei.* In Tudor times, *Benedicite and Jubilate* were sometimes sung in place of *Te Deum* and *Benedictus,* respectively. Rarely does a service include all these items, and settings for just one of the three liturgical observances are fairly common. Texts from the burial service may also be included in or constitute a "service." Settings survive also of other miscellaneous liturgical texts: litanies, *preces,* various versicles, and responses; however, these were usually musically simple and seldom included in sets designated as "services." In Elizabethan times the communion service received little musical elaboration; few musical settings survive of items other than the *Kyrie* and the *Gloria,* and the *Kyrie* settings tend to be short and simple.

The term "anthem" derives from "antiphon," and anthems seem to have had a variety of uses in the sixteenth century. By circa 1600, it had come to mean a choral composition on any sacred text other than those ordinary items that constituted "services." Biblical texts, metrical psalms, and miscellaneous texts from the Book of Common Prayer account for virtually the entire body of Tudor anthems. There is no explicit liturgical provision for the performance of anthems in the earliest prayer books, but it was apparently common practice during the Elizabethan era to include an anthem at the end of a service, a practice probably deriving from the earlier tradition of the votive antiphons that followed matins and/or compline in most cathedrals and monastic and collegiate establishments.

To a considerable extent, the composers of the earliest Anglican service music simply set English texts using the same compositional approaches they had used for Latin texts. However, the Protestant concern for intelligibility of the texts used in worship was a powerful force helping to shape the course of church music in Tudor England; indeed, many in positions of influence were in sympathy with Calvinist attitudes, and opposed church music of almost any kind, or at least practices that excluded congregational participation. Thus, from the beginning of Anglican Church music there were opposed attitudes toward the use of music in the liturgy, and very early on, two distinct types of service emerged, the short service and the great service. The short service is characterized by simplicity and brevity: settings are syllabic, textures are homophonic, and there is little or no textual repetition. Such settings bear an obvious relation to simple settings of metrical psalms that were in wide circulation for home devotional use, and some of which utilize tunes borrowed from continental Protestant sources such as the Genevan Psalter. These short services were apparently the staple repertory of cathedral and chapel choirs, whereas great services seem to have been produced mainly for special occasions; at least, they seem to have been less widely circulated, and many were beyond the capabilities of most choirs. Great services were not just longer, but often employed a full range of contrapuntal techniques, as well as division into two choral bodies, the *decani* and *cantoris* (literally, the sides "of the deacon" and "of the cantor," or right and left, respectively, when one faces the altar). By the end of the sixteenth century, "verse" technique, developed in anthems, also comes to be used in services: passages for one or more solo voices, accompanied by organ or consort of viols, alternate with passages for the full choir. Verse services enjoyed widespread use, probably, at least in part, because the reliance on soloists reduced the musical burden on the choir, and so settings of considerable elaboration could be performed without the choir being overtaxed.

The earliest surviving important source of Anglican Church music is Bodleian MSS Mus.Sch.e.420–422, the Wanley Partbooks. Its provenance is not known, but it was apparently compiled c. 1550–1552 for a choir of modest size with no treble voices (that is, no boys); the partbooks specify two countertenors and bass (the tenor book is lost). The vast majority of texts can be found in the 1549 Book of Common Prayer. Included are ten communion services, two of which are adaptations of Latin masses by John Taverner; several settings of morning and evening canticles; miscellaneous liturgical items such as sentences from the burial service and litany responses; and seventeen "antems." Most of the compositions are anonymous, but works by Tallis, Tye, Sheppard, and others have been identified. Most of the Wanley music is simple in texture and avoids melismatic text treatment, the few exceptions all seeming to be adaptations of Latin works.

The first printed music for the Anglican rite was *The Booke of Common Praier Noted* (1550), in which John Merbecke provided simple, syllabic plainchant settings, some adapted from Latin chant, some originally composed. Merbecke's settings seem to have had little use, for the appearance of the 1552 prayer book soon rendered them obsolete. A collection published by John Day in 1565, *Certaine notes set forth in fowre and three parts,* was the first published collection of Anglican polyphonic music during Elizabeth's reign, but its contents are Edwardian (several items appear also in Wanley). Day had assembled the collection and had even begun printing it in 1560, but it seems that uncertainty concerning what direction church music would take under the new queen caused him to delay publication.

Thomas Tallis stands out as the best of the first generation of Anglican composers. His English church music includes a *Short Service* that has enjoyed continuous use in the active repertoire. Also extant are isolated settings of the *Benedictus* and *Te Deum,* a litany, and about a dozen anthems. Several of Tallis's Latin motets, mostly from the *Cantiones sacrae,* were also adapted to English words.

Tallis's contemporaries include Christopher Tye, Osbert Parsley (1511–1585), Robert Parsons (c. 1530–1570), John Sheppard, Robert White (c. 1538–1574), and William Mundy (c. 1529–1591). These composers achieved a stylistic synthesis in which imitative techniques were prominent, but were not permitted to obscure the text. This style remained the norm for Anglican Church music well into the seventeenth century.

The *Short Service* by William Byrd was one of the best known of its time; stylistically, it is indebted to the *Short Service* of Tallis. His *Great Service* is one of the monuments of the late sixteenth century. Technically in five voices, it features *decani-cantori* divisions that produce passages in ten real parts, and there are also solo-full-voice contrasts specified. Byrd's English liturgical music also includes settings of *preces,* responses, and psalms, as well as a litany, and two settings of the evensong canticles, one of which makes limited use of solo voices with organ. Works that might be classified as anthems number more than sixty, but many were intended more for home devotional use than for liturgical performance, being essentially consort songs for voice and viols with brief choral sections. Of the larger anthems, *Christ rising again* was one of the first verse anthems to be printed and is remarkable for its dramatic contrasts of soloists and choir. *Sing joyfully,* a full anthem, is probably one of Byrd's last works; Byrd skillfully exploited the many word-painting opportunities afforded by its text. As with Tallis, several of Byrd's Latin motets were adapted to English words in his lifetime, though there is no evidence of Byrd's own participation in such adaptations. Especially widely circulated was *O Lord, turn thy wrath,* adapted from *Ne irascaris,* one of Byrd's finest large-scale motets.

The sacred music of Thomas Morley is little known today. There are a half-dozen anthems, a set of simple settings of sentences from the burial service (the earliest surviving such set), several psalms, two evening services, and an elaborate *Great Service.* The five-voice evening service, possibly a student work, is closely modeled on one of Byrd's services. The *Great Service* might have been compiled from movements composed at different times: the *Venite, Kyrie,* and *Creed* are for full choir; the *Te Deum* and *Benedictus* make limited use of solo verses, and the evening canticles are in elaborate verse style with imaginative contrasts of scoring.

The generation that followed William Byrd and his contemporaries were mostly active after the death of Queen Elizabeth, but their music nonetheless represents the final flowering of the Tudor style. Chief among them

A

are Byrd's pupils and younger Chapel Royal colleagues Orlando Gibbons and Thomas Tomkins, along with Thomas Weelkes in Chichester.

Gibbons ranks with Tallis and Byrd as one of the most important Anglican composers, although his surviving church music is considerably less in quantity: two services and around forty anthems constitute the principal items. The *Short Service in F* was easily the most popular work of its kind in the early seventeenth century. The other service is a verse service consisting of the two morning canticles and the two evening canticles. Of the anthems, the full anthems are generally considered to be Gibbons's finest achievements, ranging from the eight-part textures and antiphony of *O clap your hands together* to the chordal homophony of *Almighty and everlasting God.* Gibbons also made outstanding contributions to the early verse anthem repertory. *See, see, the Word is incarnate,* for example, demonstrates firm formal control over its unusually long text.

Whereas Gibbons's career was cut short by his untimely death at forty-two, Thomas Tomkins lived into his eighties, and whereas it is likely that we possess only a fraction of Gibbons's music, a large collection of the church music of Tomkins, titled *Musica Deo Sacra,* was published posthumously. Seven services and more than one hundred anthems survive, as well as "sacred madrigals" and other minor items. Less expert than either Gibbons or Byrd with the intricacies of imitation and canon, Tomkins did effectively set texts with clear dramatic or emotional content. *When David heard* manages to be both vivid and moving without resort to madrigalian chromaticism.

Thomas Weelkes is now ranked among the best madrigalists and composers of church music, but of his forty-eight known anthems, only twenty-seven survive in complete enough state to be reconstructable. Likewise, only four of the nine known services can be reconstructed. His best anthems are among the most brilliant of the period, for example, *Alleluia, I heard a voice* and *Hosanna to the Son of David.*

The tumult of the civil war was tragic for early Anglican Church music because cathedral and collegiate choir repertoires were in some cases completely destroyed in the Puritan zeal to eliminate "popish vanities." Major portions of the work of such important figures as Tallis and Weelkes are now hopelessly fragmentary, and surely much more has totally vanished. Fortunately, enough survives to allow us to see that the first generations of

Anglican composers created one of the most magnificent bodies of sacred music the Western world has seen.

BIBLIOGRAPHY

Fellowes, Edmund H. *English Cathedral Music from Edward VI to Edward VII.* 1946.

Le Huray, Peter. *Music and the Reformation in England, 1549–1600.* 1978.

Phillips, Peter. *English Sacred Music 1549–1649.* 1991.

Stevens, Denis. *Tudor Church Music.* 1966.

Charles S. Larkowski

SEE ALSO

Anthem; Anglicanism; Book of Common Prayer; Byrd, William; Merbecke, John; Morley, Thomas; Tallis, Thomas; Taverner, John; Weelkes, Thomas

Anglicanism

A term in general use since the mid-nineteenth century to describe the particular mix of doctrine, worship, and ecclesiastical polity that has characterized the Church of England and other churches in communion with it, Anglicanism has been the approved English Church since at least the time of the Reformation in the sixteenth century.

Whether it can be said that there was a genuine Anglicanism before the Reformation is a matter of controversy, and depends largely on the weight given to certain aspects of liturgical distinctiveness and juridical independence that the English Church had developed over the centuries. Post-Reformation Anglican apologists naturally stressed these as much as they could, but modern research has demonstrated that, on the whole, their claims were exaggerated. Doctrinally, there was no difference between the Churches of England and Rome, and papal authority was generally accepted in England, at least in spiritual matters.

When Henry VIII broke with the papacy in 1534, the Church of England came under his authority in all matters, both spiritual and temporal. However, although this was to be highly significant at a later stage, it made little practical difference at the time. Henry was not concerned with developing an independent theological or liturgical tradition, but only with ensuring that juridically the Church of England would no longer have to defer to Rome. Radical changes in doctrine and worship were not made until the reign of Edward VI (1547–1553), but even then it is doubtful whether the reformers were thinking in terms of establishing a distinctive type of

Christianity that could be called Anglican. Most of them were Erasmian humanists who had been influenced by Martin Luther, and their reforms paralleled what was going on in other Protestant countries at the time. Distinctive features, like the retention of the traditional hierarchy, almost certainly owed more to local circumstances than to a specific ecclesiological outlook.

Traditional Anglicanism, however, only came into being as a result of the Elizabethan Settlement (1559). At that time, the Church of England was reconstituted as a moderately Protestant body that henceforth would consciously (and not merely accidentally) retain an episcopal system of government, along with certain other aspects of pre-Reformation tradition. "Anglican" has now become the term used for those theologians and churchmen who defended this settlement, and who tried to give it theoretical justification as a *via media* between the developing extremes of post-Tridentine Catholicism and radical Protestantism. Understood in this sense, it is quite possible that "Anglicanism" was a minority movement in the Church of England for most of the period up to the collapse of the Elizabethan Settlement in 1640, although its more articulate defenders were usually backed by the crown and frequently occupied high office in the church.

There is no doubt that the views and longevity of Queen Elizabeth I played an important role in securing the 1559 settlement, and in that sense she must be numbered among the architects of classical Anglicanism. Her main aim was to secure a form of church that would be as comprehensive of the nation as possible, and it is largely because of this that comprehensiveness later became one of the main hallmarks of Anglicanism. There is great debate as to how closely the settlement conformed to her own beliefs; probably the fairest thing to say is that she found a pattern that most people in England could accept, and adjusted her own preferences accordingly. This could be why she clung so tenaciously to the settlement to the end of her life, and why she found it so difficult to sympathize with those who were unable to make similar adjustments to their consciences for the sake of the common good.

Under Elizabeth I, this type of Anglicanism was expounded and defended by Bishop John Jewel, whose 1562 *Apology* for the Church of England remains a classic statement of Anglican theology. Jewel sought to defend the church against the charge of schism by going back to the early centuries of Christianity, when Rome did not occupy a dominant position, even in the West. He tried to show that at the Reformation, the Church of England recovered independence, and thus recovered ancient rights and privileges that had been lost to the papacy during the Middle Ages. In terms of doctrine, Jewel sided with the continental reformers, and regarded their work as one of necessary purification. Once again, his touchstone was the belief and practice of the early church, up to and including the Council of Chalcedon in A.D. 451.

Jewel was equally opposed to radical Protestantism, but wrote less about it, since it did not become a major problem until shortly before his death (1571). The fight against what we now know as Puritanism was led by John Whitgift, who made it a cornerstone of his policy when he was archbishop of Canterbury (1583–1604). Although he was doctrinally a Calvinist himself, and a firm believer in predestination, Whitgift was nevertheless loyal to the polity of the English church, and defended it against Genevan-style presbyterianism. This led him to adopt what contemporaries regarded as a more "Catholic" standpoint, which could be seen in his attachment to things like liturgical vestments. It also led him to stress the importance of the Book of Common Prayer as it stood after 1559, and to reject Puritan calls for further reform of the church's worship.

At the end of the Tudor period, this establishment Anglicanism was still doctrinally Calvinist, but it was liturgically wedded to the Elizabethan compromise, which, as its critics would argue, opened the door to a shift away from Calvinism in the next century. The trend was already apparent toward the end of Elizabeth's reign, as can be seen from the writings of Bishop Richard Bancroft and of Richard Hooker. By the middle of the seventeenth century, Hooker's writings, which were mainly composed in the 1590s, had become the classical exposition of Anglicanism, but it is important to remember that this was not the case at the time they were written. To that extent, the development of Anglicanism as we now know it was a post-Tudor phenomenon.

BIBLIOGRAPHY

Avis, P. *Anglicanism and the Christian Church.* 1989.
Lake, Peter *Anglicans and Puritans? Presbyterianism and English Conformist Thought from Whitgift to Hooker.* 1988.
Neill, S. *Anglicanism.* 1977.
Rowell, G., ed. *The English Religious Tradition and the Genius of Anglicanism.* 1992.

Gerald L. Bray

A

SEE ALSO
Bancroft, Richard; Catholicism; Church of England; Hooker, Richard; Jewel, John; Lutheranism; Whitgift, John

Annates

Derived from the Latin *annus* (year), annates was the name given to the so-called "first-fruits" or first year's revenues of an ecclesiastical benefice. By a papal prerogative dating from the legatine visitations of Cardinals Otho (1237–1241) and Othobon (1265–1268), newly appointed incumbents were expected to surrender the first year of their income to the Holy See. The precise amount was supposed to be calculated according to the census of Pope Nicholas IV, which was taken in 1291, but by Tudor times this was vastly out of date and the subject of much abuse. Complaints were raised by the House of Commons in 1532; and by an act of Parliament later that year (23 Henry VIII c. 20), severe limits were imposed on the collection of annates, as part of a move to put pressure on the pope to grant Henry VIII an annulment of his marriage to Katherine of Aragon. In this purpose it failed, although there is evidence to suggest that it may have encouraged the pope to dispatch the documents necessary for the consecration of Thomas Cranmer as archbishop of Canterbury. By a further act in 1534 (25 Henry VIII c. 20), annates were annexed to the crown, and all payments to Rome ceased. This was also the occasion for a reassessment of the value of ecclesiastical benefices, which was published the following year and has come to be known as the *Valor Ecclesiasticus*. The collection of annates continued until 1703, when Queen Anne reformed the system of payments to the clergy.

BIBLIOGRAPHY
Bray, G.L. *Documents of the English Reformation.* 1994.
Gerald L. Bray

SEE ALSO
Cranmer, Thomas; Katherine of Aragon; *Valor Ecclesiasticus*

Anne of Cleves (1515–1557)

As the Franco/Imperial peace of 1539 seemed to threaten English security, Thomas Cromwell sought an Anglo/German alliance. He arranged a fourth marriage for Henry VIII with Anne of Cleves, who was born on September 22, 1539, to Duke John III, a descendant of England's Edward I, and Maria, heiress of Juliers. Anne's brother, William, who became duke in 1539, opposed Habsburg power but was Erasmian, not Lutheran, in religious belief. The negotiations for Anne, who was literate only in Low German, included a realistic painting of her by Hans Holbein the Younger.

Following courtship protocol, Henry greeted her in disguise at Rochester but afterward confessed great disappointment. Although her agents presented no documentation to prove that her precontract of marriage with Francis of Lorraine was invalid, Henry wed her on January 6, 1540. He failed to consummate the union. In July, after the Franco/Imperial threat lessened, Cromwell was executed as a traitor and a sacramentarian by authority of a parliamentary attainder. Citing the Lorraine precontract and nonconsummation of the union, convocation granted the king an annulment. Endowed with a generous settlement and ranking as his sister, Anne was required to remain in England. She died on July 16, 1557, and was buried at Westminster Abbey.

BIBLIOGRAPHY
Land Im Middlepunkt Der Machte: Die Herzogtumer Jülich-Kleve-Berg. [Exhibition catalog.] 1985.
MacEntegart, Rory. "Fatal Matrimony: Henry VIII and the Marriage to Anne of Cleves." In *Henry VIII: A European Court in England.* David Starkey, ed., pp. 140–143. 1991.
Saaler, Mary. *Anne of Cleves: Fourth Wife of Henry VIII.* 1995.
Warnicke, Retha. "Henry VIII, Anne of Cleves, and Court Protocol." *Albion,* vol. 28, pp. 565–586.
Retha Warnicke

SEE ALSO
Cromwell, Thomas; Convocation; Henry VIII; Holbein, Hans

Anthem

The anthem is, broadly understood, the Anglican counterpart of the Latin motet and thus is a setting of a sacred English text, usually intended for liturgical performance. The word itself stems from "antiphon," and was in use as early as the eleventh century. In the century or so immediately preceding the establishment of the Church of

England the term "anthem" was used either to refer to a votive antiphon, which concluded ladymass or various office services in many English cathedrals and collegiate churches, or, more generally, to mean a polyphonic work performed for some special ecclesiastical or state occasion. Anglican anthems intended for liturgical use mostly survive in choirbooks, whereas those published alongside madrigals and lute songs seem to have been intended for home devotional use.

In the Wanley Partbooks, seventeen pieces are labeled "antem." The liturgical locations of these are not indicated, nor do the Edwardian prayer books of 1549 and 1552 make explicit provision for inclusion of anthems in any service, but Elizabethan practice was to sing an anthem at the end of matins and evensong. The texts are generally biblical, as taken from various Bibles and primers then in use, or from the Book of Common Prayer itself. Several more works in Wanley are anthems, although they are not so labeled; these include offertory and postcommunion sentences, and several psalms.

The musical style of these earliest anthems is reserved. The texts are set almost entirely syllabically, there is relatively little text repetition, and familiar style (chordal homophony) predominates. When a point of imitation does appear, the melodic motive tends to be simple, and the voices enter at short time intervals. All of this stands in dramatic contrast to the Latin motets and masses of the earlier Tudor period, in which composers cultivated a style featuring elaborate melismas, rhythmic complexities, and dense textures; it is clear that Protestant ideas of intelligibility of the texts in worship were exerting considerable influence. The first Anglican generation of composers includes Christopher Tye, John Sheppard, and, most importantly, Thomas Tallis. Tallis's *Hear the Voice and Prayer* is a good example of the Edwardian anthem and was widely known in its day.

More complex styles of church music did not die, however. Queen Elizabeth's preference was for more elaborate liturgical ceremony, and the repertoire of anthems produced by the Chapel Royal during her reign tends toward more use of antiphonal division of the choir, scoring for five or more voices, as well as more intricate polyphonic textures, although syllabic setting of texts still predominates. The second half of the sixteenth century also brought the development of the verse anthem, which features passages for solo voice ("verses," perhaps so named from the psalm verses that were frequently the texts being set) with instrumental accompaniment, alternating with choral sections. Verse anthems produced for liturgical use usually used the organ, but settings calling for consort of viols (consort anthem) were also common, a fact that reveals a connection to the contemporary consort song. The influence of the metrical psalm is also apparent; some early verse anthems are simply strophic songs with the final phrase of each stanza repeated chorally. The popularity of choirboy plays seems also to have played a significant role in the verse anthem's early development. Several surviving examples are explicitly for boys' voices, and musical entertainment by the various local boy choirs was a feature of London social life. One of the earliest surviving verse anthems (1560s?) is *When as we sat in Babylon,* by Richard Farrant (d. 1581), who was master of the choristers at both Windsor and the Chapel Royal and was much involved in such entertainments. By the end of the sixteenth century, the surviving repertory indicates that verse anthems were being written in greater numbers than full anthems (the term that emerged to refer to wholly choral anthems). The verse anthem's reliance on soloists was a practical advantage, especially for less expert choirs, and the medium offered excellent opportunities for dramatic text setting.

William Byrd dominates the Elizabeth period with respect to virtually all musical genres, and he brought the Anglican anthem to a high peak. He seems to have been the first to publish verse anthems, although some are rather rudimentary, being essentially accompanied songs with a concluding choral refrain. *Christ rising again,* on the other hand, is an impressive demonstration of the possibilities of the new form. The verses are for two voices and viols, in imitative style; the choral sections provide dramatic contrasts rather than repeating and elaborating the music of the verses. Byrd's full anthems range in style from simple and syllabic (*O Lord, make thy servant Elizabeth*) to varied and brilliant (*Sing joyfully*). Many of Byrd's Latin motets were adapted to English words as well, as were Latin works of many other composers (the practice was common into the early seventeenth century).

The history of the Tudor anthem culminates in the works of Thomas Weelkes, and Byrd's pupils, Orlando Gibbons and Thomas Tomkins. All three explored more dramatic contrasts of texture and more declamatory treatments of text, and at the same time found ways to unify their forms motivically. These characteristics sound remarkably baroque, yet the style of this music is still distinctly English since contemporary Italian innovations made little headway in Britain until after Jacobean times.

A

BIBLIOGRAPHY

Fellowes, Edmund H. *English Cathedral Music from Edward VI to Edward VII.* 1946.

Le Huray, Peter. *Music and the Reformation in England, 1549–1600.* 1978.

Phillips, Peter. *English Sacred Music 1549–1649.* 1991.

Stevens, Denis. *Tudor Church Music.* 1966.

Wrightson, James, ed. *The Wanley Manuscripts.* Recent Researches in the Music of the Renaissance, pp. 99–101. 1995.

Charles S. Larkowski

SEE ALSO

Anglicanism; Anglican Church Music; Book of Common Prayer; William, Byrd; Motet; Tallis, Thomas; Weelkes, Thomas

Antichrist

The name "Antichrist" to designate the prince among Christ's enemies appears in the New Testament only in the first and second epistles of John, although many have associated him with various of the bizarre beasts described in the Book of Revelation, or with the "man of sin" mentioned in Paul's second epistle to the Thessalonians. Following the separation of the Church of England from Rome in 1534, Anglican apologists often identified the pope as the Antichrist. But in the violent debate over ecclesiastical polity that characterized Tudor England, both conformists and reformers tended to view their opposition in "Antichristian" terms. John Whitgift, archbishop of Canterbury, for example, described Presbyterians as "instruments" of Satan by which he sought to disrupt the unity of the English Church, not "the head of the Antichrist" but the tail: "for the tail of the beast (as learned men say) be false prophets" who "stir up schisms and factions . . . by pretense of zeal" and thus "seek to draw into the church the Antichrist backward." The reformers, for their part, having likewise identified the pope as the Antichrist, felt the need to cast off all vestiges of papal Catholicism—such as the episcopal hierarchy, the liturgy, and the ceremonial garments—from the Church of England.

BIBLIOGRAPHY

Emmerson, R.K. *Antichrist in the Middle Ages.* 1981.

Hill, Christopher. *Antichrist in Seventeenth Century England.* 1969.

Lake, Peter. *Anglicans and Puritans? Presbyterianism and English Conformist Thought from Whitgift to Hooker.* 1988.

Lake, Peter. "The Significance of the Elizabethan Identification of the Pope as Antichrist," *Journal of Ecclesiastical History,* vol. 31. 1980.

Mark Goldblatt

SEE ALSO

Catholicism; Church of England; Whitgift, John

Antiquarianism

Antiquarianism is an approach to the study of the past emphasizing the collection of materials about some chosen subject, perhaps a Roman institution or province. Such a collection would most likely be systematic, but the organization might well be quite loose. Where the historian tells a story in chronological order, the antiquarian may avoid both story and chronology. Again, where the historian, at least during the Renaissance, often uses his story to influence the moral or political behavior of his readers and so employs the methods of the rhetorician to accomplish his purpose, the antiquary, not bound in this fashion and so prepared to abandon stylistic elegance, feels less compunction about encumbering his work with a wide variety of documents, inscriptions, and other source materials.

Renaissance antiquarianism began in Italy, when scholars such as Flavio Biondo (1388–1463) adapted what they saw as ancient Roman (and, to a lesser extent, Greek) models. In *Roma Instaurata* (1446) and *Italia Illustrata* (1453), Biondo described the topography of ancient Rome, then of all Italy, using the writings of the ancient Romans but adding to them his own observations based on an early version of "field archeology." In these works, Biondo reconstructed the mixture of history and geography that Ptolemy had called "chorography." The early sixteenth-century English scholar, John Leland, tried to emulate Biondo by riding around England just as the monasteries were being suppressed; he recorded what he could, but died leaving only manuscript fragments. A generation later, William Lambarde, a Kentish justice of the peace, wrote up a chorography of his county. However, the greatest of the English chorographers was William Camden, whose *Britannia* (1586 and many later editions) set the fashion and the benchmark of such works for more than three centuries.

The center of Camden's *Britannia* was the Roman province; to make the work reflect current interests, Camden grouped the English counties by roughly following the British tribes found by the invading Romans. Within these subdivisions, Camden traveled along the rivers, then spread his investigation out into the countryside. At each significant stop, Camden traced the history of the location from Roman times to the present. To the volume as a whole, Camden prefaced a series of essays on British, Roman, Saxon, and Norman Britain. To accomplish all this, Camden made use of a wide variety of evidence. The history of place-names (which required that he learn Anglo-Saxon and Welsh) was supplemented by medieval charters, town records, chronicles, and genealogy. Along with this literary evidence, Camden used archaeological materials. Like Biondo, he rode along the Roman roads, working out the identity of the ancient way stations as he went. Roman and British coins provided data for the physical appearance of rulers; together with the evidence provided by inscriptions, the coins also showed the extent of the Roman penetration of the island. In all this, Camden was scrupulous in keeping antiquarianism separate from history: *Britannia,* though it contained many small histories, was not a chronological account of the history of England, or even of the Roman province. At the beginning of his labors, Camden had been assisted by predecessors like William Lambarde, and by the loan of the manuscripts of John Leland; once the book became well-known, he also received help from a growing network of men equally fascinated by the remnants of the past and eager to see them preserved. Drawings of inscriptions and other ancient remains came to him from all over the island, and it was this sort of information in particular that fueled the growth of the book from the small octavo of 1586 to the substantial, heavily illustrated folio of 1607. The expansion of *Britannia* reflected the burgeoning interest in the land of Britain, especially by an aristocracy whose homes and milieus were so carefully delineated by Camden and his followers. This Elizabethan discovery and exploration of Britain amounted to a kind of proto-nationalism, which was fueled as well by victories over Spain and by a growing insistence on the uniqueness of English institutions such as the common law.

The initial publication of *Britannia* coincided with the founding of the first Society of Antiquaries, a group of lawyers, genealogists, and historians centered in London. For twenty years, these men met to discuss such subjects as the history of English coinage, the age of castles, the antiq-

uity of parliament, and the history and nature of various royal offices like that of the earl marshal. The meetings of the society served to propagate the new antiquarian methods; they also brought to light many new documents, as the members competed to display their discoveries. Such activity, however, was not altogether disengaged from politics, for the long-standing antiquity of institutions might seem to limit the authority of the monarch. Or so King James saw the matter, and his hint of disapproval closed down the meetings. Nevertheless, antiquarian activity continued unabated throughout the seventeenth century, most especially in the countryside, and by 1695, a new, expanded edition of *Britannia* was called for, showing that the antiquarian tradition was still very much alive.

BIBLIOGRAPHY
Kendrick, T.D. *British Antiquity.* 1950.
Levine, Joseph. *Humanism and History.* 1987.
Levy, F.J. *Tudor Historical Thought.* 1967.
McKisack, May. *Medieval History in the Tudor Age.* 1971.
Momigliano, Arnaldo. "Ancient History and the Antiquarian." *Journal of the Warburg and Courtauld Institutes,* vol. 13, pp. 285–315; repr. in Arnaldo Momigliano, *Studies in Historiography,* pp. 1–39. 1966.

F.J. Levy

SEE ALSO
Camden, William; History, Writing of; Lambard, William; Leland, John; Manuscripts

Apprenticeship

Apprenticeship was a key mechanism for the transfer of skills, the regulation of the labor market, and the maintenance of social discipline. It was a predominantly male institution, and the number of formal female apprenticeships arranged through the craft guilds was declining in the sixteenth century. When women were apprenticed (and it was increasingly through the less formal means of a parish apprenticeship), it was usually to learn housewifery, some form of sewing, or petty retailing. For males, however, apprenticeship was a necessary path to the acquisition of skills and civic responsibility.

The Statute of Artificers (1563) made apprenticeship an essential qualification for anyone wishing to practice a number of named trades from that of blacksmith to merchant. The indenture of apprenticeship was a formalized

A

legal agreement that placed obligations on both of the contracting parties. The master was obliged to provide instruction as well as board, lodging, and clothing, and in return the apprentice was to serve his master, obey his commandments, keep his secrets, and avoid moral lapses such as fornication, gambling, and drunkenness. The craft guild, before which these indentures were enrolled, levied fees, limited by a statute of 1531 to 2s.6d. But the main obstacles to apprenticeship arose from the premiums required by the master that were often supplemented by bonds for the good behavior of the apprentice during his term. The size of the premium, which varied from one trade to another, tended to be higher in London than in the provinces, and was increasing in the sixteenth century. By 1600, premiums of 40s. were typical in manual crafts, while those in the distributive trades could expect to pay up to £50, and merchants upwards of £100. Sureties for good behavior were common in those trades where the apprentice was entrusted with valuable goods or large amounts of money. Some crafts like goldsmithing required that their apprentices be literate. These considerations determined the social groups from which apprentices were recruited. Typically, those in the distributive and wholesaling trades were the younger sons of gentlemen or from prosperous farming or provincial trading backgrounds, while those in the manual crafts came from the lower (but not usually the lowest) echelons of society.

Boys were typically apprenticed in their mid-to-late teens, and there was a strong presumption that men should not assume householding responsibilities until they were at least twenty-four. The Statute of Artificers (1563) required minimal terms of seven years, but in this it was simply following the long-established practice of towns like London, Chester, Coventry, York, and Lincoln. The length of the term ensured an adequate return to the master on his investment and gave the apprentice a degree of security. Many apprentices, in fact, served longer terms than the minimum required, and these variations might be governed by the state of the labor market. Guild regulations also sought to manipulate apprenticeship to control the labor market by limiting the number of apprentices a master could have at any one time.

Although the fears of the authorities about the sexual license and disorderliness represented by the young were probably exaggerated, apprenticeship was seen as a vital agency of social discipline: in the words of a memorandum on the Statute of Artificers "younge men [who] lead a ryotouse life" might be reformed for "the aged should be guides unto youth." Sixteenth-century moralists increasingly insisted on the need for regular household catechizing as a means by which apprentices could be instructed in their social obligations. The possibilities of apprenticeship as a means of socialization help explain the growing preoccupation with the compulsory apprenticeship of the children of the poor who, it was thought, might be rescued from the consequences of idleness by early training. Pauper apprenticeships arranged by the parish authorities usually began at a younger age and involved longer terms than were served by those apprenticed through the craft guilds.

The quality of relations between masters and apprentices is debated by historians. There were numerous sources of potential conflict in the household. The leisure activities of apprentices were strictly regulated; many masters were not up to the demands of their calling, giving inadequate training or maltreating their charges with over-severe correction; the position of apprentices in relation to the mistress of the household, who in spite of her gender enjoyed some authority over them, was ambiguous. In the early years of the apprentice's term he could too easily seem to his master to be a drain on resources, while in the later years the already trained apprentice anxious to set up his own business might chafe under the continued position of subordination. Tensions of this kind help to explain the high dropout rate among apprentices: fewer than half of those taken on seem to have completed their terms. But insofar as the indenture was a contract embodying reciprocal obligations, it provided a framework within which grievances on both sides could be negotiated, and both masters and apprentices are found appealing to external agencies like the craft guilds, the municipal authorities, and local justices to arbitrate disputes. Much clearly depended on individuals, for in spite of the manifest inequalities of power, there are many countervailing cases of harmonious relations between masters and apprentices. Marriage to the master's daughter was for many a means of social promotion. Others were assisted in setting up in business by bequests from their masters, while still others received recognition for their faithful service in the remission of one or two years of their terms.

BIBLIOGRAPHY

Ben-Amos, I. *Adolescence and Youth in Early Modern England.* 1994.

Griffiths, P. *Youth and Authority in Early Modern England: Formative Experiences in England 1560–1640.* 1996.

Rappaport, S. *Worlds Within Worlds: The Structures of Life in Sixteenth Century London.* 1989.

Ian W. Archer

SEE ALSO
Guilds

Arcadia

None of the classical or Renaissance "Arcadian" landscapes bears any physical resemblance to the Greek province after which they are named. Theocritos, the acknowledged "father" of pastoral, had nominally set his *Idylls* (third century B.C.), in Sicily and Cos, two rural areas he had known from his youth, but imaginatively described and inhabited by clearly unrealistic rustics. Vergil adapted his format— various types of poems separated by prose passages or links—but named his countryside "Arcadia" in the *Eclogues* (c. 42–39 B.C.). The Renaissance pastoral follows his usage. Rosenmeyer suggests that Vergil chose the name strictly for its mythic, literary, and historic allusions: Arcadia was the traditional home of the god Pan; Roman legends associated the Arcadians with the original golden age and also as the earliest settlers of Italy; and because the more nominally remote the setting, the easier for the poet to deal "openly [with] the political reality of his day." The "other" world is named "Arcadia"; but it is an imaginative landscape that permits the poet to order experience as he sees fit. (It should be noted that post-Vergilian Latin pastoralists did not use the name "Arcadia" for their landscapes; Calpurnius and Nemesianus thought "Vergil's choice of Arcadia was in fact a disclaimer of geographical realities." Vergil's Arcadian landscape was recognized by his contempories as a composite of the Po Valley and the barren hills of Italy's heel.)

The pastoral eclogue form remained all but dormant between antiquity and Jacopo Sannazaro's adaptation of Vergil's themes and techniques to the vernacular with his *Arcadia* (Naples, 1502). The work was an immediate success, with new editions appearing on the average of every two years throughout the sixteenth century. Jorge de Montemayor's *Diana* (Milan, 1559), and Gil Polo's continuation *Diana Enamorada* (Valencia, 1564), were both set in Arcadia: like Sannazaro, their focus was on love and rural pleasures and were equally popular. Sir Philip Sidney's debt to these works was recognized by his earliest readers; his major innovation is the extensive juxtaposition of "heroic" and "pastoral" elements in the *New Arcadia*.

BIBLIOGRAPHY
Kennedy, Judith M. *A Critical Edition of Yong's Translation of George of Montemayor's Diana and Gil Polo's Enamoured Diana.* 1968.

Kennedy, William J. *Jacopo Sannazaro and the Uses of Pastoral.* 1983.

Lang, A. *Theocritus, Bion, and Moschus Rendered into English Prose.* 1911.

McCanles, Michael. *The Text of Sidney's Arcadian World.* 1989.

Mills, Barriss. *The Idylls of Theokritos: A Verse Translation.* 1963; repr. 1966.

Nash, Ralph. *Jacopo Sannazaro: Arcadia & Piscatoral Eclogues.* 1966.

Robertson, Jean, ed. *Sir Philip Sidney: The Countess of Pembroke's Arcadia (The Old Arcadia).* 1973.

Rosenmeyer, Thomas G. *The Green Cabinet: Theocritus and the European Pastoral Lyric.* 1969.

Skretkowicz, Victor. *Sir Philip Sidney: The Countess of Pembroke's Arcadia (The New Arcadia).* 1987.

Gerald J. Rubio

SEE ALSO
Classical Literature, English Translations; Classical Literature, Influence of; Pastoral; Sidney, Sir Philip; Spanish Literature, Influence of

Archery

Archery was held in great reverence in Tudor England because of the successes won by the longbow in the Hundred Years' War at Crecy (1346), Poitiers (1356), and Agincourt (1415). Henry VIII, Edward VI, and Mary Stuart personally practiced archery, and Henry VIII encouraged continuation of the traditional exercise with the bow while simultaneously furthering the introduction of firearms. For Bishop Latimer in 1549 there was no doubt that the longbow was "God's chosen instrument."

A romanticized view of the triumph of the bow in the wars against France lay behind a long struggle to retain it in defiance of the modern weapons of fire, the arquebus, caliver, and musket. There was great reluctance to change. As late as 1590, 3,577 men of the Essex footbands included 1,177 archers and billmen, as well as 2,400 men armed with pikes and firearms in the modern fashion. It was not until the 1620s that the musket won the battle for adoption in England's militia.

A

BIBLIOGRAPHY

Ascham, R. *Toxophilus, The Schole of Shootinge Conteyned in Two Bookes.* STC 837 (1545); 2nd edition STC 837 (1571); 3rd edition STC 839 (1589).

Gaier, C. "L'invincibilité anglaise et le grand arc après la guerre de cent ans: un mythe tenace." *Tijdschrift voor Geschiedenis,* vol. 91. 1978.

Smythe, Sir John. *Certain Discourses Military.* J.R. Hale, ed. 1964.

David Eltis

SEE ALSO

Military History; Ordnance

Architecture

Architecture in Tudor England underwent a period of great creativity, in the face of rapidly shifting conditions for building. There was an increased interest in building as an activity appropriate for those of noble birth, as well as an interest in the intellectual and historical dimensions of architecture. John Dee wrote in his preface to John Billingsley's translation of Euclid (1570) that architecture ought to be considered a science and part of the humanist educational curriculum, and not just a manual craft. Building and the study of architecture came to have a place in the arts curriculum for young men as a subject worthy of study, and the interest is reflected in the library catalogs of the major patrons of the day. The evidence of surviving library lists shows that masons as well as patrons looked on architecture as a subject whose roots could be traced back to the ancient text of Vitruvius as well as to the current fashions for classical architecture on the continent. Yet, if patrons were alert to the intellectual and visual frameworks of classicism, when they came to build, classicism was only one architectural language used in connection with the powerful and vital native traditions of heraldry, invented ornament, and gothic forms. In this, England was similar to other northern European countries, which saw classicism as only one subset of a complex repertoire of elements that could be selected, combined, and modified to suit local taste and building practice.

The changes in design occurred in parallel to the economic, political, and social events that stimulated new construction on all levels: increasing desire for domestic comfort, changes in domestic organization and in education, and new patterns of patronage. Henry VII and Henry VIII both built extensively, but their successors built virtually nothing. Hence, over the whole of the sixteenth century there is a shift in the pattern of patronage, transferring of innovation in building from the crown to private and local patrons.

Local conditions and materials determined the developments in architecture as much as any national developments. Innovation by masons emerged out of their use of the local materials, as in the use of napped flints in the stoneless regions of Norfolk as a form of rustication, or the development of timber-framing in the west Midlands as a local specialty. New fashions in domestic architecture, such as the use of glass windows, came in the wake of increasing interest in domestic comforts.

A sudden change in the architectural history of England came with Henry VIII's break with the church of Rome and the subsequent dissolution of the monasteries through acts of Parliament in 1536 and 1539. The lands and properties entered into the hands of the aristocracy, while some of the houses became royal properties. New owners transformed the religious buildings, keeping some parts standing, using stone for new projects, and renovating residences with windows, doors, and fireplaces to accommodate new standards of domestic comfort. At Lacock Abbey, Wiltshire, Sir William Sharington incorporated the cloister of the nunnery as a courtyard corridor in his new house (1540–1553). He also added a tower with fittings as his "strong room" in the classical style then fashionable.

However, Gothic forms and structures continued to be used for religious architecture long into the seventeenth century, as this was not an area where experimentation with classical forms was deemed appropriate. Pre-Reformation Tudor England saw the construction or enlargement of many churches, together with clerical and monastic lodgings. The Prior's Lodging at Much Wenlock, Shropshire (c. 1500), is one of the most extravagant, and best preserved, of the monastic buildings of the period. Country houses later in the century incorporated such characteristics seen here as the long glazed gallery on an upper floor. New churches of the period include St. James, Barton-under-Needwood, Staffordshire (begun 1517), built by John Taylor, master of the rolls to Henry VIII. The idea of architectural structure and ornament as a medium for social display, which was already active in domestic building, is suggested here by the inscriptions and arms over the columns in the nave recounting Taylor's family history, education, and prominent career at court.

There was little new church building after the Reformation and in a period of religious turmoil, though smaller renovations continued. The classical porch at St. Leonard, Sunningwell, Oxfordshire (c. 1551), reflects an interest in classical forms, though limited to an addition to the church.

Parish churches were multifunctional buildings and often served as town halls or grammar schools well into the Elizabethan era. One of the most important architectural transformations of the church after the Reformation was the emphasis placed on the creation of seating that ordered the civic populace according to status and rank. Pews also encouraged the congregation to listen in relative comfort to the lengthy sermons of the reformed religion.

In addition to churches, individual patrons built and endowed charitable foundations, such as almshouses, hospitals, schools, or colleges. Groups, such as guilds, assumed an increasing importance in the civic life of towns as cooperative benefit societies, especially in the wake of the Black Death. The Corpus Christi Guild was one of the most active and built the timber-framed guildhall at Lavenham, Suffolk, in 1528–1529, just before the guild's suppression. Guildhalls presented a strong corporate image within the town, and were also used to ensure the continuity of the memory of guild members through the saying of masses and obsequies and the staging of pageants and festivals throughout the year.

Before the Reformation, civic festivals, especially those connected with Corpus Christi celebrations, allowed diverse members of the civic society to participate in urban ritual life. The city itself was the setting for these events, in all of their organized and informal aspects. After the Reformation the civic hall took on a new importance in many towns. A high civic culture developed, transforming many of the previously religious processions into events that emphasized civic themes. There was a new attention paid to public buildings connected with secular power. Aging halls were rebuilt, with a new emphasis on the symbolic and functional roles they served as signs of civic government. At the Much Wenlock guildhall, a jail was added in 1577 as part of the felt need for facilities connected with punishment and law enforcement.

A new and different kind of public building appeared in London in 1566 when Sir Thomas Gresham began the Royal Exchange. The English Merchant Adventurers (chartered in 1509) had their headquarters in Antwerp, and that city's remarkable bourse served as the model for London's new center for economic activity. The money for the construction came in large part from Gresham and the merchant Richard Clough, and Clough arranged to have much of the material brought from Antwerp. The building was long and four-storied. In shops on the upper stories milliners, apothecaries, goldsmiths, and booksellers sold their goods. Around the courtyard was an arcuated walkway with niches above containing statues of the English monarchs. The building was destroyed in the fire of 1666.

Triangular Lodge, Rothwell, Hertfordshire (1594–1597). The triangular ground plan and windows and many other features of the building honor the Holy Trinity. By permission of Christy Anderson.

The Tudor establishment believed strongly in the importance of formal education as preparation for public service, both religious and secular. Prior to the Reformation, this activity was centered on monastic establishments; after the dissolution, it became necessary to build many new schools. A commission under Edward VI (1548) revived a number of schools as "Edward VI Grammar Schools," and many others were newly founded by private patrons in the second half of the century. These school buildings were often long and one room deep, occasionally with lodgings for the master and additional rooms for a library and gallery. Many followed the earlier model set by schools founded before the dissolution by John Colet's at St. Paul's (founded 1509), and Cardinal Wolsey's school at Ipswich (founded 1527). Archdeacon Robert Johnson's small schoolhouse at Uppingham,

Leicestershire (1587), is typical of those still present in towns throughout England.

Colleges and the universities were the continuation of the educational system. Several new colleges in Oxford and Cambridge were founded during the Tudor period, or significantly improved through the construction of new chapels, halls, and lodgings. At Oxford, Cardinal Wolsey founded Cardinal College in 1525, which then became Christ Church. The present cathedral was originally the college chapel. In Cambridge, Lady Margaret Beaufort, mother of Henry VIII, refounded Christ's in 1505, and then in 1511 established the college of St. John's. At both, the first courts are primarily Tudor work, following the established pattern of collegiate buildings, with the hall, chapel, and lodgings opening onto a central space. When the physician John Caius refounded his college in Cambridge in 1567, he added three gateways that symbolized the intellectual progression of a student's career: the gates of Humility, Virtue, and Honor. Inspired by the ancient Roman triumphal gates, known through books, prints, and travelers' descriptions, these gates incorporate classical architectural details as a sign of humanist learning and the knowledge of ancient languages.

For Sir Thomas Tresham, one of the most avid architectural patrons of Elizabeth I's reign, buildings were also part of his public proclamation of his Catholic faith. In the town of Rothwell, Tresham commissioned the mason William Grumbold to design a market house (1578) that honored the families of Northamptonshire through the display of their arms, while a Latin inscription ensured that no one would mistake Tresham's good intentions. The Triangular Lodge (Rothwell, 1594–1597), built on Tresham's own land, was the center of his farming and rabbit industry and a potent religious statement to his faith. References to the trinity appear on the lodge—and in its plan—in every conceivable form.

In domestic architecture, changes in ordinary domestic building, both rural and urban, were slow and incremental. Most large urban houses were indistinguishable from their rural counterparts, a loosely organized group of individual buildings around a courtyard, and while these were modernized throughout the sixteenth century, there was little

Oxburgh Hall, Oxburgh, Norfolk (c. 1480). A fine Tudor manor house, built for defense as well as comfort. By permission of Christy Anderson.

change to the general type. In many towns throughout England, however, the century saw a general rebuilding of the urban structure. In Shrewsbury, for example, there was renovation or new building of housing on all levels. Timber was used as the appropriate urban material for the large amount of speculative and private housing, while stone was reserved for major civic structures such as the Market Hall (1596).

During the Tudor period the aristocracy and upper gentry added on to old houses and built many new ones, in London, but especially in the country, incorporating architectural features intended to express the builders' wealth and status. Early in the period large houses display a remarkable loyalty to local traditions, in spite of the innovations in courtly architecture of the same period. Important patrons continued to use the courtyard plan, no longer needed for defensive purposes but still expressing in symbolic form the builder's wealth and rank. Compton Wynyates, Warwickshire (1520s), has all the elements of the defensive house—moat, battlements, and tower—though these are by this date intended primarily as signs of the family's ancient status rather than for practical use. The asymmetry of the house is the result of building over a long period, and would have been less noticeable with its original forecourt buildings. The organization of the rooms was determined by the patterns of use and the traditions of hospitality kept by the family. Movement through the house was carefully controlled by a complex sequence of entrances and passages. Ornament on these houses followed the hierarchy established by planning: the most elaborate ornament, often a combination of heraldry framed by classical elements, appears near the door as a sign of the builder's status, sophistication, and ability to hire the best craftsmen.

Rural houses of the courtiers were seats of their power, both in economic and symbolic form, and help to explain the emphasis on the gatehouse in early Tudor houses. The gatehouses at Oxburgh Hall, Norfolk (1480s), and Layer Marney, Essex (1520), create imposing entrances into the forecourt that retain the language—if not the function—of defensive structures.

The architecture of the Protectorate was innovative in its use of classicism and the emphasis on a unified appearance. Edward Seymour, duke of Somerset and Lord Protector, spent lavishly on his building projects of the mid-century, though almost nothing survives. The mason John Thorpe recorded the facade and plan of Somerset House (1547–1552) along the Strand, one of the large palaces lining the road connecting London with Westminster. The new facade was symmetrically organized around a three-story gatehouse with a sequence of the classical orders, much resembling book frontispieces of the period. Columns were used over the whole of the street front, and a classical balustrade unified the roof line.

John Thynne's rebuilding of Longleat, Wiltshire (1547–1580), over a period of thirty years, resulted in a house that was remarkable in its use of the orders over the whole exterior, and in its outward-looking and symmetrical planning. In its isolated setting, Longleat was intended to be seen from a distance and to serve as a jewel marking the center of the owner's properties. At Longleat the classical orders appear on the projecting bays in a sequence from Doric to Corinthian. Classical features also appear at Kirby Hall, Northamptonshire (1570–1575), where Sir Humphrey Stafford had a giant order used around the inner courtyard, an innovative use of classicism for this date. This interest in the proportions and use of classical details coincides with the publication of John Shute's treatise, *The First and Chiefe Groundes of Architecture,* in 1563. Shute had been sent into Italy by the duke of Northumberland to study architecture and measure antique Roman columns. Following his study of Vitruvius and Serlio, Shute bases each order on a mythological figure and appropriate body type, so that Doric is Hercules, and so on. Architectural classicism is explicitly connected with the knowledge of ancient Latin texts and humanist educational principles.

The buildings and theories of the circle around Somerset were not generally followed by the next generation of architectural patrons and masons in Elizabethan England. There was a conscious turn toward the native architectural types and aesthetic principles of ingenious form and heraldic ornament. Like the courtiers of Henry VIII, the Elizabethan nobility built in order to display their own wealth and status and as part of a general interest in the visual arts. But their "prodigy houses" also glorified a monarchy that chose not to spend its own money on architecture as part of its court image. Built to entertain Elizabeth I and her retinue, they also stood for her in her absence; courtier houses served as extravagant settings for a royal portrait.

Many rooms in the house were intended as the setting for rituals of daily life in the house, such as the hall as the site for hospitality and entertainment, or the great chamber as the central room for the visiting monarch. The long gallery, most often on the upper stories, was used for walking and frequently for the display of the owner's wealth and erudition, either through the display of portraits (by the duke of Norfolk at Kenninghall), emblems (in the stucco ceiling at Blickling), fantastic ornament (as in the facet-set glass at Haddon Hall), or sententiae taken out of ancient authors (at Sir Nicholas Bacon's house at Gorhambury).

A

Building was taken up by certain families as a sign of their status and sophisticated taste, and kept pace with their increasing power at court. William Cecil, Lord Burghley, continued work at Burghley House, Cambridgeshire, from 1553 on, and then later at Theobalds, Hertfordshire, from 1564, throughout his long political career. Burghley made many additions to Burghley House, but it retains many features of houses from the previous generation, such as the courtyard, the gatehouse-like entrance façade, and a veritable forest of ornamental turrets and chimneys. Theobalds (demolished under the Commonwealth) was far larger than Burghley House, with five courtyards entered through a series of arches, loggias, and passageways. Thomas Cecil, Lord Burghley's eldest son, continued the family building tradition at his house at Wimbledon (London, 1588; demolished). The plan, strongly influenced by French models, was an "H," open to a series of terraces and gardens. Both patrons and architects in the second half of the sixteenth century were increasingly interested in the aesthetic and practical potential of symmetrical planning.

The development of Tudor architecture culminated in the work of Robert Smythson. His architectural career was built on his ability to design country houses that met the various functional and ritual needs of Elizabeth's courtiers. After his initial success at Wollaton, he did a series of projects for Elizabeth Hardwick, countess of Shrewsbury. Hardwick Hall (Derby, 1590–1598), for example, expressed the patron's, desire to impress the monarch (or any other visitor) through the building's dominating presence in the landscape, its shimmering and glass-covered surface, the carefully contrived processional route to the High Great Chamber, and its heraldic and mythological symbolism. The size of the windows—and therefore the light on the interior—increase on each floor, adding architectural priority to the symbolic importance of the rooms on the upper story. Smythson also oriented the plan in a new way for a house of the time, with the hall on the same axis as the entrance, thus eliminating the traditional circuitous planning. In every way Hardwick Hall is a revolutionary house that established new precedents for the next generation of builders.

The experience of a contemporary visitor to a great house like Hardwick was intended to play on the effect of surprise and wonder. Through its planning, ornamentation, and gardens, the house expressed the owner's control and power over his or her surroundings. Buildings were recognized as the sites of events that gave them meaning—court rituals as well as the everyday running of the estate.

BIBLIOGRAPHY
Airs, Malcolm. *The Tudor and Jacobean Country House. A Building History.* 1995.
Howard, Maurice. *The Early Tudor Country House. Architecture and Politics, 1490–1550.* 1987.
Summerson, John, gen. ed. *Architecture in Britain, 1430–1830.* 9th edition. 1993.

Christy Anderson

SEE ALSO
Cecil, William; Dee, John; Grammar Schools; Gresham, Thomas; Hardwick, Elizabeth; Monastic Orders; Royal Palaces; Universities; Wollaton Hall; Illustrations: Hardwick Hall, Triangular Lodge, Oxburgh Hall

Archpriest Controversy

Fueled by mutual suspicion, envy, and spite, the Archpriest Controversy was a dispute between some secular English Catholic priests and Jesuits over ecclesiastical organization and authority in England. By the 1590s, divisions had developed within the English Catholic mission among the Jesuits and secular clergy. Some priests, like John Mush, resented the influence that the small number of Jesuits had over the Catholic mission, while others, most notably Christopher Bagshaw, harbored personal hatred for Robert Parsons, the leading English Jesuit, and dislike for the Jesuit order in general. These secular priests came to believe that the Jesuits, led by Parsons, wanted to make the English Catholic Church an instrument of Spanish policy, and they thought that if the Jesuits could be withdrawn from England, then Elizabeth's government would grant toleration to Catholics. Parsons and Henry Garnet, the Jesuits superior in England, regarded their critics as factious and disobedient clerics who flirted dangerously with schism and apostasy.

The secular priests wanted the pope to approve their plan for a hierarchy elected by an association of the secular clergy. But in March, 1598, Enrico Cajetan, the cardinal protector of England, without consulting the secular clergy, accepted an idea proposed by Parsons, and appointed George Blackwell, a secular priest, as archpriest over the English secular clergy, but with limited authority and the right to select only six of his twelve assistants. While most secular priests submitted to Blackwell, a few refused because they thought that the office of archpriest was unprecedented and because the appointment was made by the cardinal protector, not by the pope; and Parsons's influence in the matter convinced these critics that Blackwell was merely a Jesuit stooge. Two secular priests, William Bishop and Robert Charnock, set out for Rome bearing an appeal to the pope, signed by thirty-three priests, who outlined their objections to the archpriest and asked for permission to form their own association and for the appointment of a bishop elected by the secular clergy. In response, Blackwell, asserting his authority, suspended his most vociferous opponents, John Mush and John Colleton, and asked Clement VIII to confirm his appointment. A petition, with sixty signatures, was presented to the pope in support of Blackwell, and Garnet wrote Clement denouncing the secular critics of the archpriest as factious schismatics who should be severely disciplined.

Bishop and Charnock, arriving in Rome in December 1598, lodged at the English College, where Parsons ruled as rector. Parsons imprisoned the two priests, and in April 1599, they were tried before Cardinal Cajetan and Cardinal Borghese, partisans of Blackwell, and expelled from Rome shortly after Pope Clement's confirmation of Blackwell's appointment.

The secular priests would have accepted the pope's decision, but Blackwell insisted that the appellants do penance for the sin of schism, and he approved publication of a pamphlet by the Jesuit Thomas Lister accusing the appellants of schism and disobedience to the Holy See. The seculars wanted to answer these charges in print, but in January 1600, Blackwell forbade them to publish. Colleton, meanwhile, asked for an opinion from the largely anti-Jesuit theologians of the University of Paris, who accordingly ruled in May that the seculars were not guilty of schism. Blackwell, denouncing the opinion as prejudicial to the apostolic see, forbade any priest to speak or write in support of it; and, in October, he suspended several of the appellants, including Mush and Colleton, for continuing to insist on their innocence. In response, thirty-three priests sent another appeal to Rome on November 17, 1600, detailing the archpriest's abuse of authority, accusing him of favoring the Jesuits, and asking for reform of ecclesiastical government. Pope Clement, in a brief of August 17, 1601, answered the appellants' written appeal. He exonerated them of the charge of schism and rebuked Blackwell for abusing his authority, but he chided the appellants for their disobedience, and he enjoined both sides from publishing any further controversial literature. Blackwell held back publication of the pope's brief until January 1602, giving Parsons time to publish his *Brief Apologie,* defending the archpriest, and his *A Manifestation of a Great Folly and Bad Spirit,* attacking the secular priests. Throughout 1601–1602, the appellants published their own pamphlets, harshly assailing the Jesuits and the office of archpriest, and putting forth their own ideas of ecclesiastical hierarchy and government.

The tone and volume of this brawl convinced the ministers of Elizabeth I that the Catholic missionaries were not a monolithic group conjoined in treason, and they saw that the government and the appellants could work together for a common goal: the removal of the Jesuits from England. In 1601, the government, negotiating through Richard Bancroft, bishop of London, reached an agreement with the appellant Thomas Bluet to support the priests' appeal at Rome, providing money for travel and help with the publication of their pamphlets. Thomas Bluet, John Mush, and Anthony Champney, leaving England in late September, were joined in France by the unstable John Cecil. King Henry IV of France, concerned about Jesuit support for the Spanish claim to England, instructed his ambassadors in Rome to aid the appellants. The four secular priests, arriving in Rome on February 14, 1602, presented their grievances to the Holy Office. Blackwell's supporters answered with charges that the appellants were disobedient and were seeking an unholy alliance with enemies of the Catholic faith. The ruling issued by the Holy Office on July 20, 1602, censured Blackwell for unjustly accusing the appellants of schism, ordered that he not consult the Jesuits on matters involving the English clergy, and instructed that he report directly to the pope and to the cardinal protector of England. The Holy Office, however, upheld the rule of the archpriest, and condemned the appellants' negotiations with Elizabeth's government, recommending excommunication of those who dealt with heretics. Clement VIII, in his bull of October 5, confirmed the decision of the Holy Office, but he further limited Blackwell's authority, ordering him to appoint three of the appellants as his assistants, and he again forbade both sides to publish controversial writings. Although the appellants were exonerated, they failed to get the form of ecclesiastical government they had wanted, or the removal of the Jesuits from England.

BIBLIOGRAPHY

Bennett, John. "The Archpriest Controversy." In *Miscellanea, XII.* Catholic Record Society, vol. 22. 1921.

Bossy, John. *The English Catholic Community, 1570–1850.* 1976.

A

Law, Thomas G. *A Historical Sketch of the Conflicts between Jesuits and Seculars in the Reign of Queen Elizabeth.* 1889.

———. *The Archpriest Controversy: Documents relating to the Dissensions of the Roman Catholic Clergy, 1597–1602.* Camden Society. 2 vols. 1896, 1898.

McGrath, Patrick. *Papists and Puritans under Elizabeth I.* 1967.

Meyer, Arnold O. *England and the Catholic Church under Queen Elizabeth.* J.R. McKee, Trans. 1915.

Morey, Adrian. *The Catholic Subjects of Queen Elizabeth I.* 1978.

Pollen, John H. *The Institution of the Archpriest Blackwell.* 1916.

Prichard, Arnold. *Catholic Loyalism in Elizabethan England.* 1979.

Tierney, Mark A. *Dodd's Church History of England.* Vol. 3. 1840.

John M. Currin

SEE ALSO
Bancroft, Richard; Jesuits; Parsons, Robert

Aristotelianism

Two great institutions of medieval and early modern cultural life, the university and the church, were shaped by the rediscovery of Aristotelian doctrines. From its inception in the twelfth century, the university's curriculum, forms of instruction, and conceptual vocabulary for grammar, logic, and rhetoric were derived from Aristotle. His works defined the trivium of lower disciplines as well as the higher disciplines of ethics, natural philosophy, and metaphysics. Aristotelian syllogistic logical forms and dialectical reasoning structured university exercises like the disputation. Despite sharing a common-sense Aristotelian tradition shaped by such instruction, humanists especially attacked scholasticism, which relied on Aristotelian logical forms to clarify disputed points of theology. Three waves of criticism destroyed Aristotle's intellectual dominance. Humanists attacked dialectic or Aristotelian method based on syllogistic logic; Protestants condemned the aridity of scholastic theology that applied such method to matters of faith; and finally, the practitioners of the "new science" ridiculed the mistakes of Aristotelian natural philosophy and Aristotelian metaphysics.

Aristotle's humanist critics challenged the institutionalization of the medieval studium and the enormous scholarly resources devoted to logic and dialectic, which they claimed ought to be at best a grounding for, not the end of, study, and stressed instead rhetorical and probabilistic modes of understanding. Humanists also sought to recover accurate texts, including Aristotle's, by close study and retranslation. At the headwaters of Renaissance criticism of Aristotle stands Petrarch (1304–1374). In *On his own ignorance and that of many others* (c. 1367), he sought to justify a new *rhetorica theologica* on five grounds. First, mastery of scholastic theology was not equivalent to understanding either Christian faith or Aristotle. Surely, Aristotle could not replace the message of Gospels, nor should criticism of Aristotle be considered irreligious, since Aristotelian doctrines could never be matters of faith. Second, scholasticism not only sullied religion, it diverted intellectual inquiry away from useful pursuits. Third, Petrarch challenged the privileged status granted Aristotle in elucidating theology, claiming Plato was more congenial for Christian theology; in a famous *bon mot*, Petrarch noted, "Plato is praised by the greater men, Aristotle by the bigger crowd." A more inclusive study of philosophy would lead to a greater appreciation for other philosophers—those like Plato, who preceded Aristotle, and those like Cicero, who provided moral lessons and methods of presentation congenial to Christian belief. Fourth, in a telling blow, he accuses his opponents of defending what they do not fully understand. By concentrating on logic and dialectic, they only understand part of Aristotle's works. Worse, they know their "god Aristotle" only second-hand, through unreliable (and un-Christian) commentators like Averroës. Despite the accusation of ignorance directed at him, Petrarch had at least carefully read all of Aristotle's moral works that could provide lessons in how to act virtuously. Finally, Petrarch suggests that Aristotle's authority should not be a substitute for "reason" or "experience." His opponents had stifled intellectual curiosity by becoming "Aristotelians" who blindly accepted Aristotle's authority, rather than true philosophers. The history of Renaissance Aristotelianism is the history of successive engagements by humanists, theologians, and natural philosophers with Petrarch's claims.

If Aristotle had been misunderstood by his adherents and distorted by his commentators, humanists returned to the source, the texts. Aldus Manutius printed the Greek first edition of Aristotle in Venice in 1495–1498 (excluding the texts of the Rhetoric and Poetics), following a more conventional Venetian edition of 1472–1474, which printed the medieval Latin text with the commentaries of Averroës. Such editions, new Latin translations

A

from better Greek texts, the recovery of previously unknown works like the *Rhetoric ad Herrenium,* and the winnowing out of pseudo-Aristotelian works made possible a closer scrutiny of Aristotle. The print explosion also led to a burgeoning Aristotelian literature ranging from commentaries, paraphrases, and epitomes, to moral guidebooks published in the vernacular. Combined in facing-page editions with older Latin texts, and compared with newly completed editions of Averroës' commentaries (Giunta, 1550), humanists were able to disentangle Aristotle from his Arabic commentators, as well as his early assimilation in this form by the church fathers. Problems of coherence were solved through careful comparison of passages from different works of Aristotle. Problems of Aristotelian conceptual vocabulary were addressed by publishing careful studies of the Greek texts. The problem soon became too much rather than too little Aristotle. Humanist criticism, inseparable from the scholarship required for accurate texts, also forced substantive engagement with Aristotle's philosophical system.

Petrarch's attack on scholasticism and dialectic forms a second key aspect of humanist engagement with Aristotle. For many humanists, attacking scholastic method was a means to purify theology. Lorenzo Valla (1407–1457) continued the attack on dialectic and scholasticism in his *De Dialectica.* Like Petrarch, he championed instead a *rhetorica theologica* based on the persuasive and affective modes of rhetoric, in contrast to the mistaken science of scholastic logic that had corrupted theology. Following Valla was Rudolph Agricola (1443–1485), whose reputation as a critic of dialectic was made by Desiderius Erasmus's much-delayed publication of Agricola's *De Dialectica* early in the sixteenth century. This attack on the "pseudodialecticians" was carried out with a vengeance by others of the Erasmian circle, most notably by the Spaniard Juan Luis Vives. While Valla, Agricola, and Vives were motivated by religious concerns, their criticisms extended to other issues. By attacking the centrality of syllogistic logic, they reemphasized the importance of rhetoric and challenged the existing university concentration on the teaching of dialectic. Petrus Ramus best characterizes the combination of Aristotelian critic and Protestant educational reformer. His better-known work, the *Dialecticae Institutiones* (1543), cannot be separated from his *Aristotelicae Animadversiones* of the same year in which he launched a full-scale broadside against those Parisian masters who had tied Aristotle so closely to Christian theology that to criticize one was to criticize the other. The continuation of this anti-Aristotelian, pro-Ciceronian

(and thus pro-rhetoric) humanist attack can be found in Mario Nizoli's *Of true principles and philosophical reasoning against the psuedophilosophers* (1553), republished by Leibniz in 1670. Nizoli's work more closely resembled a philosophical work in epistemology, unconcerned with religious matters.

A third humanist research program, foreshadowed by Petrarch, involved developing a greater sense of the history of philosophy and Aristotle's place in it. With the fuller recovery of classical texts, Aristotle increasingly became one philosopher among many, rather than "the philosopher," whose true measure ought to be taken in comparison with other philosophers. The use of ancient writers to aid in textual exposition, reading Aristotle along with newly printed editions of early Greek commentators like Simplicius and Theophrastus (who deserved scrutiny because they were more ancient than Averroës, and thus closer to the source) contributed to a growing sense of the historicity of Aristotle's works and the process by which his works had been assimilated by the church and university. Showing Aristotle as one philosopher among many made him an historical figure rather than an icon. Once separated from the commentaries of Averroës, Aristotle's works could be scrutinized and compared in their own right. For an Aristotelian like Pietro Pomponazzi (1462–1525), such scrutiny remained in the world of texts. In his *Of the Immortality of the Soul* (1516), he notes that doctrines claimed by Averroës to be Aristotelian and taught in the universities were "unintelligible, and monstrous, and quite foreign to Aristotle." In his *Tractatus* (1516), Pomponazzi argued that freedom to philosophize meant the right to interpret and teach pure Aristotle by closely scrutinizing Aristotle's arguments without church interference. This claim, quite radical when made, already sounded archaic by the end of the sixteenth century. A landmark book was Leonardo Bruni's *Life of Aristotle* (1429), in which Aristotle was placed in his historical context as a founder of a sect, actively teaching and engaged in quarrels with other philosophers, an earlier exemplar for the life of a humanist. Still, other humanists like George Trebizond (1395–1484) felt it necessary to write reconciliations of Aristotle and Plato. Trebizond's *Comparationes phylosophorum Aristotelis et Platonis* (Venice, 1523) demonstrates their congruence in matters deemed important for Christian faith.

The recovery of an Aristotle who was a working philosopher was continued by Franciso Patrizi of Cherzo (1529–1597), who began a "life" of Aristotle, first published as *Discussionum peripateticarum tomi primi* (Venice,

A

1571), later included as Book I of his *Discussionum peripateticarum tomi IV* (Basel, 1581). Patrizi's "life" included an accurate canon for Aristotle's writings, along with a chronological sequencing of the works, and a consideration of subsequent Peripatetic interpretations of Aristotle. When expanded, Book II developed the theme of *concordia* between philosophers, Book III outlined *discordia,* while Book IV engaged in substantive criticisms of Aristotelian doctrines. Increasingly, agreement between Plato and Aristotle, and the easy assimilation of Cicero with Aristotle was challenged by the profusion of recovered texts. Gianfrancesco della Mirandola (1469–1533) responded by rejecting the lifelong project of his famous uncle, Pico della Mirandola, of establishing concordia among Aristotle, Plato, and earlier philosophical traditions. Rather, the variety of opinions by philosophers meant that we ought to trust only the truths of Christian revelation. In his discussion of Aristotle's inconsistencies, Gianfranceso questioned the metaphysical basis, logical coherence, and physical theories of Aristotelian science, rejecting four key Aristotelian assumptions regarding the nature of motion, time, place, and vacuum, all of which became battlegrounds for the new science of the seventeenth century. More damagingly, Gianfrancesco struck at the heart of the Aristotelian claim to interpret reality by questioning Aristotle's assumption that sense impressions could adequately convey reality to the perceiver—a most corrosive attack with far-reaching consequences for emerging "new science."

While Gianfrancesco's attack on the certainty claimed by Aristotelian method led him to fideism, for others, like Descartes, the answer was to recreate grounds of certainty by other means. Other skeptics such as Henricus Agrippa, writing *Of the Vanitie and Uncertainty of the Artes* (1530; English, 1569), included Aristotle as a key target in his broadside against philosophy. Equally critical of the pretensions of dialectic, he not only showed the kaleidoscope of philosophical opinions in which Aristotle was only one voice, but engaged in *ad hominem* arguments that impugned Aristotle's moral character, especially undercutting his moral philosophy. Such arguments had a long life in the seventeenth century, when they were used and reused by natural scientists who were engaged in polemical contests against "Aristotelians." The emergence of an autonomous discipline of philosophy, hinted at by Petrarch and Pomponazzi, required the uncoupling of any necessary connection between Aristotle and Catholic theology, making the connection a matter of historical circumstance.

Juan Luis Vives influenced all subsequent critics of Aristotle by providing a compendium of humanist attacks used by seventeenth-century critics. Like Ramus (who borrowed from him), Vives attacked Aristotelian logical method and especially the excesses of scholastic theology. He wished to revise the teaching of logic, reemphasizing rhetoric and arguing for curriculum reform. Like Petrarch, he argued that Aristotle's defenders did not understand the philosopher they defended. Vives's engagement with Aristotle lasted from his first historical and philological placing of Aristotle in his *Of the Origin of Sects* (1518), through his attack in *Against the Pseudodialecticians,* climaxing in his exhaustive criticism of the encyclopedia as currently taught in *Of the Disciplines* (1531), whose best-known first part, "Of the Causes of the Corruption of the Arts in General," is a masterly attack on the shortcomings of dialectic and scholastic logic. By his late work, *De Censura de Aristotelis Operibus* (1538), Vives could thoughtfully comment on each of Aristotle's works, demonstrating his technical competence and knowledge of earlier Renaissance criticism, both substantive and philological. High praise is reserved for Aristotle's ethical works, and central philosophical difficulties of others are raised. Vives amplified other Petrarchan tropes. In his *Of the Origin of Sects,* he reiterated that a proper understanding of Aristotle requires knowledge of Greek, therefore criticizing the early commentators like Averroës. In *Against the Pseudodialecticians,* Vives claimed the Aristotelians were defending someone they did not understand, even in the limited province of Aristotle's logic. They had also failed to cultivate useful knowledge. Unlike most humanists, Vives took his own advice, making practical proposals for dealing with problems of poor relief. Like later critics, Vives acknowledges the acute observations of Aristotle's *de Animalium*—a work in which Vives claimed Aristotle had not yet let his concern for system distort his direct observation of the world. Yet the limits of the humanist program is demonstrated in Vives's inability to move from texts to direct observation of the natural world.

But while humanists raised the questions, others were concerned with the world of experience and observation. Francis Bacon, who had assimilated humanist criticism of Aristotelian logic, argued that philosophy must shift its attention to empirical observation. Bacon, like Galileo and Vives before him, praised the early Aristotle of the *de Animalium* for acuteness of observation, but criticized the "later" Aristotle for having made "his natural philosophy a mere bond servant to his logic, thereby making it contentious and well-nigh useless" (*Novum Organon*, I. c. 54). Bacon took to heart humanist criticisms of the limits of syllogistic logic and the certainty claimed for it. Echoing the humanists, Bacon was critical of Aristotle's arrogance and took a dim view of his relationship to prior philosophy, which he had arrogantly destroyed like a "Turk." Bacon was equally critical of the humanists' concentration on rhetoric, and even their excessive focus on texts. By the time Bacon wrote his *Advancement of Learning*, he condemned humanism for having become a "Ciceronianism" that substituted style for weight, a distemper of learning in which "words are studied, not things." Bacon's program was to build a system by induction from particulars for understanding the first causes of the natural world.

In summary, humanists criticized the complexity and barbarity of scholastic theology. Rhetorical and probabilistic arguments, they claimed, provided a better means for human understanding, and were a better model of human interaction and knowledge than the fallacious certainty generated by dialectical method based on syllogistic logic. The humanists developed a history of *varia philosophia*, historicizing Aristotelianism as a key, but not the only, philosophical system. Aristotle was not only one philosopher among many, but internally inconsistent as well. According to the humanists, Aristotle was wrong about matters of fact, since he had turned away from the observation of the world and forced his observations to fit his bad metaphysics. The emergence of autonomous disciplines of natural and moral philosophy was only possible after humanists helped to free Aristotelian theories from their theological encumbrances. Later critics of Aristotle incorporated humanist attacks on scholastic logic, Aristotelian metaphysics, cosmology, and natural science, and they relied heavily on humanist philological work on the Aristotelian corpus and commentaries. At the very least, later critics understood better the Aristotle they attacked because of humanist textual scholarship. They appropriated the humanists' *ad hominem* and rhetorical arguments against Aristotle to buttress their own anti-Aristotelian "scientific" claims, and increasingly defined themselves in opposition to Aristotelian metaphysics and cosmology. They relied also on humanist criticisms that had moved past attacks on dialectic to question the disciplinary foundations of the medieval university derived from the Aristotelian encyclopedia. But these changes should not be exaggerated; nor can they be downplayed. The common-sense Aristotelian structures of intellectual inquiry did not disappear overnight. Aristotelian categories and modes of intellectual practice continued to shape university instruction and intellectual inquiry, so that even those who wished to criticize Aristotle shared his common-sense outlook even as they sought to think outside it.

BIBLIOGRAPHY

Dibon, Paul. *La philosophie néierlandaise au siécle d'or.* vol. I. 1954.

Garin, Eugenio. "Le Traduzioni Umanistiche Di Aristotele Nel Secolo XV." *Atti della Societa Colombaria Fiorentina*, vol. 16 (1947–1950), pp. 55–104.

Green, Lawrence, ed. *John Rainold's Oxford Lectures on Aristotle's Rhetoric.* 1986.

Lohr, C.H. "Renaissance Latin Aristotle Commentaries." *Studies in the Renaissance*, vol. 21, pp. 228–289.

Schmitt, Charles. *John Case and Aristotelianism in Renaissance England.* 1983.

Siegel, J.E. *Rhetoric and Philosophy in Renaissance Humanism.* 1968.

Dean Kiernan

SEE ALSO

Bacon, Francis; Ciceronianism; Classical Literature, English Translations; Classical Literature, Influence of; Education; Humanism; Logic; Petrarchanism; Platonism; Ramism; Rhetoric; Science, History of; Vives, Juan Luis

Armada, Spanish

To Sir James Whitelocke, then a freshman at Oxford, Philip II of Spain's attempt to conquer England in 1588 seemed in retrospect just a minor nuisance: "That summer after was the terrible shew of the sea Armada from Spaigne, which was a little distemper to the quiet course of studies." Nevertheless, for thirty-six hours in August 1588, more than 120 ships of Philip II's Grand Fleet, carrying 20,000 troops, lay at anchor off Calais while, twenty-five miles away at Dunkirk, 30,000 veterans began to embark on their transports under the watchful eye of Alexander Farnese, duke of Parma, Europe's most successful soldier. Spain's plan called for the two forces to join and sail to the Kentish coast, landing the troops and a powerful siege train near Ramsgate; then, while Parma and his men marched rapidly on London, the Armada would sail up the Thames. Elizabeth would be captured and deposed, and an interim administration headed by Cardinal William Allen would begin to re-catholicize the kingdom while Philip II selected the new sovereign.

Armada, Spanish 37

A

Philip II had been king consort to Mary I in 1554–1558 and had sought to replace Elizabeth I with Mary Queen of Scots in 1570–1571, but then the outbreak of rebellion in the Netherlands (1572) and the annexation of Portugal (1580) diverted his resources. However, Spain's successes in these two theaters alarmed Elizabeth, and in 1585, she dispatched Sir Francis Drake with a fleet to raid the Spanish Caribbean, and Robert Dudley, earl of Leicester, with an army to assist the Dutch rebels.

These acts of aggression provoked Philip II to concentrate the energies of his entire monarchy against Elizabeth, and he worked both to secure her diplomatic isolation and to mobilize the ships, men, and munitions necessary for invasion. Everything seemed ready by summer 1588, and the Armada forced its way to the English Channel despite desperate efforts by the Royal Navy to halt its progress. As the Spanish fleet lay off Calais, however, the English sent in fireships that broke the Armada's order, allowing Elizabeth's warships to use their superior firepower to inflict serious damage on the Spaniards and to drive them into the North Sea. Strong winds then prevented the Armada from returning to the Channel, forcing it to return to Spain by circumnavigating the British Isles. Storms struck them on route, damaging the ships further so that some sank and others ran out of supplies. In the end, perhaps one-third of the fleet and one-half of the men perished.

Philip II learned several lessons from this catastrophe. Almost immediately, twelve purpose-built warships were laid down in the royal dockyards, and the design of naval guns improved. Two subsequent attempts at invasion, in 1596 and 1597, involved only forces from the Iberian Peninsula (storms drove both back before they reached the invasion area). But the cost of continuing the war with England proved crippling: Elizabeth's navy now made regular raids on the coasts of Spain, destroying property, seizing ships, taking hostages, and even (for two weeks in 1596) occupying the city of Cadiz. Meanwhile, on the high seas and in the Americas, English privateers preyed on Spanish shipping and outposts, causing huge losses and paralyzing trade; and, in the Netherlands, English troops helped the Dutch struggle for independence. When peace came in 1604, six years after Philip II's death, Spain's decline as a great power had become evident.

Nevertheless, the campaign of 1588 had been a close call. The Armada seemed to contemporaries "the largest fleet that has ever been seen in these seas since the creation of the world" (a Florentine ambassador), and "the greatest and strongest combination, to my understanding, that ever was gathered in Christendom" (Sir John Hawkins). Even after its defeat, Admiral Charles Howard (who had led the victorious navy) claimed that "All the world never saw a force such as theirs was"; while according to Sir Walter Ralegh (who had been charged to defend Cornwall from possible invasion), Elizabeth had no land forces sufficient "to encounter an armie like unto that, wherewith it was intended that the prince of Parma should have landed in England." And, indeed, London in 1588 lacked effective defenses; Elizabeth's troops, although numerous, lacked experience; and her main army mustered at Tilbury in Essex, too far from Ramsgate to have prevented Parma's landing. Under the circumstances, Sir James Whitelocke was lucky to have been able to continue his "quiet course of studies" at Oxford with only "a little distemper."

BIBLIOGRAPHY

Laughton, John K., ed. *State Papers relating to the Defeat of the Spanish Armada*. Navy Records Society, vols. 1–2. 1895.

Martin, Colin and Geoffrey Parker. *The Spanish Armada*. 1988.

Mattingly, Garret. *The Armada*. 1959.

Rasor, Eugene L. *The Spanish Armada of 1588: Historiography and Annotated Bibliography*. 1993.

Geoffrey Parker

SEE ALSO

Allen, William; Drake, Francis; Dudley, Robert; Foreign Relations and Diplomacy; Military History; Ordnance; Philip II; Privateering; Ridolfi Plot

Armin, Robert (?–1616)

Robert Armin is famous for playing the role of the fool in William Shakespeare's plays after Will Kemp left the company in 1599. Born to a Norfolk tailor, Armin received a good education and became an apprentice goldsmith, an elite occupation. He took to performance, encouraged by his small and ugly physique, and began by writing and performing ballads. Shakespearean songs are witness to Armin's musical talent. Armin learned his skills in clowning from the most famous of Elizabethan clowns, Richard Tarleton, and *Quips Upon Questions* (1600) is an intellectual reworking of extemporal comic improvisations in verse. Armin's style as a writer is convoluted and surrealistic, and relies on his gifts as a mimic. He became a player with the Company of Lord Chandos, and while touring the countryside gathered material for *Fool upon Fool* (1600), a study of six "natural" fools, handicapped individuals retained in great households to provide amusement. His play, *Two Maids of More-clacke,* was performed by boys, with Armin in the role of a "natural fool" at Christ's Hospital.

Armin joined Shakespeare's company soon after it moved to the Globe Theatre in late 1599, and his first roles included Touchstone and Feste. A series of household fools followed, the most famous being Lear's (1606). The recurrent theme is the idea made famous by Erasmus in his *Praise of Folly*—that only the fool is truly wise. This Renaissance conception of folly differs from the medieval conception of the fool as a "vice" or devil, and from Tarleton's conception of the fool as a rustic parvenu. Armin's growing intellectual concern with folly is apparent in his reworking of *Fool upon Fool,* published as *Nest of Ninnies* (1608), and his influence on Shakespeare was profound.

BIBLIOGRAPHY

Felver, C.S. *Robert Armin, Shakespeare's Fool.* 1961.

Hotson, Leslie. *Shakespeare's Motley.* 1952.

Mullini, Roberta. *Il fool nel teatro di Shakespeare.* 1983.

Wiles, David. *Shakespeare's Clown.* 1987.

David Wiles

SEE ALSO

Actors; Shakespeare, William; Tarleton, Richard; Vice, The

Arminianism

This seventeenth-century term originally denoted the opinions of a political and theological party in the Netherlands (also called the "Remonstrants") that reflected the teachings of Jacobus Arminius (1560–1609), professor of theology at Leiden from 1603–1609. Arminius, his associates, the churchman Uitenbogaert and the statesman Oldenbarnevelt, and followers such as Hugo Grotius, were critical of the emphases in Theodore Beza's, Francis Gomarus's, and William Perkins's developments of Calvin's theology of predestination and election. Arminius's theology was derived partly from the Lutherans Melanchthon and Hemmingsen, but also from Charles Perrot, the rector of the Genevan Academy, who was his teacher. The Arminians believed that God predestined to salvation those who had faith (not that God's absolute decree of election was the cause of salvation), that faith could be lost, that God's grace could be resisted, that Christ died for all (not only the elect). They also believed that the state had the right to regulate the church. In 1618, Arminianism was condemned by the Dutch Reformed Church at the Synod of Dort, but not obliterated.

Arminianism is, strictly speaking, anachronistic when used to describe English theology of the Tudor period. The debates over predestination and related issues at Cambridge in the 1590s, and the ensuing Lambeth Articles show that there were Elizabethans with views similar to those of Arminius. At that time they were in the minority in the Church of England, but they foreshadowed an increasingly important viewpoint in English theology and the English church in the seventeenth century. Repercussions of these debates, through Perkins's tract on predestination (1598), first caused Arminius to write on the subject. Some have found it useful to consider Peter Baro, professor at Cambridge from 1574 to 1596, Richard Hooker, or Launcelot Andrewes, as proto-Arminian, as, later, Andrewes and William Laud would be called Arminians. But, given the intricacy of late-sixteenth-century theological discourse and the evolution of English theology, it is difficult to define absolutely what constituted Arminianism, especially English Arminianism. Like Puritan or Bolshevik, Arminian and Arminianism were used broadly and imprecisely as terms of opprobrium. The literature shows the methodological difficulties of establishing the limits of the subject.

BIBLIOGRAPHY

Bangs, Carl. *Arminius.* 1981.

Lake, Peter. *Anglicans and Puritans?* 1988.

Tyacke, Nicholas. *Anti-Calvinists.* 1990.

White, Peter. *Predestination, policy and polemic.* 1992.

Frederick H. Shriver

SEE ALSO

Andrewes, Launcelot; Church of England; Hooker, Richard; Lambeth Articles; Laud, William; Perkins, William

Arthur Tudor, Prince of Wales (1486–1502)

The eldest son of Henry VII and Elizabeth of York and first husband of Katherine of Aragon, Arthur Tudor was born on September 19, 1486, at Winchester. At once heir to the Houses of York and Tudor, he was given the name of Britain's legendary king. At age three, Arthur was created knight of the bath, and in 1491 made a knight of the garter.

His education was rigorous, first under his chaplain, John Rede, and later with the poet laureate, Bernard André, who praised his mastery of the Latin and Greek authors.

Negotiations for his marriage to Katherine began when he was two and were finalized in the Treaty of Medina del Campo in 1498. For Ferdinand and Isabella, Katherine's marriage to the English heir would secure Henry VII's alliance against France; Henry was equally eager to have united Spain as an ally. However, threats posed to his succession by Lambert Simnel and Perkin Wabeck ensured Ferdinand's caution, while Henry was also careful not to seem a proxy of the Spanish king's wishes.

Arthur was not healthy, and to satisfy Ferdinand's doubts Arthur was made to rehearse the marriage ceremony three times before Katherine's arrival at Plymouth on October 2, 1501, with the Spanish ambassador as her proxy. The wedding took place at St. Paul's Cathedral on November 14; the couple then returned to hold court at Arthur's residence in Ludlow on the Welsh borders. But within five months, Arthur and Katherine were seriously ill, possibly due to a local outbreak of the plague. Arthur's fragile health failed and he died on May 2, 1502.

Katherine soon entered into a marriage treaty with Prince Henry, but they were married only after long delays in a papal dispensation, and Henry VII's death in 1509. In 1533, Henry had their marriage annulled, setting the dispensation aside and arguing that he had in fact committed incest with his brother's wife (citing *Leviticus* 18), contrary to Katherine's claims that Arthur had never consummated their marriage.

BIBLIOGRAPHY

Kelly, Henry A. *The Matrimonial Trials of Henry VIII.* 1976.

Mattingly, Garrett. *Catherine of Aragon*, pp. 11–49. 1941.

Scarisbrick, J.J. Henry VIII, pp. 4–8. 1968.

David W. Swain

SEE ALSO

Foreign Affairs and Diplomacy; Henry VII; Henry VIII; Katherine of Aragon; Simnel, Lambert; Warbeck, Perkin

Arthurian Legend

Sir Thomas Malory's English rendition of the Arthurian legends was published by William Caxton as *Le Morte D'Arthur* on July 31, 1485. Less than a month later, Henry Tudor seized the English throne by defeating Richard III at Bosworth, and the new Henry VII bolstered his royal claim by tracing his ancestry back to Arthur and Calwallader, the last British king. Henry named his first son Arthur and had him christened at Winchester Castle where the traditional Round Table hung. When Prince Arthur died at fifteen, the new Arthurian age his father envisioned for England did not materialize.

As Henry VIII ascended the English throne, he, too, traced his ancestry to Arthur and presented himself as the fulfillment of Merlin's prophecy that "the once and future king" would return to unite Britain. Later Tudor monarchs made less of their Arthurian heritage, but the political importance of the historical King Arthur (as presented by Geoffrey of Monmouth) limited the literary use of the Round Table stories.

Malory's Arthurian compilation was popular enough to cause concern among some early modern scholars. Juan Luis Vives, tutor to Princess Mary, condemned the tales of Tristram, Lancelot, and Arthur "whiche were written and made by suche as were ydle & knew nothinge. These bokes do hurte both man & woman, for they make them wylye & craftye, they kyndle and styr up covetousnes, inflame angre, & all beastly and filthy desyre." Roger Ascham, tutor to Princess Elizabeth, denounced romances in general but focused on *Le Morte D'Arthur*, "the whol pleasure of which booke standeth in two speciall poyntes, in open mans slaughter, and bold bawdrye: in which booke, those be counted the noblest Knightes that do kill most men without any quarrell, and commit fowlest aduoulteries by sutlest shifts." Another tutor, Nathaniel Baxter, deplored the "reading of vile & blasphemous, or at least of prophan & friuolous bokes, such as are that infamous legend of K. Arthur." Yet Baxter's pupil, Sir Philip Sidney, wrote that "honest king Arthure will never displease a souldier," and, as Ben Jonson told William Drummond, "had ane intention to have transformed all his Arcadia to the stories of King Arthure."

It was, however, Edmund Spenser who attempted, at least ostensibly, to build a literary work around King Arthur. In *The Shepheardes Calender*, Spenser's friend, E.K., scorned "fine fablers and lowd lyers, such as were the Authors of King Arthure the great," but at some point in the composition of *The Faerie Queene*, Spenser placed Arthur at the center of his work. The poet wrote to Sir Walter Ralegh, "I chose the history of King Arthur, as most fitte for the excellency of his person, being made famous by many mens former workes, and also furthest from the daunger of envy, and suspition of present time." Yet Spenser treats Arthur "before he was king" and includes only Tristram from the knights of the Round Table. Spenser's allegorized Arthur lacks the tragic power inherent in the myths and legends. John Hughes, Spenser's first editor, noted in 1715 that "we lose sight of [Arthur] too soon to consider him as the Hero of the Poem."

On the stage, King Arthur was treated in *The Misfortunes of Arthur* written by Thomas Hughes for presentation before Elizabeth in 1588. Hughes, a Cambridge M.A., tried to fit the historical Arthur of Geoffrey into the classical model of Seneca with unhappy results. While Hughes glimpsed the dramatic potential of the story, he could not transcend the devices and conventions of his prototype. The subject was worthy of Shakespeare, but there is no evidence that he knew Geoffrey, Malory, or any other worthwhile telling of the Arthurian tales.

BIBLIOGRAPHY

Bornstein, Diane. "William Caxton's Chivalric Romances and the Burgundian Renaissance in England." *English Studies,* vol. 57, pp. 1–10.

Carley, James P. "Polydore Vergil and John Leland on King Arthur: The Battle of the Books." *Interpretations,* vol. 15, no. 2, pp. 86–100.

Dean, Christopher. *Arthur of England: English Attitudes to King Arthur . . . in the Middle Ages and the Renaissance.* 1987.

Greenlaw, Edwin. *Studies in Spenser's Historical Allegory.* 1932.

Nohrnberg, James. *The Analogy of the "Faerie Queene,"* pp. 35–58. 1976.

Reiss, Edmund, Louise Horner Reiss, and Beverly Taylor, eds. *Arthurian Legend and Literature: An Annotated Bibliography.* 1984.

Barry Gaines

SEE ALSO

Ascham, Roger; Caxton, William; Spenser, Edmund; Vives, Juan Luis

Thomas Malory, *The Story of the most noble and worthy kynge Arthur.* From Copland's edition of Caxton's adaptation of Malory's *Morte d'Arthur* (1577). Three vignettes illustrate events around the birth of Arthur: center, Isgrayne kneeling before Uther in tent; upper left, Sir Ector's wife nursing Arthur; upper right, a marriage. Reproduced from the original by permission of the Henry E. Huntington Library and Art Gallery.

A

Articles of Religion

The promulgation of articles or confessions of doctrine was a characteristic activity of the Reformation period in the sixteenth century that was comparable to the creed-making in the church of the fourth and fifth centuries. These formularies were designed not only to exclude what were considered heretical notions but also to serve as a basis of negotiation for unity among the several bodies of Christians who found themselves separated by the controversies of the time.

During the reign of Henry VIII there was some discussion between Lutheran leaders and those of the Church of England on the basis of confessional standards, and some attempts were made to arrive at a common statement of faith acceptable to both sides. Henry VIII was far more Catholic than the Lutherans, and the negotiations undertaken during his reign ultimately came to nothing. Nevertheless, the Ten Articles of 1536 and the Six Articles of 1539 prepared the way for the Thirty-nine Articles, which were to stand as the final formulation of the Church of England on the major doctrinal controversies of the sixteenth century.

The Ten Articles of 1536 were adopted by convocation that year at the desire of the king as expressing his utmost concession to Protestantism. The authoritative standards of faith are defined as the Bible, the three ecumenical creeds (the Apostles', the Nicene, and the Athanasian), and the first four ecumenical councils. The three sacraments of baptism, penance, and the eucharist are upheld; the other four (confirmation, marriage, holy orders, and final anointing of the sick) are not mentioned either in approval or denial. The eucharistic presence is called both corporal and substantial, but transubstantiation goes unmentioned. Justification implies faith in Christ alone, but confession, absolution, and works of charity are also required. Images are to be retained as representative of virtue, but are not to be worshipped. The intercession of the saints may be invoked, but not because they will hear sooner than Christ. Masses and prayers for the dead are enjoined, but the idea that the bishop of Rome can deliver a soul out of purgatory is rejected.

These articles were followed in 1537 by *The Institution of the Christian Man*, a book compiled by a committee of bishops and divines. This book expounded the Apostles' Creed, the seven sacraments, the Decalogue, the Lord's Prayer, and the Ave Maria. It also dealt with certain other disputed issues, including the doctrines of justification and purgatory and the relation of the Church of England to the Roman see. The document never received the authority of the king, who used it rather to test the temper of the people. In 1543 a revised edition was published under the title *The King's Book*.

The Six Articles of 1539 were imposed by Parliament at the bidding of Henry VIII to prevent the spread of Reformation doctrines and practices and to demonstrate that the king was an orthodox Catholic—apart from his refusal to submit to the authority of Rome. These articles maintained transubstantiation, denial of which was to be punished by fire; repudiated priestly marriage; rejected communion of the laity in both bread and wine; upheld monastic vows of chastity; defended private masses; and enjoined auricular confession.

After Henry's death in 1547, Parliament repealed the Six Articles Act. Meanwhile, Thomas Cranmer had long been engaged in the preparation of articles of religion. The Lutheran Augsburg Confession of 1530 having been his primary source, he submitted his articles in 1552 by order of the council to six theologians, among whom was John Knox. The Forty-two Articles were issued in 1553, accompanied by a royal mandate of the young King Edward VI that required all clergy, schoolmasters, and members of the universities on taking their degrees to subscribe to them. Decidedly Protestant in tone, they were in fact directed as much against Protestant extremism (specifically Anabaptism) as against traditional Catholicism. Because of the restoration of the Roman Catholic faith under Mary Tudor, the Forty-two Articles were never enforced, but they later formed the basis of the Thirty-nine Articles.

The accession of Queen Elizabeth I in 1559 again brought to the fore the necessity of doctrinal definition for the Church of England. In January 1563, the Convocation of Canterbury took up the work of revising the Forty-two Articles of 1553. The articles were reduced in number to thirty-nine, and some of the more extreme "protestant" statements were eliminated. The queen herself made a few not insignificant alterations and additions primarily designed to conciliate Catholic sympathizers. The articles were approved in 1571 by statutes of Parliament, and the royal assent made them part of the law of the land. Subscription was enforced upon all clergy ordained during the reign of Queen Mary and upon all persons presented to a benefice and all candidates for ordination. The Canons of 1604 made this subscription a definite part of the church's ecclesiastical law.

The Thirty-nine Articles cover nearly all the heads of the Christian faith, especially those then under dispute with the Roman Catholics. The first five articles affirm the basic doctrines of the Trinity and the Incarnation.

Articles 6–8 set forth the sources of doctrinal authority in Anglicanism, namely, the Holy Scriptures and the historic creeds. Article 6 declares that "Holy Scripture containeth all things necessary to salvation."

The nature of man and of his salvation are the subjects of Articles 9–18; here, the Protestant doctrine of justification by faith alone is affirmed (Article 11), while the doctrines of supererogatory works, purgatory, the worship of relics, the invocation of saints, and clerical celibacy are condemned. The discussion of predestination in Articles 17 and 18, while affirming divine election, carefully avoids the strict Calvinist doctrine of reprobation.

Articles 19–36 deal with the doctrines of the church and the sacraments. The distinction is made between the visible and invisible church. The sacraments are defined as baptism and the Eucharist. The adoration of the host in the Eucharist is rejected, but the Real Presence of Christ is affirmed. All scholastic definitions of the nature of that Presence, however, are dismissed, and the doctrine of transubstantiation is declared to be "repugnant to the plain words of Scripture." Article 36 concerns the consecration of bishops and ministers.

The last three articles are addressed to the relation of Christians to the state. Article 37 concerns the royal supremacy, and affirms the Erastian principle that king has "chief power" in his dominions and that all causes, whether ecclesiastical or civil, appertain to his governance. It specifically denies that the pope has any jurisdiction in England. In addition, it defends the use of the death penalty by the civil authorities for "heinous and grievous offences," and declares that it is lawful for Christians, at the command of their magistrates, to bear weapons and serve in wars.

BIBLIOGRAPHY

Hardwick, Charles. *A History of the Articles of Religion, to which is Added a Series of Documents, from A.D. 1536 to A.D. 1615.* 1859.
Kidd, B.J. *The Thirty-Nine Articles: Their History and Explanation.* 2 vols. 2nd edition 1902.
Shepherd, Massey Hamilton, Jr. *The Oxford American Prayer Book Commentary.* 1950.

Lee W. Gibbs

SEE ALSO

Anabaptists; Calvinism; Church of England; Convocation; Cranmer, Thomas; Erastianism; Eucharist; King's Book; Knox, John; Lutheranism; Reformation, English

Artillery and Ballistics
See Ordnance

Ascham, Roger (1515 or 1516–1568)

The humanist educator Roger Ascham is best known for *The Scholemaster* (1570), a posthumously published, not-quite-complete work in two books on pedagogy and curriculum, and *Toxophilus* (1545), a treatise in dialogue form on shooting (i.e., archery). His letters, thirty-nine in English, more than 250 in Latin, many of which were collected shortly after his death as models of form and style, constitute an unrivaled source for the study of mid-century humanism. Within his extensive correspondence with the Strasbourg educator Johann Sturm, not to mention *The Scholemaster,* Ascham's distinctively English version of the Ciceronian ideal of the union of "good matter" and "good utterance" (*Works* 3:211), scriptural religion and classical learning, emerges as the dominant theme of his pedagogy.

Ascham was born in Yorkshire; little is known about his family and early education. In 1530, he matriculated at Cambridge University, just then emerging as the leading center of learning in England; here he would remain for some eighteen exciting years, becoming a fellow in 1534 (the day of his election was "*dies natalis* to me," he declares [3:235]), and eventually university orator and reader of Greek. During this formative period, the "new learning," like Protestantism, was taking deep root in a distinguished group of scholars, especially in Ascham's beloved St. John's College under the leadership of his friend and mentor, John Cheke.

At the same time, these Cambridge years pointed to a growing dilemma: how to reconcile an emotional attachment to the lifelong pursuit of learning with the necessity of finding patrons and preferment. The drama of Ascham's whole career centers on that tension, although it is clear that his repeated contrast between the desired *otium* of the academy and the feared *negotium* of court is highly idealized. Nothing in his life hit the mark so squarely as his hugely patriotic and learned *Toxophilus,* presented in 1545 to Henry VIII at Greenwich Palace as the king returned from his wars in France. A wider door to preferment may have been opening in 1548 when Ascham was called from Cambridge to court to tutor Princess Elizabeth, but within two years he somehow fell—the details are sketchy—on what he calls "the slippery floors of the bustling court" (*Letters* 43).

Thanks to well-placed friends, his career took a fortunate turn in 1550 when he was named secretary to Sir

A

Richard Morison, the new ambassador to the imperial court of the Holy Roman Emperor Charles V. Near the end of his travels he composed a strongly analytical *Report of Germany* concerning the tumult in church and state, but did not publish it (it was published posthumously [1570?]), perhaps because in 1553 he himself was negotiating the treacherous political crosscurrents of mid-Tudor England, until he could, in 1554, be confirmed as the Latin secretary for Mary I. Elizabeth I would continue him in that position until his death. His ability to accommodate himself to the realities of Mary's reign has raised repeated questions that must be answered in terms of what Ascham himself called "the manner of wayfaring men" (1:342). "I shape myself to be a courtier," he professed to one of his patrons at court (1:396), but in truth he never did overcome his aversion to that manner of life. Whatever his official obligations, his chief delight lay in the privileged moments when he and Queen Elizabeth read Latin and Greek together in her chamber. He was in the court, but not of it, and unlike such other contemporary Cambridge luminaries as John Cheke, Thomas Smith, and William Cecil, he attained neither wealth nor high position. Although his career exposes the extent to which mid-Tudor humanism is involved in matters of power and patronage, by temperament and preference he remained an educator, a Ciceronian in his doctrine of imitation, an earnest Protestant in religion, and always the nostalgic Cantabrigian.

BIBLIOGRAPHY

Giles, J.A. *The Whole Works of Roger Ascham.* 3 vols. in 4. 1864–1865.

Ryan, Lawrence V. *Roger Ascham.* 1963.

Vos, Alvin, ed. *Letters of Roger Ascham.* 1989.

Alvin Vos

SEE ALSO

Cheke, John; Education; Humanism

Aske, Robert (d. 1537)

A lawyer from the East Riding of Yorkshire and member of Gray's Inn, Robert Aske was the self-styled "chief captain" of the Pilgrimage of Grace. He was devoutly Catholic, opposed to Thomas Cromwell's religious policy and to what he regarded as unprecedented and dangerous legal innovations, and thus clearly sympathetic with the rebels' political and religious goals. Following the outbreak of the Lincolnshire rebellion in early October 1536, he took over leadership of the Yorkshire insurrection, giving it a sharper religious focus. He came up with the name "Pilgrimage of Grace," devised the banner of the Five Wounds of Christ, and wrote the Pilgrims' manifestos and oath.

By the end of October, Aske and his Pilgrim army of between 30,000 and 40,000 men controlled most of the northern third of England. The duke of Norfolk, Henry VIII's lieutenant in the north, lacking sufficient force to suppress the rebellion, played for time by negotiating with the Pilgrim leaders. Instead of marching the Pilgrim army on to London, Aske encamped it at Doncaster while he negotiated with Norfolk and sent emissaries to Henry VIII. Aske also presided over a provisional government in the north. He convened two "great councils" of Pilgrim representatives, the first at York (October 21–November 5) to discuss negotiations with Norfolk, and the second at Pontefract (December 2–4) to draft the Pilgrims' final petition, which Aske, in consultation with the other leaders, composed from grievances submitted by the Pilgrims' representatives. At Doncaster on December 6, Aske presented Norfolk the Pilgrims' petition, and the duke promised pardon and consideration of the Pilgrims' grievances. At heart a loyal subject, Aske, naively accepting Norfolk's—and Henry's—good faith, disbanded the Pilgrim army on December 8 and resigned his position as their leader.

After meeting in London with Henry VIII, Aske returned north bearing additional promises from the king. But in January 1537, insurrection flared anew in Lancashire; and while Aske urged the rebels to desist, Henry and Norfolk used the occasion as a pretext to renounce their promises. Norfolk quickly crushed the new insurrection. The Pilgrim leaders were brought to London, and in May and June tried and condemned to death. Henry ordered that the leaders be executed at the places where they had led the late rebellions. Accordingly, Aske was hanged in chains at York.

BIBLIOGRAPHY

Davies, C.S.L. "The Pilgrimage of Grace Reconsidered," *Past and Present,* vol. 41, pp. 54–76.

———. "Popular Religion and the Pilgrimage of Grace." In Anthony Fletcher and John Stevenson, eds., *Order and Disorder in Early Modern England.* 1985.

Dodds, Ruth, and Madeleine Hope. *The Pilgrimage of Grace, 1536–1537, and the Exeter Conspiracy, 1538.* 2 vols. 1915.

Elton, G.R. "Politics and the Pilgrimage of Grace." In *Studies in Tudor and Stuart Politics and Government, Vol 3: Papers and Reviews, 1973–1981.* 1983.

John M. Currin

SEE ALSO
Cromwell, Thomas; Pilgrimage of Grace

Askew, Anne (c. 1521–1546)

A Protestant convert, Anne Askew was arrested for heresy, interrogated by officials of the city of London, the church, and Henry VIII's council, and eventually burned at the stake. In The *first examinacyon* (1546) and *The lattre examinacyon* (1547), she wrote a compelling account of her interrogations, vividly representing key theological, political, and social conflicts of the English Reformation.

Askew's first publisher, John Bale, identifies her as the daughter of Sir William Askew of Lincolnshire and relates that her father forced her to marry a Master Kyme to consolidate familial land holdings. According to Bale, Kyme was a Catholic who drove Askew away once she had converted to Protestantism and had tangled with the priests in Lincoln Cathedral. Askew apparently sought a divorce, left her home and two children, and went to London, reappearing in the Reformist circle of Queen Catherine Parr. In March 1545, she was arrested for questioning on the Six Articles and interrogated by city officials and eventually by Edmund Bonner, bishop of London. Probably because of her connections to the Parr circle, which was then under direct attack from the conservative Catholic faction at court, Askew was again arrested in June 1546 and examined by the Privy Council at Greenwich and by Sir Richard Rich and Lord Chancellor Henry Wriothesley in the Tower of London. She was tortured on the rack and finally condemned and burned at Smithfield with three others. Recognizing the value of her writing for the Protestant cause, Bale published *The first examinacyon* in Wesel in November 1546, and *The lattre examinacyon* in January 1547, accompanying each with an interwoven commentary and "elucidation" of Askew as a martyr resisting Catholic tyranny. Of the subsequent five editions, only the first prints Bale's elucidation; Foxe included Askew's *Examinations in Actes and Monuments*.

In her dramatic account of her questionings, Askew depicts herself as a strong proponent of a scriptural, reformed faith arguing against worldly persecutors whom she continually baffles and enrages. Her biblical citations and her discussion of the symbolic nature of the Eucharist suggest the influence of Wycliffe, Frith, and Latimer. Her methodical undoing of her powerful opponents with irony and understatement suggests a satirical bent. She memorably represents her heroic resistance to torture and her preparation for death, exhorting her coreligionists to continue in the faith. Both *Examinations* include a remarkable woodcut of a female figure trampling a papal beast, bearing a Bible and a palm, and radiating light.

BIBLIOGRAPHY

Beilin, Elaine V., ed. *The Examinations of Anne Askew.* 1996.

———. "Anne Askew's Dialogue with Authority." In *Contending Kingdoms: Historical, Psychological, and Feminist Approaches to the Literature of Sixteenth-Century England and France,* Marie-Rose Logan and Peter Rudnytsky, eds. 1991.

———. *Redeeming Eve: Women Writers of the English Renaissance.* 1987.

Kendall, Ritchie D. *The Drama of Dissent: The Radical Poetics of Nonconformity, 1380–1590.* 1986.

King, John N. *English Reformation Literature: The Tudor Origins of the Protestant Tradition.* 1982.

McQuade, Paula. " 'Except that they had offended the Lawe': Gender and Jurisprudence in *The Examinations of Anne Askew.*" *Literature and History,* 3rd series, vol. 3, pp. 1–14.

Elaine V. Beilin

SEE ALSO
Articles of Religion; Bale, John; Bonner, Edmund; Eucharist; Parr, Catherine; Reformation, English

Astrology

Astrology was usefully defined by Christopher Heydon (1603) as "that Arte which teacheth by the motions, configurations, and influence of the Signes, starres, and celestiall Planets, to Prognosticate of the naturall effects, and mutations to come, in the elements and these inferiour and elementarie bodies." It can also be thought of more broadly as a system of belief that simply finds a relationship between the heavens and the affairs of men. In Tudor England, belief in the principles of astrology (in one form or another) was pervasive in all parts of the society, but not universal; there were those who opposed the belief and the practice. In the Tudor period the words "astrology" and "astronomy" were sometimes used interchangeably, although without confusion.

Astrology originated in classical antiquity, and, much like astronomy, achieved its most complete codification in the *Tetrabiblos* by Claudius Ptolemaeus (second century C.E.). Here, astrological belief was justified by extension from the undeniable influences of the sun on life and

A

weather, the association of the moon with tides, and the putative influence of the planets on agricultural conditions. But Ptolemy is also skeptical of its validity, noting frequent errors in astrological forecasts. The theoretical as distinct from the empirical support for astrology was premised on the earth's being at or near the center of motion of the celestial bodies; thus Copernicus's placement of the sun at the center of planetary motion in 1543 ought gravely to have disrupted what rational basis there was for astrological belief, but it had little effect on much of Tudor thought. Except for a statement of support in 1576 by Thomas Digges, the theoretical foundations of astrology were not undermined before the end of the Tudor period.

Astrology is often divided into distinct areas of practice: the judicial, which concerns the forecasting of weather, natural disasters, and the fate of nations; and natal (or genethliacal, this term first appearing in English in 1584), which prognosticates for individuals and delineates their characters, according to the state of the heavens at the moment of birth. A fourfold division adds the forecasting of the outcome of some action, based, as a nativity is, on the state of the heavens at the time an action is taken, and elections, the choosing of a propitious moment for some proposed action.

The sixteenth century produced an efflorescence of literature on astrology, at least on the Continent. Yet astrological belief and practice had become ossified; there was no revolution or reform in astrology, unlike those in astronomy, mathematics, or medicine. Indeed, astrology is unique in the culture of the period in being the only component of the mental universe not to undergo any form of change or upheaval. Indeed, for many, astrology could be a recourse for medical treatment, both physical and psychological, and astrologers were sometimes perceived by doctors as being in competition with them.

In the Tudor period, most astrological practice depended on books from the Continent. Two Italian astrologer-physicians, John Baptista Boerio and William Parron, visited the court of Henry VII; Cardanus, the great Italian mathematician and polymath, spent part of 1552 in England and Scotland; and the German Nicholas Kratzer (of whom Holbein painted a striking portrait) was an astrologer in the court of Henry VIII. Genethliacal astronomy had long encountered serious opposition from the church, which objected to its implication that free will was denied. This hostility was carried over, sometimes more intensely, by the Anglican Church after its Elizabethan establishment. The general response of astrology's defenders was to insist upon the contingent nature of its predictions; the subject, knowing what lay in store, could take actions that would alter the eventuality.

The proliferation of almanacs following the widespread adoption of the printing press promoted and reinforced a simple kind of folk astrological belief. Perhaps the first printed prognostications in England were produced by Parron around the turn of the sixteenth century, but for much of the next half century, most almanacs were continental productions, sometimes translated for the English market. What was probably the first native almanac with a prognostication appeared anonymously in 1539, and during Elizabeth's reign, English almanacs predominated, with their standard contents of calendar, planetary motions, "Zodiacal Man" (showing how the zodiacal signs related to the anatomy), and prognostication. There is an estimate that by 1600, more than 600 different almanacs had been printed in England, exempt from the Stationers' Company's limit of 1,200 to 1,500 copies for a single edition.

Among the most prominent astrological practitioners of the period, Simon Forman, for whom astrology was a profession, and the Reverend Richard Napier (1559–1634), a physician, used horoscopes for psychotherapy. At Oxford and Cambridge, some parts of astrology were subsumed under astronomy. Perhaps the most significant theorist of astrology in Tudor England was John Dee, whose interests gradually shifted from applied mathematics to occult studies, among which he might include astrology. He published a volume of astrological "aphorisms" (more like disorganized notes) as early as 1568, and in his famous *Mathematicall Preface* (1570), he ranked astrology along with astronomy, perspective, navigation, and fifteen other named subjects "derivative" from "Sciences, and Artes Mathmaticall."

The treatment of astrology in the Tudor period that is best known to literary scholars is the uninhibited assault on the Harvey brothers by Thomas Nashe in *Have with You to Saffron Walden* (1596). In 1601, John Chamber, a fellow of Eton College, published *A Treatise Against Judiciall Astrologie*. Christopher Heydon (1561–1623), a gentleman with deep interests in astronomy and astrology, jumped to the *Defence of Judiciall Astrologie* in 1603. The Chamber-Heydon dispute was a continuation of earlier arguments over the validity of judicial astrology, and did not in itself presage the decline of belief in astrology among the educated. In fact, however, the succeeding century was to witness that decline, but only after an extraordinary recrudescence in astrological practice and publication in mid-century.

A

BIBLIOGRAPHY

Allen, Don Cameron. *The Star-Crossed Renaissance: The Quarrel about Astrology and Its Influence in England.* 1941; repr. 1966.

Thomas, Keith. *Religion and the Decline of Magic,* pp. 283–385. 1971; repr. 1997.

Dee, John. *John Dee on Astronomy: Propaedeumata Aphoristica.* Wayne Shumaker, ed., J.L. Heilbron, intro. 1978.

Capp, Bernard. *Astrology and the Popular Press: English Almanacs, 1500–1800.* 1979.

Eade, J.C. *The Forgotten Sky: A Guide to Astrology in English Literature.* 1984.

Curry, Patrick, ed. *Astrology, Science and Society.* 1987.

Dunn, Richard Spencer. *The Status of Astrology in Elizabethan England, 1558–1603.* Unpublished dissertation, Cambridge University. 1992.

Adam Jared Apt

SEE ALSO

Astronomy; Dee, John; Digges, Thomas; Forman, Simon; Nashe, Thomas; Popular Literature

Astronomy

The sixteenth century witnessed the start of a revolution in astronomy in Europe. Astronomy was the first of the sciences to become mathematical, and its instrumentation was calibrated precisely; it not only described the motions of the celestial bodies but also predicted the positions of the sun, moon, and planets with a degree of precision that challenged the naked eye. Thus, astronomy had many applications for navigation, chronology, the prediction of eclipses, and astrology.

The ferment in Western European astronomy began in the late fifteenth century with the Polish astronomer Nicolaus Copernicus (1473–1543), who adhered more closely to Ptolemy's kinematic principles than Ptolemy himself did, proposing a detailed mathematical model of planetary motion that placed the sun at the center of the universe with the earth and planets revolving around it. Although Copernicus's comprehensive book expounding this astronomy, the *De Revolutionibus Orbium Caelestium,* was published in 1543, a preliminary working out of his ideas had been circulating in manuscript from at least 1514. An early brief account in England of the Copernican theory is that by Robert Recorde in his *Castle of Knowledge* (1556); later, Thomas Digges translated a part of Copernicus.

However, there was no overall program to promote astronomical activity in Tudor England, and astronomy had no English institutions to support its practitioners until the seventeenth century. It did, however, have a place in the university curriculum, partly as a survival from the liberal arts curriculum of the Middle Ages, though by the beginning of the Tudor period its presence there was almost vestigial. In the public disputations of candidates for the degree of M.A., there were occasionally set questions of an astronomical nature, but in the last decades of the sixteenth century astronomy began to regain some of its importance. Henry Savile (1549–1622), warden of Merton College, lectured on astronomy at Oxford. John Dee, the "magus" of Mortlake, promoted astronomy as a component of mathematical education in his *Mathematicall Preface.* Through the efforts of Savile and Thomas Allen (1534–1630), another Oxford mathematician and astronomer, the Bodleian Library at Oxford was, by the end of Elizabeth I's reign, well appointed with the major works in astronomy, including Copernicus and early works of Johannes Kepler, the great German astronomer (1571–1630).

That astronomy could readily be one component of the education of a scholar is clear from the example of William Camden, best known as an historian and antiquary, for he, too, pursued astronomy as a young man, making observations of the new star (supernova) of 1572 and corresponding with other, more mathematically inclined scholars well into the seventeenth century.

One force motivating continued activity in astronomy in Tudor England, although it can easily be overemphasized, was the need for improved navigational techniques. After some long initial voyages at the outset of the Tudor dynasty, England's enterprise in exploration had languished. Toward the end of Elizabeth's reign, however, the commercial activity in the farther reaches of the world increased, and the need for improved navigational techniques grew by 1587, when Camden wrote that navigation had become a national craze in England. Such researchers as Edward Wright (1561–1615) wrote treatises on the subject. University dons, like Thomas Allen and John Cheke, the first regius professor of Greek at Cambridge, are known to have constructed instruments for astronomical observation. In fact, Tudor England was truly innovative in the design and construction of astronomical instruments.

The telescope, in some form, may have been known, at least as a novelty, before the end of the sixteenth century, but its application to systematic astronomical observation awaited the labors and publicity of Galileo Galilei (1564–1642) in Italy. A variety of instruments for use with

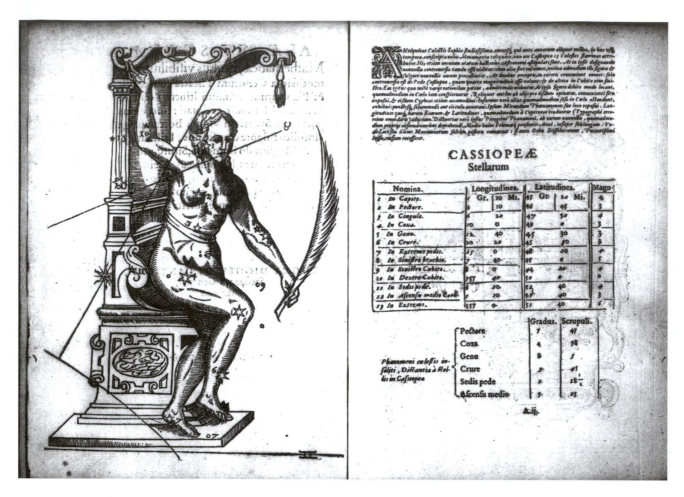

Thomas Digges, *Coordinates for the Constellation Cassiopeia.* From *Alae seu scalae mathematicae, quibus visibilium remotissima coelorum theatrea sonscendi . . . ,"* 1573. This work translated the important chapters of Book I of Copernicus's *De revolutionibus.* A supernova in this constellation in November 1572 provided a way of proving the heliocentric model. Reproduced from the original by permission of the Henry E. Huntington Library and Art Gallery.

the naked eye, however, facilitated and quantified the taking of astronomical positions in the pre-telescopic era (and for decades thereafter). The seed of instrumental tradition in England can be found in the early Tudor period, when instrument makers, notably Nicholas Kratzer ("King's Astrologer and Horologer," 1487–1550?) in 1517, were brought from the Continent. The preferred instrument of astronomical observation in Tudor England came to be the cross-staff and one of its variants, the *radius astronomicus.* The cross-staff was introduced by John Dee, after one of his excursions to the Continent, and was refined by Digges, his student, and was applied by Thomas Harriot. Digges himself designed and built a sophisticated brass *radius astronomicus,* by which he made observations of the new star of 1572; his accuracy rivaled that of the Danish astronomer Tycho Brahe (1546–1601), who was to achieve fame as the greatest European observer of his day. From 1590 to 1594, Harriot

was carrying out a program of observations of the sun's declination (celestial latitude) and of the distance of the polestar from the true pole by means of a twelve-foot-long instrument, probably an astronomer's staff, at the earl of Northumberland's London home. A later English innovation was John Blagrave's "Mathematicall Jewell" (1585), a variant of the astrolabe, an ingenious instrument for telling time by positions in the heavens that originated in antiquity.

Sir Christopher Heydon (1561–1623), of Norfolk, was one for whom astronomy was the handmaiden to astrology, although not all of his astronomical researches and readings were pursued toward astrological ends. In 1600, William Gilbert planted the seed for astrophysics when, with his *De Magnete,* he proposed that the earth itself, which he conceived to be rotating, is a magnet. The German astronomer Johannes Kepler would soon draw on this idea to provide the physical basis of his theory of celestial motions. At the

48   Astronomy

time of his publication, however, this idea would not have fitted into the category of astronomical theory; its greatest connection was, through the theory of the compass, to study the magnet's application to the problems of navigation.

For all the technical knowledge available to the learned, the kinds of astronomical knowledge occurring in literary works reflected not so much astronomical knowledge as traditional cosmology. The only known literary reference to the motion of the earth before the seventeenth century is in Sir John Davies' *Orchestra* (1596). For all this poverty of technical understanding, however, astronomical imagery, and in particular, stellar imagery, was pervasive until the later Tudor period.

BIBLIOGRAPHY

Johnson, Francis R. *Astronomical Thought in Renaissance England.* 1937; repr. 1968.

Kocher, Paul H. *Science and Religion in Elizabethan England.* 1953; repr. 1969.

Roche, John J. "The Radius Astronomicus in England." *Annals of Science,* vol. 38, pp. 1–32.

Feingold, Mordechai. *The Mathematicians' Apprenticeship: Science, Universities and Society in England, 1560–1640.* Cambridge, England 1984.

Fowler, Alastair. *Time's Purpled Masquers: Stars and the Afterlife in Renaissance English Literature.* 1996.

Russell, John L. "The Copernican System in Great Britain." In *The Reception of Copernicus' Heliocentric Theory,* Jerzy Dobrzycki, ed. 1972.

Taylor, E.G.R. *The Mathematical Practitioners of Tudor and Stuart England, 1485–1714.* 1954.

Waters, David W. *The Art of Navigation in England in Elizabethan and Early Stuart Times.* 2nd edition. 1978.

Adam Jared Apt

SEE ALSO

Astrology; Camden, William; Cheke, John; Dee, John; Digges, Thomas; Gilbert, William; Harriot, Thomas; Recorde, Robert

Atheism

A word of Greek origin that literally means "godlessness." In modern times, "atheism" usually refers to a philosophical position that seeks to explain the nature of things without recourse to belief in God. But this definition did not become common until the late seventeenth century, and in Tudor England atheism meant something rather different. The word seems to have been introduced into English by Sir John Cheke, first regius professor of Greek at Cambridge, about 1540. It was used in a wide and sometimes bewildering variety of senses, but three main ones may be distinguished here.

1. Secularism. In this sense, an atheist was a person who believed that the natural and human sciences possessed their own internal autonomy, and did not require either biblical revelation or church authority to establish their validity. The archetypal English "atheist" in this sense was Thomas Hobbes (1588–1679), who is generally regarded as having been the first person to advocate a consistent secularism in public affairs. But even Hobbes was not an atheist in the philosophical sense, and recent scholarship has tended to vindicate his protestations of religious belief.

2. Heterodoxy. This meant the denial of certain tenets of Christian belief. In the religiously charged atmosphere of the sixteenth century, when different Protestant and Catholic orthodoxies competed with one another, it was only to be expected that some people would fall short of either standard of acceptability. Denial of the Trinity (Socinianism) was the most common form of heterodoxy in the sixteenth century, and it was constantly under attack by preachers and theologians. How many Englishmen were Socinians at that time is another matter; it seems that Socinian influence did not become significant in England until the mid-seventeenth century. The word "atheist" was also applied to the Anabaptists, presumably because they rejected the established church order, though it is equally uncertain how many of them were to be found in Tudor England. As with the Socinians, their influence seems to belong more to the seventeenth century.

3. Immorality. This was by far the most common form of "atheism," as indeed it still is today. It included everything from blasphemy to immoral behavior, and was widespread in all walks of life. Preachers concentrated heavily on it, and the Puritans regarded it as their biggest single enemy. In sermon after sermon, they railed against the atheism of the times, by which they meant such matters as playing games on Sunday, absence from public worship, and swearing. Then as now, atheism of this kind was mainly a male phenomenon, and women were frequently charged with the responsibility of seeing to it that godliness was taught and practiced in the home.

Circles that were relatively free from Puritan influence were highly suspect in this regard, and the Puritan tendency to see everything in black and white tended to encourage a rebellious attitude among those who were in a position to indulge it. The theater was an obvious target for Puritan zeal,

A

and in return it tended to shelter a relatively high proportion of secularists and blasphemers. William Shakespeare, for example, though he was by no means an atheist in the modern sense, was astonishingly secular by the standards of his time, and Christopher Marlowe—notorious for his open defiance of conventional morality—was accused of atheism by Richard Baines only days before the playwright's murder.

BIBLIOGRAPHY

Berman, D. *A History of Atheism in Britain.* 1988.

Buckley, M.J. *At the Origins of Modern Atheism.* 1987.

Gerald L. Bray

SEE ALSO

Baines, Richard; Cheke, John; Marlowe, Christopher; Puritanism

Audley, Thomas (1488–1544)

Speaker of Commons and lord chancellor during the reign of Henry VIII, Sir Thomas Audley was born around 1488 in Essex. He began his parliamentary career in the early 1520s, rising quickly within Commons. He was elected a knight to the Reformation Parliament and chosen as speaker. After Thomas More's resignation in May 1532 as Lord Chancellor, Audley became lord keeper; in 1533, he became lord chancellor. He helped negotiate a treaty with the Scots in 1534 and presided over the trials of More and Anne Boleyn. Audley became baron of Walden, was given monastic lands there, and was elected a knight of the garter. He helped arrange the marriage treaty between the king and Anne of Cleves, and was later sent to tell her that Henry was divorcing her. When Thomas Cromwell fell from power, Audley did not defend him although he was indebted to him. In the opening speech of Parliament in 1542, Audley accused Katherine, Henry's next wife, of infidelity. He refounded and endowed Buckingham College, Cambridge, renaming it Magdalen. Audley died on April 30, 1544. As an ambitious, clever, and lucky Tudor parliamentarian, Audley rose from humble origins to become a wealthy and leading member of Commons; yet unlike Cromwell, Wolsey, and Thomas More, he died with his lands and prestige intact.

BIBLIOGRAPHY

Guy, John. *The Public Career of Sir Thomas More.* 1980.

Lehmberg, Stanford. "Sir Thomas Audley: A Soul as Black as Marble?" In *Tudor Men and Institutions: Studies in English Law and Government,* Arthur J. Slavin, ed. 1972.

———. *The Reformation Parliament,* 1529–1536. 1970.

Glen Bowman

SEE ALSO

Anne of Cleves; Boleyn, Anne; Cromwell, Thomas; Katherine of Aragon; More, Thomas

Aylmer, John (1521–1594)

Born at the family seat of Aylmer Hall, Norfolk, in 1521, John Aylmer received his B.A. from Cambridge in 1541 and almost immediately became chaplain to Henry Grey, duke of Suffolk. In that position he was employed as tutor to Lady Jane Grey. On June 15, 1553, he was made archdeacon of Stow in the Lincoln diocese, but after the accession of Mary I on July 19 he was deprived because of his denial of transubstantiation. He fled to Strasbourg, where he met John Foxe, the martyrologist. For the next few years, Aylmer was one of Foxe's closest collaborators. In 1559, he published a defense of female rulers in response to the attack of John Knox. This appealed to Queen Elizabeth, and in the same year he was restored to Stow. In 1562, he became archdeacon of Lincoln, and on March 24, 1577, he was consecrated bishop of London, where he remained until his death on June 3, 1594.

Aylmer was a stern disciplinarian, and this made him highly unpopular in his diocese, where the majority of ministers had Puritan leanings. When the antiestablishment Marprelate tracts appeared in 1589, Aylmer was the main butt of their satire. He was well aware of his unpopularity and sought to be transfered to another see, but all attempts to do this foundered. A good scholar but a hopeless diplomat and pastor, he is generally reckoned to have been unsuccessful during his tenure in London.

BIBLIOGRAPHY

Collinson, Patrick. *The Elizabethan Puritan Movement.* 1990.

Haugaard, W.P. *Elizabeth and the English Reformation: the Struggle for a Stable Settlement of Religion.* 1968.

Gerald L. Bray

SEE ALSO

Foxe, John; Grey, Lady Jane; Marprelate Controversy

Ayre

See Air

B

Babington, Anthony (1561–1586)

Although he had secured only vague promises of support from Catholics on the Continent, Babington was confident that Spain would come to his aid with an invasion of England. The detailed plans to murder Elizabeth and to free Mary were never clearly formed, yet the letters to and from Mary were enough to provide Walsingham with the evidence needed to bring her to trial and pursue her execution, which was carried out on February 8, 1587, as a direct result of Babington's conspiracy.

As the plot began to unravel and after the arrest of the priest John Ballard, who was instrumental in recruiting Babington to the "Enterprise," as the plot was known, Babington offered to act as a double agent and inform Walsingham of the complete details of the plot. Still unaware of the extent of Walsingham's knowledge, Babington happened to see a letter of the secretary's about himself. He made a dramatic escape from a London tavern and was able to hide in disguise in St. John's Wood with some of his fellow conspirators, eventually driven by hunger to enlist the aid of a local Catholic family.

After his arrest and imprisonment in the Tower of London, Babington fully and freely confessed, confirming the authenticity of Mary's letters. Trying to place the blame on Ballard for leading the conspiracy, which may in fact be a more accurate assessment, he also wrote to Elizabeth, asking for mercy, and offered £1,000 for his release and pardon. Elizabeth, on the other hand, is said to have asked Lord Burghley to ensure that the conspirators were executed more brutally than usual, "for more terror," though Burghley assured her that the usual methods "would be as terrible as any new device could be."

On September 20, 1586, Babington watched the execution of Ballard with calm composure, exhibiting "a signe of his former pride," and was the next to suffer. According to Camden, each conspirator was hanged briefly, then "They were all cut down, their privities cut off, bowelled alive and seeing [drawn], and quartered." Babington was last heard to whisper, *"Parce mihi, domini Jesu"* (Spare me, Lord Jesus).

BIBLIOGRAPHY

Camden, William. *The History of the Most Renowned and Victorious Princess Elizabeth, Late Queen of England.* Wallace T. MacCaffrey, ed. 1970.

Whetstone, George. *Censure Upon Notable Traitors.* 1587; repr. 1973.

James M. Dutcher

SEE ALSO
Babington Plot; Mary Queen of Scots

Babington, Gervase (c. 1550–1610)

Anglican bishop and chaplain to the earl of Pembroke, Gervase Babington was born about 1550 in Nottinghamshire and educated at Trinity College, Cambridge, where he became a fellow in 1575 before moving to Oxford, where he was incorporated M.A. in 1578. He entered the ministry and in 1580 became one of the university preachers. Selected to be one of the earl of Pembroke's family chaplains, he moved to Wilton House and began his relationship with the earl and his wife, Mary Sidney Herbert, Philip Sidney's sister.

B

His effect on the piety of Wilton was widely noted and Walter Sweeper, in the dedication of *A brief Treatis declaring the True Noble-man, and the Base Worldling* (1623) states, "In this noble House, *Babington* rules of pietie and honestie swayed, swearing was banished; yea the house keepers and inferiour servants well knew and practised the grounds of religion." Sir John Harington raised Babington's influence to the point of having helped Mary Sidney write her versification of the Psalms (a project her brother started), although his purpose was to disparage Mary Sidney rather than to praise Babington, who had left Wilton, "for it was more than a woman's skill to express the sense so rightly as she hath done in her verse, and more than she could learn from the English and Latin translations" (*Brief View*, 1653).

Of Babington's theological works the most interesting feature is not the theology, which is conventional, but his critique of late Elizabethan patronage, particularly the control that the aristocracy exerted over ecclesiastical preferment. His absorption into the powerful aristocratic patronage network made him acutely aware of this controversy. His tract, *A Very Fruitful Exposition of the Commandments,* dedicated to Pembroke in 1583, addresses the "Gentlemen in Glamorganshire," and laments "the neglect that aboundeth everywhere to furnish the rooms allotted there unto with sufficient men both for gifts and goodwill to discharge the duties of true minister." He goes on to complain of unscrupulous patrons who retain part of the stipends due to ministers and have little concern for the well-being of the church. Regardless of his disdain for the patronage system, his career advanced due to his willingness to engage in it.

Through Pembroke's influence, Babington was made the warden of St. Giles hospital at Wilton, and after 1585, he held the living of several parishes in Wiltshire. In 1588, he was installed prebendary of Wellington in the church of Hereford. The following year he was created D.D. and in 1589–1590 was collated to the office of treasurer of the church of Llandaff. Thanks to his patron, he was elected bishop of Llandaff in August 1590, and five years later, the queen installed him as bishop of Exeter. Against the counsel of the parishioners and sextons, Babington surrendered to the Crown the manor and borough of Crediton, which the Queen immediately granted to William Killigrew, one of the grooms of her chamber. She showed her gratitude by nominating him bishop of Worcester in 1597, where he remained until his death in 1610.

BIBLIOGRAPHY

Babington, Gervase. *"Works."* Miles Smith, ed. 1615; repr. 1622, 1637.

Brennan, Michael G. *Literary Patronage in the English Renaissance: the Pembroke Family.* 1988.

Copper, Charles Henry. *Athenae Cantabrigiensis.* Vol. 3, pp. 21–24. 1913.

Lamb, Mary. *Gender and Authorship in the Sidney Circle.* 1990.

Waller, G.F. *Mary Sidney, Countess of Pembroke: A Critical Study of Her Writings and Literary Milieu.* 1979.

Edward M. Cottrill

SEE ALSO

Harington, John; Patronage; Sidney, Mary

Babington Plot

The Babington Plot (1586) was a half-hearted conspiracy by a group of young English aristocrats to return England to Roman Catholicism by assassinating Elizabeth I and installing the imprisoned Mary Queen of Scots in her place. The utter failure of the plot, carefully manipulated by Secretary of State Francis Walsingham and his agents to trap Mary, directly resulted in her execution.

Walsingham's own scheme was laid in 1584 when he and William Cecil, Lord Burghley, drafted the Bond of Association to protect Elizabeth, followed the next year by Parliament's Act for the Queen's Surety. By 1585, with a strict jailer for Mary, Sir Amias Paulet, and Gilbert Gifford, a Catholic in the minor orders working for him as a double agent, Walsingham was secretly in total control of Mary's correspondence. A local brewer known as "the honest man" acted as the courier, and Walsingham's man, Thomas Phelippes, brilliantly deciphered the coded letters, even adding a forged postscript to one, before delivering them. It was Phelippes who drew a gallows mark on the letter from Mary that finally incriminated her (rightly or not) before passing it on to Walsingham.

The Babington Plot, known as the "Enterprise," was actually initiated by a priest named John Ballard, who recruited Anthony Babington. The young Babington, who was completely unaware of Walsingham's infiltration, thought that he could depend on a Spanish invasion of England and a large, spontaneous uprising of English Catholic sympathizers. His plan, outlined in a damaging letter to Mary, called for her deliverance and "the despatch of the usurping Competitor," Elizabeth, whose intended murder he refers to as "that tragicall execution."

When Walsingham had amassed enough evidence to force a trial for Mary, he began to shut down the conspiracy. Ballard was arrested and Babington, still trying to play Walsingham as, in fact, the secretary was playing him, offered to expose the plot and serve as a double agent. When finally tipped off about his own danger, Babington narrowly escaped and, with some other conspirators, eluded capture for nearly ten days, hiding in disguise in St. John's Wood.

Arrested on August 14, 1586, the conspirators were imprisoned in the Tower of London where all eventually confessed and confirmed Mary's complicity. Babington and the others who were executed on the first day were made to suffer terribly. Those executed on the second day were allowed to hang until dead, before other punishments were inflicted.

The ramifications of the plot were serious. Elizabeth seems to have wanted Mary, "The daughter of debate," dead, yet she was hesitant to authorize the execution of an anointed monarch. In her familiar pattern of pastoral rhetoric, Elizabeth claimed that she would willingly pardon Mary if "we were but two milkmaids with pails upon our arms," rather than heads of state with national and international concerns. At the same time, she had a quiet suggestion made by her junior secretary of state, William Davison, to Paulet that he "might have eased her of this burden" of deciding Mary's fate by taking the matter into his own hands. Paulet refused, so the death warrant that Elizabeth had reluctantly signed was put into force; she angrily claimed it was against her will and imprisoned Davison, who had taken the sealed death warrant to Burghley. The death of Mary Queen of Scots in 1587 was a government execution of a monarch more than a half-century before the beheading of Charles I.

Certainly, too, King Philip of Spain had been aware of the plot and its failure, and there is little doubt that the execution of Mary contributed to the amassing of the Armada, an attempted foreign invasion that came too late to help Babington or Mary and that was, ironically, to thrust Elizabeth into her greatest moment.

BIBLIOGRAPHY

Pollen, John Hungerford, S.J. *Mary Queen of Scots and the Babington Plot. Scottish History Society.* 1922.

Read, Conyers. *Mr. Secretary Walsingham and the Policy of Queen Elizabeth.* 3 vols. 1925.

Smith, Alan Gordon. *The Babington Plot.* 1936.

James M. Dutcher

SEE ALSO

Armada, Spanish; Babington, Anthony; Davison, William; Mary Queen of Scots; Walsingham, Francis

Bacon, Anthony (1558–1601)

Elder son of Nicholas Bacon, lord keeper, and brother of Francis Bacon, the well-known essayist, Anthony Bacon attended Trinity College, Cambridge, where he was tutored by John Whitgift, who later became archbishop of Canterbury. Later, Anthony and his brother attended Gray's Inn. In 1579, his uncle, Lord Burghley, suggested that Bacon undertake a continental tour in search of political intelligence. For almost thirteen years he lived abroad in Paris, Geneva, Marseilles, Bordeaux, Bearn, and Montauban, which allowed him to establish a large and complex network of impressive political contacts. Yet this period was not without hardship. Bacon's health—which had always been fragile—became extremely poor, and he managed to spend virtually all of his own and his mother's money.

In 1593, Bacon entered the service of the Robert Devereux, earl of Essex, undertaking matters of political intelligence. He also served as Essex's undersecretary, and later resided in Essex House (1595). Although Bacon supported Essex until his death—arguing that the earl was innocent of the worst charges brought against him—the queen ordered Bacon to leave Essex House before the final confrontation. (His brother, Francis, played a large part in the prosecution of Essex.)

Bacon was described by his companion, Sir Henry Wotton, as a gentleman "of impotent feet but nimble head." Many contemporary commentators characterized Bacon as an engaging, witty, sympathetic, and overly generous man. His religious liberalism was well known. Francis Bacon dedicated the first edition of his essays to his brother, although the gossip-monger John Chamberlain wrote that Anthony Bacon died "so far in debt that I think his brother is little the better by him."

BIBLIOGRAPHY

Du Maurier, Daphne. *Golden Lads: A Study of Anthony Bacon, Francis, and Their Friends.* 1975.

Harvey, Annie Jane Tennant. *Chronicles of an Old Inn; or, A Few Words about Gray's Inn.* 1887.

B

Lambeth Palace Library. *Index to the Papers of Anthony Bacon (1558–1601) in Lambeth Palace Library* (MSS. 647–662). 1974.

Ungerer, Gustav. "The French Lutenist Charles Tessier and the Essex Circle." *Renaissance Quarterly*, vol. 28, pp. 190–203.

S.P. Cerasano

SEE ALSO
Bacon, Francis; Bacon, Nicholas; Devereux, Robert; Whitgift, John

Bacon, Francis (1561–1626)

No contemporary came close to possessing Francis Bacon's combination of political power, learning, eloquence, and intellectual vision and influence. Bacon was an important literary innovator and historian. But through most of his life Bacon sought to advance the discovery of scientific principles governing the universe and humanity, principles that would master nature and transform the human condition through technology. Bacon realized that most knowledge lay undiscovered, that its discovery could provide tremendous benefits, and that discovery required a scientific method, massive state funding, and the collaboration of many researchers. He also developed a sense of his age as a critical time during which the grip of traditional ways of thinking could be broken. Bacon's two most intimate writings on his aspirations (a letter to his uncle-by-marriage, William Cecil, Lord Burghley [1592], and the autobiographical fragment of 1603, "De Interpretatione Naturae Proemium"), show the depth of his calling to build a philanthropic science. But his profound relation to modern ideas and institutions could not become apparent until after his death. And though Bacon wished to oversee programs of government research, most of his efforts were actually expended in civil service of a political and legal nature. He was directly involved in some of the most important political events of his time. While neither Bacon's civic nor intellectual efforts bore their greatest fruits until the Jacobean period, they took shape earlier.

On January 22, 1561, Bacon was born in York House, the London residence of his father, Nicholas, the lord keeper of England, an obscure yeoman's son who had become the kingdom's most powerful legal official. Bacon's mother was Nicholas's second wife, Anne Cooke, one of the most learned women of her time and daughter of Edward VI's tutor. Both Bacon's parents influenced

him with their respect for learning and Protestant zeal for godly and industrious service. Bacon entered Trinity College, Cambridge, in April of 1573, where he roomed with his one full sibling, Anthony, two years his elder. Although Anthony died in 1601, their relationship was probably the closest Francis ever experienced. In 1576, Bacon was admitted to Gray's Inn, but left the same year to travel abroad, accompanying the French ambassador, Sir Amyas Paulet, to Paris and then elsewhere in France. Dying suddenly on February 22, 1579, before his affairs were in order, Bacon's father provided this youngest of eight children £300 a year, hardly enough for a man of Bacon's background, ambition, and taste for "ceremonies and respects" (a title of one of his 1597 *Essays*). Despite his connections to the queen and her powerful minister, Cecil, like many of his peers, Bacon had considerable trouble securing a rewarding government position, so he was in debt for virtually the rest of his life, and a goldsmith had him arrested in 1598. Resuming his legal studies in 1579, Bacon was admitted as utter barrister June 27, 1582, but he retained strong ties to the Gray's Inn milieu. He kept his father's substantial lodgings there until his own death April 9, 1626. Bacon's 1606 marriage to Alice Barnham, young daughter of a London alderman, was childless. Evidence from John Aubrey suggests Bacon was primarily homosexual.

It is now known that Bacon's civic career began as early as 1581 when he became a Member of Parliament for Bossiney, Cornwall. He gradually became an influential presence and a powerful speaker, remaining thirty-seven years in the House of Commons for several different constituencies until appointed lord keeper and becoming a member of the House of Lords in 1618. The only regular state post he held before Elizabeth's death in March 1603, was the minor though prestigious one of learned counsel to the queen (from 1595). Elizabeth I did not like the signs of independent thinking Bacon had displayed in the 1593 Parliament when he earnestly advocated subjects be given a longer time to pay an unusually high royal subsidy tax. It was not until his 1597 speech in support of a royal subsidy that he really began to emerge as one of the age's greatest parliamentary champions of the royal prerogative over the common law and the rights of Parliament. In that same year he produced for the queen the first of his several proposals for rationalization of the laws, *Maxims of the Law*. Bacon's emerging political vision sought not capitulation to royal prerogative but the harmony of disparate social interests through deference to prerogative and hierarchy (as in his 1613 letters of advice to James I). He

B

wrote defenses of moderate religious toleration (1589, 1602), and of the populace against grasping gentry ("A View of the Differences in the Marches," 1606).

Bacon had a powerful patron in Robert Devereaux, the second earl of Essex; both he and Anthony were in the earl's service by 1592. But though Essex was the Queen's favorite, she resisted his headstrong importunity on Bacon's behalf. Bacon lost a bid for attorney general in 1594 to the man who was to become his lifelong enemy: Edward Coke, the leading advocate of the common law, possessed greater qualifications for the position, and would soon win the hand of the widow Bacon sought to marry, Lady Hatton. Then, what she perceived as Bacon's haughtiness peeved the queen and he lost out for solicitor-general as well (1595). When Elizabeth I had Essex arrested in 1599 for disobeying her orders not to return from Ireland, Bacon helped to reconcile the two. Essex ignored Bacon's long-standing advice to be more conciliatory toward the queen. With a touch of the sardonic, Elizabeth did give Bacon one considerable responsibility, the painful and damaging one of helping Coke prosecute Essex for treason in 1601. Yet Bacon was widely criticized for playing his role with courtroom vigor, provoking Essex into reminding the court of their former alliance. In his *Apology to Certain Imputations Concerning the Earl of Essex* (published 1604), written probably to justify his actions before the new king, Bacon attested that he would always be a better subject than a friend.

The trials of political suitorship helped inspire Bacon to record observations useful to others ready to hazard their fortunes: aphoristic, prudential precepts with little logical development that he called "essays," borrowing Montaigne's word. He claimed these works were still unfinished when he published them in 1597 to prevent the appearance of pirated editions. To these ten sophisticated, Senecan, provocative, shrewd counsels he added brief demonstrative meditations on verses of scripture (*Meditationes Sacrae*) and analyses of the truth and falsity of rhetorically colored ethical propositions (*Colors of Good and Evil*). After four editions in eight years, Bacon greatly expanded the *Essays* in 1612 and 1625; the prudential, moral, and antithetical elements of the original tripartite ensemble coalesced in these more elaborate compositions, which have had an enormous influence on prose style and remain his most popular works. The *Colors* appear again in the section on rhetoric in Bacon's encyclopedic *De Dignitate et Augmentis Scientiarum* (published 1623), and their resemblance to the "prerogative instances" of Bacon's inductive scientific method as

described in the *Novum Organum* (published 1620), is one indication that Bacon's rhetorical training and ability played an important part in his notion of scientific method. The significance of the 1597 volume in its time is suggested by contrasting it to the approximately concurrent work of another law-school rebel against stylistic regularities, John Donne. Donne's nervous, aphoristic, and irregular verse satires on the court and legal system are high-minded, covert denunciations by one apprehensive about his impending future in that compromising world; son of an insider, Bacon had plunged industriously into the labyrinth long before writing. Unbowed by his experience in public affairs, he was happy to publish his observations. He advises rather than judges, having concluded, in the terms of one of the *Meditationes Sacrae*, that the active life demands a combination of shrewdness and moral principle, of "the wisdom of the serpent" and "the innocence of the dove."

Under King James, Bacon's valuable work as learned counsel on issues such as the union of Scotland and England, as well as his parliamentary role as a prerogative man, helped him to rise at last. Having been knighted with several hundred others one afternoon in 1603, he finally became clerk of the Star Chamber (1606), solicitor general (1607), attorney general (1613), a privy councilor (1616), lord keeper (1617), and lord chancellor (1618); he was created Baron Verulam (1618) and Viscount St. Albans (1621). But, accustomed to the privileges of rank and preoccupied with the philosophical writing that he had finally made his real priority, this lord chancellor regularly accepted gifts from both sides in legal suits while apparently maintaining his judgment unswayed. A common administrative vice in which he grossly overindulged, this practice and Parliament's increasing apprehension about royal power led to his impeachment on the charge of bribery in 1621 and to the end of his public life. The alliance of serpent and dove had faltered, but Bacon's last five years saw a concentrated production of important writings, mostly related to natural history and philosophy.

Throughout the Elizabethan and the Stuart periods, England was slowly catching up to and in many cases surpassing the significant technical advances of continental Europe, and increasingly able to substitute its own goods for manufactured imports. This progress forms an important backdrop to Bacon's ideas on the reform of learning, ideas that he claimed were a product of time rather than of his own genius. Some recognized that the humanist emphasis on useful learning could be extended from statecraft and

B

rhetoric to the mechanical arts; the skeptical tradition of philosophy had been revived in Europe; Protestantism encouraged the separation of faith and reason. But no single writer or technical innovator had a decisive influence on Bacon, except possibly his chief adversary, Aristotle. As a Cambridge student, Bacon had already formed his conviction that Aristotle's philosophy, still a mainstay of the curriculum, was thoroughly unsuited to discovery or invention. He later claimed to have written his earliest work on the reform of philosophy, the lost *Temporis Partus Maximus,* as early as 1583.

A precursor to his scientific utopia, *New Atlantis* (published 1627), Bacon's contribution to a Gray's Inn holiday entertainment, *Gesta Grayorum* (1594), depicts a privy councilor to a king advocating the development of a utopian research complex including a library, a botanical garden and zoo, cabinet (for specimens and inventions), and still-house (laboratory). In 1592 and 1595, Bacon contributed to other Gray's Inn "devices" commissioned by Essex and celebrating the anniversary of Elizabeth's accession (*Of Tribute, Or Giving What is Due,* also known as *The Conference of Pleasure,* and *Love and Self-Love*). They show how much Bacon tied the success of his program of philanthropic learning to royal patronage and to courtly virtues and alliances—and also how Bacon grasped the importance of state support for collaborative research. The former device contains a stirring praise of the knowledge that can "endow the life of man with new commodities" and a critique of learning as filled with either ostentatious words and disputations (Greek philosophy and scholasticism), or with deception and random, pointless experiments (alchemy).

Between 1602 and 1605 Bacon produced a remarkable series of seminal fragments, plus his first major philosophical work, *The Advancement of Learning* (published 1605), landmark of the European Renaissance, precursor to the European Enlightenment, and intellectual culmination of the stupendous, many-faceted Elizabethan capacity to aspire. This late Elizabethan and early Jacobean legacy includes nearly all the major themes of Bacon's philosophy. Composed mostly in 1603, Book I of *The Advancement* eloquently defends learning and marshals arguments for its importance; its analysis of the "three vanities in studies" develops Bacon's 1592 critique of learning along with that in the *Meditationes Sacrae* and in two fragments: the emotional invective *Temporis Partus Masculus* (*The Masculine Birth of Time,* 1602–1603), and the pseudonymous outline *On the Interpretation of Nature* (by "Valerius Terminus," written in 1603 and probably

revised in 1605). Book II of *The Advancement,* hurriedly written in 1605 during a long adjournment of Parliament but the product of many years' research and thought, draws from these fragments' indictments of philosophy since Plato and from their discussions of the Idols of the Mind—social, psychological, linguistic, and philosophical factors that impede discovery. This work surveys all existing knowledge to discover where it can be advanced, offering a powerful and distinctively modern vision of the possible independence of the present from the past. In doing so it also provides an influential, encyclopedic classification of knowledge according to mental faculties: history (memory), poetry (imagination), philosophy (reason). Its discussion of the transmission of knowledge, including rhetoric, has been especially significant. The fragment *On the Interpretation of Nature* also represents the earliest extant outline of a six-part "instauration" of learning, Bacon's project for the renovation of all knowledge, as well as the first discussion of the centerpiece of Bacon's philosophy, his famous scientific method, induction by negation. This method emphasizes humility before nature, experiment, and the collection and classification of observations in "natural histories" by many researchers as the bases for successively broader inductive generalizations; its degree of historical significance is considerable but remains a matter of controversy. The project of instauration received its fullest explication in the *Instauratio Magna* (published 1620 and including the aphoristic work on method, the *Novum Organum*). Two important aspects of Bacon's vision touched on during this period but greatly expanded later are the gendered, exploitative relationship between scientist and nature, and the significance of scientific advancement in redemption history as the repair of the fall of humanity.

If a goal of Bacon's politics was to harmonize opposing popular, parliamentary, and monarchical interests while safeguarding royal prerogative, his philosophical vision aimed to do something analogous by systematizing particulars in a harmonious and productive hierarchy of natural laws, and by depending on humble researchers and the mechanical arts. Later in the seventeenth century his ideas were taken up enthusiastically by supporters of both the English republic and of the Restoration (including the founders of the Royal Society), each of whom emphasized different elements of Bacon's vision. The former responded more to the pragmatic emphasis, democratic implications, and redemptive framework of Bacon's philosophy, while many of the latter found a promising vision of radical change that still took social hierarchy for granted. In the seventeenth century, Bacon was already becoming a symbol of modernity, and it is in part as such that he has been revered and assaulted ever since.

BIBLIOGRAPHY

Kiernan, Michael, ed. *Sir Francis Bacon: The Essayes or Counsels, Civill and Morall.* 1985.

Peltonen, Markku, ed. *The Cambridge Companion to Bacon.* 1996.

Sessions, W.A. *Francis Bacon Revisited.* Twayne English Authors. 1996.

Solomon, Julie Robin. *Objectivity in the Making: Francis Bacon and the Politics of Inquiry.* 1998.

Spedding, James, Robert L. Ellis, and Douglas D. Heath, eds. *The Works of Francis Bacon.* 14 vols. 1857–1874; repr. 1968.

Vickers, Brian. *Francis Bacon and Renaissance Prose.* 1968.

———, ed. *Francis Bacon.* Oxford Authors. 1996.

Whitney, Charles. *Francis Bacon and Modernity.* 1986.

———. "Francis Bacon's *Instauratio:* Dominion of and over Humanity." *Journal of the History of Ideas,* vol. 50, pp. 371–390.

Wormald, B.H.G. *Francis Bacon: History, Politics and Science, 1561–1626.* 1993.

Charles Whitney

SEE ALSO

Aristotelianism; Bacon, Anthony; Bacon, Nicholas; Coke, Edward; Devereux, Robert; Donne, John; Essay; Science, History of

Bacon, Nicholas (1510–1579)

Privy councilor and lord keeper of the Great Seal, Sir Nicholas Bacon was the son of a Suffolk sheep-reeve. From this humble beginning he rose to earn a B.A. at Cambridge and then enter Gray's Inn in 1532. He reached the position of ancient in four years, an extraordinarily short time. He became a bencher in 1550 and treasurer of Gray's Inn in 1552. At Cambridge he became a convert to Protestantism and made the acquaintance of William Cecil. After the death of his first wife, Jane Ferneley, he married Anne Cooke. This union tied him even closer to William Cecil, who was married to Anne's older sister. With Thomas Cranmer as his patron, Bacon became solicitor of the Court of Augmentations in 1540. He later became attorney of the Court of Wards and earned the reputation for upholding the interests and welfare of the wards of the crown. On

Elizabeth I's succession he was made lord keeper of the Great Seal and became an influential member of the Privy Council. As lord keeper he headed the Chancery where he introduced important procedural reforms, clarified the jurisdiction of the Court of Chancery, and reorganized personnel, all of which modernized the office and made its operations more efficient. He also became the queen's voice in Parliament, where he achieved renown for his eloquent speeches. Bacon had a substantial role in the formulation of the Statute of Artificers of 1563. On the council he was firm supporter of Sir William Cecil's policies, which earned him the wrath of Robert Dudley, earl of Leicester. In 1564, Leicester used Bacon's support for Lady Jane Grey's claim to the throne to get him banished from court. His banishment lasted only a year, probably due to the intercession of Cecil, but it taught him to be more circumspect in his espousal of controversial views. As a mark of his support for Puritanism, during the 1570s, Bacon refused to help the archbishop of Canterbury, Matthew Parker, enforce statutes prescribing clerical vestments. He also helped support unlicensed Puritan preachers in prebends in Norwich Cathedral and elsewhere. For of all this, however, Bacon maintained a *politique* stance in foreign policy, carving a middle path between Puritan extremists and pro-Catholic sympathizers. He promoted the Anjou match in 1571 by writing the tract, "Discourse of the Queen's Marriage with the Duke of Anjou," which stated the case for the marriage. With the fall of the duke of Norfolk in 1572, Bacon became a major political influence in Norfolk and Suffolk. He used his authority to advance the careers of his sons and a new generation of Puritan gentry in East Anglia.

BIBLIOGRAPHY

Collinson, Patrick. "Sir Nicholas Bacon and the 'Via Media'." In *Godly Rule: Essays on English Protestantism and Puritanism.* 1983.

Elton, G.R. *The Parliament of England, 1559–1581.* 1986.

Hudson, Winthrop. *The Cambridge Connection and the Elizabethan Settlement of 1559.* 1980.

Hartley, T.E., ed. *Proceedings in the Parliaments of Elizabeth I.* 1981.

Pulman, Michael B. *The Elizabethan Privy Council in the Fifteen-Seventies.* 1971.

Tittler, Robert. *Nicholas Bacon: The Making of a Tudor Statesman.* 1976.

Robert J. Mueller

B

SEE ALSO

Alençon and Anjou, Duke de; Cecil, William; Cranmer, Thomas; Court of Wards; Grey, Lady Jane

Bainbridge, Christopher (c. 1464–1514)

Archbishop of York and later cardinal of Rome, Christopher Bainbridge was born in Westmoreland around 1464. After earning a law degree from Queen's College, Oxford, he embarked on an ecclesiastical career in the form of prebends with various cathedrals starting in 1485. The following year he was appointed provost at his alma mater and, a year later, was named treasurer of St. Paul's. Beginning in 1501, he advanced steadily to become archdeacon of Surrey, then dean of York (1503) and of Windsor (1505). Thereafter began Bainbridge's meteoric rise through the episcopacy: he was made bishop of Durham in 1507, archbishop of York a year later, and then, after Henry VIII had chosen him as his ambassador to Pope Julius II in 1509, Julius created him cardinal in 1511. He was outspoken in his tenure as papal ambassador, an advocate of king and country at a time when English interests often went unheard. His ecclesiastical duties proved more military than religious, culminating in his command of Julius's troops in a siege of Ferrara. He was poisoned, in 1514, by a chaplain in his own service; the chaplain, in turn, implicated a rival English ambassador, Silvester de Giglis, bishop of Worcester, in the murder.

BIBLIOGRAPHY

Chambers, D.S. *Cardinal Bainbridge in the Court of Rome 1509–1514*. 1965.

Mark Goldblatt

Baines, Richard (c. 1556–1594 or 1610)

Approximately three days before Christopher Marlowe's "accidental" death at Deptford on May 30, 1593, a memorandum, signed by Richard Baines, was delivered to the authorities. It was endorsed by an official as "A note Containing the opinion of one Christopher Marly Concerning his damnable Judgment of Religion, and scorn of Gods word," and contained the ominous injunction: ". . . J think all men in Cristianity ought to indevor that the mouth of so dangerous a member may be stopped." The infamous Baines note or "libel" is extant in both its original form and in a slightly altered copy that was sent to the queen. For a long time Baines was thought to have been a police spy or petty informant, but recent scholarship has shown that he was a man of some intellectual standing and had previously worked closely with Marlowe as a fellow intelligence operative. It now seems that he did not write the note of his own volition but at the suggestion of another government agent, Thomas Drury.

Baines matriculated at Cambridge University in 1568, received his B.A. in 1572/3 at Christ's College, and his M.A. at Caius in 1576. In 1579, he entered the English College at Rheims in France, a Catholic seminary that had been founded by William (later Cardinal) Allen for exiles from the strictures and persecutions of Elizabethan Protestantism. Unbeknownst to Allen, Baines was a spy in the service of Elizabeth's spymaster, Sir Francis Walsingham. Although Baines was ordained as a Catholic priest on September 21, 1581, it appears that he was working undercover for the whole of his time at Rheims, attempting to win his fellow students to Protestantism. He finally persuaded one young man to help him poison "the communal well or the soup" in order that "the whole house could be dispatched." Before Baines could carry out his plan, however, he was captured and tortured, having been betrayed by his accomplice. All this and more is known from his depositions, one an oral confession in Latin that was written down by his interrogators soon after his incarceration in the town jail on May 29, 1582, and one a written recantation in English, which Baines made on May 13, 1583, and which Allen published in *A True Report* on June 1 as part of his propaganda war. After an attempt to destroy Baines's usefulness to the Protestant cause, Allen released him later in 1583.

Following a period of inactivity, Baines resumed his work for the English authorities, but in a less prominent way. However, in January 1592, he betrayed Christopher Marlowe (for the first time) when they were chamber fellows on a mission in Flushing in the Low Countries. The "official" purpose of their mission is unknown. What is known is that they were counterfeiting currency unofficially, and that when Marlowe tried to pass off one of the coins, Baines reported Marlowe to Sir Robert Sidney, the governor of Flushing. Sidney had no choice but to arrest Marlowe and deport him to England. However, instead of being tried and punished for petty treason, Marlowe was released soon after, which has led more than one scholar to speculate as to whether Marlowe was working as an agent for the Cecils. Baines repeated the counterfeiting charge against Marlowe in his note.

It is not known exactly where and when Baines died. Scholarly debate continues as to whether he was the

Richard Baines who was executed at Tyburn for robbery the year after Marlowe's death (the Stationers' Company register records the entry to Thomas Gosson and William Blackwell of a nonextant ballad entitled the "Wofull lamentacion of Richard Banes executed at Tyburne the 6 of December 1594"), or the Richard Baines who became rector of the parish church of All Saints in Waltham, Lincolnshire, and was buried at Waltham on April 5, 1610, his wife, Barbara, bearing him a child, to be named Richard, two and a half months after his death.

BIBLIOGRAPHY

Boas, Frederick S. "Informer Against Marlowe." *Times Literary Supplement,* September 16, 1949.

Kendall, Roy. "Richard Baines and Christopher Marlowe's Milieu." *English Literary Renaissance,* vol. 24, pp. 507–552.

———. "Richard Baines and Christopher Marlowe: A Symbiotic Relationship." Dissertation, Shakespeare Institute, University of Birmingham. 1997.

Kuriyama, Constance Brown. "Marlowe's Nemesis: The Identity of Richard Baines." In *A Poet & filthy Playmaker: New Essays on Christopher Marlowe.* Kenneth Friedenreich, Roma Gill, and Constance B. Kuriyama, eds. 1988.

———. "Marlowe, Shakespeare, and the Nature of Biographical Evidence." *Studies in Literature,* vol. 20, no. 1. 1988.

Nicholl, Charles. *The Reckoning.* 1992.

Sprott, S.E. "Drury and Marlowe." *Times Literary Supplement,* August 2, 1974.

Wernham, R.B. "Christopher Marlowe at Flushing in 1592." *English Historical Review,* vol. 91, no. 359.

Roy Kendall

SEE ALSO

Allen, William; Espionage; Marlowe, Christopher; Walsingham, Francis

Baldwin, William (c. 1518–1563)

Known principally as the editor and main author of the verse narratives collected in the enormously popular *A Mirror for Magistrates* (1559), William Baldwin was a printer, poet, novelist, and preacher whose many important publications exerted a strong influence on mid-sixteenth-century English life and literature. Although the date and place of his birth are lost, we do know that he was of Welsh descent and that he may have supplicated for the B.A. at Oxford in January of 1532/3 under the name of "William Baulden." Our first confirmed biographical information is that he was, from 1547–1553, an assistant to Edward Whitchurch, a London publisher who, with Richard Grafton, printed the earliest editions of the English Bible. Like his employer, Baldwin was a supporter of the Protestant Reformation and a confirmed opponent of Roman Catholicism.

His earliest publication, a commendatory sonnet prefixed to Christopher Langton's *The Principal Parts of Physic* (April 1548), was the first English sonnet to appear in print. This was followed soon after by his four-volume series entitled *A Treatise of Moral Philosophy* (January 1547/8), a compendium of ancient philosophy that went through a total of twenty-five editions by 1651. In June 1549, he published *The Canticles or Ballads of Solomon in English Meters,* dedicated to the young King Edward VI, and three years later he translated from Latin a libelous anti-papist satire entitled *Wonderful News of the Death of Paul the Third.*

After working briefly in Edward's court as an actor and devisor of entertainments, Baldwin published his most important work of prose fiction, *Beware the Cat.* Composed in 1553 and first printed in 1570, this lengthy episodic narrative lays legitimate claim to the title of the first English novel. After the king's death, Baldwin wrote a long poem, *The Funerals of King Edward the Sixth* (1553), though in deference to Queen Mary he did not publish it until 1560, two years after Elizabeth had ascended to the throne. While working for the scrivener John Wayland, Baldwin helped prepare an edition of John Lydgate's *Fall of Princes,* to which he added a continuation entitled *A Memorial of Such Princes, as Since the Time of King Richard the Second, Have Been Unfortunate in the Realm of England.* Printed and immediately suppressed in 1554, it was issued again in 1559 under the title *A Mirror for Magistrates.* Another edition in 1563 added eight more tragedies to the original nineteen, two of which were written by Baldwin, who had organized the entire volume and written the prose links between the various sections. Eight editions of the *Mirror* were published between 1554 and 1609, making it extremely influential in shaping subsequent English history plays and English conceptions of dramatic tragedy. After the accession of Elizabeth, Baldwin was ordained deacon in 1560, then later became rector of St. Michael le Quern in Cheapside in 1561, a clerical post he held till his death of the plague in September 1563.

B

BIBLIOGRAPHY

Baldwin, William. *A Treatise of Moral Philosophie.* Facsimile Robert Wood Bowers, intro. 1967.

———, et al. *Mirror for Magistrates.* Lily B. Campbell, ed. 1938; repr. 1960.

Ringler, William A., Jr., and Michael Flachmann, eds. *Beware the Cat: The First English Novel.* 1988.

Michael Flachmann

SEE ALSO

Grafton, Richard; Lydgate, John; Prose Fiction; Whitchurch, Edward

Bale, John (1495–1563)

An extraordinarily forceful and prolific Protestant propagandist, John Bale was prominent during the early stages of the Reformation in England. In the course of his career as a cleric, antiquarian, dramatist, historian, and publisher, he mastered a diverse array of genres, including the Protestant mystery play, allegorical history play, prose tract, beast fable, Protestant saint's life, biblical commentary, polemical history, bibliography, dialogue, and autobiography. His writings left an enduring imprint on texts like the Geneva Bible, Foxe's "Book of Martyrs," and Spenser's *Faerie Queene.* He has been remembered for pioneering antiquarian research, satirical flair, and the intensity of the invective he hurled against his opponents.

Born of poor parents at Cove in Suffolk, he joined the Carmelites in Norwich as a boy, and subsequently went to Jesus College, Cambridge (B.D. 1529, D.D. later). His extensive studies of his order continued at home and abroad, and he was successively prior of three houses. Even after his conversion, probably in 1534, he continued to write about the Carmelites, prompted by John Leland, whose *Laborious Journey* he edited (1549). He left the order by 1536, married the "faithful Dorothy," and took the living of Thorndon, Suffolk. After Protestantism excited local resentment, he was rescued from prison at Greenwich by Thomas Cromwell's intervention in 1537.

Bale's literary career passed through four distinct phases in response to shifts in official political and religious policy. After an initial burst of activity under Cromwell's patronage, he fled to the Continent when Henry VIII reverted to Anglo-Catholic orthodoxy. After returning to England under the Protestant regime of Edward VI, Bale fled into a second exile when Mary I implemented a policy of Catholic reaction. Near the end of his life, he returned to England when Elizabeth I restored most of the Edwardian ecclesiastical reforms. Throughout this turbulent era, his writings were published at a steady rate by legitimate presses in England or on the Continent for smuggling into his homeland.

At the outset of his career, Bale composed many propaganda plays on behalf of Cromwell. In *King John* (1538), for example, he praises Henry VIII for supplanting the pope and embarking on a program of religious reform. His other extant plays adapt themes, conventions, and devices of the late medieval mystery and morality plays to Protestant purposes. Going into exile at the death of his patron, Bale composed religious tracts and edited writings that attacked the Church of Rome for ceremonialism, sacerdotalism, veneration of the Virgin Mary and saints, and the doctrine of transubstantiation. The most important publication of Bale's first exile is *The Image of Both Churches* (1545?), the first complete commentary on Revelation printed in the English language. It interprets Christian history as a conflict between the "true" church founded by Christ and the "false" church headed by the pope as Antichrist. The historical paradigm of the *Image* underlies most if not all of Bale's other works, including both the early and late versions of his bibliographies of British authors: *Illustrium Maioris Britanniae Scriptorum . . . Summarium* (1548) and *Scriptorum Illustrium maioris Brytanniae . . . Catalogus* (1557–1559). *Yet a Course at the Romish Fox* (1543) adapts the beast fable as a vehicle for religious propaganda. *The Acts of English Votaries* (1546) affords a tendentious history of ecclesiastical "falsity" focused on allegations that sexual license was rampant in English monastic houses. Bale edited *A Brief Chronicle concerning Sir John Oldcastle* (1544), and *The Examinations of Anne Askew* (1546–1547), a first-person narrative concerning judicial interrogation and condemnation for heresy, as Protestant saints' lives.

During Edward VI's reign, Bale's tracts included *The Apology of John Bale against a Rank Papist* (1550?) and his quasi-autobiographical *Expostulation or Complaint against the Blasphemies of a Frantic Papist of Hampshire* (1552?). A rare example of early autobiography, *The Vocation of John,* records his personal experience from the time of his appointment as an embattled missionary bishop at the see of Ossory in Ireland until his flight to the Continent on the accession of Mary I. Bale dedicated his second exile to completion of his massive bibliographical project. On his final return to England in 1560, he was the chief radical of the first reformist generation to live into the reign of Elizabeth I. He remained in England until his death in 1563.

BIBLIOGRAPHY
Bale, John. *The Complete Plays of John Bale,* 2 vols. Peter Happé, ed. 1985–1986.
———. *The Vocacyon of Johan Bale.* Peter Happé and John N. King, eds. Renaissance English Text Society, vol. 14. 1990.
Fairfield, Leslie P. *John Bale: Mythmaker for the English Reformation.* 1976.
Walker, Greg. *Plays of Persuasion: Drama and Politics at the Court of Henry VIII.* 1991.

John N. King

SEE ALSO
Askew, Anne; Cromwell, Thomas; Drama, History of; Leland, John; Marian Exiles; Reformation, English

Bales, Peter (1547–c. 1610)

Peter Bales (or Balesius) appears to have been born in London, although virtually nothing is known of his early life. Anthony á Wood relates that he resided at Gloucester Hall, Oxford, for a number of years. Undoubtedly, such a stay was in the capacity of private teacher of shorthand and calligraphy rather than student, and the several complimentary verses prefixed by Oxford students to the second edition of Bales's *Brachygraphie* may be interpreted as testimony to his success. By the mid-1570s, Bales's skills, which included such astounding accomplishments as copying of the Bible to fit the compass of a walnut, attracted the attention of Elizabeth I and her ministers, so that subsequently Bales was employed both as copyist of documents and consultant in deciphering documents. Bales's most famous accomplishment in the latter capacity was the discovery in 1586 of the Babington Plot. In 1590, he published *The Writing Schoolemaster* while dividing his time between teaching and serving various noblemen in the capacity of copyist. In 1595, Bales also won a highly publicized contest of skills with a rival penman, Daniel Johnson. Following the ascension of James I to the throne, Bales was appointed writing teacher to Prince Henry, and sought to obtain further remuneration by devising a secret cipher for the king. Not much else, however, is known of him in his last years, and even the date of his death is conjecture.

BIBLIOGRAPHY
Bales, Peter. *The Writing Schoolemaster.* 1590; 2nd edition 1597; repr. 1969, 1972. *Historical Manuscripts Commission, Salisbury Papers,* vol. 16, p. 402.

Mordechai Feingold

SEE ALSO
Babington Plot; Handwriting

Ballad

A ballad is a type of folksong that tells a story. Often combining narrative, dialogue, and lyric, it is perpetuated through oral tradition and thus will be found with numerous variants, both textual and melodic. Some remain confined to one area, while others crop up in variant forms in many countries. The typical ballad text consists of strophic quatrains: what is termed the ballad stanza ordinarily consists of fourteen stresses, with a pause after the seventh and a rhyme between the seventh and the fourteenth ("common meter"). The pause is often filled in with a stress to which a corresponding stress is added at the end ("long meter"). There are also five-, six-, and eight-phrase tunes.

Regrettably, early ballad collectors, such as Sir Walter Scott, were primarily or solely interested in the texts. Francis James Child, whose 305 ballads with their variants are considered the nucleus of English-Scottish balladry, consigned the fifty-five melodies he recorded to an appendix. It was not until the early twentieth century that Cecil Sharp, in amassing a collection of 4,977 tunes, refocused attention on the melodies. Bernard Bronson, recognizing that "ballads without tunes are as unfulfilled, as paradoxical, as songs without words," gathered together and studied the tunes associated with each of the Child ballads. Generally speaking, although ballads were always sung, tunes could and did shift freely from one text to another, while variant texts of a ballad group were not always sung to tunes from one tune family.

Traditional ballad stories usually concern one event, narrated in an utterly impersonal manner. Dialogue or the question-and-answer format, as in *Lord Randal* (Child no. 12), and *Edward* (Child no. 13), frequently moves the story forward, usually by episodic leaps. Even if historically based, ballads are not reliably factual. *Lord Randal,* for example, may have been based on a story about the presumed poisoning of the nephew of Ranulf, the sixth earl of Chester, by his wife. In the ballad, Lord Randal is poisoned by his sweetheart and comes home to his mother to die.

Ballad subjects cover a wide range. Love rewarded or unrequited or betrayed, elopement, feuds, witches, riddles, legends, knights, revenants, and shape-shifting can be found among its multitude of topics. Broadside ballads, whose texts were printed on single-sheet folios, deal

B

with social commentary, topical subjects, and moral instruction, as well as the topics of traditional ballads. More than 3,000 broadside ballad titles were entered in registers of the Guild of Stationers between 1558 and 1709, when copyright legislation was passed.

The strongly modal character of ballad tunes, however recent their sources, is sometimes evidence of considerable age. In the British-American ballad tradition, Ionian mode predominates, equally divided between authentic and plagal forms. Mixtures of Dorian, Mixolydian, and Aeolian modes are not uncommon in balladry, as are tunes based on hexatonic, or six-note, scales, usually omitting the seventh degree. Although variants among the members of a tune family may be legion, a shared core identity is often evident. Refrains adorn many ballads. Some consist of nonsense syllables, such as "Ri fol i diddle i gee wo" and "Fol the dal the di-do" from *The Cruel Mother* (Child no. 20). In *The Three Ravens* (Child no. 26), the refrain "Downe a downe, hay downe, hay downe" is interlaced with text lines. A refrain could also be a fifth repetitive line of a stanza or a burden between stanzas.

The earliest extant sources of both text and tune are often of considerably later date than the ballads themselves. Some tunes survived only because they were used as themes of variations in the Fitzwilliam Virginal Book and other Elizabethan keyboard prints and manuscripts. Other popular melodies were published in the seventeenth century by John Playford in textless arrangements for dancing, and Thomas D'Urfey included ballad tunes in *Wit and Mirth*, or *Pills to Purge Melancholy*, his 1699–1700 collection of new texts to preexisting melodies. Child had to take *Dives and Lazarus* (Child no. 56) from nineteenth-century reprints of eighteeenth-century broadsides, although there are references to it from early in Elizabeth I's reign. Although the earliest printed source of *The Three Ravens* is Thomas Ravenscroft's *Melismata* of 1611, it has been argued that an early variant adapted to pious purposes became the famous sixteenth-century *Corpus Christi Carol*. These, and other examples, of which there are many, are characteristic of a genre passed on to succeeding generations through oral tradition.

BIBLIOGRAPHY

Bronson, Bernard H. *The Traditional Tunes of the Child Ballads.* 1959–1972.
———. *The Ballad as Song.* 1969.
Chappell, William. *The Ballad Literature and Popular Music of the Olden Time.* 1855–1859; revised by F.W. Sternfeld, 1966.
Child, Francis James. *English and Scottish Popular Ballads.* 5 vols. 1882–1898.
Firth, Charles Harding. *The ballad history of the reigns of Henry VII and Henry VIII.* 1908.
Lamson, Roy. "English broadside ballad tunes (1550–1700)." Dissertation, Harvard University. 1935.
Livingston, Carole Rose. *British Broadside Ballads of the Sixteenth Century. Vol. 1: A Catalogue and Essay.* 1990.
Richmond, W. Edson. *Ballad Scholarship: An Annotated Bibliography.* Garland Folklore Bibliographies, vol. 14. 1984.
Rollins, Hyder E. *An Analytical Index to the Ballad-Entries (1557–1709) in the Registers of the Company of Stationers of London.* 1967.
Simpson, Claude. *The British Broadside Ballad and Its Music.* 1966.
Wurzbach, Natascha. *The Rise of the English Street Ballad, 1550–1650.* 1990.

Laura S. Youens

SEE ALSO
Broadsides; Carol; Keyboard Music

Bancroft, Richard (1544–1610)

When he was made bishop of London in 1597, Richard Bancroft was already well known in court circles as a leading opponent of the Puritans. Chaplain to Christopher Hatton since 1579, when Whitgift became archbishop of Canterbury in 1583, Bancroft was made his principal assistant. Bancroft had known many of the Puritan and presbyterianizing clergy while at Cambridge from 1564 to 1574, first at Christ's College (A.B. 1567), and then as tutor at Jesus for seven years. Ordained in 1574, he then became chaplain to Bishop Richard Cox of Ely, university preacher and archbishop's visitor for Ely and Peterborough, which gave him further knowledge of the activities and opinions of the Puritans in the south Midlands and East Anglia. From 1587 on he sat in the ecclesiastical court of "High Commission," which he reformed significantly. Despite the disapproval of its practice of questioning individual puritan ministers and its unpopularity with common law lawyers, it was well used by litigants because cases between parties were often handled more efficiently there than in the common law courts. Bancroft also became the principal detective in the investigation of the Marprelate tracts (1587–1589), discovering the printers and playing a large role in the trials that ensued.

Bancroft's sermon at Paul's Cross, London, in February 1589, was a notable event in the program to discredit the Puritans and vindicate the church establishment. It depicts the Puritans as a dangerous movement tending toward religious, social, and political anarchy, itself riddled with interior dissent and confusion. Most notably, in the sermon, Bancroft exalted the rule of bishops beyond the conventional contemporary argument. He did not claim directly that bishops were divinely instituted (*jure divino*), but, significantly, he omitted the traditional argument against the Presbyterians: that government by bishops was only a "thing indifferent" (adiaphora) that could be used, or not, by a "true church." Bancroft, rather, by emphasizing the apostolic origins of bishops and the continued historical usage of the office in the church, articulated a stronger theological argument than had yet been emphasized in episcopalian theory, but one which would be developed quickly in the 1590s. In 1593, two of his tracts, *Dangerous Positions,* and *A Survey of the Pretended Holy Discipline* (published anonymously), expanded some of the themes of the sermon, and reported fully the Presbyterian movement's organization. As bishop of London, he aided Robert Cecil, encouraging conflicts between Jesuits and secular priests among Roman Catholics and supporting the succession of James VI. He was made archbishop of Canterbury in 1604.

Bancroft's character and significance are controversial along ideological lines that were drawn during his lifetime. The Puritan, and then the Whig, tradition saw him as a careerist, persecutor of the godly, and an opponent of the freedoms of speech and religion. To those sympathetic to the church establishment, or cooler in their moral judgments, he was an admirably vigorous contender for Tudor ideals of law, order, and conformity, in concert with Elizabeth I and the prevailing policies at the end of her reign.

BIBLIOGRAPHY

Cargill Thompson, W.D.J. "A Reconsideration of Richard Bancroft's Paul's Cross Sermon." *Journal of Ecclesiastical History,* vol. 20, no. 2, October 1969.
Collinson, Patrick. *The Religion of Protestants.* 1982.
Lake, Peter. *Anglicans and Puritans?* 1988.
Usher, Roland G. *The Reconstruction of the English Church.* 2 vols. 1910.

Frederick H. Shriver

SEE ALSO

Adiaphora; Calvinism; High Commision, Court of; Marprelate Controversy; Saravia, Hadrian

B

Baptism

The theology of baptism was not itself a subject of controversy in the Church of England. The sacramental nature of baptism and its Scriptural foundation were accepted by Lutherans, Calvinists, Anglicans, and Roman Catholics, and the tradition of infant baptism was maintained by them. The rite of the first Book of Common Prayer was essentially that of the *Sarum Manuale,* with some touches from the Mozarabic liturgy of Spain and the addition of prayers from Luther and the Cologne Church Order of Archbishop Herman von Wied. In the second Prayer Book of 1552 it was heavily revised, to a large extent following the criticisms of Martin Bucer, and many of the medieval ceremonies considered superstitious were dropped. These included exorcism, the giving of a white robe (chrisom), anointing, and the blessing of the font. The rite remained unchanged in the Elizabethan Prayer Book of 1559.

The service was to be conducted by preference on Sundays or holy days in the presence of the congregation, following the second lesson at Matins or Evensong, although Bucer had recommended that it be celebrated at Holy Communion. The rationale for its public administration, according to the opening rubric of the service itself, was to allow the congregation to testify to the reception of the newly baptized members into the church and to remind the congregation of the profession of faith made to God at his or her own baptism. Frequently, however, newborn infants were baptized by the midwife immediately after birth. This practice was widely condemned on the grounds that "women are no ministers in the Church of God," and could not administer the sacrament.

In the fifth book of his *Of the Laws of Ecclesiastical Polity,* Richard Hooker argues that the command of Christ requiring all to be baptized must take precedence over the desirability of having the baptism publicly celebrated. The Church of England, Hooker contends, does not encourage baptism by midwives, but recognizes that those so baptized have received true baptism, for the "fruit of baptism" depends solely on the covenant and promise of God, not on the commission of the minister.

The two major controversies involving the baptismal rite in the Tudor period concerned directing questions to the infant candidates to be answered by their godparents and making the sign of the cross on the foreheads of the newly baptized, both required by The Book of Common Prayer.

In his *Censura* of the 1549 Prayer Book, Bucer argued that questioning infants was not the teaching of Scripture, and that there was no reason "why you should question

B

one who does not understand what you say and another should answer for him of his own understanding." Hooker defended the practice, pointing out that baptism implies a covenant between God and the baptized, in which God forgives sin through the Holy Spirit, and we promise to follow God's law. The church therefore requires a profession of faith and promise of obedience from all who come to be baptized, and, in the case of infants, those who present the children for baptism have the obligation to make the promises on their behalf.

The objection to the making of the sign of the cross was simply that it was not commanded in the New Testament and therefore should not be included in the rite. This was really the basis of Puritan objections to all ceremonies. They wanted no ceremonies in the church, no matter how ancient and honorable, unless they were expressly commanded in Scripture. This, defenders of the Prayer Book argued, was neither possible nor desirable, and the church was at pains to avoid superstition by explaining the meaning of the ritual acts.

BIBLIOGRAPHY

Brightman, F.E. *The English Rite.* 2 vols. 1921; repr. 1969.

Cuming, G.J. *A History of Anglican Liturgy.* 2nd edition. 1982.

Hooker, Richard. *Of the Laws of Ecclesiastical Polity,* Book V. 1597.

Manuale ad vsum percelebris ecclesie Sarisburiensis. Henry Bradshaw Society. Vol. 41. A. Jefferies Collins, ed. 1960.

Whitaker, E.C. *Martin Bucer and the Book of Common Prayer.* Alcuin Club Collections. Vol. 55. 1974.

Leonel L. Mitchell

SEE ALSO

Articles of Religion; Book of Common Prayer; Bucer, Martin; Hooker, Richard; Sarum, Use of

Barbary Company
See Joint Stock Companies

Barclay, Alexander (c. 1475–1552)

One of the first English writers to have had his works published in a nearly complete form, Alexander Barclay was a translator and poet who brought continental humanist literature and poetic forms to England, and a literary innovator whose patrons included some of the most powerful nobility of the Tudor period. Barclay is connected to such notable events as the battle of Flodden Field and the meeting at the Field of the Cloth of Gold. His writings likely influenced Skelton and Spenser.

Probably born in Scotland about the same time the printing press was first brought into England, Barclay was published by both Richard Pynson and Wynken de Worde, the two principal printers of the first part of the sixteenth century. Barclay is best known for his free translation of Sebastian Brant's German satire, *Das Narrenschiff* (1494), as *The Shyp of Folys of the Worlde,* 1508 (*The Ship of Fools*), a catalogue of fools meant to guide people toward wiser ways that also provides a picture of contemporary life. *The Dictionary of National Biography* notes that this work "pre-eminently help[ed] to bury mediaeval allegory in the grave . . . and to direct English authorship into the drama, essay, and novel of character" (1080).

Barclay's *Eclogues* are the earliest English pastorals, as well as the earliest known eclogues in English, and they anticipate Spenser, perhaps influencing both Spenser and Michael Drayton, to whom they were known. The first three of Barclay's five eclogues offer a vivid anti-court invective in support of the pastoral life, the form upholding his message; Barclay based the eclogues on Piccolomini's mid-fifteenth century *De miseriis curialum,* but transformed Piccolomini's prose into pastoral verse. Curiously, these anti-court eclogues include praise of both Henry VII and Henry VIII.

Along with Erasmus, More, and Skelton, Barclay contributed to the Tudor propaganda effort, writing in support of the English victory at Flodden Field in 1513. The English forces were lead by Thomas Howard, later duke of Norfolk, who is presumed to have been Barclay's most important patron in addition to others such as Cardinal Thomas Morton and Richard, earl of Kent. Barclay also translated Sallust's *Jugurthine War,* in which he links the Roman Marius's conquest over Jugurtha, in a prefatory letter, to Howard's success at Flodden Field. Included is a hint of warning to tyrannous "princes and governors" about the risk of violent overthrow: perhaps an early humanist suggestion of righteous disobedience.

In 1521, following the peace between England and France established at the Field of the Cloth of Gold, Barclay wrote a brief guide to the French language in what might be an early form of a traveler's companion. Regarding the suggestions that Barclay was dismissive of John Skelton's work, the evidence is thin, and the work known as *Contra Skeltonum,* said by John Bale to have been Barclay's, is lost. Also on Bale's authority, it is believed that Barclay died at Croydon and was buried on June 10, 1552, after a long and prolific life.

BIBLIOGRAPHY

Barclay, Alexander. *The Eclogues of Alexander Barclay.* Beatrice White, ed. 1928.

———. *The Gardyners Passetaunce.* Franklin B. Williams, Jr., and Howard M. Nixon, eds. 1985.

———. *The Life of St. George.* William Nelson, ed. 1955.

———. *The Mirrour of Good Maners.* Spenser Society, vol. 38. 1885; repr. 1967.

———. *The Ship of Fools.* 2 vols. T.H. Jamieson, ed. 1874; repr. 1966.

Carlson, David R. "Alexander Barclay." *Dictionary of Literary Biography.,* vol. 132. David A. Richardson, ed. 1993.

Lyall, R.J. "Tradition and Innovation in Alexander Barclay's 'Towre of Vertue and Honoure.'" *The Review of English Studies,* vol. 23, pp. 1–18.

James M. Dutcher

SEE ALSO

Brant, Sebastian; Flodden Field; Field of the Cloth of Gold; Pastoral

Barlow, William (d. 1568)

Little is known of the early years of the clergyman William Barlow. It is probable that he earned a doctorate in theology at Oxford and thereafter became prior of Blackmore. The first firm date in his biography is his resignation from Blackmore in 1509 to take the priory of Tiptree. More priories followed until, in 1525, Barlow became rector of Great Cressingham. During this period, he authored pamphlets against Cardinal Thomas Wolsey that were banned as heretical in 1529; within several years, Barlow recanted and wrote letters to Henry VIII asking him to forgive the attacks on Wolsey. These letters, along with an anti-Lutheran tract composed in 1531, made Barlow a favorite of Henry's court and helped him to more lucrative priories. In 1536, he became bishop of St. Asaph in Wales and was, almost immediately, translated to the see of St. Davids. There is no official record of his consecration—a fact that perhaps explains his extreme Erastianism: he held that a king could appoint a lawful bishop without episcopal consecration. He was made bishop of Bath and Wells in 1548 under Edward VI, but the accession of the Catholic Mary I saw his imprisonment in the Tower. He

was not executed—due, in part, to the republication of his 1531 anti-Lutheran tract—and allowed to escape to Germany. When Elizabeth I succeeded Mary, Barlow returned and, in 1559, was made bishop of Chichester, cultivating a close alliance with Archbishop Matthew Parker that lasted until Barlow's death in 1568. Among his writings are a handbook for clergy, a book of homilies, and English translations of books of the Apocrypha.

BIBLIOGRAPHY

Barnes, A.S. *Bishop Barlow and Anglican Orders.* 1922.

Garrett, Christina H. *The Marian Exiles.* 1938.

Jenkins, C. "Bishop Barlow's Consecration and Archbishop Parker's Register, with Some New Documents." *Journal of Theological Studies,* vol. 24, pp. 1–32.

Mark Goldblatt

SEE ALSO

Erastianism; Marian Exiles; Parker, Matthew; Wolsey, Thomas

Barnes, Barnabe (1571–1609)

The suggestion that Barnabe Barnes might have been the model for Shakespeare's cowardly braggart Parolles in *All's Well that Ends Well* is a little unfair to Parolles. The son of a bishop of Durham, Barnes's first publication was a rambling and interesting sequence of love poems, *Parthenophil and Parthenope* (1593), for which he is now principally remembered. This ends with the rape of the heroine, represented as a kinswoman of the dedicatee, Lord William Percy, who jokingly denied the allegations. In 1595, Barnes published the pious *A Divine Centurie of Spiritual Sonnets.* In 1591, he had accompanied Robert Devereux, the earl of Essex, on a military campaign to France in which (according to Thomas Nashe in *Have with You to Saffron-Walden*) "hee bragd . . . he slue ten men, when (fearfull cowbaby) he never heard peice shot off but hee fell flat on his face." Nashe also accuses him of being a thief. In 1598, Barnes was called before the Star Chamber Court and accused of attempting to murder a certain John Browne of Berwick, first by giving him a poisoned lemon (which was taken by someone else by mistake) and then with a cup of wine laced with mercury (which also failed). He was certainly guilty; Barnes escaped his trial by fleeing northward. In 1606, he dedicated *Foure Bookes of Offices,* a book on good government, to the new king of England, James I. He may have become a clergyman by this time. His last publication was a revised version of the play *The Devil's Charter* (1607), which had been played before

B

the king by Shakespeare's company at Whitehall in February 1607. It seems likely that its rabid anti-Catholicism was another bid for royal favor.

BIBLIOGRAPHY

Barnes, Barnabe. *Foure Bookes of Offices.* Facsimile. 1975.

Blank, Philip. *Lyric Forms in the Sonnet Sequences of Barnabe Barnes.* 1974.

Doyno, Victor A. *Barnabe Barnes, Parthenophil and Parthenophe, A Critical Edition.* 1971.

Eccles, Mark. "Barnabe Barnes." In *Thomas Lodge and Other Elizabethans,.* Charles J. Sisson, ed. 1933; repr. 1966.

Pogue, Jim C. *The Devil's Charter, A Critical Edition.* 1980.

David Farley-Hills

SEE ALSO

Nashe, Thomas; Sonnet Sequences

Baro, Peter (1534–1599)

A Frenchman born at Etampes in December 1534, Peter Baro studied law at Bourges, where he took his degree in 1556. About that time he became persuaded that Protestantism was the right form of the Christian faith, and he went to Geneva in 1560. Later he returned to France as a leader of the Reformed Church, but about the time of the St. Bartholemew's Day Massacre in 1572 he fled to England. He was admitted to Trinity College, Cambridge, where he lectured in Hebrew and theology. In 1574, he was elected Lady Margaret Professor of Divinity, a post that at that time was held for two years. Such was his reputation, however, that he continued to be elected to the chair until 1596.

Sometime about 1581 it appears that Baro began to weaken in his commitment to a full-blooded Calvinism. He began to develop views that would later be classed as Arminian, though for a long time this made little difference to his standing in the university. However, when the Lambeth Articles were published in 1595, Baro led the opposition to them in Cambridge. His hostility to strict predestinarianism meant that in November 1596, he was not reelected to his professorial chair, and he departed the university in some bitterness. He went to London, where he continued to preach and teach until his death in April 1599. He was given a magnificent funeral by Bishop Richard Bancroft, who sympathized with his theological views and was appalled at the way Baro had been treated at Cambridge.

BIBLIOGRAPHY

Tyacke, N. *Anti-Calvinists. The Rise of English Arminianism c. 1590–1640.* 1987.

White, P. *Predestination, Policy and Polemic.* 1992.

Gerald L. Bray

SEE ALSO

Arminianism; Bancroft, Richard; Calvinism; Lambeth Articles

Barrow, Henry (1550–1593)

Martyr and prolific propagandist for Elizabethan separatism, Henry Barrow was described by an incensed Archbishop John Whitgift as "hot brains" after Barrow, during an examination before the Privy Council, called Whitgift "a monster . . . even that second beast spoken of in the Revelation." That intemperate remark probably sealed Barrow's fate. Along with his co-religionist, John Greenwood, he was hanged at Tyburn on April 6, 1593, for publishing subversive religious books.

A graduate of Clare College, Cambridge, and member of Gray's Inn, London, this formerly well-connected courtier first turned to strict Puritanism, then to congregational separatism under the influence of Greenwood, whom Barrow had visited in the Clink. Imprisoned by Whitgift for separating from the Church of England, which he judged an apostate institution, Barrow remained incarcerated along with Greenwood for the remaining six years of his life, enduring numerous interrogations at Lambeth Palace.

Barrow is credited with writing the larger share of polemical tracts, letters, and treatises that the two Separatists managed to smuggle out of prison and into print abroad. Although Greenwood and Barrow denied any direct debt to the earlier writings of Robert Browne, the content of Barrowist Separatism remained in close theological accord with Brownism.

BIBLIOGRAPHY

Burrage, Champlin. *Early English Dissenters.* 1912.

Carlson, Leland H., ed. *The Writings of Henry Barrow 1587–1590.* 1962.

———. *The Writings of Henry Barrow, 1590–1591.* 1966.

———. *The Writings of John Greenwood and Henry Barrow, 1591—1593.* 1970.

Powicke, F.J. *Henry Barrow and the Exiled Church of Amsterdam.* 1900.

White, B.R. *The English Separatist Tradition.* 1971.

Stephen Brachlow

SEE ALSO
Browne, Robert; Greenwood, John

Barton, Elizabeth (1510–1534)

The "Holy Maid of Kent" was a prophetess associated with the conservative opposition to Henry VIII's divorce from Katherine of Aragon. Shortly after prophesying her own cure from epilepsy in 1526, Elizabeth Barton entered the nunnery of St. Sepulchre's in Canterbury where her mystical trances were accompanied by miracles and prophecies. Her revelations were publicized by Dr. Edward Bocking, the cellarer of Christ Church Abbey in Canterbury, and her patrons included William Warham, archbishop of Canterbury, and other leading conservative clergy. Although her reputation was such that she was able to secure audiences with Wolsey and the king, her prophecies became increasingly political, as she forecast that if Henry put aside his wife he should cease to be king within six months. Interrogated by Cromwell, Cranmer, and Latimer, she broke down and confessed in November 1533 that her prophecies were fraudulent. After publicly ridiculing her at St. Paul's Cross in London and in Canterbury, the government proceeded against her by act of attainder and she was executed in April 1534. Evangelicals capitalized on the episode to discredit Catholic superstition and to neutralize the conservative clerical establishment within Kent.

BIBLIOGRAPHY
Neame, A. *The Holy Maid of Kent: the Life of Elizabeth Barton, 1506–1534.* 1971.
Whatmore, L.E., ed. "The Sermon Against the Holy Maid of Kent." *English Historical Review,* vol. 58, pp. 463–475.

Ian W. Archer

SEE ALSO
Katharine of Aragon; Warham, William

Bastard Feudalism

Bastard feudalism is a term coined by historians to describe a set of relationships between lords and lesser men, in which cash, not land, figured prominently. In return for service to his lord, a man received a monetary payment, the privilege of wearing the lord's livery (a badge or piece of clothing that clearly denoted his loyalty), and the protection of his lord (maintenance). By retaining men through a variety of methods, noblemen established loyal retinues that bolstered their public image, helped them conduct their personal business, aided in the administration of local government, and provided the royal government with troops during war. The benefits of bastard feudalism were threefold: the aristocracy developed an effective means of recruiting the manpower needed to dominate society, lesser men were able to attach themselves to noble lords who offered them protection, and the government had a ready supply of soldiers.

Bastard feudalism survived Henry VII's legislation against retaining and the successful attempts by the Court of the Star Chamber to suppress livery and maintenance. The practice increasingly worked within the confines of the law, adapting itself to the conditions imposed by Henry VII and subsequent Tudor and early Stuart kings. The Tudor aristocracy, forced to abandon medieval forms of retaining, continued to retain men by inflating their household staff with nonresident gentry and employing more estate officials. Since Tudor lords assumed that their able-bodied male tenants would provide military service if necessary, they were able to raise significant armies from their household staff, estate officers, and tenants. Because of Tudor anti-retaining legislation, the government was able to rid bastard feudalism of its corrupt elements, thereby creating a stabilizing influence on society, while maintaining an effective means of military recruitment right up to the civil war.

BIBLIOGRAPHY
Bellamy, J.G. *Bastard Feudalism and the Law.* 1989.
Bernard, G., ed. *The Tudor Nobility.* 1992.
Hicks, Michael. *Bastard Feudalism.* 1995.
James, M.E. *Society, Politics and Culture: Studies in Early Modern England.* 1986.
Stone, Lawrence. *The Crisis of the Aristocracy, 1558–1641.* 1965.

Elizabeth G. Kunz

SEE ALSO
Henry VII; Star Chamber, Court of; Wars of the Roses

Bateman, Stephen (c. 1510–1584)

Born in Bruton, Somersetshire, Stephen Bateman (or Batman) received his LL.B in 1534 at Cambridge where he was reputed a brilliant preacher and a learned man. He earned a D.D., became a domestic chaplain to Matthew Parker, archbishop of Canterbury, and enjoyed the enviable role of collector of books for Parker's library. As a leading member of

B

Parker's team of antiquarians, Bateman was crucial in the recovery and preservation of thousands of books and manuscripts dispersed after Henry VIII's dissolution of the monasteries. On Parker's death in 1575, his invaluable collection moved to its present home, Corpus Christi College, Cambridge. After serving as rector of Merstham in 1573 and also parson of Newington Butts, both in Surrey, in 1582 Bateman was made domestic chaplain to Henry Cary, Lord Hunsdon, father of the patron of Shakespeare's acting company. Well read in contemporary mythography, natural history, theology, and the sciences, Bateman was consulted by translator Richard Robinson as an Arthurian expert. He lived for some time in Leedes, Kent, and died in 1584.

Bateman is best known as an author and translator of religious, allegorical, mythographic, and encyclopedic works. His *Batman upon Bartholome* (1582)—an augmented revision of John Trevisa's English translation of Bartholomaeus Anglicus's high medieval encyclopedia, *De proprietatibus rerum*—was probably the book Bateman was most known for in the Renaissance. Its usefulness to later writers is reflected in the often applied sobriquet, "Shakespeare's Encyclopedia." His allegorical quest poem, *The Travayled Pilgrim* (1569), is a politically modified translation of Hernando de Acuña's Spanish version of *Le Chevalier délibéré* by Olivier de la Marche. It anticipates and may well have influenced Spenser's *Faerie Queene* and Bunyan's *Pilgrim's Progress*. Burgundian and Hapsburg Catholicism in word and illustration are transformed into the triumphant history of Tudor protestantism culminating in Elizabeth I. Militant nationalism also pervades Bateman's other major work, *The Doom Warning All Men to the Judgement* (1581), once again a modified translation, this time of Conrad Lycosthenes' *Prodigiorum ac ostentorum Chronicon* (1557). This long and generously illustrated chronicle of folklore and prodigies is extended to the year 1580 by Bateman, and comments in his commonplace book (now held by Harvard University) such as, "be ware of French myce, and Spanish owles," assist the interpretation of *The Doom* as a polemic against the Spanish military threat and the proposed marriage of Elizabeth I and the duke of Alençon.

Bateman's other texts—*A Crystal Glass of Christian Reformation* (1569), *The Golden Book of Leaden Gods* (1577), *The New Arrival of the Three Graces* (c. 1580), and his preface to John Rogers's *The Displaying of a Horrible Sect of Gross and Wicked Heretics* (1578)—maintain the mythographic interests and religious biases of his major works and chastise various radical Protestant sects. Critics no longer see Bateman's works as simply source texts for

great Renaissance writers but as complex examples of preservation and revision governed by interwoven aesthetic, ideological, and pedagogical criteria.

BIBLIOGRAPHY

Greetham, D.G. "On Cultural Translation: From Patristic Repository to 'Shakespeare's Encyclopaedia.'" In *Voices in Translation: The Authority of "Olde Bokes" in Medieval Literature: Essays in Honor of Helaine Newstead.* Deborah M. Sinnreich-Levi and Gale Sigal, eds., pp. 69–84. 1992.

McNair, John R., intro. *The Doome Warning All Men to the Judgement* (1581). Facsimile edition. 1984.

Prescott, Anne Lake. "Spenser's Chivalric Restoration: From Bateman's Travayled Pylgrime to the Redcrosse Knight." *Studies in Philology*, vol. 86, pp. 166–197.

Schäfer, Jürgen. Introduction to *Batman vppon Bartholome His Booke De Proprietatibus Rerum* (1582). Facsimile edition. 1976.

Sutch, Susan Speakman, and Anne Lake Prescott. "Translation as Transformation: Olivier de la Marche's *Le Chevalier délibéré* and its Hapsburg and Elizabethan Permutations." *Comparative Literature Studies*, vol. 25, pp. 281–317.

Liam E. Semler

SEE ALSO

Alençon and Anjou, Duke de; French Literature, Influence of; Parker, Matthew

Beaton, David (c. 1494–1546)

Cardinal, archbishop, and would-be regent of Scotland, David Beaton (or Bethune) was educated at the universities of St. Andrews and Glasgow before going to Paris to study civil and canon law. After his return to Scotland in 1523, he was named abbot of Arbroath, and his connections with the French soon proved invaluable to James V: Beaton was instrumental in arranging the king's first and second marriages to Frenchwomen, thereby strengthening ties between Scotland and France. In 1528, Beaton became lord keeper of the privy seal. He was made bishop of Mirepoix in Foix in 1537 and, a year later, created cardinal by Pope Paul III. In 1539, Beaton succeeded his uncle as archbishop of St. Andrews. When James V died in 1542, Beaton produced a dubious will in which provisions had been made for a joint regency to include himself and the earls of Huntly, Argyle, and James Hamilton, second earl of Arran. The scheme failed: Arran was eventually declared governor of the kingdom. But when Arran attempted, in 1543, to arrange the marriage of James V's daughter, Mary Queen of Scots, to Edward, the son of Henry VIII—the effect of which would have been to distance Scotland and France and to bring the former under even greater English sway—Beaton raised a faction against Arran, who eventually relented. The act for which Beaton is most often remembered, however, is his persecution of George Wishart, a preacher and reformer with ties to Henry VIII and John Knox; Wishart was brought to trial and burned at the stake in 1546. Two months later, Beaton was assassinated by Wishart's friend, John Leslie.

BIBLIOGRAPHY

Forbes, F.A. *Leaders of a Forlorn Hope; a Study of the Reformation in Scotland.* 1922.

Herkless, J. *Life of David Beaton.* 1891.

Knox, John. *History of the Reformation in Scotland.* 1587.

Spottiswoode, John. *The History of the Church of Scotland.* 1655.

Mark Goldblatt

SEE ALSO

Hamilton Family; James V; Leslie, John; Wishart, George

Beaufort, Margaret (1443–1509)

The life of Margaret Beaufort is significant because she played a vital role in her family's dynastic success. A descendant of the illegitimate line of John of Gaunt, duke of Lancaster, she was born May 31, 1443, the only child of his grandson, John Beaufort, duke of Somerset, and Margaret Beauchamp of Bletsoe. A much sought-after heiress, she was betrothed first to John de la Pole, son of the duke of Suffolk. After that union was dissolved, she wed Edmond Tudor, earl of Richmond, the uterine half-brother of King Henry VI, and gave birth posthumously to their child, Henry, in 1456. She next married Henry Stafford, second son of the duke of Buckingham, and, after his death, Thomas Stanley (later earl of Derby). Having sent her son, the future Henry VII, abroad for safekeeping, she used her connections to advance his overthrow of Richard III, the last Yorkist king, in 1485. She successfully promoted the marriage of Henry to Elizabeth of York, heiress of Edward IV, to unite in their children the Yorkist and Lancastrian claims to the throne.

During her son's reign, she remained a source of dynastic strength, drawing up guidelines for funeral and lying-in

rituals and performing in family rites. Interested in scholarship, she lamented that although she had learned to read and write French and English, she knew only enough Latin to follow church services. From their French versions, she translated into English and had published two religious works, one of them authored by Thomas á Kempis. After she and her husband took vows of celibacy in 1499, and, especially after he died in 1504, she turned increasingly to her own preparations for death, relying greatly on the assistance of John Fisher, bishop of Rochester. Among her endowments were Christ's Church and St. John's at Cambridge and theology lectureships at both universities. She lived to witness the coronation of her grandson, Henry VIII, and was buried in Westminster Abbey after her death on June 29, 1509.

BIBLIOGRAPHY

Jones, Michael K., and Malcolm G. Underwood. *The King's Mother: Lady Margaret Beaufort, Countess of Richmond and Derby.* 1992.

Simon, Linda. *Of Virtue Rare: Margaret Beaufort, Matriarch of The House of Tudor.* 1982.

Warnicke, Retha. "The Lady Margaret, Countess of Richmond (d. 1509), as Seen by Bishop Fisher and Lord Morley." *Moreana,* vol. 19, no. 74, pp. 47–55.

Retha Warnicke

SEE ALSO

Elizabeth of York; Henry VII

Becon, Thomas (c. 1513–67)

A Protestant divine born in Norfolk, Thomas Becon was educated at St. John's College, Cambridge, where he commenced B.A. in 1530. He was greatly influenced at Cambridge by Hugh Latimer and George Stafford. Becon was ordained priest in 1533. His first living was the vicarage of Brenzett, near Romney in Kent. Having written in support of Reformation doctrines under the pseudonymn Theodore Basille, he was arrested and forced in 1543 to recant at Paul's Cross in London and to burn his books. He departed for the Peak of Derbyshire, then to Staffordshire and Warwickshire, and later to Leistershire, where he earned his living by teaching pupils. He continued to write during this fugitive period, and all of his books were successively proclaimed heretical. On the accession of Edward VI in 1547, he was appointed chaplain to the Lord Protector Somerset at Sheen; presented to the living of St. Stephen, Walbrook; made one of the six preachers

B

at Canterbury Cathedral and a chaplain of Thomas Cranmer's household; appointed to read divinity at Oxford; and invited to contribute to the *Book of Homilies,* for which he wrote "Against Whoredom and Uncleanness," usually known as the "Homily against Adultery." During this time he also probably influenced Cranmer to accept the "Memorial on Kneeling at Communion" (the so-called "Black Rubric"). On the accession of Mary Tudor in 1553, he was committed to the Tower by the Privy Council as a seditious preacher and ejected from his living as a married priest. On his release, he went to Strasbourg in 1554 and to Frankfurt in 1555. From 1556 to 1559, he appears to have taught at Marburg University. While abroad, he wrote *Displaying of the Popish Mass* (Basle, 1559). Meanwhile, his enemies at home issued in 1555 a proclamation denouncing as heretical the books of "Theodore Basil, otherwise called Thomas Becon." Soon after the accession of Elizabeth I, he returned to England and was reinstalled as a canon of Canterbury Cathedral in 1559; presented to the rectory of Buckland, in Hertfordshire, in 1560; to Christ Church, Newgate Street; and to the rectory of St. Dionis Backchurch in 1563. On his return, he initially expressed scruples with regard to certain "regulations" and "ritualisms," but acquiesced after a time; he was usually ready to compromise on what he regarded as "less important points." He died in 1567.

Becon's writings enjoyed wide popularity. At first they were moderate in tone, devotional in intent, and much under Lutheran influence. During and after his exile, however, they became more polemic in nature and their viewpoint closer to that of Zwingli.

BIBLIOGRAPHY

Bailey, D.S. *Thomas Becon and the Reformation of the Church in England.* 1952.

Becon, Thomas. *Works.* 3 vols. J. Ayre, ed. Parker Society. 1843–1844.

Lee W. Gibbs

SEE ALSO

Black Rubric, the; Calvinism; Cranmer, Thomas; *Homilies, Book of the*; Latimer, Hugh; Lutheranism

Bellenden Family

The Bellendens were crucial cultural and political intermediaries in early-modern Scotland. Emerging from obscurity in the sixteenth century, the family as a whole presents a model example of social and cultural mobility, representing a middling class rising in the world through legal training, loyal service to the crown, and pragmatic politics. Not of noble stock, they served the crown's interest rather than any aristocratic family in order to gain wealth and security.

Thomas Bellenden (c. 1490–1547) studied logic in Paris in 1510 under the legist and philosopher Robert Galbraith, and moved in a circle of scholars and jurists who were to occupy important posts in Reformation Scotland. He was appointed director of Chancery briefly in 1513, then again in 1539. A reform-minded royalist, he was one of the two men commissioned to discuss border affairs with the English in 1540, briefing them on James V's position in political and religious matters, including a valuable report of an early version of the one extant pre-Reformation Scots play, David Lindsay's *Ane Satyre of the Thrie Estaitis*. There were close links between the Bellendens and the kin of Gavin Douglas, the poet-clergyman, as evidenced through intermarriage, but also by Thomas Bellenden's copying a manuscript of Gavin Douglas's translation of Vergil's *Aeneid* in 1546.

Thomas's brother was John Bellenden (c. 1495–1547/8), archdeacon of Moray (1533–1538) and precentor of Glasgow (1537–1547), but best known for his translations of Hector Boece's *Scotorum Historia* (1531) and the first five books of Livy's *History of Rome*. Moreover, his vernacular poetry frames the Bannatyne Manuscript (1568), the most comprehensive Older Scots literary anthology. Judging from family documents of the Bannatynes, another family of culturally-minded legists, the Bellendens were their patron family.

Thomas Bellenden's son and heir was Sir John Bellenden of Auchnoull (d. 1577), appointed director of Chancery in 1543 and justice clerk in 1547. His subterranean political trafficking often kept precarious balances intact. He was succeeded as justice clerk by his son, Sir Lewis Bellenden (d. 1591), who in the 1580s became a close political ally of Chancellor William Maitland, and succeeded the latter's father as a lord of session (1584). As an ambassador, he negotiated James VI's marriage to Anne and sailed with the king to Denmark in 1589 to fetch her.

BIBLIOGRAPHY

van Heijnsbergen, Theo. "The Interaction between Literature and History in Queen Mary's Edinburgh: The Bannatyne Manuscript and Its Prosopographical Context."

In *The Renaissance in Scotland. Studies in Literature, Religion, History and Culture.* A.A. MacDonald, et al., pp. 183–225 [191–198]. 1994.

Sheppard, E.A. "Appendix." In *The Chronicles of Scotland Compiled by Hector Boece. Translated into Scots by John Bellenden 1531.* Vol II. Edith C. Batho and H. Winifred Husbands, eds. pp. 411–461. 1941.

Theo van Heijnsbergen

SEE ALSO

Boece, Hector; Douglas, Gavin; Hamilton Family

Bethune, David

See Beaton, David

Bible Commentary

The writing of commentaries on the Bible was an ancient practice, going back to the Jewish philosopher Philo of Alexandria (d. A.D. 50). It was introduced into the Christian Church by Origen (c. 185–c. 254) and produced a considerable body of literature during the Middle Ages. English scholars played a prominent part in this, and the commentaries of the Venerable Bede (673–735), in particular, were widely used until the Reformation. In the fourteenth century, John Wycliffe (d. 1384) developed a hermeneutic of biblical authority that was to have a great impact across Europe, influencing the early Reformers on the Continent. But it was the rise of Renaissance humanism and the outbreak of the Reformation that transformed the traditional commentary genre almost beyond recognition. Following the example of Erasmus, sixteenth-century scholars began to pay greater attention to the literal meaning of the biblical text, and limited allegorical interpretation to those parts of Scripture (e.g., the Song of Songs) where textual evidence would not support a literal reading.

Commentaries in the new style appeared in England during the 1520s, and spread rapidly. Lists of confiscated and banned books demonstrate that by 1530 commentaries by Martin Luther (1483–1546), Philipp Melanchthon (1497–1560), Martin Bucer, François Lambert (1486–1530), Andreas Althamer (c. 1500–c. 1539), Johannes Brenz (1499–1570), Wolfgang Capito (1478–1541), and Johannes Bugenhagen (1485–1558) were all circulating among intellectuals in London and Cambridge. The only contemporary Englishman whose work could be compared to these was William Tyndale, who prefaced his translations of the Bible with extensive introductions that gave the sense of the text. Tyndale could not publish his work in England, of course; most of it was printed in the Low Countries or in Germany and smuggled in from there.

In general, it can be said that the imperatives that determined the approach that these scholars took were the following. First, they had to find a principle of authority on which Christian faith and experience could be credibly grounded. Second, there was the need to expound the Bible in a way that would make its true meaning clear to nonspecialists, as well as to theologians. Finally, it was necessary to defend Protestant theological positions on the basis of Scriptural teaching. William Tyndale accepted these principles, and in general he followed Luther closely in his interpretation. However, he also had his own slant on biblical commentary, which gave a higher authority to the literal interpretation of the Old Testament. Tyndale believed that the Old Testament could be used as a guidebook for the Christian life, and that its principles might be applied to the social organization of the Christian state. This makes him an ancestor of what the seventeenth-century Puritans would call Federal, or Covenant, Theology, even though he did not live long enough to develop his ideas into a viable theological system.

After the Reformation, the main concern of the church authorities was to get English-language Bibles into the parishes, and the leading English Reformers were not engaged in commentary writing. The most we have from them are prefaces to the Bible and a number of sermons on different passages of Scripture. These are seldom original, and on the whole, they faithfully reflect their Lutheran, Zwinglian, and Calvinist models. For the edification of the clergy, the Reformers recommended Desiderius Erasmus's *Paraphrase of the Gospels*, a humanist but not a Protestant commentary. As late as the 1570s, every ordained clergyman in England was expected to own a copy of this, along with the Scriptures themselves (in both English and Latin).

The translators of the Geneva Bible (1560) offered readers a running commentary in note form, which appeared in the margins of the main text. The Calvinist and openly anti-Roman tenor of these notes caused considerable offense among the upper ranks of the court and church in England, and to some degree brought the whole idea of commentary writing into disrepute. When the Puritans proposed to King James I that a new translation

B

of the Bible be prepared (1604), James insisted that no marginal notes be included.

Bible commentaries became common in England during the 1580s, when a massive translation project made John Calvin's Commentaries and many of his sermons available in English. These were generally recognized as the best of their kind then available, and there was little incentive for English writers to produce their own work. The major exceptions to this were the Presbyterian leader Thomas Cartwright (1535–1603), who wrote commentaries on Ecclesiastes, Colossians, and Revelation, and the Separatist Henry Ainsworth (c. 1569–c. 1623), a leading rabbinical scholar who wrote on the Pentateuch, the Psalms, and the Song of Songs. Mention should also be made of Hugh Broughton, who pioneered the study of biblical chronology in his seminal work, *A Consent of Scripture* (1588). This was subsequently taken up by James Ussher (1581–1656), later (Anglican) archbishop of Armagh, who worked out that the world had been created at 9 A.M. on October 26, 4004 B.C. This date, along with many others determined by one or other of this pair, continued to appear in many English Bibles until the beginning of the twentieth century.

It is obvious from this that Bible commentary in the sixteenth century was mainly a Puritan phenomenon, and as such it had serious political implications. This was especially evident in the Old Testament, with its fierce criticisms of Israelite monarchy, which the Puritans did not hesitate to apply to the inadequacies (as they perceived them) of the English system of government.

For all these reasons, commentary writing as a distinct genre only established itself in England in the early seventeenth century, when it was often closely linked to parliamentary and Puritan opposition to the crown. It continued to be more prominent among nonconformists and dissenters than among those who conformed to the establishment, and it was not until the mid-eighteenth century that Anglicans began to write biblical commentaries that could stand comparison with the best that was being produced by others, both inside and outside the country.

BIBLIOGRAPHY

Bray, G.L. *Biblical Interpretation Past and Present.* 1996.
Gerald L. Bray

SEE ALSO

Anglicanism; Bible Translations; Broughton, Hugh; Bucer, Martin; Calvinism; Church of England; Desiderius, Erasmus; Lutheranism; Puritanism; Reformation, English; Tyndale, William

Bible Translations

Translation of the Bible into the vernacular languages of Western Europe goes back to the third century, when Latin versions were developed for use in the churches. Beginning about the year 375, Jerome produced the definitive Latin version, which ever since has been known as the *Biblia Vulgata* (Vulgate). Eventually, when the Latin of this text became a foreign language to everyone in Europe, the need for a series of new translations became acute. Moreover, the rediscovery of the Greek Bible in the fifteenth century, and the renewal of interest in Hebrew, gradually made scholars realize that the Vulgate was not an adequate translation of the original texts. Scholarship demanded a new version based on the original languages, but tradition weighed heavily in favor of the Vulgate text. The nettle was finally grasped by Desiderius Erasmus, who published his own Latin translation of the New Testament in 1516. This caused a sensation, and when the Reformation began a year later, Erasmus's principle *ad fontes* ("back to the sources") was adopted by Martin Luther and his followers.

By 1524, Luther had produced a translation of the Bible into German, and this was the model followed by other Protestant translators. In England, William Tyndale soon took up the challenge, and by 1525 he had produced his first version of the New Testament. He then went on to tackle the Old Testament as well, but apart from the Pentateuch (1530) and Jonah, he was unable to complete the task. In the meantime he revised his New Testament, and published it again in 1534. This is now regarded as the classical text, even though a further revision appeared in 1535.

Tyndale's activities were illegal; neither his name nor his translations could be mentioned openly in England. Curiously enough, this ban remained long after the Reformation, and it was not until the early seventeenth century that his work could be publicly acknowledged. However, this does not mean they were without influence. Miles Coverdale completed the task of Old Testament translation, and in 1535 published his work along with Tyndale's as the first complete modern English Bible. Although it was soon eclipsed by other translations, Coverdale's work survives in the psalms, which became (and still remain) the psalter found in the Book of Common Prayer.

Another version soon came out under the name of Tobias Matthew, the pseudonym of John Rogers (1537). By that time, Henry VIII had been persuaded that an

English-language Bible was needed, and he authorized a new translation. Coverdale played a major part in this, and in 1538 the Injunctions drawn up by Thomas Cromwell in Henry's name directed that copies of the forthcoming translation should be placed in all parish churches by Easter (April 9) 1539. The work was sent to Paris for printing, but it was seized by the Inquisition there, and publication had to be started all over again in

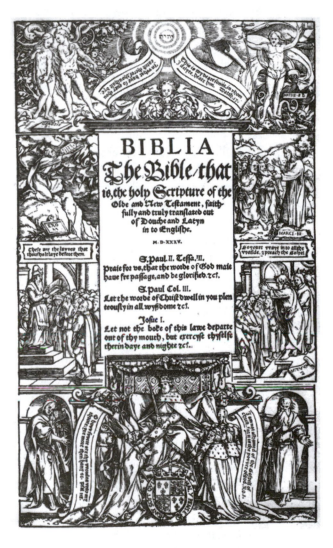

Frontispiece from *The Coverdale Bible,* 1535, probably by Holbein. On the left are scenes from the Old Testament, and on the right are those from the New Testament. At the bottom Henry VIII is depicted giving the Bible to bishops on the left, witnessed by temporal lords on the right. Ironically, Henry withheld permission for this translation to be printed in London until 1537, by which time a Protestant translation, the "Mathew" Bible of John Rogers, gained his approval. Reproduced from the original by permission of the Henry E. Huntington Library and Art Gallery.

England. The target date was extended to November 1, 1539, but demand was such that it could not be met.

A second edition was needed as early as April 1540. Archbishop Thomas Cranmer provided a preface, which became the hallmark of this translation and was included in all subsequent editions. The Great Bible, or "Cranmer's Bible," as it became known, went through a total of seven editions before publication was suspended at the end of 1541. An eighth edition appeared in 1549, and a ninth in 1553, although the accession of Mary I relegated most of it to the warehouse. Some copies of that were still available in 1558, when Elizabeth I ascended the throne, and there was a tenth (and last) edition in 1562.

By that time the situation had changed considerably, in that the English exiles at Geneva had produced their own version of the Scriptures, the New Testament in 1557 and the complete Bible in 1560. The Geneva Bible was based on the most modern critical methods, as these had been developed by John Calvin and Theodore Beza. Without a doubt, it was the most accurate version available in English, and in this respect it remained without a rival until the Authorized Version of 1611. However, the translators included substantial marginal notes that conveyed their own Calvinist and extremely anti-Roman views. The purpose was to inculcate not only the Scriptures but a particular interpretation of them, and this made the Geneva Bible unsatisfactory in the eyes of many in England.

However, the Geneva Bible was produced cheaply, and could be bought by a wide segment of the population. Within a few years it had become the popular Bible, and it did a great deal to help spread what would later be known as Puritan ideas. It also became the official Bible of the Church of Scotland in 1572. This was the Bible of William Shakespeare, and it was the version brought to America by the Pilgrims in 1620. The last edition of it appeared in 1644, by which time it was yielding its preeminence to the Authorized Version.

In response to the Geneva Bible, the bishops of the Church of England revised the Great Bible and published it in 1568. The Bishops' Bible, as this translation was known, was the one normally read in churches, but it never received official recognition and was generally unpopular. As a translation it was inferior to the Geneva Bible, so its imposition was never more than a political act. When James I ascended the throne, the Puritans proposed a new translation, to which the king readily agreed. However, he stipulated that the Bishops' Bible should be used as the primary text for the revision, and forbade the translators to add any marginal notes.

B

The work was apportioned to different committees, who in fact ranged much more widely and freely in their choice of readings than the king had envisaged. It was completed in 1611 and authorized for use in the Church of England, where it remains the official Bible even now. Within a generation, the Authorized or King James Version had ousted its rivals and become the classic English text. It is generally reckoned that about 90 percent of the New Testament comes from Tyndale, which demonstrates the essential continuity of the revision process. It is also interesting to note that it was accepted equally by all shades of theological opinion, something that had not been true of the earlier versions.

Roman Catholics had initially resisted the idea of Bible translation, but eventually they realized that it was necessary to produce their own version in order to counteract Protestantism. In 1582, they published the Rheims (Reims) New Testament, named after the place in France where it was translated. Work on the Old Testament was held up for many years because of internal dissensions among the exiles and lack of funds, but it was eventually published at Douai (Douay) in 1609. The translation was made from the Latin Vulgate, the official Catholic Bible, though it was revised in 1593. The use of the Vulgate was justified on the ground that it was a witness to an older Greek textual tradition than the one used by Desiderius Erasmus. As a result, it occasionally reflected a better Greek text, even though it was a translation. There were also a number of minor points, such as the use of the definite article in Hebrew, where the Catholic translators were more punctilious than their Protestant counterparts. The Douay Bible was consulted by King James's translators, and some of its readings found their way into the 1611 version. Nonetheless, the Douay Bible was condemned to an early demise because of its extravagant Latinity. The translators rejected terms like Passover and foreskin, which struck them as crude neologisms, preferring to say Pasch and prepuce instead. These terms meant nothing to most English people, and very soon Catholics were seeking to revise what even they realized was a poor translation.

English was not the only language spoken in the Tudor dominions, and as early as 1563 Parliament made statutory provision for a Welsh translation of the Bible. This appeared in 1588, and was periodically revised up to 1629, when it acquired its fixed form. An Irish New Testament was published in 1602, but the complete Bible was not made available until 1690, when it was too late to win the Irish people to the Protestant cause. However, this version was also used among Protestants in the Highlands of Scotland until a separate Scottish Gaelic translation finally appeared in 1807.

BIBLIOGRAPHY

Bray, G.L. *Documents of the English Reformation.* 1994.
Bruce, F.F. *The English Bible. A History of Translations.* 1961.
Tyndale, W. *New Testament.* D. Daniell, ed. 1989.
———. *Pentateuch.* D. Daniell, ed. 1992.

Gerald L. Bray

SEE ALSO

Bible Commentary; Calvinism; Coverdale, Miles; Cranmer, Thomas; Cromwell, Thomas; Erasmus, Desiderius; Injuctions, Royal; Lutheranism; Reformation, English; Rogers, John; Tyndale, William

Bilney, Thomas (c. 1495–1531)

Born in East Anglia, Thomas Bilney received his B.A. from Trinity Hall, Cambridge. After ordination as a priest, he fell under the influence of Desiderius Erasmus's Latin New Testament and subscribed to the doctrine of justification by faith based on Luther's interpretation of the Pauline epistles. He became a leader of the influential Cambridge conventicle that included such early English Protestants as Matthew Parker and Hugh Latimer. Converted by Bilney, Latimer became the spiritual leader of the first generation of English Protestants. Although Bilney received a license to preach in 1525, he ran afoul of Cardinal Thomas Wolsey for iconoclastic attacks against the use of relics and religious images, intercession of the saints, pilgrimages to shrines, and other elements of traditional religion. Bilney approved of translation of parts of the Bible into the vernacular. After a period of imprisonment in the Tower of London, he preached Lutheran doctrine in the open air because withdrawal of his preaching license denied him access to churches. For these violations he was burned to death at Norwich on August 19, 1531. Nonetheless, Bilney seems miscast as a Protestant martyr because he always maintained orthodox positions concerning the the pope, ecclesiastical hierarchy, the mass, transubstantiation, and clerical celibacy.

BIBLIOGRAPHY

Foxe, John. *Acts and Monuments* (1563). 8 vols. 1843–1849; repr. 1965.

John N. King

SEE ALSO

Erasmus, Desiderius; Latimer, Hugh; Lutheranism; Parker, Matthew; Wolsey, Thomas

Bilson, Thomas (1546/47–1616)

Bishop of Winchester and apologist for the Church of England as established under Elizabeth I, Thomas Bilson was born in Winchester and educated at Oxford, receiving his B.A. in 1566, his M.A. in 1570, his B.D. in 1579, and finally his D.D. in 1580. His ecclesiastical career began in 1576 with his installation as a prebend of Winchester, where he remained for twenty years until his consecration as bishop of Worcester in 1596. The following year, he was translated to the see at Winchester. Throughout his adult life, Bilson devoted his considerable literary energies to the defense of the Elizabethan Church. His *True Difference between Christian Subjection and Unchristian Rebellion* (1585), commissioned by the queen to justify her intention to aid Protestant Holland, is essentially an argument against Catholic recusancy; it is an argument, however, that, given the latitudes it allows for disobedience to authority, would haunt the monarchy during the reign of Charles I. Likewise, Bilson's *Perpetual Government of Christ his Church* (1593), *Effect of certain Sermons concerning the Full Redemption of Mankind by the Death and Blood of Christ Jesus* (1599), and *Survey of Christ's Sufferings and Descent into Hell* (1604) are adamant in their support of the Elizabethan Settlement but, in the final analysis, logically suspect. Long after Bilson's death, many passages in his writings were seized upon by opponents of the status quo to justify their own agendas. Dead in 1616, Bilson was interred in Westminster Abbey.

BIBLIOGRAPHY
Lake, Peter. *Anglicans and Puritans? Presbyterian and English Conformist Thought from Whitgift to Hooker*, pp. 93–99, 132–139. 1988.

Mark Goldblatt

SEE ALSO
Church of England; Recusancy

Bishops' Bible
See Bible Translations

Bishops' Book, The

The name popularly given to a work entitled *The Institution of a Christian Man*, *The Bishops' Book* was published in 1537 as a commentary on the Ten Articles of 1536. The Articles were mildly Protestant in tone, particularly on the question of justification by faith, but they said little or nothing that a loyal Catholic could not equally affirm. Archbishop Thomas Cranmer and other Protestant-leaning bishops felt that a Protestantizing commentary was needed, and extended it to cover the Ten Commandments, the Apostles' Creed, and the Lord's Prayer as well. The theology of the Bishops' Book reflects the Lutheranism then in vogue in Cranmer's circle, and at the time it was written an alliance between Luther and the Church of England still seemed to be a possibility. However, political events and Henry VIII's innate conservatism combined to thwart any moves in that direction, and after 1539 the Bishops' Book fell out of favor. It was finally replaced by the so-called King's Book in 1543.

BIBLIOGRAPHY
The Institution of a Christian Man. Facsimile of the 1537 edition. 1976.

Gerald L. Bray

SEE ALSO
Articles of Religion; Cranmer, Thomas; King's Book; Lutheranism

Black Death
See Plague

Black Rubric

A rubric originally appended to the 1552 Book of Common Prayer, the "Black Rubric" stated that the practice of kneeling at Holy Communion should not be taken to imply belief in the Real Presence of Christ in the sacrament. This was done to satisfy John Knox and others who felt that kneeling was a superstitious practice and ought to be discontinued. The rubric derives its name from the fact that it was a last-minute addition, printed in black instead of the usual red. Because it was not officially part of the Book of Common Prayer, it was omitted in 1559, and not restored until 1662, when it was included in the official text.

BIBLIOGRAPHY
Neil, C., and J.M. Willoughby. *The Tutorial Prayer Book.* 1963.

Gerald L. Bray

SEE ALSO
Book of Common Prayer; Eucharist; Knox, John

B

Blount, Charles, Lord Mountjoy (d. 1545)

The fifth baron Mountjoy, Charles Blount, was the eldest son of William Blount, the fourth baron, and his second wife, Alice Kebel. The elder Lord Mountjoy is known chiefly as a student and patron of Desiderius Erasmus, and his son, Charles, continued his work as one of the foremost sponsors of humanism in England.

The elder Mountjoy gathered an impressive assembly of scholars to instruct Charles, including John Crucius of Louvain, Peter Vulcanius of Bruges, Juan Luis Vives, and John Palsgrave. To Charles, Vives dedicated his influential *De Ratione Studii Puerilis*. A letter included in Palsgrave's 1530 grammar, *L'Eclaircissement de la Langue Francaise*, shows that Charles was taught with Lord Thomas Howard, probably the son of the second duke of Norfolk, as well as other sons of the nobility. Erasmus also took a lively interest in Charles's education, praising his developing skill in Latin. He dedicated his *Adagia* to the elder Mountjoy, and then to Charles once he succeeded his father in 1534. In 1531, Erasmus dedicated his *Livy* to Charles.

The elder Mountjoy served as chamberlain to Katherine of Aragon in 1512–1533, and Charles made his first appearance in public life as page to the queen. In 1544, he commanded part of the English force sent to France, and he was with Henry VIII at the siege of Boulogne.

Always conservative in matters of religion, Lord Mountjoy offered refuge to Richard Whitford, the humanist cleric and writer of popular devotional works, on the dissolution of the Bridgettine house at Syon. His final work, *Dyuers holy instrucyons and teachynges*, was written under his protection.

Following his marriage to Anne, the daughter of Robert, Lord Willoughby de Broke, and the births of three sons and a daughter, Lord Mountjoy turned his attention to educating the next generation. He attempted to secure Roger Ascham to instruct his son James in 1544. Ascham referred to his house as the "home of the Muses," but declined the invitation. In preparing a will before his departure for France, Mountjoy made provisions for catechism lectures in Scripture and obedience for the children of Westbury-under-the-Plain in Wiltshire. He died in 1545 and was buried at St. Mary Aldermary Church in London.

BIBLIOGRAPHY
Dowling, Maria. *Humanism in the Age of Henry VIII.* 1986.

McConica, James Kelsey. *English Humanists and Reformation Politics.* 1965.

Susan Wabuda

SEE ALSO

Erasmus, Desiderius; Humanism; Vives, Juan Luis

Bodley, Thomas (1544–1613)

The founding benefactor of the library at Oxford University that bears his name, Sir Thomas Bodley was born at Exeter on March 2, 1544, into a strongly Protestant family that, during the reign of Mary I, fled to Germany and then Geneva. There he studied under Calvin, Beza, Beroaldus, and Chevalier. Returning on the accession of Elizabeth I, Bodley studied and then taught at Oxford from 1560 to 1576. For some years thereafter he traveled in Europe and was elected to Parliament twice: for Portsmouth in 1584, and St. Germans in 1586. In the succeeding years he entered the diplomatic service, undertaking missions in Denmark, France, and the Netherlands, where in 1588 he was appointed the queen's permanent representative at The Hague. Years of increasing frustration led him to withdraw from the service of the state in 1597.

Armed with means brought to him through his marriage in 1586 to a wealthy widow, Ann Ball, Bodley returned to Oxford and, in February 1598, offered to refurnish and restock the university's library, which had been dispersed by the Protestant reformers half a century earlier. The new library, subsequently styled the Bodleian Library, opened in a single room over the vaulted divinity school in November 1602. Within three years it was equipped with one of the earliest published library catalogues, which spread the library's fame throughout the learned world. Before his death on January 29, 1613, Bodley (who was knighted in 1604), had financed two further extensions to the library, and had made an agreement with the Stationers' Company that in 1610 made his library the first library of legal deposit in Great Britain. During his life he and his librarian, Thomas James, had been very successful in "stirring up other men's benevolence" toward what was, in effect, the first national public library, and by his will he provided a handsome endowment for it.

BIBLIOGRAPHY
Catalogus Librorum Bibliothecae Quam Vir Ornatissimus Thomas Bodleius Eques Auratus in Academia Oxoniensis Nuper Instituit [The first printed catalog of the Bodleian Library]. 1605; repr. 1986.

Sturdy, David. "Bodley's Bookcases: 'This Goodly Magazine of Witte.'" *John Donne Journal,* vol. 5, pp. 267–289.

David Vaisey

SEE ALSO
Education; Literacy; Reading Practices

Boece, Hector (c. 1465–1536)

Hector Boethius (usually anglicized to Boece, probably originally Boys) was born around 1465 in Dundee, where his father may have been a burgess. He was educated at Montaigu College in Paris, gaining his M.A. in 1492. Among his contemporaries were John Mair, the great scholastic theologian, and Desiderius Erasmus, who dedicated his only volume of poems to Boece. In 1496, William Elphinstone, bishop of Aberdeen, appointed him as a teacher at his new university, King's College. Boece became principal in 1506, after taking the required degree in theology, and remained in office until his death in 1536.

His three works are *Explicatio quorundam vocabulorum ad cognitionem dialecticos opera* (1519), the *Vitae Episcoporum Aberdonesium et Murthlacensium* (1522), and the *Scotorum Historia a prima gentis origine* (1527). The first is a treatise on scholastic logic, while the second is largely a biography of Elphinstone, whose life occupies half the text, possibly modeled on Platina's *Lives of the Popes*. The *Scotorum Historia* traces the history of the Scots from their origin myth of Gathelos and Scota and their arrival in Scotland in 330 B.C. to the assassination of James I in 1437. Although Boece has been much criticized for his succession of early kings, his citation of sources no longer extant, and his rhetorical style, the *Scotorum Historia* is comparable in all three areas with contemporary humanist histories. Following Livy's example, humanist historiographers used descriptions of the past to strengthen the sense of national consciousness. For Boece, the need to present a legitimately independent Scottish nation was pressing, since, after the battle of Flodden Field (1513), Scotland was increasingly threatened by its nearest neighbors.

Despite such political pressure, however, it seems probable that the origins of the early narrative of the *Scotorum Historia* lie in earlier chronicle tradition, rather than in Boece's imagination, as is sometimes suggested. Although Veremund's account, Boece's main source for his record of the Scots between 330 B.C. and A.D. 424, may never be identified conclusively, Boece's association of it both with his patron Elphinstone and with important noblemen of the Campbell family suggests that it is unlikely to be a forgery. Moreover, the king-list that underpins Boece's narrative agrees substantially with earlier Irish and Scottish Gaelic lists and genealogies, again implying that while the rhetorical detail of Boece's account is his own addition, the underlying structure has a much earlier derivation.

The *Scotorum Historia* proved popular. Within fifteen years of its first publication, it had attracted three translators, and within fifty, a second edition had been printed (1574 and 1575). It is a source for George Buchanan's *Historia Rerum Scoticarum* and John Leslie's *De origine, moribus et rebus gestis Scotorum* (1578), and, mediated through John Bellenden's translation (1531), an important influence on Raphael Holinshed's *Chronicle,* despite its condemnation by such writers as John Leland and John Twyne. Boece's portrayal of the Scots has proven to be a central text of British humanist historiography, and as such, has an important place in the developing definitions of nationhood and history.

BIBLIOGRAPHY
Broun, Dauvit. "The Birth of Scottish History." *Scottish Historical Review,* vol. 76, pp. 4–22.
Burns, J.H. *The True Law of Kingship.* 1996.
Durkan, John. "Early Humanism and King's College." *Aberdeen University Review,* vol. 48, pp. 259–279.
MacQueen, John. "Humanism in sixteenth- and seventeenth-century literature." In *Humanism in Renaissance Scotland.* John MacQueen, ed. 1990.
Mason, Roger A. *Kingship and the Commonweal.* 1998.
Simpson, W. Douglas, ed. *University of Aberdeen Quatercentenary of the Death of Hector Boece.* 1937.

Nicola Royan

SEE ALSO
History, Writing of; Holinshed, Raphael; Humanism; Scotland, History of

Boleyn, Anne (c. 1507–1536)

Many facts about the career of Anne Boleyn, the second consort of Henry VIII, are disputed. Probably born in 1507, her life is significant because the king's determination to divorce Katherine of Aragon and marry Anne ushered in the English Reformation.

A descendant of Edward I, Anne was born to Thomas Boleyn (later earl of Wiltshire) and Elizabeth Howard, daughter of the second duke of Norfolk. Of medium height with dark hair and eyes, she lacked the sixth finger on her right hand; this and the wen on her throat and other disfigurements were attributed to her by later Catholic writers. Her siblings, George, Lord Rochford, and Mary, a mistress of Henry, were probably younger. In

B

about 1513, Anne joined the court of Margaret, regent of the Netherlands, and in 1514, attended Mary Tudor, the consort of King Louis XII of France. From his death in 1515 until about 1521, Anne resided in the households of Claude, consort of Francis I, and his sister Marguerite d'Alençon. Back at the English court, Anne won the attentions of Henry Percy, who wished to marry her.

By 1527, the king claimed that his marriage to Katherine—with whom he had only a daughter, Mary—was invalid. God had deprived him of sons, he argued, as a punishment for wedding his brother Arthur's widow. Although Pope Clement VII refused to dissolve his first marriage, Henry wed Anne on January 25, 1533. After a statute preventing the appeal of divorce cases to Rome was enacted, Thomas Cranmer, archbishop of Canterbury, declared the union with Katherine invalid. Anne was crowned queen on June 1 and gave birth to Elizabeth on September 7.

She apparently had miscarriages in 1534 and in January 1536. Some scholars have speculated that because Thomas Cromwell, the principal secretary, sought a Spanish alliance after Katherine's death in January 1536, he deserted Anne's allegedly Protestant court faction. Leading the Catholics, he manipulated the king, who was enamored with Jane Seymour, to effect Anne's downfall. The evidence that she was a Protestant is not persuasive, and it was probably her miscarriage, perhaps of a deformed fetus, that was deemed a sign of divine disfavor, which caused Henry to have her imprisoned in the Tower of London on May 2. She was accused of witchlike behavior, of incest with her brother, and of adultery with Sir Francis Weston, William Norris, William Brereton, and Mark Smeaton, who were executed. Thomas Wyatt, who may earlier have addressed sonnets to her, and Richard Page were arrested but released. As a prisoner, she recalled discouraging the flattering attentions of Norris and Weston. These admissions, which some scholars claim provide evidence of courtly love exchanges between her and the men, surely reveal a futile attempt to persuade her jailers of her innocence and her faithfulness to her husband, claims that she maintained both at her trial and in her execution speech. On May 19, after the Calais executioner beheaded her with a special sword, she was buried in St. Peter ad Vincula at the Tower. During her final days of freedom, her thoughts turned to her daughter, and she requested her chaplain, Matthew Parker, later archbishop of Canterbury, to have a special regard for her.

BIBLIOGRAPHY
Ives, Eric. *Anne Boleyn.* 1986.
Warnicke, Retha. *The Rise and Fall of Anne Boleyn: Politics at the Court of Henry VIII.* 1989.
———. "Family and Kinship Relations at the Henrician Court: The Boleyns and the Howards." In *Tudor Political Culture,* Dale Hoak, ed., pp. 31–53. 1995.

Retha Warnicke

SEE ALSO
Cranmer, Thomas; Henry VIII; Katherine of Aragon; Reformation, English

Bonner, Edmund (c. 1500–1569)

Of obscure, and possibly illegitimate birth, Edmund Bonner was at Broadgate Hall (now Pembroke College), Oxford, in 1512. He became chaplain to Cardinal Wolsey in 1529, but was not implicated in the latter's fall from grace soon afterward. In 1532, he went to Rome to protest the king's citation for the attempted annulment of his marriage. In 1535, he became archdeacon of Leicester, and in 1538, while ambassador to France, he was made Bishop of Hereford. Before he could occupy the see he was made Bishop of London (1539), where he remained for the next ten years. He was Ambassador to the Holy Roman Empire in 1542, but after the accession of Edward VI he was suspended for obstructing the royal visitation of his diocese. When he neglected to enforce the use of the Book of Common Prayer in 1549 and failed to comply with Archbishop Cranmer's instructions, he was deprived of his see on October 1, 1549. He regained it on August 5, 1553, shortly after Mary I's accession, but was again deprived on May 30, 1559, for failing to take the oath of allegiance to Elizabeth I. He was imprisoned almost immediately and remained in custody until his death on September 5, 1569. Bonner was closely associated with the repression of Protestants, both under Henry VIII and under Mary I, although it seems that he was more agent than author of persecution. In any case, he has always suffered from his association with Mary; his reputation as a persecutor has endured for more than four centuries.

BIBLIOGRAPHY
Duffy, Eamon. *The Stripping of the Altars.* 1992.
Loades, D.M. *The Reign of Mary Tudor.* 1991.

Gerald L. Bray

SEE ALSO
Book of Common Prayer; Marian Martyrs; Mary I; Wolsey, Thomas

John Foxe, *Edmund Bonner, scourging a Protestant Saint.* From *Actes and Monuments of these latter and perillous dayes,* 1563. During the reign of Mary I, Edmund Bonner gained a reputation for severity toward Protestants, although he acted under orders and was even reprimanded for leniency. Foxe depicts Bonner as almost gleefully cruel. Reproduced from the original by permission of the Henry E. Huntington Library and Art Gallery.

Book of Common Prayer

The name "Book of Common Prayer" is given to a series of prayer books used by the Church of England, and related churches of the Anglican communion, for most purposes of public worship. Prayer books are very ancient, and there was a great proliferation of them in medieval England. Different parts of the country had grown accustomed to using particular forms of worship, which are traditionally referred to as "rites." The Sarum (Salisbury) Rite was especially popular, and traces of it can be found in post-Reformation worship services.

When Henry VIII broke with the papacy in 1534, there was no immediate change in the pattern of worship. Only after the king's death (January 28, 1547) was it possible to introduce major reforms in this sphere, and

Thomas Cranmer, archbishop of Canterbury, set about composing a book of worship that could be used by everyone in England.

The first and most obvious change from the medieval service books was that the new Book of Common Prayer was in English, following the Reformation principle that worship should be conducted in a language people could understand. Versions in Latin, and later Welsh, were also produced, but the English text predominated in Tudor England.

The first Book of Common Prayer came into use on June 9, 1549, enjoined by an Act of Uniformity passed by Parliament. It was intended that every parish church in the country should conform to one pattern of worship, thereby emphasizing the unity of the church and controlling the public expression of its doctrine.

Cranmer's intention was that the Book should convey a Reformed theological position, particularly on the sensitive doctrine of the Holy Communion, but at the same time he did not want change for its own sake, and retained as much of the traditional pattern as was compatible with his theology. Soon, some Catholics in the Church of England were saying that they could use the new Book without compromising their principles, while a number of leading Protestants felt that the Book did not go far enough in stating a clearly Protestant position.

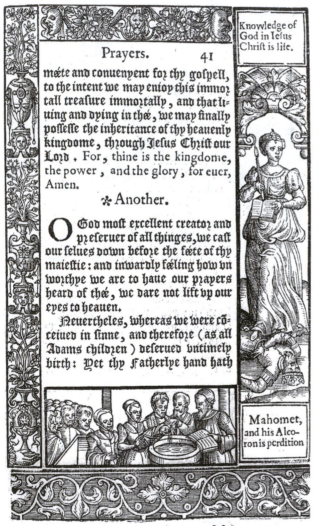

Richard Day, *A book of christian prayers*, 1578. This page contains text from a richly illustrated Elizabethan prayerbook: the lower image is of an Anglican baptism with the priest holding a Prayer Book. Reproduced from the original by permission of the Henry E. Huntington Library and Art Gallery.

Cranmer was affected by these criticisms, and soon began to prepare a second Book, which came into use, accompanied by another Act of Uniformity, on November 1, 1552. The second Book was much more clearly Protestant in tone, and Catholics could not adjust to it as they could to the first Book. The new services did not last long, however, because after the accession of Mary I, both the 1549 and the 1552 books were abolished (December 20, 1553).

The 1552 Book continued in use among the Protestant exiles on the Continent, in spite of the fact that some of the more radical reformers wanted even more changes to it. Controversy over this erupted in the English church at Frankfurt in 1555, and it is from this that the emergence of a Puritan movement is generally dated. Cranmer's execution in 1556 made the Book a monument to his memory, and when Elizabeth I ascended the throne, it was reintroduced, with a few slight changes (June 24, 1559). The most famous of these occurred in the communion service, where the words of administration used in 1549 were combined with those found in the 1552 Book. The former had stressed the objective nature of the sacrament: "The Body of our Lord Jesus Christ, which was given for thee, preserve thy body and soul unto everlasting life." The second Book had focused instead on the subjective act of reception: "Take and eat this, in remembrance that Christ died for thee, and feed on Him in thy heart by faith, with thanksgiving." By putting the two together, the 1559 Book sought a balance between these two emphases, which has been held ever since to mark the essence of the Anglican *via media*. There were subsequent, very minor, alterations in 1604, to accommodate certain Puritan objections, and in that form the Book lasted until it was outlawed by the Long Parliament (January 4, 1645).

The Book of Common Prayer contains set forms of worship for morning and evening, for Holy Communion, and for the so-called "occasional offices"—baptism, holy matrimony, and the burial of the dead. In addition, there is a service of confirmation, and a number of less-used services, such as the thanksgiving of women after childbirth, traditionally known as the churching of women. The Book also contains a short prayer (known as a "collect") for every sunday and major feast day in the year, together with Scripture readings (normally one from an epistle and one from a Gospel) appropriate for that day. The complete Psalter is also included, in the translation by Miles Coverdale (1535).

Annexed to the Book of Common Prayer, although not strictly part of it, is the "Form and Manner of Making, Ordaining and Consecrating of Bishops, Priests, and Deacons," commonly known as the "Ordinal." Also printed with the Book are the Thirty-nine Articles of 1571, a statement of doctrine that has been officially recognized as an Anglican standard since 1628. The Book of Common Prayer, the Ordinal, and the Thirty-nine Articles, together with the Homilies, are regarded as the basic confessional documents, or "formularies," of the Church of England, which may be used to decide questions of Church doctrine.

The Book of Common Prayer cannot be altered or superseded except by an act of Parliament, although its use has declined in recent years as new services in twentieth-century language have been introduced. Even so, it can still claim to be the only liturgy of the Reformation era in regular use today.

BIBLIOGRAPHY

The First and Second Prayer Books of King Edward VI. 1910 (frequently reprinted).

Booty, J., ed. *The Book of Common Prayer. 1559. The Elizabethan Prayer Book.* 1976.

Neil, C., and J.M. Willoughby. *The Tutorial Prayer Book.* 1963.

Gerald L. Bray

SEE ALSO

Anglicanism; Articles of Religion; Church of England; Coverdale, Miles; Cranmer, Thomas; Eucharist; *Homilies,* Books of; Reformation, English; Sarum, Use of; Uniformity, Acts of

Book Ownership

The main sources for book ownership in the Tudor period are library catalogues, wills, inventories, a few surviving records of purchases and sales, and the books themselves. Although the contents of some collections have been reconstructed and examined in detail, there is as yet no overall study of the subject as a whole, and any account of it is bound to be only partial.

Two forces played a leading part in shaping the ownership of books in the earlier part of the period. Printing, which preceded the Tudors in England by a decade or so, made books widely available, stimulating growth in education and in literacy. The destruction of books during the Reformation, especially manuscripts owned by religious and academic institutions, was evidently widespread and pursued with great enthusiasm. However, manuscripts went on being produced and collected throughout the period: from extant catalogues and lists, they appear generally to have been shelved or stored with printed books rather than kept separately. After the Reformation the most important institutional libraries were to be found among the colleges at Oxford and Cambridge Universities: the foundation of the Bodleian Library in Oxford in 1598 by Sir Thomas Bodley was to make it the most important public library in the country. Private collectors, like Matthew Parker, archbishop of Canterbury, or the secretary of state, Sir Thomas Smith, played an important part in preserving pre-Reformation and contemporary books and manuscripts and, by leaving their collections to Corpus Christi College and Queens' College, Cambridge, in increasing the riches of college libraries. Other public and religious institutions also benefited from the gifts of private individuals: many of the printed books of the antiquary William Camden, for example, survive in the library of Westminster Abbey, probably presented by Robert Cotton, who kept his friend's manuscripts for his own extensive collection.

The great book collectors of the period tended to be scholars, ecclesiastics, and those involved in the running of the state: courtiers, politicians, and lawyers. In the first group, figures like the Cambridge academic Gabriel Harvey, the Kentish historian and antiquary William Lambarde, the scientists John Dee and Henry Percy (1564–1632), ninth earl of Northumberland, stand out. Among ecclesiastics, the libraries of Matthew Parker, Thomas Cranmer, archbishop of Canterbury, and Lancelot Andrewes, bishop of Winchester, were notable. The Tudor monarchs, especially Henry VIII and Edward VI, laid the foundations for the Royal Library, but this was largely the creation of the Stuarts: James I bought the huge Lumley library of around 2,800 titles, the joint collection of John Lumley (1534–1609), Lord Lumley, and his father-in-law, Henry Fitzalan, twelfth earl of Arundel, which contained many of Cranmer's books, for his son, Prince Henry. The Old Royal Library eventually became part of the British Library. Among other Tudor courtiers and statesmen, the manuscripts and papers of William Cecil, Lord Burghley, are still at Hatfield House, but his printed books were sold at auction in 1687; the finely bound books owned by Robert Dudley, earl of Leicester, are widely dispersed, but the books and manuscripts of Henry Wriothesley, third earl of Southampton, are still at St. John's College, Cambridge, to which he bequeathed them. These several categories are, however, by no means watertight, and one feature of book ownership during this period is the growing use of scholarly libraries for political and religious ends. This culminated during the reign of Charles I in the closing of the library of Sir Robert Cotton (1571–1631), which had become, in effect, a public institution for those interested in the historic

B

relations between the monarch and the state. In a similar way, John Dee's library became an important resource for many of those interested in the new sciences.

At a less exalted level, the smaller libraries of Oxford and Cambridge dons can be studied through inventories of their possessions taken after their deaths: their books can reveal a certain amount about their intellectual interests. References to books in wills of ordinary citizens need to be treated with some caution as evidence of literacy, since books then (as now) evidently had a totemic as well as a practical function. In the absence of surviving documentary evidence, ownership can be reconstructed through the study of the books themselves. The most common marks of ownership were signatures; these might be accompanied by presentation inscriptions, a personal motto in English or a foreign language, or notes of prices. Printed book labels or bookplates were sometimes used, especially to mark benefactions, but were not common: personalized bindings, stamped in gilt or blind with the owner's coat of arms or badge were much more frequently used by wealthier owners. Where a book has no marks of ownership, distinctive bindings, especially those produced at Oxford and Cambridge, can reveal a certain amount about their history. In smaller private collections, books were often kept in chests; when they were shelved, especially in institutional libraries, they were usually arranged with their spines inward and might have their contents written by hand on their fore edges.

Although there was some provincial activity, especially in the university towns, the book trade was heavily concentrated in London, in particular in the area around St. Paul's Cathedral. Itinerant hawkers sold books and more ephemeral publications at local fairs, and provincial stationers might order titles from London booksellers. Some of these specialized in the import of continental books that were made widely available through the Frankfurt book fair and its catalogues. By at least the end of the sixteenth century, there was a well-established second-hand book trade. Books were sold and imported unbound, their cost determined by their format and the number of sheets of paper used in their production. The surviving evidence for book ownership in the Tudor period is substantial, but it still awaits systematic investigation.

BIBLIOGRAPHY

De Ricci, Seymour. *English Collectors of Books and Manuscripts (1530–1930) and their Marks of Ownership.* 1930.
Fehrenbach, R.J., and E.S. Leedham-Green. *Private Libraries in Renaissance England: A Collection and Catalogue of Tudor and Early Stuart Book-Lists.* Vols. 1–3. *Medieval & Renaissance Texts & Studies,* vols. 87, 105, 117. 1992–1994.
Jayne, Sears. *Library Catalogues of the English Renaissance.* 2nd edition. 1983.
Pearson, David. *Provenance Research in Book History: A Handbook.* 1994.
Wormald, Francis, and C.E. Wright, eds. *The English Library before 1700.* 1958.

H.R. Woudhuysen

SEE ALSO
Bodley, Thomas; Dee, John; Literacy; Manuscripts; Printing, Publishing, and Bookselling; Reading Practices

Books, Household
See Household Books

Boorde, Andrew (c. 1490–1549)
Born near Cuckfield, Sussex, Andrew Boorde was known to his contemporaries as a physician and an indefatigable traveler. After several years as a Carthusian monk, in 1529 Boorde received dispensation and went abroad to study medicine. During the 1530s, he traveled through France, Italy, Spain, Scotland, Germany, and the Low Countries; he also went on pilgrimage to Jerusalem. While he improved his medical knowledge at some of the best universities in Europe, Boorde also used these travels to carry out a confidential mission: he reported back to Thomas Cromwell on the state of feeling about Henry VIII abroad. Around 1542, he published his *Dietary,* which he dedicated to one of his patients, the earl of Norfolk. Two of his most important works, the *Fyrst Boke of the Introduction of Knowledge,* the first printed "handbook" of Europe, and the *Brevyary of Health,* a medical treatise, were completed around 1547. Two other books may also be attributed to him: the *Boke of Berdes* (never found but referred to by one Barnes who opposed Boorde's opinions about beards), and the *Itinerary of England or Peregrination of Doctor Boorde* (not printed until 1735). In the description of Egypt he offers in his introduction, Boorde provides the first printed specimen of the Gypsy language; he is also credited with having anticipated some of Shakespeare's later assumptions about the character of Englishmen (for instance, their fantastic dress and tendency toward treachery and deceit). In 1547–1548, Boorde was committed to the Fleet prison in London, accused of having kept three prostitutes in his chamber at Winchester. He died in prison in April 1549.

BIBLIOGRAPHY

Boorde, Andrew. *Itinerary of England or Peregrination of Doctor Boorde.* 1735.

Furnivall, F.J., ed. *The Fyrst Boke of the Introduction of Knowledge made by Andrew Borde of Physycke Doctor. A Compendyous Regyment or A Dyetary of Helth made in Mountpyllier, compiled by Andrewe Boorde of Physycke Doctour. Barnes in the Defence of the Berde: a Treatyse made, answerynge the Treatyse of Doctor Borde upon Berdes.* 1870.

Francisco J. Borge

SEE ALSO
Travel Literature

Bosworth, Battle of

The battle of Bosworth (August 22, 1485) was the decisive engagement in the second phase of the Wars of the Roses, ending with the death of England's last Plantagenet king, Richard III, and with the establishment of the Tudor dynasty by the victor, Henry Tudor, earl of Richmond, who became King Henry VII.

Provided by the French with a small flotilla of seven ships and between 500 and 1,000 men, Henry Tudor landed near Milford Haven in southwestern Wales on August 7, 1485. During the next two weeks, he marched slowly northward toward England, passing through Shrewsbury, Stafford, Litchfield, and Tamworth, reaching Atherstone on August 21. King Richard, situated at Nottingham awaiting his rival's invasion, learned of Henry's landing on August 11. Quickly assembling his forces, Richard marched to Leicester on August 19. By nightfall of Sunday, August 21, the opposing armies were encamped on Redmore Plain, between the villages of Shenton and Sutton Cheney, two miles south of the town of Market Bosworth.

Henry Tudor benefited from the unpopularity of Richard III. Gradually, a few prominent men of Wales and England, especially Sir Gilbert Talbot and Rhys ap Thomas, added their retinues to the Tudor army, bringing its size to about 5,000 men. But Henry failed to secure openly the allegiance of his stepfather, Thomas, Lord Stanley, and Lord's Stanley's brother, Sir William Stanley, who had an armed force of 3,000 men. Richard III's army was made up mostly of northerners drawn from his own affinity. It was a sizable force still, of between 8,000 and 10,000 men, well armed and mostly horsed. Although expecting Lord Stanley to support him, Richard suspected treachery, and held Stanley's son and heir, George, Lord Strange,

hostage; yet, Stanley refused the summons from the king, claiming illness. Richard's keeping Rhys ap Thomas's son hostage did not prevent Thomas from joining Henry.

Early on the morning of battle, King Richard arranged his army and artillery on a narrow plateau called Ambien Hill, which rose 400 feet in elevation from the plain. A marsh to the south and west of the hill protected Richard's flank. From this hill the king had a commanding view of the battlefield. He could see the deployment of the Tudor army, and would notice any movement by the Stanleys. But the narrowness of Ambien Hill prevented Richard from deploying his army abreast, and so it was drawn up in columns. The king's vanguard of 1,200 men, commanded by John, duke of Norfolk, was comprised mostly of archers, but with spearmen protecting the flanks. Behind Norfolk was the main "battle" of 2,000 to 3,000 men, mostly mounted, commanded by the king himself. The rear guard behind the king, of about 2,000 to 3,000 men, was commanded by Henry Percy, earl of Northumberland. Because of poor communication, topography, and the column formation of the army, Northumberland was unable, or unwilling, during the battle to engage the enemy with his rear guard. Richard's sympathizers regard this failure as an act of treason. The Tudor vanguard, commanded by John de Vere, Earl of Oxford, also consisting mostly of archers, was deployed abreast, with the right wing under Sir Gilbert Talbot, and the left wing under Sir John Savage. Through the battle, Henry Tudor remained with his bodyguard behind Oxford's vanguard. Sir William Stanley, commanding the Stanley retainers, positioned himself along "Hanging Hill," near the village of Nether Coton and about a mile from the field of battle. Lord Stanley stationed himself somewhere south of Ambien Hill and southeast of the marsh.

The engagement lasted about two hours. It began early in the morning with an ineffective exchange of artillery fire and volley of arrows. The Tudor vanguard worked its way around the marsh before advancing up Ambien Hill to engage Norfolk's troops. Along the forward slope of the hill, under the hail of arrows and of cannon fire and the onslaught of Norfolk's men, Oxford managed to deploy more fully his left and right wings, partially enveloping Norfolk's force, and putting pressure on his line. Bitter hand-to-hand combat ensued, and sometime during the fighting Norfolk was killed. Richard, seeing Norfolk's line buckling, and perhaps perceiving that William Stanley was about to join Henry, decided on an impetuously bold move. With his household retainers and personal attendants at his side, the king, battle axe in hand, galloped

B

down Ambien Hill, around Oxford's force, and charged directly toward Henry's position, which was marked by his unfurled standard. Richard struck down Sir William Brandon, the standard-bearer who was at Henry's side, and unhorsed the burly Sir John Cheney. Even after his horse had been killed under him, Richard continued fighting. Henry Tudor was in peril. At this crucial juncture, William Stanley joined the fray with his men, and King Richard perished amid the press of enemies.

The crown that Richard wore into battle was found, according to Tudor legend, resting atop a thornbush, but most likely among the spoils. Lord Stanley, who arrived at the scene when the Tudor victory was assured, placed it on Henry's head. Richard's bloody and battered body was stripped naked and flung across a horse. With a halter hung around the neck, it was brought to Leicester and put on public display for two days. The corpse was buried in Grey Friars' Church, and later given a modest tombstone by the victor. It was dug up during the dissolution of the monasteries, and the bones tossed into the river Soar.

BIBLIOGRAPHY

Bennett, Michael. *Battle of Bosworth.* 1985.

Hammond, P.W., and Anne F. Sutton. *Richard III: The Road to Bosworth Field.* 1985.

Williams, Daniel Thomas. *The Battle of Bosworth, 22 August 1485.* 1973.

John M. Currin

SEE ALSO

Henry VII; Wars of the Roses

Bourchier, John, Lord Berners (1467–1533)

Active in politics, the second Baron Berners took part in a premature attempt to enthrone Richmond, and after Henry VII's accession, Berners joined the court. He was sent on diplomatic missions to Spain and France, made chancellor of the Exchequer (1516) and deputy of Calais (1520), a post he retained until his death. At Calais, apparently, Berners began translating, "at the highe commaundement of . . . Henry the viii," Froissart's *Chronicles*. The work, published separately in two volumes by Richard Pynson (1523, 1525), is widely considered to be the first English historical writing of sustained literary excellence and, due to Berners's adherence to the English idiom, reads as if it were an original English work; it influenced the historical works of Edward Hall, Robert

Fabyan, and Raphael Holinshed, and may have been a source for William Shakespeare's *Richard II*.

Berners's *Huon of Burdeux* (published 1534) continued William Caxton's tradition of translating romances of Charlemagne. *Huon* was used by a number of Elizabethan writers: Spenser's *Faerie Queene* notes that Guyon "knighthood tooke of good Sir Huon's hand, / When with King Oberon he came to Faery land"; Robert Devereux, earl of Essex's players performed a play (now lost) based on the work in 1593–1594; Shakespeare's Oberon (*A Midsummer Night's Dream*) owes much to Berners's fairy king. Another French romance, *Arthur of Lytell Brytayne* (1555?), which Berners found to be "a fayned mat[t]er" but written with a "vertuous entent," may have influenced Spenser's "false Florimell."

Berners also translated two Spanish works (via French versions): the *Castell of Love* (published 1549), an allegorical novel by Diego de San Pedro, and Guevara's *The Golden Boke of Marcus Aurelius* (published 1534 with thirteen more editions before 1588), a collection of ornamental sentences that may have inspired the Euphuistic style in England. To Berners has also been attributed a Latin comedy, "Ite ad Vineam," which was acted at Calais, and a tract on "The Duties of the Inhabitants of Calais."

BIBLIOGRAPHY

Blake, N.F. "Lord Berners: A Survey." *Medievalia et Humanistica*, n.s., vol. 2, pp. 119–132.

Bourchier, John. *The History of the Valiant Knight Arthur of Little Britain*, E.V.U., ed. 1814.

Bulough, Geoffrey, ed. *Narrative and Dramatic Sources of Shakespeare*, vol. III. 1960.

Kane, George. "An Accident of History: Lord Berners's Translation of Froissart's *Chronicles*." *The Chaucer Review*, vol. 21, pp. 217–225.

Ker, William Paton, intro. *The Chronicle of Froissart Translated out of French by Sir John Bourchier Lord Berners*, vol. I. 1901.

Lee, S.L., intro. *The Boke of Duke Huon of Burdeux done into English by Sir John Bourchier, Lord Berners.* Early English Text Society, extra series, vols. 40, 41, 43, and 50. 1882–1887.

Kerri Lynn Thomsen

SEE ALSO

Caxton, William; Euphuism; Fabyan, Robert; Hall, Edward; History, Writing of; Holinshed, Raphael; Spanish Literature, Influence of

Bradford, John (c. 1510–1555)

Born in Manchester, John Bradford spent his early adulthood in military service and as a law student at the Inner Temple. Under the influence of Thomas Sampson, he shifted to theological study and began to distribute his wealth to the poor. Enrolling at St. Catherine's Hall, Cambridge, in 1548, he received the M.A. degree a year later by special dispensation. As a fellow of Pembroke Hall, Bradford became a friend of Martin Bucer, the eminent German theologian whom Edward VI appointed Regius Professor of Divinity at Cambridge. Ordained a deacon by Nicholas Ridley, bishop of London, Bradford served as chaplain to Ridley and King Edward. In the latter capacity, he preached at the royal court and throughout England. After the accession of Mary I, Bradford's Protestant sermons led to his imprisonment in the Tower of London, where he shared lodging with the reformist luminaries, Thomas Cranmer, Hugh Latimer, and Nicholas Ridley. His condemnation followed repeated examination by groups of bishops including Stephen Gardiner and Edmund Bonner. On June 30, 1555, he was burned to death at Smithfield. With the exception of some translations, a letter concerning parental authority, and *A Sermon of Repentance,* virtually all of his numerous publications were posthumous.

BIBLIOGRAPHY

Foxe, John. *Acts and Monuments* (1563). 8 vols. 1843–189; repr. 1965.

Townsend, Aubrey, ed. *The Writings of John Bradford.* 2 vols. 1848–1853; repr. 1979.

John N. King

SEE ALSO

Bonner, Edmund; Bucer, Martin; Gardiner, Stephen; Ridley, Nicholas

Brandon, Charles (c. 1484–1545)

Created duke of Suffolk in 1514, Charles Brandon was one of Henry VIII's leading courtiers, councilors, and military commanders. Brandon built on the achievements of his courtier family to joust and revel his way to a unique and rewarding position in the friendship of the young Henry VIII, but early in 1515 he incurred Henry's anger by marrying the king's sister, Mary Tudor (1496–1533), without royal permission. Henry forgave the couple at a price, but Cardinal Thomas Wolsey's concurrent rise to clear supremacy in the government lessened Brandon's political role, although Brandon was among those who accompanied the king at The Field of the Cloth of Gold in 1520. In the following years he faced the difficult challenge of establishing himself as a local magnate in East Anglia on the basis of the forfeited estates of Edmund de la Pole, earl of Suffolk.

In 1523, he led an Anglo-Dutch army across the Somme to threaten Paris, but was forced to withdraw by adverse conditions. During the public restlessness in 1525 and 1527–1528, he worked with Thomas Howard, duke of Norfolk, to keep Suffolk and Norfolk under control. Following Wolsey's decline and fall in 1529, renewing his political importance, Brandon became lord president of the council. But uneasy relations with Anne Boleyn and Thomas Cromwell and trouble in East Anglia between the Brandon and Howard factions made his life uncomfortable until his suppression of the Lincolnshire rising of October 1536, known as the Pilgrimage of Grace, regained him the king's favor. In the wake of the rebellion Henry ordered Brandon to reside in Lincolnshire on the estates of his ward, Catherine, Lady Willoughby (1519–1580), whom he had married after Mary's death. Land exchanges soon made him the county's greatest landowner. During his last years he led armies on the northern borders (1542–1544), in France (1544), and on the south coast (1545).

Brandon patronized some reformist clergy, but was generally conservative in religion. He was an enthusiastic builder and a patron of Holbein and of drama, perhaps including the interlude *Hick Scorner.* Although his two sons by Mary Tudor predeceased him, two daughters by a somewhat scandalous earlier marriage wed Edward, Lord Grey of Powis (1503–1551) and Thomas Stanley, Lord Monteagle (1507–1570); two of his daughters by Mary Tudor married Henry Grey, marquis of Dorset (1517–1554) and Henry Clifford, earl of Cumberland (1517–1570); and two sons by Catherine Willoughby survived him to become the second and third dukes of Suffolk, both dying in 1551.

BIBLIOGRAPHY

Gunn, S.J. *Charles Brandon, Duke of Suffolk, c. 1484–1545.* 1988.

Steven Gunn

SEE ALSO

Field of the Cloth of Gold; Mary Tudor; Pilgrimage of Grace; Pole, Edmund de la

B

Brant, Sebastian (c. 1457–1521)

A renowned humanist, writer, editor, and legal scholar in Germany, Sebastian Brant became an important influence throughout Europe due mainly to his book *Narrenschiff*, or *Ship of Fools* (1494). After he was awarded his baccalaureate degree from the University of Basel (1477), Brant began to teach and practice law in Basel in 1484, mainly conducting courses in Latin. He later earned his *Doctor Utriusque Juris* (1489) and wrote a law text, *Expositiones sive declarationes* (1490), which became a popular casebook for students. In 1501, Brant returned to his native Strasbourg as legal advisor to the city council and in 1504 was promoted to municipal secretary. Several times, Emperor Maximilian summoned Brant to Innsbruck: for legal consulting (1502), for expert advice in a matter concerning Venice (1508), and for confidential advice (1513). He was sent on a mission as mediator in the controversy on the immaculate conception in the case of Wigand Wirt (1513) and headed a delegation to Ghent to pay homage to Emperor Charles V (1520). Brant strongly advocated cultural nationalism, and as a devout Christian, he argued for action against the Turks and in the Holy Land. Until his death, Brant was active in humanist and religious circles that included, among others, Desiderius Erasmus and Martin Luther.

Brant played a significant role as an editor and translator. He edited St. Augustine's *De civitate Dei* (1489), and in 1490 is credited with the German translations of *Cato, Facetus, Moretus,* and *Thesmophagia*. He also edited *Decretum Gratiani* (1493), dealing with canon law; *Bethicae et regnie Granatae* (1494), honoring King Ferdinand of Spain; and *Librorum Francisci Petrarche* (1496), containing ten distichs by Petrarch. In 1497, Brant edited the works of Bebenburg, Hemmerlin, Methodius, and the complete Vulgate Bible. He continued, editing a legal text by Gazalupis (1500), the Fables of Aesop (1501), two illustrated devotionals (1502), a collection of Vergil (1502), and of Terence (1503), and a collection of epigrams by the poet Freidank (1508), as well as a pair of legal texts, *Layen Speigel* (1509) and *Der richterlick Clagspeigel* (1516).

Brant also wrote three important works of his own: *De Origin et converstione bonorum Regum* (1495), a recounting of Jerusalem's history, through which Brant argued the threat of the Moors and pleaded for Maximilian to make war against them; *Freiheitstafel* (1502), a collection of fifty-three short strophes describing the rooms of Strasbourg's city hall as reflections of the city's

freedom; and *Narrenschiff,* his most significant work. Intended as a type of moral handbook, each chapter of *Narrenschiff* describes a particular type of fool and is accompanied by a corresponding woodcut. Full of references to the Bible, canon law, the church fathers, and ancient history and literature, the work satirically discloses man as the central figure on earth, faced with the necessity of deciding whether he will take the path of wisdom or of folly. Few secular books can boast of so widespread an influence, not only in their own country, but throughout Europe. During Brant's lifetime, six authorized and seven unauthorized editions of *Narrenschiff* were published in a variety of languages. First appearing in England in 1509, and in later editions in 1570 and 1590, it constitutes a striking example of the infiltration of a continental literary work into English literature. *Ship of Fools* is mentioned in works by Sir Thomas More, Thomas Nashe, Robert Greene, and Robert Burton, and influenced others, including John Skelton, Robert Copland, and Samuel Rowlands.

BIBLIOGRAPHY

Van Cleve, John. *Sebastian Brant's* The Ship of Fools *in Critical Perspective, 1800–1991.* 1993.
Wilhelmi, Thomas. *Sebastian Brant: Bibliographie.* 1990.
Zeydel, Edwin H. *Sebastian Brant.* 1967.

Melinda Emmons

SEE ALSO
Canon Law; Humanism; Satire

Breton, Nicholas (c. 1545–c. 1626)

Poet, essayist, fiction writer, pamphleteer, satirist, and miscellanist, Nicholas Breton practiced every sixteenth- and seventeenth-century literary genre except drama. He is remembered, alongside his stepfather, George Gascoigne, as one of the first English authors to make his living almost entirely by writing. His father, William Breton, hailed from a noble Essex family that traced its lineage back to William the Conqueror's victorious army. Embarking on speculation of church properties confiscated during the Reformation, Breton moved his family to London before Nicholas was born. After his father's death in 1559, Breton inherited a modest fortune; however, his mother's marriage to the poet Gascoigne in 1569 diminished substantially young Nicholas's estate. Although enjoying a certain degree of privilege throughout his life, which may have included a short time in study at Oriel College, Oxford, the young Breton now required literary patrons for financial security.

His literary career commenced publicly some time around 1575, and drew attention not only to his associations with the Sidney circle but also to his employment of Petrarchan and pastoral motifs as metaphors for his newly tenuous social position. In his lyric and even some of his divine poems, the countess of Pembroke, Mary Sidney, stands as Breton's courtly lady, an ideally intellectual female whose favors remain always just beyond reach of the youthful poet. Although her distant position is a commonplace in courtly love poetry, Breton allegorically associates it with his own struggle for social reinstatement after his father's death. By the 1590s, Breton was publishing his mature works, many of which still emphasize, in the Arcadian manner that Sir Philip Sidney and Edmund Spenser recently had made fashionable, his uncertain place. *Brittons Bowre of Delights* (1591) also includes an elegy to the recently deceased Sidney, heightening his connections to the family. Probably his best poetic work can be found in *England's Helicon* (1600, 1614), and *The Passionate Shepherd* (1604), where Breton again intermingles masterfully both these pastoral conceits and personal insecurities.

By the turn of the century, Breton's work increasingly turned toward devotional poetry. His most lasting achievements in this genre attempt to ease the tensions between humanist ambition and English Protestant tradition. Often, his pondering over this struggle answers his earlier fears by directing his attentions toward the heavenly realm. Also at this time Breton begins, under the pseudonym "Pasquill," his satiric verses. Mild by his time's standards, these verses (which include some Martin Marprelate tracts) are still interesting for their recordings of contemporary colloquial language and idiom.

Despite Thomas Nashe's chastisement of Breton as a "croaking" poet, nearly all of Breton's poetry achieved immense popularity during his life. Much of this favorable reputation owes to both an orthodox religious devotion that remains free of any factionalizing impetus (although some twentieth-century critics suspect a recusant Catholicism lurking in many poems) and a reliance on the vastly successful melancholy narrator persona—a quality that also frequently appears in his satires and mixes well with his persona's feigned dilettantism.

In keeping with his poetry, Breton's equally celebrated prose exemplifies a pronounced reluctance to engage in coarseness, a common malady among his fellow writers. Some of his best-remembered work in this genre includes *Wits Trenchmour: Or, A Conference Between a Scholler and Angler* (1597), second only to Isaac Walton's *The Compleat Angler* in his ruminations over fishing; the oft-reprinted epistolary *A Poste with a Packet of Mad Letters* (1603); the character sketches *Characters upon Essaies, Morall and Divine* (1615); and the pastoral *Fantasticks* (1626). Breton's work consistently demonstrates a refined, elegant, and devoutly religious manner that simultaneously explores topics as diverse as love and virtue, duty and holiness, honor and humility, and court and country.

BIBLIOGRAPHY

Bullen, A.H. *Elizabethans*. 1924; repr. 1962.

Grosart, A.B., ed. *The Works of Nicholas Breton in Verse and Prose*. 2 vols. 1879; repr. 1966.

Kentish-Wright, Ursula, ed. *A Mad World My Masters and Other Prose Works*. 2 vols. 1929.

Robertson, Jean, ed. *Poems by Nicholas Breton*. 1952.

Rollins, Hyder E., ed. *England's Helicon* (1600, 1614). 1935.

Tannenbaum, Samuel A., and Dorothy R. Tannenbaum, eds. "Nicholas Breton." *Elizabethan Bibliographies*. vol. 1. 1947; repr. 1967.

Dana E. Aspinall

SEE ALSO

Gascoigne, George; Pastoral; Petrarchanism; Sidney, Mary; Verse Anthologies

Bright, Timothy (c. 1550–1615)

Born in Cambridge, Timothy Bright matriculated from Trinity College, Cambridge, in 1561, at age eleven, but did not take residence in the college until 1564. He graduated B.A. in 1568, one year after he had been made scholar, but left for the Continent in 1570 to pursue medical studies without completing his course for the M.A. Our next sighting of him is in Paris during the St. Bartholomew's Day Massacre, at which time he took refuge in the English embassy. Subsequently, Bright returned to Cambridge where he took the necessary examinations and was awarded the M.B. degree in 1574, a license to practice medicine the following year, and the M.D. degree in 1579. Bright practiced in Cambridge for several years, and it was there that he embarked on his career as author, publishing in 1580 *A Treatise: Wherein is Declared the Sufficiencie of English Medicines, for Cure of all Diseases* (repr. 1977). He must have also taught

B

medicine in some capacity, for he stated in the preface to his *Hygieina, Id est De Sanitate Tuenda Medicinae pars prima* (1582) that the book was published at the request of his auditors. By 1584, Bright moved to Ipswich, but he appears to have already mobilized some powerful patrons to procure for him the position of physician to St. Bartholomew Hospital. Despite the attempts of the College of Physicians to have their own candidate nominated, Bright's appointment was finalized in early 1586. The college proceeded to harass Bright, prosecuting him for practicing in London without a license, but without success, owing to Bright's powerful connections.

Not long after his arrival in London, Bright published his *A Treatise of Melancholy* (repr. 1940, 1977), which exerted considerable influence on Robert Burton's more famous work on the same subject, as well as on William Shakespeare. Also in 1586 we find Bright seeking a patent bestowing on him exclusive rights to teach, and publish on, shorthand writing. Such a patent was granted him in 1588, and he immediately published his celebrated *Characterie: An Arte of Shorte, Swifte and Secrete Writing by Character,* the first modern work on the subject. By that time, however, Bright was already contemplating abandoning medicine in favor of theology, a life change presaged in 1589 with his publication of an abridgment of John Foxe's *Book of Martyrs.* During the next two years, the governors of St. Bartholomew Hospital warned Bright several times of his neglect of duties, and eventually dismissed him in the summer of 1591. Conveniently for Bright, he had just received from Elizabeth I the living of Methley, Yorkshire, to which he added three years later the more profitable rectorship of Berwick-in Elmet. Bright practiced his new vocation until his death in 1615, without appearing again in print. He was survived by a wife, two sons, and a daughter.

BIBLIOGRAPHY

Carlton, William J. *Timothe Bright Doctor of Phisicke: a Memoir of "the Father of Modern Shorthand."* 1911.

Jordan-Smith, Paul. *Bibliographia Burtoniana; a Study of Robert Burton's* The Anatomy of Melancholy, *with a Bibliography of Burton's Writings.* 1931.

Keynes, Geoffrey. *Dr. Timothie Bright, 1550–1615; a Survey of His Life with a Bibliography of His Writings.* 1962.

Mordechai Feingold

SEE ALSO

Foxe, John; Handwriting; Medicine and Health

Bristol

With a population of about 10,000, Bristol was the leading port outside London and second only to Norwich among English provincial towns at the end of the fifteenth century. Bristol's importance was initially recognized in 1373 when it was the first provincial town to be granted county status. Its wealth was based both on a diverse manufacturing base, dominated by the cloth finishing industry, and on its internal, coastal, and overseas trade, dominated by the export of cloth and the importation of wine and other luxury goods. After the loss of Gascony in 1453, Bristol merchants had been forced to find additional markets, with the result that the Iberian Peninsula became a major partner in the cloth/wine trade. However, this was not enough to stave off economic stagnation, and the sixteenth century was a difficult period for Bristol traders and manufacturers, faced by a frequently hostile international climate and increasing competition from London monopolies and rural clothiers backed by London finance.

The overseas traders consolidated their power through the establishment of the Society of Merchant Venturers, which received its charter in 1552. This body acted to defend its members from outside competition, particularly from London, but was also instrumental in the creation of a mercantile elite within the Bristol commercial classes. The Merchant Venturers came to dominate the governance of the city, and their tightening grip on power prompted criticism from those who were excluded.

The structure of Bristol's sixteenth-century government was determined by the charter of 1499. Henceforth, Bristol was governed by an oligarchy of forty-five burgesses, self-electing and answerable to none but themselves. Office-holding was not always popular among the Bristol burgesses: in 1518, one sheriff complained that he had been forced to accept the office and had been burdened with unreasonable expenses as a result.

Inevitably, religion generated further dissent. Pre-Reformation Bristol was notorious for its Lollardy, particularly among the textile workers of Redcliffe and Temple, and during the Reformation there was an influential radical party among the burgesses. In 1533, the mayor invited Hugh Latimer to preach the Easter sermons, and his radical message provoked a "battle of the pulpits" between conservative and radical factions. In the early Tudor years Bristol was split between two ecclesiastical jurisdictions: the section north of the Avon belonged to the diocese of Worcester, while the southern suburbs lay in the diocese of Bath and Wells. This changed with the creation of the

B

diocese of Bristol in 1542, but the diocese was poorly endowed. Bristol's lay elite benefited greatly from the dissolution of the monsteries and increasingly dominated the clergy. Under Mary, Bristol witnessed between four and eight burnings—the victims drawn from the same artisanal class as their Lollard antecedents—but the elite acquiesced in her attempts to reestablish Catholicism. However, Protestantism was strongly entrenched among the upper ranks of Bristol society by 1603.

BIBLIOGRAPHY
Fleming, P.W. "The emergence of modern Bristol." In *The Making of Modern Bristol.* M. Dresser and P. Ollerenshaw, eds., pp. 1–24. 1996.
Sacks, David H. *The Widening Gate: Bristol and the Atlantic Economy, 1450–1700.* 1991.
Skeeters, M. *Community and Clergy: Bristol and the Reformation, c. 1530–c. 1570.* 1993.

Peter W. Fleming

SEE ALSO
Cloth Industry; Cloth Trade; Trade, Overseas

Broadsides

Broadsides were a popular form of print media in the Tudor age, of particular interest to students of literature, folklore, and popular culture. A broadside was a single piece of paper that came in various sizes, printed on one side (if printed on both sides, it was known as a broadsheet), often accompanied by a woodcut, and containing various kinds of texts: works of religious and moral instruction, ballad lyrics, commentaries on religious and political issues, church edicts, and state proclamations. Very often these texts were versified. Broadsides were usually sold for a half-penny, making them accessible to a wide audience. Known as the "non-books of the poor," it would be more accurate to say that broadsides were aimed at a middle-class audience, instructing them in religious and social mores, defining their social protests, teaching them popular ballads, and in all cases entertaining them. Broadsides were sold on the streets, from book stalls, door to door by traveling pedlars, in marketplaces, at city and county fairs, and at other public festivals.

Broadsides are a reminder that, for all its aspirations to art, literature can also simply be a commodity produced for and sold to a buying public. Because they were printed on a single sheet of paper, broadsides had no aspirations to being preserved and valued, much less being consid-

ered art, unlike an "official" print form such as a book. The fact that so many did survive is lucky accident: they were preserved by being pressed into service as, for example, book bindings or wallpaper.

Broadsides are found in English culture as early as the time of William Caxton, who printed one in 1477 as an advertisement for the Sarum Ordinale. Few extant copies of broadsides from the fifteenth through the first half of the sixteenth century have survived, but in the second half of the sixteenth century, broadside circulation increased enormously because there were more printers, a more organized system of distribution, and an increased public demand for edifying entertainment. Printers consequently produced thousands of broadsides, especially in the period from 1580 to 1600—enough so that printers could devote their entire trade to them without having to pursue the upper-class patronage or royal warrant that other, more "literary" works demanded. Printers were technically required to get a license for every broadside they printed from the Stationers' Company in London (incorporated in 1556), but beyond that, broadsides had no specific requirements for public consumption other than the presence of a buyer, unlike a work such as a play script, which had to be produced. Generally, broadsides were free from the threat of censorship that restricted other forms of literature; though little research has been done in the field of broadside censorship, it has been estimated that half of all the broadsides produced were never registered at all. London was the broadside printing center in England, but they were also produced in the thriving printing centers of Birmingham, Manchester, Preston, and Newcastle.

Broadsides contained an enormous range of texts, but are generally known today for their role in the development of newspapers and for their preservation of ballads. The earliest extant broadsides from the fifteenth and first half of the sixteenth century tended to be religious in nature. Many were purely devotional works or ecclesiastical documents, but increasingly in the Tudor period, they reflected and commented on the various heated public debates of the English Reformation, paving the way for a much wider variety of broadsides dating from the second half of the sixteenth century. Some of these later works recounted historical events and others contemporary events of topical interest, leading many historians to argue that broadsides were the precursor to the modern newspaper. These newspaper broadsides were normally in prose, occasionally in rhyme, and were also known as chapbooks—literally, a "cheap book" made by folding a broadside so that it formed

Broadsides 89

B

a pamphlet. With their emphasis on topicality, these broadsides were usually distinguished from tracts and religious works, which had a more scholarly focus and audience. They were especially suited for the broad dissemination of government proclamations, which were meant to be publicly posted, and though broadsides of this type were not meant to be sold, they could, and did, find their way into private ownership. Many English people got all of their information on what the government was doing through the medium of broadsides.

Broadsides are perhaps even better known today for their preservation of ballads. Though there were sixteenth-century collections of love lyrics found in pamphlet form called "garlands," they were often written by court poets, whereas broadside ballads tended to be written by, and for, a more popular audience. Many ballads were written in the Tudor ballad meter, but the range of ballad texts found in broadsides reveals a great variety of stanzaic forms and rhyme schemes; thus "ballad" was a catch-all term in Tudor culture, generally referring to some kind of a song that told some kind of a story. Broadsides grew out of the remains of professional balladry; minstrel songs as well as country folk songs found their way into broadsides, and in the sixteenth century, traditional ballads coexisted with newly composed works on topical themes.

The subjects and themes of ballads were equally diverse. Many ballads were written about topical events—natural disasters, state functions, crimes and trials, military exploits, and the like—while others were based on folk narratives handed down in the oral tradition. Love was an extremely popular theme in all of its manifestations—courtship, marriage, parting, abandonment—ranging in treatment from from serious to bawdy. Other ballads had a more didactic function, their texts dispensing advice or moral instruction on such issues as health, love and marriage, religion and morality, and so on. Ballads were an extremely popular medium, if we are to judge by the Tudor culture's response to them: in 1543, Parliament passed an act to encourage "the advancement of true religion" by purging the English realm of seditious books, ballads, and rhymes—while at the same time, the church was appropriating ballad tunes for new Reformation hymns.

The broadside ballad offers other dimensions to consider in regard to its status as a literary commodity. The woodcut illustration might be a selling point, even though it was often unrelated to the text. There is a further element of performance, as a broadside ballad was often performed by the balladmonger who was commissioned by the printer to sing or recite it to an audience in order to encourage buying. Because he might perform the various roles of the characters found in the text, broadsides are thus related to the kind of street theater common in Tudor England.

BIBLIOGRAPHY
Shepherd, Leslie. *The Broadside Ballad.* 1978.
Shaabar, Matthias A. *Some Forerunners of the Newspaper, 1476–1622.* 1929.
Würzbach, Natascha. *The Rise of the English Street Ballad, 1550–1650.* 1990.

Robert Kellerman

SEE ALSO
Ballad; Caxton, William; Didactic Poetry; Engraving and Illustration; News Quartos; Pedlars; Popular Literature; Printing, Publishing, and Bookselling

Bromley, Thomas (1530–1587)

A leading lawyer and lord chancellor from 1579 until his death, Sir Thomas Bromley was born in Shropshire to a family with strong legal connections and educated at Oxford and at the Inner Temple. He married Elizabeth, daughter of Sir Adrian Fortescue, a King's Bench justice. His legal expertise was recognized in his service as member of Parliament in 1558, 1559, and 1563; in his election to the prestigious post of recorder of London in 1566; and in his tenure of the post of solicitor general from 1569 to 1579. He was well connected in the Elizabethan establishment and his promotion to the post of lord chancellor was supported by both the earl of Leicester and Sir Christopher Hatton. As lord chancellor he presided over the trial of Mary Queen of Scots, and applied the Great Seal to the warrant for her execution. His tenure of the post was otherwise uncontroversial, and there is little sign of his pushing forward with the kind of procedural analysis that had characterized the tenure of his predecessor, Sir Nicholas Bacon. As Thomas Fuller put it, "it was difficult to come after Sir Nicholas Bacon and not to come after him."

BIBLIOGRAPHY
Jones, W.J. *The Elizabethan Court of Chancery.* 1967

Ian W. Archer

SEE ALSO
Bacon, Nicholas; King's or Queen's Bench, Court of; Mary Queen of Scots

90 Broadsides

Brooke, Arthur (?–c. 1563)

Little evidence remains to determine the facts about Arthur Brooke's brief life and canon. His biography centers on his death by drowning, which took place in the ship *Greyhound* near Rye on March 19, 1562/3. In a letter to Thomas Challoner dated May 14, 1563, Henry Cobham reports that "little Brook and some other petty gentlemen" were cast away with Sir Thomas Finch on a mission to serve the queen at Le Havre. The death was commemorated in verse by Thomas Brooke the Younger (in Arthur Brooke's posthumous translation, see below), and by George Turberville in an epitaph lamenting the fortune of the "unlucky youth." A year or so earlier, records of the Inner Temple show that Arthur Brooke probably contributed to the revels there; a Parliament held on February 4, 1561–1562 gave him "special admission, without payment, in consideration of certain plays and shows at Christmas last set forth by him."

Brooke's canon may include certain "plays and shows" as well as some occasional verse, but his known works consist of two translations: *The tragicall historye of Romeus and Juliet*, printed three times in the sixteenth century (1562, 1567, 1587), and reprinted frequently since the late eighteenth century; and *The agreement of sondry places of scripture*, published after Brooke's death in 1563. The latter, a Huguenot tract of unknown authorship, reconciles 107 pairs of short passages from the Old and New Testaments that seem to conflict (for example, "Thou shalt hate thine enemy" and "Love your enemies" [Matthew 5]). As "The Epistle to the Reader" explains, study of the Bible with "a spirit ready to be taught" finds agreement in all parts of the holy book and guards against the "many troubled spirits . . . overthrowing and corrupting the meaning of the Scriptures to confirm their opinions." In its prefatory material, *Romeus and Juliet* also testifies to Brooke's strong Protestant sympathy, a bias that his political ambition may have enhanced.

Of course, *Romeus and Juliet* influenced Shakespeare and established what C.S. Lewis has called Brooke's "shadowy immortality." Shakespeare based his early tragedy on the poem, taking details from Brooke and at times quoting his very words. Brooke's version of the popular story, translated from Pierre Boaistuau's *Histoires tragiques* (1559), contains 3,020 lines distinguished by a few inventions, poulter's measure, and enough figures of repetition to give the romantic narrative a pronounced rhetorical style. Brooke's exaggerated use of rhetoric may have invited Shakespeare to revise the typical presentation of the story. Whatever the effect, Shakespeare borrowed from the poem more than once, drawing on it for *The Two Gentlemen of Verona* and short passages elsewhere.

BIBLIOGRAPHY

Bland, D.S. "Arthur Broke, Gerard Legh and the Inner Temple." *Notes and Queries*, n.s., vol. 16, pp. 453–455.

Brooke, Arthur. *The agreemente of sondry places of scripture, tr. out of French, and nowe fyrst publyshed by A. Broke*. 1563.

———. *Brooke's* Romeus and Juliet *Being the Original of Shakespeare's* Romeo and Juliet. J.J. Munro, ed. 1908.

———. *The Tragicall Historye of Romeus and Juliet written first in Italian by Bandell, and nowe in Englishe by Ar. Br.*. In *Narrative and Dramatic Sources of Shakespeare*, vol. 1. Geoffrey Bullough, ed., pp. 269–363. 1957.

Heltzel, Virgil G. "A Poem by Arthur Brooke." *Shakespeare Quarterly*, vol. 22, pp. 77–78.

McAleer, John J. "Arthur Brooke: Elizabethan Dissembler." *Drama Critique*, vol. 2, pp. 131–140.

Jill L. Levenson

SEE ALSO

Challoner, Thomas; Shakespeare, William; Turberville, George

Broughton, Hugh (1549–1612)

A Puritan divine, accomplished Hebraist, and biblical translator, Hugh Broughton published nearly eighty works that demonstrate his interest in scriptural chronology, genealogy, exegesis, and—in opposition to Jewish reading of Scripture—his view of the Old Testament as an historical foreshadowing of the New. Reflecting Protestant emphasis on "the Word" as the key to faith and salvation, their aim is to show that "the Kingdome of God & Christ [is] the matter of all the Bible." Much of his work, though, proved controversial, and from 1589/90, he spent much of his time abroad.

Broughton came from an ancient Shropshire family. In 1569, he entered Cambridge, where he studied Hebrew and gained fellowships. In 1578, he was appointed a prebend and reader in divinity at Durham before moving to London to become a Puritan preacher and private tutor in Hebrew. In 1588, he published *A Concent of Scripture* in which he attempted to settle scriptural chronology and reveal the Bible as a work of divine inspiration and perfection throughout, "breathed from one spirit" and "certainly chained, even from the fall to the Redemption." His book was publicly attacked at Oxford by John Rainolds and at

B

Cambridge by Edward Lively, both men earning Broughton's enmity for life. He defended his work to young scholars at weekly lectures in St. Paul's until some bishops attacked the gatherings as "dangerous conventicles."

Consequently, in late 1589 or early 1590, he left for Germany, where he disputed with the archbishop of Mainz and Rabbi Elias of Frankfurt. On a later visit (1592–1603, with possibly a brief return to England in 1595) he made the acquaintance of J.C. Scaliger and disputed with Rabbi David Farrar, whose interpretation of "the fourth kingdom" and "Messias" in Daniel he was to refute in print.

In 1593, Broughton had unsuccessfully proposed to Burghley a new translation of the Bible. In 1597, he published at Middleburg *An Epistle . . . touching translating the Bible from the original.* It outlines his principles of translation that would honor the text as "sound, holy, pure" with an exact and scholarly approach, one exemplified by his own accurate and dramatically expressive translations—*Jeremiah* (1606), *Daniel* (1607), *Job* (1610)—with their erudite commentaries. His combative attitude toward those who disagreed with him ensured his exclusion from the panels of translators (headed by Rainolds) that produced the King James Bible, a translation he vehemently attacked for its inclusion of wrong renderings in the text and the consignment of correct ones to the margins. In 1599, he published his definitive refutation of the belief that Christ descended into hell.

He returned to London for a brief stay in 1603, when he preached to Prince Henry, returning later that year to Germany to become preacher to the English congregation at Middleburg, from where in 1604 he unsuccessfully petitioned King James for a pension. In 1611, he made his last return to London, there to die the following year. Broughton's exegetical style was parodied by Ben Jonson in *The Alchemist* (1610), 4.5.1–32.

BIBLIOGRAPHY

Broughton, Hugh. *Works, prefaced by a life.* John Lightfoot, ed. 1662.

Bruce, F.F. *The English Bible: A History of Translations.* 1961.

Daiches, David. *The King James Version of the English Bible.* 1941.

Levi, Peter. *The English Bible, 1534–1889.* 1974.

Norton, David. *A History of the Bible as Literature.* 2 vols. 1993.

Robinson, H. Wheeler. *The Bible in its Ancient and English Versions.* 1940.

David Freeman

SEE ALSO

Bible Translation

Browne, George (d. 1556)

The details of the early life of George Browne, archbishop of Dublin and right-hand associate of Henry VIII in the Irish reformation, are obscure. He became leader of the Austin Friars sometime before 1534, the year that the Act of Supremacy effected the separation of the English church from the church of Rome. Browne was charged with administering the oath of succession, acknowledging Henry as supreme head of the Church of England, to friars south of London. He soon gained Henry's favor by advising the poor, who were upset over the religious turmoil, to pray to Christ solely and directly—hence, without the intermediary of the Catholic Church or its saints. By 1535, Browne was made archbishop of Dublin, although he did not set foot in Ireland until the following year. His efforts at reform, including payments on, and seizure of, ecclesiastical properties, were bitterly opposed by the Irish clergy, especially Edward Staples, bishop of Meath. But Browne persisted, promulgating forms of prayer that joined the Irish to the English church under the royal supremacy. His adoption, in 1550, of the first English prayer book further solidified the union of the two churches, and Browne, now the primate of Ireland, gained gradual conformity thereafter. After the accession of the Catholic Mary I to the English throne in 1553, Browne's primacy was revoked on the grounds that he was a married man. He was provided a modest benefice until his death three years later.

BIBLIOGRAPHY

Bradshaw, B. "George Browne, First Reformation Archbishop of Dublin." In *Journal of Ecclesiastical History,* vol. 21, pp. 301–326.

Flood, W.H.G. *George Browne, First Protestant Archbishop of Dublin.* 1914.

Mark Goldblatt

SEE ALSO

Book of Common Prayer; Catholicism; Church of England; Supremacy, Act of

Browne, Robert (c. 1550–1633)

Robert Browne was the leading proponent of Separatist ecclesiology in Elizabethan England. Although active for only a few years, his name became synonymous with Separatism following the publication of *A Treatise of Reformation Without Tarrying for Anie* (1582). Browne was influenced by Thomas Cartwright's radical Puritanism at Cambridge in the early 1570s, where Browne studied at Corpus Christi College. His advanced Puritan views initially led him to denounce the prelacy and burn his episcopal license to preach.

By 1581, however, Browne had abandoned the parish system entirely and with Robert Harrison formed a small Separatist congregation in Norwich. Arrested and twice imprisoned, Browne and Harrison finally removed their congregation to Middleburg in Zeeland. But dissension soon led to congregational division. Disillusioned, Browne returned to England where he endured a brief imprisonment in 1585 for his earlier Separatist publications. Released through the intervention of his kinsman, Lord Burghley, Browne submitted to ecclesial authority, was received back into communion with the Church of England, and appointed master of St. Olave's School in Southwark.

In 1591, he was ordained and installed as rector of Thorpe-cum-Achurch in Northamptonshire. His Puritan nonconformity led to further conflict with authorities in 1617, and again in 1631, however, when he was suspended and excommunicated. Two years later Browne was imprisoned for striking a village constable and died in jail.

BIBLIOGRAPHY

Burrage, Champlin. *The True Story of Robert Browne.* 1906.

Peel, Albert, and Leland H. Carlson, eds. *The Writings of Robert Harrison and Robert Brown.* 1953.

Powicke, F.J. *Robert Browne.* 1910.

White, B.R. *The English Separatist Tradition.* 1971.

Stephen Brachlow

SEE ALSO

Cartwright, Thomas

Brownists

See Browne, Robert

Bruno, Giordano (1548–1600)

Born in Nola in southern Italy, Giordano Bruno entered the monastery of San Domenico Maggiore in Naples in 1565, and was ordained a priest in 1573. In 1576, accused of heresy, he escaped to Rome. Traveling north, Bruno reached Geneva in 1579, where he professed Protestantism while accusing the Calvinist theologians of being ignorant "pedagogues." Excommunicated, he left for France, where he taught philosophy at the University of Toulouse. From 1581 to early 1583, Bruno was in Paris where he published two Latin works on the art of memory, *De umbris idearum,* dedicated to the French king, Henri III, and *Cantus Circaeus.* The king summoned him to know if his memory techniques worked by magic or by art. Bruno demonstrated that they worked by art. Appointed as a *lecteur royale* in the service of the king, he also published in Paris a Latin work on Raymond Lull and a comedy in Italian, *Candelaio.*

On March 28, 1583, the English ambassador in Paris, Sir Henry Cobham, wrote to Sir Francis Walsingham, secretary to Elizabeth I: "Il S' Doctor Jordano Bruno Nolano, a professor in philosophy, intendeth to pass into England; whose religion I cannot commend." Bruno arrived in London carrying letters to the French ambassador, Michel de Castelnau. He remained in the French embassy as a gentleman attendant until Castelnau, who was supporting the cause of the Catholic Mary, Queen of Scots, was recalled to France in the autumn of 1585.

In June 1583, Bruno left London briefly to go to Oxford, where he debated successfully against John Underhill, soon to become vice-chancellor. Later that year, he returned to teach *de immortalitate animae and de quintuplici sphere,* probably using material from his own *Sigillus sigillorum.* These lectures were interrupted with accusations of undertaking "to set on foote the opinion of Copernicus," and also of plagiarizing from the *De vita coelitus comparanda* of the Florentine Neoplatonic philosopher, Marsilio Ficino. Bruno may have been quoting from chapter 15 of Ficino's text, which extends the phenomenon of magnetism from earth to the constellation of the Little Bear, implicitly contradicting the traditional Aristotelian-Ptolemaic cosmology based on the idea of a heavenly fifth essence far removed from the heavy earthy elements.

After his difficulties at Oxford, Bruno returned to the French embassy in London, where Fulke Greville, the friend and biographer of Sir Philip Sidney, invited him to attend a supper in order to explain his Copernicanism and "other paradoxes" of his philosophy. Bruno argued his case against two neo-Aristotelian scholars from Oxford present at the supper, and published his account of the debate in 1584 in *The Ash Wednesday Supper,* one of the major philosophical texts produced in Elizabethan England.

B

Various suggestions have been put forward as to Bruno's true role in the French embassy in London. However, all that is known with certainty of his years there is that he published two Latin works on the art of memory, *Ars reminiscendi* and *Explicatio triginta sigillorum*, as well as writing and publishing six philosophical dialogues in Italian: *The Ash Wednesday Supper; Of the cause, principle and one; Of the infinite universe and worlds; The expulsion of the triumphant beast; The cabala of the pegasean horse* and *The heroic frenzy*. Bruno's Italian dialogues proposed a post-Copernican universe of infinite dimensions, filled with numberless solar systems besides our own. He also went well beyond Ficino in positing an infinite substance composed of circular atoms as the basis of being throughout an infinite whole: a daringly unorthodox cosmology for the time, on which he attempted to found a new form of inquiry into both natural and divine truths.

Bruno's later philosophical works, written in Wittenberg in Germany, where he taught at the university, and in Prague, are largely concerned with the mind in its search for knowledge of the now infinite whole. They deal with the art of memory, Euclidean geometry, Pythagorean number symbolism, and the techniques of magic in an effort to formulate a new language with which to interpret a new world. Bruno proposed a picture logic rather than a rational mathematics as the new language, a proposal that left him at odds with the newly emerging mathematically oriented sciences, but which appears of increasing interest in our own era of computerization. The major work of his last years is the so-called Frankfurt trilogy composed of *De triptici minimo, De monade, and De immense.*

Bruno's ideas remained dangerously heretical both in the Protestant and in the Catholic Europe of his time. After his return to Italy in 1591, he was arrested by the Inquisition in Venice and subjected to a long trial. Claiming the liberty of the philosopher to follow the dictates of his reason, and refusing to recant, Bruno was burned at the stake in the Campo dei Fiori in Rome on February 17, 1600.

BIBLIOGRAPHY

Aquilecchia, Giovanni. *Schede bruniane* (1950–1991). 1993.

Ciliberto, Michele. *Giordano Bruno.* 1990.

Gatti, Hilary. *The Renaissance Drama of Knowledge: Giordano Bruno in England.* 1989.

De Léon-Jones, Karen Sylvia. *Giordano Bruno and the Kabbalah.* 1997.

Ordine, Nuccio. *Giordano Bruno and the Philosophy of the Ass.* 1996.

Yates, Frances. *Giordano Bruno and the Hermetic Tradition.* 1964.

Hillary Gatti

SEE ALSO
Astronomy; Greville, Fulke; Platonism

Bryskett, Lodowick (c. 1545–c. 1612)

Born to Antonio Bruschetto, a successful London merchant who immigrated to England from Italy around 1535, Lodowick Bryskett was the third son of five brothers and two sisters. He attended Trinity College, Cambridge, but took no degree, most likely due to his father's financial difficulties. Shortly after, Lodowick entered the household of Sir Henry Sidney, temporarily fulfilling the duties of clerk of the council of Ireland. In May of 1572, Lodowick accompanied Sidney's son Philip on a tour of Europe, returning ahead of his companions due to the death of his father in 1574.

In 1577, Bryskett was appointed as a clerk of the Chancery, a position in which he was soon succeeded by Edmund Spenser. In 1582, Bryskett received an appointment of secretary of the Munster council from Lord Grey de Wilton. Spenser was at that time acting as Lord Grey's secretary, and he and Bryskett became friends. Bryskett surrendered his office with the Munster council in March of 1600, receiving from the queen a grant of 100 pounds for the payment of debts, and an additional 100 pounds *per annum* for his maintenance. Sent abroad, Bryskett was captured and held in Flanders. By 1602, he had been returned to England and was serving as clerk of the casualties in Ireland. King James removed him from office in 1604, but by 1606 he reputedly held large estates in Cavan, Cork, and Dublin. These lands were apparently seized by rebels several years later, just before Bryskett's death sometime in 1611–1612.

Bryskett's primary work of note is his translation of the Italian philosophical treatise of Baptista Giraldo, which he entitled *A Discourse of Civill Life.* He is also apparently the author of two poems on the death of Sir Philip Sidney: *The Mourning Muse of Thestylis* and *A Pastoral Aeglogue upon the Death of Sir Philip Sidney, Knight.* Although licensed to the printer John Wolfe in August of 1587, neither poem seems to have been published outside of Edmund Spenser's collection of elegies entitled *Astrophel.* Bryskett's translation opens with a description of a party of friends gathered at Bryskett's cottage near Dublin that is particularly noteworthy. Their discussion of the Italian popularization of moral philosophy led to Spenser's, inviting Bryskett to read his translation of Giraldo's work. Also included, and of particular interest, are some of Spenser's remarks regarding the philosophical problems that arise from Bryskett's reading.

BIBLIOGRAPHY

Plomer, Henry R., and Tom Peete Cross, eds. *The Life and Correspondence of Lodowick Bryskett.* 1927.

Charles Leiby

SEE ALSO

Italian Literature, Influence of; Ireland, History of; Sidney, Sir Henry; Sidney Philip; Spenser, Edmund

Buc, George (1560–1622)

George Buc (as he always signed his surname), the son of Robert Buck, gentleman-usher to the bishop of Ely, was baptized on October 1, 1560, at Holy Trinity, Ely. He may have studied at Cambridge, though the evidence is not conclusive. By about 1580, he was in London and made an unenthusiastic attempt to study law, entering the Middle Temple in 1585. His various subsequent activities were influenced by his links to the powerful Howard family. Several times between 1587 and 1601 he traveled abroad, acting as a diplomatic courier. He served against the Armada in 1588, and took part in the raid on Cadiz in 1596 (he was dispatched home to report on it to Elizabeth I). He served briefly as M.P. in 1593 and 1597–1598, and was included in diplomatic missions to Flanders in 1601 and to Spain in 1605. King James made him a gentleman of the Privy Chamber and knighted him on July 23, 1603. He had literary and scholarly interests, writing several treatises on history and genealogy, the most famous of these being a substantial defense of King Richard III against the allegations of Tudor historians. Several manuscript copies survive, and in 1646, his great-nephew, George Buck, published a heavily revised version of it that he tried to pass off as his own work.

Buc's main interest to modern scholars lies in his capacity as master of the revels, responsible for the licensing and censoring of all plays performed on the public stage. He also supervised productions of plays, but not of masques, at court. It is not clear precisely when his connections with the Revels Office began. In the 1590s, Buc and the dramatist John Lyly were competing for a reversion of the mastership (i.e., a promise of the job at the death of its current

holder, Edmund Tilney). A letter of Lyly's dated 1597 gives the impression that Buc had won, but his reversion was not issued until June 23, 1603. He took over the mastership at Tilney's death in 1610, but to what degree he had exercised the powers of the office before that date is uncertain. He definitely began in 1606 to license plays for publication, but this may have been because Tilney would not let him do anything else. (Buc was not Tilney's nephew, though this has often been asserted, but distantly related to him through marriage, and there was bad feeling between Buc and the Tilneys because of a disputed inheritance.)

Buc's office-book, in which he recorded his activities as master, passed into the hands of one of his successors, Sir Henry Herbert, who preserved a few entries from the book but subsequently discarded it. Some drafts of Revels Office documents survive because Sir George reused the paper while composing his book on Richard III. His work as censor can be seen in two play manuscripts: *The Second Maiden's Tragedy* (anonymous but now usually attributed to Thomas Middleton), which he censored and then licensed on October 31, 1611; and Fletcher and Massinger's *Sir John van Olden Barnavelt* (1619), which was censored but does not bear a license. Buc seems to have been a careful censor, removing material that might have embarrassed the political establishment, but not unduly rigorous. In his last years as master he suffered from financial problems and insubordination from the revels officers, vividly described in a letter to Lionel Cranfield of December 13, 1621. Early in 1622 he became insane, and in March was replaced as master by Sir John Astley. He died on October 31, 1622, and was buried at Broadwater, Sussex, on November 14.

BIBLIOGRAPHY

Bawcutt, N.W. "New Revels Documents of Sir George Buc and Sir Henry Herbert, 1619–1622." *Review of English Studies,* vol. 35, pp. 316–331.

Chambers, E.K. *The Elizabethan Stage.* 4 vols. 1923.

Dutton, Richard. *Mastering the Revels: The Regulation and Censorship of English Renaissance Drama.* 1991.

Feuillerat, A. *Documents Relating to the Office of the Revels in the time of Queen Elizabeth.* In *Materialen zur Kunde des älteren englischen Dramas.* vol. 21. W. Bang, ed. 1908.

N.W. Bawcutt

SEE ALSO

Censorship; History, Writing of; Revels Office; Tilney, Edmund

B

Bucer, Martin (1491–1551)

Born at Schettstadt, Alsace, in 1491, Martin Bucer entered a monastery in 1506 against his will, and he remained there until he was dispensed from his vows in 1521. In 1518, he was in Heidelberg, where he heard Martin Luther. On leaving the monastery he went to Wittenberg, becoming one of Luther's associates. In 1523, he returned to Strasbourg, where his father had become a citizen, and was appointed a public preacher. In 1525, he was embroiled in the eucharistic debates between Luther, who believed in the real presence of Christ in the sacrament, and Huldrych Zwingli, who did not. Bucer sided with Zwingli, in spite of his earlier association with Luther, but he continually tried to find a way to reconcile the two Reformers. He managed to satisfy Luther by confessing that even unbelievers received the Body and Blood of Christ at Holy Communion, but this merely antagonized the Zwinglians and was not a lasting solution to the problem.

Political developments in Germany forced him to leave Strasbourg in 1549, and he went to England. He had already been consulted by Henry VIII about the annulment of his marriage to Katherine of Aragon, and was well known to the leaders of the English Reformation. Once in London, he became a close associate of Archbishop Thomas Cranmer, who asked him to help with the revision of the Book of Common Prayer. Some of Bucer's suggestions, though by no means all of them, were subsequently incorporated in the 1552 Book. In 1549, he was appointed Regius Professor of Divinity at Cambridge, where he lectured in 1550. His health gave way, however, and he died on February 28, 1551. He was buried in great St. Mary's Church, but his body was exhumed and burned in 1557, on the orders of Mary I.

Bucer was one of the greatest of the continental Reformers, and played a major part in the theological education of John Calvin. He also wrote a famous commentary on the Psalms. Historically speaking, he has been greatly underestimated, and it is only in recent times that his true achievement has come to be recognized.

BIBLIOGRAPHY

Hopf, C. *Martin Bucer and the English Reformation.* 1946.

Krieger, C., and M. Linchard., eds. *Martin Bucer and Sixteenth-Century Europe.* 2 vols. 1993.

Wright, D.F., ed. *Martin Bucer: Reforming Church and Community.* 1994.

Gerald L. Bray

SEE ALSO

Book of Common Prayer; Cranmer, Thomas; Eucharist; Katherine of Aragon; Lutheranism

Buchanan, George (1506–1582)

Dramatist, historian, educator, political propagandist, and foremost Latin poet of his generation, George Buchanan was born in Stirlingshire. After studying in Paris as long as his funds would allow, he returned to Scotland and received his B.A. from St. Andrews in 1525. Back in Paris, Buchanan studied Greek, earned his M.A. in 1528, and became an instructor at the Collège de Sainte-Barbe. Within a few years Buchanan left the drudgery of classroom teaching to tutor a series of young noblemen.

In the mid-1530s, offended by clerical corruption in Scotland, Buchanan satirized the Franciscan order, first in the *Somnium,* based on William Dunbar's dream/vision "How Dunbar was desyrit to be ane frier." Next, to please King James V, who requested a more caustic attack, Buchanan composed the *Franciscanus,* an ingeniously protracted catalogue of hypocrisies. In 1539, helped by the king, Buchanan fled to England to escape Cardinal David Beaton's persecution.

Thinking himself still pursued by Beaton, Buchanan sailed to France, where he accepted André de Gouvéa's invitation to join the faculty of the Collège de Guyenne in Bordeaux. There Buchanan prepared for student performances: Latin translations of Euripides' *Medea* and *Alcestis* and two original biblical tragedies, *Baptistes* and *Jephthes.*

From the mid-1540s, again in Paris, Buchanan deepened associations with leading humanists, poets, and patrons such as Théodore de Bèze, Adrien Turnèbe, Lazare de Baïf, and the Cardinal of Lorraine, Charles de Guise. In 1547, Buchanan traveled to Portugal to help found the Real Colégio das Artes in Coimbra. Sadly, the college succumbed to dissension, culminating in an inquiry into the religious beliefs of its faculty. Consequently, Buchanan was arrested by the Lisbon Inquisition in 1550 and confined to the monastery of San Bento. While interned, Buchanan translated many of the Psalms into Latin verse paraphrases, which, over time, he published to sustained acclaim.

After his release in 1552, Buchanan made his way again to Paris with a happiness that he expresses in one of his more sprightly occasional poems, "Adventus in Galliam": "At tu beata Gallia / Salve, bonarum blanda nutrix artium." He taught at the Collège de Boncourt, possibly with Marc-Antoine Muret, and renewed friendships with members of the Pléiade, especially Joachim du Bellay.

In 1558, Buchanan commemorated the marriage of Mary Stuart and the Dauphin François in an epithalamium. Three years later he followed the young, widowed queen home from France and immediately joined the Church of Scotland. Serving Mary as tutor and translator, in 1565 Buchanan wrote poems celebrating her ill-fated marriage to Henry Stuart, Lord Darnley. For the birth of their son James the next year, he composed a "Genethliacon" replete with the prescient exhortations and admonitions of a humanist counselor.

In Scotland, political and educational duties hindered Buchanan's efforts to polish and publish his writings. He was a member of the General Assembly from 1563 to 1567, and in 1566, the earl of Moray nominated him to the principalship of St. Leonard's College. The murder of Darnley and the ensuing deposition of Mary in 1567 made Buchanan propagandist to the Lennox faction. As such, in 1568–1569, he accompanied Regent Moray to England for the conferences held to examine the queen's conduct. These turbulent years produced Buchanan's *Detectio Mariae Reginae Scotorum,* reiterating crimes itemized in the English hearings; *Ane Admonitioun Direct to the Trew Lordis,* warning of the threat posed by the Hamiltons to James VI after Moray's assassination in 1570; and the *Chamaeleon,* a slashing satire on the cunning William Maitland of Lethington. Also in the wake of Moray's murder, the Privy Council directed Buchanan to oversee James VI's education. In 1577, Buchanan published his old school play *Baptistes,* adding an epistle to the young king, pointedly instructing him of the torments suffered by tyrants. A similar dedication prefaces *De jure regni apud Scotos* (1579), written as a dialogue between Buchanan and Thomas Maitland (William's younger brother) in which Buchanan defends the right of the Scottish people to resist tyranny. But as it became apparent that the aging humanist had not reared a philosopher king, Buchanan's dedicatory epistle to his longest and most controversial work, *Rerum Scoticarum Historia* (1582), expresses with little confidence the hope that moral lessons drawn from Scottish history might guide James VI where his tutor's precepts had failed. Samuel Johnson's backhanded tribute—"the only man of greatness his country ever produced"—brings to mind the melancholy mix of achievement and regret that colored Buchanan's life and times.

BIBLIOGRAPHY
Buchanan, George. *Opera Omnia.* Thomas Ruddiman, ed. 1715.
Durkan, John. *Bibliography of George Buchanan.* 1994.
McFarlane, I.D. *Buchanan.* 1981.
Phillips, James E. "George Buchanan and the Sidney Circle." *Huntington Library Quarterly,* vol. 12, pp. 23–55.
Steven Berkowitz

SEE ALSO
Beaton, David; Dunbar, William; Hamilton Family; Maitland Family; Scotland, History of; Mary Queen of Scots

Bullinger, Johann Heinrich (1504–1575)

Born at Bremgarten, near Zurich, on July 18, 1504, Johann Bullinger became a Protestant by reading the works of Martin Luther, Philipp Melanchthon, and Huldrych Zwingli. In 1529, he was appointed pastor of Bremgarten, and after Zwingli's death, succeeded him at Zurich in 1531. In 1549 he coauthored the *Consensus Tigurinus* with John Calvin. This was an agreement between the Zwinglians and the Calvinists on the vexed question of the Lord's Supper. In 1566, at the request of Frederick III, he produced the Second Helvetic Confession, a primarily Calvinist statement of faith that incorporated Zwinglian elements.

Curiously enough, no other continental reformer had as much impact on England as Bullinger had, even though he never left his native Switzerland. He corresponded with Henry VIII, Edward VI, and Elizabeth I, but his main influence was exerted through the returning Marian exiles, many of whom had received his hospitality at Zurich. He was regarded as a moderate Protestant, and his views were eagerly sought by the Elizabethan bishops. The queen herself valued his support; and when she was excommunicated by Pope Pius V (1570), it was to Bullinger that she turned for advice in drafting a reply. Bullinger died at Zurich on September 17, 1575.
Gerald L. Bray

BIBLIOGRAPHY
Harding, T., trans. and ed. *The Decades of Henry Bullinger.* 4 vols. Parker Society. 1849–1852.

SEE ALSO
Calvinism; Eucharist; Lutheranism; Marian Exiles

B

B

Burbage, James (c. 1531–1597)

Actor and theater owner, James Burbage is almost as well remembered for his familial ties as for his own involvement with the theater. Although a joiner by trade, Burbage seems to have turned player early in his life. He was connected with the Earl of Leicester's Men in 1572, 1574, and 1576. In May 1574, his name headed the list of the earl's players in a patent authorizing them to perform throughout the "Realm of England."

In 1576, having borrowed a substantial sum of money from his brother-in-law, John Brayne, Burbage constructed the Theatre in Shoreditch. Brayne's death ten years later prompted several physical confrontations between his widow (accompanied by her supporters) and the Burbage family, all which finally resulted in litigation in Chancery (1590). Margaret Brayne won the suit. Thereafter, Burbage seems to have made his career managing the theatre and planning for a private playhouse in the Blackfriars that he never used during his lifetime. Two sons—Cuthbert and Richard—each lent his own distinctive stamp to theater history. The former was holder of the theatre's lease and a theatrical manager; the latter became the principal actor in Shakespeare's company, the Lord Chamberlain's-King's Men.

Burbage lived most of his life in the parish of St. Leonard's Shoreditch, and he was buried there on February 2, 1597, leaving his wife as executrix of his estate, valued at a modest £37 14d.

BIBLIOGRAPHY

Berry, Herbert. "Handlist of Documents about the Theatre in Shoreditch." In *The First Public Playhouse: The Theatre in Shoreditch, 1576–1598*. Herbert Berry, ed., pp. 97–133. 1979.

Chambers, E.K. *The Elizabethan Stage*. Vol. II., pp. 305–306. 1923.

Ingram, William. "The Early Career of James Burbage." *The Elizabethan Theatre*, vol. 10, pp. 18–36.

Nungezer, Edwin. "James Burbage." In *A Dictionary of Actors*, pp. 66–67. 1929.

S.P. Cerasano

SEE ALSO
Burbage, Richard; Theater Companies, Adult; Theaters

Burbage, Richard (c. 1568–1619)

Actor and younger son of James Burbage, Richard Burbage seems to have been associated with the theater from childhood. It is possible that he was acting minor roles as early as 1584; but he was clearly performing by 1590 when his uncle's widow sued the Burbages for repayment of money that had been borrowed to fund the construction of the Theatre in Shoreditch. It seems to have been during the early 1590s that Richard was brought into contact with William Shakespeare. At Christmas 1594, he was summoned with two other players—Will Kemp and Shakespeare—to perform in several interludes before the queen at Greenwich Palace. Following this, Richard played a prominent part in the Lord Chamberlain's Men, remaining with the company when it obtained a royal patent in 1603 and beyond, to the end of his professional life. Contemporaries concur in assigning to Burbage the roles of Hamlet, King Lear, and Othello; to this some have added Richard III, Romeo, King Gorboduc, and Tereus ("The Plot of the Seven Deadly Sins"), Hieronimo (*The Spanish Tragedy*), and Ferdinand (*The Duchess of Malfi*). Doubtless there were many others; but they are difficult to trace with certainty.

As a servant first of the lord chamberlain and later of James I, Burbage participated frequently in the public life of the court. In 1605, Sir Walter Cope—a close friend of Robert Cecil—wrote to Cecil that Burbage proposed to perform Love's Labours Lost before Queen Anne, and that he had sent the actor to Hatfield (Cecil's home) to learn of his pleasure. On May 31, 1610, Burbage was employed by the city of London to deliver a speech (probably as Amphion, a judicious prophet) to Prince Henry in a water pageant on the Thames. So significant was Burbage's influence that the earl of Pembroke noted, shortly after his death, that he had absented himself from a play at court that "I being tender-hearted could not endure to see so soon after the loss of my old acquaintance Burbage."

Moreover, Burbage was an astute businessman. In addition to holding a half-interest in the Globe (which he apparently shared with his brother Cuthbert and a sister), he inherited the Blackfriars playhouse, a private theater, in 1597, which he leased to Henry Evans, who managed a company of boy actors. This arrangement persisted until August 1608, when a new lease divided the ownership of the playhouse between seven members of the King's Men who performed there sporadically. Additionally, for a few years after the death of James Burbage, Richard and Cuthbert assumed responsibility for the original Theater. Finally, harrassment from Giles Alleyn (the lessor of the property on which the playhouse stood) forced the owners to demolish the playhouse and move it across the Thames to Southwark where it was reconstructed as the first Globe.

In addition to his eminence as an actor Burbage seems to have been a recognized painter. Middleton's epitaph mentions "painting and playing," and Overbury questioned whether Burbage's painting "makes him an excellent player, or his playing an excellent painter." In 1613, Burbage was paid by the earl of Rutland for "painting and making" an heraldic device, Shakespeare being rewarded at the same time for some unspecified assistance he offered on the project. Three years later Rutland again paid Burbage, this time for painting the Earl's "shield and for the emblence." Part of the Cartwright collection, presented to Dulwich College, included "a woman's head on a boord done by Mr. Burbige, ye actor"; and it is likely that the contemporary portrait of Burbage is a self portrait.

Burbage married c. 1601, fathering eight children over the next sixteen years, six of whom died in childhood. The family resided in the parish of St. Leonard's Shoreditch, not far from the original Theater that his father had built. In fact, Burbage seems to have lived, for most of his life, in the same house in Holywell Street that his father owned.

Burbage was buried in March 1619, leaving £300 (according to gossip and letter writer John Chamberlain). Myriad epitaphs were written to memorialize him, many of which suggest biographical elements that are largely unprovable: that Burbage was short and fat; that he performed the roles of Edward II, Edward III, Vendice (*The Revenger's Tragedy*), Brachiano (*The White Devil*), and Frankford (*A Woman Killed with Kindness*); that he was paralyzed shortly before death. The shortest epitaph (and possibly the wittiest) was simply "Exit Burbage."

Nonetheless, much commentary, written both during his life and afterward, attests to Burbage's stature as an eminent tragedian. The characterizations of him in several actors' wills (including Augustine Phillips, William Shakespeare, and Nicholas Tooley, one of his apprentices) would lead historians to conclude that he was valued not only as a professional but also as a mentor and friend.

BIBLIOGRAPHY

Chambers, E.K. *The Elizabethan Stage.* vol. II., pp. 306–310. 1923.

Nungezer, Edwin. "Richard Burbage." In *A Dictionary of Actors.*, pp. 67–79. 1929.

S.P. Cerasano

SEE ALSO
Actors; Burbage, James; Kemp, Will; Shakespeare, William; Theater Companies, Adult; Theaters

Burleigh, Lord
See Cecil, William

Byrd, William (1543–1623)

William Byrd is considered by many to be foremost among the composers who produced works during the reigns of Elizabeth I and James I. The remarkable range and versatility of his creative talents have led many to consider him a pivotal figure, who was at once the last great composer in the long-lived tradition of Catholic polyphonic music in Britain, and the first composer of what is now considered the "golden age of music"—a period of superlative British music making that begins about midway through the rule of Elizabeth I.

Byrd's musical talents were well recognized early on. In 1563, just twenty years old, he was appointed organist and master of the choristers at Lincoln Cathedral, a position he retained until he was installed as a gentleman of the Chapel Royal in the early 1570s. It is believed that in 1572 Byrd received an extra appointment to the Chapel Royal, making him joint organist with Thomas Tallis.

Byrd's rapid rise through the ranks is aptly demonstrated by the royal license to publish music granted jointly to both him and Tallis, which assured them a monopoly on printing music in England. Their initial publication, the *Cantiones sacrae* (1575), was the first Latin church music to be published in England, and comprises the first works to be published by these two composers.

William Byrd, the great composer of the "golden age of music" during the Tudor era. Illustration reproduced by permission of the British Museum.

B

In 1593, Byrd moved to Stondon Massey in Essex near a Catholic community centered around the Petres of Ingatestone Hall. A committed lifelong Catholic, Byrd composed his Latin music for noble Catholic patrons such as Edward Paston, who continued to celebrate the Roman Catholic rite on their country estates. It was for them presumably that Byrd composed his three Mass Ordinary settings, one each for three, four, and five voices. Entirely original (not parody masses), they were printed between 1593 and 1595; the final Agnus Dei of the four-voice Mass, with its series of suspensions, is one of Byrd's most inspired works. His two volumes of *Gradualia,* which contain settings of the Proper for celebration of both the Mass and Offices, consist of one hundred items of motet sections. Byrd followed the reformed Roman Missal of 1570 and organized *Gradualia* according to a complex "cut-and-paste" scheme in which recurring texts are always sung to the same music. Crafted in intricate polyphony on an elaborate scale, these volumes are viewed as the most important contribution of this type since Heinrich Isaac's *Choralis Constantinus,* published some fifty years earlier.

The three volumes of *Cantiones sacrae* (1575, also including compositions by Thomas Tallis; 1589; and 1591) are collections of Latin motets, although not explicitly tied to the Roman Catholic liturgy. In these pieces Byrd adopted a more flexible approach toward imitative part-writing through the use of a less symmetrical patterning of voice entries and more subtle treatment of texture, which allowed him to craft his contrapuntal melodies in a more complex and interesting way. Byrd considerably extended the horizons of British music in the late sixteenth century through these freer techniques of polyphonic writing.

Three publications from the late 1580s comprise secular vocal music mixed with religious music to vernacular texts. *Psalmes, Sonets, & Songs of Sadnes and pietie of 1588,* and *Songs of sundrie natures and Psalmes, Songs, and Sonnets: some solemne, others joyfull,* both of 1589, all demonstrate a certain resistance to the importation of Italian madrigal style (*Come woeful Orpheus* from the last-named print might be a parody of the late Italian chromatic madrigal). Some of the most memorable selections from these prints, like his elegy *Ye sacred muses* on the death of his mentor, Thomas Tallis, are consort songs for solo voice and four viols. In others, such as *Though Amaryllis daunce in green,* Byrd adapted the viol parts for voices.

Byrd also contributed substantially to the development of keyboard music, which he composed in a variety of styles ranging from rich contrapuntal imitation inspired by the sacred polyphonic vocal styles then current to the more simple ornamented melody supported by chordal accompaniment favored for dance music. Pieces like his *Quadran Paven and Galliard* bring together into a single piece the breadth of his stylistic capabilities. His works survive in many manuscripts, but are notably gathered in *My Ladye Nevells Booke (1591), Parthenia or the Maydenhead of the First Musicke that Ever was Printed for the Virginalls* (1612), and in the comprehensive anthology *The Fitzwilliam Virginal Book* (1609–1619). Along with John Bull and Orlando Gibbons, Byrd created the highly stylized and mature keyboard music that brought dance music to an artistic climax during the reign of Queen Elizabeth I.

BIBLIOGRAPHY

Brett, Philip, gen. ed. *The Byrd edition.* 1976.

Fellowes, Edmund H., ed.; revised by Thurston Dart, Philip Brett, and Kenneth Elliott. *The Collected Works of William Byrd.* 1937–1971.

Howes, Frank. *William Byrd.* 1928.

Kerman, Joseph. *The Masses and motets of William Byrd.* 1981.

Neighbour, Oliver. *The Consort and Keyboard Music of William Byrd.* 1978.

Turbet, Richard. *William Byrd, a Guide to Research.* Garland Composer Resource Manuals, vol. 7. 1987.

Joseph C. Morin

SEE ALSO

Consort and Consort Song; Keyboard Music; Madrigal; Motet; Tallis, Thomas

C

Cabot, John (c. 1450–1498)

Italian merchant and explorer John Cabot made three important voyages from Bristol during the 1490s in search of a western route to Cathay that subsequently gave England a claim to the discovery of North America. Before arriving in Bristol in 1494 or 1495, Cabot traded extensively in the Mediterranean, settling in Spain about 1490, where he acquired renown as a cartographer and navigator. Failure to obtain support for a western voyage led him to Bristol, where the search for new fishing grounds was stimulating interest in Atlantic venturing. On March 5, 1496, Cabot and his three sons received a patent from Henry VII authorizing them to search for land in the west not held by a Christian ruler.

Cabot's first voyage, probably in 1496, was a failure. In 1497, sailing in the *Matthew* of fifty tons, Cabot crossed the Atlantic, making landfall either at Newfoundland or Cape Breton, which he claimed for Henry VII. He returned to England claiming that he had discovered the northern regions of Cathay. He also brought news of the rich fishing grounds off Newfoundland. Feted as a hero in London, Cabot received a gift of £10 and a pension of £20 a year from the king, who agreed to support another voyage. Cabot's last voyage, of 1498, made up of a fleet of five ships, was a disaster. Some ships may have crossed the Atlantic, but Cabot never returned to England, presumably perishing at sea. Cabot's death was a setback to further exploration in the North Atlantic. But his voyage of 1497, the first recorded English crossing of the Atlantic, was a landmark in maritime enterprise. His landfall was used later in the sixteenth century by colonial enthusiasts, such as Richard Hakluyt, to justify an English claim to the discovery of North America that served to legitimize colonization.

BIBLIOGRAPHY

Andrews, K.R. *Trade, Plunder and Settlement: Maritime Enterprise and the Genesis of the British Empire, 1480–1630.* 1984.

Williamson, J.A., ed. *The Cabot Voyages and Bristol Discovery Under Henry VII.* 1962.

John C. Appleby

SEE ALSO

Cabot, Sebastian; Colonial Development; Discovery and Exploration; Hakluyt, Richard

Cabot, Sebastian (c. 1482–1557)

The Italian explorer and cartographer Sebastian Cabot played a significant role in English maritime enterprise during the early sixteenth century, though the little evidence that survives of his career has caused considerable confusion concerning the nature of his achievement. From 1501 to 1505, he was involved with a group of Bristol and Portuguese merchants in setting out ventures to Newfoundland that combined fishing and trading with exploration. In 1508, Cabot probably led an expedition across the Atlantic in search of the Northwest Passage. Apparently his crew forced him to turn back, although he managed to complete a coasting voyage along the eastern shore of North America that went some way toward confirming and defining its continental character. Failing to get support for another voyage, in 1512, Cabot moved to Spain

C

where he was employed as a pilot in the king's service. His return to London in 1521, in an unsuccessful attempt to revive interest in the Northwest Passage, was short-lived.

In 1548, Cabot returned to England, becoming closely involved in the search for new trades. He may have been instrumental in developing English trade with Barbary and Guinea during the 1550s. He revived interest in the search for a northern passage to Cathay. In 1553, he played a leading role in the establishment of a company for the discovery of new trades, drawing up instructions for an expedition set out later in the year to search for a northeast passage. As governor of the newly incorporated Muscovy Company in 1555, Cabot continued to foster hopes of finding a northern route to Asia. Despite the failure of these hopes, and a tendency to inflate his own importance, Cabot played an important part in the diversification of English commercial and maritime enterprise at a critical time in its development.

BIBLIOGRAPHY

Andrews, K.R. *Trade, Plunder and Settlement: Maritime Enterprise and the Genesis of the British Empire, 1480–1630.* 1984.
Ruddock, A.A. "The reputation of Sebastian Cabot." *Bulletin of the Institute of Historical Research,* vol. 47, pp. 95–99.

John C. Appleby

SEE ALSO
Cabot, John; Discovery and Exploration

CAIUS, JOHN
See Medicine and Health

Calendar, Church

The church calendar marks the annual observance of major Christian feasts, fasts, and saints' days. The one adopted by the Church of England during the sixteenth century is a revision of the Western Roman tradition and was inseparably bound up with the various editions of the Book of Common Prayer (1549, 1552, and 1559).

The early Christian calendar stemmed directly from that of Judaism. Christians replaced the Jewish Sabbath with the first day of the week as the day of rest and worship in commemoration of Christ's resurrection having occurred on that day.

The early Christian liturgical year consisted of three unitive festivals: Epiphany, Easter, and Pentecost. Celebrating Christ's resurrection, Easter was the first to emerge and constituted a transformation of the Jewish *Pasch* (Passover). Commemorating the sending of the Holy Spirit fifty days after Easter, Pentecost was second to emerge and constituted a transformation of the Jewish Pentecost. The third, Epiphany, commemorated the Incarnation and constituted a transformation of ancient pagan rituals associated with the winter solstice.

In the fourth century, three new festivals were established—Christmas, Good Friday, and Ascension Day. These six early festivals of Christmas (December 25), Epiphany (January 6), Good Friday, Easter, Ascension, and Pentecost constitute the permanent structure of the church calendar.

The calendar begins with the season of Advent (the four Sundays before Christmas). The twelve days of Christmas are followed by Epiphany, and Sundays are reckoned "after Epiphany" until Septuagesima (seventieth), Sexagesima (sixtieth), and Quinquagesima (fiftieth), which receive their names from the approximate number of days before Easter. Ash Wednesday introduces the forty days of Lent with its six Sundays, and the five Sundays after Easter lead up to Ascension Day and Pentecost (or Whitsunday), the end of Eastertide. The Roman Catholic Church numbers the Sundays from Pentecost to Advent "after Pentecost," but the Church of England reckons these days after Trinity Sunday, which is observed the first Sunday following Pentecost. Sundays after Trinity continue until the first Sunday in Advent, when the church calendar begins anew.

During the Middle Ages, additional feasts multiplied so greatly that there was by the sixteenth century widespread demand for reform. The number of holy days were accordingly reduced in the Prayer Books of 1549 and 1552; only New Testament saints were acknowledged in addition to the recognition of All Saints on November 1. In 1567, some sixty-seven more holy days were added to the calendar of the Prayer Book, consisting for the most part of saints of the early, undivided church, with the addition of a number of illustrious English men and women.

BIBLIOGRAPHY

Cressy, David. *Bonfires and Bells: National Memory and the Protestant Calendar in Elizabethan and Stuart England.* 1989.
Gibbs, Lee W. *Holy Days and Holidays.* 1995.
Hatchett, Marion J. *Sanctifying Life, Time and Space: An Introduction to Liturgical Study.* 1976.

McArthur, A. Allan. *The Evolution of the Christian Year.* 1953.

Price, Charles P., and Louis Weil. *Liturgy for Living.* 1979.

Shepherd, Massey Hamilton, Jr. *The Oxford American Prayer Book Commentary.* 1959.

Lee W. Gibbs

SEE ALSO

Book of Common Prayer; Calendar, Secular; Folklore and Folk Rituals

Calendar, Secular

Throughout the Tudor period the calendar of secular events—the legal "terms" and popular holidays, commercial and agricultural schedules—was still interwoven with the liturgical year. However, the Tudor sense of calendar changed as the century progressed. A calendar that celebrated religious festivals, holy days, and saints' days was gradually succeeded by one celebrating royal and civic occasions, such as entries, triumphs, and pageants. Thus, the festive observance of Elizabeth's accession was observed on November 17, and Elizabeth's birthday, September 17, actually displaced the old feast of the Blessed Virgin's nativity.

Other calendar systems also competed in Europe and in England during the Tudor period. Because the Julian calendar was never synchronized with the "tropical" or solar year, Pope Gregory XIII instituted in 1582 a reform of the Julian calendar in which ten days were subtracted from October and leap days were established to avoid quadrennial discrepancies. England, however, like most Protestant nations, resisted this reform until the middle of the eighteenth century. As a consequence, England's official correspondence to the Continent from Elizabeth's reign onward was given double dates (December 12/22, 1635, for example) to avoid confusion. The "Old Style" calendar, generally instituted in Europe between the ninth and the thirteenth centuries, also began the new year not with January 1, but with the feast of the Annunciation or "Lady Day," March 25. In England, this calendrical practice remained generally in force until the official adoption of the "New Style" Gregorian calendar in 1752. Ben Jonson, however, contrary to usual practice even in the seventeenth century, dates some, and possibly all, of his dramatic productions in the 1616 folio edition of his dramatic works by the New Style. Although historians usually silently modernize Old Style datings, dates from January 1 through March 24 are often rendered using the competing years, such as 1593/94.

BIBLIOGRAPHY

Adams, Robert M. *The Land and Literature of England.* 1983.

Chambers, E.K. *The Elizabethan Stage.* 4 vols. 1923.

Cheney, C.R. *Handbook of Dates.* 1945.

Cressy, David. *Bonfires and Bells: National Memory and the Protestant Calendar in Elizabethan and Stuart England.* 1989.

Macey, Robert, ed. *Encyclopedia of Time.* 1994.

Strong, Roy. *Art and Power: Renaissance Festivals, 1450–1650.* 1984.

Wright, A.R. *British Calendar Customs.* 3 vols. 1936–1940.

R. Chris Hassell

SEE ALSO

Accession Day; Calendar, Church; Folklore and Folk Rituals

Calvinism

Calvinism is an ambiguous term sometimes used to designate the teaching of the French and Swiss reformer, John Calvin (1509–1564), and at other times used to designate more broadly the doctrinal system confessed by that body of Protestant churches known historically, in distinction from the Lutheran churches, as the "reformed" churches, whose greatest exponent and systematic theologian was Calvin. Calvinism in this latter sense spread outward from Switzerland to France, and along the Rhine through Germany to Holland, eastward to Bohemia and Hungary, and westward, across the channel, to Great Britain. It was a powerful movement in Scotland, especially through the advocacy of John Knox and Andrew Melville; the Scottish Reformation was predominantly Calvinist in its second and definitive phase. In the Church of England during the latter half of the sixteenth and the beginning of the seventeenth century, Calvinist doctrine was widely allied with an episcopalian form of church polity; both the Thirty-nine Articles and the Lambeth Articles were moderately Calvinist. The teachings of Calvin molded the theology *and* the polity of the Elizabethan Puritans.

The foundation of Calvinism as a theological system was elaborated chiefly in Calvin's *Institutes of the Christian Religion,* published first in 1536. His intention was to produce a persuasive apology for Protestantism as well as a coherent and

C

systematic summary of the teachings of Scripture as a whole. Throughout the rest of his life, up to the time of the fourth definitive Latin edition of 1559, Calvin amplified, revised, and polished his treatise, until it became the first major systematic presentation of Reformation theology.

The central theological idea of Calvin was the sovereignty and glory of God; predestination, whether in a supra- or infralapsarian form of God's election of sinners either to salvation or reprobation, was a corollary, not the primary focus of his theology. His emphasis on the divine omnipotence and will of God revealed the strong influence of medieval theological voluntarism (Duns Scotus) and nominalism (William of Ockham). Calvin was at one with Luther on the central tenets of the Reformation (Scripture alone as the only authority for faith and morals, justification by grace through faith alone, the priesthood of all believers, and Christian vocation), but parted company with Luther over the presence of Christ in the Lord's Supper. Calvin's "virtualist" or "receptionist" view of the real presence has not unjustly been described as an attempted compromise between Luther's doctrine of consubstantiation on the one side and Huldrych Zwingli's symbolic interpretation on the other.

Calvinism as a doctrinal system also included the structure of church order into synods and presbyteries, generally called "presbyterianism." Calvin at times in his *Institutes* seems to go beyond Luther by adding "discipline" or church polity to preaching the Word and the administration of the two sacraments—Baptism and Eucharist—as a "third mark or sign" of the true church. Around 1570, Calvin's incipient Presbyterian polity had been elaborated and elevated to the rank of a dogma by Theodore Beza, Calvin's successor at Geneva. Beza had clarified his views with specific reference to affairs in England and Scotland, where the reformed churches were peculiar in their retention of forms of episcopal government. In a letter of 1572, which became a kind of charter for the Scottish Presbyterians, Beza warned of the evils the church would suffer if it entertained "pseudoepiscopi," the dregs of the papacy. Some of his later writings asserted that the Elizabethan episcopate was "of man" and not "of God," and even implied that it was "devilish."

Beza's doctrine was absorbed at the Geneva Academy by an international band of scholars, which in 1571 included the Englishmen Thomas Cartwright and Walter Travers and the Scot Andrew Melville. These men returned to their respective countries to assume the leadership of kindred Presbyterian movements.

Presbyterianism is usually said to have made its first appearance in the series of academic lectures delivered at Cambridge in the spring of 1570 by Thomas Cartwright, then newly elected Lady Margaret professor of divinity. The controversial material in Cartwright's lectures was contained in his exposition of the model of the primitive church from the first two chapters of Acts. To apply these standards to the contemporary situation was to call for the abolition of the names and offices of archbishops, bishops, deans, and archdeacons, and for the reduction of the ministry to the apostolic offices of pastor and deacon; and to suggest that the government of the church should be restored from the usurpation of bishops' and archdeacons' officials to the minister and presbytery of every local church, and that a minister should be elected by his congregation and subsequently linked to it indissolubly. In the midst of the furor his lectures incited, he was ejected from his chair (at the end of 1570) and withdrew to Geneva.

Shortly thereafter, Walter Travers wrote the first definitive treatment of Presbyterian government, *Ecclesiasticae disciplinae . . . explicatio,* which was published simultaneously in English (translated by Thomas Cartwright) as *A full and plaine declaration of ecclesiastical discipline* in 1574.

The Elizabethan Puritans led by Cartwright and Travers agreed that spiritual and moral discipline could be rightly administered in the local church only by means of a congregational consistory, conceived as a kind of court composed of the pastor and the lay officers called elders, and in some measure representative of and responsible to the congregation. The Presbyterians insisted on the absolute necessity of this institution as alone embodying New Testament discipline, which was for them an indispensable mark of a true church.

Hitherto, congregational discipline had not been thought incompatible with the higher government of the church by Christian magistrates or bishops. The Presbyterians condemned both out of hand. The rule of magistrates was excluded by the distinction of church and commonwealth as two separate, if interdependent, spheres of authority. The rule of bishops was dismissed by claiming on biblical authority the parity of both congregations and pastors. The subordination of one church or of one minister to another was condemned by arguments closely related to those the first generation of Protestants had deployed against the primacy of the bishop of Rome.

In practice, presbyterianism differed from other polities, not so much at the congregational level as in the method it prescribed for the federation of individual congregations in the fabric of the wider church. In place of the rule of magistrates or bishops, it provided a graduated series of representative assemblies: at the lowest level was a meeting called a *classis,* composed of the ministers and elders of the churches of a convenient division (the *colloque* of French and the *presbytery* of Scottish Calvinism). Above the *classis* were provincial *synods* and national *general assemblies.* The distinguishing marks of presbyterianism are the *classis,* and the rotation of the presiding office of moderator within its membership. These institutions preserved the principle of parity and so distinguished the system from any kind of episcopal or quasi-episcopal polity. On the other hand, the power of the *classis* over the local churches, and authority residing in the ordained ministry, separated presbyterianism from the purely congregational form of church order.

Initial drafts of *The Book of Discipline* were written in 1585 and 1586; the version endorsed by the Westminster Assembly in 1644 dates from the early months of 1587. This book provided for the conduct of public worship according to the Genevan pattern, including preaching, catechizing, administering the sacraments, marriage, the maintenance and training of divinity students, and for congregational discipline, including the distribution of authority within the congregation and the mutual rights and duties of the congregations and the higher Presbyterian assemblies.

These Presbyterian notions were deeply subversive of the Erastian, monarchical constitution of the Elizabethan church and of the political structure of the Tudor state, undermining as they did all established hierarchies. They were accordingly opposed by Elizabeth, and in the last years of her reign the Presbyterians were in a radical state of decline. The dashing of Puritan hopes by James I at Hampton Court in 1604 was the final chapter in the history of the Elizabethan Puritans and of their largely abortive sixteenth-century movement for further reformation of the Church of England according to Calvinist principles.

BIBLIOGRAPHY

Bouwsma, William J. *John Calvin: A Sixteenth-Century Portrait.*1988.

Collinson, Patrick. *The Elizabethan Puritan Movement.* 1967.

Dakan, A. *Calvinism.* 1940.

Lake, Peter. *Anglicans and Puritans? Presbyterianism and English Conformist Thought from Whitgift to Hooker.* 1988.

McNeill, John T. *The History and Character of Calvinism.* 1954.

Prestwich, Menna, ed. *International Calvinism, 1541–1715.* 1985.

Wendel, François. *Calvin: The Origins and Development of His Religious Thought.* 1950; Philip Miret, trans. 1963.

Lee W. Gibbs

SEE ALSO

Articles of Religion; Church of England; Church Polity; Erastianism; Eucharist; Knox, John; Lambeth Articles; Lutheranism; Melville, Andrew; Puritanism; Sacraments; Travers, Walter

Cambridge University
See Universities

Camden, William (1551–1623)

The son of a member of the Painter-Stainers' Company, William Camden was educated in London, perhaps beginning at Christ's Hospital, certainly finishing at St. Paul's School. His poverty was such that he needed patronage to attend Oxford; the young Camden was fortunate in being taken up first by the chronicler Dr. Thomas Cooper, fellow of Magdalen College, Oxford, ultimately bishop of Winchester, and then by Dr. Thomas Thornton, fellow of Broadgates Hall (now Pembroke College), whom he followed to Christ Church College. Among Thornton's other pupils was Philip Sidney, with whom Camden struck up a friendship; and Camden also made the acquaintance of Richard Carew, the future author of the antiquarian *Survey of Cornwall.* Camden's efforts to remain in Oxford were frustrated when for religious reasons he was denied a fellowship at All Souls' College, Oxford; he left the university in 1571 without obtaining a degree. Encouraged by noble friends such as Sidney and the Goodman brothers, Camden seems to have spent the next several years exploring England until, in 1575, he procured the post of under master at Westminster School in London. For a time, Camden put his scholarly ambitions aside, but a visit to London by the great Flemish mapmaker and antiquary Abraham Ortelius rekindled his enthusiasm, with the result that *Britannia* came from the press in 1586.

Britannia was the first example in England of a new genre called chorography, the object of which was to

C

paint the true likeness of the place under discussion. For Camden, this meant adding an historical dimension to the geographical. At the foundation of Camden's book was a description of the Roman province of Britannia, based on a careful scrutiny of the all the documents concerning Britain surviving from ancient times. In addition, Camden studied the remaining traces of the Roman settlement by walking along the Roman roads, looking at ruins and inscriptions, even making use of such seemingly modern techniques as cropmarks. On top of this base, Camden drew a series of overlays, describing the various invaders of the Britanno-Roman island, a task that involved him in learning Welsh and Old English; then, dividing the counties of England into groups roughly by their place in the ancient British kingdoms, he carefully examined the whole of the British Isles. To the description of each spot, he added an account of its history, ending with notes on the great families whose seats had adorned the place. The book was an instant success, at home and abroad. The London edition of 1586 was followed by those of 1587, 1590, 1594, 1600, and 1607, each an enlargement of its predecessor; there was an edition in Frankfort in 1590; and Camden's friend, Philemon Holland, translated the work into English in 1610 (reprinted with additions, 1637). The constant enlargements were the result not only of further field trips, some done in the company of his friend, Robert Cotton, but also of contributions by a growing number of local antiquaries.

Patronage followed success: Camden was given the prebend of Ilfracombe in 1588 and became head of Westminster School in 1593; in 1597, Fulke Greville, Sidney's friend, procured for Camden the post of Clarenceux king-at-arms, a senior position in the College of Arms, which freed him from schoolteaching—though not before Camden had rewritten the school's Greek grammar textbook in a form that was to dominate English pedagogy for several centuries. Also during the years following the publication of the first *Britannia*, Camden took a leading part in the newly established Society of Antiquaries; those of his studies "left over" from papers contributed to the society and from the *Britannia* were published as *Remains of a greater work concerning Britain* (1605 and following). Then, to ease the work of his successors, he edited a series of chronicles of medieval Britain (Frankfort, 1602).

Camden had all along received help from Elizabeth I's chief minister, William Cecil, Lord Burghley, and it was this patron who placed on him the burden of writing a history of her reign. Burghley supplied Camden with documents; additionally, Camden learned a good deal about how to analyze political problems from a careful scrutiny of Burghley's memoranda. The great minister's death in 1598 suspended the project; it was restored to life by the importunate demands of James I, who wanted to have available a history exculpating his mother, Mary Queen of Scots. Camden published the first three books of the *Annales*—the section up to 1589—in 1615, but the political pressures had been so severe that he refused to send any more to the printers during his lifetime. To protect the text, he sent it for safety to a friend in France. The complete *Annales* were thus not published until 1625, the same year that saw the appearance of a translation of Books I–III. The remainder followed shortly thereafter.

Camden spent the last years of his life in retirement, keeping up a heavy correspondence with English scholars who were, quite commonly, his disciples, and with his great scholarly contemporaries on the Continent. He devoted most of his estate to the establishment of a chair of history at Oxford, surviving to this day. Camden's influence on his successors was so pervasive that it is hard to measure. Certainly, *Britannia* established the study of British antiquities so firmly that, for several centuries, progress in the discipline could be measured by the yardstick of new, totally reedited versions of the great classic, while the authority of his history of Elizabeth has so dominated the subject that serious questioning of his opinions has only just begun.

BIBLIOGRAPHY

Camden, William. *Britannia sive florentissimorum regnorum Anglicae, Scotiae, Hiberniae chorographica descriptio.* R. Gough, ed. 3 vols., 1789; 4 vols., 1806.

———. *Annales rerum anglicarum et hibernicarum regnante Elizabetha.* W.T. MacCaffrey, ed. and abbrev. 1970.

———. *Remaines of a greater worke concerning Britaine* (1605). H. Morley, ed., 1870, 1974; R.D. Dunn, ed., 1984.

———. *V. Cl. Gulielmi Camdeni epistolae.* Thomas Smith, ed. 1691.

———. *Poems by William Camden.* George Burke Johnston, ed. Texts and Studies. *Studies in Philology,* vol. 72. 1975.

Fussner, F. Smith. *The Historical Revolution.* Chap. 9. 1962.

Levy, F.J. *Tudor Historical Thought,* pp. 148–161, 279–285. 1967.

McGurk, John. "William Camden: Civil Historian or Gloriana's Propagandist?" *History Today,* vol. 38, April 1988, pp. 47–53.

Piggott, Stuart. *William Camden and the* Britannia. Reckitt Archaeological Lecture, 1957; repr. with alterations in *Ruins in a Landscape,* pp. 33–53. 1976.

Trevor-Roper, H.R. *Queen Elizabeth's First Historian.* Neale Lectures in English History. 1971.

Woolf, D.R. *The Idea of History in Early Stuart England,* pp. 115–25. 1990.

F. J. Levy

SEE ALSO

Antiquarianism; Carew, Richard; Cecil, William; Cooper, Thomas; Greville, Fulke; History, Writing of

Campion, Edmund (1540–1581)

Jesuit priest, English missionary, and Catholic martyr, Edmund Campion was born in 1540, the son of a London bookseller. At age fifteen, after completing schooling at Christ's Hospital in London, he attended St. John's College, Oxford, becoming a junior fellow in 1557 and earning the B.A. in 1561 and the M.A. in 1564. In 1568, he served as a junior proctor of the university. That same year he accepted ordination as a deacon in the Anglican Church, while keeping private his Catholic sympathies.

Campion demonstrated his gift of eloquence at an early age. He was selected to give the address of welcome on the occasion of Mary I's entry into London in 1553. At Oxford, other scholars deliberately mimicked his oratorical style. In 1566, he gave the address welcoming Queen Elizabeth to Oxford, and, in her presence, took part in a Latin disputation. The performance won him the queen's admiration and the patronage of Robert Dudley, earl of Leicester, and Sir William Cecil, Lord Burghley.

Unable to reconcile his private Catholic faith with his public Anglican profession, Campion left Oxford in 1569 for Ireland. There he became involved in the project of James Stanihurst for the restoration of a Catholic university in Dublin. The project never came to fruition, but Campion's role in so blatant a papist scheme made him a wanted man. He went into hiding, where he wrote his *History of Ireland,* which was published later as part of Raphael Holinshed's *Chronicles.* Returning secretly to London in June 1571, Campion witnessed the trial and execution of Dr. John Storey, the English Catholic expatriate who was kidnapped from Antwerp, tortured, and put to death out of spite. Campion decided at this time that he would go abroad to Douai.

Formally reconciled with the Catholic Church, Campion took the B.D. degree from the English College, and, in 1572, went on pilgrimage to Rome. He entered the Society of Jesus the following year. After serving his noviate at Brhnn in Moravia, he taught at the Jesuit school in Prague. He was ordained a priest in 1578. Two years later, at the request of William Allen, Fr. Everard Mercurian, the vicar-general of the Society of Jesus, selected Campion to join Fr. Robert Parsons and Ralph Emerson on the first Jesuit mission to England.

On the night of June 25, 1580, Campion, disguised as a jewel merchant, crossed with Emerson to Dover. He was detained briefly, but then made his way to London, to the house of Thomas Jay in Chancery Lane, where he waited for Parsons, who had arrived in England a week earlier. Elizabeth's government, alert to the mission of the Jesuits, began searching for Campion and Parsons. The two men left London to avoid capture. Before departing, Campion, at the request of Thomas Pounde, wrote his "Challenge to the Privy Council," which asserted the purely spiritual purpose of the mission to English Catholics in refutation of the charge that the Jesuits were agents of treason.

Campion, traveling incognito to the homes of Catholics throughout the Midlands, Lancashire, and Yorkshire, preached, celebrated Mass, and administered the Sacraments. As his fame spread, the government intensified the hunt for him. It sought to discredit him in a reply to his letter, written by William Charke, entitled *The Great Bragge and Challenge of M. Campion* (1581). The severe anti-Catholic legislation introduced in the Parliament of 1581 was in part a response to the prominence of Campion and Parsons.

An underground press set up by Parsons printed hastily in June 1581 Campion's *Decem Rationes,* a learned and eloquent Latin summation of Catholic doctrine and a challenge to Anglican divines to a debate. Copies of it appeared at an Oxford University commemoration service on June 27.

The following month, George Eliot, a priest-hunter who had infiltrated a Catholic household at Lyford, alerted local magistrates to Campion's presence. He was captured on July 17, along with several other seminary priests. Queen Elizabeth offered Campion pardon and favor if he would renounce Catholicism. He refused. Racked several times, Campion did not give direct evidence of any treason, but he revealed the names of those

C

who had helped him. In September, the government, hoping to discredit the Jesuit, selected some Anglican clergy to dispute publicly with him, forgetting Campion's skills at debate and oratory. The debate was called off after four sessions. Campion was tortured on the rack a second time in October, and then indicted for offenses under the treason law of Edward III. He was unable to raise his right hand to enter his plea at his arraignment on November 14. His trial was a mockery; the verdict a foregone conclusion. A large crowd stood in the rain to witness his execution at Tyburn on December 1. Campion was allowed the privilege of dying from hanging before he was disemboweled. Pope Leo XIII beatified him in 1886.

BIBLIOGRAPHY

Basset, Bernard. *The English Jesuits from Campion to Martindale.* 1967.

Challoner, Richard. *Memoirs of Missionary Priests.* John H. Pollen, ed. 1924.

Foley, Henry. *Records of the English Province of the Society of Jesus.* Vol. 1, 1877; vol. 3, 1878; vol. 7:1, 1882.

Hughes, Philip. *Rome and the Counter-Reformation.* 1942.

———. *The Reformation in England.* Vol 3: "True Religion Now Established." 1954.

McGrath, Patrick. *Papists and Puritans under Elizabeth I.* 1967.

Meyer, Arnold O. *England and the Catholic Church under Queen Elizabeth.* J.R. Mckee, trans. 1915.

More, Henry. "Historia Provinciae Anglicanae Societatis Jesu." In *The Elizabethan Jesuits.* Francis Edwards, ed. 1981.

Pollen, John H. *The English Catholics in the Reign of Queen Elizabeth.* 1920.

Reynolds, E.E. *Campion and Parsons: The Jesuit Mission of 1580–81.* 1980.

Simpson, Richard. *Edmund Campion.* 1867.

Waugh, Evelyn. *Edmund Campion.* 1935.

John M. Currin

SEE ALSO
Jesuits; Parsons, Robert

Campion, Thomas (1567–1620)

A physician, theorist, and poet, Thomas Campion was the composer of 119 lute songs. On April 27, 1586, he was admitted to Gray's Inn, one of the Inns of Court whose members presented plays and masques before distinguished audiences, including Elizabeth I and then James I. By 1595, his reputation as a poet was firmly established with the publication of his Latin poems, *Thomae Campiani poemata.* His friend Philip Rosseter published *A Booke of Ayres* in London in 1601, fully half of the collection (twenty-one songs) consisting of Campion's songs. The following year, a treatise expounding his theories of poetic structure and meters, *Observations in the Art of English Poesie,* was published, provoking Samuel Daniel to reply with a treatise of his own in 1603. His musical treatise, *A New Way of making Fowre Parts in Counter-point, by a most Familiar, and Infallible Rule,* was published a decade later, probably in 1613 or 1614. Reacting to the stylistic changes of the late Renaissance and early baroque era, Campion observed that the bass, rather than the tenor, provides the foundation on which "any man at the first sight may view in it all the other parts."

In 1606, called for the first time "Doctor of Physick," Campion contributed a poem to Barnabe Barnes's *Four Bookes of Offices.* Although his interest in medicine may have been stimulated by earlier studies at Peterhouse, Cambridge, he took his M.D. degree in February of 1605 at the University of Caen. That the air "Come let us sound with melodie" from the 1601 print imitates the procedures of *musique mesurée à l'antique* suggests that he kept abreast with contemporary French music.

From at least 1607 on, Campion provided both words and music for royal court masques. Surviving examples include *The Discription of a Maske, presented before the Kinges Majestie at White-Hall, on Twelfth Night* of 1607, *The Lords Maske,* and *The Masque of Squires.* However, most of his songs were gathered together in *Two Bookes of Ayres* of 1613 or 1614, and *The Third and Fourth Booke of Ayres* of 1617 or 1618, each printed in one volume. Alto, tenor, and bass voices were printed with many of these songs, but it is more likely that solo voice with a lute playing of the three lower voices comprised the usual performing ensemble.

Because Campion composed to his own poetry and was so sensitive to meter, his melodies match more finely than most with the rhythm and meaning of his verse. "See where she flies" from *A Booke of Ayres,* "Author of light" from *Two Bookes of Ayres,* and "Kinde are her answeres" from *The Third Booke* are excellent examples of the rhythmic flexibility and melodic sensitivity of his best work. In his call for a new edition, Christopher Wilson notes that the ideal editor should possess the "Renaissance diversity" in poetry, theory composition, Latin, and the court masque that are so abundantly evident in Campion's works.

BIBLIOGRAPHY

Davis, Walter R. *Thomas Campion.* 1987.

————, ed. *Thomas Campion: Complete Songs, Masques, and Treatises with a Selection of the Latin Verses.* 1967.

Fellowes, Edmund Horace, ed. Revised by Thurston Dart. *The English School of Lutenist Song Writers,* series 1: 1–2, 13, and series 2: 10–11.

Greer, David. "Campion the Musician." *Lute Society Journal,* vol. 9, pp. 7–16.

Lowbury, Edward. *Thomas Campion: Poet, Composer, Physician.* 1970.

Pilkington, Michael. *Campion, Dowland and the Lutenist Songwriters.* 1989.

Ratcliffe, Stephen. *Campion, on Song.* 1981.

Sabol, Andrew J. *Four Hundred Songs and Dances from the Stuart Masque: with a Supplement of Sixteen Additional Pieces.* 1982.

Vivian, Percival, ed. *Campion's Works.* 1909.

Wilson, Christopher. *Words and Notes Coupled Lovingly Together: Thomas Campion, a Critical Study.* 1989.

Laura S. Youens

SEE ALSO

Air; Barnes, Barnabe ; Daniel, Samuel; Masques; Song

Canon Law

See Law, Canon

Capital Punishment

Capital punishment was widely employed in the Tudor period. The standard method of inflicting it was by hanging, although men convicted of treason would be subjected to the barbarities of hanging *and* drawing and quartering, with female traitors being burned at the stake, as were heretics of either sex, while aristocratic traitors were beheaded. Generally, however, convicted criminals were hanged.

The number of criminal offenses carrying the death penalty was extensive. They included such common law felonies as premeditated murder (although the concept of manslaughter as a lesser offense developed over the sixteenth century), grand larceny (the theft of goods worth more than a shilling), robbery, burglary, rape, and arson. The list was augmented by statute over the sixteenth century, comprehending such offenses as witchcraft, male homosexuality, bestiality, and horse theft.

Lack of records makes it difficult to speak with any precision on the incidence of capital punishment in the late fifteenth and early sixteenth centuries; it is, however, obvious that capital punishment was frequently inflicted from the mid-sixteenth century onward. The lack of national figures means that this point has to be illustrated from county samples. At the Middlesex sessions, some 41 percent of those accused of felony in the 1550s were sentenced to death, and 50 percent in the 1570s. On the home circuit of the assizes (covering Essex, Hertfordshire, Kent, Surrey, and Sussex), 27.4 percent of accused felons were sentenced to death in the 1560s, 28.2 percent in the 1570s. These figures were matched by some very high absolute totals of felons hanged, especially when the Elizabethan regime faced social breakdown during a run of bad harvests in the late 1590s. In 1598, seventy-eight felons were capitally convicted at the assizes and quarter sessions in Devon, while in Kent, forty-five felons were sentenced to death by the assizes alone. This trend continued into the reign of James I, and it seems that the late Elizabethan and Jacobean periods saw the highest levels of capital punishment in English history. Moreover, these executions were carried out overwhelmingly for property offenses, notably grand larceny, burglary, and robbery. Surviving documentation for the Essex assizes demonstrates that 363 persons are known to have been capitally convicted for property offenses in Elizabeth's reign, compared with seventeen for various forms of homicide.

These high levels of execution were partly due to a lack of effective secondary (i.e., noncapital) punishments. However, by the closing years of Elizabeth's reign the courts were attempting to ameliorate this situation by altering the value of goods allegedly stolen to reduce thefts to noncapital petty larceny, or easing the rules restricting grants of benefit of clergy. These devices built clemency into what was a draconian penal code, and their frequent use implicitly indicates a judicial disquiet at this harshness.

Changes in capital punishment also possessed a cultural dimension. Like most punishments, executions normally took place in public, and the Tudor period witnessed an elaboration of the ceremonies that accompanied public executions. Changes in the management of the public execution, aimed at achieving maximum propaganda effect, seem to have been introduced in the well-publicized (and well-documented) treason trials of Henry VIII's reign; by the end of Elizabeth I's reign these changes were being recorded, via the sensational trial pamphlet, even in the execution of ordinary felons, notably murderers. For instance, the speech made on the scaffold by the convicted traitor or felon came to assume a central importance.

C

These speeches characteristically voiced acceptance of the offender's fate, told a tale of youthful sinfulness that led to the offense for which the speaker was suffering death, and exhorted the audience to regard the execution as a dreadful warning of the fruits of disobedience to the laws of the monarch and of God. This last point was reinforced by a growing interest of the clergy in the stage management of public executions. If post-Reformation concepts of the godly commonwealth meant that the good Christian was equated with the good citizen, there was an obvious religious point to be made when the punishment of the bad subject was being carried out.

Frequent use of capital punishment and the elaboration of the public ceremony accompanying it were, therefore, key features of the Tudor penal system. The public execution, widely recognized as one of the major ritual phenomena of eighteenth-century England, had already assumed a deep cultural significance by 1603.

BIBLIOGRAPHY

Sharpe, J.A. *Judicial Punishment in England.* 1990.
Smith, L.B. *Treason in Tudor England: Politics and Paranoia.* 1986.

James Sharpe

SEE ALSO

Crime; Criminal Law; Sexual Offenses; Treason; Witchcraft

Carew, Richard (1555–1620)

A minor poet and translator, Richard Carew had antiquarian interests in the folklore, history, and topography of his native Cornwall, and his works, though modest, won the acknowledgement of many accomplished contemporaries.

Born in the Cornish village of East Antony to a well-established family, Carew entered Christ Church, Oxford, in 1566, where he befriended both Philip Sidney and William Camden. Carew entered the Middle Temple in 1574, and three years later married Juliana Arundell. Appointed justice of the peace in 1581 and sheriff of Cornwall the following year, he also served as M.P. for Saltash in 1584–1585. As the Spanish threat intensified in 1585, Carew found himself in charge of defending the vulnerable southwestern coast, a position that occupied him through the decade's close. In 1597, Carew returned to Parliament, this time for Mitchell. The next year he was elected to the Society of Antiquaries, a forum for the topographical survey he had begun to compile as early as 1584.

Failing health placed him in virtual retirement at Antony after 1602; he was buried there upon his death in 1620.

As a translator, Carew's principal undertaking was to turn Toquato Tasso's *Gerusalemme liberata* into English *ottava rima* on the model of John Harington's great 1591 rendition of Ludovico Ariosto. Carew is supposed to have finished all twenty books of Tasso's poem, though only Books 1 to 5 of *Godfrey of Bulloigne* (as Carew titled the work) appeared in a pirated text of 1594. The remainder has not survived. Carew's text influenced Edward Fairfax's complete translation of Tasso that would eclipse his own in 1600. In 1594, Carew also released *The Examination of Man's Wits,* a translation of Juan de la Huarte's peculiar pseudoscientific treatise. Carew's own colorful imagination found original (though, unfortunately, hexameter) expression in his *A Herrings Tayle* of 1598. Inspired by Sidney's *Defence of Poetry,* Carew also offered a series of literary critical ruminations as *The Excellencie of The English Tongue,* published in the 1614 edition of Camden's *Remains.*

Camden had long admired and encouraged Carew's antiquarian interests, anticipating in repeated editions of the *Britannica* the formal release of his friend's research. *A Survey of Cornwall,* however, would wait until 1602 for Carew to complete his meticulous revisions and allow publication. The work's textured prose and quaint anecdotes represent period taste in a manner akin to Michael Drayton's *Poly-Olbion,* a poem it helped inspire.

BIBLIOGRAPHY

Carew, Richard. *Survey of Cornwall.* Thomas Tonkin, ed. 1811.
———, trans. Tasso's *Godfrey of Bulloigne.* Alexander B. Grosart, ed. Occasional Issues of Unique or Very Rare Books, vol. 15. pt. B, no. 36. 1881.
Huarte, Juan. *Examen de Ingenios. The Examination of Men's Wits (1594) Translated out of the Spanish by M. Camillo Camilli. Englished out of his Italian by Richard Carew.* Scholar's Facsimiles and Reprints. 1959.

Christopher Martin

SEE ALSO

Antiquarianism; Camden, William; Italian Literature; Influence of Spanish Literature.

Carol

The most distinctive musical genre to come out of medieval England was the carol. It could be either monophonic or polyphonic and usually consisted of verses both preceded and followed by a refrain, called a burden. Some carols are macaronic, with both English and Latin lines of text. The poems deal with all manner of subjects, although many are associated with the Virgin Mary and with Christmas.

Originally the *carole* was a French public dance song, described by Jean Renart in *Guillaume de Dole,* and by many other poets and authors. There might be a connection between the Franciscans, secular religious song, and ecclesiastical dance song: the fourteenth-century Irish bishop Richard de Ledrede, who compiled the *Red Book of Ossory,* containing celebratory Latin songs, was Franciscan. The carol was adopted by the fourteenth-century English court, whose traditions were French.

The carol served a variety of functions. There is formal evidence for the use of the carol as a processional song in church; some have burdens taken from processional litanies and hymns, and some are marked for specific liturgical occasions, such as *in die nativitatis.* Frank L. Harrison has amassed evidence that some were substitutes for the second *Benedicamus Domino* at offices after Christmas. Some carols, such as the Boar's Head carols, of which *Caput apri defero* is the most famous, were intended for secular festivals. Others were used as musical accompaniment to courtly games, most notably the holly and ivy carols, symbolizing male and female. (The well-known *The Holly and the Ivy,* although its earliest extant source dates from the eighteenth century, treats indisputably medieval themes.) Some carols were political, the earliest of which is *Deo gracias Anglia,* the "Agincourt Carol." It may have been sung at a ceremony honoring Henry V on his return to London and is also the earliest carol with two burdens, one for soloists and one for a small chorus.

Of the six principal sources of polyphonic carols, three date from the early Tudor period. British Library Additional MS 5665, the "Ritson Manuscript," dates from c. 1460 to 1510 and may have had a connection with Exeter Cathedral, since two of its carol composers, Richard Smert and John Trouluffe, worked there as vicar-choral and canon, respectively. It contains Latin motets, masses, and other English songs besides forty-four carols such as *Nowell: The borys hede,* and *Mervele noght, Josep,* all of which have double burdens. These sources do not indicate the order in which the two burdens and the verses should be sung. A group of meditative Passion carols by William Cornysh, Davy, Browne, and Banastir in the Fayrfax MS constitutes a distinctive late-fifteenth-century repertory: these may have been intended for devotional use in the household or in private chapels. British Library Additional MS 31922 also contains carols, some composed by Henry VIII. Many Tudor carols contrast two-part writing in the verses and three-part writing in the burden. Harmonically, the polyphonic carol repertory was marked from the beginning by the prominence of thirds and sixths.

The early Tudor carols modify the usual fifteenth-century format. In one new formal scheme, of which Richard Pygott's *Quid petis? o fili* from Henry VIII's manuscript is an example, each verse is set to new music. In another, it is the burden that is altered on repetition, as in *Jhesu, mercy* by John Browne (fl. c. 1490). In yet a third, the burden is not heard after its opening statement, although text and music from the burden is melded into the close of the verse, as in *Woefully araid* by William Cornysh.

One of the most famous carols is *Lully, lulla, thow littel tyne child,* the so-called "Coventry Carol." It is one of two carols from the Pageant of the Shearman and Tailors, a Corpus Christi mystery play from Coventry. The earliest known manuscript source was completed in 1534, but *Lully, lulla* and *As I out rode this enderes night* were added only in 1591. The music has proven hard to reconstruct, and there exist several solutions to its notational problems.

The carol declined in popularity after the Reformation, although William Byrd composed several for *Songs of Sundrie Natures* of 1589 and *Psalmes, Songs, and Sonnets* of 1611. The revival of carol singing began in the nineteenth century, leading the way for today's modern editions of medieval and Tudor carols.

BIBLIOGRAPHY

Bent, Margaret; Greene, Richard Leighton; Harrison, Frank Llewellyn; Stevens, John; Trowell, Brian; et al. "The English Carol." *International Musicological Society Congress Report: Ljubljana 1967.* Vol. 10, pp. 284–309.

Greene, Richard Leighton. *The Early English Carols.* 2nd edition 1977.

———. *A Selection of English Carols.*1962.

Harrison, Frank Llewellyn. "Benedicamus, Conductus, Carol: A Newly Discovered Source." *Acta musicologica,* vol. 37, pp. 35–48.

Keyte, Hugh, and Parrott, Andrew, eds. *The New Oxford Book of Carols.* 1992.

Routley, Erik.*The English Carol.* 1958.

Stevens, John. "Carols and Court Songs of the Early Tudor Period." *Proceedings of the Royal Musical Association,* vol. 77, pp. 51–61.

C

———, ed. *Early Tudor Songs and Carols.* Musica Britannica, vol. 36. 1975.

———, ed. *Medieval Carols.* Musica Britannica, vol. 4. 2nd edition 1958.

Laura S. Youens

SEE ALSO

Cornysh, William; Byrd, William; Henry VIII as Composer

Cartwright, Thomas (1535–1603)

Leader and chief theologian of the Presbyterian movement in Elizabethan England, Thomas Cartwright was elected a scholar of St. John's College, Cambridge, in 1550, but had to leave the university on the accession of Mary I in 1553. On Elizabeth's accession in 1558, he was elected to a fellowship at Trinity College, Cambridge, and became Lady Margaret professor of divinity there in 1570. In his inaugural lectures on Acts he advanced semi-Presbyterian views, and was forced to resign and flee the country. He went to Geneva, but returned to England in 1572, when he got into a protracted argument with John Whitgift over the Puritan *Admonition to the Parliament.* He was soon back in exile, but in 1585, he made his peace with Whitgift, who was by then archbishop of Canterbury, and became master of the earl of Leicester's hospital at Warwick. He remained there until 1590, when Archbishop Whitgift finally decided to uproot the Presbyterians. He was tried before both the High Commission and the Star Chamber, and was imprisoned in the Fleet for two years. From 1595 to 1601, he resided in the Channel Islands, but then he returned to Warwick, where he died on December 27, 1603. To the last he remained a preacher, and his following never deserted him.

During the 1580s, Cartwright was involved in the clandestine *classis* movement, which was an attempt to establish a covert presbyterianism within the Church of England. He always recognized that it was more important to be free to preach the Word of God than to worry about details of ceremony, and this enabled him to remain within the Church of England at a time when other Puritans were beginning to consider the path of separation as the only way to preserve their principles intact. He eventually came to accept that it was better to live with the imperfections of episcopal polity than to provoke schism in the church, but he was never able to shake his links with the presbyterianism that provoked his persecution.

BIBLIOGRAPHY

Collinson, P. *The Elizabethan Puritan Movement.* 1967.

Lake, P. *Moderate Puritans and the Elizabethan Church.* 1982.

Pearson, A.F.S. *Thomas Cartwright and Elizabethan Puritanism.* 1925.

Peel, A., and L.H. Carlson, eds. *Cartwrightiana.* 1951.

Gerald L. Bray

SEE ALSO

Admonitions Controversy; Church of England; Church Polity; Puritanism; Whitgift, John

Cary, Elizabeth (c. 1585–1539)

Best known today as the author of the first original play published in English by a woman (*The Tragedy of Mariam, Faire Queene of Jewry,* 1613), Elizabeth Cary was, like many upper-class women of her time, ambivalent about assuming the public role of author. Born in comfortable circumstances (she was the only child of a wealthy lawyer, Sir Lawrence Tanfield, and his wife, Elizabeth Symondes), Cary read voraciously in her youth, in several languages, and evidently began writing for her "private recreation," as her biography puts it, at a young age. Only two of her works, however, were printed in her lifetime: *Mariam,* most likely written between Cary's marriage to Henry Cary in 1602 and the birth of her first child in 1609; and a translation she did much later in life (*The Reply of the Most Illustrious Cardinall of Perron,* 1630), after her Catholicism had been made public, evidently against her will, in 1625. Many modern scholars believe that she also wrote one or both versions of a history of Edward II published in 1680. A number of other works by Cary are mentioned by contemporaries but are now lost: a play "set in Syracuse," a "life" of Tamburlaine, several lives of saints, and "innumerable slight things in verse."

The last phrase comes from the biography of Cary written by one of her daughters, a Catholic nun also ambivalent about assuming the public role of author; her biography of Cary, the first life in English of a female writer, remained in manuscript, in a French convent, until it was printed in 1859. The title page of *Mariam,* a verse drama in five acts based on a narrative from Josephus's Antiquities of the Jews (c. 90 C.E.), shrouds the author's identity by referring to her only as "that learned, vertuous, and truly noble, Ladie, E.C." The title page of the longer version of the narrative of Edward II says that it was "written by E.F. in the year 1627"; after 1620, when her husband became viscount of Falkland, Elizabeth Cary regularly signed her letters "Elizabeth Falkland," so the initials on the folio title page could well be hers. The shorter version of the Edward II narrative, published in octavo, claims on its title page to have been "found among the papers of, and (supposed to be Writ) by the Right Honourable Henry Viscount Faulkland, Sometime Lord Deputy of Ireland."

If one or both of the narratives about the "unfortunate" King Edward and his equally unfortunate wife Isabel are indeed by Elizabeth Cary, there is a nice historical irony in the supposition of the original printer, shared by some modern scholars, that Lord Falkland rather than his wife was the text's author. His view that women should live "quietly" as private beings was widely shared; it is articulated, as a voice of "common opinion," in the Chorus of Cary's *Mariam*. Neither Cary herself nor her heroine was governed by that view, but it undoubtedly contributed to Carys' ambivalence about assuming the public role of author. Her Chorus compares a wife's use of "public language" to an act of prostitution, a violation of the husband's right to own his wife's mind as well as her body: "For in a wife it is no worse to find / A common body than a common mind"(3.3.243–244).

Donald Foster believes he has located a funeral elegy on the duke of Buckingham by Cary, and more of her "lost" manuscripts may surface; the state of her oeuvre is far from settled. Internal and external evidence both establish her authorship of *Mariam* quite conclusively, but the only text she published in her lifetime under her own full name is, perhaps tellingly, the work of translation published in 1630. As a woman and as an intellectual who, "through reading," as her biography puts it, "grew into much doubt of her religion," Cary was socially well positioned to reflect on the problem of censorship. It is a major theme in *Mariam* (the heroine's "unbridled tongue" is a key cause of her death) and a major theme, as well, in what we can reconstruct of the story of Cary's life. Elizabeth Cary died in October 1639.

BIBLIOGRAPHY

Brashear, Lucy. "A Case for the Influence of Lady Cary's *Tragedy of Mariam* on Shakespeare's *Othello*." *Shakespeare Newsletter*, vol. 16 (1976), p. 31.

Callaghan, Dympna. "Re-reading The Tragedie of Mariam, the Faire Queene of Jewry." In *Woman, Race, Writing in the Early Modern Period*. Margo Hendricks and Patricia Parker, eds. 1996.

Cary, Elizabeth. *The Tragedy of Mariam, The Fair Queen of Jewry. With The Lady Falkland: Her Life*. Barry Weller and Margaret Ferguson, eds. 1994.

———. *The Tragedie of Mariam, The Faire Queene of Jewry* (1613). Malone Society facsimile edition. A.C. Dunstan and W.W. Greg, eds. 1914; repr. 1992, Marta Straznicky and Richard Rowland, eds.

Ferguson, Margaret. "Running on with Almost Public Voice: The Case of 'E.C.'" In *Tradition and the Talents of Women*. Florence Howe, ed. 1991.

Gutierrez, Nancy. "Valuing *Mariam*: Genre Study and Feminist Analysis." *Tulsa Studies in Women's Literature*, vol. 10, pp. 233–251.

Margaret Ferguson

SEE ALSO
Censorship

Castiglione, Baldassare
See Court; Hoby, Thomas; Platonism

Catechism, The

Prior to 1549 there was no form of religious instruction in England that could be regarded as a catechism. The idea was introduced by Thomas Cranmer in imitation of Protestant models from the Continent. In its original form, the catechism was intended as a manual of instruction for confirmation, and it was included with the confirmation rite in the Prayer Book. It had four distinct sections, of which the first was an exposition of the baptismal covenant, the second dealt with the Apostles' Creed, the third with the Ten Commandments, and the fourth with the Lord's Prayer. The Royal Injunctions of 1536 and 1538 had already commanded that these be taught to all confirmation candidates, and the catechism merely put those commands into effect, adding appropriate commentary as required.

After the Hampton Court Conference in 1604 a lengthy section was added on the Sacraments. This was subdivided into the Sacraments in general, followed by baptism and Holy Communion. At the same time, the catechism was separated from the confirmation rite and became a distinct part of the Prayer Book. This arrangement was retained in 1662, where it is printed immediately before the "Order for Confirmation." Some idea of the catechism's importance can be gained from Canon 59 of 1604, which ordered catechetical instruction on

C

every Sunday and holy day, under pain of "reproof, suspension and eventual excommunication." It long remained virtually the only religious instruction that most laypeople received, and it was still in general use in the early twentieth century. Since about 1945 it has succumbed to modern methods of education and to liturgical revision, though it remains an official part of the Book of Common Prayer.

BIBLIOGRAPHY

Neil, C. and J.M. Willoughby. *A Tutorial Prayer Book.* 1963.

Gerald L. Bray

SEE ALSO

Book of Common Prayer; Cranmer, Thomas; Injunctions, Royal

Catherine of Aragon

See Katherine of Aragon

Catholic Reformation

See Catholicism; Lutheranism; Reformation, English

Catholicism

Although in theory an organic unity, late medieval Catholicism was anything but that. United by certain basic beliefs, above all in the power of the Mass and of the Incarnation of Christ, and a range of pious practices, especially celebrating holidays, asking the saints' intercession, worshipping images and relics, and observing the cult of purgatory (a recent invention), believers were often separated not only by local variations in almost every other aspect of their belief and worship, but, more importantly—and especially in England—by politics. While the pope continued, as he had for centuries, to assert his primacy over all Western Christians, in fact his authority varied greatly from place to place and time to time. It is one of the distinctive features of English Catholicism that the pope was held in higher esteem at the end of the fifteenth century than he was, for example, in France. The first Tudor monarch, Henry VII (1485–1509), enjoyed very good relations with the papacy and probably tried—by his lights—to carry out a program of religious reform partly inspired by Rome. One of its clearest marks is the quality of the English

bench of bishops, who, although heavily weighted toward successful royal servants, may have been among the most successful in Europe in providing pastoral care.

This dual link both to the pope and to the monarch largely determined the constant evolution of Tudor Catholicism. During the reign of Henry's son, Henry VIII (1509–1547), a king who began as a conspicuously faithful son of Rome, broke with the pope and ended up replacing him in England. The young Henry not only undertook wars in alliance with the pope; he also wrote a treatise defending the seven sacraments against Martin Luther. In his devotion to them, and especially in his pronounced ritual piety, including creeping to the cross in Lent, Henry typified his subjects' attitudes. To judge by the relative ease with which the break with Rome was carried out, his notion of the relations between royal and papal power could not have been too different from that of most of his subjects.

The issue that led to the breach was Henry VIII's desire for an annulment of his marriage to Katherine of Aragon. By the mid-1520s, it had become clear that Katherine would not produce a male heir, a problem of acute concern to the new dynasty. Henry convinced himself that his lack of a son was a divine punishment for having married the woman once his brother Arthur's wife. Armed with Scriptural and legal arguments, Henry had his chief minister, Cardinal Wolsey (his eminence is another sign of England's close ties to Rome) approach the pope for an annulment. Katherine and her uncle, the emperor Charles V, resisted, but when Pope Clement VII fell into Charles's hands in 1527 during the sack of Rome, it became impossible to grant Henry's wishes. Over the next seven or eight years, Henry, with the assistance of Parliament, created the royal supremacy over the English church that gave him nearly all the authority once possessed by the pope.

Henry and his advisers quickly decided to use his new powers against the English church as an institution. Having cowed the clergy, including the bishops early on, the English government gradually decided it could make better use than the church of much of the church's property. The dissolution of the monasteries, executed over a span of three years from 1536 to 1539, did away with one of the basic institutions of medieval Catholicism. Although often not in very good shape—perhaps fifteen or twenty houses in England could be said to observe their rule rigorously—the monasteries were not only a major means of providing salvation through their prayers but also played a large economic and social role,

C

especially in the north of England. Their dissolution was one of the causes of the Pilgrimage of Grace Uprising in 1536.

Henry's new policy inspired a few other celebrated instances of resistance, especially those of Bishop John Fisher and Sir Thomas More. Both refused to take the oath of the Act of Supremacy by which English men and women were forced to recognize the new order, and both were executed for treason. But only Fisher certainly died in defense of papal primacy. More as much as said that that was *not* the reason he would not swear, and he never clearly said what had prevented him until after the fact. Nevertheless, Fisher and More would become powerful symbols of Catholic resistance.

The royal supremacy is best thought of as a revived caesaro-papism, like that exercised by the Byzantine emperors, above all Henry's "British" model, Constantine. That is, the king had virtually complete power over all aspects of religion, except that he could not himself exercise priestly functions (even though here there was room for slippage). Despite this broad control, Henry made very few changes in doctrine. Even the Act of Ten Articles (1536), once thought to be a concession for diplomatic reasons to the German Lutherans, was judged wholly Catholic by one of Henry's principal opponents, Cardinal Reginald Pole, except for its exclusion of the pope. In the last decade of his reign, Henry staunchly refused to back down on the score of the pope in the face of Roman pressure, including his excommunication in 1538, but did open the door to movement away from traditional ritual piety in the *King's Prymer* (1546).

Continuing the same slow drift, Henry put the government of England during his son Edward's minority into the hands of "advanced" Protestants. During Edward VI's reign (1547–1553), England became an officially Protestant country, through widespread iconoclasm, the abolition of the mass, and "the stripping of the altars." The introduction of the first Book of Common Prayer, largely written by Archbishop Thomas Cranmer, sparked a dangerous rebellion in the west of England (1549), but otherwise there was little outward resistance to Edward's changes. The likely reason emerges from the way in which his sister, Mary I (1553–1558), succeeded him on the throne, despite Edward's best efforts to divert the succession to Lady Jane Grey: Mary played on her legitimacy and carefully did not talk of religion in the early months, despite the fact that everyone knew she was a Catholic. In short, most English men and women were prepared to do most of what the monarch wished.

That the English had no deep attachment to the pope quickly became clear. Mary, abetted by her cousin Cardinal Pole, wished to restore papal obedience immediately, but she was met with dogged refusal both at home and abroad. For one thing, the spoils of the dissolution had wound up in at least as many Catholic as Protestant hands, and the new owners had no intention of giving their property back to the church. For another, the emperor, busy negotiating his son Philip's marriage to Mary, persuaded her to go slowly. Only in late 1554 did Charles allow Pole to enter England and reconcile the realm to Rome. England was once again publicly both Catholic and Roman.

Pole's top priority was restoring papal obedience and undoing the effects of twenty years of schism. Many of the people on whom he had to rely, including a good many bishops, did not share his enthusiasm for either. Despite her sound intentions and the good example she set by giving back a good piece of the church property still in crown hands, Mary did not succeed in finding the financial resources Pole needed. Their efforts to restore monasticism—indicative of their attachment to traditional piety—were almost entirely limited to the refoundation of Westminster Abbey. But Mary's and Pole's religion was not reactionary, as their effort to provide for preaching and catechesis—both building on Henrician and even Edwardian changes—indicates. The many reforms introduced by Pole in his legatine synod of 1556, above all the establishment of new standards of clerical discipline, point to the same conclusion, even though they could barely be put into effect before Pole lost his legatine authority in 1557. When Pole and Mary died within twenty-four hours of each other in 1558, the Catholic revival seemed to die with them.

Undoubtedly it had not yet made a great deal of progress, but the degree to which they had in fact succeeded may be measured by the resistance of the bench of bishops to the new queen Elizabeth I's timid moves away from papal obedience, even though it was missing about half its members. During the first decade of Elizabeth's reign, she did little to repress Catholicism, despite the best efforts of some of her advisers, especially Sir William Cecil, and of Parliament, which passed stringent penal laws as early as 1563. For their part, the popes, first Pius IV and then Pius V, also went slowly. This breathing space allowed Marian Catholicism to survive. When, in 1568, Mary Queen of Scots, the principal Catholic claimant to Elizabeth's throne, fled into England and was imprisoned by Elizabeth, the majority of English believers were still

C

traditional Catholics and some were ready, as the sequel showed, to resist Elizabeth's Protestant drift.

Catholic resistance burst into the open only during two periods, 1569–1573 and 1584–1596. In both cases, outside intervention was the inspiration. In the first, the pope took the lead by excommunicating Elizabeth and then, less cautiously than Paul III in the case of Henry VIII, publishing the papal bull of excommunication. Pius V tried to coordinate the bull *Regnans in excelsis* (1570), in which he threw down the gauntlet to the queen with the rising of the northern earls in 1569–1570, but the bull did not arrive in England until after the rising had been crushed. It did not help that Pius had sent agents to England, including Nicholas Morton, who apparently offered to absolve the queen's subjects of their allegiance to her. The second spell of open resistance drew on the example of the successful Catholic League in France, which helped to assassinate Henry III.

Resistance also depended heavily on the Jesuit mission to England, begun in 1580, and usually directed by the irrepressible Robert Parsons. Some argue that the Jesuits saved English Catholicism, adopting a line first put forward by Parsons, but it might be as true to say that the interminable wrangles between them and the mission priests trained at Cardinal William Allen's seminary at Douai (and between those two groups and the surviving Marian clergy) did as much harm as good. The Jesuits took a hard line on the vital question of attendance at church services, while both mission priests and Marian clergy argued that such attendance was licit as a means of survival. Events proved them right, but the Catholicism that survived into the seventeenth century was very different from even its Marian predecessor. While large tracts of the country probably remained imbued with traditional beliefs, especially in the north once again, Elizabethan Catholicism was increasingly a religion of individual gentry households. The priests sent to England frequently took up service as chaplains to the gentry rather than serving parishs, for obvious political as well as social reasons. Nonetheless, their mere presence helped to guarantee the survival of English Catholicism.

BIBLIOGRAPHY

Bossy, John. *The English Catholic Community, 1570–1850.* 1975.

Duffy, Eamon. *The Stripping of the Altars. Traditional Religion in England c. 1400–c. 1580.* 1992.

Haigh, Christopher. *English Reformations. Religion, Politics, and Society under the Tudors.* 1993.

Holmes, Peter. *Resistance and Compromise. The Political Thought of the Elizabethan Catholics.* 1982.

Knowles, David. *The Religious Orders in England.* Vol. III, *The Tudor Age.* 1959.

Loach, Jennifer. *Parliament and the Crown in the Reign of Mary Tudor.* 1986.

Loades, David. *The Reign of Mary Tudor. Politics, Government, and Religion in England, 1553–1558.* 2nd edition. 1991.

Meyer, Arnold Oskar. *England and the Catholic Church under Queen Elizabeth.* J.R. McKee, trans. 1914; repr., John Bossy, intro. 1967.

Scarisbrick, J.J. *The Reformation and the English People.* 1984.

Thomas F. Mayer

SEE ALSO

Allen, William; Articles of Religion; Clergy; Cranmer, Thomas; English College of Rome; Fisher, John; Jesuits; Katherine of Aragon; Marian Exiles; Marian Martyrs; Monastic Orders; More, Thomas; Northern Rebellion; Parsons, Robert; Pilgrimage of Grace; Recusancy; Pole, Reginald; Reformation, English; *Regnans in Excelsis;* Supremacy, Act of; Trent, Council of; Uniformity, Act of; Wolsey, Thomas

Cavendish, George (c. 1500–c.1562)

Cavendish was the elder son of Thomas Cavendish, clerk of the pipe during the reign of Henry VII. Shortly after his father's death in 1524, Cavendish married Margery, William Kemp's daughter and Sir Thomas More's niece. Although his younger brother William amassed wealth and attained knighthood under Henry VIII, George Cavendish led a quiet, simple life with the exception of the few years he served as Cardinal Thomas Wolsey's gentleman usher. In the early 1520s, Cavendish, in Wolsey's words, abandoned "his own country, wife, and children, his house and family, his rest and quietness, only to serve me." Wolsey's trust in Cavendish's loyalty was not misplaced. Even when the cardinal's inability to annul Henry VIII's marriage to Katherine of Aragon cost him the king's favor, Cavendish remained Wolsey's faithful servant until the cardinal's death at Leicester in 1530. Following interviews with the Privy Council and the king, Cavendish returned to his home in Suffolk with his pick of six horses from Wolsey's stable, five marks for traveling expenses, ten pounds in wages, and a twenty-pound reward, all granted by the king in recognition of his service. Before his death in 1561 or 1562, Cavendish again proved his devotion to the cardinal by writing the biographical *Life of Wolsey* (1558). Without denying Wolsey's shortcomings, the gentleman usher, unlike other sixteenth-century biographers, remembered his former master with kind affection as he answered "divers sundry surmises and imagined tales made of [Wolsey's] proceedings and doings" that Cavendish knew "to be most untrue." Appreciating the memoir-like quality of the *Life,* scholars have often overlooked Cavendish's failure to recall facts with complete accuracy. Indeed, it seems that in Cavendish's case, a well-crafted presentation of "truth" is more important than a flawless memory.

As recent scholarship notes, Cavendish skillfully draws on an eclectic mixture of medieval and Renaissance influences to develop structure, imagery, and characterization. As in Cavendish's ill-received *Metrical Visions* (1558), a collection of poems begun around 1552, the primary structure of the *Life* was fashioned after the medieval tradition of John Lydgate's *Fall of Princes,* a translation of Bocaccio's *De Casibus Virorum Illustrium.* The *Life* is divided into two parts. In the first, Wolsey rises to position and power (which is curtailed only by his conflict with Henry and Anne Boleyn), but in the second half, Wolsey falls into a state of humility and disgrace. The secondary structure of the biography follows yet another medieval tradition: the morality play. In this tradition, a key figure represents mankind in its spiritual struggle toward redemption. Thus, Cavendish's vivid details of Wolsey's physical illness suggest that the cardinal paid his debts for sin before his death. Imagery emphasizing Fortune further defines Wolsey's progression from sin to salvation. Before his fall, Wolsey mistakenly trusts in two images of Fortune: first a power of chance and mutability and then a spiritual entity who offers deceitful, enslaving gifts. After his fall, the cardinal struggles to understand Christian Fortune better, an instrument that accomplishes God's will. As evidence of his penance, Wolsey learns to trust in God and to appreciate the gift of poverty that Fortune offers him. Besides being an integral part of the morality play tradition, these various images of Fortune also testify to changing beliefs in mythology and Christianity from the middle ages to the Renaissance.

Likewise, many of the characteristics of Wolsey described in the *Life* reflect substantial ideological changes that occurred during the Renaissance. Cavendish's first sentence notes that the cardinal at one time "was an honest poor man's son." Wolsey's ability to attain position is evidence that the ambitious could break from medieval class rigidity and enjoy social mobility in the Renaissance. Similarly, the cardinal's distraction by opulent banquets and orchestrated theatrical processions illustrates not only a marked increase in devotion to pleasure in the sixteenth century, but also the idea of a worldwide stage on which we are all "players." Ironically, the superficial image of success that Wolsey tries to create for himself hides his true identity through much of the biography. After Wolsey's death, Cavendish himself becomes a central player not only in the biography but on the world "stage" as well. Although he intended to transmit an accurate memory of his former master by writing the *Life,* Cavendish actually created a work of such lasting historical and literary significance that he himself is memorable. Shakespeare further immortalized this faithful gentleman usher as a key Renaissance "player" by relying on the *Life* to write his own *Henry VIII.*

BIBLIOGRAPHY

Anderson, Judith. *Biographical Truth.* 1984.

Cavendish, George. *Metrical Visions.* A.S.G. Edwards, ed. 1980.

Crewe, Jonathan. "The Wolsey Paradigm." *Criticism,* vol. 30, no. 2, pp. 153–69.

Morley, Henry, intro. *The Life of Cardinal Wolsey.* George Cavendish. 1890.

Sylvester, Richard S., and Davis P. Harding, eds. *Two Early Tudor Lives.* 1962.

Wooden, Warren W. "The Art of Partisan Biography: George Cavendish's *Life of Wolsey.*" *Renaissance and Reformation,* vol. 1, pp. 24–35.

Jonathan Wright

SEE ALSO
Lydgate, John; Wolsey, Thomas

Cavendish, Thomas (1560–1592)

Naval captain, pirate, and circumnavigator of the globe, Thomas Cavendish first took to the sea in 1585 as part of Sir Walter Ralegh's attempt to plant the Virginia colony in North America. The following year he began a voyage to circumnavigate the globe, hoping to emulate the accomplishment of Sir Francis Drake. After negotiating the Strait of Magellan he plundered Spanish shipping along the Chilean, Costa Rican, and Californian coasts before turning west across the Pacific. He returned to Plymouth on September 10, 1588, with a cargo of gold and treasure that made him a rich man and each of his investors a 200

C

percent profit. His last voyage was in 1591, when he joined the fleet of John Davis to open up trade with China and Southeast Asia. However, he was not able to negotiate the strait, and was forced to turn back to England. Cavendish died on the return voyage of illness, railing against Davis and his own crew for his failure.

BIBLIOGRAPHY
Andrews, K.R. *Elizabethan Privateering.* 1964.
Williamson, J.A. *The Age of Drake.* 1946.

Robert J. Mueller

SEE ALSO
Davis, John; Discovery and Exploration; Piracy; Ralegh, Walter

Caxton, William (1415/24–1492)

The first unambiguous reference to the English printer William Caxton is the record of the payment by Robert Large in 1438 to enroll him as an apprentice in the Mercers' Company. Caxton was born between 1415 and 1424, probably in the Weald. Large, lord mayor of London in 1439, died in 1441 and bequeathed his apprentice Caxton twenty marks. By 1450, Caxton was trading as a Merchant Adventurer, for a document in Bruges records his standing surety for another English merchant. In the 1450s, he took the livery of the Mercers' Company and shortly afterward he settled in Bruges. By 1465 (and probably earlier), he was governor of the English nation there. This position underlines his wealth and the standing he enjoyed in national affairs.

He was also involved in international negotiations. In 1464, the English nation left Bruges because of a trade dispute with the duke of Burgundy, the ruler of Flanders, and settled in Utrecht (Holland). There the English merchants remained until relations between England and Burgundy were reestablished, a process in which Caxton was deeply involved. The reconciliation in 1467 was followed by the marriage of Duke Charles with Margaret, Edward IV's sister. The last reference to Caxton as governor occurs in 1470, although he may have relinquished the governorship only in 1471 when he went to Cologne.

He received permission from the Cologne authorities to reside there from July 17, 1471. He teamed up with Johannnes Veldener, a printer and type cutter, from whom he learned the craft of printing and publishing. In 1473, he returned to Bruges with Veldener and possibly

Wynkyn de Worde, who was later his principal assistant, to set up a press. With their help he printed his translation of *History of Troy,* dedicated to Margaret Duchess of Burgundy. Caxton had probably gone to Cologne especially to acquire a printing press and made the translation of *History of Troy* to provide material for it. He had evidently devised a printing policy before acquiring a press.

In Bruges he printed another of his translations and four books in French. Selling books in England from Bruges may have been more difficult than he anticipated, and in 1476, he returned to England to settle in the precincts of Westminster Abbey. In England he became a bookseller, a printer, and a publisher. As a bookseller he issued his advertisement asking potential buyers to come to his shop at the sign of the Red Pale. As a printer he printed many items at others' requests, including indulgences, liturgical texts, and grammars. As a publisher he issued books that he or others had translated, as well as original writings in English; and occasionally he published books printed on other printers' presses. He also remained a merchant who undertook various commissions for the king and who managed a thriving business. Where many other printers went bankrupt, his mercantile experience allowed him to survive comfortably, even though political circumstances in England were difficult. One of the aristocrats with whom he had a special relationship, Anthony Earl Rivers, was executed by Richard of Gloucester in 1483, and Richard was himself killed at the battle of Bosworth Field in 1485. To survive politically and financially through these difficult times was no mean feat.

Caxton's publishing policy involved providing material in English that would appeal to a secular audience. It had to be fashionable and, preferably, new. Of English poets he printed Chaucer, Gower, and Lydgate, but not Langland because of his alliterative style. Of English prose writings he printed Sir Thomas Malory's *Le Morte D'Arthur* and religious material that was general and consolatory, but not that which was specialized, such as the writings of the mystics. Most of his published output consisted of translations of French texts that he and other approved translators had made. An approved translator was either a member of the aristocracy or someone who had been commissioned by an aristocrat to make a translation. He published translations by Earl Rivers and John Tiptoft, earl of Worcester. His own translations were mostly of French prose works available in contemporary manuscripts from Flanders or in printed books. He often added prologues and epilogues to these works to make them more appealing to his clientele. Caxton also engaged in the book trade, for his name occurs as both importer and exporter in the port of London accounts. He was familiar with what was printed in northern Europe. He knew what to avoid, namely books in Latin for an academic or religious audience, because so many publishers in Europe were producing books of that type. He established his own market for which he enjoyed a monopoly: the market for books in English was not big enough for continental printers to move into.

A dispute has raged over whether Caxton led or followed the literary taste of his time. He was undoubtedly influenced by the prevailing fashion in reading, but he was able to extend that taste by providing different material in the same genres. He issued more than 100 publications between 1474 and 1492, at least twenty of which he had translated. But the quality of his printing lagged behind the best continental practice.

He died in 1492 and was buried at St. Margaret's, Westminster. He left a daughter who had married Gerard Crop, a tailor. A lawsuit after Caxton's death provides us with this information, but little is known of her and nothing is known of his wife. His business was taken over by Wynkyn de Worde, who moved to the city of London in 1500. It continued successfully until his death in 1535, though the publishing policy changed. What we know of Caxton the man can be gleaned mainly from his prologues and epilogues, although it is difficult to discern the individual behind what are no more than stock phrases. His principal claim to fame is that he was a successful businessman who recognized the opportunities offered by the new technology and was able to harness his own mercantile expertise to make the new business a success.

BIBLIOGRAPHY

Blake, N.F. *Caxton and His World.* 1969.
———. *Caxton's Own Prose.* 1973.
———. *England's First Publisher.* 1976.
———. *William Caxton: A Bibliographical Guide.* 1985.
Hellinga, Lotte. *Caxton in Focus.* 1982.
Needham, Paul. *The Printer & the Pardoner. An Unrecorded Indulgence Printed by William Caxton for the Hospital of St. Mary Rounceval, Charing Cross.* 1986.
Painter, George D. *William Caxton: A Quincentenary Biography of England's First Printer.* 1976.

N.F. Blake

SEE ALSO

Arthurian Legend; Book Ownership; French Literature, Influence of; Printing, Publishing, and Bookselling; Merchant Adventurers

CECIL, ROBERT
See William, Cecil

Cecil, Sir William, Lord Burghley (1520–1598)

Sir William Cecil (created Baron Burghley in 1571; henceforth called "Burghley") was arguably the greatest statesman not only of Tudor England but of all sixteenth-century Europe. He was Elizabeth I's de facto prime minister for the first forty years of her forty-five-year reign (1558–1603). In a century when royal ministers tended to rise and fall with astonishing alacrity, Burghley managed both to attain the highest state offices and pass on a powerful political inheritance to his second son (Sir Robert Cecil).

The obscurity of Burghley's family origins are noticeable because of his attempts to construct elaborate genealogies to justify his possession of multiple offices and great wealth. Born on or around September 18, 1520, at Bourne, Lincolnshire, to a prosperous family whose line could be traced back only as far as Burghley's grandfather, David Cecil, who attained office under King Henry VII, Burghley enrolled in St. John's College, Cambridge, in 1535, at the height the Reformation. So Burghley was what the Romans called a *novus homo* (new man), or to paraphrase a poet whose path he crossed mysteriously more than once (Christopher Marlowe), he "fetched his gentry from Oxford, not from heraldry." But in this case the fetching was from a university closely associated with radical early English Protestantism. There he met and married Mary, sister of the great Greek scholar Sir John Cheke, by whom he had his first son Thomas in 1542 (later named first earl of Exeter). Mary died in 1544, and Burghley was remarried in 1545 to Mildred Cooke. Burghley's education at Cambridge (and throughout his long life) was an appropriately classical one, especially his training in Latin and the study of Roman authors, whose political precepts he implemented for half a century.

Attending Cambridge during the heady days of the 1530s undoubtedly gave Burghley a strong interest in law. He went up to London to study at Gray's Inn in 1541, best known of the Inns of Court for grooming future ser-

C

vants of the state. Here Burghley gained the knowledge and made additional connections that facilitated his later, masterful influence on Parliament. For the Elizabethan era was an age of statutes, the bloodiest period in the history of English criminal law, and areas such as treason law were extensively refined in order to induce religious and political conformity to the new Protestant order.

It is crucial to understand that Burghley's power was rooted in early attainment of high political office by 1548, a full ten years before Elizabeth's accession. During the reign of the boy king Edward VI (1547–1553), Burghley was first secretary to Edward Seymour, Protector Somerset (1548), then principal secretary under John Dudley, duke of Northumberland, in 1551, the same year in which he was knighted. Around 1551, Burghley wrote a Latin memorandum describing the European situation as a straightforward battle between international Roman Catholicism and the Reformed religion, in which England's survival guaranteed the survival of the Protestant Reformation. Although Burghley's career seems to have faded into the shadows during the reign of the Catholic Queen Mary (1553–1558), he nonetheless continued to build important political networks at home and abroad, and was engaged by Mary's government to perform diplomatic duties. And outside this period, in 1550 and 1558, Burghley was named to the Privy Council. In effect, he was untouchable from a very early age. Burghley's most important connection, of course, was to the young Princess Elizabeth, who immediately named him to head her government when she succeeded to the throne on November 17, 1558. Burghley's great accomplishment lay in deploying his seniority and connections to build symbiotic rule among himself, the queen, and the first two or three generations of Protestant "new men" whose ambitions and energies form the basis of late Tudor government.

In little more than a decade, from 1558 to 1572, Burghley consolidated his power so well that the anonymous Catholic author of the 1572 *A Treatise of Treasons Against Q. Elizabeth* (attributed to John Leslie) could coin the phrase *"Regnum Cecilianum"* (or "Cecilian Regime"). As principal secretary from the outset of Elizabeth's reign, Burghley dominated the court by controlling its correspondence. He also supervised covert operations (such as the 1570 kidnapping of Dr. John Story from the Netherlands), and he patronized Sir Francis Walsingham to become the next dominant secretary. Burghley became master of the Court of Wards in 1561, which contributed to his cash flow and power since he could now dictate certain marriages among

the elite. In 1572, Burghley became lord treasurer, which consolidated both his personal financial position and control of court expenditures. In brief, controlling the court and its cash allowed him to build an unparalleled patronage network.

One could say that Burghley presided over major changes in the English state that linked Henry VIII's Reformation to external realignments in the burgeoning European battle for maritime supremacy over a suddenly global order. He combined Henry's break with Rome and his construction of the best European navy with the establishment of the Church of England in 1560. Burghley severed England's traditional alliance with Spain (against Franco-Scottish interests) and ushered in a new period in which England would challenge the Hapsburg Empire and other largely Catholic powers by sea and by land.

The 1560s featured Sir John Hawkins's multiple attempts to break into Portuguese dominance of the West African slave trade to the Americas, as well as extensive privateering (piracy); the onset of the Elizabethan conquest of Ireland; the capture and imprisonment of Mary Queen of Scots, followed by the 1569–1570 Northern Rebellion; and Protestant uprisings in Europe. Burghley played a key role in all these events. Following the initial northern revolt in 1569 he authorized the execution of some 700 English Catholic commoners. In 1570, Pope Pius V excommunicated Elizabeth, and thereafter the stage was set for open warfare largely between England and Spain from 1585 to 1604. But Burghley survived the deaths of numerous colleagues such as Walsingham (1590), and trained his own son Robert to assume Walsingham's position at court. The frustrations and relative impotence of the earl of Essex and his faction throughout the 1590s, never able to displace Cecilian predominance at court, culminated in Essex's abortive revolt and execution in 1601—testifying to the position that Burghley had attained and that Robert Cecil maintained after his father's death despite fierce opposition.

As a humanist statesman, Burghley was always involved with arts and letters. He was a polemicist in matters relating to state and religion: *The Execution of Justice in England* (1583) represents the height of his intellectual battle against William Cardinal Allen, the most prominent of the English Catholic exiles (see *A True, Sincere and Modest Defence of English Catholics,* 1584). Burghley was a great builder and horticulturist, obviously believing that the splendor of a statesman's houses and gardens lent prestige to their owner, as indeed they needed to do, if only for the sake of entertaining Queen Elizabeth on several of her many royal progresses.

Pamphlet wars engaged exiled English Catholics, state Protestants, and Presbyterians, among others, and Burghley's most interesting entry in this field is his forgery of a letter to the Spanish ambassador, supposedly written by an English Catholic at the time of the Armada (1588). Royal proclamations from 1591 against English Catholics, thought to emanate from Burghley, were answered in pamphlets by exiles such as Richard Verstegan. Burghley's predominance at court, resulting in his possession or control of most court offices, drew opposition even from Protestants. Edmund Spenser's "Prosopopoia: Or Mother Hubberds Tale" seems to contain a heavy satire on Burghley.

As the affairs in Ireland strained relations between the queen and the earl of Essex, and the conflict with Spain continued, Burghley grew very ill, yet continued to advise Elizabeth on the Low Countries. While he was alive, Essex was unable to gather sufficient support to oppose her, but on Burghley's death on August 4, 1598, forty years of political domination came to an end, leaving room for Essex's rebellion and factional conflict.

BIBLIOGRAPHY

Allen, William. *A True, Sincere, and Modest Defence of English Catholics* (1584). D.M. Rogers, ed. 1971.

Bartlett, Kenneth. "The English Exile Community in Italy and the Political Opposition to Queen Mary I." *Albion*, vol. 13, no. 3, pp. 223–241.

———. "Papal Policy and the English Crown, 1563–1565: The Bertano Correspondence." *Sixteenth Century Journal*, vol. 23, pp. 643–659.

Breight, Curtis C. *Surveillance, Militarism, and Drama in the Elizabethan Era.* 1996.

Canny, Nicholas. *The Elizabethan Conquest of Ireland: A Pattern Established 1565–1576.* 1976.

Cecil, William. *The Copie of a Letter Sent out of England to Don Bernardin Mendoza* (1588).

———. *The Execution of Justice in England* (1583).

Corrigan, Philip, and Derek Sayer. *The Great Arch: English State Formation as Cultural Revolution.* 1985.

Croft, Pauline. "The Reputation of Robert Cecil: Libels, Political Opinion, and Popular Awareness in the Early Seventeenth Century." *Transactions of the Royal Historical Society*, vol. 1, 6th series, pp. 43–69.

Historical Manuscripts Commission. Calendar of the Manuscripts . . . Preserved at Hatfield House. 24 vols. 1883–1976.

Leslie, John. *A Treatise of Treasons Against Q. Elizabeth, 1572.* 1975.

Pollitt, Ronald. "The Abduction of Doctor John Story and the Evolution of Elizabethan Intelligence Operations." *Sixteenth Century Journal*, vol. 14, pp. 131–156.

Read, Conyers. *Mr. Secretary Cecil and Queen Elizabeth.* 1955.

———. *Lord Burghley and Queen Elizabeth.* 1960.

———. "William Cecil and Elizabethan Public Relations." In *Elizabethan Government and Society: Essays Presented to Sir John Neale.* S.T. Bindoff et al. eds., pp. 21–55. 1961.

Roberts, Michael. "The Military Revolution, 1560–1660." In *Essays in Swedish History*, pp. 195–225. 1967.

Smith, Alan G.R., ed. *The "Anonymous Life" of William Cecil, Lord Burghley.* 1990.

Spenser, Edmund. "Prosopopoia: Or Mother Hubberds Tale." In *The Yale Edition of the Shorter Poems of Edmund Spenser.* William Oram et al. eds., pp. 327–379. 1989.

Verstegan, Richard. *An Advertisement Written to a Secretarie of My L. Treasurers of Ingland, by an Inglishe Intelligencer as he passed throughe Germanie towardes Italie* (1592).

———. *A Declaration of the True Causes of the Great Troubles, Presupposed to be Intended Against the Realme of England* (1592).

Curtis C. Breight

SEE ALSO

Mendoza, Bernardino de; Espionage; Foreign Relations and Diplomacy; Hawkins, John; Inns of Court; Privateering; Treason; Walsingham, Francis

Censorship

Censorship became an urgent issue in the sixteenth century for three reasons. First, the rapid growth of printing, paralleled by a steadily increasing rate of literacy, meant that texts could be disseminated much more widely than ever before. Second, the emergence of acting troupes able to sustain themselves professionally, either by touring or by semipermanent residence in London, meant that play texts began to circulate outside traditional contexts of control, such as the church, the trade guilds, the court, and other noble households. Third, the Reformation put an unprecedented premium on controlling the flow of ideas.

C

For both print and performance, the government evolved systems of licensing as primary mechanisms of control. They devolved their own authority on key interested parties (in print, the Stationers' Company; for performance, a limited number of licensed and patronized troupes), tying them into systems of patronage and monopoly trading so as to promote a degree of mutual self-interest between themselves and those in power. Specific censorship practices grew up within those licensing systems, backed ultimately by the authority of the monarch, the Privy Council and/or the church, sometimes with the added sanction of Parliament. But it should be noted that the most brutal cases of "censorship" in the period involved attempts to avoid the systems of licensed control altogether.

As early as 1529 there were proclamations against heretical and seditious books, and in 1533 an act to regulate the import of books from abroad. In 1538, all books were required to be licensed (with implicit precensorship) by the Privy Council or their nominees. Under Edward VI, when William Cecil acted as a press licenser, there were orders in 1547 and 1549 against Roman Catholic books of prayer and instruction. Mary I's attempts, conversely, to restrict Protestant propaganda from both home and abroad culminated in the 1557 charter of the Stationers' Company, expressly because "certain seditious books . . . are daily printed, renewing and spreading great and detestable heresies against the catholic doctrine of the holy Mother Church." Yet the charter was confirmed two years later by Elizabeth I, under Protestant auspices. A marriage of commercial self-interest and state orthodoxy had been forged, reinforced later that year by "injunctions" that books must be licensed by the queen, six of her Privy Council or certain clergymen, and the names of licensers appended at the back of the book. These were the conventions under which George Gascoigne's *An Hundreth Sundrie Flowers* (1573) and Holinshed's *Chronicles* (1577) were both censored, exception apparently being taken to quite specific passages; they were also the ones that John Stubbs tried to circumvent with his unlicensed *Discovery of a Gaping Gulf* (1579), attacking the queen's marriage plans, for which he and his publisher both lost their right hands.

In 1586, under pressure from the Stationers, whose privileges had been challenged by pirate printing, the Court of Star Chamber sought to confirm their monopoly and to forbid all printing that was not officially licensed under the authority of the church. In 1588, Archbishop John Whitgift nominated twelve clerics as official licensers, and authority from one of them was required before a printer's "copy" could be established in the Stationers' Register. Whitgift's immediate concerns were Puritan attacks on the episcopal church itself, notably the Martin Marprelate tracts, whose unlicensed printers he pursued relentlessly; one suspect, John Penry, was hanged in 1593. Yet when John Hayward's duly licensed *Life of Henry IV* (1599) became a scandal because of its dedication to the earl of Essex, the licenser, Samuel Harsnett (perhaps prudentially), excused himself on the grounds that he had not actually read it. The 1599 Bishop's Ban, which proscribed various contentious works, notably by Gabriel Harvey and Thomas Nashe, and forbade the printing of satires and epigrams, was another symptom of nervous times, and had few long-term effects. It did, however, tighten up on such works as ballads and plays being printed on licensed presses but without due authority; Shakespeare's *Richard II* (1597) is an example, though its abdication scene had in fact been censored, or prudentially cut.

Controls on theatrical performance paralleled those for print, with authorities keen to limit open religious controversy, in both public and private venues. The mystery cycles and other drama with strong Roman Catholic associations were brought under ever closer control and finally squeezed out of existence. The feast of Corpus Christi itself, to which so much of this drama was traditionally attached, was suppressed in 1548. The Mary plays from the York cycle were not performed in the 1540s; the Chester cycle was last performed in 1575, despite efforts by the city authorities to save it; in 1576, the conditions imposed on the York cycle made it unplayable; the last cycle, that at Coventry, was performed for the last time in 1579.

In 1559, Elizabeth spelled out exactly what restrictions were expected on plays:

> The Queenes Majestie doth straightly forbyd all maner Interludes to be playde eyther openly or privately, except the same be notified before hande, and licenced within any Citie or towne corporate, by the Maior or other chiefe officers of the same, and within any shyre, by suche as shalbe Lieutenauntes for the Quenes Majestie in the same shyre, or by two of the Justices of peax inhabiting within that part of the shire where any shalbe played . . . And for instruction to every of the sayde officers, her majestie doth likewise charge every of them, as they will aunswere: that they permyt none to be played wherein either matters of religion or of the governaunce of the estate of the common weale

C

shalbe handled or treated upon, but by menne of aucthoritie, learning and wisedome, nor to be handled before any audience, but of grave and discreete persons (Chambers, *Elizabethan Stage,* vol. IV, pp. 263–264).

These latter exemptions replace earlier leeway given to works in Latin, in privileged contexts such as colleges, the Inns of Court, and the court itself. The implication is that more relaxed standards of what was permissible pertained there, allowing such works as *Gorboduc* to be performed, although it transparently touched on "the governaunce of the estate of the common weale." This principle had important implications when the master of the revels became involved in dramatic censorship. In 1574, Leicester's Men received a license permitting them to perform, on the condition that their "stage playes be by the master of our Revells . . . before sene and allowed." This challenged the Common Council of London, who that year forbade plays "which shall not be firste perused and Allowed . . . by such persons as by the Lorde Maior and Court of Alderman . . . shalbe appoynted" and "wherain shalbe uttered anie wourdes, examples, or doynges of anie unchastitie, sedicion, nor suche lyke unfytt and uncomely matter."

In 1581, however, Edmund Tilney, master of the revels, received a special license, establishing the ultimate authority of the court in all theatrical matters, initially over the London region but progressively further afield. By the time of Henslowe's *diary,* he had sole responsibility for censoring plays in the capital. He read and, if necessary, "reformed" a script, to which he would attach his license. This "allowed" text was the only permitted basis for performance; the license also restricted the right to perform to the company that owned it, establishing a form of copyright. So Tilney was an ally of the acting companies, protecting them from civic authorities and regulating competition, as much as their censor. That he was licensing plays as if for court performance meant that he assessed them relatively more liberally than might otherwise be the case. The one surviving script that shows his attentions, *Sir Thomas More,* reveals no objection to the careful depiction of a man revered by some as a Catholic martyr to royal tyranny, but a determination not to allow the depiction of anti-alien riots, a sensitive issue in 1590s London. Tilney had no responsibility for censoring plays for the press, which remained with the ecclesiastical licensers. However, his successors under James I performed both functions, suggesting that, even though the two branches of censorship had evolved separately, they were not so different in spirit and function.

BIBLIOGRAPHY
Clare, J. *"Art Made Tongue-Tied by Authority": Elizabethan and Jacobean Dramatic Censorship.* 1990.
Clegg, C.S. *Press Censorship in Elizabethan England.* 1997.
Dutton, R. *Mastering the Revels: The Regulation and Censorship of English Renaissance Drama.* 1991.

Richard Dutton

SEE ALSO
Literacy; Marprelate Controversy; Printing, Publishing, and Bookselling; Revel Office; Star Chamber, Court of; Stubbs, John; Tilney, Edmund; Whitgift, John

Chaloner, Thomas (1520–1565)

The political career of Sir Thomas Chaloner's spanned the reigns of four Tudor monarchs. Famous in his own day chiefly for his Latin poetry, Chaloner is now best remembered as the first English translator of Desiderius Erasmus's *Moriae Encomium.*

A distinguished Latinist at Cambridge in the 1530s, Chaloner attended the Imperial Diet at Regensburg in 1540–1541 as secretary to Sir Henry Knyvet and the diplomatic party representing Henry VIII. He subsequently accompanied Charles V's expedition against the Moors in Algeria, although shipwreck cut short Chaloner's venture before he saw action. He attained the less adventuresome office of clerk of the Privy Council in 1545, and never thereafter left government service. Knighted in 1547 after the Musselburgh campaign against the Scots, Chaloner went on to serve as M.P. for Lancaster borough (1547), as commissioner of the peace for Middlesex (1547 and 1554), as Edward VI's resident ambassador to France (1553), as Mary I's agent at the Scottish negotiations of 1556, and as Elizabeth I's chief ambassador to Spain from 1561 to 1565. He married twice: first in 1546 to Joan Leigh, who died in 1557, and then in his last days to Audrey Frodsham. William Cecil stood as chief mourner at Chaloner's elaborate funeral at St. Paul's in 1565.

Chaloner's literary affiliations were no less substantial than his political contacts. Throughout his travels he maintained correspondence with such mid-century poets as Barnabe Googe and Thomas Sackville. His original poetic efforts include a contribution to the account of Richard II's fall in *A Myrroure for Magistrates* (1559), and the didactic epic *De republica Anglicana,* issued posthumously in 1579.

C

Chaloner rendered his greatest service to English literature, however, as a translator. His considerable skill as a Latinist—already tested in his *Of the Office of Seruauntes, a Boke Made in Latine by one Gylbertus Cognatus* (1543), and his rendition of John Cheke's Latin version of a sermon by John Chrysostom (1544)—met its supreme challenge in Erasmus's great mock-encomium. *The Praise of Folie* (1549) turns Erasmus's pointed satire into accessible English while sacrificing impressively little of the original's intricate verbal wit. The translator's announced willingness to ease "the sowre sence of the latine with some manerlier englishe worde," and deft substitution of homier English equivalents for the allusive classical proverbs that punctuate *Folly's* performance, splendidly exhibit Chaloner's excellent grasp of his author's "meerie conceited sentences." What results is both a fine translation and a delightful portrait of the period's literary wit.

BIBLIOGRAPHY

Chaloner, Thomas, trans. *The Praise of Folie.* Clarence H. Miller, ed. Early English Text Society, vol. 257. 1965.

Christopher Martin

SEE ALSO

Classical Literature, English Translations; Erasmus, Desiderius; Neo-Latin Literature

Chancery

The Chancery was one of the most amorphous institutions of the early modern era. Presided over by the lord keeper (untitled) or lord chancellor (a titled nobleman), the Chancery was a secretariat for the monarch, a department of state, and a court of law for matters in equity or common law. As a secretariat, the Chancery was an administrative center of the government, handled petitions to the monarch, and issued the original writs that commenced actions in the common law courts. The chancellor himself presided over the Privy Council and the House of Lords, serving as a major spokesman of royal policy. Under the early Tudors, the chancellor was quite close to the monarch, and was said to possess the royal conscience that allowed him to give justice to petitioners who sought remedies either within or outside of the common law. Thomas Wolsey represented the height of this development. Later, under Elizabeth I, a series of common law chancellors from Sir Nicholas Bacon to Sir Thomas Egerton developed a department of state and court of law that no longer represented the royal mind.

Thus by 1603 the Chancery functioned as an institution independent of the crown.

The chancellor wore many hats. The Tudor era witnessed the growth of the royal prerogative and the conciliar courts, and the office of chancellor was primarily responsible for both their growth and administration. From Thomas Wolsey to Thomas Egerton, chancellors presided over the Court of Star Chamber, and from Nicholas Bacon they added the presidency of the Court of High Commission, and served as lord high stewards for treason trials where the crown wanted swift justice without the complications of formal court proceedings. While the judicial nature of the office was minor under Henry VII, the conciliar and legal duties became so overwhelming that by the late Elizabethan period only career lawyers, not bishops, were seen as competent to dispense the responsibilities of the office, and common lawyers made inroads as career officials in competition with civilians.

As a court of law, the Chancery began the Tudor era with the shortest court calendar of the central courts, and ended it as one of the busiest courts in the country. The concept of the chancellor bearing the conscience of the monarch to do justice where no writ lay at common law had brought civil matters such as copyholds, trusts, and charities into this court of equity. Problems associated with the expansion of the Tudor economy, inflation, and heightened social distinctions fed the growth of equitable causes in the court. By the late 1590s, the case load had become so large that delays, abuses, and jurisdictional conflicts with other courts brought the Chancery into the vortex of political strife that marked the last years of Elizabeth's reign.

BIBLIOGRAPHY

Cioni, Maria L. *Women and Law in Elizabethan England, with Particular Reference to the Court of Chancery.* 1985.

Guy, J.A. *The Public Career of Sir Thomas More.* 1980.

Horwitz, Henry, ed. *Chancery Equity Records and Proceedings, 1600–1800.* 1995.

Jones, W.J. *The Elizabethan Court of Chancery.* 1967.

Knafla, Louis A. *Law and Politics in Jacobean England. The Tracts of Lord Chancellor Ellesmere.* 1977.

Louis A. Knafla

SEE ALSO

Bacon, Nicholas; Common Law; Economy; Egerton, Thomas; Star Chamber, Court of; Wolsey, Thomas

Chantry

Originally, the term "chantry" referred to an ecclesiastical endowment providing for the saying of Mass, in perpetuity, for the souls of the endower, his family, and friends. The term also came to mean the small chapel in which such Masses were said. The chapels were built and maintained by the initial endowment, which also paid the salary of the chantry priest. Chantries were common in England prior to the Reformation; even after an act was passed in 1546 allowing the chantries to be dissolved by the crown, Henry VIII left them largely intact. On the accession of Edward VI, however, chantries were suppressed and much of their properties and monies were siphoned off by the young king's advisers.

BIBLIOGRAPHY

Cook, George Henry. *Mediaeval Chantries and Chantry Chapels.* 1963.

Mark Goldblatt

SEE ALSO

Edward VI; Monastic Orders

CHAPBOOKS

See Broadsides

CHAPEL ROYAL

See Cornysh, William; Edwardes, Richard; Hunnis, William; Theater Companies, Boys

Chapman, George (c. 1559–1634)

The son of a yeoman, George Chapman was born in Hertfordshire and his early years are obscure. As a young man, he served in the household of Sir Ralph Sadler and fought in the Low Countries. Chapman emerged on the *fin de siècle* literary scene with *The Shadow of Night* (1594), as his bid to enter an intellectual circle. While writing remarkable poetry, Chapman supported himself producing scripts for the London stage, earning recognition as "among the best" for both comedy and tragedy. Always unlucky in his patrons, who either died (Prince Henry) or were disgraced (Essex, Ralegh, Somerset), Chapman often was in debt and, like other playwrights, in trouble with the law: hauled into court over a libelous comedy (1603), imprisoned with Ben Jonson and John Marston for satirizing Scots (1605), and in difficulty again from French complaints about *The Tragedy of Byron* (1608). Through this turbulent career, his personal obses-

sion was the translation of Homer into English, a project finished a decade before his death. Inigo Jones paid for his headstone, still to be seen at St. Giles in the Field.

In his activities as poet, dramatist, translator, and—through prefaces, dedications, and defenses—a theorist, Chapman rivaled his friend Jonson as a man of letters. Humanist in his learning, Stoic in his ethics, and Neoplatonic in his epistemology, Chapman was influenced profoundly by Marsilio Ficino, the great translator and interpreter of Plato. Chapman's difficult style has caused some scholars to link him with the Metaphysicals; however, Chapman wrote as a Neoplatonic mystagogue, using obscurity to conceal truth from the many while revealing it to the few "understanders." Rather than being paired with John Donne, Chapman should be placed in a line of visionary poets extending from Edmund Spenser, whom he saw as a competitor, through John Milton and William Blake.

Chapman's best poetry emerged during a few intense years. *The Shadow of Night,* like T.S. Eliot's *The Waste Land,* was a poetic manifesto, intimidating in its obscurity and learning (largely derived from Natalis Comes's *Mythologiae*). It consists of two "Orphic" hymns, or religious mysteries, the first lamenting the fallen human condition and the second, a complex allegory, invoking the goddess Cynthia. Another "epic hymn," *De Guiana* (1596), celebrates the emergence of Elizabethan imperialism under the Virgin Queen in an appeal for Ralegh's colonial expedition. A pair of poems attack the fashionable, Ovidian erotic narratives. *Ovid's Banquet of Sense* (1595), described by Frank Kermode as "the most difficult poem in the English language," exploits the tactic of an unreliable narrator; as the title-page emblem hints, the entire poem is a warning to distrust the senses. Chapman's continuation of Christopher Marlowe's *Hero and Leander* (1598) redirects the poem to epic metamorphosis, endowing it with moral seriousness. Neoplatonism's visual bias may account for Chapman's creative response to the print medium.

Chapman made his mark in the theater with innovative comedy, initiating the vogue for the comedy of humors, then progressing to tragicomedy (*The Gentleman Usher*) and satiric comedy in *The Widow's Tears,* a riposte to *Measure for Measure.* He followed Marlowe's *The Massacre at Paris* in choosing recent French history, rather than remote English history, as the subject for five tragedies, of which *Bussy D'Ambois,* a sensational melodrama overlaid by philosophic myth, is the best known. Like Jonson and others, he responded to

C

changes in government and political philosophy by turning to Roman tragedy (*Caesar and Pompey*). Only one court masque survives, but we have Jonson's testimony that "next himself only Fletcher and Chapman could make a Mask."

The translation of Homer began with *Seaven Bookes of the Iliades and Achilles' Shield* (1598). In *The Teares of Peace* (1609), Chapman announced his visionary inspiration by Homer to complete the project. The *Iliads* was published two years later; the *Odysses* in 1615; *The Whole Works of Homer* in 1616, followed by Museus, Hesiod, and the lesser Homerica. Chapman's feat in translating the poetic *prisca theologia* parallels that of his mentor Ficino in philosophy. Despite his unfulfilled promise to publish "my Poeme of the mysteries / Reveal'd in Homer," Chapman did not overburden his translations with learned exegesis. Scorning "word-for-word traductions," he sought to make Homer's universal truths relevant to his own era and culture. His English makes explicit the ethical and philosophical values he perceived in the original. Chapman's assertion that each epic is epitomized in the first word (*wrath* and *man*) characterizes his approach to translation: "in one, the Bodie's fervor and fashion of outward Fortitude to all possible height of Heroicall Action; in the other the Mind's inward, constant and unconquered Empire." Like other humanists, Chapman approached Greek through the filiation of Latin translations and commentaries; but questions about his fidelity to the Greek should not distract attention from his achievement as the outstanding poetic translator of the English Renaissance.

BIBLIOGRAPHY

Braunmuller, A.R. *Natural Fictions: George Chapman's Major Tragedies.* 1992.

Chapman, George. *The Plays of George Chapman: The Comedies, a Critical Edition.* Alan Holaday, ed. 1970.

———. *The Plays of George Chapman: The Tragedies.* Alan Holaday, ed. 1987.

———. *Chapman's Homer.* Allardyce Nicoll, ed. 1967.

Snare, Gerald. *The Mystification of George Chapman.* 1989.

Waddington, Raymond B. *The Mind's Eye: Method and Form in George Chapman's Narrative Poems.* 1974.

Raymond B. Waddington

SEE ALSO

Classical Literature, English Translations; Classical Literature, Influence of; Sadler, Ralph

Chapuys, Eustace (c. 1489–c. 1550)

Imperial ambassador to England on two separate tours of duty, 1529–1536 and 1542–1545, Eustace Chapuys was the descendant of a minor Savoyard family of notaries. His legal education at Turin gained him employment in the service of the bishop of Geneva, the duke de Bourbon, and finally the emperor Charles V. His diplomatic career began with his first mission to England. Charles wished him to preserve the honor of Katherine of Aragon, the emperor's aunt, without antagonizing Henry VIII and precipitating a break between England and the empire. Before long, his sympathy for Katherine became his chief motivation, however futile that proved to be. He devoted his best years to her defense and to that of her daughter, the princess Mary. A shrewd and very capable ambassador, Chapuys kept in close touch with imperial and Catholic sympathizers in England, and provided his master a close and perceptive account of affairs at court. Many considered his taste for intrigue a threat to the Henrician regime, but Henry appears to have valued his extensive knowledge of continental affairs. At the end of Henry's reign Chapuys retired to the University of Louvain, where he founded a college and spent his last years.

BIBLIOGRAPHY

Mattingly, Garrett. "A Humanist Ambassador." *Journal of Modern History,* vol. 4, pp. 175–185.

———. *Catherine of Aragon.* 1941.

Loades, David. *Mary Tudor, a Life.* 1989.

Robert Tittler

SEE ALSO

Foreign Relations and Diplomacy; Henry VIII; Katherine of Aragon

Cheke, John (1514–1557)

Born and reared in Cambridge, John Cheke received the M.A. in 1533 from St. John's College. In the 1530s, he became the central figure of a group of Cambridge humanists who later became prominent in the universities, in the church, and at court; Cheke's circle included Thomas Smith, Walter Haddon, William Cecil, and Roger Ascham. In 1540, Cheke was named the first regius professor of Greek at Cambridge. In 1542, he engaged in a controversy over the pronunciation of Greek with Stephen Gardiner, then chancellor of Cambridge, which was published in *De pronuntiatione Graecae linguaeae* (1555).

In 1544, Cheke was called to court to become one of the tutors of Edward, Prince of Wales. He remained Edward's tutor until 1552, leading him through a demanding program of classical studies. In the last years of Henry VIII's reign, Cheke dedicated to the king a series of translations from Greek into Latin, including Plutarch's *De superstitione.* Cheke's lengthy preface to this work involves discreet advocacy of further religious reform. After his pupil came to the throne as Edward VI, Cheke became a member of Parliament and began accumulating lands and sinecures. In 1549, he wrote his best-known work, *The hurt of sedition,* directed against the rebels of that year; Cheke describes at length the economic, social, and political damage he believes their actions may cause. In 1551 he was knighted. Cheke supported development of the new Prayer Book of 1552, and engaged in many other tasks related to ecclesiastical reform. He corresponded with the Reformer Martin Bucer, whom Archbishop Thomas Cranmer had welcomed to England; on Bucer's death in 1551, Cheke contributed to and probably organized the compilation of *De obitu . . . Buceri,* a memorial collection of Latin prose and Latin and Greek verse, the first such volume printed in England.

In June 1553, as Edward was dying, Cheke was appointed a secretary of state, and allowed himself to become a party to the effort to interpose Lady Jane Grey as Edward's successor. On the triumph of Queen Mary, Cheke was imprisoned, then released but stripped of his lands and offices. He went abroad in 1554. In Padua in 1554–1555 he began a treatise on the nature of the church. Another unfinished work that may date from Cheke's exile is his English translation of the Gospel of Matthew and a fragment of Mark. In 1556, Cheke was kidnapped in the Low Countries and taken to England, where he was induced to recant his Protestant beliefs. On his deathbed the following year he expressed remorse for his action.

In Cheke's work, Protestant doctrine interacts with the heritage of Erasmian humanism. Beginning with his earliest surviving letters, Cheke demonstrates his commitment to central Reformation doctrines, including utter dependence on divine grace and justification through faith. For Cheke, however, grace not only instills faith but enables the elect to lead a sanctified Christian life. Cheke echoes Erasmus in decrying overemphasis on ceremonial religion; what the Christian is above all called to is a life of active charity. Obviously, deep engagement with classical learning is also part of Cheke's humanistic inheritance. For Cheke as for Erasmus, philological knowledge is vital to the interpretation of Scripture. Eloquence guided by classical models is a means of impelling men and women toward right moral conduct. Cheke was involved in a number of humanistic linguistic projects, including those intended to raise English to the level of the classical languages. He advocated bringing quantitative meters into English. His letter (1557) prefacing Sir Thomas Hoby's translation of *The Courtyer* opposes unnecessary borrowings from foreign languages; Cheke's approach follows that of Cicero. The Gospel translation uses new-coined words from native roots in preference to borrowings, and also a rationalized spelling. The concern of Cheke and his colleagues for style and linguistic detail has been criticized as a preoccupation with verbal surface at the expense of substance. It is fair to say that Cheke attached great importance to particular classical stylistic canons, but it is clear that he understood his concern for words as a concern for rhetorical expressiveness and effectiveness.

BIBLIOGRAPHY

Ascham, Roger. *English Works.* William Aldis Wright, ed. 1904.

Cheke, John. *De pronuntiatione Graecae linguae.* Facsimile edition. *English Linguistics, 1500–1800,* vol. 81. 1968.

———. *The hurt of sedition.* Facsimile edition. 1971.

———, trans. *The Gospel According to St. Matthew and part of the first chapter of the Gospel according to St. Mark.* James Goodwin, ed. 1843.

Hudson, Winthrop. *The Cambridge Connection* and *The Elizabethan Settlement of 1559.* 1980.

Nathan, Walter Ludwig. *Sir John Cheke und der Englische Humanismus.* 1928.

Needham, Paul. "Sir John Cheke at Cambridge and Court." Unpublished dissertation, Harvard. 1971.

Vos, Alvin. "'Good Matter and Good Utterance': The Character of English Ciceronianism." *Studies in English Literature, 1500–1900,* vol. 19, pp. 3–18.

John F. McDiarmid

SEE ALSO

Erasmus, Desiderius; Grey, Lady Jane; Humanism

Chester, Robert (1566?–1640?)

English cleric, chaplain, and house-bard to Sir John Salusbury (1567–1612), of Lleweny Hall, near Denbigh, in Wales, Robert Chester might have been born in June 1566, and might have lived until May 3, 1640,

C

though this chronology is conjectural. He may also have died in 1607. Chester wrote a great amount of elaborately contrived verse, most of it at the behest of his tyrannical employer; he also undertook an epic poem on the "Life of King Arthur," but was never able to finish it. The numerous poems that Chester wrote for Salusbury fall into two groups: unpublished pieces written to celebrate various occasions in the Salusbury household and copied into the family album; and *Loues Martyr,* for which he is best known, an enormous project consisting of a long allegorical narrative poem, followed by eighty-two shorter poems. *Loues Martyr* was composed between September 1598, and August 1599, in an effort to persuade Salusbury's estranged wife, Ursula, to return to him, and so save his threatened knighthood.

As soon as Salusbury was knighted (June 1601), he arranged for the publication of *Loues Martyr,* but included as an appendix is a group of fifteen poems that had been expressly written for this volume by other authors. The title page attributes this part of the volume to "severall moderne Writers," in fact, William Shakespeare, John Marston, George Chapman, and Ben Jonson. Following four pseudonymous poems is Shakespeare's "The Phoenix and the Turtle," divided into two parts; four poems on perfection by Marston; a pair by Chapman, and the final pair by Jonson. Although these poems all touch on themes present in *Loues Martyr,* they reshape and comment, often in cruel satire, on Chester's allegory of the union of the Phoenix and the Turtle. Chester's reaction to the ridicule of *Loues Martyr* in the appendix poems may be seen in his poem "Conclusion." The occasion for these poems may be the changing fortunes of Robert Devereux, the earl of Essex, and his relationship to Elizabeth I, although critical opinion on this point differs.

The book was published in London in October 1601 (STC 5119) by Edward Blount, best known for publishing French and Italian works. Blount's strategy for marketing Salusbury's book was to advertise *Loues Martyr* as the work of an Italian poet, "Torquato Caeliano" (heavenly dove), relegating Chester's role to that of translator. Chester was allowed to sign his name to each of three short preliminary verse epistles. Salusbury authorized the inclusion in the volume of Chester's unfinished epic about King Arthur, but Blount describes this work on the title page merely as "the first Essay of a new Brytish poet."

BIBLIOGRAPHY

Brown, Carleton, ed. *Poems by Sir John Salusbury and Robert Chester.* Early English Text Society, extra series, vol. 113. 1914.

Grosart, Alexander B., ed. *The Poems of Robert Chester (1601–11) with Verse Contributions by Shakespeare, Ben Jonson, George Chapman, John Marston, etc.* 1878.

Jayne, Sears. Unpublished study of *Love's Martyr.* Huntington and Bodleian Libraries. 1990.

Matchett, William H. *The Phoenix and the Turtle: Shakespeare's Poem and Chester's* Love's Martyr. 1965.

Sears Jayne

SEE ALSO

Devereux, Robert; Shakespeare, William

Chettle, Henry (c. 1560–c. 1607)

Printer, poet, and collaborator on approximately forty-eight plays (with, among others, Thomas Dekker, Ben Jonson, and Anthony Munday), Henry Chettle is known best for his hack writing under Philip Henslowe and for his participation in Robert Greene's *Groatsworth of Wit, Bought with a Million of Repentance* (1592), which contains an early allusion to William Shakespeare. Although called by Francis Meres in *Palladis Tamia* (1598) one of "the best for Comedy amongst us" and often described as a capable writer, Chettle eked out a penurious, debt-ridden existence and died in obscurity.

Son of the London dyer Robert Chettle, Henry Chettle began his career with the stationer Thomas East as a printer's apprentice in 1577. He later joined the printers John Danter (responsible for the 1594 quarto of *Titus Andronicus* and the 1597 *Romeo and Juliet* "bad" quarto) and William Hoskins between 1589–1591. After this, Chettle may have continued printing alone or with Danter.

While working as a printer Chettle edited—and possibly even wrote—*Groatsworth,* Greene's well-studied deathbed confession. Although no conclusive evidence exists for Chettle's authorship, the publisher William Wright's disclaimer of responsibility for its first printing (he prints it "upon the perill of Henrye Chettle"), together with Chettle's own apologetic *Kind Hart's Dream* (1593), may implicate Chettle in an interesting literary hoax. In *Kind Hart's Dream,* Chettle both mollifies Greene's scandalous comments and praises the understandably maligned Shakespeare. He also vehemently denies composing *Groatsworth.*

After *Groatsworth's* publication, Chettle married and began writing plays. His participation in Anthony Munday's *Sir Thomas More* (c. 1593) is extensive and refined, yet parts were marked for omission by Edmund Tilney, the master of the revels And while the anonymous *Two Lamentable Tragedies* (c. 1594), *The Trial of Chivalry* (c. 1600), and *The Weakest Goeth to the Wall* (1600), all have been attributed to Chettle as well, only *The Tragedy of Hoffman; or, A Revenge for a Father* (1602) is certainly his. This "Danyshe tragedy," as Henslowe describes it, adequately explores the Senecan themes of a hero's ambition and his stoic defiance that flourished during Chettle's time.

Chettle's poetry includes "England's Mourning Garment" (1603), an elegy for Elizabeth I that summons several contemporary poets to join him in lamentation. Among these poets is Melicert, who may be Shakespeare. Evidence for Chettle's death around 1607 includes Dekker's *Night's Conjuring* (1607), which humorously provides Chettle rest alongside Chaucer and Spenser in Elysium.

BIBLIOGRAPHY

Ackermann, R.A., ed. *The Tragedy of Hoffman.* 1894.
Carroll, D. Allen, ed. *Greene's Groatsworth of Wit, Bought with a Million of Repentance.* 1994.
Chambers, E.K. *The Elizabethan Stage.* 4 vols. 1923.
Gabrieli, Vittorio, and Giorgio Melchiori, eds. *Sir Thomas More.* 1990.
Harrison, G.B., ed. *Kind Hart's Dream.* 1923.
Jenkins, Harold. *The Life and Work of Henry Chettle.* 1934.

Dana E. Aspinall

SEE ALSO

Dekker, Thomas; Elegy; Greene, Robert; Jonson, Ben; Munday, Anthony; Shakespeare, William; Tilney, Edmund

Childbirth

Childbearing was an obligation for Tudor married women, although continuing ambivalence about whether it should be regarded as godly or sinful was reflected in some of the clerical discourse relating to it. It was a highly feminine experience, births taking place in warm, darkened rooms among female "gossips" who were occasionally the subject of male anxieties about threatening women. Many women would be delivered in their moth-

ers' homes, and the support of other close female relatives was common. Births were managed by midwives, usually respectable women drawn from the middling sections of the community, and supposedly licensed by the ecclesiastical authorities. The purpose of licensing was to ensure that the women involved were religiously orthodox rather than medically qualified, because in the event of peril to the child's life, they were authorized (albeit with much clerical misgiving) to perform baptism. The attack of professional male medicine on the role of the midwife had not begun, and midwives were trusted members of the community. In the absence of anaesthetics childbirth could be perilous. Women stood a 1 percent chance of dying in the course of a delivery, and as they averaged six or seven pregnancies in a lifetime, their cumulative risk of dying in the childbed was about 7 percent. For the 2–4 percent of women whose births were illegitimate, childbirth was even more fraught, as they were subjected to immense pressure, at the moment of their greatest pain, to name the father. Protestant reformers launched a major campaign (albeit with limited results) to eliminate the superstitious practices that had surrounded childbirth, in particular the use of charms and holy girdles, and they promoted forms of prayer appropriate to the new reformed sensibilities. After giving birth, the woman was expected to keep to her house for a period of about a month. Her reincorporation into the community took place in the religious ceremony known as "churching." This was a site for conflict between conformists and godly radicals. Although notions of penitential cleansing had supposedly been removed from the ceremony at the Reformation, it continued to arouse the anxieties of the godly, but enjoyed apparently widespread support from the populace. Some ambivalence remained about the nature of the ceremony (was it a purification or a thanksgiving?) but it is clear that the people did not think of it in terms of pollution, but rather saw it as an occasion for celebration, often with elaborate feastings.

BIBLIOGRAPHY

Cressy, D. *Birth, Marriage, and Death: Ritual, Religion, and the Life Cycle in Tudor and Stuartt England.* 1997.
Pollock, L.A. "Childbearing and Female Bonding in Early Modern England." *Social History,* vol. 22, pp. 286–306.

Ian W. Archer

SEE ALSO

Gender; Population and Demography

C

Christopherson, John (d. 1558)

Bishop of Chichester and confessor to Mary I, John Christopherson earned an M.A. from Trinity College, Cambridge, in 1543 and was made a fellow of the college three years later, working to advance the study of Greek language and literature. The shift of the English church, after the accession of Edward VI in 1547, toward a more reformed Protestant polity caused Christopherson, whose sympathies were steadfastly Catholic, to retire to Europe for the duration of Edward's reign. He was supported by Trinity College, to which he dedicated his Latin translation of the Jewish theologian Philo. When Mary succeeded Edward in 1553, Christopherson returned to England and was named master of Trinity, becoming Mary's private chaplain and confessor. The next year he was installed as dean of Norwich and was present at the burnings, in 1555, of William Wolsey and Robert Pigot. Consecrated bishop of Chichester in 1557, Christopherson served on the commission that oversaw the exhumation, posthumous trial, and subsequent burnings of the bodies of Martin Bucer and Paul Fagius at Cambridge. When Mary died and was succeeded by Elizabeth I in 1558, Christopherson, whose participation in the Marian persecutions had brought him the everlasting enmity of Protestants, was imprisoned; he died shortly thereafter. He is also remembered as a scholar and translator of patristic writings and benefactor of Trinity College.

BIBLIOGRAPHY

Cooper, T. "John Christopherson." *Dictionary of National Biographies.* Vol. 4., pp. 293–295. 1917.

Mark Goldblatt

SEE ALSO

Bucer, Martin; Church Polity; Marian Martyrs

Church of England

Ecclesia Anglicana, the name given to the church founded among the Anglo-Saxon tribes by Augustine of Canterbury, acting as the legate of Pope Gregory the Great in 597, was known in Tudor times as the Church of England. There had been Christians in Roman Britain since the late second century, and the country was officially converted at the same time as the rest of the Roman Empire (313), but with the retreat of the legions and the Germanic invasions, Christianity receded into the Celtic parts of the British Isles. Both Celtic and Roman missionaries participated in the evangelization of the English, but after the Synod of Whitby in 664, the new church accepted the Roman obedience in which it remained until 1534.

The Anglo-Saxon church was the oldest institution of the whole English people, antedating the kingdom of England by several hundred years. But it was always closely tied to the secular rulers, and many of the decisions affecting it were taken by the *witan,* a kind of Anglo-Saxon parliament. Pope Gregory the Great had originally envisaged a church consisting of two provinces, one based at London and the other at York, along the lines of the late Roman administration of Britain. Augustine was able to establish an archbishopric at York, but London was too exposed to attack, and he was forced to withdraw to the Kentish capital of Canterbury, which has been the center of the southern province ever since. During the early Middle Ages there was considerable rivalry between the two archbishoprics (or "metropolitan sees"), but the latter eventually prevailed, and decisions taken by Canterbury were often held to extend to the whole of England, regardless of the claims of York.

After the Norman Conquest, the Church of England was reorganized to bring it into closer conformity with the Western church in general. Ecclesiastical courts were separated from civil jurisdiction in 1072, and after that time, England came to experience church-state conflicts of a type already familiar on the Continent. However, the relatively high degree of centralization that prevailed in England ensured that church and state would continue to work closely together, and when Parliament emerged in the thirteenth century, the church was fully represented in it. Bishops sat in the House of Lords, and the lower clergy were represented by proctors in the House of Commons, at least until 1340. After that date, the clergy withdrew, preferring to be represented through the two Convocations of Canterbury and York that normally met at the same time as the Parliament, although they claimed to be juridically independent of its authority.

The Church of England was hierarchically organized, in line with the Western church in general. The two provinces of Canterbury and York were subdivided into dioceses, each of which was presided over by a bishop theoretically elected by the local clergy, but who, in practice, was usually a royal nominee whose "election" was confirmed by the pope. These bishops were known as prelates, because of their promotion to higher office, and prelacy was the standard Tudor term for both the episcopate and the system of episcopacy.

A major problem with this system was that dioceses were very large, and bishops, even if they were resident in

C

them, could not supervise their affairs effectively. One of the first things Parliament did after the break with Rome (1534) was to create a number of suffragan (i.e., assistant) bishops who would be better able to administer portions of the larger dioceses. This reform was later followed by the creation of five new dioceses (1541), which was yet another attempt to deal with the problem.

Each diocese was subdivided into archdeaconries, presided over by an archdeacon, whose main task was to ensure that the property and fabric of the church were properly cared for. The archdeacon was meant to make periodic inspections and report any irregularities to the bishop, who was then supposed to take action to correct them. The inefficiency of this system is amply attested by the numerous enactments of canonical legislation designed to enforce it. Archdeaconries were in turn subdivided into rural deaneries, each of which grouped together a relatively small number of parishes. The rural dean acted as a kind of superintendent, and was supposed to ensure that services were properly (and regularly) conducted in the parishes.

Parishes were usually coterminous with the village communities that embraced the majority of the population, and each one theoretically had a resident priest who was known in law as the "incumbent" of the "benefice" or "living," because he was entitled to receive the revenues of the parish that were reserved for the support of the clergy. The incumbent might be either a rector, if he held the living in his own right, or a vicar, if he stood in for a monastery or religious house that technically owned the benefice. The owner of the benefice had the right to appoint its minister. This right was called the "advowson" (a corruption of the Latin advocatio), and was treated as private property that could be bought and sold without reference to the bishop. After the dissolution of the monasteries most of the monastic advowsons passed into the hands of lay patrons. There was no longer any real difference between rectors and vicars, although both terms have been preserved to the present day. Incumbents might hire assistant priests who were technically vicars, but who have come to be known as (assistant) "curates." After the Reformation, an attempt was made to increase the standard of teaching in the parishes by appointing "lecturers" who, with the consent of the parish priest, gave instruction in the Christian faith to the parishioners, often on Sunday afternoons. These lecturers were effectively curates, and it was among them that Puritanism took hold most rapidly in the later sixteenth century.

The medieval Church of England was fully subject to the Holy See of Rome, but it managed to compile a vast amount of local legislation that governed its everyday affairs. Provincial synods were a regular occurrence from the thirteenth century onward, and the canons that they issued form several printed volumes. In 1433, an attempt was made by William Lyndwood to reduce this to order, and his authoritative compilation of this legislation, contained in his *Provinciale,* formed the basis of English canon law in Tudor England. Throughout this period, the king was regularly involved in church affairs, and Lyndwood quite happily included two royal decrees among the legislation passed by the provincial synods. Parliament also continued to show an interest in church affairs, and occasionally legislated even against the abuse of papal power in England.

All of this was to be of great importance in the 1520s, when Henry VIII discovered that he could not obtain an annulment of his marriage to Katharine of Aragon without first seizing control of the church. Henry believed, in spite of the objections of some of his more prominent subjects like Sir Thomas More, that he was acting within his traditional rights as king. He was always very careful to make certain that whatever reforms he introduced were supported by appropriate parliamentary legislation, thereby emphasizing the fact that the church was to be subject not merely to the crown, but to the House of Lords and House of Commons as well.

At first, the convocations of the clergy did their best to resist Henry's encroachments, but they were not able to stand up against the king, and by 1534, all organized opposition had been silenced. The clergy of Canterbury voted to accept the royal supremacy on March 31 of that year; York followed suit on May 15. Only after that was legislation introduced into Parliament making the change legal (November 3, 1534). By the terms of the Act of Supremacy, Henry VIII became supreme head on earth of the Church of England, as of the other national churches within his dominions (notably the Church of Ireland). Henry also retained the title defender of the faith, which had been granted to him by the pope (1521) in appreciation for his defense of the sacraments against Luther, but which was now put to a new and very different use.

Over the next few years, Henry confiscated the extensive properties of the monasteries, which he dissolved in two stages—the smaller ones in 1536, and the larger ones in 1538. From the income thus derived, he endowed several educational foundations, founded five new dioceses, and paid a number of his supporters by allowing them to

C

purchase monastic land at modest prices. This created a gentry class with a vested interest in making certain that the old order would not be restored, and this class was to form the backbone of support for the Reformation.

After 1534, there were some attempts on the part of leading churchmen to bring the Church of England closer to the Lutherans, but these came to nothing. In 1539, Henry acted to put a stop to what he perceived was the growing Protestantism of the church, and initiated a doctrinal reaction that reaffirmed such Catholic teachings as transubstantiation and clerical celibacy. Further reform had to wait until after the king's death (January 28, 1547).

Under Edward VI , Thomas Cranmer, as archbishop of Canterbury, had a much freer hand to reform the church along Protestant lines. He introduced a reformed pattern of worship in 1549, and supplanted it with an even more Protestant document in 1552. He also composed a statement of faith called the Forty-two Articles, which was adopted by the Convocations in 1553. His one great failure was a planned reform of the canon law (*Reformatio Legum Ecclesiasticarum*), which he introduced into the House of Lords in 1553, but which was defeated by lay opposition. It is sometimes said that had he succeeded in reforming the church courts, Puritanism would never have acquired the popularity it was to attain later in the century. In this connection, it should be remembered that the ecclesiastical courts dealt not only with matters affecting church worship and discipline, but also with questions of matrimony, the probate of wills, and even charges of defamation, which was regarded as a spiritual crime.

Cranmer's work of reform came to an abrupt halt when Edward VI died and was succeeded by his Catholic sister, Mary I (1553–1558). Mary hastened to arrest Cranmer and his associates, and did everything she could to bring the church back to the Roman obedience. Pope Julius III sent a legation under the authority of Reginald, Cardinal Pole, who entered England in 1554 and received the formal submission of Parliament on November 30 of that year. Pole then embarked on a comprehensive plan of counter-reform, very much in the spirit of the Council of Trent, which had been in session since 1545, but both time and resources were lacking. When both Mary and Pole died on the same day (November 17, 1558), their cause died with them, and Elizabeth I was able to restore most of the reforms made under Edward VI.

The Church of England that emerged from the legislation of 1559 was a body that reflected the progress of the Protestant Reformation since 1534, although it avoided too close an identification with any one of the continental churches. In deference to popular feeling, Elizabeth adopted the title "Supreme Governor" (not "Supreme Head") of the Church of England, which the sovereign retains to this day, but the substance of the 1534 Act of Supremacy was left unaltered. There was a Book of Common Prayer, an Act of Uniformity enjoining a single pattern of worship on the whole country, a series of Injunctions (patterned on earlier models issued by both Henry VIII and Edward VI) that gave detailed instructions as to how parish churches were to be organized and run, and a revised confession of faith known as the Thirty-eight Articles (1563) and later as the Thirty-nine Articles (1571), which remain to this day.

The Bible was read in English, but there was no officially authorized version. The Great Bible of 1538 was replaced by the so-called Bishops' Bible (1568), but most ordinary people preferred the Geneva Bible (1560), which was much cheaper and a better translation, in spite of its marginal notes that reinforced strongly Puritan and Calvinist ideas. The coexistence of two different Bibles led the Puritans to demand a new translation when James I ascended the throne, leading to the Authorized Version (1611).

In Tudor England, the church embraced every native Englishman, and it was not possible to escape membership. Those Catholics who rejected the Reformation were known as *recusants* ("refusers"), but they were still expected to attend worship, and many did so, although they refrained from taking communion. Those who wanted a further Reformation (the so-called Puritans) organized themselves into groups within the church, but did not actually leave it. The only exceptions to this were small numbers of so-called Separatists in the 1590s, who were savagely persecuted as a result. It was in the course of the seventeenth century that Separatism became more common, particularly as many Puritans despaired of reforming the church from within and joined their ranks. In this connection, it is worth remembering that the first settlers of New England were Separatists, who were not joined by Puritans of the established Church of England until after 1630.

BIBLIOGRAPHY

Bray, Gerald L., ed. *Documents of the English Reformation*. 1994.
Dickens, A.G. *The English Reformation,* 2nd edition. 1989.
Foster, A. *The Church of England,* 1570–1640. 1994.

Moorman, J.R.H. *A History of the Church in England.* 1980.

Spalding, J.C., ed. *The Reformation of the Ecclesiastical Laws of England (Reformatio Legum Ecclesiasticarum), 1552.* Sixteenth Century Essays and Studies, vol. XIX. 1992.

Gerald L. Bray

SEE ALSO

Anglicanism; Articles of Religion; Bishop's Bible; Book of Common Prayer; Calvinism; Canon Law; Catholicism; Clergy; Convocation; Cranmer, Thomas; Defender of the Faith; Injunctions, Royal; Monastic Orders; Puritanism; Recusancy; Reformation, English; Supremacy, Act of; Trent, Council of; Uniformity, Act of

Church of Scotland

The history of the Church of Scotland did not begin with the Reformation. The church is older by several centuries than the nation, for it was only after the year 1000 that anything like the modern Scotland, with its frontier on the Tweed, emerged. King Duncan (1034–1040) was the first king to rule over a united realm; Christianity, on the other hand, had come to Scotland during the last years of the Roman occupation of Britain.

The first known Christian missionary to Scotland was the Briton, St. Ninian, who in 397 built the first stone church, Candida Casa, at Whithorn, from which he carried on a widespread mission among the Picts. The next great evangelist was St. Columba, a Scot from Ireland, who from 563 to 597 used Iona as the headquarters of his missionary labors. The Columban monks, through St. Aidan (c. 635), created a new center in northeastern England at Lindisfarne, from which they evangelized the northern English. The Celtic church represented by these men was monastic and missionary; the heads of its communities were presbyter-abbots, not bishops; it was independent of Rome and maintained peculiar usages—for example, the date of Easter was different from that of the Roman church. The declaration of the Synod of Whitby (664) in favor of the Roman Easter was a prelude to the decline of the Celtic church's influence in England and the gradual adoption of Roman usages in the north.

The Scoto-Pictish church eventually emerged as a united body under a national bishop, whose seat was at Dunkeld from the middle of the ninth century to the beginning of the tenth, when it was transferred to St. Andrews. The Romanizing of the Scottish church was completed under the influence of Queen Margaret (d. 1093), the devout exile driven from England by the Norman Conquest, and her sons, especially David I, in whose reign (1124–1153) diocesan episcopacy was extended, Roman monastic orders introduced, and many monastic houses built.

The name *ecclesia Scoticana,* Church of Scotland, first appeared officially in 1192 in a papal bull that virtually constituted the Church of Scotland. Hitherto, reference had been made only to individual bishops and their sees. The bull of Pope Celestine III declared *ecclesia Scoticana,* embracing the sees of St. Andrews, Dunblane, Glasgow, Dunkeld, Brechin, Aberdeen, Moray, Ross, and Caithness, to be the special daughter of the apostolic see, directly subject to the pope or a legate specially sent from his side. No appeal might be made to any other authority. This action of Celestine settled the vexed question of the pretensions to jurisdiction on the part of the English archbishops of Canterbury and especially of York. However, this policy left the Church in Scotland without a metropolitan of its own. It was not until 1472 that the Scottish province was established with a complete hierarchy of its own. Archdioceses, which were to last for 200 years, were set up at St. Andrews in 1472, and at Glasgow in 1492.

The Reformation in Scotland was less a movement for a new theology than for the reform of morals and a general overhaul of ecclesiastical organization. Origins of the Scottish Reformation may be discerned in the fifteenth century among the exponents of the doctrines of John Wycliffe. The first wave of the Reformation proper was Lutheran; the second was Swiss. Heretical Lutheran books were smuggled into Scotland in spite of a 1525 act of Parliament against their importation. Patrick Hamilton, who had been in Germany, was burned at the stake in 1528 at St. Andrews by Archbishop James Beaton for advocating Lutheran principles, and his heroic death increased the number of reformers. The more irenic works of Alexander Alesius were also influenced by contact with Wittenberg and Marburg, centers of Lutheranism. The policy and campaigns of Henry VIII and Edward VI added to the pro-Reformation forces but also created patriotic opposition. Cardinal Archbishop David Beaton led the anti-English party, but his responsibility for the martyrdom of George Wishart in 1546 led to his own murder shortly thereafter. Wishart's mantle fell on the shoulders of John Knox who, after labors in England, Frankfurt, and Geneva, returned to Scotland in May 1559 to lead the Calvinist party, now strongly supported by the nobles known as "the Lords of the Congregation."

C

The revolution that brought into existence "the Church of Scotland" in its modern sense came about in 1559 and 1560. The marriage of Mary Queen of Scots to the dauphin in April 1558 had greatly intensified the fear of French domination. Under Elizabeth Tudor, who became queen of England in November 1558 England once again gave help to the Scottish reformers against France and Rome. In October 1559 the Lords of the Congregation formally suspended the queen regent, Mary of Guise, from the government, and in the spring of 1560, with English help, drove out the French. This point marks the end of the war with England that had gone on intermittently for nearly 300 years, and the breaking of the old alliance with France.

The 1560 Parliament abrogated the authority of the pope in Scotland, adopted a reformed confession of faith, and forbade the celebration of the Latin mass. Although the absent Queen Mary had authorized the meeting of this Parliament, it had been forbidden to deal with religion. Its composition was therefore irregular, and its legislation was not confirmed by the queen. Mary returned to Scotland from France in August 1561, and for the next six years until she was deposed and superseded by her infant son, James VI, the reformed church was in an ambiguous and precarious legal situation.

The 1560 Parliament established the reformed church of Scotland along Presbyterian lines. It prepared a confession of faith (the "Scottish Confession"), a "Book of Discipline," and soon adopted the Anglo-Genevan "Book of Common Order" as its liturgical directory. Knox and some of his colleagues had proposed that the regional administration of the church should be in the hands of ten "superintendents," whom the Presbyterians did not like because they compromised the principle of ministerial parity and the Episcopalians did not like because they were not consecrated bishops. This all reveals that the 1560 church polity was not yet fully Presbyterian: the presbytery did not yet exist, the synod existed merely as the superintendent's diocesan synod, and both general assembly and kirk session were different in composition and in conception from the later Presbyterian organs of the same name.

After Knox's death in 1572, the mantle of leadership fell on Andrew Melville, who brought Scottish prebyterianism to its full maturity. Melville had returned to Scotland in 1574, after having spent the previous five years at Geneva. There he had fallen under the influence of Theodore Beza, whose teaching on church polity was more definite and unyielding than Calvin's.

Melville insisted that the equality of ministers must not be violated on any pretext whatsoever, and he thereby excluded both bishops and superintendents. Furthermore, the laity—whether kings, nobles, or elected magistrates—must be secluded from any voice in church affairs; instead, the church must have its own self-contained and exclusive polity, with a kirk session consisting of elders appointed for life, presbyteries and synods consisting of ministers and elders, and a general assembly no longer representing the estates of the realm but likewise confined to ministers and elders. Melville set forward this fully developed presbyterian polity in his *Second Book of Discipline,* which was approved by the General Assembly in 1578.

BIBLIOGRAPHY

Burleigh, J.H.S. *A Church History of Scotland.* 1960.
Donaldson, Gordon. *The Scottish Reformation.* 1960.
———. *Scotland: Church and Nation through Sixteen Centuries.* 1960.

Lee W. Gibbs

SEE ALSO

Alesius, Alexander; Beaton, David; Calvinism; Hamilton, Patrick; Knox, John; Melville, Andrew; Wishart, George

Church Polity

In its broadest sense, church polity is the structure of ecclesiastical laws and customs that regulate the religious and moral life of the church. Five different models or types of church polity were of importance during the Reformation era: (1) the monarchical or hierarchical, (2) the territorial or consistorial, (3) the episcopal, (4) the Presbyterian, and (5) the Congregational.

(1) The constitution of the Roman Catholic Church was monarchical and hierarchical. The pope was restricted by the constitutional jurisdiction of bishops in ecclesiastical administration. Nevertheless, there were no bishops but by papal appointment or approval, no assemblies of bishops without his calling, and no binding legislation passed without his approval. The Roman church rejected the principle of the separation of church and state. Church and state were not related as equals; the church, representing the supernatural order and appointed guardian of faith and morals, had preeminent authority. The authority of the church in this context meant the authority of its hierarchy.

(2) While divine right was claimed in Roman Catholicism for the monarchical and hierarchical system, Martin

Luther repudiated the notion of divine right in the domain of church polity. He regarded polity as resting on human discretion and practical demand. It was contrary to his emphasis on the universal priesthood of believers to exalt the pastor over the congregation as either a necessary medium of grace or an embodiment of sovereignty. He regarded aptness for teaching as the most important pastoral credential; ministration of Word and Sacraments were the essential pastoral functions. Ordination meant for him simply a solemn public recognition of the ministerial office. Luther was never opposed to the office of bishops as such. Nevertheless, episcopacy maintained only a transient existence in any part of Germany; the Scandinavian countries were exceptional in uniting Lutheranism with an episcopal form of administration.

In Germany, mitigating circumstances soon led to the emergence of evangelical princes, secular rulers who espoused the principles of the Reformation and became heirs in their own territories to the old episcopal authority. The resulting type of polity was distinctly Erastian, with the government of the church becoming largely a matter of territorial sovereignty. The princes were not expected to assume the spiritual office of adminstering the Word and the Sacraments, but in the general management of ecclesiastical affairs they were accorded a preeminent function.

The foremost organ of church administration under the temporal rulers was the consistory, which was composed of theologians and jurists appointed by the state. This body served as a tribunal to pass on disputed points of administration, to supervise property and educational interests, and to render judgment in major cases of discipline. Superintendents, who were usually pastors, were selected by the secular government to oversee neighboring pastors. In the presentation of pastors to their parishes, the deciding voice belonged to the state and to the local prince. The prerogative of local congregations was usually limited to that of approving presented candidates.

(3) The episcopal model of government that emerged in the Church of England preserved in great part the polity of the medieval church. The hierarchical constitution was maintained except for the elimination of papal authority. In the scheme for parishes, cathedral chapters, and aids to diocesan administration such as archdeacons and rural deans, much of the old system was retained. It is noteworthy, however, that English churchmen did not, in the early sixteenth century, claim divine right, or exclusive validity, for their polity as against that of other Protestant communions. The position of John Whitgift was representative of the view that predominated until the end of the 1580s: episcopacy was the pattern of the apostolic church, of great antiquity, confirmed by the best councils, allowed by the most learned fathers, and most fitting for Christian England. Whitgift never went so far as to claim that the episcopal form of polity was the only one laid down for all times in scripture. Nevertheless, largely in response to the *iuro divino* argument being espoused by the English Presbyterians, leading advocates of episcopal polity were by 1593 defending its status for divine right on grounds of scriptural exegesis, patristic authority, church history, and rational expediency.

The "royal supremacy" over the Church of England was originally asserted during the reign of Henry VIII and reaffirmed in the reign of Elizabeth I. This dominion of jurisdiction included a full complement of prerogatives that enabled the sovereign to interpose efficiently in church affairs. Convocation could not perform any real work of ecclesiastical government without commission or approval from the sovereign. The laity in general, outside of the function of Parliament in relation to the establishment, had very little part in the government of the Church of England.

(4) The Presbyterian form of polity received its initial impulse from John Calvin and the Genevan model. In Scotland, presbyterianism came to hold the status of an established religion, while in England, Presbyterian opinions were first systematically espoused by Walter Travers and Thomas Cartwright during the 1570s. Following Theodore Beza, Calvin's successor in Geneva, these Elizabethan puritans argued that presbyterianism was the only true form of church government laid down in Scripture.

In emphasizing the exclusion of all hierarchical gradations, presbyterianism stressed the parity of ministers. Another characteristic feature was the union of ministers and laymen in governing assemblies, beginning with the church consistory and moving up through regional presbyteries to provincial synods to national general assemblies. The first of these assemblies, entrusted with the supervision of the spiritual interests of the local church, was composed of the pastor and the lay officials called ruling elders. Pastor, ruling elders, and lay deacons were all elected by the local congregation. In respect to the pastor-elect, however, the approbation of the presbytery had to precede his installation.

In Calvinist theory, state and church were regarded as coordinate powers, with each having its own province; the extent of the alliance between them was determined by the possibilities of mutual cooperation and service.

C

(5) The Congregational type of church polity is a direct democracy. While the distinctive features of the congregational polity were anticipated by the Anabaptists on the Continent, it was in England at the extreme end of the Puritan reaction against prelacy that this polity was best represented in the latter part of the sixteenth century by such figures as Robert Browne, Jeremiah Burroughes, John Greenwood, and John Robinson.

The most pronounced feature of congregationalism, advocated as the form of polity laid down in Scripture and practiced in the primitive church, was the autonomy of the individual church; ecclesiastical sovereignty began and ended there. Within the individual congregation, the proper officers were the pastor, ruling lay elders, and lay deacons. As in continental Anabaptism, the principle of the separation of church and state was contained in the initial congregationalism as represented in the teachings of Robert Browne.

BIBLIOGRAPHY

Collinson, Patrick. *The Elizabethan Puritan Movement.* 1967.

Hooker, Richard. *The Folger Library Edition of the Works of Richard Hooker.* W. Speed Hill, ed. Vols. 1–5, 1977–1990. Vol. 6, 1993.

Lake, Peter. *Anglicans and Puritans? Presbyterians and English Conformist Thought from Whitgift to Hooker.* 1988.

Lee W. Gibbs

SEE ALSO

Anabaptists; Browne, Robert; Calvinism; Catholicism; Church of England; Greenwood, John; Puritanism; Reformation, English; Travers, Walter

Churchyard, Thomas (c. 1520 or 1530–1604)

Courtier, adventurer, traveler, and writer, Thomas Churchyard is one of the preeminent Renaissance self-fashioners, since much of our knowledge of his life until 1569 comes from his own apparently autobiographical poetry. Born and educated in Shrewsbury, he left for court in either 1537 or 1542–43 where he served the earl of Surrey for several years, perhaps as a page. Churchyard's first active military service was in the Scottish war of 1547, where he served at Wark Castle and was present at a battle of Pinkie (September 10). In 1548, he was with the fleet and, during the attack on St. Monance in Fife, was captured and confined in Scotland for an indefinite period. He escaped to Lawder Castle, which he apparently left

when peace was declared on March 29, 1550. He later served in Ireland; returning to England, he may have married a rich widow, Catherine Browning. By 1552, he had joined the emperor's forces at the siege of Metz, which ended January 1, 1553. Churchyard traveled down the Rhine, and served in Flanders where he was again imprisoned and escaped, but continued fighting until 1555 when he returned to England. Under Mary I, Churchyard served with Lord Grey of Wilton in the Scottish war, and was imprisoned in Paris.

After the war ended (July 6, 1560), Churchyard probably lived in London, but by 1567 he was in Antwerp where he met William of Orange, with whom he served in Flanders in 1568. Returning to England, he was granted a patent by the earl of Derby in 1571; in 1574, he was engaged to supply verses for Elizabeth's visit to Bristol; and on July 17, 1575, he received five marks for helping to provide a show for her visit to Shrewsbury (which did not take place). After serving in Ireland under Sir Henry Sidney in 1575–1576, he was employed to carry letters from Secretary Francis Walsingham to the English ambassador to Flanders, Thomas Wilson. Early in 1581, Churchyard fled England for Scotland because he had killed a man in a quarrel. Although Churchyard received money from James VI, he left Scotland in June 1581, returned to London, and was imprisoned for murder. By 1582, however, he was free, and accompanied the duke of Alençon to Antwerp. In 1584, Churchyard was a muster-master in Kent during preparations for the Spanish Armada. In 1592, he apparently followed Elizabeth I on her progress to Woodstock, and in both 1593 and 1597, Elizabeth granted him pensions.

Except for a short poem speeding Essex on his way to Ireland in 1599, he was relatively inactive from 1598 until 1602, when he and Richard Robinson published an abridged translation of Emanuel van Meteren's *Historiae Belgicae,* Churchyard providing the historical commentary and documents. He wrote a poem on Whitgift's death (February 29, 1604), and died sometime between March 29, the date of his will, and April 3, 1604, the date it was proved. At his request, Churchyard was buried next to the poet John Skelton in St. Margaret's Church in Westminster.

During a prolific literary career that began with *Davy Dycars Dreame* (1552 or 1560?) and ended only with his death, Churchyard published approximately forty-five books and pamphlets in both poetry and prose. He attempted a wide variety of genres, including court entertainments, satires, complaints, love poems, ballads, narratives, epitaphs, tragedies, as well as journalistic accounts, and he experimented with various forms and rhyme schemes. He has been praised for his neo-Chaucerian poems "Spider and the Gowt" and "Church-yards Dream," but his best known work remains "Shore's Wife," which appeared in the 1563 edition of *A Mirror for Magistrates*. Based largely on Sir Thomas More's account in *The History of Richard III,* "Shore's Wife" was highly popular until the early eighteenth century, and has been credited with beginning the vogue of the complaint; Samuel Daniel, in *The Complaint of Rosamond* (1592), admits his debt to Churchyard. Marlowe remembered lines from the poem: "They brake the boughs and shak'd the tree by sleight, / And bent the wand that might have grown full straight," when he wrote the epilogue of *Doctor Faustus*. Churchyard's work has received little sustained scholarly attention or aesthetic appreciation, and there is no complete edition of his work.

BIBLIOGRAPHY

Brown, Barbara. "Sir Thomas More and Thomas Churchyard's *Shore's Wife.*" *Yearbook of English Studies,* vol. 2, pp. 41–48.

Chalmers, George, ed. *Churchyard's Chips Concerning Scotland Being a Collection of His Pieces Relative to that Country.* 1817.

Goldwyn, Merrill Harvey. "Notes on the Biography of Thomas Churchyard." *Review of English Studies,* vol. 27, pp. 1–15.

Greimer, Roger Anthony. "The Life and Work of Thomas Churchyard." Unpublished dissertation, Northwestern University. 1965.

W.L. Godshalk

SEE ALSO

Howard, Henry; Progresses, Royal

Ciceronianism

The study and imitation of Cicero was at the heart of Renaissance humanism. The study began with Petrarch's discovery of Cicero's letters, and in them the model for a *vita activa* that countervailed the medieval *vita contemplative*. The imitation began with Petrarch's own efforts to write letters to Cicero and others. The discovery of Cicero's treatises on rhetoric, along with his political and judicial speeches, intensified both the study and imitation, and by the start of the Tudor period Ciceronian emulation was the norm throughout Europe. But as early as the fifteenth century, Angelo Poliziano had cautioned that the excitement could lead to extremism, and by the sixteenth century, reactions had begun to set in, with some Ciceronian imitators accusing others of being "servile." The parties to these debates were all imitators and students of Cicero, but by the end of the Tudor period, "Ciceronianism" had become a partisan term of opprobrium in England, and later generations of critics were left with the mistaken impression that a significant anti-Ciceronian party had existed.

Both the study and the imitation of Cicero took place within the larger context of Renaissance *imitatio*. Humanists and educators were convinced that classical Latin promised greater clarity and readability than did medieval Latin, that it would foster universal learning and thought, and improve the efficacy of Christian preaching. Thus the practice of *imitatio* was first a technical effort to recreate classical Latin, and second a literary effort to recreate classical texts in either form or content. Among classical models Cicero was preeminent. First, his rhetorical treatises and speeches demonstrated a clear relation between theory and practice, between technical proficiency and cultural impact. Second, he had long been celebrated for his own professed attention to Latin purity, breadth of practical learning, and eloquence. Third, the sheer bulk and variety of his recovered writings exceeded those of other classical writers. In a time of linguistic and cultural uncertainty, this Ciceronian corpus provided Renaissance writers with both the linguistic standards by which to measure individual proficiency in Latin and the cultural promise of what such proficiency could bring.

Renaissance imitation of Cicero was largely successful. In many circles Latin acquired or recovered flexibility, scope, and energy, and classical literary forms reappeared in fresh guises. Throughout Europe the study and pedagogy of composition derived directly from Cicero. Intensified study, however, also led to aesthetic obsession, producing massive concordances, lexicons, and efforts to write no word that had not been used or inflected as Cicero had. Desiderius Erasmus criticized such obsession in his *Ciceronianus* (Basle 1528), in which he mocked those who imitated Cicero to the exclusion of all other worthy models. Many contemporary writers took deep offense at his critical evaluation of their Latin proficiency, and French readers felt that their national honor had been insulted. The resulting literary turmoil lasted decades, and the personal vitriol obscured the serious issues on either side. Erasmus argued that Cicero needed

C

to be imitated along with a variety of other models in order to develop the larger framework for rhetoric that makes the entire enterprise worthwhile. His opponents argued that a coherent rhetorical framework could only be learned by studying one coherent author, that multiple models led to an incoherent style, and that Cicero alone offered the greatest variety and excellence to be found in a single model.

At the start of the Tudor period there were few English writers who were competent Ciceronians, but by the end nearly all educated English writers could be called such, and a number were celebrated on the Continent for their excellence. A major force was the success of Erasmus's *De copia rerum et verborum* (Paris 1512), a textbook composed originally for John Colet's school at St. Paul's. Erasmus's position in *De copia* was consistent with that in his *Ciceronianus*: *verba* (words) and *res* (things) call one another into being, and while *res* is foremost, the only path to it is the study and manipulation of *verba*. But Cicero alone was inadequate because his Latin and modes of thought could hardly anticipate the Christian Renaissance world, and Erasmus stressed judgment about the reciprocal appropriateness of *verba* and *res*. His *De copia* was adopted or adapted throughout England, and at the universities it supplemented the formal study of Cicero (now augmented with Terence, Demosthenes, and Hermogenes). The English split with Rome, however, complicated the study of both Latin and Latin letters; most continental Ciceronians were Catholics, and some of them used their eloquence in arguments with English Protestants. Bishop Hieronymous Osorius, in particular, was openly admired for his Ciceronian style, even as he was reviled for his religion and politics, and the issue of Osorius percolated in English discussions throughout the century. Christopher Haddon drew distinctions between Erasmian copiousness and Osorian loquacity (*Contra Hieronymum Osorium*, 1577), viewing that latter as excessive attention to the surface texture of Cicero's writing, with none of its underlying structure or energy, and he feared that linguistic facility could seduce loyal English into religious and political error.

Laurence Humphrey endorsed the Erasmian position in his *Interpretatio linguarum* (Basle 1559), specifying that purity was less important than decorum and intelligibility. But Humphrey insisted that Cicero's life and morals not be imitated, even if his language was, thus weakening one of the links between language and life that originally inspired Ciceronianism. Humphrey was echoed at Oxford in lectures by John Rainolds, who declared that eloquence was twofold, both of life and of utterance: "the second we learn from Cicero, the first from Christ." These interests at Oxford combined with a native English aureate tradition in Latin, and both were carried over into the vernacular during the 1580s and 1590s as the literary phenomenon of Euphuism, a self-conscious fascination for linguistically balanced phrases and clauses, balanced subjects and patterns of thought, and elaborately structured sentences. At Cambridge, Gabriel Harvey confessed himself to be a recovering Ciceronian now converted to eclecticism (*Ciceronianus*, 1577). True Ciceronianism for Harvey now meant allegiance to Cicero's idea of the orator who united in his own rhetorical practice the best his culture offered in philosophy, history, law, and letters. Harvey urged as contemporary models not only Erasmus but also Petrus Ramus, underscoring that in England, Ramist rhetoric was viewed as correlative with true Ciceronianism. The surge of Ramist rhetoric in the next century should be seen as a continuation of Ciceronianism rather than as a reaction to it; and when Francis Bacon attacks the extremes of Ciceronianism, he does so in the language of Cicero, just as Thomas Sprat's later call for a scientific language cleansed of rhetoric will be voiced in Ciceronian terms, phrases, and rhythms.

BIBLIOGRAPHY

Croll, Morris W. *Attic and Baroque Prose Style; The Anti-Ciceronian Movement.* Max J. Patrick and Robert O. Evans, eds. 1969.

Erasmus, Desiderius. *Ciceronianus.* Betty I. Knott, trans. and ed. In *Collected Works of Erasmus,* vol. 28. 1986.

———. *De Copia.* Betty I. Knott, trans. and ed. In *Collected Works of Erasmus,* vol. 24. 1978.

Green, Lawrence, ed. *John Rainold's Oxford Lectures on Aristotle's Rhetoric.* 1986.

Henderson, Judith R. "'Vain Affections': Bacon on Ciceronianism in *The Advancement of Learning.*" *English Literary Renaissance,* vol. 25, pp. 209–234.

Howell, W.S. *Logic and Rhetoric in England.* 1961.

Siegel, J.E. *Rhetoric and Philosophy in Renaissance Humanism.* 1968.

Vos, Alvin. "'Good Matter and Good Utterance': The Character of English Ciceronianism." *Studies in English Literature,* vol. 19, pp. 3–19.

Lawrence D. Green

SEE ALSO

Aristotelianism; Bacon, Francis; Classical Literature, Influence of; Classical Literature, Translation of;

Education; Erasmus, Desiderius; Euphuism; Harvey, Gabriel; Neo-Latin Literature; Petrarchanism; Ramism; Rhetoric

Cinque Ports

England's only urban confederacy, the Cinque Ports enjoyed extensive economic and judicial liberties from the crown in exchange for naval service. Located along the narrowest stretch of the Channel separating England from the Continent, these Sussex and Kent port towns were well positioned to provide transport to the Low Countries, intercept foreign commercial shipping, and repel would-be invading forces. The rights of the original Five Ports (Hastings, Romney, Hythe, Dover, and Sandwich) were of pre-Norman Conquest origin, but the confederacy only came into its own during the thirteenth century with the inclusion of the boroughs of Winchelsea and Rye. The Tudor period marked the twilight of the Cinque Ports.

The decline of the Cinque Ports in national affairs began during the later Middle Ages—largely due to French raiding during the Hundred Years' War, coastal deterioration and harbor silting, and the collapse of the North Sea herring fishery—but Tudor defense policy accelerated this descent. Henry VIII's castle-building campaign in coastal Sussex and Kent in the 1540s was a vote of no-confidence for the confederacy's fleets and crown efforts to centralize and professionalize the Tudor navy finally sealed the fate of this reservist naval force.

The elites of the Cinque Ports (known as the barons) fought to mitigate the decline, by gradually extending the burdens and benefits of service to some twenty-five additional member ports, by occasionally commuting their service to cash subsidy, and through the continual assertion of their "ancient rights" at Parliament. Unfortunately, by the sixteenth century, the barons no longer possessed the naval strength to persuade, or coerce, the crown. The Cinque Ports provided but six vessels to the fleet that opposed the Armada. Indicative of the confederacy's decline was Elizabeth I's characterization of Winchelsea in 1573 as "little London": a polite slight on the ostentatious ceremony maintained by the officials of a beleaguered port town that no longer had access to the sea.

BIBLIOGRAPHY

Murray, K.M. *The Constitutional History of the Cinque Ports.* 1935.

Rodger, N.A.M. "The Naval Service of the Cinque Ports." *English Historical Review,* vol. 111, no. 442, pp. 636–651.

David Sylvester

SEE ALSO
Trade, Overseas

CIVIL LAW
See Law, Civil

Civility

Around the year 1500, "civility" was a rare term that meant, more or less, "citizenship." By 1600, however, the word had come into regular use, like its equivalents in Latin, Italian, and French, and it had also acquired a wide range of meanings that between them gave expression to new models of social behavior. A "civil" person was someone who was well-bred, courteous, or "gentle." It was of course no accident that these terms for good behavior were associated with the upper classes, gentlemen and gentlewomen who were of good family and at home in courts. To be civil was to be the opposite of "wild," "rude," or "barbarous." The most famous book about civility, published by Desiderius Erasmus in 1530 and translated into English two years later, dealt with good manners at table and elsewhere. A related term was "discipline," in contexts that ranged from the monastic to the military. The aim of Edmund Spenser's *Faerie Queene* was what the author called "virtuous and gentle discipline," inculcating the rules of what Elizabethans sometimes called "civil life."

The contrast between the Tudor period and the later Middle Ages must not be exaggerated. What are now called the courtesy books of the fourteenth and fifteenth centuries offered precepts for good conduct. Romances of chivalry—known in French as *romans courtois*—inculcated the rules of courtesy for young noblemen. However, the Tudor period was marked by an increasing emphasis on the ideals formulated in classical texts, notably Aristotle's *Ethics* and Cicero's *Duties,* and also in texts from Renaissance Italy, especially Baldassare Castiglione's *The Courtier* (published in 1561 in the English translation by Sir Thomas Hoby), Giovanni Della Casa's *Galateo* (published in 1576 in the English translation by Robert Peterson), and Stefano Guazzo's *Civil Conversation* (translated by George Pettie and Bartholomew Young and published in 1586). These texts had more to say about the art of

C

conversation, more about politics, and more about body language than their medieval equivalents. Given the growth of London and the spread of literacy, it is likely that these books were read by a wide range of people, young and old, male and female, and from mercantile and artisan families as well as noble ones.

Underlying these texts and the new vocabulary they introduced was a social or cultural theory. Groups or whole societies as well as individuals were classified as more or less civil; civility was associated with peace, order, obedience, or "quietness." When Spenser wrote of Ireland as "reduced to perpetual civility," he probably meant that the "wild" Irish would not rebel against their English masters. In Tudor times, "policy" was virtually a synonym for civility, the two terms being derived from the Greek and Latin words for "city" (*polis* and *civitas*), with the clear implication that townspeople were better behaved, more capable of political participation, and so more human than country folk. Perhaps it was because he had heard about the great city of Cuzco that Francis Bacon found it less difficult to say that the Incas of Peru were truly civil than Spenser had in the case of the Irish. He concluded that despite some "barbarous customs," the Incas had "many parts" of civility.

The language of civility also implied a theory of history. Following Cicero, it was argued that humanity had once been completely wild and that it was gradually "civilized." This view of the process of civilization coexisted and conflicted with the opposite view in its own Christian and classical forms of the early state of humanity as a golden age or paradise that was brought to an end either by the sin of Adam and Eve or the rise of agriculture. The genre of the pastoral, whether poem, drama, or romance (Sidney's *Arcadia,* for example), depended on the idea of the noble shepherd, even if Sidney himself was sometimes less than complimentary about the manners of the common people. But it was only in the eighteenth and nineteenth centuries that the idea of the rise of civility would triumph, translated into the language of civilization and progress.

BIBLIOGRAPHY

Bryson, A. "The Rhetoric of Status: Gesture, Demeanour and the Image of the Gentleman." In *Renaissance Bodies,* L. Gent and N. Llewellyn, eds., pp. 136–153. 1990.

Elias, N. *The Civilizing Process.* 1939; English trans., 2 vols. 1981–1982.

Erasmus, Desiderius. "On Good Manners for Boys." In *Collected Works,* vol. 25, pp. 269–289. 1985.

Ferguson, A.B. *Clio Unbound,* pp. 346–414. 1979.

Pagden, Anthony. *The Fall of Natural Man.* 1982.

Peter Burke

SEE ALSO

Court; Hoby, Thomas; Sidney, Philip; Edmund Spenser

Classical Literature, English Translations

Translations figure largely in the story of Renaissance humanism. Tudor translations testify to the desire for accessible classical learning as well as an increasing confidence in the English language. The first half of the sixteenth century saw mainly the translation of school texts, moral treatises, and philosophical works: Aristotle, Cicero, Seneca, Plutarch, Cato, and others. In the middle of the century translations of fiction, poetry, and drama appeared, particularly the works of Apuleius, Heliodorus, Seneca, Ovid, Vergil, and Horace. The last quarter witnessed the appearance of some large and significant projects: Thomas North's version of Plutarch's *Lives* (1579), the first installment of George Chapman's *Homer* (1598), I.D.'s translation of Aristotle's *Politics* (1598), Livy's *Opera* (1600), and Plutarch's *Moralia* (1603), these last two by the serious and scholarly Philemon Holland.

A surprisingly large number of Tudor translations, particularly of Greek works, lie several removes from their original text, having been mediated by continental versions or redactions. The first Greek play we possess in English, Jane Lumley's manuscript translation of Euripides' *Iphigeneia in Aulide* (1555?), owes to a Latin version; George Gascoigne and Francis Kinwelmershe's version of Euripides' *Phoenissae, Jocasta* (1566), advertised on the title page as a translation, actually derives from Lodovico Dolce's Italian rendering, which is, in turn, based on a Latin translation. This intermediation occurs early and late in England. William Caxton's *Eneydos* (1490) Englished Guillaume LeRoy's French translation of an Italian text that paraphrased the *Aeneid* and Giovanni Boccaccio's *Fall of Princes.* French translations intervened between original text and the English of Thucydides's *Historia* (1550) by T. Nichols, North's Plutarch's *Lives* (1579), the *Ilias* (1581) by Arthur Hall, and Moschus's *Idyllae* (1593) by Barnabe Barnes. Homer's fiery breath directly animated Chapman's *Iliad,* or so he claimed, but it reached him through the sometimes unfortunate agency of Spondanus's Greek and Latin edition, Divus's Latin translation, Stephanus's redactions, and Scapula's lexicon.

Such intermediation did not prevent editors and translators from directly applying ancient wisdom to contemporary problems and political events. The title page of Thomas Wilson's *Demosthenes* (1570) directed its warning against Philip II of Spain ("in these dangerous days"), not Philip of Macedon. C. Watson annexed to his *Polybius* (1568) an account of the life of Henry V, because, he explains, an oration from that English history inspired him to review classical orations. For Watson, as for many Tudor readers, ancient and British history furnish lessons in the art of political rhetoric. Edmund Spenser added to his *Axiochus,* based on a Latin text, by the way, a speech spoken at a triumph at Whitehall. Philemon Holland's translation of Xenophon's *Cyropedia* (1632) concludes with Abraham Holland's account of the battle of Lepanto (1571). LeRoy's version of Aristotle's *Politics* (translated by I.D., 1598) uses copious commentary to discuss ancient principles in the context of European history.

A polemical political or religious bias shapes many translations themselves, not merely their commentary or extratextual apparatus. The scholarly translator of Horace's odes, epistles, and *Ars Poetica,* Thomas Drant, for example, in 1567 "wyped away" without a qualm Horace's "vanitie and superfluitie of matter." Jasper Heywood advertised his translation of Thyestes (*Seneca, His Tenne Tragedies,* Thomas Newton, 1581) as "faythfully Englished." Yet he added to the last act a full scene featuring Thyestes soliloquizing in hell:

> Come see the glutted guts of myne, with such a kinde of meate,
> As thou didst once for Gods prepare. Let torments all of hel
> Now fall uppon this hatefull head, that hath deservde them well.

Here the moralized universe of *de casibus* tragedy, served up in fourteeners, recontextualizes the grisly terrors of Senecan crime. Heywood turns Thyestes into a self-consciously moral exemplum, a warning to all readers to follow virtue and avoid vice. The Phaer-Twyne *Aeneid,* admired by William Webbe, George Puttenham, Francis Meres, and Barnabe Googe, likewise adds a moral ending to the ancient text. This *Aeneid* (1573, then revised) appeared to Tudor readers in thirteen books, the last being Maphaeus Vegius's supplement. This epic ends not with Aeneas's bitter fury, but with his marriage to Lavinia and the Trojans' final settlement of Italy. At the conclusion the hero completes literally his allegorical journey to heaven: Venus finally cleanses Aeneas "from contagion of

mortalitie," carries him up to heaven, and translates him "into the number of the starres."

Like all such exercises, Tudor translations of classical texts exhibit to a greater or lesser degree the problem of belatedness, the inevitable drift in meaning resulting from the progression of time and the differences in languages and cultures. Consider Chapman's poetic rendering of Hector's death (II. 22. 361–363):

> Thus death's hand closed his eyes;
> His soul flying his fair limbs to hell, mourning his destinies,
> To part so with his youth and strength.

The closing of the eyes replaces the Homeric formula, *telos thanatoio kalupse,* "the end of death enfolded [him]." Chapman substitutes a discrete funerary gesture for the stylized music of the Homeric formula, a recurring melody that contrasts the vivid and painful physicality of dying with the gentle respite offered by death's embrace. (Chapman is impatient with repetitions generally and offers variations instead.) The change from *psuche* to soul and *Haidos* to hell, words freighted with two millennia of intense discussion, shift the drama from the universal battlefield of life and death to the individual's private struggle for salvation against damnation. A distinctive feature of Homeric death is precisely the array of huge impersonal figurations that depict it and defy translation. *Potmos,* what befalls one and all, here becomes "his destinies," again a privatization and particularization emphasized by the personal possessive pronouns, "his . . . his," absent from the Greek. The translation, though technically faithful and even skillful, recreates the drama in a new and Christianized universe, ruled elsewhere not by Zeus, but by the hand of a providential God.

Despite the belatedness incident variously to all translation, Tudor translators made the ancients speak to states unborn in accents yet unknown. William Shakespeare, for example, heard Ovid's enchanting music in the original Latin and in Golding's lively rendering (*Metamorphoses,* 1567), which inspired him early and late in his career. North's rendering of Plutarch's *Lives* (1579) furnished plot and poetry for the Roman plays. Witness North's description of Cleopatra's barge:

> the poop whereof was of gold, the sails of purple, and the oars of silver, which kept stroke in rowing after the sound of the music of flutes, howboys, citherns, viols, and such other instruments as they played upon in the barge. And now for the person of herself: she was laid under a pavilion of cloth of

C

gold of tissue, apparelled and attired like the goddess Venus commonly drawn in picture; and hard by her, on either hand of her, pretty fair boys apparelled as painters do set forth god Cupid, with little fans in their hands, with the which they fanned wind upon her.

Compare this with Enobarbus's famous description in Shakespeare's *Antony and Cleopatra*:

The barge she sat in, like a burnished throne
Burnt on the water. The poop was beaten gold;
Purple the sails, and so perfumed that
The winds were lovesick with them. The oars were
silver,
Which to the tune of flutes kept stroke, and made
The water which they beat to follow faster,
As amorous of their strokes. For her own person,
It beggared all description: she did lie
In her pavilion—cloth-of-gold of tissue—
O'erpicturing that Venus where we see
The fancy outwork nature. On each side her
Stood pretty dimpled boys, like smiling Cupids,
With divers colored fans, whose wind did seem
To glow the delicate cheeks which they did cool,
And what they undid did. (*Ant.* 2.2.201–215)

North's prose translation supplies the blank-verse magic, the gold poop, purple sails, and silver oars now participating in a sensual erotic fantasy inspired by the goddess Cleopatra. Nature becomes animate and amorous in Shakespeare's lines, and the boys' innocent fanning, here simultaneously heating and cooling the queen, suggests her paradoxical mystery: "She makes hungry / Where most she satisfies" (2.2.247–248).

Shakespeare was merely the most illustrious of the many readers who heard anew the ancient voices in some 175 translations of Greek and Latin writers published in the Tudor period.

BIBLIOGRAPHY

Bate, Jonathan. *Shakespeare and Ovid.* 1994.
Bolgar, R.R. *The Classical Heritage and Its Beneficiaries.* 1954.
Bush Douglas. *Mythology and the Renaissance Tradition in English Poetry.* 2nd edition. 1963.
Greene, Thomas M. *The Light in Troy: Imitation and Discovery in Renaissance Poetry.* 1982.
Lathrop, H.B. *Translations from the Classics into English from Caxton to Chapman.* 1933.
Matthiesen, F.O. *Translation, An Elizabethan Art.* 1931.
                                             Robert S. Miola

SEE ALSO

Chapman, George; French Literature, Influence of; Gascoigne, George; Humanism; Italian Literature, Influence of; North, Thomas; Shakespeare, William; Spanish Literature, Influence of

Classical Literature, Influence of

Renaissance humanism has a story that extends well beyond the Tudor dates in both directions, well beyond the shores of England, and well beyond the boundaries of any discipline. Print technology gave new life to Greek and Roman writers, who appeared in various continental (especially Italian) *editiones principes* from 1465–1520. Renaissance recovery of classical literature exhibited at least two contradictory aims: the intention to present the past on its own terms and in its own context, and the intention to reappropriate the past for direct and practical application to the present. The latter intention frequently manifested itself in prefatory material, notes, and commentary on matters rhetorical and moral. Sometimes this commentary aggressively managed reading, directly and indirectly conforming classical text to Christian revelation. Fulgentius, Cristoforo Landino, and Pontanus, for example, reread Vergil allegorically. The interpretation of Vergil's fourth eclogue as a prophecy of Christ's nativity is only the most famous illustration of pervasively syncretic reading practices in the period. The urgent impulse to exhume and revitalize antiquity led also to fragmentation. Commonplace books abounded, arranged rhetorically or thematically. The Muses sang for the masses also in the form of dictionaries like Cooper's *Thesaurus Linguae,* with appended *Dictionarium,* handbooks like Giovanni Boccaccio's *De genealogia deorum,* emblem books like Andrea Alciati's *Emblemata,* proverb collections like Desiderius Erasmus's *Adagia,* epitomes like Florus's redaction of Livy, and mythographies like Natalis Comes's *Mythologiae.* There were also many important exercises in translation.

English humanists like John Colet, Thomas Linacre, John Cheke, Roger Ascham, Thomas Smith, and Richard Mulcaster made classical study central to elementary school and university. The imitation of antiquity began early as a pedagogical technique prescribed in such works as the *Rhetorica ad Herennium* (thought to be Cicero's) and Quintilian's *Institutio oratoria.* In grammar school, students memorized hundreds of passages and practiced reading, writing, and speaking the ancient languages. Recommended authors and texts included: (in Greek)

C

Isocrates, the New Testament, Homer, Demosthenes, Hesiod, Aesop, Euripides, catechisms, Psalms, Basil's Epistles, Dionysius of Halicarnassus, Heliodorus, Lucian, Pindar, Plutarch, the *Tabula Cebetis,* Theocritus, Xenophon; (in Latin) Cato's *Disticha,* Terence, Plautus, Cicero, Quintilian, *Ad Herennium,* Ovid, Vergil, Horace, Juvenal, Lucan, Sallust, Catullus, and such later writers as Susenbrotus, Erasmus, Palingenius, and Mantuan. Not only a pedagogical practice, *imitatio* also functioned as an aesthetic principle central to Renaissance poetics, fully explored and articulated in copious commentaries on Aristotle and Horace.

Greek always took a distant second place to Latin. For one thing, the language was more difficult to learn; Clenardus's popular textbook, with italic Greek on a crowded page and explanations in Latin, could frustrate the most dedicated student. Moreover, Tudor England, encouraged by Latin writers and St. Paul, associated Greeks with licentiousness and perfidy; this view received confirmation by the Tudor myth that traced British ancestry through Brut to that famous enemy of the Greeks, the once Trojan and future Roman Aeneas. Tudor readers and writers experienced Greek language and literature in shapes that are surprising today, often through the medium of Latin translation. The Greek New Testament was the most important text Plato appeared largely through Ficino and Neoplatonist commentary, only one spurious dialogue being available in English, the *Axiochus* (1592), translated by Edmund Spenser. The most popular Aristophanes play was the pseudo-allegorical *Plutus,* or *Wealth.* In Europe and in the East, Aeschylus's reputation rested on the Byzantine Triad—*Prometheus, Seven against Thebes,* and *Persae*—not on the *Oresteia.* Euripides appeared in various Latin versions and, Englished, in Gascoigne and Kinwelmershe's *Phoenissae,* itself based on an Italian intermediary. The sole English imprint of Sophocles in the *Short-Title Catalogue* is Thomas Watson's Latin translation of *Antigone,* replete with moralizing *thema* and *pompae* (processions). On the matter of ancient Troy, Dares and Dictys, recast in the medieval tales of Benoît de Saint-Maure and Guido delle Colonne, predominated over Homer, though Chapman's great translation was on the horizon. *The Tabula Cebetis,* a moral allegory ascribed to Cebes of Thebes, appeared in translation all over Europe.

Latin reigned as the supreme language of the Renaissance, and Latin authors provided models for imitation in every major genre. Vergil's epic *Aeneid* and its Italian progeny supplied Edmund Spenser's compendious and eclectic *Faerie Queene.* In the pastoral genre, writers imitated Vergil's *Eclogues* and its descendants, especially Mantuan, Petrarch, and Sannazaro. Vergil's elegant verse and his complex, allusive, metaphorical treatment of the green world inspired pastoral works by Alexander Barclay, Barnabe Googe, Michael Drayton, Philip Sidney, Giles Fletcher, and, most important, Spenser's *The Shepherd's Calendar* (1579). The related genre of romance, featuring fanciful, episodic tales of love and adventure, originated in Greek stories—Chariton's *Chaereas and Callirohe,* Achilles Tatius's *Clitophon and Leucippe,* Longus's *Daphnis and Chloe,* Heliodorus's *Aethiopica,* and *Apollonius of Tyre*—and in Latin ones, Petronius's *Satyricon* and Apuleius's *The Golden Ass.* These works inspired much Renaissance prose fiction and drama, including works by Thomas Lodge, George Whetstone, William Shakespeare, the parodies of Thomas Nashe, and Philip Sidney's *Arcadia.*

Satire, including forms like the epigram, elegy, and complaint, drew inspiration from Juvenal, Horace, Persius, and Martial. Sir Thomas Wyatt experimented with this genre, as did George Gascoigne in *The Steel Glass,* the first English blank verse satire. Toward the end of the century there was an explosion of verse satire beginning with Thomas Lodge, *A Fig for Momus* (1595), and continuing in Joseph Hall, *Virgidemiarum* (1598), John Marston, *The Metamorphosis of Pygmalion's Image and Certain Satires* (1598) and *The Scourge of Villainy* (1598); Everard Guilpin, *Skialethia* (1598); T.M., *Snarling Satires (Microcynicon)* (1599); Sir John Davies, *Epigrams;* and works by John Donne and Ben Jonson. These works used classical figures and techniques to ridicule contemporary expressions of London folly—amorous would-wits armed with sonnets, sartorial affectations like ruffs and silks, and contemporary fads such as smoking tobacco and dueling.

Tudor tragedy also looked to Latin models, especially to Seneca. His declamatory verse tragedies, admired by theorists like Julius Caesar Scaliger, Bartolomeo Cavalcanti, and Daniel Heinsius, provided patterns of action and rhetoric as well as dramatic conventions for all of Europe. Seneca showed later generations how drama might portray the most terrifying *scelus* (crime)—infanticide (Medea), spousal murder (Agamemnon, Hercules Furens), the eating of children's flesh (Thyestes). He also showed dramatists how characters might speak the unspeakable, how they might voice forbidden desires and passions in a superbly dramatic rhetoric of autonomous

C

and nihilistic self-creation. Sir Philip Sidney praised Thomas Sackville and Thomas Norton's *Gorboduc* (1562), arguably the first English revenge tragedy, for "climbing to the height of Seneca his style." Whether producing tragedies of revenge, tyranny, furor, or other kinds, the Tudor playwrights wrote in Seneca's gigantic shadow. Scholars have documented important specific and general indebtedness in the plays of Thomas Kyd (*The Spanish Tragedy*), Christopher Marlowe (*Tamburlaine* plays), George Chapman (the *Bussy* plays), John Marston (the *Antonio* plays), William Shakespeare (all the great tragedies and some histories), Ben Jonson (*Sejanus* and *Catiline*), and John Webster (*The Duchess of Malfi*). Seneca inspired the richest tragic achievements of the Tudor age.

Tudor writers of dramatic comedy imitated Plautus, who left behind twenty-one astonishingly varied plays, ranging from mythological travesty to farce to romance, and Terence, whose sophisticated style, rhetorical debates, and elegant Latin made him a favorite of schoolmasters. Together these two playwrights defined the structure of comic action for later generations and bequeathed as well a rich legacy of character and action. Dramatists learned from them how to organize a comedy into *protasis* (opening action), *epitasis* (tension), and *catastrophe* (resolution), with *anagnorisis* (recognition) and *peripeteia* (reversal). Looking to these models, Tudor playwrights populated their stages with classical characters like the *senex* (old man), *virgo* (girl), *servus* (slave), *miles gloriosus* (bragging soldier), *parasitus* (parasite), and *adulescens* (young man). They also adopted classical comedic dramaturgy—the use of resonant symbolic localities like the sea, brothel, and temple—and ancient dramatic devices like the lock-out, disguise, and eavesdropping, and the climactic discovery of identity. Directly or indirectly, Plautus and Terence claim as their descendants most comic playwrights in the period, especially George Gascoigne, George Peele, John Lyly, Thomas Heywood, Thomas Middleton, William Shakespeare, and Ben Jonson.

A brief generic survey like this one can only indicate major categories of classical influence. Authors like Vergil and Ovid, we should remember, appeared everywhere in Tudor literature and culture, across a variety of genres in many forms, extending from brief allusion to extended, often eristic, imitation. Influence is often indirect, the ancient voices reaching new audiences through the intermediaries of translation and adaptation. Tudor writers ranged widely and eclectically, always and unpredictably joining classical and nonclassical sources. They practiced a fluid, innovative *imitatio* that combined Greek and Roman authors with sources that were biblical, Italian, medieval, and contemporary. Such imitation of classical literature brought forth creations resonant with a rich and strange intertextuality.

BIBLIOGRAPHY

Baldwin, T.W. *William Shakspere's Small Latine and Lesse Greeke*. 2 vols. 1944.

Bolgar, R.R. *The Classical Heritage and Its Beneficiaries*. 1954.

Braden, Gordon. *Renaissance Tragedy and the Senecan Tradition: Anger's Privilege*. 1985.

Bush, Douglas. *Mythology and the Renaissance Tradition in English Poetry*. 2nd edition. 1963.

Doran, Madeleine. *Endeavors of Art: A Study of Form in Elizabethan Drama*. 1954.

Grafton, Anthony, and Lisa Jardine. *From Humanism to the Humanities: Education and the Liberal Arts in Fifteenth- and Sixteenth-Century Europe*. 1986.

Hamilton, A.C., ed. *The Spenser Encyclopedia*. 1990.

Highet, Gilbert. *The Classical Tradition: Greek and Roman Influences on Western Literature*. 1949.

Kinney, Arthur F. *Humanist Poetics*. 1986.

Kristeller, Paul Oskar, et al., eds. *Catalogus Translationum et Commentariorum: Mediaeval and Renaissance Latin Translations and Commentaries: Annotated Lists and Guides*. 1960–present.

Miola, Robert S. *Shakespeare and Classical Comedy*. 1994.

Reynolds, L.D., and N.G. Wilson. *Scribes and Scholars: A Guide to the Transmission of Latin and Greek Literature*. 1974.

Robert S. Miola

SEE ALSO

Commonplace Books; Drama, History of; Education; Gascoigne, George ; Grammar Schools; Humanism; Pastoral; Platonism; Prose Fiction; Rhetoric; Satire

Clergy

In the Tudor period the clergy underwent more profound and far-reaching changes than almost any other social group. In the early sixteenth century there were perhaps twenty-five thousand secular clergy distributed through England's approximately nine thousand parishes, and a further nine to ten thousand regular clergy in the religious houses, representing together a substantial proportion of the total adult male population. Extreme diversity characterized the early Tudor clergy. There was a fundamental distinction between the beneficed clergy—rectors and vicars with security of tenure, who received some or all of a parish's tithes—and the unbeneficed, many of whom led a precarious existence as chantry priests, fraternity chaplains, or assistant curates. Even within these two groups there was substantial variety. At the top end, well-connected graduate careerists occupied the wealthiest benefices (often in plurality) and were frequently absent from the parishes nominally in their charge as they pursued administrative tasks in the service of church or state. They had little in common with resident vicars in the poorer livings. At the lowest end of the scale, stipendiary curates often earned little more than agricultural wage laborers. Formal training for the priesthood was nonexistent: candidates for ordination merely had to persuade the presiding bishop of their legitimate birth and minimal literacy. Contemporary literary depictions of ignorant "Sir John Lacklatins" often reflect the exalted expectations of humanist reformers, or turn out to be tendentious Protestant propaganda, but it is likely that very many of the parish clergy lacked the ability to preach, or to do more than perform their basic pastoral and sacramental duties (though they must often have done so earnestly and conscientiously). The manifest shortcomings of the clergy have persuaded some historians that anticlerical feeling was rife in early Tudor England, and contributed to a readier acceptance of the Reformation, but there is little evidence of endemic lay-clerical conflict in more than a handful of local communities, and much to suggest that many lay people held the priesthood in high regard, not least the huge numbers putting themselves forward for ordination in the first three decades of the sixteenth century, most with little hope of material advancement.

The break with Rome in the mid-1530s, and the subsequent Henrician Reformation ostensibly did little to alter the status and function of the priest. Nonetheless, from the early 1530s onward, levels of recruitment to the clergy began to fall, partly as a result of growing uncertainty about the future, partly as a reaction to the monastic dissolutions of 1536–1540, which released thousands of former monks and friars onto the clerical "job market." The establishment of an avowedly Protestant regime in the reign of Edward VI heralded more dramatic changes. The new Prayer Books of 1549 and 1552, and the accompanying Ordinals, sought to transform the theological understanding of the clerical office: henceforth the parish clergyman was no longer to be a sacramental priest, whose principal duties were the saying of mass and hearing of confessions, but a preaching minister. Edwardian Protestant emphasis on the "priesthood of all believers" was perhaps given its most emphatic expression in 1549, when Parliament legalized clerical marriage, breaking a centuries-old taboo and rejecting the association of virginity with sanctity that had been so marked a feature of medieval religion. Across the country clergymen availed themselves of this opportunity in highly variable numbers: in Lancashire, only one in twenty of the beneficed clergy appears to have married; in London, one in three did so. The discrepancy may well reflect the pressures emanating from their parishioners. Ordination levels continued to slump in the Edwardian period, exacerbated by the dissolution of the chantries in 1547, which reduced career opportunities and put further pressure on the competition for benefices. The accession of Mary in 1553 meant a return to the status quo ante, but it is unlikely that the reign did much to restore battered clerical morale. The Marian regime deprived married priests and separated them from their "pretensed wives," often forcing them to perform public penance in front of their parishioners, but due to the shortage of priests it was obliged to redeploy them elsewhere. This can hardly have increased lay confidence in the clergy, nor can the fact that in many parishes, in the space of little more than twenty years, the same incumbent would have been required to announce and justify at least four dramatic changes of ecclesiastical policy.

The Elizabethan period provided an opportunity for gradual stabilization after the convulsions of the mid-century. The manpower shortage persisted throughout the 1560s, necessitating the novel expedient of appointing lay "readers" in many parishes, but by the 1570s, the crisis was abating, and in the following decades the universities, particularly the new colleges of Emmanuel and Sidney Sussex at Cambridge, were turning out increasing numbers of graduate ministers for the parishes. There is little doubt that the social and material status of the clergy rose in Elizabeth's reign, and that the clergy evolved into a more homogeneous unit, although the scale and significance of these changes should not be exaggerated. It was the disappearance of the massed ranks of the unbeneficed that did most to produce an aggregate rise in the wealth and educational standards of the clerical body, rather than any dramatic improvement in the value of benefices, or sudden transformation of the quality of the beneficed clergy. The thesis that the decades after the Elizabethan Settlement witnessed a gradual "professionalization" of the parish clergy, characterized by a less haphazard career

C

structure, more university training, greater emphasis on preaching and pastoral duties, and a growing sense of esprit de corps, is an attractive one, although one that arguably runs the risk of underestimating the importance of pastoral roles to the late medieval priesthood. "Professionalization" was in any case an extremely slow process: a uniformly graduate ministry was not achieved across much of the country until at least the 1620s. In one of its most striking features—the pattern of intermarriage between clerical families and the creation of clerical "dynasties"—it can make the clergy seem more like a self-perpetuating caste than a profession in the modern sense. The growing social standardization of the clergy in Elizabeth's reign was to some extent offset by emergent ideological fissures. "Godly" ministers who hoped for further reformation of the church established their own networks through the preaching occasions known as "prophesyings" and later as "lectures by combination," and on occasion they were able to secure appointment to high-profile stipendiary town lectureships. They evinced growing contempt for those among their profession whom they regarded as unpreaching "dumb dogs," and who sought "good fellowship" at the village ale bench.

The married, graduate minister of the late 1590s may seem to have little in common with the celibate mass-priest of the 1490s, but important elements of continuity in the form and function of the clerical office must not be forgotten. The financial underpinning of the clergy, through the system of tithes, remained virtually unchanged, and the basic pastoral duties of reciting public worship, baptizing, marrying, and burying their parishioners provided another constant. In rural areas, throughout the sixteenth century, much effort would have been spent on agricultural pursuits and the tilling of the "glebe" land. Historians determined to uncover "anticlericalism" are as likely to find it at the end of the sixteenth century as at the beginning.

BIBLIOGRAPHY

Collinson, Patrick. *The Religion of Protestants: The Church in English Society 1559–1625.* 1982.

Haigh, Christopher. "Anticlericalism and the English Reformation." In C. Haigh, ed., *The English Reformation Revised.* 1987.

Marshall, Peter. *The Catholic Priesthood and the English Reformation.* 1994.

O'Day, Rosemary. *The English Clergy: The Emergence and Consolidation of a Profession 1558–1642.* 1979.

Peter Marshall

SEE ALSO

Book of Common Prayer; Chantry; Monastic Orders; Sacraments; Sermons

Clitherow, Margaret (d. 1586)

Margaret Clitherow, daughter of Thomas Middleton, chandler and sheriff of York, was a Catholic martyr. She married, in 1571, a prosperous butcher, John Clitherow, who conformed to the established Protestant religion, even though he came from a Catholic family and his brother was a Catholic priest. Margaret converted to Catholicism around 1574, while John was serving as chamberlain of York. The zeal she exhibited for her Catholic faith came to the notice of civic authorities, who imprisoned her. While in prison, Margaret gave birth to her third child, William, and she taught herself to read. Prison did not temper Margaret's Catholicism. Following her release, she sent her eldest son, Henry, abroad to the Catholic seminary at Douai. She continued the treasonable practices of harboring priests and of attending Mass; and she employed in her household a Catholic tutor for her two other children and for the children of other Catholic families.

In March 1586, the Council of the North cracked down on Catholic activities in Yorkshire. While John was before the council explaining his wife's behavior and the departure abroad of his son, the sheriff of York raided the Clitherow home, seizing a young boy, who, when threatened with beating, revealed the hiding place for the priest's vestments, chalice, and books. Arraigned before Judge Clinch, Margaret, refusing to plead, was threatened with the penalty *peine forte et dure*. Adamant in her refusal to plead, Judge Clinch ordered that she be stripped naked, laid upon her back, and as much weight as she could bear placed on her for a duration of three days, when she was then to be pressed to death. On March 25, 1586, Margaret was taken to the Tolbooth near her prison of York Castle for execution. Spared the shame of dying totally nude, she was allowed covering for her face and private parts. She was stretched out on her back across boards that rested on a sharp stone. Some seven or eight hundred pounds of weight was placed on her, cracking her ribs and pushing them through her skin. She died within a quarter hour, though her body was left to be pressed for another five and three-quarter hours. Margaret's sons studied abroad for the priesthood, and her daughter, Anne, entered the convent of St. Ursula in Louvain. Pope Paul VI canonized Margaret Clitherow a saint in 1970.

BIBLIOGRAPHY

Morris, John. *The Troubles of Our Catholic Forefathers.* Third series. 1877.

Monro, Margaret T. *Blessed Margaret Clitherow.* 1947.

Mush, John. "An Abstracte of the Life and Martirdome of Mistres Margaret Clitherowe." In *English Recusant Literature.* D.M. Rogers, ed. Vol. 393. 1979.

SEE ALSO

Catholicism, History of; Southwed, Robert; Torture

John M. Currin

Cloth Industry

Woolen cloth was by far the most important textile manufactured in Tudor England. Plain linens were made in Lancashire and elsewhere, but on a small scale and for a limited market. Most linens, as well as a wide range of other fabrics, were imported. In contrast, the woolen textile industry earned praise from contemporaries not only for providing employment for the poor throughout the country, but also for its unique contribution to the export trade. An unknown but substantial and rising volume of cloths, perhaps half or more of output, was shipped abroad, thereby exposing the industry to an extensive network of markets in which shifts in demand could exert a powerful influence on its structure and organization. This was most apparent in the early Tudor period when exports more than doubled. These were, however, more important in some areas than others, depending largely on the kind of cloth that was produced.

There were three basic types of cloth: woolens proper, worsteds, and fabrics similar to worsted called the "new draperies" to distinguish them from the traditional woolens and worsted. In the category of woolens there were cloths of varying fineness and weight. Broadcloth was the finest, heaviest, and therefore the most expensive. Most were produced in the Weald of Kent, parts of East Anglia and in the West Country clothing region that embraced parts of Oxfordshire, the Cotswolds of Gloucestershire, Somerset, Wiltshire, and eastern Devonshire. Manufacture of coarse woolens—mainly kerseys, dozens and "cottons"—was concentrated in the West Riding of Yorkshire and Lancashire, and on a smaller scale in Westmoreland, Wales, and Devonshire. Worsted was the principal manufacture of the Norfolk textile industry centered in Norwich; and it was mainly there that the new drapery—bays, says, and many other types of "stuff"—was developed by Protestant immigrants early in Elizabeth I's reign.

The differences between the types of cloth arose mainly from the quality and character of the raw material. Fine, short staple wool went into the making of good quality woolens, while coarse, long staple wool was most suitable for worsted. Both kinds of wool were normally used in the new draperies. Access to and variations in the character of the raw material had some influence on where and what kind of cloth was manufactured. However, clothiers were not dependent on local supplies. As production increased and spread, wool was carried over great distances through the mechanism of the market town and the wool "broggers" (brokers). The key factor in the location of the industry was thus not the supply of raw materials but of labor. In the absence of technological innovation, cloth manufacture in all its stages was extremely labor-intensive, labor costs amounting to between a half and two-thirds of total production costs. The fleece was first cleaned before it was combed or carded for spinning, the yarn then passing to the weaver who worked on the two-man broadloom if the article was the standard broadcloth. The cloth was then fulled either by the traditional foot method or by the fulling mill, a process that bleached and compressed the cloth, making it stronger and more durable. For most broadcloth made for export this was the end of the process, the finishing, pressing, and dyeing being performed abroad. But even in the production of the unfinished "white" cloth many hands were required, with varying degrees of skill. Hence the trend, from the fourteenth century onward, for commercial clothmaking to shift from towns into the countryside where cheap part-time employment could be found for the whole family. The "putting-out" system, or "outworking," particularly favored its location in the densely populated dairy farming, wood-pasture regions where underemployment was the norm. The need for clear water to scour and clean the cloth and to drive the fulling mill contributed further to the decline of urban manufacture. There were exceptions, most notably the city of Worcester, which retained its high-quality broadcloth manufacture throughout the sixteenth century. The effect of the rapid expansion of the overseas cloth trade in the early Tudor period, however, was to tilt the balance decisively in favor of rural outworking.

A further consequence of export-led growth was the commercialization of cloth production. The wider and more distant the market became, the more difficult it was for the small, part-time rural worker to dispose of his cloth other than through an intermediary. That role was most likely to be taken by the more substantial clothier

C

who, in addition to manufacturing cloth in his own premises, provided the small producer with wool on credit, a loom on rental and piece-rate wages, and selling of the cloth, often on credit, to the wholesale merchant, usually in London. This capitalistic domestic system was most developed in the manufacture of broadcloth, the staple of the export trade. In Kent and Wiltshire, for example, the large or middling clothier controlled all stages of production. Wealthy and famous capitalist clothiers like William Stumpe of Malmesbury, who put to work hundreds of spinners and weavers, may have been exceptional; and some weavers were well-to-do. Most, however, lived poorly, and were normally in debt to the clothier. Where the cheaper woolens were made the self-employed weaver was much more common, as in the West Riding of Yorkshire and in Devonshire, where makers of broadcloth as well as the cheap dozens were less often under the influence of overseas markets. In Worcester, too, the small independent artisan survived, in part through the protection of the guild, as he did in Norwich, where the new drapery revived the city's fortunes after the decline of the local worsted manufacture earlier in the century. There and elsewhere the immigrant and native workers, who took up the trade later in Elizabeth I's reign, produced mainly for the domestic market until late in the century. By 1600, England saw the beginnings of a profound shift in overseas demand, as well as in native fashion, that would have major consequences for the English cloth industry in the following century.

BIBLIOGRAPHY

Coleman, D.C. *Industry in Tudor and Stuart England.* 1975.

Harte, N.B., ed. *The New Draperies in the Low Countries and England.* Pasold Studies in Textile History, vol. 10. 1997.

Kerridge, Eric. *Textile Manufactures in Early Modern England.* 1985.

Ramsay, G.D. *The English Woolen Industry, 1500–1750.* 1982.

——. *The Wiltshire Woolen Industry in the Sixteenth and Seventeenth Centuries.* 1943.

Thirsk, Joan. "Industry in the countryside." In *Essays in the Economic and Social History of Tudor and Stuart England.* F. J. Fisher, ed. 1961.

Brian Dietz

SEE ALSO

Cloth Trade; Industry and Manufacture; Trade, Overseas

Cloth Trade

Textiles were the most widely manufactured product in early modern Europe. Every region had an industry producing cloth from wool, cotton, flax, or hemp. Some mainly satisfied local needs, but many were geared to export markets, often far distant from the center of production. Of the different branches of the industry, the manufacture of woolen cloth was the most important. There were numerous kinds of cloth, varying considerably in quality and price. These, too, were produced in many different countries or regions, each exchanging its speciality for that of another. There was, on the other hand, considerable competition in the cloth trade, not only between products that were similar but also between different kinds and qualities of cloth. What the customer could afford and what was in fashion were consequently key factors in the cloth trade.

At the beginning of the Tudor period, England's contribution to this extensive and competitive market were medium-priced woolen broadcloth and coarser, cheaper woolens called kerseys, dozens, and "cottons." Most of the broadcloth was exported "white," that is, unfinished and undyed, though there was a substantial market for finished cloths in Spain and the Baltic. The cheaper cloths were all finished and dyed. Together they were the country's most valuable export, displacing raw wool as the staple commodity in the course of the fifteenth century. The market for broadcloth was the largest, and most were dispatched to Blackwell Hall, London's great cloth market. Not all the cloths were destined for abroad: the domestic market may have been the more important. The weaver, clothier, and wholesale merchant, however, became increasingly dependent on overseas demand, in particular in the Low Countries, Germany, and central Europe. From the late fifteenth century onward the Merchant Adventurers' staple at Antwerp, the emerging capital or *entrepot* of European commerce, provided the link with those markets.

Under the Tudors the cloth merchant experienced the volatility and uncertainties of a market in which demand was elastic, exchange rates fluctuated, rival manufactures were sometimes strong, sometimes weak, and fashion changed. In the early Tudor period market conditions were exceptionally favorable. Against a background of sustained growth in most branches of European trade English woolens competed well with the products of the industry in the southern Netherlands, in northern and central European markets, and with those of northern Italy where textile manufacturing was devastated by war in the early sixteenth century. Exchange rates were also favorable, particularly in the late 1540s when the debasement of the coinage and a fall in the value of the pound probably fueled the sharp rises in those years. In 1550, cloth exports were at twice the level of the 1480s, while those from London had risen from 40,074 in 1480 to 132,600. Close to 90 percent of the cloth trade was channeled through the capital, while cloth itself accounted for around 80 percent of the nation's exports. Those proportions were maintained for the rest of the century. Growth, however, was not. Shipments in 1552 were a third below their peak, and for the next two decades metropolitan cloth exports fluctuated sharply before, in more settled conditions, they stabilized at around 100,000 cloths annually. There was also stability or continuity in the geographical distribution of the market and of the types of cloth exported. Toward the end of the century roughly the same proportion of cloths was sold in the Netherlands, Germany, and central Europe as in mid-century, and the unfinished broadcloth was most in demand. The most positive aspect of the Elizabethan cloth trade was the market for finished cloths in the Baltic region. Shipments of broadcloth from East Anglia and northern kerseys approximately doubled, partly offsetting the closure of the Spanish market.

The problems facing the cloth exporter in the later Tudor period seem to have been numerous. Devaluation was followed by revaluation and the stronger pound was a factor in the difficulties the Elizabethans experienced in competing in price and quality in continental cloth markets. Contemporary opinion was that quality was sacrificed for price. If so, the problem may have been compounded by a decline in the quality of the raw material. Once famous for its fineness, English wool seems to have became more coarse as well as longer in the staple, making it less suitable for working into good-quality woolens. At the same time, the Merchant Adventurers faced growing competition in markets where demand was affected by the apparently sluggish growth in real incomes. The Italian industry staged a remarkable recovery after 1550, while cloth manufacturers in the southern Netherlands had responded to the competition of English cloths by developing fabrics known as the "new draperies." As the tide of fashion turned in favor of these light, colorful, less durable and generally cheaper says, bays, fustian, and so on (a garment made from broadcloth was expected to last a lifetime and it was much heavier than the heaviest overcoat of today) the new draperies were introduced into England by refugee

weavers in the 1560s. The coarser, longer staple wool could be used in the new draperies, as it was in the manufacture of the traditional worsteds that enjoyed a revival in the later Tudor period. But the contribution of the new draperies and worsteds to the cloth exports was slight before the seventeenth century. The mainstay of the cloth trade remained the "old drapery," and in particular the unfinished broadcloth.

BIBLIOGRAPHY

Brenner, Robert. *Merchants and Revolution. Commercial Change, Political Conflict and London's Overseas Traders, 1550–1653.* 1993.

Carus-Wilson, E.M., and O. Coleman. *England's Export Trade, 1257–1547.* 1963.

Clay, C.G.A. *Economic Expansion and Social Change in England, 1500–1700,* vol. 2. *Industry, Trade, and Government.* 1984.

Gould, J.D. *The Great Debasement.* 1970.

Harte, N.B., ed. *The New Draperies in the Low Countries and England.* Pasold Studies in Textile History, vol. 10. 1997.

Zins, H. *England and the Baltic in the Elizabethan Era.* 1972.

Brian Dietz

SEE ALSO
Economy; Merchant Adventurers; Trade, Overseas

Clothing and Costume

Contemporaries justified clothing as a means of hiding nakedness, as a protection against the elements, as a form of adornment for the body, and as a marker of social distinctions. Of these arguments the last was the most powerful. Distinctive forms of dress marked out differences of age, gender, rank, occupation, and office. Sumptuary legislation sought to maintain social boundaries by limiting the types of fabric that could be worn by persons from different social groups. Thus an act of 1510 used a mixture of income bands and status distinctions as determinants of the right to wear certain materials: gentlemen worth £100 per annum in lands and fees were permitted to wear velvet in their doublets, while persons worth upwards of £20 per annum might wear satin and damask in their doublets, but only silk or camlet in their gowns and coats. Legislation of this kind proved extremely difficult to enforce, and it was a standard complaint of the moralists that "there is such a confuse mingle mangle of

C

apparell that it is verie hard to knowe who is noble, who is worshipfull, who is a gentleman, who is not" (Phillip Stubbes, 1583).

The sumptuary codes were eroded by the speed with which fashions changed, a phenomenon remarked upon by foreign visitors like von Meteren in 1585: "the English are very inconstant and desirous of novelties, changing their fashions every year to the astonishment of many." Fashion was driven by the increasing prominence of the social elite in London as a result of the attractions of the court and the developing London "season." Competition at court encouraged novelty in dress as a means of attracting notice and favor, while within the more anonymous framework of city life, dress acquired still greater importance in making social distinctions. On the stage, actors wore as costumes clothing that had been worn at court. The thriving second-hand market in elite clothing in Birchin Lane made it easier for people of lower rank to imitate the elite, thereby fueling further innovation in fashion, as the elite sought to differentiate themselves from their inferiors. Fashionable clothing was already one of the markers of metropolitan "superiority": London fashions were eagerly followed among provincial elites, and Londoners delighted in sneering at the plain country folk "apparelled either in a coat of homespun russet or of frieze."

These pressures drove upward the amounts spent by the elite on clothing. At his death in 1588, the earl of Leicester's wardrobe included seven doublets and two cloaks valued at £543, while in the 1590s, the earl of Rutland spent up to £1,000 in a single year on his clothing. At the lower social levels expenditures were nowhere near this scale: the inventories of even wealthy gentlemen show that their clothing was rarely valued at more than £40–£50. It was remarked by the antiquarian Richard Carew (with approval) that the Cornish gentry "delight not in braverie of apparell," while the modesty of the dress of London merchants struck William Harrison. But both commentators qualified their remarks by noting the ways in which the wives of both gentlemen and merchants were in the vanguard of fashion: even in Cornwall, "the women would be verie loth to come behinde the fashion in newfanglednes of maner, if not in costlynes of mater"; while Harrison criticized the wives of London merchants for "all kind of curiosity in far greater measure than in women of higher calling." Among the poor the pressure on family budgets was such that changes of clothing could rarely be afforded. They would have recourse to the second-hand market (in London centered

on Houndsditch), or would wear the gowns frequently distributed to the poor in return for their presence at the funerals of the elite.

English fashions lagged behind those of mainland Europe. In the early sixteenth century, reflecting Italian influences mediated through France, elite males wore white silk shirts frilled and embroidered at the neck and wrists, over which they wore short tunics attached to close-fitting hose. Women's gowns had square necklines, cut low enough to show the chemise beneath; their skirts were slit in front to show an undergown through a triangular opening. From 1520, under German influences, padded puffs on decoratively slashed sleeves revealing still richer fabrics beneath became fashionable. Male tunics (or doublets) between 1520 and 1545 had knee-length skirts open at the front to display padded codpieces of implausible girth. From the 1540s the predominant influences were Spanish. The main innovations were the farthingale and the ruff. The farthingale was a conical-shaped underskirt made by stretching fabric over a series of circular hoops (of whalebone, wire, or wood) that increased in circumference as they descended from the waist. The ruff originated as a narrow, ruched band finishing the high collar of the bodice, but with the introduction of starch around 1564, they grew ever larger. For both males and females under Elizabeth I, there was an increasing emphasis on an elongated waist, wide circular ruffs, and swollen hips, sensitizing the moralists to the dangers of gender confusion. Women wore stiff high bodices with tight sleeves and excessively wide skirts, while men wore highly pointed doublets with puffed trunk hose. Although the models were drawn from Spain, the elaboration of applied decoration and the striking color schemes were taken to exceptional lengths, and English ruffs (reaching their highest point of elaboration in about 1585) often had several tiers made of different types of material. By the 1590s, however, styles were becoming less artificial and more relaxed as French influences predominated. Men adopted the falling collar in preference to the ruff and wore simpler doublets, while women transformed their bell-shaped gowns into a drum-like shape. The English remained notorious for their mixing of continental styles. George Gascoigne remarked that although the English could "mocke and scoffe at all contryes for theyr defects," yet we "doo not onlye reteyne them but do so farre exceed them: that of a Spanish Codpeece we make an English football; of an Italyan wast, an English petycoate; of a French ruffe, an English chytterling."

C

Although much of the literature of complaint about unnecessary consumption and the confusion of gender and social boundaries focused on the lower orders, their clothing was far less elaborate than the pulpit-thunderers suggested. Although some rich fabrics were incorporated into the clothing of merchants' wives, their dress was more sober than that of the court ladies. Women of yeoman stock used worsted and russet, although they might have velvet trimmings on their best kirtles and gowns. For all the difficulties of enforcing the sumptuary laws, dress remained a critical social distinction at the end of the century.

BIBLIOGRAPHY
Arnold, J. *Queen Elizabeth's Wardrobe Unlock'd.* 1988.
Ashelford, J. *Dress in the Age of Elizabeth I.* 1988.
Cunnington, C.W., and P. Cunnington. *Handbook of English Costume in the Sixteenth Century.* 2nd edition. 1970.
Stubbes, P. *The Anatomie of Abuses.* 1583.

Ian W. Archer

SEE ALSO
Social Classes; Sumptuary Laws

Coal Industry

Coal had been used in Britain since Roman times. In the Middle Ages the most important area of production stretched along the river Tyne. Coal was shipped from Newcastle to towns down the east coast, and especially to London, where complaints about smoke and soot polluting the atmosphere were first voiced in the thirteenth century. Away from the Newcastle area production remained very small scale, with part-time miners digging the coal from surface seams or from shallow bell pits. Output was low; although accurate statistics are not available it seems likely that national production could be measured in tens of thousands of tons a year at the start of the Tudor period. In the sixteenth century, production was stimulated by the growth of population and the associated rise in the prices of other fuels, especially in the later decades of the sixteenth century and early into the seventeenth. This was particularly true of charcoal, the most prized fuel for both domestic and industrial purposes. Inflation stimulated the production of coal throughout the country, although most coal-producing regions were landlocked and remained dependent on narrow, localized markets. On Tyneside, and to a lesser extent on Wearside, a massive increase in output after the middle of the century resulted when control of much of the best coal-bearing land passed into lay hands after the Reformation.

In the early sixteenth century an estimated 45,000 tons of coal were shipped down the east coast to Hull, Ipswich, and above all to London. By the end of the century, shipments (including relatively small amounts sent overseas) amounted to more than 200,000 tons a year and the London market alone absorbed some 150,000 tons each year. Indeed, by the end of Elizabeth's reign coal had become the staple fuel of the capital, much of it used for domestic heating and cooking. Increasingly, coal also became an industrial fuel, used widely in brewing and soap production and in any other trade where the noxious fuel could be kept apart from the ingredients being processed. Similarly, it was used in other parts of the country for both domestic and industrial purposes wherever it could be acquired at lower prices than alternative fuels, which was especially the case in the northeast. By the early seventeenth century, Newcastle was becoming a major center of coal-dependent industries. The town attracted glass makers and soap boilers, and large-scale salt works (boiling salt water in great cast-iron pans produced by the newly introduced blast furnace) sprang up at the mouth of the Tyne to exploit the availability of cheap, low-grade coal.

The industry also developed away from the northeast, but apart from a few coastal districts such as South Wales or the Firth of Forth, pits remained small-scale, employing only a handful of part-time workers. The great expansion of the industry in the northeast continued in the following century as England became increasingly and uniquely dependent on coal to heat its homes and fuel its industry.

BIBLIOGRAPHY
Coleman, D.C. *Industry in Tudor and Stuart England.* 1975.
Hatcher, J. *The History of the British Coal Industry, Vol. 1: Before 1700.* 1993.
Nef, J.U. *The Rise of the British Coal Industry.* 2 vols. 1932.
Stone, L. "An Elizabethan Coalmine." *Economic History Review,* 2nd series, vol. 3.

Donald Woodward

SEE ALSO
Economy; Industry and Manufacture; Metal Industries

Coal Industry   151

C

Coke, Edward (1552–1634)

One of the most important jurists and legal philosophers in English history, Sir Edward Coke's voluminous writings, especially the *Reports* or commentaries on specific legal cases and the *Institutes of the Laws of England*, influenced legal studies in the United States as well as in England through the nineteenth century.

The son of a prosperous barrister, Coke (pronounced Cook) was born in Norfolk, educated at Norwich Grammar School, Trinity College, Cambridge (a center of Protestant thought at that time), and the Inns of Court. In 1582 he married Bridget Paston, who brought him a considerable fortune but died in 1598 after bearing him ten children. In the same year an even more brilliant marriage to Lady Elizabeth Hatton, a granddaughter of Lord Burleigh and niece of Robert Cecil, cemented his alliance with one of the most politically powerful families of the late sixteenth and early seventeenth centuries, but the marriage was troubled with public disputes about property.

Coke served Elizabeth I as attorney general, a position for which Francis Bacon was also in competition. The two were to remain rivals until Bacon's public career came to an end in 1621. As attorney general, chief prosecutor for the queen and for James I in the early part of his reign, Coke prosecuted several notable cases, including that of the Robert Devereux, earl of Essex, for treason in 1601, that of Sir Walter Ralegh, also for treason, in 1603, and that of the conspirators of the Gunpowder Plot in 1605.

Under James, who knighted him in 1603, he was appointed chief justice of the Court of Common Pleas in 1606. Whereas he had been a ferociously anti-Catholic and anti-Spanish protector of the crown as prosecutor, his new role involved a wider interpretation of the law. Basing his arguments on legal precedents from Magna Carta onward, he became an ardent defender of the common law and the courts that enforced it against what he saw as encroachments, both by the ecclesiastical Court of High Commission and the Court of Chancery, and by the monarch's claims of royal prerogative. He was dismissed from his post of chief justice in 1616.

Coke nonetheless remained active in public life until 1628, reinstated in some of his administrative positions despite his opposition to the absolutist claims of James and of Charles I. As a member of the House of Commons he was one of the principal drafters in 1628 of the Petition of Right (a seminal document later for American history), which defined as "rights," among others, freedom from arrest without cause, and from imprisonment without an expeditious trial. During the last four years of his life he completed the multivolume *Reports*, based on cases that he had been collecting from the beginning of his legal career, as well as the *Institutes*. The first volume of these was a commentary on the sixteenth-century jurist Thomas Littleton's writings on land law ("Coke upon Littleton"); this became a classic text for many generations of beginning law students in England and the United States.

BIBLIOGRAPHY

Bowen, Catherine Drinker. *The Lion and the Throne: The Life and Times of Sir Edward Coke.* 1957.

Pocock, J.G.A. *The Ancient Constitution and the Feudal Law.* 2nd ed. 1987.

White, Stephen D. *Sir Edward Coke and "The Grievances of the Commonwealth," 1621–1628.* 1979.

Bridget Gellert Lyons

SEE ALSO

Chancery; Law, Common; High Commission, Court of; Treason

Colet, John (1467–1519)

London educator, theologian, and ecclesiast, John Colet was raised in a locally prominent middle-class family. Colet completed a B.A. and M.A., probably at Cambridge. As he prepared to enter the university in 1480, his father, Henry, became one of the leading wardens of the Mercers Company and an alderman in London; by 1486, Henry was named lord mayor of London for the first of two non-successive terms.

Writing in 1521, Desiderius Erasmus indicated that Colet traveled to Italy in the early 1490s to study sacred authors and improve his preaching. In Italy, Colet likely encountered writings by Italian philosophers from the Florentine Academy, especially Marsilio Ficino and Pico della Mirandola, and possibly the writers themselves, although we only have evidence of his presence in Rome. There, he joined ecclesiasts who, like himself, later gained positions of authority in the English church. Following his return to England, Colet studied divinity at Oxford, perhaps in these years focusing on the writings of Dionysius the Areopagite, not yet exposed as spurious by Colet's friend, William Grocyn. At a series of free public lectures at Oxford in the last years of the fifteenth century, Colet earned a reputation as a stirring lecturer on the Pauline epistles. Ordained a priest in 1498, he completed a doctorate in divinity by 1504, afterward leaving Oxford for London. By 1505, he was named dean of St. Paul's.

In 1499, Colet met Erasmus and the two remained friends until Colet's death. Their correspondence attests to a rich and complex relationship that involved rivalry in issues of theology and Erasmus's sometimes mercenary view of Colet as potential patron (mostly unrealized). Nevertheless, they shared attitudes about a "philosophy of Christ" centered on inward, fiducial faith manifest in belief and charitable action, together with a suspicion of external ritual; they collaborated on the curricula and pedagogy for St. Paul's School, refounded by Colet in 1510 with inherited wealth and maintained in perpetuity by the Mercers' Company; and they held a mutual interest in the "true Latin speech" and Greek of classical and patristic writers. Colet never attained the facility of Erasmus in either language, but he struggled to master Greek even in the last years of his life. In the statutes of his school, Colet carefully spells out the requirements for hiring qualified masters and surmasters (able in both Latin and Greek), regulations for the activities of the 153 boys given free education (no eating in school, no attendance at cockfights, attendance at the child bishop's sermon, the use of wax candles), and even the poor student's special duties. Scholars have often noted the inconsistency between Colet's explicit praise of the "true Roman tongue" exemplified by Vergil, Cicero, Seneca, and Ovid, and his prescription of Latin models that include only patristic and medieval Christian writers exhibiting "chaste eloquence" (Lactantius, Prudentius, Proba, Juvencus, and Mantuanus). It is hard to say when, if ever, the youth of St. Paul's would be introduced to non-Christian classics, but graduates of the school—including Thomas Lupset, Richard Pace, Thomas Starkey, and John Clement—shared a solid background in the classics, perhaps prescribed, as Colet directed, according to the "wit" of the masters.

As dean of St. Paul's, Colet often held strong convictions of human weakness and spiritual strength put to the test. In 1510, he delivered to convocation in London a sermon challenging the clerical audience to abandon worldliness and immorality witnessed in simony, nonresidence of curates and bishops, immoral investiture, clerical misuse of temporal goods, and ordinations without concern for spiritual and moral matters. He encouraged instead the frequent use of councils and the application of existing laws rather than the imposition of new ones. Due to the boldness of his stance, Colet seems to have developed important enemies, including first the bishop of London, Ralph Fitzjames, and later the archbishop of Canterbury, William Warham. In 1513, Colet's principled attack against warfare drew the attention of Henry VIII, naturally concerned that the dean of St. Paul's pacifist sermons might weaken the morale of troops soon to travel to France. In a letter, Erasmus describes the result of a private meeting between the king and dean, with the latter thereafter emphasizing the distinction between a just war and a worldly one and the former declaring, to the horror of Colet's enemies, "This is the teacher for me." Ironically, Colet preached at the installation of Thomas Wolsey as cardinal in 1515, perhaps seeing in the Yorkist butcher's son an aspiring ecclesiast rising from a commoner's background like his own. By 1517, Colet worked alongside Wolsey in the Privy Council.

Colet's works integrate humanist concerns for education in the *studia humanitatis* and eloquence with a strong Christian belief in the need for moral and spiritual action. His varied writings and activities as commentator, benefactor, educator, and ecclesiast are united by a conviction that, in the Christian era, one must look past the external, symbolic, and legalistic character of words, institutions, and acts, substituting for them a new, liberated order of spiritual existence. Paradoxically, however, this new liberty is constrained by the superiority and causal priority of the spiritual over the corporeal, with the result that the corporeal will necessarily be abandoned as one grows to spiritual perfection. His Latin commentaries on the writings of Dionysius, the epistles of St. Paul, and the heptameron reinforce this emphasis on spiritual and rhetorically moving interpretation. Colet strove to move his audience to horror at the crassness of worldliness and admiration for the mercy, power, and goodness of God and the Son. He created a Christian formulation of Cicero's idea of the virtuous orator: for Colet, the eloquent Christian must comprehend a perfect, spiritual understanding in order to speak the truth with conviction.

BIBLIOGRAPHY

Colet, John. *Opera.* John H. Lupton, trans. and ed. 1867–76; repr. 1965.

———. *Commentary on First Corinthians.* Bernard O'Kelly and C.A.L. Jarrott, trans. and eds. 1985.

Gleason, John. *John Colet.* 1989.

Jayne, Sears. *John Colet and Marsilio Ficino.* 1963.

Lupton, John H. *A Life of John Colet.* 1887.

Trapp, J.B. *Erasmus, Colet and More: The Early Tudor Humanists and Their Books.* 1991.

Daniel T. Lochman

SEE ALSO
Education; Erasmus, Desiderius; Humanism; Warham, William

C

Colonial Development

England failed to establish any effective overseas colonies during the sixteenth century. Although a number of promoters and propagandists championed colonization in the 1580s and 1590s, notably Richard Hakluyt the Younger, their ideas had limited appeal and impact. Lack of state support crippled English colonial enterprise, leaving it in the hands of a small group of private adventurers whose interest in short-term profit was inimical to the longer-term investment needed to sustain colonization. It also meant that no clear strategy for colonial development emerged during the Tudor period; instead, expediency and experiment predominated as private enterprise cautiously tested the opportunities for colonization in Ireland and North America.

Although the monarchy was reluctant to provide support for colonization, it was prepared to sanction private colonial initiatives. John Cabot's royal patent of 1496 authorized him to settle any land he discovered that was not possessed by another Christian monarch, but settlement was secondary to his search for a westward route to Asia. Henry VIII also supported John Rastell's venture of 1517. Rastell, the brother-in-law of Sir Thomas More, intended primarily to search for a passage to Cathay, but his other purpose was to establish a colony in North America. Even though the expedition disintegrated shortly after setting out, leaving Rastell stranded in Waterford, Ireland, his ideas show an unprecedented understanding of the colonial opportunities in North America. But his recognition of the value of American forests and fishing grounds was not widely shared. The inhospitable nature of the region, the apparent absence of gold and silver mines, and the dangers of the transatlantic crossing cooled interest in North America. For the next fifty years, Rastell's ideas lay dormant as English energies were channeled elsewhere.

When interest in colonization revived during the 1560s, it was focused on Ireland, where the establishment of English colonies by private adventurers was seen as an effective means of subjecting the country to Tudor rule. Under the sponsorship of the lord deputy, Sir Henry Sidney, various schemes emerged for the plantation of Ireland, though they met with little success. When Humphrey Gilbert and others attempted the colonization of Munster in 1569, the Gaelic Irish rebelled, destroying a small settlement established near Cork. In Ulster, Sir Thomas Smith's attempts to establish a colony from 1571 to 1575 also failed as a result of Irish hostility. These reverses induced caution in English policy toward Ireland, but colonization was renewed after the Munster rising of

1579. The subsequent plantation of Munster was a considerable success in the long term, although the arrival of English settlers aroused deep anxiety that led to widespread resistance and rebellion from 1594 to 1603.

Ireland played an important role in English colonial development, not least in providing a precedent for subsequent activity in North America. Colonial activity in Munster and Ulster raised serious problems concerning the mobilization and utilization of resources, problems that were to reappear across the Atlantic. But the Irish experience of adventurers like Gilbert also aroused expectations and established certain patterns of behavior whose relevance to North American settlement was questionable. Gilbert's subsequent colonizing schemes, though immature and deeply colored by hostility toward Spain, were important primarily for their recognition of North America as a field of opportunity for English settlement. In 1578, he received a patent from Elizabeth I for discovery and overseas plantation. Although his first American colonizing expedition was a disaster ending with the dispersal of his fleet off the coast of Ireland, in 1583 he crossed the Atlantic with the intention of establishing a colony in North America. The spread of sickness and poor morale among his men effectively aborted the expedition. On the voyage home Gilbert was lost at sea.

Gilbert's ideas and ambitions were taken up by his half-brother, Sir Walter Ralegh, whose attempt to establish a colony at Roanoke, an island off the coast of modern North Carolina, marks the high point of the colonial movement in Tudor England. Unfortunately, the timing for peaceful colonization was unpropitious. The outbreak of the Anglo-Spanish war in 1585 raised expectations that Roanoke might serve as a naval base for raids on Spanish shipping in the Caribbean, but the war also diverted scarce resources into privateering. At the same time it dashed hopes that the queen would support the Roanoke settlement, despite the persuasiveness of Hakluyt's *Discourse of Western Planting* (1584), a key text in the evolution of English colonial ideology that marshaled a wide range of economic, social, and political arguments in favor of state support for colonization. As a result, the two settlements established at Roanoke in 1585 and 1587 were abandoned: the first after a difficult winter during which relations between the English and Indians deteriorated to the point of conflict; the second after the crisis arising from the Armada campaign of 1588. The survivors of the first settlement returned to England in 1586; the second group of settlers were left to an obscure fate. Attracted by the lure of privateering, Ralegh made little effort to search for the "lost colonists" in the decade after 1590. The abandonment of Roanoke curtailed serious interest in colonization until the early seventeenth century. In 1597, an attempt to establish a base on the Magdalen Islands, in the gulf of the St. Lawrence River, raised the prospect of using North America as a haven for religious exiles, but the plan was given up in favor of privateering.

Despite these limited practical achievements, English colonization made some advances during the Tudor period. In Ireland it was already laying the basis for a profound social transformation. In North America it led to the acquisition of experience and knowledge, reflected in the sketches and maps of John White and the writings of Thomas Hariot, based on their experiences in the first Roanoke settlement, that was of immense potential value. And in the work of Richard Hakluyt it acquired an ideology that could be used to encourage and justify future colonial development.

BIBLIOGRAPHY

Andrews, K.R. *Trade, Plunder and Settlement: Maritime Enterprise and the Genesis of the British Empire, 1480–1630.* 1984.

Canny, N. *The Elizabethan Conquest of Ireland: A Pattern Established, 1565–1576.* 1976.

Hakluyt, R. *Discourse of Western Planting.* D.B. Quinn and A.M. Quinn, eds. 1993.

McFarlane, A. *The British in the Americas, 1480–1815.* 1994.

Quinn, D.B. *North America from Earliest Discovery to First Settlements: The Norse Voyages to 1612.* 1977.

———. *Set Fair for Roanoke: Voyages and Colonies, 1584–1606.* 1985.

Scammell, G.V. *The World Encompassed: The First European Maritime Empires c. 800–1650.* 1981.

John C. Appleby

SEE ALSO

Cabot, John; Devereux, Walter; Gilbert, Humphrey; Hakluyt, Richard; Hariot, Thomas; Ralegh, Sir Walter; Rastell, John; Sidney, Henry; Smith, Thomas

Commonplace Books

When Hamlet, learning that his uncle has murdered his father, cries out "My tables!—meet it is I set it down / That one may smile and smile and be a villain," (1.5.107–108) he refers to the practice, widespread in Tudor England, of noting down wise or pithy sayings encountered in the course of reading (or, less often, experience) in a commonplace book. Hamlet's earlier promise that:

> from the table of my memory
> I'll wipe away all trivial fond records,
> All saws of books, all forms, all pressures past
> That youth and observation copied there
> (1.5.98–101)

similarly records a frequently drawn analogy between the copying of such aphorisms in "table books" and in the mental "tables" of memory. Although the practice of reading with a commonplace book at hand in which to record notable fragments was, in part, a way of supplementing memory, commonplace books also functioned in Tudor England as a central element of humanist education that held that the gathering of such wise sayings was able to produce students who possessed both authoritative speech and a store of moral advice. Although students in school used commonplace books primarily to record proverbs, aphorisms, maxims, idiomatic expressions, and other material discovered in the course of reading classical authors, such notebooks were often used by adults for different purposes. While writers continued to record sayings as raw materials for their own works, ministers frequently copied and catalogued biblical citations for use in the composition of sermons. Courtiers often circulated manuscript books among members of a coterie that contained poems and speeches as well as sayings (e.g., the Arundel Harington Manuscript, the Devonshire Manuscript), and merchants or businessmen often included financial records, useful recipes, and family data in their notebooks (e.g., Henslow's "diary").

The name "commonplace" book, as well as the practice of keeping such a notebook, derives from the Aristotelian strategy of using "topoi" or "places" to find or "invent" arguments on topics not subject to the more rigorous proofs of logic. These places are essentially a way of classifying concepts such as "definition," "wholes," "parts," "opposites," which help a would-be speaker or writer to think about how ideas relate to each other. This system of invention through "places" was taken over by influential Roman rhetoricians and was passed on to the Renaissance by Manuel Chrysoloras, a Byzantine scholar who became an influential teacher in fourteenth-century Florence. The German scholar and teacher Rodolphus Agricola transmitted the method to northern Europe and added suggestions for organizing commonplaces under topical "headings" such as "virtue," "vice," etc., rather than the traditional Aristotelian "places."

C

The use of the commonplace book in humanist education was first introduced to England by Juan Luis Vives and reinforced by its important role in Desiderius Erasmus's *De Copia*. Erasmus's interest in Christian humanism led him to emphasize the importance of collecting morally efficacious sayings, and the notebook method became a way to ensure that impressionable students could read pagan classical works without harm. Both Vives and Erasmus use metaphors of picking flowers from among poisonous herbs, or of a bee distilling honey from dangerous plants, to emphasize the selectivity to be exercised in the educational use of the commonplace book. Erasmus further uses metaphors of fortification and engraving to express his hopes that the collection and assimilation of sententious material would have a morally transformative effect on the student.

The widespread use of the commonplace book method in grammar school education in England had a profound effect on the practices of reading and writing in the period: it encouraged fragmentary reading, with an eye for excerptible fragments rather than a narrative whole, and it encouraged the widespread citation of wise sentences that so mark both prose and poetry written in the period. Of course, published collections of proverbs, aphorisms, and quotations soon provided a ready store of such material even for those who did not have the benefit of a humanist education. Inevitably there was a backlash against this method of education and style of writing, with educators like Roger Ascham and critics like Sir Philip Sidney criticizing the superficiality to which it could lead. Nevertheless, the practice of keeping a commonplace book survived into the nineteenth century, and the taste for aphorism that it cultivated can be seen in Bacon's essays, and into the eighteenth century.

BIBLIOGRAPHY

Bolgar, R.R. *The Classical Heritage and Its Beneficiaries.* 1954.

Bushnell, Rebecca W. *A Culture of Teaching: Early Modern Humanism in Theory and Practice.* 1996.

Crane, Mary Thomas. *Framing Authority: Sayings, Self, and Society in Sixteenth-Century England.* 1993.

Crane, W.G. *Wit and Rhetoric in the Renaissance: The Formal Basis of Elizabethan Prose Style.* 1937.

Halpern, Richard. *The Poetics of Primitive Accumulation: English Renaissance Culture and the Genealogy of Capital.* 1991.

Mary Thomas Crane

SEE ALSO

Education; Erasmus, Desiderius; Grammar Schools; Henslowe, Philip; Reading Practices; Vives, Juan Luis

Common Pleas, Court of

The Common Pleas was the busiest court in the country by the accession of Henry VII. The oldest central court, it had a near-monopoly in actions by royal writ between private parties, and a large share of the burgeoning business of debt actions that increased significantly in the course of the sixteenth century. By 1600, the membranes of the court rolls were at least five times that of 1500. This was due in large part to the price revolution of the sixteenth century, wherein the 1540s, maximum value on contracts sued in the local courts brought the tradesman's bills to Westminster. Thus, in spite of the problems of the old actions, which required written documents under seal, and the problem of compurgation in an age where one's word was not necessarily his bond, Common Pleas continued to exercise an increasing role in the judicial system.

The ancient pattern of law suit involved a claim, a denial, and a counting of the facts by each party in law French. Called pleading, the sergeants who counted these facts developed a monopoly of that practice, and thus acquired control of the court and its jurisdiction. The ancient pattern of proof was by wager of law, or trial by jury. The most common method of proof in this court was wager of law, where the defendant would bear the burden of proof by bringing into court a sufficient number of worthy men (compurgators) to swear on oath that his denial was true. By the late sixteenth century, compurgators were readily available for hire outside Westminster Hall, bringing disrepute to this procedure. But since this method of proof was quick and cheap, it continued to be used well into the following century.

Its jurisdiction bound by original writ, and lacking in discretion, Common Pleas was the most vibrant court of those sitting at Westminster. Having a near-monopoly of pleas of land, debt, covenant, detinue, and account, apprentices learned their early law and court practice there. It literally teemed with human population. The court was also the most profitable one for its clerks, practitioners, and judges. Licensed to make final concords on land transactions, fines on every debt, and seizures of the goods and chattels of all persons who were outlawed, the court also returned a handsome profit to the crown.

BIBLIOGRAPHY

Baker, J.H. *The order of Serjeants-at-law.* Selden Society, supplementary series. Vol. 5. 1984.

Hastings, Margaret. *The Court of Common Pleas in Fifteenth-Century England.* 1947; repr. 1971.

Prest, W.R. *The Rise of the Barristers.* 1986.

Sutton, R. *Personal Actions at Common Law.* 1929.

Louis A. Knafla

SEE ALSO

Chancery; Exchequer; Law, Common

Conduct Books

See Civility; Marriage Manuals

Consort and Consort Song

The term "consort" comes into usage in late sixteenth-century England with a variety of meanings, but today primarily refers to a small ensemble for the performance of instrumental music composed before 1700. Our modern usage of the term also distinguishes between two types of consort: the "whole consort," which designates an ensemble consisting of instruments of the same family (e.g., consort of viols, or recorders), and the mixed or "broken consort," which refers to an ensemble of instruments of several different family types. It is to the latter type of consort that late sixteenth- and seventeenth-century English documents most readily attest, with the "classic" grouping comprising the six assorted instruments: lute, bandora (pandora), cittern, bass viol, treble viol, and flute. The bandora is a plucked string bass instrument said to have been invented in England in 1562; the cittern was a plucked string instrument in various sizes that was played with a plectrum. Consort music with this instrumental combination is described in an account of a royal entertainment for Elizabeth I at Elvetham in 1591, and is the combination of instruments for which *The First Booke of Consort Lessons* of 1599 of Thomas Morley and *Lessons for Consort* of 1609 by Philip Rosseter (1567/68–1623) were composed. In the distinctive treatment of the dances and instrumental settings of vocal pieces that survive in these collections, the flute renders the melody in a relatively straightforward fashion, the bass viol, cittern, and bandora supply the bass part and supporting chordal harmony, while the treble viol and lute provide fanciful embellishment by often trading

virtuosic ornamentation and scalar runs between one another. In addition to this specific arrangement of instruments, it is clear from other archival and literary references that mixed consorts could be made up of all sorts of combinations of different instruments, and that the occasion for which the music was being performed, rather than the music itself, dictated the instrumentation of a given ensemble. Whether performed by whole or mixed consorts, the range of sixteenth- and early seventeenth-century English instrumental ensemble music is vast, notably ranging from the extended four- and five-part contrapuntal *In nomine* settings and six-part free fantasias to the more homophonic pavan and galliard dance pairs for six instruments.

The term "consort song" is a modern one that designates a specific type of secular English song of the late sixteenth and early seventeenth centuries performed by solo voice and supporting instruments, most usually a consort of viols. These performance forces later were augmented with a vocal chorus. The consort song is important because it is seen as the preserve of a steadfast native vocal tradition that endures in the face of more popular but short-lived forms such as the Italianate madrigal and the lute song. The consort song's association with the setting

A Man Playing a Luite. From Adrien Le Roy, *Tunes in Tablature for the Lute* (1581). Douce R 129, fol. 62v. By permission of the Bodleian Library.

C

of psalms also leads it to branch off to establish the verse anthem, which is essentially a consort song of sacred function. The origins of the genre are obscure, but they are rooted in growing early Tudor preferences for the consort of viols (increasingly popular after an Italian viol consort appeared at the English court in 1540), for courtly entertainments performed solely by boys, and in the performance of part songs by solo voice with instrumental support. From its outset it seems that the consort song assumed its standard five-part texture (the top part carrying the text), with the style of the earliest surviving examples (c. 1580) being simple strophic settings, with the poetry set one note to a syllable, and with repetitions typically limited to the final line or couplet of a stanza. One popular early type was the lament (e.g., the anonymous *O Death, rock me asleep*), with many examples seemingly coming from courtly productions of Senecan plays by choirboys.

The musical significance of the consort song is immediately elevated with William Byrd's embrace of the genre in the latter part of the sixteenth century. From the outset of his involvement with this genre Byrd invested it with more musically sophisticated means of expression. While maintaining characteristic features of strophic form and syllabic settings of his models, he separated poetic lines with music, added flowing melismatic writing to the penultimate syllable of lines of text, and in his later examples (*Psalmes, Sonets and Songs* of 1588) employs rigorous use of imitative polyphony as a structural principle. He also shows more creativity and care in his treatment of text setting, with the iambic flow of the poetry mirrored by the alternation of short and long note values, but with the clever employment of syncopation so as to avoid predictability. In Byrd's hands the consort song undergoes further flexibility in its evolution, with Byrd being given some credit for establishing the genre as appropriate for setting sacred, serious, light, occasional, and elegiac texts. Although Jacobean composers such as Thomas Ravenscroft and Michael East attempted to meld the consort song with the pictorial word-setting and expressive harmonies characteristic of the more popular Italian madrigal, its resurgence in published collections after 1610 attests to its value and durability in the musical environment of a post-madrigal England.

BIBLIOGRAPHY

Brett, Phillip. "The English Consort Song, 1570–1625." *Proceedings of the Royal Music Association,* vol. 88, pp. 73–88.

Dart, Thurston, and William Coates, eds. *Jacobean Consort Music.* Musica Britannica, vol. 9. 2nd edition. 1962.

le Huray, Peter. *Music and the Reformation in England.* 1967.

Meyer, Ernest H. *Early English Chamber Music from the Middle Ages to Purcell.* 1982.

Neighbour, Oliver. *The Consort and Keyboard Music of William Byrd.* 1978.

Joseph C. Morin

SEE ALSO

Byrd, William; Campion, Edmund; Dowland, John; Jones, Robert; Madrigal; Morley, Thomas

CONSUBSTANTIATION

See Eucharist; Sacraments

Convocation

Convocation was the name given to the assemblies of the clergy in each of the provinces of Canterbury and York in the Church of England. The convocations are of ancient origin, but their historical importance dates from about 1340, when clergy (at their own request) ceased to sit in the House of Commons. Instead, they intended to govern the church through their own assemblies, which, like Parliament, consisted of Upper and Lower Houses. The Upper Houses (i.e., the bishops) also sat in the House of Lords, which provided a direct link with the secular government. The Convocation of York was always a shadowy body, and usually did little more than rubber-stamp what the Convocation of Canterbury decided. For that reason, the word is often used in the singular, to refer to Canterbury alone.

The convocations normally met the day after Parliament was convened, and ended at the same time. They claimed the right to legislate for the church, a right that was not seriously challenged until the seventeenth century. In 1529, the Convocation of Canterbury initiated a reform program designed to forestall the more radical plans of the House of Commons. For a time it seemed as if a constitutional clash was unavoidable, but in the end the convocations both gave way and accepted the royal supremacy in causes ecclesiastical. Canterbury gave its assent on March 31, 1534, and York, after some debate, on June 2. Only after that did Henry VIII proceed to pass the Act of Supremacy (November 3, 1534), which theoretically was giving Parliamentary assent to a decision already taken by the church.

By the Act for the Submission of the Clergy (25 Henry VIII, c. 19, 1534), the convocations were empowered to proceed to a revision of the canon law, but it was clearly stipulated that all their decisions would require the consent of Parliament in order to become law. In any event, nothing was done, and the convocations retreated to a subordinate role in the administration of the church. In 1640, Charles I extended the normal session of the Convocation of Canterbury in order to pass a series of canons that he knew he could not get through Parliament, but this procedure was regarded as irregular, and the legality of the canons (which were never invoked) is still a matter of debate today.

BIBLIOGRAPHY

Cardwell, E. *Synodalia*. 2 vols. 1842.

Lathbury, T. *A History of the Convocation of the Church of England.* 2nd edition. 1853.

Moore, E.G., and Timothy Briden. *Moore's Introduction to English Canon Law.* 2nd edition. 1985.

Gerald L. Bray

SEE ALSO

Canon Law; Church of England; Submission, Act of; Supremacy, Act of

Cooper, Thomas (c. 1520–1594)

Born at Oxford and educated at Magdalen College, Thomas Cooper refrained from being ordained after graduation and became a physician instead. Cooper assisted on Thomas Elyot's *Dictionary* (1538) and expanded it after Elyot's death. He also took up writing and finished off Thomas Lanquet's *Chronicle of the World,* which had been interrupted at A.D. 17. After the death of Mary I, Cooper felt it safe to seek ordination, and he was ordained in 1559. In 1562, he entered theological controversy by defending Bishop John Jewel's *Apology* against Catholic attacks. Although he wrote anonymously, everyone knew who he was, and his advancement was rapid. In 1567, he was made dean of Christ Church, Oxford, and two years later he became dean of Gloucester. He was consecrated bishop of Lincoln in 1571 and was translated to Winchester in 1584. In 1589 he engaged in controversy against the Marprelate Tracts, and the struggle against Puritanism occupied his declining years. As before, he published his work semi-anonymously; but again everyone knew who he was, and the author of the Marprelate Tracts attacked him by name. He died at Winchester on April 29, 1594. Cooper was in many ways the archetypal Elizabethan bishop, loyal to the 1559 settlement of the church and ready to engage in controversy against both Catholics and Puritans to defend its *via media.*

BIBLIOGRAPHY

Collinson, Patrick. *The Elizabethan Puritan Movement.* 1990.

Haugaard, W. P. *Elizabeth and the English Reformation: the Struggle for a Stable Settlement of Religion.* 1968.

Gerald L. Bray

SEE ALSO

Dictionaries; Jewel, John; Marprelate Controversy

COPERNICUS, NICOLAUS

See Astronomy

COPPER INDUSTRY

See Metal Industries

Cornwallis, William (1559–1614)

William Cornwallis the Younger is best remembered as an early practitioner of the informal essay. An extravagant and mostly self-educated gentleman, he was knighted during the ill-fated Essex campaign in Ireland (as was his uncle, Sir William Cornwallis the Elder) and returned to England to devote himself to reading and writing. His first essay, "Of Resolution," is his most autobiographical, a portrait of a reformed young man who has left behind his "continuall troubles" and folly under the salutary influence of Seneca and Plato. Although he does not set out to write a spiritual autobiography, at times he adopts a confessional retrospective view and the moral authority it confers. The first volume of Cornwallis's essays appeared in 1600, preceded by a dedicatory epistle by Henry Olney, who explains that unauthorized copies of Cornwallis's essays had been delivered to a printer who "would have published them unpolished & deformed without any correction; to prevent which" he published them on the author's behalf. *A Second Part of Essayes* appeared in 1601, and both were reissued in 1606 and 1610, with three final essays added to the 1610 edition. Although most literary historians regard Francis Bacon as the undisputed father of the English essay, Cornwallis may in fact deserve to be called the first English essayist. As Don Cameron Allen observes, "what Cornwallis wrote

C

in 1600 is a more finished essay than Bacon was to achieve before 1612."

Cornwallis took his inspiration from Montaigne, whom he mentions several times in his essays. He speaks of the Frenchman's writings as "a short touching of thinges" rather than "a Historie's constancie," composed in "a talking stile." Like Montaigne's, the essays of Cornwallis have the improvisatory, digressive, and eclectic character of the letter or private journal; they are by turns self-referential, confiding, and speculative in manner. His subjects include such standard Renaissance essay topics as love, ambition, praise, youth, fame, vanity, and fortune.

Cornwallis also composed a small volume of *Discourses Upon Seneca,* published in 1601. Each discourse is inspired by a line or two from a Senecan tragedy; rather like a Tudor preacher, the author explicates by dividing the verse into smaller units, first probing and then expanding on the meaning and implications of key words in a pattern that employs considerable repetition and reiteration. The speaking voice of the *Discourses* is more authoritative and formal than that of the essays, and not nearly as entertaining.

BIBLIOGRAPHY

Bennett, Roger E. "Sir William Cornwallis's Use of Montaigne." *PMLA,* vol. 48, no. 4.

Cornwallis, William. *The Essays.* Don Cameron Allen, ed. 1946.

Martha Rozett

SEE ALSO

Bacon, Francis; Essay

Cornysh, William (d. 1523)

At least three members of the Cornysh family were active as musicians at the end of the fifteenth and the beginning of the sixteenth centuries. John and William Cornysh, both of whom flourished at the end of the fifteenth century, may have been brothers, and the composer William Cornysh, who was employed as Henry VIII's master of the children of the Chapel Royal, may have been William's son.

William, like Thomas Campion, was a poet-musician. In the earliest record mentioning his name, he was paid for "a prophecy" in 1493. The following year he took the part of St. George in the Twelfth Night revels. He participated in the entertainments for Prince Arthur's marriage and was paid for composing a carol in 1502. In 1504, for unknown reasons, Cornysh was imprisoned in the Fleet, where he wrote *A Treatise bitwene Trouth and Enformacion.* It is not known how long he was incarcerated, for the next record, of September 29, 1509, is of his appointment as master of the children, a post he would hold until his death in 1523.

He continued to act at court, taking parts in *The Golden Arbour* of 1511 and *The Dangerous Fortress* and *Triumph of Love and Beauty* of 1514. In 1513, he went with the Chapel Royal to Lille, Tournai, and Thérouanne in France; he revisited France with the Chapel Royal in June of 1520 for the ceremonies of the Field of Cloth of Gold. His play describing the negotiations of Henry VIII and Charles V against the French was performed for the court in June of 1522. In a document dated the year of his death, he is called "comptroller of the petty custom of the port of London" and a draper, as well as a gentleman of the chapel.

Five of his works from the Eton Choirbook are missing, as are some Masses. What has survived are five motets (one incomplete), one Magnificat, two instrumental pieces, and sixteen English part-songs. The instrumental works and ten of the secular works were copied in Additional MS 31922. The Magnificat accords well with the prevailing elaborate style of the Eton Choirbook, but the motet *Ave Maria mater Dei* is simpler in style and closer to the secular songs. Two of these may have been derived from preexistent tunes: *A Robyn, gentyl robyn,* although deceptively simple in effect, is a three-part canon, and *My love sche morneth* also features canon in two voices. *Adew mes amours* by Cornysh is one example of the strong French influence on the repertory of Add. 31922. The sturdy *Blow thi horne hunter* is a carol, as are *Whilles lyve or breth* and *Yow and I and Amyas,* although only the burdens of the two last-named are found in the manuscript. Examples of the new, strikingly chordal style include *Adew my hartis lust, A the syghes,* and *Trolly lolly lo,* as well as *Blow thi horne.* The secular part-songs, representative of the significant change in English musical style in the early sixteenth century, are deservedly popular with audiences and performers alike.

BIBLIOGRAPHY

Anglo, Sydney. "William Cornish in a Play, Pageants, Prison and Politics." *Review of English Studies,* vol. 10, n.s., pp. 347–360.

Harrison, Frank Llewellyn. "English Polyphony (c. 1470–1540): Antiphons by Fayrfax and Cornysh." *Ars nova and the Renaissance, 1300–1540.* The New Oxford History of Music, vol. 3. 1960.

Stevens, John. *Music and Poetry in the Early Tudor Court.* 1961.

———, ed. "Music at the Court of Henry VIII." *Musica Britannica*, vol. 18. 1962.

Laura S. Youens

SEE ALSO

Carol; Eton Choirbook; Field of the Cloth of Gold; Motet

Counter-Reformation

The Counter-Reformation was the name traditionally given to a series of measures taken by the church of Rome to counter the spread of Protestantism. In recent years it has been increasingly recognized that this process entailed a far-reaching internal reformation of the Roman church, and many modern scholars therefore prefer to call it the Catholic Reformation.

The Counter-Reformation did not really begin until the newly formed Society of Jesus received papal approval on September 27, 1540, an event that was soon followed by the establishment of the Roman Inquisition (July 21, 1542). The Jesuits were an order specifically dedicated to the service of the pope and the extirpation of heresy, and their appearance marked a new militancy on the part of the Roman authorities. Attempts to come to terms with Martin Luther and the other Protestants were broken off, and a more aggressive policy was adopted instead.

This policy was developed at the Council of Trent, a gathering of all the bishops of the Roman church that opened in the northern Italian city of Trent (Trento) on December 13, 1545. Pope Paul III (1534–1549) did not attend the council in person, but charged it with the task of "uprooting heresy, restoring peace and unity, and reforming Church discipline and morals." The council got off to a slow start, and it never made much attempt to understand Protestantism or deal with it in a balanced manner. Instead, the bishops saw their task as defending Rome against Protestant attacks, and they were often disposed to canonize whatever aspect of medieval theology was most unlike what the reformers were teaching. The result was that the doctrinal pluralism of the late medieval church was narrowed down in a deliberately anti-Protestant direction.

The first phase of the council lasted until February 1, 1548, when the eighth session was suspended as a result of pressure from the emperor Charles V. In that period, the council managed to publish decrees on a number of doctrinal matters, including Scripture and tradition, orig-

inal sin, justification by faith, and the Sacraments. The second phase of the council began on May 1, 1551, and representatives from some of the Protestant states of Germany attended some of the sessions. However, the council fell victim to warfare between the Habsburgs and Henri II of France, and it had to be suspended once more on April 28, 1552.

The third and final phase of the council began on January 18, 1562 and it was formally dissolved on December 4, 1563. It was during this phase that serious reform of the clergy was undertaken, and that the groundwork was laid for the eventual publication of the revised liturgy, known ever since as the Tridentine Mass (1570).

Responsibility for implementing the council's decrees rested with the papacy, but it was not until the reign of Pius V (1566–1572) that a thoroughgoing attempt to do this was made. Once the reforms were in place, however, they determined the basic shape of Roman Catholicism as it was to be until the Second Vatican Council (1962–1965).

As far as England was concerned, the Council of Trent meant nothing until the accession of Mary I in 1553. The arrival of Reginald Cardinal Pole later in that year brought Tridentine ideas to the Tudor court, and during Mary's reign Pole did what he could to implement them. His crowning achievement was a national synod that published a series of canons on February 10, 1556. These were intended to bring about far-reaching reforms in religious education and clerical discipline, but the resources for implementing them were lacking, and when Mary and Pole both died in November 1558, little had been done.

The Counter-Reformation disappeared from England almost as soon as it had begun, but after the accession of Pius V, Catholic sympathizers in England began to organize themselves. They established seminaries on the Continent where they could train priests in the new Tridentine fashion and then smuggle them back into England. The mastermind of this was William Cardinal Allen, who founded a seminary at Douai (then in the Spanish Netherlands), which subsequently moved to Reims (France). In 1567, Mary Queen of Scots arrived in England, and was regarded by many Catholics as the rightful sovereign, since Queen Elizabeth I was technically illegitimate according to Roman canon law. The papal bull *Regnans in excelsis* (April 27, 1570), which excommunicated Elizabeth and ordered her subjects to rise in revolt against her, was a declaration of war against Protestant England, after which the full force of the Counter-Reformation would be felt. Parliament responded in 1571 with legislation that made it treason to import or publish any documents from Rome.

C

Anthony Munday, *The Execution of Richard Atkins at Rome.* Anthony Munday, an English Catholic, had been at the English College of Rome and reported on both the martyrdom of Jesuits in England and punishment of Protestants such as Richard Atkins, seen here in four vignettes illustrating his interruption of the Mass and his eventual burning. Reproduced from the original by permission of the Henry E. Huntington Library and Art Gallery.

In 1572, the Irish chiefs rose in rebellion, and Elizabeth was unable to suppress them completely until 1600. From 1577, Catholic missionary priests began to arrive in England, and they were able to form a small but dedicated band of Catholic loyalists who resisted every attempt to integrate them into the Elizabethan church. Most of these people were known to the authorities, but because they were generally well-to-do and often lived in the more remote parts of the country, they were let alone. However, if the missionaries were caught they would be tried, tortured, and executed—not for heresy, but for treason.

At first it was difficult to secure convictions because the legislation of 1571 was too vague and the Catholic missionaries were seldom (if ever) guilty of any genuinely treasonable offence. But in 1581, it was made a crime to withdraw anyone from allegiance to the Church of England, and in 1585, it became illegal simply to be a Jesuit or a seminary priest. A further Act of

1593 confined Catholics to within five miles of their residence.

Persecution of Catholics was at its height in the 1580s, and at least 187 priests were put to death. In addition, some laypeople were martyred, although the queen and Parliament always maintained that the executions were political, not religious. The failure of English Catholics to rise in support of the Spanish Armada (1588) made it clear that they were not really a political danger, and persecution diminished after that. The death of Cardinal Allen in 1594 led to splits in English Catholicism that greatly weakened it at the very time when Puritanism was poised to become a widespread popular movement. Counter-Reformation Catholicism's last gasp was the Gunpowder Plot of 1605, after which it soon ceased to have any influence.

The main impact of the Counter-Reformation on Tudor England was that it forced the queen and Parliament to define the Protestant character of the Church of England more carefully than they might otherwise have done. It also ensured that a specifically Roman form of Catholicism would continue to exist, particularly in Ireland, where it was the religion of the vast majority of the population.

BIBLIOGRAPHY

Delumeau, J. *Catholicism between Luther and Voltaire.* 1977.

Evenett, H.O. *The Spirit of the Counter Reformation.* 1968.

Jones, M.D.W. *The Counter Reformation.* 1995.

Gerald L. Bray

SEE ALSO

Allen, William; Catholicism; Church of England; English College of Rome; Clitherow, Margaret; Heresy; Jesuits; Marian Martyrs; Recusancy; Trent, Council of

Court

The court is a somewhat unstructured institution consisting of the vast network of servants and supplicants as well as counselors and officials surrounding the monarch. For the Tudor rulers, the court was a crucial tool in their dynastic success, and they used it to consolidate control over powerful subjects by making it a conduit for the political system's flow of favors and rewards. The court became the source of nearly all political and military appointments, displacing the nobility from their feudal base of power by reducing them to royal servants, and it served as an allocation system for customs operations, import and export licenses, and manufacturing monopolies. The court was also a hub of Tudor politics; because power flowed from the sovereign's person, access and patronage were crucial, and policy was complicated by factional and personal intrigue.

This blend of the private and domestic realms with public and bureaucratic activities made the atmosphere of the Tudor court especially intense. Only a few courtiers had regular contact with majesty, and given the value of proximity, many sought out offices that might otherwise seem demeaning, such as the groom of the stool. Those privileged to attend upon the monarch's most private moments, including his bowel movements, were allowed a closeness that could sometimes be turned to advantage. Gentleman pensioners served as royal bodyguards and attendants on the monarch, escorting the ruler to chapel, keeping order during receptions, and

joining royal progresses, and their ranks included sons of most of the Tudor noble families. Alternatively, such intimacy sometimes caused acute difficulties, especially when entangled in the complex sexual politics of the court. Sir Thomas Wyatt had been one of the aristocratic minions surrounding Henry VIII, but his previous affair with Anne Boleyn got him in trouble both when the king married her and when she subsequently fell from favor and was executed for adultery. Similarly, Sir Walter Ralegh acquired prominence as the captain of the guard under Elizabeth I, but his affair and marriage to one of her maids of honor led to his downfall.

Both Wyatt and Ralegh survived their difficulties, but their experience was considered typical. The court was perceived as a slippery slope whose glories were precarious and transient. The tense atmosphere of court life and the insecurities of courtiers were recurrent themes of Tudor courtly literature. This genre can be divided into two categories: the complaint, and the conduct manual outlining the rules of courtship or courtesy. Occasionally, the court is praised as the domain of the philosopher-king, where conversation sparkled and the best and the brightest had a chance to influence and advise on affairs of state, but such enthusiasm is frequently a prelude to disillusion. In his *Utopia,* Thomas More's narrative persona urges Raphael Hythlodaeus to embrace the courtly philosophy in which timing and tact are essential, but the uncompromising Hythlodaeus repudiates such courtesy as ineffectual flattery. Satires and diatribes prevail in much of the literature of the Tudor court from John Skelton's *Bowge of Court* to Walter Ralegh's putative poem "The Lie." Nevertheless, the classic conduct book, Baldessar Castiglione's *The Courtyer,* which was translated by Sir Thomas Hoby and published in England in 1561, is largely positive, and its elegant exchanges serve as models of the grace, good humor, and delicacy it prescribes. Although devoted service to the prince is paramount, courtly conversation implies "a certain equality which would not seem possible between a lord and a servant." The ideal courtier finds subtle ways to ingratiate and influence his master, using art to conceal art. Castiglione calls this apparently artless artfulness *sprezzatura,* meaning something like nonchalance.

This artful aspect of courtliness requires skill in playing a role, an attainment that is somewhat Machiavellian and can easily degenerate into fawning hypocrisy. Combined with the fierce competition and relentless self-promotion, this tendency toward pretense continued to

C

trouble those who may have also been disappointed by the meager results of all these efforts. Practical disappointments probably weighed as heavily as moral objections among those disillusioned with the court. The gifted and ambitious Sir Philip Sidney complained bitterly to his uncle, the earl of Leicester, after the queen offered him only the confiscated assets of recusant Catholics, writing "Well my Lord, your Lordship made me a courtier[;] do you think of it as seems best unto you." On the other hand, Robert Carey, the seventh and youngest son of Henry Carey, Lord Hundson, boasted that "I lived in court, had small means of my friends, and yet God so blessed me that I was ever able to keep company with the best . . . either at tilt, tourney, or barriers, in masque or balls." Sir Francis Knollys worked the system very effectively, moving from the ranks of the gentlemen pensioners under Henry VIII through household offices such as captain of the guard and vice-chamberlain to a seat on the Privy Council under Elizabeth I. On balance, the Tudor court's attractions and deficiencies derived from its fixation on the monarchy. On the one hand, its cultivation of a more docile civility and decorum was a healthy antidote to the brutality and belligerence of feudal society. Norbert Elias attributes "a new self-discipline, an incomparably stronger reserve, that is imposed on people by this new social space," treating the court as a major advance in what he calls *The Civilizing Process*. On the other hand, the court finally did not provide an adequate outlet for political ambition and idealism. Its requirement of abject devotion to the prince reduced it in the eyes of many to a sink of flattery and corruption, prompting growing estrangement during the next regime.

BIBLIOGRAPHY

Castiglione, Baldessar. *The Book of the Courtier.* Charles Singleton, trans. 1959.

Elias, Norbert. *The Civilizing Process.* Edmund Jephcott, trans. 1994.

Elton, G.R. "Tudor Government: The Points of Contact: The Court." *Transactions of the Royal Historical Society,* series 5, vol. 26, pp. 211–228.

Javitch, Daniel. *Poetry and Courtliness in Renaissance England.* 1978.

Starkey, David, ed. *The English Court: From the Wars of the Roses to the Civil War.* 1987.

Stone, Lawrence. *The Crisis of the Aristocracy, 1558–1641.* 1965.

Richard C. McCoy

SEE ALSO

Civility; Government, Central Administration of; Knollys, Sir Francis; Monopolies; Patronage; Sidney, Sir Philip; Wyatt, Sir Thomas

Courts

See Common Pleas, Court of; Exchequer; High Commission, Court of; Star Chamber, Court of

Courts, Ecclesiastical

The courts of the church were the major stabilizing factor in the history of ecclesiastical institutions in the Tudor era. Centered in the archdeaconries and the dioceses, they administered the canon law of the Roman Catholic Church. The archidiaconal courts, administered by archdeacons who were called the "bishop's eye," handled the larger number of cases litigated. Ranging in number from one to six in each county, they primarily heard cases of moral wrongs and church discipline, including disorderly conduct in church, clerical misbehavior, sexual misconduct, and defamation. Archdeacons usually took their courts to each parish twice a year. Called visitations, they often had a list of matters relating to the life of the local church: the credentials of clerics and schoolmasters, the state of the church fabric and property, and the moral and ethical conduct of the parishioners. As a rule, they avoided engagement with the religious changes of the sixteenth century. Lacking the power of arrest or imprisonment, they relied on the support of parishioners for adherence to their judgments.

The courts that represented the jurisdiction of the dioceses were called consistory courts; these tended to handle appeals from archidiaconal courts as well as matters of more weighty substance. Bishops made visitations also, and these often concerned matters central to ecclesiastical policy. Unlike archdeacons, however, bishops had the power to suspend officials and excommunicate their parishioners. The role of hierarchy in the church was revealed in its system of appeal courts. The court of Chancery for the see of York served to hear appeals from diocesan courts in its jurisdiction, while the courts of arches and audience served the same function in the see of Canterbury. In addition, the prerogative court of Canterbury had an ancient jurisdiction to hear probate cases involving property in multiple dioceses.

This system was strengthened in the reign of Elizabeth I with the creation of the Court of High Commission in

1559, a prerogative court with statutory jurisdiction of all causes concerning matters of religious disaffection. Using the *ex officio* oath to examine people with open-ended questions, it had authority to fine and imprison. The twin powers of inquisition and imprisonment brought the commission into conflict with common law courts, which used their powers of prohibition and habeas corpus to prohibit jurisdiction and release persons from jail. By the 1580s, however, the common law was extending its attacks to all church courts.

The ecclesiastical courts had a reputation for inefficiency and corruption in the early years of the Tudor era. Reforms under Henry VIII and Elizabeth strengthened the training and credentials of the judges, and defined more closely the jurisdiction of these courts. Some contemporaries in the late sixteenth century considered them to be among the most popular courts in the country, while others (primarily Puritans) contested the legitimacy of their authority in criminal matters and questioned the value of religious courts in an increasing secular society. The view that only God, and not his representatives, should judge matters of religious faith and practice would gain ground under the Stuarts.

BIBLIOGRAPHY

Helmholz, R.H. *Canon Law and the Law of England.* 1987.

Houlbrooke, Ralph. *Church Courts and the People during the English Reformation.* 1979.

Ingram, Martin. *Church Courts, Sex, and Marriage in England, 1570–1640.* 1987.

Marchant, Ronald. *The Church and the Law: Justice, Administration, and Discipline in the Diocese of York, 1560–1640.* 1987.

Usher, Roland G. *The Rise and Fall of the High Commission.* 1913; repr. 1968.

Louis A. Knafla

SEE ALSO

Canon Law; Chancery; Law, Common; Delegates, Court of; High Commission, Court of

Coverdale, Miles (1488–1568)

Born in Yorkshire and educated at Cambridge, Miles Coverdale was ordained in 1514 and entered the Austin Friars in the university city. There he was greatly influenced by Robert Barnes, who was prior of the friary from 1523 to 1526. When Barnes was arrested on charges of heresy, Coverdale left the monastery and became a traveling evangelist. About 1528, he went abroad, and is thought to have met William Tyndale at Hamburg in 1529. He is next heard of in 1535.

On December 19, 1534, Convocation petitioned the king to allow an English Bible to be prepared, and in the following year one was printed under Coverdale's name. Coverdale was soon back in England as the protégé of Thomas Cromwell, and played a major part in the publication of the Great Bible of 1538. After Cromwell's fall and Barnes's execution (1540), Coverdale left England and did not return until 1548, when he preached the sermon at the funeral of Queen Catherine Parr. In 1551, he was made bishop of Exeter, but he was deprived on the accession of Mary I, and in 1554, he left for Denmark. He returned to England in 1559, but did not resume his post at Exeter. In 1563, he was made a D.D. of Cambridge and became rector of St. Magnus in London. In 1566, he resigned his living in protest against the strictness being employed against the nascent Puritan movement. He continued to preach unofficially until his death and was buried in St. Bartholemew's Church, London, on February 19, 1568. Coverdale is remembered today mainly for his psalms, which are printed in the Book of Common Prayer (1662).

BIBLIOGRAPHY

Pearson, G., ed. *Writings and Translations of Myles Coverdale, Bishop of Exeter.* Parker Society. 1844.

Gerald L. Bray

SEE ALSO

Bible Translations; Book of Common Prayer; Convocation; Cromwell, Thomas; Parr, Catherine

Cox, Leonard (c. 1500–1599?)

Born in Thame, Oxfordshire, Cox is first encountered in 1513, when he left England on his way to study in Paris. He did not stay there for long, however, and the following year proceeded to Tübingen, where he studied with Johannes Stöffler and met Philipp Melanchthon. In 1518, Cox matriculated at Krakow, delivering an oration, *De laudibus celeberrimae Cracoviensis academiae,* which was promptly published. For the next few years he taught in two schools in Hungary as well as in Krakow, making important contributions to the introduction of humanism in these regions. While at Krakow, Cox published a short treatise delineating his

C

educational philosophy, *De erudienda iuventute* (1526), and from there he also initiated a correspondence with Desiderius Erasmus. By early 1527, Cox was back in England, and was immediately admitted B.A. at Cambridge. In February 1530, he was incorporated M.A. at Oxford and was appointed master of the grammar school in Reading, thanks to the patronage of Hugh of Faringdon, abbot of Reading, to whom two years later he dedicated *The Arte or Crafte of Rhethoryke* (repr. 1971). In 1534, Cox published a translation of Erasmus's *Paraphrase on Titus*, which he carried out, at least in part, in the hope of endearing himself to Thomas Cromwell and obtaining the mastership of the free school in Bristol. His aspiration came to naught. Following the dissolution, and the execution of Faringdon in 1539, Cox retired to teach in Caerleon, Wales. From there he attempted, once again, to gain Cromwell's patronage, dedicating to the latter in 1540 his edition of William Lily's *De octo orationis partium constructione libelus* (1540), and following it up with a letter promising to accomplish even more once in Cromwell's service. Unfortunately for Cox, Cromwell was executed two months later, so he returned to teach in Reading. In 1541, Cox also became a beneficiary of a £10 annuity from Henry VIII, which was discontinued in 1547. We lose clear sight of Cox after the publication in 1549 of a new preface to his *Paraphrase on Titus*, printed as part of the complete edition of Erasmus's *Paraphrases*. However, in 1572, Leonard Cox became the master of a grammar school in Coventry, a position he held until 1599, perhaps the year of his death.

BIBLIOGRAPHY

Emden, A.B. *A Biographical Register of the University of Oxford A.D 1501 to 1540.* 1974.

Bietenholz, Peter G., and Thomas B. Deutscher, eds. *Contemporaries of Erasmus,* vol. 1., pp. 353–354. 1985.

Breeze, Andrew. "Leonard Cox, a Welsh Humanist in Poland and Hungary." *The National Library of Wales Journal,* vol. 25, pp. 399–410.

———, and J. Glomski. "An Early British Treatise upon Education: Leonard Cox's *De erudienda iuventute.*" *Humanistica Lovaniensia,* vol. 40, pp. 112–167.

Mordechai Feingold

SEE ALSO

Bible Commentary; Cromwell, Thomas; Erasmus, Desiderius; Grammar Schools; Humanism; Lily, William

Cox, Richard (1500–1581)

Bishop of Ely and an active church reformer, Richard Cox was educated at Cambridge and then Oxford. He was appointed headmaster of Eton and gained favor with Archbishop Thomas Cranmer and Henry VIII himself, becoming chaplain to both. In 1540, he served on the commission that annulled the marriage of King Henry to Anne of Cleves, and soon thereafter Cox was appointed archdeacon of Ely, receiving preferments through the end of Henry's reign. Edward VI's accession in 1547 proved a boon for Cox, who had previously been the new king's tutor and almoner. Within a year, he became chancellor of Oxford, rector of Harrow, Middlesex, and canon of Windsor. As part of Cranmer's Windsor commission, Cox helped compile the first English communion in 1548, and the first Prayer Book in 1549—the same year he was raised to dean of Westminster. During his tenure at Oxford, which lasted until 1552, he brought such notables as Peter Martyr to the university, yet 1549 also saw Cox's participation in destructive raids on Oxford properties designed to eradicate vestiges of Catholicism: for his efforts the chancellor was given the nickname "cancellor." At the accession of Mary I in 1553, Cox was deprived of his preferments and fled to Frankfurt. There he feuded with John Knox over the proper degree of ecclesiastical reforms. The two factions became known as "Coxians" and "Knoxians"; Cox's more moderate faction prevailed, and Knox was expelled from the city. Cox returned to England at Elizabeth I's accession in 1558 and was consecrated bishop of Ely the following year. Faithful to the English *via media,* he was hard on both Catholics and Puritans during his twenty-one years at Ely. Disenchanted with Elizabeth's court after much of his see's property was confiscated, he resigned in 1580 and died a year later.

BIBLIOGRAPHY

Dixon, R.W. "Richard Cox." *Dictionary of National Biography.* Vol. 4. pp. 1337–1339. 1917.

Mark Goldblatt

SEE ALSO

Anne of Cleves; Book of Common Prayer; Catholicism; Cranmer, Thomas; Knox, John; Vermigli, Peter Martyr; Puritanism

Cranmer, Thomas (1489–1556)

Born at Aslacton, Nottinghamshire, on July 2, 1489, Thomas Cranmer received his early education at home, but in 1503, he was sent to Cambridge, where he spent eight years studying philosophy and the classics. During this time he became a disciple of Desiderius Erasmus. He took his M.A. in 1515 and was elected a fellow of Jesus College, but had to resign after his marriage. However, when his wife died in childbirth, he was reelected to the college, where he remained until 1529. In that year the plague struck Cambridge, and Cranmer fled to Waltham Abbey to escape the danger.

While he was at Waltham he became aware of the king's desire for an annulment of his marriage. When the king himself arrived at Waltham, Cranmer met Dr. Fox, the royal almoner and a leading agent in the case for the annulment. Cranmer managed to persuade Fox that it

was only necessary for the king to get the opinions of theologians in the universities who would support the view that his marriage to Katherine of Aragon was invalid, and he could proceed to the annulment without a papal dispensation. The king promptly ordered Cranmer to write a treatise on this subject, which he later defended successfully at Cambridge. In 1530, Cranmer went to Rome to press the king's case. It is indicative of his character that he was able to do this without losing the favor either of the pope or of the emperor Charles V.

In late 1532, following the death of Archbishop William Warham, the king recalled Cranmer to England and appointed him archbishop of Canterbury. The appointment was confirmed at Rome on February 22,

John Foxe, *Thomas Cranmer renouncing his recantation before his execution.* From *Actes and Monuments of these latter and perillous dayes* (1563). After watching the burning of Latimer and Ridley, Cranmer was persuaded to recant the Oath of Supremacy, theoretically submitting him to the pope as the supreme head of the church. On the occasion of Cole's sermon at Oxford, Cranmer's dramatic retraction and statement of Protestant faith undermined the strategic value of his subsequent execution. Here he is seen being pulled down by enraged friars. Reproduced from the original by permission of the Henry E. Huntington Library and Art Gallery.

C

1533, and Cranmer was consecrated on March 30. He was now totally devoted to the king's cause, and on May 23 he unilaterally pronounced the royal marriage null and void. Five days later he confirmed the king's secret marriage to Anne Boleyn, and when Princess Elizabeth was born in September, he stood godfather at her baptism.

From that time on, Cranmer was a faithful servant of the royal will. He concurred in the publication of the Ten Articles (1536), which set out the king's views on the main theological issues of the day, although he was able to influence them in a Protestant direction, especially on the vital question of justification by faith. In 1537, he published a Protestantizing commentary on the articles that is popularly known as the Bishops' Book. Henry VIII allowed him to enter into negotiations with the Lutherans, which led Cranmer to compose a confession of faith along Lutheran lines (1538), but the king would not accept any genuine movement in the direction of Protestantism. In 1539, he reversed his earlier toleration, and began to enforce traditional Catholic teaching on such matters as clerical celibacy and transubstantiation. Cranmer, who had remarried, put his wife away for the rest of Henry's reign and never publicly dissented from the king's policy.

In 1540, he was able to write a preface to the second edition of the Great Bible (1538), and in this his Protestantism was still evident, but in 1543, he was forced to preside over a commission that revised the Bishops' Book in a more Catholic direction, and which was published later that year as the King's Book. After that he was able to accomplish little until Henry died (January 28, 1547), when he became one of the regents for the young Edward VI.

At this point his Protestantism was able to blossom into full flower, and he embarked on a threefold project designed to establish the reformed faith in the Church of England. The first part of this was a reform of the church's worship, which led to the Book of Common Prayer (1549). His second, revised version of this (1552) still forms the basis of Anglican worship today. The second part of his project was a confession of faith, which appeared as the Forty-Two Articles (1553). These were later revised and are now known as the Thirty-Nine Articles, which have been the official doctrinal statement of the Church of England since 1628. The third part of his project was a thorough reform of the canon law, which he completed in 1553, but which was rejected by Parliament. Some believe that had it been implemented, there is a good chance that the Puritans, who emerged after 1555, would have been reconciled to the church's system of government.

Cranmer's activities were cut short by the death of Edward VI on July 6, 1553. Much against his will, he entered the plot to put the Protestant Lady Jane Grey on the throne, and when this failed, he was exposed to the full wrath of Queen Mary I's anger. He was arrested and committed to the Tower of London on September 8. On November 13, he was tried for treason and was convicted, although his life was spared by the queen. This did him little good, because on March 8, 1554, he was taken from the Tower and sent to Oxford, where he was obliged to defend himself against the university on charges of heresy. This he did with great learning and dignity, greatly impressing his opponents, even though the outcome was a foregone conclusion. Cranmer was kept in detention at Oxford, where nobody knew what to do with him, but on September 12, 1555, he was formally charged with heresy and put on trial. No judgement was pronounced at the time, but the whole matter was referred to Rome, where on December 11, the pope formally declared him guilty. This verdict was relayed to England, and Cranmer was formally degraded on February 14, 1556.

Cranmer had already been persuaded to sign two formal documents of recantation, and shortly after his degradation, he signed a third. Three more recantations followed in quick succession, the last on March 18, but it was to no avail. On March 21, he was led to the stake at Oxford, and as the fire was being lit, he renounced all his recantations, putting his own hand into the fire as a sign of his repentance. As so often happens, Cranmer the martyr was more powerful in death than Cranmer the theologian had been in life, and when the Protestant faith was restored in 1559, it was largely his work that was canonized as the official teaching and practice of the Church of England.

BIBLIOGRAPHY
The Works of Thomas Cranmer. 2 vols. Parker Society. 1844–46.
Brooks, P.N. Cranmer in Context. 1989.
Johnson, M., ed. Thomas Cranmer. 1990.
MacCulloch, Diarmaid. Thomas Cranmer: A Life. 1996.
Ridley, J. Thomas Cranmer. 1962.

Gerald L. Bray

SEE ALSO
Articles of Religion; Bishop's Book; Book of Common Prayer; Canon Law; Church of England; Grey, Lady Jane; Katherine of Aragon; King's Book; Reformation, English

C

Crichton, James (1560—82)

Born in Eliock House, Dumfriesshire, James Crichton (or Creighton) was the son of a Scottish advocate. The precocious youth entered St. Salvator's College, St. Andrews, in 1570, graduating B.A. and M.A. in 1574 and 1575, respectively. There he demonstrated his considerable literary talents and exceptional memory, as well as the more predictable skills, such as horsemanship and fencing, expected from a man of his social status. In 1577, Crichton left for the Continent, his first stop being Paris, where he is reputed to have successfully discharged a challenge he set at the Collège of Navarre to respond to any question proposed to him, on any topic, in any one of the twelve languages in which he claimed proficiency. A day later he won a titling match at the Louvre. After serving in the French army for two years, Crichton proceeded to Italy, again distinguishing himself in numerous public orations, Latin verses, and scholarly debates, in all of which he much delighted. His death befitted such a dashing life. Having entered in 1582 into the service of the duke of Mantua as tutor to his son, Vincenzo di Gonzaga, Crichton's skills and arrogance quickly antagonized his charge, who one night led a band of his followers to attack his tutor. According to one account, it was, in fact, the young Gonzaga who inflicted the mortal blow after Crichton, having recognized the identity of his attackers, surrendered his sword. Crichton's odes and orations were published throughout the 1580s, but have never been collected. His great fame as the perfect gentleman and scholar is owed, to a large extent, to Sir Thomas Urquhart's sometime extravagant *The Discovery of a Most Exquisite Jewel* (1652).

BIBLIOGRAPHY

Crichton, Patrick F. *The Admirable Crichton.* 1988.
Tytler, Patrick F. *Life of James Crichton of Cluny, Commonly Called the Admirable Crichton.* 1819.

Mordechai Feingold

Crime

Crime in the Tudor period has attracted serious attention among academic historians only since the 1960s; moreover, study of the history of crime under the Tudors is complicated by problems of methodology and conceptualization. Even the definition of "crime" remains problematic, for the term was virtually unknown in its modern sense in the sixteenth century; contemporaries preferred to use the categories of felony (broadly speaking, serious offenses conviction for which might lead to capital punishment) and misdemeanor.

Most of the initial work on the history of crime in this period consisted of mapping patterns of serious offenses. Unfortunately, many archives are largely missing for the early Tudor period, and survive in bulk only from the early years of the reign of Elizabeth I, and even there survival is restricted to the records of the home circuit of the assizes, which covered the counties of Essex, Hertfordshire, Kent, Surrey, and Sussex. Some records also survive for Middlesex, which enjoyed an independent jurisdiction, while the palatinates of Lancaster and Cheshire possessed courts trying serious offenses for which good records, as yet not exhaustively researched, also survive.

Lack of relevant records for the period c. 1485–1560, and the unexplored nature of those that do survive for those years, render it difficult to make categorical statements on patterns of criminality under the early Tudors. The tradition that 70,000 "rogues" were executed in the reign of Henry VIII is almost certainly an exaggeration, but it might well point to a growing problem of law and order.

One aspect of crime that does seem to have altered over the early Tudor period was the retreat of the upper classes from criminal activity. Peers and gentry were to continue to indulge in acts of violence, and to involve themselves in such offenses as poaching, long after 1603, but the "robber barons" or gentry leaders of criminal gangs that had operated in the late Middle Ages seem to have been gradually eradicated. Even the traditions of noble violence came to be diluted, with the old taste for private warfare being replaced by pursuing conflict via litigation, or through the more polite forms of violence present in the duel. The involvement of this social level in criminal acts is an issue awaiting further investigation, but there is evidence that the changing cultural values of elites during this period included a retreat from late medieval violence.

If upper-class criminality was decreasing, the socioeconomic changes of the period were providing social commentators with a new criminal stereotype in the form of the vagrant. Vagrancy was one of the major social problems of the sixteenth century, and many contemporaries saw it as a novel and dangerous one. One byproduct of this interpretation was a growing body of literature in which the vagrant was typically portrayed as a member of an organized hierarchy of wrongdoers to whom were ascribed a number of qualities considered undesirable in the model citizen: these people did not work, they had no time for organized religion, they frequented the alehouse,

C

and they were sexually promiscuous at a time when sex outside marriage was seen as sinful, and when the family was seen as the basic unit of social and political organization. In fact, evidence about vagrants from court records suggests that the contemporary literary stereotype of the criminal vagrant was overdrawn. Even so, vagrants, itinerant workers, or temporarily unemployed persons on the road between jobs did constitute one of the main groups from which thieves were drawn. Detailed research, however, is revealing that they were only one element of a much larger body of the poor who were regarded by contemporaries as increasingly delinquent and disorderly.

Those materials dealing with serious crime that have been analyzed demonstrate that it was offenses against property which, by the Elizabethan era, were most frequently tried before the courts. Figures for Sussex, for example, record 1,921 indictments at the assizes between 1559 and 1603. Of these, 1,318 were for property offenses, including 654 cases of simple larceny, twenty-six cases of theft from the person, 332 cases of theft from premises, 267 of burglary, and thirty-nine of highway robbery. These figures should be contrasted with 127 cases of homicide, and a further twenty-seven of infanticide. Other felonies included twelve accusations of rape, five of other sexual offenses, fourteen of witchcraft, and fifteen of sedition. Other offenses indicted included thirty-one assaults (assault, as a misdemeanor, would often not be tried at the assizes), sixty-six cases of poaching, 101 of vagrancy, and 205 miscellaneous cases, most of them of a petty nature. Figures from other counties show much the same pattern: on the evidence of indictments, property offenses massively outnumbered homicides, and other felonies (apart from the occasional local peculiarity such as witchcraft in Essex) were very rarely prosecuted. The records of most counties also point to a rising level of indictments for property offenses in the late 1590s; by that point English society was experiencing a number of strains, which, for the most vulnerable, at least, were compounded by a series of bad harvests. Indeed, the last part of the sixteenth century saw the establishment of that connection between dearth and high levels of property crime which was to last throughout the seventeenth and eighteenth centuries.

Although it is the serious offenses in any period that attract attention, in Tudor England petty crime was, statistically, much more common than the serious offenses tried at the assizes. As well as the quarter sessions and assizes, England possessed a wide range of local courts, many of which enjoyed a jurisdiction over minor criminal offenses. Manorial courts, whose records form one of the major sources for medieval historians, were still operating in many villages, and their juries tried a range of offenders: perpetrators of assaults, petty thieves, and local nuisance offenders. And after a decline in their fortunes in the immediate post-Reformation period, the ecclesiastical courts were also involved in attempting to discipline the English into habits of godliness; thus, they found themselves hearing not only cases involving persons failing to attend church or holding heterodox religious views, but also instances of adultery, fornication, disorder on the Sabbath, and other types of misbehavior that had offended community values. And, throughout the Tudor period, parliamentary legislation, in its efforts to regulate society more closely, imposed a growing burden of law enforcement on parish constables and justices of the peace, thereby adding to the range of criminal offenses.

In prosecuting petty offenses, parish constables, the churchwardens responsible for most presentments to the ecclesiastical courts, and manorial jurors were all drawn from the local community, and, ultimately, law enforcement depended upon their efforts. This system was obviously prone to abuse and inefficiencies; yet it seems to have operated far more effectively than might have been expected. In general, the local community was anxious to preserve its internal harmony and order, and saw prosecution before a criminal court, even the local manor court, as a means to this end. The language in which complaints against local nuisance offenders were couched is frequently full of genuine dismay at disruptive behavior. And it is likely that in many settlements the demographic changes and socioeconomic pressures of the period were creating an increased polarity between a stratum of relatively prosperous and "respectable" villagers and a body of poor who were increasingly being regarded as disorderly, ungodly, and criminally inclined. In such a situation, local officeholders such as constables, drawn as they were from the upper reaches of village society, regarded local law enforcement structures as a means of controlling their poorer neighbors.

Study of local law enforcement through the records of local courts gives a very different profile of "crime" from that provided by analysis of assize records. There were, for example, 198 presentments for wrongdoing at the manorial court of Acomb, a small village near York, between 1550 and 1600. Many of these were for the typical manorial offenses of letting cattle or pigs stray, or for allowing fences or hedges to fall into disrepair. But forty-five involved assault, about the same number for theft of wood, often from hedges, with further presentments for keeping disorderly alehouses, harboring vagrants or other undesirables, or scolding and slandering. In Kent for the years 1600–1602 there were 898 criminal suspects each year in borough and other local courts, 221 at the county quarter sessions, and about a third of that number at the assizes. 10 percent of the total were property offenses, 22 percent crimes against the person, 20 percent crimes against the peace, 22 percent moral offenses, and twenty-five public nuisance offenses. The annual crime rate in Kent, on the basis of these figures, was ninety-two offenses per 10,000 people. The tendency to use local courts for conflict resolution and the regulative thrust of the late Tudor period combined to produce numerous criminal prosecutions and a distinctive crime pattern. By the end of the sixteenth century many contemporaries felt that they were confronting a law-and-order problem of considerable dimensions.

BIBLIOGRAPHY

Cockburn, J.S., ed. *Crime in England, 1550–1800.* 1977.

Knafla, Louis A. "'Sin of all Sorts swarmeth': Criminal Litigation in an English County in the Early Seventeenth Century." In E.W. Ives and A.H. Manchester, eds. *Law, Litigants and the Legal Profession.* 1983.

Samaha, Joel. *Law and Order in Historical Perspective: The Case of Elizabethan Essex.* 1974.

Sharpe, J.A. *Crime in Early Modern England, 1550–1750.* 1984.

James Sharpe

SEE ALSO

Capital Punishment; Courts, Ecclesiastical; Criminal Law; Government, Local; Justice of the Peace; Poor Laws; Population and Demography; Sexual Offenses; Social Classes; Vagrancy; Witchcraft

Criminal Law

Criminal law was a considerable concern in the Tudor period, and its significance is now becoming more widely acknowledged as historians revise their interpretations of Tudor government. Certainly it was a commonplace among contemporary political theoreticians that among the responsibilities of an effective ruler were the punishment of criminals, the enactment of good laws, and the general maintenance of law and order.

By about 1500, most of continental Europe had adopted, or was in the process of adopting, legal codes based on Roman law, the most famous being Emperor Charles V's code of 1536, the *Carolina*. Unique among the major states of Western Europe, England maintained an individual legal system based on the common law that was expanded and modified by parliamentary statute. The English system—as some English contemporaries acknowledged—was in both ideological and practical terms more ramshackle than those of some continental states. In particular, lawyers were not normally involved in criminal trials, so criminal law remained technically underdeveloped compared to, for example, land law, from whose complexities lawyers derived considerable business. But English criminal law enjoyed a number of distinctive features. In criminal trials, the most important of these was the dependence on a jury, as opposed to a Roman law trial, which relied on an "inquisitorial" judge and the use of judicial torture to help prove criminal charges and discover criminal associates. Torture, although used in England while investigating treason, was never established as a normal part of the criminal trial process.

The criminal justice system operated by the Tudors was essentially inherited from the Middle Ages. The courts operated under a system of royal law, the common law of the subjects of England's monarchs: seigneurial jurisdictions were less powerful, and peculiar jurisdictions less common, than in many continental states. Serious crime (including such offenses as murder, grand larceny, robbery, burglary, and rape) could be tried at the assizes, quarter sessions, borough courts with a right of jail delivery, or at Westminster at the Court of King's Bench. Over the sixteenth century, however, it became accepted that cases likely to result in a capital conviction were best left to the assizes, courts presided over by royal judges sent from Westminster held twice yearly in each county.

These judges, and the local justices or urban patricians running the local courts, found themselves presiding over an ever more complex body of criminal law, for one of the major developments in Tudor legislation was the proliferation of criminal offenses through parliamentary statute. This tendency first became marked in the reign of Henry VIII, with a tightening of the treason laws. It also witnessed an extension of capital offenses under the criminal law, such as statutes against servants stealing their employers' goods (1529); imposing boiling in oil as the punishment for murder by poisoning (1530); against male homosexuality (sodomy or buggery in contemporary terms) and bestiality (1533); and against piracy (1536), theft of fish from ponds (1540), and witchcraft

C

(1542). This legislation created new offenses, and also redefined and prescribed harsher punishment for some established ones. The troubled and short reigns of Edward VI and Mary I afforded scant opportunity for further criminal legislation, but the process was renewed after the stabilization of Elizabeth I's regime. The laws against witchcraft, "buggery," and bestiality were renewed in 1563, and later statues prescribed the death penalty for pickpocketing and cutting purses (1565), rape (1575), burglary (1575), and horse theft (1594). As in Henry VIII's reign, some of these statutes created new offenses, while others (for example, those concerning rape or burglary) provided clarification for the definition and punishment of established common law offenses.

These legislative efforts were matched by the more systematic imposition of the criminal law through the courts. From the accession of Elizabeth, records from the assize courts make it possible to see how serious crime was being treated, a matter that became more urgent in the late 1590s as demographic pressure, deteriorating conditions among the poor, and a run of bad harvests created a severe problem of law and order over much of southern England. During the Tudor period the criminal courts were heavily dependent on capital punishment, but by the 1590s they became increasingly willing to bend the law to save at least some offenders from the gallows, in some cases as a result of plea bargaining. Overall, the operation of the criminal law through the courts indicated a system both flexible in its approach to offenders and selective in its use of various punishments.

The Tudor period, therefore, saw developments in criminal law in both the statute book and enforcement through the courts. Obviously, Tudor criminal law was theoretically underdeveloped, and the courts through which it was enforced were clearly based on their medieval antecedents. Nevertheless, it proved an effective framework within which the Tudor state could operate.

BIBLIOGRAPHY

Bellamy, John G. *Criminal Law and Society in Late Medieval and Tudor England.* 1984.
Harding, A. *A Social History of English Law.* 1966.
Langbein, J.H. *Prosecuting Crime in the Renaissance: England, Germany, France.* 1974.

James Sharpe

SEE ALSO

Capital Punishment; Crime; Criminal Law; King's or Queen's Bench, Court of; Sexual Offenses; Witchcraft

Cromwell, Thomas (c. 1485–1540)

Born around 1485 to Walter Cromwell, a Putney clothworker and alehouse keeper, Thomas Cromwell rose to be the dominant political agent of Henry VIII in the eight years during which the Reformation was set in motion in England. Between 1532 and 1540, he controlled the royal secretariat either directly or through men of his own household promoted into the king's government. So, too, did he effectively control the King's Council and Privy Council as well as the many financial departments either by holding office directly or dominating men who did. He thus rose from lowly origins to be earl of Essex and lord privy seal before his execution on July 28, 1540, by a bill of attainder alleging eleven charges of treason and heresy.

We know very little about his career before 1512. Contemporaries alleged he had fled his tyrannical father in 1503 and took service on the French side at Marignano. Recent research has established that he was in the service of the powerful Florentine merchant bankers Frescobaldi for some years before 1512, when he dealt in cloth at Syngsson's Mart in Middelburgh in the Netherlands. Contrary to earlier assertions that he did not return to England until around 1519, when he entered Cardinal Thomas Wolsey's service, it has been demonstrated from the Vatican archives that Cromwell was an agent in the household of Cardinal Reginald Bainbridge and was active in English ecclesiastical business before the papal Rota. This service ended with Bainbridge's death in 1514, and Cromwell returned to England early in August 1514. There, together with other of Bainbridge's relicta, Cromwell entered Wolsey's service, where manuscript evidence shows this layman in charge of important ecclesiastical business from 1515.

Doubtless Wolsey recognized Cromwell's value to a churchman at a time when England had no cardinal resident in Rome. Wolsey also must have appreciated Cromwell's mastery of business, finance, and languages—among them Latin, Italian, and French—for the new cardinal of England steadily promoted Cromwell in his own service. By 1519, Cromwell had married Elizabeth Wyckes, daughter of a prominent London clothier. He entered the House of Commons in 1523, and may have caused some stir at court, if he delivered the speech opposing the French war that survives among his papers. In 1524 he was admitted to Gray's Inn. He was also in charge of Wolsey's suppression of some thirty religious houses to provide the foundations for his grammar school at Ipswich and Cardinal's College at Oxford. By 1529, the year of Henry VIII's divorce, he had befriended religious radicals in London, and was on intimate terms with important London printers.

C

In 1531, Cromwell was a sworn royal councilor, with a special charge from the king to have in hand parliamentary business in what we now call the Reformation Parliament (1529–1536). Promoted to be the king's principal secretary early in 1533, Cromwell put his stamp on every kind of business until his fall in 1540. Without regard to the now arid controversy whether he presided over a "Revolution in Government," Cromwell managed Parliament and organized new financial agencies and fiscal courts in the wake of the dissolution of the monasteries. These and other matters of ecclesiastical reform and reorganization he managed by virtue of his powers as Henry VIII's vice-regent and vicar-general in spiritual matters. Despite the opposition to him manifested in the Pilgrimage of Grace and other northern broils in 1536–1537, Cromwell pushed for religious reform, and he put his imprimatur on the injunctions to the clergy in 1536 and 1538, the King's Book of 1537, the establishment of parish registers, and the printing projects of a markedly Lutheran character that culminated in his management of the printing of the Great Bible in 1539–1540.

Indeed, it was chiefly his zeal in pursuit of reforms running well beyond what the king himself would accept that brought Cromwell down. By 1538, Bishop Richard Sampson and others were collecting a "book of evidences" against Cromwell. While the treason charges in the attainder after his arrest on June 10, 1540, were clearly trumped up, much hard evidence supports the charges that he knowingly supported sacramentarians at Calais and other heretics and heresies at home. The reaction led in the House of Lords by the duke of Norfolk, Thomas Howard, and several bishops, chiefly Gardiner of Winchester, and signaled by the famous Act of the Six Articles, was merely the sign and token of long-accumulating troubles. Cromwell's arrest, attainder, and execution were less the result of any single failure—the Cleves marriage, the "Protestant" foreign policy, or suspected deviance in doctrine—than they were of a loss of confidence in Cromwell by the king himself, a man susceptible to persuasion in such matters, as we know from the fates of Thomas More and Thomas Wolsey. Seldom has a king been better served than Henry was by his three Thomases; and seldom has a king been less faithful to those faithful to him.

BIBLIOGRAPHY

Elton, G.R. *The Tudor Revolution in Government: Administrative Changes under Henry VIII.* 1953.
———. *Policy and Police: The Enforcement of the Reformation in the Age of Thomas Cromwell.* 1972.
———. *Reform and Renewal: Thomas Cromwell and the Commonweal.* 1973.
Slavin, Arthur J. *Thomas Cromwell on Church and Commonwealth.* 1969.
———. "The Gutenberg Galaxy and the Tudor Revolution." In *Print and Culture in the Renaissance,* pp. 90–109. 1986.
———. "Cromwell, Cranmer, and Lord Lisle: A Study in the Politics of Reform," *Albion,* vol. 9, pp. 316–336.
Arthur J. Slavin

SEE ALSO
Injunctions, Royal; Monastic Orders; Pilgrimage of Grace; Reformation, English; Treason; Wolsey, Thomas

Crowley, Robert (c. 1518–1588)

A prominent Protestant controversialist who flourished during the brief reign of Edward VI, Robert Crowley was inspired by Hugh Latimer to appeal to the king and Parliament for a radical reformation of both church and state. He was a merciless satirist of corrupt clergy, and in 1550, he published an edition of *The Vision of Piers Plowman,* which he thought was a Lollard tract. Because of this, he produced an edition that turned this quite orthodox Catholic work into a powerful weapon against monasticism and the church hierarchy. Crowley also wrote poetry in a biblical vein, in which he continued to plead for further reform of the church. He fled the country during the reign of Mary I, but returned in 1559 to become archdeacon of Hereford.

He remained in that position until 1567, when he resigned because of his refusal to accept the official policy over the question of vestments. From that time on, he became a leading spokesman for Puritanism. He died on June 18, 1588.

BIBLIOGRAPHY

Cowper, J.M., ed. *The Select Works of Robert Crowley.* Early English Text Society, extra series, vol. 15; repr. 1987.
King, J.N. *English Reformation Literature: The Tudor Origins of the Protestant Tradition.* 1982.
Norbrook, D. *Poetry and Politics in the English Renaissance.* 1984.
Gerald L. Bray

SEE ALSO
Latimer, Hugh; Puritanism; Vestiarian Controversy

Crowley, Robert   173

D

Dance Music

English dance music from the Tudor period can be found in both manuscript and printed sources of instrumental ensemble music, such as *The First Booke of Consort Lessons* by Thomas Morley. However, many dances are preserved in keyboard arrangements because the originals have disappeared. Six dance pieces, including *The emperorse pavyn* and *The kyngs pavin,* in British Library MS. Roy. App. 58, seem to allude to a visit to England by Charles V in 1522. *A hornepype* by Hugh Aston (c. 1485–1558) might have been performed at court, but not danced, since the hornpipe was not a court dance. Some of the more well-known keyboard sources include the *Fitzwilliam Virginal Book* and *My Ladye Nevells Booke* (all forty-two compositions by William Byrd). Dance sources for lute include Folger V.a.159; "Thomas Dallis Pupil's Lute Book" at Trinity College, Cambridge Dd.2.11; and Trinity College, Dublin MS. D.1.21//ii, which mixes dances with popular tunes.

That keyboard and lute arrangements were not just archaic survivals is clear because these same dance types are found in instrumental consorts intended for actual dancing. One scholar has argued that the court violins in the sixteenth century constituted a dance band and that some of its repertory was copied into the "Lumley" books (British Library MS. Roy. App. 74–76).

In the second half of the fifteenth century, the *basse danse* was danced all over Europe to polyphony improvised over a cantus firmus. However, by 1500, such older court dances as the *basse danse,* saltarello, and tordion were largely superseded in favor of new ones, particularly the pavan-galliard pair. The pavan, originally Italian, is a slower dance in duple meter; a simple choreography is provided by Thoinot Arbeau in his *Orchésographie, et traicte en forme de dialogue,* *par lequel toutes personnes peuvent facilement apprendre & practiquer l'honneste exercice des dances* of 1588, and a more complex one for professional dancers by Fabritio Caroso in *Il ballarino* of 1581. Pavans were almost invariably followed by livelier, triple-meter galliards, a variety of the *cinque-pas* or five-step pattern taken in six beats and usually ending with a jump and a "posture," or resting pose. It existed in a number of variations and choreographies, as did the branle, a group circle or line dance, which by the 1580s came in double, simple, gay, and Burgundian types.

It is known that John Bull (1562/3–1628) owned a copy of the 1596 edition of Arbeau, suggesting that this French tutor is an authoritative source for Elizabethan dances. Arbeau (Jehan Tabourot), a cleric who rose through the ranks to become vicar-general of his diocese, apparently devised his own dance tablature, matching music to the steps more precisely than anyone had before and also including helpful illustrations. Tabor rhythms are given for many dances, which include the outmoded *basse danse* and its accompanying tordion, the pavan, fifteen types of galliards, twenty-five types of branles, the courante, allemande, volte, *morisque,* canary, and *Les bouffons,* a sword dance for four men.

Caroso's *Il ballarino,* first printed in 1581, and *Nobiltà di dame* of 1600, both containing accompanying lute music, are the principal Italian sources for dances and dance etiquette. Cesare Negri's *Le gratie d'amore* of 1602 describes more complex professional dances and dances for the theater.

Given the international character of Renaissance court dance, England's proximity to France, and the prevailing influence of Italy at the end of the sixteenth century, it is not surprising that commonplace books from the Inns of Court include directions for both English and Italian dances and

D

for "The French Brawles" (branles). One troublesome term frequently encountered with regard to English dance is "measure," which may designate a dance with its own pattern of steps and music. Some references equate the measure with the alman, or allemande, a dance for which the keyboard composers exhibited a special partiality.

BIBLIOGRAPHY

Arbeau, Thoinot. *Orchesography.* Mary Stewart Evans, trans., and Julia Sutton, ed. 1967.

Brainard, Ingrid. "Dance." In *A Practical Guide to Historical Performance: The Renaissance,* pp. 209–215. 1989.

Caroso, Fabritio. *Courtly Dance of the Renaissance: A New Translation and Edition of the Nobiltà di Dame (1600).* Julia Sutton, trans. 1995.

Clark, Alexander. *Court and Country Dances of the Renaissance in England and France.* 1994.

Cunningham, James. *Dancing in the Inns of Court.* 1965.

Dolmetsch, Mabel. *Dances of England and France from 1450 to 1600.* 1949; revised 1975.

Holman, Peter. *Four and Twenty Fiddlers: The Violin at the English Court, 1540–1690.* 1993.

Kendall, G. Yvonne. "Le gratie d'amore (1602) by Cesare Negri: translation and commentary." Dissertation, Stanford University. 1985.

Little, Meredith. "Recent research in European dance, 1400–1800." *Early Music,* vol. 14, pp. 4–14.

Pugliese, Patri J., and Joseph Casazza. *Practise for Dauncinge: Some Almans and a Pavan, England, 1570–1650.* 1980.

Thomas, Bernard, and Jane Gingell. *The Renaissance Dance Book: Dances from the Sixteenth and Early Seventeenth Centuries.* 1987.

Ward, John. "The English Measure." *Early Music,* vol. 14, pp. 15–21.

Laura S. Youens

SEE ALSO

Byrd, William; Inns of Court; Keyboard Music; Morley, Thomas

Daniel, Samuel (c. 1562–1619)

Poet, historian, and dramatist, whose long career spanned the sonnet, classical tragedy, verse chronicle, and the masque, "well-languag'd" Samuel Daniel was born in Somerset, possibly to John Daniel, a music master. After studying at Oxford and traveling in France and Italy, Daniel entered the Wilton household of Mary Sidney Herbert, countess of Pembroke, as tutor to her son, William. In 1591, twenty-eight of his sonnets were appended to a pirated printing of Sir Philip Sidney's *Astrophil and Stella.* The next year, Daniel's *Delia,* his authorized edition of fifty sonnets, was dedicated to the countess along with his *Complaint of Rosamond,* whose popularity and influence were signs that Elizabethan taste was moving from didactic moralism toward an aesthetic of restrained pathos. Passion's fatal disorders reappear as a theme in Daniel's stately rhymed Senecan tragedy, *Cleopatra* (1594; revised 1599, 1607).

In 1595, Daniel published *The First Fowre Bookes of the Civile Warres Between the Two Houses of Lancaster and Yorke,* which gradually grew into an eight-book epic (completed 1609) recounting in nearly 900 staid eight-line stanzas the "tumultuous Broyles, / And Bloody factions of a mightie Land" from Richard II to Edward IV. The year 1599 saw the publication of *Daniel's Poeticall Essayes* including *A Letter from Octavia to Marcus Antonius,* a verse epistle modeled on Ovid's *Heroides* and dedicated to Margaret Clifford, countess of Cumberland, to whose daughter Anne Daniel had lately been tutor. Also printed for the first time in this volume was the verse debate *Musophilus,* a defense of the power of words and learning in a world that, as expressed by Philocosmus, has little time for the pettiness of scholars. While Musophilus says he would pursue his studies—"this holy skill" (line 576)—even in lonely integrity—"This is the thing that I was borne to do / This is my Scene, this part I must fulfill" (lines 577-578)—his final argument is that knowledge through the poet's eloquence orders the "affections" of men and rescues them from the chaos of ignorance—"the misery of darke forgetfulnesse" (line 352).

In 1601, Daniel became the first writer to bring out a volume of English poetry classically entitled *Works.* This laboriously revised collection did not, however, include any pieces written for the public stage, and so, unlike Ben Jonson's 1616 folio, was not greeted with derision. In one of the last Elizabethan literary duels, Daniel replied to Thomas Campion's pamphlet, *Observations in the Arte of English Poesie* (1602), which revived the humanist claims for quantitative blank verse. Daniel's *The Defence of Ryme* (1603), dedicated to his pupil, William Herbert, earl of Pembroke, chauvinistically redeems the rhyme and stress of English prosody. In January 1604, Daniel began his service to the court of Queen Anne with *The Vision of the Twelve Goddesses,* the first Jacobean masque. Daniel combined theater with his interest in emblems—an interest shown by his first publication, a translation of Paulus

Jovius's *Imprese* (1585). Although Daniel was appointed licenser to the Children of the Queen's Revels in 1604, the printing of his *Philotas* (1605) placed the author-censor at risk himself when the Privy Council supposed that this tragedy made reference to the Essex rebellion of 1601. But Daniel denied any seditious intent and retained court favor.

The young Daniel was hailed by Edmund Spenser in *Colin Clout's Come Home Againe* (1595) as "new shepheard late upsprong, / The which doth all afore him far surpasse." Daniel's contribution to English prosody and diction was in refining the pedantic extremes of both archaic native and classicizing foreign forces. But later, Ben Jonson made Daniel the foil to John Donne: "Daniel was a good honest man, had no children, but no poet" (*Conversations with Drummond*, 1618). In prefatory lines to one of his several corrected and augmented collected works (1607), Daniel himself, possibly responding to those who had called him both "sweete hony-dropping" and prosaic, declared that while he may have outlived fashion, his "serious labor" had gained him what he had sought above all—immortality: "I know I shalbe read, among the rest / So long as men speake english, and so long / As verse and vertue shalbe in request, / Or grace to honest industry belong" (59–62). Nevertheless, despite Daniel's gifts to humane language, his contemporary prestige, and his grand patrons, it has been Jonson's self-serving dismissal that has prevailed. Arguably, because his thoughtful poetry lacked obscurity, Daniel himself has languished in it.

BIBLIOGRAPHY

Godshalk, W.L. "Recent Studies in Samuel Daniel (1975–1990)." *English Literary Renaissance*, vol. 24, pp. 489–502.
Grosart, Alexander B., ed. *The Complete Works.* 5 vols. 1895–1896; repr. 1963.
Rees, Joan. *Samuel Daniel.* 1964.

Steven Berkowitz

SEE ALSO

Campion, Thomas; Donne, John; Herbert, William; Masque; Sidney, Mary; Sonnet; Theater Companies, Children

Darnley, Lord Henry Stuart (1545–1567)

The first husband of Mary Queen of Scots and father of James VI and I, Henry Darnley was the second but eldest surviving son of Matthew Stuart, fourth earl of Lennox, and Margaret Douglas (daughter of the sixth earl of Angus by Margaret Tudor, daughter of Henry VIII). Because of his father's activities as an English agent in 1543–45, Darnley's parents had to leave Scotland, and Darnley was born at Temple Newsam, their Yorkshire family estate, on December 7, 1545. There he was raised as a Catholic by his mother and educated by private tutors, notably John Elder, a Scottish priest. Darnley became an exceedingly tall and handsome young man, well-versed in letters and lute playing, and with a passion for hunting and other sports. He escaped to France when Elizabeth I placed the family in confinement in December 1561, but returned to court a year later when the Lennoxes were back in favor.

In 1565, Elizabeth allowed Darnley to travel to Scotland to woo Mary Queen of Scots, which resulted in their wedding on July 29, 1565, a match that brought both Mary and Darnley closer to the English throne, as Darnley stood next to Mary in the English succession. However, by the time their only child, Charles James, later James VI of Scotland and I of England, was born on June 19, 1566, the couple had already become estranged. Darnley lacked the intelligence to make the most of his propitious birth, and increasingly manifested himself as a proud, vacillating king. Mary, alarmed at Darnley's unreliability and penchant for bad company, refused to grant him the crown matrimonial. This, together with jealousy about Mary's increasing reliance on her secretary, David Rizzio, made Darnley conspire in Rizzio's murder on March 9, 1566, which was witnessed by Mary. Darnley's continued equivocation in seeking to fulfill his own ambitions soon made him universally disliked, and he was murdered on February 10, 1567, at Kirk-o'Field in Edinburgh, a conspiracy in which James Hepburn, fourth earl of Bothwell, Mary's later husband, played a major part.

BIBLIOGRAPHY

Bingham, Caroline. *Darnley. A Life of Henry Stuart, Lord Darnley, Consort of Mary Queen of Scots.* 1995.
Fraser, Antonia. *Mary Queen of Scots.* 1969.
Fraser, William. *The Lennox.* 1874.
Wormald, Jenny. *Mary Queen of Scots. A Study in Failure.* 1988.

Theo van Heijnsbergen

SEE ALSO

Hepburn, James; Mary Queen of Scots; Rizzio, David; Scotland, History of

D

Davies, John, of Hereford (c. 1565–1618)

Born in Hereford of Welsh descent, John Davies studied at Oxford and acquired such skill at handwriting that he was styled by Thomas Fuller as "Master of the Pen." Davies exercised this skill as an Oxford writing master, teaching at Magdalen College and tutoring in noble households. Also a poet, Davies published "Mirum in Modum" (1602), a philosophical poem extended by "Summa Totalis, or All in All" (1607); "Microcosmos" (1603), a poetical treatise on the body and psyche to which is appended "An Extasie" and sonnets of praise; "Humours Heau'n on Earth" (1605), the third part of which portrays the 1603 plague; "Bien Venv" (1606), which celebrates the London visit of Christian IV; "The Holy Rood" (1609), a meditation on the crucifixion; "Wittes Pilgrimage" (1610?), a collection of amorous sonnets and other poems; "The Scourge of Folly" (1611), a collection of satirical epigrams, decorated with an illustration of Wit scourging the bare buttocks of Folly, who is hoisted on Time's back; and later work including "The Muses Tears" (1613), an elegy for Prince Henry.

Through his accomplishments Davies became acquainted with the elite of his day. The dedications of his works illustrate his network of patrons: William Herbert, earl of Pembroke; Sir Robert Sidney; Edward, Lord Herbert of Cherbury; the Ladies Dorothy and Lucy Percy; Lord Ellesmere; and the countess of Derby and her three daughters. Davies' works also show a network of literary acquaintances: Michael Drayton, John Donne, George Chapman, Fulke Greville, Lady Mary Wroth, Samuel Daniel, Ben Jonson, William Shakespeare, William Ostler, Robert Armin, John Marston, Joseph Hall, Philemon Holland, Francis Beaumont, and John Fletcher.

BIBLIOGRAPHY

Davies, John. *The Complete Works of John Davies of Hereford.* 2 vols. 1873; repr. 1967.

Roslyn Knutson

SEE ALSO

Epigrams; Handwriting

Davies, John (1569–1626)

A poet and lawyer, John Davies was born in a Wiltshire family that had migrated from South Wales. Educated at Winchester and Queen's College, Oxford, he subsequently studied law at the Middle Temple. He was called to the bar in 1595, by which time he had already written one of his major poems, *Orchestra.* He was subsequently disbarred when he assaulted the fellow student to whom he had dedicated *Orchestra.* He then retired to Oxford, where he wrote his other major poem, *Nosce Teipsum,* published in 1599. In 1601, he was taken back into the Middle Temple, after which he became first solicitor general, then the attorney general for Ireland. Near the end of his life he was made the lord chief justice of the King's Bench in England, as a reward for maintaining the legality of Charles I's forced loans. He died, however, before taking office. An example of the "compleat" Renaissance gentleman, he was poet, scholar, lawyer, and administrator.

Preserving the original Greek meaning of "orchestra" as "dance," *Orchestra* is cast as a lengthy disputation between Antinous and Penelope concerning the role of the dance in the order of the world. All order in peace and war is a dance; the seven liberal arts are a dance; all social and political organizations are a dance. Invoking the aid of Love, who gives Penelope a magic mirror in which she can see the image of a future "golden age" of Elizabeth I's court with dancing courtiers, Antinous almost persuades her to dance with him. At this point, however, the poem stops. Although "unfinished," the poem is a fine example of a significant Renaissance idea, the dance as a figure of world order.

Nosce Teipsum, a philosophical poem on the subject of self-knowledge—a dominant theme in Renaissance secular and religious literature—was the most successful of Davies' poems in his lifetime and the best-known among contemporary readers. It is structured in two elegies, unified by a common speaker. Elegy I largely deals with the paradox of human nature. Deprecating human knowledge as vanity, the poet tries to direct human reasoning toward one goal, self-knowledge. The concluding lines are somber but moving: "I know my life's a paine and but a span, / I know my Sense is mockd with euery thing: / And to conclude, I know myselfe a MAN, / Which is a proud, and yet a wretched thing." Elegy 2 supplies an answer in a vision of the integration of mortal body and immortal soul: the soul as spiritual substance has an individuality of its own. The deep desire for knowledge is a desire of the soul, which can be fulfilled only in heaven. Extremely popular, *Nosce Teipsum* appeared in six editions during Davies' lifetime. For the contemporary student of Renaissance thought, it offers a clear and comprehensive poetic statement of Elizabethan popular philosophy.

Although writing poetry was not Davies' primary interest, in addition to his major poems he wrote and published a great variety of shorter pieces, religious and secular. *The Hymnes of Astraea* (1599) were written as tributes to the aging queen; other occasional verse offered tributes to other royalty and nobility, as well as occasional satiric epigrams on social types, such as the twelve six-line verse "characters" in *Yet Another Twelve Wonders of the World* (1608). But his greatest poetic achievement lies in *Orchestra* and *Nosce Teipsum*.

BIBLIOGRAPHY

Krueger, Robert, ed. *The Complete Poems of John Davies.* 1974.

Manning, R.J. "Rule and Order Strange: A Reading of Davies' *Orchestra*." *English Literary Renaissance,* vol. 15, pp. 179—194.

Norbrook, David. *Rhetoric, Ideology, and the Elizabethan World Picture.* 1994.

Sanderson, James L. *Sir John Davies.* 1975.

———, comp. "Recent Studies in Sir John Davies." *English Literary Renaissance,* vol. 4, pp. 411–417.

Sneath, E.H. *Philosophy in Poetry; A Study of Sir John Davies'* Nosce Teipsum. 1903; repr. 1969.

Charlotte Spivack

SEE ALSO

Epigram; Paradox

Davies, John (d. 1625)

Not to be confused with John Davies, the Irish attorney general and poet, or John Davis, the navigator, John Davies (or Davis) is best known for his role in the Essex rebellion. He graduated from Gloucester Hall, Oxford, in 1577, where his tutor had been Thomas Allen, and where he is reputed to have been a Catholic and to have written texts on mathematics and astrology with John Dee and Matthew Gwynne.

A military man who likely met Robert Devereux, the earl of Essex, while serving in the Netherlands with Roger Williams, or on the 1589 raid on Portugal, Davies was one of Essex's Cadiz knights and a member of his "community of honor"; and in 1598, Essex appointed him surveyor in the ordnance office in the Tower of London. In plotting rebellion, Davies commanded a place among the earl's closest advisors, and his tactical advice was to take the Tower and its munitions first. Yet this plan was abandoned, and in the actual plot Davies was left holding hostages at Essex House.

Although convicted and sentenced to death, Davies was subsequently pardoned (likely by making a full confession implicating coconspirators), and released from prison in July 1601, only six months after the rebellion. He died in 1625.

BIBLIOGRAPHY

Ashley, Roger. "War in the Ordnance Office: The Essex Connection and Sir John Davis." *Historical Research,* vol. 67, no. 164, pp. 337–345.

Calendar of State Papers Domestic, 1598–1601.

Great Britain Historical Manuscripts Commission, *Hatfield MSS.*

Lacey, Robert. *Robert, Earl of Essex: An Elizabethan Icarus.* 1971.

Matter, Joseph. *My Lords and Lady of Essex: Their State Trials.* 1969.

Thomas A. Deans

SEE ALSO

Dee, John; Devereux, Robert

Davis, John (1550?–1605)

Captain John Davis (or Davys), one of the greatest English seamen, was born about 1550 at Sandbridge and spent his youth with the Gilbert and Ralegh families. First mention of him occurs in the diary of John Dee in 1579. In 1585, he commanded an expedition organized by Adrain Gilbert to find the Northwest Passage, during which he explored the coast of Greenland. He followed this with similar voyages in 1586 and 1587, naming prominent places after his friends and places at home— Mount Ralegh, Cape Walsingham, Gilbert Sound, Cape Dyer, Exeter Sound, Davis Straits. A master navigator, he wrote *Traverse Book* in 1587, *Seaman's Secrets* in 1594 (which ran through eight editions), and *World's Hydrographical Description* in 1595. He also invented equipment for navigation, including the back staff and double quadrant.

Davis returned from the Arctic in time to join the battle against the Armada, and is thought to be the John Davis who commanded the *Black Dog*, tender to Lord Howard's flagship. In 1596 and 1597, Davis was again at sea, probably as master of Sir Walter Ralegh's ship at Cadiz and the Azores, which brought him directly under

D

the notice of Robert Devereux, the earl of Essex, at whose suggestion he afterward piloted a Dutch ship to the East Indies. His account of the voyage is addressed to Essex.

In 1600, Davis served as pilot major for the first expedition sent out by the East India Company. In 1604, he again sailed for the East India Company, but his ship was attacked by Japanese pirates near Bantam, and he was killed during the battle.

BIBLIOGRAPHY

Markham, Capt. A.H. *The Voyages and Works of John Davis.* 1880.

Miller, Helen Hill. *Captains from Devon: The Great Elizabethan Seafarers Who Won the Oceans for England.* 1985.

Thomas A. Deans

SEE ALSO

Armada, Spanish; Dee, John; Devereux, Robert; Discovery and Exploration; East India Company; Ralegh, Walter

Davison, William (c. 1541–1608)

A skilled diplomat, William Davison rose from an obscure birth to a seat on Queen Elizabeth's Privy Council. At the height of his career, though, Elizabeth and her more powerful advisors made him their scapegoat for the execution of Mary Queen of Scots.

After serving on Scottish and Dutch embassies, Davison negotiated the alliance with the States-General that led in January 1586 to the earl of Leicester's armed intervention. Although Leicester attempted to blame Davison for his acceptance of the governorship of Holland, Elizabeth rewarded the diplomat by admitting him to the Privy Council as assistant to Francis Walsingham, secretary of state.

In October 1586, Davison was appointed to the commission charged with the trial of Mary Queen of Scots; he did not attend any of its meetings. In November, Burghley sent Davison to Elizabeth with Mary's death warrant; seeking delay, she told him to hold on to it. On February 1, 1587, Elizabeth called Davison for an audience, where she read and signed the warrant. She then told him to hint to Mary's jailer, Amias Paulet, that another way be found to eliminate her. As Burghley and the council quietly and without Elizabeth's knowledge sent out the death warrant, Davison had four more audiences with the queen, where she restated her anxieties and inveighed against him and Paulet for refusing to arrange a secret assassination. On February 8, Mary was executed. An enraged Elizabeth blamed her council for executing Mary against her wishes, a claim she made to European ambassadors and, especially, to James VI of Scotland (Mary's son and Elizabeth's presumptive heir). Elizabeth had Davison sent to the Tower, charging that she had commanded him to keep the signed warrant secret and that he knew she had no intention of actually executing it. Davison was tried in Star Chamber for "misprision and contempt," fined 10,000 marks, and sentenced to imprisonment during the queen's pleasure.

Davison was released from the Tower in 1589. Elizabeth refused to hear his petitions, so he retired to a house in Stepney. He received a pension from Elizabeth and then James until his death in 1608.

BIBLIOGRAPHY

Camden, William. *The History of the Most Renowned and Victorious Elizabeth Late Queen of England, Selected Chapters.* Wallace MacCaffrey, ed. 1970.

Howell, T.B., ed. *Complete Collection of State Trials.* Vol. 1. 1816; pp. 1229–1250.

Neale, J.E. *Elizabeth I and Her Parliaments, 1584–1601.* 1957.

Nicolas, Nicholas Harris. *Life of William Davison, Secretary of State and Privy Counsellor to Queen Elizabeth.* 1823.

Rait, Robert S., and Annie I. Cameron. *King James's Secret: Negotiations between Elizabeth and James VI Relating to the Execution of Mary Queen of Scots.* 1927.

Read, Conyers. *Lord Burghley and Queen Elizabeth.* 1960.

———. *Mr. Secretary Walsingham and the Policy of Queen Elizabeth.* 3 vols. 1925.

John D. Staines

SEE ALSO

William, Cecil; Mary Queen of Scots

Day, John (1574–c. 1640)

John Day is less important as an author than as a representative man: he typifies the professional "hack" dramatist of the Elizabethan era, surviving by his wits and by his ability to produce plays that appealed to popular tastes. Although little studied, his works have much to tell us about such important topics as censorship, satire, rivalry, collaboration, and urban or "city" comedy. His life, meanwhile, is intriguing since he (like William Shakespeare) was one of the first professional creative writers in English history.

Born at Cawston, Norfolk, to a husbandman in 1574, Day completed his schooling at Ely. Admitted to Gonville and Caius College, Cambridge, in 1592, he was expelled in 1593 for stealing a book. He next appears in 1598 in the "Diary" of Philip Henslowe to whom he sold plays. Unfortunately, most of Day's works are now known only by their titles (recorded by Henslowe until 1603). Collaborators included William Haughton, Thomas Dekker, Henry Chettle, Wentworth Smith, and Richard Hathaway. Lost plays written or coauthored for the actors of the Lord Admiral's Men included *The Conquest of Brute* (1598), *Cox of Collumpton* (1599), *Thomas Merry or Beech's Tragedy* (1599), *The Spanish Moor's Tragedy* (1599/1600), *The Seven Wise Masters* (1599/1600), *The Golden Ass, or Cupid and Psyche* (1600), *Six Yeomen of the West* (1601), *The Conquest of the West Indies* (1601), *Friar Rush and the Proud Woman of Antwerp* (1601), the second part of *Tom Dough* (1602), *The Bristol Tragedy* (1602), *Merry as May Be* (1602), and *The Boss of Billingsgate* (1602/03). Lost plays collaboratively written for Worcester's Men included *The Black Dog of Newgate* (1602/03), *The Unfortunate General* (1602/03), and *Shore* (1603). Lost plays perhaps written with Thomas Dekker included *The Life and Death of Guy Earl of Warwick* (performed in 1618), *The Bellman of Paris* (licensed 1623), and *Come See a Wonder* (performed 1623). Day also wrote for the Queen's Men and Children of the Revels.

Seven works by Day survive. The earliest extant play, *The Blind Beggar of Bednal Green,* was coauthored with Chettle and Haughton in 1600–1601. *Law Tricks,* although printed in 1608, may have been performed as early as 1604. *The Travailes of Three English Brothers* (1606/07) was coauthored with William Rowley and George Wilkins. The notorious *Isle of Gulls* (1606), performed by boy actors, was suspected of satirizing James I and other Scots and has received much attention from recent critics. *Humour out of Breath* (1607/08), a comedy possibly coauthored with Wilkins, has been praised by its few readers. The first of Day's two existing nondramatic works is his prose piece *Peregrinatio Scholastica,* which exists in two different versions. His last work, *The Parliament of Bees,* consists of poetic dialogues excerpted from earlier dramas. Few of the works have been well edited; readers must depend on facsimiles or the helpful but unreliable edition prepared by A.H. Bullen.

Little is known about Day's later years. Apparently he had died by 1640, when an elegy by a friend was published. Ben Jonson had earlier dismissed Day as a "rogue" and a "base fellow," and later critics usually have regarded his works as entertaining but undistinguished. However, his writings merit more attention, if only as evidence of conditions affecting authors, texts, and audiences in the greatest era of English drama.

BIBLIOGRAPHY
Bullen, A.H., ed. *The Works of John Day.* 1881; repr. 1963.
Burns, Raymond S. "John Day." *Dictionary of Literary Biography.* Vol. 62. 1987.
Jeffs, Robin, intro. *The Works of John Day.* A.H. Bullen, ed. 1963.

Jonathan Wright

SEE ALSO
Censorship; Chettle, Henry; Dekker, Thomas; Henslow, Philip; Satire; Theater Companies, Adult

Dee, John (1527–1609)

One of Tudor England's most learned scholars, John Dee remains one of its most enigmatic characters: often considered an Elizabethan Merlin or Faustus, and even a model for Shakespeare's Prospero, Dee's scientific aspirations and achievements have (since his own day) been shadowed by his assocations with the occult. His reputation derives primarily from his position as one of the great Renaissance polymaths: his protean career ranged across the whole spectrum of disciplines and professions—from the most practical to the most speculative.

Dee was born in London on July 13, 1527. After attending Chelmsford Grammar School, he studied at St. John's College, Cambridge, and the University of Louvain—earning his B.A. and M.A., but not the doctorate implied by the label "Dr." that is customarily attached to his name. After a brief period as a fellow (and underreader in Greek) at Trinity College, Cambridge, Dee returned to London and established his household in Mortlake—a site designed not only for domestic activities but for research, containing a library, a garden, and a series of laboratories. It was here that Dee hosted an impressive group of visiting scholars and politicians, and produced works on a remarkable range of subjects, from astronomy and alchemy to cartography and calendar reform. Dee worked from this base for the rest of his life, with the exception of two significant detours: in September 1583, he left London for what would become a six-year tour of central and eastern Europe (much of it spent at the court of Emperor Rudolf II in Prague), and in 1596, he was appointed warden of

D

Manchester College, a position that occupied him (and vexed him) until 1600, when he returned to London to spend his eight or nine remaining years in what he described as frustration and poverty.

The breadth of Dee's learning was both reflected in and driven by his extraordinary personal library: perhaps the largest in Tudor England, it contained several thousand books and manuscripts in more than twenty languages, representing virutally every aspect of theoretical and practical learning. One of the typical products of this library—and Dee's use of it—was the extensive and influential preface he provided for the first English translation of Euclid's *Elements of Geometry* (1570): based on an exhaustive search of the relevant sources, this text attests to the dignity (and even divinity) of mathematics and outlines its application to a range of mechanical and mercantile activities.

Like other advocates of Renaissance "pansophism," Dee believed that his encyclopedic studies were a unified endeavor that would not only benefit his patrons and fellow citizens but would ultimately reveal the mystery of God's creation. His struggle to understand and manipulate the workings of the cosmos is represented in his early astronomical and philosophical publications; in his lifelong practice of alchemy; and in the elaborate angelic seances he turned to toward the end of his life, in search of a more direct source of divine revelation. It is these arcane studies—and the suspicions and accusations that dogged him throughout his life—that have led to Dee's reputation as the great Elizabethan "magus." It is clear, however, that this label does not do justice to Dee, to his sense of purpose, and his actual contribution to Tudor culture.

From his university years onward Dee served as a scholarly advisor to courtly and commercial groups. From the 1550s onward, he enjoyed the patronage of many prominent courtiers, and gave advice to Elizabeth I herself, not only on astrological matters, but on medical, philosophical, and political matters. During the same period he served as a geographical consultant to most of the Elizabethan voyages of exploration, ultimately becoming one of the foremost theorists of the British Empire (a phrase he is credited with coining). Even after he returned from his mysterious six-year residence at the court of Emperor Rudolf II in Prague, and entered what is often characterized as a final period of disappointment and disgrace, he remained unusually well connected and respected.

The activities that account for most of Dee's intellectual and professional work tended not to result in publications. As with many other Tudor scholars and authors,

it is a range of manuscript sources—treatises prepared for particular patrons, marginal annotations in books from his library, and biographical details from his private diaries—that yield a fuller picture of his career.

While Dee may not have been an archetypal Neoplatonic magus, he is nonetheless an exemplary Tudor figure. In looking back to the medieval as well as ahead to the modern, in combining spiritual and scientific beliefs and practices, in pursuing continental ideas while celebrating a British national ideal, and in occupying a complex socio-professional position, somewhere between court, city, and university, Dee is a fascinating representative of the transitional intellectual culture of Tudor England.

BIBLIOGRAPHY

Clulee, Nicholas H. *John Dee's Natural Philosophy: Between Science and Religion.* 1988.

French, Peter J. *John Dee: The World of an Elizabethan Magus.* 1972.

Roberts, Julian, and Andrew G. Watson. *John Dee's Library Catalogue.* 1990.

Sherman, William H. *John Dee: The Politics of Reading and Writing in the English Renaissance.* 1995.

William H. Sherman

SEE ALSO

Alchemy; Astronomy; Book Ownership; Magic; Mapmaking; Medicine and Health; Reading Practices

Defender of the Faith

In Latin, *Fidei Defensor,* this was the title granted by Pope Leo X to Henry VIII on October 11, 1521, in gratitude for Henry's learned attack on Martin Luther's doctrine of the Sacraments (*Assertion of the Seven Sacraments*). When Henry broke with the papacy in 1534 he retained the title, and his successors have borne it ever since. Today it is usually assumed that it reflects the position of the Church of England as the established church, but this is not so. The relationship between the church and the crown is (and always has been) indicated in the Royal Style by the words *by the grace of God* (*Dei gratia*), which indicate the divine source of the monarch's authority, sanctioned by the church at the coronation.

BIBLIOGRAPHY

Elton, G.R. *The Tudor Constitution.* 1982.

Gerald L. Bray

D

SEE ALSO

Church of England; Henry VIII; Lutheranism;
Sacraments

Dekker, Thomas (c. 1572–1632)

Playwright and pamphleteer, Thomas Dekker turned his hand to many genres and earned his meager wages from court and city, from public and private stages, and from the middle-class reading public of London, eager for humor, information, and moral instruction. His life, economically marginal when not desperate, is probably representative of the statistical majority of his fellow "hacks."

Earlier biographical details are scarce, but Dekker was an established playwright by 1598, when he first appears in the "Diaries" of the theater manager Philip Henslowe. His name is attached to more than sixty plays; Dekker wrote mainly in collaboration with others, his most frequent partners being Michael Drayton, Henry Chettle, and Robert Wilson. Others included lesser known figures such as Anthony Munday, John Day, and William Haughton, and the more renowned Ben Jonson, John Webster, John Middleton, Thomas Heywood, and John Ford. If, as many think, he contributed to the manuscript play *Sir Thomas More* (1595–1596?), he may also have worked with William Shakespeare.

Although Francis Meres lists Dekker as among the best writers of tragedies, he is best known for work in other genres. *Old Fortunatus* (perhaps composed 1595; revised 1599) reworks a German folktale as a moral romance in which the protagonist, magically granted his wish for wealth, ruins his own and his sons' lives. *The Shoemaker's Holiday* (1599), a romantic city comedy, combines the rise of shoemaker Simon Eyre to lord mayor of London with the love stories of a nobleman who courts a merchant's daughter and of a shoemaker separated from his bride by war. *Patient Grissil* (1599; with Chettle and Haughton) counterbalances the immensely popular tale of a forbearing wife (told earlier by Boccaccio, Chaucer, and others) with a subplot about a rebellious shrew.

Satiromastix, or the Untrussing of the Humorous Poet (1601) is Dekker's contribution to (and the last volley in) the War of the Theatres, a public quarrel among playwrights. (Shakespeare alludes to the controversy in *Hamlet* 2.2.) Responding to Jonson's attack on him in *The Poetaster* (1601), Dekker produced an amusing lampoon of Jonson as a laborious composer of verse.

Theaters were closed because of plague in early 1603, but Dekker, along with Jonson, contributed speeches to a municipal production, *The Magnificent Entertainment Given to King James,* on the occasion of the monarch's entry into London that year. Dekker also began his career as a pamphlet writer with *The Wonderful Year* (1603), a moralizing and descriptive account of the death of Elizabeth I and the London plague of 1603.

Dekker tried his hand at satire in *Westward Ho!* (1604, with Webster), written for the Boys of St. Paul's. The play apparently inspired the much superior *Eastward Ho!* (1605, by Jonson, John Marston, and George Chapman), and was followed by Dekker and Webster's *Northward Ho!* (1605), but Dekker was by temperament a writer for the popular stage. He returned to sentimental city comedy with *The Honest Whore, Parts I and II* (1604–1605, with Middleton), which follows its titular heroine out of prostitution into a search for respectability. That plot is combined with the story of a patient linendraper whose good nature confounds his foes. *The Roaring Girl* (1605, with Middleton) romantically portrays a somewhat notorious London character, Mary Frith. *The Whore of Babylon* (1606), a nostalgic patriotic allegory, celebrates England's conversion to Protestantism and the defeat of Catholic plots against Elizabeth I, including the Spanish Armada. Dekker went on to write many satirical pamphlets such as the *The Gull's Hornbook* (1609), and continued to collaborate on plays such as the topical *The Witch of Edmonton* (1621, with Rowley and Ford).

Dekker's lost plays include such intriguing titles as *The Famous Wars of Henry I* (1598, with Drayton and Chettle), *Troilus and Cressida* (1599, with Chettle), *Agamemnon* (1559, with Chettle), *Jeptha* (1602, with Munday), and *Caesar's Fall* (1602, with several others). It is regrettable that we lack this representative Renaissance playwright's work on these classical, biblical, and historical topics, because Dekker leaves a heritage of colorful prose, valuable reporting, serious moral analysis, adept verse, and vivid stage characters.

BIBLIOGRAPHY

Bowers, Fredson, ed. *The Dramatic Works of Thomas Dekker.* 4 vols. 1953–1961.

Champion, Larry S. *Thomas Dekker and the Traditions of English Drama.* 1985.

Dekker, Thomas. *The Gull's Hornbook.* 1904; repr. 1971.

D

———. *The Roaring Girl*. Paul A. Mulholland, ed. Revel's Plays. 1987.

———. *The Shoemaker's Holiday*. R.L. Smallwood and Stanley Wells, eds. Revel's Plays. 1979.

———, John Ford, and William Rowley. *The Witch of Edmonton*. Arthur F. Kinney, ed. New Mermaids. 1998.

Gasper, Julia. *The Dragon and the Dove: The Plays of Thomas Dekker*. 1990.

Grosart, Alexander B. ed. *The Non-Dramatic Works of Thomas Dekker*. 1884–1886.

Hoy, Cyrus. *Introductions, Notes, and Commentaries to Texts in The Dramatic Works of Thomas Dekker,* edited by Fredson Bowers. 4 vols. 1980.

McKluskie, Kathleen. *Dekker and Heywood: Professional Dramatists*. 1994.

Harry Keyishian

SEE ALSO

Chapman, George; Chettle, Henry; Day, John; Drama, History of; Drayton, Michael; Jonson, Ben; Marston, John; Munday, Anthony; Satire

Delegates, Court of

The name usually given to the high court of appeal in ecclesiastical cases, the Court of Delegates was set up according to the terms of the Act for the Submission of the Clergy (1534). It was made necessary because the traditional church courts functioned only up to provincial level. This meant that cases involving both the provinces of Canterbury and York had to be appealed to a higher authority. Until 1533, this had usually been taken to mean the see of Rome, but by the Act in Restraint of Appeals, which Parliament passed in that year, that option was closed. To provide for the right of appeal, a new court was established by the crown and was usually known as the High Court of Delegates. It consisted of ecclesiastical lawyers, though in the early days bishops and secular judges might be added. The court continued to function until 1833, when it was replaced by the Judicial Committee of the Privy Council.

BIBLIOGRAPHY

Duncan, G.I.O. *The High Court of Delegates*. 1971.

Gerald L. Bray

SEE ALSO

Courts, Ecclesiastical; Submission, Act of

Deloney, Thomas (d. 1600)

Famous in his own day as a ballad maker, Thomas Deloney is studied chiefly for his four works of prose fiction about shoemakers and clothiers: *Jack of Newberry* (1597), *The Gentle Craft (the first part)* (1597), *The Gentle Craft (the second part)* (1598), and *Thomas of Reading* (1597–1600). Deloney's prose narratives have attracted the attention of those literary historians who trace the origins of the novel back to Elizabethan fiction. But together with the ballads they are just as significant for the social historians who find in their pages a complex construction of England in the fitful and dynamic transition from feudalism to capitalism.

The date of Deloney's birth is unknown, but it has been speculated that he was born in Norwich in the decade just before or just after mid-century. Given the typical profile of those French Protestant refugees living in Tudor East Anglia, it is probable that his trade was silk weaving, at least until he turned his attention fully to writing. Deloney's earliest publication—translations of Latin epistles by the archbishop of Collen (1583)—shows strong Protestant leanings as well as a reasonably good education. By 1586, the year in which we know that Deloney lost an infant son, his ballads began to appear first as broadsides, then in such collections as *The Garland of Good Will* (1593). His contemporaries took notice. In the 1590s, such wits as Robert Greene, Thomas Nashe, and Gabriel Harvey mocked the balladist for his "triviall trinkets and threedbare trash." In 1595–1596, he received government pressure and jail time for "vain and presumptuous" poems expressing discontent about the influx of foreign weavers and about the dearth of corn. Perhaps because of this trouble with the Elizabethan authorities, he changed his medium to prose fiction until his death in 1600.

Most of Deloney's extant verse consists of subjects taken from chronicle accounts of medieval kings and aristocrats. Together with matter culled from the Bible or contemporary events, these tales feature a number of persons familiar to the Elizabethan reader, from Lady Godiva, Rosamond, and Shore's wife to Locrine, Bolingbroke, and Lancelot. From one ballad to another, an Elizabethan's favorite themes—for instance, fortune, friendship, marriage, and reformed religion—are set to such tunes as "the hunt is up."

But the portrait of society in these ballads is not always neatly hierarchical. On occasion, the poems intersect with the principal themes of Deloney's prose when they depict some interaction between members of the high and middling ranks of society, for example, when a forester rescues, then marries, a princess. In the so-called novels, however, this interaction is much more complex and unsettling. At one level the four narratives are meant to redress the omission of honest, productive, and charitable yeomen "by Stow, Hollinshed, Grafton, Halle, Froissart, and all the rest of those deserving writers." Accordingly, Deloney's alternative history seeks to idealize the distinctive qualities, lifestyles, and speech patterns of its neglected subject. But far from simply constituting an interest group unto themselves, Deloney's shoemakers and clothiers often surmount the aristocracy in the possession of traditionally chivalric virtues and thus represent the potential, if not quite the consummation, of a major social upheaval. Whether or not Deloney himself had radical designs is finally unclear.

The most focused example of Deloney's social experiment is *Jack of Newberry*. The stated purpose of the narrative is the restoration of the weaver's fame. Neither a miser nor a prodigal, Jack is noted for his charity, hospitality, and discretion. He is, moreover, fortunate in love, insofar as a wealthy widow, his gentle employer, elevates him through marriage, an easy transition because his "good government" makes him as worthy a master as he was a servant. Marriage has its hardships and quarrels, but as time unfolds and the widower Jack marries one of his faithful servants, the clothier is beloved of nobles, merchants, and laborers alike. In certain respects, he encroaches on noble ground: when the focus of the tale turns to war between England and Scotland, it is a splendidly armed Jack who proves most gallant and attracts the favor of the queen. When he protests his humble status as a "poor clothier, whose lands are his looms," the queen defines Jack as a social hybrid, "a clothier by trade yet a gentleman by condition." Meanwhile, a proper aristocrat, the earl of Surrey, wins the battle against the Scots. But Jack's authority with and aspirations for the upper ranks persist: he advises Henry VIII by way of fables and emblems about the danger of idle and ambitious courtiers; his picture gallery features wise and creditable men who rise above humble parentage to greatness; and in a time of hardship, he leads a campaign of clothiers against Thomas Wolsey. In this last case, however, Jack epitomizes the good Elizabethan values of a dutiful patriot protesting on behalf of a godly monarch and social order—little danger there in 1597.

Deloney's other fictions are as replete with noble characters who, through fortune's whims, must learn to work with working characters who approximate their superiors as Jack does in Deloney's *Jack of Newberry.*. *The Gentle Craft* begins in the mode of John Lyly's *Euphues,* much ado about nobles in love and, above all, in meditations about love. But soon enough the amorous hero meets a shoemaker, whence the tag: "The Gentle Craft is fittest, then, / For poore, distressed Gentlemen." Persecution, like love, leads other noble persons into the merry and honest, if also valiant and magnanimous, household of the shoemaker.

More than the novel per se, Deloney's fictions often resemble the tale collections of the day; this family resemblance is especially visible in the merry devices that characters play, but also in the dispersion of narrative focus in *Thomas of Reading* among "six worthie Yeomen" and their wives. Deloney's characters can be stock figures, but also memorable eccentrics such as women with traditionally male attributes, servants who answer in rhyme, and a vigilante who regrets his rash burial of a still living, if greedy, priest. The style of speech in these fictions runs the gamut from the highly rhetorical patterns of the melancholy lover to long sections of dialogue in the workaday dialects of the craftsmen. Given this attention to dialect, it is not surprising that philologists have mined Deloney for proverbs and grammatical forms. But it is for evidence of late feudal social dynamism and of Elizabethan narrative strategies that critics most often turn to Deloney now.

BIBLIOGRAPHY

Dorsinville, Max. "Design in Deloney's *Jack of Newbury.*" *PMLA*, vol. 88, pp. 233–239.

Jordan, Constance. "The 'Art of Clothing': Role-Playing in Deloney's Fiction." *English Literary Renaissance*, vol. 11, pp. 183–193.

Lawlis, Merritt E. *Apology for the Middle Class: The Dramatic Novels of Thomas Deloney.* 1960.

———, ed. *The Novels of Thomas Deloney.* 1961.

Mann, Francis Oscar, ed. *The Works of Thomas Deloney.* 1912.

Stevenson, Laura Caroline. *Praise and Paradox: Merchant's and Craftsmen in Elizabethan Popular Literature.* 1984.

Wright, Eugene P. Thomas Deloney. 1981.

Reid Barbour

SEE ALSO
Ballads; Broadsides; Grafton, Richard; Holinshed, Raphael; Prose Fiction; Stow, John

D

Derby, Earls of
See Stanley Family

De Vere, Edward (1550–1604)

The seventeenth earl of Oxford, poet, and chief exemplar of the Elizabethan "crisis of the aristocracy," Edward de Vere was born April 12, 1550, to John de Vere, sixteenth earl of Oxford, and Margery née Golding, half-sister of Arthur Golding. In 1558, Edward matriculated at Cambridge as "impubes," but left within a year to be educated in the household of Sir Thomas Smith.

Following John de Vere's death in 1562, Katherine, a daughter by an earlier marriage, challenged Edward's legitimacy (John's second marriage was irregular). Although Elizabeth I taunted him with bastardy, Edward succeeded as seventeenth earl of Oxford. A ward of Sir William Cecil, Oxford moved to Cecil House in the Strand, where Cecil appointed Lawrence Nowell as his tutor and drew up a daily schedule for his education. Oxford accompanied the queen to Cambridge University in 1564, and to Oxford University in 1566, accepting an honorary degree at each place. In 1564 he became the dedicatee of the first of some twenty books.

In 1567, Oxford killed an unarmed undercook with a rapier, the first of many killings that occurred within his circle of influence. On attaining his majority in 1571, he entered the House of Lords and married Cecil's daughter, Anne, then fifteen. In 1574, he crossed the Channel without license; persuaded to return, he was licensed to travel from February 1575 to April 1576 to Paris, Strasbourg, and Italy. In Venice, he took up with Virginia Padoana, a courtesan, and Orazio Cogno, a choirboy. He spent heavily, and is reported to have built a house.

Oxford's returning entourage was attacked in the Channel by pirates. When he reached England he rejected both his wife and his new daughter, born July 1575. Instead, he lived with Cogno. In 1579, a quarrel with Philip Sidney threatened violence until Elizabeth I intervened. In December 1580, Oxford accused former friends of Catholic sympathies. They returned the charge, adding murder and buggery, but Oxford remained free until March 1581, when Anne Vavasour, a maid of the queen's bedchamber, gave birth to his illegitimate son. Released in July, Oxford reconciled with his wife in December, but quarrels with Anne Vavasour's kin in 1582 and 1583 caused four deaths and several injuries, including an injury to Oxford. Disgraced and bankrupt, Oxford

was called before Elizabeth in 1585. On a pledge of future good behavior he was readmitted to court, and granted an annuity of £1,000 (which commenced in 1586).

The Armada year of 1588 was marked by his wife's death and by Oxford's refusal to take command of Harwich during wartime (he thought the post beneath him). Although Lord Burghley covered for him, Oxford never received another vote for the garter until the year of his death. Marriage to Elizabeth Trentham in 1591 or 1592 produced a son, Henry, who would succeed as eighteenth earl. From 1595 to 1599, Oxford sought the Cornwall-Devon tin monopoly in vain, but he had better luck recovering rights to Waltham Forest. He survived the plague that devastated London during the first year of James, but died from unknown causes on June 24, 1604, at his residence in Hackney.

Oxford first appeared in print in Thomas Bedingfield's *Cardano's Comforte* (1573). Beginning with Richard Edwardes's *The Paradise of Daynty Devices* (1576), he became a staple of printed verse anthologies, attracting approval from William Webbe (1586), George Puttenham (1589), and Francis Meres (1598). Of twenty poems reasonably attributed to Oxford, sixteen are certainly his, while four, including "My mynde to me a kingdome is," are doubtful. Oxford's pentameter and longer-lined verse suffers from heavy alliteration and repetition, but his tetrameter verse, like "When werte thow borne Desire," has true grace. Puttenham and Meres also praised Oxford's comedies. These were probably court masques, but Oxford served as a patron of professional acting companies. In 1580, he took over Warwick's Men, who survived as "Oxford's Men" until 1602, when they were absorbed into Worcester's Men. Among Oxford's servants were John Lyly and Anthony Munday.

BIBLIOGRAPHY

Cokayne, G.E., et al. *The Complete Peerage of England, Scotland, Ireland, Great Britain, and the United Kingdom.* 12 vols. 1910–1959.

May, Steven W., ed. "The Poems of Edward DeVere, Seventeenth Earl of Oxford, and of Robert Devereux, Second Earl of Essex." *Studies in Philology,* vol. 77, part 5. 1980.

Stone, Lawrence, *The Crisis of the Aristocracy, 1558–1641.* 1965.

Ward, Bernard. M. *The Seventeenth Earl of Oxford, 1550–1604, From Contemporary Documents.* 1928.

Alan H. Nelson

Devereux, Robert, Second Earl of Essex (1565–1601)

A controversial courtier who played a central role in national politics and cultural patronage during the 1590s, Robert Devereux was the last great favorite of Elizabeth I. Essex was a respected soldier, a leading member of the Privy Council, and aspired to be an international statesman. Unlike other favorites of the reign, he was also an aristocrat of high birth. Essex's ambition helped to galvanize England's war effort during the 1590s but also encouraged bitter factionalism within the Elizabethan regime. By the end of the decade, the changed political environment, ill health, and a growing recognition of personal failure left Essex a broken man.

Born on November 10, 1565, he inherited from Walter Devereux the heavily-indebted earldom of Essex in September 1576. As a royal ward, Essex came under the guardianship of Lord Burghley and the earls of Huntingdon and Sussex. After briefly residing with Burghley, he went up to Trinity College, Cambridge, in May 1577. He remained there until November 1581, performing the requisite public exercises for a degree and receiving an M.A. in July 1581. Following his mother's remarriage to Robert Dudley, earl of Leicester, in September 1578, Essex became increasingly associated with his step-father during the early 1580s. Under Leicester's guidance, he made a brief debut at court in September 1585, and served as colonel-general of the cavalry for Leicester's army in the Low Countries during 1586. In September 1586, Essex played a prominent role in a skirmish at Zutphen, at which Sir Philip Sidney was mortally wounded. Leicester subsequently dubbed Essex a knight banneret, ending his period of wardship.

After their return to England in late 1586, Leicester put his full weight behind advancing Essex at court, with spectacular success. By May 1587, when Leicester was promoted to lord steward, he arranged with Elizabeth for Essex to replace him as her master of the horse. Essex's meteoric rise provoked a sharp struggle with Sir Walter Ralegh, who also sought royal favor. This rivalry lasted for almost three years, briefly peaking in intensity after Leicester's death in September 1588. By late 1589, however, Essex's predominance was clear. Although he endured a brief spell of royal anger in late 1590, when it was revealed that he had secretly married Sidney's widow (probably earlier in that year), he became deeply entrenched in the queen's favor. After Christopher Hatton's death in late 1591, he was unchallenged as the chief royal favorite.

Despite his remarkable success at court, Essex was rarely comfortable there and he made regular efforts to escape to fight abroad. Most notoriously, he defied Elizabeth by secretly leaving court to join the Portugal expedition in April 1589. Although this venture provoked an outpouring of royal wrath, it helped to prove Essex's *bona fides* as a soldier and patron of military officers. Elizabeth was finally forced to recognize Essex's martial ambitions when she appointed him to command an army in Normandy between July 1591, and January 1592. Although he proved competent as a general and ultimately won grudging approval from the queen, the campaign was a failure and destroyed his naive belief that he could win political influence merely by battlefield engagements. Thereafter, he sought to establish himself as a genuine politician, specializing in foreign affairs and intelligence.

Essex was made a privy councilor in February 1593, and became a figure of international importance, but he never achieved his goal of succeeding Burghley as the queen's chief adviser. Essex sought to expand the war against Spain and to strengthen cooperation with the Dutch and Henry IV of France. More covertly, he fostered toleration for English Catholics (although he was a strong Protestant) and championed the claim of James VI of Scotland (with whom he was in regular secret contact by early 1594) as the next monarch of England. Essex's efforts to pursue these policies in the face of growing unwillingness from Elizabeth and Burghley, and concern at the scale of his ambition, gradually encouraged opposition to him. Essex's aspirations also ran headlong into Burghley's own plans for his son, Sir Robert Cecil, to become the next secretary of state. These tensions became acute in 1595, when Elizabeth's determination to withdraw English troops from France clashed with Essex's personal commitment to Henry IV. In 1596, Essex, therefore, sought to hijack the Cadiz expedition by using it to seize a permanent base in Spain, contrary to the queen's orders. Although the city was captured in spectacular fashion, the lord admiral, Charles Howard, who shared command of the venture, refused to establish a garrison there and the scheme collapsed.

Essex's frustration was compounded when Elizabeth appointed Cecil as secretary of state, while the factions

D

that had appeared within the expeditionary force soon began to emerge at court. In 1597, because of negotiations with Cecil and Ralegh, Essex commanded the Azores or "Islands" expedition. This proved a costly failure and tarnished Essex's reputation. However, he remained the leading military man in England, a status that was reinforced by his appointments as master of the ordnance on March 19, 1597, and earl marshal nine months later on December 28. Although he acted as secretary of state during Cecil's absence in early 1598, Essex's world soon began to disintegrate. Peace between France and Spain rendered his war policies obsolete, while his adamant opposition to peace between Spain and England cost him political credit. An incident in which he almost drew his sword on the queen after a furious row, followed by his secession from court, destroyed his hold on royal favor.

In August 1598, the death of Burghley and the near-collapse of English power in Ireland were further blows. Although Essex had previously avoided close involvement in Ireland, command of the large new army being sent there offered him a last chance to regain his political credibility. However, Essex's expedition to Ireland proved an expensive failure and, feeling betrayed and abandoned, he suddenly returned to court in September 1599. Arriving to find Elizabeth still in her bedchamber, Essex received a cold welcome. Before the day was out, he was arrested and charged with concluding a truce with the Irish rebels—led by Hugh O'Neill—and dereliction of duty. By now broken in spirit and health, Essex almost died at Christmas 1599. In June 1600, he was condemned by his fellow councilors and stripped of all his offices except that of master of the horse. By the end of 1600, Essex was bankrupt, paranoid, and surrounded by desperate followers who urged him to take drastic action to protect their interests and "rescue" the realm from government by their factional enemies. In contrast to his bold actions in the mid-1590s, Essex now proved remarkably indecisive in dealing with his political failure. On February 8, 1601, Essex and many of his close adherents were finally panicked into a hasty display of force on the streets of London. This confused action merely bewildered the citizens and caused him to be proclaimed a traitor. After a rapid trial, Essex was executed in the Tower on February 25, 1601.

BIBLIOGRAPHY

Hammer, P.E.J. *The Polarization of Elizabethan Politics: the Political Career of Robert Devereux, 2nd Earl of Essex, 1585–1597.* 1999.
———. "Essex and Europe: evidence from confidential instructions by the earl of Essex, 1595–1596." *English Historical Review,* vol. 111, pp. 357–381.
———. "The uses of scholarship: the secretariat of Robert Devereux, 2nd earl of Essex, c. 1585–1601." *English Historical Review,* vol. 109, pp. 26–51.
Harrison, G.B. *The Life and Death of Robert Devereux, Earl of Essex.* 1937.
Henry, L.W. "The earl of Essex as strategist and military organiser (1596–1597)." *English Historical Review,* vol. 68, pp. 363–393.
Henry, L.W. "The earl of Essex and Ireland, 1599." *Bulletin of the Institute of Historical Research,* vol. 32, pp. 1–23.
James, M. "At a crossroads of the political culture: the Essex Revolt, 1601." In *Society, Politics, and Culture: Studies in Early Modern England,* pp. 416–465. 1986.
Lacey, R. *Robert, Earl of Essex: an Elizabethan Icarus.* 1970.
Lloyd, H.A. "The Devereux inheritance." *Welsh History Review,* vol. 7, pp. 13–38.
May, S.W., ed. "The poems of Edward De Vere, seventeenth earl of Oxford and Robert Devereux, second earl of Essex." *Studies in Philology,* vol. 77, Texts and Studies issue. 1980.
McCoy, Richard C. *The Rites of Knighthood: the Politics of Elizabethan Chivalry.* Chap. 4. 1989.

Paul E. J. Hammer

SEE ALSO

Cecil, William; Devereux, Walter; Dudley, Robert; Foreign Relations and Diplomacy; Ireland, History of; O'Neill, Hugh; Ralegh, Sir Walter; Treason

Devereux, Sir Walter, First Earl of Essex (c. 1541–1576)

Best known for his attempt to establish a colony in northern Ireland, Walter Devereux, Second Viscount Hereford, first distinguished himself serving against the rebels of the Northern Rebellion and was subsequently awarded with the earldom of Essex. He was poorer than others of his rank and he determined to make his fortune by colonizing part of Ulster. Shortsighted and parsimonious in her Irish policy, Elizabeth I granted Essex land in Antrium and agreed to pay half of the expenses; Essex mortgaged some of his estates to her in order to subsidize the rest. He embarked in the summer of 1573 with a force of 1,200 men who were lured by the hope of land and wealth.

The expedition was poorly planned. Essex's ships were scattered by a storm and on reaching Ulster, the survivors quickly became disheartened, plagued by famine, sickness, and fierce Gaelic resistance. With insufficient support, Essex and his men were unable to establish themselves and retreated to the Pale, the area around Dublin ruled by the English, in May 1574; only 200 remained. Essex, recently named governor of Ulster, ordered a number of raids and resorted to harsh and sometimes treacherous methods, such as the massacre of the 600 inhabitants of Rathlin island, but success continued to elude him.

Elizabeth was alarmed at the mounting expenses, and in May 1575, the same year Essex was appointed earl marshal of Ireland, she suddenly canceled the enterprise. Essex pleaded for further funding and assistance in paying his debts, but in September of the next year he contracted dysentery and died shortly thereafter in Dublin Castle. Even after an autopsy, rumors persisted that he had been poisoned.

Essex's harsh policy only strengthened native Irish resistance and his failure demonstrated to many the hopelessness of a private enterprise colony that preceded the subjugation of the Gaelic people. Essex had four children with his wife, Lettice Knollys, including Penelope Devereux, and on his death, Essex left to his eldest son, Robert Devereux, his remaining property, his titles, and his debts.

BIBLIOGRAPHY

Devereux, Walter. *The Lives and Letters of the Devereux, Earls of Essex.* Vol. 1. 1853.

Ellis, Steven G. *Tudor Ireland: Crown, Community, and the Conflict of Cultures, 1470–1603.* 1985.

Hammer, P.E.J. *The Polarization of Elizabethan Politics: The Political Career of Robert Devereux, 2nd Earl of Essex, 1585–1597.* 1999.

Lennon, Colm. *Sixteenth Century Ireland: The Incomplete Conquest.* 1995.

R. Morgan Griffin

SEE ALSO

Colonial Development; Devereux, Robert; Ireland, History of; Knollys, Lettice; Northern Rebellion

Dictionaries

The Renaissance dictionaries were composed by the humanists themselves, the scholar-printers who used their technological expertise to spread the gospel of the "new learning." And while Chaldean, Arabic, and other exotic languages were occasionally represented in the polyglot dictionaries of the period, the focus of these learned tomes was primarily on the Latin language, and secondarily on the Greek. Print technology encouraged the production of such massive word lists, as well as the development of indices, marginal notes, cross-references, and interlinear glosses. These reference books were an essential cultural tool for future humanists, an indispensable source of myth and other arcane matters for philosopher-poets, and the basic reference guide for young schoolboys struggling with the complex vagaries of the Greek and Latin languages. They were used by all and resented by many, the fate of many good reference books.

One of the earliest Greek dictionaries, which was later translated into Latin, is attributed to one "Suidas" (compiled c. A.D. 975). It appeared in numerous editions during the Renaissance, in both Greek and Latin. But the tradition of Renaissance dictionaries (Greek-Latin, Latin-Latin, Latin-vernacular, and polyglot) begins with an Italian lexicographer, Ambrosio Calepino (c. 1435–1511), whose *Dictionarium* was first published in Reggio in 1502, and later (Basel, 1544) enhanced with an onomasticon (*Onomasticon Propriorvm Nominvm*) by the great bibliographer and encyclopedist Konrad Gesner (1516–1565). The *Dictionarium,* in turn, became the parent source for the multiple editions of Greek and Latin dictionaries by the French lexicographers and printers Robert (1503–1559), Charles (1504–1564), and Henri (1528–1598) Stephanus (the family's given name was Éstienne or Étienne). (Charles Hoole, in his famous work, *A New Discovery of the old Art of Teaching Schoole* [London, 1660], lists Charles Stephanus's Latin dictionary as one of the six sources that every school library should contain to assist students in glossing Ovid's *Metamorphoses.*)

These dictionaries were adapted in turn by Thomas Elyot, bishop of Winchester (c. 1490–1546), in his *The Dictionary of syr Thomas Eliot knyght* (first edition, 1538). Unlike the works of "Suidas," Calepino, Gesner, and the Stephanus lexicographers, the definitions of the Latin words in Sir Thomas Elyot's *The Dictionary* are in English. Many editions of this work were coedited by Thomas Cooper, who expanded some definitions and contracted others. The first of these composite editions, the *Bibliotheca Eliotae: Eliotis Librarie,* issued from the press in 1548 and quickly became the standard lexicon in England.

D

Cooper became sole author after Elyot's death and continued the tradition of drawing heavily on the Stephanus dictionaries. For example, his *Thesavrvs Lingvae Romanae & Britannicae* (London, 1565)—which is, in effect, a revision and expansion of both Elyot's *Dictionary* and Robert Stephanus's *Thesaurus Linguae Latinae*—follows Gesner's example in creating a separate onomasticon, his *Dictionarivm Historicum & Poeticum propria locorum & Personarum vocabula breuiter complectens* (*An Historical and Poetical Dictionary, Briefly Covering the Proper Names of Places and Peoples*).

Finally, Thomas Thomas (1553–1588), who became first printer to Cambridge University, put out the first edition of his *Dictionarivm Lingvae Latinae Et Anglicanae* in 1587, literally dying in the attempt. At least thirteen other posthumous editions (retitled *Dictionarium Summa Fide*) followed, the last being printed at Cambridge in 1644. Thomas's dictionary was very popular, perhaps because of the succinctness of its entries. More than any other lexicographer, Thomas borrows heavily and profitably from his predecessors, but not without some loss of significant detail.

The dictionaries have sometimes been lumped indiscriminately with other reference works of the period, particularly Lodovicus Caelius's *Lectionum Antiquarum*, Joachim Cameriarius's *Commentarii Utriusque Linguae* (*Glosses on Either Language*), Niccolò Perotti's *Cornucopiae*, Natale Conti's *Mythologiae*, and Andrea Alciato's *Emblemata*. It would perhaps be more accurate to say that these and many other reference sources are incorporated in successive editions of the dictionaries, especially in the seventeenth century.

Clearly, the dictionaries of the Renaissance made the writers of ancient Greece and Rome more accessible to the *literati* in Tudor England, and also encouraged both translation and philological analysis. And although continental humanists like Calepine and the Stephanus family were the dominant lexicographers of the age, Eliot, Cooper, and Thomas also produced scholarly dictionaries of substantial merit that were not beneath the notice of the first modern lexicographer in English, Samuel Johnson.

BIBLIOGRAPHY

Dillon, John B. "Renaissance Reference Books as Sources for Classical Myth and Geography: A Brief Survey, with an Illustration from Milton." *Proceedings, Fourth International Conference of Neo-Latin Studies*, pp. 437–450. 1985.

Kibbee, Douglas A. "The Humanist Period in Renaissance Bilingual Lexicography." *The History of Lexicography: Papers from the Dictionary Research Centre Seminar at Exeter, March 1986.* R.R.K. Hartmann, ed., pp. 137–146. 1986.

Mulryan, John. *Through a Glass Darkly: Milton's Reinvention of the Mythological Tradition.* 1996

Starnes, DeWitt T., and Ernest William Talbert. *Classical Myth and Legend in Renaissance Dictionaries: A Study of Renaissance Dictionaries in Their Relation to the Classical Learning of Contemporary English Writers.* 1955.

Steadman, John M. "Renaissance Dictionaries and Manuals as Instruments of Literary Scholarship." *New Aspects of Lexicography: Literary Criticism, Intellectual History, and Social Change.* Howard D. Weinbrot, ed., pp. 17–35. 1972.

John Mulryan

SEE ALSO

Classical Literature, Influence of; Classical Literature, Translations of; Cooper, Thomas; Elyot, Thomas; Language, History of

Didactic Poetry

According to a common prejudice, didactic poetry is an oxymoron: poetry is supposed to be at odds with plain statements of moral and other messages. Questions about the status of sermons and versified lore can be traced within the Tudor period itself: Sir Philip Sidney doubted that a writer "wrapped within the fold of the proposed subject," lacking freedom to follow "the course of his own invention," could properly be termed a poet. Such writers as Thomas Tusser, Thomas Churchyard, and the anonymous composers of broadsides may never be more than candidates for the chorus when "right poets" are being honored, but didactic poetry in the Tudor period came out of age-old traditions in both the erudite and vernacular languages, as did several kinds of cultural work. The whole purpose of print culture was didactic, driven by humanism, the Reformation, and the apparatus of central government. When George Gascoigne, Sidney, Edmund Spenser, and their followers sought to distinguish their art and its refined pleasures from the work of less expert and ambitious versifiers, they also confronted anti-poetical notions that verses not explicitly godly are idle fancies, vain use of learning, temptations to effeminacy.

Horace had advised poets to "mingle the sweet and the useful" (*Ars Poet.* 343), and this rationale was adaptable to many occasions when entertainment was under suspicion. Sidney justified the pleasures poetry offered as qualities directly appealing to the rational will and therefore conducive to virtue, adding ideas from Quintilian and interpreters of Plato to the Horatian tradition, and contributing to a debate central to humanist thought about the reconciliation of pleasure and virtue. How much sweetness, and of what kind, should be mingled in poetry with the useful didactic matter? Sidney's stance on this question of taste is indicative of his aristocratic lineage, but also of his tenuous position within the peerage, owing more to a wit erected by education than to inherited status.

If we were to separate overtly didactic poetry from that which foregrounds its "imaginative groundplot" in fiction (a dubious undertaking: where do allegories belong?), the didactic poems would constitute a massive and various portion of those written, and especially of those published, in the period. They might seem tedious and undistinguished today, but such texts had instrumental value in their time. Whether composed for an elite and learned audience, for the industrious and self-improving "middling sort," or for the illiterate and minimally literate audience reached by broadside ballads, many kinds of didactic poems, from book-length allegories (Hawes's *Pastime of Pleasure,* Spenser's *Faerie Queene*) and cautionary narratives (*A Mirror for Magistrates*) to incidental distichs and occasional poems (moral tags, aids to memory, epitaphs and obsequies), served vitally important social functions. As literary studies shift from a focus on supposedly intrinsic aesthetic values to analyses of instrumental functions such as the constituting and regulating of social groups and personal interests, didactic poetry has been moving from the margins to the foreground in studies of Tudor culture.

Most of what has traditionally counted as the period's poetry, from that of the "courtly makers" in the time of Henry VIII to the generation that included George Chapman, John Donne, and Ben Jonson, was produced and consumed either by members of an elite group of courtiers, or by men seeking access to such circles. Such poetry might voice the interests of reforming elements within the elite, but it did so by inscribing all the more deeply the criteria for inclusion and exclusion. By the end of the century, explicitly didactic poetry had become less commonplace, more learned; the business of inculcating manners and morals was more complex and devious. In courtly circles, some of the work was done by entertainment rather than explicit instruction; Sir John Davies' *Orchestra* (1596) glosses this process, by which virtue and pleasure are supposed to be reconciled. In the last ten years of Elizabeth I's reign, some of the most distinctive of the decade's great poems count as not only didactic but philosophical: *The Shadow of Night* (1594) and other poems of Chapman, Spenser's *Fowre Hymns* (1596), Samuel Daniel's *Musophilus* (1599), Davies' *Nosce Teipsum* (1599), and the poems published with Robert Chester's *Love's Martyr* (1601), including William Shakespeare's "The Phoenix and Turtle."

By contrast, less distinguished and often anonymous types of didactic poetry, which did not contribute materially to the culture of the elite, put in print a common language and some of its dialects, over against which the poets of London and the court distinguished themselves. By various means, and for several audiences, didactic poetry inculcated piety and modesty; patriotism and obedience to authority; the virtues of domesticity, thrift, and work. It reiterated an obvious order, valuable to rulers and the ruled, and sometimes challenged the status quo by remarking on pride, dishonesty, and injustice. Laborers and the "middling sort," together with some prosperous people in London and provincial centers of commerce, sometimes stood aloof from the elite culture, with interests of their own that were affirmed by this didactic poetry. The pastoral and georgic themes prominent in elite culture should be recognized as dialogically related to interests that the "baser sort" voiced in a lower stylistic register.

BIBLIOGRAPHY

Hunter, G.K. "Drab and Golden Lyrics of the Renaissance." In *Forms of Lyric; Selected Papers from the English Institute.* Reuben A. Brower, ed., pp. 1–18. 1970.

King, John N. *English Reformation Literature; The Tudor Origins of the Protestant Tradition.* 1982.

May, Steven W. *The Elizabethan Courtier Poets; The Poems and Their Contexts.* 1991.

Norbrook, David. *Poetry and Politics in the English Renaissance.* 1984.

Wilcox, Helen, Richard Todd, and Alasdair MacDonald, eds. *Sacred and Profane: Secular and Devotional Interplay in Early Modern British Literature.* 1996.

Jon Quitslund

D

Digby, Everard (c. 1550–1592)

Educated at one of the leading foundations of humanist learning in Tudor England, St. John's College, Cambridge, founded by Bishop John Fisher, Everard Digby entered St. John's as sizar in 1567 and was elected Queen Margaret fellow in 1573 and senior fellow in 1585. He proceeded M.A. in 1574 and B.D. in 1581. Although he had powerful patrons at court, such as Sir Christopher Hatton, Digby was deprived of his fellowship in 1588 for alleged breaches of the statutes, and Catholic tendencies.

Digby's major publications are his *Theoria analytica ad monarchiam scientiarum demonstrans* (1579), and *De duplici methodo libri duo unicam P. Rami methodum refutantes* (1580). Among his other claims to fame is the fact that he wrote the earliest treatise on swimming to be published in England (*De arte natandi*). *Theoria analytica* is syncretic in approach, effecting an accommodation between Platonism and Aristotelianism. Digby's epistemology combines Aristotelian syllogistic with Platonic dialectic. This in turn is overlaid by, if not infused with, a Platonist system of metaphysics. According to Digby, the formal processes of dialectic enhance our rational powers. Through the exercise of reason we can advance from contemplation of the natural world to the realm of metaphysics. Through our exercise of reason we are able to ascend toward an apprehension of the divine, that is the first principle, or being itself. Once we attain knowledge of the intelligible principles of being, we can descend to certain knowledge of the world. Furthermore, *Theoria analytica* sets out a Platonist metaphysics. For Digby, all things, including the human mind, derive from the divine ideas in the mind of God. All things are therefore blessed with a spark of the divine. Throughout, like Pico della Mirandola, Digby stresses the rational faculty in man and his ability to love God. And, like Pico, he has an optimistic view of human nature.

In both *Theoria analytica* and *De duplici methodo*, Digby takes up the challenge of Ramism, then gaining popularity at Cambridge. To the single method of Ramus he added his own "double method": composition (roughly equivalent to Aristotelian induction) and

analysis (or demonstration). In 1580, William Temple (1555–1627) attacked Digby using the pseudonym Franciscus Mildapettus. Digby replied and Temple responded in his own name. It is perhaps no coincidence that the master of St. John's at the time when Digby was deprived of his fellowship was William Whitaker, an ally of Laurence Chaderton, who was also one of the first promoters of Ramism at the university. The opposition of the Ramists also had a theological edge, since Whitaker and Chaderton were both Calvinists, whereas, as Digby's later theological writings indicate, his theological outlook was closer to Hooker.

Everard Digby, *Cutting one's toenails while swimming.* From *De arte natandi* (1587). This unique illustration is from the first comprehensive manual on swimming printed in England. Reproduced from the original by permission of the Henry E. Huntington Library and Art Gallery.

D

Digby's defense of Aristotle and opposition to Ramus do not, however, mean that he was a conservative, defending the intellectual status quo against new ideas. On the contrary, as his *Theoria analytica* shows, Digby had a wide acquaintance with philosophical sources. This was the outcome of a broad humanist acquaintance with classical sources, and is therefore not the mark of a scholastic. Digby's knowledge of Aristotelianism, was in fact, matched by his knowledge of Platonist sources, which included Plato, Plotinus, Porphyry, Iamblichus, Proclus Pseudo-Dionysius, and Hermes Trismegistus, as well as Apuleius and Alcinous. He is indebted to Ficino and Pico as well as the Christian Cabbalists, Reuchlin and Agrippa. The Aristotelians cited by Digby include Aristotle's earliest commentators, Alexander of Aphrodisias and Themistius, as well as sixteenth-century Aristotelians such as Jacob Schegk and Johannes Caesarius, and, above all, the anti-Ramists Carpentarius and Nicholas Grouchy. The combination of Platonism and Aristotelianism makes it hard to classify him as an Aristotelian, except loosely as an eclectic Aristotelian.

Theoria analytica was the first serious philosophical work to be published in post-Reformation Tudor England. It shows acquaintance with contemporary intellectual developments outside England, and was, moreover, the first English philosophical work to be addressed to a learned international audience since the Middle Ages. Digby's accommodation of Platonist metaphysics and Aristotelian dialectic is the result of a syncretic approach to ancient philosophy facilitated and nurtured by a humanist approach to antiquity. Digby's anti-Ramism is part of the opposition to the Calvinist ascendancy within the University of Cambridge. His interest in Platonism and Christian kabalah, his syncretic approach to philosophy, and his liberal, anti-Calvinist theology anticipates the Cambridge Platonists of the next century.

BIBLIOGRAPHY

Akester, S.A. (née Butters). *Life and Works of Everard Digby, c. 1551–1605.* Dissertation, Oxford. 1980.
Gilbert, N.W. *Renaissance Concepts of Method.* 1960.
Schmitt, Charles B. *John Case and Aristotelianism in Renaissance England,* pp. 47–52. 1983.
Jardine, L. "The Place of Dialectic Teaching in Sixteenth-Century Cambridge." *Studies in the Renaissance,* vol. 21, pp. 31–62.

Sarah Hutton

SEE ALSO
Aristotelianism; Humanism; Platonism; Ramism

Digges, Leonard (c. 1515–c. 1559)

Leonard Digges came from a prominent and long-established gentry family of Kent and was an important member of the first generation of English mathematical authors to publish in the vernacular. He was probably studying at Oxford in 1531; he entered Lincoln's Inn in 1537. Digges took part in Wyatt's Rebellion against the Catholic marriage of Queen Mary I in January 1554 and, after its failure, was charged with high treason and sentenced to death. However, he was pardoned in April 1554, and, on payment of a fine in 1555, recovered his lands and goods, which had been seized after his attainder.

Digges published only two works during his lifetime, a popular almanac and a short treatise on mensuration. The earliest surviving issue of the almanac is *A Prognostication of Right Good Effect, Fructfully Augmented* (1555), which had evidently been preceded by one or more editions (now lost). Many subsequent issues appeared under the title *A Prognostication Euerlasting.* The text includes astronomical and calendrical tables and information, with rules on weather as well as times for planting, grafting, and bloodletting. This miscellaneous compendium was prefaced by an apology for the mathematical sciences, defending them against charges of impiety and vanity. Digges's *Tectonicon* (1556)—which was reissued until the end of the seventeenth century—taught the measurement of land, the calculation of quantities, and the use of various instruments for carpenters, masons, and surveyors.

Digges promised several other volumes, and his *Pantometria* was published posthumously by his son, Thomas, in 1571. Its three books cover the measurement of length, area, and volume, and show Digges's familiarity with the latest continental sources. The work extends and complements *Tectonicon* through its focus on surveying and instruments, and offers the first English account of the altazimuth theodolite. Digges also wrote on arithmetic, and some surviving papers became the basis for the first book of Thomas Digges's *Stratioticos* (1579).

Digges's private studies included optics and ballistics. Although he did not devise a modern telescope, he evidently created a large (and probably unwieldy) lens-mirror combination for terrestrial viewing. In artillery and

D

Longimetria. From Leonard Digges, *Pantometria* (1571). The picture illustrates a procedure for finding the height of tall objects. By permission of the Houghton Library, Harvard University.

ballistics, Digges's researches led him to criticize many of the results announced by Niccolo Tartaglia in his *Nova scientia* (1537). His published works of the 1550s were elementary and popular, but Digges's investigative enterprise, pursued as a self-conscious combination of theory and practice, helped to set the foundation for Elizabethan practical mathematics.

BIBLIOGRAPHY

Easton, Joy B. "Leonard Digges." In *Dictionary of Scientific Biography.* 16 vols. C.C. Gillispie, ed. Vol. 4, p. 97.

Richeson, A.W. *English Land Measuring to 1800.* 1967.

Taylor, E.G.R. *The Mathematical Practitioners of Tudor and Stuart England.* 1954.

Turner, Anthony J. "The prehistory, origins, and development of the reflecting telescope." *Bollettino del Centro Internazionale A. Beltrame di Storia dello Spazio e del Tempo,* vol. 3–4, pp. 11–22.

Stephen Johnston

SEE ALSO

Astronomy; Ordnance; Wyatt's Rebellion

Digges, Thomas (c. 1546–1595)

Mathematician, military administrator, and active member of Parliament, Thomas Digges was the eldest son of the mathematical author Leonard Digges. He published both his father's work and his own independent studies of topics ranging from astronomy, geometry, and magnetism, to military mathematics and organization. Thomas's education was begun by his father and continued under John Dee. His most novel mathematical and scientific work was accomplished at the beginning of his career. He added a lengthy analysis of polyhedra to the posthumous edition of his father's *Pantometria* (1571), a text on practical geometry. In the following year he observed the new star that had appeared in the constellation of Cassiopeia and was prompted to publish *Alae seu scalae mathematicae* (1573). Addressed to a European audience of astronomers, *Alae* was Thomas's only Latin publication, offering an analysis and rectification of the mathematical and instrumental techniques available for the study of the nova. Digges concluded that the new phenomenon was indeed celestial rather than rising in the earth's atmosphere, and recent radio astronomy has shown that his observations were the most accurate then made.

Digges was the first English author to declare publicly his support for Copernicus's cosmological scheme. He had broadly hinted his acceptance of Copernican thought in *Alae,* but wondered whether additional improvements might still be required. Such hesitations no longer exist when he translated the cosmological sections of Book 1 of Copernicus's *De revolutionibus orbium caelestium* (1543) as an appendix for his father's popular almanac, *A Prognostication Everlasting.* As well as making Copernicus accessible to an English audience, Digges also made some additions, including a famous diagram that went beyond Copernicus, showing the stars extending into an infinite universe.

In 1579, Digges published *Stratioticos,* a text on military mathematics. It was dedicated to Robert Dudley, the earl of Leicester, in the expectation that he would lead an English force against the Spanish in the Netherlands. When Leicester's expedition was finally realized in 1585, Digges was appointed muster-master of the army. His military concerns are also reflected in *Pantometria* (1591).

Digges was elected M.P. in 1572, and again in 1584–1585. He served as a "man of business," speaking, drafting memoranda, and consulting with the Privy Council. He was appointed surveyor of the harbor works at Dover—one of the largest of Elizabethan technical projects—and was asked to review John Dee's proposal for reforming the calendar. Through such civic service, Digges increasingly stressed the worldly effectiveness of mathematics.

BIBLIOGRAPHY

Hall, A.R. *Ballistics in the Seventeenth Century.* 1952.

Hasler, P.W., ed. *The House of Commons, 1558–1603.* 3 vols. Vol. 2, pp. 37–39. 1981.

Johnson, F.R. *Astronomical Thought in Renaissance England.* 1937.

———, and S.V. Larkey. "Thomas Digges, the Copernican System, and the Idea of the Infinity of the Universe in 1576." *Huntington Library Bulletin,* vol. 5, pp. 69–117.

Stephen Johnston

SEE ALSO

Astronomy; Calendar, Secular; Dee, John; Digges, Leonard; Dudley, Robert; Ordnance

Diplomacy

See Foreign Relations and Diplomacy

Discipline, Ecclesiastical

See Church Polity; Courts, Ecclesiastical; Law, Canon

Discovery and Exploration

Tudor England played a secondary role in Europe's early overseas expansion. Discovery and exploration were not high priorities either for the monarchy or the merchant community, who were reluctant to support ventures whose outcome was uncertain. This lack of support for overseas discovery was reinforced during the early Tudor period by an unwillingness to challenge the prior claims of Spain and Portugal to the west or east. As a result, English adventurers were forced to operate on the fringes of Spanish and Portuguese spheres of influence in America and Asia, restricting their activities to the northwest and northeast. Although this situation changed after 1558, it was in these regions that the English made their most positive contribution to European discovery and exploration.

The initial phase of English maritime expansion is shrouded in obscurity. Fragmentary evidence has been used to support the argument for an English discovery of North America as early as 1481. At this time there was clearly some interest in Bristol in searching for the island of Brasil, which was supposed to lie to the west of Ireland. The first of these voyages, for which evidence survives, occurred in 1480. The following year, Thomas Croft, a customs official, set out with two ships laden with salt on a similar venture. It is possible that a landfall was made somewhere in the north Atlantic during this voyage, but the evidence is vague and inconclusive. Without more convincing evidence it would be safer to argue for a prolonged, but unsuccessful, attempt to find what Bristol merchants called the island of Brasil that was motivated by the search for new fishing grounds to replace the traditional fishery at Iceland, where English fishermen were facing intense German competition during the 1470s and 1480s.

This early activity, which may have continued during the 1480s, was given greater focus and ambition by the arrival in England of John Cabot during 1494 or 1495, with a plan for sailing to Cathay by a westward route. Although Cabot's first voyage was a failure, his second venture of 1497 was a landmark in the English Atlantic enterprise. Cabot achieved the first indisputable recorded crossing of the Atlantic from England, landing either at Newfoundland or Cape Breton, which he claimed for Henry VII. On his return to England Cabot insisted that he had reached the northern regions of Cathay, though news of the rich fishing grounds off Newfoundland were of more immediate interest to his Bristol backers. With the support of the king and a small group of Bristol and London merchants, Cabot set out with a much larger expedition, in 1498, from which he never returned. His death represented a severe setback, particularly as the king withdrew his support from further voyages of discovery. Geographical understanding of his achievement was recorded in Juan de la Cosa's world map of 1500, showing a "sea discovered by the English" that almost certainly refers to Cabot's voyages.

Some of Cabot's Bristol backers, together with his son, Sebastian Cabot, set out a series of exploratory voyages to North America from 1501 to 1505, in partnership with a group of Portuguese merchants. These ventures combined fishing and trade with the exploration of Newfoundland and the coasts of Labrador or New England. The widening scope of these voyages

D

probably culminated in an attempt by Sebastian to search for a northwest passage around America in 1508 and 1509. Although Cabot may have sailed as far as 67 degrees north, he was forced back by a mutinous crew. Sailing south, he completed a lengthy coasting voyage along the eastern seaboard of North America that went a long way toward confirming its continental character. Unfortunately, Cabot had found little to maintain the interest of his backers, or to arouse the excitement of the new king. In these circumstances England's pioneering role in the exploration of the North Atlantic lapsed.

Although Henry VIII lent his support over the next three decades to three ventures aimed at exploring the coast of North America, their failure was discouraging and symptomatic of the underlying limitations of English maritime enterprise. In 1517, John Rastell set out to search for the Northwest Passage with the intention also of establishing a colony in North America, but the expedition disintegrated shortly after leaving England, and he never got beyond Waterford in Ireland. Ten years later John Rut led an expedition to find the Northwest Passage. Rut may have reached the coast of Labrador, but he was forced south after meeting heavy ice in the sea, returning to England through the Caribbean after completing one of the longest English reconnaissances of the North American coastline. Finally, in 1536, Richard Hore led a disastrous expedition to Newfoundland or Labrador, during which some of the crew turned to cannibalism to stay alive. After a grueling ordeal the English seized a French ship with its supplies, and used it to return home. These cumulative and costly failures effectively ended the king's limited interest in exploration.

It took the shock of a severe depression in overseas trade during the early 1550s to revive interest in discovery, although its purpose was essentially commercial. In 1553, a company for the discovery and exploration of new lands was incorporated with unprecedented support from wealthy London merchants, courtiers, and government officials. Sebastian Cabot, governor of the new company, played a leading role in organizing the expedition set out in 1553 to search for a northeast passage to Cathay. Under the command of Sir Hugh Willoughby and Richard Chancellor, the expedition reached the Barents Sea, where it was dispersed in difficult conditions. Unable to proceed eastward, Willoughby was forced to spend the winter at Varzino, along the coast of Lapland, where he and his men died of cold and malnutrition. Chancellor, who sailed on to the White Sea, eventually reached Moscow, opening up Muscovy to English trade.

A monopoly of the trade with Russia and other regions in the northeast and northwest was granted to the Muscovy Company, which was formed in 1555. For the next thirty years the company was a major sponsor of geographical and maritime enterprise. In 1556, it sent out Stephen Borough to explore a route eastward from Vardo in Finnmark, but ice and poor conditions forced him back. These difficulties led the company into an attempt to pursue its eastern ambitions by an alternative route to Moscow and across central Asia. In 1557, Anthony Jenkinson was set out to reconnoiter this sea and land passage to Cathay. Although Jenkinson failed in his main purpose, he was able to establish commercial contact with Persia, which the company tried to develop through further expeditions in 1564, 1565, 1568, and 1581. By the time of this last expedition the company had revived its search for a northeast passage. In 1580, it sent out Arthur Pet and Charles Jackman with instructions to follow the mainland coast of northern Russia round to Cathay. Although the expedition reached the Kara Sea, it was unable to make further headway against the ice. Jackman was subsequently lost at sea in obscure circumstances.

Ironically, as the company lost interest in the northeast, renewed attempts to find a northwest passage met with insurmountable obstacles. During the 1560s, Humphrey Gilbert revived interest in the passage, but his plans for setting out an expedition to the northwest were frustrated by opposition from the Muscovy Company. By the mid-1570s, the company was persuaded to license Martin Frobisher and Michael Lok to search for the passage. With Lok's backing, and the occasional support of Elizabeth I, Frobisher led three expeditions to the Arctic between 1576 and 1580. Although these ventures failed, in 1576, Frobisher discovered new land that the queen called Meta Incognita, now identified as Baffin Island, and on his last voyage he accidentally sailed into what he named the Mistaken Straits, subsequently known as Hudson Strait. Lok's map of America of 1582 made some attempt to assimilate Frobisher's discoveries into contemporary geographical knowledge. Although it represents an important advance in English knowledge of the northwest, it was crude, inaccurate, and misleading. Continued belief in the mythical island of Frisland, supposedly lying eastward of the American mainland, created confusion over Frobisher's experience that was not cleared up until the nineteenth century.

Despite Frobisher's failure, from 1585 to 1587 John Davis led three expeditions in search of a northwest passage that were landmarks in the English exploration of the

Arctic. In 1585, Davis landed on Baffin Island, exploring the coastline south into Cumberland Sound. He extended the scope of these explorations in 1586 and 1587. On his last voyage he sailed as far as 72 degrees north, before being turned back by heavy pack ice and northerly winds. Sailing south, he reached the mouth of Hudson Strait, but he had no time to explore further. Davis returned to London optimistically believing that the discovery of the passage was very probable, but lack of support brought this sequence of ventures to an end. Serious interest in the Northwest Passage did not revive until the early seventeenth century.

The search for a passage to Cathay invigorated English overseas discovery and exploration. After 1558, however, maritime enterprise was increasingly influenced by the deterioration in Anglo-Spanish relations, which encouraged piracy and privateering at the expense of more peaceful pursuits. Hostility to Spain stimulated a wide range of maritime and colonial projects, including Francis Drake's circumnavigation of the world from 1577 to 1580. Although one of the main purposes of the venture was plunder, during the course of the voyage Drake explored the coast of modern California, which he called Nova Albion and claimed for the queen. Thereafter, he crossed the Pacific, reaching Ternate in the East Indies on his way home around the Cape of Good Hope. Drake's circumnavigation was accidental; nevertheless, in Tudor England it was an unparalleled feat of seamanship and exploration. His return to London with a rich haul of plunder inspired imitation, which came with Thomas Cavendish's circumnavigation from 1586 to 1588. It also encouraged interest in the possibility of establishing a direct trade with the East Indies by sailing around the Cape of Good Hope. After several false starts, these efforts culminated in the formation of the East India Company in 1600.

In North America, meanwhile, Sir Walter Ralegh had attempted to establish a colony at Roanoke, off the coast of modern North Carolina. In 1584, Ralegh set out with Francis Amadas and Arthur Barlowe to reconnoitre the coastline. Their favorable report was followed by the establishment of a small colony at Roanoke in 1585. Among the settlers were John White and Thomas Hariot, who were sent by Ralegh to collect information on the region. White's sketches and maps, and Hariot's written account, of the land and its people dramatically unveiled a new world to Tudor England. Based on close and careful observation, their work was a major intellectual advance in geographical and scientific discovery. Unfortunately, the Roanoke settlement had a short life. Attracted by the potential profit to be made from privateering, Ralegh abandoned colonization in 1590. Although plunder dominated English maritime enterprise for the rest of the Tudor period, in the early seventeenth century several attempts to break into the North American fur trade led to the renewed exploration of the coast of New England. In 1602, for example, Bartholomew Gosnold explored the coastline around Cape Cod, sailing south beyond the cape to an island that he called Martha's Vineyard.

Compared with Spain or Portugal, England's contribution to European discovery and exploration during the sixteenth century was limited. This was, perhaps, inevitable given the lack of sustained royal support for maritime enterprise, and the limited understanding of geographical or scientific discovery in Tudor England. Nevertheless, a small group of merchants and mariners played a significant role in the European exploration of the wider world, notably in North America. And if the short-term tangible gains seemed small, the voyages of discovery and exploration set out during the Tudor period laid the basis for subsequent colonial and commercial expansion.

BIBLIOGRAPHY

Andrews, K.R. *Trade, Plunder and Settlement: Maritime Enterprise and the Genesis of the British Empire, 1480–1630.* 1984.

Morison, S.E. *The European Discovery of America: The Northern Voyages, A.D. 500–1600.* 1971.

Quinn, D.B. *England and the Discovery of America, 1481–1620.* 1970.

———. *New American World: A Documentary History of North America to 1612.* 5 vols. 1979.

Williamson, J.A., ed. *The Cabot Voyages and Bristol Discovery under Henry VII.* 1962.

John C. Appleby

SEE ALSO

Cabot, John; Cabot, Sebastian; Colonial Development; Davis, John; Drake, Sir Francis; Frobisher, Martin; Gilbert, Humphrey; Hakluyt, Richard; Hariot, Thomas; Ralegh, Sir Walter

Dissolution of the Monasteries

See Monastic Orders

Divorce

See Marriage and Marriage Law

D

Donne, John (1572–1631)

Although John Donne published nothing during the Tudor period, by 1603 he had written a significant number of the poems that would later gain him fame: his five satires, most of his love elegies and his epigrams, a body of verse letters to friends, and at least some of the lyrics that would ultimately be grouped together as his *Songs and Sonets*. Beginning in the 1590s, he circulated at least some of his poetry in manuscript, and by the beginning of the Jacobean period Donne had a reputation among the London literati as a witty writer of verse.

Donne was born into a Roman Catholic family. His father, who died when Donne was only four years old, was a London ironmonger who descended from Welsh gentility. His mother, a great-niece of Sir Thomas More, was a member of the prominent Heywood family. Her father was John Heywood, the epigrammatist and author of interludes. Shortly after Donne's father died, his mother married John Symminges, a London physician who had been educated at Oxford. In the fall of 1584, Donne entered Hart Hall, Oxford (later absorbed into Hertford College), where he studied for about three years. Because of his Catholicism, Donne could not sign the Oath of Supremacy and left Oxford without taking a degree. For the next four years, his whereabouts is less clear. Although Izaak Walton suggests that he attended Cambridge University for a while during this period, no record of such an association exists. Perhaps, as Dennis Flynn has recently argued, Donne took part in the conflict in the Low Countries, fighting on the side of Catholic Spain, and was present at the siege of Antwerp. His first portrait, made by William Marshall in 1591, shows him in the uniform of a soldier and has a Spanish inscription.

In 1591, Donne entered Thavies Inn, and the next year he transferred to Lincoln's Inn, where he remained until 1595, preparing himself for a career in public service. While at the Inns of Court, Donne made several friends among the young sons of prominent families. They were to constitute his first literary coterie, and many of them aided him in his later years. In 1596, Donne took part in the earl of Essex's expedition against Cadiz, and the next year he was a member of the Azores Islands expedition. In 1597, he became secretary to Sir Thomas Egerton, Elizabeth I's last lord keeper, perhaps through the recommendation of Sir Thomas's sons, who had become his friends at Lincoln's Inn. Although Donne frequently railed against the corruption at court in his verse letters and satires, he obviously enjoyed his position as secretary to one of the most powerful men of the time. From his position in York House, Egerton's London residence, he closely followed the earl of Essex's disastrous campaign in Ireland, exchanging guarded verse and prose letters with his friend from his Oxford days, Henry Wotton, who was in Essex's retinue. He was at York House when Essex was imprisoned there by Elizabeth, and was an eyewitness to the Earl's downfall.

Donne was a member of Parliament for Brackley, Northampton, in the fall of 1601; and in December of that same year he committed an act that began his own downfall, marrying without her father's permission Ann More, a niece of the lord keeper. He was dismissed from Egerton's service and briefly imprisoned before the marriage was finally ratified by the archbishop of Canterbury in April of 1602. When Elizabeth I died, Donne and his wife were living with a cousin, and for more than a decade they and their growing family lived virtually a hand-to-mouth existence, depending on the generosity of friends and patrons. Donne gradually converted to the Church of England; and in 1615, at the urging of King James, he became a priest. In 1621, he was appointed dean of St. Paul's, London, a position that he held until his death in 1631. During the second half of his life he continued to write some poetry, but after his ordination he devoted most of his time to the composition of sermons and meditative prose.

Although it constitutes less than half of his work, the poetry that Donne wrote during the last decade of the Tudor period is a major achievement. In style, it challenges the prevailing Spenserianism of the era by replacing allegory and decorative language with tough intellectual argument and "plain," though still lyrical and often fantastic, expression. Its hallmarks are learned imagery, pseudological syllogisms, ingenious conceits, and an exuberant wit that discovers connections between seemingly disparate ideas and objects. Thus, in an epigram, Donne can congratulate a soldier buried under a collapsing wall for having an entire town for his tomb; in a seduction lyric he can argue that a flea on his mistress's bosom is their marriage temple; and in a love elegy he can, in disgusting detail, prove that his friend is fortunate in having a loathsome mistress. At the same time, however, Donne also addresses serious questions and writes with feeling, although such emotion is always subject to intense intellectual scrutiny. In a satire, for example, he examines the rival claims of the competing religions of his day and concludes that the best course is to "doubt wisely"; in verse letters to his male intimates, he explores the delights and the obligations of his "second religion," friendship; and in the *Songs and Sonets* he limns the pains and the satisfactions of erotic love.

Many of the poems that Donne wrote in the 1590s seem to be products of the patronage system, displays of wit designed to curry favor with the rich and powerful who controlled the avenues to public employment and financial security. Whatever their origins, however, they fascinate as expressions of intellectual feeling and emotional thought. Donne's reputation as a poet flourished during the Jacobean and Caroline periods, and many of the poets of the day learned from him and paid him homage as the monarch of wit. His "metaphysical" style displeased Reformation and Enlightenment arbiters of style, however, and for 200 years Donne was largely ignored as a poet. His reputation was revived early in the twentieth century, when his poetry was championed by T.S. Eliot and a host of academic critics, and he is now recognized as the major poet writing between Edmund Spenser and John Milton.

BIBLIOGRAPHY
Bald, R.C. *John Donne: A Life.* 1970.
Carey, John. *John Donne: Life, Mind, and Art.* 1981.
Flynn, Dennis. *John Donne and the Ancient Catholic Nobility.* 1995.
Hester, M. Thomas. *Kinde Pitty and Brave Scorn: John Donne's Satyres.* 1982.
Marotti, Arthur F. *John Donne, Coterie Poet.* 1986.
Roberts, John R. *John Donne: An Annotated Bibliography of Modern Criticism, 1912–1967.* 1973.
———, ed. *Essential Articles for the Study of John Donne's Poetry.* 1975.
———. *John Donne: An Annotated Bibliography of Modern Criticism, 1968–1978.* 1982.
Smith, A.J., ed. *John Donne: Essays in Celebration.* 1972.
Stringer, Gary A., gen. ed. *The Variorum Edition of the Poetry of John Donne.* 1995.
Summers, Claude J., and Ted-Larry Pebworth, eds. *The Eagle and the Dove: Reassessing John Donne.* 1986.

Ted-Larry Pebworth

SEE ALSO
Devereux, Robert; Egerton, Sir Thomas; Elegy; Epigrams; Heywood, John; Inns of Court; Lyric; Satire; Sonnet Sequences

Douai-Rheims Bible
See Bible Translations

Douglas Family

The Douglas family first came to prominence during the first Scottish war of independence, (1306–1314), when Sir James Douglas fought under Robert I. Their influence rested on their power base in southeastern Scotland, from which they drew resources in men and in kind, as well as on the intricate network of allegiances common in early modern Scotland. By 1485, the senior figure was Archibald, fifth earl of Angus (d. 1513), often identified as "Bell-the-Cat," a seventeenth-century sobriquet that refers inaccurately to the fifth earl's role in the first rebellion against James III in 1482, when he was allied to the king's brother, the duke of Albany. Angus was also involved in the successful rebellion of 1488, and, under James IV, managed to be both chancellor (1493–1497) and a royal prisoner on Bute (1502–1509).

Since his son was killed at the battle of Flodden Field, the sixth earl of Angus (d. 1566/7), also Archibald, was the fifth earl's grandson, and Gavin Douglas's nephew. He married the queen dowager, Margaret Tudor, in 1514. Their daughter, Lady Margaret Douglas, married the earl of Lennox and became the mother of Lord Darnley. To protect his place in government during the minority of James V, the sixth earl kidnapped the king in 1526. On reaching his majority in 1528, James took revenge: he exiled the earl and his brother George to England and had their sister Janet burned in 1537. The brothers returned during Mary's minority (1542–1561), remaining favorable to reforming and anglophile interests.

The seventh earl of Angus was George's son. He died young, leaving his son as the eighth earl (d. 1588), who later became associated with the ultra-Protestant faction. He was the ward of his uncle, James Douglas, fourth earl of Morton (executed 1581). Morton had spent two years (1548–1550) as a hostage at the court of Edward VI, where he developed an English accent. Despite Protestant sympathies, he was chancellor under Mary Stuart (1563–1566), during which time he participated in David Rizzio's murder, and after Mary's abdication (1567–1572), when he was a central figure in the King's Party. He was regent for James VI (1572–1578), and maintained his importance in government until the arrival from France in 1579 of Esmé Stuart, later earl of Lennox. He was executed in 1581, allegedly as an accessory to Henry Darnley's murder, but also to suit Lennox's political aims. The fluctuations in the Douglas's fortunes in the sixteenth century are no more extreme than those in the fifteenth century, demonstrating the precarious nature of early modern Scottish politics, even for the established nobility.

D

BIBLIOGRAPHY

Donaldson, Gordon. *All the Queen's Men: Power and Politics in Mary Stewart's Scotland.* 1983.

Donaldson, Gordon. *Scotland: James V–James VII.* 1990.

Hewitt, George R. *Scotland under Morton, 1572–1580.* 1982.

Macdougall, N.A.T. *James III: A Political Study.* 1982.

———. *James IV.* 1997.

Nicola Royan

SEE ALSO

Douglas, Gavin; Flodden Field, Battle of; James IV; James V; James VI and I; Rizzio, David ; Scotland, History of; Mary Queen of Scots

Douglas, Gavin (1475/6–1522)

Scottish poet and clergyman, Gavin Douglas was the third son of the fifth earl of Angus. He was probably born in Tantallon Castle in East Lothian, one of the homes of the powerful and ambitious Douglas family. He attended St. Andrews University (1490–1494), then studied in Paris. He was named dean of Dunkeld in 1497, and provost of St. Giles in Edinburgh (March 1503), an appointment possibly connected to his poem *The Palis of Honoure* (c. 1501), dedicated to James IV. In 1512–1513, Douglas translated Vergil's *Aeneid,* with verse prologues of his own, an achievement of international importance (it was printed in London in 1553). The English poet Henry Howard, earl of Surrey, consulted it in manuscript for his own (incomplete) translation.

Douglas rapidly filled the political vacuum created by the battle of Flodden Field and became a statesman rather than poet. His nephew, Archibald Douglas, sixth earl of Angus, in 1514 married Margaret Tudor, widow of James IV of Scotland, and Gavin Douglas's fortunes temporarily became linked to those of the queen. Invoking the support of her brother, Henry VIII, Margaret petitioned the pope to appoint Gavin Douglas abbot of Arbroath after he had been unsuccessfully nominated to the archbishopric of St. Andrews, but this was heavily contested by rival candidates. Douglas was even imprisoned (1515–1516), but was eventually appointed bishop of Dunkeld (1516). Increasingly involved in factional politics, Douglas traveled to England in 1521, where he fell victim to the plague. Although he had been befriended in London by such well-known writers as John Major and Polydore Vergil and was in contact with Cardinal Thomas Wolsey, he died an anguished exile in Lord Dacre's house in September 1522.

BIBLIOGRAPHY

Bawcutt, Priscilla. *Gavin Douglas: A Critical Study.* 1976

———, ed. *The Shorter Poems of Gavin Douglas.* Scottish Text Society. 1967.

Coldwell, David F.C., ed. *Virgil's Aeneid. Translated into Scottish Verse by Gavin Douglas, Bishop of Dunkeld.* 4 vols. Scottish Text Society. 1957–1964.

Parkinson, David, ed. *Gavin Douglas. The Palis of Honoure.* 1992.

Small, John, ed. *The Poetical Works of Gavin Douglas, Bishop of Dunkeld.* 4 vols. 1874; repr. 1970.

Scheps, Walter, and Anna J. Looney. *Middle Scots Poets. A Reference Guide to James I of Scotland, Robert Henryson, William Dunbar, and Gavin Douglas.* 1986.

Theo van Heijnsbergen

SEE ALSO

Classical Literature, Influence of; Epic; Flodden Field, Battle of; Margaret Tudor; Vergil, Polydore

Dowland, John (1563–1626)

England's greatest composer of solo lute works and ayres, John Dowland was (by his own testimony) born in 1563, possibly in Westminster. He converted to Catholicism during a stay in Paris from 1580 to 1584, although he was later to set Anglican texts, and Sir Robert Sidney, of an unimpeachably Protestant family, stood as godfather to his son, Robert. Dowland earned the bachelor of music degree in 1588 from Christ Church, Oxford; he was called Dr. Dowland in 1621, although it cannot be established from which university his doctorate was awarded. When Thomas East's *The Whole Booke of Psalmes* was published in 1592, six of Dowland's harmonizations were included. However, in 1594, Dowland failed to win an appointment as lutenist to the queen; bitterly disappointed, he went to the court of Henry Julio, duke of Brunswick, and then to the court of Moritz, landgrave of Hesse, at Kassel. Eventually reaching Florence, he befriended a group of exiled recusants plotting to assassinate Elizabeth I. Frightened by the implications of their plot, he fled to Nuremberg and disclosed all to Sir Robert Cecil. After returning to England in 1596 or 1597, he failed once again to be appointed lutenist to the queen.

In 1597, he published *The First Booke of Songes or Ayres of Foure Partes with Tableture for the Lute,* establishing the standard format for the lute ayre: melody and lute tablature on one page, with altus, tenor, and bassus vocal parts for an alternative four-part performance on the facing page. By November of 1598, he was lutenist to Christian IV of Denmark; from there he sent his wife *The Second Booke of Songs or Ayres* in 1600. He was still in Denmark in 1603 when *The Third and Last Booke of Songs* was published, but was dismissed, financially destitute, in 1606. At some time between 1609 and 1612 he entered the service of Theophilus Howard, Lord Walden, and was finally appointed one of the king's lutes in October of 1612. His fourth book of songs, *A Pilgrimes Solace,* was published that same year. However, having attained his life's ambition, he published little else. His last known performance was for the funeral ceremonies of James I in May of 1625. He died not long afterward and was buried on February 20, 1626.

A complex personality, Dowland was emotionally volatile, self-centered, and given to fits of melancholy. His music comprises eighty-four lute ayres; seventy-nine pieces for lute; fourteen harmonizations of psalms, canticles, and prayers; and thirty-three consort pieces, including the twenty-one in his collection *Lachrimae or Seaven Teares* for five viols, or violins, and lute. The "seaven teares" are fantasies on the instantly and deservedly famous *Flow my teares* from the second book of ayres, and they exhibit Dowland's typically contrapuntal approach to composition, allied with the constant use of momentary dissonance. Many of the solo lute works, only thirteen of which were printed during his lifetime, are cast in dance forms such as pavane, galliard, almain, and jig. Of his seven contrapuntal fantasies, two, *Forlorne Hope Fancye* and *Farwell,* are built upon chromatic subjects. Not unsurprisingly, despite the cheerful charm of such songs as *Fine knacks for ladies* and *Say love, if ever thou didst find,* the greatest of his ayres (*Come heavy sleepe, Sleepe wayward thoughts, Sorrow stay*) dwell on death, darkness, and tears. *In darknesse let mee dwell,* from *A Musicall Banquet* of 1610, which was edited by Dowland's son, Robert, is his masterpiece. It ends on what is now labeled an unresolved dominant and melds words, harmonies, and melody into a seamless and astonishingly original expression of profound grief.

BIBLIOGRAPHY

Dart, Thurston, and Nigel Fortune, eds. *John Dowland: Ayres for Four Voices.* Musica Britannica, vol. 6. 2nd edition. 1963.
Fellowes, Edmund H., ed.; revised by Thurston Dart. *The English lute-songs,* ser. 1: 1–2, 5–6, 10–12, 14. 1965–1969.
Poulton, Diana, and B. Lam, eds. *The Collected Lute Music of John Dowland.* 1974.
Poulton, Diana. *John Dowland.* 2nd edition. 1982.
Spink, Ian. *English Song: Dowland to Purcell.* 1984.
Tayler, David S. "The solo lute music of John Dowland." Dissertation, University of California, Berkeley. 1992.
Ward, John. "A Dowland Miscellany." *Journal of the Lute Society of America,* vol. 10, pp. 5–153.

Laura S. Yoens

SEE ALSO
Air; Consort and Consort Song; Dance Music; Song

Drake, Francis (c. 1540–1596)

One of the greatest mariners of Tudor England, Francis Drake's career illuminates many of the strengths and weaknesses of Elizabethan maritime enterprise. Born near Tavistock, he was brought up in Kent after his father, Edmund, fled the southwest following the rebellion of 1549. Drake inherited his father's staunch Protestantism, which was to be a powerful influence on his later career. Living in straitened circumstances, he spent his early years as an apprentice in the coasting and cross-channel trades. In the early 1560s, he found employment with his kinsmen, the Hawkins family of Plymouth. In 1566 and 1567, he served on two slaving voyages to Guinea and Spanish America. During the latter voyage he was made captain of the fifty-ton *Judith.* The venture ended in disaster when the expedition was caught in the harbor of San Juan de Ulua, on the coast of Mexico, by a Spanish fleet. Only two English vessels escaped, the *Minion* under John Hawkins and the *Judith.* The episode ended Hawkins's interest in slaving, strengthening the piratical tendency in English transatlantic enterprise.

Taking advantage of these circumstances, Drake led three voyages to the West Indies in 1570, 1571, and 1572. Though justified as legitimate retaliation for San Juan de Ulua, these ventures amounted to a private campaign of plunder that culminated in the seizure of the Spanish mule train transporting silver and gold across the Panama isthmus in March 1573, with the assistance of a group of French Huguenots and a band of *cimarrones,* or runaway slaves. Although much of the plunder had to be buried, and was never recovered, the proceeds from the raid amounted to about £20,000. Drake's share made him a wealthy man, but improved Anglo-Spanish relations led him to withdraw from this phase of Caribbean raiding. He maintained a low profile for the next few years. Changing commercial and political conditions, which were increasingly anti-Spanish in character, allowed him to set out in November 1577,

D

with the discreet support of Elizabeth I and the backing of prominent courtiers and naval men, on an expedition to plunder Spanish trade and settlements along the vulnerable Pacific coast of South America. He returned three years later, after the first English circumnavigation, with a huge haul of plunder. Despite Spanish protests he was knighted by the queen on April 4, 1581, and acclaimed by the public. The voyage boosted English confidence, but exacerbated tension between England and Spain.

Drake played a leading role in the subsequent maritime war with Spain. In 1585, he led a major expedition to the West Indies, pillaging and partly destroying Santo Domingo and Cartagena, and severely denting Spain's international reputation. The Cadiz expedition of 1587, in which many Spanish ships were destroyed or damaged, delayed the sailing of the Armada. During the Armada campaign itself, Drake commanded one of the four English squadrons, and served with distinction as vice admiral. But the Portugal expedition of 1589, ostensibly to destroy the survivors of the Armada, was a failure. On his last voyage, in 1595, he jointly commanded an expedition to the Caribbean with Sir John Hawkins, with the intention of seizing control of Panama. The voyage was marred by antagonism between its leaders, both of whom died during its unsuccessful course. Despite the failure of the voyage, after his death Drake became a folk hero whose exploits attained legendary status.

Drake's maritime career was remarkable. His seamanship was widely admired, though his tough and uncompromising leadership was not to everyone's liking. Ashore he became a prominent figure in the southwest, serving as M.P. in 1581, in 1584, and in 1593, when he sat on several committees concerning supply and maritime matters. He was survived by his second wife, Elizabeth Sydenham; his first wife, Mary Newman, died in 1583. There were no children by either marriage.

BIBLIOGRAPHY

Andrews, Kenneth R. *Drake's Voyages: A Reassessment of Their Place in Elizabethan Maritime Expansion.* 1967.
————. "The Aims of Drake's Expedition of 1577–1580." *American Historical Review*, vol. 73, pp. 724–741.
Corbett, J.S. *Drake and the Tudor Navy.* 2 vols. 1898.
Cummins, John. *Francis Drake: The Lives of a Hero.* 1995.
Martin, Colin, and Geoffrey Parker. *The Spanish Armada.* 1988.
Sugden, John. *Sir Francis Drake.* 1990.

John C. Appleby

Armada, Spanish; Discovery and Exploration; Foreign Relations and Diplomacy; Hawkins, John; Piracy

Drama, History of

From fifteenth-century mysteries and moralities to such Elizabethan masterpieces as *Doctor Faustus* and *Henry IV,* Tudor playwrights brought the conflict between elite and popular cultures to the English stage. By the time William Shakespeare wrote *A Midsummer Night's Dream* (c. 1594–1595), his complacent aristocrats might ridicule the mechanicals' performance of "Pyramus and Thisbe," but in the process, they lampooned their own distant origins in the craft cycles and other amateur ventures that laid the basis for the high Elizabethan theater. The drama that Shakespeare and his contemporaries inherited amalgamated high and low influences, morality plays and Senecan tragedy, rustic mummeries and courtly masques, popular romances and chronicle plays.

Because of its synthetic nature, Tudor drama resisted the conventions that neoclassical theorists upheld as the basis of fine theater. According to Sir Philip Sidney, English playwrights produced "neither right tragedies, nor right comedies." On the Continent, the court's domination of the theater ensured strict adherence to the classical unities of time, place, and action. These conventions distinguished the "verisimilitude" of elite performances from the "improbability" of romances and other popular entertainments that represented multiple locations and actions—some tragic, some comic—on a single stage. In England, however, popular dramatic traditions flourished. Within "two-hours' traffic," the typical Tudor play represented multiple actions that sprawled over several locations and encompassed months or even years. Low comic subplots punctuated the most serious actions, and, in Sidney's phrase, mingled "kings and clowns."

Critics and historians once celebrated the Tudor drama's hybrid character because it supposedly arose from an organic society whose universal belief in hierarchy neutralized conflicts among ranks, classes, occupational groups, and genders. More recent scholars have treated the sixteenth-century stage as a site of social confrontation. As Marxists, feminists, new historicists, and cultural materialists have reminded us, successive Tudor regimes recognized the drama's subversive potential. They tried to control it through the master of the revels, an official who licensed theaters, companies, and individual plays. Censorship was pervasive with respect to religion, domestic politics, and international affairs. In 1597, the Privy Council imprisoned Ben Jonson for his contributions to the allegedly seditious *Isle of Dogs*. A few years later, the council questioned the Lord Chamberlain's Men about their performance of a play about Richard II's deposition—probably Shakespeare's—on the eve of the 1601 Essex rebellion. As these examples suggest, the Tudors feared the drama as much as they respected its potential for aggrandizing their authority.

Although the censors could suppress topical allusions and overt representations of rebellion and deposition, they could not police the drama's more subtle and pervasive interrogation of Tudor power. The more scholars have come to see prolonged social crisis rather than organic harmony in the period, the more they have emphasized the drama's engagement with conflicts over social and geographic mobility, the distribution of wealth, the pace of religious reformation, the changing status of women, and the emergence of a rigidly dichotomized discourse of gender. Few of the period's plays were inherently conservative or radical. Drama often represented competing positions without necessarily advocating any single one. Even when plays like *The Play of the Weather, Tamburlaine,* or *The Taming of the Shrew* posed radical social alternatives only to contain them within a conservative framework, they publicaly disseminated subversive views. Before the devils dragged Marlowe's Faustus to hell, for example, he voiced skeptical opinions that no Elizabethan could print with impunity.

The recent emphasis on Tudor drama as a site of social conflict has encouraged revisionary accounts of its historical development. An older model explained the transition from morality plays to Marlovian and Shakespearean tragedy as the triumph of mimesis over allegory. According to this view, dramatists perfected their art by abandoning allegorical types and creating instead individualized characters. More recent theatrical historians have analyzed the drama's development as a response to larger social forces. The late medieval theater that formed the basis for sixteenth-century playwrighting, for instance, foregrounded a competition between clerical and vernacular cultures. The mystery cycles—in which guildsmen enacted such biblical episodes as Noah's flood, the Nativity, and the Passion—threatened the church's monopoly on religion by providing an opportunity for the laity to translate and interpret Scripture. Although never condemned by the church, they provoked an aesthetic backlash in the more socially conservative morality plays. In plays like *Mankind* (late 1460s),

Everyman (c. 1520), and *Mundus et Infans* (printed c. 1522), virtues pontificating in Latinate English contend against colloquial vices for possession of the human soul. Some playwrights characterized the virtues as clerics and the vices as urban ruffians.

In general, the pre-Reformation moralities pitted older, often monastic values such as economic cooperation and communal ownership against the more competitive, urban culture that produced the mysteries. *Mankind* and *Everyman,* for example, indict the acquisitiveness of a developing market economy. Later playwrights adapted the moralities' central opposition between virtues and vices to new kinds of social conflict. The interludes produced in Thomas More's humanist circle, for instance, used the basic morality plot of a central character's temptation, fall, and regeneration to celebrate new social configurations and the "new learning" that supported them. In *The Nature of the Four Elements* (c. 1518), John Rastell transformed the older, spiritual psychomachia over Mankind or Everyman's soul into a secular conflict over Humanity's education. The stakes were no longer salvation but intellectual development and the personal advancement that it underwrites in a more fluid society. The vices were no longer agents of the devil so much as impediments to scholarship, like Ignorance and Sensual Appetite. In a conspicuous turn against the medieval past, Rastell cast the outmoded scholasticism that informed the older drama as learning's greatest enemy. His preface urged his audience to abandon theology for physics, meteorology, geology, cosmology, geography, navigation, and other practical fields that would improve society and enrich their individual practitioners.

Humanist dramatists like Rastell and Henry Medwall typically celebrated education as the route to personal advancement in a newly established meritocracy. As the Tudors created a new class of low-born bureaucrats to replace aristocrats in the realm's administration, plays like the *Four Elements,* Medwall's *Nature,* and *Fulgens and Lucrece* (c. 1495, printed 1512), and *Gentylnes and Nobylyte* (probably written by John Heywood, but published by Rastell in 1525), ratified the social and political revolution by privileging individual merit over birthright. In one play after another, virtuous men from humble backgrounds triumph over decadent aristocrats. Medwall's *Nature,* for example, transforms the medieval vice Pride into the *arriviste's* stereotype of the older aristocrat whose rank cannot offset his personal ignobility. In *Fulgens and Lucrece,* the earliest surviving English play set in ancient Rome, the heroine chooses the low-born Gyas over the

D

noble Cornelius on the basis of his greater inner worth. Such plays reinforced the values of a whole *arriviste* class that owed its privileges to education and individual talent.

Not every playwright fully endorsed the new meritocracy. In *Magnyfycence* (c. 1519), John Skelton transformed the morality play into an indictment of the Tudor's dependence on newly arrived bureaucrats and advisers. Magnyfycence—a transparent cover for Henry VIII—falls into poverty and despair when he rejects his trustworthy counselor Measure and relies instead on the socially ambitious vices Countenaunce, Crafty Conveyaunce, and Clokyd Colusyon. The Catholic playwright John Heywood crafted a more subtle critique of absolutist practice in *The Play of the Weather*. When different petitioners ask Jupiter to change the weather so that it will foster their particular occupations, he prevents meteorological disaster by preserving the status quo, a mixed weather pattern that pleases one person one day and another person the next. Heywood ostensibly compliments the king by allowing his divine surrogate to solve a seemingly unresolvable conflict. But the playwright also undercuts this compliment to the king's Solomonic wisdom by making Jupiter vain and pompous. Well before the Elizabethans instituted their systematic control of the stage, the drama proved that it could challenge as well as endorse the dominant social structure.

Whereas the playwrights examined thus far typically wrote for coterie audiences associated with the court or private households, a humanist emphasis on classical learning as a route to social advancement also dominated plays written for schools, colleges, and the Inns of Court. By providing students an opportunity to advertise their verbal and rhetorical talent, such plays provided credentials for the nation's future governing, administrative, and professional classes. They were a major route for disseminating and displaying the knowledge of classical antiquity that differentiated the elite from the uneducated masses. Proficient in Latin and often knowledgeable in Greek, the students embraced Plautus and Terence as the supreme models for comedy and Seneca for tragedy. Plays like Nicholas Udall's *Ralph Roister Doister* (c. 1553) and *Gammer Gurton's Needle* popularized such comic stock characters as the *miles gloriosus,* the tricky servant, and the parasite. At the same time, tragedies like Thomas Sackville's and Thomas Norton's *Gorboduc* (performed at the Inner Temple, 1562), Thomas Preston's *Cambises* (presented before Elizabeth by members of the Inner Temple in 1562), and Thomas Hughes's *The Misfortunes of Arthur* (presented by Francis Bacon and other members

of Gray's Inn in 1588) created a taste for the five-act structure, declamatory speeches, editorializing choruses, ghosts, and gory violence particularly associated with the Roman playwright Seneca.

Although these Plautine comedies and Senecan tragedies were first performed for elite audiences, they soon influenced both the public and private theaters that flourished in London during the final decades of the Tudor century. Many of the cities leading playwrights–including John Lyly, George Peele, Robert Greene, and Marlowe—were educated at the universities or the Inns of Court. In writing for nonacademic audiences, they brought classical forms into a quintessentially Elizabethan dialogue with indigenous comic and tragic traditions. With structural debts to Roman comedy and allusions to Ovid, Cicero, and Pliny, for example, Lyly's *Endymion* (1587/88) epitomized the classical foundations of Tudor humanism. But its social comedy depends on a ludicrous contrast between Endymion's Ovidian situation as a shepherd in love with the moon and Sir Thopas's Chaucerian situation as dreamer obsessed with an erotic image of the enchantress Dipsas. By the 1580s, English drama had become the hybrid entity that neoclassical purists like Sidney scorned. It produced its complex effects through often shocking juxtapositions of classical, continental, and indigenous influences.

Lyly wrote *Endymion* for the most elite occasion imaginable, a private performance before the queen by the Boys of St. Paul's, a private children's company. In this context, its conspicuous classicism reinforced traditional class boundaries by assuming the educated audience's familiarity with Latin subtexts. But Tudor classicism acquired a more complex social valence when writers like Thomas Kyd, Marlowe, Shakespeare, and Jonson reinvented it for the public theaters. Just as the mystery cycles vernacularized scripture for an upstart laity a century earlier, plays like Thomas Lodge's *The Wounds of Civil War* (c. 1585–1589), Shakespeare's *The Comedy of Errors* (c. 1589–1593), and Jonson's *Sejanus* (performed soon after Elizabeth's death in 1603) brought classical forms, dramaturgical techniques, and plots to a socially diverse audience.

In the process, the plays also introduced London audiences to classical history and politics. The theater provided one of the avenues through which citizens could imagine greater participation in political life. The tide of English history plays that began with the Armada and lasted throughout the rest of Elizabeth's reign especially contributed to the nation's political literacy. Scholars like E.M.W. Tillyard once argued that these plays celebrated the unity that Elizabeth had brought to a nation divided in the fifteenth century by civil war and in the earlier sixteenth century by religious controversy. According to this view, their focus on medieval rebellions reaffirmed a universal belief in the sanctity of kingship, social hierarchy, and the evil of resistance to royal authority. More recent scholars have denied that the plays served as dramatized homilies against disobedience. They have noted instead how late Tudor drama resists absolutism by stressing the fallibility of individual rulers, the dependence of monarchical power on the consent of the governed, and above all, the sheer theatricality of kingship. By drawing recurrent and unsettling parallels between sovereigns and the actors who portrayed them, works like Marlowe's *Edward II* and Shakespeare's *Henriad, Richard II, Henry IV,* parts 1 and 2, and *Henry V,*) suggested that all kings were finally players and that power rested in a complex relationship with illusion. This demystification marked the first step in the nation's turn from absolutism toward the later seventeenth-century investment of sovereignty in the English people.

By the end of the sixteenth century, Tudor dramatists had attained an intertextual complexity that underwrote the rich characterizations, parallelings of action, and sudden shifts of tone and genre commonly identified as the hallmarks of the Elizabethan theater. A figure like Falstaff draws on the range of popular and elite, indigenous and neoclassical traditions examined throughout this survey. As a comic character whose bawdy puns and mockery disrupt the tragic rhythms of Shakespeare's *Henriad,* he incorporates such seemingly incongruent influences as the medieval Vice and the Plautine *miles gloriosus.* Glancing back to Chaucer and forward to Dickens, he stands, like so many other characters in late Elizabethan drama, on the boundary between two aesthetic and political representational orders, an older one that he inherited and a new one that he helped to create.

BIBLIOGRAPHY

Bevington, David. *Tudor Drama and Politics: A Critical Approach to Topical Meaning.* 1968.
Braunmuller, A.R., and Michael Hattaway, eds. *The Cambridge Companion to English Renaissance Drama.* 1990.
Bristol, Michael D. *Carnival and Theater: Plebian Culture and the Structure of Authority in Renaissance England.* 1985.
Chambers, E.K. *The Elizabethan Stage.* 4 vols. 1923.
Cohen, Walter. *Drama of a Nation: Public Theater in Renaissance England and Spain.* 1985.
Dollimore, Jonathan. *Radical Tragedy: Religion, Ideology, and Power in the Drama of Shakespeare and His Contemporaries.* 1989.
Hattaway, Michael. *Elizabethan Popular Theatre: Plays in Performance.* 1982.
Kastan, David, and Peter Stallybrass, eds. *Staging the Renaissance: Reinterpretations of Elizabethan and Jacobean Drama.* 1991.

John Watkins

SEE ALSO
Censorship; Classical Literature, Influence of; Inns of Court; Patronage; Rastell, John; Theater Companies, Adult; Theatre Companies, Boys; Theaters; individual playwrights

Drama, Staging and Performance

The opening in 1996–1997 of the reconstructed Globe Theatre on London's South Bank, following the discovery of the foundations of the Rose Theatre and the Globe near the foot of Southwark Bridge, has aroused considerable interest and even excitement among both students of Elizabethan drama and the general public.

Much research had gone into the construction of the new Globe, based as it was on a century's scholarship by such notables as E.K. Chambers, W.W. Greg, G.E. Bentley, Richard Hosley, C. Walter Hodges, Andrew Gurr, Herbert Berry, Peter Thomson, John Orrell, and others. The idea for reconstructing the Globe originated with the American actor Sam Wanamaker, who lived only long enough to see the cornerstone laid and the first bays put up. The Third Globe, as it is sometimes called (the first, built in 1599, burned down in 1613 and was rebuilt), follows as closely as possible the proportions and layout of the original theater, though not quite the size—it can hold about 1,700 spectators, whereas the original might have held as many as 3,000. It has a thatched roof over three galleries circumscribing a spacious playing area and the tiring house, where dressing rooms are located and props are stored. The large raised stage on which two colored columns support a huge canopy, or "heavens," dominates the yard, open to the sky, in which up to 700 spectators may stand. Above the stage on a line with the middle gallery are the "Lords' Room" for specially privileged spectators and spaces for musicians and balcony

D

scenes. In a small room above the heavens, a cannon overlooks the scene, discharging a shot when appropiate. (During a performance of *King Henry VIII* in 1613, a cannon shot caused the thatch to catch fire and burned down the first Globe.) On the stage, actors enter from doors on either side of the back wall, and in the middle of the wall a "discovery space" also permits entrances as well as setting out of props, such as a throne or a bed. A "trap" further permits entrances from "below" or the thrusting up of props. Around the stage in the yard stand those who pay a minimum fee–not a penny, as in Shakespeare's time, but five pounds sterling. But just as in Shakespeare's time, they stand throughout the performance, a very different experience of the action from those seated somewhat more comfortably on benches in the galleries surrounding the yard. These "groundlings" have felt much more involved with the actors and found that standing for several hours was not a serious problem (the new Globe schedules intervals after each act during most performances, unlike the uninterrupted "two hours' traffic" of Shakespeare's time).

Of course, the authenticity of the experience, whether for the groundlings or those in the galleries, is hardly exact. Four hundred years make a difference, not only in the way language is pronounced, as Helge Kokeritz and Fausto Cercignani have shown, but in many other respects. It still requires a leap of the historical imagination to return to the origins of this Globe and its forebears, which include a number of theaters erected on the South Bank and elsewhere in London in Shakespeare's period. The so-called public playhouses, moreover, were neither the first nor the only places where professional actors performed. The development of the theater and its productions already had a long history before the first playhouse, simply called The Theatre, was constructed in Shoreditch in 1576.

We need not go back as far as the medieval performances of mystery and miracle plays to understand the nature of Tudor playhouses and performances, although the history of modern drama properly begins there. By the sixteenth century, secularization had already exerted a strong influence on the drama in England and on the Continent. Using the spaces provided by innyards or booths at fairs, and by the halls of great houses and palaces, traveling troupes of players performed a variety of dramas, setting up portable platforms and scaffolding, when necessary, to do so. To avoid being arrested and punished as vagabonds, the players sought the protection of noblemen; hence, companies of players came to be known

as the Lord Admiral's Men, or the Lord Strange's Men, the Lord Pembroke's Men, and so forth. In 1583, Sir Francis Walsingham directed the master of revels to form a company comprised of the best actors in London—Robert Wilson, Richard Tarlton, John Laneham, and others. They became known as the Queen's Men and enjoyed her patronage and protection. With the accession of James in 1603, Shakespeare's company, formerly the Lord Chamberlain's Men, was newly titled the King's Men, and was one of only three companies permitted to perform in the capital. Like the late queen, her nephew enjoyed the theater, and there are records of many performances given at court in James's time as well as Elizabeth's.

Andrew Gurr is probably right in saying that when James Burbage built The Theatre he was motivated more by commerce than by art. The structure he built allowed him greater control over the audience, who now paid their penny at the door instead of to those who moved among them, hat in hand. But while we tend to think of playhouses like the Globe as the home of a single company, this was not true at first. The Curtain, built soon after and quite nearby The Theatre, and the playhouses that followed—the Rose, the Swan, the Fortune, and others—were host to various companies at various times. Shakespeare's company, for example, is known to have played at Newington Butts and the Rose as well as the Globe; the theaters were also used from time to time for purposes other than plays—for fencing matches and bearbaiting and other spectacles. Because of the city fathers' antagonism against plays and players, which they considered a corrupting influence, the large public amphitheaters had to be built outside the city walls. The small "private" ones, however, like Blackfriars or Whitefriars, originally used for companies of boys, like the choristers of St. Paul's, could be found within the city. Performances in the public theaters took place in the afternoon starting at about two o'clock to take advantage of daylight; the indoor private theaters were lit by candlelight, as were performances held at court or in the great halls of noble houses.

Acting companies varied in size, but London-based companies could include as many as twelve men and several boys; no actresses, so far as we know, appeared on the London stage until after the Restoration in 1660. Boys played the parts of women as well as children. Since many plays called for larger casts, doubling of parts was commonplace. An actor in Hamlet, for example, might play the roles of Marcellus, Voltemand, and Lucianus. Because plays ran only for a few performances—a good run might be five or six—new plays or revivals of old ones were in constant rehearsal. Players must have had extraordinary memories to perform in such repertory companies as those in Tudor England. They probably resorted to ad-libbing to some extent, as repertory actors do now when a line or cue escapes them, though the chief offenders—as Hamlet says—were the clowns, who spoke more than was set down for them once they got an audience going.

Actors rarely saw the complete text of a play. Instead, only their parts and cues were copied out for them; the bookkeeper held the complete playscript, amended and annotated during rehearsals from the fair copy of the playwright's manuscript, which the author himself might have revised and overwritten. A "plot," or outline of the action scene by scene, was posted backstage to alert both actors and prompter in the course of the play regarding entrances, props, and the like. The differences among several versions of Shakespeare's plays, such as *Romeo and Juliet, Hamlet, King Lear,* and others printed before the Folio of 1623, show how scripts could be and often were altered between composition and performance, and from original staging to later revivals. Further evidence is available from such promptbooks that survive, like that of *The Second Maiden's Tragedy,* reproduced in a Malone Society reprint.

Accounts differ regarding the style of acting in Tudor England, but it appears that the broad style, which today we would call overacting and compare to the acting in silent films, was perceived as archaic by Shakespeare's time, as both the verse and the action of "the Murder of Gonzago" in *Hamlet* indicate. Hamlet's famous advice to the players, still valuable, is a critique in part of that older style of performing and a powerful recommendation for a more natural style. The two most famous actors in the late sixteenth century, Shakespeare's fellow shareholder Richard Burbage, and the leading actor of their rival company, Edward Alleyn, probably had no single style of acting but adapted performance to the characters they played. Bottom's reference in *A Midsummer Night's Dream* to a tyrant's rant (1.2.24 ff.) doubtless has for its basis an older tradition, as does Buckingham's reference to the antics of the "deep tragedian" in *Richard III,* (3.5.5–11). On the other hand, Ben Jonson's eulogy on the boy actor who played old men so convincingly that he died young suggests the alternative style of natural playing that had become prominent by the seventeenth century. Nevertheless, what was "natural" to an Elizabethan might seem artificial today, much as some Tudor styles of writing also appear unrealistic now.

Before the theaters were built and troupes necessarily carried with them such costumes and props as they had, performances took place on essentially bare stages. But with the advent of more permanent structures, greater use of props became possible, though performances never approached the kind of staging familiar to us today or even that of productions that used the movable scenery that became available late in the seventeenth century. Compensating for this lack, costumes were elaborate and expensive, and they were typically in the fashions of the time. True, for an historical tragedy like *Julius Caesar,* something resembling a toga might be draped over contemporary dress, but the historical imagination did not take hold of theatrical presentation until well into the nineteenth century. Actors, using the language of their country and their time, costumed themselves accordingly, and this fact may lend some support to modern dress productions of Tudor plays today.

To consider the kinds of plays Elizabethan actors performed is to run through Polonius's category of tragedy, comedy, history, pastoral, and all the combinations they permit. Early in the Tudor period morality plays were still prevalent, and plays in Latin, following classical models (e.g., Seneca, Terence, Plautus), were written and performed by scholars in schools and the two universities of Oxford and Cambridge. But scholars, like the author of *Gammer Gurton's Needle,* a fellow of Christ's College, Cambridge, could also draw on popular subjects and homely characters; indeed, the mixture of the classical and native traditions of drama became one of the strengths of later Tudor drama. The first use of blank verse in a tragedy appears in Thomas Sackville and Thomas Norton's *Gorboduc* (1561), but it was not until decades later that Marlowe's "mighty line" transformed it and made it the staple of serious drama. By the 1580s and 1590s, a wide range of theatrical entertainment became available to playgoers, sponsored by such entrepreneurs as Philip Henslowe and the various acting companies, who commissioned or otherwise paid dramatists for new works. Many of the plays of the period are lost, known to us only by their titles as recorded in the Stationers Company register or elsewhere. But the plays of Robert Greene, George Peele, Thomas Kyd, George Chapman, Ben Jonson, and Thomas Dekker, as well as those by Marlowe and Shakespeare, provided audiences with a rich fare and enormous variety. Unlike classical drama or later neoclassical plays in France, Tudor drama was mixed, combining comedy and tragedy, or history and pastoral, and it seldom troubled to observe the unities of time or place.

D

Multiple plots were common, and modern criticism has shown how they usually contributed to rather than detracted from the unity of action, making plays complex rather than merely diffuse, as for example in Ben Jonson's *Every Man in His Humour* (1598). The most popular play of the period was *Mucedorus* (1588), which went through many editions and was kept in the repertory of the Globe until the closing of the theaters in 1642. The reason for its popularity is probably its rich admixture of romance, adventure, melodrama, pathos, and comedy that had enormous audience appeal.

Many, but by no means all, of the plays in Tudor drama have come down to us in single, sometimes pirated editions, although Peter Blayney has recently questioned on economic grounds whether stationers would risk publishing plays illegally. Obviously, plays were not taken seriously as works of art or intellect, if we may judge by the quality of many printed editions, which show far more carelessness than contemporary books of sermons or historical treatises. Plays were, after all, only plays, and Ben Jonson was soundly teased by his contemporaries when he published his folio of 1616 and called it *The Works of Benjamin Jonson*. The efforts of modern scholarship have helped to provide us with reasonably complete and accurate editions of these plays, but for many of them, including the major plays of Shakespeare, a definitive edition still eludes us.

BIBLIOGRAPHY

Berry, Herbert. *Shakespeare's Playhouses.* 1987.

Chambers, E.K. *The Elizabethan Stage.* 4 vols. 1923.

Evans, G. Blakemore. *Elizabethan-Jacobean Drama: The Theatre in Its Time.* 1988.

Greg, W.W. *Dramatic Documents from Elizabethan Playhouses.* 1931.

Gurr, Andrew. *The Shakespearean Stage: 1574–1642.* 1991.

Hattaway, Michael. *Elizabethan Popular Theatre.* 1982.

Hildy, Franklin J., ed. *New Issues in the Reconstruction of Shakespeare's Theatre.* 1990.

Hosley, Richard. "The Origins of the Shakespearian Playhouse." *Shakespeare Quarterly,* vol. 15, pp. 29–39.

Orrell, John. *The Quest for Shakespeare's Globe.* 1983.

Thomson, Peter. "Playhouses and Players in Shakespeare's Time." In *The Cambridge Companion to Shakespeare Studies.* Stanley Wells, ed. 1986.

Waith, Eugene. "Words and Action in Tudor and Stuart Drama." *The Elizabethan Theatre,* vol. 13, pp. 79–94.

Jay L. Halio

SEE ALSO

Actors; Alleyn, Edward; Burbage, Richard; Drama, History of; Henslowe, Philip; Jonson, Ben; Marlowe, Christopher; Shakespeare, William; Theater Companies, Adult; Theater Companies, Boys; Theaters

Drayton, Michael (1563–1631)

Hailed in his own time as the "father of our bays . . . our still reviving Spenser," Michael Drayton was among the most energetic and prolific poets of an energetic and prolific era. Drayton, who was born in Warwickshire and spent much of his youth in the household of Thomas Goodere, announced his Spenserian affiliation in his first original published poem, *Idea. The Shepherds' Garland* (1593). Clearly based on Edmund Spenser's *Shepheardes Calender*—and, through it, on Vergil's *Eclogues*—*The Shepherds' Garland* proclaims the emergence of still another "new poet," another aspiring laureate. Although, unlike Virgil or Spenser, Drayton never established himself as the ruler's poet, high ambition continued to mark his career. He wrote in many of the genres fashionable in his and the following generation: the sonnet sequence and epyllion, Ovidian elegy and familiar epistle, satire, lyric, pastoral, ode, and biblical narrative. Moved, as he tells us, by the "shouts and claps" of the public theater, he even collaborated for a few years on plays. But the majority of Drayton's work was shaped by the Elizabethan antiquarian project of recovering and representing the land and history of England. Drayton's personal ambition was thus caught up in a broadly national ambition.

Chronicle history supplies the source for a remarkable number of Drayton's works, as it did for his close contemporaries Samuel Daniel and William Shakespeare. He began with poems he was later to call "legends," moral tales of "eminent person[s]": *Piers Gaveston* (1593), *Matilda* (1594), *Robert of Normandy* (1596), and *Great Cromwell* (1607). Even these he classed as "a species of an epic or heroic poem," as if straining in whatever way possible after the Vergilian legacy. But war being the proper subject of epic, Drayton hurried to meet that challenge with *Mortimeriados* (1596), his account of the civil conflicts of the early fifteenth century, a poem he later radically revised and expanded as *The Barons' Wars* (1602). And near the end of his career he added a further epic account of war in *The Battle of Agincourt* (1627), and another legend in *The Miseries of Queen Margaret* (1627). Neither the legends nor the accounts of war could, however, compete in the favor of his contemporaries with *England's Heroical Epistles,* the

D

collection of imaginary love letters between historical figures from Henry II and Rosamond to Guilford Dudley and Lady Jane Grey that Drayton first published in 1597 and kept revising and expanding until it reached a dozen pairs of letters in the 1619 folio edition of his *Poems.* Inspired by Ovid's *Heroides, England's Heroical Epistles* combine the erotic and pathetic appeal that made Ovid the favorite ancient poet of the 1590s with a claim to history, a claim Drayton bolstered with generous annotations from the English chronicles.

Drayton's longest and most ambitious poem, his *Poly-Olbion* (1612 and 1622), also draws heavily on chronicle sources, but its generic model comes from a wholly different antiquarian kind, the chorography or topographical survey. William Camden's *Britannia,* which appeared in many ever-expanding editions from 1584 to 1610, was the prime English chorography and Drayton's most obvious source, but there were many others, whether the national surveys of Christopher Saxton, John Norden, and John Speed, or the more restricted perambulations of William Lambarde, John Stow, and Richard Carew. Perambulation is a key term here. A chorography is a work that moves from place to place, describing what it sees or what it remembers along the way. Such movement gives *Poly-Olbion* its principal narrative design. But that alone is not enough to make a poem of what characteristically took rather the form of a set of maps or a catalogue of antiquarian gleanings. So Drayton animated England, made its rivers, valleys, and hills tell their own stories and set them in opposition to one another, thus providing some of the characterization and conflict that a poem needs. The result may still fail to capture the reader's imagination. Few would agree with Angus Fletcher that "*Poly-Olbion* is, with *The Faerie Queene* and *Paradise Lost,* one of the most comprehensive and powerful English sublime poems." But, for all its dull stretches, *Poly-Olbion* does mark a bold ideological departure in English nationalist poetics from the dynastic vision of Shakespeare's English history plays to a new land-based vision, one that would support a republican as easily as a monarchic regime.

Throughout his career, Drayton had an uneasy and sometimes openly hostile relationship with the court and court culture. His choice of the rebellious Mortimer as the hero of several of his early poems points in this direction, as do his frequent complaints about coterie poets, his interest in the victims of royal ambition and lust, his satire of James I under the name of Olcon, his exclusion of the king from *Poly-Olbion,* his siting of Elizium in a pastoral realm of imagination far from the court. It can be heard, too, in the

brusque energy of his best poems, in the opening, for example, of *Idea 6*: "How many paltry, foolish, painted things, / That now in coaches trouble ev'ry street, / Shall be forgotten, whom no poet sings, / Ere they be well wrapped in their winding sheet?" Part Marlovian overreacher, part Spenserian idealist, part anti-Jacobean satirist, Drayton remained for his younger followers the voice of a braver, more heroic past: "a muse," as William Browne wrote in 1622, "in this mortality / Of virtue [who] yet survives."

BIBLIOGRAPHY

Brink, Jean R. *Michael Drayton Revisited.* 1990.

Drayton, Michael. *The Works.* William Hebel, Kathleen Tillotson, and Bernard Newdigate, eds. 5 vols. 1931–1941.

Grundy, Joan. *The Spenserian Poets.* 1969.

Hardin, Richard F. *Michael Drayton and the Passing of Elizabethan England.* 1973.

Newdigate, Bernard. *Michael Drayton and His Circle.* 1941.

Richard Helgerson

SEE ALSO

Camden, William; Carew, Richard; Daniel, Samuel; History, Writing of; Lambarde, William; Norden, John; Saxton, Christopher; Spenser, Edmund; Stow, John

Dudley, Edmund (1462?–1510)

Finance minister of Henry VII, Edmund Dudley is most often associated with Sir Richard Empson, another prominent member of Henry's chamber administration with whom he was executed by Henry VIII on August 17, 1510. Although the traditional year of his birth is 1462, Dudley might have been born as late at 1472. While there is slim evidence that he studied at Oxford, it is possible he studied at Gray's Inn, for he later lectured there on law. His entry into local and then central government came through the patronage of Sir Reginald Bray, Henry VII's most trusted minister, with whom his father, John Dudley, had a commission in Sussex in 1493. He later went on to become undersheriff of London and a speaker in Parliament in 1504. Most of Dudley's experience was gained deciding disputes in the Court of Star Chamber, particularly over commercial matters among London merchants.

The historical importance of Edmund Dudley rests on his notoriously effective enforcement of the fiscal policy of Henry VII's final years, a reputation based on Polydore Vergil's villifying account in *Anglica Historia* (1513;

D

revised 1534) and reinforced by later Tudor historians. Henry VII gained administrative independence from the medieval exchequer by appointing councilors of his personal chamber to raise revenue by exacting payments in lieu of punishments, in exchange for appointments, promotions, the waiver of customs, or to secure allegiance or good behavior. Of the group of councilors who administered Henry's increasingly harsh fiscal policy, Dudley and Empson had charge of gathering fines and forfeitures, and their notoriety is proportionate to their spectacular success in securing the king's debts, particularly during his final years. They possessed enormous power over nobles and merchants who sought the king's favor or pardon. It is certain that Dudley held private court in his home. Dudley became very wealthy, and his will suggests that he purchased forfeited lands and obtained goods such as cloth in lieu of bond payment. But it is clear that he did not make Henry VII's policy so much as enforce it zealously. He was highly valued during the king's final years and acted as an executor of his will.

Within days of Henry VII's death and his son's accession on April 24, 1509, Dudley was arrested, nominally charged with conspiracy to overthrow the king, and placed in the Tower to await trial. Even after his trial he attempted to carry out Henry VII's last wishes by writing Henry VIII a "Petition" that he pardon a long list of the late king's debtors, in order that "Restitution should be made to all persons by his grace wronged contrary to the order [of] his lawes." This list of pardoned debts was kept secret, for it would have weakened the case being built against him. During his imprisonment Dudley also wrote *The Tree of Commonwealth* for Henry VIII, a short instructional treatise outlining the responsibilities of monarchy. Among Dudley's advice to Henry is an ironic warning, "Let never christen prince folow the counsell of cruell men nor covetouse men, for the cruell counsell ever provokyth the ire of god [and] The covetouse counsell shall lose the hartes of the subjectes." It is likely that for Henry VIII the execution of his father's detested minister represented an effective and satisfying way to reject his fiscal policies and appease an angry, distrustful nobility without tarnishing the succession.

BIBLIOGRAPHY

Brodie, D.M. "Edmund Dudley: Minister of Henry VII." *Transactions of the Royal Historical Society,* 4th service, vol. 15, pp. 133–161. 1932.
Dietz, Frederick C. *English Government Finance, 1485–1558.* 2nd edition, vol. 1, pp. 33–50. 1964.
Dudley, Edmund. *The Tree of Commonwealth, a Treatise.* D.M. Brodie, ed. 1948.
Gunn, S.J. "The Accession of Henry VIII." *Historical Research,* vol. 64, pp. 278–288.
Harrison, C.J. "The Petition of Edmund Dudley." *The English Historical Review,* vol. 87, no. 342, pp. 82–99.
Horowitz, Mark R. "Richard Empson, minister of Henry VII." *Bulletin of the Institute of Historical Research,* vol. 55, pp. 35–49.
Richardson, W.C. *Tudor Chamber Administration, 1485–1547,* pp. 141–158. 1952.
Vergil, Polydore. *The Anglica Historia, A.D. 1485–1537.* Denys Hay, trans. and ed. Camden 3rd series, vol. 74, pp. 128–130, 150–152. 1950.

David W. Swain

SEE ALSO

Exchequer; Government, Central Administration of; Henry VII; Henry VIII

Dudley, John, Duke of Northumberland (c. 1504–1553)

John Dudley was the son of Edmund Dudley, executed minister of Henry VII, and Elizabeth Grey, sister and co-heir of John, Lord Lisle. While little is known of his childhood, he began a military career in 1523 under the duke of Suffolk and later served with distinction at sea. He worked assiduously to acquire landed wealth and advance himself at the court of Henry VIII, entering the peerage as Viscount Lisle in 1541. With his appointment as lord admiral and privy councilor in 1543, Dudley became one of the great officers of state. The following year he led troops into Scotland and later participated in Henry's conquest of Boulogne. When the king died in 1547, Dudley was a powerful figure at court and one of the most prominent men in the country.

The accession of the nine-year-old Edward VI offered Dudley leadership opportunities that were impossible under an adult monarch. Edward Seymour, duke of Somerset, quickly assumed the position of lord protector, and Dudley became earl of Warwick and great chamberlain. The new government embarked on a bold program of political and religious reform that was supported by Dudley, but he questioned the protector's anti-enclosure policy. During the summer of 1547 he accompanied the protector as he attempted to bring Scotland under English rule. The outbreak of rebellions throughout England in 1549 discredited the protector's leadership and allowed

Dudley to achieve greater prominence as he led an army that reoccupied Norwich and defeated a large rebel army commanded by Robert Kett. After peace had been restored, Dudley, supported by the majority of the king's council and the city of London, successfully removed the protector from power. Dudley never became lord protector, but based his authority on his office as lord president of the council and above all on a close relationship with Edward VI. Created duke of Northumberland in 1551, he presided over a government that undertook policies to maintain law and order, reform finances, and promote Protestantism. His career ended with the king's death in 1553, when the failure of a plan to transfer the throne to Lady Jane Grey led to his execution for treason. By renouncing the Protestant religion, Dudley lost his reputation among contemporary reformers, but modern scholars have rejected the legend of the "wicked duke" that exaggerated his shortcomings. His survivors included the duchess of Northumberland, Ambrose, earl of Warwick, Robert, Earl of Leicester, and Mary, mother of Sir Philip Sidney.

BIBLIOGRAPHY

Beer, Barrett L. *Northumberland: The Political Career of John Dudley, Earl of Warwick and Duke of Northumberland.* 1973.

———. "Northumberland: The Myth of the Wicked Duke and the Historical John Dudley." *Albion,* vol. 11, pp. 1–14.

Loades, David. *John Dudley, Duke of Northumberland, 1504–1553.* 1996.

Jordan, W.K. *Edward VI: The Young King.* 1968.

———. *Edward VI: The Threshold of Power.* 1970.

Barrett L. Beer

SEE ALSO

Dudley, Robert; Edward VI; Grey, Lady Jane; Henry VIII; Kett's Rebellion; Seymour, Edward

Dudley, Robert, Earl of Leicester (1532/33–1588)

The fifth of the duke of Northumberland's eight sons, Robert Dudley was one of the four of his thirteen children to survive to Elizabeth I's reign. Little is known of his youth before his marriage to Amy Robsart on June 4, 1550. In July 1553, he held King's Lynn for his father against Mary I, for which he was found guilty of treason and attainted. He was released from the Tower in the

autumn of 1554 through the intercession of Philip II and served him as master of the ordnance of the English contingent in the St. Quentin campaign of 1557. On Elizabeth's accession he was appointed master of the horse, an office he held until 1587 when he became lord steward of the household.

Although Dudley was undoubtedly the central emotional relationship of Elizabeth's adulthood and he was clearly one of her intimates by 1558, all that is known of their early relations is his later statement that they first met as children in 1541. Following the death of his wife (September 8, 1560), marriage became a distinct possibility, and one of the leading political issues of the 1560s. How seriously he rated his chances is a moot point, for about 1569 he began a long-standing affair with the widowed Douglas, Lady Sheffield, who bore him a son (the future Sir Robert Dudley) on August 7, 1574. On September 21, 1578, he married the widowed countess of Essex, who also bore him a son (Robert, Baron of Denbigh, June 6, 1581–July 19, 1584).

Despite their closeness, it was not until July 1563 that Elizabeth granted Dudley a substantial landed estate in the Midlands and Wales, and a year later (September 29, 1564) that she raised him to the earldom of Leicester. Thereafter he was possibly the leading recipient of her favor. He managed his financial affairs with care and some skill (he was an active commercial investor and improver of his estates), but his income was never sufficient to support his position at court and he was always financially dependent on the queen.

Elizabeth did not appoint Leicester a privy councilor until October 10, 1562, though he was already active in court politics, but from that time until his death he was one of her leading councilors. Given his interests, he might well have played a more active military and diplomatic role had Elizabeth been prepared to accept his absence from court. It was only in 1582 that he next went abroad (to escort the duke of Anjou to the Netherlands). In 1585, she reluctantly appointed him captain-general of her forces in the Netherlands. His two periods in the Netherlands (December 1585–November 1586, and June–December 1587) met with mixed success both politically and militarily and broke both his health and his finances. There was some feeling that he extended the authority the queen had given him there. In 1588, he took an active part in the preparations against the Armada, but the strain of commanding the army at Tilbury in July and August led to his sudden death from a malarial infection in the following month.

D

Leicester is possibly the most difficult Elizabethan to appraise. If he can no longer be regarded simply as the object of Elizabeth's misplaced affection, his eminence was nonetheless derived from her favor as much as any abilities of his own. Thanks both to his involvement at the highest level of politics and the extensive nature of his patronage, his influence permeated all levels of Elizabethan society. Although he was not a university-trained intellectual, his patronage—artistic, scientific, literary, religious, commercial, and military—reflected the genuinely broad range of his interests. His generosity was famous but, as Walsingham put it, he could also be "a shrewd enemy where he listeth." He attracted strong loyalties and strong enmities, the latter epitomized in *Leicester's Commonwealth*, the famous libel published against him in 1584.

Next to his relations with the queen his association with the Puritans has caused the most debate, for both at the time and later it has been claimed that his Puritan patronage was intended solely to serve his own political ends. But what these were has never been adequately explained, and evidence of his consistent support for the reformed church is plentiful. It included the advancing of a number of nonconformist divines as well as an extensive range of foreign Protestant contacts and friendships. He gave no support to presbyterianism, but he certainly protected a number of open Presbyterians. He may not have been a model of godly living; but, as numerous posthumous comments reveal, without his backing the spread of Puritanism would have been greatly inhibited. In this respect, as in many others, Leicester was a central shaper of the Elizabethan regime.

BIBLIOGRAPHY

Adams, Simon. *The Earl of Leicester and the Politics of Elizabethan England: Collected Essays.* 1997.
———, ed. "The Papers of Robert Dudley, Earl of Leicester, I–IV." *Archives*, vol. 20, 1992–1993; vol. 22, 1996.
———, ed. *Household Accounts and Disbursement Books of Robert Dudley, Earl of Leicester, 1558–1561, 1584–1586.* Camden Society, 5th series, vol. 6, 1995.
Collinson, Patrick. "Letters of Thomas Wood, Puritan, 1566–1577." repr. in *Godly People.* 1983.
Oosterhoff, F.G. *Leicester and the Netherlands, 1586–1587.* 1988.
Peck, Dwight C., ed. *Leicester's Commonwealth: The Copy of a Letter Written by a Master of Art of Cambridge (1584).* 1985.
Rosenberg, Eleanor. *Leicester: Patron of Letters.* 1955.
Strong, Roy C., and J.A. van Dorsten. *Leicester's Triumph.* 1964.
Wilson, Derek. *Sweet Robin: A Biography of Robert Dudley, Earl of Leicester, 1533–1588.* 1981.

Simon Adams

SEE ALSO
Alençon and Anjou, Duke of; Armada, Spanish; Elizabeth I; Patronage; Robsart, Amy

Dunbar, William (c. 1460–c.1513)

A Scottish clergyman and poet, William Dunbar was probably born c. 1460. He studied at St. Andrews University from 1477 to 1479. Repeated references in his poetry to traveling and foreign countries (France, Scandinavia) suggest he may then have gone abroad; he is not mentioned in other pre-1500 Scottish records. In 1500, he was granted an annual pension, and in 1501, he was sent to England as part of an embassy negotiating the marriage of James IV of Scotland and Margaret Tudor, daughter of Henry VII; he composed a poem on their wedding in 1503. In 1502, he acted as procurator (lawyer in lower court), and he celebrated his first mass in 1504. His poetry, ranging from court satire to devotional verse, features large among the oldest printed books in Scotland (1507–1508), and his career seems to have taken off in this period. His pension was increased and he emerged as the leading poet at James IV's court, possibly serving in Margaret's household as a scribe or clerk of some sort. He is last mentioned in official accounts just before the battle of Flodden Field in September 1513.

BIBLIOGRAPHY

Bawcutt, Priscilla. *Dunbar the Makar.* 1992.
———. ed. *William Dunbar. Selected Poems.* 1996.
Baxter, J.W. *William Dunbar.* 1952.
Gray, Douglas. "William Dunbar." In *Authors of the Middle Ages. English Writers of the Late Middle Ages.* Vol. III. M.C. Seymour, ed., pp. 173–194. 1996.
Kinsley, James. *The Poems of William Dunbar.* 1979.
Scheps, Walter, and Anna J. Looney. *Middle Scots Poets. A Reference Guide to James I of Scotland, Robert Henryson, William Dunbar, and Gavin Douglas.* 1986.

Theo van Heijnsbergen

SEE ALSO
Flodden Field, Battle of; Scotland, History of; Margaret Tudor

E

East India Company

The company had its origins in the decision of 101 London merchants in September 1599 to finance jointly a voyage by the Cape of Good Hope to the East Indies. Legal foundation was delayed until December of the following year when some 219 founding members were incorporated under the title "The governor and Company of Merchants of London trading into the East Indies." The circumstances of the foundation were inauspicious. Previous voyages eastward had been spectacular failures, in marked contrast to the enterprises of the Dutch, who had launched their own challenge to the Portuguese monopoly of direct trade with Asia five years earlier. The formation of the East India Company was essentially a defensive response by Levant Company merchants to this threat to their own trade in Oriental wares through the traditional junction of Europe and Asia in the Red Sea.

The response was not only belated; it was also unimpressive. Although the joint stock of around £70,000, which was raised in shares varying on average between £100 and £300, was a considerable sum in an English context, it was a small fraction of the far more broadly based subscription to the rival Dutch United East India Company on its establishment in 1602. Dutch investment, moreover, was permanent, whereas the English displayed less confidence by making their joint stock terminable on completion of the first voyage.

Organizational problems were also encountered in finding suitable ships and cargoes. Four vessels were eventually purchased, embarking from the Thames in February 1601. The cargoes included woolen cloths and other commodities worth £6,860. But European goods generally did not sell well in Asia and large amounts of specie were needed to secure imports. For the voyage in 1601, the company needed special permission from the government to export £21,742 worth of bullion. Imports, principally of pepper, on which the company's future depended, also posed problems. Pepper had the advantage of being of high value relative to bulk, a key consideration in such a long-distance trade. The disadvantage was the extreme volatility of the market. When the company's ships returned in September 1603 laden with more than a million pounds of pepper, the cargo created a glut in the market, and the difficulties encountered in disposing of the pepper added to the problem of persuading shareholders to invest in another voyage. Their doubts, however, were overcome, and the second voyage in 1604 was successful enough to make annual voyages thereafter routine.

BIBLIOGRAPHY

Andrews, K.R. *Trade, Plunder and Settlement: Maritime Enterprise and the Genesis of the British Empire, 1480–1630.* 1984.

Chaudhuri, K.N. *The English East India Company. The Study of an Early Joint Stock Company, 1600–1640.* 1965.

Foster, W. *England's Quest of Eastern Trade.* 1933.

Brian Dietz

SEE ALSO
Joint Stock Companies; Trade, Overseas

Eastland Company
See Joint Stock Companies

E

Economy

At the start of the Tudor regime, England was a backward rural area compared with the more developed economies and cultures of Renaissance Italy or the towns of the nearby Low Countries. Massive population losses in the middle of the fourteenth century and the subsequent ravages of epidemic disease kept the population at around two million during the fifteenth century; thinning of the population led to the abandonment of many settlements—especially in the Midlands—and the substitution of sheep for men. Although the country had a thriving woolen textile industry, whose products were in high demand on the Continent, many other industries were either underdeveloped or nonexistent.

As the period progressed many aspects of economic and social life changed. From the late fifteenth or early sixteenth centuries the population began to grow to reach four million in 1600. This was not a simple upward progression; in the late 1550s, the population was cut back savagely by a severe bout of influenza, and the harvest crisis of the mid- to late 1590s may well have reduced numbers, at least in the north of England. The birth rate seems to have been relatively high, especially in the later sixteenth century, and bubonic plague became less of a problem, being confined mainly to the towns and especially to London; but there were still many killers in a world innocent of antiseptics, anaesthetics, and antibiotics. Throughout the period the population remained predominantly rural with perhaps 90 percent living in villages, hamlets, and scattered farmsteads; apart from London, only a few towns contained 10,000 inhabitants. London reached an estimated 200,000 by 1600, but it had probably been less than half that size a century earlier and depended on a constant stream of migrants for its growth.

The increase of population was accompanied by inflation, although even today its causes are imperfectly understood. Historians are divided between those who believe that the cause was essentially monetary (an increase in the money supply chiefly due to the influx of precious metals from the New World and the debasement of the coinage in the 1540s) and those who stress real factors such as population growth. Population growth in particular helps to explain why some prices rose more substantially than others; industrial prices rose less than agricultural prices, and the price of land (rent) rose more steeply than the price of labor (wage rates). Whatever the causes of the so-called "price revolution," inflation took a heavy toll on the living standards of many toward the bottom of the social ladder; well before the middle of the sixteenth century,

laborers were complaining that they could not subsist on the wages allocated to them by government legislation. To help to remedy the situation the first Elizabethan government passed the Statute of Artificers that, among other things, allowed justices of the peace to establish local wage scales, taking into account local conditions. This did little to ameliorate the situation, and by the end of the century laborers and others dependent on their wage-earning abilities were much worse off than their great-grandfathers had been in the earlier sixteenth century. The governments of Tudor England—both central and local— became increasingly alarmed at the swollen ranks of the poor and devised new and imaginative schemes to provide additional support and protect the social fabric; this culminated at the very end of Elizabeth's reign with the passing of the great poor law acts that formed the basis for English poor relief until 1834.

Agriculture lay at the heart of the economy. The great majority of the population earned at least part of its livelihood from the soil; rural artisans—carpenters, blacksmiths, thatchers, and millers—usually owned a few animals and sometimes grew an acre or two of grain (usually corn). For most of the population the state of the harvest was of vital importance; poor weather followed by a shortfall in the harvest led to escalating prices during the following winter, and the whole economy took on a depressed air as people were forced to spend a higher proportion of their incomes on foodstuffs. In response to the growth of population and inflation, agriculture began to change. Growing numbers meant increased pressure on the land, and a process began (that continued, probably at a greater pace, in the following century) whereby more land was brought into cultivation: heathlands were colonized, woodlands cleared, and boggy areas drained. The search also began for ways to raise arable yields, although farmers were to have far more success in the seventeenth century. More commercial attitudes to the exploitation of the land also developed, stimulated in part by the dissolution of the monasteries, which placed the great bulk of the old monastic estate into lay hands within a generation or so.

Although total numbers remained relatively small, Tudor England was a labor surplus economy. Many people were underemployed; that is, they were not employed gainfully on a full-time basis. This encouraged the development of a wide range of grassroots industry to which the poor turned to eke out their meagre earnings—these included the manufacture of stockings, buttons, ribbons and lace, pins and nails, knives and other tools, vinegar, and strong spirits. At the same time there was a substantial development of heavy industry, a process in which the coal industry reigned supreme; by the end of the sixteenth century, Newcastle was a thriving industrial center shipping coal down the east coast, especially to London (which probably consumed about half of its output). Considerable advances were made in other industries: the blast furnace was introduced from the Continent early in the period and spread rapidly in the 1540s to support Henry VIII's warlike aims; the copper industry was revived in mid-century by German experts, and brass production was established; saltmaking began on a large scale on Tyneside; glassmaking was transformed in the hands of immigrant artisans; and a range of other industries were revived or established for the first time, including soapmaking and the production of alum and paper. In many of these enterprises the central government supplied active encouragement.

The English textile industry also developed during the Tudor period, although the story was not one of simple upward progress. The export of traditional woolen cloths approximately doubled between the start of the regime and the middle of the sixteenth century; these were mostly high-quality white cloths produced in Wiltshire and the surrounding counties, exported to Antwerp and finished in the Low Countries by skilled artisans. This trade collapsed temporarily in the early 1550s due to a combination of factors including the currency manipulations of the 1540s and their cessation in the eary 1550s, and the removal of privileges from the merchants of the Hanseatic League. The trade in these traditional cloths—or "old draperies" as they were known—recovered during the following decades but failed to reach their former peak before the end of the century. But some relief was granted by the development of new, more variegated cloths known as "new draperies" after the middle of the century. The new cloths, which were mostly of worsted, were produced in various parts of the country, although the most important area of production centered on Norwich; shortly after the middle of the century the city council offered religious toleration and self-determination to a group of Protestant clothworkers from the Low Countries. Within a generation or two, they had helped to stimulate the production of new cloths in the English population and had brought great prosperity to the city.

The growth of cloth exports in the first half of the sixteenth century was tied ever more closely to the important market of Antwerp. This led to a decay of English shipping, for there was little reason for London merchants to venture further afield if they could sell their wares at a single market and buy all the goods they needed at the same place. In a sense this was a strange development since the world known to Europeans had expanded enormously in the fifteenth century, thanks to the pioneering voyages of the Portuguese and, to a lesser extent, the Spanish. The English had played some part in this process; an Italian adventurer, John Cabot—backed by the merchants of Bristol—had discovered the coast of Newfoundland at the end of the fifteenth century. But English interest faltered despite the promptings of Cabot's son, Sebastian. The collapse of cloth exports in the early 1550s had a dramatic effect on English trade; from the 1550s, English merchants sought new markets for their cloth in western Europe and new sources of supply for the wines, spices, and other goods in demand at home. In the 1550s, there were pioneering voyages to the White Sea to establish trade with the Russia of Ivan the Terrible, and a regular trade with Morocco and Guinea was established. Trade with areas of southern Europe was strengthened, and the English moved more freely in both the Baltic and the Mediterranean from the 1570s. In many cases, English merchants sought to consolidate and control their gains by the establishment of monopoly merchant companies; any English merchant wishing to trade with a particular area had to join the relevant company.

Forays across the Atlantic were rarer; they were limited to the early slaving voyages of Richard Hawkins and the depredations of Elizabethan sea dogs such as Francis Drake. In particular, despite the attempts at settlement by Walter Ralegh at Roanoke in the 1580s, and the urgings of Richard Hakluyt, the English showed little enthusiasm for colonial development before the seventeenth century. In part, this was because they had been preempted by the Spanish and Portuguese; intrusion into the Spanish area of influence in particular was fraught with difficulties. In addition, the lack of interest in colonial adventures shown by both the London merchant community and by the central government dampened activity; the crown in particular was deflected by the continuing drain on reserves caused by the massive military effort needed to subdue the Irish. After the death of Elizabeth and the end of the privateering war against the Spanish, which had soaked up a great deal of London merchant capital, colonial enterprises and the development of far-distance trades made much faster headway.

The pace of change in Tudor economic life remained slow and often uncertain. Life remained essentially rural for the great bulk of the population, and for many, the way of life in 1600 was little different from that of their forebears at the end of the fifteenth century. Nevertheless,

E

the broadening of the industrial base, the early attempts to increase agricultural output, and the first faltering steps toward trade with more distant lands and the establishment of colonies there pointed the way toward a very different future.

BIBLIOGRAPHY

Clarkson, L.A. *The Pre-industrial Economy in England, 1500–1750.* 1971.

Clay, C.G.A. *Economic Expansion and Social Change: England, 1500–1700.* 2 vols. 1984.

Coleman, D.C. *The Economy of England, 1450–1750.* 1977.

Holderness, B.A. *Pre-Indusrial England: Economy and Society from 1500 to 1700.* 1976.

Donald Woodward

SEE ALSO

Agriculture; Cloth Industry; Cloth Trade; Coal Industry; Colonial Development; Discovery and Exploration; Enclosure; Government, Central Administration of; Government, Local; Immigration; Industry and Manufacture; Justice of the Peace; Metal Industries; Monastic Orders; Money, Inflation, and Moneylending; Plague; Poor Laws; Population and Demography; Privateering; Trade, Inland; Trade, Overseas

Education

Tudor England was marked by a great thirst for education. Men of all social classes wanted education for themselves and their sons for a variety of reasons: merchants, doctors, and lawyers needed education for the conduct of their business and professional affairs, while the poor realized that illiteracy was a hindrance to social and economic advancement. Prosperous yeoman farmers knew that a modicum of learning was fast becoming a prerequisite for gentle status, whereas aristocratic fathers were well aware that their sons must be educated before seeking lucrative positions in either church or state.

Women also valued education for different reasons. The ability to read and write made it possible for them to correspond with family members who lived at a distance; to enjoy the histories, romances, and devotional works that England's early printers published in inexpensive editions; and to be able to read the English-language Bibles that were produced in relatively cheap runs from 1535 on. (Between the 1470s, when mechanized printing was established in England, and the 1530s, the price of reading materials declined by approximately seven-eighths, which greatly facilitated the spread of education among both sexes and all social groups except the very poor.)

In comparison to the educational opportunities available to boys, those available to girls were strictly limited, especially after the dissolution of the nunneries by Henry VIII and the disappearance of the forty or so schools kept by them. Still, many young women of the upper and upper-middle classes became accomplished scholars with the help of tutors employed by their families. The extensive learning of Margaret More Roper, Lady Jane Grey, and the many daughters of the earl of Surrey and the duke of Somerset is well known. Later in the century that tradition was continued by Elizabeth Tanfield, the daughter of an important judge. Born in 1585, she learned to read at the age of three and began to study French the next year. By the time she was twenty she had mastered French and Italian as well as Spanish, Latin, and Hebrew. Her learning was almost as great as that of Elizabeth I, an accomplished linguist who read Greek for an hour each morning with her old tutor, Roger Ascham, until his death in 1568.

Although women could not attend the universities or the grammar schools of the age, they were nevertheless important educational patrons. By founding new schools and colleges as well as providing scholarships for poor boys who hoped to enter the church, women made an important contribution to further the spread of education. During the early sixteenth century, Lady Margaret Beaufort, the mother of Henry VII, established two new colleges at Cambridge, Christ's and St. John's. However, Christ's was nursed back into existence seven years after Lady Margaret's death by her old friend and confessor, Bishop John Fisher of Rochester, who rendered so much aid that he deserves to be considered its cofounder. Much later in the century, the countess of Sussex left an educational bequest of £5,000 that her nephew, Sir John Harington, enlarged before establishing Sidney Sussex College, Cambridge, in 1596. Queen Elizabeth gave so much aid to Jesus College, Oxford, which Dr. Hugh Price, treasurer of St. David's Cathedral, established in 1571, that she is generally considered its principal founder. During the 1580s, Queen Elizabeth established eleven scholarships for poor boys at Oxford and Cambridge, but her greatest educational work came shortly after her accession to the throne. In 1560, she established Westminster School, an outstanding grammar school for 120 boys, forty of whom were on full scholarship. On the eve of the Armada, Mrs. Joyce Frankland, widow of a rich

Hertfordshire clothier, left £400 each to Emmanuel College, Cambridge, and Lincoln and Brasenose Colleges, Oxford. To her favorite collegiate society, Gonville and Caius College, Cambridge, Mrs. Frankland bequeathed the large sum of £1,540 along with a yearly rental of £33 6s. 8d., the latter sum always to be reserved for the support of twelve poor undergraduates each year.

Although women were unusually generous with the funds at their disposal, men made a much greater contribution, owing to their more extensive resources. In addition to the three colleges that were founded through the joint action of men and women, eight of the nine new colleges established between 1496 and 1596 were founded by men. Of those nine new colleges, the most important were undoubtedly Christ Church, Oxford, and Trinity College, Cambridge, which Henry VIII endowed in 1546 with former monastic estates.

Although Henry VIII is often criticized for not doing enough for education, he was, in fact, the greatest educational patron of the century. Not only did he establish his two new colleges in 1546 but he also founded the ten original regius professorships—five at either university—in the fields of Greek, Hebrew, medicine, divinity, and law. Furthermore, he established approximately two dozen grammar schools, including the King's School at Canterbury, to take the place of monastic schools that had disappeared between 1536 and 1540.

In 1543, Henry VIII issued an important proclamation commanding all of England's schoolmasters to make exclusive use of the outstanding Latin grammar that John Lily, the first headmaster of St. Paul's School, London, produced between 1510 and 1515. After 1543, Lily's grammar quickly came into general use; and by 1549, schoolboys entering the universities were so much better prepared that the Privy Council decided to make a mastery of Latin grammar a prerequisite for admission. At that point basic Latin grammar was banned from the undergraduate curriculum and its place assigned to mathematics. In general, the reform of 1549 was intended to encourage the study not only of mathematics but also of medicine and science. Students hoping to qualify for a bachelor's degree in medicine were now required to attend at least two human dissections; and students hoping to earn a doctor's degree in medicine were required to attend an additional two.

For almost thirty years the reform of 1549 proved abortive because of the overweening interest of most students with divinity and the dearth of mathematical and scientific books at the universities. However, during the 1550s, men with an interest in such subjects began to purchase books and manuscripts that had survived the dissolution of the monasteries. While some 85 to 90 percent of the books and manuscripts owned by the religious houses were lost forever, the remainder eventually found their way into the hands of bibliophiles who, in many instances, donated them to the various colleges at Oxford and Cambridge during the 1560s and 1570s. In that way important mathematical and scientific collections took shape, collections that were adequate to support original work in medicine, mathematics, astronomy, geography, navigation, and other fields. By the last two decades of the Tudor age, the English universities were in the vanguard of the movement long known as the scientific revolution. Among the graduates of Oxford and Cambridge between 1575 and 1600 were such distinguished scientists as Edward Wright, Thomas Harriot, Thomas Hood, Nicholas Torporley, and William Oughtred. In 1599, George Abbot, who eventually became archbishop of Canterbury, produced the first geography textbook, *A Briefe Description of the Whole World.* The great physician, Dr. William Gilbert, was also a university graduate, having been trained at Cambridge before opening a lucrative practice in London in 1573. Gilbert's pioneering book on geology and magnetism, *De Magnete,* appeared in 1600.

Almost a generation before Dr. Gilbert settled in the capital, medical standards around London began to improve. This was largely owing to the Barber Surgeons Company and its great benefactor, Dr. John Caius. The Barber Surgeons Company received a royal charter in 1540. Its members could set broken bones, pull decayed teeth, and perform other simple procedures. In 1546, the Barber Surgeons Company asked Dr. Caius if he would instruct them in the techniques of human dissection. He willingly agreed, and for twenty years he gave a weekly lecture and demonstration in the company's great hall. Because Dr. Caius's lectures and demonstrations were free, they were well attended; and within several years the barber surgeons of southern and central England became much more knowledgeable about the human body and its structure. As a consequence they were able to give better medical care to the English people, and in succeeding years several barber surgeons published popular self-help books.

Dr. Caius's lectures set the standard for later public lectures on medical and scientific topics. Many were delivered in London during the reign of Queen Elizabeth, the most famous being those of Thomas Hood, who received an M.A. from Cambridge in 1581. The university mathematical lecturer in 1582, Hood settled in the capital five

E

years later and gave public lectures on mathematics, geography, and navigation at the behest of a rich patron, John, Lord Lumley. Dr. Caius's lectures may also have inspired Sir Thomas Gresham to leave a bequest in 1579 for the establishment of an institution that would sponsor such public lectures on a permanent, recurring basis. A wealthy merchant and important financial adviser to Elizabeth I, Gresham stipulated in his will that, once his widow died, his estate should be used to endow a permanent society in London that would be staffed by eminent professors in the fields of astronomy, geometry, medicine, law, rhetoric, divinity, and music. Paid £50 a year, each professor was required to give regular public lectures in Latin and English and to answer questions and conduct discussions afterward. Because Lady Gresham survived her husband for sixteen years, Gresham College did not come into being until 1596. But once it opened, it served as a clearing house for information of all kinds. For example, the first Gresham professor of geometry, Henry Briggs, who had been trained at Cambridge, soon learned about the invention of logarithms by the Scottish mathematician, John Napier. Early in the seventeenth century, Briggs traveled to Scotland twice to meet with Napier and learn his method of complex mathematical calculation. During his public lectures at Gresham College, Briggs explained logarithms to large audiences and popularized their use.

Only one other topic remains to be considered—the literacy rate. In 1533, the year of Queen Elizabeth's birth, Sir Thomas More estimated that 60 percent of England's adults were literate. But because More never journeyed more than forty miles from London, and because literacy was more widespread in the home counties than in the northern shires or the West Country, More's estimate is usually rejected as too high. During recent years, several scholars have suggested that the literacy rate was probably no more than 20 percent for men and only about half that for women.

Surviving literary evidence from the Elizabethan period indicates a much higher literacy rate than most of the recent studies suggest. Of course, literacy was somewhat greater among men than among women because of women's more restricted educational opportunities, and literacy was obviously more widespread in the neighborhood of the capital and the universities than elsewhere. Moreover, literacy seems to have been almost nonexistent among the lowest 33 percent of the population, those people who lived in abject poverty and were unable to send their children to school for even a year or buy the cheapest books and pamphlets. But for the other 67 percent of the population, those in more fortunate circumstances, literacy seems to have been extremely widespread by the end of the period. It appears that during the 1590s, around 85 percent of all adult males in the upper two-thirds of the population could read and approximately 65 percent of all females in that same group. Assuming that the number of men and women was roughly equal, approximately three-fourths of all adults in the more affluent tiers of society were literate by the last decade of the age. In other words, the literacy rate for the entire adult population, regardless of economic circumstances, was just over 50 percent (50.25 percent, to be exact). But computations of this sort are educated guesses at best because the dearth of surviving evidence causes so much to hinge on impressions. Thus it seems unlikely that the literacy rate will ever be computed to general agreement.

BIBLIOGRAPHY

Alexander, Michael V.C. *The Growth of English Education, 1348–1648.* 1990.

Charlton, Kenneth. *Education in Renaissance England.* 1965.

Cressy, David. *Education in Tudor and Stuart England.* 1975.

———. *Literacy and the Social Order: Reading and Writing in Tudor and Stuart England.* 1980.

Lawson, John, and Harold Silver. *A Social History of Education in England.* 1973.

Simon, Joan. *Education and Society in Tudor England.* 1967.

Michael V.C. Alexander

SEE ALSO

Beaufort, Margaret; Book Ownership; Grammar Schools; Gresham, Sir Thomas; Lily, John ; Literacy; Manuscripts; Reading Practices; Universities; individual educators and patrons

Edward VI (1537–1553)

The only legitimate surviving son of Henry VIII, Edward was delivered by caesarian birth on October 12, 1537, after which his mother, Jane Seymour, soon died. Never a robust child, Edward led a carefully sheltered childhood. A statute of 1544 declared him the heir to the throne, to be succeeded by his half-sisters Mary and Elizabeth. The same year saw the reorganization of his household at Hampton Court and the effective beginning of his education for the kingship: the first Tudor to be so trained. His tutors included some of the leading Protestant educators and thinkers of the day: Richard Cox, John Cheke, and Roger Ascham. By the age of fourteen, Edward had a command of Latin and French as well as some Greek, showed an impressive grasp of geography and military engineering, and kept a political diary of some importance covering the period 1547–1552. Under the patronage of his stepmother, Catherine Parr, his school became a gathering place for numerous humanist and Protestant figures of the day.

Edward's public duties as prince began at the age of nine, with responsibility for hosting the admiral of France in 1546. Though by law Edward acceded to the throne on the death of Henry VIII on January 28, 1547, this was only announced after the several days it took for his uncle, Edward Seymour, then earl of Hertford, to secure his own place as "Lord Protector." This unconstitutional act effectively allowed Hertford to dominate the Regency Council of sixteen members called for in the will of Henry VIII: an arrangement intended to last until the young king's eighteenth year. In that capacity, Hertford (shortly thereafter assuming the title of duke of Somerset) also acted as Edward's guardian, and ruled as if he, and not Edward, were king.

In the Somerset years, Edward innocently allowed himself to become entangled in the intrigues surrounding the marriage of his other uncle, the protector's brother, Thomas Seymour, to Henry VIII's widow, Catherine Parr. After Catherine's death in 1548, Thomas Seymour tried to enlist Edward's support for his plan to marry the Princess Elizabeth, a match that would have allowed him the upper hand against his brother, the protector. Edward did not support this and, pushed by Somerset, he consented to Thomas Seymour's execution in March 1549.

In October 1549, when John Dudley, earl of Warwick, began his coup against Somerset, he gained control over the king before announcing the dissolution of Somerset's protectorate. Warwick persuaded the young king to support what had transpired. Taking the title of the duke of Northumberland, Warwick eventually completed his coup by engineering Somerset's trial and execution in January 1552. Yet from the last months of 1549, he effectively ruled in Edward's name, not with Somerset's device of guardianship, but under the pretence that the king himself had come into his full powers. Under his watchful eye, Sir William Cecil and Sir William Petre acted as the king's advisors, gaining Edward's approval of actions taken by Northumberland. Sir John Gates effectively gained control, on Northumberland's behalf, of the warrants to the privy seal, further allowing the duke to do much as he wished.

Throughout these years Edward gradually assumed the role of an active king, holding court, presiding at state occasions, sending memoranda, receiving ambassadors, and "assenting" to policies placed before him. In matters of faith he supported the evangelical Protestantism that flourished under Northumberland's patronage, extended his own support to some groups, and strenuously urged the Princess Mary to abandon her Catholicism. Yet the intensity of his own religiosity seems modest, and there are some indications that he shared some of the *politique* values of his half-sister, Elizabeth, rather than the doctrinaire inclinations that Mary would pursue. He came to take a keen interest in routine matters of administration as well as such particular problems as the debasement of the coinage, the plight of the poor, and the intricacies of foreign affairs. He punctuated his interest with a constant flow of memoranda to the council and others, and seemed willing even to concern himself with the reform of administrative structure. Although some historians have attributed to him considerable initiative and independence of action on such issues, this remains a moot contention.

As an unmarried prince and then king, he served as the centerpiece of several marital schemes throughout his short life: as the projected match for Mary Stuart in 1543 and again in 1547–1548; for Lady Jane Grey in 1548 and after; and for Princess Elizabeth, daughter of Henry II of France, in 1551.

Edward's health remained a constant concern throughout his reign, although, in fact, he enjoyed long periods of good health between bouts of illness. In April 1552, he contracted what he himself described as a combination of measles and smallpox, though—as both were usually fatal at that time—this is unlikely to have been an accurate diagnosis. Although he recovered sufficiently to undertake a triumphant progress through the southern counties over the ensuing summer, he became ill in the following February (1553), and relapsed in late May with what would be his final and fatal illness.

His chief concern in these weeks seems to have been for the succession, and especially his intense determination to keep the resolutely Catholic Mary from the throne. With Northumberland's encouragement, he drafted a *Devise for the Succession* that recognized Jane Grey, newly married to Guildford Dudley, and her heirs, ahead of the succession of Mary and Elizabeth Tudor. The document had the effect of setting aside the succession that Henry VIII had willed and that Parliament had

E

approved. Ignoring the facts that a minor may not make a valid will and that no king could be free to devise the succession by will alone in any event, Edward acted with Northumberland's support and pressured his councilors and chief legal officers to accept this revised formula as part of his will. His death a few weeks later, on the evening of July 6, 1553, led to the abortive reign of Lady Jane and the rapid triumph of Mary as queen.

BIBLIOGRAPHY

Hoak, Dale E. *The King's Council in the Reign of Edward VI.* 1976.

Jordan, W.K. *Edward VI, the Young King.* 1968.

———. *Edward VI: The Threshold of Power.* 1970.

———, ed. *The Chronicle and Political Papers of King Edward VI.* 1966.

Robert Tittler

SEE ALSO

Dudley, John; Grey, Lady Jane; Mary I; Parr, Catherine; Seymour, Edward; Seymour, Thomas

Edwardes, Richard (1524–1566)

Despite considerable popularity during his lifetime, little is known about Richard Edwardes. His surviving dramatic output consists of a version of a classical work, *Damon and Pythias,* for which he is best known; "An Elegie" from *Palamon and Arcite;* and *The Paradise of Daynty Devises,* which went into many editions between 1576 and 1606. He also authored twenty-six other poems. The theme of *Damon and Pythias* is sacrifice, and the sacredness of relational ties would have resonated sharply with Tudor audiences. That it hearkens back to a classical emblem of virtue would also have contributed to its success as a dramatic narrative.

What exists of Edwardes's chronology is sparse and vague, and provides only a crude sketch of a life committed primarily to holy orders, not artistic endeavor. He was born in Somersetshire in 1524. On May 11, 1540, he was admitted to Corpus Christi College, Oxford, and received a B.A. in 1544. Soon after, he was appointed as a probationer fellow at Corpus Christi College, with a position as a lecturer in logic at Christ Church College, in 1546. He advanced to an M.A. degree in 1547 and was probably ordained between 1547 and 1550.

He became a philosopher of Christ Church, having been elected to a group known as "the theologians." He was selected as "Magistri puer regalis Capelle ad vitam" on October 27, 1561, and on November 25, 1564, he was admitted to Lincoln's Inn as an honorary fellow. Edwardes died in 1566, age forty-two, when he was master of the children of the Chapel Royal. An entry in *The Old Cheque Book of the Chapel Royal* simply states: "Richard Edwardes, Mr. of the children, the last October." Edwardes was succeeded as master by William Hunnis, who had contributed to *The Paradise of Daynty Devises.*

His dramatic life has even fewer reliable sources. It is documented that on a showing of his piece from *Palamon and Arcite* in 1566, Queen Elizabeth commended Edwardes with "a promise of rewarde." Whether it was the result of his untimely death or royal negligence that Edwardes received no largesse is not known. Any specific accounts of other dramatic works, outside of documented publishing histories, have been lost. *Damon and Pythias,* the one work in his oeuvre to preserve his name, was first reprinted by Robert Dodsley in *A Selection of Old Plays* (1744; 4th edition repr. 1964) from the 1582 edition.

BIBLIOGRAPHY

Bradner, Leicester. *The Life and Poems of Richard Edwardes.* 1924.

Edwardes, Richard. *A Paradise of Dainty Devices (1576–1606).* Hyder E. Rollins, ed. 1927.

Farmer, John S., ed. *The Dramatic Writings of Richard Edwardes, Thomas Norton, and Thomas Sackville.* 1966.

White, Jerry D. *Richard Edwardes's Damon and Pythias: A Critical Old Spelling Edition.* 1980.

Á Wood, Anthony. *Athenae Oxoniensis.* 1691.

Jon Curley

SEE ALSO

Hunnis, William; Theater Companies, Boys; Verse Anthologies

Egerton, Thomas (1540–1617)

Born in Dodleston, Cheshire, as an illegitimate son of lesser gentry, Thomas Egerton was a prime example of how one could rise from the stock of esquire, Catholic, and illegitimate, and use a law career to become one of the most titled and wealthiest men in the country. Raised by the Ravenscroft and Grosvenor families without mother or father, his Catholic stepmother, Mary Grosvenor, was a motivating factor throughout his formative years. She sent him to one of the early Tudor grammar schools, and from there to Brasenose College, Oxford, in 1556. Participating in the new extracurricular program for the professions, he left after three years for Furnivall's and Lincoln's Inn, the Inns of Court that became prominent for housing students from the West Midlands and the Welsh borderlands.

Egerton had several crises in the 1560s and 1570s that reflected Elizabethan society. As a young man without a pedigree, he was arrested and charged in Star Chamber for participating in a riot. A Catholic, he was cited several times for practicing the old faith, and eventually conformed. Two of his stepbrothers did the same as priests. Reading Desiderius Erasmus, John Calvin, and Thomas Cranmer, he became a devout Protestant by 1580. He also struggled in his early law career. Called to the bar in 1572, he litigated cases in Cheshire until he did some work for the earls of Leicester and Derby, whose patronage gave him a local office in 1578, and national office as legal counsel to the queen in 1581. He prospered there as only few others had. Solicitor general, attorney general, master of the rolls, and lord keeper by 1596, he rode to fame on his talents, winning every major post that became vacant. Ennobled as Baron Ellesmere at the accession of James I, he did not advance further until just before his death in 1617, when he was made Viscount Brackley.

The lord keeper was one of the most prominent chancellors of the early modern era. Presiding over the Chancery, Star Chamber, and House of Lords, he was seen by contemporaries as a judge who had "dignity," who used reason to make law instead of fluent and deceitful speeches. He addressed legal counsel with public grace, and nurtured young counsel in court. Having indefatigable energy, as well as a photographic mind, he was usually the first official to appear in a courtroom. An impartial judge who would suffer no fools, he earned the epitaph "l'enfant terrible." A *politique,* he strove for compromise in politics and the nation state.

Successful judge and politician, Egerton was also devoted to religion, literature, and the pastoral countryside. Once established, he patronized evangelical preachers and scholars of the liberal and fine arts, and gave major monetary gifts to Brasenose College and Lincoln's Inn. Amassing large estates, first in the West Midlands and then in the East, he always chose close relatives as his estate agents. While his first two wives predeceased him, he devoted his remaining years providing for his three children and eighteen grandchildren. A country man, he loathed London with its teeming crowds and pollution, and often fled London for an afternoon on the heath. Marrying the notable countess dowager of Derby in 1600, his personal life was never the same. Unattuned to the life of the court, and disenchanted with its politics, he

arranged for burial in his parish church of Dodleston, leaving the world in the manner in which he had found it.

BIBLIOGRAPHY

Fogle, French R. "'Such a Rural Queen': The Countess Dowager of Derby as Patron," and Louis A. Knafla, "The 'Country' Chancellor: The Patronage of Sir Thomas Egerton, Baron Ellesmere." In *Patronage in Late Renaissance England.* Fogle and Knafla, eds. 1983.

Jones, W.J. "Ellesmere and Politics, 1603–17." In *Early Stuart Studies.* Howard S. Reinmuth, ed. 1970.

Knafla, Louis A. *Law and Politics in Jacobean England. The Tracts of Lord Chancellor Ellesmere.* 1977.

Louis A. Knafla

SEE ALSO

Chancery; Inns of Court; Patronage; Star Chamber, Court of

Elegy

Tudor authors wrote many fine poems on death, including William Dunbar for the "makarirs" [poets], John Skelton on Edward IV, the earl of Surrey recalling the duke of Richmond, Nicholas Grimald on his mother, Barnabe Googe on Grimald, Barnabe Rich on William Drury, Ben Jonson on his first son, and Samuel Daniel for the earl of Devonshire. With rare exceptions, however, these were not called elegies but epitaphs, epigrams, epicedia, eclogues, laments, lays, lachrymae, monodies, funeral songs, and funeral sonnets, and were shaped by the rhetorical traditions of the lamentation and the encomium. *Tottel's Miscellany* (1557), and the graver *Paradise of Dainty Devices* (1576–1606), never use elegy as a label, despite being replete with funerary poems and love complaints. None of the English and Latin poems by John Leland and Surrey that marked the passing of Thomas Wyatt in 1542, not even those composed in Latin elegiacs, was called an elegy. After the death of Sir Philip Sidney, only two of the flood of Latin, Greek, and English verse memorials published in 1587 were called elegies, and these were in the elegiac measure (a dactylic hexameter followed by a pentameter). For William Shakespeare at the end of the sixteenth century, an elegy was still a suitor's "dire lamenting" lyric (*Two Gentlemen of Verona*), what lovesick Orlando might hang from "brambles" in the forest of Arden (*As You Like It*). That is, in the Tudor period, the word elegy most often referred to poems imitating the themes and distichs of Ovid's *Amores.*

E

Classical practice, then, was at odds with Horace's well-known observation in his *Ars Poetica* that elegiacs were first used for mourning (*querimonia*). J.C. Scaliger bridged the gap by interpreting *querimonia* as complaints of love (1561). Writing in the 1580s to defend the morality of poetry, Sidney chose to stress elegy's "rightly painting out how weak be the passions of woefulness," rather than the suspect side of this genre. George Puttenham's *Art of English Poesie* (1589) is more candid: some Latin poets "sought the favor of faire Ladies and coveted to bemone their estates at large and the perplexities of love in a certain pitious verse called Elegy." Elegies were commonly associated with Petrarchan sonnets: Francis Meres's list of English elegists (1598), "the most passionate among us to bewaile and bemoane the perplexities of love," included Surrey, Wyatt, Francis Bryan, Sidney, Sir Walter Ralegh, Edward Dyer, Edmund Spenser, Daniel, Michael Drayton, Shakespeare, George Whetstone, George Gascoigne, and Samuel Page. In addition, Barnabe Barnes (1593), Thomas Lodge (1593), Giles Fletcher (1593), and Alexander Craig (1606), all placed erotic elegies of various metrical patterns among their sonnets. Although neither ancient nor Tudor authors used elegiacs solely for poems about love, plaintive love defined a genre. George Buchanan and Thomas Campion both counted amatory elegies among their well-regarded Latin poetry. In addition, Gabriel Harvey, Spenser, and Sidney experimented with quantitative equivalents for classical elegiacs. In 1602, Campion even devised an accentual substitute called the "English Elegeick":

> Constant to none, but ever false to me,
> Traitor still to love through thy faint desires,
> No hope of pity now nor vain redresse
> Turns my griefs to tears, and renu'd laments.

"Elegy" was too evocative, however, to be squandered on morally dubious poems composed in an intractable meter. By the mid-sixteenth-century, Neo-Latin and French elegy had already developed into a more philosophical and autobiographical genre. In the first occurrence of the word in English, Skelton used "elegy" in *Philip Sparrow* of an epitaph in Latin elegiacs (c. 1508). He also composed a Latin "Elegia" on the mother of Henry VII. Thomas Elyot defined *elegia* as "a lamentable songe or verse" (1538). Awash in melancholy, Gascoigne described his *The Complaynt of Phylomene* (1576) as "an elegy, or sorrowful song." And his moralizing *The Grief of Joye* (1576), was comprised of "Certeyne Elegies." Yet Gascoigne composed an epitaph for a Captain Bourcher, not an elegy, and was himself remembered by his friend

George Whetstone in an epitaph (1577). For his several attempts at obsequies, Thomas Churchyard also preferred the title epitaph or simply sorrowful verses, as for Elizabeth I. Gradually, however, the English love complaint became a subcategory of lamentation and the term elegy was increasingly fixed to poems on death. Puttenham closed his chapter on "the form of poetical lamentations," for example, obsequies, epicedia, and monodia, noting that the "sorrowing" of love was best borne by the "limping Pentameter after a lusty Hexameter, which made it go dolorously, more than any other meter" (1589). Sir John Harington's apology for poetry simply states that the "Elegy is still mourning" (1591). Early in the century, Alexander Barclay had a poor shepherd "tell mine elegy"—indeed a "woeful elegy"—for Edward Howard (*Fourth Eclogue*, 1521?). Both *Daphnaida* (1591) (for Lady Douglas Howard) and *Astrophel* (in a gathering for Sidney published in 1595), two stanzaic memorials by Edmund Spenser that, along with "November" in the *Shepherds' Calendar*, influenced Milton's *Lycidas*, were each titled elegies. This novel use of "elegy" for a pastoral epicedium whatever its meter was accepted by only a handful of Spenserians, and the term remained in flux. William Bas's *Three Pastoral Elegies* (1602) were love poems. Indiscriminate, Michael Drayton applied the term to sonnets, satires, epistles, and epicedia. John Davies' long, didactic *Nosce Teipsum* compiled in quatrains is subtitled "Two Elegies" (1599). Meanwhile, Francis Davison was still using "elegy" just for love poems in *A Poetical Rhapsody* (1602–1621), a gathering that also included hexameters, an eclogue, and a translated epigram in "elegicall verse" for Sidney, as well as epitaphs for Henry IV of France and Elizabeth I. *England's Helicon* (1600) included mournful ditties and dumps but no pastoral elegies. While John Lane did publish an "Elegy upon the Death of Elizabeth," none of the many lamentations collected as *Sorrowes Joy* (1603) were titled elegies. After 1600, however, while the old ways of describing threnodies remained in use, "elegy" became a popular label for conventional memorial verse usually written in rhymed couplets, even if the word often required modification by "funeral." Most of John Donne's "Elegies" written at the end of the century fit William Webbe's description of the "Comical" genre, linking "Epigrams, Elegies, and delectable ditties" (1586), for they are Ovidian in wit. But Donne also used the term for several brief laments, "A Funeral Elegy" (1610) for Elizabeth Drury and an epitaph on Prince Henry (1613), whose untimely death in 1612 filled England with elegiac tributes. Still, of

Cyril Tourneur, John Webster, and Thomas Heywood, who each wrote dirges for Prince Henry, only Heywood favored the term "funeral elegy." None of the poems for Prince Henry in *Epicedium Cantabrigienses* (1612) were called elegies. Joshua Sylvester's *Lachrymae Lachrymarum, Part 2, Sundry Funerall Elegies* (1613), however, which included contributions by Donne, Edward Herbert, Henry Burton, Henry Goodyear, and others, marked a watershed. William Alexander, Robert Allyn, George Wither, and Campion all composed English epicedia called elegies for Prince Henry. The taste for personal elegies spilled over to the commemoration of the deaths of lesser notables. Murdered William Peter was memorialized in a long poem in quatrains now attributed to Shakespeare titled "A Funeral Elegy" (1612). Christopher Brooke and William Browne each published an elegy on Prince Henry (1613) and on the murdered essayist Thomas Overbury (1616). Donne's death in 1631 incited the production of English-styled elegies by Thomas Carew, Lucius Cary, Sidney Godolphin, Edward Herbert, and Izaak Walton. But, with the exception of two elegies for noblewomen in the 1630s, Ben Jonson, who also numbered "the dapper Elegie" among his lyrics, preferred epigrams and epitaphs for his severe memorial verse. By styling his own couplets on Shakespeare and Lady Winchester epitaphs, Milton resisted the fashion of writing English elegies. Milton himself wrote several Ovidian elegies in elegant Latin—two being on death— but, despite being otherwise indebted to Spenser, referred to *Lycidas* (1638; 1645) as a "monody." In 1639, Milton mourned his friend Charles Diodati in Latin hexameters called *Epitaphium Damonis*. Although loss and consolation could be the topic of a Roman or British elegist, the English pastoral elegy traces its formal origins not to Catullus, Ovid, Tibullus, and Propertius, but to Theocritus, Bion, Moschus, and Vergil, in whose bucolics we find shepherds transforming into song the heartache of love and death.

BIBLIOGRAPHY
Foster, Donald W. *Elegy by W.S.* 1989.
Pigman, G.W., III. *Grief and English Renaissance Elegy.* 1985.
Weitzmann, Francis. "Notes on the Elizabethan *Elegie.*" *PMLA,* vol. 50, pp. 435–443.

Steven Berkowitz

SEE ALSO
Classical Literature, Influence of; Epigrams; Sonnets

Elizabeth I (1533–1603)

Elizabeth Tudor's birth was a deep disappointment to her father. Henry VIII had broken with the church of Rome and decisively changed England's course religiously and politically to end his marriage with Katherine of Aragon in the hopes of finally having a son as a legitimate heir instead of his daughter Mary, Catherine's only surviving child. Instead, his second wife, Anne Boleyn, gave birth to Elizabeth on September 7, 1533, at Greenwich Palace. At first Henry proclaimed Elizabeth as his heir, but before she was three years old Henry had her mother Anne executed for adultery and treason. Elizabeth was declared illegitimate, as Mary had been earlier.

In 1536, only days after Anne Boleyn's execution, Henry married Jane Seymour, and the following year Jane gave birth to the future Edward VI, though she died soon after. Henry married three more times. Although Henry's religious policy fluctuated throughout the rest of his reign between more conservative (Catholic without the pope) and more real reform, Elizabeth's education was under such men of new learning as William Grindal and later Roger Ascham. In her teens Elizabeth became proficient in Latin, Greek, French, and Italian.

Henry died in January 1547. An act of Parliament in 1543 officially restored Mary and Elizabeth to the succession, though it did not restore their legitimacy. Elizabeth went to live with Henry's last wife, Catherine Parr, who soon made an imprudent marriage with her former suitor, Thomas Seymour, maternal uncle to the new king. In the early summer of 1548, the then pregnant Catherine Parr suggested that Elizabeth leave and set up her own household. Parr was upset by the over-familiarity that had developed between her husband and Elizabeth. Catherine Parr died after giving birth to a daughter at the end of August 1548, and Seymour engaged in a number of schemes to gain power; one of these included marrying Elizabeth. The following year the Privy Council had Seymour executed for treason. Elizabeth herself was touched by scandal and subjected to a rigorous examination; Sir Robert Tyrwhit informed her that many people believed she was pregnant by Thomas Seymour. She demanded to come to court to show herself, but Edward Seymour, duke of Somerset and lord protector, refused her request. During the rest of her brother Edward's reign, Elizabeth lived quietly, and dressed with ostentatious simplicity, thus regaining her reputation as a model of the Reformed faith.

Edward died in the summer of 1553, and his death led to a dynastic crisis. Edward disinherited both his sisters in

E

Elizabeth I. From George Puttenham, *The Arte of English Poesie* (1589). Reproduced from the original by permission of the Henry E. Huntington Library and Art Gallery.

favor of his cousin, Lady Jane Grey, recently married to the youngest son of the most powerful man of the realm, John Dudley, duke of Northumberland, who had led a coup to topple and then destroy the duke of Somerset. Without the force of Parliament, Edward's will was patently illegal; it was also highly unpopular, and Elizabeth's sister Mary succeeded to the throne without a contest. Elizabeth joined Mary in her triumphant procession through London, but she soon lost favor with her Catholic half-sister. Many of the English perceived Elizabeth as the Protestant alternative. Thomas Wyatt's rebellion of 1554 against Mary's marriage to her cousin, Philip II of Spain, caused Mary and her council to send Elizabeth to the Tower, where she was kept for two months. Elizabeth was afraid she would be executed, like her cousin Lady Jane Grey. Nothing could be proved against Elizabeth, however, and her life was spared. On Mary's death Elizabeth peacefully ascended the throne on November 17, 1558.

Many of the English, distressed by Mary's religious persecution and the losing war with France, were delighted with their new young queen, though some worried that her reign would be short and chaos would follow. Elizabeth began her reign emphasizing the theme of national unity. One of Elizabeth's first acts was to appoint William Cecil, whom she had known since the time she lived in Catherine Parr's household, as her principal secretary. Eventually, he achieved the title Lord Burghley and treasurer. It was to be a long and fruitful partnership. She had other loyal servants, including Sir Francis Walsingham, Sir Christopher Hatton, and Sir Robert Dudley.

The English Protestant community believed that Elizabeth's safe accession was God's will, and Elizabeth chose to follow the path of reform in the church settlement of 1559. There are, however, a variety of historical perspectives on how actually devout a Protestant Elizabeth actually was. The 1559 Acts of Supremacy and Uniformity made the celebration of Mass illegal and established fines for those who stayed away from the Church of England. Once the question of religious practice was settled in 1559, Elizabeth did not want any further discussion. Elizabeth wished for outward conformity, and as broadly based a religious settlement as possible. As her reign progressed she was unwilling to compromise with the growing Puritan movement, which had support in Parliament and among some of her church hierarchy. Edmund Grindal, archbishop of Canterbury, was suspended from his duties, though not actually deprived of office, over the issue of "prophesying," congregations being allowed to hold discussions on Scriptural texts. Elizabeth perceived these meetings as forums for dissatisfactions with the established church, but Grindal refused to suppress them.

Another significant issue for Elizabeth was the succession. Most of the English hoped this issue, as well as the problem of a woman ruling, would be solved when Elizabeth married and had a son. Elizabeth, however, while she played with courtship and perceived its use as a useful political tool, refused actually to marry; she also would not name an heir. The example of Henry and his succession of wives would hardly have convinced Elizabeth that marriage was an enviable estate or that even if she married she would have a surviving son or survive the rigors of childbirth herself. Elizabeth had a variety of suitors: her former brother-in-law, Philip II; the Hapsburg Archduke Charles; the Scottish earl of Arran, Eric of Sweden; and the sons of Catherine de Medici, both Henry, duke of Anjou (later Henry III), and Francis, duke of Alençon, later duke of Anjou. Robert Dudley, to whom Elizabeth eventually gave the title earl of Leicester, was also a forceful suitor for her hand. For years rumors swept around Elizabeth and Dudley, particularly after the mysterious death of his wife, Amy Robsart, in 1560. People gossiped

E

that Elizabeth was pregnant by Dudley. Later in her reign anxiety over the succession manifested itself not only in rumors that Elizabeth had illegitimate children, but that she had deliberately destroyed them, as well.

The problems of religion and the succession were interconnected, especially since Elizabeth remained unmarried and refused to name an heir. By primogeniture, Elizabeth's Catholic cousin, Mary Queen of Scots, granddaughter of Henry VIII's older sister Margaret, was the next heir. In fact, for some Catholics, Mary was the legitimate queen, since the pope had never recognized the nullity of Henry VIII's marriage to Katherine of Aragon, thus making Elizabeth a bastard. The situation became far more serious for England in 1568 when Mary Stuart fled Scotland and put herself into her cousin's hands. Elizabeth did not want to return Mary to Scotland as queen with full power, nor did she want to see the Scots execute Mary. Allowing her to go on to France or Spain might mean that Mary would return to Scotland with an army. Elizabeth kept Mary in confinement for the next nineteen years. Her presence in England undermined the delicate religious balance, leading to the Northern Rebellion in 1569 and to Elizabeth's excommunication by papal bull in 1570. During Mary's captivity there were a number of plots to assassinate Elizabeth, free the Scottish queen, and place Mary on the English throne with the aid of foreign invasion. In 1572, Thomas Howard, duke of Norfolk, was executed for his role in a plot to free Mary and marry her. In 1584, Protestants formed the Bond of Association, whose signatories threatened Mary with death if Elizabeth was assassinated. The Babington Plot of 1586 finally led to Elizabeth's reluctant decision to sign Mary's death warrant; she was executed on February 8, 1587.

The problems with Mary Stuart demonstrated the impact of religious division on international politics. There were others. The English supported the Protestants in the Netherlands against the Spanish. Mary Stuart's execution helped to convince Philip that it was righteous for Spain to conquer England and restore it to Catholicism. He also would not be invading England to help put the close ally of France, Mary Stuart, on the throne. Philip finally committed himself to the invasion; in the summer of 1588, after a number of delays, he launched the Armada.

One of the great moments of Elizabeth's reign came in August 1588, when she went to Tilbury Camp to encourage the assembled troops. Although we do not know definitely, what has come down in history as her speech at that occasion does express Elizabeth's self-identity. Elizabeth proclaimed that while she might have "the body of a weak and feeble woman, I have the heart and stomach of a king, and a king of England too, and think foul scorn that Parma or Spain, or any prince of Europe, should dare invade the borders of my realm. . . ." A combination of English naval skill and bad weather foiled the invasion.

In a number of ways, the final fifteen years of Elizabeth's reign after the defeat of the Armada were difficult. The advisors she trusted most died. To her great personal grief she lost Dudley in 1588. Walsingham died in 1590. Burghley's death in 1598 was also a great blow. The economy suffered from the drain of the long and expensive struggle in Ireland, as well as the continued support of the revolt in the Netherlands. There were bad harvests and inflation. Continued struggles with Puritans over the religious settlement were also divisive. In 1594, Elizabeth's physician, Roderigo Lopez, of Portuguese Jewish background, though outwardly an Anglican, was accused of planning to poison the queen and executed. That spring, Christopher Marlowe's *Jew of Malta* was put on frequently to sellout crowds. The anti-Jewish sentiment was paralleled by a belief that the relatively few Africans in England were one cause of the economic problems because they were taking jobs away from the English. Elizabeth issued an edict in 1601, in which she complained of the influx and ordered them transported out of the country. In fact, most of them stayed and more entered, usually not by choice, in the next century.

Another serious problem was the struggle for power of some of the younger men at court for Elizabeth's favor, such as Robert Cecil and Sir Walter Ralegh. Her relationship with her last favorite, Robert Devereux, earl of Essex, the young stepson of the earl of Leicester, was especially difficult. Alternately he cajoled and threatened the queen in an effort to gain power, seeking glory from military exploits such as the capture of Cadiz in 1596. He was, however, both profligate and unstable, and feared Robert Cecil's growing influence. In 1599, Essex led a disastrous campaign in Ireland to subdue rebels. The disgrace he faced when he returned to England without leave eventually led him to stage a rebellion against the queen in 1601. It failed, and Essex was executed.

The latter part of Elizabeth's reign was also marked by a flowering in literary cultural development. The work of such men as Edmund Spenser and William Shakespeare must have drawn inspiration from the extraordinary woman who ruled England both as a Virgin Queen and mother of her people. And while literature, and especially drama, was most remarkable, architecture, music, and

Elizabeth I 225

E

portrait painting were also flourishing. Overseas trade was expanding and there was the beginning of interest in expansion and colonial development, though this meant the beginning of involvement in the slave trade.

Elizabeth aged visibly after the Essex rebellion and his subsequent execution. She held the final Parliament of her reign that same year. Though her physicians could not name a specific complaint, by the beginning of 1603 her health began to fail, and she died on March 24, 1603. Elizabeth had always refused to name an heir, stating God would take care of England. Her cousin, James VI of Scotland, the son of Mary Stuart, peacefully ascended the throne of England after Elizabeth.

Although there were problems throughout the reign, most historians believe that Elizabeth will be remembered more for her successes than for her failures. England under Elizabeth survived as an independent nation, not dominated by any foreign power. Her religious policy was broadly based, and despite attacks on it by Puritans and Catholics, England did not suffer through the religious wars of its continental neighbors. Elizabeth's godson, Sir John Harington, suggested that the queen's success came from convincing the English people through her assurances that she loved them, and the love that she inspired in return.

BIBLIOGRAPHY

Doran, Susan. *Monarchy and Matrimony: The Courtships of Elizabeth I.* 1996.

Frye, Susan. *Elizabeth I: The Competition for Representation.* 1993.

Levin, Carole. *The Heart and Stomach of a King: Elizabeth I and the Politics of Sex and Power.* 1994.

MacCaffrey, Wallace. *Elizabeth I.* 1993.

Somerset, Anne. *Elizabeth I.* 1991.

Carole Levin

SEE ALSO

Alençon and Anjou, Duke of; Babington Plot; Boleyn, Anne; Devereux, Robert; Dudley, Robert; Foreign Relations and Diplomacy; Grey, Lady Jane; Henry VIII; Northern Rebellion; Parr, Catherine; Philip II; Ralegh, Sir Walter; Wyatt's Rebellion; Robsart, Amy; Supremacy, Act of; Uniformity, Act of

Elizabeth of York (1465–1503)

Elizabeth of York was the eldest child of Edward IV and his queen, Elizabeth Woodville-Grey, the sister of Edward V, the niece of Richard III, the wife of Henry VII, the mother of Henry VIII, and the woman for whom her granddaughter, Elizabeth I, was named. Hers was a life defined largely by these family roles rather than through political activities of her own. Her motto, "Humble and reverent," therefore seems apt. Her life, however, is paradigmatic of the rhythms of the Wars of the Roses. During her childhood, her Yorkist father, Edward IV, was forced into exile by the adherents of the Lancastrian Henry VI, and the family sought sanctuary in Westminster Abbey. When Edward victoriously returned to the throne, the family was returned to positions of wealth and power. When Edward died in 1483, the throne was seized by his brother, who became Richard III, and Elizabeth's family again took refuge in the abbey. During this period, Elizabeth's two brothers, Edward V and Richard, duke of York, were murdered in the Tower of London. Perhaps to silence rumors of responsibility for these deaths, Richard III publicly promised security to Elizabeth and her mother and her sisters once they left sanctuary. Shortly afterward, Richard wooed Elizabeth for his wife and queen. However real these plans were, they were interrupted by the return to England of the Lancastrian Henry Tudor, earl of Richmond, and the final battle of the Wars of the Roses at Bosworth Field. Henry left the battle as King Henry VII with the understanding that he marry the heiress of the Yorkist faction. He and Elizabeth of York were married on January 18, 1486. Elizabeth's coronation was held on November 25, 1486, more than a year after her husband's. By then her first child, Arthur, was two months old. Other children included Margaret, who became queen of Scotland through marriage to James IV; Henry, who succeeded his father to become Henry VIII; and Mary, who became queen of France through her marriage to Louis XII. Elizabeth died on her thirty-eighth birthday in 1503. She is buried in the Henry VII Chapel in Westminster Abbey.

BIBLIOGRAPHY

Gairdner, James. *Letters and Papers Illustrative of the Reigns of Richard III and Henry VI.* 1861.

Hall, Edward. *Chronicle Containing the History of England.* 1809 edition.

Harvey, Nancy Lenz. *Elizabeth of York: The Mother of Henry VIII.* 1973.

Nancy Lenz Harvey

SEE ALSO

Henry VII; Henry VIII; Wars of the Roses

Elyot, Thomas (c. 1490–1546)

Lexicographer, translator, and one of the most influential English humanists of the first half of the sixteenth century, Sir Thomas Elyot was the son of Sir Richard Elyot, a prosperous West Country justice, and Alice Delamere. Well-read, "well-fed," and, by his own account, largely self-taught in the liberal arts, Elyot was primarily a man of affairs. As an author, he was less a scholar and philosopher than a compiler and stylist. In trying times, Elyot was an advocate for principled counsel, but no martyr.

Before being admitted to the Middle Temple in 1510, Elyot may have attended an Inn of Chancery and was perhaps assisted in learning Greek by Thomas Linacre. Probably appointed at the request of his father, Elyot served from 1510 until 1526 as clerk of assize of the western circuit. After his father's death and his marriage to Margaret Barrow, Elyot came under Cardinal Thomas Wolsey's patronage and served as clerk for Henry VIII's Council (c. 1523–1530). In 1531, to regain royal preferment after Wolsey's fall, Elyot published his absolutist political theories and wide-ranging humanist course for the education of young aristocrats in *The Boke of the Governour*. For this, his major work—part manual of instruction, part political tract—Elyot drew on his own translation of Plutarch's *De educatione puerorum, The Education or Bringinge Up of Children* (1533?). Other sources include Plato's *Republic,* Aristotle's *Politics* and *Ethics,* Quintilian, Cicero's *De officiis, De amicitia,* and *De oratore,* writings by Francesco Patrizi and Giovanni Pontano, Castiglione's *Courtier,* and Desiderius Erasmus's *Institutio principis christiani.*

The first of the *Governour's* three books describes a hierarchical state ruled by an absolute monarch or "capital governour": "a publike weale is a body lyvyng, compacte or made of sondry astates and degrees of men, whiche is disposed by the ordre of equite and governed by the rule and moderation of reason" (I, 2). Boys born to wield authority are to be intellectually and morally trained in classical poetry, history, and philosophy, guided by reverence for Scripture, tempered by music and painting, and hardened by physical exercise. In addition to martial skills, dancing is approved for its marriage of male and female natures (I, 21). The second book advises the governors on employing their authority with affable benevolence. Chapter 12 illustrates "amitie" by Boccaccio's tale of Titus and Gisyppus, which Shakespeare may have used for *Two Gentlemen of Verona,* where friendship conquers love. The third book's discussion of justice, fortitude, magnanimity, continence, temperance, wisdom, and consultation brings out the central tension of this eclectic work: a program of ethical instruction ultimately curbs the sovereign power of the monarch. What is a "paterne to knyghtes" is also a "myrrour to princes" (*Image of Governance*).

Written for advancement or as consolation for his lack thereof, Elyot's works also share the intent of advancing the beauty and utility of the English language, borrowing from ancient models for the complexity of its syntax and increasing through translations and loanwords the richness of its vocabulary. To embody "majesty," a governor's speech should be "compendious, sententious, and delectable" (*Governour* I, 2). Common words first appearing in *The Boke of the Governour* include *tolerate, explicate, animate, analogy, acumen, hostility, education, modesty, society, elegy,* and *democracy* (Kennedy 53–57).

Supported by Thomas Cromwell, in 1531 Elyot was appointed ambassador to Charles V with the assigment of persuading the Holy Roman Emperor to accept Henry's divorce of Katherine of Aragon. Elyot's lack of zeal was soon apparent, and he was replaced by Thomas Cranmer after just a few months. In later years, Elyot feared that his friendship with Sir Thomas More made his own loyalty suspect and, although he would serve as sheriff, justice of the peace, on various commissions, and as member of Parliament, he was never again offered high office.

Elyot's *Pasquil the Playne* (1533) and *Of the Knowledge whiche Maketh a Wise Man* (1533) are Socratic dialogues that dramatize the counselor's dilemma: that flattery and dissimulation rather than wisdom and plainness are the paths to power. *The Bankette of Sapience* (1535?) was a gathering of adages from pagan and Christian sources offered for Henry VIII's pleasure and edification. *The Castell of Helthe* (1536?), also a compendium, was the first medical treatise in English to be widely circulated and recommends food and exercise by which one may restore the proper balance of the humors. In 1538, Elyot, again hoping for preferment, dedicated the first Latin-English dictionary to Henry VIII. Derived from an Italian predecessor, the dictionary has been praised as the foundation of English lexicography. With the king's encouragement, the work doubled in size and became encyclopedic as *Bibliotheca Eliotae: Eliotis Librarie* (1542). Elyot dedicated the first edition of his *The Defence of Good Women* (1540), a brief dialogue based on Boccaccio's *De claris mulieribus,* to Henry's new and soon-to-be disavowed queen, Anne of Cleves.

Besides the enduring influence Elyot had on the English ideal of the educated gentleman, which was furthered

E

by Roger Ascham and Henry Peacham, much of Elyot's importance lies in his writings being a storehouse for poets. For example, Ulysses' speech on degree in Shakespeare's *Troilus and Cressida* (I.ii.109) echoes the *Governour*'s concept of order: "take away ordre from all thynges what shulde then remayne?" (I, 1).

BIBLIOGRAPHY

Baker, Herschel. *The Dignity of Man.* 1947.

Croft, H.H.S., ed. *The Boke of the Governour.* 2 vols. 1883.

Dees, Jerome S. "Recent Studies in Elyot." *English Literary Renaissance,* vol. 6, pp. 336–344.

Fox, Alistair. "Sir Thomas Elyot and the Humanist Dilemma." In *Reassessing the Henrician Age.* Alistair Fox and John Guy, eds., pp. 52–73. 1986.

Hogrefe, Pearl. *The Life and Times of Sir Thomas Elyot, Englishman.* 1967.

Kennedy, Teresa. *Elyot, Castiglione, and the Problem of Style.* 1996.

Lehmberg, Sanford E. *Sir Thomas Elyot, Tudor Humanist.* 1960.

Steven Berkowitz

SEE ALSO

Ascham, Roger; Classical Literature, English Translations; Cromwell, Thomas; Dictionaries; Education; Humanism; More, Thomas

Emblem Books

Illustrated books known as emblem books combine moralizing texts with allegorical images in a format that has influenced wider understanding of word-image relationships in literature and the visual arts. The genre was invented in 1531, when an Augsburg printer supplied illustrative woodcuts to the collection of Latin epigrams by the Milanese lawyer, Andrea Alciato, to which the author had given the title *Emblemata,* a Greek word meaning "mosaic, or inlaid work." Alciato's *Emblematum liber* ("Book of Emblems") consists of epigrams modeled on the *Greek Anthology* in which he draws a deeper meaning from more or less visual subjects. During the next fifteen years in France this novel combination of epigrammatic text and pictorial image developed into a standard format, consisting of a sententious motto (*inscriptio*), a speaking picture (*pictura*), and an epigrammatic or explanatory poem (*subscriptio*). Several thousand editions of such emblem books were to appear over the next 250 years, with the result that the word "emblem" came to assume the meaning of "symbol" or "pictorial parable" that it now has in most European languages.

England was late on the scene, only half-dozen English emblem books having appeared before 1600, although there is good evidence that continental emblem books circulated quite widely from the 1550s onward. The earliest English emblem book is almost certainly Thomas Palmer's manuscript *Two Hundred Poosies,* composed around 1565 for presentation to Robert Dudley, earl of Leicester, but the first printed emblem book is Geffrey Whitney's *A Choice of Emblemes* (1586), compiled during Leicester's campaign in the Netherlands and printed in Leiden using borrowed woodcuts drawn from the stock of printer Christopher Plantin. Though Whitney's *picturae* are mostly borrowed, his imitations of his continental sources in the verse epigrams are inventive, and the book has an overall structure that it owes to none of its sources. Much closer to its continental source is Thomas Combe's *Theater of Fine Devices* (c. 1593), which translates a French emblem book by Guillaume de la Perrière. In 1591, a certain "P.S." translated *The Heroical Devices of M. Claudius Paradin,* to which were added the thirty-seven *Imprese* composed by the exiled Italian Gabriel Simeoni. This was a major channel through which the specific conventions

Occasion. From Guillaume de la Perriere, *Theater of Fine Devices* (1614). In this typical emblem, the picture and the poem convey the same ideas in different media. Reproduced from the original by permission of the Henry E. Huntington Library and Art Gallery.

of the Italian *impresa* were transmitted to Elizabethan England. The *impresa* (or "device") differs from the emblem, with which it was (and is) often confused, insofar as the emblem offers a generalized moral applicable to all its readers, whereas the impresa is a personal device unique to its bearer. As the poet William Drummond put it in his letter to the earl of Perth, "Emblems serve for demonstration of some general thing, and for general rule . . . an impresa is a demonstration and manifestation of some notable and excellent thought of him that conceived it, and useth it; and it belongs only to him." As opposed to the three parts of the emblem, the *impresa* consists only of motto and picture (lacking the verse *subscriptio*).

English knowledge of continental emblem theory is attested to by Samuel Daniel's *The Worthy Tract of Paulus Iovius* (1585), a translation of Paulo Giovio's *Dialogo dell'imprese* (1556). In 1588, Abraham Fraunce, a prominent member of the literary circle surrounding Sir Philip Sidney, published an *Explicatio* of "those signs, coats of arms, emblems, hieroglyphs, and devices which the Italians call *Imprese*." Fraunce's interest may suggest why so much of the writing of the English poetic renaissance centering on Sidney and Edmund Spenser should have used imagery that has widely been recognized as "emblematic."

The bimedial form of the emblem meant that it has important relationships with both literature and the visual arts, applications that have come to be known as "applied emblematics." At a time when assumptions encouraged conceptions of poetry as, in Sidney's phrase, "a speaking picture," emblem books were always likely to influence poetics. Emblems also came to have extensive interrelations with the visual arts. In the Tudor period these extend from the inclusion of (inset) personal devices in so-called "impresa portraits," to decorative painting and plasterwork, where the use of suggestive images in particular architectural *loci* may have important connections with the art of memory. They were widely used in pageants, ceremonial entries, and court festivals, including the annual accession day tournaments when courtiers, often in elaborate tiltyard or masquing costumes, delivered set speeches before Elizabeth and presented her with their *impresa* shields. These pasteboard shields were painted with symbolic devices that normally contained a message specific to the bearer's courtly circumstances and aspirations. They were subsequently hung in a famous shield gallery at Whitehall, where they became a tourist attraction for visitors. Emblem books were at an early stage of their long development in England at the time of Elizabeth I's death, but these manifold contexts suggest that they were already strongly embedded in English culture by the end of the Tudor period.

BIBLIOGRAPHY

Bath, Michael. *Speaking Pictures: English Emblem Books and Renaissance Culture.* 1994.

Daly, Peter M. *Literature in the Light of the Emblem.* 1979.

———, ed. *The English Emblem Tradition. Index Emblematicus.* 1988–.

———, and Virginia W. Callahan. *Andreas Alciatus Index Emblematicus.* 2 vols. 1985.

Freeman, Rosemary. *English Emblem Books.* 1974.

Höltgen, Karl Josef. *Aspects of the Emblem: Studies in the English Emblem Tradition and the European Context.* 1986.

Praz, Mario. *Studies in Seventeenth-century Imagery.* 1939.

Michael Bath

SEE ALSO

Daniel, Samuel; Epigrams; Fraunce, Abraham; Heraldry

Empson, Richard (d. 1510)

Finance minister to Henry VII, Richard Empson is best known for his association with Edmund Dudley, the better known of the two ministers executed by Henry VIII on August 17, 1510. Little is known about Empson's life before 1473, the year of his father's death, but thereafter Empson is associated in county records with influential members of Parliament on royal commissions. In 1475, he entered royal service as justice of the peace in Lancaster, and became attorney general for the duchy of Lancaster in 1478.

The end of Yorkist rule threatened Empson's career, but he quickly realigned his allegiances and gained the patronage of Sir Reginald Bray, Henry VII's most trusted minister. Reappointed attorney general, Empson succeeded Bray to the chancellorship of the duchy of Lancaster in 1505, becoming Henry's senior minister. Empson's association with Dudley was particularly strong during the final years of Henry's rule, when both men had prominent roles in the king's increasingly unpopular revenue policies. Both had charge of fines and forfeitures, and although it is unclear to what extent Empson profited from collecting royal debts, he earned along with Dudley the enmity of nobles and merchants alike, whose complaints were appeased by the new king. Empson was arrested only days after the accession of Henry VIII, charged along with Dudley with conspiracy against the king, and executed after a year in the Tower.

E

BIBLIOGRAPHY

Dietz, Frederick C. *English Government Finance, 1485–1558.* 2nd edition. Vol. 1, pp. 33–50. 1964.

Horowitz, Mark R. "Richard Empson, minister of Henry VII." *Bulletin of the Institute of Historical Research,* vol. 55, pp. 35–49.

Richardson, W.C. *Tudor Chamber Administration, 1485–1547.* pp. 141–58. 1952.

David W. Swain

SEE ALSO
Dudley, Edmund; Henry VII

Enclosure

Enclosure signifies the act of fencing or hedging land previously subject to common rights, thereby excluding other commoners from enjoying its natural resources. Enclosed land may be arable, meadow, pasture, or waste, but under a common-field system it is enjoyed in common by a defined group of people, usually all landholders, and often all residents of the same village, hamlet, or parish. The commoners take its bracken, furze, wood, berries, sand, peat, or herbage for grazing according to their needs, though the quantities allowed to each person may be restricted by the community's bylaws. The grazing of animals on arable fields is confined to certain weeks after harvest and in the fallow season; animal numbers on common pastures are generally restricted according to the size of each commoner's landholding. Bylaws could change allowances according to circumstances.

Enclosure might be carried out by agreement with other commoners, in which case the encloser surrendered his corresponding share in the remaining common lands. But enclosers sometimes took action without consultation; in any case, all manorial lords, by the statutes of Merton and Westminster (1235, 1284), had the right to enclose their commons so long as they left "enough" for their tenants. Disputes about what was "enough" inevitably led to endless quarrels in periods of land shortage.

Enclosure in the sixteenth century became highly controversial because of the growing demand for land. Rising food prices spurred farmers to farm more intensively, and they objected when their freedom was curtailed by common rights. After the Black Death in the mid-fourteenth century, much arable land was put under grass as a rational economic solution to a lowered demand for food. After 1500, as population recovered, it was necessary to plow it up again. But past experience had established a firm association between enclosure and the conversion of arable land to pasture, and many farmers continued to favor the opportunity to convert once their land was enclosed. Enclosure for pasture was thus assumed in popular debate, and because of food shortages and serious unemployment under the Tudors, opposition to enclosure was bitter. Public protests resulted in severe governmental measures against enclosure: commissions of enquiry were conducted in 1517, 1548, and 1565, and acts against enclosure were passed in 1489, 1515, and 1536.

In fact, both the incidence of enclosure, whether of arable or of pasture land, and its motives in each part of the country, varied greatly according to pressure on the land and the local farming system. It aroused most tension in the Midland counties of Warwickshire, Leicestershire, Northamptonshire, and Bedfordshire, but none at all in Kent, Essex, Cornwall, and Devon. Generally, it was most controversial in densely settled areas where the land was readily convertible to arable or pasture. Gradually, the government discerned the complexity of enclosure and modified restrictions on it. In 1593, a statute actually allowed enclosure, but at the wrong moment, for a series of bad harvests followed. Consent was withdrawn in 1597–1598, but land that was being converted to pasture for a few years only, in order to regain its fertility, was allowed to remain. By 1600, good harvests and falling food prices led some members of Parliament to argue that farmers should be left free to do what they liked with their land. But a final change of policy was delayed by more bad harvests, the Midland Revolt in 1607, and several bad seasons in the 1620s and 1630s, until all opposition to enclosure ended in the 1650s.

BIBLIOGRAPHY

Thirsk, Joan. *Tudor Enclosures.* Historical Association pamphlet G41. 1989.

———, ed. *Agrarian History of England and Wales, IV, 1500–1640.* 1967.

Joan Thirsk

SEE ALSO
Agriculture; Food and Diet; Population and Demography

English College at Douai
See Allen, William

E

English College of Rome

The *Venerabile Collegium Anglorum de Urbe* was formally established on April 23, 1579. Proposals for using the English Hospice of San Tommaso in Rome to train English priests were not given serious consideration until the pontificate of Gregory XIII (1572–1585), who was interested in educating priests to win back to the Catholic faith the regions of Europe lost to Protestantism. Pope Gregory and Cardinal Girolamo Morone, the protector of England, approved the plan of Owen Lewis and William Allen to house English students at the hospice. From his college at Douai, Allen in 1576 began sending students to the hospice, where they were supervised until 1578 by Gregory Martin, and then by Maurice Clenock, the warden of the hospice, who became the college's first rector.

Pope Gregory's bull formally constituting the English College provided it with annual revenues of 3,000 gold scudi, and with possession of the abbey of San Sabina, near Piacenza, which brought in additional annual revenues of 3,000 ducats. Initially, the English College had places for forty students, and these were increased by 1585 to seventy. The statutes of the college, promulgated on June 12, 1579, required that students could be no younger than fourteen years, nor older than twenty-five years, and that they be physically healthy and of good moral character. Students also had to swear fealty to the pope and to the Catholic Church and an oath to receive holy orders and return to England for the salvation of souls, at the direction of the superiors of the college. The spiritual and educational program instituted by the Jesuits was seen as preparing the students for martyrdom and followed strict courses of study and devotion as well as a spartan personal regimen.

In 1579, the English students complained that Clenock, who was Welsh, was favoring Welsh students. An Italian Jesuit, Alphonso Agazzari, was appointed its rector, with Allen's blessing. However, in 1585, after a large number of students again rebelled against the rector, complaining of the rigorous Jesuits discipline and of partiality to students who seemed inclined to join the Society of Jesus, Allen advised the pope to appoint an English rector. Agazzari was thus succeeded by a series of English Jesuit rectors, including Robert Parsons briefly in 1588–1589. Agazzari returned twice as rector, but tensions continued until Parsons returned to the college as rector in 1598. With the support of Pope Clement VIII and the cardinal protector, Enrico Cajetan, and after compromising on matters of discipline, he restored order and Jesuit control to the college.

BIBLIOGRAPHY

Foley, Henry. *Records of the English Province of the Society of Jesus.* Vol. 6, 1880; vol. 7:1, 1882; vol. 7:2, 1883.

Gasquet, Francis A. *History of the Venerable English College, Rome.* 1920.

Meyer, Arnold O. *England and the Catholic Church under Queen Elizabeth.* J.R. Mckee, trans. 1915.

Pollen, John H. *The English Catholics in the Reign of Queen Elizabeth.* 1920.

Prichard, Arnold. *Catholic Loyalism in Elizabethan England.* 1979.

Williams, Michael E. *The Venerable English College, Rome.* 1979.

John M. Currin

SEE ALSO

Allen, William; Catholicism; Jesuits; Parsons, Robert

Engraving and Illustration

Tudor engravings, whether woodcuts, line engravings on copper and other metal plates, or etchings, were primarily used to ornament and illustrate books, and comprised the most widely distributed and accessible form of representational art in Tudor England. Like other visual arts, printmaking tended to follow continental fashions, and the trade depended heavily on foreign-born practitioners, although some important native engravers began to appear late in Elizabeth's reign. Printmakers, like other artisans, were mostly anonymous; only a few achieved enough individual distinction that their names survive.

A small group of single-sheet woodcuts, devotional pieces without much aesthetic distinction, seem to have been produced in England in the fifteenth century. From the outset, however, printers in England began including woodcut illustrations and ornaments in their books, starting with William Caxton's *Mirour of the World* (1481). The second of Caxton's editions of Chaucer's *Canterbury Tales* (1483) includes appealing vignettes of many of the pilgrims. The most extensively illustrated of Caxton's early works was the endlessly popular collection of saints' lives, *The Golden Legend (Legenda Aurea),* first issued in 1493–1494 and several times reprinted; the cut representing the murder of Thomas à Becket is particularly fine.

Caxton's successors, Wynkyn de Worde and Richard Pynson, carried on his devotion to woodcut, even using some of his blocks again. Indeed, a feature of Tudor printing was the reuse of individual cuts, not only from edition to edition of the same work, but in different works, and

E

Theodore de Bry, *Sitting at Meate.* From Thomas Hariot, *A Briefe and True Report* (1590). De Bry's fine copperplate engravings for Hariot's account of the Virginia colony were based on drawings by John White, the artist on the first Roanoke Island expedition under Ralph Lane. De Bry had negotiated through Richard Hakluyt to illustrate Hariot's text. Here natives sit to dine on maize, fish, nuts, and venison. De Bry's mannerist style ennobled his subjects with classical features and sculpted musculature. Reproduced from the original by permission of the Henry E. Huntington Library and Art Gallery.

even within the same work. Thus, in the chronicle histories, each one of a handful of idealized royal portraits might serve to represent several different kings who ruled at intervals over several hundred years, then reappear in an altogether different context in a different book published a decade later. Similarly, English printers often bought worn or outmoded blocks and plates from continental printers and gave them another ten or twenty years of use.

The most artistically distinguished woodcuts produced in earlier Tudor England were the work of Hans Holbein the Younger, especially a group of four illustrations of episodes from the New Testament (scattered through three different books published in the late 1540s). Holbein's famous treatment of the Dance of Death was an important influence on the striking memento-mori bor-

ders of John Day's *Book of Christian Prayer* (1569). Other relatively sophisticated work includes the energetic, often violent images in John Foxe's *Book of Martyrs [Actes and Monuments of the English Martyrs]* (1563), John Bettes' title page for the Bishop's Bible (1568), the cuts at the beginning of each section of Edmund Spenser's *Shepheardes Calender* (1579), the illustrations of military and political episodes in John Derricke's *Image of Ireland* (1581) and in the second edition of Holinshed (1587), and the hunting scenes (incorporating a portrait of Elizabeth I enjoying a picnic lunch) from George Turberville's *Book of Fauconrie* and *Noble Art of Venerie* (both 1575).

Less skillful work appeared in dozens of books of many kinds—representations of the Temple and of priestly regalia in the Geneva Bible, images of plants and animals in herbals and bestiaries, diagrams (crude to the point of incomprehensibility) of Sir John Harington's water closet and other devices and techniques, elaborate initial letters, and many title pages, borders, and colophons.

Metal engraving did not begin to appear in England until nearly a century after its first use on the Continent. But some of the earliest examples are also among the finest, in terms of both artistic and technical quality. Thomas Geminus (like most Tudor engravers an immigrant) produced illustrations for Andreus Vesalius's *Anatomia* (1545, based on Hans Stephan van Calcar's woodcuts for the Basle edition of 1543, *De Humanis Corpore Fabrica*) that set a high standard. Another important foreign-born engraver was Franciscus Hogenberg, whose single-sheet views of the royal palace of Nonesuch and of the Royal Exchange in London are important for architectural history. Marcus Gheeraerts the Elder (also significant as a painter) illustrated Jan van der Nodt's *Theatre of Worldlings* (1569; it includes the first published work of Edmund Spenser), but is best known for his treatment in several sheets of the installation procession for the Order of the Garter, placing idealized images of nearly thirty English and foreign dignitaries in an architectural setting against a landscape background, all of considerable elegance.

Theodore de Bry recorded in many sheets a detailed view of the funeral procession of Sir Philip Sidney (1589), and his engravings after John White's drawings of many Native American figures and scenes, published as illustrations to Thomas Hariot's *Virginia* (Frankfurt, 1590), not only gave the English their first visual introduction to the exotic encounters taking place across the Atlantic, but leave us an important insight into European attitudes toward the New World. DeBry, the brothers Franciscus and Remigius Hogenberg, Augustus Ryther, and Jacobus Hondius all worked in one of the most important areas of engraving, the making of maps and views, whether for atlases and other collections, as book illustrations, or as single sheets. Ryther's series on the Spanish Armada (1588), showing eleven different phases of the battle, has some historical value. These continental artists provided models for the English cartographers John Norden and Christopher Saxton, whose maps of the British Isles, shire by shire, whether bound together as atlases or dispersed as single sheets, adorned many late Tudor and Jacobean households.

Among native English engravers, Benjamin Wright reproduced the *Arms of the Chief Corporations of England* (1596), and designed elaborate symbolic representations of celestial bodies, collected in *Astrolabium uranicum generale*

Ionica, John Shute. Wood engraving from *The First and Chiefe Groundes of Architecture* (1563). A exceptional example of the impact of Renaissance classicism on the arts in Tudor England. By permission of the Royal Institute of British Architecture.

(1596). The most productive and versatile of them, Thomas Rogers, did botanical illustrations for John Gerard's *Herball* (1597), a large single-sheet redaction of Hans Eworth's great dynastic painting, *Henry VIII and his Successors,* elaborate title pages, and an important group of portraits, including several of the aging queen, mostly full-lengths rich in symbols, with titles like *Eliza Triumphans* (1589), and *Rosa Electa* (1592).

BIBLIOGRAPHY

Hind, A.M., Margery Corbett, and Michael Norton. *Engraving in England in the Sixteenth and Seventeenth Centuries.* 3 vols. 1952–1964.

David Evett

SEE ALSO

Caxton, William; Day, John; Foxe, John ; Gerard, John; Hariot, Thomas; Holbein, Hans; Holinshed, Raphael;

E

Norden, John ; Printing, Publishing, and Bookbinding; Spenser, Edmund; Saxton, Christopher; Turberville, George

Epic

Definitions and classifications of epic poetry vary widely, and not all of them are strictly applicable to Tudor literature. The most common definition—a long narrative poem centered on one or more exploits (usually martial) of a single hero or several heroes—does not by any means cover all of the necessary works. Distinctions have been drawn between diffuse and brief epics, oral and literary epics, and primary and secondary epics, between epics composed in verse or prose, between epics based on history and on fiction, and between epics centered on secular or religious themes. Renaissance concepts of the epic were shaped not only by the example of Homer and Vergil (and, to a lesser degree, Lucan and Ovid), but, particularly in Italy, by the influence of the commentaries on Aristotle's *Poetics* around the middle of the sixteenth century.

Although the precise extent to which late Tudor conceptions of epic were influenced by neo-Aristotelian poetic theory remains questionable, Sir Philip Sidney's *Defense of Poesie* and to a lesser degree John Harington's *Briefe Apologie of Poetrie* were clearly indebted to the Aristotelian tradition. Although Torquato Tasso's *Discourses on the Heroic Poem* (1594) would in all probability not have been known to Edmund Spenser, the latter may have encountered Tasso's *Discorsi dell'Arte Poetica* (composed around 1564 and published in 1587), and Spenser certainly knew (and was influenced by) Tasso's own epic poem, *Gerusalemme Liberata*. Demanding unity of action in plot, Aristotle argued that it should have for its subject a single action, "whole and complete, with a beginning, a middle, and an end." Aristotle regarded tragedy as superior to the epic.

In Horace's *Ars Poetica*, Renaissance poets and critics encountered the principle of beginning an epic narrative *in media res*; in the *Iliad* Homer carries "the listener into the midst of the story as though it were already known." This stipulation would subsequently become a cardinal doctrine of epic theory and practice. Spenser echoes it in his letter to Sir Walter Ralegh, prefixed to *The Faerie Queene*. No less significant, however, was Horace's praise of Homer for portraying his epic hero as an exemplar of virtue.

With few exceptions, such as Henry Howard, earl of Surrey's partial translation of the *Aeneid*, the development of Tudor epic occurs relatively late in the century—actually during the final decades of Elizabeth's reign. Among the factors that encouraged its development were the influence of continental humanism in English schools and universities; the correlative emphasis on the close study and imitation of classical authors; the patriotic ambition to enrich the English language and its literature; the growing interest in English antiquities and the desire to celebrate (or in some instances critique) the national past. A further consideration (which could act either as a stimulus or a deterrent) was the widespread Renaissance conception of the epic as the foremost but also the most difficult of literary genres.

The Tudor interest in both classical and modern epic is reflected in the large number of translations published during the sixteenth century. In 1581, there appeared Arthur Hall's version of ten books of the *Iliad*, based on the French of Hagues Salel and rendered in a meter known as fourteeners. George Chapman translated the *Iliad* in heptameter couplets (1598, 1611, 1616) and the *Odyssey* in heroic couplets (1614, 1616). William Fowldes's translation of the *Batrachomyomachia*, a short burlesque epic attributed to Homer, was published in "heroical verse" in 1603, and Chapman's translation of the same work appeared in 1616.

The Earl of Surrey's blank verse rendition of Books 2 and 4 of Vergil's *Aeneid* was published in Richard Tottel's *Tottel's Miscellany* in 1557; Book 4 had already appeared in 1554, printed by John Day. Thomas Phaer's incomplete translation of the *Aeneid* into English fourteeners appeared in 1558 and 1562; the 1584 edition of Phaer's work included Thomas Twyne's translation of the last three books of the *Aeneid* in addition to Twyne's version of a thirteenth book by Mapheus Vegius. Richard Stanyhurst's translation of the first four books of the *Aeneid* in quantitative verse appeared in 1582.

Christopher Marlowe's translation of the first book of Lucan's *Pharsalia*, rendered in blank verse, was published in 1600. Arthur Golding's translation of Ovid's *Metamorphoses* was published in 1567 in fourteeners; the first four books had appeared in 1565. Thomas Underdown's English rendition of Heliodorus's *AEthiopica* appeared around 1569. Harington's rendition of Ariosto's *Orlando Furioso* into "English Heroical Verse" (*ottava rima*) came out in 1591. Edward Fairfax's translation of Tasso's *Gerusalemme Liberata* (in *ottava rima*, like its original) appeared in 1600. Chapman's translation of Musaeus's epic *Hero and Leander* was published in 1616.

Like Lucan's *Pharsalia (De Bello Civili)* on the disastrous wars between Julius Ceasar and Pompey, Samuel Daniel's poem *The Civil Wars* (published in various installments between 1595 and 1609), and Michael Drayton's *The Barons Warres in the Reigne of Edward the Second* (published with various revisions between 1603 and 1619), merit consideration as historical epics, even though none of the three could altogether meet the rigorous criteria advanced by stricter theorists of the epic genre. In various degrees both of these English poets invite comparison with Lucan in their choice of an epic subject based on national history, in their insistence on the tragic consequences of civil conflict, in their choice of such a well-established epic verse-form as *ottava rima* (though Marlowe chose blank verse as a medium for his translation of the first book of Lucan's epic), and in their respective propositions and invocations.

Du Bartas's biblical epics also found English translators. Thomas Hudson's English translation of the brief epic *Judit* appeared in 1585, and Joshua Sylvester's version in 1614. Portions of du Bartas's *Semaines* were translated into English by Sidney, Thomas Churchyard, James I, John Eliot, William Lisle, Thomas Lodge, Thomas Winter, Robert Barrett, and others. Sylvester's translation of the first and second *Semaines* into English heroic couplets appeared in 1605 as *Bartas his Divine Weekes and Workes,* but portions had been published earlier.

During the latter decades of the sixteenth century the admiration of Ovid fostered a series of erotic epyllia, or brief epics. Beginning with Thomas Lodge's *Scillaes Metamorphosis* (1589), these included Marlowe's *Hero and Leander* (1598) and Chapman's continuation of it (1598), Thomas Heywood's *Oenone and Paris* (1594), Thomas Edwards's *Cephalus and Procris* (1595), Michael Drayton's *Endimion and Phoebe: Ideas Latmus* (1595), Chapman's *Ovids Banquet of Sense* (1595), John Marston's *The Metamorphosis of Pigmalions Image* (1598), John Weever's *Faunus and Melliflora* (1600), Francis Beaumont's *Salmacis and Hermaphroditus* (1602), Phineas Fletcher's *Venus and Anchises: Britain's Ida* (1628), and James Shirley's *Narcissus or the Self-Lover* (1646). Along with Marlowe's incomplete poem, however, the only outstanding example of the Ovidian erotic epyllion is William Shakespeare's *Venus and Adonis* (1593).

Spenser's avowed intention in *The Faerie Queene* "to fashion a gentleman or noble person in vertuous and gentle discipline" and "to portraict in Arthure, before he was king, the image of a brave knight, perfected in the twelve private moral vertues, as Aristotle hath devised," along with his emphasis on the practice of other epic poets who had "ensampled a good governour and a vertuous man," reflects the neo-Aristotelian and Horatian emphasis on the epic hero as an exemplar of heroic virtue. But in describing the *Faerie Queene* as "a continued Allegory or darke conceit," Spenser was apparently also following the example of many other epic poets such as Homer. Sir John Harington followed Simone Fornari and Gioseffo Bononome in allegorizing Ariosto's *Orlando Furioso*. Torquato Tasso, in turn, wrote his own "allegoria" for *Gerusalemme Liberata*.

Renaissance views on prose as a medium for epic poetry may provide a valid context for reexamining recent arguments that Sidney intended the revised version of his romance (the incomplete *New Arcadia*) to be regarded as a heroic poem. The fact that Sidney composed his romance in a mixture of prose and verse would not, in the eyes of many of its original readers, have compromised its status as true poetry, for on the question whether verse was or was not absolutely essential to poetry Renaissance critics were significantly divided.

Even more apposite for the genre of Sidney's revised *Arcadia* was the Renaissance conception of Heliodorus's prose romance as epic poetry. In *Poetices Libri Septem* Julius Caesar Scaliger extolled the *AEthiopica* as a model epic. In *Palladis Tamia,* in a passage that echoes almost verbatim Sidney's praise of Xenophon's Cyropaedia and Heliodorus's *AEthiopica* as heroic poetry, Francis Meres expressly compares Sidney's Arcadia with both of these works as prose poems. Different as they are in many ways—in style, structure and form, and literary models— the two most important heroic poems of the Elizabethan period are romances (or romance epics) left incomplete by their authors—the *New Arcadia* and the *Faerie Queene*.

On the whole, however, Elizabethan epic poets are far from strict or consistent in their imitations of, and borrowings from, classical antiquity; and the type of neoclassical epic favored by critics, such as Julius Ceasar Scaliger and Marco Girolamo Vida, seems to have been alien to the age. The overall impression one receives from their use of classical models often appears distinctly unclassical; and their adaptations of the principles of *imitation auctorum* seem to have been marked less by scrupulous fidelity than by very considerable freedom.

BIBLIOGRAPHY

Daniel, Samuel. *The Civil Wars.* Laurence Michel, ed. 1958.

Donno, Elizabeth Story, ed. *Elizabethan Minor Epics.* 1963.

Gilbert, Allan H. *Literary Criticism, Plato to Dryden.* 1940.

E

Greenfield, Thelma N. *The Eye of Judgment: Reading the New Arcadia.* 1982.

Lawry, Jon S. *Sidney's Two "Arcadias," Pattern and Proceeding.* 1972.

Myrick, Kenneth. *Sir Philip Sidney as a Literary Craftsman.* 1935; repr. 1965.

Puttenham, George. *The Arte of English Poesie.* Gladys D. Willcock and Alice Walker, eds. 1936.

Smith, G. Gregory, ed. *Elizabethan Critical Essays.* 2 vols. 1904; repr. 1937.

Snyder, Susan, ed. *The Divine Weeks and Works of Guillaume de Saluste Sieur du Bartas.* Joshua Sylvester, trans. 2 vols. 1979.

Soens, Lewis, ed. *Sir Philip Sidney's* Defence of Poesie. 1970.

Spingarn, J.E. *A History of Literary Criticism in the Renaissance.* 2nd edition. 1908; repr. 1949.

Williams, Ralph G., ed. and trans. *The De Arte Poetica of Marco Girolamo Vida.* 1976.

John M. Steadman

SEE ALSO

Antiquarianism; Humanism; Italian Literature, Influence of; Literary Criticism; Neo-Latin Literature

Epigrams

In Tudor England, the word "epigram" designated a short poem written in the style either of the Greek Planudean or Palatine Anthologies or the Roman poet Martial. Although by the 1590s the pointed, witty, satiric style of Martial had became the dominant epigrammatic mode (exemplified in the seventeenth century by the *Epigrammes* of Ben Jonson), English writers (writing in both Latin and English) in the first half of the sixteenth century wrote epigrams largely inspired either by the aphoristic and lyric poems of the Anthology (with added influence of the late Latin *Distichs of Cato*) or by the ecclesiastical satires of the Italian *Pasquil* tradition.

In the years between 1518 and 1521, three collections of Latin epigrams were published in London, all of which seem to consciously promulgate humanist values. Thomas More's *Epigrammata* (1518) include translations or imitations of poems from the Greek Anthology, *Pasquil*-like satires against abuses in the church and epideictic poems in praise of Henry VIII that are clearly meant to further the cause of humanist reform in England. The emphasis on translation from Greek was part of the humanist program, and moralizing poems that counsel moderation and hard work repeat English humanist themes. Even the ecclesiastical satires criticize not sexual vice (as was common in the continental *Pasquil* tradition), but rather the lack of classical learning among priests. Other collections written in this early humanist Latin tradition include the epigrams of John Constable (1520), and William Lily (1521), whose poems perhaps most clearly reveal the connection between these collections and school exercises in Latin verse composition that were common in humanist schools (such as St. Paul's School) at the time. The later and more overtly Protestant poems of John Parkhurst (1573) closely resemble these three early collections. At the same time, a collection of didactic and overtly Protestant epigrams was written in English by Robert Crowley (1550), while the Catholic John Heywood published *Hundreds* of epigrams on traditional proverbs that assumed a more witty voice without, however, imitating Martialian "pointedness."

By the 1590s, however, most English writers turned to the Latin epigrams of Martial as a model for short, often satiric poems that had a witty or "pointed" conclusion. These poems were often characterized as containing the "salt" of wit rather than the "honey" of lyric, or were likened to a scorpion because of the barbed point or "sting" at the end. In the 1590s, such poems were closely connected with the fashion for (often scurrilous) verse satires, and both epigrams and satires were banned by ecclesiastical authorities in 1599. Sir John Davies' *Epigrams* (1595?), Joseph Hall's *Virgidemiarum* (1598), John Marston's *Certaine Satyres* (1598), Thomas Bastard's *Chrestoleros* (1598), and Everard Guilpin's *Skialethia* (1598) were among the collections published during this period.

The seventeenth century would see the most important collections of English epigrams, including Ben Jonson's *Epigrammes. I. Booke, The Forrest,* (1616) and *Underwood* (1640), and Robert Herrick's *Hesperides* (1648). Although writing in the tradition of Martial, Jonson insisted that his poems espoused a moral seriousness lacking in the satirical poets of the 1590s, a seriousness that might be seen as resulting from the influence of the early humanist collections. However, the wit of Jonson's poems places them clearly within the seventeenth-century epigrammatic tradition. Indeed, epigram (and related forms such as the emblem) might be considered a dominant literary mode in Stuart England, with ideals of witty pointedness influencing both prose and poetry.

BIBLIOGRAPHY
Coiro, Ann Baynes. *Robert Herrick's Hesperides and the Epigram Book Tradition.* 1988.

Crane, Mary Thomas. "*Intret Cato:* Authority and the Epigram in Sixteenth-Century England." In *Renaissance Genres: Essays on Theory, History, and Interpretation.* Barbara K. Lewalski, ed., pp. 158–186. 1986.

Hudson, Hoyt Hopewell. *The Epigram in the English Renaissance.* 1947; repr. 1966.

Mary Thomas Crane

SEE ALSO

Classical Literature, Influence of; Emblems; Guilpin, Everard; Hall, Joseph; Heywood, John; Jonson, Ben; Lily, William; Marston, John; More, Thomas; Satire

Episcopacy
See Church Polity

Erasmus, Desiderius (c. 1466/1469–1536)

The outstanding Greek and Latin scholar of his generation, Erasmus was born in or near Rotterdam on October 27 between 1466 and 1469. The illegitimate son of a cleric, he obscured the circumstances of his birth. He attended Latin grammar schools in Deventer and s'Hertogenbosch. In the hostels conducted by the Brethren of the Common Life, he was introduced to the *Devotio Moderna*, which opposed speculative theology and fostered practical charity. After his parents died of the plague, his guardians pressured him to enter the monastery. He joined the Augustinian Canons near Gouda c. 1486 and was ordained by the bishop of Utrecht in 1492. He left the monastery with permission to become Latin secretary to the bishop of Cambrai c. 1492–1495.

Erasmus began doctoral studies at the University of Paris, 1495–1499, reluctantly attending the lectures on Scotist theology, but eagerly studying Greek. William Blount, one of the youths he tutored in Latin, invited him to England around May 1499 to around January 1500. There he met the future Henry VIII and English humanists. John Colet and Thomas More introduced him to the thought of Marsilio Ficino and Giovanni Pico. Collecting classical proverbs, he dedicated expanding editions of *Adages* (1500ff.) to Blount and his son. Notable are the Horatian anti-war protest, *Dulce bellum inexpertis,* and "Sileni of Alcibiades" (1515), on Socrates and Christ.

Erasmus continued to study theology and Greek in France and the Low Countries, publishing Lorenzo Valla's pioneering work, *Annotations on the New Testament* (1505). This experience helped confirm his growing commitment to biblical studies. During his second visit to England, late 1505 to June 1506, Erasmus and More translated dialogues of the satirist Lucian from Greek into Latin (1506). The latter's spirit of mockery influenced *The Praise of Folly* and *Utopia.*

Erasmus was finally able to study Greek in Italy, 1506–1509. After crossing the Alps, he promptly applied for his D.D. from Turin. He spent a year in Bologna and another in Venice, where he published *Adages* (1508) with Aldo Manuzio. The third year he spent traveling and residing in Rome as tutor to Alexander Stewart, illegitimate son of James IV of Scotland. Like Luther in 1510–1511, Erasmus was repelled by the warrior-pope Julius II. Erasmus presumably wrote the anonymous dialogue in which St. Peter turns his unworthy successor away from heaven's gates, *Julius Excluded* (1518).

After the accession of Henry VIII, Erasmus sought patronage in England. In the home of More, 1509–1511, he wrote his most imaginative work, a mock oration by Folly praising herself. Rhapsodically, Folly builds her criticisms into a crescendo: from the family, to the academy, the state, and the church. Finally, she loses herself in ecstatic silence. Dedicated to More, *The Praise of Folly* (1511) honored the wisest fool in Christendom. From their mutual correspondence, twenty-five letters from Erasmus and twenty-four letters from More survive.

From 1511–1514, Erasmus resided at Queens' College, Cambridge, where the university chancellor, John Fisher, had invited him to serve as Lady Margaret professor of divinity and lecturer in Greek. He also helped Colet plan St. Paul's School for boys with *Method of Study* (1511), and *Abundance of Words and Matter* (1512). Two archbishops of Canterbury, first William Warham and later Thomas Cranmer, gave him a lifelong pension. He made three further trips to England: checking manuscripts, May 1515; applying for a papal dispensation, August 1516; receiving it, April 1517. Released from his monastic vows of obedience and poverty, he remained a celibate priest of the diocese of Utrecht.

Erasmus moved to Basle to work with the press of Johann Froben from 1514–1516. Three magisterial works appeared in 1516: the New Testament dedicated to Leo X, *Education of a Christian Prince* to the future Charles V, the works of Jerome to Warham. Based on late and thus inferior twelfth-century manuscripts, the 1516 New Testament contained the first Greek version ever published, plus a Latin translation and annotations. Luther used the 1519 edition and William Tyndale the 1522 edition for their vernacular New Testaments.

E

Councilor to Charles, Erasmus returned to Louvain to be near the Habsburg court, 1517–1521. As a "Praise of Wisdom," he republished *Handbook of the Christian Soldier* with a new preface (1518). This manual of lay piety combined the contemplative spirituality of Neoplatonism with the active charity of the *Devotio Moderna*. Erasmus last saw Henry VIII, Warham, and Fisher at Calais, July 1520. He dedicated to Wolsey his *Paraphrases on the Epistles of Peter and Jude* (1520). Erasmus last saw Wolsey and More at Bruges, August 1521.

Returning to Basle for his longest residence in one place, 1521–1529, Erasmus continued his pastoral and educational writings. To further international peace, he dedicated his *Paraphases on the Gospels* to the leaders of Western Christendom: Matthew to Charles V (March 1522), John to Ferdinand of Austria (February 1523), Luke to Henry VIII (August 1523), and Mark to Francis I (February 1524). His graceful *Lord's Prayer* (1523) was translated by Margaret More Roper as *A Devout Treatise upon the Paternoster* (1524?). Expanding editions of *Colloquies* (1522ff.) critiqued religious practices. Remarkable are "The Godly Feast" (1522); a Christian *Symposium*; "The Abbot and the Learned Lady" (1524), where Magdalia represents Meg Roper; and "A Pilgrimage for Religion's Sake" (1526), which recalls visits to Walsingham and Canterbury.

In addition to Catholic theologians from the Low Countries, France, Spain, and Italy, Erasmus engaged in controversy with Edward Lee, 1518–1520, future archbishop of York. After the excommunication of Luther, January 1521, Henry VIII, Wolsey, and More urged the humanist to write against the reformer. Erasmus began with the friendly colloquy, "An Examination concerning Faith" (March 1524), followed by the conciliatory *Freedom of the Will* (September 1524). Luther answered with the impassioned *Bondage of the Will* (December 1525), but did not respond to the angry *Hyperaspistes 1 and 2* (1526 and 1527).

Meanwhile, each party to "the King's Great Matter" called on Erasmus for support. At the request of Katherine of Aragon, he wrote *Institution of Christian Marriage* (1526). This sensible treatise gives better advice on choosing a spouse than addressing the issue of a male heir. Anne Boleyn's father commissioned three pastoral works: *Commentary on Psalm 22* (1530); the popular *Catechism* (1533), on the Apostles' Creed, Ten Commandments, and Lord's Prayer; *Preparation for Death* (1534), which later gave comfort to the rejected Katherine. After Basle adopted Protestantism, Erasmus moved to Catholic Freiburg-im-Breisgau, 1529–1535.

Assured of freedom of conscience, he made his last journey to Basle, 1535–1536. After Fisher and More were beheaded for treason, he finished *Ecclesiastes* (1535), the treatise on preaching that Fisher had urged him to write. Erasmus died on July 12, 1536, leaving a rich legacy. In spite of its flaws, his New Testament became the basis of Western Scripture study until the nineteenth century. His many editions of classical and patristic authors formed leaders of state and church. His pastoral and educational works were translated from Latin into the vernaculars. By royal injunction a version of his *Paraphrases on the Gospels and Acts*, (1548) was placed in every English church. His linguistic virtuosity helped shape Rabelais, Cervantes, and Shakespeare.

BIBLIOGRAPHY

Collected Works of Erasmus. 1974– (in progress).
The Colloquies of Erasmus. Craig R. Thompson, trans. 1965.
Erasmus. *Christian Humanism and the Reformation.* John C. Olin, ed. 1965.
———. *The Praise of Folly.* Clarence H. Miller, trans. 1979.
The Erasmus Reader. Erika Rummel, ed. 1990.
Halkin, Leon E. Erasmus: *A Critical Biography.* John Tonkin, trans. 1987; 1993.
Jardine, Lisa. *Erasmus, Man of Letters.* 1993.
McConica, James Kelsey. *English Humanists and Reformation Politics Under Henry VIII and Edward VI.* 1965.
Opera Omnia Desiderii Erasmi Roterodami. Amsterdam, 1969– (in progress).
Screech, M.A. *Erasmus: Ecstasy and The Praise of Folly.* 1980.
Thomson, D.F.S. trans.; H.C. Porter, ed. *Erasmus and Cambridge.* 1963.

Anne M. O'Donnel, S.N.D.

SEE ALSO
Bible Commentary; Bible Translations; Colet, John; Fisher, John; Humanism; Injunctions, Royal; Lutheranism; More, Thomas; More Roper, Margaret; Universities; Utopia

Erastianism

"Erastianism" is the belief that the church should be subject to the secular power in matters of doctrine and administration. It was named after Erastus (1524–1583), a Swiss theologian of Zwinglian persuasion, who was supposed to have taught this doctrine. The claim that he really did so is strongly contested but makes little difference to the historical development of the idea in the English context.

Erastianism in the English context is basically the belief that the church is an institution of society like any other, and must therefore be governed in the same way as other public bodies. This does not preclude a measure of internal autonomy, but it reserves to Parliament, as the representative body of the whole community, the final say in decision making.

The post-Reformation Church of England has been held to be Erastian because it recognizes the royal supremacy in causes ecclesiastical, and because it is not free to legislate on church affairs without parliamentary approval. Furthermore, the cathedral chapters are obliged to elect the bishop of the state's choice, refusal of which could until recently lead to imprisonment for contumacy.

At the same time, the bishops have always been represented in the House of Lords, where they can make their views on church affairs known. It is true that they have not always prevailed; but their influence has often been considerable, and not merely in church affairs. The clergy likewise have always enjoyed a status different from that of civil servants, as has not been the case in the Lutheran countries of Scandinavia, for instance. The church may not be independent of the state, but its supposed Erastianism should not be exaggerated.

BIBLIOGRAPHY

Rhodes, R.E., Jr. *Lay Authority and Reformation in the English Church.* 1982.

Gerald L. Bray

SEE ALSO

Church of England; Clergy; Reformation, English; Supremacy, Act of

Erskine, John, (c. 1510–1572)

Third son of the fifth Lord Erskine, John Erskine, earl of Mar, was originally destined for the church, and was already abbot of Dryburgh and commendator of Inchmahome when he succeeded his father in 1555; his two elder brothers had predeceased their father. As the sixth Lord Erskine, he was keeper of Edinburgh Castle, and as such held a key position during the Reformation struggles in 1559–1560. However, his main aim was always the prevention of civil war, and he played a strictly neutral role. He refused to subscribe to the first *Book of Discipline* in

1560 (incurring the wrath of John Knox) and, although a Protestant, he was a favorite of Mary of Guise as well as of Mary Queen of Scots because of his integrity and conciliatory disposition.

He was created earl of Mar in July 1565. In 1567, he was deprived of the captaincy of Edinburgh Castle, but his more recent position as captain of Stirling Castle (1566) was made hereditary instead, and he received the care of the young prince James, later James VI and I. Stirling Castle was the traditional nursery of royal children, and acting as their guardians and overseeing their education was almost an Erskine prerogative; John Erskine had also been one of the caretakers of the young Mary Queen of Scots.

When confronted with the choice of supporting the infant king's party or the queen's men in the years that followed Mary's enforced abdication, his position as James's caretaker made him side with the king's men. He was appointed regent of Scotland on September 5, 1571, to general acclaim, but died a natural death soon after, on October 28, 1572.

BIBLIOGRAPHY

Fraser, William. *The Red Book of Menteith.* Vol. 1, pp. 524–527. 1880.

Paton, Henry, ed. *Report on the Manuscripts of the Earl of Mar and Kellie.* 1904.

———, ed. *Supplementary Report on the Manuscripts of the Earl of Mar and Kellie.* 1930.

Theo van Heijnsbergen

SEE ALSO

James VI and I; Knox, John; Mary Queen of Scots

Espionage

The practice of using spies to gather information about domestic and foreign affairs did not originate with Tudor rule in England or with the sixteenth century in Europe. The word "espionage" itself is an eighteenth-century coinage; from the fourteenth through the seventeenth centuries, English speakers referred to "intelligence" or "espial," performed by the intelligencers, espials, or spies who provided "delations" or information on particular persons and "advertisements" of wide-ranging conspiracies at home and abroad. How and to whom intelligence was offered sets Tudor information gathering apart from the subsequent history of espionage.

Channels of information were centralized to a degree under Henry VII along with most other aspects

E

of government. Throughout the Tudor period, however, it was the patronage system that served as the vehicle for the uneven flow of information toward multiple inlets in the court and eventually the ears of the monarch. The key here was the royal council: actually larger and less centralized under Henry VII than his immediate predecessors, this body of aristocrats and new men was restored to a core of some twenty administrators by Thomas Cromwell during the later reign of Henry VIII. By Elizabeth I's time it was known, significantly, as the Privy Council, and most intelligence came from the clients, contacts, or employees of its important members. Cromwell also defined the office of principal secretary that William Cecil, Lord Burghley, in his early career, and Francis Walsingham used to solicit and coordinate much of the information and present it to the queen. Cromwell maintained a few paid spies in foreign cities, but in domestic matters he seems to have relied on casual village informing about recusancy or treasonous statements, accusations of neighbor against neighbor that came unbidden to the ears of constables and justices of the peace. Burghley targeted political conspiracies through espionage as principal secretary, and maintained a significant network of agents and clients as lord treasurer that his son, Robert Cecil, was later to build on. Walsingham began as the elder Cecil's client and became at least his equal as "spymaster" after he acceded to principal secretary. He funded his spies himself, but after the 1580s he persuaded Elizabeth to set aside money for intelligence purposes as well. It is important to realize, however, that there was no "Elizabethan secret service," and that neither Burghley nor Walsingham could ever have been at its head. Walsingham's biographer, perhaps too conservatively, counts only six "professional" spies in his employ, men who often started informing on suspected conspirators in prison before undertaking missions of infiltration in continental seminaries or communities in the north of England. Other councilors such as Burghley and Robert Dudley, earl of Leicester, patronized spies, and a separate body like the Council of the North preserved its own intelligence contacts. Servants, scholars, merchants, and ambassadors all engaged in spying; double and triple agents were common. Invisible ink and ciphers, often absurdly simple, were used in the written correspondence that remained an important means of communication. Much information was still generated by casual informing from client to patron up the chain of prestige and obligation: to have

or claim to have knowledge of a traitor or plot gave those of lower status access to greater circles and the countenance, gifts, and money they offered. Rival intelligence systems depended on the persons and personalities of their chief patrons, men who were members of the Privy Council or who could hope to become members, and threatened to dissolve when the patron left the scene. After Walsingham's death in 1590, his helper, Thomas Phelippes, apparently tried to operate alone with a private information service, but this ambitious commoner was eclipsed by the competition between Robert Cecil and Robert Devereux, second earl of Essex, both of whom had some access to the queen and craved more.

Religious surveillance was fundamental during a period when religion and politics reflected one another closely. Tied to members of the church hierarchy at the beginning of Elizabeth's reign, espionage on Roman Catholics and Puritans shaded into court spheres of influence and information. Cromwell had relied on voluntary delation from countryside and neighborhood to enforce the Reformation, and Mary I took similar means to undo it. The presence of Mary Queen of Scots in England after 1568 and the Catholic conspiracies attributed to her intensified the political nature of the Elizabethan Settlement in religion. Elizabethan statutes of uniformity gradually formalized the role of informant. A proclamation of July 1570 promised rewards for information about circulators of papal bulls and other writings and some immunity for turncoat accomplices. In 1581, one-third of the fine on recusants was offered to the informer who turned them in. Pursuivants, originally heraldic office holders in ecclesiastical households, now served the bishops as professional hunters of Catholics and nonconformists. When John Whitgift became archbishop of Canterbury in 1583, he set about the surveillance and eradication of organized Puritanism through the newly formed Court of High Commission (1580), which integrated previous church commissions on nonconformity into a virtual adjunct of the Privy Council in religious matters. In 1586, Whitgift himself was appointed to the Privy Council by Elizabeth, an appointment that cemented religious and political intelligence. Richard Bancroft, Whitgift's chaplain, molded religious espionage into a useful tool of the Court of High Commission, although he failed to track down the chief propagandist behind the Martin Marprelate tracts. Walsingham united the analysis of foreign and domestic intelligence in monitoring the infiltration of priests and snaring Mary Stuart, but he probably concocted as well as discovered information. Tudor espionage was not a smoothly running system of total surveillance. Nevertheless, its dependence on personal contacts, half truths, and the cultivation of anxiety bequeathed something to the bureaucratic culture of the nation-state.

BIBLIOGRAPHY

Archer, John Michael. *Sovereignty and Intelligence: Spying and Court Culture in the English Renaissance.* 1993.

Breight, Curtis. *Surveillance, Militarism, and Drama in the Elizabethan Era.* 1996.

Elton, G.R. *Policy and Police: The Enforcement of the Reformation in the Age of Thomas Cromwell.* 1972.

Handover, P.M. *The Second Cecil.* 1959.

Read, Conyers. *Mr. Secretary Walsingham and the Policy of Queen Elizabeth.* 3 vols. 1925.

Stone, Lawrence. *An Elizabethan: Sir Horatio Palavicino.* 1956.

John Michael Archer

SEE ALSO
Baines, Richard; Bancroft, Richard; Cecil, William; Cromwell, Thomas; Devereux, Robert; Dudley, Robert; High Commission, Court of; Justice of the Peace; Marprelate Controversy; Mary Queen of Scots; Puritanism

Essay

The invention of the essay in the late sixteenth century has been described by Rosalie Colie as "interesting" from the standpoint of genres, "for although it was immediately imitated . . . only in the eighteenth century did it become an officially noticed genre" (89). Derived from the French verb meaning "to try" or "test," the term essay was invented by Michel de Montaigne, whose three volumes of *Essais* were published in France between 1580 and 1588. Sixteenth-century allusions indicate that John Florio's English translation, published in 1603, circulated in manuscript form in the late 1590s and immediately began to inspire English experiments in the new genre.

The most original feature of Montaigne's essays was their formlessness, in marked contrast to the sonnet, the tragedy, and other highly organized kinds of writing. Personal, experimental, improvisatory, and above all seemingly unstructured, Montaigne's essays challenged the concept of literary form as the Renaissance understood it. Starting with the title, which generally employed the formula "Of _____" but often bore little relation to the text, Montaigne's essays exhibit a disarming approach toward the ostensible subject, as initially formal discussions become interspersed with or interrupted by digressions, anecdotes, and non sequiturs.

The essay's precursors include Seneca's *Epistles,* Plutarch's *Morals,* Renaissance commonplace books, and collections of *exempla* and *leciones* such as Pedro Mexia's *Silva de varia lección* (1540). Other possible influences include St. Augustine's *Confessions,* the genre of spiritual autobiography, and the writings of the reformers, which provided Montaigne and his contemporaries with a tradition of self-examination. Ted-Larry Pebworth notes that related short prose forms, such as the paradox (Donne wrote a collection of these short, humorous pieces in the 1590s) and the resolve share some characteristics with the early English essay.

According to the nineteenth-century editor Edward Arber, "the earliest publication in the technical form of Essay-writing in our language" was the anonymous "Remedies against Discontentment." The titles of these "discourses," as the author refers to them, suggest a greater resemblance to the essay than their content—for example, "Of the choice of affaires," "Of foresight," "Of the diversities of men's actions," "Of dissembling." The anonymous author clearly has not made the transition from moralist to essayist; rather than describing and exploring human behavior, he issues a series of instructions in sentences that repeatedly begin, "we ought." The "we" is a public self, and no personal comments, connections, or digressions disrupt the rational advice regarding self-government and classical allusions with which each short discourse instructs the reader.

Francis Bacon, generally regarded as the father of the English essay, published his first collection of *Essayes* in 1597; these short "fragments of my conceites," as Bacon described them in his dedicatory epistle, were revised considerably and added to in the volumes of 1612 and 1625. As E.N.S. Thompson remarks in *The Seventeenth-Century English Essay,* Bacon's method "is never that of Montaigne"; Bacon is "terse and aphoristic," while Montaigne is "diffuse and informal." Bacon proffers an authoritative, impersonal speaking subject in his essays, approaching his topics in a public manner variously akin to the orator, the preacher, or the writer of treatises and handbooks. Contrasting the two, Ann Imbrie notes that the essay takes "as the object of imitation either the individual mind and the processes of its thought (Montaigne) or the 'collective' mind and the value of its wisdom (Bacon)."

E

Montaigne's most direct English heir was William Cornwallis the Younger, whose first volume of essays appeared in 1600. A second volume came out in 1601, and both were reprinted in 1606 and 1610. Although virtually unknown and unanthologized today, Cornwallis was described by Thompson as holding a "leading position in the maturing of the English essay." W.L. Macdonald, in *Beginnings of the English Essay*, quotes freely from Cornwallis's essays in his attempt to "define" the essay as a form. Bacon, he says, "was incapable of thinking desultorily on every idea suggested by the main theme," whereas "Cornwallis's mind works in much the same way as Montaigne's." In his "Of Essaies and Bookes" Cornwallis provides a contemporary characterization of the essay that emphasizes its experimental and informal aspects: his essays, he says, are "a maner of writing wel befitting undigested motions, or a head not knowing his strength like a circumspect runner trying for a starte. . . . If they proove nothing but wordes, yet they breake not promise with the world, for they say, 'But an Essay,' like a Scrivenour trying his Pen before he ingrosseth his worke" (190).

During the years that followed the appearance of Bacon's and Cornwallis's first volumes of essays, several more collections were published: S.K. Heninger's recent bibliography lists such titles as Robert Johnson's *Essaies, or Rather Imperfect Offers* (London, 1601); Daniel Tuvill's *Essaies Politicke, and Moral* (London, 1608); William Mason's *A Handful of Essaies or Imperfect Offers* (London, 1621); and Henry Peacham's *The Truth of Our Times. Revealed out of One Mans Experience by Way of Essay* (London, 1638). These authors are generally not included in anthologies, in contrast to their contemporaries, the character-writers, who took the short essay in a rather different direction. The character sketches of Sir Thomas Overbury, Joseph Hall, and John Earle are short prose pieces that employ satirical description in the service of extended exemplary portraits of various social types: the Courtier, Puritan, Pedant, Gentleman, and so forth. They lack the autobiographical references or anecdotes of the personal essay, as do Owen Feltham's *Resolves,* another experiment in short prose. While purporting to set forth personal "resolves" or resolutions at the conclusion of each essay-like piece, Feltham reveals very little about himself, in marked contrast to Montaigne, Cornwallis, or Sir Thomas Browne, the best known of the seventeenth-century essayists, whose *Religio Medici* is as explicitly self-absorbed as Montaigne's most autobiographical essays. At its best, the early English personal essay employs an epistemological method that emphasizes receptivity to whatever comes one's way, in contrast to a method that privileges the ordering and organizing of experience prevalent in the sermons, treatises, and other more formal prose of the age.

BIBLIOGRAPHY

Bennett, Roger E. "Sir William Cornwallis's Use of Montaigne." *PMLA,* vol. 48, no. 4.

Colie, Rosalie. *The Resources of Kind: Genre-theory in the Renaissance.* 1973.

Heninger, S.K. *English Prose, Prose Fiction, and Criticism to 1660: A Guide to Information Sources.* 1975.

Imbrie, Ann. "Defining Nonfiction Genres." In *Renaissance Genres: Essays on Theory, History, and Interpretation.* Barbara K. Lewalski, ed. 1986.

Macdonald, W.L. *Beginnings of the English Essay.* 1914.

Pebworth, Ted-Larry. "Not Being, But Passing: Defining the Early English Essay." *Studies in the Literary Imagination,* vol. 10, no. 2.

Thompson, E.N.S. *The Seventeenth-Century English Essay.* 1926; repr. 1967.

Martha Rozett

SEE ALSO

Bacon, Francis; Cornwallis, William; Florio, John; Hall, Joseph

Essex, Earl of

See Devereux, Robert

Eton Choirbook

The largest and most significant source of Latin sacred polyphony from c. 1490 to 1530 is Eton College Library MS 178. This large folio choirbook was copied, probably in London in the late fifteenth century, for use at the chapel of Eton College. A daily part of life at the Eton school was the singing of an antiphon to the Virgin Mary before the students left school and then later in the evening, and it is not surprising that the Eton Choirbook originally included among its contents sixty-eight motets, almost all Marian, including fifteen settings of the *Salve regina,* twenty-four Magnificats, and one Passion setting by a total of twenty-five composers. The nine voices of one *Salve regina,* by Robert Wylkynson, are labeled according to the hierarchy of angels who would receive the Virgin Mary into heaven.

The Eton Choirbook is now missing ninety-eight leaves of 224, and only fifty-four works remain. Unique to this manuscript are the composers William Brygeman, Fawkyner, Robert Hacumplaynt, John Hampton, Holyngborne, Nicholas Huchyne, Richard Hygons, Hugh Kellyk, John Sutton, and Robert Wylkynson. John Browne, Walter Lambe, Richard Davy, Robert Wylkynson, William Cornysh, Edmond Turges, William Horwood, Fawkyner, and Kellyk are the only composers represented with two or more extant compositions.

Works from the repertories of other, nearby chapels are dominant in this source, although John Browne, who is the best represented composer with seven surviving works, may have been the John Browne from Coventry who was elected scholar of Eton in 1467. (Others believe that he was at New College, Oxford, rather than at one of the royal musical establishments.) He quotes the partsong *From stormy wyndis and grevous wethir* by Edmund Turges (born c. 1450) in his antiphon *Stabat iuxta Christi crucem*. Its text invokes the protection of the ostrich feather, emblem of Prince Arthur, Henry VII's elder son, as he began a journey. He composed one of the manuscript's three large-scale settings of the *Stabat mater*. Richard Davy's setting was probably first performed at Magdalen College, Oxford, where Davy was master of the choristers, and William Cornysh's, at court, where he was master of the children from 1509. (Davy's Passion setting according to Matthew is the earliest known Passion by a known composer.) Robert Fayrfax, gentleman of the Chapel Royal from 1497 to 1521, titled one of his Magnificats "Regale." Walter Lambe was a member of the choir of St. George's Chapel at Windsor, close to Eton; he is represented with six surviving works out of an original twelve. Wylkynson was master of the Eton choristers from 1500 to at least 1515.

Rich sonorities, lengthy melismatic melodic lines, unexpected melodic and harmonic twists, and extravagant rhythmic complexities characterize the distinctive musical style of Eton Choirbook compositions. Virtuoso music by the standards of any period, it is a unique monument to the genius of the early Tudor period.

BIBLIOGRAPHY

Harrison, Frank Llewellyn. "The Eton Choirbook: Its Background and Contents (Eton College Library Ms. 178)." *Annales musicologiques,* vol. 1, pp. 151–175.
———, ed. *The Eton Choirbook.* Musica Britannica, vols. 10–12. 1956–1961.
Williams, Carol J. "The Salve Regina Settings in the Eton Choirbook." *Miscellanea Musicologica,* vol. 10, pp. 28–37.

Laura S. Youens

SEE ALSO
Cornysh, William; Fayrfax, Robert; Motet

Eucharist

The doctrines of the eucharistic presence and sacrifice were major topics of debate, not only in England but throughout Europe in the sixteenth century. The peculiar political aspects of the English Reformation make it notoriously difficult to determine the position of the Church of England at various stages of the debate. The eucharistic theology of Archbishop Thomas Cranmer, chief architect of the Book of Common Prayer, remains a matter of serious scholarly divergence of interpretation.

Henry VIII defended both the traditional medieval Catholic doctrines of transubstantiation and the sacrifice of the Mass against Luther in his *Assertio Septem Sacramentorum,* for which he received the title "Defender of the Faith" from Pope Leo X. In the debate among the bishops in 1548, three positions on the eucharist emerged. One party, led by Stephen Gardiner, believed in the bodily presence of Christ in the eucharist. A center party, of which Nicholas Ridley was the chief representative, held that the change in the elements at consecration was entirely spiritual, and that the sacrament was the true body of Christ inwardly, spiritually, figuratively, by the power of God. They attributed this view to Retramnus, a ninth-century Augustinian and Platonist. A third party favored the views of the Zurich reformers Huldrych Zwingli and Johann Heinrich Bullinger that the identification of the elements with the body and blood of Christ was purely metaphorical and representational, a psychological aid to Christian devotion.

"The Svpper of the Lorde and the Holy Communion, commonly called the Masse" from the first prayer book of Edward VI was a compromise. It was condemned by the Zurich party as "nothing but the mass in English" and disliked but accepted by Gardiner's partly for the same reason. It could be used both by believers in transubstantiation or by believers following Ridley's position. The Zurich party were willing to use it, but considered that it did not sufficiently repudiate Roman errors and was no more than a first step. Concerning the sacrifice, there are three sacrificial offerings in the eucharistic prayer of 1549:

E

(1) the offering of prayer at the beginning of the intercessions, (2) the commemoration of the sacrifice of Christ, and (3) the self-oblation of the worshipers in union with the offering of Christ.

The most extensive critique of the 1549 eucharist came from Martin Bucer, and an extensive revision of the prayer book appeared in 1552 taking his critique into consideration. Most especially the structure of the eucharistic prayer was altered, removing the intercession from the beginning of the prayer into a separate "Prayer for the Church Militant," eliminating the *epiclesis,* or invocation of the Holy Spirit over the elements "that they may be vnto vs the bodye and bloud of . . . Iesus Christe," and removing the final paragraph, later called the prayer of oblation, to a position after the ministration of communion. The most significant effect of this change was to place the reception of communion immediately following the narrative of the institution at the place where the elevation of the host had occurred in the Latin Mass, the intention being to indicate that communion, not adoration, was the purpose of the service. Moving the language about self-offering to a place after communion also made it clear that only as united with Christ in communion was it possible for Christians to speak of offering themselves to God. Finally, the words of administration were changed from "The body of our Lord Iesus Christe . . ." to "Take and eate this, in remembraunce that Christe died for thee, and fede on him in thy heart by faith, with thankes geuying," moving from an objective to a subjective statement of Christ's presence.

A so-called "black rubric" was inserted into the 1552 book by royal authority after it had already been printed. This denies "anye reall and essenciall presence" of Christ's natural body and blood, which "are in heauen and not here." This rubric was excluded from the Elizabethan Prayer Book of 1559.

Elizabeth I's Prayer Book retained the 1552 order of the eucharist, but combined the words of administration from the two books of Edward VI to balance the objective and subjective aspects. John Jewel described a double eating in the eucharist, of the bread and wine with the bodily mouth and of the body and blood of Christ with the mouth of faith. Jewel distinguished between the sign and the thing signified, stating that the body of Christ offered to our faith in the eucharist was "the thing itself, and no figure."

Queen Elizabeth attempted to forbid controversy about the eucharist, and the verses probably written by John Donne, are often ascribed to her:

He was the Word that spake it,
he took the bread and brake it,
and what his word doth make it,
I do believe and take it.
(Hymn 322. *The Hymnal, 1982*)

Richard Hooker follows the same line: "What these elements are in themselves it skilleth not, it is enough that to me which take them they are the body and blood of Christ." Hooker draws a strict analogy between the water of baptism and the eucharistic elements. The grace for him does not reside in the elements but in their reception. They are "causes instrumental upon the receipt whereof the participation of [Christ's] body and blood ensueth," and this is accomplished by God's omnipotent power.

Hooker argues that all sides agree on five points: (1) the sacrament is "a true and a real participation of Christ," who gives his entire person to each receiver, constituting the church as his mystical body with himself as the head; (2) all who receive Christ receive also the Holy Spirit to sanctify them; (3) "what merit, force or virtue soever there is in his sacrificed body and blood, we receive fully and wholly have it by this sacrament"; (4) the effect is a real transformation of our souls and bodies from death to life, from sin to righteousness; and (5) it is by the mighty power of God, not through any inherent virtue of the sacramental elements, that we receive what Christ has promised.

However difficult it may be to sort through the earlier stages of the discussion, it is Hooker's position, not Cranmer's, that becomes the basis of subsequent Anglican eucharistic theology.

BIBLIOGRAPHY

Booty, John E., ed. *The Book of Common Prayer, 1559.* 1976.

———. Booty, John. *John Jewel as Apologist of the Church of England.* Chap. 7. 1967.

Brightman, F.E. *The English Rite.* 2 vols. 1921; repr. 1969.

Clark, Francis. *Eucharistic Sacrifice and the Reformation.* 1967.

Crockett, William R. *Eucharist: Symbol of Transformation.* 1986.

Cuming, G.J. *A History of Anglican Liturgy.* 2nd edition. 1982.

Dugmore, C.W. *The Mass and the English Reformers.* 1958.

Hooker, Richard. *Of the Laws of Ecclesiastical Polity.* Book 5. 1597.

Stevenson, Kenneth. *Eucharist and Offering.* 1986.

Whitaker, E.C. *Martin Bucer and the Book of Common Prayer.* Alcuin Club Collections, vol. 55. 1974.

Leonel L. Mitchell

SEE ALSO

Black Rubric; Book of Common Prayer; Bucer, Martin; Bullinger, Johann Heinrich; Church of England; Cranmer, Thomas; Defender of the Faith; Donne, John; Gardiner, Stephen; Hooker, Richard; Jewel, John; Reformation, English; Ridley, Nicholas; Sacraments

Euphuism

Euphuism refers to a style of writing perfected and popularized by John Lyly in his prose fiction, *Euphues* (published in two parts, in 1578 and in 1580). The style is characterized by its use of consistently parallel constructions, in which alliteration and other devices are employed to establish and maintain antithetical balance in phrasing and mainly antithetical turns of thought. Equally important to this style are, first, the persistent use of allusion to mythological and historical characters and to observations of natural history; and second, the articulation of these allusions in intricate comparisons and ingenious metaphors. However, rhetorical artifice and verbal virtuosity, by themselves, are not what distinguish the euphuistic style. At the heart of euphuism is the spirit of *élan*, an adroit play of mind that captivated Lyly's Elizabethan readers and separates his style from its imitations.

Lyly took the word euphues, used by Roger Ascham to refer to the sort of mind characterized by superior intellect and readiness to learn, and employed it to identify his literary creation (both the character and the work of prose fiction) as well balanced and beautifully proportioned. In composing this prose fiction, he drew upon and refined the modes of expression of his courtly contemporaries, formulating euphuism to provide his Elizabethan readers with the balance and proportion of a humanistic, courtly, and satiric rhetorical performance. Early in the work, in his address "To the Gentleman readers," Lyly establishes his tone of balanced courtly banter, "Gentlemen use books as gentlewomen handle their flowers, who in the morning stick them in their heads and at night straw them at their heels."

As the narrative proper begins, Lyly's style moves from simple banter to a satiric demonstration of wit in action. (He signaled his satiric intent when he subtitled this first part of *Euphues,* "The Anatomy of Wit.") Lyly's Elizabethan contemporaries were challenged to recognize the two-fold nature of wit: its humanistic and anti-humanistic potentialities. The early narrative evokes the traditional conception of wit held in the first decades of the sixteenth century by the earlier English Christian humanists, among whom was Lyly's own grandfather, William Lily. This traditional view defined wit's essence as intellectual dexterity, an aptness for expressing multifaceted knowledge with elegance and a lightness of humor. To the early English humanists, wit existed as a correlative of wisdom, the capacity to advance the mind through humanist study and thereby achieve moral growth and ultimately moral action. As wisdom's correlative, wit was established as a *sine qua non* for the shaping of the ideal humanist Englishman and courtier-counselor.

Although rooted in this early English Humanist conception, Lyly's *Euphues* actually anatomizes the later half-century Elizabethan experience that wit, too frequently, could be subverted into an instrument of personal ambition and political intrigue. In its contemporary context, the euphuistic style seems to enact the adroitness of wit exiled from wisdom, and euphuistic verbal dexterity suggests the intellect's employment of knowledge and experience in the service of self-love and self-delusion. Consequently, the power of euphuism for its Elizabethan audience resides in the understanding, shared by Lyly and his readers, that his deft execution of rhetoric and style ironically involves their own intellects in the moral ambiguities of wit.

Particularly pervasive in Lyly's style is the use of *isocolon,* successive verbal structures of equal length; *parison,* parallel syntactic structures; and *paramoion,* a repetition or similarity of sounds (e.g., alliteration) to emphasize these parallel structures. These devices make manifest, and lay out for examination, the juxtapositions and antithetical operations of wit.

In the two parts of *Euphues,* the euphuistic verbal dynamics develop within a rhetorical matrix of opposing arguments or *controversiae,* and the resulting play of possibilities involves the reader in a process of ongoing reassessment. In the first part (1578), the euphuistic narrative voice presents the youthful courtier, Euphues, in Naples, where folly holds court. It is here that he is urged by Eubulus to examine his own conscience. The young courtier's agile and multiphrased response insists upon his imperviousness to Naples' folly, noting among many analogous natural instances, "The diamond lieth in the fire and is not consumed." Near the conclusion of this first part of *Euphues,* the

E

ostensibly repentant prodigal asserts, "I will so frame myself as all youth hereafter shall . . . rejoice to see my amendment. . . . I will endeavor myself to be a mirror of Godliness hereafter," and he resolves to use his wit in the service of wisdom. However, the preceding euphuistic anatomizing of equivocal possibilities has sensitized readers to reflect upon the antithetical possibility that we are beholding "how lewdly wit [still] standeth in his own light." In 1580, Lyly published *Euphues and His England,* which presents a seemingly reformed but still noticeably self-satisfied Euphues. In this work, the euphuistic style is continued, but the sequence of opposing debates plays a more primary role, and there is a loss of stylistic sprightliness as Euphues' self-righteous certainty is translated from the profane and prodigal into a more solemn religious conviction.

In his subsequent court dramas, Lyly employed euphuism as the operative mode of rhetoric, and euphuism's nimble and graceful equivocalities aptly mirror the contemporary language of Elizabeth's court. Reasonable approximations of euphuistic style occur in the work of several of Lyly's contemporaries. In all instances, the style is to be considered euphuistic only if its alchemy of ornately and undeviatingly balanced constructions taunt the reader with the ironic ambiguities and contrarieties of human perceptions.

At the same time, an accurate understanding of the characteristics of euphuism must recognize that in its virtues are its limitations. Lyly's style was a vehicle of its time; its artfulness did not possess the depth and scope of art, and its prolific intricacies came to seem (in the words of Lyly's contemporary, Sir Philip Sidney) "a most tedious prattling."

BIBLIOGRAPHY

Barish, Jonas A. "The Prose of John Lyly." *English Literary History,* vol. 23, pp. 14–35.

Kinney, Arthur F. "Rhetoric and Fiction in Elizabethan England." In *Renaissance Eloquence.* James J. Murphy, ed., pp. 385–393. 1983.

Hunter, G.K. *John Lyly: The Humanist as Courtier.* 1962.

Lyly, John. *Euphues: The Anatomy of Wit; Euphues and His England.* Morris W. Croll and Harry Clemons, eds. 1964.

Richard Haber

SEE ALSO
Humanism; Prose Fiction; Rhetoric

Exchequer

The major financial bureaucratic office in England from the twelfth century, the Exchequer had practices that were often stigmatized as rigid and time-consuming. Situated in the old Palace of Westminster, Exchequer was divided into two parts. The Lower Exchequer or Receipt was a treasury that handled moneys and tallies. The Upper Exchequer or Exchequer of Audit was responsible for the oversight of accounts, the enforcement of statutes, and the hearing of disputes concerning the monarch's revenues. As a court of record its records were final and unchallengeable in any law court. The lord treasurer was the principal officer, but within the Exchequer there were numerous departments, effectively separate, such as the clerk of the pipe and the offices of the lord treasurer's remembrancer and the king's remembrancer. Each of the offices kept its own records, and although they may have had to cooperate for certain purposes, they were usually independent and sometimes at odds.

The Upper Exchequer oversaw many functions of central government that were eventually to become separate bureaucratic departments such as trade and industry, forestry, agriculture and fisheries, and the navy. It also oversaw aspects of local government by supervising the conduct of sheriffs, escheators, and customers, and its power to penalize those who breached statutes was critical to the effective enforcement of the royal will in the provinces.

A need for speed and secrecy often led monarchs to bypass Exchequer process in raising and accounting for revenue and expenditure in the early part of the sixteenth century. Many of the principal sources of revenue were removed from Exchequer control and allocated to special officers. In the 1530s and 1540s, a number of new courts with authority over particular areas such as land revenue and First Fruits were established, but problems of costs and overlapping jurisdiction led in 1554 to all these courts except the Court of Wards and Liveries being joined to the Exchequer. New offices such as the auditors of the prests then developed within the Exchequer with separate processes to accommodate the specific needs of these specialized jurisdictions. As Elizabeth I's reign progressed, the Exchequer also developed oversight of equity, probably to address the problems of leaseholds, but this function was rapidly adapted to meet a variety of other needs, both of the monarch and of royal accountants.

BIBLIOGRAPHY

Alsop, J.D. "The Structure of Early Tudor Finance 1509–1558," and Coleman, C., "Reorganisation of the Exchequer of Receipt." In *Revolution Reassessed.* C. Coleman and D. Starkey, eds. 1986.

Bryson, W.H. *The Equity Side of Exchequer: Its Administration, Procedures, and Records.* 1975.

Jack, S.M. "In search of the custom of the exchequer." *Parergon,* n.s., vol. 11, no. 2, pp. 89–106.

———. "English bishops as tax collectors in the sixteenth century." In *Protestants, Property, Puritans: Godly People Revisited. A Festschrift in Honour of Patrick Collinson.* S.M. Jack and B.A. Masters, eds. 1996.

Sybil M. Jack

SEE ALSO

Government, Central Administration of; Government, Local; Wards and Liveries, Court of

Exploration

See Discovery and Exploration

F

Fabyan, Robert (d. 1513)

Robert Fabyan's *New Chronicles of England and France,* probably completed around 1504 but not published by Richard Pynson until three years after the author's death, was the major intermediary between the tradition of the London city chronicle of the fifteenth century and such mid-Tudor chronicles as those of Edward Hall, Richard Grafton, and John Stow. Fabyan's bias against Margaret of Anjou, wife of Henry VI, was taken up by his successors, and ultimately found its way into William Shakespeare's portrayal. Fabyan was a member of the Drapers' Company, an alderman, and (in 1493) one of the sheriffs of the city of London, and his chronicle takes the point of view of a Londoner. Beginning with Book 7, which opens with the Norman Conquest, the English section of the chronicle largely concerns London; and from the accession of Richard I the arrangement follows that of the standard London chronicles, in which each year begins with a list of the bailiffs (or, later, the mayor and sheriffs) of the city. Fabyan, however, differed from his predecessors by alternating sections of French history with the English, and by organizing the whole chronicle into seven books representing the Seven Joys of the Virgin Mary rather than the Seven Ages of the World. Although Fabyan was an eyewitness to very little of the story he tells, he did take the trouble to consult a variety of previous authors, French and English. It has been suggested that, after finishing his *New Chronicles,* he produced another version of a city chronicle, the *Great Chronicle of London,* which remained in manuscript until this century.

BIBLIOGRAPHY

Bean, J.M.W. "The Role of Robert Fabyan in Tudor Historiography of the 'Wars of the Roses,'" In *Florilegium Columbianum. Essays in Honor of Paul Oskar Kristeller.* Karl-Ludwig Selig and Robert Somerville, eds., pp. 167–185. 1987.

Fabyan, Robert. *Prima pars cronecarum.* 2 vols. 1516; repr. as *New Chronicles of England and France.* Henry Ellis, ed. 1811.

Gransden, Antonia. *Historical Writing in England,* vol. 2, pp. 231ff., 245ff. 1982.

F.J. Levy

SEE ALSO

Grafton, Richard; Hall, Edward; History, Writing of; Stowe, John

Fairs and Markets

By the start of the Tudor period England had moved a long way from a system of largely self-supporting rural communities. Some fairs and markets, both of which drew producers and customers together, can be traced back to the Anglo-Saxon period, and by Norman times there was a sprinkling of market towns in all parts of the country. Many new markets and fairs were established by royal, manorial, and ecclesiastical authorities in the Middle Ages, and by the sixteenth century there was a dense network of these essential marketing institutions.

Day-to-day marketing was dominated by market towns with their more or less permanent shops and weekly markets. In Tudor times there were some 750 market towns in England and a further fifty in Wales; some new markets were created during the century although the total number remained below the medieval peak that had been reached before the Black Death. Most

F

towns and some villages held at least one market a week, and they were closely regulated by the town or manorial authorities; tolls were to be paid and trading was controlled by a series of orders imposed by a posse of officials. Markets allowed country dwellers to enter the towns and sell both agricultural produce and manufactured goods either to townsfolk or to other country folk. The rationale of the weekly market was that it provided a regular service for those who lived within a few miles of the town or village; many would walk to market and home again on the same day. All markets dealt in a wide range of products, although there was some tendency toward specialization in some of the larger towns. This was especially true of London, which had developed specialized markets for fish, livestock, and other products such as grain and coal.

Fairs were the focal points for trade over broader areas than the markets of most provincial towns. Although the grant of market rights to a particular town or village almost always included the right to hold fairs (usually one or two a year, although there could be as many as four or five) many fairs were not associated with a market town. Moreover, only a small part of the transactions conducted at fairs was as closely regulated as the business of the town markets; much traffic went unrecorded. The staple commodities of the majority of fairs were cattle and sheep, but horse fairs were also numerous and some were beginning to specialize in other products such as cheese, cloth, leather, or even household utensils. But all fairs catered to a wide range of customers and sellers; and, as one East Yorkshire farmer emphasized in the early seventeenth century, fairs like Beverley Great Fair—which was held in early May—were important regional events: "Thither the Londoners send their wares by water, and thither come the York grocers and others to furnish themselves with such commodities as they want." In addition, many fairs provided a wide range of entertainment—tumblers, fire-eaters, cardsharps, and the like—which contributed to the annual diet of fun and merriment.

Not all trade was conducted through markets and fairs; town and village retailers sold their products from day-to-day to local customers, and there was also a tendency for larger buyers and sellers to deal directly with each other, circumventing more regulated outlets. But it would be difficult to exaggerate the importance of fairs and markets to the common folk of Tudor England, both as producers and consumers.

BIBLIOGRAPHY

Everitt, A. "The Marketing of Agricultural Produce." In *The Agrarian History of England and Wales, IV, 1500–1640.* Joan Thirsk, ed., pp. 466–592. 1967.

Starsmore, I. *English Fairs.* 1975.

Walker, W. *Essex Fairs and Markets.* Essex Record Office, vol. 83. 1981.

Woodward, D. *The Farming and Memorandum Books of Henry Best of Elmswell.* British Academy Records of Social and Economic History, n.s., vol. 8. 1984.

Donald Woodward

SEE ALSO

Cloth Industry; Fish and Fishing; Industry and Manufacture; Metal Industries; Pedlars; London; Towns

Fairy Lore

Complexity and variety characterize Tudor conceptions of fairy lore, depending on the contexts in which fairies appear and the traditions from which they derive—folklore beliefs and/or literary representations. By the end of the sixteenth century, the influences from classical as well as medieval romance literature had become intertwined with popular superstitions and folk mythology. Edmund Spenser syncretizes fairies, elves, and nymphs in the *Aprill, Maye,* and *June* eclogues of *The Shepheardes Calender* (1579). In his play *Endimion* (1591), John Lyly also flexibly describes his stage fairies as "fayre fiendes," "Hags," "Nymphes," "prettie Ladies," and "fair babies" (4.3.26–27, 132, 166). Exposing contemporary superstitions in *The Discoverie of Witchcraft* (1584), Reginald Scot maintains "our mothers maids" have taught childhood imaginations to fear many "vaine apparitions"; he catalogs "fairies" with such different extraordinary beings as spirits, witches, elves, hags, satyrs, fauns, centaurs, dwarfs, nymphs, changelings, Robin Goodfellow, hobgoblin, Tom Thumb, the puckle, the incubus, the mare, "and such other bugs" (7.15).

Thomas Nashe, in *Pierce Pennilesse* (1592), develops Scot's general association of foreign and native spirits; he sees the contemporary English sprites as indigenous versions of the lesser deities of ancient Greece and Rome, further linking them through their familiarity with humans and their communion with night: "The Robbin-good-fellowes, Elfes, Fairies, Hobgoblins of our latter age, which idolatrous former daies and the fantasticall world of Greece ycleaped *Fawnes, Satyres, Dryades, &*

Hamadryades, did most of their merry prankes in the Night" (1:347), such as grinding malt, pinching untidy maids, dancing in rounds in meadows, and leading travelers astray. Later, in his *Terrors of the Night, or a Discourse of Apparitions* (1594), Nashe relates spirits to the four elements, as did the Neoplatonists, but he spoofingly reduces them to extremely diminutive creatures active in the engendering of mortals' dreams through melancholy (1:349–357). Although in his *Daemonologie* (1597) King James I disapproves of Scot's skepticism about witches, he shares Scot's and Nashe's view of fairies as fictions, classifying them as one of the four kinds of devils "conversing in the earth" but also likening them to Vergil's Elysian shades in the *Aeneid* (3.1; 3.5). James negates the popular belief in a king and queen of fairies who held a jolly court and acted like "naturall men and women": "That fourth kinde of spirites, which by the Gentiles was called *Diana,* and her wandring court, and amongst vs was called the *Phairie* . . . or our good neighbours, was one of the sortes of illusiones that was rifest in the time of Papistrie" (3.5). Noteworthy for functioning often as a kingdom or a court, fairies could have a king or queen or both. Oberon is the most common name for a fairy king, as in Robert Greene's play *The Scottish Historie of James the Fourth* (1598), but a fairy queen figure is usually unnamed. If named, the most frequent designation is Diana, with William Shakespeare's Titania being a patronymic derived from Ovid's *Metamorphoses* (3.173).

Difficult to define, other than as supernatural beings, Tudor fairies differ in their traits and dispositions, ranging in stature from adult-sized heroes in Edmund Spenser's epic fairyland to Shakespeare's minuscule monarch Queen Mab, as well as varying in nature from sinister to benign participants in human affairs. One of the basic differences between folkloric and literary fairies concerns moral nature. Fairies in English folklore are reputed predominately evil. The theorized origins of these spirits influence this negative view because several explanations serve to account for their natures: as devils, as angels who fell with Lucifer (though not yet into hell), as the dead, and as a rational species distinct from angels and men.

Literary fairies in the Tudor era generally undergo a positive metamorphosis, as in Shakespeare's representation of good-natured fairies in *A Midsummer Night's Dream,* fairies who could consort with day, unlike the dangerous ones of night's province to whom Horatio refers (*Hamlet,* 1.1.162–163). The favorable depiction of fairies especially occurs in literature designed to compliment a reigning monarch, as in the royal entertainments for Queen Elizabeth I at Woodstock (1575), and Elvetham (1591), and in Spenser's *Faerie Queene,* where he innovatively adapts the use of fairies found in medieval romances, such as *Huon of Bordeaux,* and in the Italian epics by Boiardo and Ariosto. This particular association of fairy with historical royalty continues seriously in the seventeenth century with Ben Jonson's masque in honor of Prince Henry, *Oberon, the Fairy Prince* (1611), but this motif later receives a new comic treatment, even political parody, in some poems featuring extremely diminutive courtly fairies fashioned by William Browne, Robert Herrick, and Michael Drayton.

Hybridity, however, tends to distinguish the Tudor era, and its literary fairies function more decoratively than focally, the chief exceptions being Spenser's romance epic and Shakespeare's *Dream.* Although fairies or their analogues appear in antiquity and in legends throughout the world, the term "fairy" dates from the Middle Ages and probably derives ultimately from the Italian *fatae,* the supernatural ladies who attended childbirths and directed the destiny of men as did the classical three Fates. "Fairy" originally referred to "fay-erie," a state of enchantment, and was transferred later to the agent or fay who wielded such power. Fairyland has numerous locations but several predominate—subterranean locales, sylvan and aquatic haunts, the middle region between air and earth, and the remotest eastern region of the known earth (often cited as India).

Given a pervasive faith in the reality of spiritual life, many in Tudor England probably believed humankind to have a variety of spiritual companions cohabiting the universe. The oral culture of popular belief in fairies was both reflected and changed in the culture of print; writers tended to present fairies as superstitious illusions, except where occult philosophy was foregrounded, as in Shakespeare's use of Ariel for Prospero's theurgy in *The Tempest.* The modern prettification of fairies bowdlerizes the older vital and dangerous fairy traditions, but the new trend takes root in the fanciful depiction of literary fairies at the close of the Tudor era. The liminality of these supernatural creatures, whether believed or disbelieved, is one of the more intriguing aspects of the Tudor world model.

BIBLIOGRAPHY

Briggs, Katherine A. *The Anatomy of Puck.* 1959.
———. *The Fairies in Tradition and Literature.* 1967

F

————. *An Encyclopedia of Fairies.* 1976.

Keightley, Thomas. *The Fairy Mythology, Illustrative of the Romance and Superstition of Various Countries.* 2nd edition. 1850.

Latham, Minor White. *The Elizabethan Fairies: The Fairies of Folklore and the Fairies of Shakespeare.* 1930.

Spence, Lewis. *The Fairy Tradition in Britain.* 1948.

Thomas, Keith. *Religion and the Decline of Magic.* 1971.

Joan Holmer

SEE ALSO

Drayton, Michael; Jonson, Ben; Lyly, John; Nashe, Thomas; Scot, Reginald; Shakespeare, William; Spenser, Edmund

Familists

See Family of Love

Family

Contemporaries used the term household interchangeably with the term family, including all living-in members and servants. Although more than 30 percent of households contained servants, the average size of the household was small, about 4.5 persons, and the dominant norm was the nuclear family. Only 1 percent of households enumerated in the Coventry census of 1523 contained adult relatives of any kind, but at the upper end of the social scale households were larger, and there might be more resident kin. The average household size conceals important differences from the modern pattern: high levels of mortality meant that remarriage was common, and therefore children of successive marriages might be residing under the same roof.

Lawrence Stone has provided a highly influential model of change within the family in this period. He sees a shift from the extended family characterized by kin solidarity, arranged marriage, and limited affection for children to the modern nuclear family based on affection within a narrow circle. Stone's model is flawed by a tendency to infer emotions from demographic facts (i.e., that high levels of mortality necessarily entailed limited levels of emotional commitment), an overdependence on elite sources, and an assumption that the elite led the way in change. More recent historians of the family have pressed into service a wider range of materials, in particular wills, ballads, and the evidence of the church courts, from which much can be inferred about social norms.

The household unit carried considerable ideological force in the Tudor period. Royal authority was conceived in paternalistic terms, while the husband/father figure was considered as enjoying kingly authority in his own household. The household was also seen by the reformers as a key unit of religious instruction, the duties of family prayers and catechizing in the household seminary being repeatedly urged. At the center of the family lay the relationship between man and wife. As Sir Thomas Smith put it, "The naturalest and first coniunction of two towards the making of a further societie of continuance is of the husaband & of the wife. . . . And without this societie of man, and woman, the kinde of man could not long endure." He added that no one was styled yeoman until he was married and had children.

England was characterized by a late age at marriage (twenty-six for women and twenty-eight for men), and by a relatively high proportion of nonmarriers (at least 10 percent and probably increasing toward the end of the century). This was because of the association of marriage with the establishment of an independent household, which meant that the young spent their late teens and early twenties in service saving up the wherewithal to set up on their own. At the upper end of the social hierarchy (both within the landed elite and among the daughters of London tradesmen), marriage ages tended to be younger.

Delayed marriage was one factor in ensuring that parental influence over marriage choices was more limited than the tight prescriptions of the moralists would lead one to believe, because many decisions were taken away from the parental home or after the death of parents. Ballads suggest a high degree of individual initiative, taking advantage of conditions of relatively free sociability between the sexes and in the making of marriage at the lower social levels. Even within the elite it seems that although parents might take the initiative in arranging a match, the children were given some say. The moralists stressed that mutual affection should be an element in any marriage, and that conjugal affection should develop out of emotions preceding the union. As the elite were drawn increasingly toward London by the end of the century, a freer marriage market may have developed, giving the young still greater leverage in their marriage choices. Nor should one necessarily assume an incompatibility between the desires of parents and the desires of their offspring. The view that marriage was essential to the maintenance of the security of the family and the continuity of its dynastic power was widely shared.

Some historians have seen the Reformation as leading to a strengthening of the patriarchal order within the family, but the truth was that the prescriptions of the moralists were riven by tensions that expressed the reality of negotiated rather than imposed power. The conduct literature combined a stress on the patriarchal authority of the husband and the necessity of wifely obedience, with a stress on the marriage as a partnership and a discussion of those respects in which the wife was a "joint governor" of the household with her husband. The reality of family relations was far more permissive than the literature would suggest. The moralists tended to underestimate the degree to which the economic functions of the household would erode the separation of spheres on which they insisted. Even within elite households, the woman was expected to play a role in estate management in her husband's absence, and the efficiency with which aristocratic widows were able to discharge their duties suggests that they had used the experience of marriage profitably. In the urban environment, although experiences diverged enormously between different occupational groups, the wife might be involved in the retailing side of her husband's business. In the countryside, there is no doubt that certain agricultural tasks were regarded as appropriate to women: some have gone so far as to claim that women enjoyed greater power in dairying villages because of their involvement in that activity. Because the household was an economic partnership, wives were more involved in decision making about the careers of offspring, for example, and when quarrels arose within the household, husbands are often found seeking compromise rather than simply trying to impose their authority.

This is not to say that relations between husbands and wives were always agreeable; the prevailing ideology allowed husbands a much greater role in the correction of "wayward" wives. Although the full effect of the common law (which gave the woman no control over the goods she brought to the marriage, albeit limited rights in the real estate she brought to the union) could be mitigated by settlements enforceable in the equity courts, the law left most women extremely vulnerable before feckless husbands. Moreover, the law made it very difficult for women to escape from an intolerable marriage. Although some reformers pressed for the right of divorce and remarriage for women whose husbands had been unfaithful or cruel, the divorce law remained extremely restrictive. Divorce could normally only be granted on grounds of precontract or marriage within the prohibited degrees. Women subjected to intolerable cruelty or confronted by adulterous husbands could seek a decree of separation, but they were unable to remarry, which in effect condemned them to putting up with the status quo. Among the poor, desertion was probably a more usual solution to this kind of problem.

But historians have probably underestimated the degree to which relationships both between husbands and wives and between parents and children were characterized by affection. The language used by husbands and wives in their correspondence suggests that ideals of romantic love were often realized. It is plainly untrue that high levels of mortality entailed a lack of emotional investment in relationships. Husbands and wives might be devastated by the loss of a spouse. While the death of an infant might be greeted more coolly, the deaths of older children, and especially adolescents, were often traumatic.

Because parents had inherited original sin, it was widely recognized that discipline and restraint were essential in the upbringing of children. But humanist impulses pushed a more optimistic view, stressing the child's potential for virtue. Thomas Elyot, for example, suggested that education should be directed to the preservation of innocence rather than the correction of sin, and explored the part played by imitation and example in the upbringing of the young. The godly and humanist discourses were reconciled in the increasing emphasis on the need for moderation in the correction of children. The oft-cited remark of the Venetian ambassador in 1497 that the practice of the English in sending their children out to service betokened a coolness in family relations has fostered the idea that children were neglected. But again, family letters and diaries reveal a different picture. In the case of apprenticeships the wishes of the young were often taken into account in finding them positions (at least that was the ideal), and parents continued to take great interest in the fortunes of their children both at school and in service. Fathers may have forged particularly strong bonds with their eldest sons (because of primogeniture), but it would be wrong to conclude that younger sons were neglected, or daughters entirely ignored, although the latter relationship was probably the most fraught of all because of the erroneous assumption that daughters would comply with the wishes of their fathers over marriage choices.

The quality of relations within the family therefore eludes easy generalization. Stone's pioneering work has been refined by historians more sensitive to the differences of social status, age, birth order, and gender. The dynamics of change, particularly humanism and the reformation, were more ambiguous than he recognized.

F

BIBLIOGRAPHY

Byrne, M. St. Clare, ed. *The Lisle Letters*. 6 vols. 1981.

Houlbrooke, R. *The English Family, 1450–1700*. 1984.

Mendelson, S., and P. Crawford. *Women in England, 1500–1800*. 1998.

O'Day, R. *The Family and Family Relationships, 1500–1900*. 1994.

Stone, L. *The Family, Sex, and Marriage in England 1500–1800*. 1977.

Ian W. Archer

SEE ALSO

Childbirth; Elyot, Thomas; Gender; Marriage Manuals; Matrimony; Population

Family of Love

A religious group founded by Hendrik Niclaes (1502–1580) about 1540, the Familists believed that after Christ's death on the cross, the human race had fallen a second time. Because of this, God had sent him, Niclaes, as another prophet who would teach the world and reconcile it once more to God. Anyone who failed to hear this call would be damned forever.

Niclaes was originally from Westphalia, but in 1531, he moved to Amsterdam, where he lived until he founded his sect. Persuaded of the corruption of Amsterdam, Niclaes moved with his disciples to Emden, where he lived as a wealthy merchant for thirty years. There he preached a kind of Christlike behavior that would eventually lead to deification (*vergoding*). The Family of Love was drawn from many strands of piety, and saw itself as the harbinger of a new age of simple Christianity, when quarrels over liturgy and doctrine would be done away with in the universal reign of brotherly love. The sect was very wealthy, and able to publish an enormous amount of literature justifying its position.

Many early Familists were Anabaptists, but after 1555, there were a number of humanist converts to the sect in Antwerp, largely due to the activities of Christoffel Plantijn. These converts modified Niclaes' original theology, dismissing his claims to be a prophet but accepting his vision of religious harmony.

In 1570, Niclaes moved to Cologne, where he organized his sect into a church along Catholic lines, complete with its own hierarchy of bishops and priests. This led to a split with the Antwerp humanists in 1573. After Niclaes's death, the sect declined, although it appears that some groups remained active in England until the eighteenth century.

English Familism was centered on Cambridgeshire and the Isle of Ely, with a particular concentration in the village of Balsham, which lies about seven miles southeast of Cambridge. The sect seems to have entered the country during the reign of Mary Tudor, when it was spread by the itinerant ministry of Christopher Vittels, a Dutchman who was bilingual and who later translated many of Niclaes's works into English (1574–1575). It seems to have appealed to a mystical strain in English society, and to have drawn on the *Devotio Moderna* and its English followers, rather than on Lollardy or early forms of Protestantism.

Little was heard of the Family of Love until Niclaes's writings began to be disseminated, which led to a major crisis, culminating in a royal proclamation (October 3, 1580), which ordered the burning of his books and the careful investigation of his followers, if they could be found. One of the ironies of this is that there were a number of Familist sympathizers at court who kept in close contact with groups in the Cambridgeshire villages. When Elizabeth visited Cambridgeshire in 1578, it seems that her itinerary was organized by Familists in her entourage, who used the occasion to cement these links still further.

Persecution of the Familists was never severe or more than sporadic, and after 1582 they lived in peace until the accession of James I, when they gained a new notoriety and were even caricatured in a play by Thomas Middleton, entitled *The Family of Love*, which may have been written as early as 1603–1604. After about 1610, however, interest in them waned once more, although there were still a few about as late as 1689. By then it seems that most of them had either joined the Quakers, who had a similar spirituality, or other dissenting religious groups.

BIBLIOGRAPHY

Hamilton, A. *The Family of Love*, Cambridge. 1981.

Marsh, C.W. *The Family of Love in English Society, 1550–1630*. 1994.

Martin, F.L. "The Family of Love in England: Conforming Millenarians." *The Sixteenth Century Journal*, vol. 3, no. 2, pp. 99–108.

Moss, J.D. "Variations on a Theme: The Family of Love in Renaissance England." *Renaissance Quarterly*, vol. 31, pp. 186–196.

Gerald Bray

SEE ALSO

Anabaptists

F

Fayrfax, Robert (1464–1521)

Born in Lincolnshire in 1464, Robert Fayrfax was named a gentleman of the Chapel Royal in 1497 and received a doctorate in music, for which he composed his *Missa O quam glorifica,* at Cambridge in 1504. In 1511, he acquired another doctorate, the first such degree in music from Oxford. With the other musicians of the Chapel Royal, he traveled to France for the Field of Cloth of Gold in 1520. Henry VIII named him a poor knight of Windsor in 1514, thereby augmenting his income, although Fayrfax continued to live at St. Alban's. He died there in October 1521.

The arms of the composer Robert Fayrfax are featured prominently at the beginning of a songbook dated c. 1500 and now called the "Fayrfax Manuscript" (British Library, Additional MS 5465). Six of his works were copied into the original corpus of the Eton Choirbook, although only a *Salve regina* remains, and such Eton Choirbook composers as John Browne, Richard Davy, Edmund Turges, Gilbert Banastir, and William Cornysh are also represented in the Fayrfax MS. Along with settings of courtly love poems in rhyme royal it features religious carols.

Fayrfax's music, not as florid as the majority of pieces in the Eton Choirbook, sounds less medieval stylistically, partly because of his predilection for harmonic movement by fourths and fifths at cadences. Twenty-nine compositions survive, five of them incomplete. They include six Masses, two Magnificats, two puzzle canons, eight polyphonic secular songs, and ten votive antiphons. The Magnificats and all but one of the Masses were copied into the Lambeth Choirbook (Lambeth Palace MS 1). All of the Masses lack the Kyrie, and all were composed for the standard five-voice texture of two boys' voices (treble and mean), countertenor, tenor, and bass. All but one are cantus-firmus Masses with the borrowed chant placed in the tenor. The *Missa O bone Jesu* shares musical material with his own antiphon setting, for which only the mean voice survives, and the *Missa Albanus,* based on a nine-note ostinato stated thirty times, shares its cantus firmus with Fayrfax's motet *O Maria Deo.*

It was undoubtedly the more modern features of Fayrfax's music that assured its circulation for almost a century after the composer's death. The contents of the Fayrfax Manuscript constitute the major part of the edition *Early Tudor Songs and Carols.*

BIBLIOGRAPHY

Fugler, Stephen. "Pre-compositional mathematical planning in Mass settings by Nicholas Ludford and Robert Fayrfax." Dissertation, University of Exeter. 1990.

Stevens, John, ed. *Early Tudor Songs and Carols.* Musica Britannica. Vol. 36. 1975.

Warren, Edwin B., ed. *Robert Fayrfax, 1464–1521: The Masses.* Corpus mensurabilis musicae. Vol. 17. 1959.

Laura S. Youens

SEE ALSO

Carol; Eton Choirbook; Cornysh, William; Field of the Cloth of Gold; Motet

Fenton, Geoffrey (c. 1539–1608)

Translator and statesman, Sir Geoffrey Fenton was probably born in Nottinghamshire around 1539, but no details are known of his childhood, although his mastery of languages suggests a very good education. Fenton's career interests parallel those of another statesman who served with him in Ireland, Sir Edmund Spenser. Although Spenser's poetic production far surpassed his, Fenton's translations of diverse French and Latin texts were highly regarded by his contemporaries, and his loyal service in Ireland earned him a knighthood in 1590.

While residing in Paris as a young man in 1567, Fenton produced his first major work—a translation from French of stories by Pierre Boaisteau and Francois de Belleforest. Fenton titled the work *Certaine Tragicall Discourses Written Out of French and Latine* and dedicated it to Lady Mary Sidney. Some of Fenton's subsequent translations may have educated him for his later political life: *A Discourse of the Civile Warres and Late Troubles in France,* (1570), *Acts of Confederence in Religion,* (1571), and his translation from a French text of Francesco Guicciardini's *History of the Wars of Italy.* Many Elizabethans believed that Guicciardini's *Storia d'Italia* was as important as Niccolo Machiavelli's *The Prince,* and there are many parallels between the two. Although Machiavelli views the masses as evil, and Guicciardini sees them as frail, Guicciardini's chief character is a "pragmatico," not unlike the Prince. Gabriel Harvey most admired the "pragmatico" of Fenton's translation, and perhaps Elizabeth I did too, for after Fenton's monumental work appeared in 1579, she appointed him to a position under the lord deputy in Ireland. In 1580, Fenton became principal secretary of the Irish Council.

In Ireland, Fenton vigilantly pursued English dominion, using both oppressive and conciliatory tactics. He advocated the murder of the earl of Desmond as the best way to end the rebellion in Munster; he assisted in the

F

torture of the Roman Catholic bishop Hurley; and he witnessed the final destruction of the Spanish Armada off the Irish coast. Fenton's more diplomatic strategies surfaced after the British lost the battle against Hugh O'Neill, earl of Tyrone, at the Yellow Ford near Armagh. Fearing Tyrone would continue his triumphant march before the British could regroup, Fenton and the Irish Council sent Tyrone a mild reprimand, reminding him that the British soldiers he had captured must remain safe. The letter infuriated Queen Elizabeth when she received a copy, and she admonished the writers for "this foul error to our dishonor."

Sir Geoffrey Fenton successfully served his own interests in Ireland as well as his queen's, and he was able to marry his daughter Katherine to the English adventurer, Richard Boyle, who had bought Sir Walter Ralegh's 40,000-acre plantation in Cork.

BIBLIOGRAPHY

Douglas, Robert Langton, ed. *Certain Tragicall Discourses of Bandello. Translated into English by Geffraie Fenton anno 1567.* Tudor Translations. Vols. 19–20. 1898; repr. 1967.

Falls, Cyril. *Elizabeth's Irish Wars.* 1950.

Gottfried, Rudolf, B. *Geoffrey Fenton's* Historie of Guicciardin. 1940.

Hinton, Edward M. *Ireland through Tudor Eyes.* 1935.

Palmer, William. *The Problem of Ireland in Tudor Foreign Policy, 1485–1603.* 1994.

Katherine Conway

SEE ALSO

Ireland, History of; Italian Literature, Influence of; O'Neill, Hugh; Spenser, Edmund

Field of the Cloth of Gold

The Field of the Cloth of Gold is the name popularly given to a meeting in June 1520 between Henry VIII of England and Francis I of France. The meeting was an extended tournament at which the two kings personally affirmed an alliance made between them in 1518 as part of an international peace agreement known as the Treaty of London. It was characterized by an extraordinary display of luxury and wealth. Attended by their courts, the two kings met in a shallow valley between the towns of Guines and Ardres in northwestern France on June 7, 1520. For two weeks they hosted jousts and other paramilitary games in which both kings performed well.

Henry VIII had built a temporary replica of a Tudor palace that housed some of the entertainments. The ground floor was brick, the upper story was wood and plaster painted to look like brick. The ornately decorated building had windows of glass, and each room was hung with rich tapestries. It impressed all observers with its ingenuity and splendor. Francis stayed in a series of large tents or pavilions, most covered with cloth of gold and decorated with *fleurs-de-lys.* The largest was held up by two huge masts lashed together, surmounted by a large painted statue of St. Michael. The two royal entourages entertained each other on numerous occasions with banquets, allegorical pageants, and masques, which all turned on themes of peace and chivalry. They also exchanged lavishly expensive gifts. Francis spent about 200,000 livres on the event; Henry's expenditure at least equaled that figure. On June 23, Cardinal Thomas Wolsey said a final mass of blessing on Anglo-French amity. Throughout the fortnight Henry and Francis treated each other with generosity and declared their mutual admiration and affection.

In fact, the two kings were always keen rivals and were at war within two years. In trying to resolve the contradiction in these events historians have dismissed the meeting as either a wasteful and half-hearted attempt at peacemaking or a huge deception perpetrated by Henry VIII prior to attacking Francis. On the evidence, neither view is convincing. Instead, the explanation lies in understanding contemporary political culture. Sixteenth-century princes were esteemed as successful warriors, as wealthy patrons, and as guardians of peace and good order. By 1520, both kings enjoyed international renown for apparently possessing these qualities, but Francis I had eclipsed Henry with his conquest of the duchy of Milan in September 1515. He now wanted Henry sidelined while he faced the newly elected Holy Roman Emperor, Charles V. Henry resented Francis's recent successes. He saw an Anglo-French alliance as a way of curbing the latter's ambitions while stealing the spotlight by proclaiming himself the guarantor of international peace. Therefore, his ostentatious generosity and his prowess in the tournaments were a warning to Francis. The impressive material and human resources that Henry had marshalled could be turned against Francis if necessary. Conversely, Francis's spectacular accommodation, costumes, and generous treatment of Henry stated that he welcomed, but did not depend on, English friendship. Rather than trying to deceive each other, the two monarchs were actually using the ideal of friendship between them to assert their own virtues and their aggressive potential in a ritualized way. The Field of the Cloth of Gold was a piece of propagandistic theater in which peace was celebrated not for its own sake but as the result of a princely agreement.

BIBLIOGRAPHY

Anglo, S. *Spectacle, Pageantry, and Early Tudor Policy.* 1969.

Richardson, G.J. "Anglo-French Political and Cultural Relations in the Reign of Henry VIII." Dissertation, London University. 1996.

Russell, J.G. *The Field of the Cloth of Gold.* 1969.

Glenn Richardson

SEE ALSO

Foreign Relations and Diplomacy; Henry VIII

Field, Richard (1561–1616)

Dean of Gloucester and Anglican apologist, Richard Field was born in Hertfordshire and educated at Oxford, where, by the time he earned his M.A. in 1584, he had already distinguished himself as a debater and lecturer. After proceeding B.D. in 1592, he was made divinity reader in Winchester Cathedral and, two years later, about the time of his marriage, he became rector of Burghclere. The quiet and relative obscurity of the position was apparently to his liking; although offered more lucrative rectories elsewhere, Field was content to remain at Burghclere. He earned his D.D. at Queen's College in 1594 and was appointed, in 1598, a chaplain in ordinary to Elizabeth I; owing largely to her favor, he was awarded the prebend of Windsor in 1602—although his official installation at Windsor was carried out in 1604 through Elizabeth's successor, James I. Field's major writing was published two years later: *Of the Church Five Bookes, by Richard Field, Doctor of Divinity.* In this, he defended the *via media* of the English church, focusing especially on what he deemed the errors and abuses of Rome; the work is often compared with Richard Hooker's *Laws,* and indeed, the two men were friends. Field was elevated, under James I, to dean of Gloucester in 1609, where he preached only a few times every year, still preferring to reside at Burghclere and Windsor. He died on November 21, 1616.

BIBLIOGRAPHY

Field, Nathaniel. *Some Short Memorials Concerning the Life of Richard Field.* 1716.

Hooper, R. "Richard Field." *Dictionary of National Biography.* Vol. 6. pp. 1274–1276. 1917.

Mark Goldblatt

SEE ALSO

Anglicanism; Hooker, Richard

Firearms

See Military History; Ordnance

First Fruits and Tenths

See Annates; *Valor Ecclesiasticus*

Fish and Fishing

Fish was important to the Tudors in providing food, recreation (as the numerous books on angling reveal), income, and employment. For the state, employment in the fishing industry was important for strategic as well as economic reasons. As *the* nursery of seamen, the industry was essential for the "maintenance of the navye," as was explained in the statute of 1563 that added Wednesday to the already numerous days on which only fish could be consumed. How effective the law was is uncertain. There is no doubt, however, that fish was a regular part of the diet of all the people. For the rich it offered variety, while for the poor, depending on where they lived, it might be one of the cheaper foods available. Newcastle apprentices, for example, complained of the monotony of a diet of salmon.

Freshwater fish was probably more widely available than sea fish, although the latter reached markets a hundred miles or so inland. Most freshwater fish was consumed locally, but in more sophisticated markets such as London, fishmongers acquired barrels of live fish over considerable distances. The capital was also a major market for sea fish from the many small ports on the east and south coast. For some of the ports, offshore fishing was merely a by-employment for communities mainly employed in agriculture. But in places like Cley and Wells in Norfolk, Southwold in Suffolk, and Rye in Sussex, the order was reversed, and fishing was the main source of employment. In 1582, it was estimated that 10,000 men and one-quarter of the country's ships were directly involved in the industry, with 30,000 more people in related activities such as curing and transportation.

Although many of the fishing vessels were small, commonly twenty tons or less, the ratio of men to tons was

F

A Booke of fishing with Hooke & Line, and of all other instruments thereunto belonging.

Another of sundrie Engines and Trappes to take Polcats, Buzards, Rattes, Mice and all other kindes of Vermine & Beasts whatsoeuer, most profitable for all Warriners, and such as delight in this kinde of sport and pastime.

Made by L. M.

LONDON.
Printed by Iohn Wolfe, and are to be solde by Edwarde White dwelling at the little North doore of Paules at the signe of the Gunne.
1599.

Leonard Mascall, from *A Booke of Fishing with Hooke and Line* (1590). This cut from the title page illustrates fishing with a pole, line, and hook, and one method of setting a trap. Mascall's text also included instruction on "sundry engines and trappes" for snaring vermin, both for pest control and "sport and pastime." By permission of the Folger Shakespeare Library.

exceptionally high; and the seasonal pattern of the fisheries on the east and south coasts kept ships at sea for the greater part of the year. At Rye, a leading fishing port, summer was the time for catching mackerel offshore. In the autumn, the herring "fair" at Yarmouth was a major event, as it was for fishermen from as far away as Lyme Regis in Dorset. Winter was spent cod fishing off Scarborough. For east coast ports, especially in East Anglia, cod drew many ships and boats to Iceland on voyages taking up to half the year. This fishery was very competitive, as was the herring fishery, and the fortunes of the North Sea industry fluctuated. In the mid-Tudor period a substantial fall in the number of ships setting out for Iceland underlay the government's attempt at social engineering

in 1563. Trade picked up after 1570 but declined toward the end of the century. The herring fishery was also affected by Dutch "busses" that appeared in increasing numbers from the mid-sixteenth century.

For the industry as a whole, compensation was to be found on the fishing banks off Newfoundland. After many years of neglect, English vessels began to make the voyage in increasing numbers from the 1570s. In 1594, about 100 sizeable ships embarked from West-Country ports early in the year, returning six to seven months later. Most of the catch, salted and wind-dried on the island, was for domestic consumption, as was Icelandic cod and the smoke-cured or salted herring. Fish was also imported from Holland and northern France to supplement domestic supplies. Toward the end of the Tudor period, however, imports were offset by shipments of Yarmouth herring and Newfoundland cod to markets in southern Europe, thereby enhancing the industry's importance to the economy.

BIBLIOGRAPHY

Cell, G.T. *English Enterprise in Newfoundland, 1577–1660.* 1969.

Davis, Ralph. *The Rise of the English Shipping Industry.* 1962.

Innis, H.A. *The Cod Fisheries.* 1954.

Jenkins, J.T. *The Herring and the Herring Fisheries.* 1928.

Williams, N.J. *The Maritime Trade of the East Anglian Ports, 1550–1590.* 1988.

Brian Dietz

SEE ALSO
Food and Diet; Shipbuilding

Fisher, John (1496–1535)

A humanist patron and Roman Catholic apologist, John Fisher was born in Yorkshire in 1469, the son of a merchant. Most of his life was spent in association with Cambridge University: B.A., 1488; M.A., 1491; fellow, 1491–1496; master, 1496–1498 (all of Michaelhouse, later absorbed into Trinity); president of Queens', 1505–1508; vice-chancellor, 1501–1504; chancellor, 1504, with life tenure, 1514. At his invitation, Desiderius Erasmus taught Greek there, 1511–1514. Using bequests from Lady Margaret Beaufort, he oversaw the foundation of Christ's, 1505, and St. John's, 1511.

Fisher was ordained priest in 1491, earned his D.D. in 1501, and was appointed bishop of Rochester in 1504. He resided in this the smallest English diocese for thirty years. He preached noteworthy sermons for the funeral of Henry VII, May 10, 1509; the Month's Mind of Lady Margaret, c. July 29, 1509, a mass thirty days after her death; the burning of Lutheran books, May 12, 1521; and the abjuration of Robert Barnes, February 11, 1526.

While humanist interests moved him to study Greek and Hebrew, Fisher published three treatises in support of the medieval belief in one Magdalene (1519). His most important work was *Assertionis Lutheranae Confutatio* (1523); its teachings on the papacy, grace, and free will were used at the Council of Trent. Fisher's longest work, *De Eucharistia* (1527), argued for transubstantiation against Oecolampadius. He defended Katherine of Aragon before the Legatine Court, June 1529, and in *De Causa Matrimonii* (1530).

In February 1531, he inserted the reservation "as far as the law of God allows" into the first proclamation of the royal supremacy. He was absent because of illness when the bishops made their unqualified submission, May 15, 1532. For not denouncing the Nun of Kent, he was accused of treason in March 1534, but only fined £300. By negotiating with the imperial ambassador Eustace Chapuys for the excommunication and deposition of Henry VIII, Fisher actually committed treason. Although it did not contain Fisher's view of the papacy as established by divine law, Henry's *Assertio septem sacramentorum* (1521) was included in Fisher's *Opera* (1597).

When Fisher and More refused to take the Oath of Succession because the preamble denied the papacy, they were imprisoned in the Tower in April 1534. Paul III named Fisher a cardinal on May 20, 1535, but this honor failed to save him from execution on June 22, 1535. Fisher was the only Henrician bishop to die for papal primacy. Emphasizing the supranational character of the church, Thomas More was similarly beheaded on July 6. The church of Rome canonized them together in 1935; their joint feast day is on June 22.

BIBLIOGRAPHY

Bradshaw, Brendan, and Eamon Duffy, eds. *Humanism, Reform, and the Reformation: The Career of Bishop John Fisher.* 1989.

Mayor, John E.B., ed. *The English Works of John Fisher.* 2nd edition. Early English Text Society. Vol. 27. 1935.

Rex, Richard. *The Theology of John Fisher.* 1991.

Anne O'Donnell, S.N.D.

SEE ALSO

Chapuys, Eustace; Council of Trent; Erasmus, Desiderius; Henry VIII; Katherine of Aragon; Lutheranism; More, Thomas; Supremacy, Act of; Universities

Fitzalan, Henry (c. 1511–1580)

Godson of Henry VIII, Henry Fitzalan, twelfth Earl of Arundel, entered service to the King as a young man. He remained at court under several subsequent monarchs, as lord chamberlain, then lord steward of the household. Throughout his career he was continually at the center of court life and politics. Consequently, Fitzalan's life was variously tumultuous and successful. His prominence brought him to the center of the succession crisis in the 1550s; and his constant willingness to clash with existing authority frequently made him susceptible to false charges for which he was imprisoned in the Tower or confined to home.

Although volatile in temper and open to suspicion as a Catholic, Fitzalan was also an asset to the crown. He served as deputy of Calais (1540), acted as field marshall in France (1544), and pacified the Sussex rebels during the Peasants' Revolt (1549). In later years Fitzalan was regarded as the leader of the old nobility.

Fitzalan died at Arundel House in the Strand, and was buried in the collegiate chapel at Arundel. A member of the Elizabethan Society of Antiquaries, he formed a substantial library, and was, briefly, chancellor of the University of Oxford. He married twice; both wives were distinguished for their classical learning.

BIBLIOGRAPHY

G[oodwin], G[ordon]. "Henry Fitzalan" In *Dictionary of National Biography*, vol. 6, pp. 88–93. 1967.

Stone, Lawrence. "Patriarchy and Paternalism in Tudor England: The Earl of Arundel and the Peasants' Revolt of 1549." *Journal of British Studies*, vol. 13, pp. 19–23.

S.P. Cerasano

SEE ALSO

Grey, Lady Jane

Fitzroy, Henry (1519–1536)

The natural son of Henry VIII and Elizabeth Blount, Henry Fitzroy's life encapsulates the desperate pressures his father felt to ensure the continuation of the Tudor dynasty. Despite his illegitimacy, the king used this son to attempt to safeguard the succession, creating him duke of Richmond and Somerset, earl of Nottingham, and raising him to be knight of the garter, all at the age of six years.

F

The duke of Richmond was always seen as a potential successor to his father, despite the presence of the legitimate Mary, daughter of Katherine of Aragon. His education was monitored by Cardinal Thomas Wolsey, and was designed for leadership. He was instructed by Richard Croke, the pioneer of Greek scholarship, as well as John Palsgrave and other humanist scholars (when he was not distracted from his studies by hawking and hunting, or by his schoolmates, who included Henry Howard, earl of Surrey). Important foreign marriages were considered for him, and in 1525, a satellite court was created for him in the north.

He was married to Surrey's sister, Mary, the only daughter of Thomas Howard, third duke of Norfolk, in November 1533. Increasingly, he was employed to represent his father's policies, attending the execution of the Carthusian monks in May 1535 and of Anne Boleyn the following year. But all of the efforts to use him as a possible heir were frustrated by his premature death in July 1536, a potent reminder of the continued fragility of the Tudor succession.

BIBLIOGRAPHY

Dowling, Maria. *Humanism in the Age of Henry VIII.* 1986.

Nichols, John Gough, ed. *Inventories of the Wardrobes, Plate, Chapel Stuff, etc., of Henry Fitzroy, Duke of Richmond.* In *Camden Miscellany,* vol. 3. 1855.

Susan Wabuda

SEE ALSO
Henry VIII

Fleming, Abraham (c. 1552–1607)

Functioning either as a compiler, indexer, or "learned corrector," and sometimes as all three, Abraham Fleming served in at least fifteen printing houses during the 1570s and 1580s. During the first dozen of these years, he was attached to the University of Cambridge where at the age of seventeen or eighteen he had become a sizar at Peterhouse (i.e., receiving an allowance), but during these years as a "student," he was also very much in touch with current literary activity in London, providing, for example, commendatory verses for Barnabe Googe's fourth edition of his translation of Marcellus Palingenius's *Zodiac of Life* in 1576, George Whetstone's *Rock of Regard* in the same year, Timothy Kendall's *Epigrams* in the next year, followed by a similar mode of tribute for

accounts of Martin Frobisher's second and third voyages in his search for a Northwest Passage. Publications such as these both developed a popular reading public and provided a means of livelihood, if sometimes tenuous, for authors and publishers alike.

Also during this period, Fleming was active as a translator, first, in a rendering of Vergil's *Bucolics* in fourteeners (1575), which specifies that the task was achieved during leftover and stolen hours and in fourteen days; this was offered, apparently, in emulation of Thomas Phaer's *Aeneid* (1558 and following), which had carefully stated the amount of time required for translating each book (e.g., Book 4: *Opus quindeci dierum*). At the very end of his career Fleming published a second version, this time "not in foolish rime" but in due proportion and measure, i.e., in unrimed verse, together with his version of the *Georgics* (or *Rurals*), both of which he dedicated to Archbishop John Whitgift (1589).

Among his other translations during the period was an abridged version of John Caius's treatise on English dogs and another of Synesius's mock-encomium on baldness (1576, 1579). Annexed to this latter was the "Tale of Hemetes," a work that had been presented before Elizabeth I at Woodstock in 1575, but appearing now with slight revision of both the Latin and the English. Writing for the *Dictionary of National Biography*, Sidney Lee, like others, assumed that it had been the work of George Gascoigne and charged Fleming with having boldly appropriated it; he was absolved of the charge in the early twentieth century when it was ascertained that Gascoigne, angling for foreign employment, had translated the anonymous tale into Latin, French, and English to demonstrate his linguistic skills.

In 1576, Fleming began his indexing career with Palingenius's *Zodiac of Life,* providing a table of both words and matter. This was to be followed by comparable indices for a large number of religious works and, increasingly, tables of commonplaces. First introduced in 1580 in his index to John Baret's quadruple dictionary (*An Alvearie*), Fleming included a listing of 200 proverbs, a genre that Erasmus earlier had made both accessible and popular on the Continent. From that date until 1585, he was to revise a number of dictionaries, augmenting them with proverbs, one example being John Withal's very popular *Short Dictionary,* which went through fifteen editions plus several issues up to 1634; to this Fleming added 600 rhythmical verses, interspersing proverbs throughout.

Also within this period he wrote a biography of William Lamb, a long-lived public benefactor who built a conduit in Holburn stocked with 120 pails to enable women to sell water. Relying only on Lamb's will, Fleming was able to spin out a memorial of his accomplishments, referring among them to a prayer book called the *Conduit of Comfort;* a work in verse and prose with this same popular title was assigned to Fleming in the Stationers' Register and appeared in 1579. Only three leaves of this edition are extant, the remainder perhaps having been thumbed to pieces; a fifth impression appeared in 1624.

This biographical memorial to Lamb was to be utilized in Fleming's most arduous undertaking, working on the publication of Raphael Holinshed's *Chronicles of England, Scotland, and Ireland* published in 1587. Consisting of roughly 3.5 million words, the three volumes (frequently bound as two) involved the efforts of others—John Hooker *alias Vowell* on Irish affairs, Francis Thynne on Scottish history, and the indefatigable John Stow on English history. Much of the text of Stow's later *Annals of England* (and their multiple editions) derives, as he acknowledges, from his efforts for Holinshed's *Chronicles*.

Overseeing the presentation of the text and inserting source materials, Fleming "sweated mightily" in its preparation, accounting for the index for the English history as well as the typographical excellence of the whole. The volumes were subjected to review by examiners appointed by the Privy Council, who demanded extensive deletions and alterations, particularly on matters referring to the volatile relations of the English and Scots. From the evidence of a Huntington Library copy containing proof corrections that can only be called "finicky," it represents a third or fourth "revise." Fleming's strenuous involvement as compiler, indexer, and learned corrector of the *Chronicles* is attested by printed and holograph inscriptions. His papers eventually came into the hands of Francis Peck, who announced in 1732 that they were ready for the press, but he seems never to have published them; so what would have been invaluable information about printing practices in the late sixteenth century, including censorship, has never come to light.

Fleming retired the next year to become chaplain to the countess of Nottingham and rector of St. Pancras Soper-Lane; though he delivered eight sermons at Paul's Cross, none of them was ever printed.

BIBLIOGRAPHY

Arber, Edward. *A Transcript of the Registers of the Company of Stationers of London, 1554–1660.* 5 vols. 1875–1894; repr. 1950.

Cooper, Charles Henry, and Thompson Cooper, eds. *Athenea Cantabrigiensis.* Vol. 2, pp. 459–464. 1861.

Donno, Elizabeth Story. "A Learned Corrector in 1586–1587." *Studies in Bibliography,* vol. 42, pp. 200–211.

———. "Some Aspects of Shakespeare's Holinshed." *Huntington Library Quarterly,* vol. 50, pp. 229–248.

Elizabeth Story Donno

SEE ALSO

Classical Literature, English Translations;Holinshed, Raphael; Printing, Publishing, and Bookselling

Flodden Field, Battle of

England's decisive defeat of Scotland at the battle of Flodden Field, September 9, 1513, destroyed a generation of Scottish leadership. An English army commanded by 70-year-old Thomas Howard, earl of Surrey, defeated Scottish forces led by King James IV at the foot of Flodden Hill, near Berwick, just below the Scottish border.

The war started in August. In June, Henry VIII had invaded France in support of Pope Julius's Holy League against Louis XII. Believing England was weak with Queen Katherine as governor of the realm, James honored Scotland's Auld Alliance with the French by invading Northumberland with massive artillery and more than 30,000 men.

For two weeks James led a giant border raid until his soldiers began to desert with booty and livestock. Meanwhile, Surrey summoned 20,000 men of the northern counties and marched to Durham and Newcastle, where he joined forces led by his son, Lord Admiral Thomas Howard, and a company of archers under Sir Edward Stanley.

Relying on pikes more than artillery, Flodden was the last medieval battle fought in England. When James camped on Flodden Hill, high above the River Till, Surrey sent a herald to bid him to battle on the plain. When James refused, Surrey crossed the Till by a bridge unknown to James and marched his forces around the Scots. James retreated to adjacent Branxton Hill and fired cannon on the English, but with little accuracy. The English successfully returned fire, driving the Scots to charge down the hill in heavy rain. Many stumbled into a bog and fell to English arrows. In two hours of hand-to-hand combat, English halberds, with their axes and hooks, proved deadlier than the Scottish long spears.

England's victory, combined with less bloody triumphs in France, made Henry at twenty-two an acknowledged

F

leader in European politics. Scotland's defeat left a government in chaos, for among the 10,000 Scottish casualties were leaders of most noble families and of the church. The king himself fell, his crown passing to his infant son. Katherine sent James's blood-stained coat to Henry in France. Contemporary accounts of the battle include the first popular English ballad, "A Ballade of the Scottysshe Kynge" by John Skelton, who portrays James as an exemplum of overweening pride. In Scotland, Jane Elliot's ballad, "The Flowers of the Forest," remains a piper's lament for the fallen.

BIBLIOGRAPHY

Gutierrez, Nancy A. "John Skelton: Courtly Maker/Popular Poet." *Journal of the Rocky Mountain Medieval and Renaissance Association,* vol. 4, pp. 59–75.

Macdougall, Norman. "'The Glory of All Princely Governing': The Kingship of James IV of Scotland." *History Today,* vol. 34, pp. 30–36.

Mackie, J.D. *A History of Scotland.* 2nd edition, revised Bruce Lenman and Geoffrey Parker, eds. 1978.

Scarisbrick, J.J. *Henry VIII.* 1968.

Gayle Gaskill

SEE ALSO

Henry VIII; James IV; Scotland, History of; John Skelton

Florio, John (c. 1553–1625)

By virtue of his resolute promotion of foreign language study, John Florio had a profound impact on Elizabethan literature. Through his robust translations he introduced many terms still used today, words like "conscientious," "tarnish," "efface," "facilitate," "regret," and "emotion." We have Florio to thank for the genitive neuter pronoun "its," which he used regularly in his writings and discussed in his dictionaries. Although fashions in rhetoric changed rapidly at the end of the sixteenth century, Florio maintained a clear vision of his two-fold mission: to enrich the English tongue and teach Italian.

Following his *First Fruites* (1578), which contained many "merry proverbs, witty sentences, and golden sayings," Florio contributed to the collection that helped turn England's attention toward overseas commerce, Richard Hakluyt's *Principall Navigations,* with his translation of Ramusio's account of Jacques Cartier's voyages (1580). But more far-reaching in its influence was Florio's

dictionary, which remained the standard one in use throughout the seventeenth century and which was the basis of successive efforts. Of the two dozen Italian grammars, dialogue manuals, and dictionaries published during the Tudor-Stuart period, four were by Florio: *First Fruites* (1578), *Second Frutes* (1591), *Worlde of Wordes* (1598), and *Queen Anna's World of Words* (1611); two more, by Giovanni Torriano, were either adaptations or augmentations of Florio's scholarship, *Italian Tutor* (1640) and *Vocabolario Inglese & Italiano* (1659).

But Florio's influence on the English language and its literature extends further still. While there can be no doubt that he read and commented on Sir Philip Sidney's *Arcadia* as it was being written, most likely he transcribed it at the same time he was working on his *Second Frutes,* and the chapter headings that are retained today originally were devised by Florio. Likewise, his companionship and literary exchanges with Giordano Bruno are well documented. And, for a time, he kept company with Edmund Spenser and Gabriel Harvey.

Florio is remembered primarily for his ebullient prose style and for his efforts to make English more serviceable and copious. So serious was he in this endeavor that he became involved in learned literary controversies of the day, and his style was imitated and ridiculed by John Eliot, John Sanford, William Cornwallis, and John Donne, among others. Florio was sufficiently visible—and evidently audible—in London society to have been a target for sport, as he was mocked in stage characters created by Ben Jonson and William Shakespeare (most notably the humorous language tutor, Holophernes, in *Love's Labors Lost,* and, to some extent, Florio's florid similes can be heard in the extended conceits of Falstaff's verbal jousting).

Like Shakespeare, Florio had a patron in Henry Wriothesley, the earl of Southampton; and like other literary luminaries of the day (including Jonson, Donne, Michael Drayton, George Chapman, and Samuel Daniel) he benefited from the patronage of Lucy Russell, countess of Bedford—at whose request, evidently, he undertook the translation of Montaigne (published first in 1603, and then again in 1613 and 1632). Although Florio's *Essayes of Montaigne* was far more rhetorically composed than the original French version (with attention to sound patterns and with words used in decorative rather than logical schemes), it had an immediate and lasting impact on its English audience. Shakespeare, Jonson, Sir Walter Ralegh, and Robert Burton, for example, were among those who owned and quoted freely from it.

Florio banked on his foreignness throughout his life and, although he was born in England and seems never to have visited Italy, he advanced foreign language study considerably. He was the son of a Florentine Protestant who fled persecution and came to England just before Edward VI's reign. In 1550, his father, Michael Angelo Florio, was preacher to a congregation of Italian Protestants in London, and for a time was patronized both by William Cecil and Archbishop Thomas Cranmer. Although his services at these great houses ended abruptly for obscure reasons, John Florio continued to have entrees into court circles and served as a tutor to the flower of Elizabethan gentry. In addition to having connections to the intertwining circles of the Dudleys, Rutlands, Sidneys, and Haringtons, for a time Florio seems to have been attached to the household of Thomas Sackville, earl of Dorset. He maintained ties to Fulke Greville, Lord Brooke; the earl of Pembroke was named executor of Florio's literary remains.

Florio made a living, and a name for himself, by trading in words at a time when no form of currency was less stable. Through his translating efforts and his making Italian available in everyday forms, Florio animated English with a new kind of instrumentality. Above all, though, it was through his collecting and recasting old saws, proverbs, and golden sayings that he made his readers aware of what sorts of knowledge perennially counted in the world, despite different and multiple ways of expressing it. The chief ornament crowning Florio's life of labor in the field of language study was that he succeeded, quite literally, in making a world of words.

BIBLIOGRAPHY

Conley, Tom. "Institutionalizing Translation: On Florio's Montaigne." *Glyph Textual Studies,* vol. 1, n.s., pp. 45–60.

Matthiessen, F.O. *Translation: An Elizabethan Art.* 1931.

del Re, Arundell. *Florio's "First Fruites."* Introduction and Notes to a Facsimile Reproduction. 1936.

Simonini, R.C. Introduction to Florio's *Second Frutes.* Scholars' Facsimiles and Reprints. 1953.

Yates, Frances, A. *John Florio: The Life of an Italian in Shakespeare's England.* 1934.

William Engel

SEE ALSO

Dictionaries; Education; Greville, Fulke; Hakluyt, Richard; Italian Literature, Influence of; Wriothesley, Henry

Folklore and Folk Rituals

From its earliest establishment in Britain, the Christian church accommodated ancient pagan practices and beliefs within its emerging structures. Bede's *Ecclesiastical History* quotes instructions from Pope Gregory in 601 to the mission at Canterbury to preserve the people's pagan temples while purifying them and redirecting their use, and to "translate" pagan ritual practices into those compatible with the new faith: animal sacrifice to demonic spirits, for example, was converted to sanctioned slaughter providing food for authorized sacred feasts. Folklore and folk rituals persisted and endured throughout the Tudor period. Rites of personal passage were considered inseparable from communal concerns: marriage, birth, and death were matters of public interest inextricably bound up with parish, town, or city commonweal, their public importance attested by such practices as posting marriage banns, charivaris, and feasting the entire community at weddings. Communal rites often coincided with and were subsumed into the festival days of the church calendar (as Hallowe'en sprites inaugurated All Saints' Day), and also with regular and cyclical political events such as the investiture of the lord mayor of London. The principal celebrants were invariably men; women took minor participatory roles as in the hobby-horse dance, or joined in the general throng of dancers or spectators.

In the hobby-horse dance, a man wearing a horse mask and a cloth-covered hoop-skirt made of lath cavorted around the village square, attempting to trap young women under the skirt, thereby guaranteeing their fecundity. Records of hobby-horse performances are extant from as early as a fourteenth-century Welsh poem: "The hobby horse was once magnificent, faultless in its appearance, in every throng. Come nearer: it is a miserable pair of lath legs, kicking stiffly. And now, assuredly, there never was a poorer enchantment wrought of flimsy woodwork" (Cawte 11). The poem's diction implies that the dance, known long before the fourteenth century, had already by then become a subject of nostalgia. Most fifteenth- and sixteenth-century references come from churchwardens' accounts from a variety of parishes, where the hobby-horse dance was used to collect significant amounts of money for the church. Consistent with the fertility aspects of the figure, the dance was frequently performed on New Year's Day. In London, records survive of the hobby-horse at midsummer pageants and at other seasons, in church, city, and court activities. Accounts of the

F

dance are found for the Midsummer Watch, the annual parade of the city militia, known from 1504 to 1545. The main features of the Midsummer Watch were eventually transferred to the Lord Mayor's Show at Michaelmas (a holiday combining political, economic, and ecclesiastic concerns), and were later recreated at court under the auspices of the master of the revels during the 1550s; by the 1570s, the hobby-horse had become associated with Whitsuntide, Shrovetide, Candlemas, and, ultimately, Christmas festivities.

Young women wound ribbons around a phallic Maypole on May Day to ensure human fertility. Harvest Home not only celebrated a bountiful harvest, as its name implies, but protected crops and livestock for the coming year. In many parishes, notably in Warwickshire, the coincidence of Harvest Home with Michaelmas was underscored by the practice known as "Beating the Bounds" ("Riding the Marches" in Scotland), wherein the parish priest led a procession around the parish borders, stopping at designated stations to reconsecrate its boundaries. Thus, folk ritual intertwined agricultural survival with that of the community's political, economic, and social identity. In London, a version of "Beating-the-Bounds" marked the investiture of the lord mayor at Michaelmas, inscribing the site for the mayor's chair of state with a border of fragrant herbs and flowers.

Seasonal entertainments marking the solstices and other climatic changes, loosely grouped as "mummers' plays" and including the Morris Dance, sword dance, and the St. George combat play, also grew out of ancient agrarian rituals of purgation, fertility, and renewal. The origins and precise forms of these performances are unrecoverable, the earliest extant records going back only to the eighteenth century, though versions of them are still performed today. Their descriptions are necessarily conjectural reconstructions, but because folk practice is characteristically conservative (changes occur in personal and place-names more than in the patterns of performances), such speculation is plausible. The Morris consisted of two teams of four men led by a percussionist, all wearing harnesses of bells on their calves or ankles, and shirtsleeves festooned with ribbons; the dance itself enacted a combat with large wooden staves, and is believed to represent the battle of winter and summer. The St. George play was more "scripted," with specific performers representing St. George, a dragon or other antagonist, a doctor to revive the wounded hero, and a mother figure (sometimes called the "Molly") to cheer on the combatants. The dance typically concluded with a *quête,* or solicitation of money from the spectators.

Not all instances of folk ritual involved such orderly displays. The best-known examples of sanctioned misrule were licensed mobs of young men impersonating Jack-a-Lent, sacking brothels in the name of Lenten sexual abstinence, and various charivari practices designed to humiliate publicly husbands of scolding wives or married couples of widely discrepant ages. Unruly women, brothels, and May-December marriages were considered threats to the sanctity and harmony of the family, as well as to its reproductive purposes, and thus to the community at large. Misrule practices significantly abated during the reign of Elizabeth I.

BIBLIOGRAPHY

Alford, Violet. *The Hobby Horse and Other Animal Masks.* 1978.

Baker, Margaret. *Folklore and Customs of Rural England.* 1974.

Barber. C.L. *Shakespeare's Festive Comedy.* 1957.

Burland, C.A. *Echoes of Magic: A Study of Seasonal Festivals through the Ages.* 1972.

Cawte, E.C. *Ritual Animal Disguise.* 1978.

Chambers, E.K. *The English Folk-Play.* 1933.

Cressy, David. *Bonfires and Bells: National Memory and the Protestant Calendar in Elizabethan and Stuart England.* 1989.

Hutton, Ronald. *The Rise and Fall of Merry England: The Ritual Year, 1400–1700.* 1994.

——— *The Stations of the Sun: A History of the Ritual Year in Britain.* 1996.

Laroque, François. *Shakespeare's Festive World: Elizabethan Seasonal Entertainment and the Professional Stage.* Janet Lloyd, trans. 1991.

Liebler, Naomi Conn. *Shakespeare's Festive Tragedy: The Ritual Foundations of Genre.* 1995.

Naomi Conn Liebler

SEE ALSO
Calendar, Church; Calender, Secular; Processions

Food and Diet

Ordinary people in Tudor England depended for virtually all their food on the produce of their own locality, and so great variations in regional diet are to be expected. But everywhere the basic foodstuff was cereals, eaten at dinner and supper in the form of pottage or porridge. Added to pottage were beans and peas; roots like onions, garlic, carrots and turnips; and green leaves and herbs gathered from the gardens, fields, and woods. Animal fat and bones gave additional nourishment and flavoring to that contrived by using plant and herbs. Meat was used frugally, though it was more generously added at certain seasons. The alternative to pottage was porridge, eaten with whey, buttermilk, or milk, and flavorings that included honey or possibly sugar.

Bread was essential when eating food that was cold and when away from home, but in the kitchen, when it was used to thicken soups or stews, cereals might just as well have been used. Water, whey, or milk were the drinks of the poorest; ale, beer, and mead ranked next in the enjoyment of all; and cider and perry were routine in areas having wild or cultivated fruit, like Worcestershire, Herefordshire, and Kent. The rich expected to drink imported wine.

Grains that were coarsely ground (or better still, only pounded) preserved some of their protein layer, and when put into pottage with pulses and other vegetables, provided sufficient nourishment to sustain a laboring family in hard work. The daily repetition of pottage would be deemed monotonous today, but variety in foods has only slowly become a convention and expectation, and in the developing modern world it is still not seen as necessary or desirable.

Regional variety was always present, and travelers noticed it, not always with pleasure. Among cereals, oats were the favored grain in northern England, where people made oatcakes, much like pancakes. Rye bread was the standard loaf in areas with gravelly soils, and it satisfied the stomach longer than wheat bread. Because it kept moist longest, it also made the longest-lasting pastry. But rye was more often mixed with wheat in family bread. Barley was the most common of all the bread cereals, since it was the most reliable crop to grow, providing both food and beer, and, if plentiful, affording animal fodder. In years of harvest failure, but not only then, beans and peas were mixed with cereals in bread, and in the worst times acorns were also; they were first boiled to remove their bitterness. Wheat flour, however, was the choice of the well-to-do, and when cleansed of all bran and ground fine, it made manchet, which was pure white and deemed the most prestigious bread of all.

All dairy produce, so-called "white meats," were considered food for the poor, and were eaten only in moderation by the rich. Meat was the food in highest esteem among all classes, and since every scrap of flesh, marrow, bone, and sinew from virtually all animals and birds, tame and wild, was cooked, something from this rich store-house came to everyone's table seasonally. Fish was obligatory on two days a week before 1550, on three days a week after 1563, and always during Lent. So the weekly round of main dishes was varied by this rule. The greatest difference between the classes lay in the proportions of meat and fish put into pottage and pies, the variety that was served from day to day, and the number of dishes served on the table at each meal. Rich families expected a large selection, knowing that the hierarchy of servants, and finally the poor at the gate, would eat all leftovers.

During this period major changes took place in what the upper classes judged to be healthy and tasty among the quality and variety of vegetables and fruits available. These had formerly been treated as poor people's fare. But attitudes were transformed by influences from Spain (especially when Katherine of Aragon, brought up in Moorish Spain, married Henry VIII); from Italy (when gentry, scholars, and merchants visited that country); and from France and the Netherlands (when middle-class immigrants arrived from the 1560s). Their tastes called for imports and better varieties of cabbages, onions, and carrots. English gentlemen and market gardeners then started to grow their own. They branched out to grow novelties like globe artichokes, Jerusalem artichokes, and asparagus, cherries, strawberries, and apricots. The taste for greenstuff and fruits is seen at banquets for nobility and gentry, and soon affected middle-class cooking in scattered towns like London and Norwich, and in counties with an old but persistent gardening tradition such as Kent, Worcestershire, and Cornwall. The homeless poor by the end of the century learned the food value of root vegetables and grew them on dung heaps outside London.

Records of overseas trade show certain food imports reaching all parts of the country in moderate quantity. Oranges and lemons arrived regularly. So did Málaga raisins and large quantities of currants; indeed, the Greeks asked themselves if the English used currants for dyeing and feeding pigs. The commonest foreign spices, apart from pepper, were ginger, mace, nutmeg, clove, and cinnamon. But poorer folk, without these extras, could savor home-grown mustard seed, their own pickled broom buds, innumerable field herbs, and vinegars of their own making.

Infinite time and trouble were spent in food preparation in large households. Pots were stirred for hours on end. Poultry was crammed. Fish were kept alive and fresh in ponds until needed. Animals were fed on tasty herbs, or hunted to death so that their meat could achieve the best flavor. Many were preserved through the winter, and

F

so beef, bacon, and pork were salted; vegetables and fruits were stored in cellars, in straw, in barrels, or pickled. Lower social classes in town and country, and in each distinctive farming region, had different resources and traditions for doing this.

Foreign influences in Elizabeth I's reign led to a fashion among rich households of making more and more elaborate confections with sugar, colorings, and flowers. Under yet another foreign influence, the distillation of herbs and other plants became a hobby and then a routine, popularizing herbal cordials and strengthening the growing connection between food as sustenance and as medicine.

BIBLIOGRAPHY

Batho, G.R. *Household Papers of Henry Percy, Ninth Earl of Northumberland, 1564–1632.* 1962.

Clark, Peter. *The English Alehouse. A Social History, 1200–1830.* 1983.

Harrison, William. *The Description of England.* Georges Edelen, ed. 1994.

Markham, Gervase. *The English Housewife.* Michael R. Best, ed. 1994.

Spurling, Hilary. *Elinor Fettiplace's Receipt Book.* 1987.

Wilson, C. Anne. *Food and Drink in Britain.* 1973.

Joan Thirsk

SEE ALSO

Fish and Fishing; Hunting; Medicine and Health; Trade, Overseas

Foreign Relations and Diplomacy

Throughout the Tudor period, England was a second-rate power in a Europe dominated by France and Spain. In the middle decades of the fifteenth century, the king of France had secured a hold on his disunited realm and defeated England in the final stages of the Hundred Years' War. By 1453, England had lost Normandy and Gascony, leaving Calais as its only continental possession. On the accession of Henry VII, France was continuing on its expansionist course. Its king, Charles VIII (1483–1498), looked set to incorporate the duchy of Brittany into his realm, as well as Flanders. French absorption of these areas was clearly against England's commercial and political interests and, consequently, Henry VII tried to prevent annexation of Brittany after the death of its duke in 1488. In 1499, he sent 6,000 men for the duchy's defense, but he was let down by his Spanish and Habsburg allies and forced to acknowledge defeat. Luckily for

him, Charles then turned his attention to Italy instead of reasserting the French claim to Flanders.

Spain had also emerged as a major power on the international stage during the late fifteenth century. The state had been born from the dynastic union of Isabella of Castile to Ferdinand of Aragon in 1579. In 1492, they captured Granada from the Moors. Thereafter, Spanish power in Europe continued to grow, thanks to a succession of dynastic accidents. Isabella and Ferdinand's grandson inherited Burgundy (which included the Netherlands) in 1516, and Austria in 1519. The same year, he was elected Holy Roman Emperor as Charles V. Spain's resources were boosted by its acquisition of a large and rich overseas empire in the Americas.

England could hardly compete with either France or Spain in terms of its manpower, revenues, or military might. Its army was relatively poorly trained and ill-equipped until the late Elizabethan period. Even its navy, which gradually developed into a fighting force, never secured mastery of the seas. In 1485, England also looked politically weak. Henry VII's usurpation made him vulnerable to the challenge of Yorkist claimants to the throne. In the early years of his reign, his relations with his fellow rulers were largely determined by his need to secure credibility for his dynasty and to prevent foreign courts from becoming havens for pretenders. With this end in view, he negotiated alliances with the rulers of France, Spain, and Scotland between 1485 and 1489. His policy, however, had only a limited success. Henry VII sought an alliance with Ferdinand and Isabella through the marriage of his eldest son, Arthur, with Katherine of Aragon, but threats to his reign delayed the marriage until 1502, shortly after which Arthur died. Margaret, duchess of Burgundy (Edward IV's sister), and her son, Archduke Philip, repeatedly aided Henry's enemies: the impostors, Lambert Simnel and Perkin Warbeck and the Yorkists, Edmund and Richard de la Pole. In addition, both Charles VIII and the Scottish king, James IV, gave hospitality and assistance to Warbeck, on occasions when their relations with Henry were tense. To counter these perils, Henry did not shrink from a show of force. He sent an army to France in October 1492 as a bargaining counter to persuade Charles to abandon the Yorkists. Similarly, he ordered a raid into Scotland in 1496 and planned a major campaign for the following year with the aim of coercing James into expelling Warbeck. In both cases Henry was successful. Against Burgundy, he applied commercial pressure, and imposed an embargo on the profitable Anglo-Netherlands cloth trade in 1493 and

1505. Neither measure was immediately successful but, in time, the rulers of Burgundy came to see that their interests lay in an alliance with Henry. By Henry's death in 1509, the threat from pretenders was negligible and England was allied to the main European rulers.

Despite its limited military resources and political weaknesses, England appeared an attractive ally to the other European powers. During the Italian wars of 1494 to 1559, the participants—France, Spain, and the Holy Roman Empire—knew that England could be useful in opening up a second front against France, and each therefore hoped to lure successive English monarchs to its side. They were disappointed in Henry VII, who chose to remain neutral, secure in the knowledge that no English interests were at stake in either Milan or Naples. Henry VIII, on the other hand, was determined to emulate his ancestor, Henry V, and win glory on the battlefield against France. In 1511, therefore, he took advantage of Habsburg-Valois rivalry to enter into an offensive alliance with Emperor Maximilian in an attempt to recover England's ancestral lands in France. Initially he won some glory in his victory at the battle of the Spurs and capture of Tournai and Thérouanne in 1513, but he held neither town permanently. Peace was made with France in 1514, but Henry soon developed a strong personal rivalry with the new French king, Francis I (1515–1547). Initially unable to find allies against Francis, he tried to overshadow his rival by posing as the peacemaker of Europe and presiding over the glittering ceremonial occasions of the Conference at London (1518) and Field of Cloth of Gold (1520). By 1521, however, Charles V was asking him to sign an offensive alliance against France, and in 1522, they agreed on terms. In the war that followed, Henry acquired neither victory nor territory. The imperialists routed Francis at the battle of Pavia (1525), but Henry was unable to benefit from his ally's success. He failed to raise the Amicable Grant—a demand for one-sixth of moveable properties and income—to finance a new invasion of France while Charles had no intention of sharing with him the fruits of his victory. In 1526, therefore, Henry turned his back on the Habsburg alliance. His decision to annul his marriage also drove a wedge between him and Charles, who was Katherine of Aragon's nephew, and in 1527, Henry signed treaties of friendship with Francis I. During the 1530s, Henry's main foreign policy concern was to keep the French alliance and prevent the launch of a Catholic crusade against England. In the early 1540s, however, Henry's thoughts turned again to continental warfare. Since his coffers were full with

ecclesiastical spoil, he had the resources to finance another campaign in France. In 1543, he signed a military alliance with Charles, and a year later he led an army into France. In this last campaign Henry captured Boulogne (1544), but at great financial cost.

Over the next six years, the town proved so difficult and expensive to defend that it was sold back to the French in 1550. An Anglo-French peace was signed the following year, and England remained neutral during a new phase of the Habsburg-Valois wars that broke out in 1552. Mary I's accession, however, seemed to place England again firmly in the Habsburg camp. Ever since Henry's divorce from Mary's mother and the break with Rome, Charles V had acted as her protector, and in 1554, she married his son, Philip. Once the Habsburg-Valois wars reopened in 1556, it was generally expected that Mary would enter the war on her husband's side. The Privy Council, however, resisted Philip's pleas for military help until April 1557, when the French raided Scarborough Castle. During the ensuing war, the Spanish alliance became very unpopular in England, and Philip was widely blamed for the French capture of Calais in January 1558. Its loss was not only a public humiliation but a strategic blow; by it, England was deprived of its last bridgehead on the Continent and its potential for mounting large-scale expeditions abroad. Elizabeth I tried to regain the town by allying with the Huguenots (Calvinists) against the French government, but the enterprise (the "Newhaven Adventure," 1562–1564) was an expensive fiasco. Thereafter, Elizabeth usually avoided overseas expeditions and never again attempted the recovery of Calais by military means.

Anglo-French hostility was the dominant feature of England's foreign relations in the first half of the sixteenth century. Not only did it lead to England's participation in European warfare but it adversely affected England's interactions with the Scottish kings who had long enjoyed a close relationship with France. In 1502, Henry VII had signed a "Perpetual Alliance" with James IV, who had married his elder sister, Margaret Tudor, in 1503, but the Scottish king had, nonetheless, remained committed to the "Auld Alliance" with the French. Consequently, no sooner had Henry set off for France in 1513 than James led an army of invasion into England. The Scots were routed and their king killed at the battle of Flodden Field. Henry made no attempt to follow up this English victory, but used his political influence to ensure that Scotland was ruled by pro-English regents of the young King James V. In the mid 1530s, however, the

F

adult James began pursuing an aggressively pro-French policy. All Henry's attempts to influence and intimidate his royal nephew failed. Consequently, when planning war against France, Henry decided to bolt his backdoor in the north before sending his army across the Channel, and in 1542, he sent troops over the border. At the battle of Solway Moss, the Scottish army capitulated. Three weeks later, James V died, leaving his baby daughter, Mary Stuart, as his heiress. Henry now planned to marry the young queen to his son, Edward, but the Scots resisted. In July 1543, their parliament refused to ratify the Treaties of Greenwich, which formally betrothed the two children, and instead renewed the "Auld Alliance." In response Henry ordered punitive action. The years 1544 and 1545 witnessed a number of brutal raids into Scotland that became known as the "Rough Wooing."

On Henry's death, Edward Seymour, Protector Somerset, invaded Scotland with a large army. He resoundingly defeated the Scots at Pinkie (September 1547), but the battle did not result in the subjugation of Scotland, as he had hoped, largely because of French intervention. In June 1548, 6,000 French troops arrived at Leith to help the Scots. They whisked Mary off to France, where she became betrothed to the dauphin, and the English policy lost direction. Nonetheless, the Scottish war continued and spread to France where Henry II's troops attacked Boulogne. Unable to afford a war on two fronts, in 1551 the English government agreed to a peace that left French garrisons in Scotland. Over the next few years the French hold on Scotland deepened, especially when Mary of Guise, the dowager queen, became regent during her daughter's absence in France. It took the Scottish Reformation and the accession of Elizabeth I to change the situation. In 1559, the Protestant Lords of the Congregation, organized in 1557 to drive out Catholics from Scotland, rebelled against the regent and turned to Elizabeth for assistance. News that French troops were setting sail for Scotland persuaded Elizabeth to act, and in February 1560, she signed the Treaty of Berwick with the Scottish lords. Her army entered Scotland to expel the French. Despite its lackluster performance, the English secured an advantagous peace. By the Treaty of Edinburgh (July 1560), the French agreed to withdraw their troops from Scotland. In addition, they accepted that Mary Stewart, who had become queen of France on the death of Henry II in July 1559 would no longer use the title and arms of the queen of England.

The Treaty of Cateau-Cambrésis in 1559 marked the end of the Habsburg-Valois wars. Although Franco-Spanish hostility continued unabated, both powers were usually too distracted by domestic difficulties to embark on an aggressive foreign policy. Indeed, during Elizabeth's reign, religious divisions created political disturbances in France, the Netherlands, and Scotland. In France, a succession of civil wars followed the death of the strong Henry II (1547–1559) and his weak successor, Francis II (1559–1560). Until 1598, France endured weak government, confessional strife, and factional unrest. Spain's position was much stronger, but Philip II (1556–1598) also experienced internal difficulties after iconoclastic riots and political protests led by Calvinists shook the Netherlands in 1566. Although Philip reacted speedily to suppress the disorder, rebellion broke out in Holland and Zeeland in 1572, and spread to the southern provinces in 1576. For the rest of his reign, Philip labored to defeat the rebels but was only successful in reestablishing Spanish power over the south. Scotland also suffered from political and religious unrest. The deposition of Mary Stuart in 1567 provoked a civil war that lasted until 1574.

As a result of these international developments, Elizabeth faced an entirely new set of problems in her relations with foreign powers. First, as a Protestant, she received urgent requests for aid from the Calvinist leaders who claimed to be taking up arms in defense of their faith. Second, she came to believe that her own security would be threatened were the Catholics to prevail in France, the Netherlands, and Scotland. In France, the leaders of the ultra-Catholics were the Guise faction, who were kinsmen of Mary Stuart, whose claim to the English throne continued after the 1560 Treaty of Edinburgh. With good reason, Elizabeth feared that their victory might well result in a French invasion on behalf of Mary's pretensions. This anxiety deepened after Mary's deposition, flight to England, and captivity there. To combat the Guises, Elizabeth offered the Huguenots loans and secret supplies of munitions, although she held back from direct military intervention on their side until 1589. At the same time, she tried to maintain a friendship with the French royal family to stop them from taking up Mary's cause. It was in this spirit that she signed the Treaty of Blois in 1572 and participated in the negotiations for an Anglo-French marriage alliance during the early 1570s.

Until the outbreak of revolt in the Netherlands, England's relations with Spain had been cool but usually harmonious; the main source of contention were the attempts of English merchants to break through the Spanish monopoly in the Indies. Although Philip scorned

Elizabeth's religion he preferred her as queen of England to Mary Stuart with her French connections. After the first Netherlands' revolt, however, Anglo-Spanish relations quickly began to deteriorate. The Spaniards believed that Elizabeth was helping the Calvinist rebels against Philip, while the English feared that the large Spanish army sent to Brussels to restore order might be used against England once it had successfully extirpated heresy in the Netherlands. In this atmosphere of mutual suspicion, small incidents blew up into major crises. Thus, the Spanish ambassador, Guerau de Spes, overreacted when he decided on the basis of very little evidence that Elizabeth was planning to confiscate treasure belonging to Spain. His call for an embargo in reprisal was heeded by his masters with devastating effects on Anglo-Spanish relations. Over the next few years, trade between the two realms stopped, Philip began to listen to conspirators against Elizabeth, while Elizabeth negotiated a protective alliance with France. Though the Anglo-Spanish breach was officially repaired in 1573, good relations were never fully restored. Nonetheless, between 1573 and 1577, Elizabeth tried to keep on good terms with Philip. She resisted the Dutch rebels' appeals for direct military aid and presented herself as neutral in the conflict. She also vetoed plans of English exploration that might lead to confrontation with the Spaniards in South America. At the same time, however, she supplied the rebels with covert assistance, which did not go unnoticed by Spain. Her aim was to secure a negotiated settlement between the two sides: one that would restore the Netherlands' ancient liberties and remove foreign troops from their soil. After 1578, however, as the rebels' position looked increasingly precarious, Elizabeth stepped up her financial and diplomatic aid. Eventually, in 1585, she signed the Treaties of Nonsuch, which committed her to sending over an army to assist the Dutch provinces still in revolt.

Elizabeth's military intervention in the Netherlands, together with the privateering expeditions of Sir Francis Drake, were highly proc ocative, leading Philip to launch an Armada against her in 1588. Its failure neither ended the Spanish threat nor concluded hostilities. On the contrary, Elizabeth's military intervention on the Continent escalated between 1589 and 1592. She kept some troops in the Netherlands and sent others to France to aid Henry of Navarre, the Huguenot leader, against the Guises and their Spanish ally. Henry gained a firmer hold over his kingdom after his conversion to Catholicism in 1593, and the danger of Spanish or Guise dominance over France consequently evaporated. A year later the Spanish

threat to the United Provinces also diminished. As a result Elizabeth disengaged from expensive continental warfare. Her military efforts concentrated, instead, on privateering raids at sea. In 1598, peace negotiations opened with Spain, but terms could not be agreed upon. To put pressure on Elizabeth, Philip III sent Spanish troops to Ireland to assist Tyrone's rebellion. Tyrone's defeat in 1601 and the surrender of the Spanish garrison at Kinsale in January 1602 paved the way for a peace settlement under James I.

BIBLIOGRAPHY

Doran, Susan. *England and Europe, 1485–1603.* 1996.
———. *Sixteenth-Century Foreign Policy.* 1998.
Gunn, Steven. "The French Wars of Henry VIII." In *The Origins of War in Early-Modern Europe.* J. Black, ed. 1987.
MacCaffrey, Wallace T. *Elizabeth I.* 1993.
———. *Elizabeth I: War and Politics, 1588–1603.* 1992.
Potter, David. "Foreign Policy." In *The Reign of Henry VIII: Politics, Policy, and Piety.* Diarmaid MacCulloch, ed. 1995.
Ramsey, G. "The Foreign Policy of Elizabeth I." In *The Reign of Elizabeth I.* Christopher Haigh, ed. 1984.
Wernham, R.B. *The Making of Elizabethan Foreign Policy.* 1980.
———. *The Return of the Armadas: The Last Years of the Elizabethan War against Spain, 1595–1603.* 1994.

Susan Doran

SEE ALSO

Armada, Spanish; Beaufort, Margaret; Cloth Trade; Elizabeth I; Field of the Cloth of Gold; Henry VII; Henry VIII; Ireland, History of; James IV; James V; James VI and I; Katherine of Aragon; Mary I; O'Neill, Hugh; Philip II; Reformation, English; Scotland, History of; Edward VI; Seymour, Edward; Simnel, Lambert; Trade, Overseas; Arthur Tudor; Warbeck, Perkin; Wars of the Roses

Forman, Simon (1552–1611)

The most popular astrologer in Elizabethan England, Simon Forman was born in Quidhampton, Wiltshire, on December 31, 1552. Aside from eighteen months in Oxford as a servant to John Thornborough, later bishop of Worcester, Forman spent his early life in Wiltshire. In 1592, he moved to London and his fortunes changed. He caught the plague, cured himself, and used his method to

F

heal other Londoners. His reputation soon spread, and his astrological services, the majority of which were for medical problems, were sought more than 1,500 times a year. His success and astrological methods attracted the attention of the London College of Physicians, and although they initially succeeded in fining and imprisoning him, Forman soon learned to avoid their attempts to curtail his practices. The college nonetheless pursued him until the end of his life, despite his moving to Lambeth at the turn of the century and obtaining a license to practice physic medicine and astronomy from Cambridge University in 1603.

On July 23, 1599, when he was forty-seven, Forman married the sixteen-year-old niece of Sir Edward Monnings, Joan Baker. With his marriage, and the birth of legitimate children (Dority, July 10, 1605–January 1, 1606, and Clement, October 27, 1606), Forman became interested in genealogy, and composed his various autobiographical tracts. In all of these he fashions himself as a magus and a gentleman.

From his early life Forman had taught himself astrology, astronomy, magic, alchemy, and medicine. These pursuits are documented in more than forty volumes of manuscripts in the Ashmole Collection at the Bodleian Library, Oxford. They contain various autobiographical accounts, more than a hundred transcriptions of alchemical texts, commonplace books, six volumes of astrological casebooks, and roughly fifteen semicomplete treatises. The most noteworthy of these are those on plague (1592 and 1607) and Forman's guide to astrological medicine (c. 1597). Despite his prolific writings, Forman only ventured into print once. This was with a pamphlet advertising a bogus method for calculating the longitude, *The Groundes of Longitude* (1591).

During the last decade of Forman's life, although the records are less detailed, his astrological and medical practice continued. The dubious nature of his employment by several court ladies is spelled out in the accounts of his association with Frances Howard and Anne Turner that emerged during their trials for the murder of Sir Thomas Overbury four years after Forman's death. This episode added "magician" and even "murderer" to the College of Physicians' appellation of Forman as a "quack." Forman also appeared twice by name in Ben Jonson's plays.

According to William Lily's account, ostensibly told to him by Forman's widow, Forman predicted the moment of his own death. He died on September 12, 1611, and was buried the same day in the church of St. Mary, Lambeth.

BIBLIOGRAPHY

Rowse, A.L. *Sex and Society in Shakespeare's Age: Simon Forman the Astrologer.* 1975.

Traister, Barbara H. "'Matrix and the pain thereof': A 16th-century gynaecological essay." *Medical History,* vol. 35, pp. 436–451.

Kassell, Lauren. "Simon Forman's Philosophy of Medicine: Medicine, Astrology, and Alchemy in London, c. 1580–1611." Dissertation, Oxford University. 1997.

Lauren Kassell

SEE ALSO

Alchemy; Astrology; Astronomy; Commonplace Books; Medicine and Health

Fortescue, John (c. 1394–c. 1476)

A distinguished constitutional and legal theorist of seminal influence in Tudor and Stuart England, Sir John Fortescue was born about 1394. He studied law in Lincoln's Inn, rapidly rising in his profession, and in 1442 was appointed by Henry VI as chief justice of the King's Bench, serving nineteen years. Caught up in the turmoil of the Wars of the Roses, once the Yorkist Edward IV had mounted the throne, Fortescue, in 1461, followed the Lancastrian Henry VI into Scottish exile. Then in 1463, he accompanied Queen Margaret and the young Prince of Wales to France. After Henry was briefly restored in 1471 and subsequently captured and killed, Fortescue, who had returned, was taken prisoner. Pardoned by Edward IV and probably becoming a member of his council, Fortescue died about 1476.

Fortescue's reputation was established by the wide circulation of his writings in manuscript. His principal works are *De natura legis naturae* (1461–1463); *De laudibus legum Angliae* (1468–1471); and the *Governance of England* (1471–1476). The importance of Fortescue in Tudor England is exemplified by the Latin publication of *De laudibus* in 1546 with twenty reprintings. It was first translated into English in 1567 with many editions before the century's end. *The Governance of England* was not published until 1714, and *De natura* in Latin and English not before 1869.

A pioneer of comparative jurisprudence and in treating the nature of the English constitution in relation to the common law, Fortescue was also a noted proponent of the law of nature. Much of the knowledge of the early jury and the legal profession is indebted to him. He opposed both absolutism and democracy, advocating the supremacy of law and parliamentary monarchy.

BIBLIOGRAPHY

Burns, J.H. "Fortescue and the Political Theory of *Dominium*." *The Historical Journal,* vol. 28, pp. 777–797.

Doe, Norman. "Fifteenth-Century Concepts of Law: Fortescue and Pecock." *History of Political Thought,* vol. 10, pp. 257–280.

Ferguson, Arthur B. *The Articulate Citizen and the English Renaissance.* 1965.

Fortescue, Sir John. *De laudibus legum Angliae.* Trans. S.B. Chrimes, ed. 1942.

———. *The Governance of England: Otherwise Called the Difference between an Absolute and a Limited Monarchy.* Charles Plummer, ed. 1885.

Fortescue, Thomas, Lord Clermont, ed. *The Works of Sir John Fortescue.* Printed for private distribution. 2 vols. 1869.

Wood, Neal. *Foundations of Political Economy: Some Early Tudor Views on State and Society.* 1994.

Neal Wood

SEE ALSO

Political Thought; Wars of the Roses

Fortification and Defense
See Military History

Fox, Richard (c. 1448–1528)

Born in Lincolnshire, Richard Fox probably attended Magdalen College, Oxford; by 1477, he was a bachelor of civil law. On July 5, 1479, he matriculated in the faculty of canon law at Louvain and later studied at Paris. By early 1485, he was in the service of the future Henry VII in Paris and later that year crossed over to England with him. Soon afterward he began to receive ecclesiastical and civil rewards for his support and service, which included a number of negotiations and diplomatic missions, including serving as executor of the wills of both Henry VII and his mother, Lady Margaret Beaufort. Keeper of the privy seal, he moved from one bishopric to another: Exeter (1487–1492), Bath and Wells (1492–1494), Durham (1494–1501), and Winchester (1501–1528). He was also chancellor of Cambridge (1498–1500) and master of Pembroke College, Cambridge (1507–1518). His most significant achievement was the planning, endowment, and construction of Corpus Christi College, Oxford, whose chief building was completed and the statutes given in 1517. Conceived in Erasmian terms of the *studia humanitatis,* Fox's college had provisions for lectureships in Greek, Latin, and divinity. In addition to other gifts to the college, Fox left the bulk of his library, rich in humanist texts. And, as well as an emphasis on Greek, Fox provided for a broadening of the canon of theological authors, with patristic theology replacing long-standing medieval authorities like Peter Lombard. Among the first lecturers under Fox at Corpus Christi were Juan Luis Vives for Greek, Nicholas Kratzer for mathematics, and John Claymond, the first president, who contributed his own books and the example of his classical scholarship. John Jewel, John Rainolds, and Richard Hooker were among the distinguished students at Corpus in the sixteenth century.

There is no scholarly edition of his works and no modern biography.

BIBLIOGRAPHY

Allen, P.S., and H.M. eds. *Letters of Richard Fox.* 1929.

Bietenholz, Peter G., and Thomas B. Deutscher, eds. *Contemporaries of Erasmus.* Vol. 2, pp. 48–49. 1986.

Emden, A.B. *A Biographical Register of the University of Oxford to A.D. 1500.* 1958.

Fowler, T. *History of Corpus Christi College.* 1893.

McConica, J.K., ed. *The History of the University of Oxford.* Vol. 3. 1986.

Schoeck, R.J. "From Erasmus to Hooker: An Overview." In *Richard Hooker and the Construction of Christian Community.* Aurthur Stephen McGrade, ed. Pp. 39–73. 1997.

Ward, G.R. *The Foundation Statutes of Bishop Fox for Corpus Christi College.* 1843.

R.J. Shoeck

SEE ALSO

Beaufort, Margaret; Henry VII; Hooker, Richard; Jewel, John; Universities; Vives, Juan Luis

Foxe, John (1517–1587)

Renowned as the compiler of a vastly influential work of the Elizabethan age, *Acts and Monuments of These Latter and Perilous Times,* John Foxe has been most often known as the Tudor martyrologist. His work became widely known when chained copies of the 1570 edition were placed in English cathedrals under order from Convocation. From the beginning it has been known popularly as the "Book of Martyrs." It contains scores of highly

F

❡ The deſcription and manner of the burning of Maiſter Wylliam Tyndall.

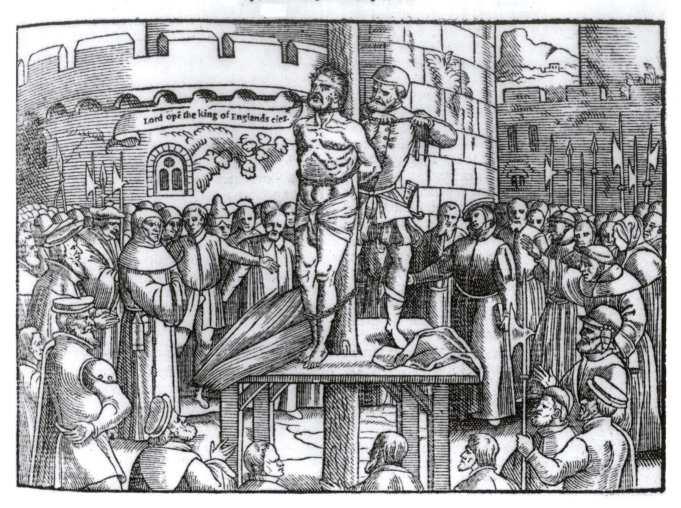

Lord opē the king of Englands eies.

The Martrydom of William Tyndall. From John Foxe, *Actes and Monuments of the English Martyrs* (1563). Reproduced from the original by permission of the Henry E. Huntington Library and Art Gallery.

charged polemical accounts of the martyrdom of Christians. Foxe alleges to have maintained faith with the "true" church of Christ as opposed to the "false" church of Antichrist under the leadership of the pope in Rome.

The narratives concerning persecutions during the recent reign of Mary I (1553–1558), the Catholic queen, are charged with nationalistic fervor that supported the reestablishment of Protestant theological doctrine in the Church of England in the reign of Elizabeth I (1558–1603). Foxe's emotional stories stirred up intense hostility against the papacy and Roman Catholicism. It has become a truism to state that if a Protestant household of England or New England were to contain no more than two books, they would have been the

English Bible and some version of Foxe's "Book of Martyrs." Methodical reading from these "holy" books was a standard practice in sixteenth- and seventeenth-century English-speaking Protestant families.

Receiving the degree of B.A. at Magdalen College, Oxford, in 1538, Foxe later left the college in opposition to the clerical vow of celibacy and compulsory membership in religious orders required of permanent fellows. During the reign of Edward VI (1547–1553), he began work as a chronicler of church history under the patronage of the duchess of Richmond, a forceful Protestant peeress. When a period of Catholic reaction ensued on the accession of Mary I, Foxe fled to the Continent, where he found havens at Strasbourg, Frankfurt, and Basel.

While abroad he published the two works that provide the foundation for the "Book of Martyrs": *Commentarii Rerum in Ecclesia Gestarum* (Strasbourg, 1554) and *Rerum in Ecclesia Gestarum* (Basel, 1559).

The onset of Mary I's persecution of Protestants, about 300 of whom were burned alive from February 1555 onward, effected a turning point in Foxe's career. Smuggled manuscript accounts of persecutions and transcripts of the dying testimonies of the martyrs came into Foxe's possession. Many of these documents passed through the hands of his fellow exile, Edmund Grindal, later archbishop of Canterbury, who urged Foxe to chronicle the Marian persecutions. The death of Queen Mary and accession of Elizabeth I in 1558 allowed for the homecoming of the Protestant exiles and renewed expectations of reforming the Church of England.

In 1563, Foxe produced the first of four increasingly lengthy editions of the "Book of Martyrs" that appeared during his lifetime. He collaborated with John Day, a zealously Protestant printer, in turning that text into one of the best-illustrated books of its age. In the popular imagination, the text is remembered for the lurid woodcuts of the "roasting" of Sir John Oldcastle, hangings of Lollards, and the seemingly countless burnings of Protestant martyrs. Foxe contrasts the historicity of his martyrologies with the incredibility of medieval legends of saints, which celebrated their subjects' alleged ability to work miracles, cures, and magical feats. In place of examples of saintly intercession, healing, and prophecy, Foxe provides alternate instances of providential intervention to deliver the faithful or work vengeance against their opponents. The suffering experience of saints is a common element in both Protestant and Catholic accounts, but Foxe and his coreligionists insist that sainthood inheres in risking even life itself to testify to faith in Christ, rather than in the marvelous elements emphasized in saints' legends. Sainthood of that kind is accessible to any elect Christian. In place of the fabulous miracle workers of medieval tradition, Foxe celebrates the little-known artisans and lowly workers who died for their faith under Mary I.

Some of the best-known narratives in the collection are those that describe the death of John Rogers, the first of the Marian martyrs; the suffering of John Hooper, bishop of Gloucester; and the recantation, reaffirmation of faith, and burning of Thomas Cranmer, archbishop of Canterbury, at Oxford University. Perhaps the most poignant of these narratives is the description of the double execution of the Protestant heroes Nicholas Ridley and the aged Hugh Latimer, also at Oxford. According to the stirring account in the second edition (1570), Latimer wore a funeral shroud to the stake, where he uttered the best-known words in the "Book of Martyrs," which are justifiably famous as a rallying cry of the English Reformation: "Be of good comfort, Master Ridley, and play the man. We shall this day light such a candle by God's grace in England, as I trust shall never be put out." That story and its accompanying woodcut left an indelible imprint on the English Protestant imagination.

BIBLIOGRAPHY
Bauckham, Richard. *Tudor Apocalypse.* 1978.
Haller, William. *The Elect Nation: The Meaning and Relevance of Foxe's "Book of Martyrs."* 1963.
King, John. "John Foxe." In *Sixteenth-Century British Nondramatic Writers.* First series. David A. Richardson, ed. *Dictionary of Literary Biography.* 1993. Vol. 132, pp. 131–40.
Wooden, Warren W. *John Foxe.* 1983.

John N. King

SEE ALSO
Convocation; Cranmer, Thomas; Day, John; Elizabeth I; Grindal, Edmund; Hooper, John; Latimer, Hugh; Marian Exiles; Marian Martyrs; Mary I; Reformation, English; Ridley, Nicholas; Rogers, John

France, Relations with England
See Foreign Relations and Diplomacy

Fraunce, Abraham (c. 1558–1633)

An intriguing figure at the forefront of the literary movements of his time, Abraham Fraunce was an adherent of the Sidney circle. He was supported in his early years by Philip Sidney, who assisted Fraunce's transition from Shrewsbury School to St. John's College, Cambridge. Having matriculated there in 1576 and taken his B.A. in 1579–1580, Fraunce became a fellow in 1580, and an M.A. in 1583. He subsequently entered Gray's Inn (1583), was admitted to the bar in 1588, and practiced thereafter as a barrister. All of Fraunce's works are dedicated to members of the Sidney family, at first to Philip Sidney, and after Philip's death, to Robert and Mary Sidney.

Fraunce's literary career spanned only five years, 1587–1592, during which he established himself a writer of English quantitative verse; as a popularizer of pastoral poetry and romance; as a writer of divine poems; and as a

F

persistent student and expositor of logic and rhetoric and of the interpretation of emblems, symbolic devices, and classical myths.

Fraunce's earliest work was *Victoria*, a Latin comedy. His first publication was *The Lamentations of Amyntas* (1587), which translates Thomas Watson's Latin *Amyntas* (1585) into English hexameter poetry. His first published work of interpretation was *Insignium, armorum, emblematum, hieroglyphicorum, et symbolorum* quae ab Italis Imprese *nominantur, explicatio* (1588). This three-volume treatise provides examples and interpretations of the enigmatic visual designs—emblems, insignia, impresas, devices—that enjoyed an extended vogue in the sixteenth and early seventeenth centuries.

Fraunce also produced two books on logic and rhetoric, developed according to the principles of Petrus Ramus (Pierre de la Ramée), who simplified earlier expositions by reducing all argumentation to one art of discourse and limited rhetoric to ornamentation. Accordingly, Fraunce produced, first, *The Lawiers Logike* (1588), which illustrates logical principles not only through examples drawn form legal cases, but also, extensively, from literary works, including Edmund Spenser's *Shepheardes Calender*. Fraunce's second Ramist volume is *The Arcadian Rhetorike* (1588), which illustrates rhetorical schemes and tropes by means of extensive quotations from pastoral poetry, quoting Vergil, Petrarch, and Tasso, among others, alongside Sidney and Spenser. Fraunce quotes one stanza (II.iv.35) from Spenser's not-yet-published *Faerie Queene*.

Fraunce's literary career reached its conclusion in the early 1590s. In *The Countess of Pembrokes Emanuel* (1591), he published hexameter poems on the life of Christ, and translations of a selection of psalms. His two final works were dedicated to the memory of Sir Philip Sidney. The first, *The Countess of Pembrokes Ivychurch* (1591), contains an adaptation of Torquato Tasso's *Aminta*, along with translations of Vergil and Heliodorus and Fraunce's own early *Lamentations*. Finally, Fraunce published *The Third Part of the Countess of Pembrokes Ivychurch, Entitled, Amintas Dale* (1592). This volume offers a selection of classical myths, drawn from Ovid's *Metamorphoses*, recounted in English hexameter poetry by a pastoral assembly of nymphs and shepherds. After each tale, an old shepherd named Elpinus interprets those myths on the varied levels—literal, historical, physical, moral, geographical, and mystical—that since late classical times had been developed in the work of continental students of myth.

Working in that tradition, Fraunce maintains in *The Third Part of the Countess of Pembrokes Ivychurch* that "[p]oeticall songs are Galeries set forth with varietie of pictures, to hold every mans eyes, Gardens stored with flowers of sundry savours, to delite every mans sence, orchyards furnished with all kindes of fruite, to please every mans mouth." For the simple reader, poetry offers "a pleasant and plausible narration"; for the more discerning, "a morall sence included therein, extolling vertue, condemning vice"; for those "of noble spirit," "hidden mysteries of naturall, astrologicall, or divine and metaphysicall philosophie."

Awareness of this conception of the nature of poetry and of Fraunce's final book remain important for modern scholars. However arcane his methods and materials might appear today, they were familiar to sixteenth- and seventeenth-century readers and authors, who employed them in their efforts both to understand literature and to write it.

BIBLIOGRAPHY

Fraunce, Abraham. *The Arcadian Rhetorike*. Ethel Seaton, ed. Luttrell Society Reprints. 1950.

———. *The Countesse of Pembrokes Emanuel*. A.B. Grosart, ed. Miscellanies of the Fuller Worthies' Library. 1870.

———. *The Lamentations of Amyntas*. In *The Lamentations of Amyntas and Amyntas*. Walter F. Staton, Jr., and Franklin M. Dickey, eds. 1967.

———. *Symbolicae Philosophiae Liber Quartus et Ultimus*. John Manning, ed., and Estelle Haan, trans. 1991.

———. *The Third Part of the Countesse of Pembrokes Yuychurch. Entitled Amintas Dale*. Gerald Snare, ed. 1975.

———. *Victoria*. G.C. Moore Smith, ed. 1906.

Pomeroy, Ralph S. "The Ramist as Fallacy Hunter: Abraham Fraunce and *The Lawiers Logike*." *Renaissance Quarterly*, vol. 40, pp. 224–246.

Darryl Gless

SEE ALSO

Ramism; Rhetoric; Sydney, Philip; Sidney, Mary; Spanish Literature, Influence of

French Literature, Influence of

France, wrote Sir Philip Sidney in sonnet 41 of *Astrophil and Stella*, was England's "sweet enemie," an oxymoron well illustrating English ambivalence. The powerful nation of the cultured Valois court and its great chateaux, of Paris and Lyons, of famed universities, was also the nation with whom England had most often fought. In early Tudor times, moreover, the crown retained Calais and Boulogne, remnants of its ancient holdings in France. No wonder that English writers paid close attention to what was going on there, that the 1580s and 1590s saw a flurry of news-quartos about events in France, and that many used French texts when assimilating classical, Spanish, and Italian literature. Thomas North's 1579 translation of Plutarch, for example, relies on that of Jacques Amyot, Alciato's *Emblemata* was best read in annotated French editions, and Matteo Bandello's Italian *novelle* came to England through versions by François de Belleforest.

Some English texts relate specifically to recent French history (several civil wars, the massacre of Protestants on August 24, 1572, the unpopular Anglo-French marriage negotiations in the 1570s): Christopher Marlowe's *Massacre at Paris* (1593?), Edmund Spenser's turncoat "Sir Burbon" (Henri IV, who became Catholic in 1593) in the 1596 *Faerie Queene,* and—more obscurely—the courtships in Shakespeare's *Love's Labor's Lost* (1594–1595) all incorporate news of the day. Some English writers, moreover, saw France for themselves. Thomas Wyatt was there on official business for Henry VIII, for example, and could have met the poet Clément Marot; and young Sidney toured France where, besides being in Paris during the massacre, he made friends with the author and statesman Philippe Du Plessis-Mornay and perhaps talked with Antoine de Baïf and Pierre de Ronsard, poets known to the English diplomatic community. Nor were friendships confined to coreligionists. True, religion could be crucial: some English Catholics (Henry Constable, for example, a poet much indebted to the witty sonneteer Philippe Desportes) moved to France, while French Protestants such as the lexicographer Claude de Sainliens ("Holyband") found safety in London's growing Huguenot community. On the whole, though, English critics of France more often mentioned its supposed fashion-driven frivolity and volatile untrustworthiness than its religion.

The influence of French writers could go unacknowledged: Robert Greene's 1584 version of Louise Labé's *Débat de Folie et d'Amour* simply says it is from the French (although the more famous Marguerite de Navarre was praised by name when Princess Elizabeth translated her *Miroir de l'âme pécheresse* in 1544 and selections from the *Heptaméron* appeared in 1597). Indeed, Thomas Lodge made several French pamphlets

his own without any indication at all. Whether openly or silently, though, the English appropriated or read a wide range of French texts. Some were encyclopedic, such as Pierre Boaistuau's work on wonders and the *Académie Française* of Pierre de la Primaudaye. On theology and moral philosophy there were works such as Duplessis-Mornay's *Vérité de la Religion Chrétienne,* translated by Philip Sidney and Arthur Golding, or the *Discourses* (1587) of François de la Noue. Some knew the cosmological and mathematical work of Oronce Finé, and for the new fashion in logic one read, like Spenser's friend Gabriel Harvey, the controversial writings of Pierre de la Ramée (Ramus). Those seeking political theory pondered the hugely influential *Methodus* and *République* of Jean Bodin or the Huguenot polemics of François Hotman, Hubert Languet, Duplessis-Mornay, and Thédore de Bäze (Beza). No educated cleric would have ignored John Calvin's writings, much translated from his elegant French, or Calvin's lieutenant in Geneva, Beza. Not all much-read works were or had been in French, for international reputations could still be made in Latin. Thomas More's friend, Guillaume de Budé (Budaeus), was especially famous for an encyclopedic study of classical culture, *De Asse,* and Beza was notorious for indecent Neo-Latin verse written in his youth.

In strictly literary terms, French impact was less important than that of the ancient world and of Italy, but it was often more immediate, thanks to proximity, travel, and a stream of French (and French-speaking Flemish) refugees. The traces are everywhere; a sophisticated taxonomy would distinguish among silent borrowings, explicit translations or imitations, deeper or more elusive influences on thought and structure, intertextual gestures and ironic or resonant juxtapositions, and momentary fashions in poetic manner.

The role of French drama in Tudor England begins with the farces that John Heywood took from French and culminates in the attempts of Mary Sidney, Samuel Daniel, and Thomas Kyd to naturalize the neoclassical tragedies of Robert Garnier. Heywood's *John John* works well in English, but French neoclassical drama did not truly catch on until the Restoration. Tudor allegorists and romance writers worked with more assimilable material, such as French versions of the *Amadis de Gaule* and pilgrimage allegories by the medieval Guillaume Deguileville (doubtless known to both Stephen Hawes and Spenser), the Flemish Jean de Cartigny (whose work was translated as *The Wandering Knight* in 1581), and the Burgundian Olivier de la Marche (whose *Chevalier Délibéré* lies behind

F

Stephen Bateman's *Travayled Pylgrime*, 1569, and Lewis Lewkenor's *Resolved Gentleman*, 1594).

Among poets, Marot drew more notice than unmixed admiration. His epigrams, pastorals, and psalm translations were known to poets from Surrey to Spenser (the "November" and "December" eclogues in *The Shepheardes Calender*, 1579, and two "Anacreontics" in the 1595 *Amoretti* paraphrase poems by Marot), although his troubles at the French court won this at least semi-Lutheran poet less respect than one might have thought. It was Ronsard whom Thomas Smith, writing to William Cecil, Lord Burghley, called "the Archipoete of fraunce." His love poetry, especially, was useful to such writers as Thomas Lodge, Giles Fletcher the Elder, and Sir Arthur Gorges, and his odes, hymns, epic *Franciade*, and the dazzle of his career attracted comment. Joachim Du Bellay, whose love poetry was also read in England, was less famous than Ronsard but perhaps more influential, thanks to Spenser's reworking his *Antiquitez de Rome* (1558) as the "Ruines of Rome" in the 1591 *Complaints*, and thus encouraging a poetic discourse that evokes time's hunger for flesh and cities, for collapsing walls, civil conflict, and the ambiguous pathos of decayed empire. Many English love poets recycled clever conceits from Desportes, but by far the most popular French poet in England was the Huguenot Guillaume de Salluste, Sieur du Bartas, whose immense popularity in England is one of literary history's curiosities. His *Divine Weeks*, mannered descriptions of the Creation and Israelite history, were translated, imitated, or quoted by scores of English writers (Sidney's version of the First Week is lost), especially Joshua Sylvester. *The Weeks* and "Uranie," a poem in which the muse of astronomy promotes a biblical poetics, reinforced a fashion for Bible-based poetry culminating in *Paradise Lost*.

The English enjoyed French prose satire, especially if directed against Catholics, like the 1581 *Stage of Popish Toyes*, taken from the writings of Henri Estienne, and the *Satyre Menippée* of Pierre Le Roy and others, mordant political commentary on the radical "Holy League" by *politique* supporters of Henri IV, was first translated in 1595. The impact of François Rabelais and Michel de Montaigne was more complex. Some, including John Eliot (whose work *Ortho-epia Gallica* takes much from Rabelais' *Gargantua et Pantagruel*), Sir John Harington, Gabriel Harvey (in the manuscript marginalia), Thomas Nashe, and Sidney, responded to Rabelais with urbane pleasure. Others cited his name with disgust, influenced by those like Calvin who thought him a scoffing atheist.

Still others, like Joseph Hall and Lodge, could borrow his humor and call him a dirty drunk. Reaction to Montaigne was less mixed and, although his chief influence came later, it was deeper. Shakespeare read him, and Bacon's *Essays* owe him something, even while being less digressively personal and disturbingly skeptical toward human reason and cultural pride. In 1603, John Florio's imaginative translation of this great French writer set a fitting cap on more than a century of Tudor attention to England's "sweet enemy."

BIBLIOGRAPHY

Kibbee, Douglas A. *For to Speke French Trewely*. Studies in the History of the Language Sciences, vol. 60. 1991.

Kirk, Andrew. *The Mirror of Confusion: The Representation of French History in English Renaissance Drama*. 1996.

Parmalee, Lisa Ferraro. *Good Newes from Fraunce: French Anti-League Propaganda in Late Elizabethan England*. 1996.

Prescott, Anne Lake. "Foreign Influences and Relations (Anglo-French Relations)." In *Critical Bibliography of French Literature II: The Sixteenth Century*. Raymond La Charité, ed. 1985.

———. "The Pearl of the Valois and Elizabeth I: Marguerite de Navarre's *Miroir* and Tudor England." In *Silent But for the Word: Tudor Women as Patrons, Translators, and Writers of Religious Works*. Margaret P. Hannay, ed. 1985.

———. *Imagining Rabelais in Renaissance England*. 1998.

Voss, Paul. "The *Faerie Queene*, 1590–1596: The Case of St. George." *The Ben Jonson Journal*, vol. 3, pp. 59–73.

Anne Lake Prescott

SEE ALSO

Bateman, Stephen; Heywood, John; Lodge, Thomas; Ramism; Sidney, Philip; Spanish Literature, Influence of; Spenser, Edmund

Frith, John (c. 1503–1533)

After receiving a B.A. at King's College, Cambridge, in 1525, John Frith became a canon at Cardinal Thomas Wolsey's recent foundation at Oxford, Cardinal College (later Christ Church). In the same year he collaborated with William Tyndale on translating the New Testament into English. After running afoul of university authorities because of his Protestant views, he joined Tyndale in the Low Countries. He then wrote a series of reformist tracts attacking Roman Catholic doctrine and ritual. They include one of the earliest antipapal books in English, *A Pistle to the Christian Reader. The Revelation of Antichrist. Antithesis Wherein are Compared Together Christ's Acts and Our Holy Father the Pope's* (Antwerp, 1529). Translated from polemics by Martin Luther and Phillip Melanchthon, the tract protected Frith with the pseudonym of Richard Brightwell and a false imprint that assigned the book to the nonexistent press of Hans Luft at "Marburg in the land of Hesse." In many other pamphlets, Frith engaged in spirited disputation with Thomas More, John Fisher, and John Rastell concerning the Eucharist and purgatory. Imprisoned on his return to England in 1532, Frith continued to write tracts before his final condemnation. He was burned to death at Smithfield on July 4, 1533.

BIBLIOGRAPHY

Clebsch, William A. *England's Earliest Protestants.* Pp. 78–136. 1964,

Foxe, John. *Acts and Monuments.*

John N. King

SEE ALSO

Eucharist; Fisher, John; Foxe, John; Lutheranism; More, Thomas; Rastell, John; Reformation, English; Tyndale, William; Wolsey, Thomas

Frobisher, Martin (c. 1535–1594)

One of the most experienced mariners in Tudor England, Sir Martin Frobisher's maritime career included piracy, exploration, and naval service. During his early years he served on several pioneering trading ventures to West Africa. From 1563 to 1573, he was involved in various semilegal enterprises, for which he was arrested three or four times on charges of piracy. Like many other sea rovers, he seems never to have been tried for these actions. During this period he was also trying to obtain support for a project to search for the Northwest Passage. In 1574, under the sponsorship of Ambrose Dudley, earl of Warwick, he acquired a license from the Muscovy Company authorizing such an expedition. With the backing of his partner, Michael Lok, a group of courtiers, and a number of prominent city merchants, Frobisher set out in 1576 with three small vessels on his first voyage in search of the passage. On his return he claimed to have discovered Frisland, a mythical island, which was confused with southern Greenland, and a new land, called Meta Incognita by

the queen, subsequently renamed Baffin Island. He also returned with quantities of ore from Meta Incognita that allegedly contained gold. This aroused considerable interest in another voyage. The queen was among a large number of new subscribers eager to profit from Frobisher's discovery.

During a second expedition in 1577, Frobisher collected a large amount of ore from Meta Incognita, but did little to explore the region in search of a passage. Despite doubts over the quality of the ore, Frobisher led a third expedition to Meta Incognita in 1578. Although he was instructed to establish a colony on the island, conditions were so difficult that this proved impossible to accomplish. Contrary winds swept Frobisher into an unknown sea that was identified as the Mistaken Straits, although it was later known as Hudson Strait. By the time of his return to London, tests had revealed that the ore was false. In these circumstances the search for the Northwest Passage came to a halt.

For the remainder of his career Frobisher was employed on various official and semiofficial ventures. In 1585, he served as vice admiral on Sir Francis Drake's expedition to the West Indies. He served with distinction during the Armada campaign of 1588, commanding one of the four Channel squadrons, for which he was knighted by the lord admiral. The following year he served on guard duty in the Channel. In 1590, he led a small expedition to the Azores as part of a wider attempt to blockade the coast of Spain. He led a relief force to Brest in 1594, but died from wounds shortly after his return to Plymouth. Although Frobisher was undoubtedly courageous, his harshness of temper led to him to quarrels with many of his contemporaries, including Drake. Ill-suited to naval command, he nevertheless played a significant role in the English exploration of the Arctic during the sixteenth century.

BIBLIOGRAPHY

Andrews, K.R. *Trade, Plunder and Settlement: Maritime Enterprise and the Genesis of the British Empire, 1480–1630.* 1984.

Corbett, J. *Drake and the Tudor Navy.* 1898.

Marsden, R.G. "The early career of Sir Martin Frobisher." *English Historical Review,* vol. 21 (1906), pp. 538–544.

John C. Appleby

SEE ALSO

Discovery and Exploration; Drake, Francis; Joint Stock Companies; Piracy

F

Fulke, William (1538–1589)

Born in London in 1538, William Fulke went to St. John's College, Cambridge, in 1555. After graduating, he went to London to study law, but in 1565, he returned to the university, where he became a lecturer in Hebrew. A follower of Thomas Cartwright, he soon became embroiled in the Vestiarian Controversy. He apparently took part in a brawl in the streets of Cambridge, and as a result was expelled from St. John's, though he was soon readmitted (March 21, 1567). He was soon accused of condoning incest, but he was acquitted and reinstated in the college for a second time. In 1578, he became master of Pembroke Hall, where he remained until his death. He was particularly active in anti-Catholic polemic, and in his later years became a leading spokesman for moderate Puritan views within the Church of England. He died at Cambridge on August 28, 1589.

BIBLIOGRAPHY

Collinson, P. *The Elizabethan Puritan Movement.* 1967.
King, John N. *English Reformation Literature: The Tudor Origins of the Protestant Tradition.* 1982.

Gerald Bray

SEE ALSO
Cartwright, Thomas; Puritanism; Vestiarian Controversy

Fulwell, Ulpian (1546–1586)

Born at Wells in Somerset, Fulwell was ordained on September 15, 1556, becoming rector of Naunton in Gloucestershire, under William Cecil's, Lord Burghley's, patronage, in 1570. He was fined for negligence over his teaching and for the inefficiency of his curate in 1576. He married twice and had seven children, six by his second wife, Mary. His interlude, *Like Will to Like,* was printed by John Allde in 1568, and popular enough to be reprinted shortly afterward (undated), and again by Edward Allde in 1587. It is notable for its Protestant tone, especially God's promise and an emphasis on the Word, and some anti-papist satire. Its early date suggests that it may have been written as part of his search for preferment. The play has some lively action, a vigorous Vice, Nichol Newfangle, and a comic Lucifer. There is no external evidence of performance, but there are detailed stage directions that show theatrical awareness. Fulwell later published *The Flower of Fame* (1575), praising the Protestant Tudor Dynasty, and *Ars Adulandi* (1576), a satire on flattery and preferment in church and state, for which he

was censured and had to make recantation. He matriculated at Oxford in 1579, and was M.A. in 1584, but died in 1586.

BIBLIOGRAPHY

Craik, T.W. *The Tudor Interlude.* 1958.
Fulwell, Ulpian. *Dramatic Works.* John S. Farmer, ed. Early English Dramatists. 1906: repr. 1966.
Happé, Peter, ed. *Two Moral Interludes.* Malone Society Reprints. 1991.

Peter Happé

SEE ALSO
Vice, The

Funerary Practices

In the sixteenth century, funerary practices were shaped by the elimination of the doctrine of purgatory by the Protestant reformers. Before the Reformation, the dead had been closely bound to the living by ritual ties. The souls of the deceased were commemorated on the seventh and thirtieth days after burial and on the first anniversary, while their names were included on the parish bede roll read out at every mass. The 1552 Prayer Book removed any notion of the burial service as a form of intercession on behalf of the dead; it was made clear that the soul went immediately to its reward, and there was no longer any need for it to be "commended" to God. It proved more difficult to eradicate elements of traditional belief from popular practices, and especially in northern England the celebration of the month's mind persisted into the 1570s, and parishioners continued to sprinkle the body with holy water and to set down the bier before crosses on its way to the grave. The burial service gave less cause for anxiety to Puritan critics of the Church of England than other elements of the Prayer Book rituals. It is true that some ministers criticized the practice whereby the clergyman would greet the body on its way into the church, but there is little sign of lay support for these criticisms. The custom of tolling bells persisted, although no longer associated with the belief that it was beneficial to the dead. Many chose to have a sermon preached at their burial, and although some of the earliest reformers were critical of the practice, it became well established in godly circles by the end of the century.

The simplification of the religious elements of the ritual did not imply any necessary reduction in funeral pomp. Although the reformers sometimes expressed unease about the cost of funerals, they recognized the propriety of socially differentiated mourning to maintain the principles of hierarchy. There remained a strong conviction that all should receive a decent burial. All would be buried in a winding sheet, while parishes often provided wooden biers for carrying the corpse, reusable coffins, and mortuary cloths or palls for hire by parishioners. But the funerals of the rich were marked by the distribution of expensive mourning cloth and the provision of elaborate hospitality to the large numbers attending. The corpse would usually be carried by servants of the deceased, and kinsfolk and friends followed closely. Poor persons wearing black would often form part of the procession, and large-scale funeral doles persisted even in metropolitan London. The high social value placed on appropriate display is indicated by the practice of open table at funeral feasts. Although the reformers denied that there were advantages in any particular place of interment for either body or soul, it was a matter in which testators continued to take a keen interest, the wealthier seeking prominent positions within the church, often close to their pews, or near the altar, the

poor being consigned to the churchyard. There is no sign that funeral expenditures declined at any social level during the sixteenth century. Among the aristocracy the costs in Elizabeth's reign were of the order of £1,000–£1,500, for the elite of London merchants £250–£300, but for humbler groups like yeomen and husbandmen only about £1–£2. Nor is there much indication in the Tudor period of the trend toward increased privacy manifested in nocturnal funerals that were to become more fashionable in the succeeding century.

BIBLIOGRAPHY

Cressy, David. *Birth, Marriage, and Death: Ritual, Religion, and the Life-Cycle in Tudor and Stuart England.* 1997.
Gittings, C. *Death, Burial, and the Individual in Early Modern England.* 1984.

Ian W. Archer

SEE ALSO
Book of Common Prayer; Reformation, English

G

Gager, William (1560–1621)

Scholar, poet, and university dramatist, William Gager wrote a series of Latin plays, all of which were performed at Christ Church, Oxford, with great success. In 1581, his tragedy, *Meleager,* was produced for a distinguished audience that included Robert Dudley, earl of Leicester, and Sir Philip Sidney. His (now lost) comedy, *Rivales,* and a tragedy (*Dido*), were performed in 1583 for the entertainment of the prince palatine of Poland. In February 1592, *Ulysses Redux* was acted. Extracts from a play based on the Oedipus story also exist. In September 1592, Gager wrote the prologue and epilogue for another comedy, *Bellum Grammaticale,* performed before Elizabeth I during her visit to Oxford. *Ulysses Redux* and *Meleager* were printed in 1592 by the University Press. (Gager seems to have supervised these printings.) The latter, dedicated to the earl of Essex, contains an epilogue addressed to the earls of Pembroke and Leicester. Gager was highly critical of the professional stage; however, throughout a series of well-known exchanges with Dr. John Rainolds, he defended the performance of plays at Oxford. Gager was also a prolific poet and translator. In his professional life he served as chancellor of the diocese of Ely and as official principal to Bishop Lancelot Andrewes.

BIBLIOGRAPHY

Chambers, E.K. *The Elizabethan Stage.* Vol. 3, pp. 317–319. 1923.

S.P. Cerasano

SEE ALSO

Neo-Latin Literature

Galilei, Galileo

See Astronomy

Games and Sports

As in other societies, forms of play affirmed the most important assumptions and beliefs of Tudor culture, such as notions of nobility, the interrelationship of sacred and profane or body and soul, and the proper society of men and women. According to Sir Thomas Elyot, author of a manual on the education of princes in the early 1530s, a gentleman should use exercise to achieve "hardness, strength, and agility" of body, to facilitate circulation of the "vital spirits" and "natural decoction" or digestion, and to prepare for war. Elyot and later authors ascribed gentility to the indoor exercises of weightlifting and tennis and to the "open" or outdoor pastimes of wrestling, running and leaping, swimming, the practice of diverse weapons, and horsemanship, especially the art of "vaunting" or leaping on a moving horse without stirrup or other technical aid. In addition, a gentleman might use hunting, hawking, and dancing in moderation, the art of the dance being viewed as preparation for marching in military formation and the partnership of men and women in the dance as an emblem of the proper relationship between the sexes in everyday life. Many authors in the second half of the sixteenth century lamented the national decline of archery and exercise of the longbow. John Stow believed the decline of archery, as a result of enclosures of the open fields in the neighborhood of London, had induced former archers to "creep" into the dicing houses and bowling alleys generally despised in public discourse. Tudor authors dismissed dice and cards as mere games of chance and schools of idleness, although chess exercised the mind and received a more favorable press. Such popular sports as bowling, football, and an early form of cricket known as stoolball appeared to celebrate animal force over the interrelationship of mind and body and were thus considered inferior exercises for gentleman.

This effort to differentiate the exercises of nobles and commoners may have been successful in the formal education of princes and the aristocracy, but, in rural parishes, poachers of diverse social rank consistently violated the statutes devised to make the hunt an aristocratic preserve, and gentlemen and their neighbors often mingled in games of stoolball, football, cards, in dances, and other pastimes. These exercises often punctuated the calendar of sacred festivals sanctioned by the church. On the festival of Shrove Tuesday, before the communal penance of Lent, "youths" participated in football matches, cockfights, and the brutal game of "throwing at cocks" secured to stakes, and "maidens" held dancing competitions for garlands. During the Christmas season, many noble households and parishes elected "lords of misrule" to supervise plays, mummeries, dances, and games of cards, and the spectacles of misrule sometimes carried profane celebrations into parish churches. These customs reflected the close proximity of sacred and profane, order and disorder, spiritual discipline and physical indulgence, characteristic of early modern Christianity. In the second half of the sixteenth century, Protestant efforts to reform the Sabbath and the sacred calendar led to bitter conflict over the use of sports in afternoons on the Sabbath and festival days. Debate over the propriety of physical exercise on the Sabbath became, among the more extreme advocates of the godly view, an assault on the perceived sinfulness of both "gentle" and "popular" pastimes, especially the violence of hunting and hawking, bearbaiting, football, and cockfights, and the avarice of dice and cards. The godly faction strove to separate the scriptural sanctity of the Sabbath from the pollution of sinful human diversions. The conflict over sports and the Sabbath continued under the early Stuarts, and the crown stated its position in the Declaration of Sports, a proclamation in favor of afternoon sports on the Sabbath and on church festivals issued in 1617, and reissued in 1633. This royal advocacy of moderate exercise on the Sabbath furnished evidence and ammunition for a militant Protestant view of the crown, most stridently expressed in Henry Burton's polemical pamphlets in the 1630s, as an enemy of godly discipline on the Sabbath in the years before the civil war.

BIBLIOGRAPHY

Brand, John, ed. *Observations on the Popular Antiquities of Great Britain.* 3 vols. 1849.

Digby, Everard. *De Arte Natandi.* 1587.

Elyot, Sir Thomas. *The Book Named the Governor.* 1531.

Gascoigne, George, and George Turberville. *The Noble Art of Venery or Hunting.* 1575.

Hutton, R. *The Rise and Fall of Merry England. The Ritual Year, 1400–1700.* 1994.

Mascall, Leonard. *A Book of Fishing with Hook and Line.* 1590.

Stow, John. *Survey of London.* 1597.

Stubbes, Philip. *Anatomy of Abuses.* 1583.

Dan Beaver

SEE ALSO

Archery; Calendar, Secular; Enclosure; Elyot, Thomas; Folklore and Folk Rituals; Hunting; Stow, John; Stubbes, Philip

Gardens

Tudor England inherited a distinguished tradition of garden-making from the English Middle Ages. Throughout the thirteenth and fourteenth centuries, gardening had flourished, encouraged notably by the repeated infusions of continental ideas, skills, practitioners, and, latterly, plants, in the wake of dynastic marriages. But the intermittent fifteenth-century civil wars resulted in a loss of gardening confidence and activity: the England of Henry VII began again, looking overseas rather than developing native gardening styles.

By the time of Elizabeth I's death, England was still imitating foreign gardens, but doing so in a more self-conscious and self-confident way. The singular nature of the late Tudor regime conditioned the number and diversity of the great Elizabethan gardens: Elizabeth's wary parsimony placed the onus for assertive building on her aristocracy, whose designs were freed by the absence of a dominant royal style. The involvement of the most senior figures in the state reveals gardening's fascination and prestige: Francis Bacon's somewhat old-fashioned essay, "Of Gardening," participates in the enthusiasm that led William Cecil, Lord Burghley, to exchange garden designs with Sir Christopher Hatton.

More modest gardening practices probably remained stable throughout the Tudor period, though evidence is slight. As usual, the uses of the land for pleasure complemented and often coincided with those for profit. Within towns, it is most likely that early Tudor gardening would have resembled that described in Pietro de' Crescenzi's *Liber ruralium commodorum* (around 1320), or Thomas Hill's *The Gardeners Labyrinth* (1577), combining limited pleasure gardening with the raising of plants for kitchen, pharmacy, and household. Gardens were enclosed, often with divisions into rectangular beds. The non-utilitarian functions of the garden are clearest in illustrations: a pergola with an elegant table, making it a garden room; carved edging boards to the raised plant beds; an arbor enclosing a bowling alley; railed paths; and intricate knots, which had become a dominant detail in gardens great and small.

The century's great changes occurred on the estates of the aristocracy and monarchy. Thornbury Castle, created by the duke of Buckingham in the 1510s, is a harbinger. Thornbury's individual elements—two enclosed gardens (one for the duke's private use), an adjacent orchard, a "newly made" park—are reminiscent of medieval English gardens; but this fateful estate was created as an ensemble of palace, gardens, and designed landscape beyond, and in that anticipates the evolution of the courtyard palace ensemble at Hampton Court, Nonsuch, and elsewhere.

Henry VIII's Hampton Court was the apogee of this early Tudor garden style, a spectacular extension of Cardinal Thomas Wolsey's already admired gardens ("so enknotted it cannot be expressed"), but—except in terms of scale—not a radical aesthetic departure. The different enclosures were dominated by the great mount, which enabled the visitor to see the patterns of the gardens from above, but also to look beyond, to the river and countryside. Decoration was characterized by rectangular beds with painted rails and numerous poles surmounted by sundials or heraldic beasts. The garden's pleasures brought constant reminders of the monarch's power and dynastic associations. Other royal gardens had similar features. The gardens of lesser nobility equally combined recreative pleasures with the assertion of social and political status.

Increasing knowledge of continental fashion, and the recognition that great houses no longer served significant defensive purposes, led to profound changes of style in later Tudor aristocratic gardens, which were also responding to the different dynamics of the Elizabethan court. Although some terracing had been a feature of medieval English gardens, the prevalence in the latter part of the sixteenth century of imposing gardens descending through wide terraces indicates the changed direction, as the garden breaks out of its traditional enclosures. The best example is that of the garden at Sir Christopher Hatton's Holdenby, for which villages were cleared, hills leveled, ponds dug, and flights of exuberant terraces constructed.

Gardeners at Work. Thomas Hill, *The Gardeners Labyrinth* (1594). By permission of the Beinecke Rare Book and Manuscript Library, Yale University.

G

Elizabethan aristocratic gardens were various in detail but similar in function. The earl of Leicester's Kenilworth had an elaborate privy garden studded with ornament; its patterns, viewed from the broad terrace overlooking it, were centered on a fine fountain carved with mythological scenes and surrounded by water jokes. This style of privy garden, impressive in its complexity (it contained a large aviary), can be found in other estates such as Nonsuch, where Henry VIII's garden had been developed and remodeled by Lords Arundel and Lumley. The wider estates at both palaces were incorporated into ensembles of house, garden, and park that were designed to be "read" allegorically. Sometimes the effect was temporary, as at Kenilworth in 1575 and Elvetham in 1592, the ensemble participating in several days of entertainment for Queen Elizabeth, when the landscape, already expressive of English history as a principal stronghold of the Lancastrian kings, was peopled with mythological figures expressing the most potent myths of Elizabeth herself. Others appear to have been constructed with a more permanent theatricality, teasing the reader through a mythological program underlying the route through the estate. At Nonsuch, the garden, banqueting houses, gates, fountains, and statues all seem to have served an epideictic function, addressing Elizabeth as Diana, the virgin huntress, chaste and fair. Lord Lumley was responding to Italian gardens, but also the gardens of the French monarchy. So was Lord Burghley's vast estate at Theobalds, the richness and complexity of which show that by the end of the century English gardening had caught up and possessed a thoroughly contemporary cultural self-consciousness.

It is easy to concentrate excessively on the symbolic qualities of Tudor gardens. To do so undervalues Tudor interest in horticulture, as well as horticulture's constant pressure on what was achievable. The gardening activity of Henry VIII and his court imposed enormous strain on the plant trade, necessitating the establishment of additional commercial nurseries. The connection between the center of power and the provision of plants continued, as Burghley patronized John Gerard, famous for his *Herbal* (1597), and Burghley's son, Robert Cecil, earl of Salisbury, supported the plant-hunting voyages of the elder John Tradescant. Hatton took an easier route, using the crown's influence to extort from the bishops of Ely their London palace, which, for centuries, had been one of the greatest and most productive garden complexes in northern Europe. The introduction of new plants from overseas was encouraged by both Protestant and Catholic bishops. By the end of the Tudor century horticultural skill had become a route to favor: the garden of the Carew family in Beddington in Surrey was remarkable for its aesthetic management of water, but more so for the famous occasion on which its owner was able to present Queen Elizabeth with freshly picked, out-of-season cherries, having contrived to hold back the ripening process. The printed garden-related texts of the period, from John Fitzherbert's *Book of Good Husbandry* (1534), through Thomas Tusser's *Hundredth Points of Good Husbandry* (1557), to Sir Hugh Plat's *Jewel House of Art and Nature* (1594), indicate the primacy of horticultural instruction, as opposed to aesthetic appreciation.

BIBLIOGRAPHY

Eyler, Ellen C. *Early English Gardens and Garden Books.* Folger Shakespeare Library. 1963.

Hill, Nicholas. *The Gardener's Labyrinth.* 1594; repr. 1982.

Johnson, George W. *A History of English Gardening, Chronological, Biographical, Literary, and Critical.* 1829; repr. 1982.

Leslie, Michael, and Timothy Raylor, eds. *Culture and Cultivation in Early Modern England: Writing and the Land.* 1992.

Strong, Roy C. *The Renaissance Garden in England.* 1979.

Tusser, Thomas. *Thomas Tusser, 1557 Floruit, his good points of Husbandry* (1571). 1557 facsimile edition. Dorothy Hartley, ed. 1931.

———. *Five Hundred Points of Good Husbandry* (1573). W. Payne and Sidney J. Herrtage, eds. English Dialect Society. Vol. 21. 1878; repr. 1965.

Michael Leslie

SEE ALSO

Agriculture; Cecil, William; Gerard, John; Hatton, Christopher; Heraldry; Kenilworth; Royal Palaces; Progresses, Royal; Tusser, Thomas

Gardiner, Stephen (c. 1483–1555)

Born at Bury St. Edmunds, Stephen Gardiner may have been illegitimate; neither the date nor the year of his birth is known with certainty. He studied at Trinity Hall, Cambridge, where he took his doctorate in civil law (1520) and in canon law (1521). In 1525, he became master of Trinity Hall, an office that he held until he was ejected in 1549. In the same year he became private secretary to

Cardinal Thomas Wolsey, and in 1527, he went to Rome on a mission from Henry VIII in search of an annulment of the king's marriage. Gardiner managed to persuade Pope Clement VII to reconsider the king's case, and for this success he was greatly admired by the king. In 1528, he became archdeacon of Norfolk, and in the following year he returned to Rome on the same mission as before. He had no success the second time, either.

Gardiner survived the fall of his patron Wolsey and in 1531 was consecrated bishop of Winchester. In 1532, he wrote the main draft of the *Reply of the Ordinaries,* a long defense of the bishops against the charges of corruption laid against them (and the church in general) by Parliament. In 1535, he abjured the Roman allegiance and wrote a defense of his position (*De vera oboedientia*), which was widely circulated in Europe and highly praised by the leading Protestant Reformers.

From 1535 to 1538, he was ambassador to France, and used his position to oppose plans for an alliance between England and the Lutherans in Germany. In 1539, he helped to draft the Act of Six Articles, which marked the beginning of anti-Lutheran reaction in England, and in the same year he was made chancellor of Cambridge University.

In 1547, he was the chief celebrant at Henry VIII's funeral, but shortly afterward he was ejected from the Council of State and deprived of his chancellorship at Cambridge. He was briefly imprisoned in 1547 for his objections to Cranmer's reforms, and he was sent to the Tower after preaching against them in 1548. In 1551, he was deprived of his bishopric.

When Mary I ascended the throne, Gardiner returned to favor, and on August 23, 1553, he was made lord high chancellor. His diplomatic skills were held in high esteem, and he rapidly became a major figure in the government. He opposed the queen's marriage to Philip II of Spain, but supported reunion with the church of Rome. He also tried to have Princess Elizabeth declared illegitimate and deprived of her right to succeed to the throne. At first he was an unenthusiastic persecutor of heretics, but by the end of 1554 he was active in prosecutions against them, and approved the reenactment of the Act of 1401 by which they were to be burned at the stake. He died at London on November 12, 1555.

BIBLIOGRAPHY

Muller, J.A. *Stephen Gardiner and the Tudor Reaction.* 1926.

Gerald Bray

SEE ALSO

Articles of Religion; Cranmer, Thomas; Henry VIII; Lutheranism; Mary I; Philip II; Reformation, English; Wolsey, Thomas

Gascoigne, George (c. 1534–1577)

Poet, translator, and prose writer, George Gascoigne, the son of Sir John Gascoigne of Cardington, Bedfordshire, and Margaret Scargill of Yorkshire, was born around 1534 and died on October 7, 1577, in Stamford, Lincolnshire. After attending Trinity College, Cambridge, he entered Gray's Inn in 1555. He served as burgess for Bedford in 1558 and 1559, was deputy almoner at Elizabeth I's coronation, and impoverished himself at court. Perpetually in financial, legal, and family troubles, on November 23, 1561, he married Elizabeth Bacon Breton, the mother of the poet Nicholas Breton. She was still married to Edward Boyes, and quarrels between the two men, in and out of court, occurred before she became Gascoigne's wife. He returned to Gray's Inn sometime before 1566, when his *Supposes* and *Jocasta* were staged as part of the Christmas to Lent revels. After trying his hand at farming at Cardington and running into further financial difficulties, he found himself in Bedford jail in 1570. He was elected once again to Parliament in 1572, this time to represent Midhurst, Sussex, but objections were raised to his election, and he did not take his seat. He tried to repair his fortunes in the Dutch wars and saw action at Flushing, Middleburgh, and Tergoes. In 1573, he changed tactics and sought patronage, in particular that of Lord Gray of Wilton, by publishing several of his works under the guise of an anonymous anthology, *A Hundreth Sundrie Flowres.* He saw further action in Holland in 1573 and spent four months in prison in Haarlem before returning to England in October 1574. In 1575, he issued an expanded edition of his works as *The Posies of George Gascoigne Esquire,* dropping the pretense of multiple authorship and presenting himself as a reformed prodigal, a warning to the youth of England. His prefatory strategies failed, and the book was censured in 1576. He continued to appeal for patronage with his writings and produced a number of edifying texts while living in Walthamstow. The earl of Leicester employed him to write an entertainment for Elizabeth during her visit to Kenilworth on July 9, 1575. Gascoigne was also present at Elizabeth's visit to Woodstock later that summer and dedicated his translation into Latin, French, and Italian of "The Tale of Hemetes the Heremyte," one of

G

the entertainments performed there, to the queen on January 1, 1576. He apparently found some favor, for he entered William Cecil, Lord Burghley's, service and sent him reports from Paris in the fall of 1576. On November 4, he witnessed the sack of Antwerp by the Spanish, an event that he movingly described three weeks later in the anonymous pamphlet, *The Spoyle of Antwerpe.* In 1577, he produced another New Year's present for Elizabeth, *The Grief of Joye,* but his death later in the year cut short his hopes for further preferment.

Gascoigne's writings reveal great versatility and innovation. *Supposes,* a free translation of Ariosto's *I Suppositi,* is the first Italian-style comedy in English and furnished the Lucentio/Bianca subplot for *The Taming of the Shrew.* Although *Jocasta,* a translation Gascoigne made with Francis Kinwelmersh from Lodovico Dolce's *Giocasta,* is not a translation from Euripides' *Phoenissae,* as it claims on its title page, it does represent the earliest version of a Greek tragedy in English. *A Hundreth Sundrie Flowres* also pioneered other kinds of writing. *The Adventures of Master F.J.,* a prose tale of adulterous intrigue interspersed with verse, has been called "the first English novel"; *F.J.* is an early—and for many the finest—example of Elizabethan fiction. The "seven Sonets in sequence" ("In haste post haste") form one of the earliest sonnet sequences in English. *The Posies* includes the first treatise on English prosody, "Certayne notes of Instruction concerning the making of verse." *The Glasse of Governement* (1575) brings Dutch pedagogic, prodigal son drama to England. Finally, *The Steele Glas* (1576), a satire annexed to the Ovidian "Complaynt of Phylomene," is one of the earliest original poems written in blank verse. Moreover, the 1573 and 1575 collections contain a wedding masque and a wide range of poems: love lyrics; moralizing verse; a long narrative in various meters of an unhappy love affair ("The delectable historie of sundry adventures passed by Dan Bartholmew of Bathe"); and an amplification of Erasmus's adage, "Dulce bellum inexpertis," which turns into a narrative of Gascoigne's adventures in the Dutch wars. Gascoigne is most engaging when recounting his experiences in a tone of wry self-deprecation and self-assertion, as in his "Wodsmanship." Admirers of this aspect of his work tend to be appalled by *The Glasse of Governement* and the moralizing prose works, *The Droomme of Doomes day* (1576), which contains a translation of Innocent III's *De contemptu mundi,* and *A delicate Diet, for daintiemouthde Droonkardes* (1576). The question of Gascoigne's moral reformation in his later works remains controversial.

BIBLIOGRAPHY

Barbour, Reid. "Recent Studies in Elizabethan Prose Fiction." *English Literary Renaissance,* vol. 25, pp. 248–276.
Cunliffe, John W., ed. *The Complete Works.* Cambridge English Classics. 1907–1910; repr. 1969.
———, ed. *Supposes and Jocasta.* 1906.
Johnson, Ronald C. *George Gascoigne.* Twayne English Authors. 1972.
Pigman, G.W. III, ed. *A Hundreth Sundrie Flowres.* Oxford English Texts (forthcoming).
Salzman, Paul. *English Prose Fiction, 1558–1700.* 1985.

G.W. Pigman III

SEE ALSO
Breton, Nicholas; Cecil, William; Italian Literature, Influence of; Kenilworth; Progresses, Royal; Prose Fiction; Sonnet Sequences; Verse Anthologies; Versification

Gender

Along with birth, age, and wealth, gender was one of the key criteria that defined the social position and role of every individual in Tudor society. Men were generally thought to differ from women both physically and more generally. Women were regarded as inferior, physically, intellectually, and morally, a belief that rested on biblical and classical authority. Medical science deriving from Galen in the second century A.D. saw the body in terms of four humours, with the typical balance in women rendering them more emotional and volatile than men. This matched the biblical account of the Fall, in which Eve had yielded readily to temptation, a teaching reinforced by St. Paul's stress on wifely obedience and his characterization of women as "the weaker vessel." Accordingly, contemporaries assigned very different roles to the two sexes, with the subordination of women enshrined in both custom and law. Preachers and magistrates agreed that the husband enjoyed a patriarchal and magisterial role as head of the household, providing for its members and responsible for their behavior, while the wife was confined to a private sphere, running the home and caring for her children. Girls were barred from all but the most elementary education, while women were restricted from trading independently by law or custom, debarred from exercising any public office, and (if married) unable to make any legal agreements in their own name.

286   Gascoigne, George

G

There was a broad acceptance of patriarchal authority. Attitudes toward gender reflected the engrained belief in hierarchy as part of the natural and God-given cosmic order. The writers of domestic conduct books, which became popular in the late Elizabethan and early Stuart period, spelled out in precise detail the respective duties of husbands and wives, while acknowledging that they were partners (if unequally) in the government of the household, and that the wise husband listened carefully to the opinions of his spouse. Assumptions about gender also reflect the contemporary popularity of binary categories, in which men represented order, reason, culture, and mind, while women stood for their opposites: disorder, emotion, nature, and body. These attitudes and assumptions help to explain why women were far more likely to be seen as gossips, scolds, and witches, for they were more easily swayed by passion and malice. Gendered assumptions also reinforced the double standard of sexual morality. Convinced that women had stronger sexual drives, men were determined to enforce strict chastity in their wives and daughters. Both men and women defined female "honesty" and reputation almost wholly in terms of sexual behavior, whereas a man's good name rested on a much wider range of attributes, and sexual lapses were often seen as unimportant.

Gender was not without its contradictions and strains. At a theoretical level, Galen had taught there was only one sex, with male and female reproductive organs essentially the same, placed outside the body in the superior male, inside and inverted in women, with maleness created by the "heat" of the individual's constitution. This implied an uncertain boundary, with potential confusion in the case of masculine women and effeminate men. It is easy to exaggerate concern over sexual identity, however. Galen's theory was largely superseded by 1600 with a view that accepted two clearly distinct sexes, each perfect in its own terms, and there is little evidence that it ever had much currency among the population at large. More important were concerns over gender identity and roles. The potential fluidity of gender was evident on the Elizabethan and early Stuart stage, with boys playing women's parts and in masques frequently cross-dressing as female characters. There was also a lively debate over new, "masculine" fashions among women in London, and a number of women were prosecuted for dressing and passing as men. But these concerns, too, can be exaggerated. The strength of traditional gendered roles is in fact underlined if it was only by masquerading as men that women could step outside them, and although Shakespearean heroines some-times dress as men and assume male roles, their female attributes (such as timidity) quickly resurface in the face of physical danger.

Nonetheless, there was widespread and genuine unease, especially in the late Elizabethan and Jacobean period, about relations between the sexes, which has been dubbed a "crisis in gender relations." Contemporaries were well aware that wives might be more intelligent and forceful than their husbands, and that male authority within the household was often precarious. A flood of jokes, ballads, satires, and plays about male cuckolds and shrewish wives testified to such concerns, while serving to reinforce traditional norms. Neighbors tolerated considerable diversity in private domestic arrangements, but couples who stepped too far and too publicly outside accepted norms were likely to face criticism and abuse. If necessary, pressure might be stepped up by mocking rhymes, horns nailed to their door (a symbol of the cuckold), "rough music" (a rowdy procession banging pots and pans outside the offenders' home), or a "skimmington," where the procession included a couple impersonating them, with the wife beating the husband. Insubordination was frequently linked with sexual fears, for it was widely assumed that a domineering wife would also be sexually unfaithful. A wife behaving suspiciously would be presented to the ecclesiastical court for suspected adultery, and if found guilty faced a humiliating public penance in which she would have to beg forgiveness, dressed in a white sheet, before all the congregation in the parish church. Other women who behaved inappropriately, for example by abusing their neighbors, might be prosecuted as scolds, and sometimes punished by being ducked or placed in the stocks.

To some extent, the widespread concern over gender relations reflected a long-standing recognition of the gap between patriarchal theory and social practice, an issue that goes back at least to Chaucer. Relations between husbands and wives inevitably varied in practice according to individual temperament and circumstance. Marital roles were also less clear-cut than in theory. Though guilds were increasingly barring women from economic activity, many wives played some part in generating family income by spinning, knitting, charring, or seasonal work on the land, which blurred the rigid distinction between the male as provider and the wife as manager. The well-documented level of concern over gender is in part the result of more available evidence, following the development of the printing press. But it did also reflect new pressures in society at large, such as a sharply rising population and

G

prices, increased poverty and unemployment, fears over crime and disorder, and large-scale migration into London, where social fluidity and gender fears were both most evident. Traditional worries over gender relationships were exacerbated by new fears over social order and stability as a whole.

Although individual women often subverted the behavioral norms regarded as appropriate to their gender, there is almost no evidence of women demanding additional rights or wider roles for their sex. In this sphere, continuity characterizes the Tudor period as a whole, and the successful reign of Elizabeth I did nothing to change wider attitudes toward gender. The queen adopted a unique persona, a compound of male, female, and divine attributes that set her apart from all her subjects, and her own views on gender were wholly traditional.

BIBLIOGRAPHY

Amussen, Susan. *An Ordered Society. Gender and Class in Early Modern England.* 1988.

Fletcher, A. *Gender, Sex and Subordination in England, 1500–1800.* 1995.

Underdown, David. "The Taming of the Scold: the Enforcement of Patriarchal Authority in Early Modern England." In *Order and Disorder in Early Modern England.* A. Fletcher and J. Stevenson, eds. 1985.

Bernard S. Capp

SEE ALSO

Childbirth; Family; Marriage Manuals; Sexual Offenses

Geneva Bible

See Bible Translations; Calvinism

Gentry

See Social Classes

Gerard, John (1545–1612)

Born in Nantwich, Cheshire, John Gerard received elementary schooling at nearby Willaston. He did not proceed to university but, becoming interested in medicine, apprenticed himself in 1562 to a London surgeon. There is little information on his movements after he obtained his freedom in 1569 other than his discovery of botany, and his rapid establishment as a noted herbalist. By the late 1570s, Gerard was serving as gardener to both William Cecil, Lord Burghley's, London and Theobald's houses, and in 1588, the herbalist attempted to use this connection to petition his patron for the opportunity to establish a botanical garden at Cambridge University, whose chancellor Burghley was, but nothing came of this. Equally unsuccessful was Gerard's suggestion a decade later that the Barber-Surgeon's Company undertake the keeping of a garden that would promote the study of medicinal plants, despite initial enthusiasm and even some subscriptions raised toward that end. For his part, Gerard kept a famous private garden in his Holborn house, publishing in 1596 a list of its more than 1,000 holdings: *Catalogus arborum, fruticum ac plantarum tam indigenarum, quam exoticarum, in horto Johannis Gerardi civis & chirugi Londinensis nascentium* (2nd edition 1599, repr. 1962). Gerard's celebrated *Herball, or Generall Historie of Plantes,* was published in 1597 (repr. 1974), containing more than 1,800 woodcuts, although most of them were reproductions and translations of Rambert Dodoens's and Matthias de L'Obel's botanical works. A second, enlarged edition, was prepared by Thomas Johnson in 1633 (repr. 1975). The last decade of his life witnessed the culmination of his professional career. Gerard served as examiner and later master of the Barber-Surgeon's Company and, following the ascension of James I to the English crown, was appointed "herbalist" to the king.

BIBLIOGRAPHY

Arber, Agnes R. *Herbals: Their Origin and Evolution. A Chapter in the History of Botany, 1470–1670.* Revised edition. 1990.

Corbett, Margery. "The Engraved Title-Page to John Gerarde's 'Herball, or Generall Historie of Plantes,' 1597." *Journal of the Society for the Bibliography of Natural History,* vol. 8, pp. 223–230.

Gerard, John. *A catalogue of plants cultivated in the garden of John Gerard, in the years 1596–1599.* 1876.

Jeffers, Robert H. *The Friends of John Gerard, 1545–1612: Surgeon and Botanist.* 1967.

Phelps, Wayne H. "John Gerard, the Herbalist." *The Library,* 5th series, vol. 2, pp. 76–80.

Waltes, Stuart M. *The Shaping of Cambridge Botany.* 1981.

Mordechai Feingold

SEE ALSO

Cecil, Sir William; Gardens; Medicine and Health

G

Gilbert, Humphrey (c. 1537–1583)

Born in Devonshire in or about 1537, Sir Humphrey Gilbert was by the remarriage of his mother a half-brother to Sir Walter Ralegh. It is thought that he was educated at Eton and Oxford and that he entered the service of Queen Elizabeth while she was still princess about the year 1554. He fought and was wounded in an expedition to aid the Huguenots in France in 1562.

In the mid-1560s, he began to take an interest in the possibility of a northern passage by sea to the East Indies, either northwest or northeast. He petitioned the queen in 1565 to sponsor an expedition and grant him a percentage of all goods brought back for ninety-nine years. He also began work on his *Discourse of a Discovery for a New Passage to Cataia,* to prove by authority, reason, experience, and circumstance that a navigable northwest passage existed: it was published ten years later (1576). Gilbert then petitioned for territorial rights within his northwest project, suing to hold and govern one-tenth of the land that was discovered.

In the meantime, Ireland offered more realistic prospects of territorial gain. Gilbert began to serve in Elizabeth's Irish wars in 1566. He joined Sir Henry Sidney in projects for settlement in Ulster and Munster. When the Irish rose in protest, Gilbert helped to put down the revolt with the utmost ferocity, massacring men, women, and children in a proudly proclaimed policy of ruling a conquered race by terror. He was knighted for his services (1570).

In 1578, Gilbert obtained a six-year license to seek out "remote heathen and barbarous lands" and to occupy and enjoy them in perpetuity. He assembled ships in the spring, maintaining an impenetrable secrecy about his destination. Eventually, five vessels left Plymouth in November but got no further than Ireland.

In 1582, a much more ambitious and elaborate scheme for conquest and settlement in North America was developed. Gilbert was to become governor and landlord of vast territories leased out to individuals and corporations. Sir Philip Sidney was assigned three million acres. Special assignments of land were to be made to Catholics to allow them freedom of worship. Gilbert's close associate Sir George Peckham headed this important Catholic project. The queen initially opposed Gilbert's going on the exploratory expedition himself, on the grounds that he was "a man noted of not good hap by sea," but she relented.

Five ships, soon reduced to four, set out in June 1583. They headed for Newfoundland, and Gilbert took possession of it for the crown. Gilbert wrote enthusiatically to Peckham of the country's potential, but others were less impressed. He then took three ships, *Delight, Squirrel,* and *Golden Hind,* on reconnaissance to the south. The largest of these, the *Delight,* was wrecked on Sable Island, and Gilbert decided to abandon the expedition. They ran into a storm on the way home, and the *Squirrel,* a tiny ship, with Gilbert aboard, was lost. Only the *Golden Hind* made it back to England.

The single full account of Gilbert's last fatal expedition is by Edward Hayes, owner of the *Golden Hind.* This account, which Richard Hakluyt printed, with its famous story of Gilbert on the deck of the *Squirrel* at the height of the storm, shouting out to the *Hind* "we are as near to Heaven by sea as by land," was largely responsible for Gilbert's enduring reputation as a Christian hero giving his life in the cause of his country's imperial future. But Hayes's narrative is a subtle and complex work, strongly critical of Gilbert, whose recklessness, obstinacy, and lack of judgement, in Hayes's view, actually impeded the cause of England's oversea empire.

BIBLIOGRAPHY

Edwards, Philip. "Edward Hayes explains away Sir Humphrey Gilbert." *Renaissance Studies,* vol. 6, pp. 270–286. 1992.
Miller, S. "Exchanging the New World: Production and Reproduction in the Newfoundland Enterprise." *Medievala et Humanistica,* n.s., no. 19, pp. 69–95. 1992.
Quinn, D.B. *The Voyages and Colonising Enterprises of Sir Humphrey Gilbert.* 2 vols. 1940.
———, and N.M. Cheshire. *The New Found Land of Stephen Parmenius.* 1972.

Philip Edwards

SEE ALSO

Colonial Development; Discovery and Exploration; Huguenots; Sidney, Henry; Sidney, Philip; Ralegh Walter

Gilbert, William (1544–1603)

Son of an Essex lawyer, William Gilbert was a Cambridge-educated physician. His London career, which included consultations for Elizabeth's navy, culminated in 1600 with his appointment as a royal physician. He published *De Magnete* ("A new natural philosophy of the magnet, magnetic bodies and the great magnet the earth")

G

in 1600, the product of many years of study. Gilbert's prominence in early modern science was secured by this work alone, but he died before he became internationally famous. The paucity of his papers directs attention to *De Magnete*, and *De Mundo* ("A new philosophy of our sublunary world, in opposition to Aristotle"), an incomplete collection of manuscripts not printed until 1651.

Traditional histories have focused justifiably on three remarkable novelties of *De Magnete*. It was the first systematic treatise on magnetism, establishing a new science that Gilbert and seventeenth-century readers called *philosophia magnetica*. Secondly, there is Gilbert's discovery of the earth's magnetism. Finally, *De Magnete* is an unprecedented piece of empiricism. Gilbert aggressively repudiated traditional, especially Aristotelian, philosophical authorities. He rested his arguments on well-designed laboratory experiments, and on the observations of practical men, notably sailors. A related novelty was the fruitful application of Gilbert's geomagnetic theory to position-finding at sea, using magnetic instruments like the compass.

Gilbert's experiments received universal acclaim. Galileo was an early admirer, but so were his Jesuit Aristotelian adversaries. The most significant experiments used natural lodestone, fashioned into a sphere (a *terrella*, or "little earth"), and miniature compass needles or *versoria*.

A Blacksmith at his Forge. From William Gilbert, *De Magnete* (1600). *Septentrio* and *auster* are Latin for *north* and *south*; the picture shows how a smith can magnetize an iron rod by pounding it with his hammer so that it will work as a compass needle. Reproduced from the original by permission of the Henry E. Huntington Library and Art Gallery.

Following a survey of past opinions, Gilbert devoted five books to five kinds of "circular magnetic motions": coition (he thought attraction too violent a term); alignment toward the north and south poles; variation from the poles (explained as the effect of magnetic landmasses); inclination, or dip below the horizon, first announced by the compass-maker Robert Norman in 1581; and rotation about the magnetic axis. In each book Gilbert built up an impressive argument by analogy for the earth's magnetism by showing that *versoria* moved over the surface of a *terrella* replicated the behavior of compasses carried on sea and land.

Book 5 predicted a correlation between inclination and latitude, and described instruments for determining it at sea. Such applications of theory to important problems ensured that Gilbert's magnetic philosophy was widely studied by state or commercially patronized practical mathematicians. They were emphasized in a prefatory address by Edward Wright, England's leading navigation expert.

Yet Gilbert's interests were overwhelmingly the traditional ones of a natural philosopher. His primary concern was to "prove" that the earth, being the mother of all magnets, had the quasi-animate faculty of self-motion or rotation about its magnetically stabilized axis. He was convinced that this refuted the Aristotelian conception of the earth (and the entire sublunary region) as a lifeless, elemental body. Consequently, Gilbert was the first carefully to distinguish magnetism, an immaterial power, from electricity, which he believed his experiments had shown to require a material medium. One distinction was that only "electrics" (Gilbert's term) repelled. According to his Neoplatonic reasoning, magnetism conferred nobility on the earth, gave it equal status with the planets, and empowered it to participate in their harmonious revolutions.

Gilbert was one of only a dozen sixteenth-century thorough-going Copernicans, although he expressed himself cautiously. His pre-Newtonian explanation of the earth's motion made his cosmology a major reason for seventeenth-century interest in his researches. Johannes Kepler seized upon it, and Galileo's ill-fated citation prompted Catholic Aristotelians such as the Jesuit Niccolo Cabeo to publish well-argued refutations, even of the earth as a lodestone (which it is not). The fact that both sides approved Gilbert's evidence but disputed his inferences testifies to the difficult emergence of experimental science.

Gilbert's reputation as an experimentalist is further complicated by *De Mundo*. It expands Gilbert's magnetic alternative to the Aristotelian philosophy of four elements into a system of physical change, matter theory, and cosmology. Yet it is not particularly experimental, and is a surprisingly typical treatise of late Renaissance nature philosophy.

The origins of Gilbert's thought and practice are probably beyond recovery. However, in 1617, Mark Ridley, a close colleague and "Gilbertino," affirmed that Edward Wright had assisted Gilbert, even writing some of the more practical chapters. Gilbert's contacts with London's maritime community doubtless cemented his rare philosophical interest in magnetism, as well as confirming his respect for practical investigative skill.

BIBLIOGRAPHY

Kelly, Mary Suzanne. *The De Mundo of William Gilbert.* 1965.

Freudenthal, Gad. "Theory of Matter and Cosmology in William Gilbert's 'De Magnete.'" *Isis,* vol. 74, pp. 22–37.

Pumfrey, Stephen. "William Gilbert's Magnetical Philosophy, 1580–1674: The Creation and Dissolution of a Discipline." Dissertation, Warburg Institute, University of London. 1987.

Roller, Duane H.D. *The "De Magnete" of William Gilbert.* 1959.

Stephen Pumfrey

SEE ALSO

Aristotelianism; Astronomy; Navigation; Science, History of

Gilpin, Bernard (1517–1583)

Called the "Apostle of the North" for his charitable works and steadfast conscience, Bernard Gilpin was born in Westmoreland and educated at Oxford where he earned an M.A. in 1542 and was concurrently admitted into holy orders. He was troubled, though, by the breach between the English and Roman churches and, receiving his B.D. in 1549, only reluctantly signed an oath affirming, in perpetuity, the validity of Anglican rites. Among the first scholars elected to Christ Church, Gilpin's studies there seem to have disabused him of his nostalgia for Roman doctrine, especially transubstantiation, which he judged a modern invention. He accepted the vicarage of Norton in 1552 and was invited to preach before Edward VI; Gilpin took as his subject the robbery of church properties—an impolitic choice, given his audience.

G

Thereafter, he resigned his benefice and was advised by Bishop Cuthbert Tunstall to travel abroad. Gilpin returned to England during Mary I's reign and was made rector of Easington and archdeacon of Durham. Appalled by the Marian persecutions, he gradually adopted a more reformed position. He was appointed to the rectory of Houghton-le-Spring where he began the charitable work that earned him his nickname. He distributed alms and fed parishioners in the impoverished northern districts of Yorkshire and Northumberland, and, with his own monies, established and supported a grammar school. After Elizabeth I's accession, he was offered the bishopric of Carlisle (1559) and the provostship of Queen's College, Oxford (1560), but declined both to remain where he felt he was more needed. The Elizabethan Settlement troubled his conscience; again he accepted the new order only reluctantly, continuing his charitable activities until his death in 1583.

BIBLIOGRAPHY

Bunting, H. *Bernard Gilpin: The Apostle of the North.* 1897.
Carleton, George. *Life of Bernard Gilpin.* 1629.
Gilpin, William. *Life of Bernard Gilpin.* 1752.

Mark Goldblatt

SEE ALSO

Catholicism; Tunstall, Cuthbert; Marian Exiles; Marian Martyrs; Mary I; Monastic Orders; Reformation, English

Goldsmiths' Work

In its broadest sense goldsmiths' work was the most important luxury art practiced in Tudor England. It ranged from precious gold hat-badges, chains, and other jeweled objects to plain utilitarian plate for the service and consumption of food. Between these extremes lay a wide range of decorated domestic wares, whose origins often lay in medieval custom, but whose form and ornament followed the fashions of the day.

In court circles throughout Europe, plate played an important role in statecraft and diplomacy. Gifts of plate were invariably exchanged between sovereigns and foreign ambassadors, and the display of sumptuous plate on tiered structures known as buffets or dressers was a standard feature of royal and aristocratic dining. Much of the most important Tudor plate was of a ceremonial nature. For example, while diners at court banquets would normally drink from goblets or bowls of precious metal, the covered cup was a mark of special dignity, reserved for the most important individuals. A covered cup was also one of the standard gifts made at court or by a benefactor to an institution. Similarly, the standing saltcellar had quasi-religious origins in the Middle Ages, but by the Renaissance had come to mark the place of honor at table, and its use was attended with carefully performed ceremonial rites. Saltcellars were made in a wide variety of forms, often incorporating other precious materials and sometimes reaching great size. The other showpieces of the Tudor goldsmith were footed bowls, ewers, and basins, and covered pouring vessels known as flagons. Church plate could also be of great magnificence until the Reformation.

Inventories from the reign of Henry VIII reveal vast holdings of gold and silver plate, especially in court circles. Almost without exception, however, these have been melted down and we know little of their appearance. A single surviving piece of royal plate from the early part of the century, a recently discovered rock crystal vase with gothic-style silver-gilt mounts of 1511, decorated with enameled roses and pomegranates, is, however, probably representative of the plate made for display on the royal buffet.

In the second and third decades of the century, royal patronage of Florentine artists led to the emergence of the Renaissance style in England. In goldsmiths' work this was given special impetus by the German artist Hans Holbein, who arrived in London in 1526. None of the plate or jewelry made to his designs survives. However, he left a rich legacy of drawings, such as that for the gold cup of 1536 made for the marriage of Henry VIII and Jane Seymour. These show a new discipline of form and range of ornament, including vase shapes, classical medallions, architectural moldings, and moresque engraving.

Plate from the second half of the century survives in greater quantities than from previous periods, but is still far from representative and is for the most part restricted to middle-ranking decorated plate. From about 1560 until the end of the century, this largely followed the currents of European Mannerism, with a decorative repertoire of embossed or engraved strapwork, fruit, and masks. Although highly skilled goldsmiths continued to work in London, especially among the immigrant community, there was a general deterioration in standards of craftsmanship in the latter part of the century that in part reflected a decline in royal patronage under Elizabeth I.

The manufacture of plate was of considerable economic importance throughout the period. In the early sixteenth century, some 400 goldsmiths were working in London alone, many of them foreign. Successful goldsmiths, their activities often bordering on banking, were among the richest citizens in the country. But pewter, costing a fraction of the price of silver, was important, too. This was the favored material for dishes and serving wares in most well-to-do households, and the high tin content of English pewter ensured it a strong export market. During the late sixteenth and early seventeenth centuries, a decorative form of pewter with cast relief decoration enjoyed some popularity. The brass industry, of great importance in the seventeenth and eighteenth centuries, was in its infancy in the Tudor period.

BIBLIOGRAPHY

Hayward, J.F. *Virtuoso Goldsmiths and the Triumph of Mannerism, 1540–1620.* 1976.

Honour, Hugh. *Goldsmiths and Silversmiths.* 1971.

Schroder, Timothy. *The National Trust Book of English Domestic Silver, 1500–1900.* 1988.

Timothy Schroder

SEE ALSO

Guilds; Holbein, Hans; Jewelry; Metal Industries

Googe, Barnabe (1540–1594)

Barnabe Googe was born in Kent or Lincolnshire in 1540 to Robert Goche and Margaret Mantell, who died a month after Googe's birth. Googe's father remarried in 1552 and died in 1557, leaving Googe an unsold ward of the court. He was a kinsman of Sir William Cecil, Lord Burghley (although no definite blood or marriage link between them has been established), who allowed him to purchase his own wardship in 1561. Later that year, Cecil sent him to France and Spain on diplomatic missions. Two years later, Googe married Mary Darrell, who bore him eight children. Under Cecil's auspices, he traveled to Ireland in 1574 to report on Essex's Ulster expedition and, in 1582, Googe was appointed provost marshall of the Presidency Court of Connaught. However, he is known mostly for his participation in refining the plain style of English lyric and for translating various popular works.

In 1557, Googe matriculated at Cambridge as a pensioner, most likely in training for government service. He left the university without a degree and resided at the London Inns of Court where he became part of the literary vanguard flourishing there. Between 1560 and 1561, he published his translation of the first six books of Palingenius's *The Zodiake of Life* (1531), an encyclopedic collection of secular ethics and scathing anti-Catholic satire. Googe continued his didactic themes in his lyric collection, *Eclogues, Epitaphs and Sonnets* (1563). Medieval didactic literature informs his aphoristic lyrics, and his amatory poems incorporate conventional themes while pronouncing moral judgment on sinful passions.

Googe is not one of the greater Tudor poets, but his collection is extraordinary for its status as the first book of published short poetry by a living author in the sixteenth century and for its "introduction" of Mantuan pastoral poetry to English readers. Along with his lyrics, Googe's "Englishing" of several popular works contributed to the worldly knowledge available in early modern English. His scientific texts include the 1577 translation of Conrad Heresbach's *Fovre Bookes of Husbandry* (1496–1576), which covers such agricultural topics as herbal medicine, livestock breeding, and naturalizing foreign plants. That year he also published Balista's *The Overthrow of Gout,* and ten years later, a tract on the drug "Terra Sigillata." His other translations are devoted to didactic subject matter.

Googe spent most of his life in financial straits, but he finally received his patrimony in 1584 on the death of his stepmother. He died in February 1594 at Alvingham, where he spent his last years.

BIBLIOGRAPHY

Googe, Barnabe. *Eclogues, Epitaphs, and Sonnets.* Judith M. Kennedy, ed. 1989.

——, trans. *The Zodiake of Life.* Marcellus Palingenius. 1947.

Peterson, Douglas L. *The English Lyric from Wyatt to Donne.* 2nd edition 1990.

Sheidley, William E. *Barnabe Googe.* Twayne English Author's Series. 1981.

Williams, John. Introduction. *English Renaissance Poetry: A Collection of Shorter Poems from Skelton to Jonson.* 2nd edition. 1990.

Catherine Maria Don Diego

SEE ALSO

Spanish Literature, Influence of; Verse Anthologies

Gosson, Stephen (1554—1624)

Born at Canterbury in 1554 (baptized April 17), Stephen Gosson was educated at the Queen's School at the Cathedral

G

School in Canterbury before entering Corpus Christi, Oxford, in 1572. At Corpus, Gosson attended lectures by John Rainoldes, who was to have no small influence on Gosson's style in his later polemical writings. After failing to graduate from Corpus, Gosson headed for London, seeking literary patronage; he tried his hand at poetry, and then playwriting (his best-known play was *Catalins Conspiracies*). He would draw on his insider's knowledge of the theater in his antitheatrical polemics.

Dissatisfaction with the present state of the theater impelled Gosson to write the first of his attacks on the stage, *The Schoole of Abuse,* published in July 1579. Gosson had not yet adopted a severe antitheatrical stance; *The Schoole of Abuse* was a critique of the misuse, as he saw it, of poetry and drama. Gosson was experimenting with style in this early text, and relied heavily on euphuistic devices learned under Rainoldes; the choice of style likely attracted the attention of humanist readers. Turning to classical sources—particularly the ideas of Plato and Plutarch—Gosson examined the ways in which the theater might provide a moral art, and become a site of instruction: "in all our recreation," he argues, "we shoulde haue an instructer at our elbows to feede the soule." This need of moral guidance is never so important as at theatrical entertainments: "Cookes did neuer shewe more crafte in their iunckets to vanquish the taste, not painters in shadowes to allure the eye, than Poets in Theaters to wounde the conscience." This utilitarian view of the theater was extended, in this work, to a wide range of literary and popular entertainments, from poetry to playing at dice; notably, the arguments here were not primarily theological.

Gosson dedicated *The Schoole of Abuse* (and the *Euphemerides,* a prose romance) to Sir Philip Sidney, but the attempt at gaining favor clearly failed. However, Gosson's polemic was widely read, in part for its style, and there were a number of responses, often quite savage in their personal attacks on Gosson. In defense, Gosson published *An Apologie of the Schoole of Abuse* along with the *Euphemerides* in November 1579. Among Gosson's champions in this dispute was Anthony Munday, who declared *The Schoole of Abuse* to be the "first blast" against plays and theaters.

Gosson left London, working as a tutor in the countryside. In 1582, in a delayed response to Thomas Lodge's *Honest Excuses* (an attack on *Schoole of Abuse*), Gosson wrote *Playes Confuted in Five Actions.* Dedicated to Sir Francis Walsingham, the text displayed a deeper opposition to the theater; the arguments here, in their complete condemnation of the stage, are more in line with the thought of Puritans and their sympathizers at court. Abandoning the euphuistic style, Gosson relied on a more logical, syllogistic structure. In *Playes Confuted,* the theater is debased by its very nature, not by abuse, and finds its source in the devil. In no kind of play does Gosson see any hope of moral instruction: "The argument of tragedies is wrath, crueltie, incest, injurie, murther eyther violent by sword, or voluntarie by poyson"; "Comedies so tickle our senses with a pleasanter vaine, that they make us louers of laughter, and pleasure, without any meane, both foes to temperance, what schooling is this?"

Gosson subsequently drew the attention of some of the more radical Protestants at court—such as Francis Walsingham—and may well have worked as a spy among the Catholics at the English College of Rome in 1584. He shortly returned to England, where he began a series of ecclesiastical appointments, including a position as lecturer as St. Dunstan's, Stepney, and culminating in his induction as Rector of St. Botolph's in April 1600. Gosson died February 13, 1624, and was buried in the chancel of the old St. Botolph's.

BIBLIOGRAPHY
Collier, John Payne, ed. *The Stage Attacked.* 1843; repr. 1966.
Gosson, Stephen. *Playes Confuted in Five Actions* (1582). 1972.
Kinney, Arthur F. "The Art of Argumentation in Stephen Gosson's Schoole of Abuse." *Studies in English Literature,* vol. 7, p. 46ff.
———. *Markets of Bawdrie: The Dramatic Criticism of Stephen Gosson.* Salzburg Studies in English Literature. 1974.
Ringler, W. *Stephen Gosson: A Biographical and Critical Study.* 1942.

Heidi J. Holder

SEE ALSO

Drama, History of; English College of Rome; Euphuism; Lodge, Thomas; Munday, Anthony; Puritanism; Walsingham, Francis

Government, Central Administration of

Although the concept that the central government of England could be separated into executive, legislative, and judicial components was not yet articulated in the Tudor period, these divisions did in fact exist and it is convenient to utilize them here.

Executive: The Monarch. In the sixteenth century the king or queen was no mere figurehead. The monarch genuinely ruled the realm, although the powers of the king or queen were as yet undefined. The monarch's word was law and there were no theoretical limits to what he or she could do; in practice, of course, popular opinion did count, for there had been instances in the Middle Ages when a king had been deposed or forced to abdicate. Both Henry VIII and Elizabeth I had an intuitive sense of just how far they could go. Their demands might appear arbitrary, but both understood the mind of the people and stopped short of any action that would alienate them. The idea of the the divine right of kings—the belief that kingship was instituted by God and that kings were God's representatives on earth—was perhaps in the air, but it was not set out fully until the reign of James I.

Kings and queens had specific powers with regard to Parliament and the church. They alone could determine when a session of Parliament should be summoned, and they might terminate a session at will, although it remained for the Stuart rulers to dissolve Parliaments whenever they began to criticize the king. The right of naming bishops and archbishops in the church was also held by the monarch. There were elections held by cathedral chapters, but for centuries the royal nominee had always been confirmed. The Reformation merely made law of what was a custom earlier.

Executive: The Council. Rulers always needed advisors. A royal council can be traced back at least as far as the Anglo-Saxon *witan.* During the late Middle Ages the council was a large body of men, most of whom were noblemen or bishops with responsibilities elsewhere. The entire body met infrequently. An inner ring of councilors, in earlier times known as the *curia regis,* gathered more often, several times each week, to deal with the actual business of government. This arrangement continued throughout the reign of Henry VII. Thomas Cromwell, Henry VIII's great minister, regularized the inner ring, giving it fixed rather than floating membership, and on his fall the inner ring began to choose officers. Historians therefore generally think of the inner ring as evolving into the Privy Council in 1540. The large council merged with the House of Lords in Parliament. Under Edward VI the group of regents for the minor king supplanted the Privy Council, and Mary I reverted to a traditional large council. But the Privy Council returned under Elizabeth and was to remain a part of the English constitution. The *Acts of the Privy Council* have been published; they make it clear that the councilors dealt with a wide variety of issues, often investigating troubling matters or ordering obedience to royal commands.

Executive: The Chancery. The Chancery was the king's secretarial bureau. Ever since the Norman Conquest the chancellor, appointed by the king, was one of the chief officers of the central government. He had custody of the Great Seal, without which important grants and writs could be not issued. His clerks and secretaries made up the Chancery office. Among the specific tasks of the Chancery was the issuing of writs summoning members of the Lords to Parliament and ordering sheriffs to hold elections for members of the House of Commons. The Chancery clerks then prepared a master list or "return" of members, naming those who were authorized to claim seats. Diplomatic documents were also issued by the Chancery.

Executive: The Principal Secretary. Until the 1530s, the king's chief advisor was generally the chancellor, who was usually a bishop or some other high-ranking cleric. Thomas Cromwell, the leading minister from 1531 to 1540, was a layman and did not become chancellor, holding the office of principal secretary instead. Elizabeth's chief advisors, William Cecil, Lord Burghley, and Sir Francis Walsingham, also held the title principal secretary. Chancellors were relegated to more ceremonial functions, such as presiding over the House of Lords, and acting as legal consultant as head of the Court of Chancery. Cromwell was lord privy seal as well as secretary, and he used the smaller seal to validate government documents. The king himself could authenticate some papers by using his seal ring, called the signet, and he validated others simply by signing them (using the so-called "sign manual," which was sometimes applied by a clerk using a dry, uninked stamp).

Executive (financial administration): The Exchequer. The Exchequer had been the principal financial bureau in England since the reign of Henry I. Its name is derived from the fact that a chequered tablecloth was used to help account for revenues paid in by the sheriffs of the various counties and by other accounting officers; counters were moved in several columns to represent pounds, shillings,

G

and pence. This simplified what would otherwise have been a difficult process, involving the use of Roman numerals and a currency that was not based on decimal units. Money (still in the form of coins, since paper money and bank drafts were not yet in use) was received in the Lower Exchequer or Exchequer of Receipt, which actually occupied the lower floor of a two-story building at Westminster. The Upper Exchequer or Exchequer of Audit or Account prepared a permanent record of all transactions, known as the pipe roll, as well as tallies, wooden sticks that served as receipts. Notches were cut into these to represent the sums of money paid in, and the tally was then struck in half, one portion being given to the sheriff or accounting officer and the other being retained in the Exchequer office. Tallies continued to be cut, though not really used, until the nineteenth century; it was an ill-advised attempt to dispose of them rapidly that led to the great fire that destroyed the Houses of Parliament in 1834.

Executive (financial administration): The King's Chamber.

Henry VII disliked the Exchequer, primarily because it had become so institutionalized that it was not amenable to direct royal control. In addition, the Exchequer's system of bookkeeping made no distinction between receipts and disbursements, so that it was not easy to ascertain the balance of cash on hand. (If the king wished to know the state of his finances, he simply looked into the chests in the Exchequer where coins were stored, to see whether they were full or empty.) Petty cash had been held in the King's Chamber for centuries, to provide for such small expenditures as rewards for messengers, but Henry VII decided to make the chamber his most important revenue bureau. Income that did not constitutionally have to be paid into the Exchequer was now received in the chamber. An improved system of accounting made it possible for Henry, who was personally interested in government finance, to monitor the state of his revenues. In fact, Henry VII himself initialed each page of the chamber accounts, occasionally correcting the arithmetic of his clerks. Under this system of "chamber administration" the Exchequer remained in existence but was of secondary importance.

Executive (financial administration): Cromwell's "Tudor revolution."

Since Henry VIII did not share his father's interest in the details of finance, the chamber sys-

tem came to an end after 1509 and the Exchequer became dominant once again. Thomas Cromwell, like Henry VII, was unhappy with the cumbersome machinery of the Exchequer and chose instead to use a variety of specialized financial bureaus, erected as part of what Sir Geoffrey Elton has called the "Tudor revolution in government." The most important of these bureaus, the Court of Augmentations, dealt with properties that had belonged to religious houses, confiscated by the government following the dissolution of the monasteries (1536–1539). The Court of First Fruits and Tenths collected annual payments from the clergy, revenues that had been paid to the papacy prior to the Reformation. The Court of General Surveyors dealt with a variety of crown lands; the Court of Wards and Liveries handled the estates of minor heirs of tenants-in-chief, who were wards of the court until they achieved maturity. In all of these financial courts Cromwell introduced modern accounting procedures and demanded efficient administration.

Executive (financial administration): The Revitalized Exchequer.

Although Cromwell himself was able to manage this multiplicity of bureaus, his system was too complex to work well following his death. Financial reforms proposed under Edward VI but not instituted until the reign of Mary made a reformed Exchequer the chief national treasury once again. Only the Wards remained outside the Exchequer; after the institution of wardship was abolished in 1646, all financial matters were handled by the Exchequer. The chief financial minister was the lord treasurer, but the duties were generally discharged by his deputy, the chancellor of the Exchequer, who is England's chief financial officer today.

Legislative: Parliament.

The legislative branch of the central government was Parliament. Representative bodies, including persons elected by various localities, can be traced back to 1265; some earlier gatherings, composed of the great magnates of church and state, had also been called parliaments. The title is derived from the French verb *parler,* to talk, and early parliaments were chiefly deliberative or advisory assemblies held by kings who wished to explain their policies to their leading subjects. Early Parliaments also functioned as courts—the official term for the assembly is still "the high court of Parliament"—in which cases involving noblemen or tenants-in-chief might be heard.

During the later Middle Ages, Parliament came to be composed of two houses, the Lords and the Commons. Noblemen and bishops of the state church (and before the Reformation, some leading abbots as well) were entitled to be summoned to sit in the Lords because of their status in society. Members of the lower house, the Commons, were elected. They were of two sorts. Each county named two knights of the shire, the right to vote being held by all men who owned a forty-shilling freehold. A number of cities and towns chose burgesses to represent them in Parliament. Here, a variety of franchises prevailed, but in most cases the right to vote belonged only to the more prominent merchants and civic leaders. At the beginning of the Tudor period the members of the Commons numbered about 200, but the size of the house rose to more than 400 by the end of Elizabeth's reign, as additional boroughs were granted representation. By 1485, Parliament was in fact mainly a legislative body, considering bills and passing acts. Parliamentary procedure developed significantly under the Tudors. The number of readings given each bill, which earlier had varied, came to be three in almost all cases. Committees were increasingly used to scrutinize proposed legislation. Conferences between the two houses became more common. Passage of legislation continued to require the assent of both houses and of the monarch; there was no way of overriding a royal veto, and the Tudors did occasionally avail themselves of the right to veto unpleasing legislation. The two houses were of about equal importance under the earlier Tudors, but by the reign of Elizabeth, the Commons—the more representative chamber—had become dominant. The parliamentary privileges of free speech, freedom of members from arrest during sessions, and free access of the speaker of the Commons to the monarch were ratified by Henry VIII at the request of Sir Thomas More, the speaker, in 1523. In practice they had existed earlier. The privilege of free speech did not convey the right to discuss whatever members wanted, for certain topics such as foreign policy and the private life of the ruler were held to be part of the royal prerogative and thus beyond the touch of Parliament. Elizabeth occasionally sent members who infringed the prerogative to contemplate their offenses in the Tower of London.

Judicial: The Central Courts. An elaborate court system was already in place at the beginning of the Tudor era. It included local courts held by justices of the peace, either individually or meeting in county groups as the quarter sessions, and regional courts held periodically by trained jurists who had been appointed justices of assize (for civil suits), or justices of gaol delivery (for criminal cases). Cases might be appealed from these bodies to the great central courts that met at Westminster, the King's Bench (criminal) and the Common Pleas (civil). All of these courts used the common law, based on customs and precedents accumulated over the centuries. Judges were appointed by the monarch and held office during his pleasure, generally for life.

Several other courts supplemented this common law system. The House of Lords, as we have seen, heard cases involving members of the nobility. During the thirteenth century the Court of Chancery developed to hear cases that were difficult to resolve at common law because of its inflexibility. Here, a second set of legal principles, called equity, was applied. The lord chancellor presided, and additional judges were appointed. By the late fifteenth century, equity had become as rigid as the common law, and some unusual cases were heard by members of the king's council sitting in the Star Chamber of Westminster Palace. By the end of Henry VII's reign this had become the Court of Star Chamber. It operated as part of the royal prerogative, doing what seemed best in each instance without reference to either common law or equity. Its speed and cheapness were originally appreciated by many subjects, but by the seventeenth century it was thought to be an oppressive arm of arbitrary royal government, and it was abolished by the Long Parliament in 1640. The Court of Requests heard the suits of poor persons who could not pay the fees required in other courts. There was also an Exchequer Court, which ajudicated disputes regarding taxation and finance. Parallel to this complex of state courts was a system of church courts, including regional or diocesan bodies and such central courts as the Prerogative Court of Canterbury. This court, which despite its name met in London, was responsible for the probate of all wills and testaments in cases where the testator owned property in more than one diocese. These ecclesiastical courts survived the Reformation; probate and questions of marriage and divorce were not taken over by secular courts until the nineteenth century.

Conclusion. A fully elaborated central government was thus in existence during the Tudor period. It related to local government in several ways. Sheriffs and justices of the peace were local officers appointed by the king or queen and were expected to enforce the dictates of the

G

central government. But they were unpaid and were not full-time officials; they could not be counted on to take action against their friends and neighbors who violated such laws as the statutes prohibiting the enclosure of farmland. Parliament was also an important point of contact between the central government and members of the politically conscious classes throughout the realm, the nobility and gentry, but it too might balk at sanctioning arbitrary policies. Royal government thus rested on concensus and the belief that the policies of the king or queen served the needs of the whole realm.

BIBLIOGRAPHY

Dean, David. *Law-Making and Society in late Elizabethan England.* 1996.

Elton, G.R. *The Tudor Constitution.* 1960.

———. *The Tudor Revolution in Government.* 1953.

Graves, Michael A.R. *The Tudor Parliaments.* 1985.

Gunn, S.J. *Early Tudor Government, 1485–1558.* 1995.

Hoak, Dale, ed. *Tudor Political Culture.* 1995.

Lehmberg, Stanford. *The Reformation Parliament, 1529–1536.* 1970.

———. *The Later Parliaments of Henry VIII, 1536–1547.* 1977.

Loades, D.M. *The Mid-Tudor Crisis, 1545–1565.* 1992.

Richardson, W.C. *Tudor Chamber Administration.* 1952.

———. *History of the Court of Augmentations.* 1961.

Tittler, Robert and Jennifer Loach, eds. *Mid-Tudor Polity, c. 1540–1560.* 1980.

Williams, Penry. *The Tudor Regime.* 1979.

Stanford Lehmberg

SEE ALSO

Chancery; Law, Common; Economy; Elizabeth I; Exchequer; Government, Local; Henry VII; Henry VIII; Justice of the Peace; King's or Queen's Bench, Court of; Monastic Orders; Money, Inflation, and Money Lending; Parliamentary History; Sheriff; Star Chamber, Court of; Wards and Liveries, Court of

Government, Local

Local government was subjected to substantial new demands during the sixteenth century and in response underwent significant developments. Those demands arose from the disruptive effects of increasing population, of inflation, and the dislocations resulting from economic development. To these should be added the need for a new type of military preparedness and the

effects of repeated religious alterations. However, it is also the case that the specific responses to all these changes were mediated through the changing perceptions within the governing elite. One aspect of this was a probably exaggerated fear of popular unrest, "the many-headed monster." But there was also a new sense of responsibility on the part of the provincial governing elites. This arose from both Renaissance and Reformation impulses. It manifested itself in the form of Christian humanism and notions of the "commonwealth," and in the idea of the godly magistrate. Both induced a new activism that was evident in the localities.

Unlike the situation in other great territorial states such as the Spanish kingdoms and France, most of the work in the localities was undertaken by local individuals rather than by "professionals" imposed by central government. However, most local appointments such as justice of the peace and sheriff were made centrally. This resulted in a mutual curiosity and familiarity on the part of individuals in central and local government. It was facilitated by the relatively limited numbers involved and the comparatively geographically compact character of England. During Elizabeth I's reign the proliferation of newsletters brought news of the court into the country while newly surveyed maps made the localities more familiar to those at court.

There were two basic units of local administration: the essentially rural "shires" or counties, and the towns. There was a greater diversity among the towns than there was among the shires. This diversity included the degree of independence from the encompassing county, the complexity of internal organization, the extent of the franchise, the existence or nonexistence of formal corporate status, and whether it was a parliamentary borough. The range was from Norwich, England's second city, which was a county in its own right, to nascent industrial centers such as Birmingham, Manchester, and Leeds, which had to settle for parochial or old forms of manorial administration that they had inherited from their rural past. The main feature of urban government was oligarchy: dominance by a small group of usually wealthy residents. The mid-Tudor period saw the creation of new boroughs on a scale not seen since the thirteenth century. However, the comparative institutional history of towns "as distinct from their economic and social history" has been neglected, and at present no satisfactory overall classification exists.

Even in 1603, there still survived a variety of anomalous "liberties" in which the "normal" pattern of administration was augmented or replaced. These included the palatinates of Chester, Durham, and Lancaster, the honor of Peveril, the West-Country stannaries, the duchy of Cornwall, the royal forests, the Cinque Ports, and the Marcher lordships. The Channel Islands and the Isle of Man also had distinct administrative arrangements, as had the residual territories in France "until their loss." However, in this respect, the key feature of the period is the reduction in the number of liberties and their insignificance compared with the situation elsewhere in Europe.

Both negative and positive factors enhanced the importance of the counties as units of local administration in this period. In the 1530s and 1540s, the dissolution of the monasteries and specific legislation both contributed to the removal of many of the liberties and immunities that had created exemptions from the norm. In 1536, the "shiring" of Wales extended English local administrative practice into the principality. The long-term aim of the Tudors to contain the independent power of the great magnates, and their conversion over the generations into courtiers, also had ramifications for local government. The "magnatial countries" of the Percys, the Howards, or the Veres had encompassed or cut across more than one county and interposed a powerful layer of influence between central government and the localities. Contrary to what is often assumed, these magnatial countries were located not only in the "backward" English peripheries, and they continued until quite late: that of the Howards in the economically advanced region of East Anglia survived until the execution of the fourth duke of Norfolk in 1572.

An anachronistic but useful distinction can be made between the crown's "private" and its "public" administration in the localities. The former encompassed its role as a substantial landowner and even its right to income from customs. Many of the officials in these areas were "semiprofessional" and salaried "however inadequately." These included receivers, feodaries, and escheators. Others were local gentry who acquired crown offices. For example, the Norfolk gentleman Nathaniel Bacon was steward of the duchy of Lancaster lands in Norfolk. The public aspect of the crown's local administration was to do primarily with its traditional activity: the delivery of justice. In the course of the sixteenth century there was added substantial new areas of economic and social regulation. Both types of work were carried out by the brief, twice-yearly visitations of the counties by the justices of assize and by the resident justices of the peace operating through quarter sessions. A key feature is that much administration was carried out through the institutions of courts and used quasi-judicial procedures.

Other new spheres of local government activity were also created. These included the regular appointment from 1585 of courtier-noblemen as lords lieutenant to oversee military preparedness in the counties. However, this did not compensate for the earlier progressive removal of resident great magnates. For most of the time effective management of military affairs in the localities was devolved to deputy lieutenants who were leading local gentry and justices of the peace. Another sphere was the imposition of religious conformity from the 1580s on, especially by the imposition of the recusancy laws.

Many of these new spheres of local government activity had been created by parliamentary legislation, but to the extent that they were given life and substance it was by local officeholders, especially the justices of the peace, under the central supervision and prompting of the Privy Council. In the peripheral areas of the west, Wales and the Marches, and in the north at various times, provincial councils sitting within these localities extended conciliar supervision.

Increasingly, local administration in Tudor England was not something divorced from central government: it was part of a dialogue between the two. The documents attest the sheer bulk of administration that increased in this period along with the volume of that dialogue. The council prodded; central courts devolved the taking of evidence; even when resident in London, justices of assize referred matters to justices of the peace within their circuits. Often, groups of justices responded with prevaricating self-interest only thinly disguised as the best interests of their "country." At other times they deluged the council or their patrons at court with news and requests on behalf of their particular localities. The occasion of the assizes and the periodic visits by local gentry to London and the court provided further opportunities for face-to-face meetings between representatives of central and local administration.

Within the counties were subordinate administrative areas known variously in different parts of the country as "hundreds," "rapes," or "wapentakes." Although little studied by historians, they retained minor judicial and administrative functions. In many counties in this period these were grouped together into larger "divisions" for the purposes of administration by the justices and deputy lieutenants. Below these were the parishes—a fundamental development was the emergence of the parish as the basic unit of secular administration. A corollary of this was that existing officials such as parish and hundred constables, churchwardens, and the latter's deputies, the

G

sidesmen or questmen, were incorporated into an increasingly complex system of county administration and came to be supervised by the justices of the peace and judges of assize. From their inception, new types of parochial officials such as supervisors of highways (1555); collectors, later overseers, of the poor (1563, 1597); and trustees of parochial charities (1601) were assumed to be part of this system. A consequence of all this was the beginning of a process in which the local manifestations of the state began to replace the local community in the provision of administration and the delivery of justice.

It has been argued that within parishes there emerged a group of habitual amateur "administrators" that coincided with the wealthier inhabitants and those inclined toward a "reformation of manners." They are said to have aligned themselves more with the values of the "godly" gentry and to have attempted to distinguish themselves from the "dissolute poor." These parochial officials came together in the vestry, the "parish council" of the day. While this may be true of some parishes, recent research suggests that it was not invariably the case.

A further feature of local government was the overlap and, increasingly, the acrimonious clash of jurisdictions. The church had its own administrative structures and diocesan and archdeaconry courts. These impinged on the lives of the laity and, if anything, they became more active in this period, especially in the area of moral regulation. At the same time, new legislation also gave jurisdiction over these offenses to the justices in quarter sessions. Similarly, the Court of Admiralty had jurisdiction within the seaboard counties. Increased commercial activity generated more business for it and brought it into competition with other local jurisdictions.

Against this picture of increased "public" administration in the localities must be set a neglected phenomenon: the deliberate resuscitation of "private" feudal and manorial rights. Originally, manorial courts had been designed to administer small, working agrarian communities (courts baron) and to provide minor local justice (courts leet). In most parts of the country, economic, social, and judicial developments had long since rendered these courts superfluous for their original purposes. However, two groups with diametrically opposed aims had a vested interest in reinvigorating them. First, the owners of manorial rights were induced to exploit them for their economic advantage. This resulted in a "financial manorialism" equivalent to the crown's own financially motivated practice of "fiscal feudalism." Second, manorial tenants sometimes used them either defensively against

innovations by their manorial lord or aggressively, when substantial tenants exploited them in pursuit of their own economic interests against both humbler tenants and their manorial lord. However, the very condition of conflict inherent in the assertion of manorial rights inevitably brought these matters within the purview of royal justice and the mechanisms of informal local arbitration, the assizes, or the central courts.

BIBLIOGRAPHY

Clark, Peter, and Paul Slack. *English Towns in Transition, 1500–1700.* 1976.

Hurstfield, Joel. "County Government, c.1530–c.1660." In *Freedom, Corruption, and Government in Elizabethan England,* pp. 236–293. 1973.

Kent, Joan R. *The English Village Constable, 1580–1642: A Social and Administrative Study.* 1986.

Morgan, Victor. "Some Types of Patronage: Mainly in Sixteenth- and Seventeenth-century England." In *Klientelsysteme im Europa der fruhen Neuzeit.* Antoni Maczak, ed. *Schriften des Historischen Kollegs,* Kolloquien 9, pp. 91–116. 1988.

Sharpe, J.A. *Crime in Early Modern England, 1550–1750,* pp. 73–93. 1984.

Slack, Paul. "Books of Orders: The Making of English Social Policy, 1577–1631." *Transactions of the Royal Historical Society,* 5th series, vol. 30, pp. 1–22.

Smith, A.G.R. *Tudor Government. New Appreciations in History.* Vol. 20. The Historical Association. 1990.

Smith, A. Hassell. *County and Court: Government and Politics in Norfolk, 1558–1603.* 1974.

Tittler, Robert. "The Incorporation of Boroughs, 1540–1558." *History,* vol. 62, pp. 24–42.

Williams, Penry. "The Crown and the Counties." In *The Reign of Elizabeth.* Christopher Haigh, ed., pp. 125–146. 1984.

———. *The Later Tudors: England, 1457–1603.* 1995; repr. 1998.

Youngs, Frederick A., Jr. "Towards petty sessions: Tudor JPs and divisions of counties." In *Tudor Rule and Revolution: Essays for G.R. Elton from His American Friends.* DeLloyd J. Guth and John W. McKenna, eds., pp. 201–216. 1982.

Victor Morgan

SEE ALSO

Cinque Ports; Government, Central Administration of; Justice of the Peace; Population and Demography; Sheriff; Towns

Gowrie Conspiracy

The attempt on King James VI of Scotland's life known as the Gowrie Conspiracy remains an unresolved controversy. The central question is whether the third earl of Gowrie, John Ruthven, and his brother, Alexander, conspired and attempted to murder King James on August 5, 1600, or if James staged the incident in order to murder them. The basic report of that day at Gowrie House in Perth (Saint-Johnstoun) comes primarily from a pamphlet published—under James's supervision—shortly after the events took place; as such, this account has been the object of debate since its publication.

Very early on the morning of Tuesday, August 5, 1600, Alexander Ruthven rode to Falkland Palace where James was preparing for a day of hunting. Claiming to be holding a prisoner in possession of a large quantity of gold, Alexander urged the king to return with him to Perth and assert a royal claim to the treasure. Skeptical at first, James eventually agreed to ride to Perth at the end of the chase, and despite Alexander's protests of the need for discretion, brought with him members of his hunting party (no more than fifteen, according to the royal account), including the earl of Mar and the duke of Lennox.

Once at Gowrie House, following dinner, Alexander lured the king to an upstairs turret chamber and held him under guard. Believing the king had set out to return to Falkland, his men assembled in the courtyard to follow when James cried out from the turret window that he was being murdered by traitors. His men charged back in, and John Ramsey, reaching the upstairs chamber first, stabbed Alexander as he was struggling with the king. The earl himself reached the upstairs room accompanied by seven of his own men. While the king was ushered to safety, his four men engaged the earl's. Despite the two-to-one odds, "it pleased God," in the words of the royal account, that the king's men should prevail. Ramsey killed Gowrie, while the other seven were driven back downstairs, severely wounded. Ramsey and his men, too, were badly injured. Mar, Lennox, and the rest finally broke through the locked door of the main staircase to find the the earl lying dead, and the king saved from harm. They all dropped to their knees, and were led by the king in giving thanks to God for his deliverance.

On his return to Falkland that same night, the king wrote a letter reporting the events to his Privy Council, and it reached the secretary of Edinburgh by nine the next morning. The story was immediately communicated to the English envoy, Nicolson, who wrote that very day to William Cecil, Lord Burghley, in England. Thus it took no more than forty-eight hours for the British crown to become advised of the treason. The Scottish Privy Council ordered Gowrie House confiscated, but a search of the property disclosed no evidence of treasonable activity by the earl or his brother. A party was sent to Direlton to arrest William and Patrick, the two youngest Ruthven brothers, but they had already fled into England.

Skepticism about the official version of events arose almost immediately, especially among certain members of the Edinburgh clergy, led by Robert Bruce. Patrick Galloway, the royal chaplain, preached a sermon on August 11 in support of the king's version, but the extent to which it settled public opinion is still questioned.

The official report, *Gowrie's Conspiracie. A Discourse of the unnaturall and vyle Conspiracie, attempted against the King's Maiesties Person, at Sanct-Johnstoun, up Twysday the Fifth of August, 1600,* was published in early September. It was appended with corroborating depositions from witnesses present at Gowrie House that day: James Wemyss, the earl's cousin, William Rynd, the earl's former tutor and confidant, and Andrew Henderson, who a few weeks earlier had become the guard in the turret room. A copy of this pamphlet was once again sent to Cecil by Nicolson on September 3. An anti-James, pro-Gowrie tract may have appeared shortly before this, but details of it are unclear.

On November 15, 1600, the Scottish Parliament declared the earl and Alexander Ruthven guilty of treason and their titles and estates forfeited, the Ruthven name abolished. A portion of the confiscated lands and titles were distributed as rewards to some of those who had come to the king's aid back in August. The 5th of August was declared a national holiday in celebration of the king's deliverance. Modern historians tend to find evidence lacking that James fabricated the entire affair to eliminate the Ruthvens, who were both his creditors and, to some degree, his rivals. At the same time, a premeditated conspiracy by the Ruthvens seems equally difficult to support based on the narratives that survive.

BIBLIOGRAPHY

Arbuckle, W.F. "The Gowrie Conspiracy." *The Scottish Historical Review,* vol. 36, nos. 121, 122, pp. 1–24, 89–110.

Clark, Arthur Melville. *Murder Under Trust or The Topical Macbeth and other Jacobean Matters.* 1981.

Lang, Andrew. *James VI and the Gowrie Mystery.* 1902.

Roughead, William. *The Riddle of the Ruthvens.* 1919.

W.T. Chmielewski

G

SEE ALSO
James VI and I

Grafton, Richard (1513–1572?)

Best known as a Protestant printer, Richard Grafton was a wealthy London merchant and member of the Grocer's Company, serving as their warden from 1555–1557. Little is known about the circumstances of his birth or education. His commercial sense and entrepreneurial spirit made him one of the sixteenth century's most important and productive printers, earning him the royal patent as king's printer during Edward VI's brief reign. Grafton also rewrote the *Chronicles* of Edward Hall and the *Chronicles* of Harding, and in 1553–1554 and 1556–1557, Richard Grafton was registered as a member of Parliament for Coventry.

Grafton began his publishing career with the first English Bible. Printed abroad, this Bible became known as the "Matthew Bible" after Thomas Matthew, the pseudonym of the theologian who annotated it, John Rogers. Thomas Cromwell secured a market for the English Bible in 1537 by requiring each curate to buy one copy, each monastery six, and each parish a folio version. Soon after, Cromwell commissioned Grafton and his associate, Edward Whitchurch, to produce the Great English Bible, but when it was being printed in Paris, officials of the French Inquisition shut down the presses and seized the sheets. After Grafton and Whitchurch fled to London, Cromwell bought the presses and had them re-assembled in London, where Grafton and Whitchurch produced the first copies in April 1539. The Great Bible frontispiece ascribed to Hans Holbein depicts Henry VIII distributing the Word of God to Thomas Cranmer and Cromwell, who distribute it to the clergy and laity. Cromwell's coat of arms, though, was cut out of the frontispiece block in 1540 when he lost favor at court. Cromwell's descent affected Grafton, who was imprisoned for six weeks for printing the English Bible and the Great Bible with only Cromwell's consent. Later, Grafton was jailed again for allegedly printing a ballad praising Cromwell after he was executed.

In 1548, Grafton rewrote Hall's *Chronicles* titled *The Union of the Two Noble and Illustre Famelies of Lancastre and Yorke,* and continued it to the end of the reign of Henry VIII. In 1562, Richard Tottel, his son-in-law, printed Grafton's *Abridgment of the Chronicles of England,* and the following year John Stow's similar work, *Summarie of English Chronicles,* appeared. In Grafton's next edition of his *Abridgment* he tried to monopolize the chronicle summary market by dedicating his text to the "Maisters and wardeins of the companie . . . of Imprinting," requesting they print no other summary or abridgement of the Chronicles, "but only this litle boke." Stow retaliated in the later edition of his *Summarie* when he accused Grafton of "mangeling Halle's worke." Grafton's revision of Harding's *Chronicles* was criticized as well by the learned George Buchanan.

Grafton and Whitchurch printed numerous church service books, the Book of Common Prayer, the *Psalter,* and the *Primer.* After Grafton became the king's printer for Edward VI, he had the patent to print the statutes, the acts of Parliament, the king's proclamations, as well as the articles and sermons. In addition to these, he printed Thomas Wilson's *Art of Rhetoric,* a *Boke of Presidentes,* an edition of Vergil and Aristotle's *Ethics,* among other important texts. Grafton's identifying device was a tun with a grafted fruit tree growing through it. He lived and worked in part of the dissolved house of the Gray Friars, the greater part of which was granted by Edward VI as a hospital for orphans called Christ's Hospital.

Grafton's misfortune came when Mary I ascended the throne in 1553. Following orders after Edward's death, Grafton printed the proclamation declaring Lady Jane Grey successor to the crown. For this, Mary had him imprisoned briefly. He lost the royal patent and never regained it after Elizabeth I became queen. Little is known of Grafton's end. Even though his third son, Richard, had his arms confirmed to him with a crest, Richard Grafton, the printer, seems to have died in reduced circumstances.

BIBLIOGRAPHY

Dibdin, Thomas Frognall. *Typographical Antiquities; or the History of Printing in England, Scotland, and Ireland.* Vol. 20. 1816.

Ellis, Henry, ed. *Chronicle of John Harding Containing an Account of Public Transactions from the Earliest Period of English History to the Beginning of the Reign of King Edward the Fourth Together with the Continuation by Richard Grafton to the Thirty-Fourth Year of King Henry the Eighth* (1562). 1812.

Handover, P.M. *Printing in London.* 1960.

Katherine Conway

SEE ALSO

Bible Translation; Cromwell, Thomas; Grey, Lady Jane; Hall, Edward; Holbein, Hans; Printing, Publishing, and Bookbinding; Rogers, John; Stowe, John; Tottel, Richard; Whitchurch, Edward

Grammar Schools

The Tudor age was a period of upheaval and massive readjustment for England's grammar schools. During the last years of Henry VIII and the brief reign of Edward VI, almost all the monastic, nunnery, and chantry schools were swept away, leaving no grammar schools in many localities. But within a generation local energies were unleashed and dozens of new, endowed schools appeared to take the place of those that had vanished. However, in 1600, there were approximately 125 fewer grammar schools than had existed a century earlier, although the schools that were founded or remained open during the Elizabethan period tended to be larger and stronger than their medieval predecessors, with better qualified and better paid teachers and slightly more diverse curriculums.

During the first decades of the sixteenth century, England had perhaps 475 or 500 grammar schools. Almost half were run by chantries, and they varied tremendously in size and quality. The average chantry school had approximately thirty to forty pupils, but in the West Country they tended to be much larger. At Chipping Camden School, there were usually between sixty and eighty pupils enrolled, while at Taunton and Crewkerne the total enrollment sometimes exceeded 120. In most cases these schools offered only rudimentary instruction in reading, writing, and arithmetic. In addition to the 220 or so chantry schools, there were approximately 135 monastic and forty nunnery schools in early Tudor England. These schools tended to be considerably smaller, averaging between eighteen and twenty pupils each. They also tended to be mediocre, although the schools maintained by Reading Abbey, Sheen Abbey, and Hyde Abbey near Winchester were highly regarded by contemporaries.

The nine secular cathedrals of the realm maintained schools that are almost as difficult to categorize in terms of quality. At York, the cathedral school usually had between sixty and seventy pupils enrolled; but that school, like the others in its class, seems to have been far from adequate. Most of the teaching was done by the organist or the songmaster, and as such it cannot have been of a high order. Three of the best schools of the age were located in London. During the mid-1440s, the collegiate churches of St. Anthony's and St. Dunstan-in-the-East, and the City of London School, were highly regarded.

During the late Middle Ages a new type of school came into being. This was the endowed grammar school, which paid a yearly stipend of at least £10 to the schoolmaster in order to attract a university graduate. The most famous of these early endowed schools was Eton, near Windsor. King Henry VI established Eton in the 1440s and linked it to his other great foundation, King's College, Cambridge, which routinely admitted Eton's better graduates for advanced work. But the most important of these early endowed schools was probably Magdalen College School, in Oxford, which was founded in 1479 by William Waynflete, bishop of Winchester, known for the excellent Latin grammars produced by its first two headmasters, John Ankwyll and John Holt.

In London, the most famous grammar school was St. Paul's School, established by John Colet, where William Lily served as headmaster from 1510 until his death in 1522. During his first few years at St. Paul's, Lily compiled his exceptional Latin grammar. Between 1515 and 1540, Lily's textbook was adopted by dozens of other schoolmasters, especially in the London area. Because Henry VIII preferred order and uniformity in all things, he issued a proclamation in 1543 commanding every schoolmaster in the realm to make exclusive use of Lily's textbook.

Ironically, as many of the grammar schools improved during the latter part of Henry VIII's reign, scores of them disappeared. Between 1536 and 1540, Parliament bowed to the king's wishes and dissolved all the religious houses in England, causing the 175 monastic and nunnery schools to vanish at a stroke. A short time later, during the autumn of 1547, the first Parliament of Edward VI decreed an end to England's thousands of chantries by Easter of 1548. As a result, approximately 80 percent of the 220 or so chantry schools disappeared also.

The loss of approximately 340 schools had mixed consequences. On the one hand, the disappearance of the forty or so nunnery schools was a disaster for the cause of female education because no other institutions appeared to take their place. In the 1550s, Thomas Becon made a stirring appeal in his *New Catechism* for the establishment of a system of well-endowed schools for girls, which would fill the void created by the disappearance of the nunnery schools. But his proposal fell on deaf ears, and it was not until James I's reign that the first academy for young women, the Ladies Hall at Deptford, Kent, was founded.

However, the disappearance of the 135-odd monastic schools was far from serious. As a group, those schools were mediocre at best; and once they disappeared, local efforts began to establish generously endowed schools for boys that were considerably better than the ones they replaced. Approximately 130 such schools are believed to

G

have been established during Elizabeth I's reign alone, including such famous institutions as Rugby, Harrow, Westminster, and the celebrated Merchants Taylors' School for 250 boys in London. By the end of the century several of those schools were providing instruction in Greek and Hebrew as well as Latin. Those three classical languages seem to have been taught first at the Merchant Taylors' School during the time of Richard Mulcaster, the original headmaster between 1561 and 1586.

Thus, by the end of the Tudor Age, England had about 360 grammar schools in all. While the schools that existed in 1603 tended to be considerably better than those of a century before, the quality of the Elizabethan grammar schools should not be exaggerated. In most places the curriculum was still limited to Latin grammar and a smattering of religion as defined by the Thirty-Nine Articles of 1563. As yet almost no science, mathematics, history, or modern foreign languages were taught, and only in the most outstanding schools had the teaching of Greek and Hebrew put down roots. Furthermore, many of the schools were so large—there were usually 360 boys enrolled at Shrewsbury School between 1563 and 1603—that the headmaster and his assistants, who seldom numbered more than three, were unable to maintain discipline without recourse to brutal punishment. The school day, beginning as early as six in the morning, was too long, holidays and vacations too short and infrequent, and the wooden benches on which the boys sat much too hard. Even worse, in most places the school building consisted of a single large room without partitions to separate the younger students from the older ones. But many of the schoolmasters were dedicated men, and given the conditions under which they worked, their improvements in grammar school education as well as the spread of literacy are remarkable.

BIBLIOGRAPHY

Carlisle, Nicholas. *A Concise Description of the Endowed Grammar Schools in England and Wales.* 2 vols. 1818.

Lawson, John. *Medieval Education and the Reformation.* 1967.

Moran, Jo Ann H. *The Growth of English Schooling, 1348–1548.* 1985.

Orme, Nicholas. *English Schools in the Middle Ages.* 1973.

———. *Education in the West of England, 1066–1548.* 1976.

Stowe, Ancel R.M. *English Grammar Schools in the Reign of Queen Elizabeth.* 1908.

Wood, Norman *The Reformation and English Education.* 1931.

Michael V.C. Alexander

SEE ALSO

Articles of Religion; Chantry; Clergy; Education; Colet, John; Monastic Orders; Social Classes; Universities

Great Bible
See Bible Translations

Greene, Robert (1558–1592)

After his death, Robert Greene became the subject of a series of accounts, some by attackers, some by defenders, and some, if title pages are honest, by Greene himself in alleged deathbed pamphlets. Despite untrustworthy details, these accounts provide a clear picture of a reckless life ending in illness and poverty at the age of thirty-four. That life had begun in 1558 in Norwich, where Greene's father was probably a saddler or an innkeeper. Greene entered St. John's, Cambridge, in 1575, and eventually received degrees from Cambridge and Oxford. He wrote his first work at Cambridge before going to London, possibly after spending time back in Norwich, where, like many of his characters, he may have abandoned a wife and child.

In London he took up the still new, and still precarious, profession of writing for profit. Greene can be linked to Thomas Nashe, Thomas Lodge, Henry Chettle, Christopher Marlowe, and others, and he claimed also to associate with prostitutes and cutpurses. Greene attacked some of his contemporaries, notably Gabriel Harvey, and his most famous words are an attack: the warning in *Greens Groats-worth of Wit* (1592) against "an vpstart Crow" who "is in his owne conceit the onely Shake-scene in a countrie." The passage as a whole describes the refusal by theatrical acquaintances to help Greene in his time of need, but no explanation for the singling out of William Shakespeare has won consensus.

The posthumous works recall events from earlier years and describe the suffering of Greene's last weeks. Gabriel Harvey also describes that suffering, claiming to have visited Greene's lodgings after his death. Not a sympathetic witness, Harvey may suppress the deathbed repentance that is the principal theme of the posthumous works. On the other hand, whether repentance took place remains uncertain, as does the very authenticity of the pamphlets.

THE DEFENCE OF
Conny catching.
OR
A CONFVTATION OF THOSE
two iniurious Pamphlets publiſhed by *R.G.* againſt
the practitioners of many Nimble-witted
and myſticall Sciences.

By Cuthbert Cunny-catcher, Licenciate in Whit-
tington Colledge.

*Qui bene latuit bene vixit, dominatur enim
fraus in omnibus.*

Printed at London by *A. I* for *Thomas Gubbins*
and are to be ſold by *Iohn Busbie*, 1592.

Cuthbert Cunny-Catcher, pseud. *The defence of Conny catching* (1592). The title is illustrated by the coney—representing the author—challenging Robert Greene in an ironic defense of his trade. Greene's pamphlets on petty crime are advertised by both title and image. Reproduced from the original by permission of the Henry E. Huntington Library and Art Gallery.

The first of Greene's more than thirty prose works was *Mamillia,* registered in 1580. One of many to imitate *Euphues,* Greene strings together ornately phrased debates, soliloquies, and letters. Slight works, the two parts of *Mamillia* nevertheless include elements that became recurrent motifs, including the contrast between rational and passionate love, the power of temptation, the dangers of rhetoric, and the gap between precept and experience. Of particular interest is the portrayal of women, for Greene not only imitates John Lyly but proclaims rivalry: his hero will learn not, like Euphues, that women are treacherous, but rather that "for inconstancie men are farre more worthie to be condemned than women to be accused." Greene would make the point often, creating a series of female paragons whose constancy is betrayed by unworthy males but remains to reward those males when they repent. Whether or not connected to Greene's biography, the motif contributes distinctively to Elizabethan discussions of men and women.

Several more works in Lyly's manner followed *Mamillia,* the most interesting being the rather grim *Planetomachia* (1585). With *Penelopes Web* (1587), Greene began to use more intricate plots based largely on romance motifs. Some works tell several stories within a frame; others present a sustained narrative that later readers would see as novelistic. These include Greene's two best-known romances, *Pandosto* (1588), and *Menaphon* (1589). *Menaphon* in particular has had admirers. Here the banished and disguised princess Sephestia is loved by her father, her son, and her husband—all of whom fail to recognize her. Despite genuine narrative energy, *Menaphon* includes lengthy discussions of love, fortune, ambition, and other issues, with characters, as often in Greene, representing attitudes or values emblematically. The work ends happily, with repentance and forgiveness, and resembles Shakespearean drama in many respects. The similarities are more obvious in *Pandosto,* for it is the source for *The Winter's Tale.* Unlike *Menaphon* (and *The Winter's Tale*), *Pandosto* has an ending both tragic and comic, and the work as a whole has a complexity not always appreciated by commentators engaged in identifying Shakespeare's improvements.

Greenes Mourning Garmen (1590) echoes the story of the prodigal son and begins a series of repentance tales, including *Never Too Late* (1590) and *Francescos Fortunes* (1590). Another new direction is represented by *A Notable Discovery of Coosnage* (1591), first in a series of coney-catching pamphlets exposing the tricks of confidence artists or petty criminals (1591–1592), which claim to record Greene's firsthand knowledge. Underworld jargon and circumstantial details lend authenticity to the portrait of urban life in the pamphlets. At the same time, borrowings from earlier writers make them sometimes seem padded and thin. The most interesting for modern readers may be *A Disputation between a Hee Conny-catcher and a Shee Conny-catcher* (1592), a two-part work notable for its frank treatment of female sexuality. In addition to the coney-catching pamphlets, Greene wrote other works during this period, including *Philomena* (1592), once greatly admired but now neglected (despite passages of considerable power and several interesting points of contact with *Othello*). Finally, there are

G

the deathbed pamphlets. Internal evidence indicates that the third one, *Greenes Vision* (1592), was written two years before—a reminder of the need for caution in discussing Greene's life and works.

The nature and extent of Greene's career in the theater is unknown. Five plays are now generally accepted as his, although his hand has been "found" in many others. The earliest was probably *Alphonsus, King of Aragon,* which awkwardly blends self-conscious imitation of Marlowe with chivalric romance. More characteristic is *Orlando Furioso,* of textual interest because the actor's part for Orlando survives. Marlovian elements again exist, especially in Sacrepant's villainy and Orlando's mad raving, but also present is the romantic tale of Orlando's distrust of the constant Angelica, who is purged of her capriciousness in Ariosto. Greene collaborated with Lodge for *A Looking Glasse for London and England,* a scriptural drama notable for its complex structure.

None of these three plays receives much attention today, and Greene's dramatic reputation rests on *Friar Bacon and Friar Bungay* and *James IV.* The former is included in many anthologies and continues to attract critical attention. Often called instrumental in the development of romantic comedy, *Bacon and Bungay* has seemed a warm and genial play to many critics, some of whom wax sentimental over Margaret of Fressingfield. Bacon's magic has also received substantial scholarly attention. The play is more complex and interesting than most appreciations of it suggest, however. It ends with reconciliation, but unresolved elements (like Lacy's cruel testing of Margaret) reproduce areas of cultural conflict. *James IV* provides still another treatment of male folly, as James, pursuing Ida despite marriage to Dorothea, manages to cause suffering for *two* surpassingly virtuous heroines. Also of interest are Ateukin (vice-figure, Machiavel, parasite) and the use of a framing device. Again, the play ends with the recognition of human frailty allowing reconciliation but no clear resolution. Greene's best works thus offer often absorbing versions of important elements in Elizabethan culture. Connections to Shakespeare are apparent, but they have made Greene's work difficult to evaluate. Other factors have not helped—his messy life, his reputation as a hack, his use of conventional motifs. Those same factors, however, place Greene firmly in historical context and may enhance his importance for a new generation of critics. Although his voice is in many ways distinctive, Greene cannot easily be seen outside a time and place, and his works are among our best tools for examining the later sixteenth century.

BIBLIOGRAPHY

Collins, J. Churton, ed. *The Plays & Poems of Robert Greene.* 2 vols. 1905.

Crupi, Charles W. *Robert Greene.* 1986.

Davis, Walter R. *Idea and Act in Elizabethan Fiction.* 1969.

Grosart, Alexander B., ed. *The Life and Complete Works in Prose and Verse of Robert Greene, M.A. Cambridge and Oxford.* 15 vols. 1881–1886; repr. 1964.

Helgerson, Richard. *The Elizabethan Prodigals.* 1976.

Jordan, John Clark. *Robert Greene.* 1915.

Newcomb, Lori Humphrey. "'Social Things': The Production of Popular Culture in the Reception of Robert Greene's *Pandosto.*" *ELH,* vol. 61, pp. 753–781.

Pruvost, René. *Robert Greene et ses Romans (1558–1592).* 1938.

Richardson, Brenda. "Robert Greene's Yorkshire Connexions: A New Hypothesis." *YES,* vol. 10, pp. 160–180.

Sanders, Norman. "The Comedy of Greene and Shakespeare." In *Early Shakespeare.* John Russell Brown and Bernard Harris, eds. 1961.

Charles W. Crupi

SEE ALSO

Chettle, Henry; Harvey, Gabriel; Lyly, John; Machiavell, The

Greenham, Richard (c. 1535–c. 1594)

Of obscure parentage, Richard Greenham (or Grenham) entered Pembroke Hall, Cambridge, in 1559, when he was already a mature student. He became a strong supporter of Thomas Cartwright, and in 1570 was inducted as rector of Dry Drayton, just outside Cambridge. From there he was able to exercise a preaching and teaching ministry that influenced several generations of undergraduates at the university. Sometime about 1588 he went to London, and in 1591 he resigned his living, to his subsequent regret. He preached against the Marprelate tracts in 1589, because he regarded them as frivolous. His chief claim to fame today is that he authored the first Puritan tract on Sunday observance (1592), a surprisingly mild and moderate defense of sabbatarianism that contrasts favorably with later Puritan writings on the subject. The date of his death is unknown, but it seems to have been sometime late in 1594.

BIBLIOGRAPHY

Collinson, Patrick. *The Elizabethan Puritan Movement.* 1967.

Gerald Bray

SEE ALSO
Cartwright, Thomas; Marprelate Controversy; Puritanism

Greenwood, John (c. 1560–1593)

Puritan clergyman-turned-Separatist under Archbishop John Whitgift's anti-Puritan measures, John Greenwood became one of the first Separatist martyrs in Elizabethan England. Silenced from preaching in Norfolk, Greenwood joined a Separatist conventicle in London with connections to several earlier Elizabethan Separatist groups. In 1587, Greenwood and twenty others were arrested and committed to the Clink. His incarceration attracted the attention of Henry Barrow, whom Whitgift also arrested for Separatism following a visit Barrow had made to Greenwood in prison. Deprived of Greenwood's leadership, the remaining London Separatists were harassed and many of them jailed by the archbishop's pursuivants. By 1593, seventeen London Separatists had died in several prisons.

From prison, Greenwood and Barrow attacked the Church of England and defended Separatism with arguments similar to those espoused by the now apostate Separatist Robert Browne. Smuggled out of prison, published in the Netherlands, and disseminated in England, their writings had the impact of luring Francis Johnson, a Puritan minister, into dialogue. After a conference with the imprisoned Separatist leaders, Johnson joined their cause and was elected pastor of the remnant of Greenwood's London congregation. In March of 1593, Greenwood and Barrow were convicted of propagating "seditious books" and hanged on April 6 at Tyburn.

BIBLIOGRAPHY
Burrage, Champlin. *Early English Dissenters.* 1912.
Carlson, Leland H. ed. *The Writings of John Greenwood, 1587–1590.* 1962.
———. *The Writings of John Greenwood and Henry Barrow, 1591–1593.* 1962.
White, B.R. *The English Separatist Tradition.* 1971.

Stephen Brachlow

SEE ALSO
Barrow, Henry; Browne, Robert; Church of England

Grenville, Richard (c. 1541–1591)

Gentleman and sea captain, Sir Richard Grenville was a leading promoter of colonization during the reign of Elizabeth I. He was also a prominent figure in county affairs in Cornwall, serving as M.P. in 1571 and 1584, and as sheriff in 1577. His earliest colonizing venture was in Ireland where, in partnership with a group of West Country gentlemen, he established a small settlement near Cork in 1569 as part of an ambitious attempt to colonize Munster on a large scale. These plans were thwarted by a rebellion of the Irish that destroyed the small English colony. In 1574, Grenville and a group of supporters from the southwest petitioned the queen for a patent to discover lands south of the equator. His interest was fixed on the river Plate region in South America, which he seems to have been planning to colonize. Although he was granted a license by Elizabeth I, it was withdrawn when she became aware of Grenville's anti-Spanish purpose.

During the 1580s, Grenville played an important role in Sir Walter Ralegh's colonizing ventures at Roanoke in North America. He commanded the first colonizing expedition of 1585, capturing a rich Spanish prize on the return voyage that probably offset the cost of the venture. The following year he led a relief expedition to Roanoke, but was delayed on the way out by the seizure of prizes. When Grenville reached Roanoke, he found the site abandoned. His decision to leave fifteen men behind as a holding force has been criticized as a fatal half-measure, which left the party to an uncertain fate in a hostile environment. He played little role in the second Roanoke colony. He was to have commanded a relief expedition to the colony in 1588, but it was halted by the queen. Thereafter, he became preoccupied with his lands in the Munster plantation. In 1591, Grenville served as vice admiral on an expedition to the Azores under the command of Lord Thomas Howard. It was here that Grenville met his death aboard the *Revenge,* in a naval action that has assumed legendary status. Although outnumbered, Grenville refused to surrender to the Spanish, battling on in hopeless circumstances for another twelve hours. His death, shortly after the surrender of the *Revenge,* was immortalized by his cousin, Ralegh. He was a brave but temperamental commander, whose career reflects the ambitions of the militant, expansionist element in Elizabethan society.

BIBLIOGRAPHY
Canny, N. *The Elizabethan Conquest of Ireland: A Pattern Established, 1565–1576.* 1976.
Corbett, J. *Drake and the Tudor Navy.* 1988.
Quinn, D.B. *Raleigh and the British Empire.* 1947.

G

———, ed. *The Roanoke Voyages, 1584–1590.* 1955.

John C. Appleby

SEE ALSO

Colonial Development; Ireland, History of; Ralegh, Walter

Gresham, Thomas (c. 1519–1579)

One of the most prominent and wealthy Tudor merchants, Sir Thomas Gresham is best known for founding the Royal Exchange and for his writings on foreign exchange. The Greshams were an old Norfolk family, and Thomas's father, Richard, arrived in London in about 1500 to be apprenticed, and was admitted to the Mercer's Company in 1507. Richard Gresham prospered by exporting cloth when European demand was increasing; he spent much time in Antwerp, was elected lord mayor of London in 1537, and had close ties with the court of Henry VIII. Thomas was born in London, and became even more successful than his father. After his university years in Cambridge, he was apprenticed to his father in 1535 and was trained both in the business of a mercer and more importantly as a royal agent. In 1551, two years after his father's death, he obtained the office of king's merchant, whereby he was required to spend much time in Antwerp procuring loans from continental bankers for the English crown as well obtaining foreign goods needed for military purposes. In addition, he kept the Privy Council informed of political developments of importance abroad. Because of the great expenses incurred by Henry VIII's wars with France, this post took up most of Gresham's time, and he left most of his own business to be conducted by his London factor.

In 1552, to help pay the king's debts, Gresham persuaded the government to issue a royal order restraining the cloth fleet from sailing to the Low Countries. This was done in order to force the Merchant Adventurers to agree to turn over the proceeds from their sale of cloth to Gresham in Antwerp, where he was able to pay the king's debts without having to exchange sterling for Flemish currency. This effectively reduced the amount of the debt that would have been paid in London, where its sheer size would have increased the demand for Flemish currency to the extent that its exchange rate with the pound would have risen. Having dealt with the repayment of the king's loans in this way, Gresham was thereafter able to obtain better interest rates on the Continent. Although he was removed from his post at the accession of Mary I when his patron Northumberland died on the scaffold, he was soon reinstated when it was discovered that loans could not be procured at as cheap a rate because of the trust invested in him by continental lenders.

Gresham continued his services of procuring loans under Elizabeth I, and spent six years in Antwerp. He worked closely with William Cecil, Lord Burghley, was knighted in 1559, and became ambassador in the Netherlands for a short time soon after. In March 1567, when Gresham was in Antwerp a final time, he reported on the first battle between the Spanish and Protestant citizens there. From this date Gresham spent much time reorganizing the queen's finances in the face of the dislocations caused by the ending of the Antwerp money market. In 1568, he opened his new exchange in London to improve the city's ability to serve as a center of the exchange of foreign credit and bills of exchange. Although he attempted to raise money in Hamburg, from 1570 he advised the Privy Council to negotiate loans with London merchants; this was the foundation of the London money market. He ceased to be the queen's agent in 1574, whereupon he was audited and was found to be £10,000 in debt to the government, but managed to circumvent the auditors by obtaining a complete discharge from the queen before the money could be demanded. He died in 1579, leaving land worth £50,000 in capital with an income of £2,670 per annum. He also left an endowment to found Gresham College, a London society for merchants and gentlemen that promoted learning in such practical sciences as mathematics, medicine, and navigation through professional lectureships. The scientific and experimental community that grew out of Gresham College later became the basis for the Royal Society of London during the Restoration.

Gresham's name is commonly applied to the economic law that states that where two media of exchange come into circulation together, the more valuable will tend to disappear because it is less expensive to pay for foreign purchases in good-quality money. This is often expressed in the dictum, "bad money drives out good," and was attributed to Gresham in 1858, although he did not formulate it. It was, in fact, a well-known phenomenon that the issue of base money by a mint would drive away good coins, and although Gresham mentioned this in his "Memorandum for the Understanding of the Exchange," he was only one of a number of authors to do so.

BIBLIOGRAPHY

Bindoff, S.T. *The Fame of Sir Thomas Gresham.* 1973.

De Roover, Raymond. *Gresham on Foreign Exchange.* 1949.

Salter, F.R. *Sir Thomas Gresham.* 1925.

Craig Muldrew

SEE ALSO

Cecil, William; Cloth Trade; Education; Merchant Adventurers; Money, Inflation, and Money Lending; Royal Exchange

Greville, Fulke (1554–1628)

Courtier in the reigns of Elizabeth I, James I, and Charles I, Fulke Greville was a frequent member of Parliament; an amateur philosopher and theologian; and a writer of secular love poems, religious and philosophical lyrics, closet dramas, verse treatises on monarchy, war, honor, learning, and religion, and a biography of Sir Philip Sidney.

Greville was born on October 3, 1554, into a prosperous Warwickshire family that enjoyed strong connections with the Dudley and Sidney families. At the age of ten he entered the grammar school at Shrewsbury, the same day as Philip Sidney. There both received a classical education, especially the study of Latin writers characteristic of a humanist education in the period. Their teacher, Thomas Ashton, also emphasized the study of Calvin's *Catechism,* and it was probably Ashton who gave the attitudes of both young men their first, strongly Protestant bent.

Greville's friendship with Sidney was the most powerful, perhaps even erotic, relationship in his life. Although they were separated in their university years—Greville going to Cambridge in 1568 and Sidney to Oxford probably the same year—their attendance at university furnished them a major qualification for service at the court of Elizabeth, where they became members of the faction, including Robert Dudley, the earl of Leicester, and Sir Francis Walsingham, that, in its embrace of a radical Protestantism in domestic and foreign policy, gradually defined itself against the increasingly *politique* William Cecil, Lord Burghley, the queen's lord treasurer and the man whose judgment she most trusted.

Beginning with a minor position as clerk of the council and signet in the Council of Wales, secured for him in 1577 by the influence of Walsingham and Sidney's father, Greville began the lifelong quest for wealth in the role of client in the system of court patronage. But his relationship with the radical Protestant faction went beyond a concern about income to an embrace of its ideology and rigorous ideals of the individual moral life and service to English and international Protestantism.

Greville's earliest love poems, eventually grouped together with short philosophical and religious poems as *Caelica,* were probably written in friendly competition with Sidney, who was composing *Astrophil and Stella* in the early 1580s, although Greville became more cynical in his love poems than Sidney and moved toward a plainer style than Sidney's in his poems on love and other subjects. But writing love poems was merely a diversion because he, like Sidney, craved employment abroad as a soldier and diplomat, ambitions mainly limited by the queen and Burghley to ceremonial functions and some minor military duties. By the time England went to war formally with Spain in 1584, they had become convinced that only an offensive war against Spain, not the limited war in the Low Countries, would address the crisis. But their attempt to join Sir Francis Drake's expedition of 1585 to attack the Spanish in the Americas was frustrated by the queen. Scaling back their ambitions, Greville received a commission from Leicester in 1585 to command 100 horse in the English army preparing for the Netherlands, only to have it revoked by the queen, and Sidney was appointed governor of Flushing in November of 1585. Sidney's departure from England to assume that position was the last time Greville saw his friend alive.

The death of Sidney at Zutphen in 1586 was, by Greville's own reckoning, the most devastating event in his life. The activist friend, whose spirit was always more daring than Greville's and on whom Greville depended for adherence to his personal and political ideals, was gone. Even though he remained loyal to the pro-war party of which the earl of Essex became the leader in the 1590s, the cautious spirit that characterized his entire career was exacerbated. He burned, for example, a play entitled *Antony and Cleopatra* because he feared it might be construed as a commentary on the relationship of Essex and Elizabeth.

Twenty-five years after Sidney's death, when Robert Cecil, Burghley's son and secretary of state, had punished Greville for his allegiance to the ideals and policy of Sidney and Essex by taking away his position as treasurer of the navy—an office he held from 1598 through 1604—and left him languishing in retirement, Greville wrote a *Life of Sir Philip Sidney* intended as a dedication of his two remaining plays, *Mustapha* and *Alaham,* and political choruses that became *A Treatise of Monarchy.* In the *Life,* he recollected and undoubtedly idealized Sidney's

G

accomplishments, giving one more expression of his grief and erecting an image of Sidney by which to judge the lives and politics of his contemporaries, hostilely with respect to Cecil and James I, and even with restraint in the largely admirable account of Elizabeth, who assumed a more prominent role in revisions he made to the *Life*. While Greville's religious and increasingly Calvinist works—the later poems in *Caelica, Fame and Honour, Wars, Human Learning,* and *Religion*—cannot be dated with certainty, it seems that a growing pessimism about government coincided with a sense that any conversion he might have experienced had to be tempered by a realization that, even if he was one of the elect, his works had not demonstrated that election.

On September 1, 1628, Greville's servant, Ralph Hayward, as Greville was "coming from stool" and before he had finished the "trussing up" of his breeches, stabbed him twice and then fatally stabbed himself. Greville died on September 30. Hayward might have felt slighted by the amount left to him in Greville's will, but more recently scholars have suggested that Hayward was seeking his revenge for slights of a master to a servant in a homosexual relationship.

Whatever the motive, Greville's death had given even more substance to the final line of the epitaph he had placed on his tomb, a black stone in a side chapel of the church in Warwick: FULKE GREVILLE / SERVANT TO QUEEN ELIZABETH / COUNCILLOR TO KING JAMES / AND FRIEND TO SIR PHILIP SIDNEY / TROPHAEUM PECCATI.

BIBLIOGRAPHY

Bullough, Geoffrey, ed. *Poems and Dramas of Fulke Greville, First Lord Brooke.* 2 vols. 1945.

Larson, Charles. *Fulke Greville.* 1980.

Rebholz, Ronald A. *The Life of Fulke Greville, First Lord Brooke.* 1971.

Rees, Joan. *Fulke Greville, Lord Brooke, 1564–1628: A Critical Biography.* 1971.

Waswo, Richard. *The Fatal Mirror: Themes and Techniques in the Poetry of Fulke Greville.* 1972.

Wilkes, G.A., ed. *Fulke Greville, Lord Brooke: The Remains, Being Poems of Monarchy and Religion.* 1965.

Ronald A. Rebholz

SEE ALSO

Cecil, William; Devereux, Robert; Dudley, Robert; Homosexuality; Philip Sidney; Francis Walsingham

Grey, Lady Jane (1537–1554)

Queen of England for nine days in July 1553, between the reigns of Edward VI and Mary I, Lady Jane Grey was the eldest child of Frances Brandon, niece of Henry VIII, and Henry Grey, marquis of Dorset (later earl of Suffolk). Her father's chaplain early taught Jane Latin and Greek and a devotion to Calvinism, which increased when she lived with the pious Protestant Dowager Queen Katherine Parr after Henry's death in 1547. Henry's will had put Jane fifth in the line to the throne, following his children and his niece, Jane's mother. By 1553, however, Edward was dying of tuberculosis and fearful of a Catholic succession. Acting on the advice of John Dudley, the duke of Northumberland and head of the council, he created a *Devise* that bypassed his sisters Mary and Elizabeth. Northumberland convinced Jane's mother to renounce her right of succession and to force Jane to marry his youngest son, Guilford.

Edward died on July 6. On July 10, Jane was proclaimed queen and—following royal tradition—was brought to the Tower to await coronation. Meanwhile, in Norfolk, Mary proclaimed herself queen. On July 11, Northumberland instructed the councilors to recognize Guilford as king, but to her husband's chagrin, Jane refused to make him king without parliamentary endorsement. On July 12, Mary formed a rival council and raised her royal standard in Suffolk with a force of 15,000 men.

Though he rightly suspected he was losing the council's support, Northumberland left the earl of Suffolk in charge and on July 14 led an armed force against Mary. On July 15, the council learned Mary's supporters were marching on Westminster, and on July 17 the council convened at the earl of Pembroke's London residence, where they turned their support to Mary. On July 19, Jane's father told her to take off her royal robes. "I much more willingly take them off than I put them on," she replied and asked to go home. For weeks she had been so sick she believed she was being poisoned.

In a month Northumberland was executed, but Suffolk was released. Jane, meanwhile, was arrested and moved to the house of the gentleman gaoler of the Tower. Despite the demands of Emperor Charles V that all traitors be executed, the new queen called Jane the innocent dupe of ruthless men. In October, Mary announced her engagement to the emperor's son, Philip II of Spain, and in November, Jane stood trial for treason, along with her husband, two of his brothers, and Archbishop Thomas Cranmer. All confessed and were condemned, but Mary planned to pardon Jane as soon as her own forthcoming marriage had produced a male heir.

In February, Sir Thomas Wyatt led a revolt against the queen's Catholic marriage. The earl of Suffolk supported him, perhaps hoping to restore Jane to the throne. Wyatt reached London, where he was arrested on February 7. Suffolk's support was completely ineffectual. Abandoned by his small force, he was arrested in Warwickshire hiding in a hollow tree.

Once more demanding death to traitors, Charles V refused to permit Philip to enter England while Jane lived, and Mary ordered her execution. Jane declared herself prepared to die and rejected Mary's offer of a reprieve if she would become Catholic. On February 12, after seeing Guilford carried to his execution on Tower Green, Jane was brought to a scaffold within the Tower, where she addressed the crowd, recited a psalm, and was blindfolded. Then she knelt, fumbled for the block, said, "Lord, into thy hands I commend my spirit," and was beheaded.

Literature has variously recast Jane Grey's story. John Foxe stressed her uncompromising faith as the model of Protestant martyrdom in *Actes and Monuments* (1563). In *The Scholemaster* (1570), Roger Ascham presented her cheerfully reading Plato in Greek. In 1579, Thomas Chaloner's Latin *Elegy* made her a beautiful young Socrates and—to stress Mary's savagery—claimed Jane died pregnant.

On the stage, *The Innocent Usurper* (1694), by John Banks, invented a love story for Jane and Guilford, and Nicholas Rowe's anti-Catholic *Tragedy of the Lady Jane Grey* (1715) showed Jane reluctantly turning from Plato to politics to save England. Historian Gilbert Burnet called her "the wonder of the age" in his *History of the Reformation* (1679–1714). Jane became the evangelical inspiration for Victorian young ladies in Harrison Ainsworth's novel *The Tower of London* (1840). Recent popular histories include Mary Luke's *Nine Days Queen* (1986) and Alison Weir's *Children of Henry VIII* (1996).

BIBLIOGRAPHY

Matthew, David. *Lady Jane Grey: The Setting of the Reign.* 1972.
Prochaska, Frank. "The Many Faces of Lady Jane Grey." *History Today,* vol. 35, pp. 34–40.
Williams, Penry. *The Later Tudors.* 1995.

Gayle Gaskill

SEE ALSO

Edward VI; Mary I; Parr, Catherine; Philip I; Wyatt's Rebellion

G

Grimald, Nicholas (c. 1520–c. 1562)

The author of many extant and lost works, Nicholas Grimald is best known for his *Christus Redivivus* (1543), a passion play with Protestant touches, *Archipropheta* (1548), a classicizing tragedy about John the Baptist, a translation of Cicero's *De Officiis* (1556), a paraphrase of Virgil's *Georgics,* and forty poems in Richard Tottel's influential *Miscellany* (1557), a collection some think Grimald helped edit. For reasons that remain unclear, a new edition soon dropped most of these verses and credited the rest to a mere "N.G."

Grimald came from an originally Italian family named Grimaldi, and his mother was Annes, or Agnes: one poem (Tottel 162) gratefully recalls her "milky paps." Then, says the same poem, after meeting Minerva and Phoebus, Grimald went to that "Parnassus," Cambridge, and later to Oxford near the "Swanfeeder Thames" while his mother's "fingers fine" made him clothes until her "last threads gan Clotho to untwine." He got his M.A. in 1544. Sympathetic to the Reformation, Grimald worked for Nicholas Ridley (the future Protestant martyr), and some of his verses are probably to the Protestant Seymour family, but when jailed by Mary Tudor's government he prudently reverted to Catholicism and gained a reputation for at best, timeserving, and at worst, treachery.

Grimald's poetry is less imaginative than the lyrics by Thomas Wyatt and Henry Howard, earl of Surrey, also found in the *Miscellany.* The very humanism that led Grimald to experiment with blank verse can weigh down his lines: "Phoebe twice took her horns, twice laid them by," says no. 129, meaning that two months had passed. But he could turn a trope, telling in "The Garden" (no. 155), for example, how "The creeping vine holds down her own bewedded elms." And he had range. If many of his lines pronounce, a little heavily, on moral and political matters, others sing of desire: "What sweet relief the showers to thirsty plants we see, / What dear delight the blooms to bees, my true love is to me," says no. 128. Grimald also kept an informed eye on continental literature, adapting some Latin epigrams that the Huguenot leader, Theodore Beza, had composed when young and basing a sonnet (no. 137, "Concerning Virgil's Aeneid") on one by Joachim du Bellay—the first trace in England of the new French La Pléiade style, albeit one that converts an erotic poem into literary encomium. Grimald's poetry sometimes sags with old-fashioned long lines and thumping alliterations ("Deep dumps do naught but dull, not meet for man but beast," says no. 138), but the work of this clever Latinist also anticipates the styles and topics of later decades.

G

BIBLIOGRAPHY

Grimald, Nicholas, trans. *Marcus Tullius Ciceroes thre bookes of duties*. Gerald O'Gorman, ed. Renaissance English Text Society. 1990.

Arens, J.C. "Du Bellay's Sonnet 'Face le ciel,' Adapted by Nicholas Grimald." *Papers in Language and Literature*, vol. 1.

Blackburn, Ruth H. *Nicholas Grimald's* Christus Redivivus: *A Protestant Resurrection Play. English Language Notes*, vol. 5, pp. 247–250.

Grimald, Nicholas. *Christus Redivivus, Archipropheta* (1556). Facsimile. Kurt Tetzeli von Rosador, ed. 1982.

Hudson, H.H. "Grimald's Translations from Beza." *Modern Language Notes*, vol. 39, pp. 388–394.

Merrill, R.L. *The Life and Poems of Nicholas Grimald.* 1925.

Norland, Howard B. "Grimald's *Archipropheta*: A Saint's Tragedy." *Journal of Medieval and Renaissance Studies*, vol. 14, pp. 63–76.

Turville-Petre, Thorlac. "Nicholas Grimald and *Alexander A.*" *English Literary Renaissance*, vol. 6, pp. 180–186.

Anne Lake Prescott

SEE ALSO

Epigrams; Neo-Latin Literature; Wyatt, Thomas

Grindal, Edmund (c. 1519–1583)

Archbishop of Canterbury under Elizabeth I, Edmund Grindal was born in Cumberland. Educated at Cambridge, he was elected a fellow of Pembroke Hall in 1538 and, three years later, received his M.A. After his ordination as deacon in 1544, he served as proctor of the university from 1548–1549. He gained the friendship of Nicholas Ridley, bishop of Rochester and a former master of Pembroke himself, who selected Grindal to argue the Protestant side in a series of theological debates. After Ridley was translated to the bishopric of London, he chose Grindal as one of his chaplains and, in 1551, made him precentor of St. Paul's. Grindal became chaplain to Edward VI the same year and was soon licensed to preach in Canterbury; by 1552, Grindal was installed as prebendary of Westminster. Edward's death the following year temporarily quashed Grindal's rumored elevation to bishop, and the crowning of the Catholic Mary I forced him to flee to the Continent; there he spent the duration of Mary's reign collaborating with John Foxe on Foxe's *Actes and Monuments*.

The accession of Elizabeth I in 1558 returned Grindal to England. He served at once on a commission to revise the liturgy, and he was the preacher chosen to explain the use of the revised Prayer Book. This won him the queen's favor, and, in the space of a single week, Grindal was made master of Pembroke Hall and bishop of London. With some pangs of conscience, he retained the two positions simultaneously—despite not setting foot in Pembroke for three years.

Grindal's actions as bishop of London pleased neither Matthew Parker, his archbishop, nor Elizabeth. Perhaps because his own position with regard to the Elizabethan Settlement was uncertain, Grindal was inconsistent in his efforts to defend and strengthen the church as established. He seemed to be especially indecisive in confronting the resistance of the Puritans, whose grievances mirrored his own Calvinist leanings. Since London was a hotbed of Puritanism, Parker translated him to the see of York in 1570, where the threat came from the Catholic end of the spectrum; here, Grindal was able to enforce uniformity with a somewhat clearer conscience. His performance at York, indeed, proved so efficient and tactful that when Parker died in 1575, Elizabeth, in a conciliatory gesture to Puritans, was persuaded to pick Grindal as his successor. She soon regretted the choice. Grindal was ordered, in 1576–1577, to put down Puritan-led gatherings called "prophesyings," but he refused, albeit politely, questioning the appropriateness of Elizabeth's intervention in such matters. He was suspended from his functions for six months, and there was talk of his permanent dismissal. His duties were gradually restored, but he was not fully empowered again until 1582. By then his health was failing, and he died on July 6, 1583.

BIBLIOGRAPHY

Collinson, Patrick. *Archbishop Grindal: The Struggle for a Reformed Church.* 1979.

Lehmberg, S.E. "Archbishop Grindal and the Prophesyings." *Historical Magazine of the Episcopal Church*, vol. 34, pp. 87–145.

Lane, Robert. "Edmund Grindal." *Dictionary of Literary Biography.* Vol. 132, pp. 154–159. 1993.

Strype, J. *History of the Life and Acts of Edmund Grindal.* 1710.

Mark Goldblatt

SEE ALSO

Elizabeth I; Foxe, John; Marian Exiles; Parker, Matthew; Puritanism; Ridley, Nicholas

G

Guest, Edmund (1518–1577)

Born at Northallerton, Yorkshire, Edmund Guest was educated at York and at Eton, and finally King's College, Cambridge, in 1536. He remained in the university, and in 1548 declared openly for the Reformation. In the following year he took the Protestant side in the great university debate over predestination. During the reign of Mary I he went into hiding and managed to escape arrest. In 1559, he was made domestic chaplain to Archbishop Matthew Parker, and soon afterward became archdeacon of Canterbury. In 1560, he was consecrated as bishop of Rochester, where he remained until called to succeed John Jewel at Salisbury in 1571. He died at Salisbury on February 28, 1577.

Guest was much liked by Queen Elizabeth I because he remained celibate, and she did everything in her power to keep him in the London area. His theology was typical of his time, being Protestant but not extreme. He played his part in church affairs, but without special distinction, and in consequence he has been largely ignored by historians.

BIBLIOGRAPHY

Haugaard, W.P. *Elizabeth and the English Reformation: The Struggle for a Stable Settlement of Religion.* 1968.
Gerald L. Bray

SEE ALSO

Jewel, John; Parker, Matthew; Reformation, English

Guilds

Guilds were in origin voluntary associations of people who, although not blood relatives, used a language of brotherhood to express their solidarity. Guilds often began as religious brotherhoods whose members secured intercessory masses for one another in the hope of speeding their passage through purgatory to heaven, and one of the key items of expenditure was the stipend of the guild chaplain. Guilds also performed a variety of social functions for their members, offering commensality through an annual feast, undertaking the arbitration of disputes among members, providing assistance to those who had fallen on hard times, and ensuring that their members received respectable funerals attended by the guild brethren.

The basis of the association was extremely varied. Entrance fees and membership dues might be set at such a level as to make one guild an exclusive social club, while another guild might express solidarity of neighborhood or common occupation. Membership of these associations was pervasive among the middling sections of society both in urban and rural areas, and it was not uncommon for individuals to be members of more than one guild. The wealthier guilds acquired property through charitable bequests charging them with the maintenance of schools, the repair of bridges, highways, and harbors, and the relief of the poor in the wider community. Such a proliferation of functions meant that elite guilds often constituted the governing body of a town.

There is no sign that these guilds were in decline on the eve of the English Reformation; but because they were so implicated in the superstitious doctrine of purgatory, religious guilds were attacked by the reformers. Edward VI's government confiscated the property of all religious guilds in its attack on the chantries in 1548, depriving local communities of valuable welfare resources, which it was often necessary for them to repurchase in the ensuing years. After the Reformation those towns that had been governed by guilds often sought incorporation, or the secular functions of the guild were maintained by bodies of feoffees overlapping in personnel with the now defunct guild's leaders.

Other guilds had evolved rather differently because of their association with particular occupational groupings. They had performed the same social and religious functions, but their potential as mechanisms for the representation of the craft's or trade's interests and as political tools within the towns was soon realized, and they tended to be less voluntary in character, as membership was often the prerequisite for the practice of a particular trade within a town. Such craft or trade guilds were highly varied in character. Most provincial towns had a couple of trading guilds, usually the mercers and drapers, and a variable number of craft guilds, which underwent regular amalgamations and splits. There were often also less formal associations among unskilled workers such as laborers, porters, waterbearers, and watermen. The structure of the London guilds differed from that of their provincial counterparts, for here the trading element had colonized a number of the more prominent guilds, which came to combine an artisan rank and file with a ruling body dominated by wholesalers. The most prestigious guilds secured formal incorporation from the crown, enabling them to hold property in their own right, to sue and be sued in the royal courts, and to hold a common seal.

Membership of a guild brought valuable economic privileges, for members usually enjoyed a monopoly of trade within the towns. The nonfree were limited to selling

G

their goods to freemen and the practice of "foreign bought and sold" subject to stiff penalties. Nor were the interests of craft producers neglected, for among the primary functions of the guilds was the protection of the small master. Limits were placed on the scale of individual enterprises by means of restrictions on the numbers of apprentices in each workshop and by confining each master to one retail outlet. Protection for journeymen was achieved by regulations requiring that masters with establishments of a particular size employ them and by strict limits on the licensing of nonfree labor. Guilds also maintained standards of production by regular searches of members' premises and by responding to the complaints of customers about shoddy workmanship. In this their own interest in maintaining the "honor" of their craft coincided with those of the town councils in protecting the consumer. Guilds were also vigorous in representing the interests of their members both before municipal authorities and in the national arenas provided by the law courts, Parliament, and the royal council. Many waged relentless campaigns against nonfree labor, seeking enhanced powers of search and control over rural producers; others sought to maximize employment opportunities for members by limiting the export of unfinished products.

The effectiveness of trade regulation is often called into question, but it is difficult to believe that the regulations would have been maintained for so long had they not served some useful purpose. In conditions of marked occupational zoning within towns, infractions were probably more easily identified; and the guilds made sophisticated use of mechanisms of consensual policing, involving the body of the craft in enforcement and making effective use of the exemplary theater of punishment. Moreover, although many of the legislative initiatives failed, it seems unlikely that cautious businessmen would have devoted what were substantial sums of money to worthless campaigns. Rather, lobbying drew attention to grievances, reinforced ties of patronage, and the persistence of guilds that pursued their campaigns over many years and in several arenas was often crowned with success.

The guilds are sometimes seen as the enemies of innovation and a brake on progress. This is to ignore their flexibility. For example, many guilds were lowering their admission fees in the late fifteenth and early sixteenth centuries long before the statutory intervention by central government. It should also be remembered that the guilds were key institutions in the transfer of skill through the apprenticeship system, and that guild rulers in crafts like

goldsmithing were willing to draw on the expertise of alien craftsmen to train native workers by licensing rather than banning their employment.

Guild constitutions were as varied as the types of guild. Smaller guilds would elect one or two searchers each year overseen by one or two guild wardens or masters, and these offices would essentially rotate among the master craftsmen. In the larger guilds the social hierarchy was more clearly articulated. Many of the London guilds had elaborated a distinction between the livery (the senior and wealthier members of the guild who alone were eligible for high office) and the yeomanry or bachelors who were more junior. The livery was often populated by wholesalers and retailers while the yeomanry was dominated by artisans. Executive power lay in the hands of a master and up to four wardens who were answerable to a court of assistants usually composed of past wardens. Liverymen sometimes enjoyed limited rights in the nomination of these officers, but many guilds had become closed oligarchies co-opting to the courts of assistants. The inevitable result was that power was concentrated in the hands of the wealthier members, but this was probably unavoidable given that officeholders not only had to devote considerable amounts of time to guild affairs, but also were expected to support the round of guild feasting from their own pockets. The force of oligarchy was blunted by the fact that the assistants shared power with the rank and file devolving functions in the regulation of the craft to the yeomanry's own representatives who nevertheless remained closely supervised by the assistants.

The inequalities of power within guilds resulted in conflict, but the lines of division were by no means straightforward. Much conflict was political in nature, turning on disputes about the abuse of power, failures of administration, and the details of internal constitutional arrangements rather than reflecting conflicts of economic interests. It was rare for the yeomanry to be pitted against the livery, because in most guilds the division was one of seniority rather than economic function. Even in the more socially differentiated guilds, there were always artisans who made it on to the livery, and there remained divisions within the ranks of the yeomanry, such as those between the journeymen and the larger masters whose interests diverged over the number of apprentices appropriate to each workshop. It was also rare for the rulers of guilds to neglect the concerns of the rank and file completely, not least because the rhetoric of brotherhood that the rulers themselves fostered could be manipulated by artisans to secure interventions on their behalf. So, although ruling bodies might be hostile to measures that limited their own activities as middlemen, they might still actively sponsor legislation against the nonfree.

Most craft and trade guilds derived their income from the fees charged to members on admission and from regular quarterage payments, supplemented by more erratic income from fines for infractions of regulations. Where the guilds enjoyed the greater political clout that came from incorporation they were attractive bodies to act as trustees for charitable resources, and the more prestigious guilds came to enjoy substantial property portfolios supporting schools, almshouses, and poor relief. The chief items of expenditure, once charitable trusts had been discharged, were on the guild's ceremonial life, civic pageantry, and subsidies for the feasts that punctuated the guild year. The larger guilds employed a clerk and beadle whose modest stipends were supplemented by the payment of fees for their services. Over the course of the century guilds became increasingly involved in the relief of poor members. Smaller guilds rented premises for their functions, but the wealthier guilds acquired their own halls, often lavishly decorated by tradesmen's standards and reflecting on the honor of the guild.

The craft guilds were predominantly masculine institutions. Although guild ordinances often assumed that women could be members, formal apprenticeship for women seems to have been declining in the sixteenth century; and those women who appeared on the membership lists were almost invariably widows carrying on their deceased husbands' businesses. This practice was easier for those engaged in the distributive trades than it was in the manual crafts where women encountered prejudices relating to the gendering of skill. Guilds also directed a substantial portion of their efforts in poor relief at the widows of members.

The craft guilds (with significant exceptions like York) were only rarely directly represented in town government, but the guilds played an important part in urban government as conduits through which councils could tap the wealth of the citizenry and arrange military levies. They were usually subject to firm control by the municipal authorities whose approval was necessary for new ordinances, and a statute of 1504 entailed growing intervention by central government that required that royal officials be involved in the approval of their ordinances. Nevertheless, in spite of their subordinate status, guilds remained vital institutions both in representing the interests of their members and in providing them with a framework of sociability.

BIBLIOGRAPHY

Unwin, G. *Industrial Organisation in the Sixteenth and Seventeenth Centuries.* 1904.

Rappaport, S. *Worlds Within Worlds: Structures of Life in Sixteenth-Century London.* 1989.

Palliser, D.M. "The Trade Gilds of Tudor York." In *Crisis and Order in English Towns, 1500–1700.* P. Clark and P. Slack, eds. 1972.

Ian W. Archer

SEE ALSO

Aliens; Apprenticeship; Chantry; Industry and Manufacture; Monopolies; Trade, Inland

Guilpin, Everard (c. 1572–c. 1608)

Everard (sometimes Edward) Guilpin (sometimes Gilpin) is remembered as the author of one book, *Skialetheia; Or, A Shadow of Truth, in Certain Epigrams and Satires,* published anonymously in 1598. We believe he wrote it because excerpts in the 1600 anthology *England's Parnassus* carry his initials. *Skialetheia* (translated from the Greek in the subtitle) contains seventy epigrams and seven formal verse satires modeled after Martial and Juvenal, the major classical influences, respectively, on Elizabethan epigram and satire.

We identify this work generally with other expressions especially audible in the 1590s in verse and prose, in books and plays, of a negative, melancholic, and malicious tone. And we group Guilpin particularly with other young writers of satiric verse, many of whom, like him, came from the universities in the 1590s to London's Inns of Court to study law and find preferment at court: John Marston (to whom Guilpin was related), John Donne (who dedicated a verse letter to Guilpin), Sir John Davies (whose epigrams closely resemble Guilpin's), and Joseph Hall (whom Guilpin seems to attack). Guilpin attended Emmanuel College, Cambridge, from 1588 to 1591, and Gray's Inn soon thereafter.

The epigrams, approximately a third of which are based on Martial's, treat subjects traditional with epigrammatists, such as loose women, absurd fashions, dishonest lawyers and merchants, fops, other eccentrics, and poetasters, and do so usually under conventional type-names such as Lais, Clodius, Matho, Licus, and so on. The verse satires (in iambic pentameter couplets of more than a hundred lines apiece) treat the following topics: Satire Prelude (*Satyre Preludium*)—on poets and poetry, attacking contemporary tastes and defending satire and

G

epigram as modes; Satire One—Hypocrisy; Two—Cosmetics; Three—Inconstancy; Four—Jealousy; Five—Vanity; and Six—Opinion.

The book's most obvious feature is its tone—the angry, crude, sputtering voice of the satirist, who was thought to be related to the half-man, half-goat satyr—a tone whose appeal derives partly in reaction to the ease and sweetness of Elizabethan lyricism. The satirist is outraged at depravities he describes in detail and must correct. A second feature is the rich allusiveness of the text. Time and again, place-names are given and references made, more or less recognizable now, to real individuals of the day.

For its tone and allusion, *Skialetheia* was called in and burned by the Bishop's Ban in 1599 along with other books considered socially disruptive. After a reference to his marriage in 1607, Guilpin disappears. He wrote one other book, we believe, also unsigned, *The Whipper of Satire His Penance* (1601), a defense of satire against one of its detractors.

BIBLIOGRAPHY
Carroll, Allen D., ed. *Skialetheia*. 1974.

D. Allen Carroll

SEE ALSO
Censorship; Classical Literature, Influence of; Davies, John; Donne, John ; Epigrams; Hall, Joseph; Marston, John; Satire; Verse Anthologies

H

Hakluyt, Richard (1552–1616)

No traveler himself, Richard Hakluyt was responsible for the most important collection of travel writings in the English language, the *Principal Navigations, Voyages, and Discoveries of the English Nation,* first published in 1589, and then in a much enlarged form in 1598–1600. Hakluyt was born in London in 1552. His name appeared in a wide variety of spellings in his own day, indicating a wide variety of pronunciations. Pronunciation today varies from "Hackle-wit" to "Hack-loo-it" and "Hacklit." Possibly Hakluyt himself pronounced it "Hackloot" or "Hacklut."

Hakluyt described how his interest in voyaging and exploration was awakened when as a schoolboy at Westminster he visited his lawyer cousin (also called Richard Hakluyt) and found on his table "certain books of cosmography, with an universal map." The young Hakluyt resolved that he would "by God's assistance prosecute that knowledge and kind of literature." Remaining at Oxford as a student of Christ Church, Hakluyt was ordained in the Church of England, and in 1583 went to Paris as chaplain and secretary to the English ambassador. He gave up his fellowship at Oxford in 1586, married, and was appointed rector at Wetheringsett in Suffolk. He had a number of additional ecclesiastical appointments, but his real life was not in the church but in advancing the maritime activities of England. He became acquainted, he wrote, "with the chiefest captains at sea, the greatest merchants, and the best mariners of our nation." He was associated with the major figures organizing oversea expansion, such as Sir Humphrey Gilbert and Sir Walter Ralegh; with the scholars who advised them, John Dee and Thomas Hariot; and with the statesmen who supported them, particularly Sir Francis Walsingham. He sought out every piece of writing (he was an excellent linguist) relating to exploration, discovery, trade, and settlement. He made it his business, especially while he was in Paris, to find out not only what every European nation had achieved across the seas, but what was being thought or planned.

At the root of his life's work lay the passion of the historian to discover and make available the documents of discovery. He spoke of restless nights and painful days, long and chargeable journeys, to rescue records "from obscurity and perishing." But to establish an archive of voyaging was not an end but a beginning. The archive was a body of knowledge contributing to "the certain and full discovery of the world," and, more immediately, providing navigators, merchants, and politicians with vital information about conditions in distant seas and territories, helping them to devise and shape their own activities. The activities Hakluyt hoped to promote were intended to enlarge English power in the New World and further English trade through settlement overseas.

England had come late to the feast of European expansion, but, Hakluyt believed, not too late. The exploits of Francis Drake, Martin Frobisher, and Richard Hawkins in the 1570s showed the mettle of the English. For Hakluyt these were only a part of a long story of English endeavour and could be the prelude to England's challenge to Spain as a world power.

Hakluyt's views on the development of England's oversea interests are best seen in his *Discourse on Western Planting,* a memorandum submitted to Queen Elizabeth I "at the request and direction" of Sir Walter Ralegh, urging her to establish colonies in North America. Basic in Hakluyt's argument is the need to expand England's trade, particularly the export of finished woolen cloth. His starting

H

point is an England in decay, needing the impetus of over-sea development to energize the young and find employment either at home or in the new colonies for people of all trades and professions—from shipwrights to astronomers. In particular, colonization would solve the pressing problem of England's "superfluous" people, the "multitude of loiterers and idle vagabonds" who spent their time pilfering and thieving. Instead of pining in prison or being hanged, they could live out useful lives in the colonies.

He paints a lyrical picture of the riches of North America, awaiting the arrival of the English to develop them. The inhabitants are not much talked of, although a main purpose of the imperial enterprise is their conversion to Christianity. In southern parts the savages will welcome them because of the cruelty of Spanish rule. And, of course, the reduction of the pride and power of Spain—"the supporter of the great Antichrist of Rome"—was in itself a sufficient reason for England to commit itself to the North American enterprise.

In making a collection of voyage-narratives, Hakluyt was not an innovator. He acknowledges his debt to G.B. Ramusio, whose *Navigationi et viaggi* appeared in 1550–1559. In England, Richard Eden and Richard Willis had made compilations of travels. But Hakluyt's work outdistanced his predecessors as William Shakespeare's English history plays outdistanced those of his competitors, and it performed a function similar to that of Shakespeare's history plays: it created a body of writing that defined the nation, giving it an identity and a sense of destiny, as was recognized at the time by Gabriel Harvey.

Divers Voyages touching the Discovery of America, Hakluyt's first compilation, published in 1582, had only a limited scope. The first edition of *Principal Navigations* in 1589 covered the entire globe and contained more than 250 items. Many of these were quite small: letters, notes, lists, and the like, but there were more than sixty substantial accounts of voyages. Although we are given the circumnavigations of Drake and Thomas Cavendish and the efforts of Frobisher and John Davis to discover the Northwest Passage, special attention is devoted to the exploration of Russia and Persia by Sir Hugh Willoughby, Anthony Jenkinson, and others.

The three volumes of the final edition of *Principal Navigations of the English Nation* published in 1598, 1599, and 1600, contain over a million and a half words, more than doubling the size of the earlier edition. While there are many accounts of failure as well as success, the work as a

whole stood for centuries as the classic repository of stories of courage, daring, and persistence in the building of the British Empire. Hakluyt's faith in the future of his country's expansion was justified and his work made a distinct contribution to that expansion. Now that the empire is no more, *Principal Navigations* remains an archive of great historical importance, and a collection of narratives of lived-through action of unique literary value.

Hakluyt continued to collect voyage-accounts, but he had no further publication, and his materials passed to Samuel Purchas, who published them in *Hakluytus Posthumus, or Purchas his Pilgrims* in 1625. Hakluyt died in 1616 and was buried in Westminster Abbey.

BIBLIOGRAPHY
Parks, G.B. *Richard Hakluyt and the English Voyages.* 1928; 2nd edition, 1961.
Quinn, D.B., ed. *The Hakluyt Handbook.* 1974.
Taylor, E.G.R., ed. *The Original Writings and Correspondence of the Two Richard Hakluyts.* 1935.

Philip Edwards

SEE ALSO
Colonial Development; Dee, John; Discovery and Exploration; Drake, Francis; Harvey, Gabriel; Hawkins, Richard; Frobisher, Martin; Hariot, Thomas; Gilbert, Humphrey; Ralegh, Walter; Travel Literature; Walsingham, Francis

Hall, Edward (1497–1547)

Edward Hall is best known for his history of fifteenth- and early sixteenth-century England, *The Union of the Two Noble and Illustrate Families of Lancaster & York* (1548), although the book was only part of a long career in the service of the city of London and in the House of Commons. Hall was born in London, the son of a well-to-do merchant, and was educated at Eton College and King's College, Cambridge (B.A., 1518); he then read law at Gray's Inn, where he ultimately attained the honor of becoming a reader (1533, 1540). His legal training led to his appointment as common serjeant of London, 1533–35, then undersheriff from 1535 until his death. He was elected a member of Parliament from the borough of Much Wenlock in 1529, and took an active part in the debates that led to the passage of Henry VIII's reformation statutes, of which he left an eyewitness record in his chronicle. He probably sat for Much Wenlock again in

1536 and perhaps 1539, then for Bridgnorth in 1542 and 1545. He consistently opposed ecclesiastical pomp and power (for him, personified in Cardinal Thomas Wolsey), a position that led him to Protestantism; no less consistently, he believed in accommodation to the royal will, a view that may have come into conflict with his religious beliefs when he took on the post of a commissioner to enforce the anti-Protestant Six Articles (1541, 1547).

Hall's *Union,* written in the vernacular and secular in tone, was a history of a sort not hitherto seen in England. Unlike his predecessors, Hall limited his subject to a relatively brief period, and organized it as a story. In accordance with his belief in the power of the royal will, Hall made the monarchs the "heroes" of his tale. Thus he began the book with a brief account of the end of Richard II's reign, entitled "An introduction into the division of the two houses of Lancaster and York," then followed it with "The unquiet time of king Henry the fourth." After recounting the adventures of Henry V and the misadventures of Henry VI, he continued with the "prosperous" reign of Edward IV and the "pitiful" life of Edward V (the elder of the princes in the Tower). Like Thomas More, Hall saw Richard III's reign as tragic; he contrasted it to the "politic governance" of Richard's successor, Henry VII. He then concluded his drama of the Wars of the Roses with the "triumphant" reign of Henry VIII, who reunited the kingdom by combining the blood of the two warring houses.

For his account of the fifteenth century, Hall was dependent on the London chronicles (such as that of Robert Fabyan), on the Latin *Anglica Historia* of Polydore Vergil, and on various French histories. In addition, perhaps influenced through an acquaintance with Fabyan, one of whose sons had been apprenticed to Hall's father, the young Hall had been collecting material on current events; his position in London also gave him access to the city's archives. Like many of his predecessors, Hall had a passion for ceremony, both urban and royal, and included lengthy and detailed descriptions of processions, tournaments, and state occasions (as, for example, the Field of the Cloth of Gold) in his history.

Around 1532, Hall's passion for his chronicle flagged somewhat, although he continued to add materials until 1544, and he never drew the manuscript to a close. Instead, he willed it to his friend, the printer Richard Grafton, who put it in order, finished it, and published it in 1548. Hall's story, both in its content and its drama, influenced all subsequent Tudor historians, and provided the foundation for William Shakespeare's account, in his

two tetralogies, of the same period. In addition, Hall's eyewitness reports provide one of the best sources for the beginnings of the Henrician Reformation.

BIBLIOGRAPHY

Bindoff, S.T., ed. *The House of Commons, 1509–1558.* 3 vols. 1981.

Ellis, Henry, ed. *The Union of the Two Noble and Illustrate Families of Lancaster & York* (1548, 1550). 1811; repr. 1965.

Levy, F.J. *Tudor Historical Thought.* 1967.

Pollard, A.F. "Edward Hall's Will and Chronicle." *Bulletin of the Institute of Historical Research,* vol. 9 (1931–1932), pp. 171–177.

Pollard, Graham. "The Bibliographical History of Hall's Chronicle." *Bulletin of the Institute of Historical Research,* vol. 10 (1932–1933), pp. 12–17.

F.J. Levy

SEE ALSO

Fabyan, Robert; Field of the Cloth of Gold; Grafton, Richard; Henry VII; Henry VIII; History, Writing of; Shakespeare, William; Vergil, Polydore

Hall, Joseph (1574–1656)

A satirist and religious writer, Joseph Hall was born to middle-class parents at Bristow Park in Ashby-de-la-Zouch, Leicestershire, in 1574. His father, John Hall, was a bailiff for the earl of Huntingdon. His mother, Winifride, was later described by Hall as unfalteringly devout in her Puritan beliefs, spending the majority of her day in private prayer. This early religious influence would not be lost on young Joseph. He attended grammar school in Ashby, engaging in a strict Puritan curriculum, an education that his mother's spiritual advisor, Anthony Gilby, had a large part in mandating. After grammar school and at the urging of his older brother, Hall was enrolled at Emmanuel College, Cambridge, in 1589. His tutor, interestingly enough, was Nathaniel Gilby, son of Anthony. Hall remained at Cambridge for the next thirteen years, and was elected fellow in 1595. He graduated B.A. in 1592, M.A. in 1596, took holy orders in 1600, received his B.D. in 1603 and D.D. in 1610. In late 1601, Hall left Cambridge to assume the rectory of Hawstead in Suffolk. Two years later he married Elizabeth Winniff. In 1607, Hall moved to Waltham Holy Cross in Essex as rector. With his influence as both preacher and writer burgeoning, Hall was appointed one of twelve

H

chaplains to Prince Henry at Richmond Palace. With his ecclesiastical career in its maturity, Hall was offered the bishopric of Gloucester in 1624, which he refused. Three years later he accepted the bishopric of Exeter.

An important figure in both religious and literary circles of late Tudor and early Stuart England, Joseph Hall has since faded into the background of present studies. A moderate Puritan attacked by Anglicans, Brownists, and Presbyterians alike, Hall responded to this criticism with his pen, producing a wide array of literary pieces; he is often referred to as the first or "father of" English satire, but his work includes pastoral poetry (now lost), religious treatises and meditations, as well as the beginnings of a new genre in familiar epistles. His thorough knowledge of classical literature and rhetoric coupled with his utterly moral and stoic countenance earned him respect in the highest political circles as a preacher, writer, thinker, and cleric. His constant faith won him both friends and patrons, and enemies and political opponents, among them John Donne, James I, and John Marston. With the outbreak of political upheaval in 1641, Hall was stripped of his bishopric, twice imprisoned in the Tower of London, and evicted from his home. He died, still writing prolifically, and was buried in a country churchyard without the reverence or ceremony due a man of such intellect and influence.

Virgidemiarum, two volumes published in 1597 and 1598, was a collection of "Toothlesse" and "Byting" formal verse satires in the Juvenalian style, the first of its kind in English. The publication and proclamation, as well as the indirect insults within the satires, apparently angered John Marston, whose volume of satires came out in 1598 openly attacking Hall. Hall's quick burst onto the literary scene was rivaled in celerity by his leave of it; there would be only one more purely literary work before Hall's escape into devotional writing. *Mundus Alter et Idem,* a prose satire recounting the travels of a Cambridge scholar in Antarctica was published in 1605, but was most likely written much earlier; about this time Hall began his experimentation with the meditation as a genre. *Meditations and Vowes, Divine and Morall* (1605), *The Arte of Meditation* (1606), and *Heaven upon Earth* (1606), were all published while he held the rectory of Hawstead in Suffolk, and they helped Hall gain more lucrative employment as chaplain to a baron and rector of Waltham Holy Cross in Essex in 1607. Hall's final two literary contributions came in 1608 when he published *Characters of Vertues and Vices* and began publishing *Epistles.*

BIBLIOGRAPHY

Kinlock, Tom Fleming. *The Life and Works of Joseph Hall, 1574–1656.* 1951.

Tourney, Leonard D. *Joseph Hall.* Twayne English Authors. 1979.

Chew, Audrey. "Joseph Hall and John Milton." *Journal of Literary History,* vol. 17, pp. 274–295.

Corthell, Ronald J. "Beginning as a Satirist: Joseph Hall's *Virgidemiarum Six Bookes.*" *Studies in English Literature, 1500–1900,* vol. 23, pp. 47–60.

———. "Joseph Hall and Protestant Meditation." *Texas Studies in Literature and Language,* vol. 20, pp. 367–385.

Jensen, Ejner J. "Hall and Marston: The Role of the Satirist." *Satire Newsletter,* vol. 4, pp. 72–83.

McCabe, Richard. *Joseph Hall: A Study in Satire and Meditation.* 1982.

Jason Drake

SEE ALSO
Marston, John; Satire

Hamilton Family

As in France, so in Scotland: great magnate families were still crucial to the politics of the realm. France had the families of Guise, Bourbon, and Montmorency; Scotland the Campbells, the Gordons, and the Hamiltons, the cadet branches of the royal house of Stuart. The point is worth emphasizing, because this contrasts with the situation in England, where kin solidarity was no longer the force it had been. To interested English observers, especially in the late sixteenth century when it became likely that a Scottish monarch would succeed Elizabeth, the power of the great Scottish families was seen as primitive and dangerous. It was, in fact, another way in which Scotland was closer to Europe than England; as with its Roman law, its Parliament that was a meeting of the three estates, so with its aristocratic kindreds: Scotland operated on a European model, and it was England that was out of line.

Nevertheless, the preeminent position of the Hamiltons had one curious feature. Although birth was the original passport to power, it also helped considerably if the leading members of the great families had some intelligence to help them along. In the case of the Hamiltons, the heads of the kin, the three earls of Arran—all called James—who held the title between 1503 and 1586, were not impressive figures. The first made no particular impact except as something of a troublemaker during the minority of James V, most notably in the most sensational brawl experienced in the streets of Edinburgh, "Cleanse the Causeway" in 1520, between the Hamiltons and their rivals for the provostship, the Douglases. The second James became regent of Scotland after the death of James V in 1542. He was one of the most dithering creatures ever to wield power in Scotland. In 1543, he supported the Protestants, to their considerable if very short-lived joy. But as even he seems to have been uncertain of what he was, he was no man to give a lead to any party, Protestant or Catholic, pro-English or pro-French. He lost the regency to the much more effective Mary of Guise, French and Catholic mother of Mary Queen of Scots, in 1554, by which time the English aggression of the 1540s had driven the Scots back to their Auld Alliance with France. Arran was an important enough figure to be wooed by the French with a French title; in 1549, he became duc de Châtelherault. But his ability never matched his lofty ambition. Nor was he fortunate in his heir. He dreamed of marrying his son to Mary Queen of Scots or to Elizabeth I, an unrealistic vision, given Elizabeth's predilection for virginity, but all the more unlikely in both cases because this unfortunate James was insane. The pattern was to be repeated in the mid-seventeenth century; James, the second marquis of Hamilton, was Charles I's closest Scottish advisor, inept and unreliable and eventually to come to grief like his royal master.

Why, then, were the Hamiltons so prominent? One reason was their proximity to the throne. James, the first earl of Arran, was the son of James Lord Hamilton and Mary, daughter of James II. In typical Hamilton fashion, they complicated their position; there was doubt over the validity of the divorce between James, first earl of Arran, and his first wife, Elizabeth Home, and therefore of the legitimacy of heirs by his second wife, Janet Beaton. This produced rivalry between them and the Stuarts, earls of Lennox, also close to the throne because of the marriage of Matthew, second earl of Lennox, to Elizabeth Hamilton, sister of the first earl; and that family's standing was enhanced by the marriage of Matthew's grandson, Matthew, fourth earl, to Margaret Douglas, daughter of James IV's widow, Margaret Tudor, and her second husband, Archibald, earl of Angus. It was through that marriage that their son, Henry, Lord Darnley, second husband of Mary Queen of Scots, had a place in the English succession. More generally, while the Hamiltons were normally regarded as heirs presumptive, there was always a shadow of doubt. But they could not be disregarded.

Moreover, the family did produce some remarkable men. One, Sir James Hamilton of Finnart, was, in fact, all too successful; highly able, highly ambitious, very close to James V and his master of works, he built not only for the king but for himself, leaving a lasting monument in his remarkable castle of Craignethan, erected to withstand artillery, and the first castle in Scotland to contain the Italian carponier, a stone-vaulted firing gallery. But he made the mistake of amassing a considerable fortune, a dangerous pursuit for a subject, even a favorite, of an avaricious king; all the Stuart monarchs were greedy for money, but none more so than James V, and in 1539, Hamilton fell from favor and on some trumped-up charge was conveniently forfeited and executed.

Another was John, bastard half-brother of James, second earl of Arran, abbot of Paisely, and last Catholic archbishop of St. Andrews, and the real power behind the regent; during his pro-English period, it was said of Arran that "What the English lords decide him to do one day, the abbot changes the next." He had a reputation as a *politique;* and indeed, it was his involvement in the power struggle between king's and queen's men after the downfall of Mary that brought him to the gallows in 1571. But he deserves much credit as a churchman. In 1549, only four years after the opening session of the Council of Trent, he held the first of three reforming councils in Scotland, the others meeting in 1552 and 1559. Scotland therefore had its Counter Reformation before its Reformation; and as late as 1559, it looked as though it would succeed.

Their other great source of strength was their massive solidarity. Ties of kin mattered in any Scottish family. Even so, the Hamiltons were singled out; the contemporary *Diurnal of Occurents* gives an account of the individual major players in sixteenth-century Scotland, but repeatedly refers to "the haill Hamiltonis" (the whole Hamiltons). Thus could they compensate for the weakness of the heads of the house; thus were they collectively impressive and massively important.

BIBLIOGRAPHY

Donaldson, G. *Scotland: James V–James VII.* 1965.
———. *All the Queen's Men.* 1983.
Lynch, M. *Scotland: A New History.* 1991.
McKean, C. "Hamilton of Finnart." *History Today,* vol. 43, January 1993, pp. 42–47.

Jenny Wormald

SEE ALSO

Darnley, Henry; Hamilton, Patrick; Scotland, History of

Hamilton, James, Earl of Arran

See Hamilton Family

H

Hamilton, Patrick (c. 1504–1528)

Patrick Hamilton was the protomartyr of Scottish Protestantism. The exact date and place of his birth are unknown. He belonged to one of the most powerful families of Scotland. In 1517, Hamilton was made abbot of Ferne in Ross-shire. He studied at Paris, where he became acquainted with the writings of Martin Luther and graduated M.A. in 1520. He left Paris in 1523 and went to Louvain, where he came under the influence of Desiderius Erasmus and the new humanism. He returned later that year to Scotland to teach in the faculty of arts at St. Andrews. In 1526, Hamilton began to show open sympathy with proscribed Lutheran doctrines, and he was called before James Beaton, archbishop of St. Andrews, who formally charged him with heresy. Hamilton fled in the spring of 1527 to Wittenberg, where he met Luther and Philipp Melanchthon. Later that year he enrolled at the new university of Marburg, where he became acquainted with William Tyndale and other leading humanists. Here he drew up a series of theses, *Loci Communes,* which were later translated into English. These theses, known as "Patrick's Places," set forth basic principles of the Reformation and became a cornerstone of Protestant theology both in Scotland and England. In the autumn of 1527 Hamilton returned to Scotland. Early the following year he was again brought before Beaton and his council. After a month's reprieve, he was condemned in a formal trial for the heresy of his Protestant views, and was burned at the stake in St. Andrews on February 29, 1528.

BIBLIOGRAPHY

Burleigh, J.H.S. *A Church History of Scotland.* 1960.
Cameron, A., ed. *Patrick Hamilton: First Scottish Martyr of the Reformation.* 1929.
Donaldson, Gordon. *The Scottish Reformation.* 1960.
Kay, D.M. *Patrick Hamilton: Scottish Martyr, 1528.* 1929.

Lee W. Gibbs

SEE ALSO

Church of Scotland; Erasmus, Desiderius; Hamilton Family; Humanism; Lutheranism; Reformation, English; Tyndale, William

Hampton Court Palace

See Royal Palaces

Handwriting

The handwriting of the Elizabethan age is distinguished by both its diversity and formality. For private communication not directed at some specific official purpose, the educated Elizabethan normally had and practiced at least two hands, and those engaged in official business usually had even more.

The most common private hand during this period, that used by almost any writer of English for ordinary matters (letters, poetic manuscripts, laundry lists, and the like) was called secretary hand. It is, to the untrained modern reader, almost illegible. However, it was a formalized script, and John Baildon and Jehan de Beauchesne produced a specimen page of it in their *Book Containing Diverse Sortes of Handes* in 1571. It was a very fast cursive script and its most unusual letter is the lower case *h,* which can resemble a rather large and badly made *y* or 3. It was, however, the workaday hand for the English until well into the seventeenth century. The educated Elizabethan also wrote an italic hand. This is a hand that has survived to the present day and was the basis for the development of italic type. It was a much clearer hand than secretary and was usually reserved for formal purposes (letters to officials, patrons, and people one needed to impress), but was also employed in literary manuscripts in much the same way that italic type is used by printers today. Italic was also regularly used by scribes in the production of fair copy manuscripts for clients and by authors producing their own fair copies. One of its most famous practitioners was the poet and scribe Ralph Crane (fl. 1625), who produced a number of dramatic manuscripts that still survive. An Elizabethan writer would usually produce drafts of his document in secretary hand and then make a clean copy in italic. However, toward the end of the period a mixed hand began to develop that had the characteristics of both secretary and italic, and during the seventeenth century this mixed version supplanted secretary.

There were also the older and more formal public hands used for specific kinds of official business. These had arisen during the Middle Ages, and some, for example chancery hand, survived into the twentieth century. The names of these hands indicate the official purposes for which they were intended: engrossing, chancery, king's remembrancer, pipe office, legal, common pleas, lord treasurers, and court (all these hands are often referred to in combination as court hand). They were all very regular, almost anticursive, and prone to have a large number of specialized abbreviations and marks of abbreviation.

The private hands adopted some of the public hands' abbreviations so that, for example, the syllable "pro" became a *p* or double *p* with the vertical member crossed, and *et caetera* became first *etc.* and finally something that resembled *&c.* Various titles were abbreviated in all hands, typically by leaving out all letters save for the first and last one or two, the latter being written as superior letters, so that, for example, Sir became *Sr,* and Lordship became *Lorp,* or even *Lp.* Although such shortcuts were, of necessity, common to all writers of the public hands, the possibilities for variations and additions in the private hands were nearly as many as there were writers of them.

By 1650, the mixed hand had so completely taken over in private use that manuscripts from then on can be quite legible to the modern reader, saving the abbreviations. Of course, as with all handwriting at all times, there were those who wrote good clear hands and those who wrote slovenly hands, though the Elizabethan age seems to have placed much more emphasis on penmanship than does our own.

BIBLIOGRAPHY

Baildon, John, and Jehan de Beauchesne. *A Book Containing Diverse Sortes of Handes.* 1571.

Dawson, Giles, and Laetitia Kennedy-Skipton. *Elizabethan Handwriting: 1500–1650.* 1966.

Hector, L.C. *The Handwriting of English Documents.* 1966.

Ison, Alf. *A Secretary Hand ABC Book.* 1982.

Munby, Lionel. *Reading Tudor and Stuart Handwriting. Learning Local History,* vol. 1. 1988.

Petty, Anthony G. *English Literary Hands from Chaucer to Dryden.* 1977.

Preston, Jean F., and Laetitia Yeandle. *English Handwriting, 1400–1650.* 1992.

Tannenbaum, Samuel A. *The Handwriting of the Renaissance.* 1930.

William Proctor Williams

SEE ALSO
Manuscripts

Hardwick, Elizabeth (c. 1527–1608)

Bess of Hardwick came of the minor gentry, but her beauty, vitality, and ambition allowed her to make a series of four marriages, each more distinguished than the last, that left her one of the richest people in England, keeper and confidante of the imprisoned Mary Queen of Scots, grandmother of a prominent claimant to the throne, and one of the great builders and patrons of the arts in this or any period. From the sons of her second marriage, to Sir William Cavendish (1547), sprang three great dynasties, dukes of Devonshire, of Newcastle, and of Portland. Her daughter Elizabeth furtively married Charles Stuart, brother to Mary's husband Henry Darnley and grandson of Margaret Tudor; they produced a daughter, Arbella, of whom Bess became guardian and who was a center of intrigue and speculation as a major claimant to the throne after Elizabeth I until her death in the Tower in 1615. Bess's fourth husband, the immensely wealthy George Talbot, earl of Shrewsbury, became custodian of Mary Queen of Scots in 1569; the

Hardwick Hall, Derbyshire (c. 1597). The finest and best preserved of the great Elizabethan country houses. By permission of Christy Anderson.

H

two women talked and embroidered together as they moved from house to house until 1584, three years before Mary's death, when rumors of an affair between Mary and Talbot and other frictions arose. Thereafter Mary had different custodians and the Shrewsburys largely lived apart.

Almost from the beginning Bess bought land and built or remodeled houses—Chatsworth, Bolsover, Worksop Manor. Her association with the architect Robert Smythson was particularly fruitful; their joint masterpiece, Hardwick Hall, still sits splendidly on its Derbyshire hilltop, known then for its extensive use of glass, and its owner's initials, three feet high, in the balustrade along the roof, proclaiming her greatness for miles around.

BIBLIOGRAPHY

Collinson, Patrick. *The English Captivity of Mary Queen of Scots.* Sheffield History Pamphlets. 1987.

Durant, David N. *Bess of Hardwick: Portrait of an Elizabethan Dynast.* 1978.

David Evett

SEE ALSO
Architecture; Mary Queen of Scots; Talbot Family; illustration for Hardwick Hall

Harington, John (1560–1612)

Translator and classicist, Sir John Harington (knighted in 1599) was the eldest son of a family with strong ties to the court. His father, also John Harington, had been active in the service of Henry VIII, and married an illegitimate daughter of the king. Harington senior was later a confidential agent of Sir Thomas Seymour. In this capacity he was able to serve Princess Elizabeth, the future queen. After his first wife's death this John Harington married Isabel, daughter of Sir John Markham, who had been lieutenant of the Tower when Harington was imprisoned there at the time of Seymour's disgrace. Isabel herself was a maid of honor to Elizabeth. Through his father's first wife, John Harington, junior, inherited estates in Somerset and Berkshire, and through his parents' connection with the queen he was made her godson, and acquired favor at court that served him well throughout her reign.

After Eton and Cambridge, the younger Harington went to Lincoln's Inn to study law. He was there in 1582 when his father died, and he left his legal studies to enter into his estate. He married Mary Rogers, daughter of a local landowner, in 1583. (They had eleven children, two of whom died at birth.) In 1586, he tried his luck as a

colonist in Ireland. In these years he was completing the large house at Kelston, Somerset, begun by his father. This boasted a fountain under which the queen dined on her visit to the house in 1592. Harington was often at court in this period, wrote satirical poems and prose, translated Ariosto, and conducted a scriptorium in his house, where a manuscript copy of Sidney's *Arcadia* was made that still survives. In 1599, the queen ordered him to Ireland with the expedition of Robert Devereux, the earl of Essex; Harington saw active service, but he came under the general cloud caused by what the queen saw as Essex's presumption, and his knighthood, bestowed by Essex in the field, was a particularly sore point. Harington draws on the experience of his two visits to Ireland in his *Short View of the State of Ireland* (1605).

Under James, Harington continued to seek preferment, in part through writings, such as his translations of the Psalms and of a book of the *Aeneid,* and his *Supplie,* or supplement to a collection of lives of English bishops. He spent a period in debtor's prison as guarantor of a debt of his uncle's, and involved himself in complex legal and financial schemes, such as a proposal to have Thomas Sutton leave his immense wealth to Charles, duke of York.

Harington's writing attracted more notoriety than fame in his lifetime and has continued to be difficult to categorize satisfactorily. His translation of Ariosto, published in 1591, seems to have begun as a court prank; a version of one salacious section of the poem circulated at court and caused the queen to banish him to the country, with the penance of translating the poem in its entirety (there are forty-six books and more than 4,000 stanzas). The translation itself is an obvious and considerable achievement, and has had an impact on writers from John Milton to Antony Powell; but a great deal of Harington's effort also went into commentary and annotation and into the physical appearance of his book, with engravings and a complicated set of marginal and end-of-canto notes, and these have proved harder to assimilate into the literary history of the period. Harington's epigrams, written mainly in the 1590s, and pioneers in a revival of the genre, were dismissed by Ben Jonson as mere "Narrations." They vary from the distinctly homely and even scatological to something more urbane and closer to Martial, Harington's acknowledged model. One of them is still widely anthologized: "Treason doth never prosper, what's the reason? / For if it prosper, none dare call it treason."

Most puzzling of all from the point of view of genre and evaluation is *The Metamorphosis of Ajax* (1596),

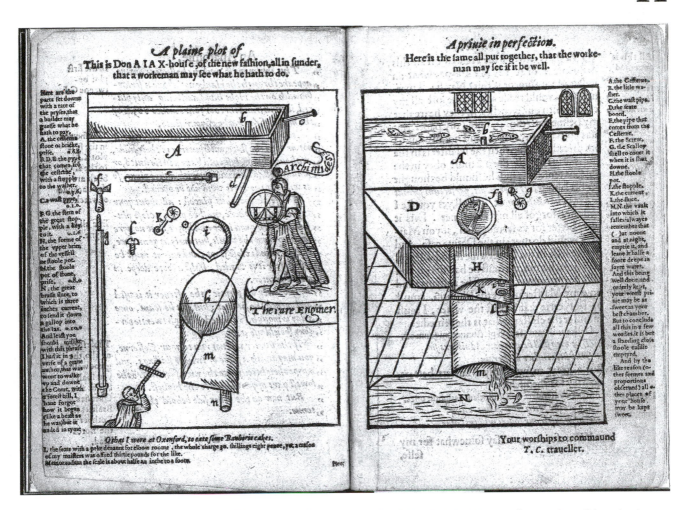

John Harington, *The Parts of a Privy*. From *The Anatomie of the metamorphosed Ajax* (1596). Harington's invention of the privy is crudely illustrated by this instructional page, with its parts illustrated, labeled, and described in the text along with their estimated cost. Archimedes, "the rare engineer," appears to hold an image of a cistern, presumably the basis for the "cesterne stone or brick pryfe" and "stoole pot." Reproduced from the original by permission of the Henry E. Huntington Library and Art Gallery.

170-plus octavo pages of anecdote, classical allusion, technical exposition, topical reference, and moralizing, based on the presentation of a new form of the privy, with a flush and a seal. There are diagrams to show how to construct the device (and there is evidence that some were actually put together and installed), but the point of Harington's book seems rather to exploit the metaphor of the reformed privy. Finally, he says, reformed souls are more important than improved sanitation, and he aims to shock Puritanical readers into acknowledging that it is hypocrisy to be aghast at the mention of excretion while freely tolerating sin.

Harington's frankness, which made it hard for his contemporaries to take him seriously, is also the basis for his continuing importance. An impulse to record the details of his own experience and attitudes, together with his privileged social position, meant that he created over the years a commentary on his times that is of exceptional interest. To him, for example, we owe the only surviving instance of an Elizabethan author's instruction to his printer (in a manuscript of the translation of *Orlando Furioso*); remarkable descriptions of Elizabeth's tormented state at the end of her life (in his letters); numerous acerbic reflections on the continuing depredations of church property after the Reformation (in his *Supplie*); a composite portrait of the high-spirited, hedonist, and rashly ambitious Sir Walter Ralegh (in the numerous epigrams involving "Paulus"); and a heartfelt account of the tedium of waiting at court (in his *Treatise on Playe*). Moreover, from the apparatus to his Ariosto, and the essays appended to his translation of Vergil, and from what we know of other activities, we can put together a detailed

H

picture of one version of the Elizabethan reader: mindful of the ultimate worthlessness of secular literature; ever alert for entertainment, and for local application; respectful of readings that moralize by way of allegory, but more interested in fictive actions as simply instructive examples of good and bad behavior; and a collector of printed plays who allows himself only a single reference to a character from Shakespeare (Falstaff, mentioned disapprovingly in an essay in his *Aeneid*).

BIBLIOGRAPHY

Cauchi, Simon. "Recent Studies in Sir John Harington." *English Literary Renaissance,* vol. 25, pp. 112–125.

Craig, D.H. *Sir John Harington.* 1985.

Croft, P.J. "Sir John Harington's Manuscript of Sir Philip Sidney's *Arcadia." Literary Autographs: Papers Read at a Clark Library Seminar.* 1983.

Harington, Sir John, trans. *Orlando Furioso in English Heroical Verse.* Robert McNulty, ed. 1972.

———, trans. *The Sixth Book of Virgil's* Aeneid. Simon Cauchi, ed. 1991.

———. *A Supplie or Addicion to the Catalogue of Bishops, to the Yeare 1608.* R.H. Miller, ed. 1979.

———. *A New Discourse of a Stale Subject, Called the Metamorphosis of Ajax.* Elizabeth Story Donno, ed. 1962.

May, Steven W. *The Elizabethan Courtier Poets: The Poems and Their Contexts.* 1991.

McClure, Norman Egbert, ed. *The Letters & Epigrams of Sir John Harington Together with* The Prayse of Private Life. 1930.

Nelson, T.G.A. "Sir John Harington and the Renaissance Debate over Allegory." *Studies in Philology,* vol. 82, pp. 359–379.

D. Hugh Craig

SEE ALSO

Classical Literature, English Translations; Devereux, Robert; Epigrams; Sidney, Philip

Hariot, Thomas (1560–1621)

Recognized by his contemporaries as a leading mathematician, astronomer, and navigational expert, Thomas Hariot remains one of the most intriguing figures of late Tudor and early Stuart England. Born into a humble Oxford family in 1560, Hariot attended St. Mary's Hall at Oxford between 1577 and 1580. After receiving his B.A. he moved to London, where he probably collaborated in the navigational enterprises of Sir Humphrey Gilbert and his half-brother, Sir Walter Raleigh, under the supervision of experts like John Dee and the two Richard Hakluyts. In 1584, Ralegh recruited Hariot to provide tutoring in matters connected with deep-sea navigation, and the following year he participated in the second voyage launched by Ralegh to the coasts of North America. Led by Richard Grenville and Ralph Lane, a party of more than 100 men was left on Roanoke Island, off North Carolina, to explore, map, and determine the possibilities of establishing the first English colony in the New World. Hariot and John White were appointed scientific observers in the expedition, and their collaboration resulted in the most influential work on the New World in late sixteenth-century England. First published in 1588, Hariot's *A Brief and True Report of the New Found Land of Virginia* stands as the most detailed description of the resources to be enjoyed in the New World and, more importantly, as one of the most influential accounts of the natives' customs and beliefs. Despite its clearly propagandistic character, the *Report* was widely circulated and its contents helped to create a feeling of optimism toward England's incipient plans of overseas expansion. The younger Richard Hakluyt also contributed to Hariot's reputation as a leading expert in New World affairs after his inclusion of the *Report* in his popular *Principal Navigations* (1589 and 1598–1600). Hakluyt's hand was also behind the four-language edition that the Flemish engraver and printer Theodore de Bry published in 1590; here Hariot's text was illustrated with plates engraved by de Bry after the watercolors that White made during the 1585–1586 voyage. Even though Hariot never left England again, his expertise allowed him to act as consultant and promoter of subsequent expeditions to the New World.

After his return from Virginia Hariot remained with Ralegh, not only as his scientific advisor but also aiding him in the management of both his English and Irish estates. While still in Ralegh's service, Hariot also started working under the patronage of Henry Percy, ninth earl of Northumberland, around 1593. His second patron was known as the "Wizard Earl" due to his interest in the new sciences, and Hariot, together with two of his fellows at Oxford, Walter Warner and Robert Hues, became known as one of the earl's "Three Magi." Soon after entering his service Hariot took up rooms at Syon House, the earl's residence, establishing his study there. Almost until the end of his life Hariot faithfully served his two powerful patrons, enjoying from both of them large pensions and grants of land that allowed him to pursue his scientific interests. But these associations also brought complications. Since 1592, Hariot was the target of repeated attacks for his supposed unorthodox doctrines; he was accused of instigating Ralegh's atheistic beliefs. He also had to suffer imprisonment at Gatehouse between late 1605 and early 1606 after Northumberland was accused of participation in the Gunpowder Plot and condemned to life in the Tower. Despite these accusations, however, Hariot was never officially investigated or condemned for charges of unorthodoxy.

With both his patrons in the Tower, Hariot managed to combine his duties toward them with a rich and fruitful scientific career. Even though he published only the *Report* during his lifetime, Hariot is now known to have pioneered in such disciplines as mathematics, optics, astronomy, ballistics, navigation, and magnetism. His only other published work, the treatise on algebra entitled *Artis Analyticae Praxis,* appeared posthumously in 1631 through the efforts of his friend Warner. In algebra, Hariot is credited with having introduced the signs for "greater than" (>) and "less than" (>); he is also responsible for popularizing the symbols for equivalence (=) and the square root ($\sqrt{}$), and for realizing the possibility of constructing a workable number system based on 2 instead of 10—a binary notation that in our time has led to the development of electronic computers. In navigation, he improved the methods of calculating latitude at sea and conducted innovative work to improve shipbuilding and the selection of vessels. In optics, he investigated theories of the atomic structure of matter by studying the refraction of light passing through media of various densities; between 1606 and 1609, Johannes Kepler corresponded with him on optical matters, admitting to the Englishman's authority in these. Around 1604, Hariot employed Christopher Tooke, a lens grinder who later on would help him in the building of telescopes, independently of Galileo. In 1607, he observed the comet later known as Halley's. As early as July 1609, Hariot conducted his first telescopic observations of the moon, which he documented with impressively detailed drawings. Closely following Galileo's published work he observed the satellites circling Jupiter, and in December 1611, he began observing sunspots, preceding Galileo, Scheiner, and others who claimed priority for themselves. Hariot can also be considered as the first astronomer to give a reasonably accurate period for the rotation of the sun.

Around 1613, Hariot started suffering the first symptoms of the nose cancer that ultimately would kill him. Tobacco, the "commodity" that he discovered in Virginia and that he so highly praised in the *Report,* ended his life on July 2, 1621. Hariot died in London while visiting Thomas Buckner, one of the men who had accompanied him to Virginia, and he was buried the following day in the church of St. Christopher's.

BIBLIOGRAPHY
Hariot, Thomas. *A Brief and True Report of the New Found Land of Virginia.* Paul Hulton, ed. 1972.
Quinn, David B. *The Roanoke Voyages, 1584–1590.* 1955.
Rukeyser, Muriel. *The Traces of Thomas Hariot.* 1970.
Shirley, John W. *Thomas Hariot: A Biography.* 1983.
———, ed. *Thomas Hariot: Renaissance Scientist.* 1974.
Stevens, Henry. *Thomas Hariot. The Mathematician, the Philosopher, and the Scholar.* 1900.

Francisco J. Borge

SEE ALSO
Astronomy; Colonial Development; Dee, John; Engraving and Illustration; Gilbert, Sir Humphrey; Grenville, Richard; Hakluyt, Richard; Lane, Ralph; Navigation; Percy Family; Ralegh, Walter

Harrison, William (1531–1593)

Best known as the author of *An Historical Description of the Island of Britain,* William Harrison was born in London in 1535 and grew up near Cheapside, where he experienced the booming mercantile culture of England's great metropolis and capital. He credits his parents for a humanist education that began at St. Paul's, continued at the Westminster School, and culminated at Christ Church, Oxford, where he earned a B.A. in 1556 and an M.A. in 1560. He shared in the religious enthusiasms and reversals of the time, embracing Roman Catholicism under the influence of the Marian dean of Christ Church, Richard Marshall, but then more lastingly inspired by the reformers and Oxford martyrs Thomas Cranmer, Nicholas Ridley, and Hugh Latimer. His conversion took place during Mary Tudor's reign, and he subsequently noted that "if that Jezebel had reigned longer," he "would not, perhaps, have escaped harm." Under the patronage of William Brooke, Lord Cobham, Harrison became rector of the small rural parish of Radwinter in Essex, and as Brooke's chaplain he also enjoyed a taste of country-house life. In 1567, Harrison obtained a second rectory, St. Olave's in London, a post that he resigned in 1571 to become vicar of Wimbish, nearer Radwinter, having in the interim married Marion Isebrande. Meanwhile, by

H

1569, he was traveling frequently to preside in the archdeacon's court. These duties were reduced to a more reasonable load in 1570, and, by 1576, he was largely retired from service in the ecclesiastical courts. After he successfully persuaded the recusant Thomas Wiseman to conform, he was asked by the Privy Council in 1578 to confer with Rooke Greene, who was, unfortunately, more resistant. In 1583, Harrison became rector of the London church of St. Thomas the Apostle; in 1586, canon of St. George's Chapel in Windsor.

An Historical Description of the Island of Britain forms the introductory section of Raphael Holinshed's *Chronicles of England, Scotland, and Ireland* (1577). With chapters on English cities, counties, universities, castles, climate, waters, woods, wild and domesticated animals, minerals, coins, laws, punishments, poor relief, antiquities, fairs and markets, as well as on the social classes, clothing, diet, housing, and furniture of English men and women, the *Description* is an invaluable contemporary account of Tudor life and institutions. Its apparent aim is to establish the national character as a prologue to the chronicle that follows, as if to reveal the transhistorical social features of a culture, its organization, and its people before their political history is particularized in the records of individual monarchs and significant events. In fact, however, with the exception of the topographical chapters that Harrison borrowed from other authors, a dominant theme of his *Description* is change. Harrison remarks the expanding economy of the Tudor years, the upward mobility of new men, and the leading indicators of rising standards of living. He brings home to his reader the material impact of his time's social, religious, political, legal, economic, and architectural transformations. In the second (1587) edition of the *Chronicles*, Harrison's *Description* is a third longer, further documenting these changes. The 1587 revision of the three-part *Description . . . of Britain* included a title change, with "Britain" applied to the first part only and with the new title *The Description of England* for parts two and three.

Harrison had precedents: Gildas, Bede, Henry of Huntingdon, Ranulf Higden, and, latterly, the prefaces of Polydore Vergil, Richard Grafton, and John Stow. But he adopted ambitious new standards of research and compilation. He admired John Leland's manuscript notes of six years of travel around England, so much so that he apologized when he himself wrote of things he did not know "by mine own travel and eyesight." He borrowed from Leland for his topographical chapters, from Stow for lists of law terms, from Thomas Harman for the language of the rogue subculture, from John Caius for material on English dogs. The *Description* was not merely an act of antiquarian compilation, however. It is enlivened by Harrison's own observations and experiences and especially by his use of oral history. In one of his most widely cited passages, he recounts that the "old men" of his village have observed three things "marvelously altered in England within their sound remembrance": the number of chimneys erected, "amendment of lodging" (more comfortable bedding), and "exchange of vessel" (pewter tableware for wooden).

In the *Description*, Harrison refers often to what he himself regarded as his more important work, a "great Chronology." Never printed, the "Chronology" survives in three manuscript volumes at the diocesan library in Derry, Ireland, among other books deposited there by his son-in-law, the bishop of Derry. Harrison included a notice of his own birth in the "Chronology" and left a more extended autobiographical note in his copy of John Bale's *Scriptorum*. He referred to the *Description* as mere "crumbs" that "fell out" from the "Chronology." The *Description* was dedicated to his patron, a tribute that was evidently returned after his death, when Cecil lobbied Brooke on behalf of one "Mr. Ketredge," and Brooke replied that the position in question was already promised to Harrison's son, Edmund.

BIBLIOGRAPHY

Edelen, Georges, ed. *The Description of England by William Harrison.* Folger Documents of Tudor and Stuart Civilization. 1968.

———. "William Harrison (1535–1593)." *Studies in the Renaissance,* vol. 9, pp. 256–272.

Furnivall, Frederick J. *Harrison's Description of England in Shakspere's Youth.* 1877–1908.

Parry, G.J.R. *A Protestant Vision: William Harrison and the Reformation of Elizabethan England.* Cambridge Studies in the History and Theory of Politics. 1987.

Patterson, Annabel. *Reading Holinshed's Chronicles.* 1994.

Lena Cowen Orlin

SEE ALSO

Economy; Grafton, Richard; History, Writing of; Holinshed, Raphael; Leland, John; Marian Martyrs; Stowe, John; Vergil, Polydore

Harsnett, Samuel (1561–1631)

Born to a family of Calvinist bakers in Colchester, Essex, Samuel Harsnett was baptized on June 21, 1561.

Under the patronage of Richard Bridgewater, Puritan fellow of King's College, he matriculated as a sizar at King's, on September 8, 1576, but then graduated B.A. (1580–1581) and M.A. (1584) from Pembroke College, where he was successively scholar, fellow, treasurer, and master (1605–1616). Shortly after being ordained, he was disciplined by the Court of High Commission for refusing the surplice (1586), and left Cambridge to be schoolmaster in Colchester. Within two years he was back at Pembroke as a member of the newly forming high church party. In 1594, he preached a controversial sermon at Paul's Cross, "Touching Divine Grace," attacking the Calvinists. Rapid preferment followed his friend Richard Bancroft's elevation to the see of London (1597). As Bancroft's senior chaplain, Harsnett managed his campaign against the practice of exorcism (1598–1604), gathering evidence, finding witnesses, and writing two books notable for witty skepticism toward alleged miracles of every kind: *A Discovery of the Fraudulent Practises of One John Darrel* (1599), attacking Puritan dispossessors of devils, and *A Declaration of Egregious Popish Impostures* (1603), attacking Catholic exorcists. Both books were widely read. William Shakespeare read *A Declaration*; it influenced *King Lear*.

Harsnett went on to a distinguished ecclesiastical career, being successively bishop of Chichester (1610–1619), Norwich (1619–1628), and archbishop of York (1628–1631). In 1628, he put the motion in the Lords that sent the Petition of Right back to Charles I for a satisfactory answer. He died on May 25, 1631, and is buried at Chigwell, Essex.

BIBLIOGRAPHY
Brownlow, F.W. *Shakespeare, Harsnett, and the Devils of Denham.* 1993.

F.W. Brownlow

SEE ALSO
Bancroft, Richard; High Commission, Court of; Shakespeare, William; Witchcraft

Harvey, Gabriel (c. 1550–1631)

A notable figure in the academic and literary culture from the 1570s to the 1590s, Gabriel Harvey was known first as a teacher and a writer of Latin, later as a pamphleteer who engaged in a famous conflict with Thomas Nashe. He is also important to modern scholars for what is left of his library—he was a wide-ranging reader who wrote many notes in the margins of his books. Though a complex and self-regarding individual, he was a perceptive and acute observer of his age. His marginal notes give us one of the most extensive portraits of any individual of his time.

Harvey was born in Saffron Walden about the year 1550, the eldest son in the large family of a prosperous rope maker. He was educated at the local grammar school, then went to nearby Cambridge for the B.A. (1570) at Christs College, then the M.A. (1573) at Pembroke College, where he was fellow. Although a gifted scholar, Harvey was apparently difficult in his dealings with others, and his second degree was delayed slightly because of opposition in his college. Yet the next year, 1574, he was made university praelector in rhetoric and became a popular lecturer. In 1577, his first three books were published. The *Ciceronianus* (lectures on the controversy over the imitation of Cicero) and his *Rhetor* (on the function and activity of the orator) were both heavily influenced by the work of the French logician Pierre de la Rameé (Petrus Ramus). The third book, *Smithus,* was a collection of poems celebrating the life of Sir Thomas Smith, the queen's secretary who had died in 1577, a patron of Harvey's who had helped him gain his fellowship at Pembroke, and possibly a kinsman.

By the late 1570s, Harvey was becoming well known as a promising academic, and it is clear he wished to model his career on that of Smith by becoming a courtier as well as a scholar. Yet he seems to have tripped along the way. On July 26, 1578, Elizabeth I paid a visit to Audley End, Lord Thomas Howard's residence near Saffron Walden. Harvey was asked to perform in a public disputation before the queen, a great honor, but he may have behaved foolishly by drawing undue attention to himself. After that, there was a slight redirection in his career. After his fellowship at Pembroke was not renewed, he became fellow at Trinity Hall. Two years later he attempted to become public orator at the university but was passed over. His publication of a very amusing and parodic correspondence in English with Edmund Spenser (whom he had met at Pembroke), the *Three Letters* of 1580, gained him some reputation as a wit; but the poem at the end, "Speculum Tuscanismi," was taken as a satire of Edward De Vere, the earl of Oxford, and got him into trouble. Four years after that, in 1584, he sought to be made master of his college, and was again passed over. He did not properly complete the doctor of civil law at Cambridge, and in 1585 applied for the degree at Oxford, while remaining a fellow at Trinity Hall. All of these rejections and redirections may have been perfectly normal in

H

themselves, but a pattern emerges of someone seeking recognition and regularly being denied it. His *Letter-book,* a notebook of drafts of his letters and various other short pieces in progress, shows his disappointment and his resentment. Yet there is, to counter the private difficulties, Spenser's sonnet of 1586, which begins, without irony, "Harvey, the happy above happiest men."

Although the complex personal quarrel played out in public against Thomas Nashe culminated in a series of extremely hostile pamphlets in the early 1590s, this quarrel had its origins in the 1580s while Harvey was still in the university and a fellow of Trinity Hall. In the late 1580s, a series of satirical Puritan pamphlets appeared under the general authorship of Martin Marprelate, attacking the Elizabethan Church. The establishment commissioned counter-propaganda. One such response was *Pap with a Hatchet* (1589), which as part of a general onslaught on Puritanism, happened to mock Harvey's correspondence with Spenser (the author is usually believed to be John Lyly). The connection may be that Robert Dudley, the earl of Leicester, Harvey's patron for awhile, supported the Puritan faction. The Ramist movement was also largely associated with Puritanism. Richard Harvey, Gabriel's brother, then attacked the anti-Martinists in his *Plaine Percevall* (1590), and soon after, in *The Lamb of God,* attacked Thomas Nashe specifically for his preface to Robert Greene's *Menaphon* published just the year before. Greene, in his *Quip for an Upstart Courtier* (1590), attacked the Harvey family generally, but he died soon after. Harvey wrote an extremely unflattering and generally mocking account of Greene's death in *Three Letters,* a collection that was withdrawn and immediately reissued as *Foure Letters.* Nashe defended Greene, his older friend and fellow writer, although in his preface to Greene's *Menaphon* he had praised Harvey's writing; Nashe's portrait of a ponderously learned, and ultimately very stupid Gabriel Harvey was begun in *Strange Newes* (1593). Harvey responded with *Pierces Supererogation* and *A New Letter of Notable Contents* (1593), portraying Nashe as an ignorant upstart. Nashe had planned to settle the battle after *Strange Newes* with a conciliatory preface to *Christes Teares* (1593), but Harvey's two pieces only inflamed him, so the following year he rewrote his preface as a further attack, and two years later published one of his best works, *Have with You to Saffron Walden* (1596). This was Nashe's final shot. A slightly later work, *The Trimming of Thomas Nashe* (1597), is often said, with no evidence whatsoever, to be by Harvey. The whole dispute had played itself out. The offical edict, by Archbishop Whitgift and Bishop Bancroft, came too late, but provided a fitting conclusion: "all Nasshes bookes and Doctor Harvyes bookes be taken wheresoeuer they maye be found and that none of theire bookes bee euer printed hereafter" (Arber 3:677).

Harvey lost his fellowship in 1591. It is not clear if he was refused a renewal or if he had already planned to leave the university, although in 1598, when the master of his college died, he again sought the position. Certainly by the 1590s he became increasingly involved with family matters and by 1596 had returned to Saffron Walden. While there are records of his local activity, he seems to have traveled in and out of London (he gives, for instance, in a manuscript note, the earliest mention of a performance of Hamlet). He died in 1631.

Harvey is often maligned as a writer. His experiments in classical meters and other verse forms are not successful. He had no sense of English verse. Nor are his writings in Latin verse especially brilliant. Yet his Latin prose writings show him to have been a lively speaker and ready to engage in the new ideas, especially Ramism. His letters with Spenser are engaging; he is a good writer of English prose. Among Harvey's greatest surviving works, however, are his two manuscript notebooks and the approximately 130 extant annotated printed books from his library, which show him to be a hardworking and wide-ranging reader who is comfortable in varying degrees with Latin, Greek, French, Italian, and Spanish, as well as English. Harvey might have used his notes for teaching; many of his marginal comments that seem pedantic in their formal self-address are sensible when seen as the words of a teacher to a literate and advanced student or group of fellow readers. Many of his books have multiple annotations, in contrasting styles, and made at different times. The impression is not just of a reader, but of a dedicated rereader, aware of the power and insight to be gained from reflective reading, but also not averse to making occasional bitter asides on how difficult these qualities were to obtain in his own life.

BIBLIOGRAPHY

Goldberg, Jonathan. "Colin to Hobbinol: Spenser's Familiar Letters." *South Atlantic Quarterly,* vol. 88, pp. 107–126

Harvey, Gabriel. *Ciceronianus.* Harold S. Wilson, ed., and Clarence A. Forbes, trans. University of Nebraska Studies in the Humanities, no. 4, November 1945.

———. *Letter-Book.* Edward John Long Scott, ed. Camden Society, n.s., vol. 33. 1884.

———. *The Works.* Alexander B. Grosart, ed. 3 vols. 1885–1886; repr. 1966.

———, and Edmund Spenser. Correspondence. In Edmund Spenser, *Poetical Works.* J.C. Smith and E. de Selincourt, eds., pp. 609–643. 1912.

Jardine, Lisa. "Gabriel Harvey: Exemplary Ramist and Pragmatic Humanist." *Revue des sciences philosophiques et theologiques,* vol. 70, pp. 36–48.

———, and Anthony Grafton. "'Studied for Action': How Gabriel Harvey Read His Livy." *Past and Present,* vol. 129, November 1990, pp. 30–78.

Smith, J.C. Moore. *Gabriel Harvey's Marginalia.* 1913.

Stern, Virginia. *Gabriel Harvey: His Life, Marginalia and Library.* 1979.

William Barker

SEE ALSO

De Vere, Edward; Dudley, Robert; Lyly, John; Marprelate Controversy; Nashe, Thomas; Ramism; Reading Practices; Rhetoric; Satire; Spenser, Edmund

Hastings, Henry, (1536–1595)

Educated alongside Edward VI and then briefly at Cambridge, Henry Hastings was profoundly influenced by evangelical Protestantism throughout his adult life. His marriage in 1553 to Catherine Dudley, the duke of Northumberland's daughter and the future earl of Leicester's sister, further cemented this Protestant connection. Nevertheless, he survived the reign of Mary I unscathed through the protection of his great uncle, Cardinal Reginald Pole.

Hastings succeeded his father as third earl of Huntingdon in June 1560, assuming responsibility for the family estates in Leicestershire and the southwest of England. When Elizabeth fell ill in 1562, Huntingdon, the senior male representative of the Yorkist line, was seen as a possible heir to the throne. This caused the queen to treat him with some suspicion and he received no royal office until the Northern Rebellion of the earls in 1569, when she made him a guardian of Mary Queen of Scots. Then, in 1572, in the aftermath of the revolt, Elizabeth appointed him president of the Council in the North, where for twenty-three years he proved a conscientious administrator, striving by all means in his power to bring the entire north of England under the control of the central government. He died unexpectedly at York on December 14, 1595.

BIBLIOGRAPHY

Cross, Claire. *The Puritan Earl: the Life of Henry Hastings, Third Earl of Huntingdon, 1536–1595.* 1966

———, ed. "The Third Earl of Huntingdon's Death-Bed: a Calvinist Example of the *Ars Moriendi.*" *Northern History,* vol. 21, pp. 80–107.

Claire Cross

SEE ALSO

Mary Queen of Scots; Northern Rebellion; Pole, Reginald

Hatton, Christopher (1540–1591)

One of the most important courtiers of Elizabeth I's reign, Christopher Hatton was born to a Northamptonshire gentry family in 1540. He studied at St. Mary Hall, Oxford, and the Inner Temple. He was not, however, called to the bar but chose a career at court. He seems to have first come to the queen's attention in 1561, at the Inner Temple masque celebrating Christmas. Three years later he became a gentleman pensioner. Active in tournaments, court entertainments, and diplomatic duties, Hatton rose to become captain of the guard in 1572 and gentleman of the Privy Chamber, vice-chamberlain and a member of the Privy Council in 1577, and finally lord chancellor in 1587, an appointment that caused much surprise and some anger among the legal profession. In the following year he was made knight of the garter. Receiving a number of grants of property and minor offices, Hatton also became high steward of Cambridge University and chancellor of Oxford. He was in constant attendance on the queen until the lord chancellorship and was on intimate terms, being visited regularly by her during a serious illness in 1573 and again at his death bed in 1591. He never married.

Hatton had considerable administrative talent. As an M.P. for Northamptonshire in the 1572 Parliament, he delivered messages from the queen and was named to a variety of committees, occasionally reporting back to the House on their work. As a privy councilor in the 1581 session of that Parliament, and in the Parliaments of 1584–1585 and 1586–1587, Hatton was an important, indeed essential, manager of government business in the Commons. This included steering through a somewhat controversial bill on the queen's safety in 1584–1585 and proceedings against Mary Queen of Scots in 1586–1587. As lord chancellor, he opened and closed the Parliament of 1589. His surviving speeches, and the comments of diarists, suggest that Hatton was an eloquent and influential speaker.

He was central to other important events of the reign. Dedicated to detecting Catholic plots, Hatton was a

H

prosecutor against Thomas Howard, fourth duke of Norfolk as well as the Babington plotters. He was credited with convincing Mary Stuart to submit to the authority of the English court that tried her, and was one of the councilors who conspired to ensure her rapid execution after the queen had signed the warrant. However, unlike others on the Privy Council, Hatton was essentially a conservative in religion and supported the anti-Puritan policies of Archbishop John Whitgift. He spoke impressively against the bill promoting a Genevan-style prayer book in the 1586–1587 Parliament.

Hatton has been described as a quintessential Renaissance man. A patron of the arts, no fewer than twelve books were dedicated to him between 1590 and 1591, including Spenser's *The Faerie Queene*. Earlier dedicatees included Barnabe Riche, John Dee, and William Byrd. The recipient of a gorgeous ceremonial suit of armor made by Jacob Halder, Hatton was the subject of several portraits, including one (possibly associated with Cornelius Ketel) in which he holds a cameo of the queen and another, with verses, celebrating his chancellorship at Oxford. Nicholas Hilliard painted him in one of his rare full-length miniatures. His emblem, the golden hind, was chosen by Sir Francis Drake for his famous voyage, in which Hatton invested. His spectacular house at Holdenby was praised for its size and symmetry. Not surprisingly, Hatton accumulated an impressive debt of more than £42,000 by the time of his death in 1591. He was buried in St. Paul's Cathedral with considerable ceremony. An elaborate and quite massive memorial was erected to him, so thoroughly diminishing those of Sir Philip Sydney and Sir Francis Walsingham that John Stow reported the quip "Philip and Francis have no Tombe / For great Christopher takes all the roome."

BIBLIOGRAPHY

Brooks, E. St. John. *Sir Christopher Hatton*. 1946.
Vines, A.G. *Neither Fire Nor Steel. Sir Christopher Hatton*. 1978.
Hasler, P.W., ed. *The History of Parliament: The House of Commons, 1558–1603*. 1981.
Fox, Alistair. "The decline of literary patronage in the 1590s." In *The Reign of Elizabeth I. Court and Culture in the Last Decade*. John Guy, ed. 1995.
Strong, Roy. *Tudor and Jacobean Portraits*. 2 vols. 1969.
Summerson, John. *Architecture in Britain, 1530–1830*. 1991.

David Dean

SEE ALSO
Babington Plot; Drake, Francis; Hilliard, Nicholas; Howard, Thomas; Mary Queen of Scots; Parliamentary History

Hawes, Stephen (d. 1523?)

Born in Suffolk and educated at Oxford, Stephen Hawes became a groom of the chamber for Henry VII in 1502. In this position he received an allowance for mourning cloth for the funeral of Henry VII's queen. His earliest and most important work, *The Passetyme of Pleasure*, was written and dedicated to Henry VII in 1506. Court records show that Hawes received a payment of 10s for *Passetyme*, which was noted in the king's private accounts as a "ballett that [Hawes] gave to the king's grace." An elaborate allegory of nearly 6,000 lines, *Passetyme* was first published in 1509 by Wynkyn de Worde, who issued a reprint with woodcuts in 1517. Hawes's relationship with De Worde appears to have been close, for Hawes was the only poet whose work De Worde published in its entirety.

In his dedication, Hawes acknowledges the influence of his teacher, John Lydgate. But language in *Passetyme* reveals more than the simple influence of a single teacher; Hawes's admiration for Chaucer is also clearly evident. In addition to *Passetyme*, Hawes invokes Chaucer in *The Exemple of Vertu* and *The Conforte*. Hawes in turn influenced Edmund Spenser, especially Book 1 of *The Faerie Queene*. In *Passetyme of Pleasure*, then, Hawes forges the link between *The Canterbury Tales* and *The Faerie Queene*.

BIBLIOGRAPHY

Copeland, Rita. "Lydgate, Hawes, and the Science of Rhetoric in the Late Middle Ages." *Modern Language Quarterly*, vol. 53, pp. 57–82.
Kaske, Carol. "How Spenser Really Used Stephen Hawes in the Legend of Holiness." In *Unfolded Tales: Essays on Renaissance Romance*. George Logan and Gordon Teskey, eds., pp. 119–136. 1989.
Lerer, Seth. "The Rhetoric of Fame: Stephen Hawes' Aureate Diction." *Spenser Studies*, vol. 5, pp. 169–184. 1984.
Spurgeon, Caroline. *Five Hundred Years of Chaucer Criticism and Allusion*. 1960.

Parmita Kapadia

SEE ALSO
Henry VII; Printing, Publishing, and Bookbinding

Hawkins, John (1532–1595)

Merchant, ship owner, and naval administrator, Sir John Hawkins was a pioneer of English attempts to break into the slave trade during the reign of Elizabeth I. As a young man he made several voyages to the Canary Islands, where he learned of the demand for African slaves in the Spanish Caribbean. Encouraged by this information, he set out four slaving expeditions from 1562 to 1568. With the backing of his father-in-law, Benjamin Gonson, treasurer of the queen's navy, and other prominent naval officials, Hawkins set out with a small fleet in 1562. He acquired more than 300 Africans in Guinea, whose sale in the West Indies brought a handsome profit. In 1564, he set out a larger expedition in which the queen and several prominent courtiers were interested. Although a success, diplomatic protests from Spain prevented him from leading a third voyage that set out in 1566 under the command of John Lovell. The voyage seems to have been unprofitable. The last venture in this sequence, set out during 1567, ended disastrously when Hawkins was caught in the Mexican port of San Juan de Ulua, in September 1568, by a fleet of Spanish ships. In the ensuing conflict only two English ships escaped capture or destruction. The disaster effectively ended English interest in the slave trade for the rest of the Tudor period, although the structure of the trade did not favor further growth at this time.

In 1577, Hawkins succeeded his father-in-law as treasurer of the navy. Although accused of negligence and maladministration by his rivals, Hawkins was an efficient administrator who is credited by modern authorities with important improvements to the design of ships. However, his official duties did not prevent him from being involved in a number of projects in which trade and plunder were combined, often in association with Francis Drake. Following the outbreak of the war with Spain in 1585 he urged the queen to adopt an ambitious oceanic strategy, although his plan for a blockade of the Spanish coast was never fully implemented. He served as a rear admiral during the Spanish Armada campaign, when he was knighted by the lord admiral, Charles Howard. In 1595, he shared the command of an expedition to the Caribbean with Drake, but died during its ill-fated course. During his career Hawkins made a major contribution to the modernization of the Elizabethan navy, although much of his administrative work was to be short-lived.

BIBLIOGRAPHY

Andrews, K.R., ed. *The Last Voyage of Drake and Hawkins.* 1972.

———. *The Spanish Caribbean: Trade and Plunder, 1530–1630.* 1978.

Loades, D. *The Tudor Navy: An Administrative, Political, and Military History.* 1992.

Oppenheim, M. *A History of the Administration of the Royal Navy and of Merchant Shipping in Relation to the Navy from 1509 to 1660.* 1896.

Williamson, J.A. *Hawkins of Plymouth.* 1949.

John C. Appleby

SEE ALSO

Armada, Spanish; Drake, Francis; Foreign Relations and Diplomacy; Howard, Charles

Hawkins, Richard (c. 1562–1622)

Sea captain and naval commander, Sir Richard Hawkins was a leading promoter of maritime enterprise during the later sixteenth century. In 1582, he served on an expedition to the Caribbean set out by his father, Sir John Hawkins. During 1585, he was a captain on Francis Drake's expedition to the West Indies. He commanded one of the queen's ships during the Spanish Armada campaign of 1588. In 1593, Hawkins was the promoter and commander of an ambitious South Seas venture. Although he later claimed that his purpose was to circumnavigate the globe on a voyage of discovery, his main aim was to plunder Spanish shipping in the Pacific. Sailing with a general commission against Spain, Hawkins entered the Pacific through the Strait of Magellan, plundering Valparaiso and seizing Spanish ships as he coasted northward. In 1594, he was captured by the Spanish off the coast of Peru, remaining a prisoner until 1602. On his return to England he became associated with a group of London merchants who were attempting to establish a contraband trade with Spanish settlers in the Caribbean. Like many others in the southwest, he found the peace with Spain unwelcome. Although he became vice admiral for Devon in 1604, his official duties did not prevent him from patronizing or dealing with English pirates who haunted the southwest in the early seventeenth century. In 1614, he was considered a suitable commander to lead a proposed expedition of the East India Company into the South Seas, although the proposal was abortive. In 1620, he served as vice admiral on Sir Robert Mansell's ill-fated expedition against the pirate base of Algiers. Hawkins's account of his 1593 voyage was published shortly after his death, and remains a valuable account of maritime life during the Tudor period.

H

BIBLIOGRAPHY

Andrews, K.R. *Trade, Plunder and Settlement: Maritime Enterprise and the Genesis of the British Empire, 1480–1630*. 1984.

Quinn, D.B., and A.N. Ryan. *England's Sea Empire, 1550–1642*. 1983.

Williamson, J.A. *Hawkins of Plymouth*. 1949.

———, ed. *The "Observations" of Sir Richard Hawkins*. 1933.

John C. Appleby

SEE ALSO

Armada, Spanish; Discovery and Exploration; Drake, Francis; East India Company; Hawkins, John; Piracy

Hayward, John (c. 1564–1627)

Scholar, lawyer, civil servant, and author, Sir John Hayward was born in Suffolk and educated at Cambridge. As a historian, he was among the first to apply the Tacitean model to English history, emphasizing the political rather than the providential, and he is now best known for his what may be his first work, *The First Part of the Life and Raigne of King Henrie the IIII* (1599), an account of the deposition and murder of Richard II and the first year of the titular monarch's reign. While modern historians debate whether Hayward had any seditious intentions in writing this history, some of the author's contemporaries were certain that he did. The timing of the book's publication, its laudatory dedication to Robert Devereux, second earl of Essex, and the subject—a childless monarch advised by flattering favorites, plagued by Irish rebellion, and overthrown by a popular earl of honor and ancient nobility—were enough to convince Elizabeth I and other members of the government that Hayward had written a veiled commentary supportive of Essex and critical of the queen. The history was on sale for only four months—its publisher, John Wolfe, claimed that "no book ever sold better"—before it was banned and all 1,500 copies of the second edition seized and burned. In July 1600, shortly after Essex was tried for insubordination and Hayward's "treasonable book" used as evidence, the historian was questioned and then imprisoned in the Tower of London. Despite his assertion that his work had been misinterpreted and that he was innocent, Hayward remained there until about the time of Elizabeth's death and James I's accession.

Hayward was more famous in his own time for the often reprinted devotional work *The Sanctuarie of a Trou-* *bled Soule* (1601), published first during his imprisonment. He came into favor under James and rose to prominence for his legal service to the crown and his authorship of several books. Hayward was knighted in 1619.

BIBLIOGRAPHY

Barroll, Leeds. "A New History for Shakespeare and His Time." *Shakespeare Quarterly*, vol. 39, pp. 441–464.

Manning, John, ed. *The First and Second Parts of John Hayward's The Life and Raigne of King Henrie IIII*. 1991.

Womersley, David. "Sir John Hayward's Tacitism." *Renaissance Studies*, vol. 6, pp. 46–59.

Woolf, D.R. *The Idea of History in Early Stuart England: Erudition, Ideology, and "The Light of Truth" from the Accession of James I to the Civil War*. 1990.

R. Morgan Griffin

SEE ALSO

Devereux, Robert; History, Writing of

Heath, Nicholas (c. 1501–1578)

A Cambridge doctor of divinity, bishop of Worcester in 1543, Nicholas Heath at first supported the Protestant reforms of Thomas Cranmer, his mentor in negotiations with the German Lutheran princes on behalf of King Henry VIII in the 1530s. But under Edward VI he grew conservative, arguing in 1548 against the new order of communion prepared for the first Book of Common Prayer. His opposition in 1550 to a new form of ordination that would exclude minor orders sent him to the Fleet prison and cost him his bishopric. On the accession of Mary he was restored to his see, appointed to the Royal Council, made archbishop of York in 1555 and lord chancellor the following year. As one of the examiners of Cranmer, he unsuccessfully urged him to declare his denial of the real presence of Christ in the Eucharist a private matter; as lord chancellor he signed the writ for his burning (1555). On Elizabeth I's accession he refused the 1559 Oath of Supremacy and was consequently deprived of his see and committed to the Tower. But he was soon released on assurance he would not meddle in church and state. He enjoyed the queen's friendship throughout a long retirement.

BIBLIOGRAPHY

Elton, G.R. *Reform and Reformation: England, 1509–1558*. 1977.

Guy, John. *Tudor England.* 1988.
Jordan, W.K. *Edward VI: The Young King.* 1968.
MacCulloch, Diarmaid. *Thomas Cranmer: A Life.* 1996.
Ridley, Jasper. *Thomas Cranmer.* 1962.

David Freeman

SEE ALSO

Book of Common Prayer; Cranmer, Thomas; Eucharist; Supremacy, Act of

Henry VII (1457–1509)

The first of the Tudors, Henry VII was born at Pembroke Castle on January 28, 1457, the posthumous son of Edmund, earl of Richmond, half-brother of King Henry VI, and of Margaret Beaufort, great-granddaughter of John of Gaunt, duke of Lancaster. Extinction of the direct Lancastrian line by battle and by murder made Henry their heir in 1471, by virtue of his Beaufort blood. His paternal uncle Jaspar, earl of Pembroke, took him to safety abroad. Henry spent the years 1471–1485 in Brittany and in France, at times a pawn in intra-European politics. In 1485, the French, hoping to neutralize England, backed Henry's campaign that culminated in his victory over Richard III at the battle of Bosworth.

In January 1486, Henry, now king, fulfilled his vow to marry Elizabeth of York; but this marriage and the imprisonment of Edward, earl of Warwick, the last legitimate male of the house of York, did not end Yorkist challenges. In 1487, Margaret of York, dowager duchess of Burgundy; John de la Pole, earl of Lincoln; and the Fitzgerald earls of Kildare and Desmond set up Lambert Simnel to impersonate Warwick. The scheme ended in a bloody Yorkist defeat at the Battle of Stoke. Four years later, another Yorkist imposture, Perkin Warbeck, paraded as Richard, duke of York, youngest son of Edward IV. This conspiracy involved Margaret of York, the Fitzgeralds in Ireland, and those disenchanted with Henry VII, especially Sir William Stanley, the lord chamberlain, who had rescued Henry at Bosworth. At various times, Warbeck had support from King Charles VIII of France, from Emperor Maximilian I and his son Archduke Philip of Burgundy, and from King James IV of Scotland. Failing to establish a foothold in Ireland, and finally expelled from Scotland in 1497, Warbeck led an abortive insurrection in Cornwall. Henry executed him and the earl of Warwick in 1499. But in 1501, Edmund de la Pole, earl of Suffolk and his brother, Richard, nephews of the Yorkist kings, fled abroad. The death of Prince Arthur in 1502 added potency to their threat; yet Henry's diplomacy succeeded in denying them foreign support. In 1506, Archduke Philip surrendered Edmund.

Dynastic security was an objective of Henry's foreign policy. He linked the Tudors to the Trastmaras of Spain with the marriage of Prince Arthur to Katherine of Aragon in 1501, and to the Stuarts of Scotland with the marriage of Margaret to James IV in 1503, which later became the basis for the Stuart claim to the English crown. Henry tried unsuccessfully for an alliance with the Habsburgs, proposing his own marriage to Margaret of Savoy, Maximilian I's sister, and of his daughter, Mary, to Charles of Burgundy, Maximilian's grandson. Plans for the marriage of Prince Henry to Katherine following Arthur's death foundered because of disputes between Henry and Ferdinand over money and Ferdinand's opposition to Mary Tudor's marriage with Charles.

Henry limited his entanglements in European politics. He went to war twice, in 1489–1492 during the Breton crisis, and invasion of Brittany violating his truce with France, and in 1496–1497 in revenge for Scottish support of Warbeck and for their invasion of northern England. His intervention in Brittany may not have been limited to keeping the duchy separate from France, for he seems also to have briefly envisioned recovery of the lost Plantagenet lands in France. Nevertheless, Henry made peace with France in 1492, renewing it in 1498. He received in turn an annual payment from the French kings. Maximilian I backed Warbeck in an attempt to overturn Henry's new relationship between England and Spain. The war of revenge against Scotland had to be abandoned because of the Western Rebellion of 1497; but in 1502, Henry obtained a peace with James IV largely on his terms, preparing the way for the marriage with Margaret.

Henry's commercial treaties with Denmark in 1489–1490 helped English trade in the Baltic, but the king could not break the Hanse's stranglehold. His treaties with Spain, Portugal, and Florence in 1489–1490, and his pressuring of Venice to allow his subjects access to Crete were meant to develop an English overseas trading network with the Mediterranean. The policy achieved partial success. The Low Countries was the most important region for English commerce; yet Henry damaged this trade with embargoes in 1493 and 1505 in order to force the Habsburgs to expel the pretenders. In 1506, Henry concluded with Archduke Philip his most successful commercial agreement. This treaty was allegedly called *Malus Intercursus* in the Low Countries because of the favorable terms granted to the English.

The tomb of Henry VII (d. 1509) and Elizabeth of York, by Pietro Torrigiano. London, Westminster Abbey. By permission of the National Monuments Records Centre, Royal Commission on the Historical Monuments of England. Crown copyright.

Henry continued Yorkist methods in restoring solvency and authority to the crown, adapting them to his own style and needs. He made the Kings chamber once more supreme in the management of crown finances. For security reasons, he established the inner Privy Chamber, which became his secret treasury. Henry increased income from crown lands, and he ruthlessly exploited his prerogative rights for profit, especially wardship. His agents even abused royal commissions investigating concealments of royal revenue by tenants-in-chief to obtain corrupt verdicts in favor of the crown. In time of war, Henry, through Parliament, tried supplementing inadequate revenues from First Fruits and Tenths with oppressive and unprecedented subsidies, provoking rebellions in Yorkshire in 1489 and in Cornwall in 1497.

Henry's council, active in administrating justice, did much of its work through special tribunals. A 1487 statute gave one tribunal jurisdiction over specific cases, such as riot. Another, called Council Learned and operating out of the duchy of Lancaster, dealt with cases involving the royal prerogative and debts, often by intimidation. Bonds and recognizances for good behavior became Henry's most notorious tool of intimidation, especially under the efficient administration of his finance ministers, William Empson and Edmund Dudley. He used them to put nobles and knights at his mercy, for by prosecuting them for debt owed from the bond, he denied them recourse to the common law courts. Henry grew rapacious and avaricious in their use later in his reign, but at the end, perhaps, he was remorseful over the abuse. He died on April 21, 1509. Henry is buried at Westminster Abbey in the chapel that bears his name.

BIBLIOGRAPHY

Arthurson, Ian. *The Perkin Warbeck Conspiracy, 1491–1499.* 1994.
Bennett, Michael. *Lambert Simnel and the Battle of Stoke.* 1987.
Chrimes, S.B. *Henry VII.* 1972.
Cooper. J.P. "Henry VII's Last Years Reconsidered." *Historical Journal,* vol. 2, pp. 103–129.
Currin, John M. "Henry VII and the Treaty of Redon (1489): Plantagenet Ambitions and Tudor Foreign Policy." *History,* vol. 81, pp. 343–358.
Elton, G. R. "Henry VII: Rapacity and Remorse." *Historical Journal,* vol. 1, pp. 21—39.
———. "Henry VII: A Restatement." *Historical Journal,* vol. 4, pp. 1—29.
Gunn, S.J. *Early Tudor Government, 1485–1558.* 1995.
Lockyer, Roger, and Andrew Thrush. *Henry VII.* 1997.
Mackie, J.D. *The Earlier Tudors, 1485–1558.* 1952.
Starkey, David. "Intimacy and Innovation: the Rise of the Privy Chamber, 1485–1547." In *The English Court from the Wars of the Roses to the Civil War.* David Starkey, ed. 1987.

John M. Currin

SEE ALSO
Arthur Tudor; Beaufort, Margaret; Bosworth, Battle of; Dudley, Edmund; Empson, Richard; Foreign Relations and Diplomacy; Government, Central Administration of; Henry VIII; Katherine of Aragon; London; Mary Tudor; de la Pole, Edmund; Privy Chamber; Trade, Overseas

Henry VIII (1491–1547)

Born at Greenwich on June 28, 1491, the future Henry VIII was the third child of Henry VII and Elizabeth of York. He was not initially destined for kingship (an unsubstantiated story promulgated by Lord Herbert of Cherbury suggested he was originally groomed for a career in the church), but the premature death of his elder brother Arthur in 1502 brought him to prominence as heir apparent. His only other surviving siblings were his sisters Margaret and Mary, who married James IV of Scotland and Louis XII of France, respectively, although Mary subsequently courted controversy and brotherly anger by contracting a love match to Henry's close friend, Charles Brandon, duke of Suffolk, when the French king died in 1515.

Henry's infamous marital history has long attracted biographers. In June 1509, he married Katherine of Aragon, his brother's widow, who bore his first child, the future Mary I, in February 1516. But he subsequently had the match annulled after a lengthy struggle with the papacy in order to marry Anne Boleyn (the mother of his second daughter, the future Elizabeth I) in January 1533, an action that was to provoke the break with Rome and initiate the Henrician Reformation. Henry's reasons for seeking this annulment were complex, combining a genuine conviction that marriage to a brother's widow contravened biblical injunction with a concern for the succession (Katherine was past childbearing age) and a desire for the younger and livelier Anne. Anne was herself rejected in May 1536: accused of multiple adultery with a number of gentlemen of the king's Privy Chamber and of incest with her brother George, Viscount Rochford, she was arrested in May 1536 and subsequently executed along with her alleged lovers, Rochford, Henry Norris, William Brereton, Sir Francis Weston, and a musician, Mark Smeaton. In the same month, Henry married his mistress, Jane Seymour, who died giving birth to the long-awaited son, the future Edward VI, in October 1537. A brief and disastrous diplomatic marriage to Anne of Cleves followed in January 1540, but this was annulled in

H

July of the same year on grounds of nonconsummation, Henry declaring himself horrified by his bride's alleged ugliness. An equally disastrous marriage to Catherine Howard, niece of Thomas Howard, duke of Norfolk, followed in July 1540, but this too was annulled when the queen was found guilty of adultery with one of the ubiquitous gentlemen of the Privy Chamber, Thomas Culpepper, and of concealing an earlier liaison with Francis Dereham prior to her marriage. All three were executed in February 1542. Henry's final marriage, in July 1543, to the twice-widowed Katherine Parr, proved more successful, although it too was not without incident. The martyrologist John Foxe describes an occasion when the queen was the subject of an accusation of heresy initiated by Bishop Stephen Gardiner and Thomas Wriothesley. But she retained the King's favor until his death on January 28, 1547, eventually marrying again, for the fourth time, to Sir Thomas Seymour, in the first year of the reign of her step son, Edward VI.

Scholars have tended to portray Henry as either a weak-willed egotist, unwilling to exert himself in the detailed business of government and subject to the dominating influence of favorites or factions, or as a monstrous tyrant, dominating his court in the manner of a despot. The truth probably lies somewhere between the two extremes. Henry was certainly more than capable of taking the lead in government. In matters of foreign policy and religious affairs, the two areas in which the reign was most distinguished, he took a close interest, drafting reports, scrutinizing the statements drawn up by his ministers, and shaping policy in the light of his own views. But his court was not monolithic, and the documentary evidence reveals the existence of debates over policy in the council chamber, in parliamentary committees, and even through the less obviously political media of prose tracts, courtly poetry, and drama.

From 1513 until 1529, Henry's chief confidant was Thomas Wolsey, who for most of his ascendancy combined the offices of lord chancellor and papal legate *a latere*. This period saw England take a leading role in peace making and power brokering on the international stage through vehicles such as the Treaty of Universal Peace of 1519 and the Calais Conference of 1521. Wolsey fell from favor in 1529, probably as the result of his failure to secure Henry a swift "divorce" from Katherine of Aragon, although some commentators felt he was the victim of a factional conspiracy. For a time thereafter Henry took the leading role in government himself, but the 1530s saw the rise of a second chief minister, the royal secretary Thomas

Cromwell, who, as Henry's vicegerent-in-spirituals, drafted and oversaw many of the chief instruments of the Henrician Reformation. Cromwell himself fell in 1540, probably a victim of Henry's need to present a more orthodox face to continental Europe during a period of diplomatic uncertainty, and no single minister was to rise to prominence for the rest of the reign.

In foreign policy, Henry's reign witnessed alternating periods of aggressive military action and high profile peacemaking. The early years of the reign were characterized by a bellicose spirit manifested most obviously in the invasion of France by an army led by the king in 1513 and the minor victories of the battle of the Spurs and the capture of Thérouanne and Tournai. But attempts to enlist continental aid for further incursions ended in expensive failure, leading to a new policy of rapprochement, resulting in the so-called Treaty of Universal Peace signed in London in 1518, and the lavish summit meeting with Francis I at the Field of Cloth of Gold in 1520. The 1520s saw a return to small-scale incursions into French territory. The ambitious attempt to exploit French disarray after the capture of Francis I by Imperial forces at Pavia in 1525 collapsed when Henry's attempts to fund an invasion by raising an inaptly named Amicable Grant from his subjects ended in popular protest. For the next seventeen years foreign policy was essentially an exercise in damage limitation, determined by the need to prevent a continental Catholic alliance against "heretical" England, but in 1543, a new invasion of France was launched in alliance with Charles V, leading to the capture of Boulogne (September 1543), while an army under Edward Seymour, earl of Hertford (the future protector Somerset), invaded Scotland and won a resounding victory at Solway Moss (November 1542). The territorial gains achieved during the reign were only modest, but Henry's policies resulted in the fortification of the major coastal towns of southern England and laid the foundations of the modern English navy.

Henry's religious position for the first two decades of his reign seemed resolutely orthodox. But the mixture of intense personal engagement with theological issues and supreme self-confidence in the rectitude of his position that led to his defense of papal authority in the *Assertion of the Seven Sacraments* (1521), which won him the honorific title Defender of the Faith, was turned against Rome in the 1530s. By 1527, at the latest, Henry was looking to divorce Katherine and marry Anne Boleyn. Attempts to achieve this foundered, however, on the refusal of Pope Clement VII to sanction a separation. What began as a diplomatic campaign to persuade Rome of Henry's right to a "divorce" grew into a more fundamental assertion of English rights to determine ecclesiastical issues domestically. The 1530s saw a series of ecclesiastical and religious reforms and the assertion of royal control over the Church of England through the mechanism of royal supremacy, given definitive form in an act of Parliament in 1534. The English clergy submitted to royal authority in May 1532, allowing Thomas Cranmer to dissolve Henry's marriage on his own authority in May 1533. A series of parliamentary acts gradually realized and enforced the break with Rome. The Act in Restraint of Annates (passed conditionally in May 1532 and definitively in April 1534) and the Act of First Fruits and Tenths (December 1534) annexed certain ecclesiastical revenues to the crown. The Act in Restraint of Appeals (March 1533) prevented recourse to the Roman courts in matters of ecclesiastical law and policy. The dissolution of the monasteries began with an act dissolving the smaller houses in the spring of 1536 and was completed with the surrender of the greater houses, ratified by the second Act of Dissolution in April 1539.

Theologically, the Church of England established its own position on the Sacraments and its opposition to "superstitious" practices such as pilgrimage, prayers to saints, and the "idolatrous" use of images, through the Act of Ten Articles (published July 1536) and Cromwell's injunctions (August 1536 and September 1538). A more conservative line was promulgated in the Act of Six Articles (April 1539), but scholarly attempts to portray this as a reversal of policy are overstated. While the public emphasis may have shifted, official policy remained reformed on many issues of substance.

The Reformation was not achieved without bloodshed, and Henry's own commitment to it, as well as his capacity for ruthlessness, may be judged from the way in which direct opposition to the reforms was suppressed. Individuals, such as Sir Thomas More and John Fisher, bishop of Rochester, were executed for opposing the royal supremacy and whole groups, such as the Carthusians, faced a similar fate or were left to starve to death in prison. Opposition to religious reform was also a major element in the popular rising known as the Pilgrimage of Grace, which swept through Lincolnshire and the northern counties of England in late 1536 and early 1537.

In many ways the term "Henrician Reformation" is precisely apt; the religious changes of the 1530s were very much Henry's initiatives, characteristic of his own personal brand of theology, a fact neatly symbolized by the policy of replacing the rood screens and "idolatrous"

A portrait miniature of Henry VIII by Lucas Horenbout (c. 1525–1527), 53 x 48 mm. By permission of the Fitzwilliam Museum, University of Cambridge.

images of saints in parish churches with the royal coat of arms. Henry's own involvement in the reforming process can be judged from his close and detailed scrutiny of the Bishops' Book (of 1537), in the drafts of which he conducted an ongoing argument with Archbishop Cranmer, endorsing reform of ceremonies but placing a more orthodox interpretation on the Sacraments, defending the concept, if not the name of purgatory, and resolutely refusing any suggestion of the Lutheran doctrine of justification by faith alone. Henry's reformation resolutely sought the via media, a middle way between the evangelical fervor of Cranmer and the more advanced reformers and the conservative instincts of bishops such as Stokesley and Gardiner and the bulk of the population in the country at large. It did so largely on grounds of political necessity. Henry's personal religious credo has been described as "Catholicism without the pope," but this understates his very real reforming instincts. He may have believed firmly in the Catholic doctrine of transubstantiation, but on the worship of images, and "superstitious" practices such as creeping to the cross, the king was significantly more radical than Roman orthodoxy would allow. But the abolition of such practices could not be

H

enacted in a vacuum. Reform, if it was to succeed, had to win the support, or at least the acquiescence, of a divided nation, and could not appear so dramatic as to alarm Catholic Europe into concerted military action to restore England to the papal fold. Hence changes were introduced piecemeal, and were always subject to qualification, even temporary reversal if circumstances dictated, and an air of studied ambiguity was carefully maintained in the attempt to prevent the complete alienation of conservatives at home and abroad. In terms of tactics as well as doctrine and temperament, then, Henry laid the foundations for the policy of careful ambivalence and doctrinal moderation that was to be the cornerstone of his daughter Elizabeth I's religious settlement, and of Anglicanism thereafter.

A final Henrician legacy, perhaps the least tangible but most influential, concerned the image of kingship itself. In the eyes of many scholars, Henry's reign saw fundamental changes to the image and substance of sovereignty in England. Memorable images of the king were created during the 1530s, chiefly by Hans Holbein, whose mural of Henry and Jane Seymour, with the king's parents, was placed in the Privy Chamber to abash visitors and inspire awe and loyalty in his courtiers. Holbein's title page to the Coverdale Bible of 1535 depicts an enthroned, god-like Henry, handing down the Word of God to his subjects. Accounts of an orchestrated propaganda campaign to promulgate a new image of monarchy probably overstate the case, but Holbein's work certainly created an image of Henry that bestrode the Tudor period and remains powerfully evocative even today.

BIBLIOGRAPHY

Bernard, G.W. "The Church of England, c. 1529–c. 1642." *History,* vol. 75, pp. 183–206.

Elton, G.R. *Reform and Reformation: England, 1509–1558.* 1977.

Hall, Edward. *Henry VIII.* C. Whibley, ed. 2 vols. 1904.

MacCulloch, D., ed. *The Reign of Henry VIII: Politics, Policy, and Piety.* 1995.

Scarisbrick, J.J. *Henry VIII.* 2nd edition. 1997.

Smith, Lacey B. *Henry VIII: The Mask of Royalty.* 1971.

Walker, Greg. *Persuasive Fictions: Faction, Faith, and Political Culture in the Reign of Henry VIII.* 1996.

Greg Walker

SEE ALSO

Anne of Cleves; Bishops' Book; Boleyn, Anne; Brandon, Charles; Church of England; Cromwell, Thomas; Defender of the Faith; Field of the Cloth of Gold; Government, Central Administration of; Holbein, Hans; Katherine of Aragon; Monastic Orders; Parr, Katherine; Pilgrimage of Grace; Privy Chamber; Reformation, English; Supremacy, Act of; Wolsey, Thomas

Henry VIII as Composer

At what age and from whom Henry learned to play organ, lute, virginals, and various wind instruments is not known. In 1513, the Milanese ambassador wrote from Tournai that he had heard Henry "play the clavicembalo and recorders in company most creditably, affording pleasure to all present." Sir Peter Carew's biographer, John Hooker, mentions that Peter and Henry delighted in singing "certain songs they called 'freeman's songs,' as *By the banks I lay* and *As I walked the wood so wild.*" By the end of his reign there were at least fifty-eight musicians on his payroll; an inventory was made of his considerable collection of instruments after his death (Harleian MS 1419).

Thirty-three compositions attributed to Henry ("The Kynge H.viij") were copied into British Library, Additional MS 31922, which probably originated in London as an anthology of the repertory at Henry's court c. 1518. Twelve of Henry's pieces (nos. 52, 54, 55, 58, 61, 72, 73, 76, 77, 80, 94, and 98) are untitled and untexted trios. (The label *Consort* in John Stevens's modern edition is anachronistic.) Quite brief, none extending beyond twenty-one measures in modern transcription, most of the trios divide into two to five brief sections. One wonders if they were used to accompany dancing, a frequent activity at court festivities. The anonymous no. 71 resembles Henry's *Pastyme with good companye.*

There are also twelve carols attributed to Henry (see list below). It is far from clear that some of these compositions are in one particular carol form, since music for either the burden or verses is absent in all of them.

Like the carol, the three-voice round, or circle canon, is a uniquely English feature of Add. MS 31922: Henry wrote two, *It is to me a right great joy* (no. 56) and *Departure is my chief pain* (no. 57). In no. 57, the three voices are augmented by a noncanonic fourth voice. For *Gentil prince de renom,* titled but untexted in Add. 31922 (no. 45), Henry did no more than to add an alto voice to a three-voice anonymous composition from Ottaviano Petrucci's *Harmonice musices Odhecaton A* of 1501, and it is suspected that he likewise composed only the alto of *Hélas madame celle que j'aime tant* (the third voice of no. 10 in Stevens's edition). The top voice of *Hélas madame* is a shortened version of a monophonic tune from the fifteenth-century Bayeux Chansonnier. The texted *Pastyme with good companye* (no. 7) shares a version of its top voice with *De mon triste desplaisir* by the French court composer Jean Richafort, whose composition might postdate Henry's. The textless *En vray amoure* (no. 81) resembles in some aspects *Alons fere nos barbes,* also printed in the *Odhecaton,* by another French court composer, Loyset Compère (c. 1445–1518). The virtuosic *Taunder naken* (no. 78) is an arrangement of a Flemish folksong, *T'andernaken op den Rijn,* but there is no known model for the four-voice, fully texted *Adieu madame et ma maistresse* (no. 9). Two works are titled *If love now reigned,* but no. 48 only adds three brief, additional sections to the five of no. 44.

Henry may have continued to compose once his religious and marital troubles began. According to Edward Hall's chronicle, he is said to have composed two five-voice masses, now lost, in 1510, and a three-voice motet *Quam pulchra es. Taundernaken* will undoubtedly remain a staple of the Renaissance instrumental repertory, and his carol *Grene growith the holy* is a miniature example of that genre at its simple, eloquent best.

Carols attributed to Henry VIII:

Grene growith the holy, no. 33 (burden only)
Whereto shuld I expresse, no. 47 (burden only)
Alas, what shall I do, no. 12
O my heart, no. 15
The time of youth, no. 23
Whoso that will all feats, no. 34
Though that men do call, no. 51
Alack alack what shall I do, no. 30
Without discord, no. 64
Though some saith that youth ruleth me, no. 66
Whoso that will for grace sue, no. 79
Lusty youth should us ensue, no. 92

BIBLIOGRAPHY

Edwards, Warwick. "The Instrumental Music of Henry VIII's Manuscript." *The Consort,* vol. 34, pp. 274–282.

Fallows, David. "Henry VIII as a Composer." In *Sundry Sorts of Music Books: Essays on The British Library Collections,* pp. 27–39. 1993.

Holman, Peter. "Music at the Court of Henry VIII." In *Henry VIII: A European Court in England.* 1991.

Stevens, John, ed. *Music at the Court of Henry VIII.* Musica Britannica, vol. 18. 1962.

——. *Music and Poetry in the Early Tudor Court.* 1961.

Laura S. Youens

SEE ALSO
Carol; Hall, Edward; Henry VIII; Motet

Henslowe, Philip (c. 1555–1616)

Theater owner, financier, entrepreneur, Philip Henslowe was the son of Edmund Henslowe of Lindfield, Sussex, who served as master of the game in Ashdown Forest and Broil Park. At an indeterminate date he gained his freedom in the London Dyers Company and married Agnes, the widow of his master, Henry Woodward. Early references to Henslowe characterize him as a businessman interested in diverse investments (starch-making, property investment, and pawnbroking) and in money-lending.

In 1587, Henslowe built the Rose playhouse in Southwark, and in 1592, he seems to have renovated the structure to accommodate a larger audience. In October of the same year Henslowe's stepdaughter married the prominent actor Edward Alleyn. From this time until his death, Henslowe and Alleyn owned and operated the most financially successful theater business of the period, which came to include the Rose, the Fortune playhouse (built in 1600), and the Bear Garden (rebuilt in 1613 as the Hope playhouse).

Over the years many acting companies performed in Henslowe's playhouses; however, his primary connection to them was as a financier. Although he came to know some of the players intimately, Henslowe was so thoroughgoing a businessman that he required them to sign bonds agreeing to specific terms of performance, and he earned his share of the profits by lending the actors money for playbooks and costumes and then collecting a percentage of the profits earned through performance. He and Alleyn also arranged for financial contracts with dramatists, paid for licenses for specific plays (required by the master of the revels), authorized payments for costumes and other theatrical necessities, and maintained the playhouses at their own cost. The last-named task brought responsibilities much more complex than simply repairing the physical structure, owing primarily to the social and political controversies that affected the theaters throughout the period. To support his activities in the theater, Henslowe's positions—first as groom of the chamber to Queen Elizabeth I, and later as gentleman sewer to King James I—brought him significant connections at court, which doubtless influenced his and

H

Alleyn's appointment as joint masters of the bears, bulls, and mastiff dogs in 1604.

Henslowe's "diary"—a memorandum book primarily containing theatrical accounts, mostly from the 1590s—is one of the most revealing theatrical documents of the English Renaissance. In it he recorded his payments to dramatists (Ben Jonson, Thomas Dekker, and Henry Chettle, among others), the titles of plays (many of them no longer extant), costume payments, performance receipts, loans, and payments to actors.

Henslowe lived all his adult life in Clink Liberty, Southwark, where he served as an overseer of the poor and as churchwarden of St. Saviour's parish. He was buried there on January 10, 1616, in the chancel of the parish church "with an afternoon knell of the great bell." In his will he set aside money to purchase mourning gowns for forty poor men to accompany his body to the burial. Shortly thereafter Henslowe's widow died, precipitating a dispute over Henslowe's estate between Alleyn and Henslowe's brother and nephew. The court settled the suit in favor of Alleyn and his wife.

In addition to his theatrical associations, Henslowe knew a broad spectrum of statesmen (not least, Sir Julius Caesar, master of the rolls and chancellor of the Exchequer), and city and parish officials, as well as the famed astrologer Simon Forman with whom he consulted twice, once over medical problems and later to purchase a magic spell to disclose which of his servants were stealing from him. Henslowe had no children, but his nephew Francis participated in theatrical affairs in a minor capacity. Henslowe's papers, including his diary, several personal letters to Edward Alleyn, and assorted legal documents, are preserved in the Wodehouse Library, Dulwich College.

BIBLIOGRAPHY

Cerasano, S.P. "Philip Henslowe, Simon Forman, and the Theatrical Community of the 1590s." *Shakespeare Quarterly*, vol. 44, pp. 145–159.

———. "Revising Philip Henslowe's Biography." *Notes and Queries*, vol. 32, pp. 66–72.

Foakes, R.A., and R.T. Rickert, eds. *Henslowe's Diary.* 1961.

Greg. W.W., ed. *Henslowe's Diary.* 2 vols. 1908.

———, ed. *The Henslowe Papers.* 1907.

S.P. Cerasano

SEE ALSO

Alleyn, Edward; Forman, Simon; Revel's Office; Theaters

Hepburn, James (c. 1536–1578)

A violent, ambitious, and reckless Scottish nobleman, James Hepburn, Protestant fourth earl of Bothwell became the lieutenant and then consort of Mary, the Catholic Queen of Scots; his ruthlessness, however, alienated all factions in the Scottish nobility, unifying them long enough to destroy him and his wife.

Despite his Protestant beliefs—family and feudal loyalties frequently outweighed religion in sixteenth-century Scotland—Bothwell remained loyal to the regent, the French Catholic Mary of Guise, during the rebellion that marked the beginning of the Scottish Reformation (1559–1560). After Mary of Guise died in 1560, Bothwell went to the French court to confer with her daughter, Mary Queen of Scots and dowager of France, who was planning to return to Scotland to claim her throne. However, Mary's control over Scotland depended on the support of Bothwell's enemy, her bastard half-brother, the Protestant James Stewart; she made James her principal minister and the earl of Moray, while Bothwell was sent into exile.

Mary's attempt to consolidate her power through a marriage to the Catholic Lord Darnley caused Moray to rebel in 1565. Bothwell was recalled from France to serve as one of the leaders of Mary's army; his daring character impressed her in contrast to her weak and ineffectual husband. In March 1566, the leading Protestant lords assassinated Mary's secretary, David Riccio (or Rizzio), and threatened to kill her if she did not grant Darnley the crown-matrimonial and let them rule Scotland in her name. Bothwell's support helped Mary defeat the coup. Although there is no evidence to support the charge that he then became her lover, he certainly became her chief lieutenant.

In the early morning of February 10, 1567, gunpowder planted under Darnley's room at Kirk-o'-Field exploded. Darnley was found dead outside the ruined building, possibly a victim of strangulation. Suspicion immediately fell on Bothwell, and Darnley's father, the earl of Lennox, demanded that he be tried for murder. On April 12, a sham trial was held: facing intimidation, Lennox, the prosecutor, refused to attend, and in his absence, a jury quickly produced a verdict of not guilty.

On April 21, Bothwell took Mary under a show of force to his castle at Dunbar. He then arranged for civil and Catholic courts to invalidate his existing marriage. On May 15, Bothwell married the queen in a Protestant ceremony. Although critics have blamed Mary's uncontrollable passion for this hasty marriage, her complete political isolation made a union with a strong consort necessary. The marriage, however, infuriated the Scottish lords and people, Catholic and Protestant alike. Bothwell and Mary raised an army to counter the opposition; the two sides met at Carberry Hill, but as negotiations dragged on, Bothwell's army deserted. Bothwell fled, while Mary surrendered and abdicated in favor of her son, James VI. A few days later, a silver casket containing Bothwell's papers was discovered in Edinburgh; despite their questionable provenance and authenticity, the "Casket Letters" would serve Mary's enemies as evidence for adultery and intent to commit murder. These letters and poems, combined with the violent, erotic, but largely imaginary adventures detailed in George Buchanan's *Ane Detectioun of the duings of Marie Quene of Scottes* (1572), have formed the basis for most of Bothwell's literary and even historical portraits.

After his flight, Bothwell formed a small pirate navy in Shetland; he was eventually forced to sail for Norway, where he was arrested and sent to the king of Denmark. Isolated in a grim Danish prison, he went insane before dying in 1578.

BIBLIOGRAPHY

Donaldson, Gordon. *Mary Queen of Scots.* 1974.

Fraser, Antonia. *Mary Queen of Scots.* 1969.

Gore-Browne, Robert. *Lord Bothwell.* 1937.

Howell, T.B., ed. *Complete Collection of State Trials,* vol. 1. 1816.

Lee, Maurice. *James Stewart, Earl of Moray: A Political Study of the Reformation in Scotland.* 1953.

Lynch, Michael, ed. *Mary Stewart, Queen in Three Kingdoms.* 1988.

Phillips, James Emerson. *Images of a Queen: Mary Stuart in Sixteenth-Century Literature.* 1964.

John D. Staines

SEE ALSO

Buchanan, George; Mary Queen of Scots, Rizzio, David; Scotland, History of

Heraldry

Although heraldry is no longer considered an educational necessity, it pervaded Tudor society. Heraldry treatises proliferated, and coats of arms were used on seals, buildings, paintings, and tombs. A nobleman might be better known by his coat of arms or heraldic badge than his face, and his arms also served to show his rank, thus attesting his membership in the upper classes of society. Even though the link between a coat of arms and its origin on the field of battle or tiltyard (where family arms were already replaced by an *ad hoc* design, the *impresa*) was increasingly tenuous, both the ethos and symbolism of chivalry helped form the ideals of the ruling classes. Tudor "governours" served more by the pen than the sword, and despite the martial ardor of a Sidney or an Essex, knights were generally made on the carpet rather than on the battlefield. Even so, the chivalric symbols that made up the coat of arms, the shield, the helm and the "crest" on top of it, supporters on either side (for peers), and the badge (also borne by retainers), served as ancestral reminders of the ruling classes' theoretical origins as well as the individual's claim to hereditary gentility. By Elizabeth's reign these claims were advanced not only on the part of ancient families but also by the rising city merchants and professional classes, including William Shakespeare's family. These new men aided their ambition by co-opting the trappings of chivalry that designated gentle status both legally and socially, and acquiring a coat of arms became an important factor in social mobility. At the height, during the 1570s and 1580s, there were nearly 1,500 grants of arms made, which, though representing a tiny percentage of the general populace, seemed a deluge to those who assumed a static social order. This assumption, clearly false in Tudor England, nonetheless would fuel satiric reactions against these armigerous "new men" and upstarts, just as it brought those officials purveying these symbols of chivalry into question.

These men were the heralds or the officers of arms at the College of Arms. The three kings of arms, garter, Clarenceux, and Norroy, were the senior officers; then came the heralds proper, then the junior officers or pursuivants. These dozen or so men were more than students of armory, for although heraldry involves learning its Anglo-French terminology, or blazon, to describe coats of arms, it also includes all a herald's activities: blazoning and recording arms, taking down pedigrees of the gentry and nobility, advising on precedence, dealing with tournaments, going on embassies, and generally serving as aides to the earl marshal or the commissioners for that office on state occasions. The right to grant arms, to make men "enobliged" as the Henrician Visitation Commission of 1530 has it, was a peculiar right of the English kings of arms not enjoyed by their French confreres. For more than a century and a half, the heralds periodically conducted a series of such visitations throughout England to register coats of arms and pedigrees and to make infamous

H

those who wrongly claimed arms and gentility; apparently the Elizabethan rise in grants of arms is mainly due to these visitations as people sought to regularize their armorial status. (Individual visitation records of counties have been published by the Harleian Society, London.) On occasion the heralds also attended the sovereign wearing their tabards of the royal arms, the "Queen's Coat"; they also wore their tabards at the heraldic funerals of peers, knights, and even "citizens" having coat armor to show that the deceased died the monarch's true subject. The heralds therefore took responsibility for marshaling these funerals, even to regulating the design and heraldic accouterments of the catafalque (or "hearse") erected in church. These somber duties were extremely lucrative and led to quarrels among the officers. Garter, whose rights extended over peers and knights of the garter, claimed the funeral of any lord mayor of London dying in office, promoting the deceased to a baron's funeral on the grounds that the mayoralty was the nation's greatest annual honor. This also lined garter's pockets as the fees for a heraldic funeral were expensive: an earl's funeral could cost as much as a year of his income, once fees for the heralds and herald painters, funeral dole, and especially all the black mourning garments were included.

Tudor heralds were a quarrelsome lot. In particular, the role of garter principal king of arms was disputed as he attempted to encroach on rights claimed by the two provincial kings, Clarenceux and Norroy kings of arms, who divided England south and north between them. Adjudicating these claims was never easy, and the contentiousness of the officers of arms would be hard to underestimate, a feature that becomes even more marked during the reign of Elizabeth's successor.

BIBLIOGRAPHY

Anglo, Sydney. *Images of Tudor Kingship.* 1992.

Day, J.F.R. "Death Be Very Proud: Sidney and Elizabethan Heraldic Funerals." In *Tudor Political Culture.* Dale Hoak, ed., pp. 179–203. 1995.

———. *Venal Heralds and Mushroom Gentlemen. The Coat of Arms: An Heraldic Quarterly,* n.s., vols. 8–9.

Moule, Thomas. *Bibliotheca Heraldica Magnae Britanniae.* 1822.

Woodcock, Thomas, and John Martin Robinson. *Oxford Guide to Heraldry.* 1988.

Wagner, Sir Anthony R. *Heralds and Heraldry in the Middle Ages.* 1956.

———. *Heralds of England.* 1967.

J.F.R. Day

SEE ALSO

Devereux, Robert; Knighthood; Sidney, Philip; Social Classes

Herbert, William (1580–1630)

Eldest son of Henry Herbert and Mary (Sidney), William Herbert, third earl of Pembroke, is often remembered as one of the Herbert brothers to whom William Shakespeare's First Folio (1623) was dedicated. Educated at home and at New College, Oxford, Herbert had Samuel Daniel as his tutor. Yet despite this auspicious beginning, Herbert's early career was marred by an indiscretion with Mary Fitton, one of Elizabeth I's maids of honor, that led to a prison sentence in the Fleet. Later, however, Herbert came into favor under James I, eventually serving as lord chamberlain and as a member of the king's council for the Virginia Company. Other positions held by Herbert included the chancellorship of Oxford University where he was memorialized in the renaming of Broadgates Hall as Pembroke Hall.

Herbert's literary and artistic interests rise above his courtly and professional achievements. He was an intimate friend of John Donne, as well as the patron of Philip Massinger and Ben Jonson. Certainly Herbert knew Shakespeare when he performed with the King's Men, a factor that has encouraged literary critics to (mis)identify him as the (unlikely) candidate for "Mr. W.H." to whom Shakespeare's sonnets are dedicated. Like his uncle, Sir Philip Sidney, Herbert wrote verse, and George Chapman inscribed a sonnet to him at the end of his translation of the *Iliad.* Inigo Jones was also in his service. In addition, Herbert performed in the masque on St. John's Day, 1604, which was presented at court for the marriage of his brother.

Clarendon characterized Herbert as the most universally esteemed man of his age. Nevertheless, he seems to have been plagued by domestic unhappiness and financial problems that left him at the time of his death approximately £80,000 in debt.

BIBLIOGRAPHY

Waller, Gary F. *The Sidney Family Romance: Mary Wroth, William Herbert, and the Early Modern Construction of Gender.* 1993.

Wilson, John Dover. *An Introduction to the Sonnets of Shakespeare for the Use of Historians and Others.* 1964.

S.P. Cerasano

SEE ALSO
Daniel; Samuel; Donne, John; Jonson, Ben; Shakespeare
William

Heresy

Heresy, or deviation from the official (orthodox) norm of
the Christian faith, is a concept as old as Christianity
itself, but in the Middle Ages it became a crime punishable
by law. In England, this was enshrined primarily in
the statute *De haeretico comburendo,* passed by Henry IV
in 1401 as a means of combating Lollardy. This statute
provided that convicted heretics should be burned at the
stake. Two other statutes, one made by Richard II in 1381
and the other by Henry V in 1414, completed the official
legislation against heresy in force at the time of the Reformation.
It cannot be said that it was ever very effective,
and the severity of the punishment seems to have done
more to prevent trials for heresy than it did to exterminate
heretics. The burning of John Frith on July 4, 1533, created
a sensation, and ushered in a new era in which several
more people met their deaths, most (like Frith himself)
because they denied the Catholic doctrine of transubstantiation.
The 1401 statute was repealed in 1534, but the
other two were reinforced.

After the Reformation, Henry VIII could not afford to
appear to be more lax on the question of heresy than the
Roman Church was. He had Parliament pass the Act of
Six Articles (1539), which detailed the charge of heresy
on six counts, all of which were matters of traditional
Catholic doctrine disputed by the reformers, and provided
capital punishment for those convicted. The most
famous victim of this act was a woman by the name of
Anne Askew, who on July 16, 1546, was executed for
denying transubstantiation. With the accession of
Edward VI, all the heresy acts were repealed (1547), and
heresy ceased to be a crime punishable by death. However,
this situation did not last, and when Mary I
ascended the throne, she did all she could to revive the
medieval statutes. This move was approved by Parliament
effective from January 20, 1555, and for the first time in
England large numbers of people were burned at the stake
for heresy. These included not only such prominent
names as Hugh Latimer and Nicholas Ridley (both on
October 16, 1555) and Thomas Cranmer (March 21,
1556), but a number of humbler folk as well. Burnings
were especially numerous in London, and caused great
public aversion to Mary and her government.

Mary's persecutions were mild by European standards,
but they shocked the English, and they were quickly
memorialized by John Foxe, who regarded all Protestant
victims from the time of Henry VIII as martyrs. After
Mary's death, the heresy legislation was once more
repealed (1559), and heresy was never again a capital or
civil crime. It continued to exist, of course, but it was
treated as a theological aberration to be judged by the
ecclesiastical courts. Catholic recusants and Puritan dissenters
were legislated against, but the restrictions placed
on them were generally far less severe than had been the
case of heretics in earlier times. Catholics who were put to
death in Elizabeth's reign suffered for political reasons, and
the same was true of the few Puritan Separatists who were
executed in the 1590s. The crucial distinction is that these
people were dissenters from the Elizabethan Settlement of
religion; their theological views did not really matter.

Genuine heresy, in the theological sense of the term,
continued to exist in such forms as Socinianism and
Familism, but it was marginal to society and easily contained.
It was not until the advent of Archbishop William
Laud in 1633 that any serious attempt was made to prosecute
heresy, and then the reaction was such that it led to
the destruction of the church courts altogether (1641).

BIBLIOGRAPHY
Brigden, S. *London and the Reformation.* 1989.
Dickens, A.G. *The English Reformation.* 2nd edition.
    1989.
Elton, G.R. *The Tudor Constitution.* 2nd edition. 1982.
                                                    Gerald Bray

SEE ALSO
Askew, Anne; Articles of Religion; Cranmer, Thomas;
Family of Love; Frith, John; Henry VIII; Latimer, Hugh;
Marian Martyrs; Recusancy; Ridley, Nicholas

Hermeticism

See Alchemy; Astrology; Bruno, Giordano; Dee, John;
Magic

Heywood, John (c. 1497–c. 1578)

John Heywood's family originated in Coventry but his
early life is obscure. He probably studied at Broadgates
Hall, Oxford, in 1513–1514, perhaps after a career as a
boy singer. By 1519, he was rewarded as a singer in the

Portrait of John Heywood. From John Heywood, *The Spider and the Flie* (1556). Reproduced from the original by permission of the Henry E. Huntington Library and Art Gallery.

king's household. For the next forty years he was connected with the court, usually associated with entertainment, mostly plays, although he also was an accomplished poet and musician. He was a popular figure, perhaps because of his ingenious and inventive wit, which is approved by several witnesses, not least John Bale, who was hardly sympathetic to his Catholic outlook.

Heywood prospered in the 1520s, becoming a freeman of the city of London in 1523. A royal pension is recorded from 1528. He now became active as a dramatist, perhaps at first in collaboration with his father-in-law, John Rastell, who had a house with a stage in Finsbury Fields from 1524.

Although the composition dates of his six extant plays elude us, the publication of most of them between February 1533 and January 1534 is significant, in a momentous period in the English Reformation. Henry VIII was married by Thomas Cranmer to the pregnant Anne Boleyn in January 1533, and his marriage with Katherine of Aragon was annulled in May. The Reformation Parliament began significant anti-Catholic legislation in March. Sir Thomas More, a relative by marriage, wrote vehemently against the changes until his confinement in the Tower in April 1534. The publication of Heywood's witty but distinctly Catholic plays may be seen as an attempt to advance his particular brand of conciliatory humor in an increasingly dangerous atmosphere.

He participated in court entertainment throughout the 1530s, being paid by Thomas Cromwell in 1539 for a (lost) *Masque of King Arthur's Knights.* He took great risks by entering a conspiracy against Cranmer in 1543, and had to make a public recantation. Specially loyal to the Princess Mary, he delivered an oration outside St. Paul's in the celebration of her accession in 1553. His reputation as a man of wit was sustained by his *Dialogue of Proverbs* (1546) and a series of books of *Epigrammes* (1550, 1555, and 1560). In *The Spider and the Flie* (1556), a political-religious allegory concerning Queen Mary I, his ingenuity was such that scholarship has not yet disentangled it.

There is no evidence of persecution by Elizabeth I, and he remained in England for the first six years of her reign, by which time some of his Catholic relatives, including William Rastell, his printer, had fled. During his subsequent exile in the Low Countries, now impoverished, he attempted to recover some of his property, but he declined to return to England, and died sometime after the death of his Jesuit son, Ellis, in October 1578.

As a dramatist Heywood has always had a reputation for wit and good humor, but in light of their political context, it now seems that a rather more serious purpose underlies the plays: one closely associated with his Catholicism and directed precisely at the crisis over the king's divorce. The differing sections of national life, each bringing pressure on the king out of factional interest, may be compared with the conflicting claims in *The Play of the Wether* (printed 1533). In most of his plays there is palpable evidence of his religious views, which can be associated, through More, with Desiderius Erasmus. Following Chaucer he ridicules pardoners, incorporating material directly from the "Prologue" to *The Canterbury Tales* in *The Pardoner and the Friar* (1533).

The theatricality of his plays subsists in the brilliant matching of different characters who are grouped around topics of dispute. In *A Play of Love* (1534), each of the characters has an attitude toward love that leads to a dazzling process of grouping and regrouping as their conflicts assemble and reassemble them in various configurations. This is not simply a matter of opposing arguments: a palpable action and a richness of performance characteristics point to the development of ideas. Thus the Vice's appearance wearing a copintank hat and exploding with fireworks has consequences on his victim as well as himself.

Johan Johan (1533), a translation from a French farce, is precisely adapted to English circumstances, and reveals in the changes made a criticism of religious hypocrisy and corruption. The characters of *The Four PP* (1544?, but perhaps published earlier) are all charlatans, although some of them have a religious profession. Their trickery shows in the competition to tell the greatest lie, an exercise that involves much religious comedy, including a visit to hell by the Pardoner.

The manuscript of *Witty and Witless,* thought to be his earliest extant play, is closer to the *Colloquies* of Erasmus than the others, and argues about salvation. It illustrates neatly Heywood's use of drama as a means of expressing the tension between opposing forces, closely related to moral values and religious belief in a time of growing controversy. But Heywood's tolerance and good humor, aimed at a court audience, afford welcome antidotes to the severity of much contemporary writing.

BIBLIOGRAPHY

Axton, Richard, and Peter Happé, eds. *The Plays of John Heywood.* 1991.

Bolwell, Robert W. *The Life and Works of John Heywood.* 1921; repr. 1966.

Farmer, John S., ed. *Proverbs, Epigrams, and Miscellanies.* Early English Drama Society. 1906; repr. 1966.

Habenicht, Rudolph E., ed. *John Heywood's A Dialogue of Proverbs.* University of California English Studies, vol. 25. 1963.

Happé, Peter, ed. *Two Moral Interludes.* Malone Society Reprints. 1991.

Kolin, Philip C. "Recent Studies in John Heywood." *English Literary Renaissance,* vol. 13, pp. 113–123.

Robinson, Vicki K. *A Critical Edition of the* Play of the Wether. 1987.

Peter Happé

SEE ALSO

Bale, John; Catholicism; Drama, History of; Epigrams; Erasmus, Desiderius; More, Thomas; Rastell, John; Rastell, William; Vice, The

High Commission, Court of

The Court of High Commission was established in 1559 to oversee the internal discipline of the Church of England. Technically there were three high commissions, one for each of the provinces of Canterbury and York, and a third one for Ireland. A fourth was added for Scotland in the early seventeenth century. But in practice the term is usually reserved for the Canterbury commission, which had power to act in both English provinces.

In theory, the right to ensure that the church maintained its discipline had been claimed by the medieval kings, and it had sometimes been exercised by them as well. But it was only after the liturgical changes of the Reformation, which brought widespread nonconformity in their wake, that a commission of the type indicated here became both necessary and powerful. The high commission had the power to inflict ecclesiastical censures such as excommunication, but it was unable to act in the purely secular sphere, for instance, by depriving convicted persons of their property. This, in practice, removed a good deal of the sting of its condemnations.

High commission initially acted in a fairly uncontroversial way, and was even rather popular. But attitudes changed after 1583, when Archbishop John Whitgift decided to use it as the chief instrument in his war against the Puritans. This inevitably involved the commission in questions of religious conscience as well as simple matters of discipline, and it lost a good deal of public sympathy as a result. High commission was little used immediately after Elizabeth I's death, but it was revived in 1610.

BIBLIOGRAPHY

Elton, G.R. *The Tudor Constitution.* 2nd edition. 1982.

Kenyon, J.P. *The Stuart Constitution.* 2nd edition. 1986.

Usher, R.G. *The Rise and Fall of High Commission.* 2nd edition. 1968.

Gerald Bray

SEE ALSO

Church Polity; Courts, Ecclesiastical; Puritanism; Reformation, English; Whitgift, John

H

Hilliard, Nicholas (1547–1619)

At a time when painting in England was dominated by continental artists, Nicholas Hilliard was one of the few English-born painters to achieve an international reputation. Like many sixteenth-century artists, he worked in a variety of media, but he is best known today for his portrait miniatures, or "limnings." He portrayed almost every Elizabethan courtier of note, as well as numerous less well-known sitters, and he established miniature painting as one of the most highly regarded branches of art in sixteenth-century England, "a thing apart from all other painting or drawing," as he described it in his treatise, *The Arte of Limning* (c. 1600). His miniatures have contributed perhaps more than any other works of art to the twentieth-century view of the Elizabethan age as a time of elaborate symbolism, mysterious allusions, colorful pageantry, and ostentatious display.

Nicholas Hilliard's portrait of George Clifford, Earl of Cumberland (c. 1590). Clifford is shown dressed as the queen's champion in a tournament. By permission of the National Maritime Museum, Greenwich.

Hilliard was born in 1547, the son of an Exeter goldsmith. In 1557, he is recorded in Geneva, in the household of John Bodley, a merchant exiled by the persecutions of Protestants under Mary I. Hilliard is presumed to have accompanied the Bodley family back to London in 1559. Here he was apprenticed as a goldsmith, being made a freeman of the Goldsmiths' Company in 1569; his first wife, Alice Brandon, was the daughter of his former master. Such training was not unusual for artists who went on to make their careers in painting, and Hilliard continued to work as a goldsmith and jeweler throughout his career. His most important commission was the design for the second Great Seal for Elizabeth I, and he was heavily occupied with portrait medals for James I toward the end of his life.

Nothing is known about Hilliard's training as a miniaturist. His earliest known works date from 1560, a self-portrait and a miniature of Edward Seymour, lord protector Somerset, a copy of a lost painting. The confident miniatures of his maturity began to appear in the 1570s; his first dated portrait miniature of Elizabeth I was painted in 1572; his long association with the queen resulted in some of his finest works.

Hilliard's training as a goldsmith and his admiration of the works of engravers such as Lucas van Leyden and Albrecht Durer were important influences on his distinctive miniature style. He avoided using shadow to create form, and the lines of his sitters' features and clothing are emphasized. Their clothing and jewelery are often as important as their facial features; Hilliard produced a number of miniatures of the queen in which the face is a repetition of a standard type, but the details of dress and jewelery are always unique. He developed elaborate illusionistic techniques for representing jewels and lace, and further stressed the flat, decorative qualities of his miniatures by the use of calligraphic inscriptions. He adapted the conventions of miniature painting inherited from his predecessors, establishing the oval rather than circular shape as standard for small portrait miniatures, and experimenting with alternatives to the usual plain blue background. Hilliard also produced a number of miniatures in a larger format in which his sitters are shown at full length in elaborate interior or landscape settings.

Hilliard made a huge and varied contribution to the cultural life of Elizabethan England, but he was plagued by financial problems. Although he was employed by the queen for many years, he did not receive a pension until 1599, and he mortgaged it only three years later to pay off debts. He was commissioned by the Goldsmiths' Company to paint a large-scale portrait of Elizabeth I in partial payment of the lease on his house. This commission and a reference in his treatise are the only evidence that he did paint in oils, but several oil portraits of the queen have been associated with him. He seems to have been involved in designing and possibly executing engravings throughout his life, and he was given a monopoly over the engraving of royal portraits by James I. However, he did not enjoy the financial privileges of this position for long, dying at the age of 72, in debt, in 1619.

BIBLIOGRAPHY

Auerbach, Erna. *Nicholas Hilliard.* 1961.

Edmond, Mary. *Hilliard and Oliver.* 1983.

Hilliard, Nicholas. *The Art of Limning.* Arthur F. Kinney and Linda Bradley Salamon, eds. 1983.

Reynolds, Graham. *The English Portrait Miniatures.* Revised edition. 1988.

Strong, Roy. *The English Renaissance Miniature.* 1983.

Catharine MacLeod

SEE ALSO

Elizabeth I; Goldsmith's Work; Jewelry; Miniature Painting; Painting

History, Writing of

As in so many other spheres, the Tudor period witnessed considerable development in thought and writing about history. At the accession of Henry VII (1509), few people other than the clergy and certain royal patrons read history; by the death of Elizabeth I (1603), the scope of historical inquiry had broadened considerably, and history, although not yet a "discipline" in anything like the modern sense, was a genre of comparable importance to poetry, widely read by the educated elite, and readily available through the medium of print.

The standard form of medieval historical writing, of which England possessed a rich tradition, was the chronicle. In the two centuries or so prior to the Tudor accession, the writing of these records of royal and ecclesiastical achievements, almost invariably arranged annalistically but sometimes in biographical format, had spread beyond the walls of monastic houses to include secular clergy and even the occasional lay, urban author such as John Harding (1378–1465?), who wrote a popular metrical chronicle devoted to *res gestae* or chivalric deeds, and Robert Fabyan (d. 1513), a Londoner who wrote in English an important set of *Chronicles of England and France.* Fabyan may also have been the author of an anonymous but later

influential work, the manuscript "Great Chronicle of London." The *Policronicon,* a popular world chronicle by the fourteenth-century monk Ranulf Higden, was the first historical work to be published by the printer William Caxton (1422?–1461). At the same time, continental influences, especially French and Burgundian, had slowly crossed the channel in the form of the chronicles of such authors as Enguerrand de Monstrelet, Jean Froissart, and, late in the fifteenth century, Philippe de Commynes.

A significant innovation in the writing of history occurred with the arrival in 1502 of the Italian Polydore Vergil (1470–1505). This papal official would spend half a century in England, during which time he wrote, in various recensions, his *Anglica Historia,* a complete Latin history of England from the earliest documented times (in Caesar's and Tacitus's accounts of Britain) to the reign of Henry VIII. The first editions of this would not appear in print until 1534, and then only outside the country, but the work was consulted in manuscript by a number of Vergil's contemporaries; it was the first full-length humanist history of England modeled on contemporary European works. It also touched off an extensive debate over the authenticity of such legendary figures as King Arthur and the Trojan Brutus.

At the same time two native Englishmen were also contributing to the genre. Sir Thomas More wrote an unfinished biography of Richard III, in Latin and English versions, that provided a useful model for later biographers, and which was unique in offering psychological insight. More immediately important was the chronicle of Edward Hall or Halle (d. 1547), a minor royal official and sometime member of Parliament, who limited his work to an account, which drew on Vergil, of *The Union of the Two Illustrious Houses of Lancaster and York,* in essence retelling the story of the Wars of the Roses from the deposition of Richard II in 1399 (a seminal event in Tudor political thought) to the restoration of legitimacy in the throne by Henry VII reuniting the two warring branches of the Plantagenet family and the subsequent triumphant reign of Vergil's patron, Henry VIII. Although Hall retained an annalistic format within his regnal chapters (a device borrowed from Vergil), his work was written in continuous prose and with such perception that it managed to transcend its chronicle form.

Hall's book was first printed in 1548. For the next two or three decades there steadily grew a lay interest in the English past. At the same time the classical curriculum of the two universities began to include Greek and Latin historians as a staple of the undergraduate diet. Hall himself

H

soon spawned imitators, such as a chronicle by Thomas Lanquet (1521–1545), and the numerous chronicles written in imitation of Hall, such as the one by Richard Grafton (d. 1572?), a printer. The most prolific chronicler of the second half of the century, however, was John Stow, a London tailor who produced several different series of *Summaries, Chronicles,* and eventually full-scale *Annals of England* in various editions, making him probably the single most widely read secular historical author of his age. The Tudor chronicle tradition culminated in the publication of Raphael Holinshed's (d. 1580) *Chronicles of England, Scotland, and Ireland* (1577). A mammoth work initiated by the printer Reyne Wolfe (d. 1573) and assembled by Holinshed in conjunction with two or three others (most notably William Harrison, the author of a prefatory *Description of England*). The inspired team of editor-writers, headed by Abraham Fleming (1552?–1607), included John Hooker (or Vowell) of Exeter (1526–1601), Stow himself, and the lawyer Francis Thynne (1545–1608), who revised the material on Scotland. In a revised and enlarged version of 1587, many late Tudor readers found the closest thing to a "definitive" history; the work furnished Elizabethan dramatists and historical poets, most notably William Shakespeare, with material and with the overarching providential structure of events (a feature of earlier works such as Vergil's) culminating in the establishment of Tudor hegemony.

Holinshed's *Chronicles* was not reprinted after 1587, and in fact the vogue for chronicles was already drawing to a close by the time his second edition appeared. Nor were most of the Tudor chronicles reprinted in the following century, the last revision of Stow appearing in 1631–1632. Two explanations are possible. First, works such as Holinshed's were extremely expensive, and the very printing press that had done so much over the century since Caxton to encourage a lay interest in the past could produce shorter works much more cheaply. Secondly, the chronicle as a literary form was being called into question. A resurgent interest in humanist historiography, including the earlier work of Vergil but also newer continental historians such as Francesco Guicciardini, increasingly appealed to the educated elite. By the 1590s, when a circle of scholars such as John Hayward (1564?–1627) associated with the second earl of Essex began to develop a newer style of "politic history," a reaction set in that favored a more politically focused, epigrammatic history, for which the ancient historian Tacitus, as edited by the Oxford classicist Sir Henry Savile (1549–1622), provided a compelling model. Just as

Protestant authors were instinctively suspicious of the "popery" inherent in medieval historians, so there is more than a hint of social snobbery in the attacks of Savile and Jacobean writers on the Tudor authors of the chronicles, who had been drawn from the urban middling sort rather than the university-trained elite. It would be a mistake, however, to discount the Tudor chronicle or view it merely as a lingering sign of medievalism, a staging post to better things. In the hands of an imaginative and perceptive writer such as Hall, it had achieved great insight into the interaction between providence and human action. And Holinshed's *Chronicles,* much-maligned over the centuries, is now viewed less as a final conservative attempt to revive an old form than as a bold and largely unimitated experiment in a multiauthored text that presented—in striking contrast to most of the seventeenth-century regnal histories that followed it—an account of the English past that was "multivocal." Seen from this perspective, its many anecdotes are less untidy digressions than a colorful tapestry of the lives of ordinary people.

The only work of comparable scope to Holinshed's to emerge from the Elizabethan period was similarly *sui generis,* though for different reasons. John Foxe (1516–1587), a Marian exile, published in 1563 his *Acts and Monuments,* a book more familiarly known as the "Book of Martyrs." Republished several times over the four decades, it became a fixture in cathedral churches, parochial libraries, and even private collections. The major Elizabethan attempt at a Protestant history of the church from Roman times, it focused in its second half on the Tudor Reformation and provided a detailed record of the persecutions and punishments of the Henrician and Marian martyrs. Foxe's own celebrated status as a writer, his religious subject, and the almost hagiographic character of his book preserved it from the same accusations of literary failure that awaited Holinshed, though Foxe, too, privileged the contribution of humble artisanal martyrs, the sort of person not traditionally deemed worthy of historical representation.

Foxe's book, like much of Holinshed, drew not only on formal historical accounts of the past (medieval authors such as Eusebius and Bede) but also on a developing interest in archival research that first appeared in ecclesiastical history. Among the most important historiographical contributions of the early Elizabethan period had been the editing and publication of a number of medieval chronicles (including pioneering work on Anglo-Saxon authors such as Bede) by a circle of scholars under the patronage and direction of Archbishop Matthew Parker (1504–1575). Not only did these scholars make the medieval record available in print; they also helped to initiate a wave of what is generally called—without its modern pejorative sense—"antiquarianism," in some senses the more erudite stepsister of Tudor narrative historical writing.

The antiquarian tradition in English writing was, of course, considerably older than Parker's circle. In the late fifteenth century, an author named William Botoner or Worcestre (1415–1482?) had made a close study of old records and of monuments and landscape part of his unpublished *Itinerary* through the southern and western parts of the kingdom. More influentially, John Leland (1506–1552?), a Henrician humanist charged with rescuing the many manuscripts held by the dissolved monastic houses, had made great strides in textual collection and editing (as had his friend and associate, John Bale, bishop of Ossory). Like Worcestre, Leland had traveled widely through the kingdom, describing its physical features, architecture, monuments, and towns. He tried, and failed, to incorporate his wide-ranging record of England's past into a formal "history"—there was no available classical model that would easily allow this "place"-oriented work to be recast chronologically. But the *Itinerary,* as the record of Leland's travels became known, remained unpublished until the early eighteenth century.

A further influence on the development of antiquarianism was the work of the heralds, the officers of the College of Arms, who were responsible for policing claims to gentility through their regular visitations of counties, and were therefore well accustomed to close inspection of public records (such as pipe rolls and close rolls) and private muniments. Leland's mode of scholarship and that of the heralds combined most forcefully in the work of the former schoolmaster, William Camden (1551–1623). Camden was not, in fact, a trained herald (although he would later be appointed to the College of Arms), but his methods closely resembled those of the heralds. In the 1580s, at the suggestion of Abraham Ortelius, a Dutch geographer, Camden undertook the *Britannia,* a description of England and, to a lesser degree, Scotland designed as Leland-style itinerary (along the ancient Roman Antonine Itineraries), but ultimately much more. First published in 1586, the work proved immediately popular among a gentry readership: so much so that Camden revised, expanded, and reissued it several more times up to 1607, and oversaw an English translation in 1610. In its various forms, the *Britannia* provided the essential published guide to the kingdom's geography, with substantial attention to its past development as Camden ferreted out the origins of local monuments and houses, and the histories of local gentry and aristocratic families. Although neither as broad in scope nor as original as Leland's earlier work (on which Camden drew heavily since he did not travel as widely), it proved, because published, even more influential on the late Tudor sense of national identity. It represented a generation of writers attempting smaller-scale, more detailed "chorographies" or descriptions of their counties or towns, beginning with the lawyer William Lambarde's (1536–1601) *Perambulation of Kent*—a work first published in 1576 and therefore developed quite independent of and prior to Camden's work—and continuing with Richard Carew's (1555-1620) Survey of Cornwall, Sampson Erdeswicke's (d. 1603) *Survey of Staffordshire,* and, perhaps most important, the chronicler John Stow's wonderfully detailed street-by-street *Survey of London,* published in 1598. The Tudor antiquaries are often thought of, even more than the prose writers such as Vergil and Holinshed, as the founders of modern English historical scholarship. It is important to note, however, that they gave considerable attention to memorializing the nondocumentary past, both the physical traces provided by ruins and old buildings, and the vigorous popular traditions, passed on orally over many generations, and used by relatively humble villagers and townsmen to explain the history of their communities. They thereby served the additional function of handing down an otherwise unrecorded wealth of historical thought among England's nonliterate masses.

The activities of many of the antiquaries came together in a unique collaborative enterprise called the Elizabethan College of Antiquaries. An informal body that involved Camden, Stow, Thynne, and many other historically minded scholars drawn from heraldry, law, and other occupations, the college met beginning in 1586 until the end of Elizabeth's reign, being revived very briefly under James I. Their "discourses," short essays on topics such as land tenures, knighthood, the coinage, and archaic words, were much consulted by seventeenth-century scholars, and, like the longer chorographies, represented an attempt to wean the study of the past away from strict attention to kings, nobility, and matters of high politics to a more comprehensive account of "things." It would be a younger generation of Jacobean scholars, most notably the lawyers Sir Henry Spelman (1564?–1641) and John Selden (1584–1654), who would apply this method of inquiry in their own subsequent investigations into topics such as the

H

history of feudal institutions and of church tithes; Selden's *Historie of Tithes* (1618), although clearly an antiquarian essay, would be the first English work to bridge the gap between antiquarianism and history proper by casting his research in a chronological form.

All of this historical writing would have had little effect had there not also developed over the course of the sixteenth century a much stronger interest in the past on the part of an expanding literate public. Recent work on readership, and in particular on library collections, demonstrates that historical titles were increasingly being included on the bookshelves of gentry, and even yeoman and merchant readers. A good deal of the minor historical literature of the period—chronicles by Grafton, Stow's shorter *Summaries,* and abridgements of history by Londoners like Anthony Munday (1557–1633)—represent a concerted attempt to make English, European, and classical history available to a wider audience than had previously been the case. This trend would continue, even more forcefully, throughout the seventeenth century, but neither the humanist-style biographies written in James I's reign (Camden's *Annales* of the reign of Elizabeth being the most famous example) nor the great antiquarian achievements of the later seventeenth century would have been conceivable without the activities of Leland, Vergil, Hall, Holinshed, and other Tudor historians.

BIBLIOGRAPHY

Baker, Herschel. *The Race of Time: Three Lectures on Renaissance Historiography.* 1967.

Ferguson, Arthur B. *Clio Unbound: Perceptions of the Social and Cultural Past in Renaissance England.* 1979.

Gransden, Antonia. *Historical Writing in England.* Vol. 2: c. 1307 *to the Early Sixteenth Century.* 1982.

Levy, F.J. *Tudor Historical Thought.* 1967.

McKisack, May. *Medieval History in the Tudor Age.* 1971.

Patterson, Annabel. *Reading Holinshed's Chronicles.* 1994.

Daniel R. Woolfe

SEE ALSO

Antiquarianism; Camden, William; Foxe, John; Hall, Edward; Holinshed, Raphael; Scotland, History of; Leland, John; Marian Martyrs; Polydore Vergil

Hoby, Lady Margaret (1571–1633)

Lady Margaret Hoby, a godly Yorkshire gentlewoman, and author of an important diary, was the daughter of Arthur and Thomasin Dakins of Linton, Yorkshire. Hoby was her well-to-do parents' only heir. Born in early 1571, she received a strongly Protestant education under the tutelage of the countess of Huntingdon, at whose estate Hoby met two of her future husbands, Walter Devereux and Thomas Sidney. She married Devereux in 1589 and the couple received the estate of Hackness, near Scarborough, as a wedding gift from her parents, Devereux's brother, Robert, the earl of Essex, and the earl of Huntingdon. Devereux was killed fighting at the siege of Rouen in 1591. In the same year, Hoby married Thomas Sidney, brother of Mary, countess of Pembroke, and Sir Philip Sidney, but he died in 1595. After the death of the earl of Huntingdon, she fought a lawsuit with his heir over the title to Hackness. In 1596, she married Thomas Posthumous Hoby, son of Sir Thomas Hoby and Lady Elizabeth Hoby Russell, and they took up residence at Hackness. They were married for thirty-seven years until her death, when Thomas Hoby erected a monument on the wall of Hackness church, a long inscription on black marble praising "her Godly manner of lyfe and conversation" (Moody 224).

Hoby's *Diary,* British Library MS Egerton 2614, is fifty-nine folio pages in italic hand and covers the years 1599 to 1605. Many entries chronicle Hoby's private prayers, spiritual self-examination, meditation, devotional reading, church attendance, psalm-singing, and household prayers. Two books inscribed with Lady Hoby's name, Philippe de Mornay's *Fowre Bookes, of the Institution, Use and Doctrine of the Holy Sacrament* (1600), and *A Treatise of the Church* (1606), represent the pious reading to which she continually refers in the *Diary* (Moody xliii, xlvii). She notes the course of her various illnesses; time spent doing needlework; kitchen and garden activities; and her care for her tenants and dependants. Hoby records her sufferings, usually from illness, probably as part of close soul-searching. She notes William Eure's hostile visit, the provocation for Thomas Hoby's famous lawsuit against the Eure family. Recording three journeys to London, she makes brief entries noting the arraignment of her former brother-in-law, the earl of Essex, and comments on Queen Elizabeth's last illness, which "wrought great sorow and dread in all good subiectes hartes" (Moody 186). Lady Margaret Hoby died at Hackness in 1633 and a chapel built in her memory by Thomas Hoby still stands.

BIBLIOGRAPHY

Fox, Evelyn. "The Diary of an Elizabethan Gentlewoman." *Transactions of the Royal Historical Society.* 3rd series. Vol. 2 (1908), pp. 153–174.

Graham, Elspeth. "Women's Writing and the Self." *Women and Literature in Britain, 1500–1700.* Helen Wilcox, ed. 1996.

Hoby, Margaret. *Diary.* Women Writers Project, Brown University. Available on the Internet at http://www.wwp.brown.edu/.

Meads, Dorothy M., ed. *The Diary of Lady Hoby.* 1930.

Moody, Joanna, ed. *The Private Life of an Elizabethan Lady: The Diary of Lady Margaret Hoby, 1599–1605.* 1998.

Wilcox, Helen. "Private Writing and Public Function: Autobiographical Texts by Renaissance English-women." In *Gloriana's Face: Women, Public and Private, in the English Renaissance.* S.P. Cerasano and Marion Wynne-Davies, eds. 1992.

Elaine V. Beilin

SEE ALSO
Devereux, Robert

Hoby, Thomas (1530–1566)

Praised by such Elizabethan exponents of indigenous English culture as Roger Ascham for "knowledge of divers tongues," Sir Thomas Hoby secured a place in English letters with his translation of Baldassare Castiglione's seminal work, *Il Cortegiano.* Hoby's rendition not only extended the book's already vast influence to an even broader English readership but also served the period as a model of vernacular prose style, elegant yet direct.

Hoby's early intimacy with continental languages was nurtured during a tour of Europe undertaken from 1547 to 1550, subsequent to his attendance at St. John's College, Cambridge. Exposure to the writing of his Strasburg host, Martin Bucer, prompted his first translation: *The gratulation of M. Martin Bucer,* a treatise celebrating the progress of English Protestantism that found speedy publication in 1549. Back home, Hoby entered the service of William, marquis of Northampton, a post he retained throughout the balance of Edward VI's reign. At Mary I's accession, Hoby again traveled abroad to Padua, where he likely completed his translation of Castiglione before returning to England in 1555. His marriage to Elizabeth Cook in 1558 produced four children. Hoby was knighted and appointed successor to Sir Thomas Smith as ambassador to France in 1566, but died that same year, shortly after his arrival in Paris.

The Courtyer of Count Baldessar Castilio, published in 1561, gave English readers access to this "storehouse of most necessary implements for the conversacion, use, and training up of mans life with Courtly demeaners." The book's anatomy of courtly manner and its culminating Neoplatonic discourse would significantly imprint the Elizabethan intellectual and poetic landscape. Yet it is Hoby's remarkable capacity to render the stylistic poise of his original—a work that largely takes rhetorical surface as its very subject—that credits his enduring status as one of England's greatest translators.

BIBLIOGRAPHY
Hoby, Sir Thomas. *The Travels and Life of Sir Thomas Hoby of Bisham Abbey, Written by Himself, 1547–1564.* Royal Historical Society. Camden Miscellany, vol. 10, no. 2. 1902.

Raleigh, Walter A., ed. *The Book of the Courtier from the Italian of Count Baldessare Castiglione: Done into English by Sir Thomas Hoby anno 1561.* Tudor Translations, first series, vol. 23. 1900; repr. 1967.

Christopher Martin

SEE ALSO
Italian Literature, Influence of

Holbein, Hans, the Younger (c. 1497–1543)

Painter, portraitist, and engraver, Hans Holbein the Younger worked in London from 1526 to 1528, and from 1532 until his death from the plague, at age 46, in 1543. These years of extraordinary accomplishment established him as the most influential portraitist in England until the advent of Van Dyck, the visual chronicler of the Caroline court, a century later. No one before Holbein could catch so exquisitely the texture of silk and fur, the play of light off a gold chain, or the nuances of emotion in the human face. His drawings and oil paintings preserve not only the outward appearance, meticulously rendered, of a generation of prominent sitters, but also an indelible impression of their inner life. Appointed as court painter to Henry VIII in 1536, Holbein created not merely images reflecting and enhancing the power of his royal patron, but the very image of Tudor kingship.

Already distinguished among the immigrant artists attracted by the newly resplendent Tudor court, Holbein enjoyed a considerable reputation as a book illustrator and painter of religious subjects as well as a portraitist. He arrived in London in 1526 with letters of introduction to the English humanist circle from Desiderius Erasmus, who had befriended the young artist in Basel, and whose

Hans Holbein's portrait of Anne of Cleves, the fourth wife of Henry VIII (c. 1539). By permission of The Board of Trustees of the Victoria and Albert Museum.

enduring image remains Holbein's portrait of the scholar at his writing desk (1523, Louvre, Paris). Having just brought out his "Dance of Death" woodcuts (1523–1526), and also having done the illustrations for a widely circulated edition of Erasmus's *Praise of Folly,* Holbein had no trouble attracting notable commissions and making connections in and out of court during those first two years in London. He painted Sir Thomas More (1527, Frick, New York) and came to know the influential royal minister Thomas Cromwell. He also became the favored painter, for both private portraits and civic commissions, of the German merchants of the Steel Yard, headquarters of the Hanseatic League in London. These patrons served him well when he returned from a Basel torn by the strife of the Reformation in 1532.

During his final period in England, although his output was large and varied, Holbein's chief continuing project was to craft and refine the image of the king. In 1535 Henry had issued the Coverdale Bible with Holbein's polemical title page showing the king handing down the Word of God to an assembly of kneeling churchmen. Holbein's successive portraits emphasize the indestructible body politic of the king rather than the increasingly bloated hulk of the man. They reveal a gradual movement, running counter to Holbein's reputation as a genius of realism, away from the psychologically probing portrait

of 1536 (Thyssen-Bornemisza Collection, Lugarno), to his bejeweled and impossibly broad-shouldered image of 1540 (Galleria Nazionale, Rome) based on Clouet's Mannerist portrait of Francis I, to the late images of an austere, hieratic monarch who projects nothing more—or less—than an impassive authority. Holbein thus sets the precedent for the official portraits of Henry's daughter Elizabeth I in the last decade of the century, images suggesting the cosmic scope of queenship while the aging Virgin Queen very nearly disappears inside her enormous collars and billowing gowns.

For the court, Holbein's most imposing image of kingship, destroyed in the fire of 1698 but surviving in a cartoon by Holbein and in several copies by later hands, must have been the wall decoration in the Privy Chamber at Whitehall (1536–1537). There the spectator ushered into the royal presence would have witnessed a careful merger of art and life: the fleshly king enthroned before a mural showing his own full-length image and that of his third wife Jane Seymour, and behind them Henry's parents, Henry VII and Elizabeth of York, the founders of the Tudor line.

Both for the beauty of its finish and the subtlety of its symbolic intrigue, Holbein's English masterpiece in the judgement of most modern viewers is *The Ambassadors* (1533, National Gallery, London), a double portrait of Jean de Dinteville and Georges de Selve, French legates to Henry's court. Ironically, the painting was scarcely known in England at the time: it followed Dinteville back to France and crossed the Channel again only at the end of the eighteenth century. Holbein's subjects here dispose themselves to either side of a table displaying the instruments of the arts and sciences. Among these objects, a celestial globe on the "upper" shelf balances a globe of the earth on the "lower," while navigational devices are positioned above a lute and a merchant's arithmetic book. The arrangement suggests the harmonies and discords between heavenly and earthly calculation. By a trick of perspective, a weird streak at the bottom of the painting resolves itself when squinted at from the side into the image of a skull—the "hollow bone" that is the meaning of Holbein's name in German. "The Ambassadors" thus combines two key Renaissance themes, a celebration of the power of the human intellect in the rational order of a world it has mastered, and a *memento mori,* an oblique reminder of death and the vanity of all things. A thorough cleaning and repair in 1995–1996 has restored this portrait, long misperceived beneath layers of glaze as somber, to its original vividness of color.

BIBLIOGRAPHY

Auerbach, Erna. *Tudor Artists.* 1954.

Rowlands, John. *Holbein: The Paintings of Hans Holbein.* 1985.

Strong, Roy. *Holbein and Henry VIII.* 1967.

Ernest Gilman

SEE ALSO

Engraving and Illustration; Erasmus, Desiderius; Henry VIII; Humanism; Painting; Privy Chamber

Holidays

See Calendar, Church; Calendar, Secular; Folklore and Folk Rituals

Holinshed, Raphael (d. 1580)

Although Raphael Holinshed is the most famous of all the Tudor chroniclers, the details of his life and career remain remarkably obscure. He is believed to be the son of Ralph Holinshed of Sutton Downes, Cheshire, and is perhaps the Holinshed who matriculated in Christ's Church, Cambridge, in 1544. Nothing certain is known of him until 1561, when he was found employed as steward to Thomas Burdet of Bromcote, Warwickshire, a position he would hold for the rest of his life. It was probably around that same time that Holinshed began his important association with the printer Reginald (or Reynar) Wolfe, assisting Wolfe in gathering historical manuscripts for a new work of world history and geography. Wolfe labored on this ambitious project for twenty-five years; however, he died before his book was ready for the press. After Wolfe's death (1573), the publishers George Bishop, John Harrison, John Hunne, and Lucas Harrison agreed to complete the project, placing Holinshed in charge of its production but, due to costs, narrowing its focus solely to histories and descriptions of the lands of the British Isles. The work that Wolfe began and Holinshed finished finally appeared in the year 1577, under the title *The Chronicles of England, Scotland, and Ireland.*

The 1577 *Chronicles* is a massive, two-volume tome of about 2,800 double-columned pages. Although Holinshed's name alone graces the title page, the work was a collaborative production in every sense of the word. Holinshed did not consider himself to be a history writer but rather a "collector" or compiler of historical materials. The historical sections of the *Chronicles* are thus chiefly a synthesis of other authors' writings, sometimes redacted

A Dying King. Raphael Holinshead, *Chronicles of England, Scotland, and Ireland* (1577). By permission of the Folger Shakespeare Library.

but often reproduced verbatim. Holinshed's editorial principle was one of inclusiveness rather than selectiveness: often he presented without comment two or more conflicting accounts of a single historical event, leaving readers to decide for themselves which account seemed most believable. In constructing the 1577 edition, Holinshed was aided by two other men: William Harrison contributed its descriptions of England and Scotland while Richard Stanyhurst wrote its description of Ireland and part of its Irish history. Although weighty, expensive, and at times contradictory in its narratives, Holinshed's *Chronicles* proved a great success, and a second edition of the work was warranted just a few years after the first one.

Holinshed died near the end of 1580, leaving all his "worldlie goodes" to Thomas Burdet. Yet two posthumous publications kept his name before the English public. The first was the new, augmented edition of the *Chronicles* (1587). The clergyman Abraham Fleming took Holinshed's place as chief editor of this version, assisted by John Hooker, alias Vowell, John Stow, and Francis Thynne. The contributions of these men increased the content of the *Chronicles* by about one-third, while the numerous moralizing asides that Fleming introduced into this edition gave it a strongly Protestant tone largely absent from the first version. This edition of the *Chronicles* famously raised the ire of Elizabeth I's Privy Council, which suppressed almost 160 pages of its text. The reasons behind the government's censorship are still unclear, though some appear to have arisen from passages deemed insulting to King James VI of Scotland, while others may have resulted from personal antipathies among members of the council.

The second work with which Holinshed was posthumously associated was the sixth edition of *A Mirror for Magistrates* (1587), the ever-expanding collection of histori-

H

cal verse tragedies that was perhaps the most widely read work of Tudor secular poetry. Holinshed is credited in this edition with commissioning a *Mirror* poem on the fifteenth-century warrior Sir Nicholas Burdet, the most famous ancestor of his employer, Thomas Burdet. Later, in two prose passages included in the collection, Holinshed himself is represented as speaking with the authors of the *Mirror* tragedies. In the first passage, he offers praise for the Burdet tragedy; in the second, he discusses two old poems on the battle of Flodden Field (1513) that he had supplied for inclusion in the *Mirror* and directs attention to some letters written by King James IV of Scotland that he had printed in the *Chronicles*.

Holinshed was responsible for several historical works during his life, including a translation of William of Malmesbury's *Historia Novella* (now lost) and an English version of Florence of Worcester's chronicle (B.L. MS. Harl. 563). However, the *Chronicles* was the only one of his writings to find its way to print, and it is on this work alone that his reputation rests. Certainly the value of the work to Elizabethan culture is undeniable. Not only was Holinshed's the most sumptuous and comprehensive of all the English chronicles, but it also played a guiding role in the development of the Tudor historical drama. Numerous playwrights of the 1580s and 1590s based their plays on narratives from Holinshed's work, including William Shakespeare, who shaped more than a dozen dramas from material from the 1577 and 1587 editions, including *King Lear, Cymbeline, Macbeth,* and all of his English history plays.

Among historians, however, the value of Holinshed's chronicle has remained a subject of controversy. Some scholars tend to fault the *Chronicles* for its seemingly indiscriminate inclusiveness and for its authors' refusal to reconcile contradictory passages, while others have argued that these "faults" are actually the greatest strengths of the work, suggesting that Holinshed and his collaborators designed the *Chronicles* as a multivocal record of the variety of English opinion and as a tool to spur critical reading practices among the members of their middle-class audience. No matter what may be the final verdict on the achievement of Holinshed's *Chronicles,* its rich and variegated store of material guarantees that it will continue to find readers among historians, literary scholars, and those interested in the early cultural history of Britain and Ireland.

BIBLIOGRAPHY

Campbell, Lily B. *Parts Added to the* Mirror for Magistrates, *by John Higgins and Thomas Blenerhasset.* 1946.

Donno, Elizabeth Story. "Some Aspects of Shakespeare's Holinshed." *Huntington Library Quarterly,* vol. 50, pp. 229–248.

Ellis, Sir Henry, ed. *Holinshed's Chronicles of England, Scotland, and Ireland.* 6 vols. 1807–1808; repr. 1965.

Kelly, H.A. *Divine Providence in the England of Shakespeare's Histories.* 1970.

Levy, F.J. *Tudor Historical Thought.* 1967.

Parry, G.J.R. "William Harrison and Holinshed's Chronicles." *Historical Journal,* vol. 27, pp. 789–810.

Patterson, Annabel. *Reading Holinshed's Chronicles.* 1994.

Scott Lucas

SEE ALSO

Censorship; Harrison, William; History, Writing of; Hooker, John; Ireland, History of; Scotland, History of; Shakespeare, William; Stanyhurst, Richard; Stow, John

Homilies, Books of

The two *Books of Homilies* or of sermons published in 1547 and 1563, respectively, were largely the work of Archbishop Thomas Cranmer for the first, and Bishop John Jewel for the second. There are twelve sermons in the first book that cover a mixture of doctrinal and disciplinary matters. The first one is an exhortation to the reading of Holy Scripture, which was a central concern of the reformers. The next three deal with original sin, salvation, and faith, while the last eight concentrate on good works and the application of Christian principles to everyday life.

There are twenty-one sermons in the second book of *Homilies,* which contains sermons on the major festivals of the Christian year. In addition, there are two sermons devoted especially to prayer: two to the Sacraments, including one on worthy reception of them, and one on matrimony. Also included are sermons on the dangers of idolatry, gluttony and drunkenness, and idleness. Two further sermons deal with the reverence that ought to be shown to the church building and the worship conducted in it, and one is devoted to the encouragement of almsgiving. The last sermon, against disobedience and wilful rebellion, was added in 1571, after Queen Elizabeth I had been excommunicated by Pope Pius V (1570).

The intention behind the publication of the *Homilies* was that they should be read Sunday by Sunday, and they are mostly subdivided into sections that could be used one at a time. The main aim was to provide a teaching resource for clergy who were not able to preach themselves. This sounds strange today, but considering the low level of education of many parish priests, who had never been taught how to preach, it was understandable at the time. The *Homilies* were also a way of ensuring that reformed doctrine would be properly communicated to ordinary people, and not reinterpreted by clergy who might not understand or sympathize with it. It is unlikely that they were ever widely used, and as time went on lecturers were appointed to parishes who could supply the deficiencies of the clergy, but they were a useful model preachers could imitate, and they are still sometimes used in the preparation of sermons today.

They also form part of the doctrinal standards, or *formularies,* of the Church of England, and as such offer a valuable source for understanding what is more briefly or obscurely expressed in the Thirty-nine Articles or in the Book of Common Prayer. It is in the *Homilies* that the Protestant character of the English Reformation is most clearly seen, and the relative neglect they have suffered in modern times has enabled a distorted view of the Elizabethan Church as a more Catholic institution than it really was to take root. In this respect, the *Homilies* offer a valuable and much needed corrective to the false impression that has too often been conveyed by those who have preferred to emphasize the structural continuities of the post-Reformation church with its medieval predecessor.

BIBLIOGRAPHY

Bond, Ronald B., ed. *Certain Sermons or Homilies* (1547), and *A Homily Against Disobedience and Wilful Rebellion* (1520). 1987.

Sermons or Homilies Appointed To Be Read in Churches. Prayer Book and Homily Society. 1833; repr. Focus Christian Ministries Trust, 1986.

Gerald Bray

SEE ALSO

Articles of Religion; Book of Common Prayer; Church of England; Clergy; Cranmer, Thomas; Jewel, John; Reformation, English; Sermons

Homosexuality

Although "homosexuality" has become since the late nineteenth century the term by which we refer to same-sex erotic relationships, the Tudor era used other terms. The principal term was "sodomy," which the *Oxford English Dictionary* locates as early as the thirteenth century and defines as "an unnatural form of sexual intercourse, esp. that of one male with another." Legal and cultural evidence reveals the problematic quality of this definition, for at moments "sodomy" can be a term to describe any imaginable form of debauchery, including heterosexual acts—or it can become a convenient term for labeling one's enemies. With unintended irony, James VI of Scotland in his advice book, *Basilicon Doron* (1599), written for Prince Henry, insists that neither sodomy nor witchcraft can ever be forgiven. Such an admonition underscores the frequent link between sodomy and other socially unacceptable activities.

The term "buggery" functions in the era as a synonym for "sodomy." The *OED* traces the term back to the fourteenth century but reveals also a possible confusion as it defines "buggery" as "abominable heresy," or "unnatural intercourse of a human being with a beast, or of men with one another, sodomy." These terms elide what seem to be clear distinctions of sexual activity. The period also used the terms "catamite," "ingle," and "Ganymede" to refer to those suspected of homosexual relationships.

However we define it, "sodomy" became a capital offense under civil law all over Europe in the sixteenth century. Parliamentary statute under Henry VIII in 1533–1534 for the first time made sodomy a felony in England. Parliament renewed this law several times under Henry and Edward VI, only to have it repealed under Mary and then reinstated under Elizabeth. Actual prosecutions for sodomy remained few: for example, the Home Counties Assizes reveal one conviction for sodomy during the 1553–1602 period. The few convictions arose from cases typically involving violence or young boys. Nicholas Udall, headmaster of Eton College, convicted of buggery in 1541, lost his position; but he lost little social or political traction, ending his career as head of Westminster School in 1554. Lax prosecution means legal indifference rather than a socially benign tolerance of homosexuality.

Social institutions inadvertently enabled possible homoerotic activities, especially the schools and colleges. In these all-male enclaves, strong same-sex ties emerged among students and between students and teachers, as the Udall case makes clear. Sleeping arrangements opened the possibility for sexual relationships, as did the households from which the young men came. Few people slept alone: masters shared beds with servants, servants with other servants, as had been the pattern in monasteries of the early Tudor period. When sexual activity occurred, it typically occurred among friends and neighbors. This contributed obviously to the difficulty in defining such activity as either sinful or illegal. On the other hand, it may have seemed natural. We

H

have no evidence that anyone in the period declared himself to be homosexual. Not only would this have been perilous, but also it seemed unnecessary; no social pressure required such public admission. Sexual preference did not define the individual.

The world of literature opens consideration of homosexual desire. Richard Barnfield's *The Affectionate Shepherd* (1594) contains, in some judgments, the most explicitly homosexual poems of the period, despite the author's seemingly orthodox life. William Shakespeare's Sonnets, written in the late Tudor period, raise issues of same-sex desire. James VI's elegiac, allegorical poem *Phoenix* (1584) bristles with the homoerotic desire that he felt for his cousin, Esmé Stuart. Many satiric tracts and poems confront the issue of homosexuality.

The all-male casts in the public theater raise uncertainties about sexuality, including transvestism. Certainly the theater becomes a major point of attack from Puritan foes, much of it based on matters of sexuality. Perhaps, on the other hand, many in the audiences went explicitly for some sexual titillation. Early in the period, John Bales's play, *Thre Lawes,* written in the 1530s, published in 1548, included the character Sodomy who, along with Idolatry, opposed the Law of Nature. A number of Shakespeare's early comedies present potential homoerotic relationships, such as those between Antonio and Bassanio in *Merchant of Venice* and Antonio and Sebastian in *Twelfth Night.* The Orlando-Rosalind courtship evokes homosexual desire when Rosalind takes on the guise and name of Ganymede.

Christopher Marlowe may be the most obvious playwright example of one who explores explicit homoerotic themes, whether in *Dido Queen of Carthage,* which opens with Ganymede on Jupiter's knee, or *Edward II,* which involves the king's love relationship with first Gaveston and then Spencer Junior. The latter play examines the intertwined politics of class and sexuality. The nobles oppose Gaveston and insist on his expulsion mainly because they resent his meteoric rise in political status, allowing the king his sexual preference. Marlowe, himself accused of homosexual behavior, offers a largely sympathetic picture of the king's relationship with his lovers.

BIBLIOGRAPHY

Bray, Alan. *Homosexuality in Renaissance England.* 1982.

DiGangi, Mario. *The Homoerotics of Early Modern Drama.* 1997.

Goldberg, Jonathan. *Sodometries: Renaissance Texts, Modern Sensibilities.* 1992.

Hutson, Lorna. *The Usurer's Daughter: Male Friendship and Fictions of Women in Sixteenth-Century England.* 1994.

Smith, Bruce R. *Homosexual Desire in Shakespeare's England: A Cultural Poetics.* 1991.

Stewart, Alan. *Close Readers: Humanism and Sodomy in Early Modern England.* 1997.

Traub, Valerie. *Desire and Anxiety: Circulations of Sexuality in Shakespearean Drama.* 1992.

David M. Bergeron

SEE ALSO

Gender; Marlowe, Christopher; Sexual Offenses; Shakespeare, William; Udall, Nicholas

Hooker, John, alias John Vowell (c. 1527–1601)

Hooker was born in Exeter of a mercantile family; both his father and grandfather had been mayors of the city. He was educated at Dr. Moreman's School in Cornwall, then at Oxford (Exeter College, or perhaps Corpus Christi College). He proceeded to Cologne to study jurisprudence and to Strasbourg for theology. By 1547, he was back in Oxford, studying civil law. Two years later, he had married and returned to his home city, which he helped defend against the West Country Catholics rebelling against the government of Edward VI. It was at this time that he met Sir Peter Carew, one of the heroes of the defense, who would be Hooker's patron and employer, and whose biography he was to write. Hooker became the first chamberlain of Exeter in 1555, and coroner by 1583; he also became a judge of the Admiralty Court in Devon in 1566. In 1568, he accompanied Sir Peter Carew to Ireland, helping him recover family lands lost more than a century before. In the course of his work for Carew, Hooker became an active (and very unpopular) member of the Irish Parliament in 1568, for whose guidance he prepared his *Order and Usage of the Keeping of a Parliament in England* (published 1572); he sat again, rather more peacefully, in 1572. Between the journeys to Ireland, Hooker was back in England, as a member of the House of Commons in 1571, during which he kept a diary; he sat in the session of 1586 as well.

While in London during his second stint in Parliament, Hooker became a member of the "team" involved in producing the second edition of Raphael Holinshed's *Chronicles*; the suggestion that he was the chief editor seems to be unfounded. Hooker did add considerably to the bulk of the revised Holinshed: a continuation of the Irish history from the place Richard Stanyhurst left off, together with a life of Sir Peter Carew, a version of the *Order and Usage*, a *Catalogue of the Bishops of Exeter*, plus a description of the city and an account of the 1549 siege. Hooker's contributions to the *Chronicles* suffered disproportionately from the censor's attentions.

Principally, however, Hooker was a local historian and antiquary, one of the first of the breed, whose emergence onto the Irish and national scenes was at best occasional. Besides the works he spliced onto the revised Holinshed, Hooker left a considerable body of manuscript material to the Exeter archives that he had had, as Chamberlain, in his keeping, including the materials for a complete description of the city of Exeter (not published until the twentieth century). His "Synopsis Chorographical of Devonshire" (written c. 1599) passed to Sir John Doddridge and was used by him and other antiquaries.

BIBLIOGRAPHY

Hasler, P.W., ed. *The House of Commons, 1558–1603.* 3 vols. 1981.

Hooker, John. *The Description of the Citie of Excester* (1575). Walter J. Harte, J.W. Schopp, and H. Tapley-Soper, eds. Devon and Cornwall Record Society, 3 vols. 1919–1947; also repr. in *Elizabethan Backgrounds.* Arthur F. Kinney, ed. 1974.

———. *The Life and Times of Sir Peter Carew, Kt.* Sir John Maclean, ed. 1857.

McKisack, May. *Medieval History in the Tudor Age.* Pp. 128–131. 1971.

Snow, Vernon F. *Parliament in Elizabethan England. John Hooker's* "Order and Usage." pp. 3–110. 1977.

F.J. Levy

SEE ALSO

Antiquarianism; History, Writing of; Holinshed, Raphael; Parliamentary History; Stanyhurst, Richard

Hooker, Richard (1554–1600)

The Anglican divine Richard Hooker was born at Heavitree near Exeter in April 1554. He was educated at Exeter grammar school. With the patronage of John Jewel, bishop of Salisbury, Hooker matriculated probably in the fall of 1569 at Corpus Christi College, Oxford. He graduated B.A. in January 1573–1574 and M.A. in July 1577, whereupon he was appointed instructor in logic. He was ordained deacon on August 14, 1579, and that same year was made a full fellow of his college and appointed to deliver the annual Hebrew lecture, a task that he continued to fulfil until his departure from Oxford. In October 1580 Hooker was expelled from the college, along with three other fellows and his former tutor and lifelong friend, John Rainolds. The expulsion occurred because he and his friends had supported Rainolds's candidacy for the office of president of Christ College. All were restored the following November after Rainolds had assumed the presidency.

Hooker was ordained to the priesthood in 1581. Around the time he left Oxford in the fall of 1584, he delivered at Paul's Cross in London a public sermon that was attacked by Puritan reformers because it undermined certain features of the Calvinist doctrine of predestination. On October 16, 1584, he was appointed rector of Drayton Beauchamp in Buckinginghamshire, but there is no evidence that he ever took up residence there. Instead, he moved into the household of John Churchman, a prosperous London merchant-tailor. On February 13, 1588, Hooker married John Churchman's daughter Joan, and he continued to reside with the Churchmans until 1595.

On March 17, 1585, Elizabeth I appointed him as master of the Temple in London, one of the principal centers of legal studies in England. At the time of this appointment, Walter Travers, a leading English advocate of presbyterianism, was reader of the Temple. Shortly after Hooker's arrival, a dispute broke out, with Hooker firmly rejecting Travers's efforts to presbyterianize the Temple. The public controversy continued for almost a year until March 1586, when John Whitgift, archbishop of Canterbury, silenced Travers. Travers appealed in a *Supplication* addressed to the queen's Privy Council, and Hooker responded by writing *An Answer to the Supplication* that he addressed to Whitgift. In the later stages of the dispute, Hooker had resolved to investigate the general principles involved in the position of the Church of England, and his great work, *Of the Lawes of Ecclesiastical Polity,* was to be the result. Although this treatise had its inception in the Temple controversy with Travers, his major opponent soon became Thomas Cartwright, who had argued the Presbyterian cause in an earlier and extended controversial exchange with Whitgift.

In 1591, in order to expedite Hooker's literary efforts, Whitgift appointed him rector of Boscombe in Wiltshire; he also made him at this time subdean of Salisbury Cathedral

H

and prebendary of Netheravon. There is no evidence that Hooker or his family ever lived at Boscombe, but records indicate that he did spend a prescribed amount of time each year at Salisbury, working at the cathedral library and conferring with the dean, John Bridges. The preface and first four books of the *Laws* were published in 1593. In 1595 the queen presented Hooker with the living at Bishopsbourne in Kent, where he moved with his family and where Book 5 of the *Laws* was completed; it was published in 1597. Book 5 was the last book of the *Laws* to be published during Hooker's lifetime. At the time of his death at Bishopsbourne on November 2, 1600, he was preparing a rebuttal to *A Christian Letter of Certain English Protestants* (1599), an anonymous puritan treatise that had attacked all five books of the *Laws* then in print. He was also still at work revising and expanding earlier drafts of the last three books of the *Laws*. Books 6 and 8 were not published until 1648, and book 7 only in 1662.

Hooker was the apologist *par excellence* of the Elizabethan Settlement of 1559, conveying his thought in a masterly Ciceronian prose style. He was the first of the defenders of the Church of England to designate clearly the middle way held by the English church between the extremes of Roman Catholicism on the one side and Genevan Protestantism and Anabaptism on the other. By modifying the Calvinist view of predestination in the direction of Arminianism, he challenged the dominant strain of theological opinion in the Elizabethan Church, conformist as well as Puritan. His emphasis on the prayers and ceremonies of the church represented a major shift in emphasis away from a vision of the ministry and public worship centered on the word and preaching to one that was more sacramental. In justifying the jurisdiction of bishops and the crown in the polity of the Church of England, he developed an essentially contractual theory of political government that would influence future political writers, especially John Locke. His defense of England as a constitutional monarchy subsumed within itself both the lay and clerical elements of the Christian commonwealth and stood for that wider integration of the spiritual and the temporal, the ecclesiastical and the secular, for which Hooker was striving throughout the *Laws*.

BIBLIOGRAPHY

Hill, W. Speed, ed. *Studies in Richard Hooker; Essays Preliminary to an Edition of His Works.* 1972.

Hooker, Richard. *The Folger Library Edition of the Works of Richard Hooker.* W. Speed Hill, ed. 6 vols. 1977–1993.

Lake, Peter. *Anglicans and Puritans? Presbyterianism and English Conformist Thought from Whitgift to Hooker.* 1988.

Sisson, C.J. *The Judicious Marriage of Mr. Hooker and the Birth of "The Laws of Ecclesiastical Polity."* 1940.

Walton, Izaak. *The Life of Mr. Rich. Hooker.* 1665; rev. 1670, 1675.

Lee W. Gibbs

SEE ALSO

Anabaptists; Arminianism; Calvinism; Cartwright, Thomas; Catholicism; Church of England; Church Polity; Jewel, John; Puritanism; Travers, Walter; Whitgift, John

Hooper, John (d. 1555)

Expelled from monastic orders during the dissolution of the monasteries, John Hooper developed into a radical Protestant reformer, bishop, martyr, and hero of the English Puritan movement. He went into exile when the Act of Six Articles (1539) imposed harshly punitive measures against Protestant reformers at the end of Henry VIII's reign. Already under the influence of Huldrych Zwingli's writings, he developed extreme theological ideas during close association with Johann Heinrich Bullinger, Zwingli's successor at Zurich. His earliest books were published at that location for export into England.

Returning from exile when the accession of Edward VI allowed for uncensored discussion by Protestants, Hooper called for abolition of clerical vestments and institution of the Lord's Supper in accordance with the Zwinglian model of a purely commemorative service. Appointed to the bishoprics of Gloucester (1551) and Worcester (1552), he tried, against local opposition, to impose Zwinglian reforms. An opponent of the theological conservatism of the first Book of Common Prayer (1549), he promoted its revision along more radically Protestant lines (1552). Burned to death as a heretic under Mary I, Hooper is memorialized as an exemplary Protestant saint in John Foxe's "Book of Martyrs."

BIBLIOGRAPHY

Hooper, John. *Early Writings.* S. Carr, ed. Parker Society. Vol. 20. 1843.

———. *Later Writings.* C. Nevison, ed. Parker Society. Vol. 21.

King, John. "John Hooper." In *Encyclopedia of the Reformation.* Hans J. Hillebrand et al., eds. 1996.

John N. King

SEE ALSO
Articles of Religion; Book of Common Prayer; Bullinger, John Heinrich; Foxe, John; Marian Martyrs; Monastic Orders; Puritanism; Suppression, Act of

Horses and Horsemanship

In the Tudor period horses served the role later played by the internal combustion engine. They transported people and goods from place to place and drove a range of machinery. They were also employed by the upper classes for recreation such as jousting, hunting, horse racing, and dressage. At the beginning of Elizabeth's reign one might obtain a horse for under a pound or pay fifty times as much. At all levels, however, horses were status symbols and horse ownership marked a basic social divide. Possession of a horse benefited the owner; apart from being able literally to look down on people on foot, it enabled him or her to travel further, more quickly and efficiently, and to move greater loads.

In the early sixteenth century the stock of horses in the country was not very good. Although foreign observers admitted that the equine population was considerable and that a relatively large proportion of the inhabitants kept horses, they also remarked on the weakness of the native breeds. According to the Venetian ambassador, writing in 1557, this was due to poor diet. Others blamed the Wars of the Roses or the dissolution of the monasteries. By the end of the century, however, the situation had been transformed. The breeds had been vastly improved and even foreign potentates were eager to acquire British horses. In this development the crown led the way. Henry VIII began breeding horses as a reaction to the poor showing of his horses in war. His successors continued his policy, importing stock from abroad, notably Flemish animals for strength and Spanish and Italian horses for riding. Through legislation and personal leadership, the crown sought to increase the size of native breeds and to foster horse breeding, especially among the upper classes. In this aim, they achieved some success. According to a descendant of Sir George Reresby of Thrybergh Hall (West Riding), Sir George's pastime "was sometimes haukes, but his cheefest was his breed of Horses, in which he was very exact."

The main breeding grounds in the country lay in pastoral regions, largely in the north and the west. Small ponies were bred on the hills and larger animals in the vales, while the biggest, most powerful horses came from the fens of East Anglia. Some horses were bred in mixed-farming areas, especially if they lay close to good grazing land, but in general, farmers there specialized in rearing horses brought in from other areas. Consequently, there was considerable movement of horses around the country. During the Tudor age, this traffic increased as demand for horses grew along with the rise in population.

To cope with the growth in the trade in horses, marketing facilities developed. Some fairs specialized in the sale of horses and attracted buyers from long distances. East Midlands fairs, for instance, were well known for their draught horses, colts, and geldings, most of which had been trained on nearby farms. Increasingly, specialist middlemen controlled the business; they alone had the time and the expertise to organize the trade on a scale larger than the purely local one. Horse dealers, for instance, were responsible for bringing to fairs many of the horses that were subsequently reared in the East Midlands. In turn, their metropolitan counterparts were prominent as purchasers when the horses were returned, fully trained, to the region's fairs. Contemporaries complained bitterly about the activities of such people, accusing them of duplicity and sharp practice, but they performed a valuable role in helping to meet the insistent demand for such an essential commodity.

Horses themselves became more varied due to the importation of different breeds and to a greater concern for suitable use. Undoubtedly, there were numerous small-scale owners who had to make do with what they had and used their animals for a multitude of tasks, but others could afford to be more choosy. Many farmers, for example, kept a saddle nag as well as a team of plow and cart horses. Draft horses, in particular, proliferated. On the farm, they were taking over from oxen, though they did not finally replace them until well into the nineteenth century. On the road, the growth of inland trade meant that more were needed to pull wagons and carts. The demand for packhorses also expanded.

The top end of the market was dominated by the upper classes. Their requirements were the most varied and sophisticated; whatever the purpose, they insisted on the best horses and paid the highest prices. To them, horses were not merely functional beasts but objects of ostentatious display. Horsemanship was an essential accomplishment to be learned by every gentleman; jousting, hunting, and dressage allowed a gentleman to show off both his skill and social refinement. An interest in dressage first developed in Henry VIII's reign, introduced by gentlemen who had learned it at Grisone's school in Naples. At a tournament at Greenwich in July 1517, Henry was one of

H

those who "performed marvellous feats, mounted on magnificent horses, which they made jump and execute other arts of horsemanship." The horses employed were the so-called "great horse," which, because they were large and well proportioned and had the fashionable convex profile of the head and nose, conformed most closely to the early Tudor image of the ideal horse. In the late sixteenth century the elite also spent a good deal of money on coaches and matched teams of horses to go with them. Their color, size, movement, and conformity were equally as important as power. After initial resistance by gentlemen, who deemed it effeminate to be seen riding in a coach, this mode of transport grew in popularity among the members of genteel society, not least because it enabled them to publicly affirm their status.

BIBLIOGRAPHY

Blundeville, Thomas. *The Fower Chiefest Offyces of Horsemanship.* 1565.

Dent, Anthony. *Horses in Shakespeare's England.* 1987.

Edwards, Peter. *The Horse Trade of Tudor and Stuart England.* 1988.

Markham, Gervase. *A Discource of Horsemanshippe.* 1593.

———. *How to Chuse, Ride, Traine, and Diet both Hunting-horses and Running Horses.* 1599.

Niemyer, Elizabeth. *The Reign of the Horse: The Horse in Print, 1500–1715.* [Exhibition catalog] Anthony Dent, intro. Folger Shakespeare Library. 1991.

Thirsk, Joan. *Horses in Early Modern England; for Service, for Pleasure, for Power.* 1978.

———. *Agrarian History of England and Wales, IV, 1500–1640.* 1967.

Turberville, George. *The Noble Art of Venerie or Hunting.* 1575.

Philip Edwards

SEE ALSO

Fairs and Markets; Industry and Manufacture; Trade, Inland; Transportation

Hospitals
See Medicine and Health

Household Books

In the domestic economy of Tudor England, a middle-class family's well-being depended on the careful management of its household and home-based business. Traditionally, farmers, tradesmen, and housewives passed their skills from generation to generation through hands-on experience and, in some families, with handwritten ledgers and commonplace books. The ledgers noted purchases and receipts; other papers recorded everything from husbandry and health hints to food and cleaning recipes. All were instructive to those who inherited them. But householders without such family records, and those who wished to improve their lot, were eager for outside advice.

With the advent of movable type, enterprising printers—householders themselves—were quick to exploit this market. By the early sixteenth century, several kinds of householders' manuals had appeared, all written by men. Some of the earliest were translated from classical or continental languages (from works by Xenophon, Nostradamus, Torquato Tasso, Salerno), but many were indigenous, reflecting middle-class English ideals. Advice was available in every form, from sermons and philosophical discourses to almanacs and ballads. Most went into many editions.

Thomas Tusser's *A Hundrethe Good Pointes of Husbandrie* (1557) became an all-time best seller, with eighteen editions in the sixteenth century alone. The first edition covered husbandry, with little mention of housewifery. The second (1562) and all later editions were expanded to include housewifery; they underscored the cooperative nature of men's and women's work. His advice took the form of rhymed proverbs. Familiar rhymes, such as "Early to bed, early to rise, / Make a man healthy, wealthy, and wise" appear in Tusser, as do: "Though husbandry seemeth, to bring in the gains, / Yet huswifry labours, seeme equal in pains. / Some respit to husbands, the wether may send, / But huswifes affaires, have never an end" (1562 edition, sig. S2).

Although husbands and wives worked as partners in a domestic economy, all manuals agreed that they had separate responsibilities under a hierarchical management scheme, with the husband in the leadership role. The wife was to supervise the younger children and house servants, but always under the direction of the husband. She was also admonished to care frugally for that which the husband provided. Management of servants and treatment of guests were addressed, as were such disparate matters as "Virtues proper to men," "The art of weaving honorable," "Beef at feasts more used for fashion than food," and "Rents" (see Tasso). By the late sixteenth century, householders' books reflected the growing influence of Protestant ethics. Authors advised strict adherence to Christian tenets, along with thrift and hard work. Idleness was considered a sin, piety an essential.

Householders were also a ready market for health manuals for home use. Along with recipes for medications, these books provided a wide variety of health hints: the proper clothing for different seasons, the correct amount of sleep, the uses of herbs, fruits, spices, and other edibles, even discussions on intercourse, impotence, and abortion. Many stressed a healthful environment and clean air. Those who discussed water recommended against drinking it unless it was boiled. Strong beliefs in astrology and the four humours colored some of the health cures. A book might list half a dozen cures for the same problem; nonetheless, cures often concluded with "God willing."

The assyse of bread what is ought to waye after the pryce of a quarter of wheete. 1544? These woodcuts illustrate a text on weighing and measuring staples such as bread, ale, firewood, coal, lath, board, timber, butter, and cheese. Upper row: left, a man kneads bread while another weighs it; right, putting loaves in an oven. Lower row: left, a man ties bundles of wood while another adjusts the scale; right, a chained dog guards utensils for making cheese: a dripping cheese cloth, pan, mold, and churn. These cuts were reused in six editions from 1555 to 1559. Reproduced from the original by permission of the Henry E. Huntington Library and Art Gallery.

The earliest English physician-author, Andrew Boorde, wrote three health books. One, *The Breviary of Helthe for all Manner of Sycknesses and Diseases* (1547), provided a narrative paragraph on each health problem, a passage on its cause, and a proposed cure. Few other university-trained doctors wrote health manuals in English, agreeing instead to conceal their knowledge in classical languages, where it would be less accessible to the public. But nonprofessionals quickly filled the public's demand for medical information in English. One, Philip Barrough, in his *Methode of Phisicke* (1583), admitted: "I shall run into the babble of our country physicians who think their art to be discredited when it is published in a base tongue and again are loath to have the secrets of their science revealed to every man" (sig. A7, 1639 edition). Thomas Elyot's *Castel of Helth* (1539), which ran to seventeen editions, discussed diet, medicines, plants, and birds. The anonymous *Treasure of Poore Men* (1526?) was an oft-reprinted recipe book of cures and cookery. John Partridge, in *The Treasurie of Commodious Conceites and Hidden Secrets commonly called The Good Huswives Closet of Provision for the Health of her Houshold* (1573), wrote of the curative values of plants, for example: "Conserve of roses . . . is good against black choller and melancholy. Conserve of white roses doth lose the belly more than the red" (B4).

Like health matters, food recipes fell within the housewife's bailiwick. Recipe books were frequently addressed to housewives, with titles such as *The Good Huswifes Jewell* by Thomas Dawson (1587), the anonymous *Good Huswifes Handmaide for the Kitchin* (1594), *The Good House-wives Treasurie* (1588), and John Partridge's *Widowes Treasure* (1582). The earliest recipe books were often pocket-sized, barely three-by-five inches, with decorative borders that further restricted the text. Yet directions for candying flowers, preserving meat, killing lice, curing an ague, and caring for cattle might be found in one volumn. Hugh Platt's *Delightes for Ladies* (1600?)

H

combined cosmetics, home remedies, and cooking recipes. *A Thousand Notable Things of Sundry Sorts* (1595), by Thomas Lupton, was a jumbled collection of cures and curiosities, from tooth care to ways to keep cats from straying. Instructions were written in a narrative form. No recipes were specific about ingredients, leaving amounts to the discretion of the reader. Highly specialized books were rare; herbals (such as those by William Turner and John Gerard) were an important and popular exception. The *Regiment of Helthe*, Thomas Paynell's 1528 translation of Salerno, emphasized the uses of herbs for good health.

Other popular householders' books were: Thomas Becon, *Works* (1560–1564); *The Book of Prittie Conceites* [1586?]; Robert Cleaver, *A Godly Forme of Housholde Government* (1598); Dudley Fenner, *The Order of Householde* (1584); Leonardo Fioravanti, *A Compendium of . . . Phisicke and Chirurgerie . . . Hidden Virtues of Sondrie Vegitables, Animalles, and Mineralls . . .* (1582); Torquato Tasso, *The Householders Philosophie* (1588); *The Treasure of Poore Men* (1526?); Richard Whitford, *A Werke for Housholders* (1530); Xenophon, *Treatise of Householde* (1532); and William Vaughan, *Naturall and Artificial Directions for Health* (1600).

BIBLIOGRAPHY

Boorde, Andrew. *The Fyrst Boke of the Introduction of Knowledge made by Andrew Borde of Physycke Doctor. A Compendyous Regyment or A Dyetary of Helth.* F.J. Furnivall, ed. 1870.

Markham, Gervase. *The English Housewife.* Michael R. Best, ed. 1994.

Tusser, Thomas. *Thomas Tusser, 1557 Floruit, His Good Points of Husbandry* (1571). 1557 edition in Facsimile. Dorothy Hartley, ed. 1931.

Wright, Louis B. "Instruction in Domestic Relations." In *Middle-Class Culture in Elizabethan England,* pp. 201–227. 1935; repr. 1958.

Suzanne W. Hull

SEE ALSO

Boorde, Andrew; Elyot, Thomas; Food and Diet; Gerard, John; Medicine and Health; Turner, William; Tusser, Thomas

Howard, Catherine (c. l521–l542)

The execution of Catherine Howard, fifth wife of Henry VIII, exemplifies the treatment deemed appropriate for queens consorts who failed to guard their reputations. Born about l521 to Jocasta Culpepper and Edmund Howard, an impoverished son of the second duke of Norfolk, she became a ward of her step-grandmother, the dowager duchess. In 1536, Catherine's music tutor taught her how to please men in a failed seduction attempt; in 1538, she entered into a precontract with Francis Dereham, which probably constituted a legal marriage because it was followed by carnal relations.

After her appointment as maiden of honor to Anne of Cleves, Catherine was attracted to Thomas Culpepper, a gentleman of the king's Privy Chamber. On July 28, 1540, shortly after the annulment of his fourth union, Henry chose to marry Catherine, whom he believed was a virgin. Her elevation to the queenship represented the returning political influence of her conservative Howard relatives at court. By springtime 1541, Jane, Viscountess Rochford, who was probably bribed, was helping Catherine arrange clandestine meetings with Culpepper. In November, Thomas Cranmer, archbishop of Canterbury, forwarded to the king rumors that had been leaked to him about her former involvement with Dereham, who was then serving as her secretary. First Dereham and then Culpepper were arrested, tortured, and executed.

After Catherine was incarcerated in Syon House and later in the Tower of London, she confessed some details of her sexual experiences, but disavowed the existence of a precontract with Dereham and corroborated Culpepper's denials that they had been lovers. The king's ministers disbelieved her, for they presumed that a sexually experienced woman would meet an admirer secretly only to pursue an illicit relationship. Beheaded on February 10, 1542, by authority of an act of attainder that charged her with adulterous treason, Catherine was buried with Lady Rochford, who was also executed, in St. Peter ad Vincula at the Tower.

BIBLIOGRAPHY

Fraser, Antonia. *The Six Wives of Henry VIII.* 1992.

Smith, Lacey Baldwin. *A Tudor Tragedy. The Life and Times of Catherine Howard.* 1961.

———. *Henry VIII: The Mask of Royalty.* 1971.

Retha Warnicke

SEE ALSO

Anne of Cleves; Cranmer, Thomas; Henry VIII; Marriage and Marriage Law

Howard, Charles, (1536–1624)

Eldest son of William Howard (first baron Howard of Effingham and lord admiral, 1553–1558) and his second wife, Margaret Gamage, Charles Howard earl of Nottingham, was thereby a first cousin to Anne Boleyn, the mother of Elizabeth I. On the accession of the queen, Howard served on diplomatic missions and as a soldier. As his first governmental mission he was sent as an ambassador to France to congratulate Francis II on his accession in 1559. In 1569, Howard was appointed general of the horse under the earl of Warwick in the suppression of the Northern Rebellion. The next year Howard commanded a squadron of ships (essentially an honor guard) for the queen of Spain as she journeyed through the English seas. But Howard's early advancement was only a glimmering of the bright future that he would come to enjoy.

The next phase of Howard's career found him in service at court, a place he never fully left until his death (although he filled a wide variety of unrelated offices). From 1573 to 1585, Howard was lord chamberlain of the household, supervising daily activities at court, in addition to which he planned the queen's summer progresses and organized both regular and seasonal entertainments. By 1572, he seems to have been knighted, and in 1574, he was installed as knight of the garter. It was during this period that he also married one of the queen's favorite ladies in waiting, Catherine Carey, daughter of Henry Carey, Lord Hunsdon. In 1586, Howard was appointed one of the commissioners for the trial of Mary Queen of Scots; and while he seems not to have been present at the trial, he was responsible for conducting some examinations in London.

In 1585, Howard vacated the office of lord chamberlain in order to assume responsibilities as lord high admiral, an appointment he held for thirty-four years. Two years later, Howard was commander-in-chief against the Spaniards and their allies. (His second-in-command was Sir Francis Drake.) He commanded the *Ark Royal* during the Armada campaign and made his name by urging the tactics of stand-off fighting rather than engaging the enemy at close quarters. Almost immediately thereafter Howard returned to court circles; however, when news of another Spanish attack surfaced he shared a joint command with Robert Devereux, earl of Essex, in the raid on Cadiz (1596). During this period animosity began to grow between Howard and Essex. The conflict continued until 1601, when Nottingham served as one of the commissioners at Essex's trial who sought the earl's execution.

In the queen's final months Howard entertained her at Arundel House. Accounts suggest that the festivities were adequate but not overly elaborate, and that the queen was disappointed with the admiral's gifts, having hoped to receive the rich tapestries made to commemorate the Armada victory. Yet Howard was ever considered the queen's faithful servant. It was to Howard that the queen named James VI of Scotland as her successor; and, following the queen's death, the Privy Council met at Howard's house in order to make arrangements to move the queen's body to London.

Throughout his life Howard's rare combination of diplomatic and managerial talents stood out. Not only was he frequently responsible for handling negotiations with foreign powers, including the treaty with Spain in 1605; but well beyond his days as lord chamberlain, Howard often entertained foreign ambassadors when they visited the court. Therefore, not surprisingly, he was patron of a company of professional actors (the Lord Admiral's Men), which performed most of Christopher Marlowe's plays and became prominent at court under its leading actor, Edward Alleyn.

In his retirement Howard continued to act as lord lieutenant of Surrey and held numerous offices connected with the royal domains, for which he was well compensated. He died at the age of eighty-eight and seems to have retained his faculties to the last. He was buried in the family vault in the church at Reigate, Surrey, but no monument marks his tomb.

BIBLIOGRAPHY

Corbett, Julian S., ed. *State Papers Relating to the Navy during the Spanish War, 1585–1587.* Navy Records Society, vol. 11. 1898.

Laughton, John K., ed. *State Papers Relating to the Defeat of the Spanish Armada.* Navy Records Society, vols. 1–2. 1895.

Kenny, Robert W. *Elizabeth's Admiral: The Political Career of Charles Howard.* 1970.

Martin, Colin, and Geoffrey Parker. *The Spanish Armada.* 1988.

S.P. Cerasano

SEE ALSO

Armada, Spanish; Devereux, Robert; James VI and I; Northern Rebellion; Progresses, Royal; Theater Companies, Adult

H

Howard, Henry (c. 1516–1547)

Poet, soldier, and courtier, Henry Howard, earl of Surrey, was heir to the third duke of Norfolk and first cousin of both Queens Anne Boleyn and Catherine Howard. By courtesy titled earl of Surrey, Howard would have been placed, had he lived, at the center of political power in the English court, but he was beheaded by Henry VIII in January 1547, in his thirtieth year, the last in the procession of victims of the Tudor king. His beheading ended a life spent at the highest levels of power in early English and European Renaissance society. He had served in the entourage of Francis I at the Louvre and Fontainebleau, and later on the war front in France with the Holy Roman Emperor Charles V. His achievement as poet rose, ironically, from this necessity to aggrandize his position at court; the paradox of the highly placed nobleman being also a gifted poet would be seen as a model by later court poets. It can be argued that Surrey became the single figure who helped most to legitimize the poet in English society, as Sir Philip Sidney confirmed in his *Defense of Poesy* when he named "the Earl of Surrey's *Lyrics*" as one of the four works of any merit in English literature, finding in them "many things tasting of a noble birth, and worthy of a noble mind."

The poems that mark the inception of Surrey's career, his 1537 sonnet and elegy on the death of his close friend, Henry Fitzroy, duke of Richmond and bastard son of Henry VIII, rose from his status at the English court. This first English sonnet and these first heroic quatrains—both Surrey's metrical inventions—may have had an ulterior purpose, whatever their display of genuine grief, to influence the king to bring the close companion of his son back into royal favor. Although the Windsor sonnet and elegy may grow out of Chaucer's *Troilus* in their laments, the new meters and language describe an experience of both noble life and courtly honor that is rendered, for the first time in English, not with allegory but with social realism. After these poems it was natural for the young Surrey to build an image of himself as courtier and warrior capable of ruling the realm with the royal family, as his father had done so powerfully and lucratively. As a result, most of Surrey's energies went not to literature but to fulfilling his role as heir by producing five children, building his spectacular Surrey House overlooking Norwich, acting as emissary for the king in court and abroad, and, especially, fighting on the fronts in Scotland and France.

From his training as a humanist (Surrey had command of five languages), he sought to express the transforma-

tions of his time, the virtual revolutions Henry VIII promulgated, in both theories and language peculiarly his own. He is responsible for two major shifts in English poetry. First, using the same metrical device of heroic quatrains he had invented for his elegy on his beloved Richmond, Surrey reinvented the idea of the poet in English society by making the figure of Thomas Wyatt into a new hero. His remarkable elegy on the older poet appeared in the autumn of 1542, written in a few weeks on the Scottish front at Solway Moss. Even more remarkably, Surrey allowed the poem to be published, a virtual canonization in print that literally figured, in a new conceptualizing of honor, the ethos that had dominated the Henrician court.

The second great shift came in Surrey's invention of blank verse. By 1540, Surrey sought a heroic meter that would make English the language of Vergil, who was for the Renaissance, as Sidney notes, the greatest of all authors. In this utterly original meter, Surrey sought a public language that would reveal the subjectivity that had marked his erotic poetry, especially the intense "The sun hath twice," which was the first poem in Tottel's *Miscellany* to make Petrarch's *capitolo* and Dante's *terza rima* English, and "When raging love," which combines for the first time in English *petrarchismo* and historicizing. Only two books have survived from Surrey's translation of the *Aeneid* (in the ransacking of the Howard palace of Kenninghall in Norfolk and Surrey House by the agents of Henry VIII in December 1546, manuscripts were doubtless lost), and in both these books voice and soliloquy predominate. Book 2 of the *Aeneid* represents Aeneas's dramatic monologue at the court of Dido, and Surrey's English dramatizes the collapse of an ancient city in fire: "Who can express the slaughter of that night, / Or tell the number of the corpses slaine, / Or can in teres bewaile them worthely? / The auncient famous citie falleth down, / That many yeres did hold such seignorie. / With senselesse bodies every strete is spred, / Eche palace, and sacred porch of the gods" (2:463–469).

Equally, Book 4 of the universal Roman epic dramatizes a lyric voice of utter subjectivity, the abandonment not in the fire of the city but in the fire of love. In unrhymed English lines, Surrey sets ten exact syllables with a varying series of stresses, generally four but often five (Surrey's long-enduring synthesis of southern European accentual verse and northern stress rhythms). The result is public language that combines the most subjective and lyric moments for outbursts—"What shall I set before, or where begin? / Juno nor Jove with just eyes this beholds" (4:485–6)—and supreme theatrical closure: "But Dido striveth to lift up againe / Her heavy eyen, and hath no power thereto: / Deepe in her brest that fixed wound doth gape. / Thrise leaning on her elbow gan she raise / Her self upward, and thrise she overthrewe / Upon the bed, ranging with wandring eyes / The skies for light, and wept when she it found? (4:917–923).

BIBLIOGRAPHY

Caldwell, E.C. "Recent Studies in Henry Howard, Earl of Surrey (1970–1989)." *English Literary Renaissance,* vol. 19, pp. 389–401.

Fishman, B. "Recent Studies in Wyatt and Surrey." *English Literary Renaissance,* vol. 1, pp. 178–191.

Nott, George F. *The Works of Henry Howard, Earl of Surrey, and Sir Thomas Wyatt, the Elder.* 1815–1816; repr. 1965.

Ridley, Florence H., ed. *The Aeneid of Henry Howard, Earl of Surrey.* University of California English Studies. Vol. 23. 1963.

Rollins, Hyder E., ed. *Tottel's Miscellany (1557–87).* 2 vols. 1966.

Sessions, William A. *Henry Howard, Earl of Surrey.* Twayne English Authors. 1986.

W.A. Sessions

SEE ALSO

Classical Literature, English Translations; Elegy; Henry VIII; Fitzroy, Henry; Italian Literature, Influence of; Petrarchanism; Sonnet Sequences; Verse Anthologies; Versification

Howard, Thomas (1538–1572)

Remembered principally for attempting to marry Mary Queen of Scots, Thomas Howard, fourth duke of Norfolk, was implicated in the Northern Rebellion (1569) and executed for his apparent complicity in the Ridolfi Plot (1570–1571) to replace Elizabeth I with Mary. Born on March 10, 1538, at Kenninghall, the country seat of the Howard family, Howard was the son of Frances Howard and Henry Howard, earl of Surrey, the soldier and poet, and grandson of Thomas Howard, the third duke of Norfolk. As a child, Howard and his siblings were tutored by Hadrianus Junius, alongside the future poet Thomas Churchyard. However, at age eight his father was executed for treason on the suspicion that he sought control of the regency of Edward VI; the eventual protector, Edward Seymour, also imprisoned his grandfather and seized Kenninghall. Howard and his siblings were put into the care of their aunt, the duchess of Richmond, who appointed John Foxe, the martyrologist, as their tutor. Howard, a lifelong Protestant, would later become Foxe's patron after the Marian exile.

On the accession of Mary I, the Howards were restored to power and Howard was reinstated as earl of Surrey, created a knight of the bath, and eventually attended on the marriage of Phillip II and Mary. On assuming his grandfather's title on August 25, 1554, Norfolk became the wealthiest and most powerful peer in the kingdom. He soon married Mary Fitzalan, daughter of the earl of Arundel, but after the birth of a son in June 1557, she failed to recover, leaving to him Arundel Castle and even more estates. His subsequent remarriage to Margaret Dudley yielded another son, Thomas, who was to become the earl of Suffolk.

As earl marshal and first peer, Norfolk was in charge of the coronation ceremonies of his cousin, Elizabeth I. This close association with the crown assured his prominence and influence; his lands in East Anglia formed his power base and provided his income. Howard's political career began in 1560 with a command of the English army in countering French influence in Scotland, successfully ending the "Auld Alliance" in the Treaty of Edinburgh. Afterward, Howard became a major voice at court, along with William Cecil (later Lord Burghley) and Robert Dudley (later the earl of Leicester) in the marriage proposals and foreign policy of Elizabeth I. Norfolk's Protestant commitments did not prevent him from favoring a Spanish alliance, no doubt influenced by his experience at court under Mary and Philip II; this position, however, put him in opposition to Cecil's policy.

Howard's second marriage ended like his first, after the birth of another son, William. In January 1567, he formed a permanent union with the Dacre family by marrying Elizabeth, Lord Dacre's widow, whose children he later married to his own. She died in childbed only nine months later. After these successive losses Norfolk did not return to court until May of 1568, when he was appointed a commmissioner to investigate the complicity of Mary Queen of Scots in the murder of her husband, Henry Stuart, Lord Darnley, by James Hepburn, fourth earl of Bothwell. The investigation took place in York, but while in Scotland on related matters, Norfolk began to entertain the idea of marriage to Mary proposed by the Scottish secretary, William Maitland, with the intent of restoring her to the throne and securing an Anglo-Scottish alliance.

H

Elizabeth I soon challenged him. Despite assuring her that "no reason could move him to like of her that hath been a competitor of the crown," he soon began to formalize arrangements for betrothal to Mary, with the secret support of Robert Dudley. Norfolk's critical error was not simply neglecting many occasions to inform the queen of his intentions, but in further alienating William Cecil, Lord Burghley, who quickly promoted suspicion that Norfolk was conspiring with the pro-Catholic northern earls to replace her with Mary Queen of Scots and restore Catholicism. Disgraced, Norfolk abruptly left court for Kenninghall; after answering the queen's summons, he was arrested and placed in the Tower for ten months, but was released after no firm evidence could be found.

Norfolk's involvement in the actual rebellion of the northern earls was incidental, but Burghley implicated him at a time when relations with Spain grew tense and Elizabeth struggled to consolidate her power and settle religious divisions. After her excommunication in 1570 by Pius V's bull *Regans in Excelsis,* it became impossible to separate Norfolk's marital intentions from perceptions of Catholic conspiracies. His popularity and status as first peer made the proposed marriage to Mary Stuart plausible, for it then became the basis of an elaborate conspiracy named after the Florentine banker, Roberto Ridolfi, with whom Norfolk had negotiated loans to support the vast costs of his career at court. Ridolfi secretly represented Pius V in England, and probably also acted as a double agent in Francis Walsingham's spy network. He was to have advised the duke of Alva, purportedly on Norfolk's behalf, to persuade the pope and Spain to invade England and Ireland and place Mary on the throne, either by assassinating Elizabeth or holding her hostage. The plot was allowed to develop long enough for Walsingham to procure incriminating evidence from the bishop of Ross (who had advised Norfolk on the marriage) and Norfolk's household. His secretary, the aging translator William Barker, made dubious and inconsistent testimony that nevertheless convicted Norfolk of treason during his trial on January 16, 1572. In his letter of defense to Elizabeth, Norfolk admitted to lapses in judgment and concealing evidence, but maintained the innocence of his marriage plans. The historical evidence supports his claim, and Elizabeth's long delay in signing his death warrant suggests she also had reservations. Yet the political and religious climate made him an absolute liability, and he went to the scaffold on June 2, 1572, with his old tutor, John Foxe, by his side.

BIBLIOGRAPHY

Edwards, Francis, S.J. *The Marvellous Chance Thomas Howard, Fourth Duke of Norfolk, and the Ridolphi Plot, 1570–72.* 1968.

Robinson, John Martin. *The Dukes of Norfolk: A Quincentennial History,* pp. 52–67. 1982.

William, Neville. *Thomas Howard, Fourth Duke of Norfolk.* 1964.

David W. Swain

SEE ALSO

Cecil, William; Mary Queen of Scots; Northern Rebellion; Ridolfi Plot; Walsingham, Francis

Huguenots

"Heugenots" is the pejorative epithet applied to French Protestants from about 1560 onwards. The origin of the name is debated, but the most likely derivation is from the German word *Eidgenossen* (confederates). This word had become current among the Protestant leagues in both Germany and Switzerland, and it seems likely that it was applied to the French as well. Certainly, Protestantism came to France from Germany, and was long associated with that country in the popular mind.

Protestantism appeared in France about 1530 and became popular in humanist circles, some of which had close connections at court. Marguerite of Navarre, the sister of King François Ier (1515–1547) protected the *Evangéliques,* as they were called, and Navarre became a stronghold of the new faith. Persecution began in 1534, when a number of Protestants had to flee Paris, among them the newly converted John Calvin. After a few years of wandering, Calvin established himself in Geneva (1541), and before long had become the acknowledged theologian of the French Protestants. When they met in Paris to draft a confession of faith (1559), it was Calvinism that was adopted. This confession was slightly revised in 1571, at La Rochelle, whence its modern name. The Confession of La Rochelle is still the main doctrinal standard of the French Reformed Church.

The growing power and influence of Protestantism worried the royal government, which began to take measures against the new faith. In 1562, a civil war broke out, which continued intermittently until 1598. Protestantism was strong in the port cities, among the provincial nobility, and in large parts of the country, especially in the south. But the central administration and the all-important city of Paris remained firmly Catholic, and this ultimately decided the fate of the Huguenots.

The most famous incident of the wars of religion was the murder of a number of leading Protestants on August 24, 1572. This so-called St. Bartholemew's Day Massacre soon became legendary, gaining the Huguenots a great deal of foreign sympathy, especially in England, where there had been a small Huguenot community since about 1560. The English ambassador in Paris opened his house to them, and many took refuge in England, giving the French Protestant community in London a visibility that it had not previously enjoyed. But sympathy did not mean support, and after an initial venture early in her reign (1559) that failed to retake Calais, Elizabeth I never allowed herself to get entangled in a French war. In 1589, the assassination of Henri III brought his cousin, Henri IV of Navarre, to the throne. Henri IV was a Protestant, and his right to succeed was hotly debated in France. Neither Paris nor Reims, the cathedral city where he should have been crowned, would admit him, and eventually Henri IV converted to Catholicism in order to save his throne.

In 1598, Henri published the Edict of Nantes, which granted a limited toleration to Protestants, but it was clear that they had lost the wars of religion and would have a difficult time surviving in the future. Catholic reaction in the seventeenth century gradually whittled away their privileges, until Louis XIV finally abolished the edict in 1685. This led to a mass exodus of Protestants, many of whom found their way to England and its colonies, where special provision was made for "stranger churches," as their places of worship were called. They established large and influential communities in both Britain and America that have retained a residual existence to the present day.

BIBLIOGRAPHY
Baumgartner, F.J. *France in the Sixteenth Century.* 1995.
Kingdon, R.M. *Geneva and the Consolidation of the French Protestant Movement, 1564–1572.* 1967.
Prestwich, M. "Calvinism in France, 1559–1629." In *International Calvinism, 1541–1715.* M. Prestwich, ed. 1985.
Rothrock, G.A. *The Huguenots: A Biography of a Minority.* 1979.

Gerald Bray

SEE ALSO
Calvinism; Catholicism; Counter Reformation; Immigration; Reformation, English

H

Humanism

The Renaissance stands as the epoch that saw the rebirth of ancient learning, marking the end of the "dark ages" that preceeded it. The dramatic changes in the arts and architecture signal a groundswell of commerce and prosperity on which this rebirth depended and the new outlook that accompanied those changes. Beginning in Italy, this rebirth spread out conceptually and geographically from its Italian urban beginnings to encompass the Christian west. The term "humanist" (*humanista*) began as university slang to denote a professional who taught the "humanities," or *studia humanitatis,* which included grammar, rhetoric, poetry, history, and moral philosophy. The term soon broadened to include their students who shared in their belief in the central importance of such studies. Our ever-expanding definition of "humanism" as both an ideal of self-transformation through literary studies, and which places the highest regard on the study and understanding of man and his condition, has its roots in the educational project of the Renaissance humanists.

Humanists believed passionately that the means for such transformation and self-knowledge could be derived from the study of the classics and mastery of the ancient languages. Humanists from the beginning pursued parallel tracks of textual scholarship and teaching. Footnote-laden, bibliography-rich modern studies, often overwhelming with their *bricolage* of titles, dates, and editions, attest to Gibbon's simple phrase: the humanists "revived the knowledge of the ancients." Humanists sought to recover classical sources, discovering and copying manuscripts, translating works, and refining the methods of translation through philological and historical criticism. The invention of printing played a key role in disseminating the fruits of the humanists' labors, as well as employment for them as translators, editors, copyists, and critics. Italian humanist educators like Guarino da Verona in Ferrara founded grammar schools of European reknown, which complimented the informal methods of education by face-to-face discussion, familiar letter, and treatise. In turn, humanist emphasis on the liberal arts influenced the statutes of the new colleges of the sixteenth-century university. By returning *ad fontes,* to the source, humanists reclaimed this treasure-house of ancient learning to be assimilated, inculcated, and applied to their world.

Humanists challenged the institutionalization of the medieval studium in the university, for it placed a mastery of dialectic, or applied syllogistic logic, at the heart of

H

undergraduate curriculum, and implied a hierarchy of disciplines that molded the arts of the *trivium*—grammar, logic, and rhetoric—to the demands of the higher disciplines of law, theology, and medicine. Scholasticism, institutionalized as the application of dialectic to clarify disputed points of theology, especially drew humanists' wrath. Early humanists like Petrarch and Lorenzo Valla hoped for a faith purified of such accretions. Humanists also rejected the implied certainty of syllogistic logic on methodological grounds. They condemned the way scholastic method deformed the disciplines by substituting logical and artificial precision for more natural and affective modes of understanding that better mirrored the way humans made sense of their world. They relentlessly criticized, as well, the diverting of intellectual inquiry to the aquisition and refinement of recondite knowledge, rather than teaching men how to live well.

Humanists championed grammar and rhetoric as a better means to inculcate useful knowledge, relying heavily on Cicero and Quintilian. Mastery of rhetoric allowed for probability or practical modes of reasoning that more closely matched human patterns of thought and interaction, as well as promising the mastery of the art of speaking publicly. The dialecticians continued medieval practices by which Aristotle's logic (mainly a mode of presentation for Aristotle) was made the whole of philosophical argumentation. They neglected (because of incomplete texts) Aristotle's own concern with problems of discovery and organization of arguments by means of topics, so that the right sort of questions could be formulated. "Discovery" or invention, stressed in the rhetorical tradition, assumed greater importance for humanists, while concern with demonstration in its many refinements waned. Humanists increasingly concerned themselves with rectifying the failure of Aristotelian or dialectical method, developing alternative methods for acquiring and organizing knowledge. Mastery of grammar and mastery of the places (*topoi*) or commonplaces of past thinkers would provide better grounds on which to base convincing arguments, and was more likely to lead to wisdom than any amount of logic-chopping. These aims overlapped and reinforced each other—the mastery of rhetoric promised the joining of eloquence and wisdom. For humanists like Desiderius Erasmus, the aim of education ought to be the development of *humanitas* and *pietas,* a joining of classical and Christian ideals. Mastery of the form and content of the humanities would develop moral men, capable in the conduct of public affairs. This humanist desire to restore the dignity and centrality of practical philosophy for the proper conduct of life found expression in a growing civic consciousness and political awareness, a civic humanism that began in the Italian city-states and spread throughout Europe.

What began for the humanists as a challenge to dialectic's preeminence provoked discussions of curriculum, and a shift in educational ideals. No longer should so much intellectual effort be devoted to the mastery of logical forms, but instead, students should master grammar and language, especially Greek and Latin. To these, northern humanists added Hebrew (for biblical sources), transforming the educational ideal of the early humanists into a necessity to master the three sacred languages, seen in institutions like the College Trilingual and later in Protestant universities. From grammar, students moved to the study of classical texts, deepening their grammatical training, but also to glean moral lessons, to be arranged in commonplace books, which the student would assimilate in the process of copying and translating. As one sixteenth-century student wrote, from Aristotle's *Politics* he seemed to receive "a twofold advantage, both a knowledge of Greek and acquaintance with moral philosophy." From Cicero's *Offices,* "a truly golden book," he derived "no less than a twofold enjoyment both from the purity of the language and the knowledge of philosophy." Such student training served those who were now less likely to pursue advanced degrees such as theology, leading to a career in the church, but were increasingly drawn into careers in commerce and public affairs, where such lessons could be used for ornamentation and to buttress arguments. Men trained in this fashion were better equipped for life at court, to argue in public assemblies, and to serve as chancellors and officers of state for the new monarchies and republics.

From the unrelenting drive to master the sources, humanists developed the tools of textual criticism still used today. Source criticism, the mastery of manuscripts, the tools of translation—indeed, the "sciences" of philology—derive from the humanists. Such tools did not respect disciplinary boundaries, and caused concern within academic specialties with institutional commitments to particular translations and particular interpretations of key texts. A legal renaissance formed a key arena for fights with incumbents over interpretation and application of the texts of the civil law. Even more explosively, humanist tools were directed at the sacred text of the Bible and the patristic and canon law texts that buttressed the institutional church. Erasmus could claim with a certain pride that he was merely a grammarian, not a theologian; yet the implications for the institutional church derived from his preface to his publication of Valla's *Annotationes* (1505) on the New Testament, and his own notes on key passages in his edition of the Greek New Testament (1516) were enormous, as he well knew. From philology developed a sense of pastness, a budding historical sense that could be directed at monuments, inscriptions, and other material objects—the beginnings of archeology, as an addition to the humanists' concern with texts and manuscripts. Humanist inquiry and textual recovery thus reshaped all the traditional disciplines, including medicine, and provided the materials (and opportunity) for the development of new disciplines. The colonizing tendencies of the humanist ideal led first to "encyclopedism," with the aim of mastery of the whole of human knowledge, an ideal that only fragmented late in the seventeenth century.

One trajectory of humanism can be traced from its beginnings as a university movement, through its widening as a cultural ideal of self-fashioning, and its institutionalization as a teaching program. Mastering the humanities became a career path for its practitioners and a means of upward mobility for its students. Humanists often worked outside the structure of the university—academics "outs" who challenged academic "ins," whose uncertain livelihood depended on freelance translating, tutoring, and patronage, but who promoted the advantages of their method in hopes of securing choice university positions. Mastery of the humanities need not necessarily lead to good or pious men, but might well be useful for one's career. As one dialogue writer noted in 1606, his aim in discoursing on the moral and intellectual virtues was only to "frame a gentleman fit for civill conversation, and to set him in the direct way that leadeth him to his civill felicitie," showing a casual disregard for the moral dilemma of service to the state presented two generations earlier by Thomas More in his preface to *Utopia*.

A second trajectory can be traced from the humanists' discovery of the historicity of all interpretation, countered by the reformer's scriptural literalism. Humanists, by challenging the close ties between syllogistic logic, medieval philosophy, and theology, and their message to return to original texts, paved the way for Protestantism's appeal to the Bible, rather than to scholastic theology. Protestant theologians took to heart humanist criticisms

of Aristotle, so Martin Luther could say in good humanist fashion, "Aristotle is to theology as darkness is to light." Yet the apparent historicity of interpretation also led to skepticism in the later sixteenth century.

Finally, Francis Bacon could turn his back on the researches of the humanists, whose concern with erudition led to a "distemper of learning where words are studied not things," signaling the shift to the study of phenomena rather than texts. Yet his historical researches, concern with "method," and his attempt to rewrite the Aristotelian *Organon* as the *Novum Organum* betray deep humanist influence. Humanism's lasting effects were in educational reform, although the humanists' intellectual profligacy soon encompassed ever more baroque and antiquarian inquiries. By the eighteenth century, George Eliot could create the character of Casaubon in *Middlemarch,* evoking his namesake, the biblical scholar Isaac Casaubon, as an archetype of the bloodless intellectual whose intellectual labors are as difficult as they are pointless.

BIBLIOGRAPHY

Dibon, Paul. *La philosophie néierlandaise au siécle d'or.* Vol. I. 1954.

Garin, Eugenio. "Le Traduzioni Umanistiche Di Aristotele Nel Secolo XV." *Atti della Societa Colombaria Fiorentina,* vol. 16 (1947–1950), pp. 55–104.

Green, Lawrence, ed. *John Rainold's Oxford Lectures on Aristotle's Rhetoric.* 1986.

Howell, W.S. *Logic and Rhetoric in England.* 1961.

McConica, James Kelsey. *English Humanists and Reformation Politics: Under Henry VIII and Edward VI.* 1965.

Schmitt, Charles. *John Case and Aristotelianism in Renaissance England.* 1983.

Siegel, J.E. *Rhetoric and Philosophy in Renaissance Humanism.* 1968.

Vos, Alvin. "'Good Matter and Good Utterance': The Character of English Ciceronianism." *Studies in English Literature,* vol. 19, pp. 3–19.

Dean Kiernan

SEE ALSO

Bacon, Francis; Ciceronianism; Classical Literature, English Translations; Classical Literature, Influence of; Education; Erasmus, Desiderius; Humanism; Logic; Rhetoric; Universities

Humors

See Medicine and Health

H

Hunnis, William (d. 1597)

Best remembered as a master of the children of the Chapel Royal, William Hunnis was a poet, musician, and gentleman of the Chapel Royal under Edward VI. Little is known about his birth or education. An active Protestant conspirator against Mary I, he was arrested and imprisoned in the Tower in March 1555. Although the record does not indicate whether he remained a prisoner after his trial in May of that year, he was reestablished after the accession of Elizabeth I in 1558. Soon thereafter he married Margaret Brigham, the well-to-do widow of his close friend, Nicholas Brigham, best known for building Chaucer's tomb at Westminster. When Margaret died in the autumn of 1559, he married a grocer's widow, became keeper of the gardens at Greenwich in 1562 and, within a few years, an elected official in the Grocer's Company. In 1566, he succeeded Richard Edwardes in the office of master of the children of the Chapel Royal. Hunnis held this position until his death, and though he received a grant of arms two years later, it appears he was in constant financial distress and died intestate.

By the time of his death in June of 1597, Hunnis had successfully rendered many of his Protestant intentions into verse; notable among his extant verses are those he contributed to the queen's entertainment at Kenilworth in July 1575, published in George Gascoigne's *Princely Pleasures at Kenilworth* (1576–1577). Among the most popular of his writings were the twelve poems contributed to Richard Edwardes's *The Paradyse of Daynty Devises,* which went into many editions between 1576 and 1606.

BIBLIOGRAPHY

Edwardes, Richard. *A Paradise of Dainty Devices (1576–1606).* Hyder E. Rollins, ed. 1927.

May, Steven. "William Hunnis and the 1577 *Paradise of Dainty Devices." Studies in Bibliography,* vol. 28, pp. 63–80.

Stopes, C.C. *William Hunnis and the Revels of the Chapel Royal: A Study of His Period and the Influences which Affected Shakespeare.* 1910; repr. 1963.

Rebecca Totaro

SEE ALSO

Edwardes, Richard; Gascoigne, George; Theater Companies, Boys; Verse Anthologies

Hunting

Hunting in its various forms was hugely popular among the upper classes of Tudor England, from the monarchs down. Indeed, contemporaries viewed an interest in hunting, hawking, fowling, and fishing as an essential mark of a gentleman and emphasized the importance of acquiring the necessary skills. Hunting was valued as a test of courage, strength, and agility, especially when hunting wild boar and stags. Not only did the sport require participants to be competent horsemen and women, a prized accomplishment in genteel society, it also offered them the chance to show it off. Hunting had the utilitarian function, too, of providing meat for the table and helping to keep down pests.

The countryside of Tudor England offered far better sport for the hunter than it does today. There was a greater stock of game and larger tracts of open land on which to hunt it, even allowing for the impact of enclosure on the wastes and common fields. One of the reasons why Henry VIII chose Cuddington (Surrey) as the site for Nonsuch Palace was the teeming wildlife of the Downs there: partridges, pheasants, hares, rabbits, foxes, and "all kyndes of vermen." Royal game was protected from hunting by anyone except the king and his companions. The upper classes also hunted in their parks. While many medieval deer parks were converted to agricultural use in the sixteenth century, a response to the growing demand for foodstuffs, others were being created. Ornamentation and a desire for greater privacy may have been the prime impulses, but hunting, hawking, and coursing could still be practiced there.

The true test for the hunter was to pit his wits—and courage—against the wild boar, though in sixteenth-century England the opportunity to do so was rapidly disappearing. A few did survive in parts of the Midlands and in the far north and west. Deer provided the mainstay of the sport. Fallow deer were the species most commonly pursued since they were spread widely around the country. Nonetheless, red deer were deemed to be superior quarry. Hare hunting was also popular. Birds and other small mammals were also caught, usually for food, while animals such as foxes, otters, badgers, wild cats, polecats, and martins were hunted as vermin, giving the participants some sport as they rid the countryside of a nuisance.

Game was normally pursued on horseback, accompanied by a pack of hounds. Various breeds of dog were used, although there was a good deal of interchangeability among them. However, mastiffs might be used for larger game, especially wild boar; and greyhounds might be used to run down hares, deer, or even foxes. Some hounds performed specialized functions: tufters and lymers flushed the game and running hounds chased the quarry until it stood at bay.

Less strenuous was the practice of hunting within the toil, a semicircular screen set up at the edge of a wood or in a park. Beaters drove the animals toward the net where onlookers waited with bows and arrows, crossbows, or firearms. Game birds might be shot at with birding or fowling pieces; but this branch of hunting remained largely the preserve of the falconer.

Hunting had a political as well as a social dimension. Because of the cost involved in maintaining parks, keeping the horses, hounds, and hawks, and paying for the army of retainers to look after them, it was an expensive sport. As a result, it was restricted to the upper classes and this gave them a unique shared experience. The feeling of belonging to an exclusive club was heightened by the employment of arcane language to define the various hunting terms. The Tudors were adept at exploiting this sentiment and used hunting as a means of cementing their ties with their subjects. They gave and received deer, venison, hawks, hounds, and hunting horses on a regular basis and used posts in their stables, kennels, and mews as a source of patronage. Invitations to a hunt were granted or withheld to show approval or disfavor, even to foreign dignitaries. Moreover, absence at hunting seems to have been the Tudor equivalent of a sick day.

George Turberville. From *The Noble Arte of Venerie or Hunting* (1575). Attributed to Turberville, this work was actually an adaptation by George Gascoigne of J. de Foulloux's *La Venerie* (1573). Here gentlemen prepare to run their dogs after game; the pose of the dogs represents them "pointing." Reproduced from the original by permission of the Henry E. Huntington Library and Art Gallery.

BIBLIOGRAPHY

Cockayne, Sir Thomas. *A Short Treatise of Hunting* (1591). W.R. Halliday, ed. 1952.

Fisher, William R. *The Forest of Essex: Its History, Laws, Administration, and Ancient Customs, and the Wild Deer which Lived in It.* 1887.

Gascoigne, George. *The Noble Arte of Venerie or Hunting* (1575; repr. 1611). 1908.

Manning, Roger B. *Hunters and Poachers: A Cultural and Social History of Unlawful Hunting in England, 1485–1640.* 1993.

Peter Edwards

H

SEE ALSO
Fish and Fishing; Patronage

Husbandmen
See Social Classes

Husbandry
See Agriculture; Household Books; Tusser, Thomas

Hymns

Two important developments in English hymnody took place during the Tudor period. The first, regarding liturgical hymns, involved the negative influence of Calvinism. Calvin opposed the use of man-made hymns in congregational worship, and the precedent set by the Genevan Church's rejection of hymns and adoption of a metrical psalmody influenced other national Protestant movements with Calvinistic leanings. Such was the case in both England and Scotland. The Scottish Church under Knox adopted Calvin's policy without variation. In England the first English Psalter of Thomas Sternhold and John Hopkins (1562) did contain a translation of the great Catholic hymn "Veni Creator Spiritus," but excluded other translations of Latin hymns that had appeared in the *Sarum Primer* of 1538 and the *Queen's Primer* of 1559. Cranmer, who was primarily responsible for the first Book of Common Prayer (1549), had, in effect, already determined the Anglican position on hymn singing. Both the first and second prayer books (1549 and 1552) omitted all translated hymns except the "Veni Creator."

The second development came late in Elizabeth I's reign, when British writers began contributing to the revival of the classical literary hymn, a revival that had begun on the Continent in the mid-fifteenth century with Enea Silvio Piccolomini's "Hymnus di Passione," an imitation of the Christian literary hymns of Prudentius in late antiquity. Subsequent continental writers—prominent among them Potano, Marullo, Flaminio, Vida, J.C. Scaliger, Joachim Du Bellay, and Pierre de Ronsard—chose objects of praise both Christian and non-Christian, the latter in imitation of the ancient *Homeric Hymns, Orphic Hymns,* and hymns by Callimachus, Cleanthes, Proclus, Julian, Horace, and Catullus. Most of these continental literary hymns are written in Latin. The best-known, by Raphael Thorius, which appeared just after the

Tudor period, celebrates the virtues of tobacco—*Hymnus Tabaci* (Leiden, 1625).

The first British examples during the Tudor period are also in Latin. While not discussing lyrical hymns or paeans (hymnic celebrations of Apollo) in the appended scholia, Richard Willes' curious handbook, *Poematum Liber* (London, 1573), does give examples of both (nos. 24 and 31). The Scottish poet, Mark Alexander Boyd, produced the first British collection of literary hymns, *Hymni* (Antwerp, 1592). Anticipating Thorius, most of these praise various flowers and plants, but the last three celebrate the spear (dedicated to James VI of Scotland), the sword, and the helmet.

The first really significant Tudor contributions to the genre, however, are written in English. George Chapman's first published work, *The Shadow of Night* (1594), consists of two literary hymns with the Latin titles, "Hymnus in Noctem" and "Hymnus in Cynthiam." These long (403 and 528 lines, respectively) pieces in five-beat couplets continue the imitations by Marullo and Ronsard of the classical, philosophical hymn, especially the *Orphic Hymns* and those by Proclus. The content is essentially Neoplatonic and is presented allegorically and obscurely in terms of Natalis Comes's system of mythography. Both hymns follow the conventional three-part structure; they invoke the muse and apostrophize the objects of celebration, develop a descriptive or narrative body, and close with the customary prayer. The first hymn construes Night in several different senses and has an explicitly satiric intention. Much of this poem is devoted to a description of the causes and conditions of man's depravity, his falling off from a primordial (Platonic) ideal self. Only poets inspired by Night can save man (ll. 308–310 and 376–377). The second hymn celebrates Queen Elizabeth as Cynthia and contains a mythical narrative of Cynthia and Euthimya (a creation of Chapman). Chapman subsequently wrote a long Christian literary hymn, "Hymne to Christ upon the Crosse" (1612), also in five-beat couplets, and includes a lyric "Hymnus ad D. Russelium defunctum" in his epicedion, *Eugenia* (ll. 1054–1171), which laments the death of William Lord Russell. Later he included the *Homeric Hymns* in his famous translation of Homer.

The most important examples of the genre in the Tudor period were, however, composed by Edmund Spenser. His long (two over and two just under 300 lines) *Four Hymns,* written in rime royal, appeared in 1596. They reflect the two basic courses that imitation of the classical literary hymn followed in the Renaissance. The first two hymns, celebrating earthly love and beauty, respectively, represent Spenser's adoption of the Marullian kind of hymn that eschewed Christian objects of praise for classical semi-philosophical themes. The latter two hymns, praising heavenly love and beauty, follow Vida and Scaliger in bringing Christian topics to the classical genre. The two earthly hymns develop elaborate fictional frames in the manner of Callimachus and Prudentius. All four are stylistically restrained and, unlike *The Faerie Queene,* are essentially free of archaic diction—leading Edmund Bolton, an anti-inkhornist and proponent of simple English diction, to single out only the *Hymns* for approval from the whole Spenserian canon (*Hypercritica,* 1618). While the earthly hymns are moderately allusive, the magnificent "Hymn of Heavenly Love," which celebrates the ministry and passion of Christ, contains not one classical allusion. On the other hand, it is the most rhetorically elaborate of all the hymns, echoing the same kind of rhetorical devices as Vida employs in his hymns "To God" and "To the Son." The "Hymn of Heavenly Beauty," the most rhetorically restrained of all the hymns, praises divine wisdom, *sapientia,* as a female personification of an attribute of Christ.

Both major critical theorists of the Tudor period discuss the literary hymn, although only briefly. George Puttenham's *Arte of English Poesie* (1589) and Sir Phillip Sidney's *Apology for Poetry* (1595) reflect some of the material and opinions in the most extensive critical discussion of the genre in the Renaissance, J.C. Scaliger's *Poetices Libri Septem* (1561)—1.3,44–45 and 3.109–118, with an additional critique of Marullo's *Hymni Naturales* on pp. 297–303. Scaliger incorporates and augments the longest critical review of the literary hymn in antiquity, that by the third-century (A.D.) sophist, Menander, in his handbook on epideictic eloquence.

BIBLIOGRAPHY

Athanassakis, Apostolos N. *The Orphic Hymns: Text, Translation, and Notes.* Graeco-Roman Religion. Vol. 4. 1977.

Booty, J., ed. *The Book of Common Prayer, 1559. The Elizabethan Prayer Book.* 1976.

Ford, Philip. *Ronsard's Hymnes: A Literary and Iconographical Study.* Medieval and Renaissance Texts and Studies. Vol. 157. 1997.

Parks, Edna D. *The Hymns and Hymn Tunes Found in the English Metrical Psalters.* 1966.

Welsford, Enid, ed. *Spenser: Fowre Hymns [and] Epithalamion: A Study of Edmund Spenser's Doctrine of Love.* 1967.

Philip B. Rollinson

SEE ALSO

Anglicanism; Book of Common Prayer; Calvinism; Chapman, George; Classical Literature, Influence of; George Puttenham; Spenser, Edmund

I

Immigration

The stream of immigrants coming into Tudor England from the Continent increased dramatically over the course of the sixteenth century, peaking during the reign of Elizabeth I. Much of this increase, as well as a shift in the nationalities that made up the majority of the newcomers, can be attributed to the unsettled conditions in Europe in the wake of the Protestant Reformation, whether in the form of religious persecution, economic displacement, or both. Except during the reign of Mary, late Tudor England appeared to many immigrants to be both a Protestant religious refuge and to hold more economic promise than did their war-torn homelands. The sudden escalation of immigrant numbers, coupled with the differences in their backgrounds and motives for immigration, forced the crown to formulate and implement new policies for maximizing the potential benefits and minimizing the potential hazards associated with their arrival and settlement.

Estimated numbers of foreign-born residents in London at the end of the fifteenth century range from 2,500 to 3,000, with merchants of Italy and the German Hanse and their households making up the vast majority of this number. Surveys conducted in Elizabeth I's reign show numbers of immigrants swelling to as many as 9,300 in 1568, but the average figure for the second half of the century was more normally around 5,000 to 6,000. This nevertheless represents a virtual doubling of the foreign population resident in the metropolis. This figure for London and its environs would have been even greater had not the crown conducted a program of settling colonies of immigrants in several towns of the eastern and southern counties, most notably Norwich, Colchester, Sandwich, and Southampton. The proportion of alien immigrants was much higher in these towns than in the capital. From the 1570s, the 3,500 to 4,000 foreigners resident in Norwich, for example, made up roughly one-third of the town's population.

The immigrants of this new, larger stream into England differed from their predecessors in more than greatly increased numbers. The preponderance of these new arrivals were skilled Dutch and Flemish artisans and craftsmen rather than wealthy merchants. Although skilled alien workers had been present in England before 1500, they had made up a small minority of the resident alien population. In the late sixteenth century the proportions were virtually reversed. These later immigrants practiced many skilled trades varying from glassblowing to gardening to making gunpowder, but most were trained in some aspect of the cloth industry, particularly in the manufacture of the textiles known collectively as the "new draperies."

Both national and local authorities recognized the potential benefits to be gained from the introduction of new commodities and technologies into the economy. One of the factors persuading the crown that the relocation of the foreigners into the provinces would be valuable—and prompting crown action—was the initiative taken by local governments in requesting the establishment of foreign settlements in their towns, usually on the grounds that decayed local economies could be revived by the introduction of the new skills brought by the immigrants. Requests were usually for aliens with expertise in the manufacture of the new draperies. The requests were almost uniformly approved since Elizabeth's ministers, particularly William Cecil, also consciously sought to improve England's position *vis-à-vis* known and potential enemies through this expansion of various skilled sectors

I

of the economy. The central government took the added step of seeking out aliens skilled in certain desirable areas, such as ordnance, mining, wire-making and other defense-related technologies, and inviting them to settle in England, usually offering as enticement patents and monopolies to protect the industries the aliens were expected to introduce.

Once committed to such a program, the crown also had to take steps to protect the foreigners against the natural economic resentment that surfaced time and again throughout the sixteenth century. Exacerbating this problem was more than a little popular hostility with strong xenophobic overtones, a hostility that expressed itself in a wide variety of ways ranging from the posting of anonymous anti-alien flysheets to outbreaks of violence in London reminiscent of the Evil May Day riots in 1517. Elizabeth's government intervened on many occasions to protect the aliens by exerting powerful influence behind the scenes or through more direct actions. This crown support eventually facilitated the assimilation of most of the immigrants, and established patterns of policy to which future governments could refer.

BIBLIOGRAPHY

Finlay, Roger. *Population and Metropolis: the Demography of London, 1580–1650.* 1981.

Pettegree, Andrew. "'Thirty years on': progress towards integration amongst the immigrant population of Elizabethan London." In *English Rural Society, 1500–1800: Essays in Honour of Joan Thirsk.* J. Chartres and D. Hey, eds. 1990.

Yungblut, Laura Hunt. *Strangers Settled Here Amongst Us: Policies, Perceptions, and the Presence of Aliens in Elizabethan England.* 1996.

Laura Hunt Yungblut

SEE ALSO

Aliens; Cloth Industry; Huguenots; Industry and Manufacture; London; Population and Demography

Industry and Manufacture

Late-medieval England was an industrial backwater, inferior to most of its continental neighbors in technology and in the scale and the range of production. Woolen cloth and, to a far lesser degree, lead, were the only English products of importance in international markets. In contrast, a wide range of processed goods, cheap everyday wares such as pins and knives, as well as more luxurious items, were imported from abroad. By the end of the sixteenth century, considerable progress had been made both in increasing the output of established industries and in establishing ones that were new: new, that is, either in the sense of complete novelty or in being put for the first time on a commercial basis. Textiles were the major industry in the early Tudor period before domestic demand stimulated growth in the metal and coal industries and elsewhere. Lead mining in the Mendips and Derbyshire and the iron industry expanded rapidly in the mid- and later sixteenth century, while coal output quadrupled between 1500 and 1600, much of the increase taking place in the northeast in the last quarter of the century. The growth rates for coal and iron were spectacular for major sectors of the preindustrial economy.

At the same time, the industrial base was considerably extended and diversified, again largely in response to domestic demand. The demonstrated effect of imported manufactures, their rapid rise in price from mid-century, a policy of protectionism adopted by the government and the arrival of skilled foreign workers early in Elizabeth I's reign encouraged investment in a wide range of import-substitute industries. The mining of copper, which was processed into brass, began in the 1560s. Other new manufactures included nails and pins, knives and tools, pots, ovens, buttons, starch, salt, soap, and paper. Almost all were influenced by foreign craftsmen. Glass manufacture affords an example of the impact on English manufacture of the diffusion of skills from the more advanced industrial regions. Before immigrant craftsmen arrived in 1567, glass of poor quality was made in minute quantities. Within a generation the home market for window glass had been captured while dependence on imported bottles and drinking glasses was much reduced. The cloth industry also benefited from the import of foreign skills through the introduction of the "new drapery," though the effects of increasing the product range of woolen cloth manufacture, which experienced some difficulty in competing in overseas markets in the second half of the sixteenth century, were to be felt later. Similarly, paper manufacture and copper mining were slow to establish themselves in the face of foreign competition. In the copper industry in particular production was small and erratic. Over the whole range of manufacturing, however, the Elizabethan innovations were a major step in the development of the "consumer society" that sustained industrial growth thereafter.

Expansion and diversification in the Tudor period are no longer seen to have required or resulted in radical changes in industrial organization or industrial processes.

In technology there were no great leaps forward, improvements in industrial processes being achieved by adjustments and modifications, each fitting into the category of "sub-invention." Many were introduced from abroad; not all were effective, and some, like the mechanically blown hearth in the mining iron industry, had been devised much earlier. For the great majority of those engaged in manufacturing, notably in the textile and leather industries, simple hand tools and a room in the house or a primitive shed outside were all that were required. Similarly, and in part because of the primitive technology that prevailed, industrial expansion did not necessitate large injections of capital. Even in the mining and metallurgical industries where untypically large, centralized places or units of production were to be found, involving relatively high levels of capital investment, fixed or true capital costs were small relative to running costs (£100 might set up a mine producing more than 2,000 tons of coal a year); and running costs, which largely consisted of wages, were in turn low relative to the value of the product. Capitalization in iron manufacture was similar, though fuel, not wages, was the major expense. The highly capitalized copper industry was perhaps the exception. But it was not a success, even in the longer term.

Over the whole range of industry, growth in the Tudor period was thus achieved largely through the multiplication of small units of production in which the key factor was the supply of cheap labor. In urban manufacture the small artisan-craftsman was a key figure. He might employ an apprentice or journeyman, but an establishment of more than two or three was exceptional. The putting-out system, whereby distributors supplied workers with raw materials to be worked up into the finished product, was also widespread in a wide range of urban manufactures, including leatherworking, one of the most important in the country in terms of employment. Putting-out, however, was more important as a means of tapping the resources of the underemployed in the countryside, where the seasonal nature of farming encouraged part-time or by-employment in manufacturing. Much of the growth in cloth manufacturing was accounted for in this way. By-employment was also characteristic of the lead industry, the medieval tradition of the miner-farmer persisting and prospering in most regions. In the coal industry the seasonal ebb and flow of activity in the small, shallow workings that remained the basic unit of production in part also reflected the agricultural calendar. From established industries putting-out and part-time employment spread to the new ones. Stocking knitting developed on that basis in the later sixteenth century, as did the making of small metalwares, such as cutlery and knives in Sheffield, Birmingham, and elsewhere. Thus, population growth in the sixteenth century was a key variable in preindustrial expansion both in respect of demand, in enlarging the market, and in supply.

BIBLIOGRAPHY

Clay, C.G.A. *Economic Expansion and Social Change: England 1500–1700.* Vol. 2: *Industry, Trade, and Government.* 1984.

Coleman, D.C. *Industry in Tudor and Stuart England.* 1975.

Hatcher, John. *The History of the British Coal Industry.* Vol. 1: *Before 1700: Towards the Age of Coal.* 1993.

Thirsk, Joan. *Economic Policy and Projects. The Development of a Consumer Society in Early Modern England.* 1978.

Brian Dietz

SEE ALSO

Cloth Industry; Coal Industry; Economy; Immigration; Metal Industries; Population and Demography; Technology and Production

Infant Mortality

See Childbirth; Population and Demography

Inflation

See Money, Inflation, and Moneylending; Price Revolution

Injunctions, Royal

Several sets of injunctions issued for the practical application of the state's ecclesiastical policies in Tudor England were together called "Royal Injunctions." The first set of injunctions was issued by Thomas Cromwell in 1536, and bore the seal of Henry VIII. Their main purpose was to ensure that the Ten Articles of that year were properly understood and applied at the parochial level. According to the injunctions, all forms of superstitious worship were to be uprooted, and great care was to be taken to ensure that the worship of the church be conducted in a dignified and orthodox manner. There were also a number of miscellaneous provisions, such as the command that a box be set up in the parish church to receive alms for poor relief.

I

The second set of injunctions appeared in 1538, also the work of Cromwell. These are famous largely because they authorized the placement of an English Bible in every parish church and imposed a system for registering baptisms, weddings, and funerals that was not superseded until 1837. When Henry VIII died, it was uncertain whether or not the authority of his injunctions would lapse; but Archbishop Thomas Cranmer took advantage of the situation to issue new injunctions of his own, under the seal of Edward VI. Most of these repeat the two sets of Henrician injunctions, although there are a number of additions, many dealing with the qualifications of the clergy sent to minister in the parishes. They also include a form of Bidding Prayer, a group of intercessory prayers to be used before sermons.

The fourth set of injunctions was issued by Mary I in 1554. They were few and short, and their only intention was to undo the Reformation as much as possible. Their authority lapsed when Mary died, and they never formed a part of the church's law.

The last and most important set of injunctions was issued in 1559, as part of Elizabeth I's settlement of religion. In the main, these repeat the Edwardian injunctions of 1547, but with a number of additions dealing with such matters as the behavior of worshippers in church, the duties of churchwardens, the censorship of books and plays, and the posture to be adopted at different points in the service, particularly the vexed question of kneeling. Annexed to them, in addition to the bidding prayers, is a special section concerning the placing of the holy table in the church. This was to be put where the altar once stood, a directive that was to cause great consternation among the Puritans, who feared that the table might be reverenced as if it were an altar.

BIBLIOGRAPHY
Bray, G.L. *Documents of the English Reformation.* 1994.
Gerald Bray

SEE ALSO
Articles of Religion; Bible Translations; Cranmer, Thomas; Cromwell, Thomas; Puritanism; Reformation, English; Sacraments

Inns of Court

Around 1470, Chief Justice Sir John Fortescue described a flourishing multicampus "academy of the laws of England" on London's western fringe. The city's legal district,

extending northward from the Thames across Fleet Street and the Strand to Holborn, grew up around the town-houses or inns *(hospicia)* of lawyers, royal officials, and statesmen. It was now dominated by four *hospicia majora,* or residential Inns of ("men of the") Court: Gray's Inn, Lincoln's Inn, Inner Temple, and Middle Temple. There were also ten lesser and subordinate Inns of Chancery (so called because some originated as hostels kept by clerks in Chancery), plus two serjeants' inns, reserved for the most senior lawyers and the judiciary. In reality, the sole common function of these private, voluntary, and somewhat informally constituted institutions was to provide lawyers and students with communal accommodation in convenient proximity to the Westminster law courts. Yet by 1602, Sir Edward Coke, another eminent jurist, could claim the Inns of Court and Chancery together as "the most famous university for the profession of law only, or of any humane science, that is in the world."

However hyperbolic, this was no empty boast. Much remains obscure about the medieval origins and early history of the Inns of Court. But during the sixteenth century these societies entered a dynamic new phase of growth, prosperity, and national prominence, unlike the Inns of Chancery, whose number actually declined to eight over the same period. These divergent fortunes reflect the success of the larger inns as multifaceted educational institutions catering to a much-expanded student clientele. By contrast, the smaller Inns of Chancery contracted to little more than lodgings for attorneys and solicitors, the lower-status "mechanical" practitioners of England's two-tiered legal profession.

Although English common law was not taught at Oxford or Cambridge, the medieval inns developed their own scholastic system of oral, disputatious "learning exercises" to supplement the would-be lawyers' private study and court attendance. Participation in these bolts, moots, and readings typically involved the argument of hypothetical cases, mimicking real-life pleadings in Westminster Hall. Competence and perseverance were rewarded by progression through each society's ranks of membership, from inner-barrister, to utter-barrister, to bencher or reader. During the early sixteenth century the common-law judges determined that only students who had been called to moot at the bar of an Inn of Court could plead before them in open court. Since a litigation boom was simultaneously enhancing demand for legal services of all kinds, the "honorable societies" (as they now called themselves) hereby gained monopoly control of a highly desirable professional qualification. Their enrollments consequently soared, with annual admissions roughly quadrupling in the century after 1500. By the end of Elizabeth I's reign the four inns together probably accommodated a total population of around 1,000 members during the four law terms.

Yet among those who flocked to the Tudor Inns of Court, practicing and would-be lawyers were easily outnumbered by young men with no firm plans for a legal career. The hope seems to have been that during their stay of a year or so they would acquire an elementary understanding of the law, and lawyers, as well as the gentlemanly accomplishments of dancing, fencing, and music, a broadening metropolitan experience, and perhaps some useful contacts. As fashionable academies for the landed and mercantile elites (although in reality far less socially exclusive than they purported to be), the Inns of Court attracted a wide cross section of the future political nation. More Elizabethan and early Stuart M.P.s seem to have attended an inn than a university in their youth. Since supervision was minimal, that experience must often have been a heady one. But besides the fleshpots, London provided unique cultural and intellectual opportunities, while the inns themselves were centers of creative writing and scholarship. Their members also staged interludes, revels, and masques, besides patronizing professional companies of players: William Shakespeare's *Comedy of Errors* was first performed at Gray's Inn, while *Twelfth Night* was staged at the Middle Temple in February 1602.

The emergence of the Inns of Court as "nursery for the greater part of the gentry of the realm" inevitably attracted official attention. Henry VIII commissioned an inquiry into their structure and government. No royal takeover bid followed, but Mary I's reign saw the first of numerous government attempts to regulate the discipline and educational functions of the societies. Religious conformity became a particular concern from the 1570s onward, when missionary Catholic priests began to target their junior members. This threat was countered in part by the appointment of preaching ministers to the chapels of Gray's Inn and Lincoln's Inn, and to the Temple Church. The famous resulting clash between the Puritan preacher Walter Travers and Richard Hooker, theological champion of the Church of England, provides a further example of the centrality of the Inns of Court to the history of Tudor England.

BIBLIOGRAPHY

Baker, J.H., and S.E. Thorne, eds. *Readings and Moots at the Inns of Court in the Fifteenth Century.* Vol. 2: *Moots and Readers' Cases.* 1990.

Brooks, C.W., ed. *The Admissions Registers of Barnard's Inn, 1620–1869.* 1995.

Fisher, R.M. "The Reformation in Microcosm? Benchers at the Inns of Court, 1530–1580." *Parergon,* n.s., vol. 6, pp. 33–61.

Prest, W.R. *The Inns of Court under Elizabeth I and the Early Stuarts, 1590–1640.* 1972.

Richardson, W.C. *A History of the Inns of Court.* 1978.

Wilfrid Prest

SEE ALSO

Coke, Edward; Law, Common; Education; Fortescue, John; Hooker, Richard; Lawyers; London; Theater Companies, Adult; Travers, Walter; Universities

Inns, Taverns, and Alehouses

Drinking houses of various descriptions were at the heart of the social life of Tudor England. The three dominant institutions—inns, taverns, and alehouses—were well established by the sixteenth century and were found in large numbers throughout the country; a survey of 1577 put the number of drinking houses at 17,595 in thirty counties. However, they served very different social groups and social and economic functions.

At the top of the scale were inns. They were usually large, fashionable establishments offering wine, ale, and beer along with food and lodging to well-to-do travelers. Inns, which began to appear in the twelfth and thirteenth centuries, were fairly numerous by Tudor times—amounting to 12 percent of the drinking houses identified in 1577—and they were usually to be found in the towns; Gloucester had twelve in 1583 and the small Leicestershire town of Lutterworth had four in the 1560s. Many were built or rebuilt on a large scale in the sixteenth and seventeenth centuries with impressive signs, often overarching the road, announcing their presence. Inns were especially large and comfortable in London and in the university towns. By the sixteenth century, innkeepers were often regarded as members of the local economic elite and their customers, who were chiefly drawn from the landed, mercantile, and professional classes, were served by a bevy of servants. The food and drink they provided were not cheap, and this discouraged more lowly prospective customers from crossing their thresholds. But inns were also important centers of economic and social exchange. In particular, merchants frequently conducted their transactions in the comfort of the inn, away from the public gaze of the marketplace, and from the sixteenth century, inns became increasingly important as centers of the national network of carrying services; in Elizabeth I's reign carriers ran weekly services from "Bosomes Inn" in St. Laurence Lane, London, to Chester. Inns also provided feasts and other entertainments for the elite, although this became more important in later centuries. Because they were the preserve of the higher orders, inns were largely free from the heavy burden of statutory controls imposed on alehouses by local and central governments.

Taverns were the least important of the Tudor drinking houses; just 339 were listed in the survey of 1577. Like the inns they catered to a relatively well-heeled clientele, although they were essentially drinking houses and rarely provided accommodation. The food they offered was relatively simple, sometimes brought in from neighboring cook-shops, but they were places of great conviviality, often noted as gambling haunts. Like the inns they were often used by merchants and others for the conduct of business.

Alehouses, the precursors of the modern "pub" or public house, were far more numerous; 15,095 were listed in the survey of 1577, and this was almost certainly an underestimate. Until recently little was known about alehouses since, unlike inns, many of which still adorn market places and high streets in the present century, few have survived, and they are rarely featured in the diaries and travelogues of the upper social groups. Moreover, they were often known by other names—tippling houses, boozing kens, or, more locally, tup-houses and beerhouses. Alehouses served the majority of the population—small farmers, artisans, craftsmen, shopkeepers, laborers, and the poor—with ale and beer, some simple food, and occasional accommodation. Although some alehouses were relatively large, with a number of rooms devoted to tippling, many were very small and shabby and lasted no more than a few years. In some parts of the country, such as Lancashire, a high proportion of alehouse keepers brewed their own beer, but in other places, such as Leicester, a relatively small number did so. Many contemporaries believed that the number of alehouses was growing fast in the later sixteenth century and, not surprisingly, elite opinion frequently condemned them; they were believed to be injurious to family life and the breeding ground for seditious opinions. However, it is likely that the great majority simply sought to forget their sad lives through drinking large amounts of strong ale or beer and competing with each other at the ubiquitous alehouse games (the forerunners of modern darts and dominoes). Attempts to regulate and control the number and

operation of alehouses remained sporadic before 1600, and we are left with the suspicion that a high proportion of the population of Tudor England—and especially the men who were the chief customers of alehouses—were in a frequent state of inebriation.

BIBLIOGRAPHY

Clark, Peter. *The English Alehouse: A Social History, 1200–1830.* 1983.

Everitt, A. "The English Urban Inn." In *Perspectives in English Urban History,* pp. 91–137. 1973.

French, R.V. *Nineteen Centuries of Drink in England.* 1884.

Hackwood, Frederick W. *Inns, Ales, and Drinking Customs of Old England.* 1909.

Monckton, H.A. *A History of the English Public House.* 1969.

Wilson, C. Anne. *Food and Drink in Britain.* 1973.

Donald Woodward

SEE ALSO
Food and Diet; Social Classes

Interior Decoration

The interiors of sixteenth-century houses, particularly those of the wealthiest classes, were not fixed in their appearance and furnishings. Contemporary inventories suggest that in the royal palaces and wealthiest houses interior decoration was splendid but temporary, created by furniture and tapestries or cheaper painted hangings that were brought together as the season or occasion demanded. In the earlier Tudor period, textiles such as wall hangings, cushion covers, and carpets (so rare and expensive they were usually thrown over tables rather than kept on the floor) were often bright, with sharp color contrasts. As the century progressed the decoration of rooms became more ambitious as they grew in size and ceilings were raised. Few sixteenth-century interiors survive intact, and many that at first appear authentic are the result of nineteenth-century re-creations using original materials and furnishings. Yet there survive interiors whose original structural features, fragments of original decoration and, in very rare cases, contents, help reconstruct their appearance in Tudor times. At Haddon Hall, Derbyshire, a sequence of rooms comprising great hall, parlor, then a staircase to the great chamber and long gallery is a good example of rooms appointed more or less richly according to their importance and showing continual modernization as the

The dining room at Haddon Hall, Derbyshire (c. 1545). A fine example of decorated panelling. By permission of the National Monuments Record.

century progressed. Lower in the social scale, the merchant's house of Paycocke at Great Coggeshall in Essex retains a modest series of paneled rooms with some original ceilings and fireplaces. Because different craftsmen were employed for walls, ceilings, fireplaces, and furnishings, these components of Tudor rooms did not always share decorative features.

The usual material for wall surfaces was plaster laid on stone, brick, or wooden laths, which was then painted with limewash. Sometimes walls were covered with roughly painted biblical, historical, or other moralistic scenes. The cycle from the 1570s depicting the story of King Hezekiah, from the Old Testament, at Hill Hall, Essex, with figures in antique or historicized costume, expresses expensive taste. Many other fragments, whether *in situ* or removed, survive from inns or smaller houses such as those at Prittleworth Manor, Hampshire, where the story of Tobias and the Angel is played out in contemporary dress, surrounded by heraldic motifs. More often, walls are decorated not with painted narrative scenes but with natural or stylized orna-

ment. Relatively sophisticated examples, such as the panels now at Loseley House, Surrey (1540s), with their courtly, fashionable, grotesque ornament (it has been suggested that these panels came from the royal palace of Nonsuch), are less prevalent than the type of decoration exemplified by the mixture of balusters and other Renaissance motifs with an older tradition of vegetable ornament, as is found at Polstead Hall, Suffolk, of about 1550.

When rooms were paneled, the most common form in the early sixteenth century involved small, plain panels fixed to battens, as in the parlor at Haddon; sometimes these panels were carved to imitate folded cloth and hence are known as "linenfold." As the century progressed, plinths, dados, and applied pilasters began to appear in paneling, giving rooms a more architectural character. Paneling was sometimes inlaid with woods of contrasting color, as seen in the room from Sizergh Castle, now in the Victoria and Albert Museum, with its illusionistic motifs. By the end of the century, fireplaces with elaborate plaster or wooden overmantels completed the architectural unity

I

within some rooms, both in houses and in public buildings such as college and town halls; usually these emphatically displayed the civic, collegiate, or private owner's heraldry.

Tapestries, the most expensive way to decorate the walls of rooms, survive in relatively small numbers. They were usually imported from the great tapestry workshops of the southern Netherlands. Tapestries from Henry VIII's collection still hang in some semblance of their original context in the great hall and great watching chamber at Hampton Court. Of the ubiquitous stained (painted) cloths, the cheapest form of wall hanging, only fragments survive, mostly in museums, though an early seventeenth-century set with figures and animals in a landscape can be found in an upstairs room at Owlpen Manor, Gloucestershire. Wall hangings were only the most prominent textiles in the room, however; among quite sparse furnishings inventories often mention carpets, bed hangings and covers, and cushions, sometimes carrying heraldic motifs.

Ceilings were initially simply left as the underside of the floors of rooms above, but sometimes the joists and the panels between were painted with heraldic or other motifs, as is seen in the parlor at Haddon and the parlor created for Prior Senhouse in his lodgings tower at Carlisle about 1507. Increasingly, however, ceilings were plastered, and toward the end of the first half of the century wooden battens were sometimes added in patterns over the plaster surface. These patterns mark the early influence in England of the illustrated books on architecture by Sebastiano Serlio. Later, ceilings were divided into geometric shapes by broad bands of plaster; plasterers could achieve a variety of curving shapes, with cusps and ogival forms, that carpenters could not. By the late sixteenth century, great hanging pendants of plaster over a wooden substructure, which mark the juncture of ribs, look back to the similar feature in wooden hammerbeam roofs of the late Middle Ages. The geometric fields between the ribs served as grounds for heraldry and abstract or figurative motifs taken from contemporary bestiaries, herbals, and emblem books.

BIBLIOGRAPHY

Blakemore, Robbie G. *Interior Decorations and Furnishings.* 1997.

Jourdain, Margaret. *English Interior Decoration, 1500–1850.* 1950.

Levey, Santina M. *An Elizabethan Inheritance: The Hardwick Hall Textiles.* 1998.

Mercer, Eric. *English Art, 1553–1625.* 1962.

Maurice Howard

SEE ALSO

Architecture; Hardwick, Elizabeth; Heraldry; Painting; Royal Palaces

Ireland, History of

Tudor Ireland was divided into three cultural zones. First, there was the narrow eastern coastal belt, centering on the Pale, the last surviving remnant of the old Anglo-Norman lordship, from which in the 1530s the reconquest began. Next, there was a broad borderland zone stretching westward and southward where the descendants of the old conquerors still held on but only at the cost of general surrender to Gaelic mores, and which, after major struggles in the 1570s and 1580s, was eventually recaptured. And finally, there was the purely Gaelic zone, comprising the farthermost parts of Munster and Connacht and all of the province of Ulster that fell to the crown only in the very last years of Elizabeth.

This geographical model and the simple narrative that it suggests have always been overly schematic. Exceptions abound: in Leinster, just a few miles from Dublin, powerful Gaelic families survived as a major threats to the Pale until the end of the century; in the west, the cities of Limerick and Galway retained such connections with Dublin as to be considered extensions of the Pale. The borderlands displayed a fluidity of cultural characteristics that defied easy categorization, while the supposed isolation of Gaelic Ulster was in reality much diluted by elaborate dynastic ties with families throughout the country and by a broad network of trade channelled through the market towns of Sligo, Cavan, and Monaghan.

Geography was indeed crucial; but the manner in which it shaped the distinctive features of the sixty or so significant lordships that constituted the political structure of the island was considerably more complex. Compact and well-centered settlements with protected frontiers enabled the great Anglo-Irish earldoms of Kildare and Ormond to retain their strength and stability, yet the too great security afforded by natural frontiers left the O'Brien lordship of Thomond a prey to chronic intra-dynastic strife. Conversely, the problems posed by particular internal geographical obstacles, such as mountain ranges or boggy terrain, compelled the Gaelic O'Neills of Tir Eoghain (Tyrone) and the Anglo-Irish Fitzgeralds of Desmond to employ such force to maintain their territorial integrity that they became two of the most powerful and feared lordships in Ireland. The success of such lordships as resorted to external aggression to preserve internal stability shaped the character of Ireland's politics in important ways. Outside intervention often fueled vicious struggles for succession, particularly in those Gaelic dynasties where primogeniture had not taken hold. But, more importantly, it furthered a tendency toward militarization in the island as a whole, as lordships threatened by aggression fought back or sought to emulate the aggressors. So it was that by the beginning of the sixteenth century, Ireland had taken on the appearance of an armed camp sustaining more than 25,000 professional soldiers on a population that was probably less than half a million. The dysfunctional effects of intensive militarization were obvious. It was, of course, extremely dangerous for the political elite; and the Gaelic annals of the period regularly record the unexpected overthrow and violent death of great men. But it was also socially and economically exhaustive.

The primitive conditions of the sixteenth-century Irish economy—the predominance of pastoralism, the low level of trade, and the ubiquity of poverty—so emphasized by late Elizabethan commentators like Fynes Moryson and Barnabe Rich, have also been greatly exaggerated. Modern research has uncovered a more complex situation, revealing evidence of a much more sophisticated society capable of handling the intricate tenurial problems presented by partible inheritance, developing a variegated agriculture, and generating in places a substantial amount of personal wealth. Such scholarship has also drawn attention to an embryonic "gentry," a freeholding class emerging from within the ruling dynasties seeking to assert its economic and political autonomy within the lordships. It was, however, precisely these economically progressive tendencies that were opposed and frustrated by the escalating numbers of unproductive military men in the lordships' private armies whose crushing demands on the economy's resources stifled development and resulted in a peasant exodus from the land, some seeking places in the great armies, others resorting to vagrancy.

The long-term implications of this clash between the conflicting forces of economic change and militaristic oppression were disastrous for the ruling dynasties, and recognizing this, most of the lordships' rulers sought a way of escaping from their dilemma by entering into larger alliances with other powerful families on the island in an effort to curtail their expenditure and maintain their authority through a strategy of collective security. This movement reached its apogee toward the close of the fifteenth century when one of the most powerful of the great dynasties, the Fitzgeralds of Kildare, established control over the royal administration in Dublin and used it to extend their own influence over all the lordships of Ireland. By the beginning of the sixteenth century Kildare authority was formidable but it was by no means complete. Opponents and recalcitrants remained, encouraged by the Kildare's closest rival, the Butler house of Ormond, and by abusing judicial and administrative office the Geraldines also provoked demands for renewed royal intervention in Ireland from a small but articulate group of reformers in the Dublin administration itself. At first, such pleadings had little effect in Whitehall, although they occasionally prompted Thomas Wolsey to interrupt Kildare's hold on the governorship. But it was only amid the crisis of Henry VIII's divorce that Whitehall, fearing foreign invasion, turned seriously to Ireland.

What happened in the 1530s was not some bold initiative to revive the English conquest, but an emergency response limited by the meager resources of the treasury and informed by a hasty consultation of the "file" comprising the various complaints presented by the Pale reformers over the previous two decades against Kildare. From this perspective a simple analysis was derived. For all its historical and cultural peculiarities, Henry and Secretary Cromwell perceived that in Ireland they were dealing with just another variant of that familiar Tudor problem: the overmighty subject. And they could see also that in the surviving structures of the royal administration in Ireland (so ably represented by the Pale reformers) they had to hand the means of applying the same policies by which the problem was even then being addressed in Wales, in the North, and at court itself. Institutional reconstruction—the reform of the offices and personnel of government, the revival and extension of assizes, and the establishment of councils in the farther provinces of the land—was the familiar and attractively gradualist prescription that they would now apply to Ireland. This was an understandable response, but it was also too simple. For, given the exceptional nature both of Ireland's historical development and England's present problems, it was inevitable that this classical solution should be complicated by a number of distinct additional factors, none of which had been addressed in the Palesmen's pleas for action, and all of which posed especially acute problems.

The first concerned the political education of the island's nobility. In England and Wales this process had been handled with considerable success through a blend of conciliation and exemplary coercion. But in Ireland, given the very different orientation of the bulk of the nobility, the task was immeasurably more difficult, and failed disastrously at the start when the Kildares, sensing the inapplicability of the policy but misreading the urgency with which it was being applied, rejected proposals for a gradual reduction of armies, and raised the standard of revolt. Henry easily crushed a rebellion the Kildares had never intended to fight, but the destruction of the most influential family in the land only deepened the crown's inherent difficulty. With the powerful Irish nobility either disaffected or untrustworthy, the advance of reform now devolved suddenly on the English viceroy alone.

The first governors placed in this predicament, Lord Leonard Grey (1536–1540) and Sir Anthony St. Leger (1540–1548, 1550, 1553–1556), sought to escape it by manipulating elements within the great dynastic alliances in order to win support for their administrations, or at least neutralize hostility. This was the intent of St. Leger's great constitutional initiative, the establishment of Ireland as a kingdom (1541), which served as a declaration to the Gaelic nobility that the crown no longer regarded them as enemies to be conquered, but as subjects of equal status to the Anglo-Irish and English peerage. There then began an energetic round of diplomatic agreements, subsidized visits to court, and generous grants and endowments, all in the manner in which the Tudors had tamed the English nobility. Yet the delicate wooing of the unstable Irish nobles was made more difficult by the absence of a real Irish king and a genuine Irish court. St. Leger's adoption of former Geraldines (now anxious to find a new patron) also left him open to charges of partiality and corruption. But the ultimate cause of his fall in 1556 was his failure to answer Whitehall's rising demands for economy, territorial security, and access to patronage, which he had quite neglected while engaged on his protracted Irish courtship. Thus the man who unseated him, the earl of Sussex (1556–1565), determined on a quite different strategy.

This mid-century change, often crudely interpreted as a shift from conciliation to conquest and explained by some poorly grounded speculations about the influence of Spanish colonial practices in America, was in reality far less dramatic. It concerned not an ideological revolution but, as Sussex himself explained, a reversal of strategic priorities. Whereas St. Leger had regarded the winning of the nobility as a necessary preliminary to institutional reform, and had failed, the crown, Sussex argued, should commence its reforms without tarrying for any. Those lords who were willing to support the reformed administration (Sussex believed they were in the majority) were to be rewarded and co-opted into its structures, while those who reneged on their promises (he anticipated only a few defections from among the Geraldines) were to be suppressed.

As it happened, Sussex was unable to deliver on the latter commitment, and his spectacular failure in relation to Shane O'Neill, the usurping lord of Tyrone, aborted his program in its earliest stages. But the priorities that he set—securing agreement at Whitehall for a specific program of institutional reform, rather than engaging with the nobility as a proxy for the monarch—were adopted, with some significant development, by his major successors as governor, Sir Henry Sidney (1566–1578, 1575–1578) and Sir John Perrot (1584–1588). Belatedly, Sidney introduced Sussex's plans for provincial councils in Munster and Connacht and summoned an Irish parliament (1569–1571) to ratify his ambitious program of social change. But in the early 1570s, Sidney also introduced the novel policy of "composition."

Often relegated to obscurity because of its early failure, "composition" in fact represented the English government's most sophisticated response to the problem of anglicizing Ireland with the meager resources at hand. Based on an understanding of the intrinsic tensions that had prevented the Irish lordships from undertaking change on their own, and on an acceptance of the failure of conventional attempts at institutional reform, "composition" sought to exploit the coercion inherent in the lordships' politics in the interests of genuine reform. Through the intense but temporary application of pressure—a large military presence—the crown would enforce detailed commutations of feudal and other informal exactions at all levels of society within the lordships into fixed payments that it would then undertake to collect in return for an annual tax. Sidney's plans were disrupted by his early recall, but in the 1580s, Perrot revived the strategy in an even more urgent fashion. In this rapid acceleration of the reform process both Sidney and Perrot anticipated trouble, and prepared for it by obtaining prior support for their actions at court and bringing with them forces sufficient to isolate or discourage local or individual dissent. Yet when serious trouble arose, it came from a quite unexpected source: the ostensibly loyal community of the English Pale.

The increased demands of the new governors for supplies substantially augmented retinues, and the subsequent misconduct of billeted soldiers and the displacement of some office-holding families all contributed to rising resentment in the Pale. But opposition grew radical only when the governors' announcement of their intention to introduce a composition of their own military exactions in the Pale precipitated a remarkably articulate and well-organized protest. Convinced that they were engaged upon a program designed to meet objectives for which the English of the Pale had long pleaded, Sidney and Perrot underestimated the Pale's resentment of such taxation without consent, and their failure to appreciate the constitutional issues involved led in the end to the collapse of their administrations. But by the mid-1580s, the Palesmen's apparent sensitivity to their rights as freeborn Englishmen was supplemented by a further imperative that had been quite absent from the Palesmen's position when they first lent their support to political reform in the 1520s and 1530s: the issue of religious reformation.

The early impact of the Reformation in Ireland is not easily measured. Despite the retrospective prejudices of historians, the constitutional and liturgical changes introduced by Parliament in 1536–1537 aroused little hostility among the laity, many of whom benefited substantially from the generous distribution of monastic property that followed shortly after. Yet from the outset the changes directly threatened the interests of one crucially important group: the secular clergy of the Pale. Though the menace faced by the religious orders was ostensibly great, it was also simple: the bulk of the monastic foundations had long since been in decline, and most were sparsely populated; almost all had granted away large lots of property to lay speculators. For the monks who remained, generous pensions were provided; none was to suffer persecution. For the secular clergy of the Pale, however, the problem was more complex. The changes entailed not a pension and retirement, but an obligation to be more active, to preach and to serve their cures while suffering a serious reduction in their paltry incomes by new clerical taxation. These pressures intensified after 1560 when the Reformation became doctrinal and the Church of Ireland was committed by the crown to a mission of conversion. But just as it lacked a court to further political reform, so Ireland lacked a university (until 1592) that might serve as a seminary to foster an indigenous reformist cadre. The clergy's conservatism, however, was based on more than mere ignorance. Though it was without a tradition in theology, an alternative schooling in canon law was deeply rooted in the Dublin diocese. Several of the pre-Reformation clergy were accomplished canonists, and in the reign of Queen Mary their numbers were deliberately strengthened. Thus when the new Elizabethan bishops attempted to resume the work of reforming the church, they found themselves facing not a corrupt and idle ministry but a reinvigorated conservative elite, expertly equipped to defend their traditional places and practices. It was the resistance of the clergy to their episcopal superiors, and the evident collapse of the episcopacy in face of this resistance, that at length prompted the most active civil administrators, Sidney and Perrot, to intervene. Thus, even as they hastened to expedite secular reform by abrupt and increasingly arbitrary measures, they embarked on a campaign to enforce religious conformity directly upon the laity. And in doing so they unwittingly provided a focus for the pervasive discontent of the Pale, and made the defense of "the old religion" the collective badge of allegiance of the old colonial community against the manifold threat of the new.

At back of this fatal combination of constitutional and religious challenge by which the governors had alienated their closest allies, there lay a further political pressure that had been underestimated: the problem of government finance. It had been assumed that the revival of English rule could be attained with only a modest increase in expenditure; for once the nobility had been won over, it seemed reasonable to expect that the Irish government should return to the state of self-sufficiency that had prevailed under Kildare. The disasters of the 1530s exploded such hopes, and even St. Leger's eirenic style failed to cut costs or raise revenues. The programs of his successors necessarily entailed substantial increases in expenditure, which they sought to secure by preparing costings and timetables in advance. Characteristically, they underestimated. The treasury failed to pay out the sums that had been agreed, and their regimes rapidly fell into debt. Formal credit was not available, so they resorted to informal measures: by requisitioning supplies, billeting troops without pay, and through a series of exactions known collectively as "the cess," they sought to make good the shortfall in their own budgets by having the country, temporarily at least, foot the bill. Such exploitation provoked widespread discontent, and successive governors sought genuinely to find a solution to the problem of supply, most notably in the policy of "composition." But in the wake of repeated failures to find a centrally controlled solution, the governors tended in practice to resign responsibility altogether and to delegate the matter to their subordinate officers, the captains of the garrisons they had posted throughout the country.

Left to themselves, these supposed representatives of reform survived simply by adapting themselves to the protection rackets already in operation in the country.

I

This ready acceptance of the mores they were appointed to change, of course, undercut the reformist claims of their superiors, and as their numbers increased, so the hostility of the native protectors with whom they were in competition began to grow. Micro-wars between military professionals had begun to appear by mid-century, and grew more serious thereafter. In Ulster, the private activities of the soldiers, notably Nicholas Bagenal, contributed greatly to the failure of St. Leger's settlement in Tyrone and the rise of Shane O'Neill. In the midlands the abuses of the garrison commanders appointed by Sussex to oversee a general resettlement of the territory ruined any chance of constructing an exemplary English colony among the native lordships. In Munster the conduct of Sidney's unofficial agents, Warham St. Leger and Sir Peter Carew, provoked an unprecedented union of the armies of Ormond and Desmond in revolt in the late 1560s. And in the late 1570s, Sidney's appointees in Munster and Connacht stirred even more serious rebellion in both provinces.

It was at that point that this unacknowledged war between native and English professionals was transformed by the return of Desmond's exiled army commander, James Fitzmaurice Fitzgerald, in 1579. Although he came only with a small force and was soon killed, Fitzmaurice's manifesto of revolt identified the plight of the old military elite now under attack from spurious English reform with that of the clergy and laity whose traditional religious practices were now threatened by aggressive reformation. The freebooters and the heretics were together destroying the true English culture in Ireland that had hitherto been preserved by the old colonial community. Fitzmaurice's pseudo-loyalist claims broadened the basis of his protest considerably by providing a larger conceptual frame within which the clergy, the native soldiers, the Palesmen, and erstwhile supporters of reform could all be encompassed. His explanation at first persuaded few to follow him into rebellion, but fear that widespread revolt was imminent frightened the new viceroy, Arthur Grey (1580), into an abandonment of due process and a ruthless period of military repression that seemed to confirm Fitzmaurice's claims. Grey's terror was short-lived, but its effects endured. In the Pale resistance became general: defiant recusancy provided the best means of barring newcomers from entry into the old community through marriage. The English government undertook by the widespread application of martial law the confiscation of suspected rebel lands and goods, and the sale of pardon, making good in the country just when the traditional

modes of entry were being closed off. Thus an open conflict appeared between the old colonials and a new professional or "servitor" interest determined to supplant them as the true representatives of English rule in Ireland.

The operations of the servitors as a distinct political interest first became evident in the mid-1580s in their attempts to reshape government plans for the settlement of Desmond's lands following the suppression of the revolt in which Fitzmaurice had precipitated. Initially the plantation of Munster was envisaged as a modest scheme, with Perrot and the earl of Ormond (to whom the suppression of the revolt had largely been due) favoring dispossession of only the leading rebels. But following intense pressure in Dublin and Whitehall, the servitors secured authority for a far more widespread confiscation that made large amounts of Munster land available for colonial investment. The rapacity of the Munster plantation sowed deep roots of resentment. But the servitors' most serious impact was felt in Ulster where inadvertently they were considerably aided by Perrot himself. In an energetic spurt in the mid-1580s, Perrot attempted what he hoped would be a permanent settlement of Ulster that included the recognition of a permanent Scottish colony, the ordering of Tyrone (including the creation of Hugh O'Neill as earl of Tyrone), the appointment of sheriffs, and the introduction of composition in most of the lordships. All of this required a significant increase in the crown's military presence in the province, but when Perrot was suddenly recalled in 1588 (because of his troubles in the Pale and Munster), his successor, Sir William Fitzwilliam (1588–1594), allowed the new Ulster soldiers either to forage on their own or replaced them with others with no commitment to reform. The activities of these abandoned soldiers provided the clearest justification of the military caste's claim to be the people's only defense against unrestrained English exploitation. Having barely escaped redundancy, the Irish soldiers rose up in 1593–1594, seeking the overthrow of supporters of composition all over Ulster and dragging the lords, Tyrone included, into their rebellion.

The long war that followed marked a culmination of the conflict between the new and old men of war, and in it the promoters of peace on both sides were squeezed out. The collapse of the English presence in Ulster in 1598 temporarily gave the Irish military men the upper hand, and encouraged rebellion all over the island. But when they were forced to march south to rescue a besieged Spanish expeditionary force at Kinsale (1601), they overstretched their resources and their power was broken. Victory thus went to the servitors, and though the generous peace of Mellifont (1603) represented a genuine attempt to return to the status quo before 1594, the servitors worked effectively in their localities to undermine all further efforts at reconciliation through reform. In doing so they were led by a new governor, Arthur Chichester, himself a former servitor, and by a distinctive interpretation of the previous century (proffered in its most radical form in Edmund Spenser's *View of the Present State of Ireland,* 1596) that discounted the moral and intellectual failures recorded by history and justified the inevitability of its outcome by citing the supposedly immutable characteristics of the people as determined by climate and by geography.

BIBLIOGRAPHY

Bradshaw, Brendan. *The Irish Constitutional Revolution of the Sixteenth Century.* 1979.

Brady, Ciaran, and R. Gillespie. *Natives and Newcomers: Essays on the Making of Irish Colonial Society.* 1986.

———. *The Chief Governors: The Rise and Fall of Reform Government in Tudor Ireland.* 1994.

Canny, Nicholas. *The Elizabethan Conquest of Ireland: A Pattern Established.* 1976.

Ellis, Steven. *Tudor Ireland: Crown, Community, and the Clash of Cultures.* 1986.

———. *Tudor Frontiers and Noble Power: The Making of the British State.* 1996.

Lennon, Colm. *Sixteenth Century Ireland: The Incomplete Conquest.* 1994.

Morgan, Hiram. *Tyrone's Rebellion.* 1993.

Nicholls, Kenneth. *Gaelic and Gaelicised Ireland in the Later Middle Ages.* 1972.

Ciaran Brady

SEE ALSO

Colonial Development; Foreign Relations and Diplomacy; Henry VIII; Moryson, Fynes; O'Neill, Hugh; Sidney, Henry; Spenser, Edmund

Iron Industry
See Metal Industries

Italian Literature, Influence of

The continental humanism that flourished in the early sixteenth century, and made a distinct impact on the court of Henry VIII through such figures as Desiderius Erasmus, Thomas More, and John Colet, had deep Italian roots. The origins of humanism lead back to the revival of classical literature in Italian city-states such as Florence in the fourteenth century and to such figures as Petrarch and Boccaccio, who combined a passion for ancient literature with their own efforts to produce works in the vernacular. Dante, of course, preceded them in the latter pursuit; but he became an instructive casualty of Renaissance culture, whose ever-intensifying classicism increasingly decried the "gothicism" of his *Commedia.* Florence's triple crown of Dante, Boccaccio, and Petrarch did not survive as a Renaissance canon. Ariosto replaced Dante as the supreme narrative poet in Italian, and Tasso mounted an undeniable challenge to Ariosto's preeminence in the late sixteenth century. Boccaccio likewise suffered, if not a falling off in reputation, increasing neglect and a consequent slip from prominence. But the recrudesence of Petrarchan sonnetteering in France and England assured that Italian exemplar an ironic triumph over time inasmuch as the very title of his songbook, *Rerum vulgarum fragmenta,* indicates the lower status to which he consigned his vernacular lyrics.

Thus, as Tudor literature began to adapt humanist principles to the production of vernacular works and Italian models set the standards that English authors sought to meet, Ariosto, Tasso, and Petrarch became especially decisive exemplars. Sir Thomas Wyatt and the earl of Surrey domesticated the Italian sonnet, whose pervasive influence culminated in the outpouring of such verse after the publication of Sir Philip Sidney's Petrarchan sequence, *Astrophil and Stella,* in 1591. Wyatt, moreover, made notable experiments with other Italian forms and traditions. The *ottava rima* of the narrative framework of his *Paraphrase of the Penitential Psalms* reproduces the stanza of Italian epic romance. The *terza rima* of the Psalms themselves perhaps ultimately derives from the form Dante immortalized, but its employment in Wyatt's epistolary satires reveals a clear affinity with the cinquecento revival of Horatian satire by Ariosto and his inheritor, Luigi Alamanni. This Florentine political exile's tenth satire serves as the direct model for Wyatt's "Mine own John Poins."

Although undeniably immense, the Italian influence on Tudor literature harbors a central paradox. While the literary accomplishments of such poets as Petrarch and Ariosto set important standards of excellence for English vernacular poetry, as Sidney's *Astrophil and Stella* and Edmund Spenser's *The Faerie Queene* (1590–1596) amply testify, the Catholic culture of Italy and the church of Rome constitute the primary enemy of Protestant England as Tudor writers seek to represent that nation. The

I

foil of Anglo-Roman religious hostilities routinely sets off Anglo-Italian intertextuality, as Spenser's "Book of Holiness," for example, abundantly reveals. The Saracens of *Orlando Furioso* are based on moorish "infidels" from North Africa and Spain who championed Islam against Charlemagne's Christian empire. Translated into the terms of Spenser's Elizabethan allegory, they become signs of heresy typical of Roman "papistry" or of elements within the English Church that resist reform. Their connection with their historical counterparts is tenuous at the very most. Even Sidney's Petrarchism frequently enacts a self-serving strategy of splitting the difference between literary and ethical imitation that ironically reflects English skill at appropriating Italian forms while substantively contesting the arguments conventionally associated with them. For example, in borrowing the sonnet form and Neoplatonic thematics of the Petrarchan pre-text "Chi vuol veder quantunque po natura" (*Rime* 248), Sidney's "Who will in fairest book of nature know" (*AS* 71) sustains the idealism of the Italian model through its penultimate line. But the final line dramatically records a failure to accomplish the high-minded aspirations of the original and thus wittily undoes their apparent superiority by exposing their false foundations in all-too-human neediness.

In *The Unfortunate Traveller* by Thomas Nashe (1594), an Italian journey occupies the major portion of Jack Wilton's peregrinations and reveals the fundamental challenge posed by Italian culture in Tudor England. Jack's exposure to the wickeness of Italy offers an extremely lurid vision of the final stage in a humanistic education, the Grand Tour, and contains pointed satire of such literary fashions as sonnetteering and romantic chivalry. Ascham had already decried such travels along with the dangerous blandishments of romance, but Nashe's picture of violence, depravity, and folly in Venice, Florence, Rome, and Bologna goes into sordid detail and includes a fulsome denunciation of travel from the banished English earl who manages to liberate Jack from the hangman's noose.

Despite such attitudes the Italian influence remained strong as the Tudor century drew to a close. Spenser was particularly responsive to Torquato Tasso's various accomplishments. Besides virtually translating substantial excerpts from *Gerusalemme Liberata* in the episode of the Bower of Bliss (*FQ* 2.12), his borrowing from Tasso to voice discontent with life at court (*FQ* 6.9) reveals an awareness not only of Tasso's literary example but also of his reputation for misfortunes and personal distress as a courtier. The 1594 stage production in London of *Tasso's*

Melancholy (now lost) indicates the widespread sense of consequence attached to this Italian poet's experience. Further, his influence permeates Spenser's *Amoretti*, where well over a dozen sonnets derive from Tasso's *Rime*. Likewise, Samuel Daniel follows Tasso's example in a few sonnets in *Delia* (1592), and his translation of the chorus on the golden age from Tasso's *Aminta* is an early sign of the impact that pastoral drama will have on English vernacular efforts to inherit the tragicomic tradition often mediated by *Il Pastor Fido,* the more elaborate successor to Tasso's play by his fellow courtier in Ferrara, Giambattista Guarini. Thomas Watson had previously offered Neo-Latin reprises of the experiences nominally attributed to Tasso's protagonist in *Amyntas* and *Amintae gaudia.* Abraham Fraunce translated the former into English hexameters and dedicated them to the countess of Pembroke. After Watson's death (and shortly before his own), Christopher Marlowe wrote (in Latin) a dedication to the countess of Pembroke for Watson's *Amintae gaudia* (1593). Such Tudor transmission of the myth that Tasso's pastoral drama made famous indicates the vitality of an Italian influence that would ultimately achieve its most notable expression in Milton's *Comus* (1634).

BIBLIOGRAPHY

Brand, C.P. Tasso: *A Study of the Poet and His Contribution to English Literature.* 1965.

Clubb, Louise G. *Italian Drama in Shakespeare's Time.* 1989.

Dubrow, Heather. *Echoes of Desire: Petrarchanism and Its Counterdiscourses.* 1995.

Hough, Graham. *A Preface to* The Faerie Queene. 1962.

Javitch, Daniel. *Proclaiming a Classic: The Canonization of* Orlando Furioso. 1990.

Kennedy, William J. *Authorizing Petrarch.* 1994.

Kirkpatrick, Robin. *English and Italian Literature from Dante to Shakespeare.* 1995.

Lawrence Rhu

SEE ALSO

Daniel, Samuel; Epic; Fraunce, Abraham; Howard, Henry; Humanism; Literary Criticism; Nashe, Thomas; Petrarchanism; Sidney, Philip; Sonnet Sequences; Spenser, Edmund

Italy, Relations with England
See Foreign Relations and Diplomacy

J

James IV (1473–1513)

James IV was born on March 17, 1473, and was raised by his mother, Margaret of Denmark. His father, James III, was a highly unpopular monarch, and, at age fourteen, the young prince James joined a group of nobles who took arms against his father's rule. On James III's death in battle, these nobles placed the fifteen-year-old James IV on the throne (June 24, 1488).

During his time in power, James IV earned a reputation as an able administrator, a friend to learning and the arts, and a firm ruler who could keep powerful magnates in check. Relations with England dominated his foreign policy. In 1495, hostilities flared between James and England's Henry VII when James supported Perkin Warbeck's attempt to claim the English throne. After Warbeck's failure, James negotiated peace with England and sealed it by marrying Henry VII's daughter, Margaret Tudor (June 8, 1503). Relative amity existed between the two nations until 1513, when James, in support of France, entered into war against Henry VIII. On September 9, 1513, James met English troops at Flodden Field, where he was slain in battle. His infant son James V was crowned twelve days later.

BIBLIOGRAPHY

Macdougall, Norman. *James IV.* 1989.
Mackie, R.L. *King James IV: A Brief Survey of His Life and Times.* 1958.
———, ed. *The Letters of James the Fourth, 1505–1513.* 1953.

Scott Lucas

SEE ALSO

Flodden Field, Battle of; Henry VII; Henry VIII; Margaret Tudor; Scotland, History of; Warbeck, Perkin

James V (1513–42)

James V was one of the most impressive and ruthlessly successful members of a successful line of Stuart kings. From the early fifteenth century, the house of Stuart had claimed for itself European importance far greater than its material and geographic position justified. No one ran this line more effectively than James V, who had the wit to seize the opportunities offered in the 1530s by the new element of religious struggle within Europe. Whereas his father, James IV, had been caught between the warring nations of England and France, and paid for it with his life when he supported the French and offered battle to the English, James V played one against the other with great skill, while exerting financial pressure on the papacy with unscrupulous insouciance. The Scottish king was now a real prize in the marriage market. Charles V, hoping to divert him from the "Auld Alliance" with France, offered his sister, Mary of Hungary. Another possibility, which might have had remarkable consequences, was Clement VII's formidable kinswoman, Catherine de Medici, future wife of Henri II and a dominant force in French politics. James himself wanted a French bride, but not any French bride. Offers of anyone less than a daughter of François I produced crocodile tears from the Scottish king over his inability to sustain the Auld Alliance, an approach that brought him, in 1537, the princess Madeleine. Her death within six months of the marriage left him free to try again; this time, he fought off competition from his uncle, Henry VIII of England, and married Marie de Guise, daughter of one of the most powerful French aristocratic houses and a lady who clearly found the king of Scots a safer marital bet than his brother of England.

His relations with England, in this instance and more generally, were equally profitable. Pressure from the English

J

king on his nephew to break with Rome allowed him to appeal to the pope as a loyal Catholic in desperate need of money; he was allowed to extort huge sums in clerical taxation from the church. Part of this was spent in establishing Scotland's supreme civil court, the College of Justice; more, along with two lavish dowries, went to his glorious buildings at Falkland, Stirling, Holyrood, and Linlithgow. Visual splendor was something that he took seriously to enhance royal prestige. And the European influence on his buildings made its own impressive point.

The problem of his own religious conviction defies solution. He certainly weakened the church, not only through his savage taxation but also by intruding his bastard children into major benefices, a policy with which a worried papacy was forced to comply. Yet repeated legislation, especially in the Parliament of 1541, showed both his awareness of the need for internal reform and his determination to uphold the Catholic Church. Only after his death were early Scottish Protestants able to make any headway.

In view of his dazzling successes, that death came as a sad irony. Henry VIII, infuriated beyond bearing by his wholly undutiful nephew, attacked Scotland as well as France in 1542. The Scots army, once again fighting on behalf of France, was defeated at Solway Moss, just as it had been at the battle of Flodden Field in 1513. The carnage was much less great. But three weeks after the battle James V, aged thirty, his infant sons both dead, father only of a baby daughter, succumbed to what was apparently nervous exhaustion, turned his face to the wall, and died.

BIBLIOGRAPHY

Donaldson, G. *Scotland: James V–James VII.* 1965.

Edington, Carol. *Court and Culture in Renaissance Scotland: Sir David Lindsay of the Mount.* 1994.

Sanderson, M.H.B. *Cardinal of Scotland: David Beaton, c. 1494–1546.* 1986.

Williams, J.H., ed. *Stewart Style, 1513–1542: Essays on the Court of James V.* 1996.

Wormald, J. *Court, Kirk, and Community: Scotland, 1470–1625.* 1981.

Jenny Wormald

SEE ALSO

Beaton, David; Foreign Relations and Diplomacy; Henry VIII; James IV; Scotland, Church of; Scotland, History of

James VI and I (1567–1625)

James VI was crowned king at the age of one by those who had deposed his mother Mary a month earlier. There would be another long minority; and its early years were beset by the civil war between king's men and queen's men, that lasted until 1573. It was another decade before James began his personal rule. He had to preside over a kingdom riven with religious as well as political division. Traditionally, his main problem was an aristocracy which had too much power; and indeed, the fact that in successive minorities power had devolved inevitably on the nobles, and the continuing localism of Scottish society to an extent unusual in the kingdoms of Europe, did mean that the balance between royal authority and noble power was itself out of line. But this was not his main problem. James understood very well the importance of the relationship between the crown and the aristocracy—"the armes, the executers of your lawes," as he told his son, Henry—and used it to advantage. Problems he faced were with individual nobles: Bothwell, Gowrie, and Huntly. In his clashes with them, the crown would always win, for the crown always had majority support. His main problem was, in fact, with the Melvillians, Andrew Melville and his followers, the extreme Presbyterians who denied him authority over the kirk. Here, victory was much less certain; it took two decades for the James I to assert his own view of the kirk, to establish bishops alongside the courts of the church, and to defeat the Melvillians. It was done by patient and skillful wooing of moderates in the kirk, by careful manipulation of the General Assembly, the highest court of the kirk, and by isolating his leading opponents.

What James displayed, in the years of his personal rule before 1603, was a remarkable talent for managing men, debating with them, and entering personally into the arena of Parliament, council, and assembly. Only in one area was he a failure; in Scotland, as later in his wealthier English kingdom, he was a notorious and irredeemable spendthrift. But if his financial officials tore their hair, and his clerical opponents rent their garments, in the main he gained respect and even affection from subjects who recognized that a very able king of Scotland was likely to succeed to the English throne, and yet—unlike his mother—never behaved as if his kingdom of Scotland were second-best. Like most of his Stuart predecessors, he had a lofty idea of the importance of being king of Scots; it is not sufficiently appreciated that, far from dancing to Elizabeth's tune, he consistently offended the English queen by making it all too clear to her that he was an independent monarch, with policies of his own.

He was also remarkable in that he was not only a king. He was a scholar, theologian, political theorist, and poet of merit. In a Scotland where the reformers had an impressive vision of a godly and educated society, even his clerical opponents could find in this grounds for irritated respect; he could argue with them to effect. Yet if he was the great royal exponent of the theory of divine right kingship, he was always in practice the pragmatic politician. His academic and political success in Scotland before 1603, his talent for inspiring affection, were to stand him in good stead as the absentee king of Scots after 1603. After 1603, he retained his interest in his northern kingdom, to its delight and to the fury of his southern one. It was his final achievement: he staved off the chill of Stuart neglect for their northern kingdom that was to become all too obvious after 1625.

BIBLIOGRAPHY

Donaldson, G. *Scotland: James V–James VII.* 1965.
Lee, M., Jr. *John Maitland of Thirlstane and the Foundation of the Stewart Despotism in Scotland.* 1959.
———. *Government by Pen: Scotland under James VI and I.* 1980.
———. *Great Britain's Solomon: James VI and I in His Three Kingdoms.* 1990.
Smith, A.G.R., ed. *The Reign of James VI and I.* 1973.
Willson, D.H. *King James VI and I.* 1956.
Wormald, J. *Court, Kirk, and Community: Scotland, 1470–1625.* 1981.

Jenny Wormald

SEE ALSO

Elizabeth I; Mary Queen of Scots; Melville, Andrew; Scotland, Church of; Scotland, History of

Jest Books

The "merry jests" that blossomed in the 1520s and 1530s were broadly comic tales rejoicing in farts, petty revenges, and buffetings about the pate; single jests in verse, such as *A Merry Jest How a Sergeant Would Learn to be a Friar;* collected jests in prose, such as *A Hundred Merry Tales;* and one collection of verse jests, *Widow Edith.* Tudor verse jests often have titles beginning with "how," use mainly tetrameter, dimeter, or ballad stanza, and are dense with formulaic tags like "many a" and "by reason and right"

and oaths by real and invented saints, redolent of oral tradition. Both verse and prose jests favor trickster heroes, slapstick humor, and scatology.

Verse jests ebbed away by mid-century. After 1590, many new prose jest collections saw print, including *Dobson's Dry Bobs, Pleasant Conceits of Old Hobson, The Cobbler of Canterbury, Tarlton's Jests,* and *Jack of Dover.* Allusions to *A Hundred Merry Tales, A Man Called Howlglas,* and *Scoggin's Jests* suggest that earlier Tudor jest books remained available. In William Shakespeare's *Much Ado About Nothing,* Benedick accuses Beatrice of mining her wit from *A Hundred Merry Tales.*

Although the jests' vulgarity seems to align them with "popular culture," and many regard these earthy romps as emanating from the "folk," a letter penned in 1603 reports that Queen Elizabeth listened to *A Hundred Merry Tales* on her deathbed, and jest books were, in fact, promulgated by Renaissance humanists. Jest collections, or *facetiae,* formed part of the humanist program from the beginning. Petrarch's collection included an elephant joke. Another of humanism's founding fathers, Poggio Bracciolini, compiled an extensive collection, *Facetiae.* Desiderius Erasmus framed a jest collection as a dialogue; Baldassare Castiglione devoted Book 2 of *The Courtier* to jesting. Other publishers of humanist jest included the Germans Nachtgall, Bebel, and Gast, the Belgian Barlandus, and the Italians Beccadelli, Piccolomini, Carbone, Domenichi, Pontano, and Cortesi. The Tudor jest book *Tales and Quick Answers* imitates continental humanist collections, drawing most of its jests from Poggio and Erasmus; *A Hundred Merry Tales* borrows less, but still aims at educated readers—many of its jokes require knowledge of Latin. Serious writers like Hugh Latimer drew on jest books in humanistic and theological works. A member of Thomas More's household wrote *Widow Edith,* and More's brother-in-law, John Rastell, was the printer of *A Hundred Merry Tales,* which several scholars have suspected More of writing. More himself published a verse jest in 1516.

Intellectuals gave educational, social, or medical reasons for purveying jokes: jests were useful to orators, essential to a gentleman's conversation, necessary to health. Such rationalizations suggest qualms: the jests *are* frivolous, vulgar, and cruel. The personnel of humanist jests are socially a cut above those in jest books not represented explicitly in humanist terms (legates and ambassadors rather than shoemakers and millers). But in individual jests, little distinguishes between the humanist

J

jesting of Poggio, Erasmus, or Castiglione and that in collections we dub "popular," such as *A Hundred Merry Tales* or *A Man Called Howlglas*. Poggio and Erasmus purvey fart jokes and scatological jests. Though "jokes" are an accepted folklore genre, even folklorists trace them to Renaissance humanists, not the folk. Though most of the jests predate humanism—in Cicero, in medieval sermon *exempla,* in folktale—it was humanists who gathered them, isolated them as a genre, printed them, and gave them intellectual rationales. As Joanna Lipking writes, "Even in classical times, the joke had a subsidiary role within other traditions, not an independent life of its own. It is above all a Renaissance form" (14).

From Poggio's time to Castiglione's, jesting's class valence was patrician. Like the major jest theorist Cicero, Renaissance humanists offered jesting as a tool to help the well-born and educated win arguments (judicial or social), ornament writings, or showcase elegant social graces among aristocratic peers. Running alongside this jesting *inter pares* was a didactic tradition of jesting in sermons preached by educated clergy to an unlettered laity; socially, these jests flowed downward. The rhetorician Thomas Wilson advised in 1553 that jests delight the "rude and ignorant": "Talk altogether of most grave matters . . . and you shall see the ignorant . . . fall asleep . . . The multitude must needs be made merry." Some late Tudor writers described conflict between high-culture products like Cicero's works and low-culture items like *Scoggin's Jests:* Gabriel Harvey complained, in 1593, that "Ciceronians" were undermined by "Scogginists"; the more jesters, "the less of Cambridge, or Oxford." Harvey himself read many jest books; the educated of his day scoffed at jest books, but read them as a kind of harmless slumming. The elite, however, were no longer *producing* jest books by the 1590s. Hived off into a lower cultural category, jest books were now seen as emanating from the masses. Perhaps because codes of civility imposed increasing refinement on the elite, vulgar jests became an embarrassment, and jest books were disowned by the classes that earlier sponsored them.

BIBLIOGRAPHY

Bowen, Barbara C. *One Hundred Renaissance Jokes: An Anthology.* 1988.

Hazlitt, William. *Shakespeare Jest-Books.* 3 vols. 1864.

Lipking, Joanna. *Traditions of the "Facetiae" and Their Influence in Tudor England.* Dissertation, Columbia University. 1970.

Wilson, F.P. "The English Jestbooks of the Sixteenth and Early Seventeenth Century." *Huntington Library Quarterly,* vol. 2, pp. 121–158.

Woodbridge, Linda. "Appendix B: English Renaissance Jest Books." *Placeless in the Renaissance: Placelessness, Mobility, and Identity in English Renaissance Literature.* Forthcoming.

Linda Woodbridge

SEE ALSO

Civility; Folklore and Folk Rituals; Harvey, Gabriel; Humanism; Popular Literature; Social Classes; Wilson, Thomas

Jesuits

The Society of Jesus, founded by Ignatius de Loyola and approved by Pope Paul III in 1540, undertook missions for the conversion to the Catholic faith of those regarded as infidels and heretics. Following the accession of Mary I in 1553, Loyola hoped that his Jesuits would be invited into England, but Reginald Cardinal Pole, the primate of England, did not want them because they did not fit well into his plans for reform. The Jesuits had to wait until 1580 to begin a mission in England, six years after the seminary priests of Douai had begun their work. William Allen, founder of the English College at Douai and spiritual father of the seminary priests, admired the Jesuits and wanted them involved in the English mission. An English Jesuit, Robert Parsons, wished for this as well. Everard Mercurian, the vicar-general of the Society of Jesus, agreeing, albeit reluctantly, appointed Parsons in April, 1580, to head the first Jesuit mission to England; and he ordered Edmund Campion to join Parsons and a group of seminary priests on the mission.

The Jesuit mission purposely concentrated on the gentry, for they seemed best positioned in society to protect priests and Catholic servants, and their support would be necessary if England were to be won back to the Catholic faith. This approach, however, contributed to making English Catholicism narrowly seigniorial. The missionaries were instructed to work within the established political order, tending only to the pastoral care and instruction of English Catholics. In keeping with the spiritual purpose of the mission, Parsons received from the pope a "rescript" suspending the 1570 bull excommunicating and deposing Elizabeth I. This mission achieved limited success, and much notoriety, and ended with Campion's capture in July, 1581, and with Parsons's departure from England the following month. In 1584, William Weston took over as superior of the Jesuit mission in England, and later wrote an account of his activities. In 1586, Henry Garnet and Robert Southwell, two of the most able missionaries, arrived. Following Weston's capture in 1586, Garnet served as superior until his capture in 1605. Southwell was captured, tortured, and executed in 1595. John Gerard, also author of an autobiographical description of his mission, entered England in 1588, and in 1597 won distinction as one of the few prisoners ever to have escaped from the Tower of London.

The Jesuits formed only a small part of the Catholic mission. By the 1590s, there were fourteen Jesuits in England, four of whom were in prison, but there were more than 400 secular priests; and while Campion and Southwell are two of the most famous Elizabethan Catholic martyrs, only six Jesuits were executed, compared with 154 secular priests and lay Catholics. Garnet, however, organized an underground agency that placed newly arrived seminary priest in Catholic households, mostly in the south and near London, and he helped provide for their maintenance. Father Garnet kept control over his Jesuits, convening them from time to time for spiritual retreats, where they renewed their vows and discussed their work.

English Jesuits received education and spiritual formation at seminaries in Italy, France, Austria, Bohemia, southern Germany and the Low Countries. The order had great influence over the education of English secular clergy at the colleges of Douai and Rome. Allen put his students at Douai through Loyola's *Spiritual Exercises*, and he approved the Jesuit takeover of the English College of Rome. Many of the English Jesuits were recruited through these colleges. Parsons established the first English Jesuit school at Eu, in Normany, transferring it later to St. Omer. This school, the forerunner of Stonyhurst College, educated many distinguished Catholic laymen and provided priests for the English mission. Parsons also established Jesuit seminaries and centers in Spain, and left an indelible Jesuit imprint on the English College of Rome during his tenure as rector.

The English government, along with many English Catholics, did not regard the Jesuit mission as politically innocuous, despite Jesuit claims to the contrary. The Jesuits' defense of equivocation convinced the government that their denials of connivance in plots were lies. In reaction to the mission of 1580–1581, the government strengthened penalties against Catholics. In 1582, a proclamation, confirmed by statute in 1585, made it treason to be a Jesuit or a seminarian. Hanging, drawing, and quartering was the penalty imposed on priests, but many seminarians and Jesuits were simply imprisoned. The pro-Spanish activities of Allen and Parsons further convinced the government that seminarians and Jesuits were indeed traitors and Spanish agents, and were so denounced by proclamation in 1591. The government assumed Jesuit complicity in plots against the queen. In 1584, the captured Scottish Jesuit, William Crichton, revealed schemes for the invasion of England and the liberation of Mary Queen of Scots. No evidence was produced showing Jesuit participation in the Babington Plot of 1586, but the government believed otherwise. In 1594, the government executed the Jesuit Henry Walpole for alleged involvement in the Lopez Plot, in which the Portugese Jewish Dr. Roderigo Lopez, personal physician to Queen Elizabeth I, was accused of poisoning her. The government also suspected that Walpole's brother, Richard, was implicated in the Squire Plot of 1598.

The Jesuits' separate organization and the pro-Spanish activities of Parsons intensified conflict between the Jesuits and secular clergy in England and at the English College of Rome. The rivalry at the prison of Wisbech in 1594–1598 between the Jesuit Weston and the secular Christopher Bagshaw became a public scandal. Some secular clergy vociferously opposed the appointment of George Blackwell, a secular priest, as archpriest in 1598 because they regarded him as a Jesuit lackey. The English and French governments tried to exploit this quarrel, supporting the so-called Appellants against the Jesuits. Despite the hostility of the secular Catholic clergy and persecution by the government, the mission in England had grown by the turn of the seventeenth century, with fifty-three English and Scottish Jesuits by 1610. The vicar-general made the English mission a vice-province in 1619, and a province in 1623.

BIBLIOGRAPHY

Basset, Bernard. *The English Jesuits from Campion to Martindale.* 1968.

Caraman, Philip, ed. *William Weston: The Autobiography of an Elizabethan.* 1955.

———, ed. *John Gerard: The Autobiography of an Elizabethan.* 1956.

Edwards, Francis. *The Jesuits in England.* 1985.

Foley, Henry. *Records of the English Province of the Society of Jesus.* Vol 1, 1877; vol. 2, 1878; vol. 3, 1878; vol. 7:1, 1882; vol 7:2, 1883.

J

Law, Thomas G. *A Historical Sketch of the Conflicts between Jesuits and Seculars in the Reign of Queen Elizabeth.* 1889.

McCoog, Thomas M. "The Establishment of the English Province of the Society of Jesus." *Recusant History,* vol. 17, pp. 121–139.

———. *English and Welsh Jesuits, 1555–1650.* Catholic Record Society. Vol. 74, 1994; vol. 75, 1995.

More, Henry. "Historia Provinciae Anglicanae Societatis Jesu." In Francis Edwards, ed. *The Elizabethan Jesuits.* 1981.

Taunton, Ethelred. *The History of the Jesuits in England, 1580–1773.* 1901.

John M. Currin

SEE ALSO

Allen, William; Archpriest Controversy; Babington Plot; Campion, Edmund; Catholicism; English College of Rome; Gerard, John; Mary I; Mary Queen of Scots; Parsons, Robert; Reginald Pole; *Regnans in Excelsis;* Treason

Jewel, John (1522–1571)

Born at Berrynarbor, Devonshire, on May 24, 1522, John Jewel was educated locally until 1535, when he was sent to Merton College, Oxford. There he studied theology in the first years of the Henrician Reformation, and in 1539, he was elected a scholar of Corpus Christi College, Oxford. He became a fellow of Corpus in 1542, and took his M.A. in 1545. He was an outstanding lecturer in the university and a deeply dedicated scholar. When Peter Martyr Vermigli went to Oxford in 1547, Jewel became one of his most devoted disciples, and it was from him that he received his wide knowledge of the continental Reformation.

When Mary I ascended the throne in 1553, Jewel was deprived of his fellowship, and took refuge in what is now Pembroke College. He was courageous enough to act as notary for Thomas Cranmer and Nicholas Ridley in 1554, when they were both in prison, but later he signed a series of Catholic articles in hope of saving his own skin. This did not work, however, and Jewel was forced to flee to the Continent. He went to Frankfurt, where he found himself in the middle of the dispute between Richard Cox and John Knox over the desirability of pushing the English Reformation still further in the direction of Calvin's Geneva. Jewel sided with the moderate party led by Cox,

but he soon left Frankfurt to rejoin his old master Vermigli, first at Strasbourg, and later at Zurich.

He returned to England in March, 1559, and on January 21, 1560, he was consecrated bishop of Salisbury. He had already earned a reputation as a Protestant controversialist in his disputes with the Marian bishops who resisted the Reformation, and the fruits of his labors soon appeared in print as *An Apology for the Church of England* (1562). This first systematic exposition of Anglican claims against Rome has formed the basis for all subsequent controversy on this subject. Jewel defended the doctrine and practice of the English Church against the charges of disorder and heresy leveled by the Roman party, and he tried to explain why a conciliar solution such as that adopted at Trent was insufficient to bring about a real reform of the Anglican church. He also expressed the belief, later to become a commonplace of Anglican theology, that the first six centuries of Christianity were a golden age of doctrinal and liturgical purity that the Church of England sought to recover as the basis for a truly ecumenical church union.

Jewel was soon attacked by an Oxford contemporary of his, Thomas Harding (1516–1572), who refused to conform to the Elizabethan Settlement and fled to Louvain, where he wrote a detailed refutation of Jewel's *Apology.* Jewel replied to this in 1565 and again, following yet another attack from the same party, in 1567. Harding tried to prolong the dispute, but Jewel would not be drawn out further. The attacks were intemperate, and Jewel's replies are models of restraint and good judgement. They also provide us with a detailed explanation of the positions he first set out in the *Apology,* in spite of a certain tediousness of detail in the overall presentation.

In doctrinal terms, Jewel was a Calvinist, but he saw the importance of establishing a broad consensus in the Church of England and rejected the more extreme claims of the emerging Puritans. In 1565, he was made a doctor of divinity at Oxford, but his failing health prevented him from realizing any really ambitious academic projects. His last major act was to supervise the publication of the Thirty-nine Articles in 1571. On returning to Salisbury he undertook a visitation of the diocese that sapped his strength, and he died at the village of Monkton Farleigh on September 23, 1571.

BIBLIOGRAPHY

Booty, John E. *John Jewel as Apologist of the Church of England.* 1963.

Collinson, Patrick. *The Elizabethan Puritan Movement.* 1990.

Haugaard, W.P. *Elizabeth and the English Reformation: The Struggle for a Stable Settlement of Religion.* 1968.

Jewel, John. *The Works of John Jewel.* 4 vols. 1845–1850.

Southgate, W.M. *John Jewel and the Problem of Doctrinal Authority.* 1962.

Gerald Bray

SEE ALSO

Anglicanism; Articles of Religion; Church of England; Cranmer, Thomas; Knox, John; Marian Exiles; Vermigli, Peter Martyr; Puritanism; Ridley, Nicholas

Jewelry

Henry VIII and his children loved jewelry, and their example inspired courtiers, the higher clergy, and all citizens who desired to appear as persons of consequence to buy and wear it. Sumptuary laws attempted to confine specific categories of jewels to particular classes, but proved so ineffective that Philip Stubbes, in the *Anatomy of Abuses* (1585), complained that it was impossible to tell "who is noble, who is worshipful, who is a gentleman and who is not." The scale of demand enriched indigenous goldsmiths such as Robert Adamas and Nicholas Herrick as well as a thriving colony of immigrants. Their products were worn not just as means of asserting rank and wealth but also to express intellectual, spiritual, and dynastic concepts. Those close to the monarchy wore jewels enameled with the Tudor livery colors, green and white, bearing the badge of the rose and incorporating royal portraits—medals, cameos, or miniatures. The elite appointed to the Order of the Garter commissioned jeweled insignia with the motto and the image of St. George. Members of the great families proudly displayed jewels ornamented with their coats of arms, crests, and badges. All liked ciphers or monograms as links in chains, as pendants, and in rings.

Devotional jewelry followed late medieval conventions until the law of 1571 officially abolished the rosary, reliquaries, and the Agnus Dei. Crosses remained popular and so did the sacred monogram, IHS. There were also jewels wrought in enameled gold with scenes from the Old and New Testaments whose English origin is confirmed by inscriptions from the vernacular Bible.

The culture of the Renaissance brought a revival of the courtly art of engraving gemstones into cameos and intaglios, which the Tudors adopted for royal portraits and badges for the Knights of the Garter, as well as for illustrations from mythology and classical history. Motifs derived from Roman art include pediments, volutes, nymphs, satyrs, and putti. Early in the period a balance was kept between stones and setting, but later the emphasis shifted toward the display of stones, and by 1600, the role of the setting was reduced to no more than a framework.

People wore jewels from top to toe. At first men wore badges embossed with storytelling scenes in their hats, but by the end of the period these little sculptural masterpieces had been superseded by jeweled aigrettes (tufts of feathers) or bands of gems. Similarly, the borders or biliments worn by women gave way to pearls strung into lace-like patterns called attires, or bodkins headed with stones or pearls. Earrings only came into fashion from the 1560s and were not always worn in pairs. For the neck there were collars of gems in enameled gold mounts alternating with groups of pearls, or chains wrought from gold in a variety of patterns. Bracelets were often individualized by clasps bearing ciphers or coats of arms. The

Enameled cover for Prayer Book. The book would have been hung as a jewel from a girdle or belt. By permission of Diana Scarisbrick.

J

Hieronimo Custodis, *Elizabeth Brydges* (1589). Portrait of a Tudor lady bedecked with jewels. By kind permission of the Marquess of Tavistock and the trustees of the Bedford Estate.

lockets or pendants that hung from the neck, girdle, or from ribbons attached to sleeves, bodice, or skirt, illustrated with a devotional, classical, or dynastic theme, or set with a gem, were framed decoratively, like pictures. Of all the luxury items—fur pieces with gold sable heads, fans, pomanders to scent the foul air, toothpicks, and whistles—the most English was the prayer book with enameled gold covers attached to the girdle.

Rings were worn in greater profusion than on the Continent. The diverse types included signets for business; marriage and love rings with the symbols of hearts, hands, or twin hoops; locket rings enclosing portraits; and *memento mori* rings with skulls and admonitory inscriptions. Those with gems—diamonds, rubies, turquoises—were not only prized for their intrinsic value but for the magical and healing properties attributed to them. Cramp rings, protecting the wearer against epilepsy, blessed by the Tudor monarchs on Good Friday at a special ceremony, were eagerly sought after both at home and abroad.

BIBLIOGRAPHY

Armstrong, Nancy J. *Jewellry: An Historical Survey of British Styles and Jewels.* 1973.
Hackenbroch, Y. *Renaissance Jewellry.* 1979.
Scarisbrick, Diana. *Tudor and Jacobean Jewellry.* 1995.
———. *Jewellry in Britain, 1066–1837.* 1994.
———. *Rings: Symbols of Wealth, Power, and Affection.* 1993.

Diana Scarisbrick

SEE ALSO

Clothing and Costume; Goldsmiths' Work; Stubbes, Philip; Sumptuary Laws

Jews

Despite the blanket claims of Victorian historians (and of their modern successors) that there were few or no Jews in early modern England, archival research over the past century makes it clear that small numbers of Jews began drifting back into England almost immediately after the expulsion of 1290 and in larger numbers during the Tudor years. The expulsion of Jews from Spain in 1492, followed by the forced conversion and then expulsion of Jews from Portugal, provided a strong impetus to the migration into England of individual Jews and gradually to the establishment of small Maranno communities in both London and Bristol (it is important to note, however, that the total number of Jews in England at any one time probably did not exceed 150 or so).

As early as 1492, the Spanish ambassador was complaining to English authorities about Spanish Jews living in London. From similar reports—and from Iberian Inquisition records—it is possible to piece together some of the activities of the Marrano communities. For example, according to the prisoner of war Pedro de Santa Cruz, repatriated to Madrid in 1588, it "is public and notorious in London" that "by race they are all Jews, and it is notorious that in their own homes they live as such observing their Jewish rites." We know from other testimony that these Jews observed such holidays as Passover and Yom Kippur; the community was well enough established that Salomon Cormano, the envoy of the Jewish duke of Metilli, had no difficulty finding fellow Jews to pray with during his official visit to London in 1592.

Among the Jews residing in England during the Tudor period were Roderigo Lopez, Elizabeth I's physician, who was put to death in 1594 for conspiring against the queen. There were also court musicians of Italian descent—the Lupos, Bassanos, and Comys—brought over by Henry VIII. Occasionally, a Jew was officially invited into the country: Marco Raphael, who resided in England for three years, was brought from Italy by Henry VIII in an unsuccessful attempt to justify Henry's divorce of Queen Katherine of Aragon. Another Jew, Yehudah Menda, from Barbary, had been living in England for five years when he was publicly converted by John Foxe in 1577 at All Hallow's Church in London (Foxe's sermon, along with an English translation of Menda's confession of faith, were published together the following year). One of the few Jews who was not of Iberian descent, Joachim Gaunse of Prague, who served as Sir Walter Ralegh's "mineral man" on the Roanoke expedition, fell afoul of local authorities in Bristol when, in an argument with a local clergyman, he spoke disparagingly of Jesus ("there was but one God, who had no wife nor child").

Most of the Jews living in England were more careful than Gaunse about advertising their religious beliefs; rather, as Marannos, many were already skilled at disguising their religious identity. Consequently, little record exists of most of the resident Jews during the Tudor years, except for those who had trouble with the law or those who converted and entered the Domus Conversorum, a converts' house on Chancery Lane, where a small handful of poor Jewish converts could be found through most of this period. Among some of the nameless Jews residing in England were the one who helped Thomas Bodley with the cataloguing of Hebrew books; another who was taken from England by Sir James Lancaster as his servant and translator in his East Indies voyage of 1601; and a third whose help was enlisted in deciphering a Hebrew letter sent to Hugh Broughton from Constantinople in 1596.

The physical presence of this small number of Jews among the many thousands of aliens living in sixteenth-century London matters far less than Elizabethan preoccupation with Jewish questions, ranging from theories of racial and national difference to questions about the Ten Lost Tribes and the role of the conversion and restitution of the Jews in millennial thought. Were the Jews physically and racially different? Did those who converted lose all trace of their Jewishness? Could one be both Jewish and English? Were the Jews in their diaspora still a nation, and if so, should they be restored to the homeland? The wide-ranging interest in these and other Jewish questions found its way into works of Elizabethans as diverse as William Shakespeare, John Donne, Francis Bacon, Thomas Nashe, Andrew Willet, and Thomas Lodge.

BIBLIOGRAPHY
Katz, David S. *Jews in the History of England: 1485–1850.* 1994.
———. *Philo-Semitism and the Readmission of the Jews to England, 1603–1655.* 1982.
Roth, Cecil. *A History of the Jews in England.* 1940; 3rd edition, 1960.
Shapiro, James. *Shakespeare and the Jews.* 1996.

James Shapiro

SEE ALSO
Aliens; Bodley, Thomas; Broughton, Hugh; Foxe, John; Immigration

Joint-Stock Companies

The Tudors are credited with being the first to finance commercial and industrial enterprises on the basis of a corporate joint-stock, though more primitive precedents can be found in medieval Italy and elsewhere on the Continent. The English version was essentially a fusion of key elements of two traditional forms of business organization: the partnership or "firm," the members trading on a joint account; and the regulated company, that provided the model of perpetual succession, a clear legal personality which enabled the company to enjoy exclusive trading rights by royal charter. The joint stock company also borrowed its management structure from the regulated company. The functions, however, of the governors, courts of assistants, and officials of the new institution were fundamentally different. They managed the company's affairs on behalf of the shareholders in the manner of a board of directors, rather than providing a framework of regulations for the conduct of business by individual members. Various explanations can be offered for the innovation. Joint-stock enterprises were normally high risk or innovative, or both, and the capital needed, especially if the ratio of fixed assets to circulating capital was high, might be beyond the resources of a partnership, whose size was limited by the liability of each member, however small his investment, for the others' debts. Only those who were prepared to be active in management to protect their investment were likely to become a partner, thereby effectively restricting investment in commercial undertakings to merchants who were well known to each other. The resources of an informal, shifting group of investors would be put under particular strain if the capital was locked up for a long period of time. And in the more permanent structure of the company, stockholdings could be

J

more readily transferred than in a partnership, where the consent of all members was required.

The risks attendant on long-distance voyages were probably the key consideration when the first experiments were made in the 1550s. A joint stock was formed in 1553 to finance voyages to West Africa. The enterprise initially resembled that of a partnership in that there were relatively few stockholders, and each voyage was financed separately: that is, the joint stock was terminable, rather than permanent. In addition, the stockholders did not seek monopoly rights and incorporation until 1584, when they formed the Barbary Company. The Muscovy or Russia Company, which was granted its charter in 1555, was in every respect a more sophisticated model for large-scale, permanent associations of capital. More than 200 shareholders, including a substantial group from outside trading circles, raised close to £50,000 in the first ten years, and the joint stock was continuous for about twenty more. Fixed assets were kept low, the Moscovy company abandoning shipowning in favor of chartering soon after its foundation. When the Turkey/Levant Company was formed in 1581, the desire to spread risks and protection costs probably weighed most heavily with the small number of members—only twelve were named in the charter. The same concerns undoubtedly underlay the formation of the East India Company in 1600, although that company's capital requirements, fixed as well as circulating, were unprecedentedly high and the time scale uniquely long.

When the joint stock principle was applied to industry the circumstances were exceptional. Two monopoly companies were incorporated in 1568: the Mineral and Battery Works to manufacture wrought copper, brass, and wire; and the Mines Royal to mine gold, silver, copper, and quicksilver in Wales and western England. Both were notable for the small number of shares of issued (thirty-six and twenty-four, respectively), the high denomination and, in the case of the mining company, the prominence of German members, who brought capital as well as expertise. Membership was subsequently widened by the division of shares into fractions. Although fixed capital expenditure on, for example, workshops and furnaces, was prominent in both enterprises, in the case of the Mines Royal protection of the crown's mineral rights, which would otherwise have been at risk, was paramount.

The longevity and success of the East India Company—the last to be established in Elizabeth I's reign—should not obscure the fact that in 1600, corporate associations of capital were still in a highly experimental stage; nor that their contribution to commerce and industry had so far been limited and unconvincing. Confidence in the institution is not suggested by the tendency of members to abandon or dilute the joint stock when the risks and protection costs had been reduced to levels acceptable to individuals or partnerships. Thus the Turkey/Levant Company had opted for a regulated trade before its charter was renewed in 1592. The Muscovy merchants persisted with joint stock, but from the 1580s onward it was made terminable, as in the case of the West African voyages. Moreover, by that time most non-mercantile investors had withdrawn and members were permitted to trade privately, a concession that brought the Muscovy Company even closer to the status of a regulated company. This it duly became soon after the death of Queen Elizabeth. The ambiguity and uncertainty surrounding the experiments was further revealed in the formation of the East India Company. Even though the undertaking could only be financed corporately, the charter gives no indication of the East India Company's status (nor had that of the Muscovy Company); and despite the need for a long perspective, which the rival Dutch East India Company recognized, the joint stock was made terminable. The distinctions between the new institution, the regulated company, and the partnership remained blurred. The law, too, was slow to come to terms with the innovation, in particular on the question of liability. Many years were to elapse before the question was even addressed. Similarly, although shares were transferable, how this might take place was unclear, and a stock market as such was still far distant. When this emerged the organization was well entrenched in the commercial world; but not in industry. The Mineral and Battery Works and the Mines Royal had shown little promise, and though they survived well into the seventeenth century, the future of industrial finance and organization clearly lay with the partnership and the family firm.

BIBLIOGRAPHY

Chaudhuri, K.N. *The English East India Company.* 1965.
Rees, William. *Industry before the Industrial Revolution.* Vol. 2. 1968.
Scott, W.R. *The Constitution and Finance of English, Scottish and Irish Joint-Stock Companies to 1720.* Vol. 1. 1912.
Willan, T.S. *The Early History of the Russia Company, 1553–1603.* 1956.

Brian Dietz

SEE ALSO
East India Company; Industry and Manufacture; Coal Industry; Metal Industries; Monopolies; Regulated Companies; Trade, Overseas

Jones, Robert (fl. 1597–1615)

Robert Jones was one of a large group of composers known for their secular songs and ayres at the beginning of the seventeenth century. While the circumstances of his birth and death are uncertain, Jones received a bachelor of music degree from St. Edmund College, Oxford, in 1597, reportedly after sixteen years of study. In addition to his own five collections of lute songs and one book of madrigals, he also contributed to *The Triumphes of Oriana* of 1601. His career centered around the royal court, where, in 1610, he and three partners (Philip Rosseter, Philip Kingham, and Ralph Reeve) were awarded a patent to "practice and ex'[er]cise in the quality of playing [a group of children] by the name of Children of the Revells of the Queene within the white ffryers." This group, a semiprofessional company organized in 1603, staged choirboy plays. These performances, begun as an amateur enterprise including music, were originally for the instruction of the boys, but quickly became popular forms of public entertainment. The partnership continued for several years, and the last mention of Jones dates from 1615, when the same four men were issued a permit to build a permanent house for the group. However, civic protests against the theater led to its demolition.

Jones published five books of ayres from 1600 to 1610. Many of these songs, particularly in the third and fourth books, were apparently composed first as four-part works and then adapted to solo form. Only two part-books survive from his 1607 collection of madrigals, but several of the pieces are complete in surviving manuscripts, allowing for judgments to be made about his style of madrigal composition.

Jones faced considerable criticism of his works during his lifetime, and he published colorfully-worded rebuttals in the forewords of his later publications. Critical judgments largely centered around the dissonant nature of his music, a quality made more extreme by the large number of printing errors in the fourth and fifth books, respectively titled *A Musicall Dreame* and *The Muses Gardin for Delights*. However, he had clearly learned much from John Dowland, and his best songs are memorably melodious and either charmingly light (*Love is a bable*), or impressively melancholy (*When wil the fountain*).

BIBLIOGRAPHY
Cuts, J.P. "A Reconsideration of the Willow Song." *Journal of the American Musicological Society*, vol. 10, pp. 14–24.

Fellowes, Edmund H. "The Texts of the Song Bookes of Robert Jones." *Music and Letters*, vol. 8, pp. 25–37.

Seng, Peter J. *The Vocal Songs in the Plays of Shakespeare: A Critical History*. 1967.

Sommerock, Ulrich. *Das englische Lautenlied (1597–1622). Eine literaturwissenschaftliche musikologische Untersuchung*. 1990.

Teplow, Deborah. "Lyra Viol Accompaniment in Robert Jones' Second Booke of Songs and Ayres (1601)." *Journal of the Viola da Gamba Society of America*, vol. 23, pp. 6–18.

Karen M. Bryan

SEE ALSO
Air; Dowland, John; Madrigal; Song; Theater Companies, Boys

Jonson, Ben (1572–1637)

A poet, dramatist, and classicist, Jonson was born in London and educated at the Westminster School (c. 1583–1589). His father, a minister originally from Scotland, died before his birth. After his mother remarried, Jonson was adopted by his stepfather, who apprenticed him to the bricklayer's guild. Jonson's education enabled him to escape the life of a workingman; his writing allowed him to work in the theater; his poetry finally gave him access to patronage at court, although this last and major phase of his career developed, after the Tudor period, in the reign of James I (1603–1625). Jonson's early experience included military service in the Netherlands (1591–1592), where he claimed to have killed an opponent in single combat. Afterward, in London, he married Anne Lewis (c. 1594–1595), and then began to work for the theatrical manager Philip Henslowe as actor and playwright (1597). Theater work, however, led to other violence. In 1598, he killed a fellow actor, Gabriel Spencer, in a quarrel and received a prison term, from which he was released under benefit of clergy (gained by translating a Latin psalm). While imprisoned, he adopted Roman Catholicism, a faith that he held for a decade. He was also marked in another way—being branded at the base of one thumb with a "T," to indicate that another offense would lead to hanging at Tyburn.

These biographical elements indicate major concerns in Jonson's career. He was a London poet, depicting the

J

urban scene. The quarto of *Every Man In His Humour* (1601; acted 1598), locates the play in Florence; the character names are Italian. But the 1616 Folio shifts the scene to London, and gives the characters English names. The revised play was dedicated to Jonson's schoolmaster at Westminster College, William Camden, a noted antiquarian scholar, who constituted a model of learning. Throughout his career, Jonson advocated the virtues of work as prologue, not alternative, to inspiration; good poets, the elegy to William Shakespeare affirms (1623), are made as well as born. They need not spring from aristocratic birth but can fashion themselves as Jonson himself did——most literally in his respelling of the name Johnson. Violence also appears in Jonson's work. His difficult, prickly character; his experience of army life and professional quarrels; his learned assertiveness: all join in the sharp satires he composed for the stage. The satire was so sharp that Jonson's work, with that by John Marston, Thomas Dekker, and Bishop Hall, led to the so-called "war of the theaters" and then to their temporary closure by the government. Here character or personality intersects with literary coteries, the traditional institution of the state, and the new institution of public theaters. Tudor England had witnessed bitter controversial debates in print; but, presented on stage, they owned a visual and rhetorical immediacy that was disturbing in early modern society. At his career's start, Jonson completed Thomas Nashe's play, *The Isle of Dogs* (a spit of land in the Thames, to the east of London, where the queen's hounds were kenneled). That play's satirical allusions led to imprisonment in 1597. In *Poetaster* (1601), a "comicall satyre," Jonson added to satirical attack the authority of Augustan Rome, putting on stage in the context of quarreling poets the figures of Augustus, Horace, and Vergil. Whatever favor this work earned was not enough to save Jonson from another prison term in 1604–1605. Then, with Chapman and Marston, he was imprisoned for reflections in *Eastward Ho!* on the national character of the Scots, the kings's accent, and the new government's sale of titles—a harsh lesson in responsibility for literary texts.

Jonson began as an actor, but his talents lay in writing scripts for other actors. (The later quarrel with Inigo Jones would turn on issues of text as against spectacle in the masque.) Jonson's first dramatic success was *Every Man In His Humour* (performed 1598; quarto, 1601; folio, 1616). The play was acted by the Lord Chamberlain's Men, with Shakespeare apparently in the role (later named) of Knowell. A sequel, *Every Man Out of His Humour*, took advantage of this success, and in 1599–1600 was performed at the newly built Globe Theater. The emphasis on "humours" points to Jonson's innovation in comic drama, a theory of character construction that aligns, however loosely, several traditions of thought and dramatic practice. Medieval ideas of human physiology and the label types in Plautine comedy underwrote the simplified or "affected" character, joining quasi-scientific, ethical, and literary views of character. This mixture of ideas allowed Jonson to view character as immersed in—and shaped by—the physical body; as subject to both ethical evaluation and comic laughter; and as carrying the dignity of classical traditions. This approach to character found its setting in urban scenes in contrast to the Shakespearean practice of removal to a "green world" of natural liberty. The contrast between Jonson's practice with static characters and Shakespeare's with dynamic characters is real, although the contrast is replicated in a number of stories and anecdotes that emphasize personal rivalry or seemingly fundamental differences between the "art" of Jonson and the "naturalness" of his rival and colleague. Whether the differences between two great dramatists form so simple an opposition may be questioned. Jonson's major contribution to English drama rests in a series of remarkably constructed comic plays that aim at anatomies of a present world rather than narratives of one elsewhere. Jonsonian comedy requires judgment; its audience must distinguish those characters who are victims of their bodies from those who pretend to such conditions for cunning reasons. No one has bettered the taut intersection in comedy and satire between folly and fraud.

Jonson's learning rested on a grammar school education and on an intense period of study at the end of the 1590s. The latter began, under the prompt of government censorship, as a search for classical justifications of satire; it ended in the self-creation of "a man of vast erudition" (Riggs, 58). Jonson's classicism emerges then from study to practice in the first of two tragedies set in ancient Rome. *Cataline* did not appear until 1611, but *Sejanus* was acted in 1603 by the King's Men, with Shakespeare (apparently) in the role of Tiberius. The story of the rise and fall of a favorite of the emperor is from Tacitus (*The Annals*), but it is checked against other historical accounts. The play is filled with the factions, spies, and informants of imperial court life, and then as now, suspicions have arisen of topical references. When Jonson published the play in quarto (1605), he provided marginalia that directed his reader to numerous sources.

It seems clear that he wished to join the seriousness of tragedy to the dignity of historical writing. Yet the "Englishing" of Roman history allowed Jonson to engage the classical past without resorting to the obvious anachronisms of Shakespeare. Throughout his career, he sought to dignify literary work by aligning it with other professions and institutions. In his doctrine of literary imitation, the poet is a mediator between history and culture. He must know what to appropriate and how to shape it. Jonson did so by shaping plays and poems of a distinctive individuality—those "strange poems," he said to the countess of Rutland, "which as yet / Had not their form touched by an English wit" (*The Forest,* XII, 81–82). By touching poetic forms with his English wit, he set poetic standards for the next century that spliced classical traditions and a distinctive individuality.

BIBLIOGRAPHY

Jackson, Gabriele Bernhard. *Vision and Judgment in Ben Jonson's Drama.* 1968.

Jonson, Ben. *Works.* C.H. Herford, Percy Simpson, and Evelyn Simpson, eds. 11 vols. 1925–1952.

Kay, W. David. *Ben Jonson: A Literary Life.* 1995.

Maus, Katherine Eisaman. *Ben Jonson and the Roman Frame of Mind.* 1984.

Orgel, Stephen. *The Jonsonian Masque.* 1965.

Riggs, David. *Ben Jonson: A Life.* 1989.

Michael Holahan

SEE ALSO

Chapman, George; Classical Literature, Influence of; Drama, History of; Marston, John; Nashe, Thomas; Satire; Shakespeare, William ; Theater Companies, Adult

Justice of the Peace

Justices were local gentry appointed by the crown to mainly county-based Commissions of the Peace—familiarly referred to as "the bench." In addition, some urban corporations and the universities were also issued with commissions, although these J.P.s did not in every instance exercise the full range of powers or always bear the appellation of "justice." Originating in the fourteenth century, the office underwent substantial development during the sixteenth century and became the main focus of local administration and justice. The justices operated through the court of quarter sessions. To the judicial core of their activities were added new administrative responsibilities and, some have argued, the Commission of the Peace also became the focus of the political and social life of the counties. Among numerous other things, J.P.s became responsible for overseeing poor relief, the supply of the markets, local wage rates, and apprenticeship. These developments were reflected in two parallel sets of changes.

Especially in Elizabeth I's reign there was an elaboration of their organizational arrangements, in part to accommodate their new administrative remit. This involved the creation of new structures and procedures in addition to their quarterly meetings. While the precise arrangements varied from one county to another, most came to meet in "divisions" of counties in petty sessions; and there was also more out-of-sessions activity by pairs of or individual justices. Records were better preserved and many counties rebuilt their main place of meeting, the "shirehouse." The records were the formal responsibility of a designated J.P., the *custos rotulorum* (keeper of the rolls). The management of their work was assisted by an official, the clerk of the peace, but especially busy justices also began to employ private clerks to oversee their activities.

Changes in the character of the bench and of its justices included a remorseless increase in the number of J.P.s and inflation of the quorum: those reputed to be legally qualified whose presence was required for certain types of business. Numbers varied according to the size of counties but in some they rose from around twenty c. 1500 to around sixty c. 1600. Under Elizabeth in most counties J.P.s became independent of control by great local magnates. Their independence and articulacy was also amplified by their enhanced education, which reflected increased attendance at university.

Historians have not always recognized that the individuals who were justices were also issued with numerous other commissions and *ad hoc* responsibilities (e.g., for the subsidy or musters). For those subject to their authority, and probably for some justices, it cannot always have been easy in every instance to distinguish precisely in what capacity they were acting.

In pursuit of more control in the localities at various times the central government contemplated either replacing J.P.s or finding ways of making them more responsive. Nothing came of these rumblings, but there were periodic purges to reduce numbers or to remove Catholics or "drones." Toward the end of Elizabeth I's reign there were experiments with "contracting out" aspects of government to informers and patentees who,as a result, came into conflict with the justices.

J

BIBLIOGRAPHY

Elton, G.R. *The Tudor Constitution.* 2nd edition 1982.

Gleason, J.H. *The Justices of the Peace in England, 1558–1640.* 1969.

Heal, Felicity, and Clive Holmes. *The Gentry in England and Wales, 1500–1700,* pp. 166–189. 1994.

Morgan, Victor. "The Elizabethan shirehouse at Norwich." In *Counties and Communities: Essays on East Anglian History Presented to Hassell Smith.* Carole Rawcliffe, Roger Virgoe, and Richard Wilson, eds. Center of East Anglian Studies. pp. 149–160. 1996.

Smith, A. Hassell. *County and Court: Government and Politics in Norfolk, 1558–1603.* 1974.

———, Gillian M. Baker, R.W. Kenny, Jane Key, Victor Morgan, and Barry Taylor, eds. *The Papers of Nathaniel Bacon of Stiffkey, 1556–.* 4 Vols. to date (in progress). Norfolk Record Society and the Center of East Anglian Studies. 1979–.

Victor Morgan

SEE ALSO

Apprenticeship; Government, Local; Lawyers; Poor Laws

K

Katherine of Aragon (1485–1536)

Katherine of Aragon is mostly remembered for her pride in her lineage, for her devotion to the Catholic faith, and for her refusal to accept Henry VIII's conclusion that they had been united in an illicit marriage. Her perseverance and determination form the backdrop to the English Reformation.

The fifth child of Isabella of Castile and Ferdinand of Aragon, she was born December 16, 1485. Besides receiving the usual instruction for women, she was also tutored in the classics by leading humanists. In 1501, she traveled to England and, on November 14, married Arthur, Prince of Wales, the fifteen-year-old heir of Henry VII, who died at Ludlow Castle in April 1502. When later this marriage became a matter of legal debate, she persisted in denying that it had been consummated. In 1503, she was betrothed to his younger brother Henry, but, on the eve of his fourteenth birthday, he protested against these vows at the request of his father, who had begun to reconsider the value of the Spanish alliance.

Shortly after his accession in 1509, Henry VIII married Katherine, who was six years his senior, and their double coronation was held on June 24. Subsequently, the queen had about seven pregnancies that produced in 1516 one surviving child, Mary, whose humanist education she helped to supervise. Katherine protested the ennoblement of Henry's namesake illegitimate son as duke of Richmond in 1525, the same year that Mary was recognized as Princess of Wales. By 1527, Henry had determined to divorce his consort and to marry Anne Boleyn. The authority for his decision was Leviticus 20:21, which warns that a man who takes his brother's wife will be childless. Henry believed the warning applied to his marriage because of the death of his infant sons, but for the biblical verse to carry legal weight, Katherine's marriage to his brother had to have been consummated.

In 1527, Cardinal Thomas Wolsey held secret sessions inquiring into the validity of the royal marriage, and in 1528, Pope Clement VII sent Lorenzo, Cardinal Campeggio, to England to settle the controversy. Had Katherine been willing to enter a nunnery, as Campeggio suggested, canonical law could have permitted Henry's remarriage. Having rejected this solution, she was summoned to the Cardinals' legatine court, which was permanently recessed on July 31, 1529, without reaching a verdict. Campeggio left England and Wolsey fell from power, but King Henry VIII was no closer to the remedy he sought. He banished Katherine from court in 1531.

Because she refused to recognize the authority of the Reformation statutes, her final years were spent in a scaled-down household, separated from her daughter. Having resisted being addressed as dowager princess of Wales after Thomas Cranmer, archbishop of Canterbury, pronounced her royal marriage invalid, she also protested the removal of Mary from the succession. Uncompromising to the end, she died of natural causes and was buried at Peterborough Abbey on January 29, 1536, amid rumors circulating abroad that she had been poisoned.

BIBLIOGRAPHY

Dowling, Maria. *Humanism in the Age of Henry VIII.* 1986.

Loades, David. *Mary Tudor.* 1989.

Mattingly, Garrett. *Catherine of Aragon.* 1941.

Scarisbrick, J.J. *Henry VIII.* 1968.

Warnicke, Retha. *Women of the English Renaissance and Reformation.* 1983.

Retha Warnicke

Kemp, William (d. 1603–1609?)

Actor, clown, dancer, William Kemp made his mark as a player with the Lord Chamberlain's Men, in clown's roles such as Dogberry *(Much Ado About Nothing)* and Peter *(Romeo and Juliet)*. Yet much of his career was spent peregrinating among several acting companies and at least several countries other than England.

Both Kemp's origins and his ending are obscure. It has been conjectured variously that he was the son of a printer or a gentleman's servant; likewise, that he was "William Kempe, a man," buried from St. Saviour's Southwark in 1603. The commonality of his name makes him difficult to trace. What seems reasonably certain, however, is that the earliest reference to Kemp is as "my lord of Leicester's jesting player," which occurs in a letter written by Sir Philip Sidney in 1586. Here Kemp is thought to have been one of Leicester's players, also serving as a messenger, who occasonally carried dispatches from the Low Countries to London.

From the Netherlands Kemp apparently went to Elsinore, where he appears on the payroll as "Wilhelm Kempe, instrumentist." By 1590, Kemp was established in London as a clown and the artistic heir of Richard Tarlton. In 1593, he toured the provinces with Lord Strange's Men. He remained with that company (later the Chamberlain's Men) for six years; and despite the fact that Kemp was one of the original seven shareholders in the new Globe theater, he apparently sold his share soon after the lease was signed in 1599. Nevertheless, Kemp's inclusion among the actors listed in the Jonson Folio (1616) and the First Folio of Shakespeare's plays(1623) suggests that his career with the Chamberlain's Men was temporary, albeit distinguished.

Next, Kemp decided to dance his way from London to Norwich. This venture earned him a good deal of money from bets and gifts, as well as an annuity of 40s. from the mayor of Norwich. The journey was recorded in a contemporary account, *Kempe's Nine Daies Wonder* (1600). Thereafter, Kemp performed in Italy and Germany, returning by early 1603 to join Worcester's Men, who were performing at Philip Henslowe's Rose playhouse. Throughout his life Kemp was best known on the public stage for his jigs (sketches with song and dance, often obscene) and "merriments" (improvised passages of witty repartee). Thomas

Dekker speaks of Kemp as being deceased in 1609, although it is possible he died as early as 1603.

BIBLIOGRAPHY
Baskervill, C.R. *The Elizabethan Jig.* 1929.
Chambers, E.K. *The Elizabethan Stage.* Vol. 2, pp. 325–327. 1923.
Mann, David. *The Elizabethan Player.* 1991.
Nungezer, Edwin. *A Dictionary of Actors.* Pp. 215–222. 1929.
Wiles, David. *Shakespeare's Clowns.* 1987.

S.P. Cerasano

Kenilworth, Castle and Lordship

Linked to the earldom of Leicester in the thirteenth century, Kenilworth Castle became during the following two centuries the administrative center of the duchy of Lancaster and a major royal residence. Situated on a natural mound with a large, artificial lake to the south and west side, Kenilworth was granted to Lord Robert Dudley in July 1563, a year prior to his creation as earl of Leicester, by Elizabeth I. During the next twenty-five years he created a substantial landed estate in Warwickshire centered on Kenilworth, and engaged in a major rebuilding and modernization of the castle itself to make it more suitable for entertaining and housing guests. In addition, he expanded the grounds by relocating the nearby village of Blackwell in 1570, and stocked the surrounding woodlands with deer. Although he did not visit Kenilworth until 1566, from 1570 he visited annually until 1586, with the single exception of 1583. Elizabeth herself visited on four occasions, during the progresses of 1566, 1568, 1572, and, most famously, 1575, described in a letter attributed to Robert Laneham. The significance of the entertainments has been widely debated; 1566 to 1575 was the period of the greatest of the royal progresses, and Kenilworth's prominence may reflect Leicester's encouragement of this political and social activity.

BIBLIOGRAPHY
Adams, Simon. "'Because I am of that Country & mynde to plant myself there': Robert Dudley, Earl of Leicester and the West Midlands." *Midland History,* vol. 20, pp. 21–74.

K

him and his followers in that aim. A degree of strife
between upper gentry and local officials on the one hand,
and the lesser gentry, yeomanry, and lesser peasantry on
the other, formed an inexact balance of loyalties. Many
rebels expressed a strongly reactionary view of local governance, wishing to defend traditional patterns of land use,
"good lordship," and similar behavior against the inroads
of change. Religious elements emerged as well: concerns
for the corruption of the clergy and endorsement of
Protestant ideas became widespread.

In retrospect, the rebellion may be seen as a call for a
more constructive social and economic policy at a time of
sharply accelerated social change, as a harbinger of popular Protestantism in one of the most doctrinally precocious areas of the realm, and as an expression of popular
support for due process in government. Its most dramatic
effect on national affairs was to help precipitate Warwick's
ouster of Somerset as the effective head of state in the
name of Edward VI.

IOGRAPHY

Beer, Barrett L. *Rebellion and Riot, Popular Disorder in England during the Reign of Edward VI.* 1982.
Bindoff, S.T. *Kett's Rebellion.* 1949.
Cornwall, J. *Revolt of the Peasantry, 1549.* 1977.
Land, Stephen K. *Kett's Rebellion, the Norfolk Rising of 1549.* 1977.
MacCulloch, D. "Kett's Rebellion in Context." *Past and Present,* vol. 84, pp. 36–59.
Sotherton, Nicholas. *The Commoyson in Norfolk, 1549.* Susan Yaxley, ed. 1987.

Robert Tittler

SEE ALSO
Agrarian Uprisings; Dudley, John; Edward VI;
Enclosures; Government, Local; Seymour, Edward

Keyboard Music

Tudor keyboard music was composed for two types of
instruments. The first type was the virginal or harpsichord: a single-keyboard instrument whose strings are
plucked by small quills, producing a shimmering, silvery
tone. The virginal appears to have been the favorite instrument of the English monarchy, whose players included
Elizabeth of York (wife of Henry VII), Katherine of
Aragon (first wife of Henry VIII), Henry VIII, Mary
Tudor, and Queen Elizabeth. Following royal fashion,

——. *Household Accounts and Disbursement Books of Robert Dudley, Earl of Leicester, 1558–1561.* Camden Society. 5th series. Vol. 6. 1995.
Bergeron, David M. *English Civic Pageantry, 1558–1642.* 1971.
Furnivall, F.J., ed. *Captain Cox, His Ballads and Books, or Robert Laneham's Letter. Ballad Society.* Vol. 7. 1871; repr. as *Robert Laneham's Letter.* Shakespeare Society. Series 6, no. 14. 1907.
Nichols, John. *The Progresses and Public Processions of Queen Elizabeth.* 3 vols. 1823.
Thompson, M.W. *Kenilworth Castle.* English Heritage. 1991.

S.L. Adams

SEE ALSO
Dudley, Robert; Elizabeth I; Progresses, Royal

Kett's Rebellion

Named for its eventual leader, the affluent Wymondham,
Norfolk, yeoman Robert Kett, Kett's Rebellion was the
largest of several risings that occurred in East Anglia in
1549. It began with anti-enclosure riots in Attleborough
in June, took form in the Wymondham marketplace in
early July, and peaked with the seige and occupation of
the city of Norwich later that month. Ignoring several
offers of pardon, which may or may not have been sincere, the rebels were eventually routed by a force of some
12,000 troops, including foreign mercenaries and led by
John Dudley, the earl of Warwick, in the last week of
August. As many as 3,000 rebels may have been killed in
Warwick's assault on their final positions, first at Mouse-
hold Heath and then at Dussindale. Kett and up to 300 of
his supporters were executed for treason.

Kett's Rebellion arose in a climate of widespread agrarian tension, to which economic, social, and religious
changes all contributed. In addition, the widespread and
innocent belief that Edward Seymour, ruling as lord protector Somerset, intended to protect the peasantry from
seigniorial exploitation lent courage where it might normally have been lacking. Violence first broke out in support of what appeared to be a government move against
enclosures. The rising rapidly attracted support from several social groups representing a number of pressing concerns, spreading geographically as it did so. Kett himself
emerged as a natural leader, sympathizing with the anti-
enclosure sentiment and throwing down hedges on his
own lands. He also hoped to expose corruption in local

English society took up the virginal. A small single-keyboard harpsichord with its strings were positioned at right angles to the keys rather than parallel with them, the English virginal or virginals (both terms denote one instrument) was distinguished from its continental counterparts by a wider range. The English used the term "virginals" indiscriminately for all plucked-string instruments. The second type of instrument was the organ, typically with one or two keyboards (without pedals) and registers, or pipes, producing a soft, clear, and stately tone deemed appropriate for liturgical celebration.

Keyboard music in Tudor England developed and flourished alongside that of other European countries; however, English composers set themselves apart from their contemporaries in that they were the first to create a genre of keyboard music distinctly for plucked-string keyboards as opposed to organ. In doing so they were at the forefront of developing an idiomatic harpsichord style that lasted well into the seventeenth century. These innovative keyboard techniques are in evidence from c. 1530 in pieces such as *A hornepype* by Hugh Aston, and *My Lady Careys Dompe* and *The Short Measure of My Lady Wynkfylds Rownde,* both anonymous, which survive in the British Library, MS Royal Appendix 58. All three pieces, which are dances, are hallmarked by broken-chord, ostinato basses in the left-hand part contrasted with lively improvisatory-like writing in the right-hand part. Similar compositions are still found some forty years later in the Dublin Virginal Manuscript, which contains a collection of thirty anonymous dances. In addition to the broken-chord bass, the pieces in the Dublin Virginal Manuscript exhibit varied repetitions, or "divisions," which later become a standard feature of virginal music. The first book of virginal music published in Britain is *Parthenia or the Maydenhead of the First Musicke that Ever was Printed for the Virginalls* (1612). The most exhaustive collection is the Fitzwilliam Virginal Book; compiled between 1609 and 1619 by Francis Tregian, a recusant imprisoned in the Fleet, it is an anthology containing more than 290 pieces that samples virginal repertory ranging over 100 years. Works by Thomas Tallis, William Byrd, John Bull, Orlando Gibbons, and Thomas Tomkins, among others, represent consecutive generations of the great school of virginalists spanning the mid-sixteenth through mid-seventeenth centuries. The Fitzwilliam Virginal Book also bears witness to the increasing popularity of secular compositions, where settings of song tunes, fantasias, genre pieces, and variations now take their place alongside dances such as almans, gigs, pavins, and galliards. Also notable within this collection is the wide range of styles now typical of the virginal idiom, which run from liturgically influenced contrapuntal imitation as developed by Byrd, and the rudimentary block chord accompaniment supporting a simple melody, to the virtuosic techniques of Bull and Giles Farnaby, who greatly extended virginal technique.

Also characteristic of English keyboard music is the repertory for organ, much of which was written by those who composed for virginal as well. In contrast to the virginal repertoire, however, these works tend to be composed in a more archaic style that leans toward vocal music then prominent in the church. Compositional procedures range from simple transcriptions of Latin and English motets to pieces based on plainchant that is used in innovative and various ways. While the general style of organ music is reserved, the latter type of organ composition offered composers the greatest of creative possibilities, for the plainchant might be rendered as long equal notes that support a fanciful upper contrapuntal line, as in some of the *In nomine* settings; or the plainchant might itself be decorated rhythmically or melodically, as in some *Felix namque* settings; or still further, the plainchant might be so highly embellished or paraphrased so loosely that it is nearly unrecognizable, as with John Redford's *Criste qui lux.* The most outstanding composers are Redford, Thomas Preston, Tallis, William Blitheman, and Byrd, whose works appear in British Library, MS Royal Appendix 56, and in the *Mulliner Book.*

BIBLIOGRAPHY

Caldwell, John, ed. *Early Tudor Organ Music: Music for the Office.* Early English Church Music. Vol. 6. 1965.

———. *English Keyboard Music before the Nineteenth Century.* 1973.

———. *Tudor Keyboard Music, c. 1520–1580.* Musica Britannica. Vol. 66. 1995.

Dart, Thurston. *John Bull. Keyboard Music.* Musica Britannica. Vols. 14, 19. 1970.

Fuller-Maitland, John Alexander, and Squire, William Barclay, eds. *The Fitzwilliam Virginal Book.* 2 vols. 1965.

Langley, Robin, ed. *Early Tudor Organ Music: An Anthology from Tudor and Stuart Times.* 1986.

Stevens, Denis, ed. *Early Tudor Organ Music: Music for the Mass.* Early English Church Music. Vol. 10. 1969.

———. *The Mulliner Book.* Musica Britannica. Vol. 1. 1951.

Joseph C. Morin

K at top right.

K

SEE ALSO

Byrd, William; Henry VIII as Composer; Music, History of; Preston, Thomas; Tallis, Thomas

King's Book, The

The King's Book was the name popularly given to a volume whose actual title is *A Necessary Doctrine and Erudition for any Christian Man*. It was published under the personal supervision of King Henry VIII in 1543, as part of his program to curb what he saw as the excesses of the Reformation. In particular, it was designed to be a replacement for the so-called Bishops' Book of 1537, which interpreted the Ten Articles of 1536 in a Protestant direction.

By 1543, Henry had become alarmed at the spread of Protestant ideas, and he was more than ever determined to maintain as Catholic a Church of England as the circumstances would allow. He had already admonished those who denied transubstantiation and clergy who had married; now it was the turn of the church's catechetical instruction to be purged. The pattern of the work follows that of the Bishops' Book, with the same themes being covered, though from a more conservative angle.

The King's Book died a natural death at the same time as the king Edward VI, though it was occasionally revived later by High Church Anglicans, who were in sympathy with its teachings. However, it can safely be said that the King's Book never exercised much influence on the Church of England, and after 1547 it was all but forgotten.

BIBLIOGRAPHY

A Necessary Doctrine and Erudition for any Christian Man. 1895; repr. 1932.

Gerald Bray

SEE ALSO
Anglicanism; Articles of Religion; Bishops' Book; Henry VIII; Reformation, English

King's or Queen's Bench, Court of

The King's Bench had precedence over the common law courts because it was the court that had traveled with the king and heard justice before him in the formative years of the common law. It possessed the writ of error that allowed it to hear appeals on questions of judicial error, and the writ of *certiorari*, which allowed it to call up the record of any other court for review and judgment. Its original jurisdiction was primarily over wrongs that alleged violation of the king's peace. Serving both the crown and private parties, it had two distinct administrative sides that often made its work cumbersome and inefficient. Losing business from the reign of Henry VII to Henry VIII, the future of the court lay in the Bill of Middlesex that began its modern development in the 1540s.

The Tudor era was significant in that it enabled the King's Bench to break the monopoly of the Court of Common Pleas in cases of contract. The transformation occurred by framing a claim for goods as a wrong that demanded damages. The device was the Bill of Middlesex. Trespasses, or wrongs, could come to either King's Bench or Common Pleas. But since King's Bench could hear trespasses without writs, it could accept a direct complaint and order the sheriff of that county to send the defendant to King's Bench. The problem was when defendants fled the county and could not be found. Since the Bench sat in Middlesex, where it had perpetual jurisdiction of arrest, a plaintiff could complain that the defendant was in Middlesex, a writ would go to the sheriff to arrest him, and the sheriff would report that he was not there. Then an order (a *latitat*) would go to the sheriff of the county or counties where the defendant was thought to be located for his arrest and conveyance to the marshal of Middlesex, and incarceration in the court's Marshalsea prison.

The Bill of Middlesex brought arrest, trial, and judgment in quick order. But it was also open to abuse, offering intriguing possibilities to vexatious litigants. Coupled with the new actions on the case that emerged from trespass to torts such as negligence, nuisance, and defamation, the court's business rose significantly during the reign of Elizabeth I. By 1600, its caseload had increased ten times from 1500, and its profits increased six times from 1553. The person who profited most, however, was the prothonotary, whose intimate knowledge of possible process and procedure enabled him to control the work of the court and hire a horde of clerks to assist him. Abuses were clearly perceived at an early date. A statute of 1585 created the Court of Exchequer Chamber, whose original purpose was to correct errors of the King's Bench. Nonetheless, the court underwent a renewal that was nothing less than a legal reformation.

BIBLIOGRAPHY
Baker, John. "Origins of the 'Doctrine' of Consideration, 1535–1585." In *On the Laws and Customs of England.* M.S. Arnold, et al., eds., pp. 336–358. 1981.

Baker, J.H. *The Reports of Sir John Spelman.* Selden Society. Vols. 93–94. 1976–1977.

Blatcher, Marjorie. *The Court of King's Bench, 1450–1550.* 1978.

Meekings, C.A.F. "King's Bench Bills." In *Legal Records and the Historian.* J.H. Baker, ed., pp. 97–139. 1977.

Simpson, A.W.B. *History of the Common Law of Contract: The Rise of Assumpsit.* 1975.

Louis A. Knafla

SEE ALSO

Common Pleas, Court of; Government, Central Administration of; Law, Common; Sheriff

Knighthood

The Anglo-Saxon word "knight" is linked to the German word *"knecht"* or servant, and the exchange of a royal honor for service to the sovereign remains a key element of Tudor knighthood. In *De Republica Anglorum,* a treatise on government in "the realm of England" written during the reign of Elizabeth I, Sir Thomas Smith describes the knight as "the second sort of gentlemen" and a member of the minor nobility. In contrast to dukes, earls, barons, and other members of the major nobility, "no man is a knight by succession." Knights are not born but made "either before the battle to encourage them the more to adventure their lives, or after the conflict, as advancement for their hardiness and manhood already showed" either by the king or his commanders. Smith allows that the distinction may be conferred for services rendered beyond the battlefield, conceding that by his time it has become a recognition of social and economic status: "So be knights in England [chosen] most commonly, according to the yearly revenue of their lands being able to maintain that estate." Men of wealth constituted the natural ruling class of their local communities. They often became members of Parliament and justices of the peace, and their position and authority were formally recognized by the award of a knighthood. Being non-hereditary, such a distinction was the gift of the monarch, and it was used to reward favorites, compel allegiance, and enlist the resources of Tudor England's elite.

As several historians have noted, the Tudor monarchy put an end to the anarchy of the Wars of the Roses by securing a near-monopoly on violence. The civil wars of the fifteenth century had pitted a group of overmighty noble subjects against a weak monarchy, as well as one another. Henry VII and his successors managed to suppress potential noble adversaries by centralizing control over honors and rewards, gradually transforming feudal warriors into docile courtiers. At the same time, political writers were redefining notions of knighthood as a form of intellectual and civil service. The author of *The Book of the Governor* (1531), Sir Thomas Elyot, insisted that "a knight hath received that honor not only to defend with the sword Christ's faith and his proper country . . . but also, and that most chiefly, by the mean of his dignity . . . he should more effectually with his learning and wit assail vice and error, most pernicious enemies to Christian men, having thereunto for his sword and spear, his tongue and pen." An emblem of this less belligerent version of service is presented by the poet, George Gascoigne, who depicts himself kneeling devoutly before Elizabeth, with lance and pen in hand.

Nevertheless, for many Tudor subjects, knighthood's origins on the battlefield remained definitive. Lord Willoughby de Eresby was typical in his boast, reported in Robert Naunton's memoir of Elizabeth's court, that "he could neither creep nor crouch, neither was the court his element, for indeed he was a great soldier." For him and many others, honor was rooted in a warrior code. Sir Thomas Smith also compares the English knight to the Roman *"equites"* and French *"cavalier,"* meaning horsemen. In all these societies, the knight's prosperity enables him to keep a horse and arms and ride into battle, giving

Knights Fighting with Sword and Dagger. From Sir William Segar, *Book of Honour and Arms* (1589). Reproduced from the original by permission of the Henry E. Huntington Library and Art Gallery.

him a decided military advantage. This chivalric and martial component of knighthood remained just as important in Tudor England, and it was a source of tension and difficulty in thinking about nobility. Before 1558, most Englishmen earned their chivalric honors in battle, Lawrence Stone estimating that more than two-thirds of the 600 English knights of Elizabeth's reign were created during the wars with France under Henry VIII, Edward VI, and Mary I. Elizabeth I was less well disposed toward men of war as well as more parsimonious in bestowing honors, and the number of knights dropped by half during the early decades of her reign, but they increased again during the campaigns of her final years. As Stone points out, nearly a quarter were the creations of her troublesome favorite, Robert Devereux, the earl of Essex. Essex saw himself as a great military leader, determined to prevail over the timorous indecision of the queen and her councilors, and he also regarded himself as the defender of the ancient nobility. His enthusiasm for war prompted conflicts over policy, and his generosity with knighthoods undercut the queen's control by making him a rival source of honors. These tensions erupted in an abortive military coup in 1601 supported by a group of discontented noblemen and knights loyal to the earl, and, after its suppression, he was tried and executed. Despite admiration for Essex and resentment of Elizabeth I, few supported him. Fear of a return to the feudal anarchy of an earlier time further undercut militaristic conceptions of knighthood.

Those disorders were depicted in William Shakespeare's history plays covering the Wars of the Roses, one of which was revived on the eve of the Essex rebellion. *Richard II* not only shows the deposition of a weak king and his corrupt courtiers, but it also begins with stirring scenes of the "rites of knighthood" in which the king's noble adversary seeks to vindicate his honor through trial by combat; Shakespeare's pun recognizes that ostentatious belligerence and self-esteem were also considered essential "rights of knighthood." Tournaments and other chivalric rituals remained a prominent feature of Tudor courtly ceremonial, notably celebrations of the accession day of Queen Elizabeth, and they combined tributes to the monarch with displays of martial prowess and noble grandeur. Works like Edmund Spenser's *Faerie Queene* also aimed to reconcile the conflicts between the loyal service and belligerent honor required of a knight.

BIBLIOGRAPHY

Anglo, Sydney. *Spectacle, Pageantry, and Early Tudor Policy.* 1969.

McCoy, Richard. *The Rites of Knighthood: The Literature and Politics of Elizabethan Chivalry.* 1989.

Smith, Sir Thomas. *De Republica Anglorum.* Mary Dewar, ed. 1982.

Stone, Lawrence. *The Crisis of the Aristocracy, 1558–1641.* 1965.

Strong, Sir Roy. *The Cult of Elizabeth.* 1977.

Young, Alan. *Tudor and Jacobean Tournaments.* 1987.

Richard C. McCoy

SEE ALSO

Accession Day; Devereux, Robert; Elizabeth I; Elyot, Thomas; Gascoigne, George; Henry VII; Heraldry; Justice of the Peace; Smith, Sir Thomas; Shakespeare, William; Spenser, Edmund; Wars of the Roses

Knollys, Francis (c. 1514–1596)

Privy councilor and senior official of the royal household, Sir Francis Knollys began his career of royal service in the household of Henry VIII. He rose to become a gentleman pensioner in 1539 and the master of the horse to Prince Edward by 1547. Around 1540, he married Katherine Carey, the daughter of Sir William Carey and Mary Boleyn, a former mistress of Henry VIII and sister to Anne Boleyn. During Edward VI's reign he became a Protestant, and under Mary I, he left England to become an exile in Frankfurt and Basle where his religious beliefs became radicalized. On Elizabeth I's succession he returned to England as a staunch Puritan. His wife being the new queen's first cousin, he was made vice-chamberlain of the household and a member of the Privy Council, but his ability led to greater preferment and responsibilities. In 1565, he became captain of the guard, and in 1567, treasurer of the chamber. The following year Knollys was put in charge of the confinement of Mary Queen of Scots while Elizabeth I and her Privy Council determined her long-term status in the kingdom. However, he perceived the task as a largely thankless one and even considered leaving government service over it. His reward came in 1570 when Elizabeth appointed him treasurer of the household. As treasurer he worked with William Cecil, Lord Burghley, to reform household provisioning practices, such as purveyance, but was unsuccessful. He had a tense working relationship with both Sir James Croft, the controller of the household, and with members of the board of greencloth who accused him of corruption and malfeasance, crimes of which he was almost certainly guilty. Only his close relationship to

Elizabeth saved him from disgrace. Elizabeth later lost some trust in him, especially over his long-standing quarrel with John Whitgift concerning the archbishop's subscription campaign against Puritan ministers and his *iure divino* theory of episcopacy. However, it was with Queen Elizabeth's support that Knollys was made a knight of the garter in 1593, a signal honor to cap his long, loyal years in royal service.

BIBLIOGRAPHY

Cargill Thompson, W.D.G. "Sir Francis Knollys' Campaign Against the *Jure Divino* Theory of Episcopacy." In *Studies in the Reformation: Luther to Hooker.* C.W. Dugmore, ed. 1980.

Fraser, Antonia. *Mary Queen of Scots.* 1969.

Mueller, Robert J. "Service to the Sovereign: A Prosopographical Study of the Royal Household, Court, and Privy Council of Elizabeth I of England through an Examination of the Careers of Sir Francis Knollys, Sir James Croft, and Francis Russell, Earl of Bedford." Dissertation, University of California, Santa Barbara. 1993.

Proceedings in the Parliaments of Elizabeth I. T.E. Hartley, ed. 1981.

Pulman, Michael B. *The Elizabethan Privy Council in the Fifteen-Seventies.* 1971.

Robert J. Mueller

SEE ALSO

Cecil, William; Government, Central Administration of; Mary Queen of Scots; Puritanism; Royal Household; Whitgift, John

Knollys, Lettice, Countess of Leicester (c. 1540–1634)

Maid of honor to Elizabeth I, Lettice Knollys was the daughter of Sir Francis Knollys and his wife, Catherine (Carey). Her mother was first cousin to the queen, and this accounts for Lettice's appointment as a maid of the Privy Chamber on Elizabeth's accession to the throne. By 1562, she married Walter Devereux, later earl of Essex, and bore him four children, including his heir, Robert, who became the second earl. A favorite of the queen early in the reign, Lettice resided frequently at court. There she excited the interest of Robert Dudley, earl of Leicester. There were rumors of an indecent affair between the two in the mid-1570s, and as a result, when Essex died of illness in Ireland in 1576, some unfairly suspected Leicester

of poisoning him. In September 1578, pregnant with his child, she married Leicester in a secret ceremony that was insisted upon by her father. When the queen discovered this fact she considered it the worst form of betrayal, and banished both from the court. Leicester eventually regained the queen's favor, but Lettice never did. She was denied access to the court for nearly twenty years. On Leicester's death in 1588, she married Sir Christopher Blount with, some said, inordinate haste. In 1598, at the urging of her son, Robert Devereux, earl of Essex, Lettice was finally allowed back into the queen's presence and the two exchanged kisses. However, the reconciliation was short-lived. After the Essex rebellion in 1601, when both her son and third husband were executed for their roles, Lettice retired to her estates. She emerged in 1603 to fight (and win) a case in Star Chamber against Douglas, Lady Sheffield, who asserted that she had married the earl of Leicester before Lettice, and as such her illegitimate son by that union had claim to the earldoms of Leicester and Warwick. She died at the age of 92.

BIBLIOGRAPHY

Doran, Susan. *Monarchy and Matrimony: The Courtships of Elizabeth I.* 1996.

Kendall, Alan. *Robert Dudley, Earl of Leicester.* 1980.

Somerset, Anne. *Ladies-in-Waiting.* 1984.

Robert J. Mueller

SEE ALSO

Elizabeth I; Devereux, Robert; Devereux, Walter; Dudley, Robert; Knollys, Francis

Knox, John (c. 1513–1572)

Scottish Protestant reformer, John Knox was born in or near Haddington, East Lothian, between 1505 and 1515. Knox's early life is obscure. He was educated at the University of Glasgow and possibly at St. Andrews. He received minor orders, and was perhaps ordained to the priesthood in 1536. During the next few years he was notary apostolic in the archdiocese of St. Andrews. About 1544, he became a tutor for the children of some East Lothian lairds. Soon after, under the influence of George Wishart, Knox embraced the principles of the Reformation. At the time of Wishart's arrest on charges of heresy, Knox was in attendance and tried to protect the preacher. After Wishart's execution in March 1546, some disaffected gentry assassinated Archbishop James Beaton and occupied the archepiscopal castle at St. Andrews. In April

1547, Knox joined this group and became preacher at St. Andrews. When the castle fell to the French in July 1547, Knox was taken captive and remained a prisoner aboard a French galley for nineteen months. His release was arranged by the English early in 1549. He made his way to England and became a licensed preacher, first at Berwick, then at Newcastle, and finally in London. In 1551, he was made a chaplain to Edward VI. While serving in that capacity he assisted in making final revisions to the Second Prayer Book (1552); he is credited with responsibility for the so-called "Black Rubric," which explained that the act of kneeling meant no idolatrous adoration of the bread and wine. He was also one of six theologians who prepared the final recension of the Forty-Two Articles, which was signed by Edward VI on June 12, 1553, less than a month before the young king's death. In 1552, Knox had been supported to no avail by the duke of Northumberland for the bishopric of Rochester; Knox declared that he declined the office because it still savored too much of Roman practice. In 1553, he accepted the post as a preacher to Buckinghamshire.

On the succession of Mary Tudor, Knox fled to the Continent. He eventually found refuge in Geneva. In November 1554, Knox accepted the call to be one of the pastors of the English refugees at Frankfurt-on-Maine, but was expelled after a dispute arising over use of the Edwardian Book of Common Prayer. Knox returned to Geneva. There was a short visit to Scotland in 1555, during a brief period of religious toleration to Protestants. The political and religious climate soon changed, however, and Knox once again took refuge in Geneva in 1556, where he became preacher to the English congregation. In 1558, he published several tracts, including one that asserted the right of the common people to depose and punish tyrants. Also among these tracts was *The First Blast of the Trumpet against the Monstrous Regiment of Women,* a violent diatribe against Mary of Guise, propounding the view that government by a woman is contrary to the law of nature and to divine command. This pamphlet, which appeared shortly before the accession of Elizabeth I, was taken as a personal insult by the new queen. Knox tried in vain to explain, while Elizabeth expressed her hostility by refusing to let him pass through England on his way back to Scotland in 1559.

Knox arrived back in Scotland on May 2, 1559, and assumed leadership of the reforming party. After the death of Mary of Guise (June 1560), the whole resistance of the Catholic and French party collapsed. Knox's powerful preaching contributed significantly to the 1560 Scottish Parliament's abolishment of papal jurisdiciton, adoption of a reformed Confession of Faith, and prohibition against the celebration of Latin masses. Knox also played a vital role in the writing of three major documents of the Scottish Reformation of 1560: the *Scottish Confession,* which was a summation of reformed doctrine; the *First Book of Discipline,* never adopted by Parliament, which attempted to apply the Presbyterian polity worked out by Calvin in Geneva to a whole kingdom; and the *Book of Common Order,* which was approved by the General Assembly in 1564 and became the worship book of the Church of Scotland. About this same time, his only theological work, a high Calvinist *Treatise on Predestination* (1560), appeared in Geneva.

In the same year Knox was appointed minister at Edinburgh. After Mary Stuart's return to Scotland in 1561, he preached from the pulpit of the collegiate kirk of St. Giles vehement sermons against the private masses being celebrated on her behalf and against the general worldliness of her court; the queen summoned him several times for the interviews so vividly described in his principal work, *History of the Reformation of Religion within the Realm of Scotland* (first edition 1587, first complete edition 1644). After Mary's forced abdication in 1567, Knox preached the sermon at the coronation of James VI. Following the murder of the regent Lord Murray in 1570, Knox's political power diminished. In 1571, he left Edinburgh for St. Andrews, where his weekly sermons greatly influenced the young university student Andrew Melville, and then returned once more in 1572 to Edinburgh, where he continued to preach until his death on November 24 of that year.

BIBLIOGRAPHY

Knox, John. *History of the Reformation of Religion within the Realm of Scotland.* W.C. Dickinson, ed. 2 vols. 1949.

Knox, John. *Works.* D. Laing, ed. 6 vols. 1846–1864.

Lang, A. *John Knox and the Reformation.* 1905.

McEwen, James S. *The Faith of John Knox.* 1961.

Ridley, Jasper. *John Knox.* 1968.

Shaw, Duncan, ed. *John Knox: A Quartercentenary Reappraisal.* 1975.

Lee W. Gibbs

SEE ALSO

Articles of Religion; Black Rubric; Book of Common Prayer; Calvinism; Church Polity; Church of Scotland; Marian Exiles; Melville, Andrew; Wishart, George

Kyd, Thomas (1558–1594)

A nearly anonymous Elizabethan writer, Thomas Kyd is more famous for the works attributed to him and the writers he has been associated with than for the few works that definitely can be ascribed to him. During his lifetime no work with his full name on the title page appeared, and three works attributed to him were published with only the initials T.K. Just one work, the second edition of his translation of Robert Garnier's *Cornélie,* which appeared one year after his death, contained his name on the title page.

The son of Anna and Francis Kyd, a scrivener, Thomas was baptized at St. Mary Woolnoth Church on November 6, 1558. At the age of seven, Kyd entered the Merchant Taylors' School, where three or four years earlier Edmund Spenser had begun his schooling. Kyd's future career as dramatist must have been aided by the headmaster Richard Mulcaster, who used drama as an essential part of the curriculum and maintained a boys' company which sometimes appeared in court performances.

It is not known how long he remained at the school, nor is there any evidence that he received a university education. He may have written plays for the Queen's Company between 1585 and 1587, and in 1587, as he revealed in his letters to Sir John Puckering, Kyd joined the service of an unnamed lord. Four years later, in 1591, he shared a room with Christopher Marlowe when they wrote for this same lord. His painful association with a writer whom Kyd hated became even more painful two years later on May 12, 1593, when Kyd was arrested and tortured because of his earlier relationship with Marlowe. It is this incident along with its aftermath that has given Kyd his greatest notoriety.

The Privy Council investigators came to Kyd's lodging in search of xenophobic ballads that had been posted around the city. One of the most malicious of these libels, which threatened "to shedd . . . blood per Tamberlaine," had been hung on the walls of the Dutch Churchyard at St. Paul's, so perhaps the authorities intended to investigate Marlowe and his known associates. But instead of the libels, they found a partial transcription of a proto-Unitarian treatise, *The Fall of the Late Arrian* (1549), which Kyd claimed belonged to Marlowe and had been shuffled among his "waste and idle papers" when they wrote together. Despite his protestations, Kyd was tortured, presumably for the "atheistic" beliefs contained in the incriminating disputation. Marlowe, in turn, was arrested on May 18, and after denying all charges, he was released on May 20. Ten days later, he was killed under

mysterious circumstances at a Deptford inn. For his unwilling role in this matter, Kyd has been branded as the cowardly betrayer of Marlowe, although the circumstances surrounding the chain of events have never been adequately explained.

After his release from incarceration, Kyd wrote two letters to Sir John Puckering, the keeper of the royal seal, asking for his help in being reinstated with his former patron, who had disavowed the disgraced writer. In these letters, Kyd gave his assessment of Marlowe's obnoxious and violent personality, listing some of his "monstruous opinions," which were similar to the charges of atheism leveled at Marlowe by Richard Baines.

Having failed to regain his former position, Kyd finished the translation of Garnier's *Cornélie,* and in the dedication to the countess of Sussex, he referred to the "bitter times and privie broken passions that I endured in the writing of it." He promised her a translation of Garnier's *Porcie,* but he died before it was completed and was buried on August 15, 1594, in St. Mary Colchurch. He died heavily in debt, and his parents legally renounced the administration of his estate. The church and the churchyard subsequently were burned in the Great Fire of London in 1666, and, appropriately, considering Kyd's shadowy life, no trace of the original grave remains.

Kyd's literary career is equally conjectural and anonymous. He is primarily remembered for his putative authorship of *The Spanish Tragedy,* one of the most popular and influential of Elizabethan revenge tragedies. But the play was published anonymously in 1592, and there is only one attribution of it to Kyd made eighteen years after his death by Thomas Heywood in *An Apology for Actors* (1612). However, Heywood's ascription itself went unnoticed until 1773, when Thomas Hawkins mentioned it in *The Origin of the English Drama.* In effect, for almost the first 200 years of its existence, *The Spanish Tragedy* was considered an anonymous play.

From Kyd's putative authorship of *The Spanish Tragedy,* other works connected with this play have been attributed to him. Kyd has been associated with that hoariest of literary chestnuts, the *Ur-Hamlet.* In his preface to Robert Greene's *Menaphon* (1589), Thomas Nashe alluded to a Senecan dramatist who "will afford you whole Hamlets, . . . handfulls of tragical speaches," and "like the Kidde in Aesop" leaps from one occupation to another. On the basis of this enigmatic passage, some early scholars argued that Nashe was alluding to Kyd as a Senecan dramatist who had written an *Ur-Hamlet,* but current scholarship dismisses this identification as spurious.

Philip Henslowe's "diary" lists a comic forepiece, "Spain's Comedy," as preceding the performance of *The Spanish Tragedy* on at least four occasions in 1592; in 1605, a version of this forepiece was published as *The First Part of Hieronimo,* a pastiche that most critics do not credit to Kyd. The anonymous play *Soliman and Perseda* (1592) has also been attributed to Kyd on the basis of its appearance in small as the revenge playlet Hieronimo devises to kill his son's murderers. Finally, two works involving sensational murders, *The Murder of John Brewen* and *Arden of Faversham,* have formerly been ascribed to Kyd on a slender basis of proof that most critics now dismiss.

The only play that can definitely be attributed to Kyd is his translation of Robert Garnier's *Cornélie* (1574). Kyd's capable translation of this Senecan play set in the time of the Roman civil wars places him in the neoclassical circle of Mary Sidney, countess of Pembroke, who had translated Garnier's *Marc Antonio* in 1590. Although *Cornelia* contains passages similar to some in *The Spanish Tragedy,* its decorous Senecanism, replete with long declamations and reported violence, distances it from the revenge tragedy's sensationalism and eclectic blend of popular, religious, and classical motifs.

Another work that can most probably be credited to Kyd is the translation of Torquato Tasso's *Padre di Famiglia* as *The Housholders Philosophie* (1588). In the rigorous simplicity and clarity of their styles, both of Kyd's translations emphasize the importance of classical order and controlled sentiment and probably come closest of all the works attributed to him to revealing his essential personality as workmanlike, orderly, and crafty, qualities that earned from his contemporaries the appellation of "industrious Kyd."

BIBLIOGRAPHY

Ardolino, Frank. *Thomas Kyd's Mystery Play: Myth and Ritual in "The Spanish Tragedy."* 1985.

———. *Apocalypse and Armada in Kyd's "Spanish Tragedy."* 1995.

Freeman, Arthur. *Thomas Kyd: Facts and Problems.* 1967.

Hill, Eugene D. "Senecan and Vergilian Perspectives in *The Spanish Tragedy.*" *English Literary Renaissance,* vol. 15, pp. 143–165.

Hunter, G.K. "Ironies of Justice in *The Spanish Tragedy.*" *Renaissance Drama,* vol. 8, pp. 89–104.

Frank Ardolino

SEE ALSO

Baines, Richard; Drama, History of; French Literature, Influence of; Marlowe, Christopher; Mulcaster, Richard; Puckering, John; Senecanism

L

Lambarde, William (1536–1601)

An antiquary, legal historian, lawyer, justice of the peace, and administrator at the county and national levels of the judiciary, William Lambarde was one of the most significant figures in the development of Tudor historiography, politics, and law. Born in London of a wealthy merchant family, Lambarde took up residence in Kent, the county with which he remained intimately associated in public and private life. No records of Lambarde's education survive prior to his admittance to Lincoln's Inn in 1556. He became a barrister in 1567, and was subsequently honored by Lincoln Inn's members, who made him an associate of the bench in 1579 and a bencher in 1597.

Lambarde may have represented Aldborough in the House of Commons during the sessions of 1563 and 1566. If so, then he is responsible for the "learned oration" of November 8, 1566, in which "Mr. Lambert" spoke out against the Elizabeth I's refusal to consider a petition involving her marriage and the succession question.

In 1576, Lambarde established the College of Queen Elizabeth in East Greenwich, a charitable institution for the poor. He was appointed to the Commission of the Peace in Kent in 1579, and in 1580 became justice of the peace for the county. In recognition of his legal expertise, Lambarde, along with certain other members of the Inns of Court, was asked by the Privy Council in 1588 to study the statutes and recommend changes in them for the next parliamentary session.

Lambarde's knowledge of the law was also recognized in the appointments he received late in his life. He became a deputy in the Alienations Office in 1589, a master of Chancery in 1592, and a deputy keeper of the rolls in 1597. At the queen's request he was appointed keeper of the records in the Tower of London in 1601. It was to Lambarde in August 1601, when he presented her with his *Pandecta Rotulorum,* or catalog of the Tower documents, that Elizabeth I famously said, "I am Richard II, know ye not that?" and concluded their meeting by bidding him "Farewell, good and honest Lambarde."

As a student at Lincoln's Inn, Lambarde was urged by the antiquary Laurence Nowell to publish *Archaionomia* (1568), a compilation of Anglo-Saxon legal terms and customary laws with Latin translations. Directly related to contemporary debates over religious, legal, and political precedents and liberties declared to obtain by virtue of usage and custom since time immemorial, the study of Britain's ancient past continued to inform Lambarde's writings. His *Perambulation of Kent* (1576) was the first history of an English county. His *Dictionarium Angliae Topographicum et Historicum* focused as well on England's Anglo-Saxon heritage but was set aside when Lambarde received a copy of William Camden's *Britannia* and remained unpublished until 1730.

The product of his judicial experiences in Kent, Lambarde's *Eirenarcha: Or of the Office of the Justices of Peace* was first printed in January 1582. Intended, in Lambarde's own words of 1588, to "somewhat further the good endeavor of such gentlemen [J.P.s] as be not trained up in the continual study of the laws," this handbook provided its readers with a much-needed knowledge of criminal law and the powers, procedures, written forms, and precedents essential to the administration of justice. Revised and enlarged for the edition of 1588 and appearing in eight more editions by 1619, *Eirenarcha* became the finest and most serviceable of the

L

sixteenth-century manuals for J.P.s. Similar concerns about legal procedure led Lambarde to write *The Duties of Constables, Borsholders, Tithing-men and such other low and lay Ministers of the Peace* (1583), a much-printed handbook last issued in 1640. His *Archeion* (1635), a commentary on the history of the high courts of England, is notable for its treatment of the Star Chamber and its balanced view of legal prerogatives.

A glimpse into Lambarde's own responsibilities and actions as J.P. from 1580 to 1588 may be found in his *Ephemeris*. His eloquent, often-impassioned charges, or instructions, to juries and special commissions yield further insight into Lambarde's beliefs about the operation and function of the law. His compilation of cases from Chancery rolls also helped form the basis for *Cary's Reports*.

BIBLIOGRAPHY

Alsop, J.D., and W.M. Stevens. "William Lambarde and the Elizabethan Polity." *Studies in Medieval and Renaissance History*, vol. 8, pp. 231–265.

Dunkel, Wilbur. *William Lambarde, Elizabethan Jurist, 1536–1601.* 1965.

Lambarde, William. *Archeion.* Charles H. McIlwain and Paul L. Ward, eds. 1957.

Read, Conyers, ed. *William Lambarde and Local Government: His "Ephemeris" and Twenty-nine Charges to Juries and Commissions.* 1962.

Warnicke, Retha M. *William Lambarde: Elizabethan Antiquary, 1536–1601.* 1973.

Barry Nass

SEE ALSO

Antiquarianism; Criminal Law; History, Writing of; Inns of Court; Justice of the Peace; Lawyers; Star Chamber, Court of

Lambeth Articles

The nine Lambeth articles, dealing with doctrines pertaining to predestination and election, were meant to silence opposition to the dominant "Calvinist" party at Cambridge. They were approved by John Whitgift, archbishop of Canterbury, at his palace at Lambeth in 1595. A sermon by William Barrett, in which he argued that predestination depends upon individual faith and rejection of sin, and that none can be assured of salvation, was the immediate cause. But it reflected controversy of some years' standing, between Peter Baro, the Lady Margaret

Professor of Divinity, and the Regius Professor, William Whitaker. Whitaker and his allies brought about Barrett's recantation, but the affair escalated, and, attempting to bring peace, Whitgift held a conference with Whitaker and Barrett at Lambeth from which the final text of the articles emerged.

When Elizabeth I learned of the articles from William Cecil, Lord Burlghley, she opposed them, misunderstanding Whitgift's intentions. He had intended the articles only for the private use of the university authorities, to prevent further disputes. For him, they were "true and correspondent to the doctrine . . . of the Church of England," but not "laws and decrees," and "in teaching of them . . . discretion and moderation [were to] be used." They were never published, but they remained well known to the university theologians.

Speaking as they do of the certainty of predestination and election to salvation only through the "will of the good pleasure of God," that "true faith . . . is not lost [by] the elect," that "saving grace is not granted . . . to all," the articles have been considered to be "rigidly" or "moderately" Calvinist. But Whitgift had modified Whitaker's articles in a more moderate direction with the advice of Lancelot Andrewes and Hadrian Saravia before giving approval for their limited and discreet use. Peter Baro, the "proto-Arminian" and Barrett's mentor, who knew that they were directed at him, claimed to agree with the articles; nevertheless, he publicly expressed ideas that Whitaker and his group strongly opposed. But as Victoria Miller (p. 53) has put it, "what the Lambeth Articles did not say is as important and controversial as what they did say . . . it was inevitable that the debate over their interpretation would continue."

BIBLIOGRAPHY

Dawley, Powel M. *John Whitgift and the English Reformation.* 1954.

Lake, Peter. *Moderate Puritans and the Elizabethan Church.* 1988.

Miller, Victoria C. *The Lambeth Articles.* 1994.

Porter, Harry C. *Reformation and Reaction in Tudor Cambridge.* 1958.

White, Peter. *Predestination, Policy, and Polemic.* 1992.

Frederick H. Shriver

SEE ALSO

Andrewes, Lancelot; Arminianism; Baro, Peter; Calvinism; Cecil, William; Saravia, Hadrian; Whitgift, John

Land and Landscape

The use and appearance of land under the Tudors underwent transformations after 1500, when the country was still a mosaic of different practices and cultures reflected in the material world. Without losing sight of its variety, the landscape can be divided into three types: champion, woodland, and upland. Champion dominated the Midland plain, running up to the northeast coast and down to the coast of mid-Hampshire. This country was characterized by nucleated settlement, the English villages of postcards, and open farming—between two and four fields farmed communally, divided into strips with each farmer tending to a scatter of strips in each field. The woodland lay to the southeast of the champion and to the northwest, covering Herefordshire, Shropshire, and stretching down to Devon. Here, settlement tended to be more scattered, with hamlets and farmhouses within more concentrated, smaller fields, farmed using less communal methods. To the north and west lay the upland zone, stretching from Northumbria, through the Pennines and central Wales, to Cornwall. The champion and woodland were dominated by arable farming, the primary purpose of livestock being to provide manure. In the poorer soils of the uplands, arable land was concentrated in the valleys since the landscape was dominated by huge moorland commons used for cattle and sheep and supporting a relatively small population.

Within these three regions, two other variations must be borne in mind. The wetlands carried their own differences due to their prolonged battles with the sea. The most famous wetlands were the Fens of East Anglia, but similar landscapes could be found in Somerset, north Lincolnshire, and elsewhere. Here, small arable patches proved very fertile and could be assisted by unstinted common rights, adding fish, wildfowl, and eels to the diet. Areas of forest, on the other hand, were defined by forest law intended to protect royal hunting. The result was not thick, uninhabited woodland but land that had certain constraints on arable practices. The forest land tended to have larger commons, scattered settlement, and small concentrations of manufacturing.

The primary change in the rural landscape was enclosure, a move from communal land to concentrated, individually owned fields—farming "in severalty." In the uplands many of the commons were enclosed, shown by dry-stone walling running across the moors. In the champion region many open fields were divided and hedged, often involving a depopulating move from arable to pastoral farming. In Wales, changes in land law transformed the system, usually in favor of new English landowners. In the proto-industrial landscape the growing iron industry can be seen in the "hammer-ponds" created to provide power to drive the bellows and mechanical hammers as in the Weald, Warwickshire, and Pembrokeshire. The transformation of the forest and fens was scarcely anticipated and the scale of the Stuart draining of the fens was unimaginable.

Although it hardly amounted to an agricultural revolution, the sixteenth century saw a substantial number of innovations in agricultural practice. In part, these were a consequence of the growing market created by a rising population. Within enclosed fields "up-and-down" husbandry was introduced. Instead of some fields being kept under regular cultivation with occasional fallows and others under permanent pasture, the roles were circulated, thus improving soil and allowing for more livestock. There were also two related changes in production. With growing urban markets, areas of specialization could emerge, especially around London, where the demand for particular vegetables could turn horticulture into agriculture. Thus, Battersea was the center for asparagus, Fulham for parsnips, and so on. Similarly, industrial demands could encourage farmers to produce flax and hemp to be sold to clothiers, incidentally providing the sources of paint, soap, and rope.

The Tudor landscape was predominantly a rural landscape, with but a fraction of the population living in what to us would be small towns. Norwich was the second largest town in 1550, with a population of 15,000. Towns tended to be much more open and more closely tied to the agricultural environment than in our experience, but this was starting to change, anticipating the urban renaissance of the following century. The primary purpose of towns was marketing, a role that was growing in importance as regional specializations interacted with improving roads in this era. In accordance with this use, a great deal of attention was paid to the architecture of the marketplace, with shops, market halls, and inns standing out as the primary sites of the exchange of goods.

Within the league of urban places, London was *sui generis*. The capital fulfilled the same exchange role as the provincial towns but with an immeasurably greater concentration of economic, judicial, and governmental interests. Its population, largely fueled by immigrants, rose from 120,000 in 1550 to 200,000 in 1600, higher in proportionate terms as well as in numbers. London could be seen as three cities. The ancient city of London in the east with its expanding suburbs was the economic focus.

L

Westminster contained judicial and political interests concentrated on the royal enclave of Whitehall, vastly expanded by Henry VIII after the fall of Thomas Wolsey. South of the river was Southwark, a growing and uncontrolled arena of theaters, brothels, and bear-baiting (and touching on the archiepiscopal palace of Lambeth).

By the end of Elizabeth's reign, England was almost a different country from that of her grandfather. The agricultural regions had changed in practice and appearance, with the upland less open and pockets of mining and manufacture emerging, the champion less dominated by open fields and with newly hedged private land preserving the patterns of plowing under newly planted grass for pasture, and the woodland of the southeast turned over to manufacturing and specialized crops to feed the London market. Towns had changed from the independence of boroughs to provide goods for the wider market and a site for the almost theatrical display of the lower gentry. London was gradually moving up the European league of cities in terms of size and significance.

BIBLIOGRAPHY
Beier, A.L., and R. Finley, eds. *London, 1500–1800*. 1986.
Crossley, David. *Post-Medieval Archaeology in Britain*. 1990.
Jack, Sybil M. *Towns in Tudor and Stuart Britain*. 1996.
Johnson, Matthew. *An Archaeology of Capitalism*. 1996.
Reed, Michael. *The Age of Exuberance, 1500–1700*. 1986.
Thirsk, Joan, ed. *The Agrarian History of England. Vol. 4: 1500–1640*. 1967.

Tom Webster

SEE ALSO
Agriculture; Economy; Enclosure; Industry and Manufacture; London; Population and Demography; Southwark; Towns

Lane, Ralph (c. 1530–1603)

Even though Ireland was the scene of most of his military career, the earliest record of Sir Ralph Lane is as the first governor of Sir Walter Ralegh's Virginia. Not much is known about Lane's activities before 1570, when he emerges as one of the purchasers of the "Carick Sidney," Sir Henry Sidney's ship. As early as 1571, Lane served as an agent of the queen, aiding in the investigation of unlawful imports. He also seems to have conducted privateering enterprises throughout the 1570s. In 1583, Lane was called on to build fortifications in Ireland,

becoming equerry of the great stable, a minor post in the royal household under the master of the horse. After two years in County Kerry, where he managed to accumulate a considerable estate, Lane was summoned to join the second New World expedition organized by Ralegh under the military command of Sir Richard Grenville and the scientific supervision of John White and Thomas Harriot. Once in Virginia—on the coast of modern North Carolina—Grenville returned to England, and Lane was left as governor of the colony with more than 100 men. After a year plagued with hardships, Lane's colony was finally rescued by Sir Francis Drake, and they returned to England on July 27, 1586. According to Lane's own record—published in Richard Hakluyt's 1589 *Principall Navigations*—the time this group of Englishmen spent in the New World was a continuous struggle against the hostile native inhabitants and the ever-present danger of starvation. Lane expresses his frustration at their failure to find valuable commodities and uses his narrative to counter criticism at home against his poor record as governor of the colony. In 1588, Lane also wrote the preface for Thomas Harriot's *A Briefe and True Report of the New Found Land of Virginia*, paradoxically a much more optimistic account of the English colonial experience in Virginia.

Between December 1587 and April 1588, Lane was employed in reviewing the county militia in East Anglia, and he also helped Ralegh and Grenville with the elaboration of a report on coastal defense. In 1589 and 1590, he took part in expeditions led by Drake and John Hawkins to the coast of Portugal. Around 1592, he reentered the Irish service as muster-master of the army in Munster, and on October 15, 1593, the lord deputy in Ireland, Sir William Fitzwilliam, knighted him in recognition for his services to the English crown. Lane spent the last ten years of his life on military affairs in Ireland, working to secure English possessions against the Irish rebels. He died in October 1603 and was buried in St. Patrick's Church, Dublin.

BIBLIOGRAPHY
Andrews, Kenneth R. *Trade, Plunder and Settlement: Maritime Enterprise and the Genesis of the British Empire, 1480–1630*. 1984.
Fuller, Mary C. *Voyages in Print: English Travel to America, 1576–1624*. 1995.
Hakluyt, Richard. *The Principall Navigations, Voyages, and Discoveries of the English Nation*. 1589. 2nd edition 1598–1600; repr., 12 vols., 1903–1905.

Harriot, Thomas. *A Briefe and True Report of the New Found Land of Virginia.* 1588; Facsimile. 1903.

Quinn, David B. *The Elizabethans and the Irish.* 1966.

———. *The Roanoke Voyages, 1584–1590.* 1955.

Francisco J. Borge

SEE ALSO

Colonial Development; Drake, Francis; Grenville, Richard; Hakluyt, Richard; Harriot, Thomas; Hawkins, John; Ralegh, Walter; Sidney, Henry

Language, History of

Middle English, known largely to modern readers through Chaucer, is recognizably English at a very much earlier stage than its present state. As long ago as 1580, Sir Philip Sidney, in *An Apologie for Poetrie,* expressed a sense of a vast linguistic distance between his generation of writers and Chaucer, their most revered English ancestor, marveling that he "in that mistie time could see so clearly. . . . Yet had he great wants, fitte to be forgiuen in so reuerent antiquity." The chief of those "wants" was thought to be metrical, since Elizabethans had already forgotten that in earlier pronunciation the final *e* was a heard syllable. Even so, while English had by Tudor times passed through the major shifts from Old English, many more limited changes were still taking place in all dimensions of the language. This means that English was in a state of transition, as it always is, but vestiges of the old and the rapid introduction of the new were more noticeable than has been true since the later seventeenth century, by which time linguistic standards were largely in place.

Old English grammatical inflections had virtually disappeared, but some were still in process of changing. Examples are transformation of *thou* and *ye,* pronouns originally denoting singular and plural, into marks to distinguish intimate from formal address; overlapping of the old genitive *es, is, ys* with *his,* making phrases like *Mars his heart;* confusions between *his,* earlier used for neuter as well as masculine possessives, and the newly introduced *its* (faintly suggesting personification); the gradual restriction of the relative pronoun *which* to things, where once it was also used for persons (blurring distinctions between animate and inanimate beings). Much more significant is the fact that the disappearance of inflections allowed writers to try out the expressive effects of shifting words among different grammatical relations (prevented in Old English by inflections). Shakespeare used as intransitive verbs such adjectives as *happy, false, honest, mad* ("to be

disturb'd, would mad or man or beast," bringing together the causal act and its effect); such nouns as *child, fever, witch, tongue* ("how might she tongue me," figuring the physicality of speech).

Punctuation in this fluid stage of English supported the flexibility made possible by its grammar. What few marks they had were the full stop or period; the colon; the question mark; and the virgule or oblique stroke, gradually being replaced by the comma. Since they were thought of mainly as marks of "breathing" or pauses—suggesting that reading aloud was conceived as the standard practice—they were themselves used irregularly or were easily ignored. Such freedoms invited expressive ambiguities, as in two lines from Shakespeare's Sonnet 129 as it was first printed: "Had, hauing, and in quest, to haue extreme" (typically read now in modernized texts as "Had, having, and in quest to have, extreme"); and "Before a ioy proposd behind a dreame" (modernized "Before, a joy proposed, behind, a dream"). Similarly multiple readings also arose from the absence of quotation marks and of apostrophes for possessives.

Spelling, with its mixed-up relation to pronunciation, was in a state of much greater disorderliness widely recognized and deplored by sixteenth-century writers of language. With the help of printing, Tudor English hardened into convention many antiquated spellings that had ceased to represent pronunciation as spelling was theoretically supposed to do: for instance, the consonants no longer sounded in *night, through, knife, gnat.* Other words were spelled more nearly as they were pronounced, but pronunciation even by the end of the century had not been standardized, so that regional differences showed up, especially in the choice of vowels. This variety supplied writers with the possibilities of double meanings no longer available in standardized modern spelling. Some favorites among poets were: *hart/heart; sonne/sunne; travell/travaile.* All of these inconsistencies in spelling and punctuation encouraged in writers, printers, and their readers a general indifference to consistency, so that in Shakespeare's Sonnet 18 as first printed, the same word could be spelled one way in the first line, another in line 4: "Summers day" and "Sommers lease." Printers sometimes exploited the prevailing acceptance of inconsistent spellings to compensate for shortages of type or to justify (end flush right) line endings.

The transitional state of Tudor English is most vivid in its vocabulary. Many old words survived, for instance *rood* for the *cross, crossrow* for the *alphabet.* Some were revived by English purists like Sir John Cheke, who

L

brought back *mooned* for *lunatic,* and by lovers of archaic-sounding words with a Chaucerian aura such as Edmund Spenser, who liked to write *bellibone* for *fair young woman.* Still other old words survived, but shifted semantic range: *religion,* earlier the term for the observation of rites, became synonymous with belief. At the same time, various potent cultural changes contributed to the absorption of vast numbers of new words: the spread of printing, bringing more books within reach of more readers, not all of whom knew Latin; the revival of classical learning, encouraging vernacular translations of Latin and Greek writings; the Protestant emphasis on Bible reading and interpretation; the increase in foreign travel and trade. Many of the imported words have become so entrenched that it is hard to imagine how English got along without them. Some examples are from Latin: *relaxation, imitation, invitation, frequent;* from French *entrance, appropriate, insane, explore.* Other borrowings considered pedantic raised outcries against so-called inkhorn terms; Gabriel Harvey objected to such words as "Ingenuitie," "artificiallitie," and "negotiation," and to phrases like "Conscious mind" and "addicted to Theory." While this rapid absorption of richly mixed words added to the vagaries of spelling and of other linguistic dimensions, it also contributed to the energy and excitement that characterizes much sixteenth-century writing.

The vigorous blend of preservation and novelty that constituted the changing state of Tudor English encouraged a new self-consciousness about the English language (the earliest extant English grammar was printed in 1586, the earliest dictionary of English words in 1604) and a growing national pride in its state and reputation. The first book printed in English, c. 1475, William Caxton's translation from French of the *Recuyell of the Historyes of Troye,* contained his apology for the state of "symple and rude englissh" contrasted with "the fayr language of frenshe." In 1595, Richard Carew challenged the supremacy of Latin and Greek authors in *The Excellencie of the English Tongue* by holding high "the miracle of our age Sir *Philip Sydney*" for embodying "all in all for prose and verse."

BIBLIOGRAPHY

Barber, Charles. *Early Modern English.* 1976.
Ferry, Anne. *The Art of Naming.* 1988.
Jespersen, Otto. *Growth and Structure of the English Language.* 9th edition. 1982.
Partridge, A.C. *Tudor to Augustan English.* 1966.

Anne Ferry

SEE ALSO

Carew, Richard; Caxton, William; Classical Literature, English Translations; Dictionaries; Education; Harvey, Gabriel; Humanism; Literacy; Printing; Reading Practices; Rhetoric; Shakespeare, William; Sidney, Philip

Latimer, Hugh (c. 1485–1555)

The outstanding homiletic genius of the English reformation, Hugh Latimer was born into humble rural circumstances in the village of Thurcaston, Leicestershire. He studied at Cambridge, taking his B.A. and becoming a fellow of Clare Hall in 1510. The university licensed him to preach, but, through the influence of "little [Thomas] Bilney," "or rather Saint Bilney," he "forsook the schooldoctors and such fooleries" and adopted Protestant principles. In 1525, his refusal to preach against Martin Luther led to conflict with Cardinal Thomas Wolsey, and in 1532, he was censured by convocation. When Thomas Cranmer became archbishop of Canterbury, Latimer returned to favor, and in 1535, he was appointed bishop of Worcester. Unable to comply with Henry VIII's attempt to halt the process of reform through the Six Articles, he resigned in 1539, and, following a year's imprisonment in the Tower, he was forbidden to preach. In 1546, he was again imprisoned, but was released on the accession of Edward VI, before whom, even though he refused to return to the episcopal bench, he preached regularly. On Mary I's accession in 1553 he was committed to the Tower. In 1554, in the company of Nicholas Ridley and Cranmer, he was sent to Oxford to answer charges of heresy. The next year he was martyred by burning, his witness being immortalized by John Foxe in his *Book of Martyrs,* which has Latimer say, approaching the pyre: "Be of good comfort, master Ridley, and play the man. We shall this day light such a candle, by God's grace in England, as I trust shall never be put out."

For Latimer, Christian ministry was above all else a matter of preaching: "Take away preaching, and take away salvation" he declared. He understood preaching to be the subject of the parable of the sower (Luke 8) and took Luke 9:62 to refer not (as traditionally glossed) to "monkery" but to "diligent preaching of the word of God." Neglect of his office was for him a signal mark of unreformed Christianity: "Paul was no sitting bishop, but a walking and a preaching bishop." The concern of Latimer's sermons to awaken his hearers from the spiritual torpor of unthinking formalism is characteristically Protestant, but the socially and politically disturbing

A table deſcribing the burning of biſhop Ridley and father Latimer at Oxford, D. Smith there preaching at the time of their ſuffering.

Si corp⁹ meũ tradam igni caritatẽ autẽ non habeĩ nihil vtilitatis⁹ &c.

Smith.

Latimer. Ridley. In man⁹ tuas domine

Father of heuẽ receũ my ſoule

My. Ridley I wil remember your ſuite.

L. Williã

John Foxe, *The Burning of Bishops Hugh Latimer and Nicholas Ridley.* From *Actes and Monuments of these latter and perillous dayes,* 1563. This famous illustration records the burning of Latimer and Ridley in October 1555, outside Balliol College, Oxford. Present was Thomas Cranmer, who would soon follow them to the stake. Reproduced from the original by permission of the Henry E. Huntington Library and Art Gallery

thrust of their excoriating attacks on the worldliness of bishops, the moral turpitude of the court, the corruption of the judicial system, and the oppression of the poor by the rich is distinctively his. What fires his sermons is not the challenge of explaining doctrine but outrage at an oppressive and exploitative system. This can sound radical

notes: "The poorest ploughman is in Christ equal with the greatest prince that is." He was untroubled that such sentiments brought him into conflict with church and state, for, on the authority of the Old Testament prophets and of Jesus himself ("noted to be a stirrer up of the people against the emperor; and . . . contented to be called

L

seditious"), he argued that preaching was inevitably politically engaged and subversive. To distance himself from the ecclesiastical and state authorities who are his target, Latimer adopts the persona of the outsider, a poor countryman, whose manner has nothing of the learning of the schools or the sophistication of the court about it. He is a fund of anecdotes, autobiographical reminiscences, stories, gossip, and news, all recounted in a colloquial, unbuttoned style. His sermons are digressive and formless: the language of authentic Christian commitment is demotic, unruly, apparently unpremeditated.

Latimer's sermons were collected by his devoted servant Augustine Bernher and published by him in successively enlarged editions in 1562, 1571–1572, and 1578. The forty-four extant sermons were published by the Parker Society in two volumes in 1844–1845.

BIBLIOGRAPHY

Blench, J.W. *Preaching in England in the Late Fifteenth and Sixteenth Centuries.* 1964.

Chester, Allan G. *Hugh Latimer, Apostle to the English.* 1954.

Darby, Harold S. *Hugh Latimer.* 1954.

Loades, D.M. *The Oxford Martyrs.* 1970.

N.H. Keeble

SEE ALSO

Articles of Religion; Bilney, Thomas; Convocation; Cranmer, Thomas; Foxe, John; Heresy; Marian Martyrs; Reformation, English; Sermons; Wolsey, Thomas

Law, Canon

Canon law is the law of the church. Although it had roots in antiquity, the canon law applied in later medieval England was the product of the Gregorian reform movement and the scholarly Renaissance of the twelfth century. Its basic texts were found in the *Corpus iuris canonici,* a multivolume collection that contained the *Decretum Gratiani* (c. 1140), the *Decretales* of Pope Gregory IX (1234), the *Liber sextus* of Pope Boniface VIII (1298), and a few smaller, later collections of the canons of church councils and papal decretals. It was coupled with the Roman law to create what is called the *ius commune,* and with the Roman law it was extensively commented on by medieval jurists in works of juristic detail and ingenuity often ridiculed by sixteenth-century humanists for their repetition and pedantry. The canon law was taught in English universities, and it was applied in the courts of the church and also in some measure in courts of equity. Its procedure differed from that of the English common law in several ways, most obviously in its sophisticated law of evidence and lack of trial by jury.

In practice, the church's law governed significant areas of English life in the Tudor period and beyond. Marriage and divorce, defamation, tithes and ecclesiastical taxation, last wills and testaments, and large numbers of "morals offenses" fell under the jurisdiction of ecclesiastical courts. Henry VIII's divorce from Katherine of Aragon, for example, was heard under the canon law, although the actual sentence went contrary to the decision of the papacy. Wide-ranging jurisdiction over the laity thus existed in addition to regulation of the clergy and supervision of matters of religious dissent such as heresy and blasphemy.

Since most of the canon law was contained in papal decisions and since it included many texts that stressed the authority of the papacy, it seems natural that it should have been swept aside in Protestant England. There is some support in the historical record for this supposition. Building on developments that began in the 1480s, the royal courts interfered more frequently in the exercise of ecclesiastical jurisdiction than they had earlier. The canon law faculties at Oxford and Cambridge were abolished under Henry VIII and not revived; only the civil law faculty remained. The authority of the canon law was made subject to parliamentary statutes, the customs of the realm, and the king's prerogative rights. It was also subjected to bitter attacks from many quarters, including arguments that it be abolished and its jurisdiction transferred to the temporal courts. There was also a serious proposal that it be replaced in toto by a new compilation, called the *Reformatio Legum Ecclesiasticarum,* that was produced by a royal commission.

In the end, however, the canon law managed to maintain a large share of its authority in England. The *Reformatio* was not adopted. No statute was passed to restrict spiritual jurisdiction in any serious way. The civilians (as the lawyers who practiced in the courts of the church and Admiralty were called) managed to maintain their traditional contacts with the learned world of the continental *ius commune.* And the increasing stability of the Elizabethan regime allowed the courts of the church to survive largely intact. Although it is sometimes said, not without reason, that England has produced no great canonists, sixteenth-century civilians like Henry Swinburne, Francis Clerke, and Richard Cosin wrote works on the law of the English church that made a real contribution to the preservation of canonical learning in England.

BIBLIOGRAPHY

Helmholz, R.H. *Roman Canon Law in Reformation England.* 1990.

Kemp, E.W. *An Introduction to Canon Law in the Church of England.* 1957.

R.H. Helmholz

SEE ALSO

Courts, Ecclesiastical; Law, Common; *Reformation Legum Ecclesiasticarum*

Law, Civil

Civil law was practiced in the conciliar, equity, and ecclesiastical courts. Derived from Roman civil law, it evolved in England through the ecclesiastical courts and the Chancery, where ecclesiastical chancellors used it to supplement the common law of the central courts and the customary law of local ones. Under the Tudors, civil law spread to the conciliar courts of the counties palatine of Lancaster, Durham, and Chester, to the equity courts of Admiralty and Requests, and to the prerogative court of Star Chamber. Henry VIII promoted the teaching and practice of civil law, and some members of his council had a desire to see it expand at the expense of common law. While these ideas were short-lived, regius professorships of civil law were created at Oxford and Cambridge; new conciliar courts of Augmentations, and Wards and Liveries, were established with civil law process in 1536 and 1540 to administer new royal lands; the High Commission was created in 1559 as an ecclesiastical counterpart to Star Chamber for high crimes against the church; and throughout the century the civil law process of Chancery, Requests, and Star Chamber expanded greatly.

Codified for Rome, civil law had developed in England as part of the universal Catholic Church. Taught in the universities with masters and doctoral degrees, civil lawyers (civilians) were prominent in both secular and religious society. In 1511, the civilians formed a society, and in 1565, they incorporated their own Inn of Court named Doctors' Commons. Benefiting from the growth of a litigious society in Elizabeth's reign, they filled the ranks of practitioners in the prerogative, conciliar, and equity courts. However, once the common law profession overexpanded by the turn of the century, civilians and common lawyers waged a bitter war of attrition that did not end until the abolition of the prerogative and conciliar courts in the 1640s.

The procedure and substance of the civil law underwent considerable change in the course of the sixteenth century, especially in courts of equity. Civil law was "written" law. Its substance was developed for each individual court, and procedure was its unifying element. Suits were commenced by "bills," simple statements in English of the claims or wrongs alleged. Defendants made "answers," where they denied or counterclaimed. Plaintiffs responded with "replications" and defendants replied with "rejoinders." Once the issue was joined in these written pleadings, the court's clerks devised interrogatories to examine parties and relevant witnesses. The depositions sworn provided the evidence for the court to make its judgement. An increasing professionalization of civil law in the sixteenth century led to more polished pleadings. By the 1590s, the writing of dictionaries, treatises, and law reports developed precedents modeling civil law along common law forms of evidence. Thus, by the early seventeenth century, courts of equity were considered by some to have a status comparable to common law, and elements of civil law practice were influencing the common law.

BIBLIOGRAPHY

Barton, J.L. *St. German's Doctor and Student.* Selden Society. Vol. 91. 1974.

Helmholz, R.H. *Roman Canon Law in Reformation England.* 1974.

Kemp, Eric Waldram. *An Introduction to Canon Law in the Church of England.* 1957.

Levack, Brian. *The Civil Lawyers in England, 1603–1641.* 1973.

Pritchard, M.J., and D.E.C. Yale, eds. *Hale and Fleetwood on Admiralty Jurisdiction.* Selden Society. Vol. 108. 1993.

Louis A. Knafla

SEE ALSO

Canon Law; Chancery; Law, Common; Courts, Ecclesiastical; Government, Central Administration of; High Commission, Court of; Inns of Court; Lawyers; Star Chamber, Court of; Wards, Court of

Law, Common

By the reign of Henry VII, the three central common law courts of Kings's Bench, Common Pleas, and Exchequer had at least a century of development as independent courts situated in Westminster Hall, Middlesex. The term

L

"common law," however, was not always used in such a strict sense. The main floor of the hall housed the Chancery as well as King's Bench and Common Pleas; chambers beyond it upstairs housed the courts of Exchequer, duchy of Lancaster, and Star Chamber; and beyond that was the White Hall, which housed the courts of Requests, and Wards and Liveries. Thus common and civil law courts functioned alongside one another. While each court had its own licensed "bar" of barristers, attorneys and solicitors roamed the hallways advising clients of the opportunities that lay before them for the litigation of their causes.

According to Sir John Davies, the common law was nothing more than a secular "common course" of suing in the customary courts of England, central or local. The central courts of common law, moreover, were also represented in the countryside with commissions of *nisi prius* for civil causes and of jail delivery for criminal ones, both of which were presided over by common law judges riding on the assize circuits. Indeed, common law procedure was incorporated into the framework of local courts that heard the same civil and criminal suits, albeit of lesser values, in county and borough quarter sessions, and town courts. In this regard, the common law can be seen as "English" law derived from customs that originated at least from Anglo-Saxon times, and adjudicated by a common course of hearing disputes.

Technically, however, the term common law had a very specific meaning for the barristers, clerks, and judges who comprised the common law courts. It referred to actions instigated by Latin writs according to set forms issued by the Chancery, pleadings made in Law French, and notes of all motions and proceedings recorded in Latin on plea rolls made of sheepskin. While the common law courts had drawn upon, and incorporated, matters from local, customary courts, "common lawyers" were quite jealous of their precedence and alleged antiquity. This was due to the fact that common lawyers were educated at the Inns of Court and of Chancery located in the adjoining borough of Holborn. These common law schools had established their independence, and monopoly of common law education, in the fourteenth century. Only their graduates were eligible to practice before these courts or to serve on their benches as well as at their bars.

In civil actions, the procedures involved laying an original writ, pleading the issue, finding the burden of proof, and giving judgment. The original writs prescribed the form of action required for each party to pursue a claim, and the evidence was pleaded in court orally by barristers who had been admitted to its practice. The courts, however, were open only during the four legal terms of winter, spring, summer, and autumn, which were approximately a month each. Mesne writs were available to excuse one's absence and delay proceedings significantly. The purpose of pleading was to reduce the case to a single point on which judgment would be given. The major forms of proof were wager of law, which was predominant in Common Pleas, and trial by jury, prominent in King's Bench. Since juries were difficult to organize in London for parties from the distant countryside, many cases were dismissed to be heard in their locality by local juries in commissions of *nisi prius*. This enabled influence and corruption to assist in the resolution of disputes. Judgments were given by the bench, which prided itself on identifying and following the ancient precedents of the law available in manuscript copies of year books.

The sixteenth century witnessed major changes in civil actions at common law. With regard to the writs, the King's Bench authored the advent of the "legal fiction," which offered parties better remedies than the Common Pleas. Plaintiffs, in the course of the century, were able to allege quasi-criminal circumstances to use the criminal action of trespass in King's Bench for civil actions concerning personal and real property. Trespass allowed claims for damages, a swifter process, and jury trials for proof. This enabled King's Bench to move from a superior court with a light calendar to one of the busiest courts in the country, and common law courts to expand at the expense of local ones. It also led to parties filing alternative and cross-suits in other courts, bringing common law courts into conflict with courts of equity that used Roman civil law procedure, and ecclesiastical courts using Roman canon law procedure. By 1603, the attorneys and solicitors who flogged such suits were being mocked as "pettyfoggers and vipers of the commonwealth," and the legal system as a whole was being accused of sponsoring "frivolous litigation" to line its pockets.

With regard to pleading, written pleadings began to replace oral ones during the reign of Henry VIII. First, this enabled pleadings to become much longer, and therefore more costly for the litigants. Second, it also allowed errors to be more decisive, as an error in fact could be demurred with the whole case hinging on the resolution of that fact. Third, wager of law became professionalized with compurgators (hired to testify) readily available outside Westminster Hall, thereby bringing disrepute to this method of proof. The advent of written pleadings, however, brought a qualitative element to the

Portrait of Henry VIII by Hans Holbein the Younger (1497–1543). Galleria Nazionale d'Arte Antica, Rome. Courtesy Scala/Art Resource, N.Y.

Lucas de Heere (1534–1584), *The Family of Henry VIII : An Allegory of the Tudor Succession*, c. 1570–1575 (panel). Sudeley Castle, Gloucestershire. Courtesy The Bridgeman Art Library.

Portrait of three Tudor children. Rafael Valls Gallery, London.
Courtesy The Bridgeman Art Library.

Travel cutlery and bag of Queen Elizabeth I. Alnwick Castle, Alnwick, Great Britain. Photograph © Erich Lessing. Courtesy Art Resource, N.Y.

Funeral procession of Queen Elizabeth I in 1603. Anonymous, sixteenth century. British Museum, London. Courtesy Art Resource, N.Y.

Federic Zuccaro (1540–1609). Portrait of Elizabeth I of England. Pinacoteca Nazionale, Siena, Italy.
Courtesy Scala/Art Resource, N.Y.

law. In the early Tudor period, the increasing number of demurrers enabled such cases to be handled more expeditiously, and sparked a literature on the land law. And in the late Tudor period, motions of *non obstante* and special verdicts allowed the development of trespass actions on the case that gave rise to new doctrines of contract law (assumpsit). By 1600, facts were pleaded first, motions came at the end, and as in modern law substance now controlled procedure.

Finally, with regard to judgment, the old year books began to be printed in the reign of Henry VII, making precedents of pleading more readily available. In the reign of Elizabeth I, the new "modern report" emerged in printed form in both Latin and English translation. Focusing more on precedents for legal issues than for pleading, this new and expanding legal literature gave the common lawyer profession a richer body of information on which to build and rebuild legal precedent. Books of entries were being written for forms and guides to good pleading, and legal treatises published on specialty branches of the law. Altogether, the century witnessed a legal renaissance in the practice and learning of the common law, of which the first part of Sir Edward Coke's thirteen volumes of reports in 1600 marked the dawn of the modern era.

The criminal side of the common law changed just as dramatically in the course of the century. The consolidation of county government under the rural gentry enabled the assize justices to hold their commissions of jail delivery on a consistent, semiannual basis. The spreading authority of the Tudor monarchy gave power to the sheriffs, clerks, and justices of the peace to enforce writs of arrest, the rebuilding of county jails, imprisonment for trial, and the summoning of witnesses and juries for the prosecution of alleged offenders. Moreover, assize judges sharpened the procedure of their courts in a way that allowed them to dispose of most criminal cases in less than ten minutes each by the end of the century. Tudor statutes, from Henry VIII through Elizabeth, increased the rigor of the criminal law by giving increased powers to officials, creating new criminal offenses, and expanding the crimes subject to capital punishment. Like the civil side, collections of criminal statutes and laws were published, treatises composed on the duties and responsibilities of officials and justices, and a jurisprudence began to develop that articulated a conceptual development of the criminal side of the common law.

The common law was under attack from the civil law in the 1530s, as Henry VIII's Privy Council demonstrated a preference for civil law procedures and the ideology of a law that was more beholden to the monarch. This attack was short-lived. Changes in common law procedures, the expansion of the forms of action, the assimilation of local customs, and a movement away from continental European institutions to a revival of native traditions enabled the common law to emerge as one of England's distinct institutions by the end of the century. It meant, however, that law reform would never occur from outside the institution. Firmly in the hands of its practitioners, the common law would guard its ground jealously and evolve from within rather than from without.

BIBLIOGRAPHY

Baker, J.H. *The Legal Profession and the Common Law.* 1986.

———. *The Reports of Sir John Spelman.* Selden Society. Vols. 93–94. 1976–1977.

Brooks, C.W. *Pettyfoggers and Vipers of the Commonwealth: the "Lower Branch" of the Legal Profession in Early Modern England.* 1986.

Cockburn, J.S. *A History of English Assizes, 1558–1714.* 1972.

Ives, E.W. *The Common Lawyers in Pre-Reformation England.* 1983.

Prest, Wilfrid R. *The Inns of Court under Elizabeth I and the Early Stuarts, 1590–1640.* 1972.

Louis A. Knafla

SEE ALSO

Chancery; Crime; Coke, Edward; Common Pleas, Court of; Courts, Ecclesiastical; Davies, John; Exchequer; Government, Central Administration of; Henry VII; Henry VIII; Inns of Court; Justice of the Peace; King's or Queen's Bench, Court of; Law, Civil; Sheriff; Star Chamber, Court of; Wards, Court of

Lawyers

Lawyers in sixteenth-century England were such a varied group that it is disputable whether they should be accounted a profession. The common lawyers were the largest and most flourishing group. They had acquired a powerful institutional base in the key central courts of King's Bench, Common Pleas, and the Exchequer, and judges from these courts toured the country on the twice-yearly assizes. The civil lawyers comprised the advocates, proctors, and judges in ecclesiastical courts or in the court of Admiralty. Their prestige suffered in the Tudor period

L

as a result of the Reformation, and challenges to their jurisdiction from the common lawyers.

But there was a high degree of differentiation among the practitioners of both the common and the civil law. At the head of each group were high-status practitioners. Among the civil lawyers, the university-trained doctors of civil law served in the archbishop's court in London and before the high courts of Admiralty and chivalry, and enjoyed their own exclusive social facility in London, the Doctor's Commons. At the pinnacle of the common law were the serjeants-at-law appointed by royal writ who enjoyed the monopoly right to plead before the Court of Common Pleas and from among whom the judges were chosen. Below them, and also enjoying an elite status among practitioners, were the apprentices, men who had reached the higher ranks of the Inns of Court, fully fledged advocates below the degree of serjeant. While it is true that the distinction between the upper and lower branches of the profession was not as developed as it was to become in the following century (it was only in 1591 that the judges ruled that only those admitted to the degree of utter-barrister should enjoy the right of audience), there was a broad (and growing) distinction between the high-status groups and the proctors and attorneys at the lower levels, who saw litigation through its various stages in the common law and civil law courts, respectively. Practitioners in this latter group were more likely to have acquired their knowledge through legal practice (especially as clerks, or service with another practitioner) rather than formal training. Thus, whereas at the upper ranks the Inns of Court retained tight control over access to legal practice, at the lower levels the key to practice was being a sworn officer of a particular court.

Some local practitioners enjoyed connections with the royal courts in London, or with the Inns of Court, but many did not. Those who held local manorial courts as stewards were often local landowners with a smattering of legal expertise, or men who had been trained through service in a magnate household. Urban courts often provided a venue for legal practice by men who lacked metropolitan connections. Other legal services were offered by scriveners, who would draw up legal instruments like bonds for debt, mortgages, conveyances, and indentures, overlapping in their functions with attorneys. Over the course of the period the semi-professional provincial practitioners were increasingly displaced by attorneys with London connections. This reflected a number of developments: the growth of central court litigation (the number of cases in King's Bench increased four-fold between 1560 and 1580); the policy of the judiciary (which insisted that only lawyers attached to the central courts should become involved in the new business); and the growing sense of vocational pride among the London lawyers who attacked the ignorant and unlearned.

The enormous expansion in litigation over the century fueled an increase in the number of legal practitioners. Admissions to the Inns of Court grew from about fifty per annum in 1500 to 300 per annum in the 1620s. Although many of these were not committed to a legal career, there was an increase in the number of students called to the bar, from less than 100 in the 1560s to more than 400 in the 1590s. Whereas there were about 200 attorneys attached to the central courts of King's Bench and Common Pleas in 1500, by 1600 there were 1,000. The number of pleaders in Westminster Hall increased from between 80 and 150 in 1500 to between 400 and 450 in the 1630s.

There was an increasing polarization between the upper and lower ranks of legal practitioners in the sixteenth century. Because of the role of the Inns of Court as finishing schools for the gentry, they adopted policies designed to enhance their social exclusiveness. Attorneys were excluded from the Inns, and attorneys and solicitors were prohibited from being called to the bar. This was matched by the decision of Doctor's Commons in 1570 to exclude proctors from its ranks. Nevertheless, the practice of the law remained an important social escalator. It has been estimated that probably no more than 50 percent of those called to the bar in the later sixteenth century were recruited from gentry backgrounds, and if anything, the bar was both bigger and more socially variegated in 1600 than it had been a century earlier or, indeed, a century later.

Lawyers were ubiquitous in Tudor England. The major government departments such as the Exchequer were courts; the key points of contact between local and central government were the assize courts; and the counties were administered through the courts held by the justices of the peace. Studies of local jurisdictions have revealed the extraordinarily broad social range of litigants, and a high level of popular participation in jury service. Legal values therefore permeated popular culture, and the medium of most disputes was legalistic. This explains much of the ambivalence of popular attitudes toward lawyers, seen both as parasites promoting quarrels for their own financial gain, and as the providers of essential services to their communities.

BIBLIOGRAPHY

Brooks, C.W. *Pettyfoggers and Vipers of the Common-wealth: the "Lower Branch" of the Legal Profession in Early Modern England.* 1986.

Ives, E.W. *The Common Lawyers of Pre-Reformation England.* 1983.

Prest, Wilfrid, ed. *The Common Lawyers in Early Modern Europe and America.* 1981.

———. *The Rise of the Barristers: A Social History of the English Bar, 1590–1640.* 1986.

Ian W. Archer

SEE ALSO

Common Pleas, Court of; Exchequer; Inns of Court; Law, Civil; Law, Common; Justice of the Peace; King's or Queen's Bench, Court of

Leicester, Earl of

See Dudley, Robert

Leland, John (c. 1503–1551)

Library keeper to Henry VIII, John Leland envisioned and began a project to catalogue antiquities throughout England and Wales; he also produced a substantial body of Latin poetry. Born in London sometime between 1503 and 1506, Leland was educated at St. Paul's School, where he studied under schoolmaster William Lily and may have met Desiderius Erasmus, and at Christ's College, Cambridge, from which he took a B.A. in 1521–1522. He then held a position as tutor to the sixth son of Thomas Howard, second duke of Norfolk. After Howard's death in 1524, Leland continued his studies at Oxford, perhaps at All Soul's. After leaving Oxford, he traveled to Paris where he lived for about three years, studying under Francis Sylvius and associating with a group of eminent humanists including Guillaume Budé, Paolo Emilio, Jacques LeFèvre D'Etaples, and Jean Ruel. Around 1529, Leland returned to England permanently. He held several positions in the church and seems to have associated with the humanists John Colet, William Grocyn, Thomas Linacre, and Thomas More.

By 1530, Leland had been appointed library keeper to Henry VIII. Although he did not, as some scholars have argued, hold the official position of "king's antiquary," Leland did consider himself an antiquary and used his appointment to begin an historical work that catalogued not only the manuscript remains of Britain's past but also the archaeological remains—including artifacts, coins, and inscriptions—and organized them by county. Probably the first to envision such a project, Leland valued not only the Roman past but also the Celtic and Anglo-Saxon, emphasizing the need to study the languages and artifacts of these cultures as well. From around 1534 to 1543, Leland traveled extensively throughout the kingdom, making detailed notes on topography, significant architectural sites, archaeological remains, and manuscript holdings. After the dissolution of the monasteries, Leland also procured significant manuscripts for the Royal Library.

Leland's work led him into a quarrel with Polydore Vergil over the historicity of King Arthur. In the *Anglica historia,* first printed in 1534, Vergil had attacked the Arthur stories as inaccurate. Leland responded with a defense of the historicity of Arthur, writing, in about 1536, the *Codrus sive laus et defensio Gallofridi Arturii contra Polydorum Vergilium,* originally a chapter in his *Commentarii de Scriptoribus Britannicis,* and later a more fully developed version of the argument in his *Assertio inclytissimi Arturii regis Britanniae* (1544). Although modern scholarship does not support his position, Leland became one of the first scholars to employ modern techniques. He relied not only on the authority of manuscripts but also on etymologies and archaeological remains. Moreover, the *Assertio* remained popular throughout the sixteenth century, influencing, among other works, Edmund Spenser's *The Faerie Queene* and Michael Drayton's *Poly-Olbion.*

Also a poet, Leland wrote many Latin poems, although most were not published in his lifetime. Leland's stay in Paris was particularly productive. His most significant poems include *Naeniae in mortem Thomae Viati* (1542), commemorating the death of Thomas Wyatt, whom Leland knew; *Genethliacon . . . Eaduerdi principis Cambriae* (written in 1537, first published in 1543) to celebrate the birth of Edward VI; and *Cygnia cantio* (first published in 1545), a celebration of the Thames and the master of Greenwich palace, Henry VIII.

Leland became insane in 1547, and the Privy Council entrusted him to the care of his brother; he died in 1552. Although Leland was unable to finish his antiquarian work during his lifetime, it served as a model for—as well as provided much material for—Camden's *Britannia,* which continued to be read well into the eighteenth century. A collection of more than 250 poems, edited by the poet Thomas Newton, was printed in 1589. Thomas Hearne first published both Leland's *Itinerary* (9 vols., 1710–1712) and *Collectanea* (6 vols., 1715).

L

BIBLIOGRAPHY

Carley, James P. "John Leland in Paris." *Studies in Philology*, vol. 83, pp. 1–50.

———. "Polydore Vergil and John Leland on King Arthur: The Battle of the Books." *Interpretations*, vol. 15, pp. 86–100.

Leland, John. *The Itinerary of John Leland in or about the Years 1535–1543*. Lucy Toulmin Smith, ed. 5 vols. 1907–1910; repr. 1964.

Levine, Joseph M. "The Antiquarian Enterprise, 1500–1800." In *Humanism and History: Origins of Modern English Historiography*, pp. 73–106. 1987.

Ross, Trevor. "Dissolution and the Making of the English Literary Canon: The Catalogues of Leland and Bale." *Renaissance and Reformation*, vol. 15, pp. 57–80.

Barclay Green

SEE ALSO

Antiquarianism; Arthurian Legend; Book Ownership; Camden, William; History, Writing of; Humanism; Lily, William; Neo-Latin Literature; Vergil, Polydore

Leslie, John (1527–1596)

Bishop of Ross, John Leslie was born on September 29, 1527, in Kinguissie, Iverness-shire, and graduated M.A. from King's College, Aberdeen. In 1549, he went to Paris to study theology, and then to Poitiers to study canon and civil law, returning in 1554 to Scotland. In 1558, he was ordained priest and inducted into the parsonage, canonry, and prebend of Oyne. He strongly opposed the Reformation, and in 1561 took part in a disputation at Edinburgh with John Knox and other Reformers. Later that year, after the death of Francis II, Leslie was commissioned by northern Scottish nobles to go to France to invite Mary Queen of Scots to assume the throne of Scotland as a Catholic sovereign.

In 1562, he was appointed professor of canon law in King's College at Aberdeen, and chosen a member of the Privy Council in 1565. In February 1566, he was made abbot of Lindores, and in April he was confirmed as bishop of Ross. Leslie had become the queen's chief adviser both in ecclesiastical policy and personal matters, and through all the convuluted events of her reign he remained unswervingly faithful to her cause. After Mary's flight to England and her imprisonment in 1569, she appointed him as her ambassador to Elizabeth I to negotiate her release and restoration to the throne; he was simultaneously engaged in various Scottish and foreign intrigues on her behalf.

In 1571, Leslie was imprisoned at Ely and then in the Tower for complicity in the Ridolfi Plot, which projected the marriage of Mary with the duke of Norfolk. On his release, he went to Paris in 1574, and to Rome the following year. In 1578, he published at Rome *De Origine, Moribus, et Rebus Gestis Scotorum*. That same year he departed for Paris. In 1579, he was appointed suffragan bishop and vicar-general of Rouen, and in 1593, bishop of Coutances in Normandy. Unable because of unsettled political conditions to reach his last diocese, he spent his last years at a monastery of Augustinian Canons at Guirtenburg, near Brussels, where he died May 30, 1596.

BIBLIOGRAPHY

Donaldson, Gordon. *The Scottish Reformation*. 1960.

Ross, John. *Narratives of the Progress of Events: Catholics under Mary Stuart and James VI*. 2 vols. 1888–1895.

Lee W. Gibbs

SEE ALSO

Knox, John; Mary Queen of Scots; Ridolfi Plot

Levant Company

See Joint Stock Companies; Regulated Companies

Liberties

See Government, Local; London

Lily, William (c. 1468–1522)

Humanist teacher and grammarian, William Lily was born in Odiham, Hampshire, the godson of William Grocyn. In 1486, he entered Magdalen College, Oxford; there is no record of his having received a degree. Perhaps in 1488 Lily traveled to the Mediterranean. He went on a pilgrimage to Jerusalem and spent time at Rhodes, where he studied Greek. In 1490, he was at Rome, where he attended the lectures of Pomponius Laetus and Giovanni Sulpizio. He may have returned to England by 1492, when a William Lily was presented to the rectory of Holcot in Northamptonshire, which he resigned in 1495. By the early 1500s, Lily was one of the circle of humanists in London including Grocyn, Linacre, and More. More and Lily jointly produced a set of Latin translations of eighteen

William Lily, *Schoolboys Picking Fruit.* From Lily's *Latin Grammar,* 1574. The official grammar school textbook after 1543, "Lily's Grammar" was consistently illustrated with versions of an image of schoolboys picking fruit, presumably from the Tree of Knowledge. Reproduced by permission of The Folger Shakespeare Library.

Latin verses inculcating good schoolroom manners. These Latin grammars, authorized in the 1540s for use in all English schools, remained standard texts well into the eighteenth century.

Lily as high master was provided with a house and an extraordinarily generous salary. His pupils included Thomas Lupset, John Leland, William Paget, and Anthony Denny. St. Paul's gained a high reputation and served as a model for other English schools founded in succeeding years. Probably in 1520, Lily was drawn into a controversy by the grammarian Robert Whittinton. To some extent this may have reflected a difference in conceptions of grammar: Whittinton was critical of the emphasis on imitation as opposed to rules. Verse invectives against Whittinton by Lily and his ally, William Horman, were printed in two volumes in 1521 under the title *Antibossicon.* In addition, Lily wrote Latin verse throughout his career; a small set of his *Epigrammata* was printed in 1522, and other poems survive in British Library MS Harl. 540.

Lily's large family was decimated in an outbreak of plague some time before his own death late in 1522. His daughter, Dionysia, was married to John Ritwise, the second high master of St. Paul's; Lily's son, George, became a scholar and the chaplain of Reginald Pole; Lily's grandson, John, was the author of *Euphues* (1578). Lily enjoyed a high reputation as a grammarian throughout the sixteenth century and beyond.

Greek epigrams, first published in 1518 and reprinted frequently thereafter.

By 1510, John Colet had chosen Lily to be the first high master for his new foundation of St. Paul's School. Along with Desiderius Erasmus and John Colet, Lily produced a set of humanist textbooks for use at the school; Lily's contributions included a short Latin syntax written in English, a syntax in Latin drafted by Lily and heavily revised by Erasmus, and a pair of Latin poems on accidence. In general, Lily's texts present grammatical rules as concisely as possible, in keeping with the conviction expressed by Colet that Latin was to be learned more through imitation of good authors than through conning rules. Linguistic training was to be accompanied by religious and moral instruction; the Colet-Lily texts also include Lily's *"Carmen de moribus,"* simple

BIBLIOGRAPHY

Allen, C.G. "The Sources of 'Lily's Latin Grammar': A Review of the Facts and Some Further Suggestions." *The Library,* 5th series, vol. 9, pp. 85–100.

Carlson, David R. *English Humanist Books: Writers and Patrons, Manuscript and Print, 1475–1525.* 1993.

———. "The 'Grammarians' War' 1519–1521: Humanist Careerism in Early Tudor England, and Printing." *Medievalia et Humanistica,* n.s., vol. 18, pp. 157–181.

Flynn, Vincent J. "The Grammatical Writings of William Lily, ?1468–?1523." *Papers of the Bibliographical Society of America,* vol. 37, pp. 85–113.

———, ed. *A Shorte introduction of Grammar* (1567). Facsimile. 1945.

Lily, George. *"Virorum aliquot in Britannia . . . Elogia.11."* In Paolo Giovio. *Descriptio Britanniae, Scotiae, Hyberniae et Orchadum.* 1548.

More, St. Thomas. *Latin Poems in The Yale Edition of the Complete Works of St. Thomas More.* Vol. 3. Leicester Bradner et al., eds. 1984.

L

Trapp, J.B. "William Lily." *Contemporaries of Erasmus.* Peter G. Bietenholz, ed. 1986.

John F. McDiarmid

SEE ALSO

Colet, John; Education; Epigrams; Grammar Schools; Humanism; Leland, John; Lyly, John; More, Thomas

Linacre, Thomas (c. 1460–1524)

The humanist, scholar, and physician Thomas Linacre may have been born and gone to school in Canterbury. He was at Oxford by 1481, and was elected a fellow of All Souls in 1484. In 1487 he traveled to Italy. At Florence he studied Greek and Latin authors under Angelo Poliziano and Demetrius Chalcondylas. In 1490–1491 he was at Rome. Thereafter he studied medicine at Padua, receiving the degree of M.D. in 1496. Linacre became a member of the circle of Aldus Manutius in Venice; Aldus wrote highly of him as an exemplar of British classical learning, and printed his Latin translation of *De sphaera,* attributed to Proclus, in 1499. By that time, Linacre was back in England, apparently seeking employment as a tutor of Henry VII's son, Arthur; this effort seems not to have succeeded. Linacre then joined the group of humanists in London that also included William Grocyn and Thomas More.

At the accession of Henry VIII, Linacre was appointed a royal physician, and his fortunes were soon enhanced by the income from a stream of ecclesiastical preferments that continued for the rest of his life. He was ordained a deacon in 1520. As a physician, Linacre treated not only the king but also leading figures at court such as Thomas Wolsey and friends such as Desiderius Erasmus. In 1518, he was the principal founder of the College of Physicians; he remained its president until his death. He also endowed two lectureships in medicine at Oxford and one at Cambridge. Beginning in 1517, he published a series of Latin translations of works of Galen, printed at first in Paris and later in England; it included *De sanitate tuenda* (1517), *Methodus medendi* (1519), *De temperamentis,* with *De inaeguali intemperie* (1521), *De pulsuum usu* (1522?), *De naturalibus facultatibus* (1523), and *De symptomatum differentiis* with *De symptomatum causis* (1524). Linacre's translations exemplify his command both of Latin style and of Greek.

His other publications were original works on Latin grammar. Linacre had provided a grammar for use at Colet's St. Paul's School, which Colet declined to adopt. An edition perhaps from 1515 survives of Linacre's *Progymnasmata grammatices vulgarian* written in English. Another grammar in English, *Rudimenta grammatices* (c. 1523), was dedicated to Princess Mary, whom Linacre had been appointed to tutor. His long Latin treatise, *De emendata structure Latini sermonis,* was printed posthumously in 1524. His conception of two syntactic *genera,* the *iustum* and the *figuratum,* and of elliptical constructions as a type of the latter, influenced the grammatical system of Sanctius (1587) and through him the seventeenth-century Port-Royal grammarians. Almost all of Linacre's works were frequently reprinted on the Continent through much of the sixteenth century. In poor health for the last several years of his life, Linacre died on October 20, 1524.

BIBLIOGRAPHY

Erasmus, Desiderius. *Correspondence.* In *The Complete Works of Erasmus.* Vols. 1 and 2. Trans. R.A.B. Mynors, and D.F.S. Thomson, annot. Wallace K. Ferguson, ed. Letters 118, 227. 1974, 1975.

Jensen, Kristian. *"De emendata structure Latini sermonis:* The Latin Grammar of Thomas Linacre." *Journal of the Warburg and Courtauld Institutes,* vol. 49, pp. 106–125.

Maddison, Francis, Margaret Pelling, and Charles Webster, eds. *Essays on the Life and Works of Thomas Linacre.* 1977.

Padley, G.A. *Grammatical Theory in Western Europe, 1500–1700.* 1976.

Scaglione, Aldo. *The Classical Theory of Composition from Its Origins to the Present.* 1972.

Schmitt, Charles B. "Thomas Linacre." In *Contemporaries of Erasmus.* Peter G. Bietenholz, ed. 1986.

John F. McDiarmid

SEE ALSO

Colet, John; Education; Erasmus, Desiderius; Grammar Schools; Humanism; Medicine and Health

Literacy

The Tudor age saw the beginnings of a momentous shift from the closely restricted reading and writing of the Middle Ages to the mass literacy that we today regard almost as a birthright. Sixteenth-century literacy was not as simple as the ability to read and write, but was made up of several skills that are best seen as bands in a spectrum rather than discrete categories. Reading of print or writing was possible at two levels. Some people could decipher texts, read them aloud, and memorize them—although their critical understanding may have been questionable. Those with better education and a deeper immersion in printed and written culture could comprehend the text with greater precision, reading and thinking silently to themselves. However, "reading" was not restricted to written or printed words alone. People gathered information from looking, interpreting pictures and prints in broadsheets and pamphlets, or watching and participating in plays and processions. If they wanted to transmit their own thoughts other than through speech they had to learn to write, or compose—an advanced skill that required considerable training and practice, and which effectively marked "full" literacy for most people. The other, more common, level of writing was, in fact, copying: writing without necessarily understanding. It was at this stage that people learned to sign their names on documents, and this ability is commonly used as an indicator that someone could read and understand printed and written texts in the language of everyday life (the vernacular). A small minority of men could also copy or compose in Latin, the international language of learning in the sixteenth century. Because the distinction between literate and oral culture was narrow and ill-defined, even those who had none of these skills were not culturally isolated, for they could listen to a priest's sermons or a friend reading aloud. The catechism was a powerful tool of religious instruction precisely because it bridged the gap between oral and literate learning. Religious conversion could come to those who only heard, saw, and memorized. Within this broad spectrum of skills, few were wholly "illiterate," even in 1500.

The literacy we can measure was stratified by social and economic position, place of residence, and gender. In northern England, for instance, the illiteracy of the gentry

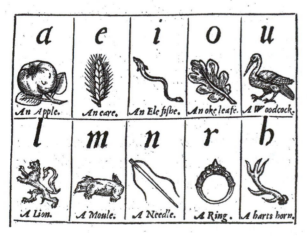

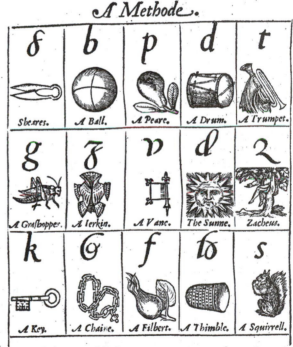

Illustrated Alphabet, from John Hart, *A Method . . . To Read English* (1570). Reproduced by permission of The Folger Shakespeare Library.

L

fell from about 30 percent in 1530 to nearly zero in 1600, while that of day laborers stayed well above 90 percent throughout. People living in towns were always better able to sign their names, and by this measure men as a whole were far more literate than women. While the drive for literacy was given fresh impetus by the Reformation and an English Bible in every church, a growth in literacy was not uniquely a product of Protestantism; its effects were felt only slowly and combined with other factors to influence literacy. As much as Bible reading, stage plays, music and processions, and hymn-singing remained through Elizabeth's reign a regular and primary expression of devotion and emotional religious experience for many Protestants. In addition to religious change, spreading commercialization was the most important factor contributing to widespread literacy. As inland trade began to centralize around the bigger cities and overseas trade relations were formalized, correspondence and record-keeping became essential to merchants at all levels.

These factors encouraged people either to seek out education or to teach themselves, possibly with help from literate friends and neighbors. With the dissolution of the monasteries, the loss of monastic, nunnery, and chantry schools forced communities and cities to found and even endow grammar schools. Most were of higher quality than those they replaced; the standardization of grammars such as William Lily's ensured a more consistent and rigorous curriculum, and the humanist education of well-paid schoolmasters ensured more literate instruction. One loss, though, was in the education of women; nunnery schools were not replaced, and it is possible that women as a whole had less access to education after the English Reformation. Less prestigious lower or elementary schools, variously known as "dame," "hedge," or corner schools, also proliferated. By 1603 half the parishes in the more developed areas of south and east England would have had a settled school. Nevertheless, self-education remained especially important for those living in isolated regions or for disadvantaged groups such as women and the poor.

As many as half a million volumes may have been published in the Tudor era, reflecting a desire for the printed word but also making that medium more a part of economic, social, cultural, and political life. Our image of the printed word in the sixteenth century is dominated by the Bible and by the prominent works of figures such as John Foxe, Thomas More, or Francis Bacon. Far more common was popular literature in the form of pamphlets and broadsheets. Rich in imagery, they generally consisted of

words with woodcut or copperplate illustrations. They were widely and cheaply available by the Elizabethan age and, entertaining as well as edifying, they commanded large (if unquantifiable) audiences among the common people.

By the end of the sixteenth century, writing was used more extensively to keep commercial records, record commonplaces, and write spiritual autobiographies; and personal letters survive in greater abundance than ever before. By many measures, England was a much more literate country in 1603 than it had been at the accession of Henry VII.

BIBLIOGRAPHY

Collinson, P. *From Iconoclasm to Iconophobia: The Cultural Impact of the Second English Reformation.* 1986.

Cressy, D. *Literacy and the Social Order. Reading and Writing in Tudor and Stuart England.* 1980.

Houston, R.A. *Literacy in Early Modern Europe: Culture and Education, 1500–1800.* 1989.

O'Day, R. *Education and Society, 1500–1800. The Social Foundations of Education in Early Modern Britain.* 1982.

Watt, T. *Cheap Print and Popular Piety, 1550–1640.* 1991.

R.A. Houston

SEE ALSO

Book Ownership; Catechism, The; Education; Grammar Schools; Printing, Publishing, and Bookbinding; Reading Practices

Literary Criticism

Literary criticism establishes criteria for evaluating literary works. In the sixteenth century it included prescriptive guidelines for the composition of literary works as well. Before any serious discussion began in England, the criteria of literary criticism had been debated in Italy, derived in part from classical texts. Aristotle's *Poetics* became known in England only in the 1550s, quoted from Italian translations and commentaries as well as from the Greek—for example, Francesco Robortello, *In librum Aristotelis de arte poetia explicationes* (1548), which included the Greek text, the Latin translation, and commentary, and Lodovico Castelvetro, *Poetica d'Aristotele vulgarizzata e sposta* (1570). Probably the most important single text for literary criticism of the time was Horace's *Ars Poetica,* commented on by Renaissance scholars who in turn took their orientation from ancient commentaries like those by Donatus, Evanthius, Demetrius, and Macrobius. Its popularity also rested on its rhetorical orientation.

The identification of rhetoric and poetic already established in the Middle Ages continued throughout the sixteenth century. In fact, rhetoric was the only classical discipline that had evolved a functional model of composition and style. Critical thinking relied on rhetoric, because its code of rules was applicable to speech as well as to literature. Although Sir Philip Sidney's knowledge of Neoplatonism seems to have made him aware of the essential difference between rhetoric and poetry, at this stage of literary criticism only rhetoric allowed poets and critics to understand what words and figures could express and what effects they could achieve. Apart from the textbooks of rhetoric, Latin schoolbooks contained important treatises that served as a basis for literary criticism—for example, Donatus, in the fourth century, had written an *Ars Grammatica* that contained examples from the Latin classics, especially Vergil. Together with the rhetorical rules concerning structure and style, such grammars provided the basis for literary criticism.

The enthusiastic reception of Renaissance learning in England took a decidedly pedagogical coloring in *The Schoolmaster* by Roger Ascham. The notion of imitation he recommends actually aims at re-creation or productive imitation that excludes slavish copying and encourages variations and development of models. The wide range of exercises in imitation demands close reading and analysis and potentially provides insight into literary composition and the characteristics of authors, including the ways classical authors imitated their predecessors. Ascham considers the social aspect of dramatic mimesis, the relationship between subject and style, and the poetical language of ancient authors. He criticizes Roman dramatists for their unpolished language and advises students to study Greek and its authors. In spite of such enlightened ideas, the modeling on the ancients also turns into a source of blindness as far as the English language was concerned. Rhyme, not to be found with the Greeks, becomes anathema for Ascham and the quantitative meters of the ancients the epitome of poetical development.

But there was dissent. George Gascoigne, in *Certayne Notes of Instruction Concerning the Making of Verse or Ryme in English* (1575), was the first writer and critic to present a formal treatise on English prosody and to argue for accentual meters. His favorable view of rhyme as natural to the English language also betrays a reserve toward the classics as undisputed norm. His critical model derives from rhetoric, where he finds the terms to describe the production of poetry starting with a fine invention from which appropriate words should flow to make a delectable poem. His requirements include regularity of lines, natural speech rhythm, rhyming with reason, moderation as to rhetorical figures, no obsolete or unusual words, and clarity. His chief end is naturalness.

It was the memory of John Skelton's satirical rhymes and the popularity of rhyme among the vulgus that moved Thomas Campion, in *Observations in the Art of English Poesie* (1602), to base his arguments for quantitative meter and his opposition to rhyme on musical criteria, which makes more sense but is no argument against rhyme. Samuel Daniel, in *A Defence of Ryme* (1603), vigorously attacks the claims of superiority of Latin and Greek and insists on the virtues and achievements of different cultures. He insists on the independent prosodic system of the English language and defends rhyme because of its musicality and grace. Sensibly, he reminds his readers that the important issue is not quantity but invention.

The passport of rhetoric did not protect literature from fundamental attacks. Rhetoric itself was made the weapon against poetry in Stephen Gosson's *The Schoole of Abuse* (1579). Its Ciceronian style betrays the hand of a former Oxford playwright who turned allegiances and reversed the notion of the sugar-coated pill to refute the claims to moral improvement by the defenders of poetry. Although Gosson's attack became the most famous of its kind, it was only one among many, many from the Puritans, that took offense at immorality. Ironically dedicated to Sir Philip Sidney, the essay was rebutted, among others, by Thomas Lodge in his *Defence of Poetry* (1579).

More important than Gosson's provocation itself was Sir Philip Sidney's *Apology for Poetry* (1580–1583). Sidney provides an elegant, rhetorically polished manifesto of the origin and ends of literature. His defense rests on the definition of the literary work as grounded in the poet's idea or fore-conceit, not to be confused with an abstraction (as in neoclassicism) but an archetypal image embodied in words that the poet sees in his mind. Sidney complements this concept by his definition of literature as imitation being "a representing, counterfeiting, or figuring forth . . . a speaking picture" of the poet's idea. Taking up the attack against poetry, Sidney lays special emphasis on the moral efficacy of the great works of literature. He argues that there is a quality to the imaginative work that makes it ethically superior to all other arts. His belief that delight in itself leads to goodness, that even the

L

most hardened criminal wants to be delighted and so, without realizing it, has to see the form of goodness, provides literature at once with an idealistic as well as an anthropological foundation. Sidney also demands persuasiveness in (love) poetry, emotional truth as well as forcibleness, *energia,* finding the English language suitable both for accentual and quantitative measures and points to its great musical potential. Every word should have its natural seat; it should be familiar and not affecting antiquity, a criticism aimed at Edmund Spenser's *Shepherds Calender.* In contemporary drama he criticizes the disregard of the unities of time and place as well as a mingling of the genres.

Less apologetic in tone and structure, George Puttenham's *The Arte of English Poesie* (1589) is the most comprehensive treatise of literary criticism of the period. Like Sidney, Puttenham looks on antiquity as a proof of the value, dignity, and utility of literature. Book 1 contains an historical account of the different kinds of poetry with a notable regard to its social value, praising Sir Thomas Wyatt and the Earl of Surrey, Sidney, and Spenser. In Book 2, "On Proportion Poetical," Puttenham argues for the inherent suitability of English for accentual meters, and especially for rhyming. His explanations of the symphonic quality of rhyme testify to his insight into the harmonious proportions and the musical qualities of poetical language. Book 3, "On Ornament," is largely rhetorical. Puttenham distinguishes two basic categories of ornament in poetry, the first, *enargia,* being decorative, the second, *energia,* emotive and lending efficacy or forcefulness. Puttenham's division of rhetorical figures into auricular and sensable corresponds to the rhetorical distinction of syntactic and semantic figures (tropes). The aim he attributes to them is characteristic of the Elizabethan endeavours of art: that art should imitate nature and not appear as art. Puttenham's discussion of individual figures still is an important source for the Elizabethan understanding of rhetorical figures in literature.

Literary criticism of the Tudor period issuing from educational concerns as much as from ideological battles about the arts, especially drama, became a syncretistic body of notions concerning the function of literature. At the same time, the recognition that literature is also a craft made writers aware of aspects like genre, structure, prosody, types of images, and aesthetic and psychological impact. Critical debate remained under the influence of rhetoric, based on the humanistic conviction that the word is a mirror of the mind and literature expressive of its highest concepts.

BIBLIOGRAPHY

Atkins, J.W.H. *English Literary Criticism: The Renascence.* 1947.

Blamires, Harry. *A History of Literary Criticism.* 1991.

Hardison, O.B., ed. *English Literary Criticism.* 1963.

Kinney, Arthur F. *Humanist Poetics: Thought, Rhetoric, and Fiction in Sixteenth-Century England.* 1986.

Lanham, Richard A. *The Motives of Eloquence: Literary Rhetoric in the Renaissance.* 1976.

Plett, Heinrich F., ed. *Renaissance-Poetik/Renaissance Poetics.* 1994.

Saintsbury, George A. *History of English Criticism.* 1911.

Smith, G.G., ed. *Elizabethan Critical Essays.* 1904.

Vickers, B. "Rhetoric and Poetics." In C.B. Schmitt et al., eds. *The Cambridge History of Renaissance Philosophy.* 1988.

Lothar Cerny

SEE ALSO

Ascham, Roger; Campion, Thomas; Daniel, Samuel; Gascoigne, George; Gosson, Stephen; Lodge, Thomas; Platonism; Puttenham, George; Rhetoric; Sidney, Philip; Skelton, John

Literary Influences

See Classical Literature, Influence of; French Literature, Influence of; Italian Literature, Influence of; Spanish Literature, Influence of; Petrarchanism

Liturgical Year

See Calendar, Church

Liturgy

Liturgy formally refers to a body of rites appointed for public worship, and especially to the Eucharist. The liturgy in use during the reigns of Henry VII, Henry VIII, and Mary I was the Latin liturgy of the Roman rite. At the beginning of the sixteenth century, this was one of a number of local uses, Sarum and York being the most significant. After Henry VIII's break with Rome, the Sarum Use was enforced throughout the Province of Canterbury, and it was the Sarum books that were reprinted under Mary when the Latin rite was reintroduced.

Liturgy was most frequently used in discussions during the Tudor period to refer to the Book of Common Prayer, issued in 1549 and imposed on all of England by a parliamentary Act of Uniformity. This book was a revision, simplification, and translation into English of the Latin liturgy, with some material from Martin Luther and the Cologne Church Order of Archishop Herman von Wied, of which Martin Bucer wrote the liturgical sections. It had as its avowed purpose the imposition of a uniform liturgy on the whole realm and was largely the work of Thomas Cranmer, archbishop of Canterbury. The book was criticized by both Catholics and Protestants. A formal critique was published by Martin Bucer, and a new and highly revised edition appeared in 1552, after the fall of Somerset as lord protector. The traditional view is that 1549 represents the Catholic tradition of the Church of England in continuity with the Middle Ages, while 1552 represents its Protestant tradition springing from the Reformation. Cranmer's own understanding of what he was about remains a matter of serious scholarly disagreement.

In 1553, under Mary, the Latin liturgy was reintroduced, along with papal obedience. The English exiles at Frankfurt continued the liturgical debate of Edward IV's reign, the conservatives under Richard Cox wishing to retain the use of the Book of Common Prayer (1552), and their opponents under John Knox wishing to revise the liturgy to make it more nearly conformable with that of Calvin's Geneva and other continental reformed churches.

In 1559, under Elizabeth I, a third edition of the Book of Common Prayer was introduced, accompanied by its own Act of Uniformity. The Elizabethan Prayer Book was that of 1552 with few but significant alterations in the direction of 1549.

The "ornaments rubric" directed the retention and use of those ornaments and vestments as were used "by the authoritie of Parliament, in the second year of the reigne of King Edw. VI." The exact meaning of the rubric was litigated extensively in the nineteenth century. Under Elizabeth I, its force was mitigated by the Advertisements of Archbishop Matthew Parker in 1566, which required only the use of the surplice in parish churches and the cope in cathedrals. Even this requirement was resisted by many of the reform-minded clergy, whose opposition to the use of vestments rested on principle and was not confined to objection to specific vestments. The black gown favored by the reformed, often called a Geneva gown, was not considered a vestment, but the ordinary street dress of the clergy.

The words of administration of Holy Communion were altered to combine the words of 1549 with those of 1552, balancing the objective "The Body of our Lord Jesus Christ . . ." with the more subjective "Take and eate this, in remembrance that Christe died for thee, and fede on him in thy heart by faith, with thankes geuyng."

Almost all aspects of the liturgy of the Book of Common Prayer were attacked by those who came to be called Puritans. Their objections were set forth in vivid detail in the *Admonition to Parliament* of 1572. The principal objection to the Liturgy was that it retained too much of the pre-Reformation service, "culled and picked out of that popish dunghill, the portuise and mass-book, full of all abominations," and differed too much from the liturgies of other reformed churches. The most comprehensive answer was Book 5 of Richard Hooker's *Of the Laws of Ecclesiastical Polity,* published in 1597, which defended the Elizabethan Prayer Book almost page by page.

"No man," Hooker writes, "hath hitherto been so impious as plainly and directly to condemn prayer." The condemnation of set forms of common prayer as superstitious he considers a stratagem of Satan, pointing out that set forms of prayer are found in Scripture, such as the priestly benediction in Numbers 6:23 and the Lord's Prayer, as well as the Psalms and other canticles in both the Old and New Testaments. He recognizes that his opponents have backed down from a complete condemnation of set forms to a condemnation of the Prayer Book specifically. He argues that it is wrong to condemn things simply because they are like the Roman Church. "Some things they do in that they are men, in that they are wise men and Christian men some things . . . ," and that only in those things that they do in error is it wrong to follow them. When their choice is better and more ancient than that of the reformed churches, "we had rather follow the perfections of them we like not, than in defects resemble those whom we love." Specifically, Hooker argues, it is better to have prescript forms everyone is bound to follow than the kind of direction offered by the Puritans, "a form for men to use if they list, or otherwise to change as pleaseth themselves." He also sides with Rome in asserting that common prayer is itself a duty to be performed much more frequently than sermons can be preached, as manifested in the services of daily morning and evening prayer, over against the form of reformed prayer allowed by his opponents, which provides only what is to be done before and after the preaching of sermons, with which the entirety of public worship is confused. He concludes: "We cannot be induced to prefer their reformed form of prayer before our own, what church soever we resemble therein."

L

The liturgical question was not resolved and became a primary issue of the Anglican-Puritan controversy of the seventeenth century, which erupted into the civil war.

BIBLIOGRAPHY

Booty, John E. ed. The Book of Common Prayer, 1559. 1976.

Brightman, F.E. *The English Rite.* 2 vols. 1921; repr. 1969.

Cuming, G.J. *A History of Anglican Liturgy.* 2nd edition. 1982.

Hooker, Richard. *Of the Laws of Ecclesiastical Polity.* Book 5. 1597.

von Wied, Herman. *Einfaltigs Bedenken* [Cologne Church Order]. In A.L. Richter. *Die evangelischen Kirchenordnungen des sechzehnten Jahrhunderts.* Vol. 2, pp. 30–54. 1847; trans. *A Simple and Religious Consultation.* 1547, 1548. [No modern edition; communion service in Cuming, pp. 268–304.]

Leonel L. Mitchell

SEE ALSO

Admonition Controversy; Anglicanism; Book of Common Prayer; Bucer, Martin; Cox, Richard; Cranmer, Thomas; Eucharist; Hooker, Richard; Ornaments Rubric; Parker, Matthew; Puritanism; Reformation, English; Sarum, Use of; Vestiarian Controversy

Lodge, Thomas (1558–1625)

Best known as the author of the prose romance *Rosalynde. Euphues golden legacie* (1590), which provided the basis for William Shakespeare's *As You Like It* (1599), Thomas Lodge is also the author of a number of other prose fictions, poetry, satires, literary criticism, prose tracts, religious works, two plays (one coauthored with Robert Greene), and translations.

Lodge was the second son born into the family of Sir Thomas Lodge, a prosperous grocer who was bankrupted during his term as lord mayor of London in 1562. Consequently, Lodge spent much of his childhood in a house oppressed by debt, poverty, and litigation. He entered the Merchant Taylors' School in 1571, where he was a pupil of Richard Mulcaster. In 1573, he entered Trinity College, Oxford, where he obtained a B.A. in 1577. On April 26, 1578, he entered Lincoln's Inn, although he seems already to have been more interested in literature than the law. His failure to be a diligent law student probably

resulted in his losing the modest inheritance left him by his mother, who died in 1579; he was completely ignored in his father's will. (For details on his early life and his financial problems, see his *Alarum Against Usurers.*) The 1580s seem to have been a restless decade for Lodge: in the mid-1580s, he voyaged to the Azores and the Canary Islands with a Captain Clarke, as is alluded to in the dedication to Lord Hunsdon that prefaces *Rosalynde.* In 1591, he sailed with Sir Thomas Cavendish to South America (an experience referred to in the dedication to *A Margarite of America*). The early- to mid-1590s were a productive literary period for Lodge, but he seems to have endured continuing financial problems and to have developed an increasingly Roman Catholic religious sensibility. Although it is unclear when he became a Catholic, in 1597 he traveled to Avignon to study medicine. He returned as a physician to London, where he practiced, largely serving members of the recusant population, until his death from the plague in 1625.

During the course of his literary career, Lodge's works seem to become less interested in the purely fictional and romantic and increasingly interested in moral and spiritual redemption. His early works include a defense of plays written in response to the attacks of Stephen Gosson, possibly called (the existing copy is missing a title page) *Honest Excuses* (1579); *An Alarum against Usurers* (1580), a fictional account of youthful economic woes; *Scillaes Metamorphosis* (1589), a collection of poetry that includes "Glaucis and Scylla," a poem that has been called the first example of the English epyllion and which is imitated, both in its use of a classical subject and its formal structure, by Shakespeare in his *Venus and Adonis* (1593); and *Rosalynde* (1590), a work strongly influenced by John Lyly's *Euphues: The Anatomy of Wit* (1578), and often seen, along with Sir Philip Sidney's *Arcadia,* as one of the two best examples of the prose pastoral romance produced during the period. After the publication of *Rosalynde,* which concludes with the restoration of the rightful duke to his kingdom and the union of the happy lovers, Lodge's work becomes darker and more realistic. Although his plots often remain largely improbable, he becomes more concerned with historical verisimilitude, drawing on historical figures and incidents, as he does in the prose fictions *The Famous, True, and Historicall Life of Robert Second Duke of Normandy* (1591), *The Life and Death of William Longbeard* (1593), and *A Margarite of America* (1596). He claims, for example, not to have written *A Margarite,* but rather to have found the manuscript during his travels with Cavendish "in the librarie of the Iesuits . . . in the Spanish tongue" (*Works* 3:4). His drama and his nonfictional prose also reflect a growing concern not only for the concerns of history but with satire, moral reform, and religious issues. His two plays, *The Wounds of Civill War* (1594) and *A Looking Glasse, for London and Englande* (1586?), with Robert Greene, both reveal a concern for human sinfulness and cultural decay. *Catharos: Diogenes in his Singularitie* (1591), is a classical dialogue that urges moral reform; *A Fig for Momus* (1595) presents a collection of classically inspired verse epistles, satires, and eclogues that criticize general follies of the age; *The Divel conjured* (1596) presents an exhortation to follow Christ; and *Wits Miserie, and the Worlds Madnesse: Discovering the Devils Inarnat of this Age* (1596), is a discourse on the presence of the Seven Deadly Sins in early modern culture. *Prosopopeia: Containing the Teares of the holy, blessed, and sanctified Marie, the Mother of God* (1596), which has been called Lodge's most Roman Catholic work, is intended, as its dedicatory epistle states, to provide "holy motives of meditation" (*Works* 3:5). After Lodge returned from France, he turned his literary interests to translation of works that he found consistent with his religious beliefs and concern for devout and virtuous behavior, producing translations of selections by Luis de Granada, the prose works of Seneca, the Jewish history of Josephus, and the poetry of du Bartas. His translation of *The Famous and Memorable Works of Josephus* (1602) was particularly well received during the period. The remaining works he wrote after his return from France are all medical, discussing such subjects as advice on how to avoid the plague and remedies for common illnesses.

BIBLIOGRAPHY:
Cuvelier, Eliane. *Thomas Lodge Témoin de son Temps.* 1984.
Davis, Walter R. *Idea and Act in Elizabethan Fiction.* 1969.
Helgerson, Richard. *Elizabethan Prodigals.* 1976.
Kinney, Arthur F. *Humanist Poetics: Thought, Rhetoric, and Fiction in Sixteenth-Century England.* 1986.
Paradise, N. Burton. *Thomas Lodge: The History of an Elizabethan.* 1931.
Sisson, Charles J., ed. *Thomas Lodge and Other Elizabethans.* 1933.
Tenney, Edward Andrews. *Thomas Lodge.* 1935.
Walker, Alice. *The Life of Thomas Lodge.* 1933.

Constance C. Relihan

SEE ALSO
Cavendish, Thomas; Euphuism; Gosson, Stephen; Greene, Robert; Literary Criticism; John Lyly; Richard Mulcaster; Prose Fiction; Satire

Logic

At the start of the Tudor period the terms logic and dialectic were used interchangeably, and both originally were tied to the arts of discussion. During the medieval period, for example, Petrus Hispanus began his widely circulated *Summulae logicales* (c. 1230) by conflating the two disciplines as the art of discussing any subject. But over time logic became more closely associated with formal discussions within the scholarly or theological community, while dialectic was associated with the informal reasoning of rhetorical encounter, and much discussion during the English Tudor period attempted to separate the two disciplines or articulate a more satisfactory relationship between them.

Dialectic was the original Greek term for both studies, and during the Tudor period logicians and dialecticians alike returned to Greek sources. Plato had celebrated dialectic as a form of questioning to find common ground and differences among terms. Aristotle elaborated dialectic as a variety of informal procedures to attack or defend an opinion by arguing either side, and in his *Analytics* developed formal procedures for distinguishing between rationally certain and uncertain statements. Stoic dialectic next defined dialectic as procedures for resolving ambiguities in language, so that valid propositional inferences could constitute truth claims. During the medieval period these three ideas about dialectic (by now also called logic) were all used in establishing the truth of contested claims in philosophy and theology.

Medieval and Renaissance training in dialectic began early in a student's education. By the end of the first year of university studies a student would have been required to attack a problematic proposition set by a master, and then to defend such a proposition, before advancing as a sophister. Advanced studies proceeded in a similar fashion, with the presiding master summarizing and settling the disputed question. Theologians used increasingly sophisticated procedures to demonstrate the rational certainty of doctrinal positions, while some logicians developed techniques of discrimination that went far beyond Aristotle's original ideas or interests in syllogisms, rigorously examining the properties of terms and the formal aspects of the structures that manipulated those terms.

L

What happens, for example, when one considers a category in terms of "all" of its members, as opposed to "every one" of them, or "each" of them? To what extent are class terms "supposed" to refer to individual and unusual instances of that class, and what happens when such terms are used in different ways?

Oxford logicians had been innovators in systematic theory during the thirteenth century, but by the start of the Tudor period the spirit of innovation had slackened and dialectical practice had become routine. Until 1530, all of the texts published in England are either reprints of basic school texts such as *Libellus sophistarum ad usum Oxoniensem and ad usum Cantabrigiensem,* or editions of medieval authors such as Albertus Magnus and Walter Burley, or standard treatments of scholastic subjects. But on the Continent the situation had been changing, with the circulation and printing of fresh Greek treatises by Aristotle, with two significant results for England.

First, logicians were able to turn directly to Aristotelian treatises, thus bypassing the interpretive studies by medieval commentators, and in the process a great number of the medieval additions to the subject of logic (such as "supposition theory") all but disappeared. John Seton's *Dialectica* (1545) was based directly on Aristotle, and it was published repeatedly throughout the period, as was Thomas Wilson's popular English version *Rule of Reason* (1551). So also at the universities there was a resurgence of Aristotelian logic at the expense of medieval scholastic approaches, based in large part on continental treatises. By the end of the Tudor period English logicians were again contributing, beginning with John Case's *Summa veterum interpretum* (1584), followed by Griffin Powel (1594), and Robert Sanderson (1602). Even scholastic logic had a revival of sorts. Peter Lombard's medieval work had been rejected at Oxford in 1564 as a Catholic abuse and corruption, but in the 1590s, Thomas Aquinas and Duns Scotus were again studied. In general, the failure of scholastic logic to support Catholic theology meant that loyal Englishmen could resuscitate scholastic logic with safety.

The second result was tied to the first, and amounted to a rethinking under the impress of humanism of what constituted logic or dialectic. Scholastic logic had long been assailed by detractors as arid, self-contained, and irrelevant, and with the continental rediscovery of classical treatises came a new appreciation for the kinds of reasoning that were used in more ordinary discourse. Where scholastic approaches viewed logic as instrumental for the timeless world of theology, or as a theoretical subject in its own right, humanist approaches viewed it as instrumental for the present world of men and letters. Lorenzo Valla argued in *Repastinatio dialecticae et philosophiae* (1439) that reasoning in language was more dependent on grammar than on the formal validity of syllogisms, while Rudolf Agricola, in *De inventions dialectica* (1479, printed 1515), provided a "topic-logic" that combined a simplified Aristotelian syllogistic with the probabilistic reasoning and associational proceeding of Aristotle's *Topics* and *Rhetoric.* The result of both was a dialectic that blurred the distinctions between rational certainty and uncertainty by insisting that the same techniques could be used for both the logic of science and the logic of probability. In England this conflation took two related forms. One, articulated by Juan Luis Vives, was that knowledge can never be more than probabilistic, so that certainty is no more than a very high degree of probability. The other, articulated by Petrus Ramus, insisted on the reverse, that probability was no more than a relaxed form of certainty. The categories of logic for Ramus reflected the true nature of human thought processes, so that if discourse followed the dictates of natural reason, persuasion would necessarily follow.

Scholastic logic in England thus was assailed on two additional fronts, by the skepticism of Vives and by the informal certitude of Ramus. Ramist dialectic drew heavily on simplified concepts from Aristotle, which made it possible to present these concepts in a more orderly ("methodical") manner than did Aristotle himself, proceeding from general to specific, usually in a series of dichotomous divisions. Ramus's dialectic was published in both Latin and English in 1574, although continental editions had been used earlier, and immediately the kinds of controversy that had swirled about Ramus on the Continent were repeated in England. Ramist imitators or advocates included Everard Digby (*De duplici methodo,* 1580, and other treatises) and Abraham Fraunce (*The Lawiers Logike,* 1588); detractors included William Temple (*Admonitio de unica P. Rami methodo,* 1580, and other treatises) and Nathaniel Baxter (*Quaestiones et responsa in Petri Rami dialecticam,* 1585). Many of these treatises were also printed abroad, and a host of continental combatants were imported into England. These several controversies led to a reinvigoration of Aristotelian logic in England. At the universities Aristotelian logic flourished, now stripped of many medieval subjects and concerns. Outside of the universities treatises on Aristotelian logic increasingly presented their materials in a more "methodical" fashion and usually added discussions about method in logic, effectively combining Aristotelian with Ramist approaches.

BIBLIOGRAPHY

Guerlac, Rita, trans. and ed. *Juan Luis Vives Against the Pseudodialecticians.* 1979.

Howell, W.S. *Logic and Rhetoric in England.* 1961.

McConica, James, ed. *The Collegiate University.* 1986.

Ong, Walter J., S.J. *Ramus and Talon Inventory.* 1958.

————. *Ramus, Method and the Decay of Dialogue.* 1974.

Schmitt, Charles. *John Case and Aristotelianism in Renaissance England.* 1983.

Siegel, J.E. *Rhetoric and Philosophy in Renaissance Humanism.* 1968.

Vives, Juan Luis. *Declamationes Sullanae.* Edward V. George, trans. 1988.

Lawrence D. Green

SEE ALSO

Aristotelianism; Classical Literature, Influence of; Digby, Everard; Education; Fraunce, Abraham; Humanism; Ramism; Rhetoric; Universities; Vives, Juan Luis; Wilson, Thomas

Lok, Henry (c. 1553–c.1608)

Third son of Henry Lok, a London mercer, and nephew to the traveler Michael Lok, Henry Lok's mother, Anne Vaughan, was the translator of Calvin's *Sermons upon the Song that Ezechias made after he had been sick and afflicted by the Hand of God* into English verse. Lok spent some years at Oxford, but apparently never matriculated. He married Ann Moyle of Cornwall, who bore him two sons, Henry and Charles. In 1591, one of Lok's sonnets appeared in James VI of Scotland's *Essays of a Prentice.* After several petitions for the appointments in the collectorship of Devon and as the Keeper of the queen's bears and mastiffs, Lok was finally employed as one of Sir Robert Cecil's agents in 1599. Falling out of favor with Cecil and into debt, Lok was imprisoned in the Westminster Gatehouse in 1606, and again in 1608 in the Clink in Southwark.

Lok's major literary work was his *Sundry Christian Passions,* printed in 1593, but no longer extant. The book is a collection of some 328 religious sonnets dedicated to fifty-six different persons, a grand effort at obtaining multiple patronage. A selection of Lok's poems also appeared in *Ecclesiasticus,* published in 1597. Furthermore, Lok produced verse translations of Ecclesiastes and the Psalms of David, and contributed to a rendering of the Psalms by Cosworth. Contemporary responses to Lok's efforts were less than enthusiastic, consisting of evaluations such as that which appears in *The Return from Parnassus* (1601), in which Lok's work was deemed suitable "to lie in some old nooks amongst old boots and shoes." Nevertheless, Lok produced a considerable volume of religious sonnets and sonnet sequences before his death sometime after his imprisonment in Southwark.

BIBLIOGRAPHY

Leishman, J.B., ed. *The Three Parnassus Plays (1598–1601).* 1949.

Saunders, J.W. *A Biographical Dictionary of Renaissance Poets and Dramatists, 1520–1650.* 1983.

Charles Leiby

SEE ALSO

Sonnet Sequences; Verse Anthologies

London

The capital of England experienced remarkable growth from the 1520s onward. Its population grew from probably 60,000 in 1500 to 200,000 by 1600, dwarfing its nearest rivals in England (Norwich 15,000; Bristol 12,000; York 11,500), and placing it among the largest of European cities (in 1600, only Paris, Milan, Venice, Naples, Palermo, Rome, Lisbon, and Istanbul had populations over 100,000). Because high levels of infant and child mortality cancelled out the effects of relatively high fertility, London's population could only be sustained by regular immigration, and it has been estimated that it required about 6,000 immigrants each year to sustain the levels of growth of the later sixteenth century. Probably only about 20 percent of the adult inhabitants of London had been born there. The immigration to the capital seems to have been dominated by those seeking to better themselves. By 1600, between 4,000 and 5,000 young men (usually in their late teens or early twenties) were arriving in London each year to begin apprenticeships, training under the supervision of a master for a minimum of seven years.

London's prominence derived from two features of its urban role—as a port and as a capital. As a port, London developed in the early sixteenth century as a satellite of the continental entrepot of Antwerp, exchanging broadcloths and kerseys for luxury goods that were widely available there, and absorbing much of the trade of the provincial outports. Whereas about 40,000 cloths were exported from London each year in the 1490s, by the 1540s the figure was 108,000. By that date the capital handled 88 percent of the country's cloth exports and probably 75 percent of all trade, while the cloth-related guilds

L

accounted for around 40 percent of the freemen. Although the growth in cloth exports faltered in the late sixteenth century with the increasing difficulties of the Antwerp market, London entered a new phase of "import-led" growth in trade, particularly with the return of English merchants to the Mediterranean. New industries such as sugar refining and silk weaving were among the consequences of the expansion in overseas trade, and shipbuilding became more important in the late sixteenth century.

As a capital, London was a beneficiary of Tudor centralization and the cultural shifts that turned it into a theater of aristocratic display. The royal court attracted crowds seeking patronage, and their increasing settlement in the western suburbs encouraged the development of a London season and the entertainment industry that sustained it. Another key development was the increasing recourse to the law courts: whereas in 1560 there were about 5,000 cases at an advanced stage in the central common law courts of King's Bench and Common Pleas, by the beginning of the reign of James I the figure was more than 23,000. The effect of this on levels of demand in the capital can be judged by the fact that during term time when the courts were sitting, the city consumed 13 percent more grain than during the vacation periods. It was to this demand for aristocratic luxury that the capital's expanding luxury industries catered.

London's close relationship with the crown was soured in the reign of Henry VII by the capital's residual Yorkist sympathies. The king's ostentatious patronage of the Merchant Taylors, the failure of the charter of 1505 to guarantee the city's right to appoint to key offices, and his hounding of individual aldermen through the courts, proved deeply unpopular in the capital, and the demise of William Empson and Edmund Dudley was greeted with relief in London. There remained some potential flashpoints: periods of aggressive fiscal activity such as 1522–1525, and the political uncertainties of the later 1530s led to higher levels of royal interference, but the relationship was basically one of mutual interdependence. City merchants appreciated that their fortunes were dependent on the chartered privileges granted to trading companies like the Merchant Adventurers, while the crown depended on London to pay customs revenue and to act as a security for loans obtained on the continental money markets. These mutual interests ensured that the changes in religion of the mid-Tudor period were negotiated without serious friction.

The authority of the corporation was compromised by the pockets of territory attached to monastic houses exempt from its jurisdiction. At the dissolution of the monastic orders the aldermen petitioned the crown to purchase these liberties, but Henry VIII dismissed their offer, and the disputed areas passed into the hands of laymen who tried to maintain their exempt status in the face of repeated litigation from the aldermen. Other liberties attached to the Tower, the Inns of Court, and the duchy of Lancaster in the Savoy. The location of much of the capital's growth in areas beyond the corporation's control in the Middlesex and Surrey suburbs was the cause of further problems. A stream of largely ineffective royal proclamations from 1580, reinforced by a statute of 1593, tried to prevent new building in the vicinity of the capital. The guilds found it difficult to maintain their privileges in the suburbs, and the coordination of the kaleidoscope of jurisdictions often fell to the Privy Council. Problems of order were more acute in these areas: prostitution flourished in Clerkenwell and Whitechapel, and the theaters were located in areas outside the control of the city fathers. The only major advance in the authority of the corporation over the suburbs was the acquisition of two manors in Southwark in 1550 that came to constitute the ward of Bridge Without, but this still left the Clink and Paris Garden outside the jurisdiction of the aldermen.

The constitution of the city was oligarchic. Power was concentrated in the hands of the twenty-five (twenty-six after 1550) aldermen, each representing one of the city's wards. Although nominated by the wards the court had the right of veto; and once elected they held office for life or until allowed to resign. The lord mayor who presided over the court and disposed of much discretionary power in his own right was elected annually from among the aldermen but usually according to a principle of seniority. The aldermen were assisted by a Court of Common Council of up to 212 representatives that was responsible for the approval of legislation and the authorization of taxes on the inhabitants. But legislation was usually initiated by the aldermen, although their powers with respect to taxes raised through the livery companies were unclear. Aldermen tended to be recruited from among the wealthiest wholesalers; the Court of Common Council broadened the range of businessmen represented, but by not very much, as the court was overwhelmingly dominated by tradesmen in the top 10 percent income bracket.

However, power was diffused downward to the 112 parishes, twenty-six wards, and fifty-five livery companies, and London enjoyed dense substructures of participatory government. It has been estimated that as many as one in ten of the city's householders were holding some

L

kind of local office in any given year. Parishes and livery companies became important foci for the loyalties of their members, providing services such as poor relief and the arbitration of disputes, as well as channels through which grievances could be represented to the elite. Moreover, after the liberalization of entry fees to the livery companies in the early sixteenth century, the ranks of the freemen swelled, so that up to three-quarters of the adult males enjoyed the privileges of citizenship. Citizens enjoyed freedom from tolls throughout England and a monopoly of retail trade in the capital, as well as having the right to vote in elections for ward officials. These privileges were vigorously defended in Parliament and the law courts against aliens and against English nonfreemen.

London society was not as sharply polarized as is sometimes claimed. Wage levels were higher than in the countryside; its lack of dependence on a key staple industry meant that it was not so vulnerable to short-term crises; within the guilds there existed opportunities for social mobility; most businesses were small-scale workshops of self-employed craft masters with no more than a couple of apprentices and perhaps one journeyman. But the location of much population growth in the poorer suburbs where housing quality was low and disease levels higher suggests that the proportion of poor in the capital was increasing. By the 1590s, London was facing serious social problems, but an impressive set of policies had been devised to meet them. The city had successfully secured properties from dissolved monastic orders between 1547 and 1552 to establish a coordinated program of hospitals supplemented by parochial rating. The livery companies financed the purchase of buffer stocks of corn that were used to keep prices down in years of harvest failure. Initiatives of this kind helped to ensure that the levels of disorder were relatively low. Although tensions between aliens and freemen threatened to produce a repetition of the violence of Evil May Day (1517) on several occasions in the later sixteenth century, the success of the aldermen in negotiating periods of acute social tension like the 1590s without a more serious conflagration testifies to the capital's fundamental orderliness.

BIBLIOGRAPHY

Archer, I.W. *The Pursuit of Stability: Social Relations in Elizabethan London.* 1991.

Brigden, S. *London and the Reformation.* 1989.

Rappaport, S. *Worlds Within Worlds: The Structures of Life in Sixteenth-Century London.* 1989.

Ian W. Archer

SEE ALSO

Aliens; Apprenticeship; Bristol; Cloth Trade; Economy; Dudley, Edmund; Empson, Richard; Government, Central Administration of; Guilds; Henry VII; Henry VIII; Immigration; Inns of Court; Law, Common; Merchant Adventurers; Merchant Taylors; Monastic Orders; Patronage; Population and Demography; Southwark; Towns; Trade, Overseas

Longland, John (1473–1547)

Born in Oxfordshire, John Longland, bishop of London, was educated at Magdalen College, Oxford, where he became a fellow and, in 1505, principal of Magdalen Hall. Concurrently, he had been ordained priest in 1500 and, four years later, made rector of Woodham Ferrers in Essex. After he earned his D.D. in 1511, more preferments followed: he was made dean of Salisbury and prebend of North Kelsey in 1514, and canon at Windsor in 1519. Gaining Henry VIII's favor, he was appointed the king's confessor and lord almoner in 1521. That same year, he was consecrated bishop of Lincoln. He proved an unwavering supporter of royal supremacy, as well as a severe represser of dissent—in 1531, he set up a commission to search booksellers' stalls at Oxford for heretical texts. Not surprisingly, when he was named chancellor of Oxford the following year, he was pelted with stones. Still, he did not resign. After the Act of Supremacy (1534) severed the Church of England from Rome, Longland issued strict injunctions that his clergy conform and suppress all references to papal authority. Even though his harsh treatment of dissenters ensured his unpopularity, Longland also undertook charitable works; his character and learning were praised by Sir Thomas More. Longland died on May 7, 1547.

BIBLIOGRAPHY

Wharhirst, Gwendolen. *The Reformation in the Diocese of Lincoln as Illustrated by the Life and Work of Bishop Longland.* 1939.

Mark Goldblatt

SEE ALSO

Heresy; Reformation, English; Supremacy, Act of

Lopez, Roderigo

See Elizabeth I; Jews

L

Low Countries, Relations with England
See Foreign Relations and Diplomacy

Lute Song
See Campion, Thomas; Dowland, John; Jones, Robert

Lutheranism

Prior to the appearance of Protestantism in England, continental humanists such as Desiderius Erasmus of Rotterdam had promoted the concepts and scholarship of the "new learning" there. This led some churchmen to employ humanist techniques of education as a means to overcome ignorance of Christian doctrine and to reform various ecclesiastical corruptions. Although these reformers sought only a cleansing of the Catholic church, their contacts with continental scholars introduced some of them to Lutheran theology, which demanded a critical examination of traditional doctrine on the basis of Scripture alone. German theologians rejected papal authority and made justification through faith alone the cardinal principle of their beliefs, and early in the sixteenth century many of Martin Luther's works began to circulate illegally in England. There, scholars acquainted with the proto-Protestant teachings of John Wycliffe (c. 1328–1384) and the Lollards received Luther's teachings enthusiastically and became, thereby, the fathers of English Protestantism.

Cambridge University was the birthplace of the English Reformation since scholars such as Thomas Bilney, Robert Barnes, and Thomas Cranmer studied Luther's writings and the New Testament, which William Tyndale had rendered into English. Their clandestine meetings at the White Horse Inn began as an effort to combat ecclesiastical corruptions and abuses of authority; but some members of the circle embraced Luther's belief about sin and salvation and thereby, in the view of their reformed church, became heretics. Theological studies at Cambridge eventually split the group because of disagreement about Luther's teaching that the human will is unable and unwilling to seek God until the Holy Spirit first regenerates it. Erasmus and Luther in 1524–1525 published opposing treatises on this subject, Erasmus defending the traditional Roman Catholic position. Scholars who accepted Luther's doctrine of human inability to contribute anything to salvation became Protestant reformers, while those who agreed with Erasmus remained Catholics.

The government of Henry VIII proscribed the reading of Protestant literature, and when Thomas Bilney, Robert Barnes, and others assailed corruptions in the church, the episcopate moved to suppress them. Barnes (1495–1540) seems to have been the first Cambridge scholar to preach objectional doctrines, and Cardinal Thomas Wolsey arrested him for distributing Tyndale's New Testament. Barnes, however, escaped to Wittenberg, where he completed his development as a Lutheran theologian. Tyndale preceded Barnes in going to Germany, and there, in 1526, produced the first edition of his English New Testament. While in Germany Tyndale wrote the *Parable of the Wicked Mammon*, which explains justification through faith alone in Lutheran terms. Tyndale accepted Luther's teachings in general and transmitted them to England, although he disagreed with Luther's understanding of the sacraments and developed some themes that were distinctively Lollard in character.

John Rogers was another important link in the transmission of Luther's ideas to England. While serving as chaplain to English merchants in Antwerp, Rogers met Tyndale and soon moved to Wittenberg to become a pastor to English refugees. He returned to England when the accession of Edward VI (1547–1553) made Protestants welcome there, and he completed the translation of the Old Testament that Tyndale had left unfinished due to his martyrdom. The prefaces and marginal notes of this version of the Bible are clearly Lutheran in character.

Lutheran theological statements appeared in English translations thanks to Richard Taverner (c. 1505–1575), who made the *Augsburg Confession of Faith* with Philipp Melanchthon's *Apology* available to English readers in 1536. English dogmatic declarations such as the Ten Articles, the Bishops' Book, and the Thirty-nine Articles of Religion reflect the influence of German Lutheranism, although Reformed theology from Switzerland and south Germany had a powerful effect in forming the final contours of English Protestantism.

Another of Taverner's contributions to the Reformation was his translation of *Common Places,* a textbook on dogmatics by the German theologian Erasmus Sarcerius that he published to help clergymen with a poor grasp of theology. He circulated some of Sarcerius's sermons too, the doctrinal character of which is obviously Lutheran.

Reformed theology became dominant in English Protestantism during Edward VI's reign, but Archbishop Cranmer's Book of Common Prayer shows the persistence of a specifically Lutheran influence, especially in the order for baptism and marriage. The Reformed persuasion about the sacraments, however, prevailed, and eventually some editors removed from Lutheran books the sections that deal with the sacraments. The recession of Lutheran teachings before the rising tide of Reformed theology appears to have been due to the flight of Protestant leaders to Switzerland during the persecutions for which Mary Tudor (1553–1558) was responsible. Some of these refugees became bishops in the Church of England during the reign of Elizabeth I (1558–1603), and in that position they promoted the distinctively Calvinistic doctrines they had adopted while in exile. The Church of England under Elizabeth I therefore espoused a system of doctrine that was Reformed rather than Lutheran. Nevertheless, the foundations of the English Reformation were the work of Luther's English disciples.

BIBLIOGRAPHY

Jacobs, Henry E. *The Lutheran Movement in England.* 1890.

McGoldrick, James E. *Luther's English Connection.* 1979.

Smeeton, Donald D. *Lollard Themes in the Reformation Theology of William Tyndale.* 1986.

Trueman, Carl R. *Luther's Legacy.* 1994.

James E. McGoldrick

SEE ALSO

Articles of Religion; Bible Translation; Bilney, Thomas; Bishops' Book; Calvinism; Cranmer, Thomas; Erasmus, Desiderius; Henry VIII; Heresy; Humanism; Marian Exiles; Reformation, English; Rogers, John; Sacraments; Tyndale, William; Wolsey, Thomas

Lyly, John (c.1554–1606)

John Lyly's career demonstrates the disappointments of the academic humanist in the latter part of the sixteenth century who seeks a position of responsibility in an Elizabethan court that values him only as an entertainer. Despite his disappointments, however, Lyly was to become celebrated as one of a group of writers, later called the "University Wits," who graduated from Oxford and Cambridge in the 1570s and 1580s and sought their fortunes in London. Grandson to William Lily, the renowned humanist educator identified with "Lily's Grammar," John Lyly was born probably in 1554 and reared in Canterbury. By 1571, he had matriculated at Magdalen College, Oxford, where Gabriel Harvey describes him as "the fiddlestick of Oxford," suggesting that Lyly may sometimes have slighted his studies and indulged his playful tempera-

ment. He received the bachelor of arts degree from Oxford in 1573, the master of arts degree in 1575, and the M.A. from Cambridge in 1579. In May 1574, Lyly wrote to William Cecil, Lord Burghley, seeking support in obtaining a fellowship at Oxford, apparently in hopes of an academic career.

Although the fellowship failed to materialize, the correspondence reveals Lyly's ties to the influential Burghley, later strengthened by his marriage to a Burghley relative, Beatrice Brown, in 1583. By approximately 1576, Lyly was living in London; apparently making acquaintance with other writers, such as Edmund Spenser, Thomas Watson, George Peele, and George Buc; and burnishing his reputation as "witty, comical, and facetious." In 1578, he published his popular and widely imitated prose fiction, *Euphues: The Anatomy of Wit,* and in 1580 its sequel, *Euphues and His England.* With his Burghley connections and his *bellelettristic* credentials, Lyly, by 1582, had become the secretary to the literary and mercurial Edward de Vere, earl of Oxford. In the early 1580s, Lyly, in the new role of dramatist, joined with the earl and a company of boy choristers to produce plays at the private theater in Blackfriars. From the 1580s to the early 1590s, he wrote some eight comedies, mostly intended for performance not only in the commercial private theater, but also at Elizabeth's court. By garnering the queen's favor, Lyly hoped for preferment to a livelihood, in particular, the position of master of the revels. Although he never received such a substantial office, he was awarded several minor positions in St. Paul's Choir School and the Revels Office. Lyly's pen also had its polemical uses, for in 1589, Lyly was induced to write *Pap with a Hatchet,* a satirical defense of Anglican bishops against the underground Puritan pamphleteers known as "Martin Marprelate."

Lyly had flourished under the earl of Oxford, but by 1592, the earl had retired from court, the boys' acting companies had been suppressed, and Lyly's fortunes had gone into eclipse. Even though he was elected to Parliament in 1589 and three times subsequently, Lyly suffered in his later years from impecuniousness, and his letters to the queen and court figures lament the official neglect of him. In such pleas, scholars have seen the erosion in Elizabeth I's reign of the humanist dream of advancement through learning, wit, and eloquence. Was Lyly unjustly ignored? The evidence seems equivocal, for Lyly's services to Burghley, Oxford, and even Elizabeth are blemished by minor accusations against him, and Lyly, for his own part, later judged that he had too much "played the fool." John Lyly died in 1606.

L

Euphues: The Anatomy of Wit went through twelve editions in Lyly's lifetime, including four in its first year. The prose style itself made the work famous and came to be know as Euphuism, a fashion of speech that conquered the court and became the most popular (and parodied) manner of prose in the Elizabethan age. The style possesses a distinctive cadence, sound, syntax, and rhetoric. The typical euphuistic sentence blooms with profuse clauses and phrases marshaled in parallel and antithetical relation, receives augmentation by alliteration and assonance (and even rhyme), and amplifies its ideas with natural and (elsewhere) mythological allusions. The style's virtuosity occurs in its apparently inexhaustible supply of vivid, almost self-generating pairs of likenesses and contrasts, but the bright artifice also betrays a deeply ironic perspicacity, often aimed at human self-deception. Expansive in its references to myth, history, and nature, Lyly's Euphuism offers a complex, even paradoxical, representation of life and the world.

Euphues tells the prodigal son story of young man who leaves Athens (i.e., Oxford) for the courtly society of Naples (i.e., London), where he rejects the wisdom of the elderly Eubulus and gives himself to folly. After swearing friendship to Philautus, Euphues wins away from him the affection of the beautiful Lucilla, who subsequently betrays Euphues, too—whereupon Euphues abandons society in favor of contemplation. Through dialogue, commentary, and epistles, the work explores familiar Elizabethan oppositions, such as between wit and wisdom, age and youth, education and experience, love and lust, friendship and selfishness, society and solitude. *Euphues and His England* (1580) greatly improves on its predecessor, critics agree, by employing its homiletic material to advance the tale. *Euphues and His England* follows Euphues and Philautus to England, where the latter pursues ill-fated and then successful courtships. Recanting *Euphues's* misogyny and isolationism, the second work takes love as its particular focus, with debates that recall those of Castiglione's *The Courtier*.

Love was also the great subject of both Lyly's fiction and drama, and he so enlivened romantic comedy as a theatrical genre that he can be seen as its virtual inventor. Particularly in his earlier plays—*Campaspe* (c. 1583), *Sappho and Phao* (c. 1583), *Gallathea* (c. 1585), and *Endymion* (c. 1588)—calibrated for the tastes of Elizabeth's court, Lyly learned to dramatize the hesitations, griefs, and exuberances of love. His love theme gives new prominence to female characters and greatly heightens the titillations of cross-dressing, that is, of boy actors playing females. Written for performance by boys choristers, Lyly's dramas make comic capital on the sexual and physical incongruities of their actors and abound with singing, dancing, spectacle, and even onstage transformations. The plays' frequently fantastical settings, furthermore, invite a delightful array of characters, including philosophers, pages, gods, generals, aristocrats, apprentices, artisans, witches, foresters, nymphs, and bumpkins.

For all its charm, Lyly's drama has often been taken as "static" and "intellectual," given to the exploration of central questions ("What is love?") rearticulated through ever-widening sets of characters and circumstances. Correspondingly, critics have identified Lyly as a court dramatist allegorizing court personages or flattering the queen. That characterization weakens, however, when applied to Lyly's later plays, such as *Midas* (c. 1589), *Mother Bombie* (c. 1589), *Love's Metamorphosis* (c. 1590), and *The Woman in the Moon,* with their darkened tones and broad interests. Lyly's plays, furthermore, employ comic devices comparable to those of public theater, draw on the popular stage romances that preceded his, adapt euphuistic style to the physical immediacy of the stage, and express a theatrical dynamism, humor, and ambiguity too easily obscured when the plays are treated as courtly, static, and intellectual.

Elizabethan prose style and dramatic practice did not develop along the paths charted by Lyly, but he influenced both. Succeeding playwrights favored realistic plays written for adult companies—and Lyly's fantasias never achieved a wide theatrical following anyway—but the plays of Robert Greene, William Shakespeare, Ben Jonson, and others often recall Lylyan dramaturgy, and many later playwrights embrace from Lyly the tribulations of romantic love and the erotic ambiguities of cross-dressed players. Lyly's literary achievement, despite his personal disappointments, suggests how richly interlaced were the strands of Elizabethan popular, courtly, and humanistic culture.

BIBLIOGRAPHY

Bond, R.W. *The Complete Works of John Lyly.* 3 vols. 1902.

Donovan, Kevin J. "Recent Studies in John Lyly (1969–1990)." *English Literary Renaissance*, vol. 22, pp. 435–450.

Houppert, Joseph W. *John Lyly.* 1975.

Hunter, G.K. *John Lyly: The Humanist as Courtier.* 1962.

Pincombe, Michael. *The Plays of John Lyly: Eros and Eliza.* 1996.

Saccio, Peter. *The Court Comedies of John Lyly: A Study in Allegorical Dramaturgy.* 1969.

Kent Cartwright

SEE ALSO

Buc, George; De Vere, Edward; Euphuism; Harvey, Gabriel; Lily, William; Marprelate Controversy; Peele, George; Revels Office; Spenser, Edmund; Theater Companies, Boys

Lyric

The status of the lyric was problematic for its writers and theorists in the English Renaissance, and not because it was often stated to have a humble or middling place in the hierarchy of poetic genres. When Aristotle included the lyric in the canon of poetic genres, he both established it as a major literary mode and left problems for subsequent literary theorists to resolve, one important problem centering on his concept of poetry as imitation. He had asserted in his *Poetics* that poetry is a form of imitation; in particular, he had claimed, it is imitative of the actions of men (see, respectively, *Poetics* 1447a and 1448a). Exactly how the lyric is imitative he did not specify. One result of his not doing so was that literary theorists of the Italian Renaissance tried to solve the problem for themselves. Some defended the lyric's inclusion in the canon of poetic genres by arguing that it imitates thoughts and feelings, or that in a lyric the poet imitates himself, projecting in verse a representation of his perceptions, emotions, and attitudes. But while that particular debate about the status of the lyric deeply concerned Italian theorists, and was not without interest to Tudor and Stuart writers on or of the lyric, the status of the lyric was debated with a different emphasis by the English.

The problem of mimesis was not, of course, ignored by them. Sir Philip Sidney, for example, dealt with it astutely in his *An Apology for Poetry,* perhaps more so than did any other writer of the English Renaissance. Referring to Aristotle's concept that poetry is "an arte of imitation," then elaborating on it by applying the authoritative Horatian dicta that poetry is a picture in words (*"ut pictura poesis"*) and that it delights and instructs (*"delectando pariterque monendo"*), Sidney claimed that poets imitate "the inconceiuable excellencies of GOD," or forms of knowledge, or forms of their own inventing. Among such poets he numbered the writers of lyrics. For Sidney, however, the status of the lyric did not depend on its capacity or incapacity to imitate (for he chose to take as a given that it does do so) but on what it imitates. Writing of "Songs and Sonnets," the latter term meaning "little songs" rather than exclusively the sonnet as we know it, he identified God as the lyric's best subject and sexual desire as a far inferior one. The lyric of his day was lowered in status, Sidney implied, because contemporary lyric poets had chosen and were choosing to compose verse that was erotic instead of theocentric. That Sidney himself contributed notably and at times self-questioningly to the store of current love verse is not at issue here. What matters more is that his disquiet over profane love as the subject of lyric verse—and it is, unsurprisingly enough, one of the great subjects of the Tudor and Stuart lyric—had been anticipated, and would be echoed, by many other voices in early modern England.

How widespread and long-lasting such disquiet was can be seen clearly if one glances at *The Court of Venus,* the earliest known miscellany of Tudor lyric verse (c. 1530s), and *Tottel's Miscellany* (1557), the forerunners of the many miscellanies containing lyric verse that were to appear in England during the last half of the sixteenth century (as might be expected, lyric verse did not always dominate the Tudor miscellanies). *The Court of Venus* included some lyrics by Sir Thomas Wyatt (1503–1542); much more of his verse, in fact the greater part of it, was printed with forty poems by Henry Howard, earl of Surrey, in *Tottel's Miscellany.* In reaction against the secularity of earlier Tudor verse John Hall composed *The Court of Virtue* (printed 1565), his work's title suggesting parody of, and an attempt to provide a moral counter to, *The Court of Venus.* Hall fulfilled the promise of his work's title by devoutly rewriting some of Wyatt's love lyrics and by fashioning morally correct counterparts to various of the poems in the two miscellanies preceding his own. It is worth mentioning that the full title of *Tottel's Miscellany,* that shorter version incorporating the name of the volume's publisher, began *Songs and Sonnets . . .*—to which Sidney was no doubt alluding when disparaging lyrics of profane love. But if Hall's response to verse of that kind was unusual in extent, he was not the only writer to anticipate or to affirm Sidney's disparagement of it. Robert Southwell and others would also write sacred parodies of profane love lyrics. In Tudor and Stuart times, the status of lyric verse was recurrently questioned because so often the lyric had profane rather than sacred love as its subject, yet that questioning proved, of course, to be inconclusive.

Wyatt and Surrey are conventionally regarded as the most important of the early Tudor lyricists. They wrote lyrics concerning love, politics, and the interaction of the

L

two, as well as lyrics of moral counsel and religious lyrics. Reviewing their achievements, George Puttenham claimed in his *The Arte of English Poesie* (1589) that "they greatly polished our rude & homely maner of vulgar Poesie, from that it had bene before, and for that cause may iustly be sayd the first reformers of our English/meetre and stile." He attributed that to their introducing aspects of contemporary "Italian Poesie" into English verse. It is true that they did so. Wyatt brought in, for example, the Petrarchan sonnet and *strambotti* imitative of Serafino's. Surrey, too, composed sonnets modeled on Petrarch's. On the other hand, Wyatt wrote lyrics in the traditions of fifteenth-century English gnomic verse and courtly love verse, and often he derived his metrics from the native metrical practices of his English predecessors. Richard Tottel smoothed out—and marred—the metrical flow of some poems by Wyatt that were included in the *Miscellany*. Surrey created an English form for the sonnet, the form that William Shakespeare would use, and wrote the most innovative paraphrases of the Psalms before those by Sidney and his sister, Mary Sidney, countess of Pembroke. Via Sidney's *Astrophil and Stella* (1590, written c. 1581–1582), Wyatt's introduction of the Petrarchan sonnet into England would prove especially fruitful in the last decade of the sixteenth century, when sonnet sequences such as Shakespeare's *Sonnets* and Edmund Spenser's *Amoretti* were composed. Surrey gave to his successors, perhaps most notably to Sidney, models of lucid and polished versification. Moreover, both Wyatt and Surrey showed to subsequent courtly lyricists ways in which various selves could be constructed and displayed in relation to the different aspects and demands of life at court.

Tottel's Miscellany offered, then, major poetic examples in the mid-century to those interested in the lyric; and the miscellany itself was a successful publishing venture, for Tottel's collection was frequently reprinted. Further miscellanies appeared, from *A Handefull of Pleasant Delites* (1566) and *The Gorgeous Gallery of Gallant Inventions* (1578) to *England's Helicon* (1600) and beyond. Yet despite all the poetic activity that, in the mid-century, followed the printing of *Tottel's Miscellany*, the lyrics of only one poet have attracted extensive critical attention, those of George Gascoigne. The range of his lyric verse resembles that of his more courtly predecessors; from his less privileged social position, he too fashioned powerful representations of his dealings—and of his hopes to have dealings—with the courtly world.

In the last twenty or so years of the sixteenth century a new impetus was given to the writing of lyrics. *The Shepheardes Calender* of Edmund Spenser was printed in 1579.

Sidney's verse in his pastoral romance *Arcadia* and his *Astrophil and Stella* were written, though not printed, at much the same time. Spenser's intricate pastorals drew him acclaim as "the new poet" and were imitated by Michael Drayton, William Basse, Phineas Fletcher, and William Browne, to name only his poems' more immediate admirers. Sidney's poems for his *Arcadia* expressed his capacity for wide experimentation with meter (classical and vernacular) and with stanzaic form. As was noted earlier, his sonnets would set the fashion for sonnet sequences in the 1590s, when Spenser's *Amoretti*, as well as that poet's long celebratory lyrics *Epithalamion* and *Prothalamion*, would appear. It is around this time, from 1576, that Sir Walter Ralegh apparently began to write his lyrics, which at first link mid-century verse to the newer poetry. The verse from his later years images in a poetic of dissonance the precariousness and failures of his courtly career.

But in the verse of Sidney, Shakespeare, and Thomas Campion, the Elizabethan lyric seems to approximate most nearly the condition of music, irrespective of actual musical settings. The lyrics of Shakespeare were written for his plays and so, like other lyrics in plays or masques, are usually both interludes in the dramatic action and commentaries on it. Many are love poems or poems of love with pastoral settings ("Who is Silvia?" for example), the latter mode of lyric being very popular in the last half of the sixteenth century; some are poems of moral advice (such as "All that glisters . . ."); some are pastoral lyrics (as is "Under the greenwood tree"); there are satirical lyrics, charms, and fantastic or grotesque fragments. They offer an almost infinite variety of theme and of form. In *The Merry Wives of Windsor*, Sir Hugh Evans sings a song that amusingly mingles one of the time's most famous love lyrics—"Come live with me . . . ," by Shakespeare's rival, Christopher Marlowe (1564–1593)—with Psalm 137. The last of the three poets mentioned, Thomas Campion, was both a poet and a musician. Like Sidney, he was a theorist as well as a writer of the lyric and experimented with classical meters. Although his Petrarchan love poems, such as "Rose-cheeked Laura, come," have received most comment he also composed moving religious poems, such as "Never weather-beaten sail. . . ." Yet if one were to consider the religious lyric, excluding the versified psalm, throughout the sixteenth century, Robert Southwell might be singled out as its most innovative practitioner. Southwell was a Jesuit priest, and as part of his mission to England's priestless Catholics he wrote sacred parodies of profane love verse, poems of moral counsel and encouragement, and poems concerning repentance. He adopted the style of mid-century gnomic verse, refigured the Petrarchan rhetoric of love, and introduced into English religious verse elements of Jesuit religious rhetoric, which can be startlingly seen in his famous meditative lyric "The burning Babe."

There were other debates concerning the lyric. Should lyrics be written in classical or in vernacular meters? Should rhyme be used or not? Those questions were debated vigorously in works ranging from Roger Ascham's *Schoolmaster* (1570) to Samuel Daniel's *A Defense of Rime* (1603). There were experiments, too, in writing unrhymed lyric verse in classical meters; Sidney's experiments seem to have been the most wide-ranging. But as we know, from that debate (and however successful the attempts to impose classical measures on English verse) the vernacular meters and rhyme emerged victorious.

The influence of Spenser's pastorals continued, like that of Sidney's *Astrophil and Stella* and of his biblical paraphrases, well into the seventeenth century. However, it was the verse of two younger poets who began writing in the 1590s that came to dominate the modes and idioms of the Stuart lyric. John Donne and Ben Jonson did not, of course, turn wholly from the ways in which the preceding generation of poets had written. Each drew on the Petrarchan language of love, for example (though neither wrote a Petrarch-derived sonnet sequence), and each could write a lyric as mellifluous as any to be found in a miscellany or a play. Nor were the two without other things in common as writers of lyrics. The epigram seems to have been, frequently for each, the basic unit of poetic design; each often used in his poems the diction and rhythms of conversational speech. For all that, as poets they were markedly different from their immediate predecessors and from one another. In his lyrics, Donne frequently deployed conceits—catachrestic images—to suggest his speakers' unique visions of experience and their skeptical analyses of it; the speakers of his secular love lyrics—the *Elegies* and *Songs and Sonnets*—were often modeled on Ovid's narrators in the *Amores* and in the *Metamorphoses* rather than on Petrarch's speaker in the *Rime;* often in his lyrics he unfolded utopian or dystopian fictions. Jonson, in his lyrics, infrequently used catachrestic images, preferring to fashion his verse with a neoclassical perspicuity of both diction and form; his lyrics acknowledged the authority of the mythographers and of *The Greek Anthology,* of Martial and of Horace, rather than that of Petrarch; he at times made himself a fully realized character in his lyrics, representing his physical traits as well as his attitudes and values. To Donne and Jonson, primarily though not solely, the Stuart lyricists would be greatly indebted.

BIBLIOGRAPHY
Dubrow, Heather. *Echoes of Desire: English Petrarchism and Its Counterdiscourses.* 1995.
Greene, Roland A. *Post-Petrarchism: Origins and Innovations of the Western Lyric.* 1991.
Greene, Thomas M. *The Light in Troy: Imitation and Discovery in Renaissance Poetry.* 1982.
Peterson, Douglas. *The English Lyric from Wyatt to Donne: A History of the Plain and Eloquent Styles.* 2nd edition. 1990.
Roche, Thomas P., Jr. *Petrarch and the English Sonnet Sequences.* 1989.

A.D. Cousins

SEE ALSO
Campion, Thomas; Daniel, Samuel; Donne, John; Gascoigne, George; Howard, Henry; Jonson, Ben; Petrarchanism; Puttenham, George; Shakespeare, William; Spenser, Edmund; Sidney, Mary; Sidney, Philip; Sonnet Sequences; Southwell, Robert; Tottel, Richard; Verse Anthologies; Versification

M

Machiavell, The

The term "Machiavell" (spelled variously) anglicizes the name of Niccolo Machiavelli, Italian political writer and dramatist, and author of *The Prince* and *The Discourses.* In Tudor political, religious, and literary discourse, the Machiavell represented an unsavory political type linked to Machiavelli's dominant English reputation as an advocate of force and fraud. In Christopher Marlowe's *The Jew of Malta,* a choric character named "Machevill" describes himself as one who believes that religion is "but a childish toy," that "there is no sin but ignorance," and that "might first made kings, and laws were then most sure / When like the Draco's / they were writ in blood" (*The Jew of Malta,* ll. 14–21). To these supposedly "Machiavellian" characteristics of atheism, bloodiness, and a belief that "might makes right" were often added persuasive rhetoric, "policy" or devious manipulation of others to achieve one's own ends, and hypocrisy.

The appearance of the Machiavell in Tudor plays and prose follows the complicated history of Machiavelli's English reception. While Innocent Gentillet's anti-Machiavellian tract *Discours sure les moyens de bien governer . . . Contre Nicolas Machiavel* (published in French and Latin in 1577 and translated into English in 1602) most thoroughly depicted Machiavelli as promoting tyranny and atheism, both anti-Machiavellian ideas and Machiavelli's own works circulated in many forms in the sixteenth century, a situation creating often quite contradictory notions of Machiavellianism. Well before the first English translations of *The Prince* in 1640 and *The Discourses* in 1636, Englishmen (including Henry Howard, earl of Surrey, Thomas Smith, and Christopher Hatton) owned and read Italian editions of Machiavelli's works. A

French edition also appeared in 1570, and English translations of *The Prince* also circulated in manuscript form. Recent scholarship on the sixteenth-century English reception of Machiavelli in this period has pointed to an appreciation of both Machiavellian republicanism and the Italian's rhetorical interpretation of politics at the same time the accusations proliferated (in conjunction with an virulent strain of anti-Italian feeling) that Machiavelli advocated tyranny and political practices of immorality, deception, violence, and ungodliness.

In Tudor plays, the negative traits associated with Machiavelli's political thought merged in different settings with the existing dramatic types of the Senecan tyrant and the Vice to create the stage Machiavell. The tyrants of Seneca's plays, especially Atreus in *Thyestes,* Lycus in *Hercules Furens,* Nero in *Octavia,* and Eteocles in *Phoenissae* (as well as in their Italian Renaissance descendants) shaped a theatrical image of the villainous and ambitious ruler who uses deceit and violence in grasping for absolute power: as Eteocles puts it, these are characters who believe that *"imperia pretio quolibet constant bene"* (sovereignty is well bought at any price). At the same time, the Vice of the vernacular morality plays offered an alternative model for casting the "Machiavell" type, not as the figure of the prince but rather in the role of the evil plotter or revenger. The traits of the Vice, such at Titivillus on *Mankind,* Ambidexter in *Cambyses* ("one that with both hands finely can play"), and Hypocrisy in *Lusty Juventus,* which included evil intent, manipulation of the innocent, and hypocrisy, defined the stage action of the "Machiavellian" abuses of rhetoric and "policy."

Some characters in Tudor plays, such as Barabas in *The Jew of Malta,* are explicitly identified as Machiavells, but

M

scholars have identified as Machiavells many villains who have several characteristics of the type without being specifically named as such. In some cases, the Machiavell's role is political, and he is, or seeks to become, a tyrant. The most notorious example is William Shakespeare's Richard of Gloucester, who in *3 Henry VI* promises "to set the murtherous machiavil to school," and indeed proceeds to do so in his campaign of murder, persuasion, and crafty deceit in *Richard III*. Similar "politicians" in Tudor plays include the Duke of Guise in Marlowe's *Massacre of Paris,* Mortimer in Marlowe's *Edward II,* Muly Mahomet in George Peele's *The Battle of Alcazar,* and Selimus in Robert Greene's *Tragical Reign of Selimus* (Greene also lets loose an extended condemnation of "Machiavel" in *A Groatsworth of Wit*). Other Machiavells, resembling Barabas, are less political and tend more to seek their own gain or revenge against more powerful foes. Like Barabas, too, these Machiavells often bear the mark of cultural difference or alienation, labeled as Italians, Spaniards, or Moors: for example, Aaron in Shakespeare's *Titus Andronicus,* Eleazar in the anonymous *Lust's Dominion,* and Lorenzo in Thomas Kyd's *The Spanish Tragedy.* Machiavells also appear in prose narrative: a notable example is the Captain in Thomas Nashe's *The Unfortunate Traveler* (1597), whom Jack Wilton persuades to be a "miraculous politician," with disastrous consequences. Nashe's Captain also represents another variation on the type, which is the failed or parodic Machiavell; in this family of foolish Machiavells are found Gostanzo in George Chapman's *All Fools* and Sir Politick Would-be in Ben Jonson's *Volpone.* The image of the Machiavell persisted in seventeenth-century literature, either in this parodic form or in the more complex villains such as Iago in Shakespeare's *Othello,* Flamineo in John Webster's *The White Devil,* and Gondomar in Thomas Middleton's *A Game at Chess.*

BIBLIOGRAPHY

Bawcutt, N.W. "Machiavelli and Marlowe's *Jew of Malta.*" *Renaissance Drama,* vol. 3, pp. 3–49.

Gasquet, Emile. *Le Courant Machiavelian dans la Pensee et la Litterature Anglaises du XVI Siecle.* 1974.

Kahn, Victoria. *Machiavellian Rhetoric: From the Counter-Reformation to Milton.* 1994.

Praz, Mario. "Machiavelli and the Elizabethans." *Proceedings of the British Academy,* vol. 13, pp. 49–97.

Raab, Felix. *The English Face of Machiavelli: A Changing Interpretation, 1500–1700.* 1964.

Scott, Margaret. "Machiavelli and the Machiavel." *Renaissance Drama,* vol. 15, pp. 147–74.

Rebecca Bushnell

SEE ALSO

Chapman, George; Drama, History of; Greene, Robert; Jonson, Ben; Kyd, Thomas; Marlowe, Christopher; Nashe, Thomas; Peele, George; Political Thought; Shakespeare, William; Vice, The

Machyn, Henry (c. 1498–1563)

A merchant tailor and supplier of funeral ornaments, Henry Machyn kept a diary from 1550 until 1563, a matter-of-fact chronology with little indication of his thoughts. Machyn rarely refers to himself in the diary and always does so in the third person. Even the births and deaths of family members are related in a detached, impersonal style.

Apparently fascinated by crime and punishment, Machyn describes pilloryings, charivaris, and executions for the full range of Tudor sins and crimes. He takes equal note of both "low" and "high" cases, describing minor cases of prostitution and the notorious murder of Arden of Faversham alongside the trials and executions attending Wyatt's Rebellion and the shift in power from Somerset to Northumberland.

Machyn's diary provides important evidence for the reaction of ordinary Londoners to the religious upheavals of the mid-century. Certain entries point toward his conservatism and attachment to the church of Rome. He repeatedly records the loss of Roman ceremonies under Elizabeth I and writes with "gret wondur" of an official burning of religious images. He once did penance for spreading a rumor that a French Protestant preacher "was taken with a wenche," and he notes acerbically that another Elizabethan preacher "had a wyf and viij chylderyn."

Machyn's diary ends on August 8, 1563. His parish register records his death on October 11, 1563; he probably died in an epidemic of plague. From his exhaustive study of Machyn's orthography, Wijk concluded that Machyn was born and raised in southeastern Yorkshire, but his diary ensures that he will be known to history as a Londoner.

BIBLIOGRAPHY

Nichols, John Gough, ed. *The Diary of Henry Machyn, Citizen and Merchant-Taylor of London, from* A.D. *1550 to* A.D. *1563.* 1848.

Wijk, Axel. *The Orthography and Pronunciation of Henry Machyn, the London Diarist.* 1937.

Zachary Lesser

Madrigal

Like the lute ayre, the English madrigal flourished for
only a brief time. The English court had employed Italian
musicians since the early sixteenth century, and Thomas
Hoby's translation of Castiglione's *Il Cortegiano* had
helped to spark English interest in Italian culture, as had
Thomas Watson in 1582 with his *Hekatompathia,* the
first published English sonnets, paraphrases of Petrarch,
Serafino dall'Aquila, and Politian, among others. The
composers modeled their works after the Italian madrigal
of the later sixteenth century, composed by Luca Marenzio (c. 1553–1599) and Giaches de Wert (1535–1596),
among others. The English madrigal was, however, tempered by the earlier tradition of English secular song and
by the fact that there was no body of English poetry to
match that of Petrarch, Tasso, Ariosto, Guarini, and others. Loath for whatever reasons to use the poetry of
Edmund Spenser and Sir Walter Ralegh (Orlando Gibbons is exceptional in this regard), English madrigalists
mostly set texts written solely to be sung.

One of the most famous examples of the English imitating Italian models is the collection *The Triumphes of
Oriana,* published in 1601 in honor of Elizabeth I (Oriana was the British princess beloved of Amadis of Gaul).
Edited by Thomas Morley, who contributed *Hard by a
crystal fountain* (modeled after Giovanni Croce's *Ove tra
l'herbe*) and *Arise, awake, awake,* it was inspired by *Il Tri-
onfo di Dori* of 1592, commissioned by Leonardo Sanudo,
a wealthy Venetian, as a gift for his bride. It consists of
five- and six-voice madrigals by twenty-three composers,
each ending with the refrain "Thus sang the shepherds
and nymphs of Diana: Long live fair Oriana." It is worth
noting that neither Byrd nor Gibbons contributed; neither was very interested in the madrigal genre. Byrd's two
1590 settings of *This sweet and merry month of May* are
exceptions to his usual disdain for the madrigal.

Elizabethan composers were influenced by several Italian types other than the madrigal. Morley, not as drawn
to the serious madrigal as others, and more indebted to
Italy besides, reworked seven balletti composed by Giovanni Gastoldi (d. 1572), improving them markedly in
the process, seen in the comparison of *Sing we and chant
it* to *A lieta vita.* The balletto, consisting of strophic texts
set homophonically with nonsense syllables marking the
ends of sections, contributed the fa-la-la refrains so many
associate with Elizabethan vocal music. Another lighter
Italian type for which Morley showed a decided proclivity
is the canzonetto, each of whose strophes usually fall in
two repeated sections or AABCC form. In all, Morley
published five collections of canzonets, balletts, and light
madrigals. His two-voice collection of 1595 is unusual
since the Italians never wrote canzonettas for so few
voices, although in it Morley borrows from Felice Anerio
(c. 1560–1614). Generally, English madrigalists were
more interested in the three- and especially four-voice
madrigal than were the Italians.

The basic conservatism of the English madrigalists is
evident in the care with which they employ chromaticism, and also in its rarity. Most composers wrote only
one or two strikingly chromatic madrigals: Thomas
Tomkins' *Weepe no more thou sorry boy,* Weelkes's *Thule
the period of cosmography* and *Cease sorrowes now,* Giles
Farnaby's *Construe my meaning,* Francis Pilkington's *Care
for thy soul,* and Wilbye's *Oft have I vowde* are among the
few examples. The basic conventions of word-painting—
including passages of rapidly moving notes for wind, running, and happiness; triple time for dancing; the
appropriate intervallic motion for mountains, valleys,
descending, and ascending; the stepwise falling fourth for
tears—are found in the English madrigal, although,
again, never to the extent evident in their Italian counterparts. The English were reluctant to break up the musical
flow of a work for musical depictions of individual words.

The best of those whom Kerman labels as serious
madrigalists are Thomas Weelkes and John Wilbye.
Weelkes, more daring than Wilbye, did not use translations of Italian texts and is one of the few to use the
cadence with both the raised and lowered seventh degree,
a false relation quite common in earlier Tudor music.
Wilbye, whose first book of madrigals (1598), uses translated Italian texts and was clearly cognizant of Morley's
canzonet style. Another excellent madrigalist, distinguished for his serious approach and exceptional literary
taste, was John Ward (1571–1638?). He published only
one book of madrigals, for three to six voices, praised for
their expressive use of both dissonance and word-painting
(*Come sable night* is an excellent example). Opinions vary
regarding the one book of madrigals published by
Thomas Tomkins (1572–1656) in 1622, with some holding such works as *Yet againe, as soon revived* and *Too much
I once lamented* as highlights of the madrigal's last years.

It is typical of this genre's decline, as rapid as its ascent,
that Tomkins and Ward each published only one book of

M

madrigals. George Kirbye (d. 1634); John Bennet (fl. 1599–1614), whose *Weepe O mine eyes* is a miniature masterpiece; John Farmer (b. 1570?), whose *Faire Phyllis I saw sitting all alone* is one of the most famous madrigals; Farnaby (c. 1563–1630); Robert Jones, and other even more minor figures also contributed only one collection each. With the increasing popularity of the lute ayre, the madrigal was soon eclipsed, although Edmund H. Fellowes' edition has done much to popularize the genre with modern audiences.

BIBLIOGRAPHY

Fellowes, Edmund H. *English Madrigal Verse, 1588–1632.* 3rd edition; revised 1967.

———. *The English Madrigal Composers.* 2nd edition. 1948.

———, ed. *The English Madrigal School.* 36 vols. 1913–1924; revised by Thurston Dart. *The English Madrigalists.* 1956–1976.

Kerman, Joseph. *The Elizabethan Madrigal: A Comparative Study.* 1962.

Roche, Jerome. *The Madrigal.* 1972.

Laura S. Youens

SEE ALSO

Air; Byrd, William; Hoby, Thomas; Italian Literature, Influence of; Morley, Thomas; Petrarchanism; Weekes, Thomas; Wilbye, John

Magic

Magic was one of the key elements in the intellectual world of Renaissance Europe, England included. In the fifteenth and sixteenth centuries, what modern terminology would describe as magic was part of a philosophical outlook that aimed at understanding and controlling nature, and which was, in many respects, inextricably connected with what modern observers would call science. Magic had been an important strand in medieval intellectual activity, and the mystical and the occult were given a tremendous boost in the second half of the fifteenth century with the circulation of key texts brought into western Europe after the fall of Constantinople, notably those attributed to the apocryphal ancient Egyptian thinker Hermes Trismegistus and the associated rise of Neoplatonic speculation.

These influences were probably more strongly at work in continental Europe than in the relatively isolated intellectual world of late medieval England, although

manuscript magical texts preserved in both the Bodleian and the British Libraries demonstrate that this new interest in the occult was present in England. It should be stressed that for the magical practitioners who pored over such texts, magic was regarded as a learned and esoteric pursuit, the product of high culture and elite scholarship. The Renaissance ideal of the magical practitioner was the magus, the man of immense learning and moral probity, a type presented in the character of Prospero in Shakespeare's *The Tempest*. The importance of this tradition of learned magic was demonstrated by the degree to which magical and occult elements were manifest in a number of intellectual activities. The practice of medicine, for example, involved not only diagnosis of illness and prescription of treatment in the modern fashion, but also the assistance of effecting a cure by the use of charms or the casting of horoscopes to determine the most propitious time for treatment. Astrology, indeed, was a respected science, and the predictions of learned astrologers were taken seriously at court. Alchemy, another esoteric science, was practiced by a few adepts, and achieved a decidedly mystical tinge. Mathematics comprehended not just the manipulation of numbers, but also the mystical contemplation of numbers as a means of unlocking the secrets of the universe. The nature of the connections between magic and the occult and what modern thinking would categorize as science is ideally illustrated in the career of John Dee, who managed to operate both as a serious mathematician and as a man who tried to raise angels in hopes of contacting the spirit world.

Some of the broader implications of this flourishing of magical and occult influences, especially within the context of Neoplatonism, can be seen in the development of mystical elements around the Gloriana cult, which revered Queen Elizabeth. The forces of nature were now not merely considered in the abstract, but were harnessed and, largely through the medium of symbols and emblems, used to express the power of the English monarchy. Thus a strand of philosophical magic came to have a considerable impact on the mobilization of the propaganda images of Elizabeth I, and looking at a royal portrait or reading some of the poetry of her reign involves the observer in the decoding of esoteric and magical messages.

But magic was not just part of a benign philosophical system. It also had its malevolent side, and this, too, could be seen at work on a high political level. From the late fourteenth century onward, English monarchs had thought that among the threats leveled against them were treasonous plots involving magic and sorcery, and the reigns of the Tudors saw a continuation of this trend. Henry VII confronted one such plot, part of an attempt aimed at replacing him with the pretender Perkin Warbeck in 1496, while allegations of sorcery and witchcraft were among the many allegations directed at Anne Boleyn at the time of her trial in 1540. Such fears continued through the mid-Tudor period into the reign of Elizabeth I, and fear of treason through sorcery was an occasional concern of the Privy Council during her reign.

These problems on the level of political culture were mirrored by the development of witchcraft as a secular crime. The first statute against witchcraft came in 1542. There is little evidence that this statute was enforced, and it was supplanted by another of 1563. Following this legislation, the prosecution of alleged witches occurred in most parts of England, although the fragmentary records preclude systematic analysis of the phenomenon. However, intensive study of witchcraft in Essex, a well-documented county in this respect, reveals steady prosecution for witchcraft throughout Elizabeth's reign, rising to a peak in the 1580s. Many of these prosecutions are linked to village disputes made more numerous and acrimonious by the socioeconomic changes of the period. Most of the accusations revolved around *maleficium,* the doing of harm by the witch, especially the infliction of death or illness on adult human beings, children, or farm livestock. Surviving documentation from the Essex assizes demonstrates that during Elizabeth's reign, 304 indictments for witchcraft were brought against 184 witches, of whom fifty-five were executed. Ninety percent of those accused were women.

The Elizabethan period also witnessed the publication of a number of large works on witchcraft, among them Henry Holland's *Treatise against Witchcraft* (1590), William Perkin's *Discourse of the Damned Art of Witchcraft* (published posthumously in 1608), and an unrelentingly skeptical tract, Reginald Scot's *Discoverie of Witchcraft* (1584). These full-scale treatises were complemented by a series of shorter tracts, some of them mere pamphlets, describing individual witchcraft trials for the benefit of a sensation-hungry readership; the first such tract, describing a trial in Essex, was printed in 1566.

Recent research has emphasized the significance and widespread nature of "good" witches, most often known at the time as cunning (skillful or knowledgeable) men or women. These cunning folk were widely consulted and provided medical services, combining folk remedies with magical charms, helped (again by magic) to find stolen goods or identify thieves, revealed the identity of future husbands to serving maids, and offered advice on countermeasures to persons who thought themselves to be bewitched. Most of them operated firmly in the context of folk magic, although a few had some education and access to the paraphernalia of the learned occult practitioner. Although many cunning folk were brought before local courts, they were usually only lightly punished. These magical practitioners were to remain a feature of English life until well into the nineteenth century. Magic, therefore, pervaded all layers of Tudor society, from the monarch's court to the isolated rural settlement.

BIBLIOGRAPHY

Macfarlane, Alan. *Witchcraft in Tudor and Stuart England: A Regional and Comparative Study.* 1970.

Sharpe, J.A. *Instruments of Darkness: Witchcraft in England, 1550–1750.* 1996.

Thomas, Keith. *Religion and the Decline of Magic: Studies in Popular Beliefs in Sixteenth and Seventeenth-Century England.* 1971.

Yates, Frances. *The Occult Tradition in the Elizabethan Age.* 1979.

James Sharpe

SEE ALSO

Alchemy; Astrology; Bruno, Giordano; Dee, John; Folklore and Folk Rituals; Witchcraft

Maitland Family

Their nonaristocratic background made the Maitland family royalist in instinct but practical in politics, and they helped create a national commonwealth in Scotland that was not based on religious creed or family considerations but instead on a rational politics of tolerance.

Sir Richard Maitland (1496–1586) of Lethington probably completed a legal education in France before serving under three consecutive Scottish monarchs as lord of Session (1554–1584) and as keeper of the privy seal (1562–1567) under Mary Queen of Scots. Throughout this period, he was respected by all political and religious factions for his mildness of temper and his moderate views. He was also a historiographer and poet, and his family preserved two famous literary anthologies containing many unique Older Scots texts.

His eldest son, William Maitland of Lethington (c. 1528–1573), was appointed secretary of state in 1558 and became one of Mary's ablest politicians. His politics,

M

aimed at securing Anglo-Scottish union, were misrepresented by sixteenth-century historiograpers, who labeled him a "chameleon" (George Buchanan's term) and "Mychell Wylie," a localized version of "Machiavelli." After Mary's abdication in 1567, he joined the king's party, but soon returned to the queen's party, and was among the last to surrender in 1573 when its last stronghold, Edinburgh Castle, fell. He is rumored to have hastened his own death soon after this by taking poison.

William's younger brother, John Maitland of Thirlestane (1543–1595), was likewise an extremely gifted statesman and Protestant royalist who advocated Anglo-Scottish unity. John was at St. Andrews University in 1555 and completed his education in France. Made commendator of Coldingham and keeper of the privy seal in 1567, and lord of session in 1568, he was imprisoned in the 1570s for his Marian activities but was rehabilitated in 1581. Appointed privy councilor in 1583, he was secretary from 1584 to 1591 and chancellor from 1587 until his death, becoming the most important figure in James VI's governments in this period. He was created Lord Thirlestane in 1590. He always made James's succession to the English throne his main priority, and set up a system of government that relied on officials recruited from the ranks of the burgesses and lower gentry and that shifted power away from nobility and kirk toward king and Privy Council. As his biographer says, Thirlestane "trained a successor" in the king himself. "The wisest man in Scotland," according to many, his sharpness was feared by Randolph, the English ambassador in Edinburgh, yet the political ideas of the Maitland brothers were welcomed almost affectionately by Elizabeth I and William Cecil. He left a small body of vernacular and Neo-Latin verse.

A third brother, Thomas Maitland (c. 1545–1572), matriculated at St. Andrews in 1559 and went on to Paris c. 1563. Returning to Scotland, he eventually joined the Marian cause and in December 1569 wrote a vernacular satire on an imaginary meeting of Protestant leaders ("The Pretendit Conference"); he also wrote Neo-Latin poems. In George Buchanan's *De Jure Regni apud Scotos*, a fictional debate intended to justify the deposition of Mary Queen of Scots, Maitland is cast as one of the debating scholars, but he immediately made it known he had no hand in this work. Traveling in Italy, he died suddenly in 1572.

BIBLIOGRAPHY

Bain, Joseph, ed. *The Poems of Sir Richard Maitland of Lethingtoun, Knight.* 1830.

Blake, William. *William Maitland of Lethington, 1528–1573: A Study of the Policy of Moderation in the Scottish Reformation.* 1990.

Lee, Maurice, Jr. *John Maitland of Thirlestane and the Foundation of the Stewart Despotism in Scotland.* 1959.

———. "Sir Richard Maitland of Lethington: A Christian Laird in the Age of the Reformation." In *Action and Conviction in Early Modern Europe.* Theodore K. Rabb and Jerold E. Seigel, eds., pp. 117–132. 1969.

McKechnie, William S. "Thomas Maitland." *Scottish Historical Review,* vol. 4, pp. 274–293.

Russel, E. *Maitland of Lethington. The Minister of Mary Stuart.* 1912.

Skelton, John. *Maitland of Lethington and the Scotland of Mary Stuart:. A History.* 2 vols. 1887–1888.

Theo van Heijnsbergen

SEE ALSO
James IV; Mary Queen of Scots; Scotland, History of

Manners, Roger, Fifth Earl of Rutland (1576–1612)

Rutland was raised as a ward of William Cecil, Lord Burghley. He attended Queens' College, Cambridge, briefly, then followed his tutor (John Jegon) to Corpus Christi College. In February 1595, he became M.A. Either in Burghley's care, or at college, Rutland befriended Henry Wriothesley, earl of Southampton. On leaving university, Rutland traveled extensively abroad (1595–1598), following which he entered Gray's Inn. Throughout his life, Rutland seems to have cultivated the friendship of learned men. He sponsored Ben Jonson's masque "Metamorphosed Gypsies" at Belvoir for James I, who stayed with Rutland on his progress southward.

The second half of Rutland's short life was marred by political strife. Rutland served with the Robert Devereux, earl of Essex, in Ireland (where he was knighted, 1599); and he and his two brothers became close friends of Essex. Despite the fact that the Elizabeth I recalled Rutland from Ireland, Rutland recovered quickly, serving with the Dutch army in the company of the earl of Northumberland. Soon thereafter, Rutland and his brothers all became involved in the Essex rebellion (1601). Rutland was arrested at Essex House, and imprisoned in the Tower; however, he later gave evidence against Southampton and escaped with a £10,000 fine.

James I restored Rutland's honors and made him a knight of the bath at his coronation. The king also sent

Rutland on a mission to Christian IV, king of Denmark, to present him with the Order of the Garter. Rutland accumulated many honors throughout his career, but his days were numbered. He died in 1612, aged thirty-six, of unknown causes. He married Elizabeth, sister of Sir Philip Sidney, who died in 1615 without children. In 1906, a theory was proposed in Germany, and later in France, that Rutland wrote William Shakespeare's plays.

BIBLIOGRAPHY

Akrigg, G.P.V. *Shakespeare and the Earl of Southampton.* 1968.

Bacon, Francis. "Advice to the Earl of Rutland Upon His Travels (1597)." In *Francis Bacon.* Brian Vickers, ed. pp. 69–80. 1996.

Bostelmann, Lewis Frederick. *Rutland.* 1911.

Demblon, Célestin. *Lord Rutland est Shakespeare.* 1912.

Sykes, Claud W. *Alias William Shakespeare?* 1947.

S.P. Cerasano

SEE ALSO

Cecil, William; Devereux, Robert; Wriothesley, Henry

Manuscripts

As in all literate societies, manuscripts occupied a central role in the everyday life of Tudor England. It was by means of documents that business, property-conveyancing, and financial transactions were secured; through letters that communication between individuals over a distance was made possible; in notebooks, ledgers, registers, and household books that accounts and records could be kept and regulated and such practical things as cooking recipes and medicinal prescriptions preserved; and by means of a variety of written instruments and commissions that government, civic, legal, ecclesiastical, military, and other affairs could effectively be pursued, at both a national and local level.

In a society where literacy was still the prerogative of a minority of the population, those people privileged to learn writing were confined either to the upper, educated classes, or to those sections of the middle classes who came to recognize that writing was itself a source of power—the latter including clerks (the derivation of this term from "clerics," indicating a time when writing was largely the prerogative of the church) and professional scribes, some of whom belonged to a London guild, the Worshipful Company of Scriveners, dating back to the mid-fourteenth century.

Although other forms of script prevailed in specialized areas (highly formal "court hands," derived from medieval models, were used by certain legal scribes, most notably the ornate-looking "Chancery" script, for example), in most schools, boys were taught to write two kinds of script. One, widely prevalent for general, all-purpose use, was what was known as "secretary" script. Descended from western European "Gothic" script and introduced from France in the late fourteenth century, secretary—which seems to modern readers an archaic, not readily legible script—developed as a peculiarly English variety until the early decades of the seventeenth century, traces of some of its distinctive letter forms (such as the inverted or double-stroke "e") surviving virtually into the eighteenth century. The other—to us somewhat more familiar—script, widespread from the late fifteenth century onward, was, as its name implies, imported from Italy: namely the characteristically Renaissance or humanistic script "italic" (sometimes referred to as "Italian" or "Roman" and derived from the lettering of the ancient Romans). Literate men generally had command of both scripts—perhaps using italic for Latin, secretary for English, for instance, although the two might sometimes alternate for particular effects (with italic perhaps adopted also for proper names, headings or incipits, and special points of emphasis). While masters of italic (such as Roger Ascham) could produce exemplary calligraphy in this script, some aristocratic gentlemen (Sir Philip Sidney and Robert Devereux, earl of Essex, for instance) chose not just to write only in italic, but in their own cursive, "rugged" version of it. It is also clear that italic was generally the only script taught to women. It was evidently considered an appropriately "fair hand"—elegant and detached from the everyday business world of secretary—though the writing accomplishment of Tudor women does vary considerably, and a sense of semiliteracy is sometimes discerned even in high-born ladies of the period (for instance, in the untutored spelling, virtually phonetic, found in the letters of Sir Walter Ralegh's wife, Bess Throckmorton).

As for writing materials, letters and most general writings were produced then, as now, on paper—most of it (made from linen or cotton rags) imported from France, or occasionally Italy, and relatively expensive. Various legal documents—indentures, manorial rolls, royal letters patent by which the sovereign conferred rights on individuals, and sometimes wills, inventories, and other formal legal, ecclesiastical, or Exchequer documents, as well as certain high-prestige literary manuscripts prepared for

M

presentation—continued to be produced on the even more expensive materials of parchment, made from the skin of sheep (or sometimes goat or calf), or vellum (technically high-quality parchment made specifically from calf, though the term is often used indiscriminately). Although parchment, like paper, can discolor, molder, or perish through exposure to humidity, fungus, bacteria, dust, or rodents, the vast quantity of existing Tudor documents on parchment in the public records and elsewhere tends to support contemporary assumptions that particularly important documents, including those testifying to individuals' serious intentions and legal rights, were best entrusted to parchment, which had the better chance of resisting the ravages of time.

Besides using ink made by this period from gall and iron sulphate (usually copper) with an admixtre of gum arabic—the most favored color in general use being black (although oxidation and other chemical changes may sometimes affect ink colors as they survive today)—a Tudor scribe would write with quills made from feathers, most commonly from the wing feathers of geese, requiring frequent sharpening (with a "pen-knife"). The ink was contained in an inkwell, perhaps within an inkstand or "standish," or carried in a portable container known as an "ink horn" with the quill in a "penner." Before the development of blotting paper (which seems to have gotten off to a slow start in the 1570s), the ink on the page might be dried with the use of "pin dust" shaken from a perforated pot (like a saltcellar but with a concave top) known as a "sander" (a name derived from the powdered resin "gum-sandarach") or "pounce pot" (pounce being a finely ground chalky substance that absorbed grease). In more carefully prepared documents, the text might be regulated and kept evenly spaced by first drawing lines across the page (if in pencil they could be rubbed out afterward), and it seems that a device was occasionally used by professional scribes to facilitate the process of marking out the lines: a kind of metal spur with a multipointed wheel could be rolled up each side of the page, leaving a series of regularly spaced pinpricks that could then be joined by the use of a ruler. A ruler would also be used in some literary texts to mark off margins, sometimes on all four sides of each page to form a frame within which the text could be centered, although margins might also be used for sidenotes as well as for folio or page numbers—whether numbers were given to each leaf (*folio*) or to each side of the leaf (*page*).

Naturally, different kinds of documents demanded different standards of accuracy and layout. Where a serious attempt at neatness and precision is being made, textual corrections (where mechanical transcription errors are amended) or revisions (where the actual text is changed) can be found in various forms. Sometimes the error is simply overwritten with the new word(s); sometimes it is first erased by scraping clean (perhaps with a knife or abrasive surface); sometimes the correction or revision is interlineated; written directly over the mistaken words that may or may not themselves be crossed out or deleted. In very rare cases, new text may be written on tiny pieces of paper neatly pasted over the original text. In professionally prepared and bound literary texts, it is not uncommon to find (from the evidence of remaining stubs) instances where original leaves have been neatly excised because the scribe botched his copy and preferred to start that part again on a new leaf.

While letters and documents, on both paper and parchment, could come in all shapes and sizes as occasion warranted—some letters patent, for instance, occupying parchment skins well over a yard square (many with huge pendent circular seals attached by plaited cords and encased in fitted boxes known as "skippets"), and manorial rolls might comprise a series of membranes stitched together running to thirty yards or more—the most common size of paper encountered is folio size (approximately twelve by eight inches, but this is variable). This format is produced when a single broadsheet is folded in two (to form a *bifolium*), each of the two hinged leaves being a "folio" (and in part recognized as such because the chainlines left by wires in the original paper mould are vertical, like watermarks). The single bifolium was the most common form used for personal letters, the outside of the integral second leaf bearing the address, and the whole thing folded up with the address panel exposed, perhaps sealed with wax (perhaps bearing the impression of a personal armorial stamped on the wax while still hot by a separate seal-matrix or ring); these wax seals would also leave tears in the letter when it was torn open by the recipient, an eventuality that experienced writers might eventually learn to anticipate by judiciously leaving space around the part of the sheet likely to get ripped away. Manuscript books, apparently known as "paper books" when they (originally) comprised blank pages, were formed from a series of gatherings, or quires, of bifolia. Alternatively, smaller "bifolia" and manuscript books could be made if the folio leaves were folded in half and then cut to "quarto-size" (approximately eight by six inches, the chainlines then being horizontal), or—for such things as notebooks—folded yet again to "octavo-size" (where the chainlines become vertical again).

Besides business, official administration, and legal matters, manuscripts were used not only for personal notebooks and commonplace books (in which copies or extracts from reading matter were recorded), but also for all the kinds of creative writing that we call "literature" in its traditional sense. In this respect, too, the Tudor period was very much a "manuscript culture," as the Middle Ages had been, despite the advent and proliferation of the printing press after the 1450s. For a variety of cultural, social, and sometimes class reasons, both ladies and gentlemen of the educated classes might prefer to confine their writings to a strictly limited and exclusive circle of readers—within their own family, or among a few close personal friends, or within a privileged group of like-minded people (such as courtiers, clerics, students, or lawyers)—or, in the case of some polemical material (of a religious or political nature), to specifically targeted figures. While the writers might choose to produce autograph presentation copies for select individuals, scribes and amanuenses might be enlisted to produce further copies, and as these were distributed, yet further copies might be made outside the original writer's immediate circle if the work in question attracted sufficient interest. The sheer quantity of Tudor poems, romances, tracts and discourses, translations, devotional and other writings that survive in manuscript, and which, clearly, were never intended originally to be published in print (though some were later), testifies to the vitality of this culture and, indeed, includes much of the best-known literature of the period. The poetry of Sir Thomas Wyatt, for instance, was still preserved in a partly autograph manuscript volume, as well as in several verse miscellanies associated with court circles and predating Richard Tottel's printed *Miscellany* of 1557. Sidney's *Arcadia*, preserved in two versions in various contemporary manuscript copies commissioned by fellow-aristocrats, was published only posthumously, in 1590, by his sister, Mary Sidney, countess of Pembroke.

While examples such as these are justly famous, the relatively recent discovery and editing of such remarkable Tudor documents as the Lisle Letters (published by Muriel St. Clare Byrne in 1981) exemplify the wealth of extant unpublished material in this period, and indicate what may yet be found in British public records and in libraries and collections around the world.

BIBLIOGRAPHY

Beal, Peter, comp. *Index of English Literary Manuscripts, Vol. 1: 1450–1625.* 1980.

———, and Jeremy Griffiths, eds. *English Manuscript Studies, 1100–1700.* 1989.
Braswell, Laurel Nichols. *Western Manuscripts from Classical Antiquity to the Renaissance: A Handbook.* 1981.
Marotti, Arthur F. *Manuscript, Print, and the English Renaissance Lyric.* 1995.
Preston, Jean F., and Laetitia Yeandle. *English Handwriting, 1400–1650.* 1992.
Woudhuysen, H.R. *Sir Philip Sidney and the Circulation of Manuscripts, 1558–1640.* 1996.

Peter Beal

SEE ALSO
Commonplace Books; Handwriting; Literacy; Printing, Publishing, and Bookbinding; Verse Anthologies

Mapmaking

By 1500, little was left of the English mapping tradition that in the thirteenth and fourteenth century had produced some of the most remarkable mapping of medieval Europe, universal, national, and regional. There were regional pockets of map-consciousness where pictorial sketch maps of small areas, drawn to shape but not to scale, were occasionally produced. Similar maps, clarifying legal disputes, were beginning to be produced in law courts. Some Bristol merchants were familiar with the work of Mediterranean chartmakers. Large cosmographical and terrestrial maps were occasionally used in court festivities inspired by Burgundian models. By 1600, in contrast, maps and mapmaking were commonplace.

Major change first became apparent at court from 1520 due to the influence of a humanist court circle associated with the Bavarian mathematician Nicolaus Kratzer, Henry VIII's astronomer and instrument maker, which was interested in the practical application of mathematical theories through mapping. The major impetus, however, came from Henry VIII himself. Faced by the threat of invasion in the wake of his break with Rome and enriched by the wealth of the dissolved monasteries, in the later 1530s he commissioned a large-scale cartographic survey of the coasts and of the individual forts and ports of his kingdom. Numerous manuscript maps or "plats" were generated. Under pressure from a demanding and increasingly knowledgeable sovereign, the maps became ever more sophisticated. Many were drawn to scale by native Englishmen like John Rogers and Richard Lee. By the early 1540s, Henry was commissioning plats for purposes of internal administration, thereby forcing

M

an awareness of the administrative utility of maps on ruling groups throughout the kingdom.

Because of decreasing wealth this royal impetus could not be maintained later in the century, although the more important English forts and harbors continued to be regularly surveyed and mapped, particularly after 1580. The realization of the value of maps as a tool for subjugation and settlement also ensured that government funds were available for the mapping of Ireland. From being a virtual *terra incognita* in 1550 it had become one of the most thoroughly mapped areas of Europe, albeit in manuscript, by 1600.

Parallel with these developments went the continuing association between mapping and north European humanism, classical studies, the emergence of mathematics and geography as academic disciplines, and patriotism. Already apparent in the 1530s in the work of John Leland (though no significant maps by him survive), it found expression over the following decades in the maps of Great Britain and its regions created by the Tudor antiquaries Laurence Nowell, William Lambarde, and John Norden, the Welshman Humphrey Lhuyd, the Scot John Elder, the Yorkshire cleric John Rudd, the Kentish squires of the Digges family, and the herald William Smith, all of whom seem to have had access to the royal library and the plats of the Henrician survey at Whitehall.

The humanist-patriotic impulse found its greatest expression in the work of John Rudd's former assistant, Christopher Saxton. His atlas of maps of the English counties (1579), and his great wall map of Britain (1583), created with government support, are a summation of English patriotism put at the service of the Elizabethan state. Other distinguished maps included Nowell's manuscript maps of the British Isles of the 1560s, including his more detailed maps of England with "Anglo-Saxon" place names; Lhuyd's maps of England and Wales and "Welsh" map of Wales alone (first published by Ortelius in 1573); Norden's manuscript county maps with explanatory text starting in the 1590s; and William Smith's uncompleted series of county maps and town plans of the later 1580s and 1590s. Plans of towns such as Norwich, Cambridge, and Dover by William Cunningham, Richard Lyne, and Thomas Digges illustrate other aspects of the antiquaries' work, while the same patriotic mentality underlay Anthony Jenkinson's map of Muscovy of 1562 and the maps of the English colony of Virginia in the 1580s by John White and Thomas Hariot.

The commencement of a native hydrographic tradition was hindered by the reluctance of English mariners to use charts and by the domination of the *genre* by such foreign pilots and chartmakers as Jean Rotz of Normandy or Diogo Homem or Portugal. It was only from the 1560s that Englishmen, notably William Borough, began to produce charts. He was followed, in the 1580s, by such skilled hydrographers as Robert Norman and Richard Poulter and instrument makers like Thomas Hood. By the 1590s, Francis Drake and his fellow sailors had English charts aboard their ships. These charts, often created in the warren of alleys lining the port of London east of the Tower, marked the start of a school that was to continue for more than a century.

On land, the earliest surviving estate map to be drawn to scale was created by an Essex lawyer, Israel Amyce, in 1576. The demand was fueled by pride of ownership, an active land market, and a growing awareness of the utility of maps for management. Within two decades Saxton and Ralph Agas, as well as the founding fathers of mapping dynasties such as the Nordens, Treswells, and Walkers, were earning a good living from producing large-scale manuscript maps of varying sizes and formats (including atlases) for legal, economic, and social purposes for ambitious squires and powerful colleges and corporations.

A trickle of small printed maps, usually illustrating texts, appeared from 1535 when a map of Canaan, perhaps based on John Rudd's work, illustrated Coverdale's Bible. Almost all English mapping, however, remained in manuscript. The English print and book trade lacked the technological capacity and the commercial infrastructure to compete with the Netherlandish map printers and publishers based in Antwerp before 1579. Though the emigré Netherlander Thomas Gemini and the Huguenot Thomas Godet (Godehede) published a few small sheet maps in the 1550s and 1560s, most Englishmen had to have their work printed abroad. The first large printed wall maps of London (c. 1555) and of Britain (Mercator, 1564), and the first printed atlas of the British coasts (Waghenaer, 1584), were engraved and published in the Netherlands. A spate of maps were engraved and published in London between 1576 and 1595 by Protestant emigrés from Antwerp. The first terrestrial and celestial globes in England, created by the Huguenot Emery Molyneux and engraved by the Netherlander Jodocus Hondius appeared in 1592. But Hondius's departure for the northern Netherlands in 1595, English mapmakers again found themselves compelled, for another century, to send their work abroad for publication.

BIBLIOGRAPHY

Barber, P.M. "England I: Pageantry, Defense, and Government: Maps at Court to 1550," and "England II: Monarchs, Ministers, and Maps, 1550–1625." In *Monarchs, Ministers and Maps.* David Buisseret, ed, pp. 26–98. 1992.

———. "Les Iles Britanniques." In *Gerardi Mercatoris Atlas Europae.* Marcel Watelet, ed., pp. 41–77. 1994.

Harvey, P.D.A. *Maps in Tudor England.* 1993.

———. "Estate Surveyors and the Spread of the Scale-Map in England, 1550–1580." *Landscape History,* vol. 15, pp. 37–49.

Taylor, E.G.R. *The Haven-Finding Art.* 1956.

Tyacke, Sarah, ed. *English Map-Making, 1500–1650.* 1983.

———, and John Huddy. *Christopher Saxton and Tudor Mapmaking.* 1980.

Peter Barber

SEE ALSO

Agas, Ralph; Diggs, Leonard; Digges, Thomas; Hariot, Thomas; Henry VIII; Huguenots; Navigation; Norden, John; Printing, Publishing, and Bookbinding; Saxton, Christopher

Margaret of York, Duchess of Burgundy (1446–1503)

Daughter of Richard, duke of York, and brother of Edward IV, Margaret was married in 1468 to Charles, duke of Burgundy, cementing a political alliance between Burgundy and the house of York. Her assistance was of vital importance to Edward IV in recovering his throne in 1471, as she worked to reconcile Edward with his brother, the duke of Clarence. She was widowed in 1477, and apart from a brief visit to England in 1480 remained resident in the Netherlands for the rest of her life. With no children of her own she took a keen interest in the fortunes of her nephews and nieces. But she was never reconciled to Henry VII's regime in spite of his marriage to her niece, Elizabeth of York. Her court at Malines became a center of Yorkist plotting against the fragile Tudor regime. In 1487, she financed a force of up to 2,000 German mercenaries who launched an invasion of England in support of Lambert Simnel, the impersonator of Edward, earl of Warwick, recently proclaimed in Dublin as Edward VI. They attracted little support in England and were defeated at the battle of Stoke. Margaret continued to be a thorn in Henry's side, from 1492 sponsoring Perkin Warbeck's impersonation of Richard, duke of York, the younger of the princes in the Tower, and committing resources to his series of incursions into England. Her freedom of maneuver was curtailed because of the desire of Maximilian, duke of Burgundy, for Henry's support against France, which resulted in the key treaty, the Intercursus Magnus, in 1496. But she remained a central figure in the life of the Burgundian court and deserves also to be remembered for her artistic patronage, including her early sponsorship of the printer William Caxton.

BIBLIOGRAPHY

Arthurson, Ian. *The Perkin Warbeck Conspiracy, 1491–1499.* 1994.

Weightman, C. *Margaret of York, Duchess of Burgundy, 1446–1503.* 1989.

Ian W. Archer

SEE ALSO

Henry VII; Simnel, Lambert; Warbeck, Perkin

Margaret Tudor (1489–1541)

Eldest daughter of Henry VII, Margaret Tudor was born at Westminster on November 29, 1489. At age thirteen, she was wed to James IV of Scotland and sent to live with him in Edinburgh in 1503. The ten years Margaret spent with James were generally happy ones, despite two brushes with death caused by complications with pregnancies.

On the loss of her husband in 1513, Margaret became regent during the minority of her infant son, James V (the only one of her six children destined to survive childhood). Unfortunately, Margaret alienated many of Scotland's nobles by favoring England in foreign policy and by marrying Archibald Douglas, earl of Angus (1514). John Stuart, duke of Albany, successfully challenged Margaret's regency and replaced her in power in 1515.

With Albany ascendant, Margaret fled to England, where she gave birth to Margaret Douglas, the future countess of Lennox and mother of Henry, Lord Darnley. Albany allowed Queen Margaret to return to Scotland in 1517, at which time she threw herself into the bitter factionalism of Scottish politics. After several years of changing sides and political maneuvering, she briefly gained possession of the king in 1524, but lost control of him to her estranged husband Angus. She divorced Angus three years later and married Henry Stuart, a man long rumored to be her paramour.

M

In June 1528, James threw off Angus's influence and recalled his mother to his side. Margaret remained on good terms with her son until 1535, when he discovered that Margaret had been betraying government secrets to the English. In 1538, James's wife, Mary of Lorraine, reconciled the king with his mother, and Margaret's last years were spent pleasantly at court. She died at age fifty-two on October 18, 1541.

BIBLIOGRAPHY

Buchanan, Patricia. *Margaret Tudor Queen of Scots.* 1985.

Chapman, Hester. *The Sisters of Henry VIII.* 1969.

Donaldson, Gordon. *Scotland, James V to James VII.* 1965.

Leslie, John. *The Historie of Scotland.* J. Dalrymple et al., trans. 1888–1895.

Lindsay, Robert of Pitscottie. *The Historie and Cronicles of Scotland, 1437–1575.* 1899.

Scott Lucas

SEE ALSO

Douglas Family; Henry VII; James IV and V; Scotland, History of

Marian Exiles

"Marian Exiles" is the name given to those Protestants, mostly clergymen and ordinands, who fled England to escape persecution under Mary I (July 19, 1553–November 17, 1558). Mary's accession to the throne did not pass uneventfully, in that a number of Protestants would have preferred Lady Jane Grey as their sovereign, and some of them actually tried to install her after the death of Edward VI on July 6, 1553. This attempt failed, but it gave Mary a good excuse for persecuting the Protestant leadership. A number of prominent figures, including Archbishop Thomas Cranmer, were arrested, and others found it prudent to go into hiding. Eventually, many of these made their way to the Continent, where they formed exile communities in sympathetic Protestant cities.

From the standpoint of later history, the most important congregations were at Frankfurt-am-Main and Geneva. The Frankfurt congregation was established by William Whittingham, who arrived there in June 1554. He remodeled the 1552 prayer book along more Calvinist lines, and summoned John Knox to come from Geneva as their leader. However, there was a group at Frankfurt that did not like this turn of events, and when Dr. Richard Cox, vice-chancellor of Oxford under Edward VI, arrived in March 1555, they chose him as their leader to dispute with the Knoxians. Cox argued for the retention of the 1552 Prayer Book unaltered; after some bitter wrangling, he and his followers were able to persuade the city authorities to expel the Knoxians. The latter retired to Geneva, but the event has gone down in history as the first skirmish in what was to become the classical battle between the establishment and the Puritan factions in the Elizabethan Church.

The Genevan congregation, now reconstituted with Knox at its head, set about preparing a new translation of the Bible, which appeared in 1560. When Mary died, the exiles returned to England, and the moderates among them were quickly reintegrated into the Anglican Church, where some of them received high office. Knox could not be compromised, however, and returned to Scotland with English support to introduce the Reformation in his native land. Thus the period of exile sowed the seeds not only of the Scottish Reformation, but also of the religious link with England that paved the way for the accession of the Scottish King James VI to the English throne in 1603 and the eventual union of the two kingdoms in 1707.

BIBLIOGRAPHY

Garrett, C.H. *The Marian Exiles.* 1938.

Loades, D. *The Reign of Mary Tudor.* 1979.

Gerald Bray

SEE ALSO

Book of Common Prayer; Calvinism; Church of Scotland; Cox, Richard; Cranmer, Thomas; Grey, Lady Jane; Knox, John; Mary I; Puritanism; Whittingham, William

Marian Martyrs

John Foxe's *Acts and Monuments* (commonly called the "Book of Martyrs"), in editions from 1563 on, brought the English what was for 400 years the accepted version of the Marian persecution. Today we realize that we must examine Foxe's reliability carefully, but Elizabethan readers had no reason to suspect him. He provides voluminous details, including martyrs' personal statements, letters, official documents, court transcripts, and eyewitness accounts. Foxe compiles and presents all available material, recording interrogations, executions, and escapes. The nearly 300 martyrs range from the Christ-like bishops Hugh Latimer and Nicholas Ridley to the illiterate fisherman Rawlins White to Elizabeth I herself. Such a mass of incidents and details makes *Actes and Monuments* seem like war reportage, recording an enemy's progress through the country. Reliable or not, Foxe's technique is effective.

Foxe is also effective in personalizing the martyrs. In the memoirs, transcripts, and eyewitness accounts we hear various distinct, sympathetic voices. Further, Foxe presents characters such as Edmund Bonner, bishop of London under Mary I, with an astonishingly even hand. One comes away with the impression that most Marian bishops would have preferred not to burn people. They felt obligated to do so for the welfare of the Roman faithful and of England. They offered the martyrs repeated chances to recant, only reluctantly consigning them to the fire. Foxe tells us relatively little of the Roman faithful. The martyrs are persecuted by the church bureaucracy, not by their peers. Those few times that lay people oppose a martyr, we find them appearing among a crowd, not as individuals. This gives the impression that the whole of England was Protestant except for the church hierarchy.

One of Foxe's most powerful strategies is his constant repetition of reformist theological commonplaces. Reading Foxe provided his audience with a home-study course in generic reformation theology derived from the very words and acts of the new "saints" themselves. Hence the "Book of Martyrs" was fundamental in unifying the conventions of acceptable mass discourse while standardizing images of the people and reform clergy in opposition to the "papists." It was thus a useful tool in Queen Elizabeth's attempt to establish a coherent and stable society.

Surprising for modern readers is the quantity of humor that Foxe builds into the text. The martyrs usually humiliate their interrogators with superior knowledge, wit, and courage. The bishops' discomfiture makes excellent satire. The stupidity of subordinate officials of church, court, and prison is still standard fare in English humor, and scenes such as a prisoner escaping while two bishops argue over the Eucharist remain hilarious.

Also noteworthy is that many of the martyrs, actual and intended, are women, among them Lady Jane Grey and Princess (later Queen) Elizabeth. The women are uniformly self-sufficient, assertive, well read, witty, and courageous; they are intellectually competitive and take great pleasure in outwitting their educated, masculine, authoritative "betters." They usually present themselves as types of Christ before Pilate. The women have a certain joy of martyrdom about them and are often fearlessly aware of the fire. By contrast, the men often require support in the weakness of their flesh. Thomas Cranmer recants from fear, retracts from shame, and holds his hand in the flames as penance. All of the martyrs submit to but will not obey those whom they clearly identify as their spiritual and intellectual inferiors. The bishops wield only earthly power, far inferior to that of God. And it is God's power, truth, and word that the martyrs believe will carry them into heaven as saints.

BIBLIOGRAPHY
Bauckham, Richard. *Tudor Apocalypse.* 1978.
Christianson, Paul. *Reformers and Babylon: English Apocalyptic Vision from the Reformation to the Eve of the Civil War.* 1978.
Foxe, John. *Acts and Monuments of the English Martyrs.* 8 vols. 2nd edition. 1843–1849; repr. 1965.
Haller, William. *The Elect Nation: The Meaning and Relevance of Foxe's "Book of Martyrs."* 1963.
Loades, David M. *The Oxford Martyrs.* 1970.
Olsen, V. Norskov. *John Foxe and the Elizabethan Church.* 1973.

Wayne DeYoung

SEE ALSO
Bonner, Edmund; Cranmer, Thomas; Foxe, John; Grey, Lady Jane; Latimer, Hugh; Mary I; Ridley, Nicholas

Markets
See Fairs and Markets

Marlowe, Christopher (1564–1593)

The greatest theatrical contemporary of the young William Shakespeare, Christopher Marlowe was probably the more prominent of the two during the late 1580s and early 1590s. His early success, joined to his controversial reputation and the fact of their birth within two months of each other, has led some to portray Marlowe as Shakespeare's unruly rival. Marlowe created violent and spectacular dramas whose exotic heroes fascinated his age with their prodigious and often amoral energies. But Marlowe's works, including his narrative poetry, are also complex in their astonishing juxtapositions of aesthetic refinement and blunt cruelty, of limitless aspiration and sardonic deflation, showing a remarkable and disturbing range.

Marlowe was baptized in Canterbury, where he attended the King's School. In 1580, he entered Christ

M

Church, Cambridge, supported by a scholarship intended to prepare young men for an ecclesiastical career. Marlowe chose a different path, though precisely where it took him is at times unclear. His work reflects wide reading in the classics and theology, but his extended absences from the university attracted suspicion. He received his degree only after the unusual intervention in 1587 by the Privy Council, which disabused Cambridge officials of rumors about Marlowe's travel plans to Rheims, informing them he had "done Her Majesty good service" and should not "be defamed by those that are ignorant in th' affairs he went about." From this defense, modern scholars have deduced that the university suspected Marlowe of subversive collaboration with English Catholics abroad, mistaking his true activities, namely his participation in Sir Francis Walsingham's spy network. He was later reputed to be a member of a small group of avant-garde intellectuals, the "School of Night," to whom he delivered an "atheist lecture." Whether the group even existed is unclear. He was also arrested for his part in a fatal brawl, charged with counterfeiting in the Netherlands, with assaulting two constables in London, and associated repeatedly, though inconclusively, with heretical views. His involvement in covert activities probably led to his untimely death six years after graduation.

Marlowe produced seven boldly imaginative plays whose precise dates are uncertain and whose textual problems are sometimes an issue. Two of the plays are now studied primarily by specialists: *Dido Queen of Carthage,* written in apparent collaboration with Thomas Nashe and drawn loosely from Virgil's *Aeneid,* and *The Massacre at Paris* (c. 1593), on the 1572 massacre of French Huguenots.

His first popular successes were *Tamburlaine the Great, Parts One and Two* (c. 1587–1588). A poor Scythian shepherd who becomes a world conqueror, Tamburlaine projects the ideal of human autonomy into a fantasy of omnipotence. With irresistible will and brutal victories he ascends to power without suffering the morally appropriate, tragic punishment a sixteenth-century audience might have expected. Paralleling Tamburlaine's aspiring mind, Marlowe's Prologue to *Part One* mocks the "jiggling veins of rhyming mother wits" of his predecessors, promising instead a new stage language, "threatening the world with high astounding terms." Marlowe's blank verse (unrhymed iambic pentameter), later praised by Ben Jonson as "Marlowe's mighty line," invented a rhetoric of endless striving that, complemented by sensational staging, made *Tamburlaine* a success and prompted a sequel.

Part Two returns the defiant imperialist to the stage, together with a wide world of exotic place-names to be invoked and conquered. In *Part One,* a captured emperor is led about in a cage and used as a living footstool, and innocent virgins are slaughtered outside Damascus; but in *Part Two,* two kings are harnessed to their conqueror's chariot, whipped to the cry of "Holla, ye pampered jades of Asia!" and the entire population of Babylon is ordered drowned. Along with this excess, the "arch-monarch of the world" is forced in *Part Two* to confront external constraints on his seemingly limitless desire, despite his best effort to redefine failure as a higher kind of victory. Whether his ultimate death delivers the divine retribution missing from *Part One,* or parodies it, remains a matter of critical debate.

So extreme is the action of these plays that scholars consider them veering close to tragic farce. This feeling becomes more palpable in Marlowe's next major effort, *The Jew of Malta* (c. 1589). Once again a central protagonist would reshape the world after his own imagination, but now heroic eloquence gives way to greed and irony; the dream of redrawing a world map becomes the hunger to "enclose infinite riches in a little room." Barabas the Jew is stripped of his wealth by the Christian governor Ferneze in order to pay a tribute due the Turks. For the rest of the play, Barabas exacts revenge with murderous ingenuity—provoking a deadly duel, poisoning nuns, betraying Christians to Turks and Turks to Christians—until he is trapped by his own contrivance and boiled alive. A striking feature of the play is how it simultaneously exploits and interrogates stereotypes of Elizabethan anti-Semitism. Barabas was probably played by Edward Alleyn with a huge, artificial nose, gloating over his gold and gems, then recounting an improbably extensive career of heartless crime. Yet the play also suggests that Barabas is the very embodiment of the culture that reviles him as an outsider. Indeed, the play begins with the spirit of "Machiavel," who declares religion to be a "childish toy" and regards political order as based on might rather than right. Barabas, he tells us, is created in his own image, but the action shows us an unscrupulous Machiavellianism motivating most of its characters.

Barabas himself is an elusive figure, yet he yearns fitfully for a partner. *Edward II* (c. 1592) focuses more intently on the longing for companionship. Its protagonist is a king who would sacrifice all if left "some nook or corner" in which "to frolic with my dearest Gaveston," his homosexual favorite. New for Marlowe is a suffering and often passive hero who luxuriates in and is manipulated by his taste for erotic self-indulgence and his need for personal intimacy. Edward's psychological drama is played out within a political context by another feature new to Marlowe, the setting of English history. Restructuring material drawn from Holinshed's *Chronicles,* the work is an important instance of English history dramatized as tragedy, a perspective that was influenced by and in turn influenced Shakespeare. Surrounded by enemies, Edward is temporarily victorious after Gaveston is murdered about halfway through the play, but eventually falls prey to his haughty and ambitious barons, meeting with a grimly ironic, sadistic death.

Marlowe's most famous play, and possibly his last, is *Doctor Faustus* (c. 1588–1593), a tragic vision of intellectual ambition. Frustrated by the limits of traditional studies, Faustus longs for the power promised by some Renaissance philosophers and turns to magic to become a "demigod." Faustus hopes to stretch his dominion "as far as doth the mind of man." Selling his soul for twenty-four years of power, Faustus is taken on a tour of the universe, but too many of his deeds on earth shrink to stagy amusements or carnal indulgences: slapstick tormenting of the pope, fetching grapes for the duchess of Vanholt, calling up the "shadows" of classical greats to amuse the emperor and later a succuba in the shape of Helen of Troy to be his paramour. What remains crucial is Faustus being hemmed in by an overwhelming, sometimes inscrutable moral cosmos that renders his rebellious energy as futile, even absurd. Faustus's eloquent and anguished soliloquy during his final hour before endless damnation leaves the audience to "wonder at unlawful things," but some have felt that behind the wonder lies an increasing pessimism on Marlowe's part about the possibilities of human achievement.

Marlowe also produced a smaller but significant body of nondramatic poetry. There are two translations, both probably produced at Cambridge: *All Ovids Elegies,* a translation of Ovid's erotic *Amores* in heroic couplets; and *Lucans First Booke,* a blank-verse translation of the first book of Lucan's epic *De bello civili* (or *Pharsalia*). Marlowe's short lyric, "The Passionate Shepherd to His Love," was widely popular, imitated, and answered, most notably by Sir Walter Ralegh and John Donne. *Hero and Leander* is Marlowe's masterpiece. Drawn from the well-known myth, the poem concerns the love of two beautiful youths at the boundary of naiveté and desire. With a continual shifting of tone and focus by a sophisticated narrator—highlighting by turns ingenious artifice, hyperbole, sympathy, detached irony, hetero-

and homosexual sensuality, and ruthless cruelty—Marlowe shapes one of the subtlest erotic poems of the English Renaissance. The work breaks off on the morning after consummation, but the abrupt ending at the brink of an already prefigured tragedy is consistent with the complex ambivalence of the whole. George Chapman continued the poem in a serious and moral manner, bringing the pair to their legendary "love-deaths."

Marlowe's own death has assumed legendary status for modern scholars. In 1594, he died in Deptford of a stab wound above the eye and into the brain, which, according to the official account, was inflicted in self-defense by one Ingram Frizer in a quarrel over a tavern bill. Modern research into Frizer and the two witnesses of the assault, as well as unlikely elements in the story itself, have led some biographers to suspect that Marlowe was assassinated. Adding to this suspicion are charges made against Marlowe around the time of his death by the playwright Thomas Kyd (under torture) and the informer Richard Baines, who concluded that Marlowe's mouth might "be stopped." They portray Marlowe as an outrageous blasphemer, a witty and fearless advocate of atheism and homosexuality whose "monstruous opinions" required his arrest and daily reporting to the Privy Council. Whatever the truth of Marlowe's end, its mystery helps fuel modern debates about the character of his work, which critics have read either as moral admonitions about the consequences of egocentrism or as explosive heterodoxy. But above all it is Marlowe's preoccupation with the boundaries of his culture that ensures his importance for understanding Tudor literary, political, religious, and emotional life.

BIBLIOGRAPHY

Altman, Joel. *The Tudor Play of Mind: Rhetorical Inquiry and the Development of Elizabethan Drama.* 1978.

Bartels, Emily. *Spectacles of Strangeness: Imperialism, Alienation, and Marlowe.* 1993.

Bevington, David M. *From "Mankind" to Marlowe, Growth of Structure in the Popular Drama of Tudor England.* 1962.

Cole, Douglas W. *Suffering and Evil in the Plays of Marlowe.* 1962.

Eliot, T.S. "Christopher Marlowe." In *Selected Essays, 1917–1932.* 1932.

Gill, Roma, ed. *The Complete Works of Christopher Marlowe.* Vols. 1–5 (ongoing). 1987–1998.

Hammer, Paul E.J. "A Reckoning Reframed: The 'Murder' of Christopher Marlowe Revisited." *English Literary Renaissance,* vol. 26, pp. 225–242.

M

Hill, Eugene D. "Marlowe's 'More Excellent and Admirable Methode' of Parody in *Tamburlaine I.*" *Renaissance Papers.* 1995.

Keach, William. *Elizabethan Erotic Narratives: Irony and Pathos in the Ovidian Poetry of Shakespeare, Marlowe, and Their Contemporaries.* 1977.

Kendall, Roy. "Richard Baines and Christopher Marlowe's Milieu." *English Literary Renaissance,* vol. 24, pp. 507–552.

———. "Richard Baines and Christopher Marlowe: A Symbiotic Relationship." Dissertation, Shakespeare Institute, University of Birmingham. 1997.

Kernan, Alvin, ed. *Two Renaissance Mythmakers: Christopher Marlowe and Ben Jonson.* 1977.

Levin, Harry. *The Overreacher: A Study of Christopher Marlowe.* 1952.

Nicholl, Charles. *The Reckoning: The Murder of Christopher Marlowe.* 1992.

Steane, J.B. *Marlowe: A Critical Study.* 1964.

Weil, Judith. *Christopher Marlowe: Merlin's Prophet.* 1977.

Wilson, F.P. *Marlowe and the Early Shakespeare.* 1954.

Ronald Levao

SEE ALSO

Alleyn, Richard; Atheism; Baines, Richard; Drama, History of; Espionage; Holinshed, Raphael; Homosexuality; Kyd, Thomas; Machiavell, The; Magic; Shakespeare, William; Walsingham, Francis

Marprelate Controversy

A dispute over Presbyterianism provoked the publication of a series of tracts under the pseudonym of Martin Marprelate. Those involved in this venture had long advocated further reform of the Church of England to introduce a Presbyterian form of church government and a firmly Calvinistic theology. For many years they had engaged in fairly open debate with supporters of the episcopal establishment, but after the consecration of John Whitgift to the see of Canterbury (1583), it became clear that Puritanism in all its forms would suffer increasing persecution.

A number of more moderate Presbyterians made their peace with episcopacy, but the extremists would not be placated. Toward the end of 1588, they gave vent to their frustration in a series of provocative pamphlets attacking the whole episcopal system and calling for a thorough overhaul of the Anglican Church. The pamphlets were issued under the name of Martin Marprelate, whose true identity remains unknown. They were, however, printed by the dedicated Presbyterian Robert Waldegrave and his associates. We also know that Waldegrave had recently printed a number of sermons and tracts by John Penry and John Udall, two of the more radical Puritan preachers of the time. It also seems likely that the later tracts were written by Job Throckmorton, another Puritan preacher who moved in the same circles, and who may have contributed something to the earlier tracts as well.

The Marprelate Tracts, combining satire and invective, targeted leading figures in the church, including Archbishop Whitgift, Bishop John Aylmer of London, and Bishop Thomas Cooper of Winchester. The attacks were vicious and unfair, yet the mud thrown by Marprelate sticks to these figures to this day. The tracts aroused the anger of everyone in a position of responsibility, including many leading Puritans who were basically sympathetic to their position. The Marprelate group was forced into hiding, and spent most of the next year traveling about the Midlands. They were never caught, but the tracts ceased to appear after the end of 1589.

The Marprelate tracts instigated a furious counterattack by the episcopal party. This began on February 9, 1589, when Richard Bancroft preached his now famous sermon at Paul's Cross denouncing the Puritans and even going so far as to claim that episcopacy was of divine institution and therefore essential to the nature of the Anglican Church. This was a novel idea in the Church of England, but it was soon to become a hallmark of the anti-Calvinist High Church party; it has left its mark on all subsequent Anglican theology.

More immediately, the Marprelate crisis stirred the High Commission into action, and a number of Puritan ministers were fined and imprisoned over the following few years. Effectively this signaled the end of peaceful coexistence between Presbyterians and Episcopalians in the Church of England, and paved the way for the controversies of the next century, which eventually ended in civil war.

The seven extant Marprelate Tracts are *The Epistle, The Epitome, The Mineral Conclusions, Hay any Work for Cooper?, Martin Junior, Martin Senior,* and *The Protestation.* They proved so effective that the bishops were forced to employ leading writers of the time in their attempt to counter them. A burlesque in verse, *A Whip for an Ape,* may be the work of John Lyly, and a dialogue called *Mar-Martin* has been attributed to Thomas Nashe. Both appeared in 1589. Lyly probably wrote *Pappe with a Hatchet* soon afterward in the process of precipitating yet

M

another controversy by challenging Gabriel Harvey to join in the debates. Harvey did so by writing *Advertisement to Papp-Hatchet* (1593), in which he blamed both sides in the Marprelate controversy almost equally. Harvey's brother Richard thereupon attacked Robert Greene along with Lyly and Nashe. Greene's reply started an exchange of satires lasting for several years that became known as the Greene-Nashe-Harvey controversy.

Meanwhile, Martin Marprelate retreated into obscurity, although his name was revived briefly during the civil war, when an anonymous Martin Marpriest produced *Hay any Work* (1641) and a *Dialogue* (1643), as well as four uninspired attacks on the bishops (1645).

BIBLIOGRAPHY

Carlson, Leland H. *Martin Marprelate, Gentleman. Master Job Throckmorton Laid Open in His Colours.* 1981.
Collinson, Patrick. *The Elizabethan Puritan Movement.* 1967.
McGrath, P. *Papists and Puritans under Elizabeth I.* 1967.
Pierce, W., ed. *The Marprelate Tracts.* 1911.

Gerald Bray

SEE ALSO

Anglicanism; Aylmer, John; Bancroft, Richard; Calvinism; Church of England; Church Polity; Cooper, Thomas; Greene, Robert; Harvey, Gabriel; High Commission, Court of; Lyly, John; Nashe, Thomas; Puritanism; Whitgift, John

Marriage and Marriage Law

The Tudor Church adhered throughout the period to the definition of marriage as decreed by Pope Alexander III (1159–1581) who defined a marriage as created by a freely given exchange of vows between the happy couple. Such vows could be of two kinds. The promise to marry couched in the present tense, *per verba de praesenti*, immediately created a legally binding union, enforceable in a church court. The vow expressed in the future tense, *per verba de futuro,* was less binding and could be terminated later by the couple. It became binding, however, if sexual intercourse took place subsequently. *De futuro* vows might also be dependent on the fulfillment of necessary conditions such as payment of a dowry. In Tudor England, therefore, neither a wedding ceremony nor even carnal knowledge were necessarily needed to create a marriage. Tudor marriage law around 1600 was summarized by Henry Swinburne (c. 1563–1623) in *A treatise of*

Spousals or Matrimonial Contracts (c. 1600; pub. 1686): "A present and perfect consent alone maketh matrimony, without either public solemnization or carnal copulation, for neither is the one nor the other the essence of matrimony, but consent only." England's marriage law defied attempts at reform both during and after the English Reformation, and it became increasingly anachronistic in sixteenth-century Europe. Catholic marriage law, for example, was reformed at the Council of Trent in 1563, when the legal validity of so-called private contracts to marry was abolished in favor of those conducted in church.

Since promises to marry carried considerable legal weight, disappointed or betrayed partners could get such contracts enforced in church courts. Such "marriage contract disputes" were, however, brought with decreasing frequency in the Tudor period for reasons that remain unclear. The decline, however, probably reflects increasing success of the English Church in emphasizing the importance of the marriage ceremony in the "marriage process," the increasing reluctance of judges to enforce prior contracts, and possibly a real decline in their formal use in courtship in some parts of England.

The extent to which individuals had the freedom to choose their own marriage partners has been much debated by historians of the family. Among the aristocracy, most young people were pawns in the dynastic, financial, and political plans of their families. Most individuals, however, having left home in their mid- to late teens, had more say in their choice of partner. The law of marriage, too, obviously facilitated freedom of choice, but in practice, most couples were prudent, not entering into binding unions until some realistic prospect of economic independence was achievable, often in their mid- to late twenties, usually to a partner of similar social status. Marriage was taken extremely seriously in Tudor England and the failure of partners to honor prior promises reflected the considerable pressures of family and friends to make a socially and economically acceptable match.

The making of marriage was conducted, even at humble social levels, with some formality. Courtships were often long, drawn-out affairs. Go-betweens were frequently employed, and gifts of symbolic meaning, such as rings or broken coins, were often exchanged; the actual exchanges of vows often took place with some ceremony and merrymaking. In the last half of the sixteenth century perhaps a third of all English brides were pregnant at the time of their church wedding, indicating that barriers to sexual intercourse dropped when vows had been exchanged. It has been

M

suggested recently that in some regions of England, particularly in the more remote pastoral highlands, exceptional rates of bridal pregnancy and bastardy indicate that the formal espousal rather than the church ceremony continued to define marriage in such communities.

In addition to an anachronistic marriage law, Tudor couples essentially got the worst of both confessional worlds, since divorce, allowed by many Protestant nations after the Reformation, was never permitted under the Tudors. At best, unhappy couples could seek in the church courts a judicial separation from bed and board, *a mensa et thoro,* which did not permit remarriage. Grounds for such a case were usually adultery or cruelty. Alternatively, one might seek an annulment on grounds such as the existence of a prior contract or the permanent impotence of the male partner. In practice, however, few couples took either route. The most common method of escape lay in desertion. Among the poor this was relatively common. In Warwick in the 1580s, some 14 percent of poor households were headed by abandoned women. High death rates, however, meant an early release for many individuals: the average marriage in early modern England lasted only twenty years or so before it was terminated by the death of a partner. Once bitten, however, Tudor widows and widowers seem to have been far from shy. Remarriage rates were at their highest ever in the middle of the sixteenth century, when some 30 percent of those marrying were doing so for the second or subsequent time.

In the 1540s, the first decade in which it can be measured accurately, the crude annual marriage rate was exceptionally high, at between twelve and fifteen per 1,000 people. This unparalleled enthusiasm for the married state was displayed not in particularly early marriage, which for most spinsters (outside the aristocracy) lay in the mid-twenties, but in uniquely low rates of celibacy. Historical demographers have estimated that only some 5 percent of individuals born in the middle of the sixteenth century never married. The economy of Tudor England, however, could not sustain the rapid rates of population growth that such enthusiasm for marriage produced. For those lacking the resources, obtaining a partner became increasingly problematic in the second half of the Tudor period. Tudor inflation, for example, meant dowry inflation. By the end of the period aristocratic brides brought dowries four times bigger than their counterparts in the late fifteenth century, and recent research now suggests that comparable, if not greater, inflation of dowries took place among more humble yeomen and husbandmen. In

this and other ways, falling real wages in the later sixteenth century increasingly prevented the poor, the under- or unemployed, from marrying at all; by consequence, of those born just after the end of the Tudor period, some 20 percent or so never married. Since relatively few babies were born illegitimate (without a preceding church wedding ceremony), this meant that the falling living standards of the later sixteenth century, by restricting entry into marriage, actually reduced the fertility of the population and hence brought the rate of population growth down to a sustainable level.

BIBLIOGRAPHY

Ingram, M. *The Church Courts, Sex and Marriage in England, 1570–1640.* 1987.

Carlson, E.J. *Marriage and the English Reformation.* 1994.

O'Hara, D. *The Making of Marriage in Sixteenth-Century Kent.* 1999.

Jeremy Boulton

SEE ALSO

Childbirth; Council of Trent; Gender; Marriage Manuals; Matrimony; Population and Demography

Marriage Manuals

Traditionally, upper-class Tudor marriages were arranged by parents or kin, with wealth, class, and social position taking precedence over any notion of romance. But the growing affluence among tradesmen made their children more attractive as matrimonial partners to the gentry; intermarriages between classes began to increase. Meanwhile, Protestantism grew in authority, and marriage supplanted, in religious importance, the celibacy favored by the Catholic Church. These changes, on top of the complications of arranged marriages, raised serious questions about marital rules and roles. Marriage sermons and manuals on proper domestic life provided answers and became favorites of the emerging middle class.

Agrippa's *Commendation of Matrimony* (1540), for example, stated that the purpose of marriage was to give man a companion in an unbreakable union. Other books assumed that the goal of matrimony was procreation. Some discussed civil, biblical, and ecclesiastical laws relating to marriage. The manuals agreed that marriage made man and woman "one," with the husband acting as the public representative for both. Marriage partners were expected to recognize the dominance and superiority of the husband, the submission and inferiority of the woman.

The wife was admonished to love and obey her husband; the husband, to care for and be gentle with his wife. The wife's chastity and her thrifty household management were stressed. Prayer and trust in God were considered essential to a good marriage. One book, *A Godly Exhortation* (1584), attributed to Richard Greenham, recommended prayer before intercourse to prevent evil children.

Although marriages in the upper classes were arranged, most manuals agreed that a man or woman should not be coerced into a marriage. But neither should they marry without the consent of parents. Several books cautioned widows to seek the advice of male relatives before considering remarriage, widowhood being the one time when a woman had more control over her own life. One such sermon was Andrew Kingsmill's *A Godly Advise . . . Touching Marriage* (1574). Other sermons published in the sixteenth century include a translation of Joannes Oecolampadius, *A Sarmon . . . to Young Men and Maydens* [1548?]; Charles Gibbon, *A Work Worth the Reading;* and Henry Smith, *A Preparation to Marriage* (1591). Early in the seventeenth century *Counsel to the Husband: To the Wife Instruction* (1608), William Whately's *A Bride-bush or a Wedding Sermon* (1617), and Robert Wilkinson's *The Merchant Royall* (1607) were popular sermons. Marriage advice is also found in A., *A Passionate Morrice* (1593); Thomas Becon, "The Boke of Matrimony" in his *Works* (1569–64); Miles Coverdale's translation of Johann Heinrich Bullinger's *A Christen State of Matrimony;* two marriage essays by Desiderius Erasmus; *Gods Arithmeticke* (1597) by Francis Meres; Torquato Tasso's *Of Mariage and Wiving* (1599); and Edmund Tilney's *A Brief and Pleasant Discourse of Duties in Mariage called The Flower of Friendship* (1568).

BIBLIOGRAPHY

Ingram, M. *The Church Courts, Sex, and Marriage in England, 1570–1640.* 1987.

Carlson, E.J. *Marriage and the English Reformation.* 1994.

O'Hara, D. *The Making of Marriage in Sixteenth Century Kent.* 1999.

Suzanne W. Hull

SEE ALSO

Bullinger, Johann Heinrich; Gender; Marriage and Marriage Law; Matrimony; Tilney, Edmund

Marston, John (1576–1634)

Born in 1576 and christened at Wardington, John Marston most likely grew up in Coventry, where his father practiced law and served as steward of the city. Marston entered Brasenose College, Oxford, in 1591, and received his B.A. on February 6, 1594. By 1595, he was residing in the Middle Temple in London's Inns of Court, where he shared his father's chambers. Much to his father's disappointment, however, Marston balked at the idea of practicing law, instead preferring to exhibit his sharp argumentative style in the literary realm. His first published work, a verse satire written under the name W. Kinsayder and entitled *The Metamorphosis of Pigmalions Image and Certaine Satires* (1598), attacked Joseph Hall, a Cambridge don and future bishop of Exeter and Norwich. Hall may have responded to these attacks on his newly published *Virgidemiarum* by inserting a contemptuous epigram in copies of Marston's verses circulating at Cambridge. Marston retaliated with *The Scourge of Villanie.* Other writers soon took sides in the argument, and the contest expanded into a debate about the merits and uses of satire. The archbishop of Canterbury, however, cut short this initial stage of Marston's career as a satirist, judging the poems subversive and ordering them burned in 1599.

Just before the Order for Conflagration, Marston had found a second outlet for his satiric talents in the theater, having earned payment for an unidentified play written for the boy's company at St. Paul's. By the end of 1599, he had revised *Histriomastix* for the same company, thereby instigating yet another public literary debate. Marston's representation of Ben Jonson as Chrysoganus in the play prompted Jonson to satirize *Histriomastix in Every Man Out of his Humour;* Marston responded by mocking Jonson via the character Brabant Senior in his next play, *Jack Drum's Entertainment* (1600). Jonson in turn goaded Marston through Hedon in *Cynthia's Revels* (1600) and, most pointedly, through Crispinus in *The Poetaster* (1601). Marston answered through Lampatho Doria in *What You Will* (1601), but his most vivid reply came in the form of the arrogant and pedantic Horace in *Satiromastix* (1602), written in conjunction with Thomas Dekker. While engaged in this exchange, Marston also managed to write both *Antonio and Mellida* (1599) and its tragic sequel, *Antonio's Revenge* (1600), as well as a poem published in the "Divers Poetical Essays" appended to Robert Chester's *Love's Martyr.*

The debate with Jonson disappeared as quickly as it had surfaced, and by 1603, Marston was writing prefatory verses for Jonson's *Sejanus* and dedicating his own hugely successful *The Malcontent* (1604) to the senior

M

playwright. During this period, Marston also bought a sixth share of the Children of the Queen's Revels company (1604), composed the popular *The Dutch Curtezan* (1605), and married Mary Wilkes, the daughter of Reverend William Wilkes, one of King James's favorite chaplains. Marston's work, moreover, remained embroiled in controversy. While living in his father-in-law's house, Marston's plays turned their attention to satirizing the king. Duke Ganzago in *The Parasitaster, or The Fawne* (1604–1606) may have been modeled after James. In 1605, passages most likely written by Marston in *Eastward Hoe!* left collaborators Jonson and George Chapman—and possibly even Marston himself—imprisoned for criticizing the Scots. Not surprisingly, Marston's friendship with Jonson faded again. In 1606, Marston attempted to surpass Jonson's *Sejanus* with the Roman tragedy *The Wonder of Women, or The Tragedie of Sophonisba*. In addition, he composed two royal entertainments, the *City Spectacle* for James I and the king of Denmark and the *Entertainment for the Dowager-Coutness of Darby*.

By 1608, Marston's charmed relationship to the king had collapsed. In March, the appearance of a play offensive to James, and another offensive to the French court, left London's theaters closed. Though the former play—which portrayed the king as a bad-tempered drunk and mocked his plan to mine silver in Scotland—has not been identified, most historians and critics hold Marston responsible for its production. On June 8, 1608, he was summoned before the Privy Council and committed to Newgate for an unspecified offense. No record of the charge or his date of release has been located.

By 1609, Marston had abandoned the stage in favor of the church. On September 24, he was ordained as deacon in the parish church of Stanton Harcourt, Oxfordshire; on December 24, he became a priest there. Fifteen years later, his wife gave birth to their only son, who died in infancy. Marston's literary works, meanwhile, remained popular. In 1613, William Barksted completed and printed *The Insatiate Countess,* a play Marston presumably began in 1608. A volume of Marston's complete works appeared in 1633 as well, although Marston insisted his name be removed from subsequent editions. He died June 25, 1634, and was buried, at his request, in the Middle Temple.

BIBLIOGRAPHY

Chambers, E.K. *The Elizabethan Stage.* 1923.
Finkelpearl, Philip J. *John Marston of the Middle Temple: An Elizabethan Dramatist in His Social Setting.* 1969.
Fleay, Frederick Gard. *A Biographical Chronicle of the English Drama, 1559–1642.* 1891.
Ingram, R.W. *John Marston.* Twayne English Author Series. 1978.
Tucker, Kenneth. *John Marston: A Reference Guide.* 1985.

Hillary Nunn

SEE ALSO
Dekker, Thomas; Hall, Joseph; Inns of Court; Jonson, Ben; Satire

Martyr, Peter

See Vermigli, Peter Martyr

Mary I (1516–1558)

Mary Tudor, the only child of Henry VIII and Katherine of Aragon to survive infancy, was born on February 18, 1516. She received a humanist education and was reared as a devout Catholic deeply attached to her mother. Although Henry gave her a household in Ludlow as Princess of Wales in 1525, his obsessive desire for a male heir, his abandonment of her mother, and his marital exploits thereafter afforded Mary an insecure youth and an uncertain future. After an abortive attempt by the duke of Northumberland and others to overturn Henry's last will and replace Mary with the Protestant Lady Jane Grey, a ploy that unfolded between July 6 and July 19, 1553, she succeeded her half-brother Edward VI as queen.

In the early months of her reign she constructed a council comprised largely of experienced Protestants who had served her predecessors on the one hand (some of whom had initially opposed her own accession) and Catholics loyal to her but less experienced at court on the other. A year after her accession, and in spite of Wyatt's Rebellion in opposition to the match, she married Philip II of Spain in July 1554. Philip was not liked in England and spent little time there. To the relief of many who feared the perpetuation of Spanish influence, the marriage produced no children. Philip played little part in English affairs, but succeeded in encouraging Mary to bring England into the war with France (1557–1559) which, right or wrong, has been counted a mistake on her part.

Much of Mary's attention remained drawn to the task of restoring Roman Catholicism as the officially sanctioned faith. With the help of Cardinal Reginald Pole she managed to restore England as a Catholic state without restoring the lands and properties of the traditional counter the currency debasements of her predecessors, amalgamated several revenue courts, and tried to strengthen the governing authority of the middling and larger towns. Though relatively large, her Privy Council proved less faction-ridden than once thought. It remained reasonably effective and may be credited with administrative continuity and some degree of innovation.

Assessing Mary's record as a Catholic queen in what became a Protestant realm has been a more polemical exercise than with most monarchs. In addition to the conflict wrought by religious transition, it was also her misfortune to reign at a time of economic and social stress and to die in her sixth year as queen, aged 42, on November 17, 1558. Certainly her rule had its successes as well as its failures, though the tenor of the times, the strains of ruling as a woman in a patriarchal system, and the personal tragedy of her unhappy and childless marriage proved powerful encumbrances. Having tried to build for the long run, many of her policies were doomed either to failure or to be credited to her successor, Elizabeth I.

BIBLIOGRAPHY

Harbison, E. Harris. *Rival Ambassadors at the Court of Queen Mary.* 1940.
Loades, D.M. *Mary Tudor, a Life.* 1989.
———. *The Reign of Mary Tudor, Politics, Government, and Religion in England, 1553–1558.* 1979.
Tittler, Robert. *The Reign of Mary I.* 2nd edition. 1991.

Robert Tittler

SEE ALSO

Catholicism; Elizabeth I; Henry VIII; Katherine of Aragon; Grey, Lady Jane; Marian Exiles; Marian Martyrs; Philip II; Wyatt's Rebellion

Mary I, from T.T., *A Booke Containing the True Portraiture of the Kings of England* (1579). Reproduced from the original by permission of the Henry E. Huntington Library and Art Gallery.

Catholic Church, which had been confiscated and resold under her father and brother. She took a number of positive steps to encourage a return to Catholic worship where it had been forsaken, concentrating especially on rebuilding a Catholic clergy. However, between 1555 and her death three years later, her impatience at continued expressions of Protestant zeal, and perhaps the pressures of her own steadily declining health, led her to the martyrdom of some 300 Protestants. Others migrated abroad, to carry out their teaching and their lives in more secure and sympathetic environments. This policy has stained her reputation for all time, but the sum of her religious policies did arrest the further decline of Catholic belief and sustained its traditions well into the reign of her halfsister Elizabeth.

In social and economic affairs Mary's government took a number of innovative steps to reverse the inflation, budgetary deficits, poverty, and trade crises of the day. She explored the commercial potential of Russian, African, and Baltic markets, revised the customs system, strove to

Mary Queen of Scots (1542–1587)

Mary Queen of Scots is one of the great romantic figures of history. She was also one of the most inept monarchs ever to sit on the Scottish throne. Queen from the age of one week, she lived for forty-four years, and ruled for only six of them, 1561–1567. Her reign began with a lengthy minority, not a new phenomenon in Scotland, but one infinitely complicated by religious reformation and diplomatic upheaval. Her regents and leading subjects had somehow to cope with successive English armies sent up by Henry VIII and Edward Seymour, protector Somerset, in pursuit of Mary as a bride for Edward VI, the murderous policy known as the "Rough Wooing." In 1548, Mary

M

was sent to France for her own safety, and there she lived, marrying the French dauphin in 1558. In 1559–1560, the pro-French and Catholic policy of her mother, Mary of Guise, the Scottish regent, was overturned by the Protestant lords; and Protestant triumph meant turning away from Scotland's traditional ally, France, to her traditional enemy, Protestant England.

When, in December 1560, Mary's husband died, her obvious move would have been to return to her kingdom of Scotland, and, as a Catholic, reverse the very recent Protestant success. What she actually did was to remain in France, seeking another husband who would keep her in happy and irresponsible luxury in Europe. Only in August 1561 did she give up hope and come back to begin her personal rule. From 1561–1565, she was little more than a decorative figurehead in a government managed by her bastard half-brother, James, earl of Moray, and her brilliant secretary, William Maitland of Lethington, Protestants both. Her Catholic subjects despaired as their Catholic queen allowed the infant Protestant kirk to establish itself. Her lack of zeal for her faith can only be explained in terms of her obsessive desire to be named as Elizabeth's heir. This most Scottish figure of legend, in fact, rated Scotland low in her priorities; her past in France, and her hoped-for future in England were of much more importance to her.

She continued to fail to find a husband until in 1565 she married Henry Stuart, Lord Darnley, a lightweight and drunkard, but with the advantages of being handsome, vaguely Catholic, and having a place in the English succession. It was the beginning of disaster. The next two years witnessed incoherent royal policy, as she temporarily and belatedly showed some enthusiasm for her Catholic subjects only to veer away from them again. It was a period dominated by scandal: first, the murder of her Italian secretary and rumored lover, David Rizzio, and then, much more spectacularly, of Darnley himself, in which she was almost certainly involved. This led directly to her third and fatal marriage to James Hepburn, earl of Bothwell, aristocratic rogue elephant and the main candidate for the role of murderer of her second husband.

Her one achievement in these dreadful years was to produce a son, James, who fortunately inherited neither of his parents' mental or emotional characteristics. By 1567, she was expendable; and after the Bothwell marriage, with virtually no allies left, she was deposed. She fled to England, where she indulged in a series of ill-conceived plots, ultimately forcing the agonized Elizabeth to execute her in 1587.

Her failure was not because she was a woman ruling in a man's world; the sixteenth century produced some remarkable women rulers. Nor was she the Catholic martyr of legend, despite her efforts to portray herself as such at her death. She was not even particularly romantic. Rather, she was a tragic figure: a woman born to a position she was quite unable to fulfill.

BIBLIOGRAPHY
Donaldson, G. *All the Queen's Men.* 1983.
Fraser, A. *Mary Queen of Scots.* 1969.
Lee, M., Jr. *James Stewart, Earl of Moray.* 1953.
Lynch, M., ed. *Mary Stewart: Queen in Three Kingdoms.* 1988.
Wormald, J. *Mary Queen of Scots: A Study in Failure.* 1988.

Jenny Wormald

SEE ALSO
Edward VI; Henry VIII; Hepburn, James; James VI and I; Rizzio, David; Seymour, Edward; Stuart, Henry

Mary Tudor, Queen of France and Duchess of Suffolk (1496–1533)

The third daughter of Henry VII and Elizabeth of York, Mary was betrothed in 1508 to Charles, archduke of Burgundy, but the marriage never took place, as the Anglo-imperial alliance came under strain in 1514 when the Emperor Maximilian made a separate truce with the French. As Henry VIII swung in a pro-French direction, Mary's marriage was again used to secure diplomatic advantage, and she was married to the fifty-two-year-old Louis XII of France in October 1514. The union was neither happy—Louis dismissed all her English servants—nor long-lived, for he died a few months later. Mary then fell in love with Charles Brandon, duke of Suffolk, sent to congratulate the new French king on his accession, and although Henry seems to have been favorable to the match, he was angered by the haste with which the couple moved to marry. For a brief period Brandon was in disfavor, and the king asked for the return of half her dowry and a payment of £24,000 in installments of £2,000 per annum. In the years ahead Brandon was sometimes suspected of pro-French leanings because of his dependence on French goodwill for the continued payment of his wife's dower, which formed a key component of their income. Mary's two sons by Brandon died young, but a daughter, Frances, the mother of Lady Jane Grey, survived. Mary was close to the king and played an important role in court ceremonial, but she was widely believed to be sympathetic to Katherine of Aragon, and one contemporary thought that she had died of grief over Katherine's tribulations.

BIBLIOGRAPHY
Richardson, W.C. *Mary Tudor, the White Queen.* 1970.
Gunn, S.J. *Charles Brandon, Duke of Suffolk, 1484–1545.* 1988.

Ian W. Archer

SEE ALSO
Brandon, Charles

Masques

The English masque, derived from Italian and French entertainments, was a performance of disguised nobility that featured spectacle and dance and often ended with the masquers dancing with the audience. In its most accomplished form, the text of a masque was only ten or twelve pages long, but the production—with its music, dancing, pageantry, and spectacular scenic effects—could last three hours. At the heart of the form was a central dance known as the revels, which often followed the masque. Although the form was much more established in the seventeenth century, when it became a frequent court entertainment, its development is well documented during the Tudor period.

The masque form may be traced back to mummings and disguisings in the reign of Richard II (1377–1399), during which the monarch was given symbolic gifts. A perfomance called a masque was prepared by William Newark, Master of the the Chapel, to celebrate the wedding of Henry VII's son Prince Arthur to Katherine of Aragon in 1501. Masquers took partners from among the ladies of the court for the first time in 1512. After 1515 symbolic pageants under Henry VIII added speeches that would be developed in later masques. William Crane, Master of the Chapel, joined the performances, now often with some dialogue, to indispensable court dances that would later be formalized in the revels. An example is Henry VIII's entertainment for a visit of French ambassadors at Greenwich, *Riches and Love,* presented on May 6, 1527.

In the reign of Edward VI (1547–1553) the playwrights John Heywood and Nicholas Udall wrote disguisings that featured allegory and spectacle, but only titles survive for what were by then called "masques." An extant comment on such a performance in 1551 reports that the masques were of apes and bagpipes, of cats, of Greek worthies, and of "medyoxes," performers who were "double visaged, th'one syde like a man. th'other lyke death." The same year Edward VI revived the office of Lord of Misrule and appointed George Ferrers to the post.

The masque became an important element of Elizabeth's court and the entertainments staged for her by the nobility during her frequent progresses. However, Henry Goldingham's entertainment for Elizabeth in 1578 is called "an excellent princely maske," even though nobility were not involved and no revels followed at the end. Staging details survive from another masque performed at court by the gentlemen of Gray's Inn at Shrovetide (March 3 or 4) in 1595. This performance at Whitehall was staged on a simple scaffold with an adamantine rock at one end; the stage had no curtain and no proscenium arch. The rock itself, from which the masquers entered, may have been little more than a canvas flap large enough to conceal eight persons.

The best of the Elizabethan masques are considered "literary" and many were published after performance. The earliest is a wedding masque composed in 1572 by George Gascoigne and published in his *Posies* in 1575. He composed a later entertainment for Elizabeth's visit to Kenilworth Castle in July 1575, which he published in 1576; an eyewitness account of the show survives in a letter from the courtier Robert Laneham to a friend in London. Perhaps the most interesting example of masque pageantry was "the deliverie of the Ladie of the Lake" in a show presented by William Hunnis. Certainly the highest achievement of Elizabethan literary masques is Sir Philip Sidney's *The Lady of May* (1579), not published until the 1598 folio of Sidney's works. Centered on the monarch, this entertainment has the forester Therion and the shepherd Espilus compete for the queen's attention and favor.

As an important and frequent form, however, the masque awaited the work of Ben Jonson and Inigo Jones and flourished at the courts of James VI and I and, especially, the court of Queen Anne of Denmark in the early years of the Stuart reign.

BIBLIOGRAPHY
Limon, Jerzy. *The Masque of Stuart Culture.* 1990.
Orgel, Stephen. *Ben Jonson: Selected Masques.* 1970.
———. *The Jonsonian Masque.* 1965.
———. "Sidney's Experiment in Pastoral." *Journal of the Warburg and Courtauld Institutes,* vol. 26, pp. 198–203.

M

Sidney, Sir Philip. *The Lady of May.* In *Works of Sir Philip Sidney. Miscellaneous Prose.* Katherine Duncan-Jones, ed. 1973.

The Editors

SEE ALSO
Gascoigne, George; Heywood, John; Hunnis, William; Jonson, Ben; Kenilworth; Progresses, Royal; Udall, Nicholas

Masterless Men
See Crime; Vagrants

Mathematics
See Dee, John; Digges, Leonard; Hariot, Thomas; and Navigation

Matrimony
The marriage rite of the Book of Common Prayer was based on that in the Sarum *Manual,* in which the vows and bestowal of the ring were already in English, with some material from the Cologne Church Order of Archbishop Herman von Wied. The service was almost unchanged through the three Tudor versions of the Book of Common Prayer, save that the 1549 edition included the giving of gold and silver to the bride as well as the giving of a ring.

The service begins with a formal address to the couple declaring the purposes of marriage: 1) procreation, 2) avoidance of fornication, and 3) mutual society, help, and comfort. This is followed by a solemn betrothal, to which the couple in turn reply, "I will." The bride is given away, and the formal exchange of vows takes place. The ring is then placed on the bride's left hand with the words "With this ring I thee wed: [This gold and silver I give thee:] with my body I thee worship: and with all my worldly goods I thee endow." According to John Hooker, the custom of giving gold and silver goes back to the Saxons. They are described by Thomas Cranmer in the rite as "tokens of spousage" and identified with the jewelry and bracelets given by Isaac to Rebecca "for tokens of theyr matrimonie." Hooker also defended the phrase "with my body I thee worship," which had been attacked in the *Admonition to Parliament* as "popish," causing the groom "to make an idol of his wife." First, according to Hooker, it distinguishes lawful marital intercourse from "unlawful copulation" which "doth pollute

and dishonour both parties," and, second, it positively describes the authority over each other's bodies that husband and wife have, according to 1 Corinthians 7:4.

The giving of the ring itself was condemned in the *Admonition* as the sacramental sign of the alleged sacrament of matrimony. The Prayer Book rite specifically defends the giving of the ring in the prayer that immediately follows its giving. It prays that the couple may "surely performe and kepe the vowe and couenant betwixt them made, *whereof this ring geuen, and receiued, is a token and pledge.*" Hooker similarly defends it as a traditional pledge of mutual love, of faith and fidelity that is by intention endless, "a pledge of conjunction of heart and mind agreed upon between them."

The prayer for the couple is followed by the priest's reciting the formula from Matthew 9:16, "Those whom God hath joined together, let no man put assunder," and pronouncing them man and wife. The theological sequence is that the couple exchange their vows, the church prays for God's blessing on them, and the priest declares the couple married. The marriage is thus the action of God and the couple, the minister's role being confined to voicing the church's prayer and pronouncing the marriage accomplished.

The minister then adds the nuptial blessing, consisting of two blessings, psalms, and various prayers. The service concludes with a rubric requiring the couple to receive communion the same day, a requirement also condemned by the *Admonition* as simply continuing the papist insistence that mass accompany all religious rites. Hooker defends the practice as "a custom so religious and so holy, that if the Church of England be blameable in this respect it is not for suffering it to be so much but rather for not providing that it may be more put in use." The clear implication of Hooker's reply, as other evidence clearly establishes, is that the rule was not enforced, and newly married couples frequently did not communicate. The apparent expectation of the liturgy was that weddings would be public celebrations on Sundays or holy days when the couple would communicate at a public service.

BIBLIOGRAPHY
Brightman, F.E. *The English Rite.* 2 vols. 1921; repr. 1969.
Hooker, Richard. *Of the Laws of Ecclesiastical Polity.* Book 5, lxxiii.
Manuale ad vsum percelebris ecclesie Sarisburiensis. A. Jefferies Collins, ed. Henry Bradshaw Society. Vol. 91. 1960.

Procter, Francis, and Walter Howard Frere. *A New History of the Book of Common Prayer*, pp. 608–622. 1958.

Stevenson, Kenneth. *Nuptial Blessing.* Alcuin Club Collections. Vol. 64, pp. 134–143.

von Wied, Herman. *Einfaltigs Bedenken* [Cologne Church Order]. In A.L. Richter. *Die Evangelischen Kirchenordnungen des Sechszehnten Jahrhunderts.* Vol. 2, pp. 30–54. 1847. English trans. *A Simple and Religious Consultation.* 1547, 1548; no modern edition.

Leonel L. Mitchell

SEE ALSO

Admonitions Controversy; Book of Common Prayer; Marriage Manuals; Marriage and Marriage Law; Sarum, Use of

Mayne, Cuthbert (1543–1577)

Cuthbert Mayne, the first of the Catholic seminary priests to be executed, was born in Youlston, near Barnstaple, in 1543. At the insistence of his uncle, a devout Anglican, Mayne was ordained a minister at the age of eighteen or nineteen. He studied at St. Alban Hall, Oxford, before becoming chaplain at St. John's College, where he earned the B.A. in 1566 and the M.A. in 1570. While at St. John's, he befriended Gregory Martin and Edmund Campion, and privately embraced Catholicism. His friends wrote him from Douai, urging him to come over. One of their letters fell into the hands of the bishop of London, who ordered Mayne's arrest. Mayne, in Cornwall at the time, fled overseas to Douai. Ordained a priest in 1575, he returned to England the following spring. He resided in the household of Sir Francis Tregian in Golden, near Truro, disguised as Tregian's steward, and went about ministering to local Catholics.

In the summer of 1577, the sheriff, Sir Richard Grenville, ordered a suppression of Catholic activities in Cornwall, arresting Mayne during a search of Golden. Mayne was discovered wearing under his doublet the Agnus Dei, a wax disc with the image of the lamb on the obverse and the arms of the pope on the reverse; and among his papers was found a copy of an expired papal bull of indulgence for the Jubilee of 1575. He was condemned under the treason act of 1571 for bringing into England bulls from Rome, and convicted of upholding the pope's authority, of saying Mass, and of wearing the Agnus Dei. Because Mayne had in his possession only a copy of an expired papal bull, there was some doubt whether the treason statute applied in his case, and it was unclear at the time if his other offenses constituted treason. Mayne's case was referred to the Privy Council, which received a divided opinion from the judges. The council decided that an example should be made of Mayne, and accordingly he was hanged, drawn, and quartered at Launceston on November 29, 1577. One of his quarters was put on display at Barnstaple as a warning to local Catholics. Cuthbert Mayne was beatified by Pope Leo XIII in 1886.

BIBLIOGRAPHY

Boyan, Pearl A., and George R. Lamb. *Francis Tregian: Cornish Recusant.* 1955.

Challoner, Richard. *Memoirs of Missionary Priests.* John H. Pollen, ed. 1924.

McGrath, Patrick. *Papists and Puritans under Elizabeth I.* 1967.

Rowse, A.L. *Tudor Cornwall.* 1941.

John M. Currin

SEE ALSO

Campion, Edmund; Grenville, Richard; Recusancy; Treason

Medicine and Health

During the Tudor period, classical ideas and attitudes about medicine and health became widely adopted among the English gentry and nobility, even in the councils of the crown; but many innovations came at the expense of friction with customary opinion and local autonomy. While most people continued to rely on friends and neighbors for assistance when needed, participating in treatments of herbs and animals, rituals and sayings, foreign and ancient learning became the most respected form of medical advice among the educated.

There had been some importation of humanist learning and institutions in the fifteenth century, but it was only during the relative peace of the Tudor ascendancy that medical humanism established itself securely in England. For instance, one of the foremost humanists of his generation was the learned physician Thomas Linacre, an outstanding classical scholar and grammarian, as well as a botanist and physician. A learned cleric and fellow of All Souls College, Oxford, Linacre traveled to the source of the new learning, Italy, when in 1487 he accompanied William Sellyng to Rome (who went on behalf of Henry VII). Starting in 1488, he spent two years in Florence studying Greek with Demetrius Chalcondylas and Angelo

M

Poliziano, two of the foremost humanists of the day; and after further time in Rome, Linacre studied in Venice and Padua, where he took a medical doctorate in 1496. He remained in Italy until 1499, becoming a friend of the renowned Ermolao Barbaro and a translator and editor of Aristotle's *Meteorologica*—an important medical as well as philosophical text—for the famed humanist printer Aldus Manutius. After his return to England, he instructed Thomas More in Greek, among other scholarly activities. He gained an appointment as physician to the new king, Henry VIII, in 1509, as well as various church benefices. Later, he became physician to the princess (and future queen) Mary I, tutor to Prince Arthur, a canon in the church, cofounder and president of the London College of Physicians, founder of a lectureship in physic at St. John's College, Cambridge, and of a lectureship at Merton College, Oxford, and translator and editor of medical, philosophical, and grammatical works. Among other endeavors, Linacre's work in translating much of Galen into Latin was especially notable.

The classical medical principles advanced by Linacre and other learned physicians of the sixteenth century taught that the task of the physician was the maintenance of health and the prolongation of life. As that connoisseur of virtue and good advice, Sir Thomas Elyot explained to his readers in *The castle of helth* (1541), the science of physic "being well understood, truly experienced, and discretely ordered, doth conserve health. . . ." He went on to discuss—in a way that physicians like Linacre would have approved—the effects on health of the things natural (elements, temperaments, humors, etc.), and the appropriate quantity and quality of food, habits, diet, and exercise. So far, he dealt with how to preserve health. Only in Book 3 did he turn to what to do (again by way of dietetics and regimen) when an excess of one or more humors caused health to weaken. He discussed diseases caused by nonnaturals only in Book 4, but again mostly from the perspective of how to restore a proper balance by diet.

Thus, the pinnacle of early sixteenth-century medical writing was not a list of cures for various diseases but a manual of advice about health. Medical advice like Elyot's, based on the classical teachings being renewed by people like Linacre, became fairly common in vernacular treatises. Not long after Elyot, for instance, Andrew Boorde, a former monk who had taken up physic when forced out of the church during the Reformation, published *A Compendyous Regyment or a Dyetary of healthe made in Mountpyllyer* (1547), dedicated to his patron,

Thomas Howard, duke of Norfolk. The rules of health he discussed began with where to situate a house, how to plan and construct it, how to organize a household, what to eat and drink and what to avoid, and what exercise to take. As Boorde's title suggested, these ideals of learned physic had been best restored by medical humanists abroad, being newly imported to England. As he argued, too, physicians, who had earned a doctorate in a university faculty of medicine, were the best advisers on how to live in accordance with nature, since they had studied it deeply ("physic" was from the Greek word for nature, *phusis*). These most learned counselors on health could go more deeply into the ways in which their clients' individual constitutions or temperaments could be best regulated to live harmoniously; that is, they advised on how the particulars of any one person's nature could best be harmonized with nature generally. Because learned Tudor physicians placed so much stress on the value of deep and grave study, they complained loudly about those who practiced without having an education. For example, early in Elizabeth I's reign, John Securis, a physician of Salisbury who had studied with the famed medical humanist Sylvius in Paris, took his lead from a reading of Hippocrates (*A Detection and Querimonie of the daily enormities and abuses committed in physick*, 1566): a good practitioner must be of long study, of good color and comely countenance, of sound body, esteemed by the common people and suspected of no excesses, and generally of a respectable character. In addition, because learned physic was founded on the study of "logic and natural philosophy," which properly could be obtained only through university study, it was unthinkable that merely reading books on medicine in the vernacular could be sufficient to make men into knowledgeable (or "cunnyng") physicians. Sound judgment was needed for good medical practice. An advanced education gave a man more than mere knowledge; it gave him "science." The end of a university education was not merely to supply the student with information; rather, it was also to develop the character of the future physician, from which his judgment would flow.

For the public good, then, continental medical humanists had also worked increasingly closely with municipal and princely governments to gain supervisory rights over other practitioners. One of the first signs that their values had a growing influence with the English government was the "Act Concerning Physicians and Surgeons" (3 Hen.VIII.c.11) passed by Parliament in 1511–1512. The act complained that while physic and surgery took both "great learning and ripe experience," they were "daily within this realm exercised by a great multitude of ignorant persons . . . [including] smiths, weavers and women" who undertook bold and difficult cures, sometimes using sorcery and witchcraft and sometimes applying inappropriate or dangerous medicines, "to the high displeasure of God, great infamie to the faculties, and greavous hurt, damage and destruction of many of the king's liege people." Parliament therefore ordered the bishops or their vicars general, together with several learned physicians and surgeons of their diocese, to examine and license medical practitioners, who would be fined 5£ per month for practicing illicitly. Cardinal Thomas Wolsey further promoted the interests of academic medical learning by supporting the efforts to found a College of Physicians in London. Humanists had argued that learning was necessary for guiding the generality of royal subjects toward the common good (the "commonwealth"). During an epidemic of plague in 1518, the scholarly papal legate and lord chancellor secured the aid of the learned physicians of London by arranging for them to be incorporated into the London College of Physicians. Formed around a corps of three royal physicians and three London physicians (including Linacre), the crown's express desire was to encourage the emulation of medical scholars, or members of the "faculty," as the charter put it. In order to fight the avaricious and credulous practice of undisciplined medicine, the college obtained the right to limit the practice of physic in London and within seven miles of its walls to its members under penalty of a fine of 5£ per month. Five years later, the charter gained the approbation of Parliament (14 & 15 Hen.VIII.c.5), which additionally required "such as shall be admitted to exercise physic" in the dioceses of England—other than graduates of Oxford and Cambridge—to travel to London to obtain letters testimonial of the members of the college before being licensed by the bishops. Under Thomas Cromwell the physicians gained no new legal rights, but about the time that he fell in 1540 they obtained further privileges by act of Parliament (32 Hen.VIII.c.40). These laws and privileges gave learned physicians and their allies clear duties and responsibilities to watch over the character and behavior of all other practitioners.

At the same time the physicians obtained the last of these acts, the learned surgeons also obtained new privileges. They combined with the barbers in a United Company of Barber Surgeons, memorialized in Holbein's large painting depicting Henry VIII handing them their charter.

The act of Parliament confirming the charter (32 Hen. VIII. c.42) exempted the surgeons, like the physicians, from various municipal offices, allowed them to obtain the bodies of four malefactors each year for their public anatomies, forbade the barbers to practice surgery (except tooth-drawing) and surgeons to dabble in barbering, and allowed nobles to exempt their own household barbers and surgeons from the requirement to join the company. The surgeons showed themselves up-to-date scholars by instituting an anatomical lectureship for the guild (usually held by a learned physician) and supporting the publication of learned medical books.

It would appear that the physicians and surgeons soon set about trying to police the practitioners of London and beyond. The sketchy records of the early years of the College of Physicians first mentioned empirics being fined for practice without the college's license in December of 1541, when the Court of Exchequer acted twice. It would seem that the surgeons were even more active. The result was more parliamentary legislation, this time in the form of "An Act that persons being no common Surgeons may minister medicines outward" (34 & 35 Hen.VIII.c.8), sometimes later called the "quacks' charter." It complained that "the Company and Fellowship of Surgeons of London, minding only their own lucre, and nothing the profit or ease of the diseased or patient, have sued, troubled and vexed divers honest persons aswell men as women, whom God hath endowed with the knowledge of the nature, kind, and operation of certain herbs, roots and waters" who took no money but ministered to the poor "only for neighborhood and God's sake and of pity and charity." To remedy these abuses, Parliament allowed "to every person being the King's subject having knowledge and experience of the nature" of the things mentioned "to practice, use and minister in and to any outward sore" and other outward swellings and diseases "according to their cunning, experience, and knowledge . . . without vexation, trouble, penalty, or loss of their goods." Although the act was clearly directed at the surgeons rather than the physicians, it was invoked in later years against the legal activities of the college as well.

The later years of the Henrician reformation also saw medical institutions operated by the church turned over to secular authorities. The dissolution of the monasteries meant that many charitable foundations became crown properties, to be sold off or neglected. The list of hospitals in John Stow's *Survey of London* (1598) includes a host of entries that end with the remark "suppressed by King Henry VIII." A few survived, however. For example, the

M

London Priory of St. Bartholomew's was suppressed during the second act of dissolution (1539), but the house it operated for the care of the sick poor continued to serve local needs as best it could. Already in 1538, acknowledging the importance of the hospitals to the well-being of the residents, the city of London had petitioned the king to grant them the hospital and its endowments. Henry VIII refounded the hospital of St. Bartholomew's in 1544 (although stripped of all the lands and properties that had previously supported it); a year later, four aldermen and eight common councilmen of the city were appointed to negotiate the settlement of it; and in December 1546, the hospital (together with the lunatic asylum of Bethlehem) was newly chartered as a municipal institution. Edward VI followed his father's example by restoring St. Thomas's Hospital (which had closed in 1540), and on his deathbed in 1553 chartered it together with Christ's Hospital (which became an orphanage) and Bridewell (which developed into a workhouse), together with the revenues of the Palace of the Savoy (which led to the dissolution of St. John's Hospital in the Savoy), as royal hospitals, which were given to the city. (St. Bart's and Bethlehem were added to the other "royal" London institutions in 1557.)

Almost from the beginning, these hospitals had paid surgeons on hand, and by the mid-1560s, both St. Bart's and St. Thomas's had regularly appointed and salaried physicians as well; the two may have been able to care for as many as 300 of the sick poor in London. St. John's Hospital in the Savoy was refounded by Queen Mary and King Philip, struggled to survive, and finally perished in the seventeenth century. Similar stories, with few long-term successes, could be told about hospitals in other locales throughout England. Aside from the efforts to revive some London hospitals at the end of his reign, Edward's years show little evidence of interest in governing medical affairs, nor do they exhibit any records of activity on the part of the medical corporations. The accession of Linacre's former pupil, Mary, in 1554 brought renewed activity, however. Cardinal Reginald Pole, Queen Mary's chief minister, was also quite learned in medicine, having studied with Linacre himself. The College of Physicians therefore quickly obtained a parliamentary act giving it the right to commit those who offended its statutes to prison (1 Mariae, St.2.c.9). The act also warned that "all Justices, Mayors, Sheriffs, Bailiffs, Constables, and other Ministers and Officers" in London and within seven miles were to help the college in these actions or else "to run in contempt of the Queen's Majesty her heirs and successors."

The work of the early English humanists and the encouragement of the crown and other patrons resulted in an efflorescence of classical medical learning in the middle and second half of the century. English physicians such as John Clement (c. 1510–1570)—and his wife, Margaret Giggs—and John Caius (1510–1573), became known throughout Europe as superb editors of Galenic manuscripts. Clement and Caius, like Clement's friend and patron, Sir Thomas More, remained Catholic as well. Caius served as physician to Edward VI, Mary, and Elizabeth. In 1555, following the accession of Mary, Caius became president of the College of Physicians and reinvigorated it: he waged war on empirics; he got Cardinal Pole to support the college's demand that medical degrees not be awarded at Oxford and Cambridge without the students having followed a prescribed course of study; he laid down rules for governing the internal business of the college; and he obtained the right to claim the bodies of four executed criminals a year for college anatomies. Under the learned Dr. Caius the college continued to stand as a bastion of medical humanism. While an excellent natural historian and philologist and fine anatomist, Caius objected to Andreas Vesalius's influential criticisms of Galen. In late October and early November of 1560, he also forced John Geynes (D.M., Oxford, 1535) to sign a document recanting his opinion that Galen had erred before admission to the college, which Geynes finally did only after a three-day formal disputation with Caius.

The encouragement of medical learning had its effect on medical teaching at Oxford and Cambridge. In addition to the lectureships founded by Linacre, Cardinal Wolsey established three lectureships in medicine, which were attached to Corpus College, Oxford, until his planned Cardinal College could be instituted. When Henry VIII endowed a series of lectureships at Oxford and Cambridge, medicine was among them. The second person to hold Wolsey's lectureship, John Warner, also became the first regius professor of medicine at Oxford in 1546; anatomy teaching from human dissection seems to have been occurring at about the same time there, formalized in the Tomlins readership in anatomy at the end of the century (usually also held by the regius professor). In refounding Gonville College at Cambridge, Caius obtained the right to anatomize the bodies of executed criminals, allowing dissections to be undertaken at his college in the last quarter of the century. Endowments also began to encourage students of medicine. The scholarship founded by Archbishop Matthew Parker, for example, supported a student of medicine from Kent who had been educated at the

King's School: in 1593, the scholarship went to support the young William Harvey at Cambridge. The encouragement of the study of physic at the two English universities resulted in over 170 M.B.s or M.D.s graduating from Oxford and about the same from Cambridge. By the end of the sixteenth century, then, England was turning out many excellent medical scholars of its own. Nevertheless, a pattern of intellectual and religious conservatism tending toward Catholic humanism appears to have continued through the first years of Elizabeth's reign. The London College of Physicians continued to act as a learned brotherhood and to prosecute empirics, but Caius stepped down from the presidency of the college in 1564 to see to his work at Gonville (and Caius) College, and was finally removed from his office of physician to Elizabeth in 1568 because of his Catholicism. In 1572, the London surgeons objected in the Lord Mayor's Court to the college fining them for applying inward remedies in a hearing, and they had an array of royal authorities appear in their support. While Caius came from Cambridge to defend the college's statutory authority successfully, the college's records almost cease afterward. The message had come through clearly: while not revoking the college's charter, the crown had given warning, and the college for many years thereafter seems to have ceased trying to rule over other practitioners. Still, during the more conservative period of the end of Elizabeth's reign, matters were restored: the college revived its juridical powers at the end of the 1580s by grant of a "privilege" from Sir Francis Walsingham. During the 1590s, one group in particular that the college began to prosecute in significant numbers was, again, the surgeons, who objected strenuously, not only against the college but also against crown officers and most of the royal judges.

The doctrines of health and physic associated with classical medicine therefore came to England with the encouragement of humanists and their patrons under the Henries, and under Mary and the early and late years of Elizabeth's reign. Laws and institutions, lectureships and scholarships, were all created to support the study of medical learning. Classical teachings about how to live in harmony with nature to avoid sickness and to prolong life earned applause from the public, even becoming basic tenets of books written in the vernacular. The Tudor period, then, helped to promote the growth of the medical learning that began to make England renowned.

BIBLIOGRAPHY

Clark, George N. *A History of the Royal College of Physicians of London.* 1964–1966.

Lewis, Gillian. "The Faculty of Medicine." In *History of the University of Oxford.* Vol. 3: *The Collegiate University.* J.K. McConica, ed., pp. 213–256. 1986.

Medvei, Victor Cornelius, and John L. Thornton. *The Royal Hospital of Saint Bartholomew, 1123–1973.* 1974.

Nutton, Vivian. "John Caius and the Linacre Tradition." *Medical History,* vol. 23, pp. 373–391.

———. *John Caius and the Manuscripts of Galen.* 1987.

Wear, Andrew, R.K. French, and I.M. Lonie, eds. *The Medical Renaissance of the Sixteenth Century.* 1985.

Webster, Charles, ed. *Health, Medicine, and Mortality in the Sixteenth Century.* 1979.

Webster, Charles, Francis Maddison, and Margaret Pelling, eds. *Essays on the Life and Works of Thomas Linacre, c. 1460–1524.* 1977.

Young, Sidney. *Annals of the Barber-Surgeons of London.* 1890.

Harold J. Cook

SEE ALSO

Boorde, Andrew; Classical Literature, Influence of; Elyot, Thomas; Humanism; Linacre, Thomas; Monastic Orders; Plague; Pole, Reginald; Science, History of; Stow, John; Wolsey, Thomas

Melville, Andrew (1545–1622)

Presbyterian reformer and theologian, Andrew Melville was born at Baldovy and educated at the Montrose grammar school. In 1559, he entered St. Mary's College at St. Andrews. In 1564, he went to Paris to study Greek, oriental languages, mathematics, and law. While in Paris he attended the lectures of Peter Ramus, whose philosopical method and pedagogy he afterward introduced into the Scottish universities. In 1566, he studied civil law at Poitiers where he was made regent in the College of St. Marceon. In 1569, political troubles in France involving the Huguenots forced him to seek refuge in Geneva, where he was welcomed by Theodore Beza and appointed to the chair of humanity in the academy. On returning to Scotland in 1574, Melville was appointed principal of Glasgow University where he introduced educational reforms that included a new plan of studies and the establishment of new chairs in languages, science, philosophy, and theology. In 1577, he received the additional charge of Govan, near Glasgow, where he preached every Sunday.

Meanwhile, Melville was active in ecclesiastical affairs. He directed a major attack against remaining forms of

M

episcopacy. The first *Book of Discipline* (1561) had permitted a quasi-episcopacy in the form of "superintendents." Melville was appointed in 1575 to the General Assembly's committee for drafting the scheme of church government set forth in the second *Book of Discipline* (1575). Inspired by the Genevan model, this document discarded the last traces of prelacy in the Church of Scotland and set forth a full-blown Presbyterian system of church government. To the gradation of church courts was assigned a jurisdiction independent of the civil magistrate.

Melville's ideas of university reform were not restricted to Glasgow. In 1575, he assisted in drafting a new constitution for Aberdeen; in 1578, he was appointed by the Scottish Parliament a commissioner for the visitation of St. Andrews; and in 1580, a royal letter requested the approval of the assembly in the translation of Melville to St. Andrews as principal of St. Mary's College. Chairs at St. Andrews were at once offered (in vain) to Thomas Cartwright and Walter Travers.

When elected moderator of the General Assembly in 1582, Melville prosecuted Robert Montgomery, one of the so-called "tulchan" bishops. Refusal to recognize the authority of these bishops brought him into conflict with James VI, whose position was summarized in the principle "No Bishops, no King!" James was seeking a settlement in Scotland similar to that achieved in England under Elizabeth I. It was in this context that Melville delivered to the 1582 General Assembly an opening sermon that denounced the doctrine of the ecclesiastical supremacy of the crown. Retained as moderator, he was appointed by the assembly to serve on a commission to visit James VI at Perth with a remonstrance and petition. In February 1584, Melville was charged by the Privy Council in Edinburgh with treason. He fled to England to escape imprisonment and possible death. In July, he was well received at Oxford and Cambridge by Puritan leaders (including John Rainolds and William Whitaker) and by men of letters. In 1585, he returned to Scotland, where he acted as a ruling elder in the kirk-session of St. Andrews, resumed his lectures at the university in 1586, was again elected moderator of the General Assembly in 1587 and 1594, and became rector of St. Andrews in 1590. His attacks on new power given by the 1597 General Assembly to the king in ecclesiastical affairs and on the prohibition of the clergy from preaching on matters of state led to the deprivation of his rectorship in 1597, but as a consolation he was made dean of the theological faculty at St. Andrews in 1599.

Melville openly supported the accession of James to the English throne and favored a legislative union of the two kingdoms. But he soon again incurred the royal displeasure by insisting on the right of a free General Assembly and was summoned to London in 1606. He penned a sarcastic Latin poem on Anglican worship in response to which he was charged before the Privy Council and confined to the Tower in 1607, where he was imprisoned for four years. During this time, he corresponded with friends in Scotland. He was released in 1611 on condition that he accept the chair of biblical theology in the University of Sédan in France, where he taught for the last eleven years of his life.

BIBLIOGRAPHY

Burleigh, J.H.S. *A Church History of Scotland.* 1960.
Donaldson, Gordon. *The Scottish Reformation.* 1960.
McCri, T. *Life of Andrew Melville.* 2nd edition. 2 vols. 1824.

Lee W. Gibbs

SEE ALSO

Cartwright, Thomas; Church of Scotland; Church Polity; Huguenots; Ramism; Travers, Walter; Whitaker, William

De Mendoza, Bernardino (c. 1540–1604)

Born in Guadalajara, 1540, into one of the most influential Spanish families of the period, Bernardino de Mendoza distinguished himself as a soldier and a shrewd diplomat. After obtaining a B.A. in 1556 and an M.A. in 1557 from the University of Alcalá, Mendoza decided to pursue a military career in North Africa and the Netherlands. His fighting gained him acceptance into the Order of Santiago. After noting his remarkable diplomatic skills on different occasions, Philip II appointed him ambassador to the court of Elizabeth I in March 1578.

The six years that Mendoza remained in this post marked the turning point in the relations between the two countries. Even though he was sent to England with orders against interfering with English policy, he soon started advocating for a direct Spanish intervention against the Protestant queen. The tension created by the situation of English Catholics under Elizabeth I, the progressive involvement of England in the Netherlands, the protection offered to Don Antonio, the Portuguese pretender, and, most importantly, the aftermath of Sir Francis Drake's 1577–1580 voyage of circumnavigation, led Mendoza to confront the English queen repeatedly and to turn from diplomacy to conspiracy. Mendoza was a very important instrument in the planning of the Throckmorton Plot, one of the many Catholic conspiracies that intended to overthrow Elizabeth I and place the imprisoned Mary Queen of Scots on the English throne. After the plot was discovered by Sir Francis Walsingham in November 1583, Mendoza was declared persona non grata in England and was forced to leave the country in January 1584. On his departure, the wounded Spanish diplomat is reported to have said: "Don Bernardino de Mendoza was born not to disturb kingdoms but to conquer them."

Mendoza tried to live by his promise. In November 1584, he was appointed Spanish ambassador in France, a post that he used, among other things, to gather information about English activities and to continue working for the fall of Elizabeth I. In France, Mendoza was instrumental in the activities of the Catholic League against the French Huguenots and the Valois monarchy. In 1586, he was implicated in the Babington Plot, whose discovery ultimately led to the execution of Mary Queen of Scots in February 1587. He also played an important role in the attack of the Spanish Armada in the summer of 1588.

When Mendoza left France in January 1591, he was almost blind. Back in Madrid he spent his last years in seclusion. He died at the Monastery of San Bernardino on August 3, 1604.

BIBLIOGRAPHY

Elton, G.R. *England Under the Tudors.* 1974.

Haynes, Alan. *Invisible Power. The Elizabethan Secret Services, 1570–1603.* 1992.

Jensen, De Lamar. *Diplomacy and Dogmatism. Bernardino de Mendoza and the French Catholic League.* 1964.

MacCaffrey, Wallace T. *Queen Elizabeth and the Making of Policy, 1572–1588.* 1981.

Mattingly, Garrett. *Renaissance Diplomacy.* 1955.

de Mendoza, Bernardino. *Theorique and Practise of Warre.* Sir Edward Hoby, trans. 1597.

Francisco J. Borge

SEE ALSO

Armada, Spanish; Babington Plot; Drake, Francis; Elizabeth I; Espionage; Foreign Relations and Diplomacy; Mary Queen of Scots; Philip II; Throckmorton Plot; Walsingham, Francis

Merbecke, John (c. 1505–c.1585)

One of the earliest contributors of music designed specifically for the Anglican Church, John Merbecke (or Marbecke) centered his career at St. George's Chapel,

Windsor, where he served as clerk and organist. His only absence from his post came in 1543–1544 when he was arrested and tried for treason. Convicted of expressing contempt for the Mass and of possessing heretical documents, he was sentenced to death, but was granted clemency by Henry VIII on the intercession of the bishop of Winchester.

After his pardon, Merbecke was restored to his position, although he was exempted from performance of his duties after 1550. It was during this time that he embraced the Anglican faith and concentrated on music for the new church. *The Booke of Common Praier Noted* of 1550 was designed for use in parish churches and consisted of monophonic settings for *The First Booke of Common Prayer* of 1549. Merbecke gave examples of the manner in which psalms and canticles in English could be sung to Gregorian psalm tones. This edition was short-lived and indeed was made obsolete in 1552 by the publication of *The Second Booke of Common Prayer.* Merbecke then abandoned musical composition for theological and literary works, including a complete concordance of the English Bible (1550) and a verse biography of King David (1579). In 1571 he was named as chantry priest at Windsor and awarded a stipend.

BIBLIOGRAPHY

Hugh Aston, John Marbeck, Osbert Parsley. Tudor Church Music. Vol. 10. 1929.

Hunt, J. Eric. "Merbecke: His Life and Times." *The Gregorian,* vol. 36, pp. 4–15.

Leaver, Robin A., ed. *The Work of John Marbeck.* 1978.

Le Huray, Peter G. *Music and the Reformation in England, 1549–1660.* 1978.

Karen M. Bryan

SEE ALSO

Anglicanism; Book of Common Prayer

Merchant Adventurers

Groups of merchants who traded with the Netherlands in the fifteenth century coalesced as the Merchant Adventurers to become the most powerful and wealthy commercial organization in Tudor England. Full union as a regulated company was effectively achieved in the reign of Henry VII, when their privileges were recognized both by the city of London and by the crown. Formal incorporation was delayed until 1564, but the Elizabethan charter merely confirmed the company's commanding position in the

M

commercial life of the country. This was built on the monopoly of trade—wool excepted—with the Low Countries at a time when Antwerp, the company's staple or "mart town," had became the undisputed commercial and financial capital of Europe.

This link with Antwerp particularly favored London, and as the company prospered the concentration of the nation's trade between the Thames and the Scheldt gave metropolitan members effective control of its affairs. The "English House" in Antwerp, where the governor resided, was the notional seat of government, and provincial members were entitled to hold courts in Newcastle, York, and elsewhere. Real power, however, lay in the city, where the wealthiest members filled the office of Governor and the Court of Assistants, consolidating their position through the strict enforcement of company laws and ordinances. Those concerning admission and the "stint" were particularly effective in promoting oligarchy within the company. The means of entry, whether by patrimony, apprenticeship, or redemption (purchase), and the stint, which limited the number of woolen cloths members might export according to length of membership, served the interests of the ruling elite, which numbered not more than a hundred in mid-Tudor London. At the end of the century, when the nominal membership was put at 3,500, the effective membership was said to be not more than 200.

The emergence of such a powerful vested interest group inevitably attracted criticism from within as well as outside the company. But even in the vulnerable situation the Adventurers found themselves in the 1550s and 1560s, when trade throughout Europe was severely disrupted, they had little difficulty in protecting themselves. Indeed, the difficulties were seen to strengthen the arguments for regulated trade generally and that of the Merchant Adventurers in particular. The crown also valued the various financial services they rendered, then and later. In return, it was supportive not only of the company against critics at home, but also of the campaign against foreign merchants: in particular the German Hansards whose privileges were curtailed. The decline in alien exports thereafter cushioned the company from the worst effects of the collapse of the Antwerp market in the late 1560s and early 1570s. The staple was moved to Hamburg in 1569, remaining there until 1578, when it moved to Emden, where the Adventurers stayed until 1587 before moving to Stade. Trade was also permitted in Middelburg, where the staple was relocated in 1598 when the Adventurers were expelled from Germany. These were difficult times for the company at home as well as abroad.

Members continued to trade in Germany in breach of their own regulations, while independent traders or "interlopers" made significant inroads on their monopoly. Moreover, since unregulated trade kept up exports, the government was unusually ambiguous in its response to the company's complaints. But in the longer term the most serious challenge to its position came from legitimate traders who capitalized on the difficulties they encountered in securing imports at their German staples after the breach with Antwerp. Those problems underlay the emergence of the import-led companies, most notably the Levant and East India Company, that were soon to rival the Adventurers in wealth, influence, and prestige.

BIBLIOGRAPHY

Bisson, Douglas R. *The Merchant Adventurers of England. The Company and the Crown, 1474–1564.* 1993.

Carus-Wilson, E.M. *Medieval Merchant Ventures.* 1954.

Ramsay, G.D. *The City of London in International Politics at the Accession of Elizabeth Tudor.* 1975.

Brian Dietz

SEE ALSO

Cloth Trade; East India Company; Economy; Henry VII; Joint Stock Companies; London; Monopolies; Regulated Companies; Trade, Overseas

Merchant Taylors

One of the so-called "Great Twelve" livery companies of the city of London, the Merchant Taylors received its first charter in 1327, and was incorporated (enabling members to hold lands in their own right) in 1408. Originally called the Guild of Taylors and Linen Armourers, it enjoyed a remarkable advance in status under the Tudors, as Henry VII, himself a member, promoted merchant-tailor candidates for civic office and in 1503 granted the company a charter, under the pretentious title of Merchant Taylors. The vigorous opposition to this charter, led by the Taylors' long-standing rivals, the Drapers' Company, proved unavailing. The new title reflected the increasing prominence of merchant members of the company as the cloth trade expanded, undermining the company's association with the craft of tailoring. By the end of the century at least half the liverymen (members of the company of senior status) were merchants, and another third were domestic cloth dealers.

Prominent members associated with the craft, like Walter Fish, tailor to Elizabeth I, were much rarer. The company alternated with the Skinners in the sixth and seventh positions in the order of precedence among the "Great Twelve," and by the later Elizabethan period had displaced the Mercers as the largest contributor to civic loans and levies. Its political prominence in city affairs was reflected in the fact that in the sixteenth century it provided six lord mayors, whereas in the previous century there had been only one. The company's premises in Threadneedle Street, acquired in 1347 and rebuilt in the fourteenth and fifteenth centuries, were among the most spacious in the city, able to accommodate an enormous and lavish banquet for King James VI and I in 1607. During the Tudor period the Merchant Taylors became the largest London guild, accounting for 13 percent of admissions to the freedom of the city in the mid-sixteenth century, and numbering about 3,500 members by the 1590s.

Since by the custom of the city a man could practice any trade, and not just that to which he had been apprenticed, the company's members were engaged in a variety of crafts. There was, for example, a substantial group of members engaged in the dressing of cloths, and this resulted in clashes with the Clothworkers' Company, whose efforts to gain monopoly control over clothworking in the capital were successfully rebuffed by the Merchant Taylors in 1551 and 1566. However, the company remained committed to the defense of the interests of working tailors. For example, in the years after 1599, the rulers supported the efforts of the artisans to secure the expulsion from the city of tailors not free of the company. Although they were largely excluded from the ruling Court of Assistants for entry to which wealth sufficient to fund the company's cycle of feasting was a requirement, many of the functions pertaining to the regulation of the craft were devolved onto the junior section of the company, the so-called Bachelors' Company or yeomanry, originating in the early fifteenth century, and ruled over by four wardens substitute and their sixteen colleagues. They undertook regular searches of the craft and administered an increasing volume of poor relief funded by membership dues. The relative lack of involvement by the ruling Court of Assistants in the regulation of the craft reflected not only their rather different business interests, but also the burdens of administering an enhanced property portfolio. Although the Reformation had been a fraught time for the Merchant Taylors as the properties that had supported chantry priests praying for the souls of deceased members (now designated as "superstitious uses") were confiscated in 1548, these lands were repurchased in 1550 for £2006.2s.6d. The company's charitable activities extended in scope with the growing prominence of wealthy merchants and cloth dealers such as Richard Hilles, the early evangelical who made the key donation of £500 that established the Merchant Taylors' School in the parish of St. Lawrence Pountney in 1560, and Robert Dowe, a customs official, who funded a remarkable series of charities beginning in 1589.

BIBLIOGRAPHY

Clode, C.M. *The Early History of the Guild of Merchant Taylors.* 2 vols. 1888.

———. *Memorials of the Guild of Merchant Taylors.* 1875.

Ian W. Archer

SEE ALSO
Cloth Trade; Guilds

Merchants

See Merchant Adventurers; Merchant Taylors; Social Classes; Trade, Overseas

Meres, Francis (1565–1647)

A Cambridge graduate who died a rector in Rutland, Francis Meres kept a commonplace book while living in London around 1583. Its publication was to overshadow his first book, *Gods Arithmetic,* written for episcopal preferment, for Meres was the first to go on record extolling William Shakespeare's greatness. *Palladis Tamia: Wits Treasury* (1598) compared Shakespeare to Ovid for his poetry, and to Plautus and Seneca for his plays. Also under the heading "comparatiue discourse of our English Poets," Meres indicated those who were enjoying revived popularity, including Chaucer, Gower, and Lydgate—although Chaucer is "accounted the God of English Poets." While some are praised as "Latine Poets," the higher praise is reserved for those who "mightily enriched" the English tongue: Sir Philip Sidney, Edmund Spenser, Samuel Daniel, Michael Drayton, William Warner, William Shakespeare, Christopher Marlowe, and George Chapman. It is in this context that Shakespeare is singled out for further treatment, and his plays up to 1598 are listed (including a tantalizing reference to a lost play entitled *Loue labours wonne).* Useful though Meres' work is to modern scholars, as a commonplace collection it was hardly outstanding (most of the similes are translated from Desiderius Erasmus, and the anecdotes often

M

from Ravisius Textor). Still, for a book of this type, it circulated widely and was reprinted twice.

BIBLIOGRAPHY
Meres, Francis. *Palladis Tamia (1598)*. Don Cameron Allen, intro. Scholars' Facsimiles and Reprints. 1938.
William Engel

SEE ALSO
Commonplace Books; Shakespeare, William

Metal Industries and Mining

There is an established and common perception that the metal mining and smelting industries of England and Wales went through a process of almost revolutionary change sometime during the later Tudor period. This is usually explained in terms of a flow of new and improved technology introduced to Britain by foreign experts, principally German. Until recently, that view prevailed for all parts of the industry—iron, copper, lead and tin—and to all regions. Recent research, however, stresses instead changing demand and domestically generated improvements in technique. Less importance is now accorded as well to the Mines Royal and Mineral and Battery Works. Most of the important technical changes that took place—underpinning the increases in output and fundamentally changing the organizational structure of the industry—occurred in the smelting rather than the mining sector. Throughout the Tudor period, mining methods for all of the minerals remained essentially the same; simple, labor-intensive, they in no significant way improved on medieval techniques. Instead, most of the extra ore output was produced by the simple multiplication of miners and mines—and possibly by more consistent work hours. It was improvements in furnace design and operation, enabling the working of poorer ores at lower cost, that proved the truly strategic changes in the industry.

In 1485, the production of iron in England and Wales was at a low level, dependent on antiquated bloomery techniques. The industry was highly dispersed, dominated by small-scale units producing for essentially local markets. From the 1490s, however, it began to undergo a process of increasingly rapid change, led by a revival of production in the Weald of southeast England. Craftsmen skilled in the use of new blast furnace technology began to immigrate into that area from the Pays de Bray iron-making districts of France, just across the channel, following a decline in the French industry. As well as an expanding pool of skilled labor, the Weald also enjoyed the benefits of a highly elastic demand for iron, generated by a combination of local arms manufacturers, regional smiths, and, most importantly, the expansion of trade to and through London. In addition, wealthy local estate owners were prepared to invest heavily in the industry and carefully promote the coppicing of up to a quarter of a million acres of local woodland. In 1520, there were two large-scale blast furnace sites in the district, and by 1548, that number had increased to twenty-four. Although slowing slightly, the rate of expansion remained at a high level during the third quarter of the century, and by 1574, the number of blast furnaces had more than doubled to fifty-two. Together with the output of the remaining bloomeries, this had probably increased the iron output of the Weald from around 6,000 tons annually in 1550 to around 12,000 tons by the mid-1570s. Some of the pig iron output of the blast furnaces was used for casting, particularly in the burgeoning cannon-founding industry, but most was sent to neighboring finery forges for conversion into bar iron for trade within and outside of the area. The very success of the new technology in the Weald soon began to cause local problems by driving up the cost of charcoal fuel and creating a shortage of good water access sites. This began the diffusion of blast furnaces to other parts of the country. In the 1560s, the first works were started in the Midlands, near Cannock, and by 1600, successful enterprises were also established in south and central Wales. By the early seventeenth century the main period of expansion was over and production began to level off, but the Tudor period as a whole had seen a true revolution in this highly strategic sector of industry.

The performance of the copper industry was far less successful. Various attempts had been made to mine copper in several parts of Britain during the medieval period, but all had met with commercial failure because of an inability to smelt it to satisfactory levels of purity. The desire to rectify that problem was strong, coming partly from the English crown, which was anxious to secure domestic supplies of strategic copper, bronze, and brass, and partly from German merchants and mining firms who were making good profits from the Tyrolean, Mansfeld, and Hungarian copper trades and were anxious to explore the undeveloped British resources. In continental Europe, copper was also often found in association with silver, and the prospect of raising the output of that metal no doubt further heightened interest by both parties. The main attempt to import the necessary skills to establish a successful copper industry centered around the crown's grant of monopoly privileges to the Hochstetters and their associates, from a successful Augsberg mining house, in the 1560s. After some preliminary investigations, the Company of Mines Royal was formed to mine, smelt, and refine copper and precious metals, and the Mineral and Battery Works to manufacture brass. However, little was achieved and no significant and durable industry was established. In Cumberland, among the Mines Royal's most successful operations, production averaged less than thirty-five tons a year in the 1560s and 1570s, and fell off considerably toward the end of the century, while all of the copper from Cornish and Welsh operations was smelted at the Aberdulais smelter, which had a capacity of no more than seventy tons per annum and was closed sometime before 1610. Demand for copper in England, even in the armaments industry, remained low and sluggish, while ample supplies of good-quality foreign metal could be obtained at low prices from central Europe and Scandinavia. The dismal record of Tudor copper production was matched by the failure to establish a successful brass industry.

The progress of the lead industry resulted primarily from domestically developed technological improvements, again principally in the smelting sector. Small-scale production was highly diffused throughout England and Wales at the end of the fifteenth century, with simple mining and smelting techniques providing essentially part-time, seasonal employment. Two major producers dominated the industry, however: the Mendip area of Somerset and the Peak district of Derbyshire. Both of these mining fields underwent radical technological change from the mid-sixteenth century with the introduction of the foot blast furnace, a simple and crude device by comparison with the new iron-smelting technology, but one that equally revolutionized the structure and output of the industry in these districts and put it on a more regular and sustained footing. This new furnace was first developed in the Mendips in the 1540s and 1550s and was taken to Derbyshire, probably by the earl of Shrewsbury, in the 1570s. Estimates suggest that the average annual production of pig lead in the Peak increased from around 300 to 500 tons per annum in the first four decades of the century, to around 1,000 tons by 1580, and to 3,000 tons by 1600. As in the Weald, the successful adoption of new technology appears to have been facilitated by the introduction of more vigour, enterprise, and large-scale capital into the industry by local estate owners, gentry, and lead merchants. Expansion of production was guaranteed by favorable movements in the European lead market. After the collapse of lead prices in the 1540s and 1550s, engendered by the flooding of the market with English monastic lead, many European mines suspended production. When prices recovered, British producers, exploiting their new technology and often higher-quality ores, were able to seize the initiative and supply a rapidly increasing international demand for lead more efficiently than their competitors. Many sectors of the lead industry were also fortunate in finding associated refinable quantities of silver to boost the value of their ores.

The only important part of the British metals industry not to see significant new activity during this period was tin. That ancient industry, centered in Cornwall and Devon, had been trading its comparatively scarce product into Europe from classical antiquity, but was at about the same level of output in 1603 as in 1489, some 550 to 600 tons of white tin per annum. The fundamental problem appears to have been the lack of significant technological innovation, in either mining or smelting, to offset rising production costs as underground mining replaced surface streaming as the principal method of extracting tin ore. Moreover, market development was restricted by the near-monopoly control that the tin merchants had established in the industry.

BIBLIOGRAPHY

Burt, Roger. "The International Diffusion of Technology during the Early Modern Period: The Case of the British Non-Ferrous Mining Industry." *Economic History Review,* vol. 44, pp. 249–271.

Cleere, Henry, and David Crossley. *The Iron Industry of the Weald.* 1985.

Donald, M.B. *Elizabethan Copper: The History of the Company of Mines Royal 1568–1605.* 1955.

Gough, J.W. *The Mines of Mendip.* 2nd edition. 1967.

Hammersley, G. "Technique or Economy? The Rise and Decline of the Early English Copper Industry." *Business History,* vol. 15, part 1, pp. 1–27.

Hamilton Jenkin, A.K. *The Cornish Miner.* 2nd edition. 1948.

Kiernan, David. *The Derbyshire Lead Industry in the Sixteenth Century.* Derbyshire Record Society. 1989.

Roger Burt

SEE ALSO

Coal Industry; Industry and Manufacture; Trade, Inland; Trade, Overseas; Technology

M

Metalwork

See Goldsmith's Work; Jewelry

Midwives

See Childbirth

Mildmay, Walter (c. 1520–1589)

Described as a man "well-versed in accounts," Walter Mildmay's financial skills were the basis of his rise to become one of Elizabeth I's principal advisors. Helped early in his career by his elder brother, Thomas, his first important appointment in 1543 was as joint auditor of the king's military and naval works and of all moneys advanced in prest. He was named general surveyor of augmentations on the reorganization of that court in 1547. At Elizabeth I's accession he was made chancellor of the Exchequer, and on the death of Richard Sackville in 1566, he also took the position of undertreasurer, which gave him a formal role in both Upper and Lower Exchequer.

In 1559, Mildmay was the only member of the commission to which Elizabeth confided the direction of the national finances who was not a privy Councilor. His main role concerned land revenue, war, and prest accounts. In 1566, he joined the Privy Council and began to be more widely involved in matters of state such as foreign relations. After the death of William Paulet, Sir William Cecil's appointment as lord treasurer in 1572 saw a change in Exchequer practice, and Mildmay's major responsibility thereafter for the detailed management of the institution is clear. He also became a spokesman for the crown in Parliament and an important influence in Northamptonshire where he built up a substantial landed estate around his house at Apethorpe. His strong religious convictions led him in 1584–1585 to obtain the queen's license to erect Emmanuel College in Cambridge, which opened shortly before his death in 1589.

BIBLIOGRAPHY

Lehmberg, S.E. *Sir Walter Mildmay and Tudor Government*. 1964.
Richardson, W.C. *History of the Court of Augmentations*. 1961.

Sybil M. Jack

SEE ALSO

Cecil, William; Elizabeth I; Exchequer; Parliamentary History; Paulet, William

Military History

Writing in 1937, Sir Charles Oman considered the sixteenth century the least interesting period in English military history. The reason for Oman's opinion is clear enough. There was no episode to grip the historical imagination in the same way as the Hundred Years' War and the English Civil War in the surrounding centuries.

However, the century did prove to be a period of change in which England abandoned the bow as a front-line weapon and embraced a new hierarchy of ranks, a new approach to training, and a completely revised approach to the conduct of siege warfare. These developments amounted to a belated attempt to catch up with the best of continental practice, adopting firearms and pikes. In addition, a new system of organization based on their use was developed, as well as new techniques of geometrical defensive construction, as witnessed in the rebuilding of Berwick in the 1550s and after. While only 7 percent of Henry VIII's native troops had firearms during his invasion of France in 1544, it is nevertheless futile to find a date when England went over to modern weapons. In fact, for most of the century, the government employed both new and old, such that in 1569, Cornwall was happily paying for a mixture of bows, bills, and the English version of the arquebus, the caliver.

As late as 1538–1540, fortresses were being constructed by the Tudor government that made no use of the *trace italienne*, the advanced geometrical defensive design perfected in Italy, by then in regular use north of the Alps. But later, Berwick was rebuilt by Mary Tudor using this more advanced technique, the work being completed under Elizabeth I with the supervision of Italian experts Jacopo Contio and Giovanni Portinari. By the end of the century, Genbelli was being employed to rework Carisbrooke Castle and, later, Plymouth. But until then, English soldiers had little opportunity to familiarize themselves with the state-of-the-art defenses being constructed in Europe until their involvement in the wars against Philip of Spain brought them in numbers to France and the Netherlands. One homegrown expert, Paul Ive, could not merely explain the new art of fortification in print, but was also at work at Falmouth and in Ireland, putting continental military design into practice many decades after it had become standard across the Channel.

England may have been behind the most advanced European countries in embracing military change, but was usually ahead of the Irish rebels, until in the 1590s Hugh O'Neill, second earl of Tyrone, showed they could learn as fast, adopting firearms as well as continental-style earthworks and tactics. He had had an opportunity to learn his trade in English service, but was most informed by his contacts with Spain. Apart from Ireland there were few countries as militarily backward as England in western Europe.

In 1572–1573 training was adopted in the English militia, as a response to the new European tactics. Before that time training in England had been in weapons, not in formations of pikemen and marksmen, whose complicated interaction now required the issuance of training manuals and a new organization of rank structure to provide instruction in the new tactics. The new ranks of sergeant, camp master, colonel, corporal, and sergeant-major came into general use in the second half of the sixteenth century, long after continental armies had first adopted them. Just as the bow and bill continued alongside the more modern weapons well into the final third of the century, the antiquated rank of "vintener" or commander of twenty men continued in use alongside the continental rank of corporal.

English military activity in the sixteenth century included the campaigns of Henry VIII against Scotland and France, the suppression of rebellions against the Tudors, the loss of Calais under Mary and the operations in Scotland under Edward Seymour, protector Somerset, and Elizabeth I, not to mention the same monarch's struggle with Spain from 1585 onward. With the exception of English operations in the Netherlands alongside the Dutch rebels and the suppression of Tyrone's rebellion in Elizabethan Ireland, there were few opportunities for English officers to experience continuous hostilities in the same place for any great length of time. Those who wished to learn their trade often signed on to continental armies, after the fashion of Sir Roger Williams, who served in the Spanish army of Flanders for several years in the 1570s. England's chief weakness in the military field was lack of experience until the wars with Philip II provided it in full. Seventy-seven of the 100 years from 1485 to 1585 were spent at peace. As Captain John Shute pointed out in 1598, a good captain could not be made in the life of a butterfly. Long years of experience or a period of systematic training were required. Sir Roger Williams did his best to acquaint his contemporaries with continental methods, as did William Garrard, Giles Clayton, and a number of other writers.

England also lacked a substantial standing army. The yeomen of the guard and a few scattered garrisons in England and Ireland and at Calais provided a small core of professional soldiers. Schemes were floated in the reigns of

Soldiers Battering Down a Door, from Flavius Vegetius, *The Foure Bookes . . . of Martial Policye* (1572). Reproduced from the original by permission of the Henry E. Huntington Library and Art Gallery.

Henry VIII, Edward VI, and Elizabeth, which, had they been implemented, would have generated a standing army of many thousand men. But nothing came of them. A Venetian observer felt that the English problem was not lack of courage but an absence of training and experience. Lazarus von Schwendi agreed when he inspected England in the 1550s, remarking that it would be no problem to conquer the backward English with 12,000 trained soldiers. As late as 1578, Captain Barnabe Riche found England lucky not to have been put to the test of invasion, considering its chronic lack of experienced officers. It has been argued that if in 1588 the duke of Parma's experienced soldiers had managed to cross the Channel, they would have made swift work of England's county militias, who, although they made up a third of a million men, were largely untrained.

Curiously, the trained part of the country's militia, some 26,000 men in 1588, represented a higher quality of soldier than that sent abroad on expeditions. The militiamen could use their influence to avoid the risk of death or injury abroad. Barnabe Riche noticed the English tendency "to scour both town and country of rogues and vagabonds." In other countries "where they use the service of malefactors,

M

they admit them not for soldiers, but they send them to their galleys and other places of like slavery. . . ." The corruption did not end in the counties. Captains in the field often helped themselves to their men's pay. Officially, they were entitled to embezzle six men's wages out of every company of a hundred men. Sir Thomas North, the moralizing translator of Plutarch's *Lives,* was notorious for pocketing his men's pay to finance his lifestyle, and leaving his men in a state of misery. It is surprising that English troops achieved as much as they did in the sixteenth century.

Yet sieges were a particular problem for Tudor armies, for here the introduction of more powerful artillery and new defensive designs rewarded an advanced approach. Henry VIII managed to take Boulogne in 1544, and Elizabeth eventually took Leith early in her reign, but in both cases the operations were slow and in the latter case incompetently managed. The assault at Corunna in 1549 went badly wrong when a mine caused a tower to fall on the English troops as they raced to assault the upper town.

Yet the worst catastrophes during sieges were defensive, at Le Havre in 1562–1563 and at Calais in 1558. The English commanders failed to hold strong positions against well-practiced and intelligently led French advances, though plague and undermanning, respectively, provided some explanation for the great losses. As late as 1587, the state of the cannons on the earl of Leicester's expedition to the Netherlands was so poor that some collapsed through neglect, while the lack of skill of the gunners shocked Leicester's deputy, Sir John Norris. But success was not always elusive, as the successful Anglo-Dutch defense of Bergen-op-Zoom in 1588 demonstrated. The strong English contingent in Maurice of Orange's Dutch field army helped win back several towns for the states in strenuous siege warfare from 1590–1594. The path to greater technical competence in siege warfare was slow.

English armies fought few engagements in the sixteenth century. Flodden Field (1513), Solway Moss (1542), and Pinkie (1547) were considerable successes against Scottish forces. Ironically the Scots, who had embraced modernity in the form of pike formations at Flodden, were massacred by the traditional English late-medieval weapons, longbows and bills. Firepower had a role to play at Pinkie, but older weapons still featured heavily. On the Continent, English troops won the battle of Spurs—scarcely a "battle"—with almost no fighting in 1513, but they appeared too late for the battle of St. Quentin (1557). In the wars against Philip II they were more involved in siege warfare than open conflict, although innumerable skirmishes occurred in the context of

this static warfare, like the fight over a supply column that cost Sir Philip Sidney his life at Zutphen. In Ireland, disaster struck at the battle of Yellow Ford in 1598, but before Elizabeth's reign was out, new leadership had crushed O'Neill's rebels in the field. Gradually, English armies reached a higher standard in the fighting in the Netherlands and elsewhere.

Strategic theory is one area of military affairs that has rarely been considered by early modern historians. But we have a Tudor study of this kind, Matthew Sutcliffe's *The Practice, Proceedings, and Lawes of Armes* (1593), which, although largely devoted to the most miscellaneous matters, does set forth a theory based on study of ancient histories and the military dilemmas of his own time, drawing conclusions about the size of armies and the relative advantages of strategic attack and defense.

English literature of war in the sixteenth century is mostly devoted to infantry training, reflecting the needs of the moment, as Elizabethan England struggled to bring its militia up to a continental standard. For this is the great theme of the century, that a proud country came to realize that it had fallen considerably behind its more powerful neighbors. England thus struggled to draw abreast of the latest military developments, a process almost complete by the end of the last Tudor reign.

BIBLIOGRAPHY

Boynton, L.O. *The Elizabethan Militia, 1558–1638.* 1966.

Bruce, A. *A Bibliography of British Military History from the Roman Invasions to the Restoration, 1660.* 1981.

Duffy, Christopher. *Siege Warfare. The Fortress in Early Modern Europe, 1494–1660.* 1979.

Eltis, David. *The Military Revolution in Sixteenth-Century Europe.* 1995.

Evans, J.X., ed. *The Works of Sir Roger Williams.* 1972.

Oman, C.W.C. *A History of the Art of War in the Sixteenth Century.* 1937.

Parker, Geoffrey. *The Military Revolution. Military Innovation and the Rise of the West, 1500–1800.* 1988.

Smythe, Sir John. *Certain Discourses Military.* J.R. Hale, ed. 1964.

David Eltis

SEE ALSO

Archery; Armada, Spanish; Flodden Field; Foreign Relations and Diplomacy; North, Thomas; O'Neill, Hugh; Ordnance; Philip II; Seymour, Edward; Sidney, Philip

Miniature Painting

Miniature painting—that is, the production of images using the techniques and media of manuscript illumination, but independent of the pages of a manuscript—is usually regarded as a sixteenth-century invention. Small independent images of various kinds, including portraits, existed before the sixteenth century; however, the earliest known references to detached miniatures are from the early 1500s in the Netherlands, and the earliest surviving miniatures were produced during the 1520s in England and France. Although the dominance of portraiture as subject matter and the round shape and small size of the early miniatures clearly indicate the influence of Renaissance interest in coins and medals, the most important influence on early miniatures was manuscript illumination. A tradition of round portraits in illuminations was already established, and the artists to whom the earliest surviving miniatures are attributed, Jean Clouet (d. 1541) in France and Lucas Horenbout (c. 1490–1544) in England, both produced portraits on the pages of manuscripts that closely resemble others produced as separate, independent objects.

Lucas Horenbout, from Ghent, settled in England with members of his family, including his father, Gerard, a manuscript illuminator, in the 1520s. An illuminated letter on letters patent of 1524 containing a portrait of Henry VIII has been convincingly attributed to Lucas Horenbout, as have five detached portrait miniatures of the king that can be dated c. 1525–1527 and appear to be by the same hand. These images are round, with a blue background, showing the king's head and shoulders only, with the head turned three-quarters to one side. The soft, light, and rather flat modeling is distinctive and close in style to the works of Ghent illuminators. A group of about twenty miniatures has been attributed to Horenbout on grounds of style; they are predominantly portraits of the king and his immediate circle. Payments to Horenbout are recorded in the king's accounts from 1525 until his death, and his large annual salary of £33 6s indicates the esteem in which he was held.

At the same time that Horenbout was depicting the king in this form, portrait miniatures were also being produced in the French court. In 1526, Marguerite d'Alençon sent miniatures of François I and his sons mounted in lockets to Henry VIII. These were probably by Jean Clouet. The stir that these gifts caused in the English court suggests that such objects were relatively unfamiliar, but it is unclear whether these miniatures stimulated Horenbout to develop the art form in England, or whether he was already producing miniatures by this date.

According to Carel van Mander, Horenbout passed on his knowledge of miniature painting to Hans Holbein. Holbein is better known for his portrait drawings and oil paintings, and only a small group of miniatures can be attributed with confidence to him, but these are generally regarded as among the most accomplished of all works in this medium. While it is usually assumed that Horenbout, like the later Elizabethan miniaturists, painted his miniature portraits from life, it may be that Holbein worked his miniatures up from preparatory drawings: his drawing of Lady Audley is closely related to his miniature of the same sitter. Holbein's miniature style is marked by an extraordinary economy and confidence in the modeling, and a remarkable ability to respond to different kinds of commissions, from intimate portraits of the sons of the duke of Suffolk to a formal portrait of the king's bride, Anne of Cleves.

Holbein and Horenbout were succeeded by a number of miniaturists whose oeuvres are as yet undefined. Notable among them was Levina Teerlinc (c. 1510/20–1576), the daughter of Simon Benninck, an important Bruges illuminator. Teerlinc is recorded as having received the very large annual salary of £40 from the court, and as having given a miniature to Mary I and nine miniatures to Elizabeth I as New Year's gifts. A number of these were scenes showing the queen among a crowd of people. It may be possible to associate a scene of the Maundy Thursday ceremony of foot washing with Teerlinc; a cluster of other, rather weak portrait miniatures has been attributed to her, but on very tenuous grounds.

Miniature painting in the later Elizabethan period was dominated by two figures: Nicholas Hilliard and Isaac Oliver (c. 1560–1617). Hilliard was trained as a goldsmith, and his interest in jewels, precious metals, and surface decoration was an important influence on the distinctive style he developed in his portrait miniatures. Hilliard's sitters ranged from the queen herself and important members of the court to city merchants. He effected the shift from round to oval format as the dominant shape for portrait miniatures, and he experimented with size and composition, producing a number of spectacular full-length portrait miniatures with elaborate interior or landscape settings. His treatise, *The Arte of Limning* (c. 1600), is an important source of information about theoretical and practical aspects of miniature painting.

Isaac Oliver's French origins were an important influence on his career as a miniaturist. Although his family was in London by about 1568, Oliver only became a denizen of England in 1606. He was an important member of the

M

community of immigrant artists living and working in and around London. Oliver's miniatures represent a more direct response to continental mannerism than Hilliard's in both style and subject. He developed a style that is distinguished from Hilliard's by its more sombre tones, softer, stippled modeling, and dark shadows. In addition to his numerous portraits, Oliver produced sophisticated miniatures and drawings of religious and mythological scenes. He does not seem to have been particularly favored by Elizabeth I, or by James I, but James's queen, Anne of Denmark, and his son Henry, prince of Wales, responded to his avant-garde style, both appointing him their official "limner" or miniaturist.

During the Tudor period miniature painting developed as a specialized, distinct art form, with its own conventions and etiquette. Although many miniatures have presumably been lost, it seems from the surviving evidence that over the century the patronage of miniature painters expanded from a courtly clientele to a broad cross section of the moneyed classes. The subject matter and composition of miniatures also became more diverse, and the 1590s saw the establishment of the larger cabinet miniature as a more elaborate alternative to the small oval portrait. These larger miniatures were presumably displayed on the wall; there are records of smaller portrait miniatures having been kept in turned ivory boxes or wrapped in paper, but during Elizabeth's reign they were frequently set in elaborate enamel and jeweled cases and worn on clothing. The growth of demand for miniatures does not seem to have jeopardized their special status; the fact that they were regarded as particularly precious objects is reflected by Hilliard's statement that the painting of miniatures was a suitable occupation for gentlemen—a radical suggestion in an age when painters generally had a low place in the social hierarchy.

BIBLIOGRAPHY

Hilliard, Nicholas. *The Art of Limning.* Arthur F. Kinney and Linda Bradley Salamon, eds. 1983.

Reynolds, Graham. *English Portrait Miniatures.* Revised edition. 1988.

Strong, Roy. *The English Renaissance Miniature.* 1983.

———, and V.J. Murrell. *Artists of the Tudor Court.* 1983.

Catharine MacLeod

SEE ALSO

Goldsmith's Work; Hilliard, Nicholas; Holbein, Hans; Illustration and Engraving; Painting

Mining

See Coal Industry; Metal Industries

Miscellanies

See Tottel, Richard; Verse Anthologies

Moffet, Thomas (1553–1604)

Internationally renowned physician, entomologist, and author, Thomas Moffet is best known for his compendious *Insectorum theatrum* (c. 1591, publ. 1634, trans. 1658 as *The Theater of Insects*). He was largely responsible for the introduction of Paracelsian medicine into England, with patrons including Lord Willoughby, Sir Philip Sidney, and the earls of Essex and Pembroke. As a member of the Mary Sidney, countess of Pembroke's literary circle, he composed the first Vergilian georgic poem in English, *The Silkewormes and their Flies* (1599), the first biography of Sir Philip Sidney, *Nobilis* (1593, publ. 1941), and the witty dietary treatise, *Healths Improvement* (c. 1595, publ. 1655 and 1746). His works, pre-Baconian and rhetorical, combine observation and common sense with respect for ancient authority.

Known in Europe as "Anglo-Scotus" for his Scottish descent, Moffet was brought up the son of a London guildsman and educated at Cambridge (B.A. Caius, 1572, M.A. Trinity, 1576). He studied medicine at Basle under Theodore Zwinger and Felix Platter, graduating M.D. in 1579 only after a confrontation with the university authorities over his espousal of Paracelsian principles and his attack on Erastus. On his return to England in 1580, he struggled to gain acceptance by the London College of Physicians, which he criticized for complacency and obscurantism in an Erasmian dialogue, *De jure et praestantia chymicorum medicamentorum* (1584). Eventually he became a fellow and censor and played a leading role in the compilation of the *Pharmacopoeia Londinensis* (publ. 1618). In 1592, he retired to Wilton under the patronage of the earl of Pembroke and established himself as a man of letters. He was elected M.P. for Wilton in 1597.

As an entomologist, Moffet was the direct heir of his friend, Thomas Penny. He received illustrations from John White in Virginia and specimens from Joachim Camerarius in Nuremberg. He attempted also to introduce the silk industry into England, a project subsequently revived by James I.

BIBLIOGRAPHY

Debus, Allen G. *The English Paracelsians.* 1966.

Houliston, Victor. "Sleepers Awake: Thomas Moffet's Challenge to the College of Physicians of London, 1584." *Medical History,* vol. 33, pp. 235–246.

Moffet, Thomas. *Insectorum Sive Minimorum Animalium Theatrum.* (1634). *The Theater of Insects; or, Lesser Living Creatures.* John Rowland, trans. In Edward Topsell, *The History of Four-Footed Beasts and Serpents and Insects.* 1658.

———. *Nobilis; or, a View of the Life and Death of a Sidney, and Lessus Lugubrius.* Virgil B. Heltzel and Hoyt H. Hudsom, trans. and eds. 1940.

———. *The Silkewormes and Their Flies: Lively Described in Verse* (1599). Victor Houliston, ed. Medieval and Renaissance Texts and Studies. 1989.

Raven, Charles E. *English Naturalists from Neckam to Ray.* 1947.

Scoular, Kitty W. *Natural Magic: Studies in the Preservation of Nature in English Poetry from Spenser to Marvell.* 1965.

Victor Houliston

SEE ALSO

Medicine and Health; Sidney, Mary

Monastic Orders

By the time the Tudors ruled, the glory days of English monasticism were long past. The coming of the friars, the devastations of the Black Death, and the advent of new avenues of lay piety, such as confraternities, had lessened the appeal of monastic life, but had not ended it. There were about 800 religious houses in early Tudor England, and more than half of these belonged to men and women of the various monastic orders. The 1536 Act of Suppression (27 Henry VIII, c. 28) identified 350 autonomous monasteries. Of these, 163 were "greater" monasteries, with annual income of above £200 and more than twelve inmates; 187 were "lesser" monasteries. The Austin Canons, or Augustinians, held forty-eight of the greater houses and 111 of the lesser; the Benedictines, fifty-two and sixteen; the Cistercians, thirty-six and twenty-six; the Premonstratensian Canons, eight and twenty-two; the Cluniacs, ten and three; the Carthusians, seven and two; and the Gilbertines, seven of the lesser. The were approximately 126 convents, mostly lesser houses; seventy-three of them were Benedictine; twenty-six, Cistercian; thirteen, Austin Canoness; nine, Gilbertine; two, Cluniac; two, Premonstratensian; and one, Bridgettine. These abbeys of monks and nuns held about half the total wealth of the church in England, revenues of approximately £136,300 annually, almost nine-tenths of it belonging to houses of men.

The depiction of English monasteries full of lewd and indolent monks was the product of propaganda used to prepare the way for their dissolution; yet there is no denying that monastic life in early Tudor England was for the most part spiritually tepid. The ideal of the monastic orders, enshrined in their rules, was that men and women would withdraw from the world and live a common life of prayer; and the labor each member engaged in for the support of the community was not to contravene. But over the centuries, many of the monasteries had grown into large enterprises, and the time that the monks needed to invest in the business of their monasteries undermined the daily routine of common prayer. Other monasteries dwindled and had too few inmates for any communal life at all. Financial pressures, brought on by heavy taxation and by economic failures, had contributed to the decay and disorder of many houses, resulting in reductions of stipends of food and clothing for the inmates and of payments in cash or in kind for the poor. The abbots of the greater houses began living apart from their communities, in their own manor houses. They traveled from manor to manor supervising the estates of their monasteries; and they became involved in secular affairs, serving on commissions of the peace, attending sessions of Parliament, and in a few cases, going abroad on diplomatic missions.

Apart from their spiritual and economic functions, monastic houses provided a variety of social services. They gave alms to the poor, although it seems not in large amounts; they offered hospitality to travelers, which could drain a house's resources; they provided a place for the surplus daughters and younger sons of the gentry; they furnished a home for some of the elderly, and a hospital for the care of the sick; and they gave poor boys at least some education.

Sexual immorality was not among the common problems found in monasteries and convents. Most of the difficulties involved lax discipline, disobedience, and violations of the rule; absences of members from prayer, from Mass, and from common meals; administrative negligence, including neglect of the buildings; abuse of authority; and failure to educate novices and younger canons and canonesses. Monasteries were open to secularizing influences through the lay people that lived

M

within their walls as servants and as corodies. At the time of the dissolution, there were 25,000 lay men and women and 7,000 religious inhabiting the various houses of the monastic orders.

Returning the monks and nuns to the strict observance of their rules was seen as the answer to reforming the monastic orders. To this end, Bishop Richard Fox translated and published the Rule of St. Benedict. Thomas Wolsey, under his legatine authority, imposed a new, rigorous book of statutes on the Benedictines. He forced out old and incompetent superiors of religious houses, replacing them with men and women of piety who could provide stern spiritual discipline and order. Wolsey suppressed two dozen lesser houses, in obvious decay with few inmates, using their wealth as endowments for his colleges; and he planned to combine twelve other lesser monasteries with larger houses.

Monasticism was affected by a change in spirituality, by a shift away from communal piety to the interior, personal piety of the *Devotio Moderna*. The monastic orders that were the most vibrant were those that engaged in this more personal piety, most notably the Carthusians, whose monks lived in private cells, spending their time alone with God, in personal prayer and in contemplation, coming together only for Mass and for meetings of the chapter. John Colet and Thomas More considered joining the Carthusian London Charterhouse. The Bridgettine community at Syon, associated with the Carthusian monastery at Sheen, also practiced the *Devotio Moderna*. Richard Whitford, a monk at Syon, former chaplain to Bishop Fox and a friend of More, published for the pious laity works and translations that expressed this sort of spirituality. The spiritual fortitude of these orders was displayed by the martyrdoms of the Carthusian monks, led by John Houghton, prior of the London Charterhouse, and of Richard Reynolds, a monk from Syon, who were brutally hanged at Tyburn in 1535 for refusing to recognize Henry VIII as supreme head of the church in England.

The dissolution of the monasteries between 1536 and 1540 brought defiance from a few other monks, and they too suffered severe punishment in return. In a few places, local people took action, some of it violent, to protect the monasteries. The rebels of the Pilgrimage of Grace in 1536 demanded repeal of the Act of Suppression. Most monks, however, calmly accepted the end of the monastic orders in England. Many were given pensions; some found places in parishes and in chantries; others, employment in a craft or trade; and a few, especially the abbots, prospered as bishops in Henry's church. But the unlucky monks who could find no other employment, the nuns who had no family to care for them, and the old and infirm who no longer had the support of their communities fell through the cracks of Tudor society.

Hardly any of the monastic houses were restored under Mary I. Thanks to royal patronage, the Benedictines returned to Westminster Abbey, and the Bridgettines to the abbey at Syon. Following the accession of Elizabeth I, the monks were again expelled from Westminster. Most of the Bridgettine nuns went abroad. A few settled in Lyford, and were there as late as 1581.

BIBLIOGRAPHY

Baskerville, Geoffrey. *English Monks and the Supression of the Monasteries.* 1939.

Gasquet, Francis A. *Henry VIII and the English Monasteries.* 6th edition. 2 vols. 1902.

Hughes, Philip. *The Reformation in England. Vol. 1: The King's Proceedings.* 1951.

Knowles, David. *The Religious Orders in England. Vol. 3: The Tudor Age.* 1959.

Savine, Alexander. *English Monasteries on the Eve of Dissolution.* 1909.

Thomson, John A.F. *The Early Tudor Church and Society, 1485–1529.* 1993.

Woodward, George W.O. *The Dissolution of the Monasteries.* 1966.

Youings, Joyce. *The Dissolution of the Monasteries.* 1971.

John M. Currin

SEE ALSO

Chantry; Elizabeth I; Fox, Richard; Henry VIII; Mary I; Pilgrimage of Grace; Reformation, English; Supremacy, Act of; Wolsey, Thomas

Money, Inflation, and Moneylending

The monetary system of sixteenth-century England was composed of both gold and silver coins. Other European states also often used copper for coins of small denomination, but the English mint did not produce copper farthings until the reign of James I, and then only a small amount. The highest denomination was the pound sterling (actually only a unit of "money of account" as no pound coin was minted), which was subdivided into 20 shillings, and each shilling into 12 pence. Coins were generally minted in units of shillings and pence, but the mark was valued at 13s, 4d, and farthings were worth only a quarter of a penny. The value of the coinage was based on

Raphael Holinshead, *The Minting of Coins,* from *The Chronicles of England, Scotlande, and Irelande* (1577). This illustration of the melting of bullion, weighing of coise, and craftsmen striking the mintage first appears in *The History of Scotlande* and is repeated seven times in the *Chronicles.* Reprinted from the original by permission of the Henry E. Huntington Library and Art Gallery.

the market value of the amount of gold or silver in the alloys used to produce the coins, and thus the value of coins of different denominations depended on their size. The fineness of the alloy was sanctioned by the monarch, and the role of the mint was to ensure that each unit of currency contained enough gold or silver. Counterfeiting coins was deemed high treason.

The bimetallic nature of the currency meant that the ratio of gold and silver coins could rise and fall according to changes in supply and demand in different countries. In the sixteenth century this meant that silver was much more plentiful in England than gold. Also, because gold was rarer than silver this meant that gold coins were always of a greater value than silver ones (the ratio fluctuated around 12/1). In practice, gold coins were circulated much less widely because most were reserved for large-scale transactions (ten shillings represented a few week's wages for a day laborer). Silver thus was the standard circulating

M

medium, and smaller denominations such as shillings, pence, half pence, and three-farthings were minted in silver alloy. There was never enough small change, however, partly because inflation meant that the size of very small denominations became reduced to impractically small discs that were hard to keep in a purse or pocket.

By 1544, the value of the circulating currency was only £1.23 million. In the last forty years of Elizabeth's reign this increased to £3.5 million, but this still amounted to only 14 shillings per person in 1590. Because of this scarcity of gold and silver, credit in its various forms was always a more dominant means of transacting exchanges in the economy. In early modern economic thought, as writers such as Gerard de Malynes pointed out, money was conceived of as the *measure* rather than the *means* of exchange in its function as a medium of pricing. Most transactions based on credits were either conducted orally or recorded in account books, and canceled sometime in the future when a reciprocal debt was incurred. The use of sealed bonds as payment in larger exchanges also increased dramatically in the late sixteenth century. By 1600, it is improbable that money was used in more than one-tenth to one-fifteenth of exchanges.

The English coinage also suffered from problems that affected its value and made monetary transactions more difficult. The greatest abuse initiated by private individuals was the clipping of coins, which involved cutting a thin sliver of gold or silver from the edge of a coin with shears, and then flattening it. The extra could then be melted down to make a profit, which was often the only way some poor people could obtain cash. As a result the value of the gold and silver in coins was normally worth less than their face value, which meant that coins often had to be weighed before they would be accepted. This encouraged the hoarding of good coins by merchants and tradesmen and moneylenders, thus further reducing the volume in circulation. Henry VIII's debasement of the currency for 1546–1551 also did much to damage trust in the government's commitment to maintain the intrinsic value of the currency. In an attempt to both address the shortage of coins and to make a profit, existing coins were called in and the bullion content was reduced by adding copper while keeping the face value the same. As a result, the official government-sanctioned value of the coinage was now greater than the value of its actual gold and silver content. The new coins were not used in exchange by people at the official rate, but rather at the market rate of their silver content. Consequently, prices rose in mone-

tary terms, causing economic dislocation, as anyone paying in old coins lost by the transaction.

Inflation. Although the debasement of the coinage caused short, rapid inflation in the 1550s, the period from approximately 1500 to 1640 experienced a continuous, European-wide, long-term rise in prices, which is often termed "the price revolution." Prices of grain and meat increased seven-fold between 1490 and 1640, with the most dramatic rises occurring in the late sixteenth century. The prices of industrial products and cloth, however, rose at a much slower rate, and only went up approximately three-fold in the same period. Sir Thomas Smith in the first version of his *Discourse of the Common Weal* (1549) initially blamed the debasements of the coinage in the 1540s, arguing that "the alteration of the coin" was the original cause of the inflation because of the sudden increase in the money supply without a concurrent increase in the amount of goods to be bought. Later, in a passage he added in 1581, he also blamed the influx of "infinite sums of gold and silver," from America that began to flow into Europe at almost the same time as prices began to rise. This view has been repeated many times since, and came to be the standard explanation until the second half of the twentieth century.

Such monetary explanations were based on the fact that the value of gold and silver was dependent on their scarcity. It was reasoned that as gold and silver became more plentiful in Europe, according to the laws of supply and demand in the marketplace, the price of the metals would drop, thereby making coins worth less in intrinsic terms. Thus, their exchange value would also drop as a measure of prices if most goods continued to hold relatively the same value. These views held up until research in the 1950s into demographic trends, and the relationship between the purchasing power of wages and the actual prices of different commodities, raised serious questions about the coherence of this explanation. Most importantly, it was discovered that the movement of prices for different commodities was by no means uniform, which would be expected in a purely monetary explanation. The prices of industrial goods, for instance, went up half as much as the price of food, and the price of labor went up even less. Furthermore, when enough statistics became available to measure change by decade, it was seen that prices had started to rise substantially before the greatest increases of the import of bullion into Europe. Even more problematic was the fact that jumps in price did not correspond to currency changes brought about by the debasement and subsequent revaluation.

The current dominant explanation for the inflation of prices now holds that it was caused primarily by demographic factors. Supply, especially of foodstuffs, was unable to meet the growing demand created by a continually increasing population, thus driving up the prices of items that were most in demand. This explanation has strong support from the fact that movements in prices followed the demographic pattern of population change very closely. The fact that the price of food went up much more than other goods is also evidence for this explanation because population growth placed the most pressure on agriculture.

Moneylending. Although credit was widespread in transactions, there were still many situations where cash was needed. Money was needed to pay the remaining balance of accounts; it was used in transactions between strangers; to pay rents, tithes, and taxes; and often merchants needed cash to pay for goods bought overseas, or to complete bargains in cases where bills of exchange might not be acceptable. As a result, the demand for cash increased as the economy grew, and prices went up. This led to an increase in moneylending and the charging of high interest rates. Moneylending was termed usury because it was essentially the charging of a fee for the loan, or *use* of a precious commodity—money—and as the economy grew the charging of interest on loans became a source of much social controversy.

In medieval theory the charging of interest for such a loan was considered a "dry exchange," which meant that the gold and silver, or bond representing gold and silver, being loaned by the usurer was having an extra cost added to the price it already had as a commodity in its own right. In this way the moneylender was seen to be taking advantage of inequalities in the system of exchange by charging a fee for its use by those individuals who lacked money, when it should have been circulating freely, allowing the market to function in a natural way. As a result the charging of interest was officially an offense. Also, because lending on a small scale to one's poorer neighbors was seen to be a duty of Christian charity, usury was seen to be a highly antisocial activity. It also kept scarce coins out of circulation in the moneylender's chests until someone could afford to borrow them. But in reality the propensity to hoard good money as it became more valuable meant that the charging of interest was increasingly the only means of ensuring that money was returned into circulation. Thus,

the scarcity of money ensured that demand created a market in which interest was inevitably charged for its use. As a result, following a long debate in which the economic necessity of interest rates was increasingly justified by some writers, an official maximum interest rate of 10 percent was sanctioned by statute in 1571, and the market rate of interest soon fell to the legal rate as the threat of punishment was removed from lending at interest.

BIBLIOGRAPHY

Braudel, F., and F. Spooner. "Princes in Europe from 1450–1750." In *The Cambridge Economic History of Europe.* Vol. 4. 1967.

Challis, C.E. *The Tudor Coinage.* 1978.

———. *Currency and the Economy in Tudor and Early Stuart England.* 1989.

Brown, H. Phelps, and S.V. Hopkins. *A Perspective of Wages and Prices.* 1981.

Outhwaite, R.B. *Inflation in Tudor and Stuart England.* 1969.

Craig Muldrew

SEE ALSO

Agriculture; Cloth Trade; Economy; Gresham, Thomas; Industry and Manufacture; Smith, Thomas; Trade, Overseas

Monopolies

Tudor monopolies took two forms, corporate and individual. Companies with exclusive rights to trade in areas or commodities designated by the crown were a feature of overseas trade throughout the sixteenth century. Corporate industrial monopolies, such as the Mineral and Battery Works, were exceptional.

Monopoly in manufacturing was largely confined to grants by patent to individuals. The first was made in 1551, a precedent for the awards that proliferated early in Elizabeth I's reign when they were associated in particular with the secretary of state, William Cecil, and his policy of protectionism, and with the arrival from the Continent of Protestant refugees who brought the requisite skills. By protecting the immigrants and native "projectors" from competition the patents encouraged import substitution, with all the economic benefits that that would bring. In 1561–1570, twelve patents were granted for various chemical processes, including the making of soap and alum, and six for mechanical inventions, including a dredging machine, furnaces, and ovens. In the next decade

M

ten monopolies were added. This "constructive phase," as it has been called, extended to the 1580s, the success of import substitution in those years owing something to the patents. The manufacture of fine glassware was one successful outcome, especially that of crystal glass under the patent granted to a Venetian craftsman in 1574. There were, on the other hand, failures; and there were also successes that owed nothing to protectionism: tapestry-making, for example. A notable failure was the patent for the manufacture of white salt by the evaporation of sea water that was intended to reduce dependence on imports from France. The original patentee (1562), an Italian, soon went bankrupt, and his successor, a Flemish immigrant, fared no better. In subsequent versions of the patent the holders, who included Secretary Cecil, had the highest expectations, as did the crown, which at one stage envisaged a state monopoly of salt production. Instead, the patent became inactive until it was revived in 1585 in a form that signified the beginnings of a new phase in the system, one that has attracted the description "scandalous."

From about that time, economic interests were subordinated to those of importuning politicians and to the dubious exercise of royal patronage. Patents were commonly renewed, the beneficiaries often being connected with the court, as were those who were rewarded with patents that were new, but for established manufactures like starch and playing cards. The value of such patents lay not in manufacture but in the control of the distribution of other people's products. This was illustrated by the salt patent that, on its renewal, degenerated into an exclusive right to sell salt in Hull and other ports on the east coast, most of the salt being shipped from Scotland. Virtually all the patents of this period were of the same character: that is, they were parasitic rather than productive, advantageous to the crown as a cost-free form of patronage, and to the recipient, but of no obvious benefit to anyone outside court circles. On the contrary, the system was blamed for raising prices, as was complained of the salt patent.

The patentee's privileges also conflicted at numerous points with the rights and privileges of municipal corporations and trade and craft guilds. Critics of the same monopoly observed that by the charters of the towns involved, only freemen authorized by the corporation were entitled to trade within the borough. Similarly, the patent to manufacture white paper, issued in 1589, gave the holder the right to collect rags in the city of London, in contravention of the corporation's own jurisdiction in such matters. Similarly, most monopolies of distribution invaded the rights and privileges of a trade or craft guild.

The starch monopoly, for example, was vigorously opposed by the London Grocers' Company whose trade it was. Other examples include the playing card monopoly that led to the *cause celebre,* Darcy versus Allen, which arose in 1601 when the defendant was charged with continuing to trade in breach of the plaintiff's patent. Shortly before the court action the question of monopolies had been raised in a higher forum when members of the House of Commons made an exceptionally forthright attack on the system. One member listed twenty-five patents. Another asked if there was one on bread. In the course of the debate monopolies were blamed for the drastic price rises of the 1590s. But economic arguments were subordinate to political and constitutional ones.

Patents of all kinds were symptomatic of the perceived decline in court life and politics in the queen's last years; and her right to issue them was questioned in such a way that the royal prerogative was invoked to fend off the attack. The outcome was that while the prerogative remained intact, significant concessions were made with the withdrawal of the more obnoxious patents and the promise to put others to the test of the law.

BIBLIOGRAPHY

Donald, M.B. *Elizabethan Monopolies.* 1961.
Gough, J.W. *The Rise of the Entrepreneur.* 1969.
Price, W.H. *The English Patents of Monopoly.* 1913.
Thirsk, Joan. *Economic Policy and Projects: The Development of a Consumer Society in Early Modern England.* 1978.

Brian Dietz

SEE ALSO

Cecil, William; Economy; Elizabeth I; Immigration; Industry and Manufacture; Patronage; Trade, Overseas

Montaigne, Michel de

See Essay, The; Florio, John; French Literature, Influence of; Pyrrhonism

More, Thomas (c. 1478–1535)

Thomas More is a central figure in any account of Tudor England by virtue of his writings, his extraordinary judicial and political career, and the strong, if enigmatic, personality and character that culminated in his martyrdom. He early achieved fame for his wit and wisdom; and his many humanist, polemical, and spiritual works, some in

Latin, some in English, are an indispensable part of the culture of sixteenth-century England and continental Europe, while he remains world famous as the author of *Utopia.* Long a public figure who became Henry VIII's lord chancellor at a time of political and religious crisis, More was knighted in 1521, beheaded in 1535, and canonized in 1935. A humanist and brilliant intellectual; a poet, jester, and storyteller who loved Lucian; a fierce polemicist; an ascetic; a loving father and genial host; an educator; a politician; a man of conscience and a man of faith: the many facets of his being continue to engage admirers and detractors alike, and More's person, works, and ideas are the subject of countless interpretations.

The first son of a successful lawyer, More began his formal education at St. Anthony's School in London. Time spent as a page in the household of John Morton, then lord chancellor of England and archbishop of Canterbury, gave him an early opportunity to observe the political life of England at firsthand. More subsequently attended Oxford University and the Inns of Court and began to practice law around 1501; in 1510 he became undersheriff of London. He tested his vocation for the spiritual life early, living within the precincts of the London Charterhouse and participating in the Carthusian monks' life of austere devotion for several years before he married Jane Colt (late 1504 or early 1505). By 1499, he was also part of a circle of humanists, persons who shared scholarly, educational, and literary ideals based on the study of classical languages and culture. Emphasizing the learning of grammar, rhetoric, history, poetry, and ethics, the humanists opposed the late Scholastic emphasis on dialectic, and they were concerned with moral and social problems. They were often involved in education; More oversaw the humanist education of his children and other students in what came to be known as the "school of More," and his first daughter, Margaret Roper, was renowned as a woman of letters.

More's earliest writings all show a humanistic bent. Around 1501, he delivered a series of lectures on St. Augustine's *City of God* from an historical and philosophical, rather than a purely theological, perspective. Around 1505, he translated Gianfrancesco Pico's biography of his uncle, Count Giovanni Pico della Mirandola, a well-known Italian humanist and philosopher, from Latin into English. In 1506, More's translations of four of Lucian's works from Greek into Latin and More's own rejoinder to one of Lucian's declamations appeared as part of *Opuscula,* a joint effort with Desiderius Erasmus, who later dedicated his *Moriae Encomium (Praise of Folly)* to More and became northern Europe's leading classical and patristic

scholar and humanist. A Lucianic impulse appears in much of More's humanist writing, which values irony, drama, and seriocomic wit, and the *Opuscula* helped to establish his reputation.

The literary works that followed—the *History of Richard III, Utopia,* and *Epigrams,* all written or published between 1513 and 1518, even as More's professional and public responsibilities increased—constitute his major humanist works. More wrote two versions of *Richard III,* one in Latin and one in English, neither a translation of the other; he left both unfinished. The Latin version, first published in 1565, is the more compact, but both versions offer dramatic, ironic, and psychologically acute studies of the exercise of power and factional politics in recent English history. Reworking classical historical models, other literary works, and oral sources, More created a powerful, albeit controversial, portrait of Richard III that deeply influenced William Shakespeare's *The Tragedy of King Richard the Third.*

Utopia (1516), which has given its name to the literary form that More invented, is his most influential work. Written in Latin, it was first translated into English by Ralph Robynson (1551). There is no agreement about its meaning; it has been read as a *jeu d'esprit,* a blueprint for an actual society or social reform, a cry for justice, or a catalyst for thought about urgent and fundamental sociopolitical issues. It is both a political and philosophical discourse, presented by way of dialogue, and a seriocomic work of fiction. Plato's *Republic* and *Laws,* Aristotle, Lucian's satires and *True History,* Cicero, Seneca, Pliny, the Bible, the church fathers, travel accounts by More's contemporaries, and the *Adages* of Erasmus are just some of many different texts and writers More used and transformed. Book 1, a dialogue between "More" (a persona of the author), Peter Giles, and the mysterious Raphael Hythlodaeus, world traveler, advances a radical critique of actual societies, centered in England, and asks how and if change can be effected. Book 2 describes Utopia, a fictive society where all goods are held in common, which is both "nowhere" and an island located in the southern hemisphere of the New World. According to Raphael Hythlodaeus, who has been there, Utopia is the best (indeed the one true) commonwealth, despite certain problems and incongruities, because it alone is concerned with the common good. Surrounding these two books is the *parerga,* a collection of material that includes an important prefatory letter. The *parerga* reinforces Utopia's putative reality, frames the two books, and invites the reader's responses. Like More's

M

other major works, *Utopia* is dialogic, polysemous, and deeply ironic: at issue are the most basic questions about the purpose and structure of society, the relation between nature and nurture, the use and abuse of power, the terrifying injustice that characterizes all known societies, and whether or not community and the common good are possible in this world.

More's Latin epigrams, first published as a collection with Erasmus's in the third edition of *Utopia* (1518), are also social, dramatic, and psychological; with the translations from Lucian and *Utopia*, they established More's fame as a humanist in Renaissance Europe, and they were much imitated. His epigrams on political subjects, among them the difference between the good king and the tyrant, are especially significant. Five Latin essays in epistolary form that More wrote between 1515 and 1520, four in defense of humanism and one defending his own Latin poetry, round out his first, humanist period.

While still undersheriff of London, More twice served as royal ambassador for Henry VIII. He formally entered the king's service in 1517 as Latin secretary, diplomat, and orator. His steady rise in public office culminated in his appointment to the lord chancellorship in 1529, following the downfall of Thomas Wolsey, whose foreign policy and attempts to obtain the king's divorce from Katherine of Aragon had failed. In 1522, More began a meditative treatise in English on the four last things (death, judgment, hell, and heaven) that foreshadows his later, devotional writings. Otherwise, his writing during the 1520s and early 1530s is occasional and polemical, as he turned from humanist issues to theological controversies. In the first of two Latin polemics, the *Responsio ad Lutherum* (1523), More defended King Henry VIII's book asserting the seven Sacraments from Luther's attacks. Rejecting Luther's insistence upon only the Scripture, More upheld the authority of the Catholic Church, inspired by the Holy Spirit and its traditions, both written and unwritten. A second Latin polemic (1526), directed against a Lutheran pastor, Johann Bugenhagen, attacks the idea of justification by faith alone. More was increasingly active in attempts to suppress and prevent heresy in England, and on March 7, 1528, the bishop of London, Cuthbert Tunstall, authorized him to read heretical books and refute them in English, thus initiating the second phase of his written anti-heresy campaign. By far the largest amount of More's writing consists of counterattacks on the Protestant reformers, including William Tyndale and John Frith, and anticlerical writers, notably Christopher Saint German. Between 1529 and 1534, More published

eight works in English, all written in haste and under great pressure. As he continued his attacks on the reformers, he became increasingly defensive. His best work is the first, *A Dialogue of Sir Thomas More,* now called *A Dialogue Concerning Heresies.* Here More put his understanding of drama and dialogue to good use; he imagined four extensive conversations between the narrator, a busy court official and concerned father figure, and the messenger, a young man who has some sympathy with Lutheran ideas but comes to understand the Catholic Church's position.

More privately opposed the king's "great matter," his divorce, which became entangled with issues affecting both the church and secular authority. By 1532, he was increasingly at odds with the policies of Thomas Cromwell and the king, who claimed the title of Supreme Head of the Church in England. On May 16, 1532, the day after the clergy made their submission to Henry VIII, More resigned as lord chancellor and ostensibly withdrew from public life. He remained a figure of high visibility, however, and became even more active in his verbal warfare against the Reformers. On March 23, 1534, Parliament passed the Act of Succession, which declared Henry's marriage to Katherine null and his marriage to Anne Boleyn lawful. More refused to sign the Oath of Allegiance that endorsed this and other acts and statutes passed by Parliament since 1529, including the Act of Supremacy and the Act of Treasons. He was imprisoned in April 1534, convicted of treason on July 1, 1535, and executed on July 6. Dying as a martyr—at the end of his trial More declared that the Act of Supremacy was "directly repugnant to the laws of God and His Holy Church"—he was canonized by the Roman Catholic Church 400 years later.

More's last works, which are focused on Christ's passion and speak to his wish to live his life in conformity with Christ's, are called his Tower works, although probably he wrote the first one, "A Treatise upon the Passion," before he was imprisoned. The acknowledged masterpiece of this period is *A Dialogue of Comfort against Tribulation* (1533), which is set in Hungary before the second invasion of the Turks in 1529. Antony, an older man, and his young nephew, Vincent, struggle for consolation and comfort as they explore the nature and meaning of tribulations that include persecution for the faith. The last part of the dialogue becomes a meditation on the Passion and death of Christ. More's last major Tower work, *De Tristitia Christi (The Sadness of Christ),* is a commentary on the biblical narrative of Christ's Passion. It breaks off just as Jesus is being taken into custody; particularly moving are More's reflections on martyrdom, including Christ's speech to the fearful martyr.

In the course of his life More was engaged in virtually all of the most fundamental and controversial issues of his day, whether social, intellectual, literary, political, economic, or religious. So often writing at a time of crisis, whether for society, the church, or self, he explored the human condition and pondered its reformation from multiple perspectives. Comic, dramatic, ironic, subtle, and inventive, More was at his best as a writer when he turned to the letter and the dialogue, and most readers would agree that *Utopia, A Dialogue Concerning Heresies,* and *A Dialogue of Comfort Against Tribulation* are his greatest works. But many might argue that More's greatest work was himself. Few men understood the nature of power as well as he, and fewer were willing to pay the cost of defying its representation in Henry VIII in the name of conscience and faith. He is someone to whom biographers are irresistably drawn, he continues to influence persons in diverse arenas, and countless persons venerate him as a saint. In the phrase used early to describe him, More remains a man for all seasons.

BIBLIOGRAPHY

Baker-Smith, Dominic. *More's "Utopia."* 1991.

Guy, J.P. *The Public Career of Sir Thomas More.* 1980.

Hexter, J.H. *More's "Utopia": The Biography of an Idea.* 1965.

Marius, Richard. *Thomas More.* 1984.

More, Sir Thomas. *The Correspondence of Sir Thomas More.* Elizabeth Frances Rogers, ed. 1947.

More, Thomas. *Utopia: Latin Text and English Translation.* George M. Logan, Robert M. Adams, and Clarence H. Miller, eds. 1995.

More, St. Thomas. *The Yale Edition of the Complete Works of St. Thomas More.* Richard S. Sylvester and Clarence H. Miller, executive eds. 15 volumes. 1963–1997.

Sylvester, Richard S., and Germain P. Marc'hadour, eds. *Essential Articles for the Study of Thomas More.* 1977.

Elizabeth McCutcheon

SEE ALSO

Boleyn, Anne; Classical Literature, English Translations; Cromwell, Thomas; Education; Epigrams; Erasmus, Desiderius; Frith, John; Henry VIII; Humanism; Katherine of Aragon; Lutheranism; Morton, John, of the Clergy; Neo-Latin Literature; Reformation, English; Roper, Margaret; Submission; Supremacy, Acts of; Tunstall, Cuthbert; Tyndale, William; Utopia; Wolsey, Thomas

Morley, Thomas (c. 1557–1602)

One of the most diverse and influential of Elizabethan composers, Thomas Morley was born in Norwich in 1557 or 1558, the son of a brewer. In 1583, he was named master of the choristers and organist at Norwich Cathedral. When he published his *A Plaine and Easie Introduction to Practicall Musicke,* he dedicated it to William Byrd, whom he calls his master. It is not known, however, when he would have studied with Byrd, although the years 1572–1574 have been suggested. Like his teacher, Morley seems to have been a Catholic, albeit one who was paid to spy on other Catholics.

Morley left Norwich in the spring of 1587. He may have been hired as virginals teacher by Edward Paston, a musically literate squire at Thorpe-by-Norwich with an impressive library that included partbooks of Italian madrigals. Morley earned a bachelor of music degree at Oxford in 1588, and by early 1589 at the latest he was organist at St. Paul's in London. In 1592, he was sworn in as a gentleman of the Chapel Royal. His first of eleven publication, *Canzonets, or Little Short Songs to Three Voyces,* appeared the following year.

Byrd's monopoly on music printing expired in 1596, and Morley applied for the patent, which was granted to him in September 1598. His right to print metrical psalter was hotly disputed, with the House of Commons ultimately ruling on the issue. There has been much speculation over the the possibility of a connection between Morley and William Shakespeare, both living in 1598 in the same parish of St. Helen's, Bishopsgate. Morley composed *It Was a Lover and His Lass,* published in *The First Booke of Ayeres* in 1600, but that is the only Shakespeare lyric he set. He had been in poor health for years, alluding in the preface to *A Plaine and Easie Introduction* to being "compelled to keep at home," but he did not resign from the Chapel Royal until 1602. It is thought that he died in early October of 1602.

Although it was Nicholas Yonge who published *Musica Transalpina,* it is Morley who was largely responsible for the English vogue for Italian music. *Madrigalls to Foure Voyces: the First Booke* of 1594 marks the first time the term "madrigal" was used by an English composer for original compositions to English words. *The First Booke of Canzonets to Two Voyces* and *the First Booke of Balletts to Five voyces,* both of 1595, consist largely of reworkings arranged after popular Italian works by Felice Anerio and Giovanni Gastoldi. He refers frequently to Italian music and musical practice in *A Plaine and Easie Introduction,* which was printed along with *Canzonets or Little Short Aers to Five and Six Voices* in 1597. The Italian anthology

M

Canzonets, Or little short songs to foure voyces was also published in 1597, and was followed by a similar anthology, *Madrigals to five voyces,* in 1598. In 1601, he was the guiding spirit behind *The Triumphes of Oriana;* the year of his probable death saw expanded new editions of both the three-voice canzonets and the four-voice madrigals.

He composed in several more native genres. *The First Booke of Consort Lessons* of 1599 consists of twenty-one arrangements of popular, theater, and dance tunes arranged for the uniquely English consort of treble and bass viols, flute, lute, cittern, and bandora (*Joyne Hands* is based on his three-voice canzonet *See, see, myne owne sweet jewell*). He turned to the lute ayre for his last original print, which includes gems such as *It was a lover and his lass.* In his motets, four of which were printed in *A Plaine and Easie Introduction,* and in his services, he shows how well he had learned from his teacher to write sacred music. His setting of the Anglican Prayer Book's seven funeral sentences was the standard for royal funerals for at least a century.

Even had Morley not been such an assured composer in so many genres, he would be remembered for the 1597 tutor. Cast as a dialogue between the music master and the pupil Philomathes, its range is protean (although Morley spends little time with the modes), its organization logical, and its style lively.

BIBLIOGRAPHY

Brown, David. "The Styles and Chronology of Thomas Morley's Motets." *Music and Letters,* vol. 41, pp. 216–222.

———. "Thomas Morley and the Catholics: Some Speculations." *Monthly Musical Record,* vol. 89, pp. 53–61.

Greer, David. "The Lute Songs of Thomas Morley." *Lute Society Journal,* vol. 8, pp. 25–37.

Kerman, Joseph. *The Elizabethan Madrigal: A Comparative Study.* 1962.

Morley, Thomas. *A Plain and Easy Introduction to Practical Music.* Alec Harman, ed. 2nd edition. 1962.

Laura S. Youens

SEE ALSO
Air; Byrd, William; Consort and Consort Song; Madrigal; Motet

Morton, John (c.1420–1500)

Archbishop of Canterbury and cardinal of Rome, John Morton was born in Dorset and educated at Cerne Abbey, then at Oxford where he earned a doctorate of civil law—the practice of which required his ordination. He became commissary for the university in 1446 but soon moved to London to practice ecclesiastical law. There he gained the patronage of Thomas Bourchier, archbishop of Canterbury, who secured his admission to the Privy Council. Preferments followed: he became in 1450 subdean of Lincoln; in 1453, principal of Peckwater Inn at Oxford; in 1458, prebend of Salisbury and Lincoln. In the Wars of the Roses, Morton supported the Lancastrians against the Yorkists, and, over the next ten years, his fortunes rose and fell with the changing tides of the struggle for the crown. Still, when Edward IV, of the house of York, triumphed in 1471, Morton, aided by his old friend Bourchier, managed to win the favor of the new king. Morton was made rector of St. Dunstan's-in-the-East in 1472 and received prebends the next two years. After serving as Edward's envoy to Hungary in 1474, he returned to England and became archdeacon of Winchester and Chester in the same year. Four years later, he was consecrated bishop of Ely, and in 1483, Morton was named executor of Edward's will; he was, however, undermined by the plot that brought Richard III to the throne. Petitions from his alma mater probably spared Morton's life, but he was confined in the Tower before being released to the custody of an ally, the duke of Buckingham. Morton, in turn, was instrumental in Buckingham's conspiracy to replace Richard with the earl of Richmond—later Henry VII—of the house of Lancaster, at one juncture saving the earl's life. Rapid advancements followed Henry's victory: Morton succeeded Bourchier as archbishop of Canterbury in 1486 and became lord chancellor in 1487; then, at Henry's request, the pope made Morton a cardinal in 1493. His final honor came two years later when he was named chancellor of Oxford. Morton is also well known as an important "character" in Thomas More's *Utopia.* He died on September 15, 1500.

BIBLIOGRAPHY
Jenkins, Claude. *Cardinal Morton's Register.* 1924.

Mark Goldblatt

SEE ALSO
Henry VII; More, Thomas; Wars of the Roses

Moryson, Fynes (1566–1630)

Fynes Moryson is known for a single book, *An Itinerary, Containing His Ten Years' Travel through the Twelve Dominions of Germany, Bohmerland, Switzerland, Nether-*

land, *Denmark, Poland, Italy, Turkey, France, England, Scotland, and Ireland*—a book whose production took up most of Moryson's adult life.

The third son of a Lincolnshire gentleman, Moryson was educated at Peterhouse, Cambridge, where he was elected fellow in 1587. But already he was thinking of traveling, and after several years preparation, he left in 1591 on a journey that, with one brief return home, would keep him abroad until 1597. For more than two years, he traveled at a leisurely pace through northern Europe. He then spent eighteen months in Italy, before making a quicker acquaintance with France and the Middle East. During the next few years, with time off for a trip to Scotland, Moryson ordered and digested the notes from his travels. But in 1600, he set out again, this time for Ireland, where he had secured a post as secretary to the new English commander, Charles Blount, Lord Mountjoy, in whose service he remained until Mountjoy's death in 1606. Of the remaining twenty years of Moryson's life, all but the last few were spent working on his *Itinerary*.

As published in 1617, the *Itinerary* is divided into three parts. The first is a day-by-day account of Moryson's European and Mideastern travels. The second, also in the form of a journal, gives Moryson's version of Mountjoy's Irish campaign. And the third, more analytical in its organization, opens with a discussion of travel in general, followed by a description of the geographical situation, apparel, and political order of each of Moryson's twelve dominions. This third part, with numerous additional headings, continues in a bulky manuscript (now in the library of Corpus Christi College, Oxford) that was licensed for publication in 1626 but only appeared—and then in a much abridged version—in 1903.

A careful observer and accurate reporter, Moryson was something of a cultural chameleon, who happily adopted foreign customs and who for convenience or safety would readily pass himself off as a German, Frenchman, or Italian. Moryson's book is, however, as thickly crammed with the results of his many years of reading as of his travels. This combination of experience and learning, rendered in uncluttered prose, makes Moryson's *Itinerary* one of the most attractive and enduringly useful travel books of early modern England.

BIBLIOGRAPHY

Moryson, Fynes. *The Itinerary*. 4 vols. James MacLehose, ed. 1907.

———. *Shakespeare's Europe*. Charles Hughes, ed. 1903.

Richard Helgerson

SEE ALSO

Ireland, History of; Travel Literature

Motet

That the Latin motet flourished in England in the earlier Tudor period, before the Anglican reforms of the 1540s, is unsurprising. That a significant body of motets also comes from Elizabethan times is more remarkable; it is most remarkable of all that a late Tudor composer, William Byrd, was able to bring the motet to an artistic climax in a Protestant country.

The first important source of Tudor motets is Windsor, Eton College Library, MS 178, and the favored motet type through the reign of Henry VIII was the votive antiphon. The texts of votive antiphons, usually freely assembled, celebrated a saint, often the Virgin Mary, and were sung at devotional services late in the day. Most were in two lengthy parts with frequent contrasts in vocal texture.

The most important English composers of motets in the early sixteenth century were Robert Fayrfax and John Taverner (d. 1545), who, however, apparently composed no music after c. 1530. Votive antiphons by Fayrfax are included in the Eton collection, but his style reflects the early sixteenth-century tendency toward simpler textures and rhythms, as well as increased use of imitation. Taverner seems to have pioneered in England the choral setting of Office responsories; earlier composers set only the sections that in plainsong had been performed by soloists, whereas Taverner's three settings of *Dum transisset sabbatum* for Easter Matins are complete choral settings.

Thomas Tallis and Christopher Tye are preeminent among the composers of the mid-century. Their careers encompassed years of great turbulence and change with respect to music and liturgy. Protestant ideas began to have a discernible influence on English church music by the 1530s, when Tallis and Tye were commencing their active careers. Especially important was the increased concern for intelligibility of text, and although examples of votive antiphons and other sacred compositions that are stylistically akin to the older Eton manner may still be found, the trend was overwhelmingly toward simplicity of expression: syllabic text setting, more frequent use of homophonic textures, and avoidance of rhythmic complexity. At the same time, Tallis, Tye, and their contemporaries mastered the imitative and canonic techniques of Josquin de Pres and his followers on the Continent; thus, English music, while retaining a certain unique character, became less isolated from the European mainstream.

M

The setting of Latin texts by no means ceased when Anglican services were instituted in 1549 and then reinstituted under the terms of the Elizabethan Settlement of 1558. Elizabeth I herself seems to have had what later would be termed "High Church" preferences, and the use of Latin was expressly sanctioned for the choirs of Oxford, Cambridge, Westminster Abbey, and the Chapel Royal. Moreover, nonliturgical motets were published for private use and were certainly performed at home, just as were madrigals or settings of metrical Psalms in English.

Tallis is rightly credited with being the finest of the composers who laid the foundations of Anglican Church music, but it is his Latin compositions that fully reveal his stature. Although few of his works can be dated with any certainty, settings of liturgical texts from the Sarum liturgy probably predate the institution of English-language services in 1549. A few may date from the reign of Mary Tudor. These earlier motets are mostly votive antiphons and Office responsories and hymns. Especially noteworthy is *Gaude gloriosa*, a Marian antiphon with large-scale sectional contrasts of scoring that are masterfully coordinated in a convincing overall formal plan. Tallis's later motets, most of them published in 1575 in *Cantiones Sacrae*, are mostly nonliturgical. The choice of texts seems to reflect a trend toward personal expression—in this, too, the English were somewhat belatedly catching up with earlier continental practice. *In jejunio* is characterized by simplicity of text setting and texture, but the harmony ranges widely and expressively. At the other extreme is *Miserere nostri*, a *tour de force* of canonic technique: against a free tenor, the two upper voices sing in canon at the unison, while the first alto part is sung by three other voices, doubly augmented, inverted and augmented, and inverted and triply augmented. Standing somewhat apart from Tallis's other motets is the famous forty-voice *Spem in alium*, for eight five-part choirs. This work was perhaps written in emulation of a forty-voice motet by Alessandro Striggio, who visited England in 1567.

William Byrd dominates the late Tudor period and the earlier seventeenth century as well. Byrd's Catholicism was no secret. He and others of his family were repeatedly cited for recusancy, but Elizabeth's appreciation of his musical services apparently outweighed such factors, and Byrd's position at the Chapel Royal is not known to have ever been in danger. A sizable portion of Byrd's considerable output of Latin motets was published in five collections: three volumes of *Cantiones Sacrae* (1575, 1589, and 1591), and two volumes entitled *Gradualia* (1605 and 1607, reissued in 1610). As the titles imply, the earlier collections are mainly nonliturgical with a predominance of Psalm excerpts and paraphrases and other scriptural texts. Byrd's text choices not only continue the trend toward emotional expression; texts of tribulation and protest clearly make reference to the plight of Catholicism in Protestant England. *Vide, Domine,* from the 1589 collection, may be taken as an example—"See, Lord, our affliction, and may you not forsake us in an evil time; more than Jerusalem is laid waste—" This is a "free" text, perhaps written by one of Byrd's acquaintances in the Catholic community. Other texts in the same vein are scriptural, or were compiled from various scriptural and liturgical sources. The 100 motet sections of the *Gradualia*, on the other hand, are liturgical, consisting of Propers for selected feasts of the Proper of the Time (the inclusion of items for All Saints would have been for Catholics an unmistakeable reference to Catholic martyrs), Marian feasts, and Marian votive masses. The 1605 collection includes settings of the Litany and of the "turbarum voces" (crowd passages) of the Passion Gospel for Good Friday. Byrd followed the reformed Roman Missal of 1570 and organized *Gradualia* according to a complex "cut-and-paste" scheme in which recurring texts are always sung to the same music.

In his Latin motets, Byrd demonstrates a mastery of composition comparable to that of Orlande de Lassus or Giovanni Pierluigi da Palestrina. The motets of the three *Cantiones* volumes tend to be grand in scope, with much repetition of text as each new point of imitation is extensively developed. Some works are constructed with elaborate canonic or cantus-firmus schemes, but, on the whole, Byrd's motets are less likely than those of Tallis to rely on rigid structural devices. The *Gradualia* motets are more compact, either because Byrd chose to indulge in less text repetition or because the text itself is brief. In the finest of these works, Byrd achieved a remarkable union of text and music, such as in the justly famous *Ave verum corpus*, whose magnificent effect is achieved almost entirely through sensitive declamation and masterful sense of harmonic color and motion rather than contrapuntal devices or word painting.

With Byrd the history of the Tudor motet ends. Two contemporaries, Peter Philips and Richard Dering, produced significant bodies of Latin motets, but they were Catholics who spent their careers on the Continent, and their music shows little trace of English style.

BIBLIOGRAPHY

Benham, Hugh. *Latin Church Music in England, c.1460–1575.* 1977.

Fellowes, Edmund H. *English Cathedral Music from Edward VI to Edward VII.* 1946.

Hoffman, May, and Morehen, John, comps. *Latin Music in British Sources c. 1485–c. 1610.* Early English Church Music Supplementary Volumes. Vol. 2. 1987.

Le Huray, Peter. *Music and the Reformation in England, 1549–1600.* 1978.

Phillips, Peter. *English Sacred Music, 1549–1649.* 1991.

Stevens, Denis. *Tudor Church Music.* 1966.

Charles S. Larkowski

SEE ALSO

Byrd, William; Fayrfax, Robert; Tallis, Thomas; Tye, Christopher

Mulcaster, Richard (c. 1531–1611)

The boldest educational thinker of the Tudor period, Richard Mulcaster was born in Cumberland about 1531, the eldest surviving son of a prominent landowner. Educated at Eton (1544–1548) and Cambridge, where he received his A.B. in 1554, Mulcaster briefly served as Latin secretary to the great London physician Dr. John Caius. In 1555, the quarrelsome Caius accused Mulcaster of theft, whereupon Mulcaster left the capital and matriculated at Christ Church, Oxford, where he received his M.A. in December 1556 and probably took holy orders. For the next two years he remained at Oxford to continue his study of Greek and Hebrew. Shortly after Mary I's death on November 17, 1558, his father's influence led to his election as the junior burgess for Carlisle during the first parliament of Elizabeth I. During that session of 1559, Mulcaster became friendly with Richard Hilles, a rich merchant who helped found the London Merchant Taylors' School in 1561.

Probably through Hilles' influence, Mulcaster was appointed the first headmaster of that school, an institution for 250 boys. Assisted by three ushers, Mulcaster received a stipend of only £10 annually, although a free house was provided for him and his family. (In May 1560, Mulcaster married Katherine Ashley, the daughter of a London grocer, and within several years they produced at least six children, causing Hilles to pay Mulcaster a yearly supplement of £10 out of his own pocket until his death in 1578.) Mulcaster taught his students Greek and Hebrew as well as Latin; he had them write

original verses in the vernacular; he stressed music, dancing, and competitive sports to a much greater degree than any other schoolmaster of the age; and he often had his students perform the ancient plays they studied. Indeed, Mulcaster's boys are known to have appeared before Elizabeth I on eight different occasions between 1572 and 1586.

Mulcaster remained at the Merchant Taylors' School until 1586, when he resigned and opened a boarding school on the outskirts of London for the children of rich families. Six years later he joined the staff of a small school in Milk Street, and between 1596 and 1608, he was the headmaster of St. Paul's School, an institution for 153 boys that dated from 1510. During the last years of his life, Archbishop John Whitgift granted Mulcaster two lucrative positions in the church, the vicarage of Cranbrook, Kent, and the prebend of Yatesbury in the diocese of Salisbury. On February 23, 1596, Elizabeth I appointed him to the wealthy rectory of Stanford Rivers, Essex, where he died on April 15, 1611.

The greatest teacher of his generation, Mulcaster believed that education should be readily available to children of all social classes. He is chiefly remembered for his books of 1581 and 1582, *Positions: Wherein Those Primitive Circumstances Be Examined, Which Are Necessarie for the Training up of Children,* and *The First Part of the Elementarie Which Entreateth Chefelie of the Right Writing of Our English Tung.* He proposed the use of graded readers designed especially for young children, the adoption of a new curriculum in a carefully structured sequence of subjects, and various improvements to spelling and orthography so that the English language would be easier for children to understand and master. Although he advocated what amounted to universal education for both boys and girls on the elementary level, in regard to the grammar, or secondary, schools, Mulcaster thought that the existing grammar schools should be restricted to boys. Although he favored secondary education for qualified girls, he maintained that completely separate schools should be established for them.

Probably Mulcaster's most radical proposals pertained to the universities, where he called for the existing colleges to be completely reorganized. Indeed, he hoped to see the existing colleges reduced by more than 50 percent and amalgamated into only seven—three (foreign languages, mathematics, and philosophy) for entering students, and the other four (law, medicine, theology, or education) for more advanced ones.

M

It is revealing that Mulcaster envisaged a separate college of education for the training of primary- and grammar-school teachers. He considered their work of crucial importance for society and hoped to see them treated with greater dignity and respect. Indeed, he proposed that their salaries be sharply increased, so that the teachers of young children would receive more remuneration than professors at the universities. But the Elizabethans ignored that and his many other radical proposals.

BIBLIOGRAPHY

Brown, J. Howard. *Elizabethan Schooldays.* 1933.

Charlton, Kenneth. "The Teaching Profession in Sixteenth- and Seventeenth-Century England." In *History and Education.* Paul Nash, ed. 1970.

DeMolen, Richard L. *Richard Mulcaster (c. 1531–1611) and Educational Reform in the Renaissance.* 1991.

McDonnell, Michael. *A History of St. Paul's School.* 1909.

Michael V.C. Alexander

SEE ALSO

Education; Grammar Schools; Merchant Taylors; Theater Companies, Boys; Universities

Munday, Anthony (1560–1633)

A prolific and wide-ranging author whose writing career spanned fifty-five years, Anthony Munday was the son of a stationer and freeman of the Drapers' Company who died prior to January 1571, leaving Anthony an orphan. In 1576, Munday was apprenticed to John Allde, becoming a freeman of the Drapers' Company in 1585. A Catholic who acquired the patronage of Edward de Vere, seventeenth earl of Oxford, Munday spent three months in 1579 in the English College at Rome, and began publishing regularly after returning to England. In the 1581 climate of harsh persecution of Catholics, Munday wrote reports on the trial and execution of Edmund Campion and other priests that expressed the viewpoint of the Protestant state government. He worked as an intelligencer for the rackmaster Richard Topcliffe during the 1580s; for Sir Thomas Heneage, treasurer of the chamber, who paid messengers until his death in 1595; and for the bishop of London in 1606, following the Gunpowder Plot. In 1587, Elizabeth I granted him several leases in reversion of crown property in consideration of his good and faithful service. From 1588 to 1596, he signed his publications "Anthony Munday, Messenger of Her Majesties Chamber"; beginning in 1596, he identified himself as "Anthony Munday, citizen and draper."

Between 1588 and 1596, he translated several chivalric romances from French. During 1590–1601, he was the single author or collaborator of at least fifteen plays, principally for the Admiral's Men. Henry Chettle, Thomas Dekker, Michael Drayton, Thomas Middleton, and William Shakespeare are among the authors who wrote collaboratively with him. From 1605 to 1623, he wrote fifteen Lord Mayor's Shows and published eight of them. In 1618 and 1633, he updated and revised John Stow's *Survey of London.* As a professional writer working across many genres, he also edited collections of poetry and sermons, wrote a rhetoric, and compiled a chronicle history of England.

Not university educated and of the middling sort, Munday needed to work for his income. Operating with a keen eye for the topical and marketable, he tended to take on projects that he could serialize or repeat. He sold books to a variety of printers—John and Edward Allde, John Charlewood, Thomas Creede, John Danter, John Wolfe, George Purslowe, and William Jaggard. His career also illustrates aspects of the situation and predicament of the English Catholic author who chose loyalty and conformity, not exile. Embedded in his work is a Catholic sensibility, allusiveness, and equivocation, which in various respects and circumstances shares an ideological and religious perspective with Protestant nonconformists. His sustained public prominence is a consequence of his skill in locating himself institutionally in relation to the court, theater, and city.

Munday's five children were baptized at St. Giles without Cripplegate. *The Survey of London* (1633) prints the inscription on his tombstone.

BIBLIOGRAPHY

Bergeron, David. "Thomas Middleton and Anthony Munday: Artistic Rivalry?" *Studies in English Literature,* vol. 36, pp. 461–479.

Eccles, Mark. "Anthony Munday." In *Studies in the English Renaissance Drama in Memory of Karl Julius Holzknech.* Josephine Bennett, Oscar Cargill, and Vernon Hall, Jr., eds., pp. 95–105. 1959.

———. "Brief Lives: Tudor and Stuart Authors." *Studies in Philology,* vol. 79, pp. 98–100 (1–135).

Kenny, Anthony. "Antony Mundy in Rome." *Recusant History,* vol. 6, pp. 158–162.

Turner, Celeste. *Anthony Munday: An Elizabethan Man of Letters.* 1928.

M

———. "Young Anthony Munday Again." *Studies in Philology*, vol. 56, pp. 150–168.
Williams, Michael E. *The Venerable English College, Rome, 1579–1979*, pp. 12–13. 1979.

Donna B. Hamilton

SEE ALSO

Campion, Edmund; Chettle, Henry; Dekker, Thomas; De Vere, Edward; English College of Rome; Espionage; Processions, Lord Mayor's; Recusancy; Shakespeare, William; Stow, John

Muscovy Company

See Joint Stock Companies

Music, History of

The Flemish music theorist Johannes Tinctoris wrote in *Proportionale musices* that English musicians of the early fifteenth century, John Dunstaple (d. 1453) chief among them, had created a new art of music. Then he criticized their successors for their more conservative approach, especially when compared to their French contemporaries Johannes Ockeghem, Antoine Busnois, and others. However, during the reign of Henry VII and the early years of Henry VIII, English music made its own unique transition to the Renaissance, primarily with sacred choral music characterized by luxuriant polyphony and lucid cantus-firmus structure. The Chapel Royal added to its roster, while other choral institutions such as the chapels of St. George at Windsor, St. Stephen at Westminster, and the educational foundations at Eton; King's College, Cambridge; Magdalen College and Cardinal College, Oxford, were founded or expanded in numbers.

Their choirs sang festal masses (mostly on a cantus firmus) intended for ceremonial occasions, votive antiphons, and settings of the even-numbered verses of the vespers canticle *Magnificat* composed in a highly elaborate ornamental style with arching melismas, cross rhythms, and a virtuosic character that was not copied on the Continent as the style of the earlier fifteenth century had been. In the polyphonic masses, the opening *Kyrie* is generally omitted, since many Kyries in the Sarum rite were troped.

The repertories of the Eton Choirbook, Caius College Book, and Lambeth Choirbook, covering the years from c. 1460 to c. 1520, are the major sources of this florid style.

Compositions are often scored for larger numbers of voices than one finds in comparable continental sources. For the Tudor period, the normal scoring for vocal music, as described retrospectively by Charles Butler in 1636, was five voices labeled treble, mean, countertenor, tenor, and bass. The nonimitative texture that characterizes the works of earlier composers such as Edward Higgons and Gilbert Banastir shifts to more use of imitation in the compositions of William Cornysh and Robert Fayrfax. The most prolific composer of masses was Nicholas Ludford, a younger contemporary of Fayrfax; his seven three-voice masses constitute the only complete set of ladymasses for each day of the week. They are all based on squares, which are now supposed to be counterpoints or basses to original *cantus firmi*. John Taverner's works sum up the achievements of this distinctive period in English sacred music and point the way toward the musical changes ushered in with the Reformation. Those masses and antiphons presumed to be earlier, such as the *M. Corona spinea*, are ornate works for larger numbers of voices, while the later compositions are less florid and complex. One distinctively native feature of English choral music is the use of cross relations. A common manifestation of the liking for such dissonances is the so-called English cadence, which Thomas Morley later decried, despite his frequent use of it. It features the deliberate clash of a sharp leading tone with a falling flat seventh in another voice.

The carol, a purely English type, first appeared about the second quarter of the fifteenth century. A strophic song on any subject, with a burden sung at the beginning and end of each verse, its text is either in English or in macaronic English and Latin. During the period of the Eton Choirbook repertory, the carol moved into the court repertory with texts that could be occasional or courtly as well as sacred. The manuscript British Library, Add. 31922, which preserves court repertory from the early years of Henry VIII's reign, contains not only carols, but also secular works in other forms, some of which are imitations or adaptations of the French chanson. Its textless compositions may have been used for dancing or dinner music: an inventory made shortly after his death shows that Henry owned a substantial number of keyboards, crumhorns, lutes, flutes, recorders, viols, shawms, sackbuts, and other instruments. Add. 31922 links the older, native ornateness of the late fifteenth century with evidence of more contemporary simplicity and directness. It is also valuable as a document of life at Henry VIII's court at a time when he actively promoted the arts. Once he was

M

embroiled in the divorce controversy, his energies were diverted away from the pageantry and artistic patronage of the earlier years.

The dissolution of the monasteries in 1539–1540 began several decades of confusion, exemplified by the fact that votive antiphons continued to be composed through Henry VIII's last years and Mary's reign as well. In addition, Latin polyphony could be sung in various venues, despite the abolition of the Sarum rite, so Latin-texted music continued to be composed. William Mundy (c. 1530–before 1591), Robert Parsons (d. 1570), Osbert Parsley (1511–1585), and, best of all, Thomas Tallis, are among that generation of composers whose work falls on both sides of the Reformational divide.

Although not every chantry or secularized community destroyed its Latin service books, the first edition of the Book of Common Prayer with, finally, the establishment of a liturgy would wait until 1549. The revised edition of 1552, with minor changes, would be the standard through Elizabeth's reign. The observance of services (matins, evensong, and Holy Communion) rarely resulted in full musical settings. Short services were the staples of the repertory. They were more homophonic and syllabic than were the great services, which utilized the standard divisions of the cathedral choirs into right- and left-hand groups (*decani* and *cantoris*) and were elaborately polyphonic. It was common for services to end with an anthem, an optional choral setting of a sacred English text other than those of the ordinary of the service.

Instrumental music flourished in Tudor England, although there are only a limited number of sources before the outpouring of instrumental compositions at the end of the sixteenth and the opening decades of the seventeenth centuries. One unique genre was the *In nomine,* in which polyphonic lines were set around a cantus firmus from the Sanctus of John Taverner's *Missa Gloria tibi Trinitatis.* Another typically English instrumental type is the fantasia, consisting of a series of imitative points. At the end of the era, Thomas Morley established a five-part mixed consort group of flute with plucked and bowed string instruments. The music of the English virginalists and organists exerted a profound influence on early Baroque keyboard music on the Continent, as Jan Pieterszoon Sweelinck's works attest. One significant source of mid-sixteenth-century keyboard music is the Mulliner Book (British Library, Add. 30513) with pieces by John Redford, John Blitheman, and Tallis, copied between 1550 and 1575. In later keyboard sources, such as the Fitzwilliam Virginal Book and My Ladye Nevell's Book, cantus-firmus keyboard pieces give way later in the century to variations sets (some of them quite virtuosic), dances, and short program pieces.

With the exception of Thomas Mulliner's arrangements of the mid-century and a few other sources, English secular song was preserved only sporadically from the period of Add. 31922 to the last decade of the sixteenth century. However, during the last three decades of England's musical Renaissance, English composers, with Thomas Morley at the head, transformed the Italian madrigal, balletto, and canzonetta into their own property. With the runaway success in 1588 of *Musica transalpina,* Italian madrigals with the texts translated into English, musicians had a model for secular music that was more up-to-date than the carol and yet could be amalgamated with the older tradition of secular song. Although William Byrd disdained the new English madrigal, others, most notably Thomas Morley, John Wilbye, and Thomas Weelkes, made outstanding contributions to a genre generally less extravagant but of no lesser quality than the Italian madrigal repertory.

The madrigal was soon replaced by the lute ayre, which was often made available in two formats, one pairing the vocal soloist with a lute accompaniment, the other wholly vocal. John Dowland, indisputably the greatest of the lutenist songwriters, wrote songs drenched in the gloom made fashionable by Robert Burton's *The Anatomy of Melancholy.* The infectious cheerfulness of some of Thomas Campion's and Robert Jones's lute ayres represents the other emotional extreme.

With the deaths of Byrd, Dowland, and Gibbons, a musical era ended. Thomas Tomkins would continue English Renaissance style for another generation, but with the introduction of the direction "in stylo recitativo" in the masque *The Vision of Delight* (1617), it was clear that the new baroque style from Italy had begun to alter the course of English music.

BIBLIOGRAPHY

Ashbee, Andrew. *Records of English Court Music.* 1986.

Flood, William Henry Grattan. *Early Tudor Composers: Biographical Sketches of Thirty-two Musicians and Composers of the Period 1485–1555.* 1925.

Harrison, Frank Llewellyn. *Music in Medieval Britain.* 2nd edition. 1963.

Hughes, Don Anselm, and Gerald Abraham, eds. *Ars Nova and the Renaissance, 1300–1540;* Gerald Abraham, ed. *The Age of Humanism, 1540–1630.* The New Oxford History of Music. Vols. 3 and 4. 1960 and 1968.

Kerman, Joseph. *The Elizabethan Madrigal: A Comparative Study.* 1962.

Le Huray, Peter. *Music and the Reformation in England, 1549–1600.* 1978.

Pulver, Jeffrey. *A Biographical Dictionary of Old English Music.* 1927.

Stevens, Denis. *Tudor Church Music.* 1966.

Wulstan, David. *Tudor Music.* 1986.

Laura S. Youens

SEE ALSO

Air; Book of Common Prayer; Carol; Consort and Consort Music; Dance Music; Eton Choirbook; Keyboard Music; Madrigal; Motet; Sarum, Use of; Song

N

Nashe, Thomas (1567–1601)

One of the most brilliantly entertaining writers of his generation, Thomas Nashe was a pamphleteer par excellence, a professional writer who observed Elizabethan life and letters from a position inside it. Primarily addressed to topical and local issues, his quick-witted criticisms of church and civic authorities not only made it difficult for him to find patrons and credit but also put him at the center of several Elizabethan controversies and scandals. Consistently, he wrote in the first person and repeatedly he evoked his own precarious position to call attention to the trials and hazards of writing and the strictures of censorship. Influenced by Pietro Aretino, Nashe shared with Rabelais a preoccupation with bodily grotesquerie; his writings exhibit a highly colloquial, spontaneous use of idiom and an extraordinary emphasis on the materiality of language. In *A Groatsworth of Wit* (1592?), Robert Greene praised Nashe as "young Juvenal, that biting satirist," words that, while summarizing his Elizabethan reputation, fall short of encompassing his talents for rhetorical license and as a virtuoso writer of vivid, often luminous, prose.

The youngest son of a curate, Nashe was baptized at the parish church of Lowestoft in November 1567 and, in October 1582, matriculated as a sizar at St. John's College, Cambridge, where he obtained his B.A. In 1586, he withdrew, possibly because he lacked funds, before attaining an M.A. After touring France and Italy briefly, he settled in London by 1588, where his acquaintance with the circle that included Greene, Thomas Lodge, Samuel Daniel, and Christopher Marlowe resulted in his first publication, a preface to Greene's *Menaphon*, addressed "to the Gentlemen Students of both Universities" (1589), which offered a scathing review of contemporary writers, among them

Thomas Kyd. This initial foray into literary criticism and the trials of authorship, Nashe's signature themes, was followed by *The Anatomie of Absurditie* (1589), a railing monologue on worldly "abuses" and the follies of the literary marketplace, including those of the Puritan Philip Stubbes, author of *Anatomie of Abuses* (1583). In his first real bid for patronage, Nashe dedicated his book to Sir Charles Blount, a commander in the Low Countries, whose failure to acknowledge the compliment perhaps convinced Nashe to abandon conventional routes to literary prominence and instead to rely on his popularity with a reading public.

Perhaps traceable to his family's religious persuasion, Nashe's hatred for Puritanism appeared full-blown in his contributions to the Martin Marprelate controversy. Although it is difficult to assign precise authorship to these pamphlets, *A Countercuffe given to Martin Junior . . .*, *The Returne of the renouned Cavaliero Pasquil . . .* (both 1589), and *The First Parte of Pasquil's Apologie . . .* (1590), bear Nashe's pseudonym, "Pasquil"; and another, *An Almond for a Parrat* (1590), dedicated to the comic actor William Kemp, not only publicly identified the Martinist conspirators but also won Nashe credit, in Archbishop John Whitgift's words, for stopping "Martin's and his fellows' mouths." Certainly writers of the ensuing generation accounted Nashe most responsible for unsettling the Martinists; among others, John Taylor's pamphlet (1640) charging the sectaries of Charles I's reign with similar abuses evoked "Tom Nash his ghost."

As the Marprelate controversy waned, Nashe turned to other literary ventures. In 1591, Thomas Newman commissioned him to edit a pirated edition of Sir Philip Sidney's *Astrophil and Stella,* but it was quickly withdrawn, and when Newman's revised edition appeared, Nashe's contributions were suppressed. The following autumn, however, saw the publication of *Pierce Pennilesse his Supplication to the Divell* (1592), a carnivalesque, confessional exposé of contemporary vices in which Nashe, styling himself "Pierce Penniless," expresses the down-at-heel condition that dogged him throughout his life. Extremely popular, his satire was reprinted six times that year and even translated into French; its success prompted imitators and, posthumously, an anonymous sequel that Thomas Dekker, protecting Nashe's reputation, criticized in *Newes from Hell Brought by the Divells Carrier* (1606).

Just as his fellow writers had defended Nashe, he was quick to answer accusations against his friends and to speak his own part in such quarrels. A case in point is his long-lasting controversy with the Harvey family. When Richard Harvey, the astrologer and divine, libeled him, as well as Greene and Lyly, Nashe retaliated in *A wonderful, strange, and miraculous Astrologicall Prognostication for this year of our Lord God 1591, by Adam Fouleweather, student in Asse-tronomy* (1591); and his *Strange Newes* (1592) even more vigorously denounced Gabriel Harvey's attack on Greene. Although Harvey's reply, Pierce's *Supererogation* (1593), insinuated that Nashe's writing was dangerously subversive, Nashe backed away from this private "war" in his next publication, *Christes Tears over Jerusalem* (1593), a didactic tract charging civic authorities with abuses of public funds in which Nashe, adopting the persona of St. Augustine, warns that the fall of Jerusalem prefigures that of London. Dedicated to Elizabeth Carey, *Christes Tears* bids "a hundred unfortunate farewels to fantasticall satirisme" and expresses a desire to make peace with Harvey. In a second edition, however, Nashe withdrew his repentent stance, once again lashing out at his opponent. Not unexpectedly, *Christes Tears* also provoked London's lord mayor and city council to take action against Nashe; released through the Carey family's intervention, he went with them to Carisbrooke Castle on the Isle of Wight, where he stayed until early 1594.

Later that year, two publications, both licensed in 1593, appeared. In *The Terrors of the Night, or a Discourse of Apparitions* (1594), dedicated to Elizabeth Carey's daughter and notable for praising Samuel Daniel's *Delia*, Nashe writes of demons and spirits and explains dreams as a sort of carnivalesque chaos, confounding states, places, and sexes. And in his self-styled "phantasticall Treatise," *The Unfortunate Traveller, or the Life of Jack Wilton* (1594), dedicated to Lord Henry Wriothesley, the earl of Southampton, Nashe claims to write in "a cleane different vaine." Exactly what that "vaine" is has puzzled

readers, who have classified it alternatively as picaresque, burlesque, parodic Arthurian romance, jest-book, and prototypical realistic novel, or some combination of all these. Whatever the case, Nashe's unconventional history of a page boy's knavish adventures in France and Italy, in which figures such as Henry Howard, the earl Surrey, Desiderius Erasmus, and Sir Thomas More mingle with Italianate villains, Zadok the Jew and a courtesan called Tabitha the Temptress, is filled with lively set pieces that fulfill its author's promise to offer "variety of mirth."

After the publication of *Unfortunate Traveller*, Nashe returned to the Harvey matter with *Have With You to Saffron Walden* (1596), a mock-oration, mock-biography that represents both Harvey and Nashe (in his Pierce Penniless persona) as tricksters who violate decorum in order to delight spectators. During this same interval, he may also have made additions to Marlowe's unfinished *Dido Queene of Carthage;* certainly by 1596, he was working on a comedy, *The Isle of Dogs.* Although the play, which apparently attacked corrupt political practices, does not survive, it was, when staged, declared seditious, and the Privy Council searched Nashe's lodgings, seized his papers, and submitted them to Richard Topcliffe, the government agent responsible for prosecuting treasonous acts. Although Nashe may have been ordered to prison, he was apparently able to avoid punishment by fleeing to Yarmouth in autumn 1597, and his last pamphlet, *Lenten Stuffe* (1599), is an idiosyncratic history of that city that departs from the usual celebration of great deeds and great men to focus on Yarmouth's resourceful populace. Dedicated to a mock-patron, Henry King, a tobacconist and author, it offers a burlesque panegyric on the "red herring" and includes a parodic retelling of Marlowe's *Hero and Leander.*

In June 1599, as part of a general attempt by church and state authorities to suppress works considered libelous, disaffected, or hostile to public order, Bishops Whitgift and Cooper issued a decree calling in and prohibiting Nashe's books as well as Harvey's. Aimed primarily at his pamphlets, that order probably did not include *The Choise of Valentines* (1592?), a vividly pornographic piece of "scandalous" erotica dedicated to Lord Strange, Marlowe's patron. Known as "Nashe's Dildo," the poem, one of many such "toies for private Gentlemen" apparently written for profit, survived only in manuscript until privately printed in 1899. Nashe's other venture into poetic literature, the masque-like *A Pleasant Comedie, called Summers Last Will and Testament* (1600), written eight years earlier and probably acted privately, ironically enough, at Whitgift's household near Croydon, was his final publication.

In it, Will Summers, Henry VIII's famous jester, figures as chorus in a pageant of the seasons that explores the incompatibility between the discourses of a traditional "natural" prosperity and an emergent economic individualism. Since the attempt to come to terms with that contradiction traces through much of Nashe's writing, *Summers Last Will* seems a fit epitaph for the brilliant figure who, perhaps even before its publication, had disappeared from London's literary scene. Exactly when, where, and how Nashe died and where he is buried remains unknown.

BIBLIOGRAPHY

Crewe, Jonathan V. *Unredeemed Rhetoric: Thomas Nashe and the Scandal of Authorship.* 1982.

Hibbard, G.R. *Thomas Nashe: A Critical Introduction.* 1962.

Hutson, Lorna. *Thomas Nashe in Context.* 1989.

Kinney, Arthur F. *Humanist Poetics: Thought, Rhetoric, and Fiction in Sixteenth-Century England.* 1986.

McKerrow, Ronald B., ed. *The Works of Thomas Nashe.* F.P. Wilson, revised 1958.

Nicholl, Charles. *A Cup of News: The Life of Thomas Nashe.* 1984.

Barbara Hodgdon

SEE ALSO

Censorship; Daniel, Samuel; Dekker, Thomas; Greene, Robert; Harvey, Gabriel; Lodge, Thomas; Kyd, Thomas; Marlowe, Christopher; Marprelate Controversy; Pornography; Satire; Stubbes, Philip

Navy

See Armada, Spanish; Howard, Charles; Military History; Privateering; Shipbuilding

Neo-Latin Literature

Neo-Latin Literature was all-pervasive in Tudor England. No one who went to a grammar school, or who read any sort of learned book at all, could possibly have avoided some knowledge of it. Probably at least 10 percent of known English publications in this period were in Latin. Far more English-language publications were trivial or ephemeral, while Latin books tended to be more substantial and made to last, so their significance surpasses their mere numerical proportion, impressive as that already is. And a large proportion of those Latin books were "modern" writings, rather than reprintings of classical or medieval texts. Very few major personal or institutional libraries were without a substantial Neo-Latin collection. Neo-Latin literature also circulated very widely in manuscript form, and indeed, this was the prevalent way in which readers encountered newly written Latin poetry, often copying poems that appealed to them in their personal miscellanies or commonplace books.

Latin was, and long remained, overwhelmingly the most popular medium for serious works on technical subjects, such as law, medicine, and natural or moral philosophy. This was partly to reach a learned audience in a language with which the majority of potential readers were familiar, and which avoided the fluidity and vagueness of a still-developing vernacular. Anyone seeking an international reputation had little choice but to use Latin: those sixteenth-century Europeans who troubled to learn the vernacular of a lively, growing, but still relatively insignificant island at the Continent's northern edge were rare indeed.

Imaginative literature is, of course, another matter. But here too, Latin remained a perfectly reasonable choice, if no longer the only one. Literary prose in Latin flourished, Thomas More's *Utopia* being perhaps the most accomplished and influential such work. Rhetoric was studied and practiced in Latin and could form the matter of literary controversy; the debate on Ciceronianism, for example, put the competing claims of an ornate style against a more flexible Latin one. Gabriel Harvey's "Ciceronianus" (1577) offers a personal account of his intellectual development from an extreme to a more moderate Ciceronian.

Many new Latin plays were written, and they were performed at both universities. Among the finest playwrights were William Alabaster and William Gager. Another was Matthew Gwinne (c. 1558–1627), of St. John's College, Oxford, who was also one of England's leading physicians and professor at Gresham College. His Latin "Music speech" (1582) shows yet another side of his character, vigorously defending the status of an art of which he professes his own ignorance. International humanist scholars, such as the Scotsman George Buchanan, played a significant part in Britain's culture.

At the start of the Tudor age, British Neo-Latin had barely begun to develop from its medieval origins and absorb the more sophisticated techniques of the Renaissance. John Skelton is perhaps the first really major English poet who might be called a Neo-Latin writer, although there is much about his use of the language that is still medieval, including his fondness for macaronic writing that mixes English and Latin. It was primarily for his Latin that he obtained the title of "Laureate," a distinction that

N

he tried, rather unsuccessfully, to extend to his purely English works.

There was an explosion of Neo-Latin poetry under Elizabeth I: sacred and secular, from epic to epigram, and in a wide range of classical meters. The Welshman John Owen (1564–1622) gained a national and international reputation for his Latin epigrams that early exceeded the fame of William Shakespeare. As in the case of Gwinne and his circle, it is often through Neo-Latin occasional poetry that we can trace links among intellectuals, scholars, and humanists. A common fashion was the adorning of books with liminary verses (from Latin "limen," threshold), in which an author's learned friends stand on the threshold of his work to praise it.

A related, and even more socially significant, genre was that of the university verse collection. The first such printed work came in 1551, with laments on the death of a "nobile par fratrum" [noble pair of brothers], Henry and Charles Brandon, carried off together by fever before they could complete their studies. "*En brevem pompam, lubricamque scenam*" [Look at (life's) brief pomp and shifting scene . . .] sang Laurence Humphrey, one of the most significant of Elizabethan scholars. There were further volumes in the 1560s and 1570s, but the tradition really became entrenched with the various books of 1587 mourning the death of Sir Philip Sidney in the previous year. Thereafter it continued virtually unbroken until 1763, nourished by the verses of several thousand British Latin poets.

Neo-Latin oratory, play-writing, and versifying were all central parts of the lavish celebrations on Queen Elizabeth's visits to Oxford (1566, 1592) and Cambridge (1564), her only two universities, places that could now boast poets to match or surpass the members of any continental institution. The manuscript of poems presented to her in 1564, now in the Cambridge University Library, contains fine specimens of italic calligraphy, and as many as 315 sets of verses (all but two in learned languages) from 255 individual university authors. Abraham Hartwell also commemorated the event in a very long printed Latin poem ("Regina Literata," 1565).

Inevitably, the university poets were all men. But women, too, participated in Neo-Latin culture, and there were a substantial number of learned ladies (as well as Elizabeth herself) who were fully capable of enjoying and composing Latin verse. Jane Weston (1582–1612) composed splendid Latin poetry in Prague; as a Latin poet, she could obtain a contemporary European reputation that far surpassed Shakespeare's, or that of any English vernacular author. The accession of James I was by no means the end of the story. Neo-Latin remained in many ways a central part of British intellectual culture for the next two centuries, a great tradition of which the foundations are firmly in Tudor England.

BIBLIOGRAPHY

Binns, J.W. *Intellectual Culture in Elizabethan and Jacobean England: The Latin Writings of the Age.* 1990.

Bradner, L. *Musae Anglicanae: a History of Anglo-Latin Poetry, 1500–1925.* 1940.

Hardin, R.F. "Recent Studies in Neo-Latin Literature." *English Literary Renaissance,* vol. 24, pp. 660–698.

Ijsewijn, J. *A Companion to Neo-Latin Studies.* 1977; 2nd edition, in two parts, in *Humanistica Lovaniensia.*

Money, D.K. *The English Horace: Anthony Alsop and the Tradition of British Latin Verse.* 1998.

David K. Money

SEE ALSO

Alabaster, William; Buchanan, George; Ciceronianism; Classical Literature, Influence of; Commonplace Books; Epic; Epigrams; Gager, William; Grammar Schools; Handwriting; Harvey, Gabriel; Manuscripts; Medicine and Health; More, Thomas; Printing, Publishing, and Bookbinding; Progresses, Royal; Rhetoric; Skelton, John

New World

See Colonial Development; Discovery and Exploration; Travel Literature

News Quartos

As the name implies, news quartos differed in kind from the myriad single-sheet broadsides and ballads circulating throughout Tudor England. The quickly produced news quartos, printed in book format, often in black letter, averaged eight pages in length. The emphasis on current news differentiates the quartos from works of fiction or prose essays. Although the term "news" related to many events, government proscription forbade the printing of virtually all domestic or political news. Most news pamphlets, therefore, focused on natural disasters, witchcraft trials, monstrous births, or other sensational events.

Between 1590–1593, a unique group of news quartos covering the rising fortunes of French King Henri of Navarre appeared in England. Printer, publisher, and entrepreneur John Wolfe developed this series of quartos into a highly visible medium; thousands of quartos circulated during this period. The reports covered Navarre's exploits, and the heroics of the English forces sent to help him, in considerable detail. War news provided valuable information to readers: the narratives often included dates, times, troop movements, and towns captured. The stories did not mention defeats or setbacks. This group of news quartos, published with unusual regularity and continuity, can be seen as the first English serial publication.

Publishers and printers of the quartos frequently employed marketing strategies to attract readers: bold title pages or woodcut illustrations served as covers, appealing to both literate and semiliterate customers. As the most available form of news, the quartos played a significant role in forming public opinion, especially in foreign policy. Direct references to the events in France appear in William Shakespeare, Christopher Marlowe, Edmund Spenser, and other writers. The proliferation of news quartos covering the events in France was short-lived; Henri's re-conversion to Catholicism in 1593 abruptly ended the English fascination with the king and all subsequent news stories concerning his activities.

BIBLIOGRAPHY

Collins, Douglas C. *A Handlist of News Pamphlets, 1590–1610.* 1943.

Huffman, Clifford C. *Elizabethan Impressions: John Wolfe and His Press.* 1988.

Parmelee, Lisa Ferraro. *Good Newes from Fraunce: French Anti-League Propaganda in Late Elizabethan England.* 1996.

Voss, Paul J. "The Unfortunate Theater of France: Shakespeare, Marlowe, and the Elizabethan News Quarto, 1589–95." Dissertation, University of California, Riverside. 1995.

Paul J. Voss

SEE ALSO

Broadsides; Popular Literature; Printing, Publishing, and Bookbinding; Wolfe, John

Nonsuch Palace

See Royal Palaces

Norden, John (c. 1547–1625)

Born in Somerset, John Norden trained as a lawyer at Oxford before becoming a land surveyor. Although he composed twenty-four religious tracts in the course of his adult life, he is best known for his county maps, forming parts of his projected *Speculum Britanniae*, for his estate maps, and for his theoretical writings on surveying. The *Speculum* was intended to be a detailed, written survey of all the English counties, with notes on their history, antiquities, topography, and economy. It was traditional in scope except that it was to be accompanied by county maps with linked gazetteers. Between 1591 and 1604, he produced accounts of eight counties (Northamptonshire, Middlesex, Essex, Surrey, Sussex, Hampshire, Hertfordshire, and Cornwall), some of which appeared in printed form, until the ending of the minimal government support that he had been receiving led him to abandon the project. The maps were derived from Saxton's maps of the 1570s, but with corrections and more detail. They were the first printed English local maps to have locational grids and, in some cases, to show roads, betraying the influence of German models. In 1600, Norden published an influential panorama of London and Westminster that now survives in only one copy (Lagardie Collection, National Library of Sweden, Stockholm). Norden's earliest estate maps date from 1593, but it was only after 1604 that he began to concentrate on them. He became perhaps the most prolific of the first generation of English estate mappers, but his methods were traditional—he made little use of the theodolite, preferring the plane table—and the majority of his numerous surveys were not accompanied by maps. Much of his work was carried out for private patrons, but as surveyor of crown woods and forests in the south of England (1600–1625), and particularly as surveyor of the duchy of Cornwall, he undertook numerous estate surveys for James I and his sons Henry and Charles as successive dukes of Cornwall. Through his work he substantially increased the revenue from the royal estates, as well as ensuring a comfortable life for himself. In parallel with this he created official maps of northern Ireland compiled from existing maps in connection with the Protestant colonies "planted" following the subjugation of Ulster. His *Preparatiue to his Speculum* (1596) and particularly his *Surveyor's Dialogue* (1607), which argues for the value of surveyors to tenants and landowners alike, contain valuable information on contemporary mapping practices.

BIBLIOGRAPHY

Kitchen, Frank. "John Norden (c. 1547–1625): Estate Surveyor, Topographer, County Mapmaker and Devotional Writer." *Imago Mundi,* vol. 49, pp. 1–18.

N

Lawrence, Heather. "John Norden and His Colleagues: Surveyors of Crown Lands." *The Cartographical Journal,* vol. 22, pp. 54–56.

Ravenhill, William. *John Norden's Manuscript Maps of Cornwall and Its Nine Hundreds.* 1972.

Peter Barber

SEE ALSO

Agas, Ralph; Mapmaking; Saxton, Christopher

Norfolk, Duke of

See Howard, Thomas

North, Thomas (c. 1535–c.1601)

Even had William Shakespeare not relied so extensively on *The Lives of the Noble Grecians and Romanes* for the raw material of his Roman plays, Sir Thomas North's great translation of Plutarch would still enjoy recognition as one of the Elizabethan age's foremost literary accomplishments. Alongside Arthur Golding's Ovid, John Harington's Ariosto, Edward Fairfax's Tasso, George Chapman's Homer, and the King James version of the Bible, North's text stands forth as an especially dazzling product of the English Renaissance's translational skill. In bringing Plutarch to life for the contemporary national audience, North also managed to forge an influential stylistic paradigm, indicating the high level to which English prose expression might artfully aspire.

Since only a scattered handful of recorded dates have survived, Thomas North's biography remains a difficult one to chart precisely. His admission to Lincoln's Inn in 1557 places his birth toward the middle of the 1530s; since the pension he was awarded by the queen in 1601 is the last official reference we have to North's career, he is presumed to have died shortly thereafter. We know that he traveled to France in 1574 as part of his elder brother Roger's diplomatic mission to Henry III, and served as captain during the Spanish threat of the 1580s in charge of a command of troops from Ely. North married twice, first to Elizabeth Colville and then to Judith Vesey. In the early 1590s, he was elevated to the status of knight, and occupied various public offices in Cambridge county and town over the course of that decade.

The published work affords us a firmer chronology. In 1557, he issued his translation of Marcus Aurelius's meditations, as *The Diall of Princes.* Allegedly "Englysshed oute of the Frenche," the translation likely relied upon the original Spanish of Antonio Guevara's adaptation, the *Libro aureo.* North's text would supersede John Bourchier's earlier English version of the work, and go through four editions by 1619. His next effort—another curious instance of North's practical skill with "layered" translation—was a rendering of Antonio Francesco Doni's Italian version of collected "oriental tales," published in 1570 as *The Morall Philosophie of Doni.* This work also enjoyed a favorable reception, seeing a second edition in 1601.

Nine years after the Doni translation, North released his final work, the *Lives.* Once again using an intermediary source, the French version of Plutarch issued in 1559 by Jacques Amyot, he set the classical biographer's monumental *agon* of Greek and Roman cultural excellence before the English audience with brilliance and clarity. As Amyot had observed in a prefatory essay that North also translates, "Plutarkes peculiar maner of inditing, which is rather sharpe, learned, and short, than plaine, polished, and easie," had excluded even many of those skilled in Greek from the *Lives'* celebrated historical, political, and ethical insights. For the next century, North's English, at once colloquial and refined, provided his countrymen with such coveted access. In addition to whatever moral edification North's widely popular work may have afforded, it seems likely that the "good and faithful service" cited by Elizabeth to justify the pension she awarded him referred chiefly to the substantial literary achievement of his Plutarch; it more consequentially provided dramatists of the age with a resource from which to adapt their images of the titanic political figures who would populate the stages of Tudor and Jacobean tragedy. Most notably, Shakespeare's *Julius Caesar, Coriolanus, and Antony and Cleopatra* draw directly on North's version. Six more editions appeared before the so-called Dryden translation finally superseded North's text in the 1680s.

BIBLIOGRAPHY

Carr, R.H. *Plutarch's Life of Julius Ceasar; in North's Translation.* 1908.

Colvile, K.N., ed. *The Diall of Princes: by Don Anthony of Guevara: tr. by Sir Thomas North.* [Selections] The Scholar's Library, vol. 1. 1919.

Christopher Martin

SEE ALSO

Classical Literature, English Translations, Spanish Literature, Influence of

N

Northern Rebellion

The Northern Rebellion (1569) grew out of two loosely connected schemes: a court-centered plot to marry Thomas Howard, the fourth duke of Norfolk, to Mary Queen of Scots; and a plan, led by the earls of Northumberland and Westmorland and encouraged by the Spanish ambassador, Guerau de Spes, to restore Catholicism in England and to liberate Mary Stuart and confirm her as Elizabeth I's successor. Rebellion, however, was not on the immediate agenda until the failure of the court plot triggered it. In mid-September, the disgraced Norfolk fled the court to his estates, unnerving the northern earls and convincing Elizabeth that an uprising was at hand. In fact, the earls were reluctant to commit to rebellion, despite pressure from Catholic activists. Throughout October, however, the earls came under increasing official scrutiny, and their growing desperation finally pushed them into action. On November 14, the rebels took Durham, where they destroyed the cathedral's Protestant books, overturned the communion table, and had a Mass said. They then marched south toward Tutbury, where Mary Stuart was held. The rebel force of 3,800 footmen and 1,600 horsemen (mostly retainers and tenants of the two earls) reached Bramham Moor on November 22. Two days later, with massive royal forces approaching, and having learned that Mary Stuart was to be moved to more secure quarters in Coventry, the earls began a retreat. The rebels took Barnard Castle in mid-December, but royal forces were closing in. The earls disbanded their foot troops and fled northwest, crossing the border into Scotland shortly after Christmas. In February, there was a brief resurgence of revolt under Leonard Dacre, which was defeated in the Northern Rebellion's only significant military engagement.

The royal armies, 10,000 strong, ravaged the north, and 450 rank-and-file rebels were executed (although this fell short of the 700 executions the queen had ordered). Nine of them were leaders (including Henry Percy, eighth earl of Northumberland, who was betrayed to the earl of Moray, the Scottish regent, and returned to England). The remaining rebel leaders were eventually abandoned by the Marian supporters sheltering them because of cross-border reprisals by English forces. They escaped to the Netherlands.

The underlying causes of the rebellion were complex, including political issues (such as opposition to the Elizabethan state's increasing marginalization of the northern nobility), as well as religious ones. Its aftermath was far-reaching—new restrictions against Catholics were enacted, English influence and intervention in Scottish affairs increased, and the state cemented its control of the north.

BIBLIOGRAPHY

Fletcher, Anthony, and Diarmaid MacCulloch. *Tudor Rebellions.* 4th edition. 1997.

MacCaffrey, Wallace. *The Shaping of the Elizabethan Regime.* 1968.

Pollitt, Ronald. "The Defeat of the Northern Rebellion and the Shaping of Anglo-Scottish Relations." *The Scottish Historical Review,* vol. 64, pp. 1–21.

Reid, R.R. *The King's Council in the North.* 1975.

Williams, Neville. *Thomas Howard, Fourth Duke of Norfolk.* 1964.

Candace Lines

SEE ALSO

Catholicism; Hastings, Henry; Howard, Thomas; Mary Queen of Scots; Percy Family; Ridolphi Plot

Northumberland, Duke of

See Dudley, John

Northumberland, Earls of

See Percy Family

Norton, Thomas (1532–1584)

Lawyer, parliamentarian, poet, and playwright, Thomas Norton was born in Bedfordshire. He was educated at Cambridge, and in 1555 he married the daughter of Thomas Cranmer, archbishop of Canterbury. Three years later he entered Parliament, where he became noted for his violent anti-Catholicism. In 1581, he was appointed by the bishop of London as licenser of the press and also the official censor of Catholics, responsible both for examining them in their beliefs and in overseeing their punishment. It was in this capacity that he gained the informal title of "Rackmaster General." His pro-Calvinist views were also extreme, and he was later imprisoned in the Tower.

His literary career included translation as well as poetry and drama. He translated twenty-six Psalms, Nowell's *Catechism,* and a Latin letter by Peter Martyr to Edward Seymour, duke of Somerset, but he is best known for his translation of Calvin's *Institutes* in 1570.

N

To students of English literature he is familiar as coauthor (along with Thomas Sackville) of the first English tragedy, *Gorboduc,* first performed in a lavish production at the Inner Temple on Twelfth Night in 1562. Norton, then aged twenty-nine, wrote the first three acts of the play. *Gorboduc* is a landmark drama in many ways, introducing blank verse and such Senecan techniques as the use of dumb shows, the figure of the ghost and the theme of revenge. Philip Sidney, in his *Defense of Poetry,* praised it for style but objected to its failure to follow the classical unities of time and place. The play is concerned with the dangers facing a kingdom without a clearly named successor to the throne; Norton, as a member of the parliamentary commission appointed to consider the limitation of succession, had strongly recommended the queen's marriage.

He continued to be active politically after his brief career in playwrighting. He went to Rome to seek information about Catholics and also began publishing controversial tracts against the Roman Catholic Church. In 1584, he was briefly confined to the Tower for his openly expressed dissatisfaction with the episcopal establishment. Shortly after his release he died at his home in Bedfordshire.

BIBLIOGRAPHY

Cauthen, Irby B., ed. *Gorboduc or Ferrex and Porrex.* 1970.

Cunliffe, John. *Early English Classical Tragedies.* 1912.

Dust, Philip, and W.D. Wolf. "Recent Studies in Early Tudor Drama: *Gorboduc, Ralph Roister Doister, Gammer Gurton's Needle, and Cambises.*" *English Literary Renaissance,* vol. 8, pp. 107–119.

Graves, Michael A. *Thomas Norton: The Parliament Man.* 1994.

Charlotte Spivak

SEE ALSO
Censorship; Cranmer, Thomas; Drama, History of; Sackville, Thomas; Sidney, Philip

Nowell, Alexander (c. 1507–1602)

Born at Whalley, Lancashire, about 1507, Alexander Novell entered Brasenose College, Oxford, at the age of thirteen and became a fellow of the college in 1526. He remained there for a number of years, but in 1543, he was appointed master of Westminster School and moved to London. In 1553, he was elected to the House of Commons as the member for Looe (Cornwall), but he was disqualified on the grounds that he was in holy orders. Soon afterward he fled to the Continent to escape possible arrest under Mary I.

Among the English exiles in Frankfurt, Nowell was recognized as a Presbyterian sympathizer, but his position was moderate and he reconciled himself to the Elizabethan Settlement in 1559, when he was made archdeacon of Middlesex. In 1560, he was appointed dean of St. Paul's Cathedral in London, and he remained there for the rest of his life.

Throughout his time at St. Paul's, Nowell maintained his moderate Puritan approach, which occasionally got him into trouble with Queen Elizabeth I. At the same time, he was prepared to invoke the law against Puritan extremists, and he served on a number of commissions set up for that purpose.

His chief claim to fame rests on the three catechisms he wrote, all of which proved immensely popular and were reprinted at regular intervals until the early nineteenth century. They present his Protestant theology in an easily accessible form, and were widely used for theological instruction.

BIBLIOGRAPHY

Nowell, A. *A catechisme or first instruction and learning of Christian religion (1570).* Thomas Norton, trans. Scholars' Facsimiles and Reprints. 1975.

Gerald Bray

SEE ALSO
Catechism; Marian Exiles; Puritanism

O'Donnell, Hugh Roe, Lord of Connell (1571?–1602)

One of the key figures of the Irish uprisings of the 1590s, Hugh Roe O'Donnell, also known as Red Hugh and Ruaidh Ui O'Domhnaill, was born about 1571 to a prestigious Irish family in Donegal. As a youth in 1587, he was captured by the English and held hostage in Dublin; he escaped and was recaptured, and escaped again in 1591, at which time his father surrendered his chieftancy, making him lord of Connell (also known as earl of Tyrconnel).

O'Donnell formally submitted to Sir William Fitzwilliam in 1592, but secretly applied to Philip II of Spain for assistance and allied with Hugh O'Neill, earl of Tyrone, in uprisings against the English. Described as fiery and flamboyant, O'Donnell, often collaborating with other families, won several victories over the following years and demanded land and the restoration of Catholicism, in response to which Elizabeth, in 1596, expressed her displeasure over such "presumptuous and disloyal petitions." In 1598, O'Donnell assisted Tyrone in a stunning defeat of Sir Henry Bagenal and the English forces at Yellow Ford.

After some losses, O'Donnell linked up with Tyrone again in 1601, with many anticipated Spanish ships en route to Kinsale for support. But in what turned out to be a devastating blow to Irish rebellion, he and Tyrone were defeated at the battle of Kinsale by Charles Blount, eighth Lord Mountjoy, Essex's replacement in Ireland. O'Donnell took a ship for Spain and died on September 9, 1602, in Simancas, probably poisoned by James Blake, an English agent of Sir George Carew.

BIBLIOGRAPHY

Doherty, J.E., and D.J. Hickey. *A Chronology of Irish History Since 1500.* 1990.

Silke, John. "The Last Will of Red Hugh O'Donnell." *Studia Hibernica,* vol. 24 (1984–88), pp. 51–60.

Walsh, Paul, ed. and trans. *Beatha Aodha Ruaidh Ui Dhomhnaill: The Life of Hugh Roe O'Donnell.* 1948.

Thomas A. Deans

SEE ALSO

Ireland, History of; O'Neill, Hugh; Philip II

O'Neill, Hugh, Second Earl of Tyrone (c. 1550–1616)

One of the most intelligent, ambitious, and powerful Gaelic lords of the Tudor period, Hugh O'Neill led the Irish confederate forces in the Nine Years' War. He opposed the English attempts to destroy the Gaelic lordships and centralize the Irish government, a scheme that would have eliminated his own authority, and used the language of national revolt and religious war to incite the Irish people to rebellion. His surrender in 1603 completed the crown's military conquest of Ireland.

Hugh was born into the prominent O'Neill family but made a ward of the English after his father's death. He was raised from an early age by a family of English settlers in the Pale, and apparently not at court, as is often claimed. After Hugh, baron of Dungannon, returned to his native Tyrone, he was a useful ally to the crown in the troublesome region, especially given his familiarity with both English and Gaelic culture, and was awarded the earldom of Tyrone in 1585. But he was not an English pawn. Hugh carefully fostered connec-

O

tions with other Gaelic lords and families, most importantly Hugh Roe O'Donnell, lord of Tyrconnell, and gradually expanded his territory. In 1593, Tyrone claimed the title of O'Neill, making him the most powerful lord in Ulster.

The Dublin government gradually became concerned with Tyrone's growing strength and tried to curb his power, refusing to recognize formally his preeminence in Ulster. By the outbreak of the Nine Years' War in 1593, Dublin had alienated an ally, and Tyrone was in contact with Spain and building up a disciplined and well-equipped army. Although Tyrone at first attempted to avoid direct conflict, by 1595 he had organized a confederacy of Gaelic lords and was in open revolt against the crown. The fighting was sporadic until 1598, when Tyrone, O'Donnell, and the confederate forces won a decisive victory, annihilating an English army led by Tyrone's English rival Sir Henry Bagenal at the battle of Yellow Ford. Their success alarmed the English and precipitated revolt in Leinster and military collapse in Munster. The crown was further humiliated the next year, when the expedition commanded by Robert Devereux, second earl of Essex in 1599, was beaten before even encountering Tyrone, and a hasty truce was concluded.

However, Tyrone's position worsened with the arrival of Charles Blount, Lord Mountjoy. The confederate forces were accustomed to guerrilla warfare, and in 1602, Mountjoy defeated them in a pitched battle at Kinsale when they attempted to relieve the besieged Spanish reinforcements. Tyrone fled but surrendered the next year to generous terms; Mountjoy allowed him to maintain most of his lordship. Tyrone did not rebel again. In 1607, fearing arrest by the government, he fled to Rome and remained there until his death.

BIBLIOGRAPHY

Ellis, Steven G. *Tudor Ireland: Crown, Community, and the Conflict of Cultures, 1470–1603.* 1985.

Lennon, Colm. *Sixteenth-Century Ireland: The Incomplete Conquest.* 1995.

Morgan, Hiram. *Tyrone's Rebellion: The Outbreak of the Nine Years' War in Tudor Ireland.* 1993.

R. Morgan Griffin

SEE ALSO

Devereux, Robert; Ireland, History of; O'Donnell, Hugh Roe

Occult Sciences

See Alchemy; Astrology; Magic; Witchcraft

Ordinal

The Ordinal is the name of two very different books. It was the proper name of the book known popularly as the Pie, which contained the directions or rubrics for the performance of the Latin services. In the preface to the 1549 Prayer Book, Thomas Cranmer complained of the complexity of the rules, "that many times, there was more busines to fynd out what should be read, then to read it when it was founde out."

More commonly, the Ordinal refers to "The forme and maner of makyng and consecratyng of Archebisshoppes, Bisshoppes, Priestes and Deacons," first published in 1550, and subsequently revised and printed with the Book of Common Prayer whenever it was reissued. Its preface expresses an intention to continue, use, and esteem the orders of bishop, priest, and deacon, as thay have been from "the Apostles tyme." The ordination was "by Publique praier with imposicion of handes." The only substantive difference among Tudor ordinals was that in 1550, the newly ordained priest was given a Bible and a chalice and paten and the newly consecrated bishop a Bible and the pastoral staff, while in 1552 and 1559, they received only the Bible. The ordination rites of the Anglican Church today are still called the Ordinal.

BIBLIOGRAPHY

Bradshaw, Paul. *The Anglican Ordinal.* Alcuin Club Collections, vol. 53. 1971.

Brightman, F.E. *The English Rite.* 2 vols. 1921; repr. 1969.

Cuming, G.J. *A History of Anglican Liturgy.* 2nd edition. 1982.

Ordinale Sarvm sive Directorivm sacerdotvm : (liber, quem Pica Sarum vulgo vocitat clerus). W. Cooke and C. Wordsworth, eds. Henry Bradshaw Society. Vols. 20 and 22. 1901, 1902.

Leonel L. Mitchell

SEE ALSO

Book of Common Prayer

Ordnance (Artillery and Ballistics)

Gunpowder was probably first used for military purposes in Europe early in the fourteenth century. Many of the early weapons were made of wrought iron, each tube built up from iron strips or bars forged together and strengthened by hoops (analogous to the technology of the wooden barrel from which the tube takes its name). Such guns were typically loaded at the breech end and provided with a detachable chamber for the powder.

O

From the end of the fifteenth century muzzle-loading guns cast from bronze increasingly replaced wrought-iron artillery. These bronze guns, manufactured by adapting the techniques of bell founders, were mounted on wheeled carriages; they were more mobile than the giant forged bombards of the fifteenth century and yet stronger and less prone to fatally explosive failure. The beginnings of Tudor rule coincided with this technological shift which, to contemporaries, signaled a revolution in the art of war: high-walled medieval castles could be quickly reduced by the new artillery and new forms of fortification were devised to resist the gunpowder siege train.

Whereas the English followed rather than led this transformation in artillery and military architecture, they played a more prominent role in the reshaping of combat at sea. Under Henry VIII, naval warships were systematically provided with heavy cast guns that could fire broadside through gun ports running along one or more decks of the ship. The distinctive naval gun carriage also seems to have been developed in England during Henry VIII's reign. Rather than the two large wheels and trailing tailpiece of a siege gun, the new sea carriage consisted of a wooden bed provided with four small solid wheels. This compact design enabled the guns to be quickly maneuvered and reloaded and was vital to the high rate of fire for which English sea gunners were noted. By the time of the Spanish Armada in 1588, the English navy's tactics had been adapted to artillery warfare: they avoided close engagement and boarding, seeking to inflict damage from a distance.

There was also English innovation in the manufacture of cast guns. Although bronze remained the preferred material, Henry VIII's encouragement of arms manufacture led to the development of iron as an alternative. Cast-iron guns, produced principally in the Weald of Kent and Sussex, were substantially cheaper than their bronze counterparts. However, their cost advantage was partly offset by their quality. They were more prone to casting flaws and, to secure safe handling, were often made heavier and thicker than equivalent bronze pieces.

The weapons themselves were manufactured in many sizes and shapes. Guns were identified and classified by name; the cannon and demicannon represented the heavy end of a scale that passed through culverins, sakers, and minions, and included smaller and lighter pieces such as the falcon and the falconet. Each piece would bear a family resemblance in weight and proportions to others in the same category, but standardization was impossible: after casting, the mold for each gun had to be broken open in order to remove the piece inside it.

The principal ammunition fired by these guns was iron shot. Stone balls had been standard in the fifteenth century and were still used, but stone-throwing guns (perriers) became less common through the sixteenth century. A range of other ammunition such as chain shot was favored for antipersonnel use and for disabling the rigging of enemy ships.

Most heavy guns were fired at point-blank range, with the gun set up to shoot horizontally. However, it was early recognized that greater range could be achieved by elevating the gun above the line of the horizon. Niccolo Tartaglia's *Nova scientia* (1537) provided the first published account of the relation between elevation and range of shot. This Italian text combined natural philosophy and mathematics and became the major point of reference for later ballistic discussions of the sixteenth century. Elizabethan authors such as William Bourne (1578) and Cyprian Lucar (1588) drew on and adapted Tartaglia's work, describing the path of the shot as proceeding initially in a straight line, followed by a curved section, and then a final vertical descent to the ground.

While artillery texts provided recipes for gunpowder and discussed the necessary routines for priming and firing a gun, ballistics was recognized as the most mathematically challenging aspect of the art. While not achieving the success of Galileo's work on the parabolic character of the path of an ideal projectile (published in 1638), several English mathematicians conducted independent research on ballistic problems. The mathematical author Leonard Digges carried out a program of trials as early as the 1540s and rejected many of Tartaglia's conclusions. Although his work remained unpublished, his son, Thomas Digges, printed a series of questions on artillery in 1579 that went beyond Tartaglia's account of ballistics. The most sophisticated Elizabethan studies of ballistics were conducted by Thomas Digges's younger contemporary, Thomas Hariot. Hariot's account of artillery trajectories sought to incorporate air resistance into the geometry of the projectile's path. However, his work remained in manuscript and had no impact on the mainstream of military literature, which continued to follow the theories of Tartaglia.

BIBLIOGRAPHY

Hall, A.R. *Ballistics in the Seventeenth Century.* 1952.
Kennard, A.N. *Gunfounding and Gunfounders.* 1986.
Martin, Colin, and Geoffrey Parker. *The Spanish Armada.* 1988.
Webb, Henry J. *Elizabethan Military Science: The Books and the Practice.* 1965.

Stephen Johnston

O

SEE ALSO
Armada, Spanish; Digges, Leonard; Digges, Thomas; Hariot, Thomas; Industry and Manufacture; Military History

Ornaments Rubric

An "Ornament Rubric" is a rubric attached to the Order for Holy Communion in the Book of Common Prayer specifying that the vestments worn by the celebrant and other ministers should be those that were worn in the second year of King Edward VI (1548–1549). In the 1662 Prayer Book, the rubric is virtually identical in wording to the 1559 Act of Uniformity (1 Elizabeth I c. 2), but this was not true of the form of words used in earlier versions of the Prayer Book.

In 1549, an equivalent rubric had directed that the celebrating priest should wear a white alb, with a vestment or cope. Assistants were to be in albs also, although without additional vestments. In 1552, the rubric was altered to say that the celebrating minister should wear only a surplice, and not the other vestments.

In 1559, the rubric was altered to conform to the Act of Uniformity enacted the same year, though not using the exact wording of the statute. The issue is clouded, however, in that Injunction 30, issued simultaneously by the queen's command, interprets the act to refer to the vestments that were worn in the *last* year of Edward VI, and Injunction 47 orders that any remaining vestments or copes be surrendered to the ecclesiastical authorities.

It seems that in Elizabethan times it was the Injunctions that were obeyed, and the statute was interpreted accordingly. The only exception seems to have been that copes were retained in cathedrals, royal chapels, and the like. But in the ritualist controversies of the nineteenth century the issue was revived, and the 1559 rubric was held to justify the reintroduction of sacramental vestments. This led to fierce controversy and to a certain rewriting of history, according to which sacramental vestments had not been abandoned in 1559, even though there is little evidence to justify such a conclusion.

BIBLIOGRAPHY
Neil, C., and J.M. Willoughby. *The Tutorial Prayer Book.* 1963.

Gerald Bray

SEE ALSO
Book of Common Prayer; Injunctions, Royal; Uniformity, Act of

Overall, John (1560–1619)

Born in Suffolk, John Overall, bishop of Norwich, was educated at Cambridge, where he earned a B.A. in 1579 and an M.A. in 1582. His association with the university continued, in the form of various advancements, through his ordination in 1592. He received his D.D. four years later and was elected regius professor of theology; his election as a moderate Calvinist was considered a sign of protest against the severe Calvinism of the Lambeth Articles of 1595, and he made no secret of his disapproval of their tenets—a disapproval that echoed Elizabeth I's. Overall was made dean of St. Paul's in 1602, and he played a crucial role in the settlement of church polity that followed the queen's death. He gained the favor of the new king, James I, with a speech given at the Hampton Court conference in 1604 on the subject of predestination; at the conference, Overall took on the task of revising the catechism of the Book of Common Prayer, adding a section on the Sacraments. The following year he became prolocutor of the lower house in the Convocation of Canterbury and compiled a set of canons on the relations of church and state; the canons were passed, but James suppressed them because they seemed to imply divine authority for successful rebellions. Nevertheless, Overall retained the king's favor and took part in the 1611 translation of the Bible. He was elected bishop of Coventry in 1614 and translated to Norwich in 1618. He died the following year.

BIBLIOGRAPHY
Blaxland, B. "John Overall." *Dictionary of English Church History,* p. 429. 1912.

Mark Goldblatt

SEE ALSO
Book of Common Prayer; Calvinism; Church Polity; Lambeth Articles

Oxford, Earl of
See De Vere, Edward

Oxford University
See Universities

P

Pageantry

See Accession Day; Progresses, Royal; Processions, Lord Mayor's

Paget, William, Lord Beaudesert (1506–1563)

The obscurity of William Paget's lineage caused Henry Howard, the earl of Surrey, to slander him as a "Catchpoll" in 1547; his father was variously a barber, shearman, and clothworker. But Paget was more fortunate in his education. At St. Paul's school he studied under the humanist William Lily and acquired valuable friends, Thomas Wriothesley and Anthony Denny among them. He was then admitted to Trinity Hall, Cambridge, presumably to read civil law. The master of Trinity was Stephen Gardiner, and Paget lived in his household after a period in Paris. It was through Gardiner's influence that he entered crown service in 1528 as clerk of the signet, a lucrative office owing to its provision of fees. He was probably elected to Parliament in 1529. However, Paget's duties were interrupted by several diplomatic missions in France (successfully securing from Orleans University a condemnation of Henry VIII's papal summons) and in Germany, where he discussed England's contribution to the Schmalkaldic League with the landgrave of Hesse. The decline of favor for Gardiner forced Paget to transfer his allegiance to Thomas Cromwell, but he managed this with characteristic skill and returned to Germany in 1534. Paget then served as the first clerk of Cromwell's newly formalized Privy Council, himself becoming a councilor in 1543.

The final years of Henry VIII's reign saw Paget at his most influential. As principal secretary from 1543, he became Henry's chief intermediary with his subjects.

Though moderate in his own religion, he was the pivot of the reformist courtiers whose control of the Privy Chamber proved crucial to the politics of Edward VI's accession. Paget secured the execution of the earl of Surrey, and Henry's will was written under his direction; he also testified to the "unfulfilled gifts clause" that allowed the regency council to award posthumously grants supposedly intended by the late king. Paget expected his advice to be heeded in return for his support for the elevation of Edward Seymour, and his increasingly impassioned letters form an excellent source for Somerset's government, given the irregular production and survival of records during the Protectorate. He became Lord Paget of Beaudesert following Warwick's coup d'etat, but fell from favor in 1551 amid accusations of corrupt administration of the duchy of Lancaster that were probably false. Paget's influence was restored somewhat in Mary's reign, when he conducted clandestine talks to minimize opposition to the Spanish marriage, but his clash with Stephen Gardiner over the persecution of heresy damaged his credit with the queen. Although remaining a councilor under Elizabeth, he held no further office.

BIBLIOGRAPHY

Beer, B.L., and S.M. Jack, eds. *The Letters of William, Lord Paget of Beaudesert.* Camden Miscellany. 1974.

Gammon, S.R. *Statesman and Schemer: William, First Lord Paget.* 1973.

Ives, Eric W. "Henry VIII's Will—A Forensic Conundrum." *Historical Journal,* vol. 35. 1992.

Miller, H. "Henry VIII's Unwritten Will: Grants of Lands and Honours in 1547." In *Wealth and Power in Tudor England.* Eric W. Ives et al., eds. 1978.

J.P.D. Cooper

P

SEE ALSO
Cromwell, Thomas; Edward VI; Gardiner, Stephen; Henry VIII; Howard, Henry; Lily, William; Seymour, Edward

Painter, William (c. 1540–1594)

William Painter enjoyed what seems to have been a colorful Elizabethan life as schoolmaster, government munitions official, best-selling humanist translator, and, apparently, embezzler. For literary history, Painter's importance rests on his *Palace of Pleasure* (1566), a prose translation of tales largely from classical authors, Boccaccio, and contemporary sixteenth-century writers, which launched a vogue for Italian novellas and became an important source of narratives for Renaissance dramatists. Born circa 1540 (perhaps before), Painter matriculated at Cambridge University in 1554, and by 1560 had become headmaster of Sevenoaks School. He was ordained a deacon in the same year, and in 1561, he assumed the position of clerk of the ordnance in the Tower of London. His patron in that appointment may have been Ambrose Dudley, earl of Warwick, who was master of the ordnance and to whom *The Palace of Pleasure* was dedicated. Despite his modest income as ordnance clerk, Painter amassed considerable wealth, including two manors. In 1586, he and two associates were charged with embezzling military supplies, for example, gunpowder presumably misappropriated from the queen's inventory and sold back to the state. First acknowledging some guilt, Painter later resisted certain of the charges and managed to retain his position as clerk for rest of his life.

The first volume of *The Palace of Pleasure,* containing sixty translated tales, was such a success that Painter brought out his second volume of thirty-four tales the next year, in 1567. The first volume went through three editions in nine years, and Painter's total number of tales was enlarged eventually to 101. Painter's sources range from classical writers such as Livy, to Boccaccio in the fourteenth century, to his later Renaissance imitators, Margaret of Navarre and Matteo Bandello of Italy. *The Palace of Pleasure* was so successful that it launched a vogue for Italian tales of manners, morals, adventures, intrigues, and passions, and inspired further translations of novellas by Geoffrey Fenton (1567) and George Pettie (1576). Painter aims his stories at a cross section of readers and declares his purpose to be instruction and delight, but Roger Ascham, in *The Scholemaster* (1570), apparently attacks *The Palace of Pleasure* as he rails against "fonde bookes, of late translated out of Italian into English, sold in every shop in London, commended by honest titles the soner to corrupt honest maners." Ascham notwithstanding, Painter presents himself as a moralist, commenting freely on behavior—often concerning women—and taking his characters as positive or negative examples. If Painter's discernments do not always hit their mark, the translations are enlivened, nonetheless, by his dramatic sense, fondness for detail, admiration for vivid speech, and appreciation for the sudden turns and ironies of fortune. Such qualities may have attracted dramatists to *The Palace of Pleasure,* since it was rummaged for narratives by decades of playwrights, including William Shakespeare, John Webster, John Marston, Philip Massinger, and Francis Beaumont and John Fletcher.

BIBLIOGRAPHY
Painter, William. *The Palace of Pleasure.* Joseph Jacobs, ed. 3 vols. 1966.

Kent Cartwright

SEE ALSO
Ascham, Roger; Fenton, Geoffrey; Italian Literature, Influence of; Pettie, George; Prose Fiction

Painting

Tudor England was a culture rich in imagery, both flat and three-dimensional. Even after the Reformation, there were paintings in churches, and through the century they hung in council chambers, dining halls, bedchambers, and private studies. Although it is mainly portraits that have survived, painters produced a wide variety of painted images: decorative and ornamental work on walls and painted unframed hangings, pictures of animals and other still-life subjects, religious imagery including biblical narratives, map-like depictions of battles, heraldry, miniature work on vellum, and the limned miniature portrait characteristic of the age. Although the visual style of English painting changed over the course of the period, attempts to subject it to the Italianate canon of Renaissance, Mannerist, and baroque have not proved fruitful, partly because the contemporary language about art in England could not suggest subtle stylistic differences. Paintings were judged more in terms of their value according to the cost of materials used and how effectively they communicated power and status. Rather than stylistic categories, other useful ways of looking at Tudor paintings examine the practice of painting and its historical context: the content of the pictures and how this changed after the Reformation; the place of foreign artists, particularly in London and at the court, in terms of England's relations with Protestant and Catholic powers; the social status of the artists; and the technical expertise commanded by painters, distinguishing them from other workers producing luxury goods.

Even portraiture is a wider category than generally supposed in that the replication of likeness was but one of the burdens placed on portraitists. The individual portrait might make sense only in the context of family power and status; it might owe its existence to an occasion such as the birth of an heir or a marriage and take its place among the ranks of ancestors in a space such as the long gallery. Tudor portraits also included complex symbolic and narrative referents to events in their subjects' lives to make it clear that the sitters were worthy of portraiture by their deeds or social position, thus steering clear of the charge of idolatry associated with the images of saints common before the Reformation. Portraiture, already a popular genre, was almost certainly given a boost after the Reformation, as other traditional subjects were entered on the prohibited lists. Indeed, very few extant later Tudor paintings took the subjects central to late medieval spirituality, such as the miracles of the saints or the Holy Trinity. Post-Reformation religious painting tended generally to be overtly didactic and moralizing: scenes of charity and narratives of fidelity from biblical texts. Old Testament battles symbolized the fight of the Tudor commonwealth against foreign continental tyranny such as that of Philip II of Spain. Biblical heroes (for example, Jephthah) returning to lead their people exemplified virtue and the punishment of sin. Group portraits in supposedly domestic settings were usually symbolic rather than naturalistic; typically, they create fictional spaces and references, as in Holbein's lost dynastic wall-painting, in which Tudor sovereigns are shown grouped around an altar-like plinth for the display of an inscription, or *The Cobham Family* (Longleat House, Wiltshire), where classical architecture appears like the coats-of-arms found on contemporary monuments. In several group portraits, long-dead spouses and ancestors appear alongside the living. In portraits of the monarch especially, there were highly developed conventions of posing, with the head profile used as a referent to imperial imagery on coins. Such pictures can be lively, subtle, and powerful.

There was an increasingly active London art market with numbers of painters on hand to satisfy it, and a less well-documented provincial painting world. A little is known about certain provincial painters, such as Richard

Marcus Gheeraerts the Younger, *Sir Thomas Lee* (1594). The bare legs and uncultivated landscape commemorate Lee's service in the Irish wars. By permission of the Tate Gallery, London.

Adams at Ludlow. Many painters were immigrants, and some became denizens, for example Cornelius Gelison, recorded as working in Colchester in 1571, having spent thirty-one years in England. Indeed, many of the most famous names were foreigners who worked under strict control of the court and around London. Documentary research suggests that there were waves of immigration. Under Henry VIII came a group of Italians, Netherlanders, and Germans, most famously Hans Holbein; many of them had little impact outside court circles. Other painters from various backgrounds followed in mid-century, some of them overtaken by the rapid changes of English foreign and cultural policy as the counter reform of the Catholic Queen Mary I was followed by an emerging Anglican Protestantism under Queen Elizabeth I; a case in point is the Antwerp-born Hans Eworth, who was largely identified with Catholic patrons and suffered a setback in his position after 1558. Finally, there was the wave of Protestant immigrants from the Low Countries pushed out of their homelands by religious oppression in the 1560s, including whole families of painters such as the De Critz and the Johnsons (Jansens). But the chief office of serjeant-painter at court was always given to an Englishman, like George Gower; this position involved some commissions on panel but mostly work on hangings, heraldry, and the decoration of an extraordinary range of royal furniture.

For the most part, painters were treated like other skilled workmen. In London, the illuminators and panel painters joined the cloth painters in the Painter-Stainers Company from 1502. The freemen of the London Painters-Stainers Company were classed as Face, History, and Arms of House painters. The state papers reveal that the company was in hot dispute with the Plasterers in 1601 and, in 1587, with the College of Heralds, who despised them as mere mechanicals. There was a great deal of overlap with other allied tradesmen such as masons, who were sometimes members of the Painter-Stainers. Many heralds lived by painting, most famously William Segar, who portrayed many court figures around 1600; Randle Holme, a polymathic family of heralds from Chester, turned out numbers of commemorative panels.

Payments to painters were often less than to other skilled tradespeople; for example, they earned less than the goldsmiths or embroiderers. In London, the painters had their workshops in communities alongside other visual artists on the western fringes of the city "from Temple-bar along to Charing Cross." Around 1600, a "Painter for the art of limning" might earn £40 per annum. Work seems to have been priced on the basis of size, the value of the materials used, and to a lesser extent, the renown of the artist.

Lord Cobham and his Family (British School, 1567). By permission of the Marquess of Bath, Longleat House, Warminster, Wiltshire.

Toward the end of the period in certain educated circles, a neoclassical ideology started to challenge the classification of painters as mere artisans; for instance, contemporary painters were compared with their famous ancient forebears or Renaissance counterparts. Henry Peacham treated painting in his directions for gentle living simply because it was a noble activity among the ancients and forbidden to the lower orders, and the miniaturist Nicholas Hilliard insisted on the gentility of his profession. Some of these arguments were based on the mathematical training that painters were thought to require, an education that set them alongside surveyors and engineers.

In general, encyclopedists regarded painting as a useful activity; thus the Oxford Aristotelian John Case (in his preface to Richard Haydocke's translation of G.P. Lomazzo's book on art theory) finds uses for painting in medicine, botany, geometry, cosmography, historical illustration, military engineering, and natural and moral philosophy. Painters were directly addressed by the authors and translators of architectural handbooks like those by John Shute and Hans Blum.

Technical questions about Tudor painting can be answered by increasingly sophisticated scientific research and by historical research in the surviving recipe books and manuscripts. Painters, like illuminators, gilders, and other visual artists, had to work in comparatively private, dust-free environments. During the sixteenth century, the standard medium was oil on oak, a technique that originated in the Netherlands. The surface of the panel was prepared for maximum smoothness to allow jewel-like colors to sit glossily on the surface. Toward 1600, canvas slowly supplanted panel, but many portraits continued to show meticulous surface detail nevertheless. Painting in miniature was a technique close to manuscript illumination. The technical skill of the painter was sometimes well rewarded; in 1612, Abraham Verderdort was paid £10 for the hands and faces of Prince Henry's funeral effigy, compared to the fee of £9 paid to Richard Norris for the wooden effigy complete with jointed limbs.

When doing figurative work, Tudor painters started at the head, "that principal of the body." Work in a wide range of colors followed preparatory drawings on paper or vellum. Some artists, such as Holbein, transferred the image directly from drawing to underpainting using a technique known as pouncing. Some were well practiced in perspective—though many were not—and many Tudor painters took tremendous care over costume, precisely recording details of fold, pattern, stitch, and hue. A sitter's costume could denote both the contemporary and the exotic (as in the portrait of Sir Thomas Lee), and was a powerful purveyor of meaning in Tudor painting. There were a few standard sizes and shapes for framed paintings to hang on walls, and a great deal of painting was done to be set on furniture. In the second half of the sixteenth century, larger portraits became more common.

In Tudor society the legitimacy of painting was disputed. Some thought it an activity of low intellectual status, simply offering modest entertainment to the sense of sight. Poets sometimes stressed how inadequate painting was to show a woman's beauty. A harder line was taken by some Puritans who regarded painting's attempt to replicate God's creation as potentially sinful and idolatrous. In these quarters painting was regarded as among cosmetics so often associated with sinful pride and therefore condemnable because of the "abuses and deceits of the painters." A substantial number of commentators felt that painting was not entirely respectable and were somewhat suspicious of its surfaceness, its superfluity: "it is but a Counterfait, which wanteth much of the Perfection of Principle." In one literary metaphor, painters taught the innocent how cunning might lurk in the fashion rather than can be expressed in the making; in another, "mere painting" set a varnish over "true substance."

These sensitivities about image-making were offset by the stress placed on its utilitarian qualities. Some argued that visual pleasure was in itself useful, for pictures delighted the eyes and adorned rooms. But full-length, late Elizabethan portraits are primarily displays of the public roles of the sitter: for men, such aspects as soldiering, the law, the court (where the capacity to pretend in art as if it were life was essential), the worlds of scholarship and politics; for women, as the virtuous spouse or chaste daughter engaged in domestic duties of educating and childbearing and charitable works. Knowledge about the visual attributes of male public roles has made it easier for historians to identify male sitters than their female counterparts. Many paintings were given as gifts, to make the absent present; this was especially true with the miniature. Also present although absent from real life were long-dead monarchs, many of whom were displayed in ranks in family galleries across the country.

The basic elements of painting were the line drawn by the pencil and the form set in with color to enliven the image, to make it more natural. The careful selection and mixing of appropriate colors was an essential skill for the painter. Works that simply employed the manual skills of copying were sometimes less well regarded.

P

Copies of paintings abounded but, for the most part, were held to be inferior to the original. Some educated observers noted that to copy paintings was an ancient practice. In other respects, the attempt to revive ancient painting was somewhat hit and miss. The naked figure (rare in Tudor painting) was a sign less of the idealized nude in its purest antique or Italianate form than of masculine action in the public domain (*Sir Thomas Lee,* Tate Gallery, London).

Painters, like poets, were expected to combine manual or technical skills with the use of their intellectual faculties, especially the imagination properly subject to and governed by reason. It was noted that ancient painters had relied on their wit and intelligence. However, the painters of propagandistic pieces, like the depictions of heroic Protestant stands against Catholic oppression (*Edward VI and the Pope,* National Portrait Gallery, London), must have been required to follow a relatively narrow brief. Such pictures often employed verbal texts in the form of captions or commentaries, again suggesting the painter's status as one who supplied visual equivalents of verbal thoughts.

Despite such occasional references, there was no fully developed conceptual vocabulary for painting, although some terms are common. "Curious" implied "effectively crafted," as in the "most curyous pictures" that Walter Hancock could paint. Indeed, Tudor paintings were often kept as if they were curios in the modern sense, curtained for private contemplation or boxed for minute examination.

BIBLIOGRAPHY

Hearn, Karen. *Dynasties. Painting in Tudor and Jacobean England, 1530–1630.* 1995.
Howard, Maurice. *The Tudor Image.* 1995.
Mercer, Erik. *English Art, 1553–1625.* 1962.
Maurice Howard and Nigel Llewellyn

SEE ALSO
Hilliard, Nicholas; Holbein, Hans; Interior Decoration; Miniature Painting

Palaces, Royal
See Royal Palaces

Paracelsus
See Alchemy

Paradox

Paradoxical thought and expression were increasingly common in Tudor England, thanks to a variety of literary, religious, and social influences. The word "paradox" implies a violation of common sense or a contradiction of widely accepted assumptions. In this respect Christianity itself is an especially paradoxical faith, particularly because of its doctrines of the Trinity, creation from nothing, virgin birth, God incarnate, glorious crucifixion, death, and resurrection, and death as the door to eternal life. By itself, the pervasive influence of Christianity would have made a taste for paradox nearly inevitable to the Tudor mind.

The importance of paradox in Tudor culture was also encouraged, however, by the period's growing interest in ancient Greek and Roman classics and in the thought of the Italian Renaissance. Cicero's *Stoic Paradoxes* were the most widely read of the relevant classical texts, but paradoxical thinking was also encouraged by the influence of ancient Greek skeptics such as Pyrrhon, and especially Sextus Empiricus. Pico della Mirandola, the fifteenth-century Italian philosopher, had relied on paradoxical thinking to reconcile seemingly contradictory modes of thought, while the whole Renaissance effort to blend classicism and Christianity made for a richly paradoxical culture. Bruno, Castiglione, and Paracelsus have also been seen (by Gruden) as feeding the appetite for paradox, and sixteenth-century humanists, both in and out of England, were also strongly drawn to paradox in thought and expression. As its title suggests, Desiderius Erasmus's celebrated *Praise of Folly* was a work rooted in paradox, but perhaps the most obviously influential literary paradoxes were composed by Ortensio Lando (c. 1512–c. 1553), whose *Paradossi* (1543) were translated by Anthony Munday in 1593. Other significant examples of paradoxical writing, either in original English or in translation, came from Cornelius Agrippa (1486–1553), Phillipe DuPlessis-Mornay (1549–1623), Edward Dyer (1543–1607), Thomas Scott (1538–1594), John Harington, Thomas Nashe, and, most significantly, John Donne. In the 1590s, Donne not only composed a collection of prose *Paradoxes* but also began writing his famously paradoxical poetry.

In many of his poems Donne was mocking literary conventions promoted by the great Italian poet Francesco Petrarca (1304–1374), but Petrarchan poetry was already thoroughly paradoxical, showing a strong taste for irony, oxymorons, and ambiguities of all sorts. Tudor writers influenced by Petrarch's sonnets included Sir Thomas Wyatt, Henry Howard, earl of Surrey, Sir Philip Sidney,

Edmund Spenser, and William Shakespeare. As numerous critics have noted, love is a subject that inevitably (and especially) lends itself to paradoxical treatment, and it is difficult to imagine a more paradoxical poem than Shakespeare's Sonnet 138. Love of paradox pervades the writing of Shakespeare and many of his contemporaries.

In Tudor culture, paradoxes could be (and were) used to display wit or discover its limits; to endorse orthodoxy or probe received ideas; to conduct serious debate, play mental games, or explore mental depths; to circumvent censorship or celebrate religious or political power; to vent skepticism or promote faith; to express, inspire, or even mock wonder; and to advertise intellectual skill or cultivate intellectual and spiritual humility. Fittingly, then, paradoxes in this period had paradoxical sources, attractions, and effects, and thus provide both a glimpse and embodiment of the larger culture's complexity.

BIBLIOGRAPHY

Colie, Rosalie L. *Paradoxia Epidemica: The Renaissance Tradition of Paradox.* 1966.

Donne, John. *Paradoxes and Problems.* Helen Peters, ed. 1980.

Geraldine, Sister M. "Erasmus and the Tradition of Paradox." *Studies in Philology,* vol. 61, pp. 41–63.

Grudin, Robert. *Mighty Opposites: Shakespeare and Renaissance Contrariety.* 1979.

Jones-Davies, M.T., ed. *Le Paradoxe au Temps de la Renaissance.* 1982.

Malloch, A.E. "The Techniques and Function of the Renaissance Paradox." *Studies in Philology,* vol. 53, pp. 191–203.

Vickers, Brian. "'King Lear'" and Renaissance Paradoxes." *Modern Language Review,* vol. 63, pp. 305–314.

Robert C. Evans

SEE ALSO

Ciceronianism; Donne, John; Erasmus, Desiderius; Petrarchanism; Pyrrhonism; Shakespeare, William; Skepticism

Parker, Matthew (1504–1575)

Born at Norwich on August 6, 1504, Matthew Parker enrolled in Corpus Christi College, Cambridge, in 1522. In 1527, he was ordained and became a fellow of Corpus. In 1535, he was asked to be private chaplain to Queen Anne Boleyn, a task he undertook with some reluctance. He was accused of heresy in 1539, but the charges were dismissed as frivolous and he returned to academic life at Cambridge. In 1544, he became master of Corpus and in the following year was made vice-chancellor of the university. When Martin Bucer came to Cambridge in 1549, Parker immediately befriended him, and the two men were closely associated until Bucer's death.

Parker became dean of Lincoln in 1552, but when Mary I ascended the throne he was deprived of his preferment and went into hiding. He escaped arrest, and in 1559 was persuaded, after some opposition on his part, to become archbishop of Canterbury. His was the first post-Reformation consecration, and he was well aware of the fact that many Catholics would regard the ceremony as illegitimate. This led him to compose an extensive treatise on the subject, which became a major pillar in the defense of Anglican orders.

As archbishop, it was Parker's task to restructure the Church of England, and most of his energy was taken up with this. The immediate cause of dissent was his requirement for clergy to wear vestments. At the queen's request, Parker drew up a series of *Advertisements* designed to regulate clerical dress. He presented this to the queen for her signature, but she refused on two separate occasions, and Parker eventually issued them under his own authority (March 12, 1566). He could not have done this without the queen's permission, however, and the *Advertisements* were regarded as having legal force. Apparently Elizabeth sensed that the measures, of which she personally approved, would provoke opposition, and she preferred the resentment to be directed against Parker rather than against herself.

Parker was subsequently engaged in the preparation of a new translation of the Bible that appeared in 1568 and is known as the Bishops' Bible. It was used in churches, but although it was clearly inferior to its main rival, the Geneva Bible of 1560, King James I insisted that it be used as the main basis for the Authorized Version of 1611.

In 1570, Parker's reformation of the statutes of the University of Cambridge marked a revolution in the university's way of life. Parker was a major scholar, and was very influential in the revival of the study of Old English, among other things. He was a major benefactor of his college and university, and the Parker Library at Corpus remains his principal monument. Parker died at Lambeth Palace on May 17, 1575.

BIBLIOGRAPHY

Bruce, J., and T.T. Perowne, eds. *Correspondence of Matthew Parker.* Parker Society. 1853.

P

Hudson, W.S. *The Cambridge Connection and the Elizabethan Settlement of 1559.* 1980.

Strype, J. *The Life and Acts of Matthew Parker.* 1821.

Gerald Bray

SEE ALSO

Advertisements, Book of; Anglicanism; Bible Translation; Bucer, Martin; Church of England

Parliamentary History

Parliament came of age during the reigns of the Tudor monarchs. In the middle of the sixteenth century the House of Commons moved from its old meeting place in the chapter house of Westminster Abbey into the chapel of St. Stephen's in the palace of Westminster, taking up permanent residence alongside the House of Lords in the precincts of the royal palaces. As important as this development was, however, what really distinguishes the Tudor Parliaments from their medieval predecessors is that the Tudor monarchs chose to deepen Parliament's role in the governing of the nation, especially after 1529. Henry VII, like the Yorkists Edward IV and Richard III before him, used parliamentary legislation to manage the nobility through acts of attainder (statutes declaring someone guilty of high treason) and restitution. Henry also used Parliament to levy taxes for the expenses of war, and when his son, Henry VIII, needed money to pay for his invasion of France, he was granted a new income tax known as the subsidy. It became a fixture of almost every Parliament thereafter, even in peaceful times.

When Henry VIII decided to secure his divorce from Katherine of Aragon, Parliament assumed an even greater role in governing the realm. The ongoing crisis required frequent meetings of the Parliament elected in 1529; it met no fewer than seven times between 1529 and 1536. Later dubbed by historians the "Reformation Parliament," it carried out, on a piecemeal basis, the separation of England from Rome. This included laws making Henry supreme head of the church, transferring clerical taxes to the crown, denying legal appeals to Rome, and initiating the dissolution of the monasteries. Other important laws were related to these changes, notably acts establishing a law of succession, oaths of obedience to the crown, and a law of treason. Much of this was carried out under the watchful eye of the king's chief minister, Thomas Cromwell.

Henry remarked in 1542 that he was no more powerful than when he stood with his Parliament. In using Parliament to legislate the royal supremacy, he obliged his successors to use statute law to make any further changes. As a consequence, Edward VI and Mary Tudor called on Parliament to legitimize the religious changes that they required. Moreover, the novelties of the young king, dominated by his two uncles, Edward Seymour, duke of Somerset, and John Dudley, duke of Northumberland, and a female ruler, encouraged frequent meetings of Parliament: eleven sessions in twelve years. The necessity of making changes through statute law also ensured that Parliament would be a significant arena for opposition. In 1555, when Mary desired a bill seizing the property of the Protestants who had fled abroad, the measure was defeated when her opponents locked the doors of Commons and forced a vote when many of the bill's supporters were absent. Parliament's important political role was reflected in Thomas Seymour's plan to launch his coup d'etat against his brother, protector Somerset, there and once again when Mary's marriage treaty with Philip II of Spain was confirmed by statute.

The period from the 1540s into the 1560s were years of economic hardship, and humanist writers saw Parliament as the perfect arena for their proposals on social and economic reform. Of course, Parliament has always legislated on such matters. Henry VII's Parliaments had passed laws on enclosure, and in 1536, a new poor law was introduced, but the 1550s saw a dramatic increase in the variety and number of such measures. These included laws against enclosure, prohibiting exports, fixing wages, governing specific manufactures, and regulating trades. As with religious legislation, once a law was enacted on a particular issue any who desired changes thereafter were forced to lobby for repeal by, or a new act of, Parliament. By Elizabeth's reign then, Parliament's role as the supreme legislative body was guaranteed.

Elizabeth I may have called fewer Parliaments relative to Edward and Mary, but they played an equally important role in her reign. Statutes regulating social and economic affairs continued to be passed, some of which, such as the Statute of Artificers of 1563 and the poor law of 1601, had a profound and lasting effect on the lives of English men and women. In her first Parliament, in 1559, acts of supremacy and uniformity reestablished Protestantism as the official faith, albeit in a more moderate form and over some opposition. Those who became frustrated with the slowness of ecclesiastical reform, the radical Protestants known as Puritans fought hard campaigns to reduce or even abolish the authority of bishops, eliminate certain rites and ceremonies, and even replace the Book of Common Prayer with a Genevan version. They found broader support, even from the government, for their desires to impose restrictions on Elizabeth's Catholic subjects.

Politics was thus never absent from parliamentary agendas. In 1572, proceedings against Thomas Howard, fourth duke of Norfolk, who had conspired to marry Mary Queen of Scots, were discussed. In 1586–1587, debates were held over Mary's fate and whether to join the Protestant cause in the Netherlands. Protests were made over corrupt court practices, such as purveyance (1589) and the granting of monopolies to courtiers (1597–1598, 1601). In all of these matters Elizabeth took advice only as she saw fit, determined to put limits on what M.P.s and peers could discuss when it came to matters of state.

Despite such tensions, and a degree of opposition to certain royal policies in specific Parliaments, it is clear that, on the whole, Tudor monarchs and Parliaments worked relatively well together, certainly compared to the fractured Parliaments of the Lancastrian period and the troubled assemblies of the Stuarts. In considering their history it is important to set aside any assumption that the conflict which occurred between monarch and Parliament in the mid-seventeenth century necessarily meant that the Tudor Parliaments were also on the brink of breakdown.

That this would be the case might be expected because of the actual structure of Parliament. It consisted of three parts: crown, Lords, and Commons. No law could be instituted without the agreement of all three. The monarch had effective control over Parliament simply because he or she summoned and dissolved Parliament at will. Monarchs also had the right to veto any bill. The House of Lords, consisting of the bishops (and abbots in the pre-Reformation Parliaments) and lay peers, assisted by the judges, was the older and most prestigious chamber. It consisted, in Elizabeth's reign, of some seventy to eighty men who sat by right of their receiving a writ of summons. The bishops had the added task, during Parliament, of attending the Convocation of Canterbury, which issued canons governing the church. The House of Commons, known as the lower house, was much larger than Lords, with 462 members at the end of Elizabeth's reign, summoned by writs of election. Very few elections were actually contested. Members of both houses had the right to initiate bills, debate them, and influence their provisions. Both houses had to approve a measure before it could proceed to the royal assent.

The legislative record of the Tudor Parliaments is impressive. Elizabeth's Parliaments usually produced between thirty and thirty-five acts. Some bills originated with the government, but most were promoted by towns,

corporations, guilds, and individuals who drafted bills and lobbied for them. The records of London's regulated and joint stock companies, for example, reveal that they paid extra fees and gave presents to officials such as clerks, entertained M.P.s at dinner, and rewarded them for speeches delivered in the House.

Hundreds of bills—nearly 75 percent—were introduced in the Tudor House of Commons; most failed to get beyond that chamber to Lords. Fewer bills were initiated in the upper house, but they enjoyed a higher success rate. There are many reasons for a bill's failure. Inefficiency, poor drafting, lack of attendance, and lack of time could all be responsible. Bills also failed because they were actively opposed. Conflict in Parliament did not only occur over matters of state and religion; "lesser" issues such as industry and manufacture, fishing, roads, and property disputes could cause great hostility and consume the parliamentary timetable. In addition, some bills were not initiated with a serious intent that they would become law. In such cases Parliament was a convenient place to be seen to be making statements or to raise problems for which solutions were also being sought elsewhere, as in the courts or Privy Council.

The formalization of procedures, such as reading a bill three times before it could be put to a vote for passage, regularly committing bills, rules of debate, the conduct of conferences between the two houses and methods of amending bills, were important and long-lasting contributions of the Tudor assemblies to the history of Parliament. Another indication of the importance of Parliament in the life of the nation can be seen in studies of the nature of Parliament and its procedures by John Hooker, William Lambarde, and Sir Thomas Smith.

The monarch had enormous control over the timing, duration, and legislative proceedings of Parliament. Tudor monarchs could also influence proceedings by nominating the lord chancellor, who chaired Lords, and the speaker, who chaired Commons. The Privy Council, as members of the government, sat in both houses to manage official business and head off complaints or opposition. The crown also had considerable patronage at its disposal. This meant that "men-of-business" could be counted on to help and, besides this, a number of M.P.s were elected, or selected, through royal patronage, control over the sheriff who ran the election process, or the influence of councilors and peers, especially in nominating borough representatives. Indeed, the very composition of both houses could be altered by the monarch. In Commons, new seats could be created through the

P

incorporation of boroughs, giving them the right to send M.P.s; by this means Commons grew from 296 to 462 during the course of the sixteenth century. In Lords, someone could miss out on a summons, be told to stay away, or sent off on other royal business. A dramatic example can be found in 1559 when, in order to secure the church settlement, Elizabeth imprisoned two of the most antagonistic bishops.

Yet the monarch was dependent on Parliament for key legislation and, even more important as the century proceeded, on the right to levy taxes. Parliamentary subsidies were the main reason why monarchs bothered with Parliaments. This made Parliament more of a marketplace than it might have been, and since, in England, the nobility paid taxes as well as those represented in Commons, there was a common ground of concern between the two chambers that few European assemblies shared. There were also important patron-client relations between the two houses of Parliament. Thus not only were the two houses a considerable force to be reckoned with, but the crown was dependent on members for good government in the localities.

Parliament thus existed because everyone needed it. For the crown it was an essential "point-of-contact" between center and locality; for the localities it provided the opportunity to resolve local problems and lobby both court and government about local matters and influence policy. The English Parliament also served the needs of individuals, notably in the settling of acrimonious property disputes among the gentry and nobility, and in the naturalization of aliens. In recent years it is the process of lawmaking, the range of laws considered, and the lobbying of interest groups that has received attention from historians. This has revised the work of an earlier generation of historians, notably Sir John Neale, who emphasized the importance of opposition and conflict between the monarch and the House of Commons. Revisionism may have gone too far in claiming that Tudor Parliaments were characterized by consensus, but there is no doubt that their existence contributed greatly to the stability of the Tudor regime.

BIBLIOGRAPHY

Dean, D.M., and N.L. Jones, eds. *Parliament in Elizabethan England.* 1990.
Elton, G.R. *The Parliament of England, 1559–1581.* 1986.
Graves, M.A.R. *Tudor Parliaments.* 1985.
———. *Early Tudor Parliaments, 1485–1558.* 1990.
———. *Elizabethan Parliaments, 1559–1601.* 2nd edition. 1996.
Hartley, T.E. *Elizabeth's Parliaments. Queen, Lords, and Commons, 1559–1601.* 1992.
Loach, J. *Parliament under the Tudors.* 1991.
Neale, J.E. *Elizabeth I and Her Parliaments, 1559–1581,* and *Elizabeth I and Her Parliaments, 1584–1601.* 1953, 1957; repr. 1971.

David M. Dean

SEE ALSO

Cromwell, Thomas; Dudley, John; Edward VI; Elizabeth I; Henry VII; Henry VIII; Hooker, John; Government, Central Administrative of; Government, Local; Lambarde, William; Mary I; Monastic Orders; Poor Laws; Reformation, English; Seymour, Edward; Seymour, Thomas; Smith, Thomas

Parr, Catherine (c. 1512–1548)

Sixth wife to Henry VIII, Catherine Parr has won praise as a benign stepmother and as a Protestant, but her life was more complicated than these traditional characterizations allow. Born about 1512 to Sir Thomas Parr, a descendant of Edward III, and Maud Greene, Catherine survived two husbands, Edward Borough and John Neville, Lord Latimer, to marry the king on July 12, 1543.

Although no evidence for John Foxe's statement in the *Book of Martyrs* that she was a Protestant can be traced to Henry's lifetime, her later views do seem to reflect some Lutheran concepts. Foxe further reported that a conservative religious faction conspired to have her arrested for encouraging Protestantism at court but that her quick acknowledgement of the king's religious authority led him to rescue her from this disgrace. This court intrigue was probably a failed scheme in the ongoing struggle for control of the regency of her stepson, the future Edward VI. Her scholarly interests included studying Latin, promoting the translation of Desiderius Erasmus's *Paraphrases,* publishing three devotional works, and encouraging her stepchildren's education.

With Edward's succession in January 1547, his uncle, Edward Seymour, duke of Somerset, was named lord protector, while another uncle, Thomas Seymour, became the king's surrogate father when he married Queen Catherine Parr, whom he had planned to wed before Henry's intervention in 1543. Maintaining close ties with Princess Elizabeth and Lady Jane Grey, two royal claimants who resided with her, she unsuccessfully sought

P

Princess Mary's approval of her marriage. She also supported her new husband's challenge for power by competing with the protector's wife for the crown jewels and for precedence at court. Her life as queen dowager was brief, for on September 5, 1548, she succumbed to puerperal fever after giving birth to a daughter, Mary. Catherine was buried at St. Mary's Church, adjoining Sudeley Castle in Gloucestershire.

BIBLIOGRAPHY

James, Susan. "The Devotional Writings of Queen Catherine Parr." *Transactions of the Cumberland and Westmorland Antiquarian and Archaeological Society,* vol. 82, pp. 135–39.

———. "Queen Kateryn Parr, 1512–1548." *Transactions of the Cumberland and Westmorland Antiquarian and Archaeological Society,* vol. 88, pp. 107–19.

Loades, David. *The Politics of Marriage: Henry VIII and His Queens.* 1994.

Mueller, Janel, intro. *Katherine Parr.* "Prayers or Medytacions" and "Lamentations of a Sinner." *In The Early Modern Englishwoman: A Facsimile Library of Essential Works.* Vol. 3, part 1: *Printed Writings, 1500–1640.* 1996.

Warnicke, Retha. *Women of the English Renaissance and Reformation.* 1983.

Retha Warnicke

SEE ALSO

Edward VI; Foxe, John; Grey, Lady Jane; Henry VIII; Seymour, Edward; Seymour, Thomas

Parry, Robert (1563–c. 1614)

A Welsh gentleman-poet, Robert Parry was the youngest son in a family of Denbighshire gentry. Parry made his living as secretary to Judge Henry Townshend (c. 1540–1621), the English circuit judge for Denbighshire. Parry's known writings, all in English, include *Moderatus* (1595), a prose romance with twenty interspersed poems; and *Sinetes Passions* (1597), a collection of ninety-nine poems purporting to record, in separate sections, Parry's own amours and those of his "Patron," Sir John Salusbury (1567–1612). "Sinetes" is a transliteration of the Greek word *cynetes,* huntsman. Two manuscript poems are copied into the Salusbury family album (Oxford, Christ Church MS 184), but not included in *Sinetes Passions.* These two poems are printed as poems no. 9 and no. 24 in Carleton Brown's edition of the poems of Salusbury

(1914). Finally, Parry left a manuscript *Diary* covering the years 1558–1613 (Aberystwyth, National Library of Wales MS Plas Nantglyn no. 1). It should be noticed that Parry did not write the translations called *The Mirrour of Knighthood,* though they are often ascribed to him.

The work commonly referred to as Parry's *Diary* is actually a yearbook. It was originally designed as a record of mistreatment of Catholics under the regime of Elizabeth I, and accordingly begins in 1558. For the years 1558 to 1592, Parry took most of his information verbatim from John Stow's *Annales of England* (1592), interpolating only a few family events, such as his own birth, and local events relevant to his theme. From 1592 onward, Parry used the yearbook in much more random fashion. Laid into the book at 1600 is an interesting journal that Parry kept during a trip to Italy in that year. The years 1606 and 1609 are ominously blank, reflecting the fact that in 1606, as a consequence of the anti-recusant hysteria following the Gunpowder Plot, Parry was dismissed from his position and stripped of his property, and he and his wife were placed under permanent house arrest. They entrusted their ten-year-old son, Ffoulk, to the Jesuit underground, who took him to safety in France and gave him the pseudonym John Portland. Parry died at the age of fifty-one.

BIBLIOGRAPHY

Atkinson, D.L. "On the authorship of the translations of *The Mirrour of Knighthood.*" *MLQ,* vol. 6 (1945), pp. 3–12, 175–186.

Foulkes-Roberts, A., ed. *Diary* [excerpt]. *Archaeologia Cambrensis,* 6th series, vol. 15 (1915), pp. 109–139.

Jayne, S. *The Poetry of Robert Parry.* Unpublished MS, Huntington Library. 1991.

Sears Jayne

SEE ALSO

Stow, John

Parry, William (d. 1585)

A gentleman's younger son, William Parry's failed social ambitions and Catholic sympathies led him into treason against Queen Elizabeth. To escape the many debts he incurred at court, Parry became a spy among the English Catholic exiles; he enjoyed Lord Burghley's confidence throughout the 1570s, even as he became a secret Catholic. In 1580, he was sentenced to death for attacking his chief creditor, but received Elizabeth's pardon.

Parry, William   531

P

Despairing of his advancement, however, Parry returned to the Continent in 1582. He met with Catholic conspirators and sought the pope's sanction for an assassination. Yet, on his return to England in January 1584, he went immediately to court to reveal the plot to kill Elizabeth and place Mary Queen of Scots on the throne. His hopes for reward, though, were not fulfilled.

Parry was elected to the new Parliament. In December 1584, he denounced an anti-Catholic bill in Commons; the rabidly anti-Jesuit Parliament had him arrested, but Elizabeth released him. Six weeks later, Edmund Neville, with whom Parry had discussed his plot, informed on him. Parry was arrested for high treason and wrote a full confession. He pleaded guilty at his trial in February 1585, but then recanted his confession. He was convicted nonetheless. Although Parry maintained his innocence on the scaffold, his tangled life became a favorite story in propaganda against Catholics and Mary Queen of Scots.

BIBLIOGRAPHY

Howell, T.B., ed. *Complete Collection of State Trials.* Vol. 1. 1816.

Neale, J.E. *Elizabeth I and Her Parliaments, 1584–1601.* 1957.

Read, Conyers. *Lord Burghley and Queen Elizabeth.* 1960.

Smith, Lacey Baldwin. *Treason in Tudor England, 1603–1640: Politics and Paranoia.* 1986.

John D. Staines

SEE ALSO

Jesuits; Marian Exiles

Parsons, Robert (1546–1610)

Jesuit missionary and polemicist, Robert Parsons (or Persons) was born at Nether Stowey, Somerset, in 1546, the sixth of eleven children of a blacksmith. After attending school at Stogursey and at Taunton, he went up to St. Mary's Hall, Oxford, in 1564, and moved to Balliol College two years later. In 1568, he received the B.A. and won election as a fellow of the college. He took the M.A. four years later.

Because of Parsons's Catholic sympathies, Edmund Campion, then a proctor of the university, arranged for him to receive his degree without taking the Oath of Supremacy. Although Parsons had to swear to the oath in the end, he declined to take Anglican ordination, even though he had been elected chaplain-fellow of his college. Hostility to Catholic sympathizers forced him to leave

Balliol briefly in 1569. Parsons thought of studying law, but soon he was able to return to the college as tutor, bursar, and dean. Although very popular with his students, Parsons quarreled frequently with the fellows, including Christopher Bagshaw, who later became a Catholic priest but remained Parsons's implacable enemy. Parsons's collegiate foes charged him with popery as well as with Calvinism, with embezzlement, and with being born out of wedlock, which, under the statutes of the college, barred him from holding a fellowship. The charges of embezzlement and bastardy were false, but Parsons Catholic sympathies left him isolated. He resigned from the college in February 1574.

Later that spring, Parsons sold land that had been given to him and left England to study medicine at Padua. At Louvain, he underwent the Jesuit spiritual exercises and was received into the Catholic Church. He took a break from his medical studies to attend the jubilee of 1575 in Rome. In July, after a brief period of spiritual anguish, he entered the Society of Jesus, and was ordained a priest in 1578.

Parsons favored the sending of Jesuit missionaries into England, and in April 1580, he and Campion were selected to go there with several secular priests. Parsons, disguised as a soldier, landed at Dover on June 12 and proceeded to London. At Southwick, he presided over a synod of the underground Catholic clergy and explained the nonpolitical purpose of the mission. Leaving London, he traveled through the counties of Northampton, Derby, Worcester, Hereford, and Gloucester, preaching, administering the Sacraments, and winning converts from among the gentry. Elizabeth's government stepped up its hunt for Parsons and Campion, and enacted harsh measures against recusants, those protecting priests, and converts to Catholicism. Meanwhile, Parsons set up an underground Catholic press, first at East Ham, Essex, and then at Stonor Park, near Henley. He published works of piety and polemics that were circulated in shops and private homes, and even at court. Parsons published at this time *Brief Censure upon Two Books,* a reply to the government's response to Campion's letter, and *A Brief Discourse Containing Certain Reasons Why Catholics Refuse to Go to Church.* Following Campion's capture in July, Parsons left England for Rouen.

During the winter of 1581–1582, Parsons wrote his *De Persecutione Anglicana* and completed the first part of his *Book of Resolution, or the Christian Directory.* At Eu, near Dieppe, he established a school for English boys, transferring it to St. Omer in 1588. Parsons also began scheming with the duke of Guise and with the supporters of Mary Queen of Scots for Spanish aid and papal support, first for an invasion of England from Scotland led by the duke of Lennox, and then, after Lennox's fall in 1582, for a Spanish invasion of England, led by the duke of Parma. The Scottish Jesuit, William Crichton, the messenger between the duke of Guise and the duke of Lennox, received his instructions from Parsons. During the next three years, Parsons, working closely with William Allen, traveled to Spain, Paris, Rome, and Flanders, organizing support for the invasion of England and tending to the needs of the missionaries. He published *Leicester's Commonwealth* anonymously in 1584, a libel against Elizabeth's favorite, which argued for toleration of Catholics and championed the claim of Mary Queen of Scots to the English throne.

King Philip II and Pope Gregory XIII, however, seemed reluctant to support the "Enterprise of England," by which infiltrating Catholics with outside help would restore Roman Catholicism as the nation's religion. In 1585, Parsons joined Allen in Rome, where the two men tried to persuade the new pope, Sixtus V, to endorse the project. Parsons took his final vows in 1587, and the following year became rector of the English College of Rome. He also helped his friend Allen obtain the red hat. Parsons continued to advise Philip on the proposed invasion, and after the execution of Mary Queen of Scots in 1587, he marshaled arguments in favor of Philip II's claim to the English throne.

In late 1588, at the request of the vicar-general of the Society of Jesus, Parsons traveled to Spain on behalf of the order to discuss with Philip the king's proposed visitations of Jesuit houses. While in Spain, Parsons urged the sending of another armada, but warned that its success depended on a strong Catholic party in England. To strengthen the Jesuit role in the mission, Parsons established, between 1589–1592, two Jesuit seminaries in Spain, St. Albans at Valladolid and St. Gregory's at Seville; and in 1591–1592, he organized at San Lucar, near Seville, and at Madrid, centers for the dispatch of missionaries to England.

In November 1591, Elizabeth's government, by proclamation, condemned Parsons by name for his pro-Spanish activities, and Parsons, under the name Philopater, responded in a pamphlet, *Responsio ad Edictum Elizabethae,* in which he asserted that the power of the pope to depose princes was a doctrine of the faith. Parsons followed in 1594 with his *Conference about the next Succession,* published under the name John Doleman, in which he asserted the right of resistance for subjects in

the cause of true religion, and argued for the claim of the Infanta Isabel to the English throne. In his unpublished "Memorial for the Reformation of England," which was given to the Infanta, Parsons proposed a program to be enacted by Parliament for the restoration of Catholicism in England, including establishment of the Inquisition. These writings angered loyal English Catholics and secular priests as well as Elizabeth I's government.

In 1598, Parsons, resuming his post as rector of the English College of Rome, put down a revolt against the Jesuits. His appointment of George Blackwell as archpriest of the English clergy provoked a long, bitter quarrel with some of the secular priests, including Bagshaw. The priests appealed to the pope, and Parsons treated the appellants who came to Rome with great severity. In 1602, he published his *Brief Apology,* a defense of Archpriest Blackwell, and a harsh denunciation of his critics, entitled *A Manifestation of the Great Folly and Bad Spirit, of Certain in England which Call Themselves Secular Priests.* Although he suffered a defeat in the Archpriest Controversy, Parsons remained influential as prefect of the Jesuit mission and as rector of the English College of Rome; and he continued publishing theological polemics, writing a total of thirty-two works in twenty-nine years. Parsons died in Rome on April 15, 1610. He was buried next to Cardinal Allen in the chapel of the English College.

BIBLIOGRAPHY

Clancy, Thomas H. *Papist Pamphleteers. The Allen-Persons Party and the Political Thought of the Counter Reformation in England, 1572–1615.* 1964.

Hicks. Leo. *Letters and Memorials of Father Robert Persons, S.J., 1578–1588.* Catholic Record Society. Vol. 39. 1942.

———. "The Foundation of the College of St. Omer." *Archivum historicum Societatis Jesu,* vol. 19, pp. 146–180.

———. "Robert Parsons, S.J., and the *Book of Succession.*" *Recusant History,* vol. 4, pp. 104–137.

Pollen, John H. "The Memoirs of Father Robert Persons." In *Miscellanea, II.* Catholic Record Society. Vol. 2. 1906. *Miscellanea, IV.* Vol. 4. 1907.

———. *Annals of the English College, Seville, with an Account of Four other Foundations from 1589 to 1595, an Unfinished Memoir Written by Father Robert Persons, S.J., in 1610.* Catholic Record Society. Vol. 14. 1914.

Reynolds, E.E. *Campion and Parsons: The Jesuit Mission of 1580–81.* 1980.

P

Rowse, Alfred L. "Father Parsons the Jesuit." In *Eminent Elizabethans*. 1983.

Scarisbrick, J.J. "Robert Persons's Plans for the 'True' Reformation England." In *Historical Perspectives: Studies in English Thought and Society in Honour of J.H. Plumb*. Neil McKendrick, ed. 1974.

Taunton, Ethelred. *The History of the Jesuits in England, 1580–1773*. 1901.

John M. Currin

SEE ALSO

Allen, William; Archpriest Controversy; Campion, Edmund; English College of Rome; Jesuits; Phillip II; Recusancy; Supremacy, Oath of

Pastoral

As a theme found in various genres of Renaissance literature, the pastoral flourished in Tudor England. The pastoral may be defined broadly as a literary theme that praises the virtues of country life in various ways: by comparing the simplicity of country life to the complexity of urban life; by comparing the contemplative life, devoted to art and productive leisure to the active life, concerned with everyday human affairs; or by comparing the "natural" world of higher aspiration to the "artificial" world of the city, market, and court. The pastoral often looks backward to a "golden age" of superior values, located somewhere in the near past, as a means to critique the present-day world.

Renaissance pastoral poetry is thus often located in a landscape populated by shepherds and rustics, pipers and singers, and has two major sources. The first is classical Latin literature, particularly the pastoral poetry of Vergil, Ovid, Seneca, and Juvenal. Theocritus is acknowledged as the father of pastoral poetry and was the model for Vergil's pastoral poetry, whose Eclogues were the most influential on Renaissance poetry. The Eclogues, a set of idyllic poems praising country life, draw on Theocritus's poems but deepen their themes, not only describing the country life of shepherds but also reflecting on it and examining its implications.

The second source is Christian literature. The Bible provided a rich mine of pastoral images and themes with specifically Christian connotations, beginning with the Creation in the Old Testament. The Garden of Eden in *Genesis* represented a literal paradise until man fell into sin; in addition, the *Song of Songs* is largely pastoral, as are many of the Psalms. In the New Testament, the image of Christ as the Good Shepherd tending His flock, and as the Paschal Lamb of God, draws on typical pastoral imagery, and the birth of Christ was first witnessed by shepherds as well.

Pastoral was not unknown in the Middle Ages; there are, for example, *pastourelles* written in medieval French, and in England the medieval drama *The Second Shepherd's Play* draws on Christian pastoral. But pastoral in Tudor England was typically based on Italian models, especially those of Baptista Spagnuoli (better known as Mantuan), which were found in Elizabethan schoolbooks. Following classical tradition, pastoral was considered a low form of poetry, inferior to forms such as the epic. However, as George Puttenham observed in his *Arte of English Poesie* (1589), though pastoral was to be written in a low style in accordance with the rules of decorum, it was nevertheless possible to write of great matters through "the veil of homely persons."

Pastoral thrives as a literary theme when society is in the process of being transformed rather than when it has been transformed and the world of the rural past is only a memory. Pastoral appealed to Tudor England because it was a society in transition, becoming a major European power, witnessing the rise of London as a major city, and planting the roots of the later industrial revolution in its mining, weaving, and trading industries; at the same time, the countryside was never far from the average Englishman. In addition, Renaissance explorers discovered human societies in the Americas living in what were considered primitive, more "natural" states than those living in Europe, which further offered the English a means for comparing their own society to one not devoted to commerce, culture, and political power.

At its best, the pastoral is a sophisticated form, written not from the point of view of rustics but rather from that of courtiers and urbanites reflecting on rusticity. Edmund Spenser's *The Shepheardes Calender* (1579), a series of eclogues examining various aspects of the pastoral, was the first important English pastoral poem. It assimilated both rustic language, in keeping with rhetorical decorum, with a sophisticated examination of various values. Spenser's shepherds sometimes speak rustically, sometimes poetically, suggesting that any number of identities could be located in the pastoral. This feature of the pastoral as a masquerade—a place where one could find oneself by becoming assuming the persona of somebody else—figures prominently in the literature of recreation, literally to the Renaissance mind "re-creation," a place where one is "re-created." This theme permeates *The Shepheardes Calender* and various books of Spenser's epic, *The Faerie*

P

Queene, as well as such William Shakespeare plays as *As You Like It, Cymbeline, The Winter's Tale;* Sir Philip Sidney's prose romance *Arcadia;* and various court masques and other pastoral dramas.

The pastoral offered English Renaissance poets various other issues to explore. One would be what the Tudors might have called "the good life" or *otium,* the state of content espoused in classical poetry. The vision of a perfect, or at least perfectible, society was often set in a mythical Arcadia (the name is derived from Vergil), which represented humankind's highest potential, to which one could retreat for recreation. The pastoral offered a world where active ambition, as found in Christopher Marlowe's *Tamburlaine* and *Doctor Faustus,* for example, was shunned in favor of the contemplative life.

Because pastoral offers a retreat from the world of human affairs, romantic love can be explored in Arcadia, as it is in Sidney's *Arcadia;* Shakespeare's romantic comedies, as well as his narrative poem *Venus and Adonis;* Marlowe's *Hero and Leander;* and hundreds of love lyrics by greater and lesser poets, Marlowe's and Sir Walter Ralegh's lyric exchange between the nymph and the shepherd being but one example. Other poetic forms of the English Renaissance are related to the pastoral: the blazon, a cataloging of a woman's beauties, is often unsophisticated, befitting a shepherd rather than a courtier; and the *carpe diem* poem has been interpreted as the poet's attempt to enjoy his "natural" instincts, free from the artifice of the social world.

Perhaps the major issue that pastoral can raise is this conflict between Art and Nature, usually framed as the conflict between the "artificial" modern world and the more "natural" rustic world. The relationship between Art and Nature is complex in pastoral. Some works advocate the superiority of Nature over Art, especially when comparing it to the corruption found in the city and the court, often interpreted in the Christian tradition as the state from which man has fallen. At the same time, human nature could be perfected by such arts as law and education, so that Art could improve human nature.

A final theme is the pastoral as the place where a poet discovers and refines his poetic vocation. Vergil considered the pastoral the first step in a poet's vocation, the highest being the epic, as he moved toward self-discovery by means of his poetic discipline. This theme permeates Sidney's *Arcadia,* for example, as the work serves in part as the means for Sidney to explore his ideas about English versification. Furthermore, Arcadia could function as a place to test one's engagement and vocation (poetic and otherwise) in the world, in order to return eventually to

October, from Edmund Spenser, *The Shepheardes Calendar* (1579). Reproduced from the original by permission of the Henry E. Huntington Library and Art Gallery.

the real world, as do the courtiers of Arcadia, those in Shakespeare's comedies, and many of the characters in *The Faerie Queene.*

Tudor pastoral set the stage for later English pastoral poetry, especially poetry drawing on the Christian pastoral tradition. Seventeenth-century devotional poets who drew on the pastoral in their lyrics include John Donne, George Herbert, Thomas Traherne, Henry Vaughan, Andrew Marvell, and, of course, John Milton, especially in such works as *Comus* and his epic of the fall of man, *Paradise Lost.*

BIBLIOGRAPHY

Barrell, John, and John Bull, eds. *The Penguin Book of English Pastoral Verse.* 1982.
Kermode, Frank, ed. *English Pastoral Poetry.* 1972.
Marinelli, Peter. *Pastoral.* 1971.
Smith, Hallett. *Elizabethan Poetry.* 1968.

Robert Kellerman

P

Patents
See Monopolies

Patronage

Patronage was a system by which a wealthy or powerful individual (the patron) afforded protection, support, or a livelihood to a talented but socially inferior member of society. In return the patron received a combination of service and loyalty. In a hierarchical society patronage was a basic mechanism for harnessing the abilities of those born outside the social elite. It was thus an extremely flexible system permeating most areas of life in Tudor England, but its influence over politics, the arts, and the church merit the most attention.

The monarch and his or her immediate family were usually the most important patrons as they possessed the greatest wealth, and were held in the highest prestige. Their immediate associates and the wider court circle were also in a position to be powerful patrons at a national level. Across the country, aristocratic households and urban elites also exercised a patronal function, albeit on a smaller scale. The success of the Tudors in establishing the monarchy in a more powerful position than had their late-medieval forebears greatly increased the importance of royal patronage. As the royal court grew in size and importance during the sixteenth century, it became the most important focus for patronage in England. The monarch alone had the wealth to commission large-scale building works, and the prestige to attract famous continental artists.

Traditionally, Henry VIII has been seen as the greatest patron of the arts among the Tudor monarchs. His expenditure on palaces was prodigious and he attracted the painter Hans Holbein to his court. Nevertheless, it has been shown that Henry VII was the first monarch to appoint a royal librarian, the first to appoint a king's painter, and the first to retain a troupe of actors, the King's Players. His granddaughter, Elizabeth I, was a very different sort of royal patron. Her reign is usually remembered for its literary achievements, rather than architectural or artistic triumphs. Royal patronage, however,

played only a small part in this. Writers such as Sir Philip Sidney, Edmund Spenser, and William Shakespeare all began their careers supported by other patrons. Spenser received little reward for his epic *The Faerie Queene* although it extolled the queen. Even Sir Walter Ralegh's *Ocean to Cynthia* appears to have been written to regain lost favor.

Patronage of the arts became increasingly important in the Tudor period. The greatest stimulus was the assimilation of artistic sensibility into notions of gentility. Though not unknown in the medieval period it became more acceptable—and ultimately essential—for a gentleman or aristocrat to appreciate the visual arts, along with prose, poetry, and plays. The princely courts of Renaissance Italy were an important influence in this respect. Though some members of the nobility and gentry participated as writers, particularly of poetry, most kept their interest at arm's length, and functioned as consumers, or if they could afford it or were sufficiently interested, as patrons. Robert Dudley, the earl of Leicester, was a notable patron in this capacity during the first half of the reign of Elizabeth I. This new interest in artistic activity among the elite developed alongside an increasingly sophisticated concept of the creative importance of the individual. Emanating from Renaissance Italy, this idea increasingly led to painters, sculptors, architects, writers, and dramatists becoming famous in their own right. This development altered the relationship between patrons and artists. Thus by the end of the sixteenth century, dramatists such as Shakespeare worked within companies of players nominally under the patronage of great noblemen or court figures, but in reality no longer dependent on their patrons in any practical sense.

Patronage in politics, on the other hand, was as important at the end of the Tudor period as it had been in 1485. Tudor monarchs often placed well-educated but low-born individuals in important administrative roles. Without any formal system of examinations, appointees to such posts were chosen on the basis of their reputation and the favor they enjoyed. Thomas Wolsey was perhaps the most spectacular example of the way in which royal patronage could pluck a talented individual from an obscure and poverty-stricken background and raise him to become the king's greatest minister. He in turn sponsored the early career of Thomas Cromwell. This exercise of royal patronage could irritate the nobility, who saw themselves as the monarch's natural councilors. The rise of Wolsey and Cromwell provoked discontent, while the importance of the low-born William Cecil was cited as a grievance by the rebellious earls of Northumberland and Westmorland in 1569. Royal patronage could also provoke discontent in other ways. Robert Devereux, earl of Essex, discovered that the withdrawal of royal favor in the aftermath of his failed lord lieutenancy in Ireland in 1600 left him unable to divert royal patronage to reward his own supporters.

Royal or court patronage could be important in the career of any cleric, but in the religious sphere patronage also had a wider impact. Perhaps the most widespread type of patronage in Tudor England was lay control of presentations to clerical livings. This right (the advowson) was considered a form of property and could be sold, bequeathed, or given away. Such rights had existed for centuries, but during the Henrician Reformation many more advowsons were dispersed to the laity along with other monastic property. Lay patronage aroused considerable hostility among those dissatisfied with the pace of religious reform. The slow spread of an educated preaching clergy could be blamed on the failings of lay patrons. Outside the mainstream, lay patronage was an outrage to Presbyterians such as Thomas Cartwright, and separatists such as Henry Barrow. Anglican apologists had no answer to their critics' main charge that there was no scriptural precedent for lay patronage. They could, however, counter that there was likewise no support for an elected clergy. The twin threats of clerical tyranny and social upheaval were more frequently highlighted. In this sphere, more than any other, an attack on the established system of patronage was an attack on the social hierarchy, and thus, despite attempts at reform, the system endured into the seventeenth century.

Although not neglected, historians have generally devoted far more attention to the workings and effects of patronage in Stuart England than they have in the Tudor period. Nevertheless, Henry VIII's role in importing Renaissance ideas into England has attracted attention. More concerted interest has been expressed in literary patronage in Elizabethan England, as scholars have sought to understand the pressures acting on poets and dramatists later in the reign.

BIBLIOGRAPHY
Briggs, J. *This Stage-Play World. English Literature and Its Background, 1580–1625.* 1983.
Fox, A. *Politics and Literature in the Reigns of Henry VII and Henry VIII.* 1989.
Lytle, G.F., and Orgel, S., eds. *Patronage in the Renaissance.* 1981.

Jason W.R. Dorsett

SEE ALSO
Barrow, Henry; Cartwright, Thomas; Cecil, Robert; Court; Cromwell, Thomas; Devereux, Robert; Dudley, Robert; Elizabeth I; Henry VII; Henry VIII; Holbein, Hans; Social Classes; Wolsey, Thomas

Paul's Cross Sermons

Paul's Cross, outside St. Paul's Cathedral in London, was a public place for preaching during much of the sixteenth and seventeenth centuries. Sermons were preached there every week on Sunday mornings, and were, in effect, government pronouncements. The preachers were carefully chosen by the bishop of London or by another state official, and the bishop was held responsible for the content of the sermons preached. Many preachers were virtually told in advance what to say, and great care was taken to ensure that no unsound views would be heard. Queen Elizabeth I took a close interest in Paul's Cross; toward the end of her reign, she often vetoed suggested preachers who would have been too radical for her tastes.

Paul's Cross sermons were frequently printed and circulated around the country, where they were often preached again by local clergymen. It was even possible for new directions in theology to be voiced at Paul's Cross for the first time, as when Richard Bancroft asserted the divine right of episcopacy against the rising tide of Puritanism (1589). When royal authority collapsed in London in 1642, Parliament granted the lord mayor and aldermen of the city the right to appoint preachers. But by then preaching was no longer controlled anywhere, and the importance of Paul's Cross rapidly declined. After the Restoration in 1660, it ceased to be used for preaching altogether.

BIBLIOGRAPHY
Maclure, M. *The Paul's Cross Sermons, 1534–1642.* 1958.
Gerald Bray

SEE ALSO
Bancroft, Richard; Puritanism; Sermons; St. Paul's Cathedral

Paulet, William, First Marquis of Winchester (d. 1572)

Probably born in the early 1480s, the eldest son of a Hampshire gentleman, William Paulet served three times as sheriff of Hampshire, but his main career was as one of

P

the monarchs' men of finance at court. He found favor with four successive Tudors, which he allegedly explained in old age by claiming he sprang from the willow, not the oak. Under Henry VIII, he was first master of the wards with Thomas Englefield from 1526, later controller and then briefly treasurer of the royal household, and finally chamberlain and great master under Edward VI until late 1549 when—following John Dudley, earl of Northumberland's coup—he became lord treasurer, a position he held during the reigns of Mary I and Elizabeth I. Although he has no reputation as a soldier, Paulet was involved with the raising, management, and victualling of nearly every English army and navy between 1540 and 1572. He had a special interest in the borders with Scotland and in the Isle of Wight, which he appears to have attempted to make into a family fief with extensive powers to levy musters, appoint officers, repair castles, and take timber. In 1551, he was created marquis of Winchester.

Winchester had strong, traditional views about royal financial management and was deeply opposed to farming the customs or other revenue sources, which brought him into conflict with other members of the Privy Council as well as the king. His relationship with Northumberland in Edward VI's reign was strained; despite his Catholic sympathies, his relationship with Mary I was not cordial, and although, under Elizabeth I, he had a good working relationship with William Cecil, their policies were very different. As Lord Treasurer, Winchester was never named to the commissions on financial matters that Edward, Mary, and Elizabeth set up to deal with individual problems, and his hostility to some of the reports they produced prevented their implementation.

Winchester had close relationships with the principal London merchants who handled the sensitive business of overseas loans and transfers. Although notionally in charge of the Exchequer and the considerable patronage within it, he had no specific functions and frequently had difficulty in obliging his subordinates, who held tenured positions, to obey his orders. Thus he had a long-running feud with Sir John Baker (d. 1558), the under-treasurer. He was nevertheless active in many different areas as a matter of policy, such as his concerns over crown land revenue. On occasion he evidently undertook more than he had warrant for, which may explain the large sum for which he had to account to the queen in 1568. Nevertheless, his long familiarity with the complex management of revenue and expenditure accounts made him invaluable to the crown as a skilled manipulator of inadequate resources in times of war, and he remained lord treasurer until his death in 1572.

BIBLIOGRAPHY

Calendar of State Papers, Domestic. Vols. 10, 11, 12, 46.

Dietz, F.C. *English Public Finance, 1485–1641.* 2nd edition. 2 vols. 1921, 1932; repr. 1964.

———. *The Exchequer in Elizabeth's Reign.* Smith College Studies in History. Vol. 8, no. 2. 1923.

Ramsay, G.D. *The City of London in International Politics at the Accession of Elizabeth Tudor.* 1975.

Sybil M. Jack

SEE ALSO

Cecil, William; Exchequer; Government, Central Administration of; Money, Inflation, and Moneylending; Wards, Court of

Pedlars

Pedlars, or "petty chapmen," were ubiquitous in premodern societies such as Tudor England and played important roles in western economies until recent times. In the late Middle Ages they were numerous, selling caps, cutlasses, girdles, gloves, musical instruments, pewter pots, purses, and vests. In the Tudor period they mainly sold haberdashery such as the things carried by the petty-chapman Autolycus in *The Winter's Tale*—tape, lace, silk, thread, "toys for your head." In the early modern era they were just one element in a large army of migrating workers that included apprentices, a great variety of artisans, domestic and farm servants, entertainers, harvesters, healers, and sailors and soldiers.

During the medieval period, pedlars were largely unregulated, but during the sixteenth century they, along with many other itinerant trades, were criminalized in vagrancy legislation. In 1547, Parliament passed an act ordering petty-chapmen to be licensed by two justices of the peace and to be restricted to limited, agreed routes. The statute took a negative view of pedlars, describing them as "more hurtful than necessary to the common wealth," and a similar line was taken in legislation of 1572 and 1597, which listed unlicensed petty-chapmen among vagrants to be punished. The Tudor authorities abhorred petty-chapmen because they threatened local guild monopolies, but also because, like vagabonds, they lived in virtual perpetual motion, a way of life perceived to foster crime and sedition. How far the detailed provisions of the 1547 statute were enforced remains questionable, and in any case it was repealed in 1604. Pedlars were arrested as vagrants, but their numbers probably increased both absolutely and relatively in the itinerant workforce. In the

P

Tudor period they accounted for one in fourteen of vagrants whose occupations were known, but under the early Stuarts the proportion was almost one in ten.

Despite their low standing with the authorities, pedlars varied greatly in wealth, conducted business with all ranks of society, and had a significant impact on the economy. Some petty-chapmen were possibly well-off, such as a Lichfield dealer who in 1577 carried a gross of lace and 5,000 pins and claimed he had £8 in a purse when it was stolen at a Chester fair. Others were little more than miserable beggars, selling small quantities of thread and ribbons, which purchasers bought out of guilt or to rid themselves of the importunate vendor. Petty-chapmen hawked their goods to all social classes. Some reported sales at gentry country houses. In the Stuart period their trading bolstered the expansion of commercially produced clothing into the countryside in what has been termed the "great reclothing of rural England." For all their alleged faults, it seems that pedlars actually played a part in advancing English capitalism.

BIBLIOGRAPHY

Beier, A.L. *Masterless Men: the Vagrancy Problem in England, 1560–1640.* 1985; repr. 1987.

Jusserand, J.J. *English Wayfaring Life in the Middle Ages.* 1889; repr. 1961.

Spufford, Margaret. *The Great Reclothing of Rural England. Petty Chapmen and their Wares in the Seventeenth Century.* 1984.

A.L. Beier

SEE ALSO

Cloth Trade; Crime; Monopolies; Vagrants

Peele, George (1556–1596)

Born in London, George Peele was the son of James Peele, a citizen of London and for many years clerk of Christ's Hospital. George attended Christ's Hospital school from 1565 to 1570. In 1571, he entered Broadgates Hall (later Pembroke College), Oxford, but received his B.A. from Christ Church in 1577 and his M.A. in 1579. Peele was a proper "university wit," well known as a poet and translator of Greek plays, although none of the translations have survived. In 1580, he married Ann Christian, daughter of an Oxford merchant, and thanks to her dowry came into a considerable sum of money. He moved to London in 1581, but returned to Oxford in 1583 to assist in the production of William Gager's comedy *Rivales* and his tragedy

Dido. Peele seems to have acted as well, whether for a living is not certain. Thomas Dekker in *A Knight's Conjuring* (1607) presents him as a companion of Christopher Marlowe and Robert Greene. Some of his poems were included in popular anthologies such as *The Phoenix Nest* (1593), *England's Helicon,* and *England's Parnassus* (both 1600). His reputation was not sufficient, however, to save him from having to write commendatory verses to attract financial support from aristocratic patrons. Toward the end of his life when his career had waned and he was virtually starving, he used his poem "Tale of Troy," probably written while at Oxford between 1579 and 1581, to ask Burghley, then Lord Treasurer, for money.

Peele's earliest play, *The Arraygnement of Paris,* was published in 1584, but performed probably in 1583 during the Christmas revels. It needed a relatively large cast of at least fourteen to fifteen characters. Peele was identified as its author by Thomas Nashe in his letter "To the Gentlemen Students," serving as preface to Greene's *Menaphon* (1589). Peele had first used the familiar classical and medieval material relating to Paris's choice and the story of Troy, including the *Iliad,* the *Aeneid,* and, especially, Ovid's *Heroides* and *Metamorphoses,* Apuleius's *Golden Ass,* Chaucer's *Troilus and Criseyde,* and William Caxton's *Recuyell of the Historyes of Troye* for his poem. Peele integrates the heterogeneous elements into the unified plot of a sophisticated pastoral comedy of ideas that provides an accomplished example of court entertainment. By turning the fifth act into a compliment to the queen, he gives the play an outcome that relieves him from the necessity of following the tragic end of the story of Troy.

Perhaps the most accomplished and structurally the most complex of Peele's plays, *The Old Wives Tale* (1593?), exhibits a frame-like structure, moving from Madge's narrative to scenic representation. Much like the *Araygnement of Paris,* Peele combines motifs and themes from folktales, legends, and romances (such as Greene's *Orlando Furioso* and Apuleius's *Golden Ass*) in interlinking episodes into a drama in which the world of the imagination and enchantment constantly overlap with that of reason and reality. Balanced opposites form the structural principle of the play in terms of character, social hierarchy, and plot development, and display Peele's sympathetic wit as well as his satirical sharpness.

In *The Battle of Alcazar* (1594), which may not have come down in its original form, Peele is dramatically innovative. He introduces a presenter or narrator, an epic device to structure material about the conflict between Portugal and Spain over the succession to the throne, an

P

issue of great popular interest in view of the aged Elizabeth I. The play also draws on popular English antipathy toward Spain. The epic narrator allows Peele to unite the complex plot movement. He evades the linear structure of *Tamburlaine* but follows that play in its exotic setting, its high rhetoric, and the use of Senecan revenge motifs and dumb shows.

Edward I was probably acted under the name *Longshanks* after it was printed in 1593. Even more than Peele's other dramatic works, *Edward I* encompasses a variety of actions and episodes, including the chronicle material relating to Edward and the Welsh and Scottish rebellions, the unhistorical Queen Elinor, and the Robin Hood story. The play was a commercial success due to its portrait of a model king, and to the use of violence and deceit as the common means of politics.

The relationship between the private and public lives of the anointed monarch, as well as the question of succession, are the topics of *The Love of King David and Fair Bethsabe* (1599), Peele's only dramatic handling of a religious topic. Here he turns the subject of David into an indirect defense of poetry, pointing out the dignity of his own calling in the epic opening of the play.

Peele's verse pamphlet and pageants show him at his most eager to please his aristocratic patrons. *Polyhymnia* (1590) provides a description of tilting on the occasion of the earl of Cumberland's taking office from Sir Henry Lee and includes an interesting reference to the earl of Essex as Sir Philip Sidney's successor. Following the culture of royal praise, encouraged by Elizabeth to keep the country at peace and her rule secure, Peele weaves the conventional image of the queen as Astreea into his pageant *Descensus Astreeae* (1591), as well as *Anglorum Feriae, Englandes Hollydayes* (1595?). He does so with great rhetorical skill, a feature of all his work that was parodied by his contemporaries but can compare with Marlowe's high rhetoric. Only in comparison to William Shakespeare does he look like a "silver poet." Despite his reputation, Peele died in 1596, ill and impoverished, leaving an oeuvre of court and popular plays, pageants, and poetry whose formal variety obviously appealed to a varied audience.

BIBLIOGRAPHY

Berek, Peter. "Tamburlaine's Weak Sons: Imitation as Interpretation before 1593." *Renaissance Drama,* vol. 13, pp. 55–82.

Braunmuller, A.R. *George Peele.* Twayne English Authors. 1983.

Cheffaud, P.H. *George Peele.* 1913.

Peele, George. *The Old Wive's Tale.* Patricia Binnie, ed. Revel's Plays. 1980.

Prouty, Charles Tyler, ed. *The Life and Works of George Peele.* 3 vols. 1952–1970.

Purcell, Sally, ed. *George Peele.* 1972.

Lothar Cerny

SEE ALSO

Dekker, Thomas; Gager, William; Greene, Robert; Marlowe, Christopher; Spanish Literature, Influence of

Peerage

See Knighthood; Social Classes

Penry, John (1559–1593)

Born in Brecknockshire, Wales, in 1559, John Penry entered Peterhouse, Cambridge, in 1580. While at Cambridge he became an extreme Puritan, and when he went to Oxford in 1586, he refused to be ordained. He was an accomplished preacher in Welsh as well as in English, and in 1586, he sent a petition to the Elizabeth I and Parliament, asking for further reform of the Welsh Church. His increasing political activity led him into publishing, and in 1588, he purchased the printing press on which the famous Marprelate Tracts were to be printed. Penry was undoubtedly closely connected with these tracts, and they certainly reflected his views, though whether he actually wrote any of them has never been established.

In the hunt for the authors of the tracts, Penry inevitably came under suspicion, and on January 29, 1590, his house was searched. Nothing incriminating was found, but he found it advisable to escape to Scotland, where he was well received. In September 1592, he returned to London, where he lived incognito for many months. Eventually he was spotted and arrested on March 22, 1593. He was tried for treason and sentenced to death, even though he pleaded his innocence and loyalty to the queen. For a time it seemed as if he might be pardoned, but on May 29, 1593, he was suddenly executed. To the end of his days he remained a passionate advocate of Welsh Church reform, and later generations of Welsh nonconformists regarded him as their founding father.

BIBLIOGRAPHY

Collinson, P. *The Elizabethan Puritan Movement.* 1967.

Gerald Bray

P

SEE ALSO
Marprelate Controversy, Puritanism

Percy Family

The Percys of Northumberland were one one England's most prominent families, notable especially for their influence in the North and the frequency with which they rebelled against the established government. Their memorialization in William Shakespeare's history plays, particularly through the character of Hotspur (Sir Henry Percy, 1364–1403), has made their participation in the Wars of the Roses legendary.

Henry Percy (sixth earl) led a short life daunted by misfortune. He began as a page in Thomas Wolsey's household and subsequently accrued a series of honors. Yet he was ill, burdened with debt, and was in constant disgreement with his wife (Mary Talbot, daughter of the fourth earl of Shrewsbury), who finally returned to her family. The marriage was probably doomed from the beginning. As a young man Percy fell desperately in love with (the as yet unattached) Anne Boleyn. Their liaison was severed by Wolsey, but their attachment was to last a lifetime. Ironically, perhaps, Percy was one of the peers who signed a letter encouraging the pope to hurry Henry VIII's divorce from Katherine of Aragon; and in 1536, he was one of those present in court for Anne Boleyn's trial. When he saw her he became ill and had to leave the room. During the proceedings Anne claimed that she and Percy, while young, had entered into a nuptial precontract, a factor that she hoped would save her life and her daughter's. Percy allowed the claim even though it was probably false. When he died he was without issue, and the title passed to his nephew, Thomas.

Henry Percy (eighth earl) was the son of Thomas Percy (seventh earl), who was executed as a chief actor in the Northern Rebellion. His early career was distinguished by military service in the Scots border wars and in France. During the Northern Rebellion (1569) he joined the royal forces and fought against his brother. For this he gained Elizabeth I's favor; however, family tradition reasserted itself when Percy decided, in 1571, to become a servant of Mary Queen of Scots. He was arrested and sent to the Tower where he was subsequently imprisoned twice more, for various treasonable offenses. He died in the Tower on June 21, 1585, having been shot through the heart. Catholics claimed that he had been murdered, and for some time rumors circulated that Sir Christopher Hatton had contrived the death.

The best-known member of the Percy family during the late sixteenth century was Henry Percy, ninth earl of Northumberland, dubbed "The Wizard Earl" for his interests in science. He was educated in the Protestant faith and traveled to the Continent where he became friendly with Charles Paget, the agent of Mary Queen of Scots; however, he defended this assocation strongly, alleging that religion did not enter into their discussions. During this period Northumberland read widely in continental literature, purchased art, and took up interests in alchemy and astrology. Among other items he purchased a crystal globe. Military accomplishments followed when Northumberland served under the earl of Leicester in the Low Countries, and later in the fleet that defeated the Spanish Armada. He was installed as a knight of the garter, carried the insignia of the garter to Henry IV of France (1596), and was nominated a general of the army (1599).

Two minor members of the Percy family greatly influenced the fate of the ninth earl. Dorothy (Devereux) Percy (1564/5–1619) was the sister of Robert Devereux, second earl of Essex and of Penelope Rich. Dorothy first eloped with Sir Thomas Perrot, which infuriated the queen; then, upon his death, she married the ninth earl of Northumberland, with whom she was periodically incompatible. She was a staunch supporter of James VI's succession, on one occasion declaring that she would "eat the hearts" of his opponents "in salt."

Thomas Percy, a distant relation of the ninth earl, played an indeterminate role in aiding the conspiracy that led to the Gunpowder Plot (1605). Possibly he served as a double agent. It was information provided to Robert Cecil by Percy that led to Cecil's allegation that the ninth earl was the leader of the conspirators. For these allegations, Northumberland was sent to the Tower for fifteen years, during which time he gathered around him various mathematicians, astrologers, and alchemists, as well as an impressive library. Finally he was released in 1621. He returned to his estate at Petworth where he died and was buried in the church. His portrait was painted by Van Dyck.

BIBLIOGRAPHY

Batho, G.R., ed. *Household Papers of Henry Percy, Ninth Earl of Northumberland.* Royal Historical Society. 1962.

Broce, Gerald, and Richard M. Wunderli. "The Funeral of Henry Percy, Sixth Earl of Northumberland." *Albion,* vol. 22, pp. 199–215.

P

Clucas, Stephan. "'Noble Virtue in Extremes': Henry Percy, Ninth Earl of Northumberland, Patronage and the Politics of Stoic Consolation." *Renaissance Studies,* vol. 9, pp. 267–291.

Davies, Kathleen M. *Henry Percy and Henry VIII.* 1967.

Gunn, S.J. "Henry Percy, Sixth Earl of Northumberland, and the Fall of the House of Percy, 1527–1537." In *The Tudor Nobility.* G.W. Bernard, ed. 1992.

Massa, Daniel. "Giordano Bruno's Ideas in Seventeenth-Century England." *Journal of the History of Ideas,* vol. 38, pp. 227–242.

Nicholls, Mark. "The 'Wizard Earl' in Star Chamber: The Trial of the Earl of Northumberland, June, 1606." *Historical Journal,* vol. 30, pp. 173–189.

Peacock, John. "The 'Wizard Earl' Portrayed by Hilliard and Van Dyck." *Art History,* vol. 8, pp. 139–157.

Pollard, Anthony. "Percies, Nevilles, and the Wars of the Roses." *History Today,* vol. 43, pp. 42–48.

Ricci, Saverio. "Giordano Bruno e il 'Northumberland Circle', 1600–1630." *Rinascimento,* vol. 25, pp. 335–355.

Stedman, Douglas C. *The Percies of Northumberland.* 1913.

S.P. Cerasano

SEE ALSO

Boleyn, Anne; Armada, Spanish; Hatton, Christopher; Mary Queen of Scots; Northern Rebellion; Wars of the Roses

Perkins, William (1558–1602)

One of the leading divines and greatest preachers of the Elizabethan era, William Perkins was born in 1558 at Marston Jabbett in the parish of Bulkington in Warwickshire. In 1577, he matriculated at Christ's College, Cambridge, where he came under the influence of the Puritan and Ramist Laurence Chaderton. He was suddenly converted one day from his notorious recklessness and drunkenness by hearing a woman in the street allude to him as "drunken Perkins" and hold him up as a figure of terror to her recalcitrant child. In 1584, he commenced M.A. and was elected a fellow of his college, a position he held until 1594. He was appointed lecturer at Great St. Andrews, where members of the university and the townspeople came in great numbers to hear him. From this pulpit he helped to mold a generation of Cambridge students with his Puritan principles. He preached an experiential religion that addressed not only the intellect but the whole person, including the affections of his hearers. In a sermon delivered in January 1586/87 in his college chapel, Perkins attacked kneeling at communion and facing toward the east as Romanist. Cited by the vice-chancellor and other university officials, he was required to qualify some of his reported remarks while retracting others. He seems thereafter to have used more cautious language in his public discourses. Nevetheless, he had been and remained throughout his life moderate in his Puritanism. Whether he disapproved of subscription is doubtful; according to Thomas Fuller he generally evaded the question. Although he repeatedly called for further reformation of the church, and in spite of his uneasiness over what he regarded as superstitious and idolatrous remnants of Roman ceremonies in the ritual of the English Church, he condoned the church as less than perfect. He distinctly taught that separatists were "far from the spirit of Christ and his Apostles." He died in 1602.

Perkins's reputation as a theologian grew in tandem with his fame as a preacher. As a high Calvinist, especially in his doctrine of predestination, he took pains to attack what he perceived as Roman Pelagianism and Protestant Arminianism. He was one of the earliest Reformed theologians to develop the concept of covenant as a systematizing principle of his theology, and he was among the first and most important of the Protestant English casuists, who wrote on "Cases of Conscience." His works, published in numerous editions and translated into many languages, were held in the highest repute by theologians with Calvinist sympathies, making him the most widely read of all English divines during the late sixteenth and seventeenth centuries.

BIBLIOGRAPHY

Breward, I. "The Significance of William Perkins." *Journal of Religious History,* 1966, pp. 113–128.

Perkins, William. *Opera.* 3 vols. 1612–1613.

Porter, H.C. *Reformation and Reaction in Tudor Cambridge.* 1958.

Lee W. Gibbs

SEE ALSO

Arminianism; Calvinism; Puritanism; Reformation, English; Sermons

Persons, Robert

See Parsons, Robert

Petrarchanism

Petrarchanism, also known as Petrarchism, is a literary term to describe the pervasive influence of the vernacular poetry of Francesco Petrarca (1304–1374) on European poetry and painting from 1400–1700. Although Petrarch wrote prolifically in Latin, including an unfinished epic, *Africa*, it is his two works in Italian that changed the whole course of European lyric poetry. The *Canzoniere*, or *Rime sparse*, was the first sonnet sequence proper, and the *Trionfi*, six narrative poems in the *terza rima* meter of Dante's *Commedia*, were based on the Roman military triumph, a literary appropriation already exploited by Ovid in *Amores,* I.ii. The *Canzoniere* and the *Trionfi* were often printed together in early editions, as well as in the manuscript tradition; Petrarch may have considered them a single work.

Both poems tell the same story of Petrarch's falling in love on April 6, 1327, with a woman called Laura, who did not respond to his love and who died on the same day—April 6, 1348. Petrarch continued to write poetry to her until the last years of his life. We are uncertain about the existence and the identity of Laura, but it has been suggested that she was a Laura de Noves, a married woman who lived in Avignon, the mother of eleven children, at the same time that Petrarch was attached to the papal court, then resident in Avignon.

The *Canzoniere* tells the story in a series of 366 poems, 317 of them sonnets, interposed with *canzoni, ballate, madrigali,* and *sestine.* The *Trionfi* tell the story as a series of triumphs, beginning with the Triumph of Love (Petrarch becomes a victim of the god of love), followed by the Triumph of Chastity (Laura's rejection of his love), followed by the Triumph of Death (Laura's), followed by the Triumphs of Fame, of Time, and of Eternity, each succeeding triumph canceling out the preceding victory. The paradigm of these triumphs is nothing more than the conventional eschatology of fourteenth-century Christian morality and suggests that the *Canzoniere* should also be considered under the same rubric.

However we interpret the *Canzoniere* and the *Trionfi*, there can be no question that they were the formative influence on lyric poetry of the Renaissance. In Italy they were immediately taken up as models of the purity of the Tuscan tongue; the most important theoretician of this argument was Pietro Bembo (1470–1547), in his *Prose della volgar lingua* (1525), who gave the crown to Petrarch over Dante and Boccaccio.

What we now call Petrarchanism is a fabrication of literary historians, who draw together the sources for both Dante and Petrarch by concocting a school of poetics, called the *dolce stil nuovo,* a literary term derived from Dante's *Purgatorio,* 24.57ff., where the poet Bonagiunta Orbicciani da Lucca praises Dante for the first *canzone* in *La vita Nuova* ("Donne ch'avete intelletto d'amore"), citing its sweetness and its newness as the qualities that separate Dante from Bonagiunta and his predecessors Guittone d'Arezzo and the originator of the sonnet, Giacomo da Lentino. Petrarch concocts a literary heritage for himself in *Canzoniere* 70, in which each of the five stanzas ends with the first line of an earlier poet—Arnaut Daniel (?), Guido Cavalcanti, Dante, Cino da Pistoia—and the first line of Petrarch's own first *canzone,* "Nel dolce tempo de la prima etade." What unites all these poets, whether there was a "school" or not, is love as the subject of their poetry, the glorification of a woman as the object of their poetry, with the final end of winning her sexually. What sets Dante and Petrarch apart from the earlier poets is their unremitting tenacity in besieging their Beatrice and Laura even beyond death; they push the conventions of what used to be called "courtly love" to its philosophical limits: the conflict of human desire with divine love. Dante and Petrarch transform their desire into a new apprehension of what the loved object is and hence resolve the conflict. The earlier poets merely suffer and write beautifully about their sufferings at the hands of the tyrant, the cruel fair, although they too are probably writing within the same ironic tradition.

Critics in general read the "narrative" of the *Canzoniere* through the lens of nineteenth-century romanticism, giving sympathy to the sad plight of a poet-lover in pursuit of an unavailable love, although he may have wanted his reader to perceive a distance between the outpourings of his fictive self and his own intentions. Nevertheless, the essence of Petrarchanism is the analysis of human desire, its objects, and its ends. That the sonnet sequences do not end with success for the poet-lover is less important for the reader than that we understand the inappropriateness of his pursuit and his illogical idolatry.

Petrarchanism has often been identified with the *blazon,* a short poem enumerating and praising the physical attributes of the lady—the hair, the eyes, the nose, the mouth, the breasts—but in point of fact, Petrarch never wrote such a poem, although the possibilities of creating such a pastiche existed in Petrarch. The *blason* had its origin with Clement Marot's *Blason du beau tetin,* which initiated a vogue that resulted in an anthology, *Blaisons anatomiques du corps feminin* (1536). The *blason* could be either encomiastic or satiric. Examples in English are Edmund Spenser's *Amoretti,* 7 and 15 (encomiastic), and

P

William Shakespeare's Sonnet 130 (satiric). It is a mistake to call Shakespeare's sonnet "anti-Petrarchan" because it merely uses devices evident in Petrarch and formalized by the French for comic effect.

More central to the concept of Petrarchanism is the elaboration of "contrarieties" such as *burning* and *freezing* to depict the plight of the poet-lover. These are given in abundance in Petrarch 134: *Pace non trovo,* which was endlessly imitated by most later sonneteers. All of the outpourings of praise or blame for a lady by all the lovesick poets of the Renaissance can be justly called Petrarchan, which goes far to justify Byron's wicked epithet for Petrarch as "the Platonic pimp of all posterity."

BIBLIOGRAPHY

Forster, Leonard. *The Icy Fire: Five Studies in European Petrarchism.* 1969.

Greene, Roland. *Post-Petrarchism: Origins and Innovations of the Western Lyric Sequence.* 1991.

Greene, Thomas M. *The Light in Troy: Imitation and Discovery in Renaissance Poetry.* 1982.

Roche, Thomas P., Jr. *Petrarch and the English Sonnet Sequences.* 1989.

Watson, George. *The English Petrarchists: A Critical Bibliography of the "Canzoniere."* 1967.

Wilkins, Ernest Hatch. "A General Survey of Renaissance Petrarchism." In *Studies in the Life and Works of Petrarch.* 1955.

————. *The Invention of the Sonnet and other Studies in Italian Literature.* 1959.

Thomas P. Roche

SEE ALSO

Italian Literature, Influence of; Literary Criticism; Lyric; Shakespeare, William; Spenser, Edmund

Pettie, George (1548–1589)

The fourth child of a prominent Oxfordshire family, George Pettie matriculated at Christ Church, Oxford, in 1564, graduated with a B.A. in 1569, and spent several subsequent years abroad traveling and serving a military stint. After returning to England, he published *A Petite Pallace of Pettie his Pleasure* (1576), a title given by his publisher, Richard Watkins, perhaps to suggest its debt to William Painter's *Palace of Pleasure* (1566). In the dedication "To the gentle Gentlewomen readers," one "R.B." remarks that the twelve tales of this collection were written copies of oral discourses intended for the edification of gentlewomen. Including such tales as "Tereus and Progne," "Admetus and Alcest," and Pygmalion, *The Petite Pallace* nonchalantly adapts familiar classical tales to Elizabethan amatory debates, *exempla,* proverbs, and *sententiae* that feature Pettie's circle of friends in classical guise.

In its time *A Petite Palace* remained widely popular. Licensed in 1576 and published soon afterward (the first edition is not dated), it saw at least six editions, possibly seven, by 1613. However, after its brief mention in a 1660 prose treatise (noticed by Hazlitt in 1867) and his great-uncle Anthony Wood's somewhat disparaging remark that its "neat stile" made it "more fit to be read by a Schoolboy, or rustical amorotto, than by a Gent. of mode or language," *A Petite Palace* faded from critical interest until twentieth-century scholars rehabilitated it for its rhetorical ornamentation, particularly its novel use of euphuism. Although Pettie, in order "to purchase [him]selfe some better fame by some better woorke," had also translated Stefano Guazzo in the first three books of his *Civile Conversation of M. Steeven Guazzo* (1581), it is nevertheless his earlier work that has purchased him comparably more—though still scant—critical attention. His influence on the euphuistic styles of John Lyly, Robert Greene, George Peele, Stephen Gosson, and Thomas Lodge secures his critical reputation as, in John Dover Wilson's words, a "euphuist before *Euphues.*"

BIBLIOGRAPHY

Borinski, Ludwig. "The Origin of the Euphuistic Novel and Its Significance for Shakespeare." In *Studies in Honor of T.W. Baldwin.* Don Cameron Allen, ed., pp. 38–52. 1958.

Bush, Douglas. *"The Petite Palace of Pettie his Pleasure." Journal of English and Germanic Philology,* vol. 27, pp. 162–169.

————. "Pettie's Petty Pilfering from Poets." *Philological Quarterly,* vol. 5, October 1926, pp. 325–329.

Hartman, Herbert, ed. *A Petite Pallace of Pettie his Pleasure: Containing many pretie Histories.* 1938.

Hornát, Jaroslav. *Anglická renesanční próza: eufuistická beletrie od Pettieho Paláce Potechy do Greenova Pandosto* [Renaissance Prose in England: Euphuistic Fiction from Pettie's *Palace of Pleasure* to Greene's *Pandosto*]. Acta Universitatis Carolinae, Philologica, Monographia 33. 1970.

Sullivan, Edward, ed. *The Civile Conversation of M. Steeven Guazzo.* The Tudor Translations, 2nd series. Charles Whibley VII, ed. 1925.

Eric Daigre

SEE ALSO

Euphuism; Gosson, Stephen; Greene, Robert; Lyly, John; Painter, William; Peele, George

Phaer, Thomas (c.1510–1560)

Born in Wales around 1510, Thomas Phaer studied at Oxford and at Lincoln's Inn. His legal training enabled him to become solicitor of the Council of the Welsh Marches. Turning to medicine, probably in his late twenties, he took an M.D. (having specialized in the study of poisons) from Oxford in March 1559. His two professional careers issued in popular works on law and medicine (*Newe Boke of Presidents,* 1543; *The Regiment of Life,* 1544), and the first work in English on paediatrics (*A Book of Children,* 1544). A loyal Welshman, he composed "Owen Glendower" for *The Mirror for Magistrates* (1559). He is chiefly remembered for his translation into English fourteeners of the first nine and part of the tenth books of Vergil's *Aeneid.* This translation, of which seven books appeared in 1558 and nine in 1562, was completed by Thomas Twyne in 1573. It was the most influential translation of Vergil in the English Renaissance, going through eight editions by 1620.

The translation has a boisterous Englishness, often imposing (as Golding does on Ovid) English mores and *milieux* on its original, as when the Sibyl transforms the Cyclops into vigorous blacksmiths: "I spie from hence the chimneis tops / Of *Ciclops* boistous walls, I see their gates their forges shopps" (VI. 666–667). The work is allied to the linguistic nationalism of John Cheke, and aims to generate a distinctively English heroical style, in which words of chiefly Anglo-Saxon origin are deflected into the word order of Latinate oratory. Its dedication to Mary I in the edition of 1558 betokens its ambition as a national epic, and incidentally marks it as the production of a lifelong Catholic. Phaer influenced subsequent epic writers: he used the phrase "fairy queenes" (VIII. 336) three decades before Spenser. Arthur Hall declares in his preface to his ten books of the Iliad that he was "abashed looking on M. Phaer's Heroicall Virgill." Chapman initially adopted fourteeners for his Homer (as well as following Phaer in recording how many days each book took him to translate). The critics who labored to create a national canon of English verse in the 1580s and 1590s (George Puttenham, Thomas Nashe, and William Webbe) accord Phaer generous praise, Puttenham describing his Vergil as "excellently well translated." By 1600, there are signs that the Phaer style, cluttered with alliteration and clashing archaism, was found touchingly old-fashioned. The player king's speech in William Shakespeare's *Hamlet* shows signs of a pastiche of Phaer's Vergilian manner; but for all its antiquity the speech does move the player king to tears and Hamlet to one of his finest soliloquies. Phaer died in 1560, but not without literary heirs.

BIBLIOGRAPHY

Bowers, Rick. "Thomas Phaer and the London Literati." *Notes and Queries,* vol. 239, pp. 33–35.

Burrow, Colin. "Virgil in English Translation." *The Cambridge Companion to Virgil.* Charles Martindale, ed. 1997.

Campbell, Lily B., ed. *The Mirror for Magistrates.* 1938.

Lally, Steven, ed. *The Aeneid of Thomas Phaer and Thomas Twyne. The Renaissance Imagination,* vol. 20. 1987.

Taylor, Anthony Brian. "Bottom's 'Hopping' Heart and Thomas Phaer: The Influence of the Early Translators on 'Pyramus and Thisbe.'" *Notes and Queries,* vol. 240, pp. 309–315.

Colin Burrow

SEE ALSO

Cheke, John; Classical Literature, English Translations; Classical Literature, Influence of; Epic; Language, History of; Puttenham, George

Philip II (1527–1598)

Philip was born in Valladolid on May 21, 1527, to Isabel, the Portuguese queen of King Carlos I, who was also the Holy Roman Emperor Charles V. He was, and remained, his father's only legitimate son, a fact of great significance both for his upbringing and his future career. His father was only intermittently present during his childhood and adolescence, and his mother died in 1539, when he was twelve. He received a normal aristocratic education, and was reasonably apt, but had no liking for scholarship. At fourteen he was declared of age, and began to assume public responsibilities. Two years later, in 1543, he was named regent during one of his father's prolonged and frequent absences. Although brought up entirely in Spain, and speaking only Latin and Castilian, he was summoned in 1548 to join the emperor in the Low Countries, and spent three years there, visiting Germany and parts of northern Italy, an experience that had a profound impact on him. Charles was hoping to settle the imperial succession upon him,

P

in addition to that of Spain, which was his birthright. However, he did not make a good impression, and his father's plans were frustrated.

In 1553, the emperor seized the opportunity created by the succession of Mary Tudor to the English throne to negotiate a marriage between her and Philip as a part of his grand strategy, both against France and for the security of the Low Countries. Philip spent a frustrating year in England, and was nominally its king until Mary's death in November 1558. The union failed any dynastic purpose, but facilitated the peaceful handover of power in the Netherlands from Charles to Philip in August 1555.

In 1559, after his father's death, Philip brought his long and exhausting wars with France to an end, and returned permanently to Spain. As king of Spain, his priorities were guided by his father's advice: the defense of his patrimony and the Catholic faith. These policies were to entail a lifelong struggle against the Ottoman Turks and the Barbary corsairs, and over thirty years of war with the Netherlanders and the English. His only unequivocal success was to secure the Portugese succession in 1580. He suffered many defeats, but protected the integrity and religion of Spain. Only later did it become clear that this was at the cost of the physical and psychological exhaustion of the country.

Philip's private life was beset by grief. His first wife, Maria of Portugal, whom he married when he was sixteen, died in childbirth two years later, and his second marriage, to Mary of England, was a political match of little emotional significance. To his third wife, Elizabeth of Valois, he was deeply attached, and that marriage lasted nine years, until she too died in childbed. In the same year, 1568, Philip also lost his only son, Don Carlos. His last marriage, to Anna of Austria, lasted ten years from 1570 to 1580, and she bore him four sons, of whom only one survived. After her death he became increasingly solitary, and began to multiply his religious exercises. Always pious, he became increasingly obsessed with his faith, and found his only emotional outlet in the affection of his two daughters by Elizabeth, Isobel and Catalina. He died after a protracted and painful illness, in September 1598, and was succeeded peacefully by his surviving son, the Infante Philip. As king, he had been immensely industrious and dutiful, but lacking in the vision that might have enabled him to conceive radical solutions to his intractable problems. As a man, he was unsympathetically regarded, both in his own time and since, being given little credit for the emotional depth and artistic sensibilities that he undoubtedly possessed.

BIBLIOGRAPHY

Bouza Alvarez, Fernando, ed. *Cartas de Felip II a Sus Hijas.* 1988.
Boyden, James M. *The Courtier and the King: Ruy Gomez da Silva, Philip II, and the Court of Spain.* 1995.
Gachard, L.P. *Don Carlos et Philippe II.* 1867.
Kamen, Henry. *Philip II.* 1997.
Parker, Geoffrey. *The Dutch Revolt.* 1977.
Rodriguez Salgado, M-J. *The Changing Face of Empire: Charles V, Philip II, and Habsburg Authority, 1551–1559.* 1988.

David Loades

SEE ALSO

Armada, Spanish; Foreign Relations and Diplomacy; Mary I

Philpot, John (1516–1555)

Born in Hampshire, John Philpot received a fellowship at New College, Oxford, and the degree of B.C.L. He went abroad after passage of the Act of Six Articles (1539), harshly punitive legislation designed to silence Protestant sympathizers, only to return several years later. As archdeacon of Winchester Cathedral, he had a contentious relationship with the bishop, John Ponet. According to Ponet's chaplain, John Bale, it was due to Philpot's good offices that Edward VI appointed Bale to the bishopric of Ossory in Ireland in 1552. Philpot's combination of political connections and reformist credentials may be noted in his gift of a manuscript translation of a Protestant treatise to Edward Seymour, duke of Somerset, and formerly protector of the realm (British Library, MS Royal 17 C. IX), around 1550–1551. Philpot's opposition to transubstantiation and other Roman Catholic doctrines led to his arrest and condemnation under Mary I. On December 18, 1555, he was burned to death at Smithfield. With the exception of a Latin account of the proceedings of convocation, his confessional writings were published posthumously. They included the accounts of his heresy examinations and an appeal to Mary I and Philip that Foxe transcribed in the "Book of Martyrs."

BIBLIOGRAPHY

Bale, John. *The Vocacyon of Johan Bale.* Peter Happé and John N. King, eds. Renaissance English Text Society. Vol. 14. 1989.
Foxe, John. *Acts and Monuments.*

John N. King

SEE ALSO
Articles of Religion; Bale, John; Marian Martyrs; Ponet, John; Seymour, Edward

Physicians, College of
See Medicine and Health

Pilgrimage of Grace

The series of revolts in Lincolnshire and northern England in late 1536 and early 1537 (collectively but incorrectly called the Pilgrimage of Grace) were the most dangerous challenge to Henry VIII's regime. It was also the moment at which the early Reformation in England is seen at its most unpopular. While the events of the Pilgrimage are well known, their interpretation remains a matter of contention. An attempt to read the revolts as arising from oppressive taxation and fears for the commonwealth is at best a partial explanation. The view that saw the revolts as arising out of an aristocratic "Aragonese" or pro-Marian conspiracy has found no recent advocates.

The most recent interpretations see the Pilgrimage fomented in the atmosphere of rumor, fear, and apprehension current in the late summer of 1536. The coincidence of the Ten Articles and Injunctions of 1536 (with their coolness toward the whole range of Sacraments, and their lack of enthusiasm for purgatory and intercessionary masses) and the dissolution of the smaller monasteries made credible wild reports about the taxation of the Sacraments, the closure of parish churches, and the seizure of church goods. The revolts were undoubtedly popular because ordinary people rallied to the defense of traditional religion and the gentry followed. The untold story of the Pilgrimage is the way in which the gentry secured the leadership of the movement and managed to persuade the rank and file to accept a pottage of royal promises as a victory and worthy outcome for their endeavors.

The Pilgrimage was not a distinctively northern movement, but a rebellion that, having started in Lincolnshire, spread northward. It began in Louth, on October 2, 1536. Over the following few days it spread into the other smaller Lincolnshire towns. Lincoln was entered on October 6 and the king was petitioned on October 9. After that the gentry refused to allow the rebels to proceed further until they had the king's answer to their petitions, and the rebels dispersed toward the end of that week. From Lincolnshire the rebellion spread over the Humber into Yorkshire. It is clear enough that the first Yorkshire rebels saw themselves as rising in solidarity with Lincolnshire. Among them was the lawyer Robert Aske, who was sufficiently convinced by the Lincoln articles to spread the rebellion. It was only when the Lincolnshire movement collapsed that he adopted the title of the Pilgrimage of Grace. Aske gathered a sizeable force that entered York on October 16, then took the indefensible royal castle at Pontefract and the nobles and gentry who had taken refuge there.

An independent center of the Pilgrimage also developed around Richmond in the North Riding of Yorkshire and spread in all directions. The pilgrims' consolidated force then advanced toward Doncaster where a much smaller force was assembling under the dukes of Norfolk, Thomas Howard, and Shrewsbury, George Talbot. At negotiations there on October 27, both armies were disbanded. Emissaries on behalf of the pilgrims were sent to the king with new articles to avoid a military clash that Norfolk would almost certainly have lost. But the king rejected these articles as too general. At subsequent congregations of the pilgrims (dominated by gentry), more detailed articles were drafted that were put to the duke of Norfolk at Doncaster on December 6. Rather than consider these, Norfolk conceded a free pardon and the promise of a Parliament during 1537. This was accepted by the gentry, although the Commons were dissatisfied and suspicious. On December 8, Aske persuaded the pilgrims to return home, but the first few months of 1537 saw continued outbreaks of disorder as attempts were made to rebuild the 1536 movement. Martial law was imposed by the king and Norfolk, resulting in forty-seven hangings in Lincolnshire and many more in Yorkshire before the rebellion ended.

These final revolts arose from popular fears for the future of parochial religion coupled with local concerns for the dispossessed religious. Thus the Pontefract articles and the clerical opinions made on December 3–4 went much further by denouncing the whole direction of government policy after 1529. They reveal a rejection of the royal supremacy, considerable doubts about the schism with Rome, the divorce, and the succession. They held that the right to raise clerical taxation belonged to convocation alone and requested that the liberties of the church be restored. In these articles and throughout the movement, a particular animus was directed toward Thomas Cromwell and his circle.

BIBLIOGRAPHY
Bush, M. *The Pilgrimage of Grace. A Study of the Rebel Armies of October, 1536.* 1996.

P

Davies, C.S.L. "Popular religion and the Pilgrimage of Grace." In *Order and Disorder in Early Modern England*. A. Fletcher and J. Stevenson, eds. 1986.

Dodds, M.H., and R. Dodds. *The Pilgrimage of Grace, 1536–1537 and the Exeter Conspiracy, 1538*. 2 vols. 1915.

Elton, G.R. "Politics and the Pilgrimage of Grace." In *Studies in Tudor and Stuart Politics and Government*, III. 1983.

Hoyle, R.W. *The Pilgrimage of Grace, 1536–1537*. 1999.

Robert W. Hoyle

SEE ALSO

Articles of Religion; Aske, Robert; Cromwell, Thomas; Henry VIII; Injunctions, Royal; Monastic Orders; Reformation, English; Talbot Family

Pilkington, James (c. 1520–1576)

A scion of the well-known Lancashire family, James Pilkington was educated at Cambridge, where he was made a fellow of St. John's College in 1539. Ten years later he took the Protestant side in the university debate over transubstantiation, and in 1550, he was made president of his college. In 1554, he was forced to flee to the Continent, going first to Basel and later to Frankfurt. He was there when Elizabeth I ascended the throne, and he returned to England immediately to become a member of the commission appointed to revise the 1552 Book of Common Prayer. In 1559, he was made regius professor of divinity at Cambridge, the post that had recently been occupied by Martin Bucer. In 1561, he was consecrated as bishop of Durham, and left Cambridge for the north. Once there, he was a strong defender of the rights of his see, which was one of the wealthiest and most independent in England. In particular, he became famous for his opposition to any sign of encroachment by the queen's officials. He died in his palace at Bishop Auckland on January 23, 1576. Like other bishops of his time, Pilkington was a confirmed Protestant in his theology, but not a Puritan extremist. His writings were reprinted in the nineteenth century; but on the whole, he has been neglected by subsequent historians.

BIBLIOGRAPHY

Scholefield, J., ed. *Works of Bishop Pilkington*. Parker Society. 1842.

Haugaard, W.P. *Elizabeth and the English Reformation: The Struggle for a Stable Settlement of Religion*. 1968.

Gerald Bray

SEE ALSO

Book of Common Prayer; Bucer, Martin

Piracy

An endemic problem in many parts of England, Wales, and Ireland during the Tudor period and led by skilled seamen such as John Callice, one of the most notorious pirates operating in the sixteenth century, piracy became an organized business with widespread economic ramifications. Encouraged by the growth of international trade, which provided a profitable target for maritime robbery, English pirates roamed the seas in search of prey, progressively extending the scope of their operations. From the 1530s to the 1560s, the North Sea and Channel were regularly infested by large numbers of pirates; at least 400 were known to be active in these waters in 1563. Thereafter, they extended their raids to the Caribbean in the 1570s, and to the Mediterranean in the 1580s.

The spread of piracy was fostered by poverty, unemployment, and chronic underemployment within the maritime community. The life- and work-cycles of mariners, the low pay, and irregular employment encouraged many to seek alternative work aboard pirate ships, as contemporary commentators such as Richard Hakluyt pointed out. Rural poverty and dislocation, brought on by bad harvests and rising prices, also led landsmen from diverse backgrounds to seek a living from piracy. The combination of social and economic distress with international conflict in western Europe created a fertile breeding ground for lawlessness at sea. Maritime conflicts encouraged large-scale legalized plunder in the form of privateering, which possessed an inherent piratical tendency. The immature development of international law made it impossible to unravel the confusion between piracy and privateering, particularly as monarchs were often prepared to connive at piratical activity for the sake of economic or military gain. Indeed, the deterioration in Anglo-Spanish relations after 1558 enabled many pirates to cloak their actions in a patriotic dress. The young Francis Drake, who pioneered transatlantic piratical enterprise in the Caribbean during the early 1570s, became a popular hero in Tudor England, inspiring a growing number of ambitious young men to join in the plunder of Spanish America. The outbreak of war between England and Spain in 1585 provided a legitimate outlet for these adventurers, enabling them to operate as lawfully commissioned privateers. But the sea war degenerated into a mad scramble for plunder, provoking a storm of protest from neutral states against the seizure of their shipping. So serious was the situation that in 1601, the queen was forced to issue a proclamation prohibiting English privateers from entering the Mediterranean.

For most of the Tudor period government attempts to deal with the problem of piracy were spasmodic, half-hearted, and ineffective. Naval expeditions were set out in 1556, 1572, and 1576 to apprehend pirates. Periodically, proclamations were issued by the crown against sea rovers. And commissions for investigating and suppressing piracy were established in the coastal shires in 1563 and 1577. But the impact of these measures was limited by the unreliability of royal officers who, from the lord admiral down, were often prepared to wink at piracy; by the willingness of officials in the port towns to do business with pirates; and by the assistance many pirates received from prominent gentry families, such as the Careys in the Isle of Wight or the Killigrews in Cornwall. The deeper problem was the state's ambivalent response to piracy, which meant that when pirates were captured, many escaped punishment: John Callice, captured off Yarmouth in 1577, was pardoned by the crown and subsequently set out in 1582 with a commission to take pirates. As this example suggests, the Tudor regime was more concerned with controlling the level of maritime lawlessness than with its eradication. In such circumstances piracy was able to survive and flourish throughout the sixteenth century.

BIBLIOGRAPHY

Andrews, K.R. *The Spanish Caribbean: Trade and Plunder, 1530–1630.* 1978.

———. *Trade, Plunder and Settlement: Maritime Enterprise and the Genesis of the British Empire, 1480–1630.* 1984.

Cordingley, D., and J. Falconer. *Pirates: Fact and Fiction.* 1992.

Ewen, C.L. *The Golden Chalice: A Documented Narrative of an Elizabethan Pirate.* 1939.

Marx, J. *Pirates and Privateers of the Caribbean.* 1992.

Oppenheim, M. *A History of the Administration of the Royal Navy and of Merchant Shipping in Relation to the Navy from 1509 to 1660.* 1896.

John C. Appleby

SEE ALSO

Drake, Francis; Hakluyt, Richard; Privateering; Trade, Overseas

Pius V

See Regnans in Excelsis

Plague

After the first devastating plague epidemic in 1348, Europe suffered a succession of irregular but frequent outbreaks of varying severity over the next three centuries. In England, the disease was probably not endemic: waves of infection generally spread from port towns, often London, into the country before subsiding after a decade or so. Contemporaries used a variety of names for the disease, including "pestilence," "mortality," "epidemic," and "plague"; but they understood it to be a special affliction of divine and natural origin.

Many observers noted two forms of the disease. The more common form, today called "bubonic" plague, presented signs including sudden coldness, prickly sensations, lethargy, fever, blisters, blood in the urine and bowels, and painful swellings ("buboes") in the groin, armpits, and under the ears. This form could last several days, and although death was frequent, recovery was possible. The second form, "pneumonic" plague, invaded the lungs, causing chest pains, a bloody cough, and labored breathing; it invariably killed within two days. Modern epidemiologists attribute the outbreaks to the bacillus *Yersinia pestis,* an internal parasite of wild rodents, spread by infected fleas or by inhaling bacilli directly. Because contemporaries witnessed other victims drop dead with no symptoms at all, some historians have posited a third form, "septicaemic" plague, but this remains controversial.

In chronicles, devotional literature, and medical treatises, contemporaries explained the disease in terms of a chain of supernatural and natural causes. The disease was widely believed to be divine punishment for personal and communal sins, as the use of the terms "pestilence" and "plague" indicate (e.g., *Exodus* 7ff.; *Ecclesiasticus* 23:12; *2 Samuel* 24:15–19). Communities, therefore, performed penitential processions of relics and recited prayers to saints to beg for protection and forgiveness.

With the English Reformation, such practices were censored: the last public plague procession in London was held in 1543. Still, special Prayer Books were printed, and in 1563 and 1569, Londoners were encouraged to pray regularly, attend church daily, and fast. Medical texts, too, noted the supernatural cause of plague—many clerics also practiced medicine—but they tended to emphasize the workings of divine providence through natural causes.

P

Using concepts derived from the ancient Greek tradition, learned physicians explained that epidemic disease was caused by corruption of the air due to malign conjunctions of planets that drew from the earth poisonous vapors and produced unhealthful, damp, and warm southerly winds. On a smaller scale, miasmas could be caused by stagnant pools, unburied corpses, or the stink of graveyards. According to physicians, the disease could also be transmitted from person to person by the vapors from plague sores and infected bedding and clothing. The corrupted air infected the body (from the Latin verb *inficere* meaning "to dye") through the lungs and pores by mixing with the blood and poisoning the principal organs—the heart, liver, and brain. Swellings resulted from the active effort of the organ to expel the poisonous matter, which the physician could help the body discharge with the traditional techniques of phlebotomy, diet, and medicines (most famously theriac, or "treacle"). To prevent illness, medical authors suggested lighting fires and incense to dispel infected air, holding pomanders to the nose when in contact with infected people or belongings, keeping shut windows facing southerly winds, and if possible, fleeing the infected area altogether. (This last advice continued to create controversy regarding the duties of Christian doctors, clerics, rulers, and subjects.) The market for learned medical advice grew throughout the century: more than 150 medical books in English were published between 1486 and 1604, most during Elizabeth I's reign.

A century and a half after the first plague outbreak, England's economic depression began to lift and its population increase. After 1479, the outbreaks became less frequent and more localized, hitting some towns hard while sparing others. Although the population grew overall (it doubled over the next 200 years), Tudor England experienced high death rates and sickness, with frequent short-term crises of epidemic disease, often causing the doubling or tripling of mortality rates and the disruption of economic and civic life. Larger towns were affected most: Exeter, Bristol, and Norwich each suffered more than one serious epidemic during 1535–1555. Another three major outbreaks between 1565 and 1626 killed 15 percent or more of the inhabitants. Along with the plague, other new and deadly diseases attacked England through the century, including "gaol fever" and "sweating sickness." The worst disaster of the period was caused by epidemics of "burning" and "spotted" fevers in 1556–1557, following two years of bad harvests; in 1558–1559, a "new ague" erupted, causing even greater mortality. As a result, between 1556 and 1560, England's population decreased by at least 6 percent.

Through the sixteenth century, learned advisors interested in promoting the "commonweal" urged the crown to view the plague as a problem requiring collective action. Inspired by continental models, crown policy aimed to control the movement of people, arguing that "unruliness" and "disorder" spread the disease, not corrupted air. In 1518, Henry VIII's councilor Cardinal Wolsey founded the College of Physicians of London to enforce standards of medical practice "for the common good," and the crown urged the city to mark infected houses and detain their inhabitants. But city fathers were reluctant to enforce the policy, preferring to rely on charitable institutions and philanthropy for the relief of the sick. Stimulated by similar concerns that produced the poor laws of the 1570s, the crown issued the Plague Orders of 1578, whose far-reaching provisions included the burning of victims' clothes and bedding, and the control of burial times to limit the number of participants. The insistence that infected houses be locked up for at least six weeks with all members of the family, whether sick or not, and that watchmen enforce the isolation especially aroused controversy: both Puritans and advocates of Paracelsian medicine, emphasizing the spiritual aspects of disease, maintained that the government orders were ineffective and uncharitable. Others argued from experience that household quarantine increased infection. Nevertheless, these provisions remained English policy between 1578 and 1665, with the increasing cooperation of civic leaders and the support of the religious establishment. Although apprehension about widespread disease continued, by the early seventeenth century it seemed clear to authorities that the plague was largely a problem of the poorer urban parishes.

BIBLIOGRAPHY

Dobson, Mary J. *Contours of Death and Disease in Early Modern England.* 1997.

Horrox, Rosemary, ed. *The Black Death.* 1994.

Shrewsbury, J.D.F. *A History of Bubonic Plague in the British Isles.* 1971.

Slack, Paul. *The Impact of Plague in Tudor and Stuart England.* 1985.

Webster, Charles, ed. *Health, Medicine, and Mortality in the Sixteenth Century.* 1979.

Ralph Drayton

SEE ALSO

Medicine and Health; Population and Demography

Platonism

It was in the Renaissance that the philosophy of Plato became more fully available in western Europe than at any time since classical antiquity. During the medieval period, Plato had been known directly through only a handful of dialogues, or indirectly through the writings of figures such as St. Augustine. In the Renaissance, humanist studies in the classical languages made possible the Latin translation by Marsilio Ficino (1433–1499) of thirty-six extant dialogues (published 1484), together with the Aldine Greek edition of 1513. At the same time, editions and translations of important later Platonists, such as Plotinus (1492), and interest in Platonizing church fathers, such as Origen, ensured a Christianized reading of Plato's writings, where the views of the later Platonists were influential. Two characteristic features of the Renaissance interpretation of Plato may be singled out, both of them deriving from Ficino: on the one hand, theological Platonism, where apparent parallels between Platonism and Christian doctrine were emphasized in such a way as to make him a fit philosopher for the Christian culture of Renaissance Europe. Plato was interpreted as an ancient sage, whose teachings on the immortality of the soul and on moral conduct meant that he deserved to be respected as an ancient theologian (*priscus theologus*). A second development was Platonic love, with its concomitant theory of the spiritual function of beauty. Deriving from Ficino's commentary on Plato's *Symposium*, this was popularised by the *trattati d'amore*, such as the speech by Pietro Bembo in the fourth book of Baldasar Castiglione's *Il Cortegiano* (1528), through which it was influential in court circles. Although Plato never displaced Aristotle as the dominant philosopher of university study, Platonism was influential throughout the court culture of Renaissance Europe.

Platonism was not a dominant strand in Tudor thought and culture, as used to be supposed. Tudor Platonism may be contrasted with the early interest in Plato in mid-fifteenth-century England, when Humphrey, duke of Gloucester, had been patron of the Latin translators of Plato, Leonardo Bruni, and Pier Candido Decembrio. The efflorescence of Platonizing thought and culture in early Stuart times comes in striking contrast to the more tentative interest of the Tudors in Plato. In the early sixteenth century, Plato's works were acquired by the new foundations of humanism in Tudor England, such as Corpus Christi College, Oxford, and St. John's College, Cambridge. The influence of Platonism in England might have been stronger had Cardinal Wolsey's plans for educational development not been lost with his fall from power. Cardinal College, his projected collegiate foundation at Oxford, was to have had transcriptions of all of Cardinal Bessarion's Greek manuscripts. This project, however, came to nothing. But visiting humanists such as Desiderius Erasmus and Juan Luis Vives helped to foster an interest in Plato. Among Tudor humanists, both Roger Ascham and John Aylmer were interested in Platonism, but their knowledge of the dialogues was limited. Aylmer's pupil, Lady Jane Grey, is another example of humanist-inspired, but exceptional acquaintance with Plato. Although Sir Thomas More did not visit Italy, he too was sufficiently interested in the Platonizing humanists of Italy to make a translation of the life of Giovanni Pico della Mirandola (1510); More also draws on Plato's *Republic* in *Utopia* (1516).

The impact of the new, theologically minded interest in Plato is evident in the work of the humanist and friend of Erasmus, John Colet, who corresponded with Marcello Ficino. But with the disruptions of the Reformation, there was little further development until the end of the century, with Thomas Jackson (1579–1640) of Corpus Christi College, Oxford. Jackson anticipates the Cambridge Platonists of the next century, but he did not publish before 1613. Acquaintance with Platonic teachings can be also be discerned in unlikely places, such as in the writings of the Oxford Aristotelian, John Case. The only serious work of philosophy to draw significantly on Platonism was the *Theoria analytica* of Everard Digby.

The only English translation of Plato to appear in Tudor times was the pseudo-Platonic dialogue *Axiochus* (London, 1592). The only dialogue to be printed in Greek was the *Menexenus* (Cambridge, 1587). This contrasts vividly with contemporary France, where there were numerous editions and translations. Indeed, France was an important mediator of Platonism to Tudor England. In 1578, the Hugenots, Henri Estienne and Jean de Serres, dedicated their edition of Plato's works to Queen Elizabeth I. And translations of compendia and surveys, like Du Plessis Mornay's *De la verité de la religion chretienne* (translated by Sir Philip Sidney) made possible an acquaintance with Platonism unavailable from local sources. A nonacademic strain of Platonism was disseminated through translations of Castiglione: one Latin (Bartholomew Clerke's *De curiali sive aulico libri quattuor* of 1571), and an English one by Thomas Hoby (*The Courtyer,* 1561) that enjoyed wide popularity. This courtly Platonism made its greatest impact in literature, where Castiglione's book combined with the influence of French poets like Du Bellay and the Pléiade. Edmund

P

Spenser drew on a range of Platonic sources in his *Faerie Queene,* and especially in the *Four Hymnes.* Platonic love was also celebrated in lyric poetry, notably sonnet sequences like Spenser's *Amoretti* and Michael Drayton's *Idea,* and, with a comic touch, in Sidney's *Astrophil and Stella* and George Chapman's *Hero and Leander.*

BIBLIOGRAPHY

Baldwin, C., and S. Hutton, eds. *Platonism and the English Imagination.* 1994.
Ellrodt, R. *Neoplatonism in the Poetry of Spenser.* 1960.
Hankins, J. *Plato and the Italian Renaissance.* 2 vols. 1990.
Jayne, S. *John Colet and Marsilio Ficino.* 1963.
———. *Plato in Renaissance England.* 1995.
Nelson, J.C. *Renaissance Theory of Love.* 1958.

Sarah Hutton

SEE ALSO

Ascham, Roger; Classical Literature, English Translations; Colet, John; Digby, Everard; Erasmus, Desiderius; Humanism; More, Thomas; Sidney, Philip; Spenser, Edmund; Vives, Juan Luis

de la Pole, Edmund, Earl of Suffolk (c. 1472–1513)

The second son of John de la Pole, duke of Suffolk, and Elizabeth, the sister of Edward IV, Edmund de la Pole was a potential Yorkist claimant and security threat to the Tudors. He was loyal during the early years, appearing regularly at court and serving on the French campaign of 1492, but his inheritance was diminished by the act of attainder against his brother, John de la Pole, earl of Lincoln. In 1499, he fled the country, possibly fearing reprisals for a murder he had committed. Although he was persuaded to return, he remained suspicious of Henry VII and in 1501 fled again with his brother Richard to the court of the Emperor Maximilian to foment conspiracy. Much of Henry's diplomatic energies in the ensuing years were directed to securing his extradiction from Flanders. It was only the chance of adverse winds that brought the Archduke Philip to England in 1506 that gave Henry the opportunity to work his charms to secure a promise from Philip that he would cause Edmund to be handed over. Although Edmund's life was spared in accordance with Henry VII's promise to Philip, he languished in the Tower until Louis XII's recognition of his brother as Richard IV during war with England in 1513 underlined the family's dynastic aspirations and resulted in Edmund's summary execution.

BIBLIOGRAPHY

Chrimes, S.B. *Henry VII.* 1972.
Lockyer, Roger, and Andrew Thrush. *Henry VII.* 1997.

Ian W. Archer

SEE ALSO

Henry VII

Pole, Reginald (1500–1558)

European religious and political figure, Reginald Pole was the grandson of the duke of Clarence, which made him a Plantagenet cousin of Henry VIII. Pole began his career as the client of Henry, who paid for his education in Italy, mainly at Padua. Beginning in the early 1530s, Henry and Pole fell out, and in 1536, Pole wrote a scathing attack on Henry, *Pro ecclesiasticae unitatis defensione [Defense of the unity of the Church].* Shortly thereafter, Pole became a cardinal and entered the papal diplomatic service. In the conclave of 1549–1550, he came within one vote of election as pope. The winner, Julius III, made Pole one of his closest associates, protecting him from the Inquisition and giving him almost free reign for the reconciliation of England (and for peace between the king of France and the emperor) after the accession of Mary I in 1553. Pole returned to England as both papal legate and later archbishop of Canterbury, and he was mainly, although not exclusively, responsible for Mary's religious policy. Perhaps the high point of his direction of it came in the London synod of 1556, which laid down many reforms later adopted by the Council of Trent, especially the establishment of synods for the education of the clergy. In 1557, Pope Paul IV engaged in a war with Mary's husband, Philip II, and used it as an opportunity to attack Pole as well. His legations were revoked, and he was recalled to Rome, where it is very likely he would have been charged with heresy, as his close ally Cardinal Giovanni Morone and other of their associates were. With his authority reduced to that of archbishop (even the archbishop's traditional legatine authority had been withdrawn), Pole's reforming efforts largely came to a halt in the last eighteen months of Mary's reign. His possiblities for success already limited by shortage of money and the institutional difficulties of the church, Pole had only an ephemeral impact on English religion.

BIBLIOGRAPHY

Fenlon, Dermot. *Heresy and Obedience in Tridentine Italy: Cardinal Pole and the Counter Reformation.* 1972.

Haile, Martin [Marie Hallé]. *The Life of Reginald Pole.* 1911.

Pole, Reginald. *Pro ecclesiasticae unitatis defensione* (1539). Joseph G. Dwyer, trans. *Pole's Defense of the Unity of the Church.* 1965.

Thomas F. Mayer

SEE ALSO

Catholicism; Counter Reformation; Mary I; Philip II; Trent, Council of

Political Thought

Political thought in Tudor England turned on certain central concepts, most of which coexisted uneasily. Most important were the twin ideas of kingdom and community, the first emphasizing the monarchy, the second its subjects, a difficult and insufficiently studied concept. Just as some monarchs embraced the idea of imperial kingship as a means of enhancing their power, so some subjects yearned to become free-acting citizens and went so far as to propose turning England into a republic. Very often they acted under external stimuli, especially from Italy, with increasing frequency in the form of Machiavelli's ideas of the republic. Ordinarily the tension between kingdom and commonwealth turned on struggles over the meaning of counsel and who could best give it. This debate was intrinsically linked to that over true nobility, one of the most hotly contested concepts between the defenders of the nobility as an estate and those who thought it depended on virtue. Sir Thomas Elyot's *Boke Named the Governor* (originally published 1531), one of the most popular works of political thought in the sixteenth century, tried to resolve the dispute through a complete eductional program designed to equip the nobility with the virtues necessary for governing.

Despite the implicit assault on the notion of hierarchy presented by the idea of a nobility by virtue, everyone assumed an unchanging order. (This assumption made possible the constant appeal to example, especially from classical sources.) No matter the strength of that order, however, the concept was permanently unstable. The same holds for another pair of major ideas, honor and conscience. Honor as the virtue par excellence of an aristocratic society emphasizing external behavior had unavoidably to stand in a tense relationship to conscience, conceived as an internal organ of judgment. The tensions between these concepts produced movement in no very clear direction. Most of the time attention was focused on the center, especially on the monarch and on Parliament, in large part because the idiom of much discourse was law, and when not law, theology, an almost equally "centralized" discipline. Literary reflection on politics was also largely the preserve of persons attached to the monarchy or at least the metropolis. There were comparatively few people like William Harrison, working out a thorough critique of aristocratic government in the fastnesses of Essex, or John Barston, town clerk of Tewkesbury, which was (in his eyes) a flourishing republic. The biggest exception to this generalization about centralization is the dispersal of traveling companies of players and those who wrote for them, such as John Bale, whose most famous play, *King Johan,* argued virulently in favor of royal supremacy as the only means to preserve the commonwealth from clerical depradations.

Centralization did not cancel competing strands in either law or theology, nor in the realm of "imaginary" literature. Civil and Roman law challenged common law, despite its apparent dominance, as did just a touch of canonist thinking that survived the Henrician Reformation. Theology was even more confused by a range of possible modes, including Thomist, nominalist, a wide variety of reformed, and, later, Catholic. Despite this fluidity, no one uncoupled politics from either law or religion, not even the Machiavellians, however ruthlessly they might advise princes to establish their rights, as in the so-called "Machiavellian Treatise" attributed to, but certainly not by, Stephen Gardiner. Foreign ideas always infiltrated, above all from Italy and France, with Germany of much less importance, except perhaps during the reign of Edward VI. But the bedrock of Tudor political thought came from Aristotle, whose description of ideal types of government and of the virtuous citizen underpinned nearly every piece of Tudor reflection on government.

When Edmund Dudley wrote his *Tree of the Commonwealth* (1509), while awaiting execution under Henry VIII for presumptive abuse of his administrative power under Henry VII, he employed most of the commonplaces of sixteenth-century political thought, most importantly an organic (but inflexible) metaphor for civil society. Despite his stress on the nobility, Dudley hoped that his work would win him a reprieve from the monarch who had condemned him, but such an emphasis on the king's power is also a constant. As Dudley's fellow lawyer Sir John Fortescue had earlier insisted, however, the king was hedged around by natural and divine laws in his *dominium regale et politicum.* Fortescue, chief justice of the Court of King's Bench, probably derived much of his

P

understanding of higher laws from Thomas Aquinas, while his insistence on custom and the power of common law was homegrown. This hybridization of common law with other kinds of law and theology continued throughout the sixteenth century. When the common lawyer Christopher St. Germain (c. 1460–1540) in his *Dialogue of doctor and student* talked about higher laws, which he also thought restrained the king, he relied on the notion of conscience, making explicit reference to the nominalist theologian Jean Gerson. St. Germain was also very clear that the church was subject to the monarch, an idea reinforced at nearly the same time as he wrote by the publication of the *Dialogus inter militem et clericum,* which, if not by William of Ockham, at least contained his ideas about the superiority of the secular order.

Henry VIII from the first intended some kind of theocracy, embracing a revived imperial crown in the mid-1510s, and as the pace of his reformation increased, he leaned more and more toward Byzantine caesaropapism. As the implications of his wishes, spelled out by his chief minister Thomas Cromwell, became clear and opened a breach with Rome, the question of obligation first became urgent. Richard Morison wrote a series of tracts against the Pilgrimage of Grace (1536) in which he emphasized the divinely sanctioned duty of the commons to obey the king, and the episcopal bench contributed defenses written in Latin of a scripturally grounded supremacy, while two other bishops, Cuthbert Tunstall and John Stokesley, argued from law and theology against Morison's former patron and Henry's most dangerous opponent, Reginald Pole (*De unitate* [1536], explicitly aimed at Richard Sampson, author of the *Oratio,* one of the first defenses of Henrician supremacy). Despite their superficially profound differences, all these writers shared many more common assumptions than divided them, especially the necessity of counsel to any monarch (Pole's pope was no more an absolute monarch than Morison's king), and all continued to believe that some kind of conciliar body could resolve their differences.

This emphasis on conciliar government was made most explicit in another work by a writer once in Pole's circle, Thomas Starkey, whose *Dialogue between Pole and Lupset* proposed to reform the English commonwealth on the model of Venice. The *Dialogue* marked the first moment in an extended engagement with Venetian institutions by Englishmen. Without benefit of much foreign stimulus, a vein of more imaginative reflection on politics opened during Henry's reign, especially in Sir Thomas More's *Utopia* and in the satire of John Skelton. *Utopia* is

one of the great classics of political thought, but its vision of the ideal society was pegged to England, whether in its direct criticisms of the barbarity of the common law or of English ideas of property, or above all in its open criticism of Henry's exaggerated claims to sovereignty, an idea foreign to the Utopians. More, who made a very successful career in royal service, gave a great deal of thought to the problem of counsel, both in *Utopia* and in his unfinished *History of Richard III,* and concluded that faction was the greatest evil of political society. That More lost his head on Tower Hill provided a stark contrast to the image of a harmonious society projected in his works. Yet that vision was never challenged, however much disagreement there might be about who was in charge and the precise obligations of those beneath them.

It is significant that More's tightly disciplined *Utopia* was translated into English during Edward VI's reign, perhaps the moment of most open debate about the political order. Obedience continued to be key, but now some of the most important "forward" reformers, above all the German Martin Bucer, proposed to put in place a system to enforce discipline and obedience. Bucer's *De regno Christi* (1550) was dedicated to the king and argued for reformation through royal supremacy, to be executed through a special council for religious affairs. Bishops were to become strictly religious authorities, supervisors of and examples for the new discipline. Bucer's scheme proved as abortive as the rest of the Edwardian reformation when the king's death in 1553 brought his older sister, Mary, to the throne. It is of great importance that a reasonably well-coordinated effort to prevent her accession collapsed quickly: the idea of order and legitimacy proved too strong. Mary's restoration of Catholicism raised once more the question of obligation, and some of those who fled into exile, especially John Knox and the former bishop John Ponet (in his *Short Treatise of Politic Power* [1556]), dared to justify regicide by private individuals in the name of religion. Curiously enough, the regime, in which Pole played a central part, offered little direct response. Instead, Mary and her council put their faith in the law, and the draconian enforcement of conformity through executions. It is more than ironic that Pole had also to defend himself against the pope's charges that he was a heretic, and did so by appealing to a collective headship. The test of true allegiance was becoming religious.

Religion and the powers of the monarchy attracted constant reflection during Elizabeth I's rule. The most profound challenge to a revived Henrician order came from the extreme Calvinists, among them Knox, who argued that subjects could force princes to change wicked laws. Anglican loyalists, especially John Jewel, replied that the visible church must be subject to a visible head, the monarch. During the Vestiarian Controversy in the late 1560s and 1570s, Anthony Gilby (d. 1585) argued that subjects had to "restrain the prince's authority to bounds and limits" drawn from Scripture. In 1570, Edward Dering bluntly put the same point to the queen herself, concluding that "if princes and magistrates will be still rebellious [to God's will], what is that to us?" In the early 1580s, Sir Philip Sidney incorporated strongly Protestant ideas into his not always thinly veiled criticism of royal despotism in *Arcadia*. Many Catholics, taking their turn in exile, put forward similar claims about resistance, and the Jesuit Robert Parsons forcefully made the not uncommon point that the crown was elective. These debates almost always turned on the idea of conscience, and the issue became the degree that conscience could be coerced. Some, like the Presbyterian Thomas Cartwright, made it a separate realm that secular authorities could not touch. Others, relying on the *locus classicus* of Romans 13:1–5, insisted that subjects were bound in conscience to obey the monarch. In a tamer form, the idea that subjects collectively could impose their will on the sovereign cropped up repeatedly, at one point almost becoming government policy in the form of the Bond of Association (1584), designed to ensure Elizabeth's safety by threatening collective vengeance on Mary Queen of Scots or her son should they kill Elizabeth. It is very likely that this and other radical steps under Elizabeth had something to do with the fact that the ruler was a woman, whose independence many of her subjects had great difficulty understanding. Elizabeth defended herself through her mastery of imagery, especially in consciously portraying herself as Gloriana, or in more scriptural terms, as Deborah.

Almost at the end of the century, Richard Hooker wrote his comprehensive *Of the Lawes of Ecclesiastical Politie* (published between 1593 and 1662), which can stand as a summary of Tudor political thought. For Hooker, the community was primary. In common with the radicals, he stressed consent, but removed any right of resistance. Rather, the ruler had a "chiefty" or "principality" of "ecclesiastical dominion." As for most other Tudor thinkers, the mean was Hooker's goal, although not all agreed with him that episcopacy provided it. Above all, the goal was order, and Hooker demonstrated to his satisfaction that the political replicated the eternal order.

BIBLIOGRAPHY

Allen, J.W. *History of Political Thought in the Sixteenth Century.* 1928.

Holmes, Peter. *Resistance and Compromise. The Political Thought of the Elizabethan Catholics.* 1982.

Lake, Peter. *Anglicans and Puritans? Presbyterianism and English Conformist Thought from Whitgift to Hooker.* 1988.

Mayer, Thomas F. "Tournai and Tyranny: Imperial Kingship and Critical Humanism." *Historical Journal,* vol. 34, pp. 257–277.

Peltonen, Markku. *Classical Humanism and Republicanism in English Political Thought, 1570–1640.* 1995.

Skinner, Quentin. *Foundations of Modern Political Thought.* Vol. 2: *The Age of Reformation.* 1978.

———. *Reason and Rhetoric in the Philosophy of Hobbes.* 1996.

Trinterud, L.J., ed. *Elizabethan Puritanism.* 1971.

Worden, Blair. *The Sound of Virtue: Philip Sydney's Arcadia and Elizabethan Politics.* 1996.

Thomas F. Mayer

SEE ALSO

Bale, John; Bucer, Martin; Cartwright, Thomas; Cromwell, Thomas; Dudley, Edmund; Elyot, Thomas; Fortescue, John; Government, Central Administration of; Harrison, William; Hooker, Richard; Jewel, John; Knox, John; More, Thomas; Parsons, Robert; Pilgrimage of Grace; Pole, Reginald; Ponet, John; Starkey, Thomas; Tunstall, Cuthbert; Vestiarian Controversy

Ponet, John (c. 1514–1556)

Edwardian reformer, Marian exile, and a writer of theological and political thought, Ponet was born around 1514 in Kent of unknown parentage. He earned a B.A. from Queens' College, Cambridge, in 1532. While there he studied Greek with Thomas Smith and John Cheke, two leading humanists who were also Protestants. Ponet mastered mathematics, constructing a sundial for Henry VIII. In the mid-1530s he began a dual career as both academic and cleric. He served as a Greek lecturer, bursar, and dean at Queens' while holding several minor ecclesiastical appointments. After leaving Cambridge, Ponet worked at Lambeth Palace as Archbishop Cranmer's assistant. In 1549, Ponet translated Ochino's anti-papal drama *A Tragedy* (or *Dialogue*) and wrote "A Defense for Marriage of Priests," one of the most detailed apologies for clerical marriage in Edwardian England. Cranmer had Ponet and John

P

Hooper preach the Lenten sermons of 1550 at Paul's Cross; the only surviving of Ponet's homilies is "A Notable Sermon Concerning the Right Use of the Lord's Supper." In this, Ponet argued that Christ's presence in the Sacrament is primarily spiritual. Around this time, Ponet was appointed bishop of Rochester; in 1551, Ponet was elevated to Winchester, one of the highest ecclesiastical posts in England. While there he designed a Latin catechism, *Catechismus Brevis;* the English translation is called *A Short Catechism.* While at Winchester Ponet had to deal with an embarrassing marriage to a woman who was already married to a butcher. He then married Maria Heywood. After Edward's death in 1553, many Protestants fled to the Continent. Before going to Strasbourg, Ponet seemingly participated in the ill-fated Wyatt's Rebellion and, perhaps, was briefly imprisoned. He lost his post at Winchester to Stephen Gardiner. While at Strasbourg Ponet penned three works. One is *An Apology* (1556), a theological polemic. He also wrote *Diallacticon.* Printed in 1557, this scholarly work elaborates on Ponet's spiritual interpretation of Christ's presence in the Lord's Supper. Ponet's greatest contribution, however, was *A Short Treatise of Politic Power.* This book offers the first detailed defense of tyrannicide since John of Salisbury's *Policraticus,* written during Henry II's reign. Ponet looked to the nobility to remove Mary I, whom he believed promoted idolatry and martyred the faithful. Ponet appealed to nationalism, apocalyptic ideas, social and economic justice, and other eclectic themes in order to convince England to repent of its sins. Ponet died of illness, perhaps plague, in 1556. His defense of regicide, though, became popular again the 1640s, during the civil war.

BIBLIOGRAPHY

Bowman, Glen. "John Ponet: Political Theologian of the English Reformation." Dissertation, University of Minnesota. 1997.

Hudson, Winthrop. *John Ponet, Advocate of Limited Monarchy.* 1942.

Glen Bowman

SEE ALSO

Catechism; Cheke, John; Cranmer, Thomas; Gardiner, Stephen; Hooper, John; Marian Exiles; Mary I; Smith, Thomas; Wyatt's Rebellion

Poor Laws

Codified in 1597–1601, the Elizabethan poor law was the culmination of more than a century of legislative and local experimentation in social welfare provision. It embodied three principles, which (with the addition of the 1662 Settlement Act, designed to remedy confusion over entitlement to relief in individual parishes), were to underpin relief of poverty in England and Wales until 1834. Each of its three provisions applied to a separate category of poverty in contemporary understanding: corporal punishment for the thriftless; doles in cash or kind for the impotent; provision of work for the under- or unemployed. Although these policies had been prefigured earlier in the sixteenth century (the 1547 "Slavery Act" stipulated even more brutal physical penalties for vagrants; poor rates, compulsory in London from 1547 and in Norwich from 1549, were extended to all parishes in 1572; local employment schemes were attempted in Essex as early as the 1560s), it was only in the 1590s that a coordinating structure for this comprehensive social policy was erected. The poor laws themselves were, moreover, only the central plank in a wider platform of social policies designed to regulate the condition and conduct of the poor: the parliamentary sessions that produced the legislation of 1597–1601 also produced a plethora of regulative statutes (e.g., against drunkenness, swearing, and profanation of the Sabbath) intended not only to relieve but also to reform the poor.

The timing of this legislative impulse can be explained largely as a political response to economic crisis. From the 1520s onward, demographic expansion was the engine of economic transformation, driving land hunger, enclosure, tenurial change, and price inflation. The consequences for individuals, families, and the local communities in which they lived were profound: economic differentiation, increasing burdens of debt, immiseration, and destitution. When compounded by the short-term dislocations of harvest failure or trade depression in the 1590s and 1620s, this nascent market economy suffered severely, and the attendant social tension was evident in sporadic (though regionally specific) starvation, widespread vagrancy, lengthening jail calendars of prosecuted thieves, and projected insurrection. The Privy Council correspondence of the 1590s demonstrates governmental concern about these issues, and the resulting legislation was designed not only to manage the crisis through discipline but also to vindicate the paternalistic credentials of the Tudor regime.

The nature of the newly codified welfare provision is, however, to be explained by a more complex combination of factors. The contemporary understanding of social and economic change was explicitly moral. In the absence of an autonomous science of economics, both governors and governed perceived price-inflation, industrial depression, and dearth in terms of providential judgement on human moral failings. The most advanced economic thinking of the time contrasted nostalgia for the mutual interdependence of all subjects in an organic social order (or "commonwealth") with the perceived contemporary expansion of individualistic private self-interest ("commodity"). In attempting to preserve this organic unity, Tudor thinkers relied on a traditional binary opposition: the healing of the genuinely diseased members of the body politic; the amputation of its corrupt or malignant limbs. The treatment of the impotent and thriftless was therefore conditioned by these medieval commonplaces, inflected with the humanist rhetoric of commonwealth reform. The discovery (especially in the urban censuses of the mid sixteenth century) of a third group—the laboring poor—was particularly troubling in this intellectual context. The gradual recognition that a substantial proportion of those in need were suffering neither from misfortune nor moral lassitude but from low wages propelled governors to consider provision for this pool of badly managed labor. The changing understanding of the causes of poverty was, moreover, compounded by the cultural ramifications of the Reformation. Although traditional ideals of charity and hospitality endured well into the seventeenth century, the combination of economic and religious change at the local level caused their fragmentation and marginalization, and each came to imply a moral judgment about the moral worth of the recipient. Finally, the changing ambitions of the Tudor state are evident in the desire not only to relieve but also to regulate the poor: above all, the Elizabethan poor laws were contrived to maintain social order, and were therefore ultimately a political achievement.

As might be expected of a social policy so fundamentally dependent on local initiatives, the effectiveness with which the poor laws were enforced varied enormously, not only from region to region but also from parish to parish. The whipping and incarceration of vagrants in houses of correction was sporadic, and depended on the conscientiousness of parish constables and the efficiency of magistrates in providing the required places of incarceration. Most northern counties lacked a bridewell (required by law as early as 1576) until the 1610s. The introduction of compulsory poor rates, assessed, collected, and distributed by local overseers, began in some parishes before the 1590s, but only seems to have become widespread by the 1630s. Much, of course, depended on the local economic context, since the system presupposed the existence not only of the casualties of economic change who required pensions and doles but also of the beneficiaries who would be both able and willing to pay the poor rates. The overseers' account books of many parishes demonstrate the system's extraordinary sensitivity to local need, with rates doubling and even tripling from one year to the next to take account of economic crises. For many, the parish dole was not only a critical component in the economy of makeshifts of the poor, it was their only lifeline in years of dearth. But the benevolence and sympathy of rate-payers and overseers for those who enjoyed recognition as members of the local community (both in moral and geographical terms) was counterbalanced by its grudging and often hostile attitude to outsiders and deviants. Poor relief could be withheld, from those (drunkards, bastard-bearers, swearers) who failed to live up to expected standards of behavior, at the discretion of the overseer. The most ambitious provision of the policy, the schemes of work for the laboring poor, was by far the least successful, with many overseers' accounts revealing only short-lived experiments with parish stocks, usually in the 1630s under the terms of the Caroline Book of Orders.

Although the Tudor poor laws were the product of profoundly conservative thinking, they constituted the only national system of welfare in early modern Europe, and their implications were sufficiently innovative to form the centerpiece of English local government for more than two centuries. The poor laws could never have reversed economic trends, and they were not intended to do so; they nonetheless succeeded in moderating the social rigor of those trends, and demonstrated that the paternalism of the Tudor state was no dead letter.

BIBLIOGRAPHY

Beier, A.L. "Poverty and Progress in Early Modern England." In *The First Modern Society: Essays in English History in Honour of Lawrence Stone.* A.L. Beier, David Cannadine, and James L. Rosenheim, eds., pp. 201–240. 1989.

Leonard, E.M. *The Early History of English Poor Relief.* 1990.

McIntosh, Marjorie K. "Local Responses to the Poor in Late Medieval and Tudor England." *Continuity & Change,* vol. 3, pp. 209–245.

Newman-Brown, W. "The Receipt of Poor Relief and Family Situation: Aldenham, Hertfordshire,

P

1630–1690." In *Land, Kinship, and Life-Cycle*. R.M. Smith, ed., pp. 405–422. 1984.

Slack, Paul. *Poverty and Policy in Tudor and Stuart England*. 1988.

———. *The English Poor Law: 1531–1782*. Economic History Society. 1990; repr. 1995.

Wales, Tim. "Poverty, Poor Relief, and the Life-Cycle: Some Evidence from Seventeenth-Century Norfolk." In *Land, Kinship, and Life-Cycle*. R.M. Smith, ed., pp. 351–404. 1984.

Steven Hindle

SEE ALSO

Crime; Criminal Law; Government, Local; London; Money, Inflation, and Moneylending; Popham, John; Population and Demography; Social Classes; Towns; Vagrants

Popham, John (c. 1531–1607)

An eminent jurist and parliamentarian, Sir John Popham was speaker of the House of Commons and holder of the highest legal offices of the crown, eventually becoming lord chief justice in 1592, when he was knighted. He was known for his severity toward thieves and prostitutes and the persecution of Catholics.

Born into a well-connected family in Somerset, he attended Balliol College, Oxford, and the Middle Temple, London. According to Aubrey, he kept "profligate company" in his youth before undertaking an exemplary study of the law. Having won distinction as a special pleader, he was made a privy councilor in 1571. In the same year he began a ten-year parliamentary career when he was returned M.P. for Bristol, where he was recorder (legal advisor). Among the bills he helped draft was one that put the poor to work to prevent idleness, anticipating an act he was to draft as lord chief justice to banish vagrants beyond the seas. Later still, in 1606, he procured patents for two companies for the colonial development of Virginia.

In 1579, Popham was created solicitor general, and speaker the following year. To the queen's question as to what had passed in his first session as speaker he offered his celebrated reply, "If it please your Majesty, seven weeks." He was appointed attorney general in 1581 when he significantly ruled that the Presbyterian Thomas Cartwright's *Book of Discipline* was not seditious as he intended to "exercise [it] with the peace of the church and the law of the land." As lord chief justice, he presided at

trials of high treason, notably of the earl of Essex (1600), Sir Walter Ralegh (1603), and the Jesuit Henry Garnet (1606). The trials were hopelessly weighted against the accused: Popham denied Ralegh's request that he confront Sir Henry Cobham, his incriminator, explaining "That there must not be such a gap opened for the destruction of the King"; at Essex's trial, Ralegh turned state's witness and described to the court the imprisonment of himself and other officers of state at Essex House the day of the earl's attempted insurrection. Before Garnet's trial he hunted down, tried, and sentenced to death a number of Catholic priests and lay persons.

Described by Aubrey as a "huge, heavie, ugly man," and praised by Sir Edward Coke for his "universal and admirable experience and knowledge of all business which concerned the commonwealth," Popham died in 1607, leaving a considerable fortune.

BIBLIOGRAPHY

Aubrey, John. *Brief Lives*. Oliver Lawson Dick, ed. 1949.

Caraman, Philip. *Henry Garnet 1555–1606 and the Gunpowder Plot*. 1964.

Collinson, Patrick. *The Elizabethan Puritan Movement*. 1967.

Fosse, Edward. *The Judges of England*. Vol. 6. 1857.

Hargraves, Francis. *A Complete Collection of State Trials*. 4th edition. vol. 1. 1776.

Stephen, H.L., ed. *State Trials: Political and Social*. Vol. 1. 1899.

David Freeman

SEE ALSO

Cartwright, Thomas; Colonial Development; Devereux, Robert; Poor Laws; Ralegh, Walter; Vagrancy

Popular Literature

Popular literature in the Tudor period comprises such a diversity of forms and modes that it is difficult to generalize about its nature or functions. The term here denotes printed matter largely devoted to the tastes and economic means of the less educated; but cultural historians have recently questioned the binary division between elite and popular in this period, and have emphasized that the reading of "popular" literature was not exclusive to a particular social group.

The dissemination of Protestant values encouraged the spread of literacy, but even so it was largely confined to 50 percent or so of the adult male population (less outside

London), although the number of readers from the "middling sort" and the lower socioeconomic groups was increasing all the time. The dissemination of popular literature outside London relied on a network of chapmen, traveling ballad sellers and pedlars. In the city the end of the period saw the growth of an Elizabethan Grub Street, and the appearance of the first men to make (or attempt to make) a living purely by the pen. A number of these writers were well educated, but though they tended to address themselves to the "gentlemen readers," their work clearly reached the socially humbler. The conditions for professional authorship were not yet in place, but they were beginning to be established.

The cheapest and most widespread forms of popular literature, however, tended to be anonymous or pseudonymous. Ballads were disseminated in enormous numbers, only a small proportion of which have survived. The broadside ballad itself is perhaps the typical kind of popular and ephemeral literature: in printed form it was cheap and easily obtainable, often illustrated; its range of subject matter was wide, covering topical themes of politics and religion, as well as less historically specific ones of heroism, adventure, love, and crime; it had little commercial, though much cultural, value. It exemplifies the interaction between oral and literate culture typical of the time.

Almanacs and prognostications, also generally anonymous, constitute a minor but intriguing subgenre; they were widely popular, and disseminated simple scientific information along with apocalyptic eschatology. For a time they exceeded all other categories of printed book or pamphlet in their annual sales. Burlesque almanacs and comic prognostications began to appear from the middle of the sixteenth century. They mock astrologers' predictions as banal truisms, and on this basis some of them construct modestly satirical accounts of social and moral behavior. Later they came to be used as a vehicle for political propaganda.

Jest books, another popular subgenre, form a link between the fictional tastes of the period and those of the Middle Ages, since many of the anecdotes compiled in them, even when grouped around a contemporary figure such as Richard Tarlton or George Peele, derive from stories that had been in circulation for centuries. The recycling of such materials testifies to the growing market for simple recreational texts; their subject matter often connects them with the rogue fiction and cony-catching pamphlets so characteristic of the second half of the period. Much rogue literature claims utilitarian justification and is presented by means of strategies to prove its authenticity.

Robert Record, *The Castle of Knowledge* (1579). Record authored several enormously popular books that provided instruction in basic mathematics and popular science. On this title page, Urania (left), illuminated by the sun, holds a compass representing rational knowledge; the blind goddess Fortune (right), illuminated by the changeable moon, pulls cord tied to "The wheele of Fortune." God's providence, revealed by rational means in nature, counters the ignorance of an irrational trust in Fortune. Reproduced from the original by permission of the Henry E. Huntington Library and Art Gallery.

In fact, however, much of it is presented as new material although it is taken from earlier texts, and compromises its authenticating strategies by a clear interest in fictionalizing. But the existence of an extensive underclass on the fringes of organized society, both in the country and in the city, was a reality documented in popular literature and in the drama. Rogue fictions express not just anxiety about marginal groups but also fascination with them; and the world of vagrants and petty criminals often reveals a subversive similarity, in its organization and "laws," to a respectable society with structures designed to privilege some members and disadvantage others.

P

A strain of unease with existing forms of social organization and a sense of widespread injustice runs through much of this popular literature, although it exists alongside a strong conservative emphasis on the preservation of traditional values. Pamphlets dealing with plague, a phenomenon endemic in London, or with prison life, regularly highlight the gulf between rich and poor revealed in circumstances that throw into relief the vulnerability of the masses in a society without any organized system of social welfare. But writers on plague exhibit the familiar tension between the need for rational investigation of the phenomenon as a material occurrence in order to find practical solutions and the quietist resolution to accept suffering as part of divine design.

But there was also a growing demand for simple topical printed material reflecting and also explaining the material conditions of everyday life, though the recording of real-life events is mediated by the appeal to the emotions in an emphasis on strangeness, wonder, horror, or fear. Censorship was strict, and domestic news was severely restricted in its handling of political matters or the activities of those in power. The subjects of news pamphlets were commonly sensational and usually approached in a didactic spirit; accounts of crimes and prodigious events were shaped so as to demonstrate the dire consequences of ungodly behavior and the guiding providence of God.

Print controversies were deliberately generated also at times to capitalize on the appetite for topical issues, and themselves generated more and more material; the controversies over women, the flyting between Thomas Nashe and Gabriel Harvey, and the anonymous Whipper pamphlets (pamphlets that attack like "whips" and that were unsigned satiric verse exchanges between Edward Gilpin and Nicholas Breton and some unknown author in 1601), all exemplify this trend. Such series are characterized by their spontaneous, improvisional style; they function as displays of wit, often ribald, gossipy, carnivalesque, always intimate in tone. They illustrate the instability of the author-function in the period in their multidirectional viewpoints and flexibility of perspective. In an age when the concept of literary property was hardly formulated, there are high levels of anonymous and pseudonymous writing, of borrowing, plagiarism, and the recycling of familiar material. In any case, many of the printed texts derive from oral forms collectively originated and formulated over periods of time through a process of accretion and accumulation.

Much of this pamphleteering can be categorized loosely as social satire or moralistic literature that has affinities with sermon as well as earlier literature. The persona of the satirist or castigator of social evils is sometimes modeled on that of Lucianic or Menippean satire. Medieval satiric traditions such as the Seven Deadly Sins or the Satire of Estates persisted, and the preacher often provided a model for the role of pamphlet moralizer. Themes for satire and moralizing were familiar from classical and medieval writing, but took on a new inflection from the anti-prodigal discourse of the sixteenth century, hence the prominence in Seven Deadly Sins satire of pride and gluttony, both depicted in terms of conspicuous consumption and the indecorous display of wealth. The conservative moral values of the satirist underlie attacks on extravagant clothing, especially when influenced by foreign fashions, and the use of cosmetics, but the particular emphases of such satire need to be studied in the light of attitudes toward a developing consumer society.

Indeed, this was an age of social transition when popular writers were much concerned with the erosion of traditional values, and especially of class boundaries. Pamphleteers lament the decay of hospitality and express fear of "upstart" or prodigal behavior. The theme of country-city antagonism that informs accounts of young heirs coming up to London from the country and being exploited by city sharks becomes prominent in the second half of the century. Pamphlet satire is often shaped around the portraits of distinctive types, and figures familiar from medieval satire are joined by those who embody preoccupations, particularly economic ones, of the Tudor age: the politic bankrupt, the merchant's extravagant wife, the spendthrift heir, the tobacco-taker. The cultivation of social self-awareness, like so many other facets of Tudor popular literature, marks the growth of early modern culture.

BIBLIOGRAPHY

Capp, Bernard. *Astrology and the Popular Press: English Almanacs 1500–1800.* 1979.

Clark, Sandra. *The Elizabethan Pamphleteers: Popular Moralistic Pamphlets, 1580–1640.* 1983.

Hutson, Lorna. *Thomas Nashe in Context.* 1989.

Judges, A.V., ed. *The Elizabethan Underworld: A Collection of Tudor and Early Stuart Tracts and Ballads Telling of the Lives and Misdoings of Vagabonds, Rogues, and Cozeners.* 1930.

Kinney, Arthur F. *Rogues, Vagabonds, and Sturdy Beggars.* 1990.

Miller, Edwin Havilland. *The Professional Writer in Elizabethan England.* 1959.

Shaaber, M.A. *Some Forerunners of the Newspaper in England, 1476–1622.* 1929.

Sheavyn, Phoebe. *The Literary Profession in the Elizabethan Age.* 2nd edition, revised by J.W. Saunders. 1967.

Watt, Tessa. *Cheap Print and Popular Piety, 1550–1640.* 1991.

Wilson, F.P. "The English Jestbooks of the Sixteenth and Early Seventeenth Centuries." In *Shakespearean and Other Studies by F.P. Wilson.* Helen Gardner, ed. 1969.

Wurzbach, Natascha. *The Rise of the English Street Ballad, 1550–1650.* 1990.

Sandra Clark

SEE ALSO

Ballad; Broadsides; Censorship; Harvey, Gabriel; Jest Books; Nashe, Thomas; News Quartos; Peele, George; Plague; Printing, Publishing and Bookselling; Satire; Social Classes; Tarlton, Richard; Vagrants

Population and Demography

The Tudors ruled in what was essentially a nonstatistical century. Official records were kept for very specific religious or fiscal purposes rather than because of any general belief that they were beneficial. For this reason our knowledge of population history is far from complete. Parish registers began to be kept in some parishes during the 1530s, but the geographical coverage, survival, and completeness of information are highly variable in the sixteenth century. Lack of consistently and accurately recorded vital events inhibit our knowledge of sixteenth-century population. In spite of these problems, the resourceful use of flawed and imperfect data has revolutionized our understanding of demography and its social context in recent years.

Population structures and the dynamics of change in Tudor England are in some ways familiar to modern readers and in other ways very different. Taxation schedules and listings indicate that average household size was comparatively small at between four and five people; composition was simple with husband, wife, and unmarried children comprising the average household. Household formation depended on economic independence—young newlyweds set up their own homes rather than joining extended families. England's population was very young: a third were aged 15 years or less.

The best estimates we have are that England had approximately 2 million inhabitants when Henry VII ascended the throne, 2.8 million people at Henry VIII's death, and 4.1 million at the end of the Tudor era. Almost all of these lived and worked on the land. Just 3 percent lived in towns of 10,000 or more inhabitants in 1500, and 6 percent in 1600, more than half of these being Londoners. With 200,000 dwellers in 1600, London was one of the largest cities in Europe and fourteen times larger than the next city, Norwich. London had a preponderance of males because of apprentice immigration, but in other towns there were more females than males and a higher proportion of female-headed households compared with rural areas. Towns created unique employment opportunities for women.

With poor hygiene and overcrowded housing, even the small towns were unhealthy places to live. Across England, life expectancy was short by modern standards: a little over thirty years in 1500, a little under forty years in 1600. That does not mean that everyone died at that age. The real difference between the sixteenth century and the present lies in the age structure of mortality. A third of all deaths occurred among those aged twenty or younger in sixteenth-century England, compared with 2 percent today. Of every 1,000 children born in those days, 160 would die before their first birthday. However, those who survived until age thirty could, on average, expect at least a further thirty years of life. The reason for the very different mortality patterns then lies in the prevalence of killer diseases in Tudor England. Smallpox, influenza, typhoid, and typhus were just some of the prevalent diseases over which contemporary medicine had no control. Perhaps a fifth of London's population died in a plague epidemic of 1563. Plague is a high-profile disease that commentators were likely to record because of its symptoms and urban focus, but it was not equally serious everywhere, and only 10 percent of all deaths can be attributed to it.

Because the pattern of mortality was so very different in the sixteenth century it used to be assumed that this was the principal motor of demographic change. Swinging mortality crises could wipe out large numbers in a few months. Short-term fluctuations could be extreme, as in the late 1550s when an influenza epidemic reduced population by more than 5 percent. With low agricultural productivity and grossly unequal wealth distribution, not everyone had enough to eat. Famines grew worryingly common in Elizabeth's reign, and those of 1594, and again 1596–1598, were particularly severe in the north and west of England. Yet, fatal shortages of food were never a national problem, and in spite of these crises, however caused, people were living longer on average in 1600 than in 1500.

P

The absence of serious national famines does not mean that the Tudors presided over a golden age. There was much poverty throughout the period, and after roughly 1570, there is clear evidence that England had too many people to support with its backward and relatively inflexible economy. Inflation rose and real wages fell, impoverishing many more people. Yet, this was not really a Malthusian regime where population grew until it was reined in by savage mortality crises. There was slack elsewhere in the demographic regime and, while adjustments were slow, they did produce results. The economy did change, notably with improvements in agriculture and the growth of foreign trade as the seventeenth century dawned. As economic opportunities contracted in the late sixteenth century, men and women began to marry younger, reducing the number of children they had and thus easing population growth rates. In some senses Tudors were the victims of natural forces, such as disease, over which they had no control, but in others they adjusted intelligently and vigorously to the opportunities before them in a way that gave them one of the highest average living standards in Europe.

Aspects of the demographic regime help to explain this relatively favorable situation. Women married for the first time in their mid-twenties and roughly one in ten never married. Fertility was "natural" in the sense that there was no widespread use of contraception. Yet the average birth interval was thirty months (largely because of prolonged breast-feeding), and the average woman would generally bear no more than six children before menopause. High mortality meant remarriage was very common, with perhaps a quarter of all marriages being remarriages during Elizabeth's reign. Fertility was thus relatively low. It could vary, and there are certain distinctive features of procreation that deserve mention. Regional variations in illegitimacy and prenuptial pregnancy may indicate different courtship and marriage patterns across England. Illegitimacy was much higher in the north and west than in the south and east before c. 1650, but still well under 5 percent of all births. For England as a whole, nearly a quarter of all brides had conceived before marriage.

A final way in which population could be adjusted to resources both locally and nationally was by the movement of people. Tudor England was far from being a closed and immobile society. Geographical mobility within was extensive from an early date. Apprentices moved from all over England to London, and there was considerable short-distance (and frequent) movement by farm servants, mostly young single people of both sexes aged fifteen to twenty-four who made up one-sixth of the population at any one time. Vagrancy came to be seen as a serious problem from the 1570s onward. Finally, emigration to Ireland picked up as the century wore on, although it is not clear if emigration was the result of pressure of population on resources or simply that opportunities were perceived to be better there, especially for farmers and skilled craftsmen.

BIBLIOGRAPHY

Houston, R.A. *The Population History of Britain and Ireland, 1500–1750.* 2nd edition. 1995.

Wrigley, E.A., and R.S. Schofield. *The Population History of England, 1541–1871. A Reconstruction.* 2nd edition. 1989.

———. *Son of Population History.* 1997.

R.A. Houston

SEE ALSO

Childbirth; Economy; London; Marriage and Marriage Law; Money, Inflation, and Moneylending; Plague; Towns; Vagrancy

Pornography

While the word pornography is not extant in the Tudor lexical world, products that we (and early moderns) would define as such did exist. If we move beyond the literal meaning of "writing about whores" to a broader definition of pornography as writing that depicts sexual activity with a range of aims from arousal to laughter, then we can view a spectrum of works. Joseph Hall in *Virgidemiarum* (1597) claims that the muses in his native land used to be vestal maids, but now ". . . is *Pernassus* turned to the stewes: / And on Bay-stockes the wanton Myrtle growes. / *Cytheron* hill's become a Brothel-bed." Tudor commentators place the works of this "Brothel-bed" on a scale ranging from the "obscene" (the most direct depictions of sexual activity) and the "wanton" (indirect, more subtle presentations of such activity) to the "bawdy" (comic presentations). And moralists, theologians, and satirists writing on literature are in remarkable agreement about the works that constitute the pornographic canon. It is a body of literature seen as informed by a classical tradition made up of particular writings of Ovid and Martial and reinvigorated, with even more graphic presentation, by Italian practitioners of the Renaissance, most notably Poggio (known for his *Facetiae* or jests); Pietro Aretino (infamous for his *Ragionamenti*, or dialogues, and his *sonetti lussuriosi*, sonnets written to accompany lascivious drawings by Guilio Romano, almost

P

always referred to in Tudor accounts as Aretino's *posizioni* or positions); the writers of paradoxical encomia (Francesco Berni in praise of peaches, Francesco Bini in praise of the French disease, Francesco Molza in praise of figs).

The English corpus is seen to be made up also of collections of jests we would characterize as bawdy, the verses of epigrammatists who do more than "glance at *Lesbia's* deed," writers of paradoxical encomia (Sir John Harington in his *Metamorphosis of Ajax*), and purveyors of outright salaciousness, particularly Thomas Nashe in his "Choise of Valentines" (also referred to as "Nashe's Dildo"). It is a keynote of such attacks on this literature that English creators exceed their classical and Italian predecessors in the degree of explicitness of their works. Gabriel Harvey is representative of such an attribution in his attacks on Nashe. Also consistently noted is an audience for such works with an "itching" to be "tickled" or "scratched." The creators or collectors of such works certainly are themselves conscious of the tradition in which they work. Collections of jests from 1525 until well into the seventeenth century (see *Shakespeare Jest-Books*, W. Carew Hazlett, ed, repr. 1964) recycle or rework standard bawdy jokes (with a particularly English bent toward the scatological). Epigrammatists Sir John Harington (in widely read manuscripts), Sir John Davies (*Epigrams,* c. 1595), and Everard Guilpin (*Skialetheia,* 1598) are important figures for a tradition that also survives robustly into the seventeenth century. Thomas Nashe, styling himself the "English Aretino," is seen as the chief purveyor of pornography through his "Choise of Valentines" (known only in manuscript, but widely referred to), a work that describes in detail the poet's encounter with a whore whom he cannot satisfy, driving her to the use of her dildo. Nashe is also known for his scabrous attacks on Harvey. It should also be noted that Pietro Aretino, justly regarded as the first creator of modern pornography in his *Ragionamenti,* was readily available to English readers, as his works were being printed and sold in London in the 1580s by John Wolfe (with fictitious places of publication, i.e., *Bengodi,* "Enjoy yourself"). By 1598, thanks to John Florio's Italian-English dictionary, *A Worlde of Wordes,* English definitions for Italian words associated with sexuality or words with sexual connotations were easily accessible to English readers.

BIBLIOGRAPHY

Dworkin, Andrea. *Pornography: Men Possessing Women.* 1979

Frantz, David O. *Festum Voluptatis: A Study of Renaissance Erotica.* 1989.

Goffen, Rona. *Titian's Women.* 1997.

Hunt, Lynn, ed. *The Invention of Pornography.* 1993.

Thompson, Roger. *Unfit for Modest Ears.* 1979.

David O. Frantz

SEE ALSO

Davies, John; Epigrams; Florio, John; Guilpin, Everard; Hall, Joseph; Harington, John; Harvey, Gabriel; Jest Books; Nashe, Thomas

Porter, Henry (d.1599)

Little reliable information survives about the life of Henry Porter, a playwright active at the turn of the sixteenth century. Some have suspected, on the grounds of the "Gent." on his surviving play's title page and his reference to himself as a "poor scholar," that Porter was a university man. The only biographical certainty is that Porter died in a duel with John Day on June 7, 1599. Francis Meres lists him among the best of Britain's comic dramatists, and Philip Henslowe's diary links him to such lost plays as *Love Prevented, Hot Anger Soon Cold* (possibly an alternative title for *Two Angry Women of Abington*), and *Two Merry Women of Abington.* Porter is also associated with the lost historical drama *The Spencers.* Porter's reputation now rests entirely on his single extant play, *The Two Angry Women of Abington,* printed in quarto in 1599. A comedy of humours with similarities to *The Merry Wives of Windsor, Two Angry Women* concerns a heated quarrel between two country wives, Mrs. Barnes and Mrs. Goursey, and the efforts of their husbands and children to heal the rift with a marriage between families. Beneath this comedy of feuding neighbors is an examination of women's ambivalence about marriage, portrayed in the wives' anxieties about their husbands' infidelities and in daughter Mall Barnes's extraordinary frankness about sexual double standards, all set in motion by Mr. Barnes's innocent question, "hast thou a mind to marry?" Equally notable are the play's contentious servants, particularly the sententious Nicholas Proverbs and vainglorious Dick Coomes. The play's fourth act is a lively extended night scene, or "nocturnal," in which all lose their way, and it suggests Porter's talent for multiplying and choreographing supposes. The play was of sufficient popularity for Henslowe to finance a sequel in 1598.

BIBLIOGRAPHY

Gurr, Andrew. "Intertexuality at Windsor." *Shakespeare Quarterly,* vol. 38, pp. 189–200.

P

Lawrence, William J. "The Elizabethan Nocturnal." *Pre-Restoration Stage Studies*. 1927.

Nosworthy, J.M. "Henry Porter." *English*, vol. 6, pp. 65–69.

Porter, Henry. *The Two Angry Women of Abington*. Alexander Dyce, ed. 1841.

Douglas Lanier

SEE ALSO

Day, John; Henslowe, Philip; Meres, Francis

Poynings, Edward (1459–1521)

A soldier and a statesman, Edward Poynings led a failed insurrection against Richard III in support of the earl of Buckingham in 1483, after which he fled to the Continent and took up the cause of Henry Tudor, earl of Richmond. Poynings landed with the future Henry VII at Milford Haven in August 1485, at which time Henry immediately made him a knight banneret.

During the reigns of both Henry VII and Henry VIII, Poynings led numerous military and political expeditions at home and across Europe, often in the Netherlands. For his efforts, he eventually became a knight of the garter, a Privy Council member, warden of the Cinque Ports, and comptroller of the royal household.

His most renowned mission was to Ireland, a Yorkist stronghold, in October 1494. As lord deputy of Ireland under the future Henry VIII, then three years old, Poynings imprisoned the viceroy of Ireland, Gerald Fitzgerald, the eighth earl of Kildare, who had supported two Yorkist pretenders to the throne, Lambert Simnel and Perkin Warbeck. Poynings also summoned a meeting of the Irish Parliament at Drogheda, which passed a measure making Ireland subject to all laws passed in England before 1494, as well as two important acts subsequently referred to as Poynings' Law. These prescribed that no Parliament in Ireland could be summoned without prior approval of the English sovereign and that no acts of the Irish Parliament were valid unless previously submitted and approved by the English sovereign. Not until 1782 did the Irish Parliament regain its independence with the repeal of Poynings' Law.

BIBLIOGRAPHY

Edwards, R. Dudley, and T.W. Moody. "The History of Poynings' Law: Part 1, 1494–1615." *Irish Historical Studies*, vol. 2, pp. 415–424.

Quinn, David B. "The Early Interpretation of Poynings' Law, 1494–1534." *Irish Historical Studies*, vol. 2, pp. 241–254.

Alan B. Farmer

SEE ALSO

Cinque Ports; Henry VII; Ireland, History of; Simnel, Lambert; Warbeck, Perkin

Praemunire

A Latin word meaning "to fore-arm," "praemunire" is used to indicate a legal procedure designed to prevent appeals being taken to a higher court outside the king of England's jurisdiction. The only higher court in existence was the Papal Curia in Rome, though any ecclesiastical jurisdiction claiming exemption from the king's laws would also be included.

The first Statute of *Praemunire* was enacted in 1353 (27 Edward III s. 1). It followed naturally from an earlier Statute of Provisors (1351) that aimed to eliminate the pope's right of presentation to ecclesiastical benefices in England. It was not very effective, however, and in 1390, a second Statute of Provisors was enacted, to be followed three years later by a second Statute of *Praemunire* (16 Richard II c. 5). Like its predecessor, it did not prove to be very effective either, and by 1500, it had generally been forgotten.

It thus came as something of a surprise when Henry VIII, in his battle against the church, decided to resurrect the statutes as a way of compelling the English clergy to profess allegiance to him instead of going over his authority to Rome. From Henry's point of view, appealing to the fourteenth-century statutes had the great merit of appearing to respect constitutional legality. Certainly no one could have accused him of inventing these laws merely to suit his immediate needs. On the other hand, it was generally understood that the statutes had fallen into disuse, and that Henry was seeking to revive them for purposes very different from those originally intended. In the end, Henry won his battle, and *Praemunire* can therefore be regarded as one of the instruments by which the Church of England was separated from the jurisdiction of Rome in the years 1529–1534.

BIBLIOGRAPHY

Bray, G.L. *Documents of the English Reformation*. 1994.

Gerald Bray

SEE ALSO
Church of England; Henry VIII; Reformation, English

Predestination
See Calvinism

Presbyterianism
See Calvinism; Church Polity

Preston, Thomas (1537–1598)

Thomas Preston is the putative author of *A lamentable tragedy mixedful of pleasant mirth, conteyning the life of Cambises king of Percia.* Published in 1569, *Cambises* is an important example of the episodic popular drama of this period, its thirty-eight parts divided on the title page for a traveling company of eight to perform. Critics have been divided over the authorship of the work; one possibility is that Preston was an unknown itinerant playwright-actor.

However, the author is probably a Cambridge scholar who was born in 1537 in Buckinghamshire, educated at Eton, and a graduate of Kings College (B.A., 1557; M.A., 1561). The inscription on this Thomas Preston's tombstone indicates that he was married and had a significant reputation both for his scholarship and the favor he had received from Elizabeth I. He was a doctor of law and a man renowned for his eloquence, but there is no mention of him as a playwright either here or by any contemporary. He wrote four works in Latin that can be positively identified as his. In 1560, he contributed a short poem to the Cambridge collection of poetry written on the occasion of the posthumous restoration of honors to Martin Bucer and Paul Fagius. In 1571, his "In obitum D. Nicolai Carri oratoris, & medici excellentissimi" appears in Nicholas Carr's *Demosthenes.* In 1564, Preston favorably impressed Queen Elizabeth, who referred to him as her scholar on her visit to Cambridge when he was one of four disputants in the Philosophy Act, negating the position, "Monarchi est optimus status reipublicae." During this visit he also performed in *Dido* and at her departure delivered an oration, "Ortatio in Discessu Regina." Several contemporaries commented on his skill and method of delivery, including Anthony á Wood, since Preston "acted so admirably well in the Tragedy of *Dido* . . . and did so genteely and gracefully dispute before her, that she [Elizabeth] gave him 20 £ per An. for so doing." Preston later went on to become master of Trinity Hall at Cambridge, and during 1589–1590, vice-chancellor of the university. He died in 1598 and was buried in the chapel at Trinity Hall.

BIBLIOGRAPHY

Armstrong, William A. "The Authorship and Political Meaning of *Cambises.*" *The Elizabethan Stage,* vol. 36, pp. 289–299.

Bevington, David M. *From "Mankind" to Marlow: Growth of Structure in the Popular Drama of Tudor England.* 1962.

Chambers, E.K. *The Elizabethan Stage.* 1923.

Dust, Philip, and William D. Wolf. "Recent Studies in Early Tudor Drama: *Gorboduc, Ralph Roister Doister, Gammer Gurton's Needle,* and *Cambises.*" *English Literary Renaissance,* vol. 8, pp. 107–119 (116–118).

Hill, Eugene D. "The First Elizabethan Tragedy: A Contextual Reading of *Cambises.*" *Studies in Philology,* vol. 89, pp. 404–433.

Johnson, Robert Carl. "Critical Edition of Thomas Preston's *Cambises.*" *Salzburg Studies in English Literature,* vol. 23. 1975.

Manly, J.M. "The Children of the Chapel Royal and Their Masters." In *The Cambridge History of English Literature,* Vol. 6: *The Drama to 1642, Part 2.* A.W. Ward and A. R. Waller, eds. pp. 314–329. 1907–1917.

Norland, Howard B. "'Lamentable Tragedy Mixed Ful of Pleasant Mirth': The Enigma of *Cambises.*" *Comparative Drama,* vol. 26, pp. 330–342.

Robert Carl Johnson

SEE ALSO
Drama, History of

Price Revolution

The term "price revolution" refers to the long-term inflation in prices that began in approximately 1500 and continued through the sixteenth century to 1650. Prices of grain and meat increased seven-fold between 1490 and 1640, with the most dramatic increases occurring in the late sixteenth century. Prices of industrial products and cloth, however, rose at a much slower rate, approximately three-fold in the same period. After 1650, prices stabilized for the next 100 years, and some actually dropped in a period of deflation in the late seventeenth century.

The inflation of prices in Tudor England was part of a European-wide phenomenon, long considered to have

P

been caused by monetary factors; specifically, gold and silver from America began to flow into Europe at almost the same time prices began to rise. Contemporary explanations for inflation were dominated by monetary factors; Sir Thomas Smith, in the first version of his *Discourse of the Common Weal* (1549), blamed the debasement of the coinage in the 1540s, arguing that "the alteration of the coin" was the original cause of the inflation because of the sudden increase in the money supply without a concurrent increase in the amount of goods to be bought. Later, in a passage he added in 1581, he also blamed the influx of "infinite sums of gold and silver, which are gathered from the Indies and other countries." Gerard de Malynes repeated this view at length in his *Lex Mercatoria* (1622), and this came to be the standard explanation until the second half of the twentieth century.

The assumptions behind these explanations rested on the fact that almost all currency took the form of gold or—more commonly—silver coins, and that the value of these coins was based on their size and the amount of precious metal in their alloy. The value of gold and silver depended on their scarcity, and price was governed by an international market for these scarce metals. It was reasoned that as gold and silver became more plentiful in Europe the price of the metals would drop, thereby making coins worth less. This meant that their exchange value would also drop as a measure of prices if most goods continued to hold relatively the same value.

These views held up until research into demographic trends and the relationship between the purchasing power of wages and the actual prices of different commodities began to be published in the 1950s, raising serious questions about the coherence of this explanation. Most importantly, scholars discovered that the change in prices for different commodities was by no means uniform, which would be expected in a purely monetary explanation. The prices of industrial goods, for instance, went up only half as much as the price of food, as also did the price of labor. Furthermore, when measured in averages by decade, prices began to rise before the greatest increases of importation of bullion into Europe, going up by 33 percent in the 1520s. Even more problematic is the fact that jumps in price did not correspond to currency changes brought about by debasement and subsequent revaluation. Although prices did go up by 34 percent in the 1540s over the average of the previous decade, the greatest percentage price rise in the whole period from 1500 to 1640 occurred in the 1550s, when prices went up by 50 percent. But in 1551, the value of the debased silver currency (almost all the circulating currency at the time) was halved in value overnight by Edward VI in an attempt to bring it more into line with its intrinsic silver value, which should have reduced inflation if it had truly been caused by Henry VIII's debasement of the currency; instead, the opposite occurred.

The current explanation for the inflation of prices now holds that it was caused primarily by demographic factors. Scholars argue that, for technological and social reasons, supply was unable to meet the growing demand for food, clothing, and housing created by increasing population. Thus, the rise in prices occurred as supply and demand in the marketplace drove highest the prices of items in greatest demand. This explanation derives strong support from the fact that changes in prices followed the demographic pattern of population change very closely. Population began to rise noticeably in the 1520s and stopped by the 1660s, actually dropping somewhat in the Restoration period, and prices followed suit. The fact that the price of food went up much more than other goods also supports this explanation; population growth placed pressure on agriculture to increase its productivity, and this was difficult to achieve given contemporary technology and customs of landholding. Food production throughout the period remained most dependent on the quality of the weather, and a bad harvest could drive up prices enormously.

Most transactions were done on credit, which is why the rapid fluctuations in the amount of money between 1540 and 1565 had so little effect on the pattern of prices. Credit was based on trust, and as long as trust could be extended, credit remained flexible enough to expand to meet economic needs. The economy grew faster than the money supply, and population growth created demand-driven inflation that caused prices to increase more rapidly than the money supply; thus, the demand for money exceeded its supply. Even with an increase in coinage the amount of coins in circulation only rose from about nine shillings per person in 1544 to about fourteen shillings in 1590. Had there been no inflation, this growth of only about 60 percent would not have been sufficient to meet the needs of the rapidly expanding market economy. But between 1540 and 1600, food prices also more than trebled, while industrial prices doubled. As a result, by the end of the sixteenth century, the demand for money had probably increased approximately 500 percent, while the supply had only expanded by 60 percent.

Throughout the century the money supply was both insufficient and unreliable, and the supply of gold and silver was never large enough to meet the needs of the economy. Although money was the measure of economic transactions, in its actual use it was only the lubricant that oiled the much larger machinery of credit. What existed was a credit economy in which everything was measured by monetary prices, but where money was not the primary means of exchange.

BIBLIOGRAPHY

Braudel, F., and F. Spooner. "Prices in Europe from 1450–1750." In *The Cambridge Economic History of Europe*. Vol. 4. 1967.

Brown, H. Phelps, and S.V. Hopkins. *A Perspective of Wages and Prices*. 1981.

Challis, C.E. *The Tudor Coinage*. 1978.

Clay, C.G.A. *Economic Expansion and Social Change: England, 1500–1700*. Vol. I. 1984.

Kerridge, Eric. *Money and Banking in Early Modern England*. 1988.

Outhwaite, R.B. *Inflation in Tudor and Stuart England*. 1969.

Craig Muldrew

SEE ALSO

Agriculture; Economy; Money, Inflation, and Moneylending; Population and Demography

Printing, Publishing, and Bookselling

The invention of moveable type and the consequent production of multiple copies of comparatively inexpensive books constituted both a mechanical and an intellectual revolution. Previous to the invention of the printing press, the only way of reproducing any writing was to copy it out letter by letter. This process was by necessity costly in time, labor, and money. Consequently, only such writings were made into multiple copies as were deemed worth the effort. The exciting practical and intellectual possibilities presented by the printing press were immediately apparent. Here at last was a field in which the "moderns" (present-day people) could accomplish something that the "ancients" (the writers and inventors of Greece and Rome) had not been able to do—to outwit time by being able to pass on what they deemed important to future ages. For the first time in history, multiple copies of a writing could be disseminated in uniform, corrected, and nearly identical copies.

The inventor of a practicable process of printing by moveable type was Johann Gensfleisch zum Gutenberg of Mainz (1394–1468), who provided various shorter printed documents in the early 1450s while he was working on his great project, the "Gutenberg" Bible (1455–1456). From Mainz, printing presses radiated across Europe to the important urban centers: Cologne (1464), Basel (1466), Rome (1467), Venice (1469), and then on to Paris, Utrecht, Milan, Florence, Lyons, Valencia, Budapest, Cracow, Bruges, Westminster, Rostock, Geneva, Pilsen, London, Leipzig, Odense, and Stockholm before 1500. Printed works produced from Gutenberg to 1500, when the process was in its infancy, have been labeled "incunabula" (in the cradle). Although their production was small compared with what was to come in the sixteenth century, the outpouring of these early presses constituted a volume of reading matter without precedent. For some this presented great opportunity; others viewed it with grave apprehension.

The printing press itself is a relatively simple machine. The set pages of type were placed in a tray that could be slid under the upper plate ("platen") of the press. To hold the paper in the proper position during the actual moment of imposition, the printers used a frame of two hinged leaves, each covered with parchment: the upper leaf (the "frisket") had openings that matched the size of the pages to be printed. The blank sheet was laid on the lower frame (the "tympan") and fixed on pins to keep it from moving. The frisket then was lowered over the tympan and the frame folded again over the inked type. The entire unit then was rolled under the platen, which was lowered to make the impression.

In 1476, William Caxton brought printing to England, opening a bookshop near the church in Westminster, Parliament, and the court itself. At approximately the same time, he set up his press in the Almonry, west of the Abbey in present-day Tothill Street. The earliest surviving work from this press is an indulgence probably printed early in December 1476. The first book was the *History of Jason*, Caxton's translation of Raoul Lefevre's *Histoire de Jason* early in 1477; the second was Earl Rivers's translation of *Dicts or Sayeingis of the Philosophers* late in 1477. Caxton had been a mercer and official of the English colony in Bruges for thirty years before taking up printing. He evidently continued his relations with the Yorkist court when he returned to England, for he retained the favor not only of Edward IV but also of Richard III and Henry VII as well. Caxton died in 1492, having published nearly 100 books, seventy-four of them in English and twenty of them his own translations. After his death, his press was taken over by his assistant,

P

Wynkyn de Worde, a native of Alsace; about two-thirds of his works were texts for grammar-school boys. In 1500, he moved his shop to the city of London, joining other printers working in the environs of St. Paul's Cathedral where the printing trade would be centered for nearly 500 years.

In contrast to the new craft of printing, bookbinding was an ancient craft and continued to be practiced in essentially the same way as leaves of paper or vellum had been bound into volumes of manuscript writings. Unlike printing, binding was not in any way mechanized, and each book, large or small, had to be treated as a separate item. When the book was printed, and all of the sheets had dried, the binder assembled the individual sheets, collating his volume in the alphabetical order of the signatures on each sheet. When the sheets were properly ordered, they then could be folded: once for folio, twice for quarto, three times for octavo. By examining the signatures, the binder could check that the folds were made in the proper direction so that the pages would run consecutively. If it was a small book—a pamphlet of a play quarto, for instance—the left margin could be stabbed twice and the sheets sewn together. Once sewn, smaller books would be trimmed in part for neatness, but essentially because the top and fore edges of the folded leaves had to be trimmed to be turned and read. With a folio book, each quire of gathered and folded sheets would be sewn through the center of each fold to the cords forming the spine of the book. Here trimming would be for neatness only. Most books were sold sewn but not bound, leaving the purchaser to decide whether to bind them and what kind of binding to use—a practice still common into the early nineteenth century. In the case of larger books, only some complete sets of sheets would be gathered, folded, and sewn, leaving the balance to await further demand.

It should be remembered that manuscript books continued to be made long after the vast majority of books were printed. There were both writers and consumers who continued to prefer (and to be willing to pay for) handwritten copies of works. Indeed, there was a certain snobbish appeal to possessing individually made books. Well into the seventeenth century there was active employment for scribes who would not sully works by the mass-media method of print. Special occasions such as a presentation copy of a work also demanded the elegance and luxury of a unique manuscript copy.

Caxton had printed literature and devotional books, De Worde mostly textbooks. Their successors and competitors rapidly expanded their offerings to serve the legal, clerical, and business demands and eventually included items of wider appeal such as almanacs, ballads, and plays—all within the first half-century of printing. Although protection of native English craftsmen, enacted into law in 1534, did protect jobs by keeping out foreign artisans, it also resulted in English printing being technically and artistically inferior to the best work being done on the Continent. However, English printers did improve their offerings, making them more sophisticated. In 1495, De Worde first printed on English-made paper; in 1509, Pynson introduced Roman type (rather than black letter); in 1517, De Worde first used Greek characters and, in 1518, Arabic and Hebrew.

By 1500, vernacular Bibles had been printed (in Protestant territories) in German, Italian, Dutch, French, Danish, Russian, Bohemian, and Spanish; but in England, Henry VIII's conservatism forbade printing an English translation. William Tyndale had been driven into exile in Antwerp (where he was executed) and his translation finally published there by Miles Coverdale in 1537. It was not until 1539, when, under the influence of Lord Chancellor Thomas Cromwell and Archbishop of Canterbury Thomas Cranmer, Henry VIII allowed Coverdale's new translation to be published as the "Great Bible." This was followed in 1560 by the "Geneva Bible" (first published in Geneva by Marian exiles with Calvinist marginalia) and in 1568 by the "Bishop's Bible."

Even before the advent of printing, craftsmen engaged in making books: scribes, illustrators, bookbinders, and booksellers had banded themselves into a guild as the Company of Stationers. The company soon, out of sheer numbers, came to be controlled by the printers; and it was they who pressured the government to keep out foreign competition. Like all guilds, the Stationers regulated standards of work and production of their craft. In 1557, the Stationers went further, securing a royal charter from Mary I, taking control of printing and publishing as an industry. Henceforth it was the company, not economics, that decided how many presses a printer could have, the number of copies of an edition he might print before redistributing his type (up to 1500), and the number of journeymen and apprentices he could have. For their own records (no doubt partially to keep peace among their members), the Stationers Company established a register in which a printer or a bookseller might record his ownership of a title or his intention to publish it. Although inscription in the *Stationer's Register* constituted a somewhat nebulous form of copyright, many books were not registered and registration was not required for legal publication. Just because

P

a published book does not have a corresponding entry in the *Stationer's Register* does not mean that it was a "piracy." An unregistered book usually means no more than that the owner saw no reason to pay a fee to register it.

From Gutenberg on, printers had trouble amassing enough capital to pay for printing and assembling the entire run of a book before realizing any income from it. Most printers, including Gutenberg, took on partners who supplied additional cash. Eventually the moneylending partners became the publishers and were identified on title pages: "Printed *by* [the printer] *for* [the publisher] and are to be sold at the sign of [the shop of the bookseller]." Such precise documentation of the persons responsible for the book, necessary both for ownership and for bringing purchasers to the correct place, also facilitated governmental censorship. In a time when ecclesiastic matters were vital and where attacks on one portion of the power structure usually were perceived as an attack on all segments, it was logical that the bishop of London was designated to license material for the press. Controls, of course, were only as stringent as the controller made them. Times of acute religious and political controversy occasioned surreptitious publications and presses—and consequent confiscations and prosecutions. But in general, events and ideas during the Tudor reigns were chronicled by the vast expansion of the printing trade.

Among the important results of the spread of printing was the increasing standardization of spelling and punctuation. Important as this was for the spread of the use and comprehension of the language, this accomplishment pales before those of sheer preservation of all manner of records. Printing facilitated the spread of reading and knowledge to a degree never before possible.

BIBLIOGRAPHY

Aldis, Harry G. *The Printed Book.* 1951.
Bennett, H.S. *English Books and Readers, 1475 to 1557.* 1952.
———. *English Books and Readers, 1558 to 1603.* 1965.
Blayney, Peter W.M. *The Bookshops in Paul's Cross Churchyard.* 1990.
McKerrow, R.B. *An Introduction to Bibliography for Literary Students.* 1927.
Munby, F.A. *Publishing and Bookselling from the Earliest Times to the Present Day.* 1954.
Rostenberg, Leona. *Literary, Political, Scientific, Religious and Legal Publishing, Printing, and Bookselling in England, 1551–1700.* 1965.
Steinberg, S.H. *Five Hundred Years of Printing.* 1974.

Williams, George Walton. *The Craft of Printing and the Publication of Shakespeare's Works.* 1985.

William B. Long

SEE ALSO
Bible Translations; Caxton, William; Censorship; Humanism; Manuscripts; Reading Practices

Prisons
See Criminal Law; Southwark; Vagrants

Privateering

Privateering originated as a legal means of redress whereby merchants whose property had been seized by foreign princes or their subjects were authorized to set out ships to seek compensation through maritime predation. In theory it was subject to strict control. Regulations developed during the Tudor period meant that merchants were supposed to provide proof of loss before receiving a commission, or letter of reprisal, from the lord admiral. Such commissions usually authorized merchants to seize foreign ships or goods to cover the amount of their losses. In addition, all captured vessels were to be returned to England, where the High Court of Admiralty would adjudge them as lawful prize. These legal procedures were supposed to distinguish lawfully commissioned privateering from piracy, although the distinction was often in danger of breaking down as a result of political expediency. In practice, privateering was unregulated for most of the sixteenth century.

At a time when the royal navy was small, Tudor monarchs encouraged privateering during wartime as a means of weakening the enemy. During Henry VIII's wars with France, the crown issued proclamations enabling merchants and others to set out privateers with little government control. In consequence, many privateers indulged in unrestrained plunder of neutral shipping, arousing diplomatic protest and retaliation. The leaders of this campaign during the 1540s included William Hawkins of Plymouth and Robert Reneger of Southampton. Reneger's seizure of a rich treasure ship returning from the Spanish Indies in 1545 provoked a major diplomatic quarrel, but it also encouraged others to join in the war in hope of similar success.

The activities of Reneger and Hawkins provided a powerful precedent for their successors in the Elizabethan period, when privateering emerged as a major business. As Anglo-Spanish relations deteriorated during the 1560s

Privateering   569

P

and 1570s, privateering was encouraged by a combination of profit, patriotism, and Protestantism. In these circumstances privateering became the main form of maritime activity during the ensuing war with Spain from 1585 to 1603. Each year, between 100 and 200 vessels put to sea in search of plunder, set out by syndicates of merchants and shipowners, and a smaller group of gentry and aristocrats. As the war progressed, London merchants such as John Watts came to dominate, and reap most profit from, the business. Although the profit from privateering varied considerably, the booty returned to England amounted to about £200,000 a year, much of it exotic cargoes of American sugar or eastern spices.

The significance of Elizabethan privateering was wide-ranging. The seizure of Spanish shipping weakened the maritime economy of Spain, damaging its imperial defenses in the Caribbean. At the same time the influx of rich Spanish-American cargoes provided some compensation to English merchants for the loss of their markets in Spain. But success at sea was not evenly shared. Many adventurers lost heavily on privateering, including the earl of Cumberland, who sold off much of his landed estates in a fruitless quest for profit and honor. Across the Atlantic, privateering diverted English interest away from colonization to the detriment of the colony at Roanoke. But it also stimulated a shipbuilding boom, and enabled mariners like Christopher Newport to acquire extensive experience of the Atlantic and Caribbean. After 1603, this experience, and the profits made by promoters such as Watts, were to be used in the resumption of colonial enterprise in Virginia and in the development of English trade with the East Indies. In these ways privateering played a formative role in the emergence of an English seaborne empire during the first half of the seventeenth century.

BIBLIOGRAPHY

Andrews, K.R. *Elizabethan Privateering: English Privateering During the Spanish War, 1585–1603.* 1964.

———. *The Spanish Caribbean: Trade and Plunder, 1530–1630.* 1978.

———. *Trade, Plunder and Settlement: Maritime Enterprise and the Genesis of the British Empire, 1480–1630.* 1984.

Connell-Smith, G. *Forerunners of Drake.* 1954.

Quinn, D.B., and A.N. Ryan. *England's Sea Empire, 1550–1642.* 1983.

Williamson, G.C. *George, Third Earl of Cumberland (1558–1605): His Life and His Voyages.* 1920.

John C. Appleby

SEE ALSO
Colonial Development; Piracy; Shipbuilding; Trade, Overseas

Privy Chamber

Set apart by Henry VII as a refuge from the Presence Chamber or great hall, the Privy Chamber became for Henry VIII a series of rooms, in whatever palace he resided, for personal indulgence and a major center of governance. After the king's bedchamber, those admitted to the Privy Chamber enjoyed the most restricted access to the king. Henry VII enjoyed administrative detail, and brought much of his administration under his direct supervision in the chamber. It had no such function under Edward VI, Mary I, or Elizabeth I. Holbein's drawing of Henry VIII dining with his gentlemen of the Privy Chamber is the most famous depiction of its activity, and his huge mural of Henry with straddled legs and upright phallus dominated the wall of the Privy Chamber at Whitehall Palace until it was whitewashed by Oliver Cromwell. By 1519, Henry VIII's gentlemen of the Privy Chamber grew undisciplined, and Thomas Wolsey exiled most and then attempted to restrain all those who remained with the Eltham Ordinances of 1526. In 1533 and 1539, Thomas Cromwell tried to gain control of this proximity to the king, but in 1547, Sir Anthony Denny, as chief gentleman of the Privy Chamber and groom of the stool, controlled the dying Henry VIII and his signature stamp and helped to determine the succession.

As the center of court life, the Privy Chamber became under Henry VIII a principal location for ceremonial display. The young Edward VI ruled for too short a time to establish a ceremonial tradition, while under Mary I this function was restrained. But with the accession of Elizabeth I the Privy Chamber grew to reflect the Queen's unique reign: additional gentleman and lords of the chamber were appointed; their system of patronage ensured a flourishing musical and dramatic life at court; and the question of succession made access to the queen's chamber a privilege of her power.

BIBLIOGRAPHY

Elton, G.R. *The Tudor Revolution in Government.* 1959.

Richardson, W.C. *Tudor Chamber Administration, 1485–1547.* 1952.

Starkey, David. *The Reign of Henry VIII: Personalities and Politics.* 1985.

———. "Intimacy and Innovation: The Rise of the Privy Chamber, 1485–1547." In *The English Court from the Wars of the Roses to the Civil War.* David Starkey, ed. 1987.

Williams, Neville. *Henry VIII and His Court.* 1971.

Williams, Penry. *The Later Tudors: England 1547–1603,* pp. 124–31. 1995.

W.A. Sessions and Peter R. Moore

SEE ALSO

Elizabeth I; Government, Central Administration of; Holbein, Hans; Henry VIII; Royal Household; Royal Palaces; Wolsey, Thomas

Privy Council

See Government, Central Administration of

Processions, Lord Mayor's

Since the establishment of an elective office of mayor of the city of London in the thirteenth century, the mayor on inauguration day (October 29) would process from the Guildhall to the Thames River and move by barge to Westminster where he would take the oath of office. He would then return to the city. By the late Tudor period dramatic entertainment, sponsored by the mayor's guild, began to be presented along the processional route.

At the beginning of the fifteenth century the London guilds became responsible for setting the Midsummer Watch on June 24 and 29 . In 1504, pageant entertainment for this occasion included a procession and dramatic representations mainly of biblical and religious subjects, recalling the medieval heritage of the guilds. But these shows declined in the middle of the century because the guilds' attention shifted to the inauguration of the new mayor. Henry Machyn's *Diary* provides for 1553 the first report of a lord mayor's show, the name for this new procession that regularly included some kind of dramatic entertainment. In the more elaborate pageants, drama occurred not only along the route of the mayor's return to the city but also on the river.

In the early Elizabethan lord mayor's shows, religious and biblical subject matter prevails. But increasingly, allegorical and historical figures appear, the latter typically drawn from the city's or guild's history. In 1561, the first show for which speeches appear in guild records, the mythological figures Orpheus, Amphion, and Arion join the biblical character David in celebrating the power of music, especially the harp, thereby honoring the new mayor, Sir William Harper.

The year 1585 marks an important development in the mayoral pageants. For the first time an established dramatist wrote the entertainment, and a published text of the pageant survives. George Peele wrote the show, called simply, *The Device of the Pageant Borne before Wolstan Dixi;* the text contains only the speeches—no descriptions of characters or theatrical directions. Several characters represent London, frequently portrayed in later pageants. The initial speaker, riding on the back of a lynx, sign of the sponsoring Skinners guild, offers an interpretation in praise of London and the qualities necessary for the city's well-being. Speakers urge the mayor to help preserve the kingdom and the sovereign, thereby ensuring London's good health.

The Fishmongers chose Thomas Nelson to write the pageant for 1590, the printed text known simply as *The Device of the Pageant.* Nelson places his emphasis on allegorical figures and personages from actual English history. Initially sounding the theme of peace, Nelson pursues it through the speeches of Peace of England, Wisdom, Policy, God's Truth, Plenty, Loyalty, and Concord. Nelson gives concrete reality to the conflict between peace and discord by representing the historical event of the Jack Straw-Wat Tyler rebellion, part of the Peasants' Revolt of 1381. The three principal figures, Richard II, Jack Straw, and the mayor, William Walworth, appear in the pageant, which finally celebrates the bravery of Walworth, who saved the king.

Peele's *Descensus Astraeae* (1591), the first to have a specific title but the last text of the Tudor period, includes for the first time a speech delivered on the Thames as the mayor went to Westminster. The speaker congratulates the mayor, bids him beautify the city with good deeds, and keep his oath inviolate. When the procession returned to the city, the mayor encountered a tableau of Astraea, who stood atop of the device, carrying her sheephook and watching her flock. In Astraea, Peele clearly intends Elizabeth I. The central theatrical device was a fountain over which Astraea presided, assisted by the Graces and the Theological Graces against the forces of Superstition and Ignorance. Each part of the pageant underscores the beneficial effect of Astraea's descent.

Anthony Munday wrote the last lord mayor's show of the Tudor era in 1602, but no text survives.

BIBLIOGRAPHY

Bergeron, David M. *English Civic Pageantry, 1558–1642.* 1971.

P

Fairholt, Frederick W. *Lord Mayors' Pageants.* 2 vols. 1843–1844.

Wickham, Glynne. *Early English Stages, 1300 to 1660.* 2 vols. 1959–1963.

Withington, Robert. *English Pageantry: An Historical Outline.* 2 vols. 1918–1920.

David M. Bergeron

SEE ALSO
Guilds; Machyn, Henry; Munday, Anthony; Peele, George

Progresses, Royal

When English sovereigns tour the kingdom, typically in the summer, we call these journeys "progresses." For example, Henry VII made a provincial tour of York in 1486, trying to secure his political position. But Elizabeth I's reign raises the progress to a high art, in part because the queen made so many journeys and also because of the involvement of skilled writers, such as Thomas Churchyard, John Lyly, George Gascoigne, and Philip Sidney. These progresses served political, economic, and practical purposes, ranging from escaping an unhealthy London to mollifying a disgruntled nobleman. They become significant theatrical events when some consciously planned entertainment occurred, typically outdoors on the estates of a nobleman. Mythology and pastoral dominated the subject matter, all designed to honor and praise the sovereign, who, in Elizabeth's case, became likened to Deborah, Phoebe, and the Fairy Queen.

As the queen visited provincial estates, the nobleman offered lavish hospitality, which might stretch out for days, including banquets, dramatic shows, and hunting. An idealized, remote world came into being, thanks to the active imagination of dramatists who wrote this occasional drama. In such a world Elizabeth presided, sometimes actively participating in the fiction, adding another dimension to the progress as drama.

In 1575, Elizabeth traveled to Kenilworth Castle, the estate of Robert Dudley, the earl of Leicester, where she remained from July 9 until July 27. Arriving on a late Saturday evening, Elizabeth encountered ten Sybils, a porter resembling Hercules, gifts from various gods left on the bridge, and the Lady of the Lake, who floated to land on a moveable island. The world of romance and mythology celebrate the theme of Elizabeth's power. After a day of hunting on Monday, Elizabeth suddenly met a "Savage Man," a role written and performed by Gascoigne, who offered verses in praise of her. On such progresses the sovereign might meet all kinds of creatures in seemingly spontaneous dramatic moments. Citizens from Coventry came one day to perform their "Hok Tuesday" play about the battle of 1002 between the English and Danes. Later in the visit, the Lady of the Lake appeared again, this time accompanied by Arion, who rode on the back of a mechanical dolphin inside of which a consort of musicians performed. As Elizabeth left Kenilworth, Sylvanus, in the person of Gascoigne, appeared and addressed her as he ran alongside her horse, emphasizing the sadness of the gods at her departure. Throughout, Elizabeth emerges as a liberating and regenerating force.

At Wanstead, a manor house belonging to Leicester, Philip Sidney presented his *The Lady of May* in 1578. Walking in the park, Elizabeth suddenly encountered a distraught woman whose daughter, the May Lady, must choose between two suitors, Espilus and Therion. As the debate opened, the participants asked the queen to make the final judgment, which she did, choosing Espilus as being the more worthy of the May Lady. This progress pageant explicitly depended on the queen's involvement. In a less direct way she also participated in the great Elvetham progress pageant of 1591, occurring on the estate of the earl of Hertford. Here, at a specially created crescent-shaped pond, Elizabeth witnessed an elaborate mock battle between the wood gods, led by Sylvanus, and the sea gods, led by Nereus. Eventually Nereus noticed the queen, whose power as peacemaker he celebrates. Her simple presence stills the battle, bringing in her person a dramatic force that alters events.

Elizabeth's transforming power informed the progresses of 1592, as she traveled to Quarrendon, Bisham, Sudeley, and Rycote. At Sudeley Castle the conflict between Daphne and Apollo subsided when Daphne fled to Elizabeth for help. At Harefield Place in 1602, this last progress pageant celebrated the queen's cosmic power as she met the allegorical figures Time and Place. By intention and extravagance these progress pageants compliment the sovereign.

BIBLIOGRAPHY

Anglo, Sydney. *Spectacle, Pageantry, and Early Tudor Policy.* 1969.

Bergeron, David M. *English Civic Pageantry, 1558–1642.* 1971.

———, ed. *Pageantry in the Shakespearean Theater.* 1985.

Griffin, Alice V. *Pageantry on the Shakespearean Stage.* 1951.

Nichols, John. *The Progresses and Public Processions of Queen Elizabeth*. 3 vols. 1823.

Wilson, Jean, ed. *Entertainments for Elizabeth I.* 1980.

David M. Bergeron

SEE ALSO

Churchyard, Thomas; Dudley, Robert; Elizabeth I; Gascoigne, George ; Kenilworth; Sidney, Philip

Prophesyings

See Barton, Elizabeth; Grindal, Edmund; Puritanism

Prose Fiction

Tudor prose fiction is a category of convenience that enables the modern reader to navigate a way through a spectacularly varied collection of literary works directed at a variety of audiences. It includes such diverse works as cony-catching pamphlets (tales of tricksters, early conmen), sophisticated romances like Sir Philip Sidney's *Arcadia*, a self-conscious and ironical narrative like George Gascoigne's *Adventures of Master F.J.*, as well as a simple, chivalric love story like Emanuel Forde's *Ornatus and Artesia*.

Tudor fiction might be said to begin with Sir Thomas More's *Utopia* (1516), a philosophical tale about an imaginary island. The other candidate is William Baldwin's *Beware the Cat* (written 1553). Although very different in style, both works illustrate the connections between Tudor humanism and prose fiction. Indeed, recent critical work has emphasized the complex relationship between the themes of Tudor novellas and stories and the growing influence of humanism, as well as tensions among humanist ideas. This is evident in William Painter's *The Palace of Pleasure* (1566) and Geoffrey Fenton's *Tragical Discourses* (1567),which are collections of translations and adaptations of European novellas and stories. The short narrative achieved greatest sophistication in George Pettie's *Petite Palace of Pettie his Pleasure* (1576), where the stories (essentially from classical sources) are connected through Pettie's witty narrative voice. The short narrative remained a popular genre, especially in the form of tales linked structurally or thematically, such as Barnabe Riche's *Rich His Farewell to Military Profession* (1581) or Robert Greene's *Planetomachia* (1585) and *Penelope's Web* (1587).

While writers like Pettie and Greene may have appealed to women especially, it is difficult to determine the exact readership for these works; different genres of prose fiction developed alongside each other, and it is possible that they were written for different audiences. Cony-catching pamphlets like John Awdeley's *Fraternity of Vagabonds* (1561) and Thomas Harman's *Caveat for Common Cursitors* (1566) achieved considerable popularity at the same time as the collections of Painter, Fenton, and Pettie. Indeed, prose fiction of all kinds increased in popularity during the second half of the sixteenth century; about three times as many fiction titles appeared in the second half of the sixteenth century as in the previous seventy-five years, paralleling the general rise in literacy. By the end of the sixteenth century a range of fictional types was evident, each the product of a growing tradition.

In the 1570s, along with Pettie's collection, two works of fiction are of special merit: George Gascoigne's *The Adventures of Master F.J.* (1573; revised 1575), and John Lyly's *Euphues: The Anatomy of Wit* (1578). Gascoigne's dryly ironic tale of an egotist's love affair had no real imitators. Narrated by a friend—who may be the protagonist disguised—and set within other frameworks, it is perhaps the most sophisticated work of Tudor prose fiction, apart from Sidney's *Arcadia,* and it is also the most accessible for a modern reader. *Euphues,* on the other hand, was extremely popular during the sixteenth century, but is much further removed from modern narrative conventions. Lyly's complex prose style, known as euphuism, was meant to establish an elaborate and courtly vernacular similar to other specialized European court languages. Both the style and content of *Euphues* were imitated by many writers for the next decade, and Lyly also wrote a sequel, *Euphues and His England* (1580).

By the end of the 1570s, the prose narrative was available to writers as a form that could encompass a wide variety of themes and ideas. At this time Sidney probably began writing the first version of his *Arcadia* (around 1578–1580). Now known as the *Old Arcadia*, this fiction is a romance in five "acts" with eclogues between each act, combining the genres of pastoral and chivalric romance. In 1583, he began revising the *Arcadia,* turning it into an elaborate, retrospective narrative, with a complex series of interwoven, subsidiary narratives. This revision was left incomplete at his death. The *Arcadia* ultimately provided a much more powerful model than *Euphues* for Tudor fiction, and indeed for the romance mode throughout the seventeenth century.

The variety of approaches to prose fiction in the 1580s can be illustrated by the career of Robert Greene, who published nineteen works of fiction between the euphuistic *Mamillia* in 1583 and the picaresque *Black Book's Messenger* (1592). He wrote collections of stories, romances, and euphuistic tales, as well as a type of autobiographical

P

fiction late in his career. Greene published two particularly accomplished romances: *Menaphon* (1589), which is in many ways typical of the accomplished hybrid romance form, and *Pandosto* (1588), most famous for providing William Shakespeare with the source for *The Winter's Tale*. It is worth noting that prose fiction provided the source for a number of Elizabethan plays; Shakespeare's other major use of a fictional source is Thomas Lodge's *Rosalynde* (1590) for *As You Like It*.

In the 1590s, two writers virtually added two new genres to fiction: Thomas Nashe and Thomas Deloney. Like Gascoigne and Lyly in the 1570s, the first was a unique voice who quickly fell into comparative oblivion, while the second remained in print (and imitated) for most of the following century. Thomas Nashe's *The Unfortunate Traveller* (1594) combines all sorts of genres—jest book, sermon, satire, travel narrative, historical fiction, revenge tale, tragedy, tragicomedy—into a pseudo-autobiographical story told by the effervescent voice of the page Jack Wilton. Nashe's unique prose style, full of neologisms, ensures that style is almost as important in *The Unfortunate Traveller* as it is in *Euphues*. Long seen as in some ways linked to the picaresque novel, *The Unfortunate Traveller* is now seen as an important example of the nature of rhetoric in Elizabethan society.

At the very end of the century, Thomas Deloney produced three works of fiction that examine the increasingly important world of Elizabethan merchants and craftsmen. *Jack of Newbury* (1597) is a rags-to-riches story of a weaver set in the time of Henry VIII and based very loosely on a real figure. The two parts of *The Gentle Craft* (c. 1598) center on shoemakers, and was used by Thomas Dekker for his play *The Shoemaker's Holiday* (1600). *Thomas of Reading* (c. 1599), likewise concerned with merchants and craftsmen, is a darker narrative with some psychological interest.

Deloney has long been a favorite writer for those who sought the origins on the novel in Tudor prose fiction. Such a teleological view distorted the nature of prose fiction in a period that did not value highly very many of the features that came to constitute the realist novel. In recent years a number of studies have approached early fiction on its own terms and values. It is perhaps most useful of all to acknowledge the immense vitality of all the different forms of prose fiction in the last three decades of the sixteenth century. This is partly because the general energy apparent in Elizabethan prose fiction generated a vital range of experiments in narrative structure and style.

The different kinds of fiction were not wholly distinct from each other: popular works and courtly works influenced each other, and within single works, different modes often intermingled. A good example is Henry Chettle's *Piers Plainness Seven Years' Prenticeship* (1595). Piers actually moves in three distinct worlds that parallel three distinct styles and narrative modes: a pastoral realm, a picaresque world in which he undertakes his apprenticeship, and the world of the court. Another author of fiction in mixed modes is Thomas Lodge. Besides Rosalynde, Lodge wrote historical fiction and euphuistic romance, but his last work of fiction, *A Margerite of America* (1596), is again a complex hybrid: a violent, dark romance that combines elements of romance with the mode of the continental novella.

BIBLIOGRAPHY

Davis, Walter. *Idea and Act in Elizabethan Fiction.* 1969.
Helgerson, Richard. *Elizabethan Prodigals.* 1976.
Hutson, Lorna. *The Usurer's Daughter.* 1994.
Kinney, Arthur F. *Humanist Poetics.* 1986.
Lucas, Caroline. *Writing for Women.* 1989.
Margolies, David. *Novel and Society in Elizabethan England.* 1985.
Salzman, Paul. *English Prose Fiction, 1558–1700.* 1985.
Schlauch, Margaret. *Antecendents of the English Novel.* 1963.

Paul Salzman

SEE ALSO

Baldwin, William; Chettle, Henry; Deloney, Thomas; Euphuism; Fenton, Geoffrey; Gascoigne, George; Greene, Robert; Lodge, Thomas; Lyly, John; More, Thomas; Nashe, Thomas; Painter, William; Pettie, George; Romance; Sidney, Philip; Utopia

Prostitution
See Sexual Offenses; Southwark

Protector Somerset
See Edward VI; Seymour, Edward

Puckering, John (c. 1544–1596)

Speaker of the House of Commons and lord keeper of the great seal, Sir John Puckering gained his training in the common law from Lincoln's Inn. He became a circuit court justice in Carmarthen in 1577, a serjeant-at-law in 1580, and queen's serjeant in 1588. During this time he made powerful friends in the government, including

William Cecil, Lord Burghley. In his first election to Parliament in 1584 he was made speaker of the House of Commons, but it turned out to be a largely thankless task. The session was marred, from the government's standpoint, by the introduction of religious bills by Puritan members of Parliament. Elizabeth I called Puckering to her to give him an order personally prohibiting M.P.s from discussing religion. This act resulted in some members calling for Puckering's ouster from the speakership for going to the queen without the permission of the House of Commons. Puckering used stalling tactics to evade reading the proffered religious bills, but in the end had to give in. By the end of the session it was clear that Puckering and the Privy Council had lost control of the session. Regardless of this failure, Puckering was again elected speaker in 1586. This session was concerned with condemning Mary Queen of Scots, but after her execution the Puritan Anthony Cope introduced his "bill and book," which called for replacing the Prayer Book with a Genevan service. Puckering called in vain for members to refrain from this kind of legislation, reminding them of Elizabeth's prohibition. This merely began a debate on freedom of speech by Peter Wentworth. Puckering ended the debate and had Wentworth sent to the Tower. In 1592, Elizabeth appointed Puckering to be her lord keeper of the great seal, a position that also gave him a seat on the Privy Council.

BIBLIOGRAPHY
Hasler, P.W., ed. *The House of Commons, 1559–1601.* 1981.
Neale, J.E. *The Elizabethan House of Commons.* 1950.
———. *Elizabeth I and Her Parliaments, 1584–1601.* 1957.

Robert J. Mueller

SEE ALSO
Cecil, William; Parliamentary History; Wentworth, Peter

Puritanism

"Puritan" is the term used to identify that element in the Church of England that desired a "purer" church than the one devised by Elizabeth I and her ministers in the 1559 settlement. The term is a controversial one because it cannot be defined precisely, and some modern scholars would like to abandon it altogether. On the other hand, there is no doubt that there was a large segment of the church that was unhappy with the post-Reformation status quo and sought to alter it in a more radical direction.

Even if there was little internal unity within this group, the word "Puritan" has normally been used to describe them as a group.

Part of the difficulty stems from the fact that the word was mainly used pejoratively by those who disliked the thought of reform. It is attested as early as 1565, when the Catholic exile Thomas Stapleton used it to refer to all Protestants without distinction. Because of this negative tone, almost nobody was prepared to use it of himself in Elizabethan times, and it appears as a self-description only rarely after that. The Puritans preferred to call themselves the "godly," "professors," or the "elect," terms that had a more positive, though equally exclusive, ring about them.

As a theological movement, Puritanism can be traced to those Marian exiles who followed John Knox to Geneva in late 1555. There they sat at the feet of John Calvin, learning his ideas of what a holy church and commonwealth ought to look like. A number of these people returned to England in 1559, where they were welcomed by the authorities and offered posts in the church. However, they were unhappy with what they thought of as the half-Reformed compromise that Elizabeth I was proposing and wanted a more thoroughgoing Reformation along Genevan lines. Some, like Knox himself, would not compromise, but others were prepared to bide their time until Elizabeth was firmly established on the throne.

In 1565, movement began to overturn the 1559 settlement, when a number of ministers protested against the need to wear clerical vestments. The so-called Vestiarian Controversy eventually fizzled out, but not before Archbishop Matthew Parker had issued a series of *Advertisements* (1566) in which he upheld the wearing of vestments and gave further directions for maintaining decorum in worship. When the queen was excommunicated by the pope in 1570, there were hopes that she might veer toward a more Calvinistic position, and John Foxe, among others, was active in trying to encourage her in that direction. However, in 1571, the queen reaffirmed the Articles of Religion adopted in 1563, and refused to sanction the *Reformatio Legum Ecclesiasticarum (Reformation of the Ecclesiastical Laws)* that had been drawn up by Thomas Cranmer and others in the reign of Edward VI. Instead, she issued a few new canons that did little but uphold the status quo.

It was after these events that the radical faction in the church realized that more direct action was required. In 1572, they presented two *Admonitions* to Parliament, in which they outlined a plan of radical reform. The *Admonitions* caused a great stir, and for a generation they were regarded as the chief platform of Puritanism. When

Richard Hooker set out in the 1590s to answer the Puritans with a defense of the Elizabethan Settlement, he took these *Admonitions* as his starting point. The authors of the *Admonitions* wanted to abandon clerical vestments, simplify church services, allow *ex tempore* prayer alongside the Prayer Book, and provide for a properly educated ministry. To them the clergy were primarily teachers of the faith, not celebrants of the holy mysteries, and this explains their devotion to sermons and to learning in general.

One way in which the Puritans advanced their cause was by supplying parishes with lecturers, university graduates trained in theology. These men assisted the clergy in teaching the Christian faith, usually on Sunday afternoons. This brought them into direct conflict with traditional village life, where Sunday afternoons had been the time normally devoted to social church gatherings known as church-ales, and sports. The Puritans were deeply opposed to these distractions, as they saw them, although it was not until the 1590s that they began to denounce such activities as a profanation of the Sabbath. Even so, the lines were clearly drawn between those who were serious about their religion and those who were not, and the concept of the "godly" was born.

The Puritans have often been pictured as a narrow-minded elite determined to force everyone into their particular mold, but this is an inaccurate picture of them. Generally speaking, they did not try to reform the ungodly, or even to keep them out of church. Their main concern was to make their version of godliness prevail as the accepted social norm. The hope was that the ungodly would then see the error of their ways and voluntarily repent of them. Having been unsuccessfully coerced themselves, the Puritans understood that such tactics would not work, and they were seldom tried.

The secret of Puritanism was that it was a spiritual movement in which the internal witness of the Holy Spirit was what really counted. A person who was filled with the Spirit might manifest this in any number of different ways, and there was great variety among the Puritans themselves. Some were mainly concerned to find good preaching, while others wanted simple worship or what would today be called a "charismatic" type of spirituality. Most were quite content to remain within the national church, hoping to reform it gradually, but in the 1590s there were growing numbers of Separatists, who felt that they would only achieve their aims by breaking with the established church altogether. These Separatists were regarded as traitors to the crown, and were severely repressed in the last years of Elizabeth I's reign.

Most Puritans held a strong doctrine of divine election and predestination, combined with an understanding that they were among those who were so chosen. Modern research has demonstrated that election and predestination were generally accepted by almost all shades of opinion in the church at the time, so that these doctrines cannot be considered Puritan in any narrow sense. Where the Puritans differed from the majority was not in their theology but in the way in which they applied that theology to themselves. Puritans took God's calling personally, and had little doubt that they were truly saved. This gave them a responsibility to spread the Gospel to what they called the "dark corners" of the land, and encouraged them to see their opponents as the Antichrist. Normally, this was the pope, but it could be extended to cover anyone who tried to thwart their intentions.

The conviction that they were light-bearers was a strong one, and recurs frequently in Puritan writings. For example, those who sailed to America wanted to establish a colony that would be "a beacon on a hill"—a model society that lesser mortals would envy and be stirred to emulate. In a similar vein, John Robinson, the leader of the Mayflower Pilgrims, told his flock that the Lord "had yet more light to break forth out of his Holy Word" as they set sail for the New World.

After 1572, various Puritan groups began to organize themselves within the Church of England, and before long there was a network of ministers who were functioning along semi-Presbyterian lines. Their great champion was Thomas Cartwright, who taught at Cambridge and helped to make that university a bastion of Puritanism. During these years most of Calvin's major works were translated into English, so that Puritan ministers had a theological library readily available to help them in their task. Edmund Grindal, archbishop of Canterbury from 1576 to 1583, was sympathetic to the Puritan cause, and did what he could to encourage their preaching ministry (known to contemporaries as "prophesying"), but the queen would not tolerate this and effectively silenced Grindal in 1577. When he died, she appointed John Whitgift (1583–1604) to succeed him, on the understanding that he would do all he could to uproot Puritanism from the church.

Whitgift tried a mixture of the carrot and the stick. His Articles of 1583 demanded complete conformity to the Prayer Book and the general practice of the Church of England, but theologically Whitgift was just as Calvinistic as the Puritans were, and in his disputes with Cartwright and others, he was able to convince them that their scruples over secondary matters were not worth the divisions they were causing in the church. In 1585, Cartwright disbanded the nascent Presbyterian groups that he had helped to organize, and it looked as though the Puritans might be reconciled to the establishment. Given the danger that Elizabeth might easily be succeeded on the throne by the Catholic Mary Queen of Scots, and that Philip II of Spain was threatening to invade the country and depose the "heretic" queen, it is easy to understand why both sides recognized the need for Protestant unity.

But when Mary was executed (1587), and the Spanish Armada was defeated (1588), the danger seemed to have passed, and divisions soon reappeared. On the Puritan side, a series of anonymous tracts appeared (1589) under the pseudonym of Martin Marprelate. These were a savage attack on the episcopate, and caused immense turmoil in the church establishment, which was never able to discover who the true authors of the tracts were. At the same time, Richard Bancroft, the bishop of London, preached a sermon at Paul's Cross in London, in which he denounced Puritanism in all its forms and virtually declared war on it.

Polarization grew worse during the 1590s, as the more radical Puritans became Separatists and were subjected to persecution by the authorities. Some left the country in protest and went to Holland, but most stayed at home, hoping that if James VI of Scotland should succeed to the English throne, the Puritan cause would triumph. James, the son of Mary Queen of Scots, had been brought up as a Presbyterian, and there were many in England who hoped that he would introduce that form of church government once he ascended the throne.

Elizabeth I died on March 24, 1603, and both James I and the Puritans were soon hard at work trying to establish their positions. On his way south to claim the throne, James was presented with the so-called Millenary Petition (April 28, 1603), which claimed the support of a thousand ministers, and which presented him with a series of Puritan demands. This in turn led to the Hampton Court Conference (January 12–18, 1604), at which Puritans and establishment figures like Whitgift (who died shortly afterward) and Bancroft tried to hammer out their differences. The resulting compromise favored the establishment, as the Canons of 1604 make clear, but most of the Puritans seemed to be reasonably satisfied at the outcome as well. During James's reign there was general peace in the country, even though the king was much less sympathetic to the Puritans than they had originally hoped he would be.

It was only when his son Charles I (1625–1649) ascended the throne and openly favored the anti-Puritan elements within the church that conflict became inevitable. The Puritans, allied with Parliament and others who were unhappy with Charles's misrule, defeated the king in the civil war, and in 1649 were given an opportunity to establish their godly commonwealth at long last. Unfortunately, it was at that point that internal divisions among the Puritans were revealed, and it became apparent that their social program could not be realized. In 1660, the monarchy and the Church of England were restored, and Puritanism was persecuted once more. Only in 1689 was toleration secured, but the majority of Puritans formally left the national church to form different dissenting denominations, most of which have continued in existence up to the present.

BIBLIOGRAPHY

Collinson, P. *The Elizabethan Puritan Movement.* 1967.
Durston, C., and J. Eales, eds. *The Culture of English Puritanism, 1560–1700.* 1996.
Lake, P. *Anglicans and Puritans? Presbyterianism and English Conformist Thought from Whitgift to Hooker.* 1988.
Trinterud, L.J. *Elizabethan Puritanism.* 1971.

Gerald Bray

SEE ALSO
Admonitions Controversy; *Advertisements, Book of;* Bancroft, Richard; Calvinism; Cartwright, Thomas; Church of England; Grindal, Edmund; Hooker, Richard; James VI and I; Knox, John; Marian Exiles; Marprelate Controversy; Parker, Matthew; Paul's Cross Sermons; *Reformation Legum Ecclesiasticarum;* Stapleton, Thomas; Vestiarian Controversy; Whitgift, John

Puttenham, George (c. 1529–1590)

Puttenham is the figure to whom the anonymous authorship of *The Arte of English Poesie* (1589) has been most frequently attributed. In 1614, Edmund Bolton described the book as having been written by "one of the queen's gentlemen pensioners, Puttenham," a plausible ascription (and partly corroborated by a MS note written by Sir John Harington in 1591), but Harington and Bolton may have been referring either to George Puttenham or to his older brother, Richard (c. 1520–c. 1601), and, in fact, the case for George's authorship of the *Arte* is only slightly better than the case for Richard's. The only significant work that may be confidently attributed to George is *A Justificacion of Queene Elizabeth in Relacion to the Affaire of Mary*

P

Queene of Scottes, which has excited interest only because its author may also have written the *Arte.*

Nephews of Sir Thomas Elyot, both George and Richard were dogged by legal and political difficulties. Richard was convicted of rape in 1561 and spent most of the succeeding decade abroad, without royal license; he was imprisoned for what is designated a second time between 1583 and 1587; and he was also in prison when he made out his will in 1597. George, for his part, was implicated in a putative plot on Lord Burghley's life in 1570, and he was summoned before the Privy Council and then imprisoned in 1578 for failure to pay his wife's allowance. Richard Puttenham joined in the proceedings against his brother in 1579, but the dispute was soon settled, and George seems to have subsided into relative respectability. By contrast, however, the author of *The Arte of English Poesie* represents himself as a much less unruly figure, as a well-traveled courtier, the familiar companion of witty aristocrats and ingenious poets, and himself the author of comedies, interludes, romances, a collection of poems in praise of Elizabeth, a mythographic treatise, and a history of the English language.

The *Arte* was written in stages, its earliest strata dating from the late 1560s, with substantial additions between about 1585 and 1589. The treatise is divided into three books, the first concerned with the cultural history of poetry and its various genres; the second, with verse structure; the third and longest, with "ornament," the various tropes and figures. The book is a cultural landmark if only for its unprecedented confidence in the state of vernacular literary culture. Modern poetry is being written, the author tells us, and it is continuous and consistent with ancient poetry; he confirms that consistency both by translating ancient rhetorical terminology into modern equivalents and by offering modern instances of ancient verse forms, figures, and tropes.

For all its confidence, the *Arte* is nonetheless fundamentally polemical, like the Italian and French treatises that anticipate it. The meticulous articulation of the regularities of syllable count, accent, rhyme scheme, and stanzaic form that may be observed in sixteenth-century English poetry supports the central argument "that there may be an Art of our English Poesie, aswell as there is of the Latine and Greeke" (5). The author is especially apologetic when he turns to confront the centrality of rhyme in English prosody, for he knows it to be a feature of the vernacular poetry of those "nations of the world . . . whom the Latines and Greekes in speciall called barbarous" (10).

The best he can offer to counter the stigma attached to rhyme in Greek and Latin prosody is to claim the antiquity and ubiquity of rhyme, and its use in ancient Hebrew and Chaldean poetry as well as in contemporary European and Amerindian literature. It is a half-hearted apologia, since the author regards rarity and artificiality as the leading marks of excellence, and the fact that rhyming apparently "comes naturally" to all peoples is something of an embarrassment—hence the author's special interest in complex rhyme schemes, in shaped poems, and in difficult figures and tropes, those highly artificial features that overshadow the regularities of simple rhyming.

The discussion of English metrics in the *Arte* initiates what became a mainstream project for subsequent analysts of English poetry, the attempt to adjust the prosodic claims of eye and ear. This is clearest in the author's discussion of the short-lived campaign of several Elizabethan poets—"a nice & scholasticall curiositie" (113) he calls it—to adapt the classical system of quantitative metrics for vernacular poetry. In the classical metrical system pronunciation was guided and shaped by orthography, and Puttenham registers this as an obstacle to English quantitative poetry, for he insists that the rules of English versification must always conform to the norms of pronunciation. By his deference to speech, and particularly by his insistence that syllable prominence is something to be gauged by the amateur ear, Puttenham becomes the progenitor of most modern theories of English versification, which emphasize the tensions and accommodations between metrical accent and speech stress, pattern, and pronunciation.

The *Arte* gives unprecedented explicitness to the cultural centralization that had been going on in England since the middle of the fifteenth century. The author promotes "the usuall speach of the Court, and that of London and the shires lying about London within lx. myles" as a national literary language, and denigrates the language used "in the marches and frontiers, or in port townes." This campaign is more than antiprovincial; it is also what we might call proto-Cavalier, since he would also have English poets reject the cultural idioms of "Universities where Schollers use much peevish affectation of words out of primative languages, or finally, in any uplandish village or corner of a Realme, where is no resort but of poore rusticall or uncivill people: neither shall he follow the speach of a craftes man or carter, or other of the inferiour sort, though he be inhabitant or bred in the best towne and Citie in this Realme" (144–145). This preference for courtly idioms explains why Camden described

P

the author of the *Arte* as that "gentleman which proved that poets were the first politicians": the *Arte* regularly associates the courtiership and poetry, for each requires a highly developed aptitude for elegant indirection.

BIBLIOGRAPHY

Arber, Edward, ed. *The Arte of English Poesie.* 1869.

Atkins, J.W.H. *English Literary Criticism: The Renascence,* pp. 156–178. 1947.

Croft, H.H.S., ed. *The Boke Named the Governour.* 2 vols. 1880. Vol. 1, pp. clxxxi–clxxxix.

Javitch, Daniel. "Poetry and Court Conduct: Puttenham's Arte of English Poesie in the Light of Castiglione's Cortegiano." *Modern Language Notes,* vol. 87, pp. 865–882.

Kegl, Rosemary. "Those Terrible Aproaches": Sexuality, Social Mobility, and Resisting the Courtliness of Puttenham's *The Arte of English Poesie.*" *English Literary Renaissance,* vol. 20, pp. 179–208.

Ward, B.M. "The Authorship of *The Arte of English Poesie:* A Suggestion." *Review of English Studies,* vol. 1, pp. 284–308.

Willcox, Gladys Doidge, and Alice Walker, eds. *The Arte of English Poesie.* 1936.

Joseph Loewenstein

SEE ALSO

Literary Criticism; Rhetoric; Versification

Pyrrhonism

Of the two traditions of skepticism in European philosophy, Pyrrhonism constitutes the more radical, since it denies not merely the possibility of certain knowledge but doubts even that judgement. The Greek skeptical philosopher, Pyrrho of Elis (c. 360–352 B.C.E.), never committed his ideas to writing, so they are known only at secondhand. The most important source for them is the *Outlines of Pyrrhonism* by the second-century philosopher, Sextus Empiricus, the only Pyrrhonian skeptic whose works survived. Pyrrho's thought was also known in the recension by Diogenes Laertius in his *Lives of the Philosophers.*

Largely unknown in the Middle Ages, the works of Sextus began to appear in manuscript form in the fifteenth century. The first printing of a work by Sextus was of the *Outlines of Pyrrhonism* in the Latin translation of Henri Estienne in 1562. This was followed in 1569 by the edition of Gentian Hervet that included both the *Outlines*

and *Against the Mathematicians.* (There was no Greek printing of Sextus's works until 1621.) Hervet's interest in Pyrrhonism was as a weapon for refuting heretics, especially Calvinism. Prior to this, the most important reader of Sextus was Gianfrancesco Pico della Mirandola. Pico's *Examen vanitatis doctrinae gentium* (1520) discusses Sextus in books 2 and 3 as part of a wide-ranging attack on pagan philosophy. Henry Cornelius Agrippa's *De incertitudine et vanitate scientiarum* (1526) shows knowledge of Pyrrhonism, probably derived from Diogenes Laertius. The work as a whole is not so much skeptical as fideistic and antiintellectual. This work was very popular and was translated into English in 1569. Agrippa had an impact on Michel de Montaigne (1533–1592), the thinker on whom Pyrrhonism made the deepest impact, and who contributed greatly to the secular dissemination of skepticism in the sixteenth century. Montaigne's Pyrrhonism is most fully apparent in the *Apology for Raymond Sebond* (written 1675–1680), published in the second book of his *Essais* (1580).

John Florio's translation of the *Essays* (1603) was important for disseminating Montaigne's ideas in Renaissance England. It should, of course, not be forgotten that texts in Latin were as accessible to educated people in Tudor times as English translations. The writings of Sextus were not widely known in Tudor England, although they were not unknown—John Dee, for example, possessed a copy. Vernacular interest in Pyrrhonism is evident from an English translation of Sextus known to Thomas Nashe and attributed to Sir Walter Ralegh. The greatest impact of Pyrrhonism on English thought was not registered until the seventeenth century, when it had a shaping influence on William Chillingworth and Ralph Cudworth.

BIBLIOGRAPHY

Copenhaver, B.P., and C.B. Schmitt. *Renaissance Philosophy.* 1992.

Le Franc, Paul. *Sir Walter Raleigh, Ecrivain.* 1968.

Popkin, R.H. *The History of Scepticism from Erasmus to Descartes.* 1968.

Schmitt, C.B. *Gianfrancesco Pico della Mirandola.* 1967.

Strathman, E.A. *Sir Walter Raleigh. A Study in Elizabethan Skepticism.* 1951.

Sarah Hutton

SEE ALSO

Calvinism; Classical Literature, Influence of; Classical Literature, English Translations; Florio, John; Ralegh, Walter; Skepticism

R

Radcliffe, Thomas, Third Earl of Sussex (c. 1526–1583)

Sir Thomas Radcliffe inherited the titles of Lord Fitzwalter in 1542 and third earl of Sussex in 1557. His first important political appointment was lord deputy of Ireland (1556–1564). He became lord president of the Council of the North (1568), a privy councilor (1570), and lord chamberlain (1572).

In Ireland, he tried unsuccessfully to expel the Scots from Antrim and subdue the Gaelic chieftains. His overall plan was to settle English garrisons on Irish lands close to the Pale, and establish military precedents further afield, but his only major success was the plantation of Leix and Offaly. His policies aroused widespread hostility, and gentlemen in the Pale accused him of maladministration. He retired from his post in 1564 in semidisgrace. At court, he worked closely with William Cecil and Thomas Howard, the duke of Norfolk, until 1568 to promote a Habsburg marriage for the queen, but his visit to Vienna in 1567 to negotiate a matrimonial treaty ended in failure. During the Northern Rebellion, the queen suspected his loyalty, but he recovered her favor after carrying out successful punitive raids into Scotland. As a privy councilor, he initiated and supported the Anjou matrimonial scheme (1578–1581) and opposed both England's military intervention in the Netherlands and financial aid to the Huguenots. These policies led him into disagreements with Robert Dudley, the earl of Leicester, whom he also disliked on personal grounds.

BIBLIOGRAPHY

Brady, Ciaran. *The Chief Governors: The Rise and Fall of Reform Government in Tudor Ireland, 1536–1588.* 1994.

Doran, Susan. "The Political Career of Thomas Radcliffe, Third Earl of Sussex (1526?–1583)." Dissertation, University of London. 1977.

———. *Monarchy and Matrimony: The Courtships of Elizabeth I.* 1996.

Susan Doran

SEE ALSO

Alençon and Anjou, Duke of; Cecil, William; Howard, Thomas; Ireland, History of; Northern Rebellion

Rainolde, Richard (c. 1530–1606)

Protestant humanist, rhetorician, and cleric, Richard Rainolde was born around 1530 in Essex. Little is known of his early life until 1546, when he entered St. John's College, Cambridge, as a sizar. The next year he became a scholar on the Lady Margaret Foundation, and in 1548, he transferred to Trinity College. He received his B.A. in 1550, was made a fellow of Trinity in 1551, and proceeded M.A. in 1553. The education he received was thus strongly Protestant and humanist in orientation. There are no records of Rainolde during the Marian years.

Rainolde's three extant works all appeared during the 1560s. The first, *The Foundacion of Rhetorike,* appeared in 1563 from the press of John Kingston, who in that same year reissued Thomas Wilson's *Arte of Rhetorique,* and Rainolde proposes his own treatise as preparation for Wilson's work. Rainolde's *Foundacion* is an English adaptation of Aphthonius's *Progymnasmata,* a fourth-century series of graduated exercises in written and oral composition. Rainolde expands upon Aphthonius's exercises, domesticates Reinhard Lorich's Latin commentary on the

R

Progymnasmata, and offers model orations that stress Protestant and English political themes. Rainolde also produced *A Chronicle of All the Noble Emperors of the Romans* (entered 1566/1567, published 1571), and "De statu nobilium virorum et principum" (BL Harleian MS 973). Both works used historical material to exemplify Tudor ideas about political order and stability, the first showing divine intervention in political affairs, the second defending monarchy and attacking the papacy. Rainolde sought noble patronage with all three of these works, but finally received none.

In 1567, Rainolde received permission to complete his degree in medicine, but instead of doing so he obtained letters of introduction from Cambridge to go to Russia, and may have gone. He became rector at Stapleford-Abbots (Essex) in 1568, and at Lambourne in 1569. In his *Chronicle* he had signed himself "Doctour of Physick," and in 1571, the College of Physicians imprisoned and fined him for being unlearned and practicing without a license. In 1578, he received a third living at West Thurrock, and the next year he was summoned to London by Bishop John Aylmer to answer certain charges. Rainolde, his wife, and the local constable assaulted the process server, and all were committed to Marshalsea prison until their release by the Privy Council. The remainder of his life was spent in local clerical duties. He died in Essex in 1606.

BIBLIOGRAPHY

Howell, W.S. *Logic and Rhetoric in England.* 1961.

Lawrence D. Green

SEE ALSO

Rhetoric; Wilson, Thomas

Ralegh, Walter (1554–1618)

The youngest son of a moderately prosperous family of rural Devonshire, Sir Walter Ralegh became one of Elizabeth I's most highly regarded favorites. His prominence at court allowed him to exert considerable leadership in English overseas exploration and colonization, as well as on foreign affairs generally. His wide-ranging intellectual pursuits included medicine, mathematics, history, geography, and literature, although he is most remembered today for his achievements as a man of letters in prose and verse.

While much has been made of Ralegh's dramatic self-promotion in gaining and maintaining royal favor during his Elizabethan career, it is easy to overlook a common theme in nearly all of these endeavors, his life-long involvement with English Protestant resistance to Catholic, and particularly Spanish, threats to national sovereignty.

Ralegh's boyhood and education are subjects of conjecture. In 1569, while still in his teens, he served with other members of his family among the English volunteers fighting for the Huguenot cause in France. He began his education at Oriel College, Oxford, no later than 1572, but left the university without taking a degree to seek his fortune in London. He enrolled first at Lyon's Inn, one of the Inns of Chancery, then transferred in 1575 to the Middle Temple, one of the Inns of Court and a fashionable gentleman's address whether or not he studied law very seriously during these years. His associates included such soldier-poets as George Gascoigne and George Whetstone. During these years, Ralegh seems to have gained little or no preferment at court or among noble patrons. Late in 1578, he sailed on an expedition commanded by his half-brother, Sir Humphrey Gilbert. Ralegh's ship engaged a Spanish vessel but was repulsed, and the Privy Council fined the participants in this unauthorized voyage.

By mid-1579, he had found a place in the entourage of Edward de Vere, seventeenth earl of Oxford, but soon fell out with his patron. Quarrels with established courtiers led to several imprisonments in the following year, yet on July 11, 1580, Elizabeth's lord deputy of Ireland, Arthur, Lord Grey of Wilton, appointed Ralegh the captain of 100 men bound for Ireland. This overseas expedition culminated in his emergence as an important public figure, just as his second expedition to Guiana in 1617 led to his final imprisonment and execution.

In November, the lord deputy's army forced the surrender of a Spanish and Italian garrison at Smerwick whose defenders were then slaughtered. Ralegh's men were among the first to enter the fort, where they found papers revealing Catholic plans for the overthrow of England's Protestant government. Ralegh's biographers have failed to note that he returned to London in December 1580 to testify about these documents before the Privy Council. Afterward, he corresponded with Lord Burghley and the earl of Leicester from Ireland, and while he probably did not meet Elizabeth on this occasion, he received the honorary sinecure of esquire of the body extraordinary to the queen. Clearly, this journey laid the foundation for his spectacular rise to favor at court when he returned to England in the following year.

Ralegh certainly made contact with the queen shortly after arriving in London late in 1581. She postponed his return to his duties in Ireland, and he was soon recognized as a prominent royal favorite. With favor came rewards: patents to license wine sellers and export broadcloths; a knighthood early in 1585, plus the offices of lord lieutenant of Cornwall and vice admiral for Devon and Cornwall. In the same year he was appointed lord warden of the Stannaries, the valuable tin-mining enterprise in southwest England. The queen granted Ralegh significant estates in Munster, Ireland, in 1586, and in the following year he became captain of her guard.

In all, Ralegh enjoyed a full decade of high royal favor. He directed his position and wealth primarily toward two closely related goals. He organized and largely financed a small fleet that preyed on Spanish shipping and disrupted trade with Spain. Second, Ralegh promoted the first attempts at English colonial development in the New World in direct competition with Spain's overseas empire. The voyages he sponsored in 1584 and 1585 founded an English colony on Roanoke Island; Ralegh dubbed the entire area Virginia in honor of the Virgin Queen. The Spanish Armada, however, subsequently tied up English shipping, and his settlement had vanished by the time a relief expedition reached the outpost in 1590. Ralegh never abandoned the idea of an English colony in North America, and he sent expeditions to search for his colonists as late as 1602.

Ralegh's hold on Elizabeth's favor was challenged in the spring of 1587 when twenty-year-old Robert Devereux, second earl of Essex, returned to England from military service in the Netherlands. Essex became the queen's premier favorite, and for the next dozen years Ralegh alternately competed and cooperated with the earl in his efforts to maintain his sovereign's regard. Allegedly "chased from the court" by Essex in the summer of 1589, Ralegh spent several months overseeing his Irish estates. He returned in December, apparently in the company of Edmund Spenser, whose *Faerie Queene* he helped to introduce to the queen and her court. Essex did not absolutely gain the upper hand in this rivalry until 1592, when Elizabeth learned that Ralegh had married her gentlewoman of the Privy Chamber, Elizabeth Throckmorton. Both were imprisoned in the Tower in July; Ralegh was released in September to take charge of a crown emergency. The Portuguese carrack, the *Madre de Dios,* had been captured and brought to Dartmouth, where Ralegh's influence and organizational skills ensured that royal interests in the dispersal of its immensely valuable cargo were protected. For the next five years, Ralegh was banished from court and the queen's presence. Yet he retained his offices, including that of captain of the guard along with his other royal patents, and in 1593, he served in Parliament for the third time.

Aside from his letters, Ralegh's extant writings before the disgrace of 1592 include a single prose work and perhaps a score of lyrics. His earliest datable verse is the commendatory poem before George Gascoigne's *The Steele Glas* (1576). Love poems such as "Calling to mind," "Farewell false love," and "Fortune hath taken thee away" were probably outgrowths of his semi-amorous courtship of the queen; certainly the latter poem falls within this category, for she replied to it with reassuring answering verses. His elegy for Sir Philip Sidney ("To praise thy life") was published in *The Phoenix Nest* (1593), and reprinted in Spenser's *Colin Clouts Come Home Againe* (1595). Meanwhile, Ralegh had written two commendatory poems for Spenser's *Faerie Queene* (1590), the first of which elevates the genre to the status of fine art.

In late 1591 appeared his *Report of the Truth of the fight about the Iles of Açores,* an anonymous account of the last fight of *The Revenge.* The queen's ship had been commanded by Sir Richard Grenville, Ralegh's distant kinsman and a colleague in his maritime enterprises. Grenville lost the ship and his own life trying to sail through a Spanish war fleet rather than outrun it. Ralegh's propagandistic tract glorified English heroism during the battle and diluted this loss of a single ship in the overall panorama of English naval victories over Spain from Drake's initial raids through the defeat of the Great Armada in 1587.

His five years of disgrace motivated and perhaps gave Ralegh leisure for further writing. Of first importance are the four "Cynthia" poems preserved at Hatfield House in unique, holograph copies. They address his relationship with Elizabeth in more than 500 lines of verse, much of it pastoral complaint that allegedly constitutes Books 21 and 22 of an otherwise lost poem dedicated to the queen. His "Succession" tract, also preserved in manuscript at Hatfield House, amounts to a prose counterpart of the "Cynthia" poems. Another autograph fragment, the tract expresses his despair over the loss of royal favor while defending the queen's policy of not naming her successor. In contrast with the discouraged but conciliatory tone of these works, Ralegh's satiric poem, "The Lie," attacks the immorality and hypocrisy of the Elizabethan "establishment" at all levels.

Ralegh's disfavor led to his most active personal involvement in the enterprises he had formerly directed

R

from London and the court. He explored Guiana on the northern coast of South America in 1595 in search of gold and gems, but with an eye as well toward eventual English colonization. Ralegh promoted his plan with publication of *The Discoverie of the Large, Rich, and Bewtiful Empyre of Guiana* (1595). Again, however, the war with Spain interrupted his colonial ambitions. He distinguished himself during the summer of 1596 on the "Cadiz" raid, an expedition jointly commanded by Essex and Lord Admiral Charles Howard. Ralegh's ship was the first to enter the Spanish harbor and engage the enemy warships, and he was wounded in the firefight. His account of the battle has survived in letters to the earl of Northumberland and to his cousin, Sir Arthur Gorges. As Spain prepared to avenge this victory, the English war council sought Ralegh's advice on how best to deal with the crisis. His "Opinion" and the untitled "Offensive" tract outline his strategy for aggressive military measures against Spain.

Ralegh's heroism at Cadiz did not alleviate at once the royal displeasure; not until June of 1597, with Essex's concurrence, did Elizabeth restore Ralegh to favor and the personal exercise once more of his duties as captain of the guard. That same summer, however, he sailed as third in command on the "Islands Voyage," again under the leadership of Essex and vice admiral Lord Thomas Howard. This was but one of a number of English efforts to intercept the Spanish treasure fleet sailing from the Carribean, attempts that always ended in failure. On his own initiative, Ralegh led a successful assault on the fortress at Fayal in the Azores. Nothing substantial was gained by this gesture, however, and he narrowly missed a court-martial for thus upstaging his superiors.

During the last five years of Elizabeth's reign, Ralegh participated only occasionally in military affairs in order to concentrate on courtiership and national politics. He continued to finance and direct quasi-piratical naval expeditions as well as voyages to the New World, but statesmanship increasingly occupied his time. He took an active role in Elizabeth's last two Parliaments, and was appointed to entertain visiting ambassadors on several occasions. Still, his ambition to be a member of the Privy Council or to gain higher office in the royal household went unfulfilled. He did, however, receive the governorship of the Isle of Jersey in August 1600, a charge that regularly took him away from London and the center of power.

Ralegh's rivalry with Essex came to an end in February 1601, when the earl attempted a coup d'etat that was quickly suppressed by the government. Ralegh brought forty of the guard to assist in the siege of Essex House in London, after which the principal conspirators were placed under arrest, tried, and executed.

With Essex out of the way, Ralegh nevertheless maintained only a secondary degree of influence at court and in the government at large. His closest associates during these years, Lord Cobham and the earl of Northumberland, were but moderately influential peers; with Ralegh, both would face lengthy imprisonments early in the reign of Elizabeth's successor, King James I. In fact, the ambitions of both Essex and Ralegh had long been checked by the formidable political power of Elizabeth's principal secretary during the last decade of her reign, Sir Robert Cecil, son of Lord Treasurer Burghley. The Cecils and Raleghs had been on excellent terms during most of this period, with Cecil's son Will spending considerable time in the Ralegh household, a playmate of Ralegh's eldest son, "Wat." Yet Cecil used his influence with the queen to ensure that Ralegh gained no significant power, while his secret correspondence with James VI of Scotland caused Ralegh's future sovereign to distrust him. Their common interests in learning and poetry could not overcome this predisposition, nor could Ralegh's belligerent foreign policy be reconciled with James's desire to negotiate peace with Spain. Within months of the king's accession in 1603, Ralegh began thirteen years of imprisonment on the ludicrous charge of plotting the Spanish conquest of England.

From the Tower, Ralegh continued to promote his plan to exploit the mineral resources of Guiana. James released him in 1616 to lead an expedition to the area, now partially occupied by Spanish colonists. Ralegh's voyage was a failure in all respects. In the assault on a Spanish outpost, "Wat" Ralegh was killed, and Sir Walter returned to England where he was beheaded, October 29, 1618, to appease Spain's objections to his intrusion into territory he had claimed for England during Elizabeth's reign.

BIBLIOGRAPHY

Edwards, Edward. *The Life of Sir Walter Ralegh.* 2 vols. 1868.
Lefrance, Pierre. *Sir Walter Ralegh Écrivain.* 1968.
———. "Un Inédit de Ralegh Sur La Succession." *Études Anglaises,* vol. 13, pp. 42–46.
May, Steven W. *Sir Walter Ralegh.* 1989.
Ralegh, Sir Walter. *The Works of Sir Walter Ralegh.* 1829; repr., 1965.
———. *The Discoverie of the large and bewtiful Empire of Guiana.* V.T. Harlow, ed. 1928.

R

Rudick, Michael, ed. *The Poems of Sir Walter Ralegh: An Historical Edition.* Medieval & Renaissance Texts & Studies. 1998.

Wallace, Willard M. *Sir Walter Raleigh.* 1959.

Steven W. May

SEE ALSO

Colonial Development; Devereux, Robert; de Vere, Edward; Discovery and Exploration; Elizabeth I; Foreign Relations and Diplomacy; Gascoigne, George; Gilbert, Humphrey; Grenville, Richard; Howard, Charles; Spenser, Edmund

Ramism

The works of Pierre de la Ramée (1515–1572)—better known by his Latinized name, Petrus Ramus—had a decisive if relatively short-lived influence on the curriculum of universities in the British Isles in the later sixteenth and early seventeenth centuries. Based in Paris, his programmatic reform of the curriculum became popular throughout Europe, particularly following his "martyrdom" in the St. Bartholomew's Day Massacre in 1572. While Ramus had not specifically rejected all of Aristotle's works and, indeed, owed much to him, he had freely criticized the scholastic approaches to the *Organon.* By applying humanist methods and emphasizing the original sources rather than later accretions, Ramus radically overhauled Aristotelian logic by abandoning the predicables, reorganizing the categories, and reducing the importance of the syllogism. His fundamental break with Aristotle came, however, in his declaration that there was only one system of logic rather than Aristotle's two, and in his specific rejection of metaphysics. The core of Ramus's reform lay in his understanding of the relationship of logic/dialectic and rhetoric, ideas outlined in the most famous of his many works: *Training in Dialectic and the Remarks on Aristotle.* There he advocated the shifting of two parts of rhetoric—invention and judgment—to dialectic, and the enhanced role of dialectic within logic. However, his definitions of these categories were very fluid—often changing as a response to criticism of his works. It was, however, in his advocacy of his highly controversial "Method" that Ramus achieved his greatest fame. Although by no means an original conception, Ramus managed to popularize his dichotomization, a methodology that significantly simplified the learning process. Ramus should perhaps be lauded more for his publicity skills than for any originality of thought. He

himself was anxious to argue that his revision was not original but had its roots in earlier works of Aristotle, Plato, and Cicero, though his most obvious debt was to a more contemporary source—Rudolph Agricola.

Huguenots such as Thomas Vautrollier played an important role in disseminating Ramist ideas in England—as did contacts between Sir Philip Sidney and the Wechel press, the chief publishers of Ramist works. The first official publication in England was by a Scot, Roland MacKilwein, in 1574, but it is clear that knowledge of Ramus's reforms was available in the British Isles as early as the 1550s, when Roger Ascham made somewhat disparaging remarks concerning it to Johann Sturm. By the 1570s, however, Ramism had become very much the vogue, especially at Cambridge, where men like Laurence Chaderton and Gabriel Harvey popularized key Ramist concepts. Throughout the 1570s and 1580s, debates were held within the university between supporters of Ramism, such as William Temple, and opponents, such as Everard Digby. Ramus's simplification of logic may account for the popularity of his *Dialectica,* especially among younger students, while the biblicism of English Ramists such as William Perkins, Dudley Fenner, and George Downham may have rendered the novelty of the approach more palatable to divines. In Scotland, Ramism was popularized by Andrew Melville in his influential university reforms in Glasgow, Aberdeen, and St. Andrews, while at Edinburgh the chief instigator of Ramism was Robert Rollock. Representatives from both Scottish and English universities played a part in introducing Ramism to Ireland. Trinity College, Dublin, founded in 1592, proved to be one of the last outposts of Ramism in the British Isles. An investigation of the early intellectual interests of members of Trinity College reveals, above all, the dominance of the Ramist curriculum in the late sixteenth- and early seventeenth-century college. Ramism dominated not only the book collecting habits but also the way books were read. This interest in Ramism was an all-pervasive one, and was not confined to the sections of the trivium most commonly associated with the Ramist challenge. Ramist authors also proved popular in fields other than the trivium—in the quadrivial subjects of mathematics and music, and indeed other areas such as politics, ethics, and history. Trinity College, Dublin continued to cling to an already outmoded program for a number of reasons. Above all, the self-perception of the college as a Puritan foundation, albeit of a moderate kind, influenced early members of the college in their choice of a Ramist curriculum. As such it formed part of a Puritan nexus of colleges

R

at Cambridge, such as Emmanuel (1584) and Sidney Sussex (1596), colleges whose members had also embraced Ramism as a useful guide to the curriculum.

A correlation between Ramism and Puritanism, both notoriously difficult areas to define, is evidenced in a study of colleges most closely connected with Ramist doctrines. To the Puritan, the Ramist nexus of thought offered a new, simpler method that could be utilized by preachers. Coupled with its appeal as a rebellion against the "old philosophy," and the fact that its founder had died a martyr's death for his Calvinist beliefs, Ramism was assured a hearing in Calvinist circles in England and the Continent. The simplicity of the Ramist approach was much appreciated by Puritans, whose attitude to studies was that they were means to an end—divinity—rather than an end in themselves. By applying a single method to all areas of knowledge, the Ramist method offered a relatively quick and easy approach to the seven liberal arts and their related disciplines. Ramism reached the height of its influence in England and Scotland in the 1580s, and in Ireland in the 1590s and 1600s. The rise of neo-Aristotelianism in the early Stuart era led to the decline of this simplification of Aristotelianism.

BIBLIOGRAPHY
Howell, W.S. *Logic and Rhetoric in England*. 1961.
McConica, James, ed. *The Collegiate University*. 1986.
Ong, Walter J., S.J. *Ramus and Talon Inventory*. 1958.
———. *Ramus, Method and the Decay of Dialogue*. 1974.

Mordechai Feingold

SEE ALSO
Aristotelianism; Ascham, Roger; Calvinism; Digby, Everard; Education; Fraunce, Abraham; Harvey, Gabriel; Huegenots; Logic; Melville, Andrew; Puritanism; Reading Practices

Rastell, John (c. 1475–1536)

A lawyer, printer, businessman, dramatist, historian, and religious controversialist, Rastell was active in the intellectual, social, and religious life of his day. Related to Sir Thomas More through marriage, and member of the More circle of humanists, Rastell shared their belief that the works of the mind should be available to all people. He printed treatises and tracts of many kinds, as well as plays and jest books. Of his own writings, he is best known for three interludes ascribed to him: *The Four Elementis* (1517), *Of Gentylnes and Nobylyte* (1525), *Calisto*

and Melebea (1525), and two prose works, *The pastyme of people* (1529) and *A new boke of Puragatory* (1530).

Rastell, probably born in Coventry, may have attended Oxford for a time, then read law at the Middle Temple. He married Thomas More's sister, Elizabeth, in 1496. They had three children, William, John, and Joan. Joan, later the wife of John Heywood, was grandmother to John Donne. William took over the printing business from his father in the early 1530s, when the latter became involved in legal and religious controversy. In 1510, when Rastell moved to London to set up his print shop, he was befriended by Sir Edward Belknap, privy councilor to both Henry VII and Henry VIII. Belknap secured various employment for Rastell, including a post as overseer for unloading ordinance at the Tower of London, and designer of the roofs of the banqueting hall at the Field of the Cloth of Gold (1520). Belknap also arranged for the lands and debts of Richard Hunne to be passed on to Rastell. Hunne had refused to pay tithes to the clergy, was imprisoned, and either committed suicide or was murdered. Rastell had to fight many legal battles to keep the properties. Ironically, after his later conversion to Protestantism, he too refused to pay tithes and was imprisoned in 1535. He wrote his will in the Tower on April 20, 1536, and died there sometime later.

Rastell launched a failed attempt at exploring the new world in 1517, but his crew mutinied and left him in Ireland; he prepared a pageant for Charles V, Holy Roman Emperor, in l522, and in 1524 built the earliest stage in England at his home in Finsbury. But it was as a printer that Rastell made his mark. One assumes it was his association with More that led him into a profession where he felt he could best serve in the disseminating of ideas. He had been raised in a family where social involvement was the norm; he had joined a guild before leaving Coventry, further evidence of his wish to serve the community. Indeed, "service" could be said to best typify his lifelong activities. His writings were meant to serve the public by exposing them to ideas and to history.

A significant detail in *The Four Elementis* occurs in the opening lines spoken by a Messenger who calls for an expansion of printing in English so that all people can be aware of what the best clerks are thinking and discovering. The Messenger calls for translations of Latin books and those in other languages so that "all subtle science" might be learned in English.

Rastell's interludes are entertaining and educational dramatic debates of issues that can be understood through common sense and reason, thus appealing to a broad audience. *The Four Elementis* mixes song, dance, bawdy jokes, and broad humor with the serious message that an individual must achieve a balance between physical desire and his intellect if he is going to experience self-realization and honor God. *Calisto and Melebea* is more dramatic than the debate interludes; it has to do with attempted seduction of Melebea and her salvation through common sense and merciful authority. It is a translation of a much longer work (originally in Spanish, although Rastell relied on a French version), *La Celestina,* with some new material added by the translator. The language of Courtly Love in *Calisto* turns out to be a fiction that can sway a young woman into thinking that promiscuity can be given respectability. But she learns that such language is dangerous and can lead to the loss of one's virtue and soul.

Of Gentylness and Nobylyte is a debate among a Knight, a Merchant, and a Plowman concerning what constitutes a true gentleman, what qualities are necessary to be a nobleman, and how these relate to the qualifications for rulers. The debate is punctuated with comic brawls, and bawdy oaths and jokes. Rastell uses the debate form to explore ideas and to allow his audience to see the strengths and flaws of each character. The play points out the paradox that important, secular questions are open-ended.

Rastell's *The pastyme of people* offers a history of England from its mythological beginnings to the reign of Richard III. *A new boke of Purgatory* is his entry into religious controversy. The pastyme is a chronological history that relies on Robert Fabyan's *Cronycles* (1516), as well as previous accounts by Bede, Brute, and Geoffrey of Monmouth.

In 1529, Simon Fish wrote *A Supplycacyon for the Beggars,* in which he faulted clerics who got rich taking tithes. He argued that paying clergy to pray for souls in purgatory, a place whose existence he believed lacked biblical foundation, was wrong. More responded to Fish in his *The Supplicacyon of soules* (1529). Rastell, too, joined in with *A new boke of Purgatory,* in which he set out to prove by "natural reason and good philosophy" the existence of purgatory. His book did not gain much attention at first, but then John Frith, a Cambridge reformer influenced by William Tyndale, published his response, *A disputacion of purgatorye* (1533), while a prisoner in the Tower. Frith refuted Rastell's natural reason argument to such an extent that the latter converted to Protestantism and became zealot enough to try to convert the monks at Charter House in London. Rastell, who had fallen into disfavor with Thomas Cromwell, also alienated himself from Archbishop Thomas Cranmer, who presided at his trial for refusal to pay tithes. Rastell died in the Tower a broken man.

John Rastell had his greatest impact on his contemporaries as a printer and writer. He published not only works of his own but also those of Henry Medwall, John Skelton, Sir Thomas More, and many others. His goal of bringing knowledge to men and women of all types marks him as an important force for learning in the sixteenth century. Rastell is best known today for his interludes, but his prose works reveal a great deal about him and need to be reexamined.

BIBLIOGRAPHY

Axton, Richard, ed. *Three Rastell Plays.* 1979.

Cameron, Kenneth W. *Authorship and Sources of "Gentleness and Nobility."* 1941.

Geritz, Albert J, and Amos Lee Lane. *John Rastell.* 1983.

Reed, A.W. *Early Tudor Drama.* 1926.

Edmund Hayes

SEE ALSO

Cranmer, Thomas; Drama, History of; Fabyan, Robert; Field of the Cloth of Gold; Frith, John; Spanish Literature, Influence of; More, Thomas; Printing, Publishing, and Bookselling; Skelton, John

Rastell, William (1508–1565)

Like his father, John, William Rastell was both a lawyer and a printer. A nephew of Thomas More through his mother, Elizabeth (More's sister), William was a close contemporary of his More cousins, and doubtless an intimate of the family. He is reported to have studied at Oxford beginning in 1525, but he took no degree. In 1527, he worked on a show at Greenwich called *The Father of Heaven,* his father's device for entertaining French ambassadors. Having mastered the craft of printing, perhaps as his father's assistant in 1527 and 1528, he established shops in Fleet Street against the Conduit (by 1531), and in Fleet Street in St. Bride's Churchyard (by 1533), the latter perhaps in the residence of his brother-in-law, John Heywood. Two imprints appeared under his own name in 1529, the year of his majority; six followed in 1530, four(?) in 1531, three in 1532, twelve in 1533, and seven in 1534.

In the face of More's arrest in 1534 and his execution in 1535, William remained Catholic while his father turned Protestant. Both stopped printing. Already admitted to Lincoln's Inn on September 12, 1532, William devoted the rest of his professional life to law. Called to the bar in 1539, he became pensioner of Lincoln's Inn in

R

1545, autumn reader and bencher in 1546, keeper of the black book in 1548, and treasurer in 1549.

In 1544, a time of personal prosperity, Rastell married Winifred, the young daughter of the physician, John Clement (who had once been tutor to More's children), and Margaret née Giggs (who had been raised in More's household). On December 21, 1549, provoked by the ascendency of radical Protestantism, Rastell, Winifred, and the Clements fled to Louvain. Winifred's death on July 17, 1553, and Mary Tudor's accession at almost the same time gave Rastell a double incentive to return to London and to Lincoln's Inn, where he resumed as treasurer in 1555. He joined a commission for inquisition into heresy on October 8, 1556, and on October 16, he became serjeant-at-law. On October 27, 1558, he was raised to the bench.

Rastell retained his office following Elizabeth's accession on November 17, 1558, but the strain of religious difference provoked a second flight to Louvain on January 3, 1563, again with Winifred's parents in tow. John Heywood, and his wife Joan (William's elder sister), followed in July 1564. Rastell died on August 27, 1565, and was buried in the church of St. Peter next to his child bride.

Nonliterary titles from William Rastell's brief printing career include eight works of religious controversy by Thomas More and three from other writers, several legal reference works, and two sermons by John Fisher in one volume. *Julius Cesars Commentaryes . . . as much as concernyth thys Realm of England* is paired with another historical work focusing on England, *Fabyans Cronycle* (2nd edition, continued to Henry VII). Rastell's literary titles include *Tullius de Amicitia, in Englysh; Book of a Hundred Riddles;* and five plays from the "More Circle": Henry Medwall's *Nature* (John Rastell had earlier printed Medwall's *Fulgens and Lucrece*), and four plays by John Heywood: *A Mery Play Betwene Johan Johan the Husband etc., A Mery Play betwene the Pardoner and the Frere etc., The Play of the Wether,* and *A Play of Love.*

Rastell had resumed book production on his return from exile in 1553 as an editor of legal texts. In 1557, having long preserved the memory and papers of his patron-uncle, Rastell published in folio, with a dedication to Queen Mary, *The Workes of Sir T. More . . . Wrytten by him in the Englysh Tonge.*

BIBLIOGRAPHY

Axton, Marie. *The Queen's Two Bodies: Drama and the Elizabethan Succession.* Royal Historical Society. Pp. 16–17, 45. 1977.

Duff, E. Gordon. *A Century of the English Book Trade,* p. 130. 1905.

Reed, A.W. *Early Tudor Drama: Medwall, the Rastells, Heywood, and the More Circle,* pp. 72–93. 1926.

Alan H. Nelson

SEE ALSO

Heywood, John; Inns of Court; More, Thomas; Printing, Publishing, and Bookselling

Reading Practices

The activity of reading in Tudor England was transformed by three major developments that contributed to the wide circulation and active interpretation of texts. First, the Tudor period coincided with the birth of print culture in Europe, which brought a dramatic increase in the availability and affordability of texts. Second, under the Tudors, English culture felt the belated impact of Humanism, a movement that fostered new methods and standards of textual scholarship (both biblical and classical) and put a greater emphasis on textual application (both personal and political). And third, Henry VIII's break with Roman Catholicism began a period of religious reformation in England that intensified the use of and debate over religious texts at nearly every level of society. Along with gradually increasing levels of literacy and access to education, these factors meant that texts played a more active role in the lives of a larger percentage of the population than ever before.

Some Tudor readers were in a position to "read for pleasure," and there was some trade in "entertaining" material among the most and the least literate. While this motive is perhaps the most familiar function associated with the Tudor texts commonly read by modern readers, most early modern texts and readings seem committed either to more instrumental or to more devotional ends. Adapting the techniques inherited from the Middle Ages, and those imported from continental humanism, the readers of Tudor England developed a set of practices that allowed them to manage a rapidly growing body of textual information and to apply it to their personal and professional conduct, and in some cases, to their own writings.

Perhaps the most important of these was the habit of creating "commonplace books." The technique of keeping books in which to enter notable passages, often according to a set of preconceived categories or topics (known as *loci communes*—hence "common places"), was

R

a central feature of the program developed by Desiderius Erasmus and his contemporaries. Such books were considered a valuable resource—a "storehouse"—for the future needs of readers, providing them with an abundance of material, as well as a categorical framework, to employ in a discourse or a composition on any subject. It is easy to see, in this context, the extent to which reading was connected to writing and speaking in Tudor England.

Throughout the Tudor period the use of commonplace books remained pervasive, and became increasingly associated with the collection of literary and epistolary miscellanies. The period has left many collections in which material is selected for later reference. Special volumes were even printed for this purpose—some with blank pages, some with printed headings, and some already complete with selected passages.

Another indication of the interaction between texts and readers in Tudor books was the use of marginal notations, or "marginalia," in the texts themselves. This, too, was a widespread practice in the Renaissance: a common feature of biblical, classical, and medieval texts, marginalia died out only gradually (and never completely) after the advent of print culture. Tudor authors and publishers increasingly relied on printed marginal notes to influence the reader's understanding of the text. In this way, marginal notes could be set alongside—on the one hand—the efforts of censors and commentators attempting to control the proliferation of texts and interpretations, and—on the other—the development of an apparatus designed to make texts clearer and easier to use. Like their medieval predecessors, however, Renaissance readers frequently entered their own notes in both manuscript and printed texts—identifying and storing useful passages, registering reactions, or preparing them for later publication. A considerable proportion of the Tudor texts that come down to us bear contemporary handwritten marginalia, and these notes provide extensive evidence of the ways in which particular books were read by individuals with a broad range of capacities and needs, and—more generally—of the role of those books in the intellectual, spiritual, and social lives of their readers.

Finally, Tudor readers encountered texts in a variety of domestic, professional, and communal settings. While the period did see the growing dominance of silent reading and the expansion of private libraries, this should not obscure the fact that, for Tudor readers, reading was primarily an interpersonal activity. Private libraries were rarely places of isolation, and the majority of the population would have encountered their texts in more obviously social contexts: studied in schoolrooms, read aloud in households, performed or preached in churches, recited, sung, or posted in public spaces, including inns and taverns, or dramatized on the stage.

BIBLIOGRAPHY
Grafton, Anthony. *Commerce with the Classics: Ancient Books and Renaissance Readers.* 1997.
Kintgen, Eugene. *Reading in Tudor England.* 1996.
Moss, Ann. *Printed Commonplace-Books and the Structuring of Renaissance Thought.* 1996.
Sherman, William H. *John Dee: The Politics of Reading and Writing in the English Renaissance.* 1995.
Watt, Tessa. *Cheap Print and Popular Piety, 1550–1640.* 1991.

William H. Sherman

SEE ALSO
Book Ownership; Commonplace Books; Dee, John; Humanism; Literacy; Manuscripts; Printing, Publishing, and Bookselling

Rebellions and Uprisings
See Agrarian Uprisings; Kett's Rebellion; Northern Rebellion; Pilgrimage of Grace; Wyatt's Rebellion

Recorde, Robert (c. 1512–1558)
The author of the first series of mathematical textbooks in English, Robert Recorde was born in Tenby, Pembrokeshire, and studied at Oxford. Graduating B.A. in 1531, he was elected a fellow of All Souls that year and vacated the position in 1535. He is reported to have taught mathematics at Oxford and presumably practiced medicine there. He later moved to Cambridge where he received an M.D. in 1545. Recorde's only nonmathematical publication—a short medical treatise on *The Urinal of Physick* (1547)—evidently arose from his career as physician. His later years were marked by administrative troubles and the political turbulence of the period. He served as an administrator of mint works and mining at Bristol and in Ireland but was recalled in both cases. After an unsuccessful lawsuit against the earl of Pembroke, he is last seen as a debtor in the King's Bench prison, where his will was written.

Learned contemporaries knew Recorde as a student of Greek and of Anglo-Saxon and British history, and his library provided a manuscript resource for bibliophile

R

scholars such as John Bale, but he is primarily remembered for his mathematical texts. Recorde's first publication, *The Grounde of Artes* (1543), was an elementary introduction to arithmetic written in dialogue form. The book was enlarged in 1552 and continued to be edited long after his death, passing through at least forty-five editions before 1699.

Recorde intended that the mathematical student should follow an orderly and methodical course of study, and the next step after arithmetic was provided by *The Pathway to Knowledge* (1551), an introduction to geometry that simplified the first four books of Euclid's *Elements*. Furnished with the basics of geometry, the student could then pass on to the spherical astronomy of *The Castle of Knowledge* (1556). Recorde drew on and critically reviewed a wide range of Greek and Latin sources in compiling this astronomical textbook, while also offering instructions on the actual construction of an armillary sphere.

More sophisticated and controversial issues of astronomy were perhaps intended for a projected but unpublished work, *The Treasure of Knowledge*. Likewise, the progression from the elementary geometry of the *Pathway to Knowledge* was left incomplete: Recorde announced a text called *The Gate of Knowledge,* on practical geometry and measurement by the quadrant, but this has not survived. However, Recorde's final publication did supplement the basic arithmetic of *The Grounde of Artes*. In *The Whetstone of Witte* (1557), he provided more advanced arithmetic and some algebra. He introduced the plus and minus signs for the first time in England and devised the equal sign still used today.

Recorde's mathematical works were not intended to contribute novel results but to form an accessible and readable introduction to mathematics, especially for those unskilled in Latin. Recorde's significance lies in his status as the first major English textbook writer and in his promotion of the idea of the mathematical sciences as a broad field encompassing practical arts such as surveying and navigation.

BIBLIOGRAPHY

Easton, Joy B. "Robert Recorde." In *Dictionary of Scientific Biography.* 16 vols. C.C. Gillispie, ed. Vol. 11, pp. 338–340. 1970–1980.

Emden, A.B. *A Biographical Register of the University of Oxford, A.D. 1501–1540.* Pp. 480, 735. 1974.

Howson, Geoffrey. *A History of Mathematics Education in England.* Chap. 1. 1982.

Johnson, Francis R., and Sanford V. Larkey. "Robert Recorde's mathematical teaching and the anti-Aristotelian movement." *Huntington Library Bulletin,* vol. 7 (1935), pp. 59–87.

Stephen Johnston

SEE ALSO
Education; Navigation; Science, History of

Recusancy

The Act of Uniformity (1 Elizabeth, c. 2) imposed a fine of one shilling a week on those who absented themselves from the legally prescribed services of the Church of England. This absence from Anglican services, known as recusancy, came to denote Roman Catholic absentees. It was once thought that there were few true recusants during the first decade of Elizabeth I's reign—that, with the exception of those in strongly conservative counties such as Lancashire, most Catholics were willing to attend Anglican services in public and worship as Catholics in private. It is now acknowledged that there were numerous recusants scattered throughout the kingdom at the start of Elizabeth's reign, that their numbers increased during the 1560s, and that these recusants served as a base of support for the activities of the Catholic missionaries.

At first, punishment of recusants was left to local officials, but country gentlemen and parish churchwardens were reluctant to charge their neighbors with recusancy; and the process of appointing more loyal, zealous Protestants as justices of the peace and as assize judges in place of Catholics and Catholic sympathizers was slow. Elizabeth's government implemented stronger measures in reaction to the steady increase in recusancy, to the rebellion of 1569, to the publication of the papal bull *Regnans in excelsis* in 1570, and to the arrival of the seminarian and Jesuit missionaries in the mid-1570s and early 1580s. In August 1575, the Privy Council, no longer content to leave the problem of recusancy to local officials, summoned leading Catholic gentlemen to London to meet with a committee of bishops and to answer before the council. Those who submitted and conformed were allowed to return home, but the obdurate were imprisoned. Catholics who had failed to conform by the following June were ordered to meet with their local bishop, forbidden to have guests frequent their homes, and compelled to post bonds ensuring their return to prison at Michaelmas term. The council also ordered a census of recusants taken in each diocese, in the two universities, and in the Inns of Court. In 1581, act

R

23 Elizabeth, c. 1 increased the fine for recusancy to £20 a month, and in 1583, the government, bypassing the ordinary institutions for penal law enforcement, appointed special recusancy commissioners, with broad authority to examine individuals. To get past the solidarity among the country gentry, the government employed paid informers to ferret out recusants. Catholics were isolated further when, in 1579, the obligation to swear the Oath of Supremacy was extended to all officials and professionals, including schoolmasters, lawyers, and justices of the peace.

Catholic gentlemen evaded heavy fines for recusancy by means of trusts and feoffment-to-use, and so, in 1586, the government, in 29 Elizabeth, c. 6, outlawed such conveyances by recusants and allowed the crown to seize a recusant's goods and two-thirds of his land until he had paid the fine, conformed, or died. Later, those husbands who conformed were made liable for the fines of their recusant wives. Enacted in 1593, 35 Elizabeth, c. 2, required recusants with land to stay within five miles of their homes, and those without land to remain within five miles of their customary or family dwelling, with expulsion from England as penalty for violations. Consideration was given also to taking Catholic children from their parents and placing them in Protestant homes to be reared as Protestants at the expense of their parents. Despite the severity of the 1593 act, the government ceased fearing Catholics as a grave internal threat, and policy toward recusants in the 1590s concentrated on isolating them socially and politically and on exploiting them financially. Catholics had their horses seized for the queen's use, and a special levy was imposed on them for the support of light cavalry in Ireland.

The government's actions against recusants were of limited success. Most Catholic families suffered from fines and the loss of offices; but few were ruined, for the undervaluing of estates and legal devices for the conveyance of property helped limit the loss of wealth. Few recusants were fined as heavily as Sir Thomas Treshman, who paid £8,000 between 1581 and 1605; and few suffered long years of imprisonment, like Thomas Pounde, or a painful execution, like Margaret Clitherow. Under Elizabeth I, of the estimated 30,000 to 40,000 English and Welsh lay Catholics, sixty-three were executed and ninety-eight died in prison. In the north, in the traditionally Catholic regions of England and those far from London, recusancy increased despite the government's harsh measures. In the West Riding of Yorkshire, presentments for recusancy rose from 271 in 1575–1580 to 1,136 in 1603–1604; in Lancashire they grew from 304 in 1578 to 3,516 in 1604. The government's stepped-up effort to uncover recusancy accounted for only part of the increase. In the south, however, the number of Catholics steadily declined to a scattering of a few noble and gentry households. Books and the preaching of seminary priests and Jesuits on the sinfulness of attendance at Anglican services stiffened the recusant resolve of many Catholics, although there were a few who argued that conformity in certain circumstances was not a sin. Many Catholics vacillated between periods of recusancy and occasional conformity. Isolated, the English Catholic community became introspective, and developed its own rich literary tradition as a source of spiritual refreshment and moral support.

BIBLIOGRAPHY

Aveling, J.C.H. *The Handle and the Axe. The Catholic Recusants in England from the Reformation to Emancipation.* 1976.

Bossy, John. *The English Catholic Community, 1570–1850.* 1976.

Haigh, Christopher. *Reformation and Resistance in Tudor Lancashire.* 1975.

———. *English Reformations. Religion, Politics, and Society under the Tudors.* 1993.

Holmes, Peter. *Resistance and Compromise: The Political Thought of English Catholics.* 1982.

LaRocca, John L. "Time, Death, and the Next Generation: The Early Elizabethan Recusancy Policy, 1558–1574." *Albion,* vol. 14, pp. 103–117.

MacCulloch, Diarmaid. *Suffolk and the Tudors: Politics and Religion in an English County, 1500–1603.* 1986.

Magee, Brian. *The English Recusants.* 1938.

Manning, Brian. *Religion and Society in Elizabethan Sussex.* 1969.

Morey, Adrian. *The Catholic Subjects of Elizabeth I.* 1978.

Prichard, Arnold. *Catholic Loyalism in Elizabethan England.* 1979.

Trimble, William R. *The Catholic Laity in Elizabethan England, 1558–1603.* 1964.

John M. Currin

SEE ALSO

Catholicism; Clitherow, Margaret; *Regnans in Excelsis;* Supremacy, Act of; Uniformity, Act of

Reformatio Legum Ecclesiasticarum

"Reformatio Legum Ecclesiasticarum" is Latin for *Reformation of the Ecclesiastical Laws,* the name given to the

R

revised canon law drawn up by a committee under the direction of Archbishop Thomas Cranmer and presented by him to Parliament in March 1553. It was not passed in the House of Lords, and the whole project lapsed with the accession of Mary I, although John Foxe tried unsuccessfully to revive it in 1570.

When Parliament abolished the juridical authority of the pope in 1534, it made statutory provision (25 Henry VIII c. 19) for a new canon law, to be drawn up by a committee of sixteen laymen and sixteen clergy. Pending reform, the ecclesiastical courts were to continue to accept the medieval canons as these were then received in England. What precisely this meant is still a matter of dispute. The canons contained in William Lyndwood's *Provinciale* (1433) were certainly regarded as valid, as were the Legatine Constitutions of Cardinals Otho (1237) and Othobon (1268), and it is no coincidence that all of these appeared in an English translation in 1534. It is less certain to what extent the Roman *Corpus Iuris Canonici* was received in England at that time, although the Anglican Church courts have generally continued to admit its validity, at least in so far as it supplements English legislation and does not contradict it.

Nothing happened to the reform project at the time, and in 1544, the same provision was repeated in another statute (35 Henry VIII c. 16). Other things continued to take priority, but eventually the committee prepared a draft by 1552. The text printed by Foxe claims to have been the final form of the text, although it differs in a number of respects from the 1552 draft. Whether Cranmer made these revisions or they were added later (perhaps even by Foxe himself) is a matter of controversy.

The *Reformatio* never became part of English ecclesiastical law, and it has had little influence. It is sometimes thought that if it had been adopted in place of the medieval canons, Puritanism might not have arisen or taken the form that it did. Certainly the *Reformatio* would have given England a comprehensive system of canon law far in advance of its time. Instead, English canon law has continued to admit the medieval precedents mentioned above, and it was not properly codified until 1969. On the other hand, the *Reformatio* was occasionally cited in eighteenth- and nineteenth-century ecclesiastical cases, which shows that it had not been forgotten. Its importance for understanding Thomas Cranmer's policies, if not English law, has been increasingly recognized in recent years. No English translation of the complete text exists, although one of the 1552 draft has recently been published (1992).

BIBLIOGRAPHY

Cardwell, E. *The Reformation of the Ecclesiastical Laws.* 1850.

Helmholz, R. *Roman Canon Law in Reformation England.* 1990.

Spalding, James C. *The Reformation of the Ecclesiastical Laws of England, 1552. Sixteenth Century Essays and Studies,* vol. 19. 1992.

Gerald Bray

SEE ALSO

Canon Law; Cranmer, Thomas; Foxe, John; Puritanism

Reformation in England

The interpretation of the English Reformation has been a subject of debate for four centuries. Although disagreements extend even to its chronological framework, the Reformation may be seen as framed by the reigns of Henry VIII and Elizabeth I, with one qualification: its crowning cultural achievement, the "King James" Version of the vernacular Bible, the culmination of work begun in the 1520s, emerged eight years after Elizabeth's death.

In the Reformation, as in much of its national history, England both participated in a defining European phenomenon and developed characteristics distinct from continental patterns. England's Church became Protestant—if the elusive word "Protestant" is defined by the repudiation of papal authority, with its corollary appeal to the authority of Holy Scripture and to a doctrine of justification akin to that set forth by Martin Luther. Yet this Protestantism retained seeds of continuity with medieval Catholicism that other European Protestants, in varying degrees, lacked. Such seeds drew the continued attacks of its most militant reformers, occasionally encouraged Roman Catholics to envision England's return to the papal fold, and, in the long run, produced a form of Christian faith and practice sufficiently distinctive to take its place alongside the Lutheran, Reformed, Anabaptist, and Roman Catholic traditions that constituted the corporate descendants of the medieval Western Church.

During the thirty years after 1530, no fewer than five changes in religion established by law marked the course of the Reformation. When Henry VIII had come to the throne, the prevailing religion was already being challenged by two movements: one local, covert, and supported largely by lowly townsfolk; the other international, manifest, and patronized by the highest levels of ecclesiastical and lay society. Lollardy, tracing its origin to the fourteenth-century John Wycliffe, subsisted in loosely related coteries who read their Bible in English from forbidden manuscripts and denied the priestly authority of the clergy. Renaissance humanism had struck as deep roots in English as in any European soil. Before and after Henry's accession, Dean John Colet of St. Paul's Cathedral with his friends, the young lawyer Thomas More and the periodic Dutch visitor Desiderius Erasmus, shared a zeal for the biblical studies engendered by their humanistic ones. Circles in court and the universities discussed the "new learning" and its implications for the reform of church teaching and life. Thus Lollardy and humanism both fostered dissatisfaction with the religious status quo.

As elsewhere in Europe, two governing hierarchies—temporal and spiritual—ruled in England. The hierarchies could meld with one another; Thomas Wolsey was unique only in the extent of his power when, in Henry's second decade, he combined the highest offices of church and state, serving as lord chancellor as well as archbishop of York and special papal legate. Early in that decade, Leo X (1513–1521) excommunicated Martin Luther, who, in turn, publicly burned not only the offensive papal bull, but also a copy of the canon law that united the Western Church under papal leadership. Johann Gutenberg's movable type, three-quarters of a century old, facilitated the flow of Lutheran discourse across the North Sea. Also appearing in England before the end of the decade were works emanating from Zurich and Basle, where a "Reformed" theology was developing. The audacious challenges to established religious authority were read with mixtures of relish and horror whether readers were drawn to these challenges, outraged at what they judged heresy, or merely piqued by curiosity. English merchants and clerics living and traveling abroad drank the heady wine of the new teachings. In 1524, a young scholarly priest, William Tyndale, sought the freedom of the Continent expressly to prepare a vernacular English Bible. As they became aware of these new religious currents, Lollards judged they had found powerful religious allies. Humanists were divided between those like More and Erasmus, who read in their Bibles a message of Christian unity and opposed the sundering of the Western Church, and those convinced that scriptural teachings demanded reform even at the cost of Western unity.

Church and government authorities responded negatively to the rumblings of the continental Reformation. The bishop of London publicly burned Tyndale's New Testament; the archbishop of Canterbury was futile in his attempt to buy up all surviving copies. The anti-Lutheran work *Assertio Septum Sacramentorum* bore Henry's name as author, and, in appreciation, Leo X granted Henry and his successors the title "Defender of the Faith." Thomas More, who had risen in royal service while Wolsey was Henry's chief minister and had aided the king in composing the book, took an increasingly active role in suppressing the continental "heresies." The first two priests to die in England for their Reformation convictions—John Frith (primarily as a consequence of More's initiative) and Thomas Bilney—went to the stake in the very years that More's own conscience was struggling with Henry's anticipated break with Rome.

Under Henry the church's juridical links with Rome were broken. Otherwise, new measures were only suggestive of future doctrinal and liturgical changes. Concern for religious reform and national self-interest underlay the motivations for an independent English Church, but the king, determined to shed Katherine of Aragon in order to marry Anne Boleyn, precipitated its implementation. The nascent concept that national sovereignty resided in king-in-Parliament, grasped by Cardinal Wolsey's protégé, Thomas Cromwell, provided the engine for the four-year series of parliamentary acts that culminated in 1534 with the declaration that England's king is "the only supreme head in earth of the Church of England, called *Anglicana Ecclesia*." Concurrent clerical convocations affirmed that, according to the Scriptures, the bishop of Rome had no "greater jurisdiction in England than any other foreign bishop." In some English eyes, the church had returned to its ancient pristine condition when it had been "sufficient and meet of itself" to manage its own affairs. The judgment of others, that England had betrayed the unity of Christendom, was reflected in the martyrdoms of More and the respected bishop John Fisher. Parliament expressly declared that ecclesiastical independence did not imply any intention "to decline or vary from . . . Christ's Church" concerning "the Catholic faith of Christendom." Yet Henry designated Thomas Cranmer to be archbishop of Canterbury, a priest touched by Lutheranism through his reading at Cambridge and his experience in Germany. By 1540, English monasteries, embedded in English society since the sixth century, disappeared, their wealth to be employed for the public good as the king might define it. If the dissolution of the monasteries was the most significant *social* consequence of the break with Rome, Miles Coverdale's "Great Bible," which drew heavily on the work of Tyndale, was the most significant *religious* consequence. When Henry in 1538 ordered it to be placed in parish churches where "parishioners may most commodiously

R

resort to the same and read it," the theologically conservative monarch supplied the foundation for a new piety and doctrinal change. Otherwise, changes were few; most folk practiced Christianity much as they had when Henry came to the throne.

When the nine-year-old Edward VI ascended the throne in 1547, the ruling Privy Council designated by Henry included a majority who favored reformation. Under Lord Protector Edward Seymour's leadership, in tandem with that of Archbishop Cranmer, religious change began to be mandated in the king's name. Initially, the council prescribed homilies for nonpreaching clergy and ordered a greater use of English in parish worship. Homilies concerning Holy Scripture and justification reflected continental Reformation teachings. By abolishing chantries for requiem masses and other church endowments, Parliament transferred a second block of properties into royal and private treasuries. Within two years, Parliament authorized the full-fledged English liturgy of the 1549 Book of Common Prayer to replace Latin rites.

After John Dudley seized control of the council, further measures moved the church closer to the continental Reformers. Just as the country was becoming accustomed to the new vernacular forms of worship, they were replaced by those of the second 1552 Prayer Book, more markedly identifiable with the continental Reformation. Convocation and Parliament formally sanctioned clerical marriage. Reform-minded bishops were appointed to replace those unwilling to support changing norms. A new doctrinal stance was underscored in 1553 by the forty-two Articles of Religion. Edward's death in 1553 abruptly halted the reforming trajectory of the English Church, which in six years had moved from Henry's national Catholicism through two sequential stages of religious reform.

Mary Tudor interpreted the widespread rejoicing that greeted her accession and the consequent fall of the unpopular Dudley as a mandate to return to the "old religion" that "God and the world" knew she had "ever professed from her infancy." Within a year and a half, successive Parliaments repealed the legislation of Edward and Henry, and Cardinal Reginald Pole absolved the nation from its sin of schism from the Roman see.

Married clergy, the Prayer Book, even vernacular Bibles disappeared from public view, and only the largely untouched transfers of property remained of the reforms of the two preceding reigns. The revival of heresy laws brought nearly 300 martyrs to the stake. Some folk practiced their religion in secret, as Lollards had once done; others fled abroad to Protestant havens. Outwardly, Mary's five-year reign restored religious practices to those of the earlier years of her father's reign. Contrary to her deepest hopes, however, many came to identify the Roman obedience with the stench of the burning flesh of Protestant martyrs, with her unpopular marriage to Philip of Spain, and, near the end of the reign, with the loss of Calais. Dying in 1558, Mary, like her brother, had not reigned long enough to stabilize the religion she would have replanted in English society and in English hearts.

From Elizabeth's first week as queen, she demonstrated a consistent determination to repudiate papal authority once again. After the queen's death, Francis Bacon commented that "within the compass of one year she did so establish and settle all matters belonging to the church, as she departed not one hair's breadth from them to the end of her life." Parliament passed legislation that recognized the sovereign as "supreme governor" of the English Church and prescribed a third Book of Common Prayer largely based on Edward's second book, but with a few conservative modifications. Elizabeth issued a set of injunctions governing various details of church life, and these, together with the 1559 Prayer Book and royal supremacy, undergirded religious policy throughout her reign.

Although all European governments continued to support established churches with coercive authority, religious dissent became more widespread. In England, outside the communion of the established church, a small and dedicated band of Roman Catholic priests ministered to isolated nobility and gentry who, with their dependent households, clung to the "old ways." For the most part, these laity were loyal subjects who, suffering legal disabilities and fines, were often suspected of treasonable support of Spanish or French intrigues or of locally hatched plots to assassinate the queen.

Although militant Protestants occasionally separated from the church, most zealous clergy and their lay adherents continued in its communion while they embraced the Reformed teachings of the churches of Zurich and John Calvin's Geneva. From Elizabeth's first year, some viewed the 1559 Elizabethan Settlement as an interim measure, leading to fuller reform. Militants looked forward hopefully to the 1563 clerical convocation, but all that emerged was a conservative revision of the now Thirty-nine Articles of Religion. In those parishes and university colleges where those who became known as "Puritans" held sway, doctrinal, liturgical, and disciplinary structures of the English Church were bent as close to Reformed models as circumstances permitted. In town councils, court, and Parliament, Puritans lobbied to restructure forms and practices to patterns they believed dictated by the New Testament. Although they could often muster significant support in the House of Commons, Elizabeth repeatedly frustrated such attempts to modify the settlement. Although initial disputes centered on liturgical and vestiarian issues, from 1572 on, a well-organized minority among Puritans worked to replace the established episcopal ministry with Presbyterian structures.

Theologically, the Elizabethan Church is perhaps best typified by two writers active in the last decade of the century: William Perkins, a Cambridge don whose writings helped to shape the rigidly predestinarian international Calvinism of the next century, and Richard Hooker, whose *Of the Laws of Ecclesiastical Polity* pointed to the future of the English Church in its theological articulation of a Christianity implicit in the Elizabethan Settlement. By the queen's death in 1603 she left a church whose character had been shaped by settlement, by the external struggle with Roman Catholics, and by the internal tensions between its supporters and those who judged the Reformation still unfinished in England.

BIBLIOGRAPHY

Collinson, Patrick. *The Elizabethan Puritan Movement.* 1967.

———. *The Religion of Protestants: The Church in English Society, 1559–1625.* 1982.

Davies, Horton. *Worship and Theology in England from Cranmer to Hooker.* 1970.

Dickens, A.G. *The English Reformation.* 1964.

Haigh, Christopher, ed. *The English Reformation Revised.* 1987.

———. *English Reformations: Religion, Politics, and Society under the Tudors.* 1993.

Hughes, Philip. *The Reformation in England.* 3 vols. 1951–1954.

Lake, P. *Anglicans and Puritans? Presbyterianism and English Conformist Thought from Whitgift to Hooker.* 1988.

McGrath, Patrick. *Papists and Puritans under Elizabeth I.* 1967.

O'Day, Rosemary. *The Debate on the English Reformation.* 1986.

Scarisbrick, J.J. *The Reformation and the English People.* 1984.

William P. Haugaard

SEE ALSO

Anglicanism; Articles of Religion; Bible Translations; Bilney, Thomas; Book of Common Prayer; Calvinism; Colet, John; Convocation; Counter Reformation; Coverdale, Miles; Erasmus, Desiderius; Elizabeth I; Fisher, John; Frith, John; Henry VIII; Hooker, Richard; Katherine of Aragon; Lutheranism; Mary I; More, Thomas; Perkins, William; Pole, Reginald; Puritanism; Recusancy; Seymour, Edward; Tyndale, William; Wolsey, Thomas

Regnans in Excelsis

Regnans in Excelsis are the opening words of the papal bull of excommunication against Queen Elizabeth I. When Elizabeth ascended to the throne (November 17, 1558) the Church of England was in restored communion with Rome; despite the queen's evident leanings toward Protestantism, this situation remained officially unchanged. During the 1560s, however, Roman attitudes hardened, and by 1567, a Catholic college at Douai (France) was training missionaries for the British Isles. Pope Pius V (1566–1572) was an extremist who believed that his duty was to extirpate heresy and schism wherever he found them. In spite of advice from his cardinals and from Catholic ambassadors to the Holy See, Pius proceeded to excommunicate Elizabeth (February 25, 1570).

The extremely severe terms of the bull of excommunication provoked a strongly negative reaction among the Catholic powers of Europe. Elizabeth was formally deposed, and her subjects were encouraged to rebel against her. The fact that her proposed successor was the Catholic Mary Queen of Scots, presented a genuine political danger, and there were many plots against Elizabeth in the 1570s and 1580s, among them the Ridolfi Plot (1570–1571), which brought down Mary's suitor, Thomas Howard, the fourth duke of Norfolk.

The bull forced papal loyalists in England to break with the national church, and gave the queen a ready excuse to pass laws against Catholicism, which had become politically subversive. A number of Catholic activists were subsequently put to death, but more for political than for purely religious reasons.

Today, the bull is a dead letter in practice, but it has never been repudiated, and to some extent it remains an obstacle to reunion between the Anglican and Roman Catholic Churches.

BIBLIOGRAPHY

Elton, G.R. *The Tudor Constitution.* 2nd edition. 1982.

R

Jewel, John. "A View of a Seditious Bull." In *The Work of John Jewel*. 4 vols. John Ayre, ed. Parker Society. Vol. 23. 1845–1850; repr. 1968.

MacCaffrey, Wallace. *Elizabeth I*. 1993.

Gerald Bray

SEE ALSO

Elizabeth I; Church of England; Howard, Thomas; Mary Queen of Scots; Reformation, English

Regulated Companies

A distinctive feature of foreign trade at the end of the Tudor era was that most English merchants, especially those of London, belonged to a company, either regulated or joint stock, founded by royal charter with a monopoly of trade either with a territorial unit, or, less commonly, in a particular commodity. In 1600, of the major continental markets, only France was a "free trade" area. Elsewhere, independent traders or "interlopers" were rigorously excluded. Of the two types of company, the older and much more important was the so-called "regulated" company that had evolved in the late Middle Ages out of the less formal associations or "fellowships" of merchants, these in turn having their roots in the ancient craft guilds or livery companies—Mercers, Haberdashers, and the rest—which had become largely irrelevant to the conduct of trade in the late Middle Ages. In the early Tudor period there were two regulated companies: the Merchants of the Staple, who exported raw wool, and the Merchant Adventurers, who exported woolen cloth to the Low Countries. As the trade in cloth grew at the expense of wool, the Adventurers, rather than the Staplers, provided the model for incorporation when the widening geographical framework of Elizabethan trade led to the formation of new companies with exclusive rights to trade in the new markets. The Eastland Company was incorporated in 1579 to regulate trade in the Baltic. In the next decade the monopoly of trade in the Mediterranean was granted by the crown to the Turkey Company, a joint stock company on its foundation in 1581 but regulated by the time of the renewal of its charter in 1592, and to the Venice Company (1583), the two companies merging in 1592 to form the Levant Company. Spain also became a monopoly trading area in 1577 when the Spanish Company was formed, reviving an earlier, short-lived attempt to regulate trade with the Iberian Peninsula.

The function and purpose of the regulated company were to license members to trade, either on their own account or in partnership, and to regulate their conduct. As licensing authority, the company was typically exclusive. Retailers were kept out, entry being restricted to wholesale merchants who had served an apprenticeship. In the case of the Eastland Company, merchants seeking membership were further required to have at least eleven year's experience in the Baltic trade. Entry fees could also be charged and set at levels that preserved the exclusiveness of the company. Those who gained admission were required to observe the regulations in the charter, with additions or modifications agreed by the governing body, normally comprising a general court, representing members, a governor and deputy governor, and a court of assistants. How detailed, restrictive, and effective the regulations were varied from company to company. Those of the Merchant Adventurers and the Eastland Company were the most comprehensive and detailed, covering every aspect of the member's conduct, moral as well as commercial. Thus the Adventurers shipped their cloths in fleets, paying freight rates set by the Merchant Adventurers Company. Space on board, times of sailing, and the days when sales could be made on arrival were corporate decisions. How many cloths each Adventurer could sell were limited by the "stint," which took into account his standing in the Merchant Adventurers Company and how long he had been a member. If resident abroad, he and his servants were told where they might lodge and how they should behave. Those who transgressed in any way were liable to be fined, imprisoned, or, in the last resort, disenfranchised. The threats were not idle. The Adventurers and the Eastland Company had the considerable advantage of limiting trade to one place or "staple," where the governor or his deputy kept a close eye on members and apprentices. The Spanish Company, lacking a staple, was significantly less successful in enforcing regulations.

When company trade was extended in Elizabeth I's reign the advantages seemed clear. For the merchant community, collective action and representation strengthened its position in dealings with governments at home and abroad, while for the crown the companies could be used as an extension of the state, providing diplomatic or consular services to supplement or even substitute for its own. There was also an increasingly important financial dimension to the relationship between crown and company. From the mid-sixteenth century onward, the Merchant Adventurers in particular provided valuable financial services. Economic arguments in favor of company trade concentrated on the perceived effect of a free market on prices. Too many sellers would depress the quality of cloth exports, while too many buyers, lacking skills, training, and experience, would force up the price of import goods. Free trade, even in a limited sense, would have seemed an extraordinary notion to the Tudors. The case for well-ordered company trade, as against "loose, distracted, and disorderly trade," seemed in particular to be strengthened by the extremely disturbed conditions of foreign trade in the mid-sixteenth century. Although the Elizabethan companies were formed in more settled times, they were in part a defensive response to the disorder of those years.

Regulated companies were not, however, without their critics. Independent traders resented their monopoly and their jurisdiction over interlopers. Clothiers complained that monopolistic merchants paid them too low a price, while clothworkers condemned the Merchant Adventurers for denying them employment by shipping unfinished cloths. There were divisions, too, within the companies: in particular between metropolitan and provincial members. The disproportionate wealth of the Londoners, their influence with the crown, and the location of corporate government in the city ensured that they controlled the companies' affairs, and they used that position to promote their own ends. They were in provincial eyes "monopolists within a monopoly."

That tendency also attracted criticism within the city, where lesser merchants resented the concentration of wealth and business in the hands of a small elite. In 1579, they joined forces with merchants in Hull, who had earlier complained that the London-based companies had brought "the whole trade of merchandise . . . to the City of London," in an attempt to exclude Merchant Adventurers from membership of the Eastland Company, thinking, with some justification, that cross-membership of trading companies further encouraged oligopoly. They were unsuccessful, and it was not until James I's reign that the tide began to turn against company trade, and then largely because the mutually supportive relationship between the Tudors and the companies was undermined by the policies of the early Stuarts.

BIBLIOGRAPHY
Croft, Pauline. *The Spanish Company.* 1973.
Ramsay, G.D. *The City of London in International Politics at the Accession of Elizabeth Tudor.* 1975.
Willan, T.S. *Studies in Elizabethan Foreign Trade.* 1959.
Wood, A.C. *A History of the Levant Company.* 1935.
Zins, H. *England and the Baltic in the Elizabethan Era.* 1972.

Brian Dietz

R

SEE ALSO
Cloth Trade; Joint Stock Companies; Merchant Adventurers; Monopolies; Trade, Overseas

Religious Toleration
See Toleration, Religious

Revels Office
The revels became a formal office of the royal household, under the lord chamberlain, in 1545 when a master (Sir Thomas Cawarden), clerk-comptroller, and clerk were all appointed by patent. This gave substance to various temporary arrangements under the early Tudors, when minor court officials acted as master of the revels for major entertainments; Sir Henry Guildford held the post from 1510 to at least 1527, aided by a yeoman of the tents—the offices of the revels and the tents overlapped a good deal, and close connections persisted until 1642.

Under Cawarden and his successor, Sir Thomas Benger (master 1560–1572), the revels settled into a regular role of planning court entertainment under the direction of the Privy Council, being responsible for the quality of performances and their costs. From 1560, it was located in the dissolved St. John's Priory in Clerkenwell; its duties included hiring and supervising all workmen required to handle stages, costumes, and lighting; procuring necessary materials; storing and cleaning costumes; assisting at productions; and accounting for all expenditures. The busiest time was the yearly revels season, from November 1 to Shrove Tuesday, when there were between eight and fourteen shows in the royal palaces; but special shows might be required for important visitors, and until about 1580, the revels were also responsible for entertainment during Elizabeth I's summer progresses.

At Benger's death the office was in disarray, and no master was appointed; the clerk, Thomas Blagrave, was acting master from 1573–1577, while Lord Treasurer Burghley undertook a thorough review of the office, with a view to keeping costs down. Among his solutions was the appointment as master of a "man of credit," a role filled by Edmund Tilney, a relative and client of Lord William Howard, lord chamberlain 1558–1572, and of his son, Lord Charles Howard, best remembered as lord admiral 1585–1619. Tilney was confirmed by patent in 1579 and served until his death in 1610.

Tilney's strategy was to rely on the professional actors then establishing a permanent presence in London. Plays

R

had been imported for some time, from both the adult companies and the boys of the choir schools. The revels accounts for a 1571 record of six plays, "being chosen out of many, and found to be the best that were to be had, the same being often perused and necessarily corrected and amended." Sometimes the master failed to "amend" adequately; in 1573, Mulcaster's boys brought *Timoclea at the Siege of Thebes* to court, where it was found so tedious that the masque due to follow it was canceled. In *A Midsummer Night's Dream* (1600Q) we see that Philostrate, Theseus's master of the revels, has perused everything available (that is, seen it in dress rehearsal), and done his best to reform it, but there was nothing suitable. Yet perusing the scripts of professional actors could be a service to them; in 1574, Leicester's Men had it written into their patent that their plays should be "seen and allowed" by the master, a precaution against civic authorities denying them performance. This was the beginning of a symbiosis between the master and the elite of the acting profession.

Tilney's reliance on the best professionals put an end to problems of quality, as well as dramatically reducing costs compared with the shows, principally masques, which the court had created for itself earlier in the reign. And he largely eliminated competition between aristocrats patronizing the actors by creating in 1583 a premier troupe, the Queen's Men, who dominated court performances for the rest of the decade. His authority for this was a special commission in 1581, which gave him sweeping powers to impress workmen he needed and over all "shows, plays, players and playmakers, together with their playing places, to order and reform, authorize and put down, as shall be thought meet or unmeet unto himself."

In practice Tilney mainly dealt with companies likely to perform at court. Between 1594 and 1600, this may only have been the Lord Chamberlain's and Lord Admiral's Men; in 1598, the Privy Council made these the only companies allowed regularly to perform around London, under Tilney's authority, on the pretext that they were rehearsing for court performance. In reality, such restrictions were the price they paid for protection from city authorities, who repeatedly tried to eliminate the actors altogether. The revival of the boy companies shortly thereafter, under different patents but still under Tilney's control, expanded the cartel but did not breach the principle. Tilney was seen as the actors' protector more than their regulator; in 1592, the lord mayor had negotiated to buy him out, but it came to nothing.

Tilney made a steady income from licensing the "allowed" companies themselves, their theaters, and their plays for performance; but he was also a serious-minded censor. The manuscript of *Sir Thomas More* shows his concern about the depiction of anti-alien riots at a time when there was similar unrest in the city. He seems to have been less concerned to impose any political or ideological orthodoxy, if topical issues were treated with discretion. The revels office provided exactly the stability and protection that allowed late Elizabethan theater to flourish as it did.

BIBLIOGRAPHY

Chambers, E.K. *The Elizabethan Stage*. 4 vols. 1923.

Dutton, Richard. *Mastering the Revels: The Regulation and Censorship of English Renaissance Drama*. 1991.

Feuillerat, A. *Documents Relating to the Office of the Revels in the time of Queen Elizabeth*. In *Materialen zur Kunde des älteren englischen Dramas*. Vol. 21. W. Bang, ed. 1908.

Streitberger, W.R. *Edmond Tyllney, Master of the Revels and Censor of Plays: A Descriptive Index to His Manual on Europe*. 1986.

Richard Dutton

SEE ALSO

Cecil, William; Censorship; Howard, Charles; Progresses, Royal; Theater Companies, Adults; Theater Companies, Boys; Tilney, Edmund

Rhetoric

The goal of rhetoric in the Tudor period was the mastery of spoken or written language to affect a particular audience in an intended and predictable manner. Mastery entailed an analysis of language in its relation to human psychology, the use of formal procedures for turning theory into practice, and the education of others in both theory and practice. The focus on particular audiences, rather than a universal audience, recognized that listeners or readers could be differentiated and grouped according to their interests in a given topic or problem, and that the particulars of their immediate social situation would shape their psychology as a group. Not every intention could be realized with every audience, and students learned to judge whether it was reasonable to expect a particular audience to respond as intended to a particular use of language.

Rhetoric emerged as the central educational discipline in the Renaissance, studied in the simplest provincial classroom and the university lecture hall. At its most basic level it involved widely available training in practical techniques of manipulating language, while at advanced levels it was an increasingly sophisticated theoretical enterprise. Widespread rhetorical education helped cement Tudor society with shared understandings of how individuals should communicate, since it trained students both in how to control language and in what to expect of the language of others. Speakers could use this shared understanding to facilitate orderly communication by speaking just as anticipated, or they could manipulate those same audience expectations to achieve surprising or subtle literary effects. The impact of rhetorical education can be seen in the regularization of mundane mercantile communication, the construction of sermons, and the writing of letters, and in the late Elizabethan love of language—with its wordplay, startling comparisons, cadences, rhythms, and memorable sound patterns.

Throughout the medieval period classical Latin rhetoric had been understood to comprise five major studies: *inventio* (the ferreting out of material worth discussing), *dispositio* (the strategic ordering of larger units of discourse), *elocutio* (the shaping of smaller units of discourse for psychological effect), *actio* (controlling voice and gesture), and *memoria* (holding ideas or tropes in the memory). But these classical studies survived only in brief or schematic forms, and in the medieval period had been adapted to more immediate needs in constructing sermons (*ars praedicandi*), letter writing (*ars dictaminis*), teaching of grammar, and producing and appreciating poetry. These medieval rhetorical traditions continued throughout the Renaissance, and when complete classical treatises were discovered they were first seen as buttressing and expanding these traditions. In particular, the discovery of the richly textured world of Cicero's letters, and the fullness of Roman culture found in Cicero's *De oratore*, supplied the original sense of context and purpose missing from the remnant classical prescriptions, so that the medieval treatises and commentaries on Cicero seemed to have more point and greater promise. But soon the recovered classical texts simply replaced the medieval studies as Renaissance writers choose to grapple directly with the original materials, and the revivified classical models offered new promise for early humanists as a civilizing force, both as an alternative to violence in a violent era, and as a means of engendering a sense of community and shared enterprise.

In Tudor England, rhetoric was largely derivative of continental movements. England did not participate in the great intellectual excitement in the Trecento and Quattrocento, when Latin treatises by Cicero and Quintilian, and Greek treatises by Aristotle and Hermogenes, became available in Italy in a series of discoveries. Instead, classical rhetoric arrived in England as a body of recovered knowledge, and English rhetoricians followed the lead of continental theorists and educators; rhetorical treatises and schoolbooks were imported from the Continent throughout the Tudor period and they provided the models for rhetorical works written and published in England. Such innovations as offered by writers in England were either accommodations to local conditions or, increasingly, accommodations to the developing English language. The first treatise on rhetoric printed in England was the *Margarita eloquentiae* (1479 and 1480; also published in epitome) by Lorenzo Traversagni, who reshaped the pseudo-Ciceronian *Rhetorica ad Herennium* for the cultural and political needs of English ecclesiasts. The first treatise published in English was *The Arte or Crafte of Rethoryke* (1530, c. 1535) by Leonard Cox, who translated and substituted English examples in Melanchthon's *Institutiones rhetoricae* (Strasbourg 1524), itself a reworking of Ciceronian rhetoric. Traversagni was an Italian Franciscan teaching at Cambridge, and Cox had just spent a decade lecturing in Poland and elsewhere on the Continent. Together they demonstrate the international and humanistic character of Tudor rhetoric from its inception, along with the early English bias for ecclesiastical and broadly cultural rhetoric, rather than for the political and judicial rhetoric of classical models.

Rhetorical genres inherited from the medieval period also showed indebtedness to Continental thinking. In letter writing, the early Tudor period was dominated by Latin manuals such as those by Brandolinus (Basle 1498) and Erasmus (Basle 1519), both published together in London (1573). Even more popular were the treatises by Macropedius (Antwerp 1543) and Hegendorf (Basle 1549), published repeatedly in London after 1576. The ready availability of Cicero's letters, and their extensive publication in England after 1570 as models for practical emulation, encouraged the idea of letter writing as humane engagement with the larger culture, an idea promoted by such vernacular works as William Fulwood's *The enimie of idleness* (1568, 1571, 1578, 1582, 1586, 1593, 1598, 1607, 1612, 1621), William Fiston's *The welspring of wittie conceites* (1584), and Angel Day's *The English secretorie* (1586, 1592, 1595, 1599, 1607, 1614, 1621, 1625, 1635). More pragmatic approaches ranged from formularies of legal letter writing to Walter Darell's *Certaine letters verie necessarie for servingmen* (1578) and John Browne's "A briefe forme of all such letters as you shall neede to write thoroughout your whole voyage" in

R

The marchants avizo (1589, 1590 [twice], 1591, 1607, 1616, 1640). By the end of the century, exemplars and collections of letters abounded, and while many advertised themselves as being for critical use in instruction and emulation, some were valued as much for their entertainment value, as with Nicholas Breton's *A poste with a madde packet of letters* (1602), frequently reprinted and vastly expanded in the seventeenth century.

The arts of preaching were also shaped by continental ideas in rhetoric, and particularly those that had been accommodated to Protestant perspectives. Treatises by Johannes Reuchlin (Pforsheim 1504), Melanchthon (Ulm 1529) and Johannes Aepinus (Wittenburg 1537), all circulated in England before being printed in London (1570). Erasmus (*Ecclesiastae,* Basle 1535) outlined a more flexible rhetoric for constructing sermons, while both Niels Hemmingsen (*Ecclesiasten,* Wittenberg 1552) and Andreas Hyperius (*De formandis,* Marburg 1553) reorganized the types of sermons to reflect changes in theological goals with different audiences; Erasmus circulated widely in continental editions, while both Hemmingsen and Hyperius were available in English translations by the 1570s. By the end of the period, materials ranged from prescriptions such as Leonard Wright's *A patterne for pastors* (1589 [four issues], 1596, 1615, 1637) to discussions attending to the dynamics of rhetorical efficacy, such as Matthew Sutcliffe's *Of doctours, and their office* (1590, 1591). The traffic with the Continent was not all one-way; *De concionatore* by the English Catholic Robert Turner was published exclusively on the Continent (Ingolstadt 1599, 1602, 1609; Cologne 1615, 1625, 1629), while William Perkins's *Prophetica, sive de sacra et unica ratione concionandi* (Cambridge 1592) was reprinted extensively on the Continent (Basle 1602; Hanau 1602; Geneva 1611, 1624; Amsterdam 1606, 1609).

Much of the impetus for Tudor rhetoric came from Oxford and Cambridge, particularly as a training ground for English writers. Classical rhetoric was studied at both universities, for the most part using continental editions and translations. Cicero's rhetorical treatises began to be printed in England in the 1570s, but they always appeared with continental commentaries, and Aristotle's *Rhetoric* would not be printed in England or translated into English until the seventeenth century. Other classical writers were available only from the Continent, with the notable exception of Aphthonius, available in six Tudor printings after 1572. Aphthonius, however, was used in grammar schools rather than at the universities, as were grammatical handbooks with lists of figures from Donatus, printed from 1502 onward. University scholarship on rhetoric was also notable for advertising its European filiation; John Rainolds lectured on Aristotle at Oxford during the 1570s, adopting perspectives from Rudolf Agricola and Juan Luis Vives; Gabriel Harvey lectured on Cicero and style at Cambridge, adopting perspectives from Petrus Ramus. In general, the efforts by Tudor writers to understand classical materials were hampered by the many non-classical rhetorical needs of their own time, which invited them to read things into classical texts or simply misread them in terms of their own experience. They were further hampered by the common belief that all classical writers were saying more or less the same things for more than 800 years in a seamless progression from Greece to Rome. This latter belief led, on the one hand, to complex efforts to reconcile vastly different classical writers with one another, and on the other, to reductive popular versions of rhetoric that sought the least common denominator among conflicting sources.

Conversely, what hampered Tudor writers in scholarly understanding aided them in adapting classical theories and practices for their own immediate needs and purposes. Only a few Tudor writers after Traversagni and Cox attempted to deal with all five constituent studies of *inventio, dispositio, elocutio, actio,* and *memoria.* Thomas Wilson adjusted all five for use by English gentry and Protestant preachers (*The Arte of Rhetorique,* 1553, 1560, 1562, 1563, 1567, 1580, 1584, 1585); William Thorne produced a complete Latin rhetoric intended for university graduates (*Ducente Deo,* 1592), and Henri Perri published a complete Welsh rhetoric (*Egluryn phraethineb,* 1595). Much more common than complete programs, however, were schoolbooks and analytical works that dealt with one or two of the Ciceronian categories, and by far the most common studies addressed *elocutio.* Classical *inventio* and *dispositio* had been formulated in terms of the genres of political and judicial oratory, so that they required extensive modification before they could be grafted onto Tudor political and judicial traditions. But *elocutio* could be easily adapted to both Renaissance Latin and English vernacular: the techniques of manipulating language on the local level could be taught starting at a very early age; it was easy to see the results in either public or private discourse; and the theory of *elocutio* could be made to yield many of the psychological insights of the Ciceronian program without the technicalities of *inventio* and *dispositio.*

The original impetus for studying *elocutio* was first to gain control of basic Latin and then to match eloquence with philosophy. Works on *elocutio* ranged from prescriptions on tropes and figures to variation and *copia,* and to theoretical studies of the relations between language and belief. The most basic and hence most widespread Tudor understanding of tropes and figures came through grammatical treatises. Thomas Linacre's *De constructionis figuris* (1524) went through thirty continental editions; his *Figures of construction* (1525) went through an additional twenty-five; William Lily's *De figuris* was published more than 125 times before 1700. *Elocutio* was also readily extracted from the larger Ciceronian program and taught by itself. Digests by Mosellanus (Frankfurt 1516), Susenbrotus (Zurich 1535), Macropedius (Dillingen 1561), and others were available in continental editions; they all had numerous printings in England starting in the 1570s, and seem to have been more widely read than English products by Richard Sherry (1550, 1555) or Henry Peacham (1577, 1593).

Two major forces complicated the study of *elocutio,* Erasmian *copia* and Ramism. Desiderius Erasmus first composed *De duplici copia verborum ac rerum* (Paris 1512) for use at St. Paul's School, but it quickly became one of the most widely disseminated rhetorical treatises in Europe. *De copia* often was received as a lively rearrangement of standard ideas of elegant variation, notable primarily for a curricular presentation that progressed from simple manipulations toward complex strategies. It was printed in England many times, beginning in 1528 and always with continental commentaries. It was also frequently digested and printed alongside other writers on *elocutio;* Meier, for example, produced a digest of *De copia* (Leipzig 1525) that was printed in England with Petrus Mosellanus's digest of Ciceronian *elocutio* (1573, 1577).

The case was much the same in England with the curricular innovations of Petrus Ramus (Pierre de la Ramee). Ramus elaborated on ideas found earlier in Rudolf Agricola on the relations between dialectic and rhetoric, and in his own writings he reassigned the classical subject areas of *inventio, dispositio,* and *memoria* exclusively to the discipline of dialectic. Ramus then collaborated with Talaeus (Omer Talon) to produce a school text on rhetoric (Paris 1549), which consisted solely of *elocutio* and a very short treatment of *actio;* Latin editions were printed in England during the 1590s. Dudley Fenner translated both Ramus and Talaeus in *The artes of logike and rhethorike, plainelie set foorth* (1584 [four issues], 1588, 1651, 1681); Abraham Fraunce translated Talaeus as *The Arcadian rhetorike: or the praecepts of rhetorike made plaine by examples* (1588), drawing his examples from

Philip Sidney; and Charles Butler revised Talaeus as *Ramae rhetoricae libri duo* (1597, 1598, 1600), a schoolbook that went into many editions in the next century. As these titles show, Ramist rhetoric was received in Tudor England as a curricular clarification, and when taken as intended with Ramist dialectic, it covered pretty much the same ground as the Ciceronian five-part study. But where Erasmian *copia* proceeded by accumulation, association, and modification, Ramist *elocutio* presented large conceptual categories, which were then progressively dichotomized until enough subsidiary categories were generated to account for nearly all the tropes and figures of classical rhetoric.

The Erasmian and Ramist approaches could both be accommodated to traditional Tudor studies of *elocutio* because neither changed things very much on the practical level. But the two differed markedly in their underlying principles and outlooks. Erasmus's idea of *copia* correlated with his theological ideas about how to engage the fullness of God's creation; finding new ways to manipulate language led to new kinds of thoughts in a continuous unfolding of possibilities, so that very few things on this earth could be understood in their totality. Erasmian *copia* made it possible to be comfortable with uncertainty by embracing possibility as a fundamental mode of human understanding. By contrast, the Ramist approach attempted to replace uncertainty with certainty; it postulated invariable criteria for determining categories, for establishing hierarchies among those categories, and for moving within those hierarchies. Once those criteria were accepted, the details of a discourse fell into place with complete certitude, and Ramus demonstrated that kind of certitude through his own analyses of speeches by Cicero. Thus, while the approaches of Erasmus and Ramus seemed to change little at the level of stylistic detail, their understandings of the entire rhetorical enterprise differed widely, with Erasmus urging alternative visions and Ramus asserting singularity. In turbulent seventeenth-century England, one or the other of these divergent understandings of rhetoric tended to be adopted by partisans who had already divided along religious and political lines that stressed either skeptical acceptance or self-confident rectitude.

BIBLIOGRAPHY

Erasmus, Desiderius. *Ciceronianus.* Betty I. Knott, trans. and ed. In *Collected Works of Erasmus.* Vol. 28. 1986.
———. *De Copia.* Betty I. Knott, trans. and ed. In *Collected Works of Erasmus.* Vol. 24. 1978.

R

Green, Lawrence, ed. *John Rainold's Oxford Lectures on Aristotle's Rhetoric.* 1986.

Howell, W.S. *Logic and Rhetoric in England.* 1961.

McConica, James, ed. *The Collegiate University.* 1986.

Ong, Walter J., S.J. *Ramus and Talon Inventory.* 1954.

———. *Ramus, Method and the Decay of Dialogue.* 1974.

Siegel, J.E. *Rhetoric and Philosophy in Renaissance Humanism.* 1968.

Vos, Alvin. "'Good Matter and Good Utterance': The Character of English Ciceronianism." *Studies in English Literature*, vol. 19, pp. 3–19.

Lawrence D. Green

SEE ALSO

Ciceronianism; Cox, Richard; Education; Erasmus, Desiderius; Fraunce, Abraham; Grammar Schools; Logic; Ramism; Wilson, Thomas

Rich, Lord Richard (c. 1496–1567)

Second son of Richard Rich and Joan Dudley, Richard Rich was born in Hampshire, studied at Cambridge, and entered the Middle Temple to study law. He is best known for his role in prosecuting Sir Thomas More and Bishop John Fisher for noncompliance with the Acts of Supremacy and Sucession by providing the key condemning evidence at their trials. Although he undoubtedly perjured himself, Rich testified that both men had denied the royal supremacy in his presence while in the Tower. After Fisher and More were executed, Rich benefited from the dissolution of the monasteries, and by 1538 was a privy councilor.

A dedicated royal servant, Rich successfully served each of the last four Tudor monarchs, switching his religious allegiance accordingly. He served as lord chancellor under Edward VI, and in 1548 was created Baron Rich of Leeze, Essex. He died June 12, 1567.

BIBLIOGRAPHY

Guy, John A. *Tudor England.* 1988.

Marius, Richard. *Thomas More: A Biography.* 1984.

Gregory P. Ripple

SEE ALSO

Fisher, John; More, Thomas; Supremacy, Act of

Riche, Barnabe (1542–1617)

Best known for his collection of tales entitled *Barnabe Riche His Farewell to Military Profession* (1581), Barnabe

Riche was himself a soldier. Riche expressed some ambivalence about the value of his fictions, especially when he judged them in relation to his more "serious" work on military conduct, on the troubles in Ireland, and on the faults of a society overrun with corrupt lawyers, parasites, whores, and hypocrites. On occasion, his two-tier scheme of literary values has been reflected by his twentieth-century students: the more didactic works have always attracted Irish and military historians while literary scholars have squabbled over whether his derivative fictions deserve their careful attention. Over the last twenty-five years, however, students of Elizabethan prose have followed William Shakespeare's lead in finding that Riche's fictions—his *Farewell*, but also his *Adventures of Brusanus* (1592, composed 1584–1585), and *Don Simonides* (in two parts, 1581 and 1584)—vividly refashion the narrative conventions of the day.

Born in 1542, Riche launched his military career some twenty years later in Le Havre. This unhappy enterprise was followed in 1565 by another—privateering, one resulting in debt and a prison sentence (1570). Thereafter seeking military action in Ireland, Riche also fought against Spain in the Low Countries. Also during the 1570s, Riche's first books appeared on his two favorite subjects: the value of military discipline and (as a corollary to its neglect) the present "miserable condition" of an Ireland undone by excessive leniency and corruption. In his "vacant tyme" from military action, however, he temporarily shifted his literary attention from camp to court, that is, from humanist contributions to the wisdom and might of England to the more "dainty fare" of romances and novellas. Riche composed the *Farewell* before July 1579, and his other fictions in the early 1580s. His satirical vein was opened during these years as well: in 1582, he based an anti-Catholic polemic, *A True Report*, on the sensational confessions of a woman at Chester Cathedral.

Riche's frequent reports on abuses in Ireland gained him a pension from the queen in 1586, but nearly lost him his life in 1592, when he was attacked by men hired by the archbishop of Dublin to silence him. Having left Ireland for safety, he continued for the rest of his life to write about that country in *A Short Survey of Ireland* (1609) and *A New Description of Ireland* (1610). But in the new century, with one lawsuit after another on his hands and the eventual loss of his pension, Riche favored the "serious" and "bitter" social satire found in *Faultes Faults* (1606), *Opinion Diefied* (1613), *The Honestie of This Age* (1614), and *My Ladies Looking Glasse* (1616).

Appropriately, his last work was *The Irish Hubbub* (1617), which exposes in both England and Ireland "all the most lewd and idle vices."

The soldierly persona of Riche's most famous work, the *Farewell,* explains at some length his transition from martial to courtly discourse. Addressing gentlewomen, he notes that the life of the witty lover is easier than that of the soldier. But the persona admits his incompetence in the "pretty" vein of amorous "histories"; and in an epistle to fellow soldiers, he mocks the very court culture that he would enter—a culture that, after all, shows no appreciation for the hardened and loyal soldier.

Of the eight stories in the collection, three "are Italian histories written likewise for pleasure by master L.B.," Lodowick Bryskett. The others move between the sprawling wonders of romance and the curt, clever intrigues of the novella. The first and longest of the stories—"Sappho Duke of Mantona"—shares the most with Hellenistic, chivalric, and hagiographic romance, featuring a noble and virtuous family dispersed and mightily tested by adversity and misfortune, yet finally reunited in a joyous scene of revelation and nuptials. Like "Sappho," "Of Apolonius and Silla" begins with a moral—in this case, the irrational errors caused by love—and offers a romantic tale of Christians at war with Turks, of unfortunate travels, and of the mistaken identities made famous by Shakespeare's use of the tale in *Twelfth Night.* Unlike the first romance, however, the second is more swiftly told and, Riche tells his reader, establishes a standard for the "celerity" of all the rest. The tale furthest from romance is the fifth: "Of Two Brethren and Their Wives." According to the conventions of French and English novellas, there is a moral for readers to consider: men should be wary of choosing bad wives. But the wit of the tale derives from the promiscuous wife's clever strategies for concealing her various adulteries and then, with the help of her soldier-lover, for exacting revenge on the physician and lawyer with whom she has dallied. Mistress Dorothy turns honest in the end, but not before redirecting the collection away from the loyal, patient, and chaste wives of the romantic tales toward the sexual trickery of the fabliau. In one final defensive maneuver, Riche's conclusion consigns the "novels" to the shelf of nugatory fashion, exhorting men to leave "such superficial follies" and to contribute to the welfare of their nation.

Riche's more extended prose fictions—*The Adventures of Brusanus* and the two parts of *Don Simonides*—take place on the "highe way of experience" traveled by their heroes. Brusanus is a voluptuous prince whose father—having failed to talk him out of his vices—rearranges financial matters so that the prodigal son is compelled to travel in search of wisdom and virtue. Along the way Brusanus learns from a disguised king, a proud courtier, and an honest soldier, among others; finds himself in the middle of a love triangle; and—after wars, misfortunes, and wanderings—is reconciled with his beloved in one of the three nuptials crowning the happy ending. Just so, Don Simonides, a thwarted Spanish lover, travels in search of some philosophical relief from his pain. He tends to find it in wildernesses where other distraught lovers offer him set speeches and emblems of their misfortunes. In cities from Italy to England, he meets a number of wise folk, from honest soldiers and ancient fathers to characters made fashionable in the stylized prose of John Lyly. At long last back at home, he finds that the once-chaste object of his melancholy obsession is married to "an olde doating Citizen" and withal that love and women must be repudiated for "more orderly studies"—no doubt exemplified in the moral, colonial, and military service paid by Riche to his England. All in all, then, Riche's "novels" epitomize Tudor humanist uncertainty over whether such fictions cause or combat the social and spiritual ills of a Protestant nation.

Setting aside protest against the serious study of Riche, some scholars have traced Riche's literary debts while others have examined his persona's mediation between Mars and Venus. Lately, however, scholarship has focused on Riche's articulation of what his most recent editor has called the "finite number of generic categories and social transactions that constitute the whole of the social fabric." In the narrative habits of his fiction, that is, Riche crystallizes some noteworthy mental habits of the Elizabethans when they set out to construct ideals of political authority, society, and family.

BIBLIOGRAPHY

Beecher, Donald. "Barnabe Riche." *Dictionary of Literary Biography,* vol. 136, pp. 283–387.

———, ed. *Barnabe Riche His Farewell to Military Profession.* 1992.

Cranfill, Thomas M. "Barnaby Rich: An Elizabethan Reviser at Work." *Studies in Philology,* vol. 46, pp. 411–418.

———, ed. *Rich's Farewell to Military Profession.* 1581.

———, and Dorothy Hart Bruce. *Barnaby Rich: A Short Biography.* 1953.

Cunningham, Peter, ed. *The Honestie of This Age . . . by Barnaby Rich.* 1844.

R

Helgerson, Richard. "Lyly, Greene, Sidney, and Barnaby Rich's Brusanus." *Huntington Library Quarterly,* vol. 36, pp. 105–118.

Jorgensen, Paul A. "Barnaby Rich: Soldierly Suitor and Honest Critic of Women." *Shakespeare Quarterly,* vol. 7, pp. 183–188.

Lievsay, John Leon. "A Word about Barnaby Rich." *Journal of English and Germanic Philology,* vol. 55, pp. 381–192.

Relihan, Constance C. *Fashioning Authority: The Development of Elizabethan Novelistic Discourse.* 1994.

Wolf, Melvin H., ed. *"Faultes Faults and Nothing Else but Faultes" (1606), by Barnaby Rich.* 1965.

Reid Barbour

SEE ALSO

Lodowick Bryskett; Ireland, History of; Lily, John; Prose Fiction

Ridley, Nicholas (c. 1500–1555)

Bishop of London and Marian martyr, Nicholas Ridley was born in Northumberland and educated at Cambridge, where he was elected fellow of Pembroke Hall in 1524 and, two years later, earned his M.A. He went to Paris to continue his studies, then returned to his alma mater, in 1530, to become junior treasurer of the college. There he acquired a reputation as a scholar and formidable debater and, in 1534, served as proctor of the university, often traveling to London to protest threatened cutbacks of academic privileges. He eventually became chaplain to the university. Around this time, he struck up a friendship with Thomas Cranmer and, in 1537, was appointed chaplain to the archbishop; the next year, Cranmer made Ridley vicar of Herne, Kent. After he earned a D.D. in 1540, preferments followed in rapid succession: master of Pembroke Hall (also 1540), chaplain to Prince Edward and canon of Canterbury (both 1541), and canon of Westminster (1545). During this period, too, Ridley experienced a gradual disillusionment with Catholic dogma—in particular, with the doctrine of transubstantiation. Ridley favored John Calvin's virtualist interpretation of the Eucharist, and Cranmer henceforth adopted Ridley's views as his own. Edward VI's accession in 1547 provided greater opportunities for Ridley; that year, he traveled from diocese to diocese preaching reformed doctrine, gained a second vicarage, and was elevated to bishop of Rochester. The following year, he helped compile the first edition of the English Prayer Book, and, in 1550, he was created bishop of London—tirelessly promoting reformed policies all the while. Not surprisingly, he worked against the accession of Mary I, a Catholic; when she succeeded Edward, Ridley was arrested and sent to the Tower of London. In 1554, still under arrest, he was summoned to defend his views before a hostile Oxford audience and, after refusing to recant, was excommunicated. Again and again, he refused to adapt his views to the Catholic orthodoxy. Finally, having been excommunicated a second time, he was burned at the stake on October 16, 1555, alongside Hugh Latimer and Cramner.

BIBLIOGRAPHY

Bromiley, Geoffrey W. *Nicholas Ridley, 1500–1555, Scholar, Bishop, Theologian, Martyr.* 1953.

Ridley, Gloucester. *Life of Nicholas Ridley.* 1763.

Ridley, Jasper Godwin. *Nicholas Ridley: A Biography.* 1957.

Mark Goldblatt

SEE ALSO

Book of Common Prayer; Cranmer, Thomas; Edward VI; Latimer, Hugh; Mary I

Ridolfi Plot

The Ridolfi Plot (1570–1571) was one of several attempts during the early 1570s by the Spanish government and English Catholics to depose Elizabeth I and enthrone Mary Queen of Scots in her stead. The principal participants in the plot were Mary, Thomas Howard, the duke of Norfolk, Guerau de Spes, the Spanish ambassador, Philip II of Spain, Pope Pius V, and Roberti di Ridolfi. Masterminded by Ridolfi, a Florentine banker who lived in London, the plot called for the duke of Alba to send an army of more than 6,000 men from the Spanish Netherlands to Harwich or Portsmouth. From there, the rebel army would march to London, where they would be joined by the duke of Norfolk and other Catholic noblemen. The army would then rescue Queen Mary from captivity, or alternatively, seize Elizabeth and hold her hostage in return for Mary's safe delivery. If the situation required it, Elizabeth would be assassinated. In any case, the Catholic faith would be restored in England, and Mary and Norfolk would jointly rule over both England and Scotland. The plot was foiled when Sir William Cecil, Elizabeth's principal secretary, intercepted some letters that Ridolfi had written to Norfolk. Armed with this knowledge of a

Spanish plot to depose England's queen, Cecil and Elizabeth expelled the Spanish ambassador, de Spes, causing a serious breach in Anglo-Spanish diplomacy.

Although the plot was detected before it ever seriously threatened Elizabeth's sovereignty, it significantly affected England's foreign and domestic policy throughout the 1570s. England's highest ranking nobleman, the duke of Norfolk, was executed on treason charges after a day-long trial (June 2, 1572). Although Elizabeth had been willing to forgive Norfolk's participation in the Northern Rebellion (1569), when she discovered how deeply he was involved in this second plot, she reluctantly agreed to prosecute him on capital charges. The plot also altered Elizabeth's attitude toward Mary. Throughout 1570 and 1571, Elizabeth was negotiating with the Scottish nobility to restore Mary to her throne. When Elizabeth discovered that her kinswoman was involved in yet another attempt against her life, however, she abandoned these negotiations. Elizabeth never again spoke of restoring Mary as queen. Finally, the discovery of yet another attempt to place a Catholic on the throne exacerbated Elizabethan anti-Catholicism. Together with the publication of the papal bull *Regnans in Excelsis* (1570), by which Pius V excommunicated Elizabeth, the Ridolfi Plot contributed to the growing popular perception that English Catholics represented a serious threat to national sovereignty and needed to be watched closely. Soon after the discovery of the plot, Elizabeth and her government tightened the measures against English Catholics, passing a new treason statute that made it treason to publish the papal bull in England and enacting a series of increasingly severe penal laws.

BIBLIOGRAPHY
Bellamy, John. *The Tudor Law of Treason.* 1979.
Neale, J.E. *Queen Elizabeth.* 1992.
Guy, John. *Tudor England.* 1990.

Paula McQuade

SEE ALSO
Elizabeth I; Cecil, William; Howard, Thomas; Mary Queen of Scots; Northern Rebellion; *Regans in Excelsis;* Treason

Rizzio, David (c. 1533–1566)

An Italian, David Rizzio, or Riccio, first entered the court of Mary Queen of Scots in 1561 as a musician. In late 1564, he was appointed the queen's French secretary, and was the primary negotiator of the marriage between Mary and Henry Stuart, Lord Darnley, in 1565.

Rizzio assumed the duties of secretary at a critical juncture in the queen's reign. With the Protestant earl of Moray in exile in England after the Chaseabout raid, Mary resolved to control her own political destiny. She began to flirt with a more actively Catholic policy, urging her nobles to attend Mass and increasing diplomatic contact with the papacy and other Catholic powers. This was at best, however, a half-hearted effort that only succeeded in alienating Protestants and disappointing Catholics. Moreover, Mary continued her trend of distancing herself from her council. Even before the Chaseabout, Mary's closest advisers were to be found in the royal household, not in the council chamber, the household dominated by Rizzio.

Opponents of these policies of the queen found Rizzio an easy target. To Protestants, the queen's secretary was a papal agent charged with ensuring the return of Scotland to the Roman fold. Members of the council, Catholics and Protestants alike, were jealous of Rizzio's influence over Mary. They viewed him as a base-born foreigner promoted to a position above his station. His arrogant and pretentious disposition furthered his unpopularity. His close relationship with the queen fueled rumors, almost certainly untrue, of sexual impropriety. Darnley, who had been increasingly excluded from political decisions, came to detest Rizzio for holding the power and position he coveted. By the end of 1565, only Mary protected her secretary.

In March 1566, Mary attempted to consolidate her new political independence by summoning the Chaseabout rebels to stand trial in Scotland. Unknown to the queen, Darnley had conspired with Moray and the exiled Protestant lords to regain their positions in Scotland. Their primary target was Mary's Italian secretary. On March 9, Darnley, Patrick Lord Ruthven, James Douglas, earl of Morton, and others interrupted a private supper party in the queen's chamber at Holyrood, and stabbed Rizzio to death in the presence of the queen, who was six months pregnant.

The deed done, Moray returned to Scotland intending to take power. Mary managed to escape, however, and found refuge in the castle of James Hepburn, fourth earl of Bothwell. There, in June, she bore a son, the future James VI and I. The murder of Rizzio, however, marked the close of any independent governing by the queen. Less than a year later, Bothwell's murder of Darnley brought on the final great crisis of her reign.

R

BIBLIOGRAPHY

Goodare, Julian. "Queen Mary's Catholic Interlude." In *Mary Stewart: Queen in Three Kingdoms.* M. Lynch, ed. 1988.

Wormald, Jenny. *Mary Queen of Scots: A Study in Failure.* 1988.

Gregory P. Ripple

SEE ALSO

Hepburn, James; James VI and I; Mary Queen of Scots; Henry Stuart

Robsart, Amy, Lady Dudley (1531/2–1560)

Little is known of Amy, daughter of Sir John Robsart of Siderstone, Norfolk, prior to her marriage to Lord Robert Dudley, possibly in June of 1550, and only fragments thereafter. The reasons for their marriage and the nature of their personal relations remain matters of speculation. At the end of Mary I's reign, she was living at Throcking, Hertsfordshire. In May 1559 she visited London for a month, then possibly went to Warwickshire and ultimately to Cumnor near Oxford, where she died from a fall. Given gossip of divorce, seclusion, or poisoning, speculation of murder was rife and haunted her husband until his death. The best modern theory is that she died of advanced breast cancer.

BIBLIOGRAPHY

Adams, Simon. *The Earl of Leicester and the Politics of Elizabethan England: Collected Essays.* 1997.

———, ed. "The Papers of Robert Dudley, Earl of Leicester, I–IV." *Archives,* vol. 20, 1992–1993; vol. 22, 1996.

Adlard, George. *Amy Robsart and the Earl of Leicester: A Critical Inquiry into the Authenticity of the Various Statements in Relation to the Death of Amy Robsart.* 1870.

Wilson, Derek. *Sweet Robin: A Biography of Robert Dudley, Earl of Leicester, 1533–1588.* 1981.

S.L. Adams

SEE ALSO

Robert Dudley

Rogers, Daniel (c. 1538–1591)

Diplomat, Latinist, and literary go-between for humanist friends, Daniel Rogers was born in Wittenberg to Adriana de Weiden and John Rogers, the first Marian martyr. He came to England with his family in 1548 and was naturalized in 1552. After his father's death in 1555, he returned to Wittenberg, where he studied with Philip Melanchthon. Elizabeth I's accession cleared Rogers's way back to England, and he received his B.A. from Oxford University in 1561.

Well connected to other Marian exiles whose careers would also be built on their foreign experiences and Protestant loyalties, Rogers would depend for preferment on his ingratiating zeal, linguistic gifts, and his privileged but not uncultivated familiarity with writers, printers, and religious and political leaders. Elizabeth's French secretary, Nicasius Yetswiert, an old Flemish friend of his father's who would become Rogers's father-in-law, introduced the young scholar to court. From letters and occasional verse, it appears next that Rogers studied Greek in Paris with Jean Dorat, was driven for a time to his mother's Antwerp by the French wars of religion, but was back enjoying Parisian cultural life in 1565 or 1566. Rogers may have served earlier ambassadors to France—Sir Nicholas Throckmorton and Sir Thomas Hoby are addressed in his epigrams—but in 1568, Sir Henry Norris wrote to William Cecil that a "well learned" Rogers was warning of dangers to Huguenot leaders and treasonous plots against England. The next year Rogers was tutoring Norris's son and had begun sending his own lengthy dispatches to Cecil. When in 1570 Sir Francis Walsingham relieved Norris, Rogers continued on as his courier. Rogers missed the massacre of St. Bartholomew, as he seems to have spent 1572 in England pursuing antiquarian interests and touring Ireland gathering notes for a long poem on the history and characteristics of the island.

By the end of 1574, Rogers had resumed his work as intelligencer, and during the next six years he would cross the channel frequently, making several circuits through the embattled Low Countries and Germany. In 1575, he was commissioned to secure compensation for English merchants whose goods had been seized in Flanders and, while still reporting to Thomas Wilson in Brussels, became Elizabeth's envoy to William, Prince of Orange. Following Sir Philip Sidney's embassy to Emperor Rudolph II in 1577, Rogers's primary assignment was to advance the Protestant League with Prince William and Count Casimir of the Palatinate. While some questioned whether he had the capacity for serious financial or political deal making, Elizabeth was glad to use Rogers's low rank to dodge firm commitments. Rogers's negotiations ended in 1580 when, on a mission to the duke of Saxony and the emperor, he was seized by a band of imperial horsemen near Kleve and held hostage for four bitter years.

Back in England, perhaps dispirited by Elizabeth's indecisive policies, then by the assassination of Prince William, as well as by the burden of discharging the debt incurred by his own ransom, Rogers declined to play a part in Leicester's Netherlands campaign. In 1587, urged by his old friend, the educator Johann Sturm, Rogers married Susan Yetswiert and, in the same year, was finally rewarded for his service to the court by being appointed clerk of the Privy Council. During 1587–1588 he twice represented Elizabeth in Denmark, each time patching anti-Spanish accords.

To the disappointment of William Camden and Abraham Ortelius, a distant cousin, Rogers never completed his study of Roman Britain nor that of Ireland, *Hibernia,* but, befitting a life spent fostering relationships, he left numerous letters, hundreds of commendatory poems, and one slender volume of Latin verse praising Antwerp (1565). While of limited artistry, Rogers's daybook poetry has biographical and historical value. One of his poems movingly presents his father's last prayer as he was burned at the stake in front of his family. Several lament the murder of Peter Ramus. Still others describe a string of English cities through which Rogers toured. In 1575, Rogers wrote the first poem to address Sir Philip Sidney, and in 1579, he again celebrated the charismatic young courtier who would sustain the political hopes of the new religion. At the close of this long Latin elegy, Rogers requests that he may be counted with Fulke Greville and Edward Dyer among Sidney's virtuous and talented companions. We may believe that the cosmopolitan Rogers, who was friends with members of the Pléiade, George Buchanan, Hubert Languet, Paulus Melissus, Charles Utenhove, and Janus Dousa, could also claim a certain degree of intimacy with Sidney's coterie of avant-garde poets, which included Edmund Spenser and Gabriel Harvey.

BIBLIOGRAPHY

Chester, Joseph Lemuel. *John Rogers.* 1861
Levy, F.J. "Daniel Rogers as Antiquary." *Bibliotheque d'Humanisme et Renaissance,* vol. 27, pp. 444–462.
Phillips, James E. "Daniel Rogers: A Neo-Latin Link between the Pleiade and Sidney's *Areopagus.*" In *Neo-Latin Poetry of the Sixteenth and Seventeenth Centuries.* James E. Phillips, Don Cameron Allen, and William Matthews, eds. Pp. 5–28. 1965.
Van Dorsten, J.A. *Poets, Patrons, and Professors: Sir Philip Sidney, Daniel Rogers, and the Leiden Humanists.* 1962.
Steven Berkowitz

SEE ALSO

Antiquarianism; Camden, William; Espionage; Foreign Relations and Diplomacy; Hoby, Thomas; Huguenots; Marian Exiles; Rogers, John; Sidney, Philip; Throckmorton, Nicholas; Walsingham, Francis; Wilson, Thomas

Rogers, John (c. 1500–1555)

Remembered chiefly as the first Protestant martyr to be executed under Mary I, John Rogers was ordained a Roman Catholic priest, but converted to Protestantism under the influence of William Tyndale, whom he met in Antwerp by early 1535. When Tyndale was arrested in spring of that year, Rogers continued his project of publishing a complete English Bible. Within a year he gathered Tyndale's manuscript translation of the Old Testment from Genesis to 2 Chronicles, the remainder of the Old Testament and Apocrypha from the Coverdale Bible (Cologne?, 1535), and Tyndale's published translation of the New Testament (Worms, c. 1526) into the Bible dedicated to Henry VIII by "Thomas Matthew," a pseudonym. He added preliminary material and marginalia that make up the first Bible commentary printed in English. First printed in Antwerp in 1537 by Matthias Crom on behalf of Richard Grafton and Edward Whitchurch, the Matthew Bible remained in print until 1551. The text underlies the Great Bible (1539), Bishops' Bible (1568), and the Authorized Version (1611). The recipient of clerical appointments under Edward VI, Rogers's preaching of anti-Catholic sermons under Lady Jane Grey and Mary I led to his burning at Smithfield on February 4, 1555.

BIBLIOGRAPHY

Foxe, John. *Acts and Monuments of the English Martyrs.* 8 vols. 2nd edition. 1843–1849; repr. 1965.
John N. King

SEE ALSO

Bible Translations; Marian Martyrs; Tyndale, William

Romance

Romances were very popular throughout the Tudor period. Sidney's *Arcadia* (1590) and Spenser's *Faerie Queene* (1590, 1596), one in prose and verse, the other in

R

verse alone, are fundamentally romances, despite their epic trappings. Both were left in one way or another incomplete at their author's deaths, but there are sufficient hints as to their planned endings. Other romances include Lyly's *Euphues* (1578, 1580), Lodge's *Rosalynde* (1590), and the twenty romances of Greene.

Although usually self-conscious about genre, Spenser and Sidney in their respective theoretical manifestos, the prefatory *Letter to Raleigh* (1590) and the *Defense of Poetry* (1595), fail to distinguish romance from epic and romance-epic, grouping them all as heroic (Sidney) or historical (Spenser), tracing predecessors in *Amadis de Gaula* (Sidney) and the narratives of Homer, Vergil, Ariosto, Tasso (Spenser), Heliodorus (Sidney), and Xenophon.

Sidney's *Arcadia* incorporates seamlessly all the available kinds of romance: chivalric, whether medieval or Renaissance-Italian, and classical, Roman or Greek. Classical romance includes, in the pastoral vein, Longus's *Daphnis and Chloe* and, in the heroic, Heliodorus's *Aethiopica*. In the Renaissance, the pastoral romance was imitated in Italian by Sannazaro's *Arcadia* and in Spanish by Montemayor's *Diana*. *The Faerie Queene* stresses allegory and Greek romance. Chivalric romances available to Tudor readers include Malory's *Le Mort Darthur* (fifteenth century) and the vast, rambling, many-authored Spanish *Amadis de Gaula* (sixteenth century). The Renaissance Italian chivalric romance known as romance-epic included Ariosto's *Orlando Furioso* and Tasso's *Gerusalemme Liberata*, along with several predecessors; with their accompanying commentaries, they represent one major and conspicuous model for Spenser but have a negligible influence on Sidney.

A minimal prescription for the plot is the focus on love and the testing of the hero's worth by physical combat; accordingly, the ingredients of *The Faerie Queene* are "fierce warres and faithful loves," as Spenser announces—echoing Ariosto—in his general proem. Romances vary in length. If they are long, as in these two examples, the plots incorporate deferrals and flashbacks. Romance structure is also episodic. It neglects "horizontal" laws of causation—those familiar from ordinary existence. Rather, the causation is "vertical." Things turn out the way somebody wants them to: the author may shape them into an allegory; society wants a reenactment of its rituals; the aristocracy wants to see itself glamorized. Incidents partake of the erotic, the violent, the coincidental, and the mysterious; in Spenser and his poetic ancestors they may also be fantastic, but in *Arcadia*, wonder is evoked only by extraordinary and

sometimes crossed human efforts such as the "resurrection" of Basilius, supposedly poisoned with what was really only a sleeping potion.

It is in the major and at least potentially positive value it places on sexual love that romance differs most clearly from epic. The romance formula for the man is "love does always bring forth bounteous [virtuous] deeds" (*Faerie Queene* III.i.49). On rare occasions, it is inverted—drastically by Ariosto, whose hero runs mad for love, and by Sidney, whose lovers, for most of the *Arcadia*, neglect their public careers to win their ladies and are reduced, one to a shepherd, the other to the guise of an Amazon woman. Even Spenser inverts it once when Timias, rejected by his lady, abandons his career and becomes a wildman (IV.vii–viii)—an incident anticipated in medieval romance (e.g., Malory XI–XII). The romance formula for the couple is "none but the brave deserve the fair" and vice versa (e.g., *Faerie Queene* IV.v.1). Romance tends to end happily for the hero and heroine. To merit this outcome, despite Sidney's theoretical endorsement of poetic justice in the *Defense,* protagonists do not have to be perfect; it may be the result of luck or mercy. In these cases, romance evokes wonder at the world around the heroes more than at the magnitude of their deeds.

Accordingly, many romance protagonists, though high-minded, occasionally commit sins and make mistakes. The *dramatis personae* consist of young heroes and heroines—the men athletic and all (except, temporarily, for Sidney's Parthenia) good-looking; older people exist only to interact (for better or worse) with the young—and double-dyed villains. The latter are necessary evils because romance oscillates between the idyllic world and the nightmare world, between the *locus amoenus* (friendly place of pastoral) or the harmonious court and the dungeon or the cave. In *Arcadia,* this polarization of character is less sharp, with many shades of grey between Euarchus and Cecropia; thus *Arcadia* stands one step closer to the novel on the continuum from romance to realism.

In setting, romance is temporally, spatially, or socially (for most readers) remote; *The Faerie Queene* is set in Fairyland, Sidney's *Arcadia,* like its classical forebears, in pre-Christian Mediterranean lands. The pitched battles and wider issues of epic are not central. The main characters are aristocratic; lower classes are scorned. Both romances were dedicated to women; romance heroines excel not in motherhood, which gets little attention, but in chastity and endurance of suffering. Spenser, moreover, has a female knight who with her magic lance conquers all men but her future lover, whereas the Amazon in Sidney is only apparently female; Sidney demonstrates authentic female achievement instead in the arena of philosophy when Pamela refutes her aunt's atheism.

Roger Ascham (1570) had criticized Malory, and by implication the whole genre, saying, "the whole pleasure of [this] book standeth in two special points, in open manslaughter and bold bawdry." As if in acknowledgement of Ascham's charges, Sidney, while he vigorously defended the usefulness of fiction in general, referred to *Arcadia* as "my toyful book[es]" and on his deathbed ordered that it be burned, and Spenser has his spokesman Contemplation categorically condemn both combat and love (I.x.60, 62). Spenser strives in Book 1 to escape these limitations of romance. He promises to "moralize" his "fierce warres and faithfull loues" (I Proem). The quest is to kill a dragon, not a man; the heroine is pure and symbolizes true religion; and extramarital sex is painted in the blackest of terms. This redemption is brought about, according to the *Letter*, by allegory—his other generic label for his poem. Most romancers insert moral judgments. Sidney defends the moral utility of fiction in general, provided it has ideal imitation and poetic justice.

BIBLIOGRAPHY

Beer, Gillian. *The Romance*. 1970.
Frye, Northrop. *The Anatomy of Criticism*. 1957.
———. *The Secular Scripture*. 1976.
Hamilton, A.C. "Elizabethan Prose Fiction and Some Trends in Recent Criticism." *Rennaissance Quarterly*, vol. 37, pp. 21–33.
———. "Elizabethan Romance: The Example of Prose Fiction." *ELH*, vol. 49, pp. 287–299.
———. "Sidney's *Arcadia* as Prose Fiction." *English Literary Renaissance*, vol. 2, pp. 29–60.
———, and Donald Cheney et al., eds. William J. Kennedy, "Heroic Poem before Spenser," and Patricia Parker, "Romance." In *Spenser Encyclopedia*. 1990.

Carol Kaske

SEE ALSO

Arcadia; Ascham, Roger; Epic; Greene, Robert; Lodge, Thomas; Lyly, John; Pastoral; Sidney, Philip; Spanish Literature, Influence of; Spenser, Edmund

Roper, Margaret More (1505–1544)

Margaret Roper is known both as Thomas More's daughter and as a learned woman whose humanist education, designed and overseen by her father, brought her fame throughout Europe and advanced the idea of the education of women. Desiderius Erasmus's colloquy between an ignorant abbot and the learned woman (1524) singles out the "More girls" in England, and the learned young woman almost certainly is based on Margaret Roper. She also has claims as a writer; her translation of Erasmus's *Precatio Dominica* is almost unprecedented as a work written by a woman and published in the early sixteenth century.

Roper was the first child and oldest daughter of Thomas More and Jane Colt More, his first wife. Educated at home, she soon became an exemplar of the new humanist learning. On July 2, 1521, when she was not quite sixteen, she married William Roper, a lawyer, subsequently clerk of the pleas or prothonotary; their first child was born in 1523. Like her father, Margaret Roper oversaw her children's education; one of her daughters, Mary Clarke, later Basset, also became a woman of letters, translating *De Tristitia*, one of More's Tower works, into English.

Margaret Roper was the stellar pupil in what is sometimes called the "school of More": a group that included More's four children, his wards, foster daughter, stepdaughter, other relatives, husbands and wives of the pupils, and friends. More's letter to Roper's tutor, William Gonell (1518?), is a major statement about his ideas of the education for women—ideas that are more liberal than those of later humanists. He wanted to develop both the mind and the conscience of each student, whether male or female, and he stressed the importance of disputation and eloquence. The curriculum was a rigorous one, grounded in a mastery of Latin and Greek and embracing the humane and liberal arts, medicine, and theology. More encouraged a system of double translation; Margaret Roper composed dialogues, disputations, declamations, epistles, and poems.

Most of her early writings are lost, but *A Devout Treatise upon the "Pater Noster,"* her translation of Erasmus's commentary on the Lord's Prayer (*Precatio Dominica*, 1523), appeared in print around 1524; there were three editions by the early 1530s. The translator is not named, but the title page identifies her as a "yong vertuous and well lerned gentylwoman of .xix. yere of age." Richard Hyrde, another family tutor, wrote the dedicatory letter to her cousin, Frances Staverton, arguing for the cause of women's education, refuting charges that Latin learning would corrupt women, praising Roper and her prose, and calling on Staverton and other women to emulate the translator.

Margaret Roper became More's personal representative after he was imprisoned in the Tower of London in

R

1534. Their correspondence was both personal and political: Roper saved (and probably privately circulated) his letters to her, in which he recorded conversations, interrogations, and attempts at intimidation. An important dialogue-letter to her stepsister, Alice Alington, perhaps written in collaboration with More, constitutes an apologetic for his refusal to swear to the oath accompanying the Act of Succession. Also extant are two letters to her father, further evidence of her learning and daughterly affection.

BIBLIOGRAPHY
Benson, Pamela Joseph. *The Invention of the Renaissance Woman.* 1992.
McCutcheon, Elizabeth. "Margaret More Roper: The Learned Woman in Tudor England." In *Women Writers of the Renaissance and Reformation.* Katharina M. Wilson, ed. Pp. 449–480. 1987.
More, Thomas. *The Correspondence of Sir Thomas More.* Elizabeth Frances Rogers, ed. 1947.
Reynolds, E.E. *Margaret Roper: Eldest Daughter of St. Thomas More.* 1960.
Roper, Margaret More. *A Devout Treatise upon the "Pater Noster."* Richard L. DeMolen, ed. In *Erasmus of Rotterdam: A Quincentennial Symposium.* Richard L. Demolen, ed. Pp. 93–124, 139–146. 1971.
Verbrugge, Rita M. "Margaret More Roper's Personal Expression in the *Devout Treatise upon the 'Pater Noster.'"* In *Silent But for the Word: Tudor Women as Patrons, Translators, and Writers of Religious Works.* Margaret Patterson Hannay, ed. Pp. 30–42, 260–264. 1985.

Elizabeth McCutcheon

SEE ALSO
Education; Humanism; More, Thomas

Royal Exchange

Built at the personal expense of the Merchant Adventurer Sir Thomas Gresham, the Royal Exchange was a four-storied building in Cornhill, London, constructed between 1566 and 1570. It was erected primarily as a means of communication so that merchants might have a single place in which to meet and exchange information on domestic and foreign prices and on political developments that might affect trade. Previously, according to John Stow, merchants as well as tradesmen and strangers had met twice daily on Lombard Street to make their bargains, but they were often hindered in finding each other because of poor weather, and as one contemporary put it, had to walk "when it raineth, more like pedlars than merchants."

The new Royal Exchange was based on the already existing example in Antwerp built in 1531. Gresham had acted as the "king's merchant" in Antwerp, then the center of the European cloth trade and credit system. In the 1560s, Gresham offered to build the exchange at his own expense if the aldermen would provide a site. The twelve principal livery companies together with the Merchant Adventurers contributed enough money to purchase the site in Cornhill. About sixty houses were torn down, and the foundation stone was laid by Gresham on June 7, 1566, and construction finished in 1570. The completed building consisted of an enclosed central piazza, along the edges of which ran loggias where the merchants could walk sheltered from inclement weather. Above these were numerous, small, rented shops, the profits from which were used to help defray the cost of the building. The whole structure was surmounted by a bell tower used to signal the opening of the front gates of the exchange in the morning so that trading could begin.

The timing of the building was fortuitous, because of the Protestant riots in Antwerp in 1566 leading to a full-scale revolt the next year, and the subsequent occupation of Antwerp by a Spanish army under the duke of Alva. The ensuing disruptions in the cloth trade made the Royal Exchange in London vital; business moved to the English capital to avoid the uncertainties of religious warfare. The Royal Exchange eventually became the center of north European finance, and one of the most important social meeting places in the city, the place where the merchant elite gathered, where news and gossip were exchanged, and where fashionable goods were sold.

BIBLIOGRAPHY
Bindoff, S.T. *The Fame of Sir Thomas Gresham.* 1973.
Braudel, Fernand. *The Wheels of Commerce.* 1982.
Saunders, Ann. *The Royal Exchange.* 1991.

Craig Muldrew

SEE ALSO
Cloth Trade; Gresham, Thomas; Merchant Adventurers; Money, Inflation, and Moneylending; Trade, Overseas

Royal Family

During the Tudor period the royal family was seldom a functional unit. Normal family life was disrupted by

Henry VIII's numerous marriages and divorces. His son, Edward VI, did not live long enough to marry or have children. Philip II, the Spanish husband of Henry's elder daughter, Mary I, spent little time in England, and Mary had no offspring. Elizabeth I, the last of the Tudor monarchs, never married and boasted of her virginity.

Ordinary family life prevailed only during the reign of Henry VII and in the earlier years of Henry VIII's rule. Although the marriage between Henry VII and Elizabeth of York was obviously dynastic and political, intended to unite the rival Lancastrian and Yorkist branches of the royal family, the husband and wife developed a genuine fondness for each other, and Henry appears to have been crushed by Elizabeth's death in 1503, six years before his own. He never remarried, although he did have an ambassador in Italy investigate at least one candidate for his hand. The king and queen had been blessed with four children; information about their childhood is limited, but they seem to have been brought up under affectionate circumstances, and the boys, at least, were given excellent humanistic educations.

The death of the older son, Arthur, in 1502, and the departure of the older daughter, Margaret, following her marriage to King James IV of Scotland in 1503, must have contributed to the sense of isolation and remorse that characterized Henry VII's last years, but his children Henry and Mary remained at court. His mother, Lady Margaret Beaufort, did not die until 1509; she took an active role in religious and educational philanthropies, enhancing the popularity of the Tudor dynasty.

Although Henry VIII's first marriage, to the Spanish Princess Katherine of Aragon, ended in divorce in 1533, Henry and Katherine lived together happily from 1509 until 1527. They had no sons—a devastating matter for Henry VIII, who was concerned to establish the succession of his heirs—but their daughter Mary enjoyed a relatively normal childhood and a better education than was usual for women, partly at the hands of the Spanish humanist Juan Luis Vives. After Henry's marriage to Anne Boleyn, Mary was declared illegitimate and sent away from court, and when Anne Boleyn was divorced and beheaded, her daughter Elizabeth suffered a like fate. Henry's son, Edward, never knew his mother, for Jane Seymour died of complications following his birth. It remained for the king's sixth and last wife, Catherine Parr, to bring Edward, Mary, and Elizabeth together and to attempt to give them some sense of motherly affection.

This was really the end of the Tudor family as a functioning unit. Mary and Elizabeth were sent off to separate country houses during Edward's reign, and the young king had no relatives at court except his uncle, Edward Seymour, protector Somerset, who served as regent from 1547 to 1549 but was never close to Edward personally. Partly because of their religious differences, Mary and Elizabeth seldom saw each other during Mary's reign. Philip II made some show of acting jointly with Mary in 1554 and 1555, but he returned to Spain in 1555 and came back to England only briefly in 1557. Mary's belief that she was pregnant proved to be a bitter delusion. There were no more royal children at court until the seventeenth century; Elizabeth's position as the Virgin Queen was an isolated and, at least in her later life, lonely one. She did regard James VI, her "cousin of Scotland," as the most suitable heir to her throne, and she corresponded with him about matters of statecraft in her last years, but they never met. Nor, despite fictionalized accounts to the contrary, did Elizabeth ever actually meet Mary Queen of Scots.

Since the fourteenth century it had been customary for the king's oldest son to be created Prince of Wales. Henry VII followed this tradition; his son Arthur was Prince of Wales from 1489 until his death in 1502, and Henry VIII held the title from 1504 until his succession to the throne in 1509. Edward VI was never created Prince of Wales, perhaps because he was not thought to be old enough during his father's lifetime, so the title remained in abeyance until the reign of James I. His son Henry was Prince of Wales prior to his death in 1612, and Charles I held the title before his accession to the throne in 1625.

BIBLIOGRAPHY
Chrimes, S.B. *Henry VII.* 1972.
Jordan, W.K. *Edward VI: The Young King.* 2 vols. 1968.
Loades, David. *Mary Tudor.* 1989.
MacCaffrey, Wallace. *Elizabeth I.* 1993.
Scarisbrick, J.J. *Henry VIII.* 1968.
Walker, Greg. *Persuasive Fictions: Faction, Faith, and Political Culture in the Reign of Henry VIII.* 1996.

Stanford Lehmberg

SEE ALSO
Beaufort, Margaret; Edward VI; Elizabeth I; Elizabeth of York; Henry VII; Henry VIII; James IV and VI; Mary I; Mary Queen of Scots; Catherine Parr; Seymour, Edward; Vives, Juan Luis

Royal Household

A continuing body from Saxon times to the present, the royal household was originally the government of the

R

kingdom of England. Over time, various compartments of the household were transformed into departments of state, such as the Chancery, Treasury, and Exchequer, until the household became merely a small part of the national government. The Tudor royal household consisted of the Chamber, under the lord chamberlain; the Household, under the lord steward; the Stables, under the master of the horse; and the Queen's Chamber (the king's children might also have separate households). In 1509, at the start of the reign of Henry VIII, these four entities employed a staff of around 650. The chamberlain's domain ("above stairs") was divided into three suites: the Guard Chamber, the Presence (or Outer) Chamber, and the Privy Chamber, which were established wherever the monarch was in residence. The chamberlain's staff of more than 200 servants were those who personally served the monarch, such as gentlemen, esquires, grooms, pages, ushers, messengers, servers, cupbearers, carvers, physicians, barbers, entertainers, and musicians (of whom Elizabeth I had sixty to seventy). The Chamber included the Yeomen of the Guard (foot soldiers) and, after 1539, the Gentlemen Pensioners or Spears (horsemen), while the chamberlain often had authority over the Chapel and its staff. Under Henry VIII the Gentlemen of the Privy Chamber achieved a degree of political power largely free from the chamberlain's control. The steward ruled about 220 servants "below stairs," with more than a score of offices reporting to him: the kitchen, bake-house, pantry, cellar, buttery, larder, spicery, wafery, pastry, confectionery, accatary (which purchased provisions, especially meat and fish), poultry, boiling-house, pitcher-house, ewery (for storing linens), scalding-house, laundry, scullery, chandlery, woodyard, porters, and almonry. The steward's responsibilities included procuring food, drink, fuel, and all other supplies, not only for the household but also for perhaps a thousand or more courtiers and their servants who might be in attendance on the monarch. Driven by inflation, the steward's annual expenditure across the sixteenth century, the largest single component in the royal budget in peacetime, grew from under £20,000 to more than £40,000. The steward's professional staff of purveyors and accountants were often used outside the household (to its detriment) on such tasks as victualing the army and navy. The master of the Horse ran the royal stables with a staff of about sixty men. The Queen's Chamber paralleled the organization of the king's, employing about 150 persons in 1509. The Queen's Chamber, of course, did not exist when there was no consort.

The functional and financial efficiency of the household varied over the years. Henry VII, who created the Privy Chamber and the Yeomen, regularly audited the accounts himself. Henry VIII was more interested in splendor, and his household soon became bloated and corrupt. Cardinal Wolsey's Eltham Ordinances of 1526 slashed much of the waste but failed to create a strong central authority. That problem was rectified by Thomas Cromwell, whose 1539 reforms directed that the principal officers and accountants who made up the governing Board of Green Cloth meet daily instead of annually, while the lord steward (whose title was changed to Lord Great Master of the Household from 1540-54) was made supreme over both Household and Chamber; this organization lasted until 1782. During the latter part of Elizabeth's reign, William Cecil, Lord Treasurer Burghley, waged a constant battle against the household's tendency to slide into inefficiency and corruption.

Aside from its two military companies, the household as a whole could transform itself into a powerful fighting force. When Henry VIII invaded France in 1544, the bulk of his own division of 3,159 horse and 9,688 foot was raised by the Privy Council and the household, where each servant produced his quota. Privy councilors and other officers of state brought men in the scores or hundreds, the seventy-two gentlemen pensioners raised 385 additional horsemen, each royal physician recruited three or four soldiers, the pages of the bed and robes contributed five, and so on down to the stable hands, each of whom mustered one or two more fighting men.

The overlap between governmental and household functions, or the process by which the English government grew out of the royal household, may be seen in eight offices more or less under the jurisdiction of the chamberlain: the Armory, Ordnance, Mint, Works, Great Wardrobe, Tents, Toils, and Revels. Their masters were members of the household, but their headquarters and finances were apart from it. Several of these clearly filled governmental functions from a modern point of view, but the monarch was not yet willing to relinquish a degree of personal control over them. On the other hand, the Revels Office was responsible for court entertainments, and its master became the licensor of public plays under Elizabeth, a role retained by the lord chamberlain until 1968.

BIBLIOGRAPHY

Elton, G.R. *The Tudor Revolution in Government.* 1959.
Gunn, S.J. *Early Tudor Government, 1485–1558.* 1995.

Richardson, W.C. *Tudor Chamber Administration, 1485–1547.* 1952.

Williams, Neville. *Henry VIII and His Court.* 1971.

Williams, Penry. *The Later Tudors: England 1547–1603.* Pp. 124–131. 1995.

Peter R. Moore and W.A. Sessions

SEE ALSO

Chancery; Cromwell, Thomas; Elizabeth I; Exchequer; Government, Central Administration of; Henry VII; Henry VIII; Privy Chamber; Revel's Office; Wolsey, Thomas

Royal Palaces

The Tudors had only one royal palace, the palace of Westminster. The rest of their many other residences were titled manor or castle. To distinguish them as royal, however, all the residential buildings are normally called palaces. The number of English palaces was at a peak during the reign of Henry VIII, through monastic wealth the richest and most prolific builder ever to sit on the throne. Monarchs required many houses because the court was constantly on the move, although it became less constantly peripatetic later in the period. The itinerary of Henry VII was initially organized around the large monastic establishments in which the court regularly stayed. But he became a substantial builder in the latter part of his reign, and left just over a score of houses, including the virtually new Thames valley residences at Greenwich and Richmond. Henry VIII acquired more than one house for each year of his reign, leaving the crown with a portfolio of about sixty residences. But the history of Tudor royal domestic construction and acquisition ends in 1547. None of Henry's children undertook significant building commissions; it was as much as they could or would do to maintain and modernize the palaces of their predecessors, and Elizabeth I in particular relied on the houses built by her great courtiers, which could entertain the court at minimum royal expense.

Broadly speaking, there were two categories of house. The principal residences in the Thames valley were intended for wintertime use when the entire court followed the ruler from place to place. They were large, brick-built houses with many courtyards and could accommodate the full court of 800 or so. Greenwich was the most visited, followed by Whitehall and Windsor Castle. Richmond and Hampton Court were also included in this group. During Elizabeth's reign, these became the "standing" houses, kept permanently at the ready with furnishings on site. The other group, some fifty in the 1540s, were small manor houses in areas of good hunting from Woking and Canterbury to York. They were used during summer for hunting parties, progresses, or residences for members of the royal family.

Only a few Tudor royal houses were wholly or even largely new contructions. Most were more or less extensive rebuildings of ancient royal houses, such as Richmond or Westminster, were modified episcopal palaces such as Hampton Court or The More, or were houses formerly belonging to courtiers, such as Beddingon or Oatlands. The only large house to be contructed on a new site was Nonsuch, built by Henry VIII in the late 1530s. Yet building works were incessant, even under Edward, Mary, and Elizabeth, as older houses were continually modified and improved.

The construction and maintenance of the royal palaces was in the hands of the monarch's Office of Works. The Office that Henry VII inherited in 1485 was largely that of the fourteenth century, with a Westminster base dealing with the London houses (except Windsor, which had its own staff), and provincial offices in Wales, the southeast, and the north. Although the main task of the Westminster office was maintenance, it also undertook commissions for new buildings, for which special units were set up and then disbanded.

The Tudor period saw several refinements and modifications of this system. The first major change came in 1532 when the post of surveyor was granted to a craftsman, James Nedeham, a former master carpenter rather than an administrator. This choice reflected the enormous building campaigns of the 1530s and 1540s, when the task of the surveyor shifted from administration of a maintenance organization toward the design and supervision of major new works. The second development was an administrative and physical centralization of the Westminster office during the surveyorship of Lawrence Bradshaw (1547–1560). This change, which effectively created a board to oversee the royal works, put the office onto a footing better suited to conditions under Elizabeth, where the initiative for domestic building passed from the crown to the great magnates, and the office again concentrated its efforts on maintenance.

Although Elizabeth built little new (Windsor Castle was her only extravagence, and a small one at that), she followed her predecessors in ensuring that the palaces were always in the vanguard of fashion. Whether patronizing work in the late perpendicular Gothic of Henry VII's reign, the early northern Renaissance styles of the

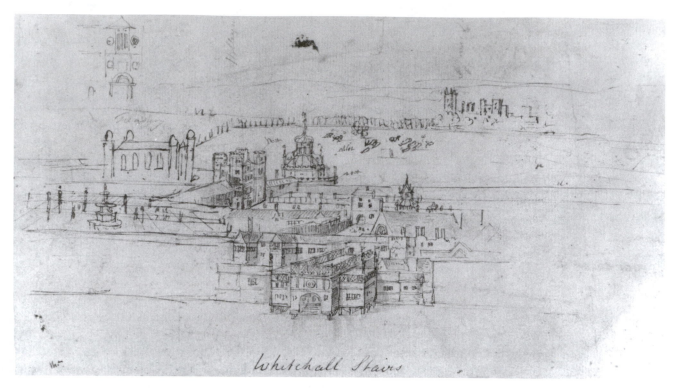

Antonis Wynegaerd, *Whitehall Palace* (c. 1558), London. By permission of the Ashmolean Museum, Oxford.

later part of Henry VIII's, or the Mannerist extravagences of Elizabeth's, the monarchy never lagged stylistically behind other English patrons. This meant, however, that Italianate neoclassicism is no more widely evident in external aspects of the surviving projects of the Tudor monarchs than in Tudor building generally, for while there is some debate about the interaction of foreign and domestic influences on the buildings of the Tudor rulers, it is generally accepted that the overall pattern, plan, and external appearances of the palaces were laid out by the Office of Works and its master craftsmen, and that many or even most of the latter were from northern Europe.

Externally, Tudor royal buildings were characterized by their extensive use of brick, sometimes enlivened by terracotta. Window and door apertures, string courses, and dressings were of stone. Whole facades were generally washed with red ochre and the joints of the brickwork picked out in white. The great hunting lodge built by Henry VIII at Nonsuch is the principal exception; its exterior was covered in panels of stuccowork of Italian or French making. But even Nonsuch had turrets and battlements, and the majority of houses continued to be moated, recalling a more turbulent past.

As regards interior decoration, modern historians are at a significant disadvantage because after nearly four centuries of subsequent redecoration no Tudor work has survived intact. Even the interiors at Hampton Court are only pale reflections of the chambers described in the works accounts. Paintings and drawings must be interpreted with care, but great canvasses like the anonymous *Family of Henry VIII* (Royal Collection, Hampton Court), and Holbein's Whitehall cartoon (National Portrait Gallery, London), give some indication. Although these works display some Renaissance architectural features such as pilasters and moldings, the primary vehicle of display was textile, especially rich silks—cloth of gold or velvet in the smaller, more private rooms, and multiple sets of tapestries in the great public rooms. Henry VIII left his children more than 2,000 tapestries. Furniture was generally utilitarian, apart from throne chairs, canopies, and state beds.

In the plan of these houses the Tudor period spans the transition from the medieval arrangement, wherein the monarch was the leader of a peripatetic war band, living fairly publicly in a few rooms, to a more modern system with a less strenuous itinerary, a greater expectation of privacy, and more extensive accommodations. Hence, from the mid-1520s on, royal palaces became increasingly extensive and sophisticated, providing the monarchs with more numerous rooms of more specialized types.

The plan of the parts of the palace occupied by the royal family that emerged during the 1530s divided the principal rooms into the public outward chambers, the restricted privy chambers, and the private secret chambers. Each area was controlled by specific household ordinances with differing degrees of control over access. This plan dominated English palace planning well into the eighteenth century. Only the kitchen and offices remained much as they had been in the fifteenth century.

The spaces within a palace corresponded to the areas of responsibility held by the great officers of the household. The lord steward ruled over the kitchens and service areas, the lord chamberlain over the public areas, the dean of the chapel over the household chapel, and the master of the horse over the stables. The privy chambers were supervised by the groom of the stool, chief of the monarch's personal servants. The stables were normally sited at a short distance from the palace (those at Hampton Court survive), and the kitchens, with a staff of about 200, on the north side of the house.

Just as a more settled and leisured lifestyle led to an elaboration of the monarch's domestic quarters, so it allowed a whole new area of royal building to open up. By the end of the seventeenth century, no palace was complete without some facilities for indoor sports. Henry VII constructed a recreation complex with tennis courts and bowling alleys at Richmond Palace at the turn of the sixteenth century. The most extensive was built by Henry VIII at Whitehall in the 1530s, including four tennis courts, a bowling alley, and a cockpit.

Only remnants of these recreational buildings survive—the shell of a tennis court at Hampton Court and a few walls at Whitehall. Their fate typifies that of royal residences as a whole: because of destruction and alteration it is not possible to see or even reconstruct much Tudor royal work. The great buildings at Richmond, Greenwich, Westminster, Whitehall, and Nonsuch were largely destroyed, although excavations have made it possible to learn much about them. Substantial remains exist at Hampton Court Palace, St. James Palace, and Windsor Castle. But none of these can fully reveal either the stylistic or the functional complexity of these great buildings.

BIBLIOGRAPHY

Summerson, John. *Architecture in Britain, 1530 to 1830.* 1991.

Thurley, Simon. *The Royal Palaces of Tudor England.* 1993.

Simon Thurley

SEE ALSO

Architecture; Henry VII; Henry VIII; Interior Decoration; Painting; Privy Chamber; Royal Household

Roydon, Matthew (d. 1622)

A late Elizabethan poet, Matthew Roydon's fame rests more on his associations than on his surviving poetry. Graduating from Oxford in 1580, Roydon is typically linked with other university-educated writers of his generation. His earliest works are commendatory verses for fellow university graduates, Thomas Watson and George Peckham. His contemporary reputation was such that Robert Greene singles him out for praise in his preface to *Menaphon* (1587), and Francis Meres compares him to the best Italian poets in *Palladis Tamia* (1598). Both link him to Thomas Achelley and George Peele. By the 1590s, Roydon is associated with other literary figures, notably Christopher Marlowe and George Chapman. Dedicating *Ovids Banquet of Sence* (1595) to Roydon, Chapman admires his intellect, capable of "sound[ing] the philosophical conceits, that my new pen so seriously courteth."

Although Greene speaks of Roydon's "Comike inventions," he is now remembered primarily for "An Elegie, or friends passion, for his Astrophill," a lament for Philip Sidney. Roydon touchingly mythologizes the circumstances of Sidney's death: fearful that Astrophil might displace him in the pantheon, Mars invents firearms to slay him. The poem was, Greene suggests, widely admired. First published in *The Phoenix Nest* (1593), although circulated earlier, it was reprinted in *Colin Clout's Come Home Againe* (1595).

BIBLIOGRAPHY

Rollins, Hyder E., ed. *The Phoenix Nest* (1593). 1931.

Douglas Lanier

SEE ALSO

Chapman, George; Greene, Robert; Meres, Francis; Sidney, Philip

Russell, John, Earl of Bedford (c. 1485–1555)

John Russell was born into a Dorset gentry family that had risen to prominence through trade, advantageous marriage, and royal service. He came to the crown's attention in 1506 when his impressive command of foreign languages enabled him to welcome Archduke Philip of the Netherlands, whose ship had unexpectedly

R

been blown into Weymouth Bay. Russell subsequently became a prominent courtier and ambassador, attending Louis XII's marriage to Princess Mary in 1514, and accompanying Henry VIII to the Field of the Cloth of Gold. In the 1520s, Russell traveled extensively in France and Italy on diplomatic missions, sometimes in disguise; he witnessed the battle of Pavia and twice met the pope. He also held several military commands, losing an eye at Morlaix in 1522. Having successfully transferred his allegiance from Thomas Wolsey to Thomas Cromwell, Russell was given the Admiralty in 1540 and created lord privy seal in 1542. He was a close companion of Henry VIII, especially in the king's last years, and entertained him at Chenies in Buckinghamshire in 1542. With the fall of the marquis of Exeter, Russell was dubbed a baron and granted substantial monastic land, the high stewardship of the duchy of Cornwall, and the presidency of the short-lived Council of the West. However, his nonresidence in that region contributed to the western rising of 1549, and his early timidity in suppressing it undoubtedly increased its magnitude. He was also implicated in the slaughter of prisoners. His subsequent defection from protector Somerset to the earl of Warwick won him the earldom of Bedford in 1550. But he swiftly abandoned Jane Grey for Princess Mary in 1553, and his malleable religion enabled him to remain a privy councilor under the queen until his death in March 1555. A sketch of Russell by Holbein survives in the queen's collection.

BIBLIOGRAPHY

Willen, Diane. *John Russell, First Earl of Bedford: One of the King's Men.* 1981.

Youings, J. "The Council of the West." *Transactions of the Royal Historical Society,* 5th series, vol. 10. 1960.

Pocock, N. *Troubles Connected with the Prayer Book of 1549.* Camden Society. 1884.

J.P.D. Cooper

SEE ALSO

Cromwell, Thomas; Dudley, John; Field of the Cloth of Gold; Henry VIII; Lady Jane Grey; Seymour, Edward

Ruthven, John, Earl of Gowrie
See Gowrie Conspiracy

S

Sackville, Thomas (1536–1608)

A distinguished Elizabethan statesman who lived to be seventy-two years old, Thomas Sackville served Elizabeth I with exceptional devotion. His fame, however, rests on his youthful writings, completed by the time he was twenty-five, rather than on his lifetime of service. He conducted the affairs of state with remarkable competence and graciousness, but without the driving ambition of a William Cecil or an earl of Essex, resulting in a reputation that was honored in his time but seems muted in ours. On the other hand, his youthful productions—the "Induction" to *A Mirror for Magistrates*, the *Complaint of Henry, Duke of Buckingham*, and *Gorboduc*—highly praised in his lifetime, give him a literary fame that persists. Sackville was primarily a statesman whose interests were mainly political, and his political, religious, and moral attitudes are clearly seen in his youthful writings.

Sackville's ancestor, Herbrand de Sackville, came to England with William the Conqueror, and from him through Sir Richard Sackville, Thomas's father, were generations of knights. Thomas Sackville and Elizabeth I had a common ancestor, Sir William Boleyn, whose daughter was Sackville's grandmother and whose son was the father of Anne Boleyn. Born in 1536 at Buckhurst in the parish of Withyam, Sussex, Sackville attended Oxford University and at the age of nineteen was admitted to the Inner Temple. He did not take the degree of barrister; he was preparing himself to be a courtier and the head of a household. The Inner Temple is closely bound to Sackville's literary career because *Gorboduc* was first presented there in 1562.

Before that date Sackville was already sitting as a member of Elizabeth's first Parliament of 1558. In 1563, he was sent to Italy and France on diplomatic business for the queen. His father's death in 1566 left Thomas in charge of a vast inheritance. A year later he was knighted and raised to the peerage as Lord Buckhurst. In the years that followed, Sackville was asked to go on delicate missions for the queen and to serve in offices that required political wisdom and tact, including an attempt to forward negotiations for the marriage of Elizabeth to the duke of Anjou. He was appointed commissioner of the state trial of Thomas Howard, duke of Norfolk, accused of high treason for attempting to marry Mary Queen of Scots. Fourteen years later, in 1586, Sackville was sent to announce the sentence of death to Mary. In 1587, Elizabeth dispatched him on his most important political assignment, to examine affairs in the Low Countries, particularly the earl of Leicester's conduct, a mission from which he was recalled because he followed Elizabeth's instructions too closely, alienating Leicester, the queen's favorite. Although he had performed his duty faithfully and often brilliantly, he was banished from court, experiencing the turning of the same wheel of Fortune he had treated poetically in his younger years. This was the only time in his long career that he suffered the queen's displeasure. When Leicester died in 1588, Sackville was restored to the queen's favor, and asked to deal with the Low Countries in 1589, and again in 1596 and 1598.

From 1588 on, the honors bestowed on Sackville were high: lord chancellor of Oxford University in 1591; lord treasurer in 1599; lord high steward in 1601. Having written about the fall of princes as a young man, Sackville the statesman served as the lawful instrument of their fall, presiding at the trials of Essex and his fellow conspirators. Sackville was appointed lord treasurer for life by King James I in 1603, and in the following year was created earl

S

of Dorset. As he advanced in years his health became progressively poorer; he often lived with great pain. At times he avoided taking remedies for fear they would interfere with his country's business. In 1608, he died suddenly while at the council table. As a statesman Sackville spent a lifetime serving his country with skill in diplomacy, with unswerving devotion, displaying gentleness of character. Early in that life he managed to make his important and lasting contribution to his country's literature.

Nothing permits us to date precisely Sackville's poems, the "Induction" and the *Complaint*, but external and internal evidence points to a reasonable speculation that both poems were written before the 1559 edition of *A Mirror for Magistrates* was published. Because the *Complaint* could not fit into the editor's chronological scheme for that edition (Richard II through Edward IV), it was saved for a future edition, and was published in 1563, along with the "Induction," which was meant to be the introduction to a collection of tragical narratives but actually stands alone as an independent poem, introducing only one narrative, Buckingham's *Complaint,* with which it has obvious connections. Although Sackville is a didactic poet in a didactic collection, the "Induction" is more a descriptive mood piece than a didactic pronouncement on the fall of princes. Sackville wants his tragical presentation to serve as a lesson to those princes alive—the "mirrour" forever reflecting—but he expends his poetic energy on description, on mood and atmosphere, not on moral reflection. The theme of mutability is felt more than it is pondered. In true Renaissance fashion he turns for inspiration to Vergil, Seneca, Dante, Chaucer, Lydgate, and Surrey, producing perhaps the finest poem written between Chaucer and Spenser. His rhyme-royal stanzas, making effective use of alliteration and repetition, brilliantly vivify his medieval allegorical figures, allowing us to feel the theme of mutability because the poem stresses the sensuous, the physical, the concrete rather than the allegorical and doctrinal. The poet-narrator responds emotionally to the figures he meets; his journey to the underworld fills us with a sense of mystery and, at times, horror. The "Induction" is a high poetic accomplishment, forcing us to believe that we lost a major poet when England gained a devoted statesman.

The *Complaint,* like the "Induction" written in Chaucer's Troilus stanza, is a logical continuation of the "Induction" in that the fallen prince, Buckingham, appears at the end of the "Induction" ready to make his lament against Fortune. As a monologue, the *Complaint* differs from the "Induction," which contains dialogue and the interplay of characters. The atmosphere of grief, so strongly felt in the "Induction," also hangs over Buckingham's lament but seems less important to the poem because the didactic intent is stated again and again. The *Complaint* contains more maxims, more exempla, less description, less color and variety. The mirror in the *Complaint* is always reflecting in order to affect the mind, to teach. It achieves its purpose admirably. Buckingham's monologue—telling how he aided Richard III in his rise to the crown, how he rebelled against Richard, how he was betrayed by his friend Banaster and was led to his death—has a sustained tone, many poetic excellences, and moral significance. The poem's themes of revenge, fortune, and retribution, together with its atmosphere of mortality and the depiction of a sympathetic, tragic, historic figure, anticipate the greatness of Elizabethan tragedy.

A more significant anticipation is the play, *Gorboduc,* which Sackville wrote with Thomas Norton for performance at the Inner Temple on January 6, 1562, and repeated for the queen at Whitehall on January 18. Most scholars accept the title page's ascription of the first three acts to Norton, the last two to Sackville, but the consistency of both parts is so impressive that the entire play must be considered the work of both men. Not surprisingly, *Gorboduc* expresses political ideas and has a didactic thrust. It is written by two men actively concerned with the political life of their country, and performed before the queen, aiming to instruct Elizabeth about specific political issues, especially the uncertain succession and the need for rulers to listen to good advice. Because the dramatists placed their political ideas in a story from British legendary history, *Gorboduc* has the distinction of being the first English chronicle play. Sackville and Norton turned to the English chronicles for their story of King Gorboduc who, against the advice of good councilors, divides England between his two sons, Ferrex and Porrex, unleashing evil human impulses that cause family and nation to suffer. The dramatists raised the history play to a more formal and artistic level by turning to Seneca—five-act structure, choruses, sense of decorum, emphasis on the revenge theme that produces a cohesion based on cause and effect—at the same time that the play is attached to the native tradition, displaying aspects of the morality plays and introducing a dumb show before each act. Most important, for the first time Sackville and Norton use blank verse as a medium for an acted play. *Gorboduc* has a secure place in the history of English drama—the first "regular" tragedy, the first chronicle history, the first play in blank verse.

BIBLIOGRAPHY

Bacquet, Paul. *Thomas Sackville, L'Homme et L'Oeuvre.* 1966.

Berlin, Normand. *Thomas Sackville.* 1974.

Cauthen Jr., Irby, ed. *Gorboduc; or Ferrex and Porrex.* 1970.

Hearsey, Marguerite, ed. *The Complaint of Henry, Duke of Buckingham.* 1936.

Swart, Jacobus. *Thomas Sackville, A Study in Sixteenth-Century Poetry.* 1948.

Normand Berlin

SEE ALSO

Duke of Alençon and Anjou; Devereux, Robert; Drama, History of; Dudley, Robert; Howard, Thomas; Norton, Thomas

Sacraments

Outward and visible signs of an inward and spiritual grace, the sacraments have been at the center of much of the conflict between Protestants and Roman Catholics, and in some cases even between different Protestant groups. The word *sacrament* means *oath,* and was first used in a Christian sense by Tertullian (c. A.D. 200). It later came to be regarded as the Latin equivalent of the Greek word *mysterion* (mystery), although this is not strictly correct. The Roman Church did not properly expound the meaning of its sacraments until November 22, 1439, when, in the context of a proposed union with the Armenian Church, they were explicitly stated to be seven in number, and their precise nature was defined. It was this document, despite its apparent obscurity, that was used by Catholic traditionalists when defending their faith against the Protestant reformers.

Rome divided its Seven Sacraments into two groups. The first consisted of baptism, confirmation, penance, Holy Communion, and extreme unction, all of which could (and should) be received by every Christian. The second group consisted of holy orders and matrimony, which were mutually exclusive. A Christian could either be ordained or marry, but not both. In addition, penance and Holy Communion were meant to be repeated, even daily, whereas the other sacraments were normally not repeatable. Extreme unction could be administered a second time if the recipient recovered from what was thought to be a fatal illness, and a person could remarry after the death of a spouse, but both of these were regarded as exceptional cases.

The Reformers preserved the theological category of sacrament, but changed its meaning. For them, only those rites that Christ had specifically instituted as visible means of preaching the Gospel could properly be called by this term. This reduced the number of sacraments to two: baptism and Holy Communion. The other five traditional rites were relegated to a secondary status, and both penance and extreme unction fell into virtual disuse. Looking at the sacraments individually, we find the following:

Baptism continued to be administered to infants within a few days of birth, and there was virtually no change from medieval practice. There may have been some pressure in England, as there was on the Continent, to abandon the baptism of infants and restrict it to confessing believers, but there is no trace of an English Baptist movement before about 1607.

Holy Communion, also called the *Eucharist* (thanksgiving), the *Mass* (by Catholics) and the *Lord's Supper* (by Protestants), was the main focus of debate during the Reformation. The Catholic doctrine, made official at the Fourth Lateran Council (1215), was that when the priest consecrated the elements of bread and wine, they were miraculously changed in their substance to the Body and Blood of Christ, although their "accidents" (outward appearance) were left unaltered. Martin Luther rejected this, but continued to believe that Christ was spiritually present "in, with and under" the elements of bread and wine. This doctrine is now usually called *consubstantiation,* to distinguish it from the *transubstantiation* of Rome. Huldrych Zwingli, on the other hand, denied any presence of Christ in the sacramental elements, and regarded the communion as a symbolic memorial of Christ's Passion and death.

The English Reformers are often thought to have been closer to Zwingli than to either Luther or Rome, and this is probably true, although they were less focused on the elements themselves. The evidence of the Book of Common Prayer suggests that Archbishop Thomas Cranmer was mainly concerned with the *action* involved in the representation of Christ's death; he wanted worshippers to feel that they had access to the saving benefits of Christ's suffering. This could be achieved by a faithful restatement of what Christ's sacrifice on the cross had achieved, and by an invitation to the communicant to participate in that achievement, which was promised to anyone who would receive the consecrated elements in the faith that Christ died for him. This doctrine is traditionally known as *receptionism,* although in fact it is too subtle to be reduced to a simple formula.

S

The Reformers also rejected the medieval notion that it was sufficient for the communicant to receive the bread and not the wine, and restored the cup to the laity. *Confirmation* continued to be practiced much as it had always been, although the Reformers tended to administer it at a later age than was customary in the Roman Church, thereby allowing more time for the believer to mature in his faith. *Penance,* as a series of outward acts designed to demonstrate sorrow for wrongs committed, was generally abandoned by the Reformers in favor of *repentance,* which was thought of as an inward and spiritual change of heart leading to a changed life. *Extreme unction,* popularly known as the last rites, was generally abandoned, although it was not formally rejected by the Reformers.

Holy orders were retained, and the Church of England continued to claim that its ordinations took place in the apostolic succession, a claim rejected by Rome. According to the Ordinal (1550), a man could be made deacon at twenty-three, priest at twenty-four, and bishop at thirty. Once conferred, orders were indelible and could not be renounced, even if they were no longer actively exercised. Men in holy orders were disqualified from certain social functions; they could not sit in the House of Commons or serve on a jury, for example. On the other hand, bishops sat in the House of Lords and the lower clergy were represented in the convocations of the provinces of Canterbury and York.

Holy matrimony continued to be regarded as a sacred, lifelong union, and there was no recognized divorce. Remarriage could therefore take place only after the death of one of the spouses. The ban on clerical marriage, imposed by the First Lateran Council (1123), was not formally lifted until an act of Parliament was passed to allow it (1549), and this legislation was soon repealed (1553). Under Elizabeth I, clerical marriage was tolerated without being officially sanctioned; and it is significant that the Puritans demanded the restoration of the 1549 act of Parliament when James I ascended the throne in 1603.

BIBLIOGRAPHY

Collinson, Patrick. *The Elizabethan Puritan Movement.* 1967.

Ingram, M. *Church Courts, Sex, and Marriage in England, 1570–1640.* 1987.

Martos, J. *Doors to the Sacred.* 2nd edition. 1991.

Stevenson, K. *Covenant of Grace Renewed: A Vision of the Eucharist in the Seventeenth Century.* 1994.

Gerald Bray

SEE ALSO

Book of Common Prayer; Catholicism; Clergy; Eucharist; Marriage and Marriage Law; Ordinal; Puritanism; Reformation, English

Sadler, Ralph (1507–1587)

Ralph Sadler benefited from an administrative apprenticeship in the household of Thomas Cromwell, into whose service he was delivered as a boy. Given the lack of a formal bureaucracy, Sadler's work as Cromwell's secretary involved him in public as well as private affairs, and prepared him for the job of principal secretary in 1540. He filled this post jointly with Thomas Wriothesley until 1543, and served as a privy councilor and M.P. Sadler's proximity to the king left him well placed to benefit from the workings of the patronage system: by 1547, he had escaped his modest origins to rival the richest commoners in the kingdom, owning property in twenty-five counties. From 1537, he was active in Anglo-Scots diplomacy; his particular concern was to weaken the influence of Cardinal David Beaton. However, his 1543 negotiations for the marriage of Prince Edward and Princess Mary failed amid Sadler's complaints of the beastliness of the Scots. He was much less active in public affairs under Edward VI, and Mary I dropped him from her council, presumably for his religion. But he was rapidly recalled under Elizabeth, and played a prominent role in responding to the flight of Mary Queen of Scots.

BIBLIOGRAPHY

Slavin, Arthur J. *Politics and Profit: A Study of Sir Ralph Sadler, 1507–1547.* 1966.

J.P.D. Cooper

SEE ALSO

Cromwell, Thomas; Mary Queen of Scots; Wriothesley, Thomas

Sandys, Edwin (c. 1516–1588)

Born in Lancashire, Edwin Sandys, archbishop of York, was educated at St. John's College, Cambridge, from which he graduated B.A. in 1539, proceeding M.A. in 1541, and B.D. in 1547. He was appointed master of Catherine Hall that same year, vicar of Caversham the next, and canon of Peterborough in 1549—the year he earned his D.D. By 1553, he had become vice-chancellor of Cambridge University, but he supported the cause of the Protestant Lady Jane Grey as successor to Edward VI over the Catholic Mary Tudor; upon Mary I's accession, Sandys was briefly imprisoned in the Tower and escaped to Europe for the duration of Mary's reign. He returned to England after Elizabeth I came to power and, in 1559, became bishop of Worcester. He made enemies among Catholic sympathizers, arguing, at the convocation of 1562, against using the sign of the cross in baptism. In 1565, he served as a translator of the Bishops' Bible. He was, in 1570, made bishop of London where, despite his personal sympathies, he felt compelled to defend the established church against Puritan critics like Thomas Cartwright (whose arrest warrant he signed in 1573), as well as against Catholic recusants. In 1576, Sandys was created archbishop of York. There he found a dangerous enemy in Sir Robert Stapleton, who arranged, in 1581, to sneak a woman into Sandys's bedroom, then to have her husband burst in on the two of them; Stapleton blackmailed Sandys until the demands became too great— Sandys eventually exposed the plot and was himself cleared. Three years later, he helped to secure the appointment of Richard Hooker, the English Church's greatest apologist, as master of the Temple. Sandys died on July 10, 1588.

BIBLIOGRAPHY
Bloxam, Matthew. *On the Sepulchral Effigy of Archbishop Sandys in Minster Church, Southwell, Nottinghamshire.* 1870.

Mark Goldblatt

SEE ALSO
Bible Translations; Cartwright, Thomas; Grey Lady, Jane; Hooker, Richard; Recusancy

Saravia, Hadrian (c. 1532–1613)

Born in Flanders, Hadrian Saravia was a leader of the Dutch churches in the Netherlands and England in the 1560s and 1570s. In Leiden as minister and professor from 1574, he was probably falsely associated with a plot to place the city under the earl of Leicester's direct control. He fled to England where he was immediately beneficed. His work, entitled *De diversis ministrorum evangeliis gradibus* (London, 1590), was important to John Whitgift and Richard Bancroft in their efforts to discredit the Puritans. In that work, Saravia argued that the office of bishop, founded by the apostles, was superior to that of presbyter in its ruling authority. He based

his arguments on Jesus' appointment of the seventy disciples (Luke 10:1) as distinct from that of the twelve apostles (*ibid.* 9:1,2), questioning many of Theodore Beza's interpretations of the New Testament. Consequently, the office of bishop was "an apostolic tradition and *divine institution,*" not merely a "custom," as Anglican apologists had claimed. These views were influential, particularly with Richard Hooker, whom he knew intimately. Although Hooker and other Anglican theologians would differ in their understanding of *jure divino* (divine right), Saravia was the first to give a thorough justification for episcopacy as a divine institution. He also advised Whitgift on the text of the Lambeth Articles. Canon of Canterbury in 1595, he lived there until his death, writing and publishing other theological works.

BIBLIOGRAPHY
Nijenhuis, Willem. *Adrianus Saravia.* 1980.

Frederick H. Shriver

SEE ALSO
Anglicanism; Bancroft, Richard; Church Polity; Hooker, Richard; Lambeth Articles; Puritanism; Whitgift, John

Sarum, Use of

The Use of Sarum became the prevailing liturgical and musical form in which the Latin liturgy was celebrated in late medieval and early Tudor England. In 1058, the dioceses of Sherborne and Ramsbury were united, and in 1075, the new see was transferred to Old Sarum. There St. Osmund, the second bishop, established a cathedral chapter of secular canons according to the Norman model, and probably compiled its first guidelines, the *Institution*. In 1218, Bishop Richard Poore moved the see to "New Sarum" or Salisbury: he also was responsible for the *Consuetudinary* (governing individual roles) and probably the first Ordinal (governing ritual actions). Revised in the mid-fourteenth century (the "New Use"), the Ordinal was later abridged into a *Pica* or "Pie," which was printed in 1487. Sarum liturgy shows influences from Bec, Bayeux, Rouen, and Evreux.

Rich in both ceremony and music, the Use of Sarum was adopted by important secular churches and cathedrals such as Exeter and London in the fourteenth century. Although other Uses (York, Lincoln, and others) continued, by the fifteenth century most of England and much of Scotland, Ireland, and Wales followed Sarum. During the Hundred Year's War, the Chapel Royal and various

S

ducal chapels spread Sarum's influence on the Continent, and, as the result of a royal marriage in 1385, its influence extended even to Portugal. Sarum books were readily available from insular ateliers and later from continental printers. A Sarum liturgy involved well-regulated and lavish ceremonial with many impressive processions. There were special feasts (e.g., St. Osmund, the feast of relics) and a few unique prayers and chants, such as *Venit ad Petrum* instead of *Ubi caritas* on Maundy Thursday. Sarum has some unique notational and performance traditions, and both its chant and its polyphony show a tendency toward use of the musical interval of a third. There is a repertoire of troped chants, of sequences, and of polyphonic settings of the *Benedicamus Domino*. In the fifteenth century, one also finds the daily "ladymass" (Marian votive mass), a rich repertoire of votive antiphons, and rubrics specifying polyphony for certain major feasts.

Despite John XXII's condemnation of polyphony in 1322, the English Church continued to develop its unique discant or harmony. Eventually called "faburden," this sweet sound was a major constituent of the "contenance angloise" that was popularized on the Continent through the works of John Dunstapl (c. 1380/1390–1453) and others. Late fourteenth- and early fifteenth-century examples are found in the Old Hall manuscript (British Museum, Additional MS 57950). Early Tudor polyphonic music for the Use of Sarum by Robert Fayrfax, William Cornysh, and others is found in a few extant choir books, the most important of which is the Eton Choirbook. This polyphony shows significant changes in meter and texture, but less use of imitation than do continental counterparts. Sometimes early Tudor compositions were based on a cantus firmus drawn from a faburden or a "square" (counterpoint) to a chant rather than on the original chant itself. John Taverner, Christopher Tye, Thomas Tallis, and William Byrd wrote works that were either based on Sarum chants or written for the Sarum liturgy.

Despite his break with Rome, Henry VIII permitted only minor liturgical changes. He did, however, commission Archbishop Thomas Cranmer to develop an English litany (paraliturgical procession rite) asking for divine assistance in the wars with France and Scotland. This 1544 litany was based on the Sarum litany "In Times of Need" and set to adapted Sarum chant. Although officially abolished by Edward VI in 1547 and again by Elizabeth I in 1559, the Use of Sarum became, along with Miles Coverdale's Great Bible, one of the major sources of the Anglican liturgy. The Edwardian Book of Common Prayer (1548 and 1552) eliminated many feasts, as well as

the minor hours of the divine office (the major hours were combined into the Anglican matins and evensong). In changing high and low masses into the Great Service and the Short Service, the reformers replaced the Kyrie with the Ten Commandments, eliminated or replaced the Proper chants (introit, gradual, etc.), and replaced the theological emphasis on sacrifice with an emphasis on communal commemoration. For these reformed rites, John Merbecke's *The Booke of Common Praier Noted* (1550) provided simplified chant based on Sarum models. Choral music and even organ music was severely curtailed, and simple congregational singing on Cranmer's principle of "for every syllable a note" was emphasized. Under Elizabeth I, restrictions on choral singing were mitigated, and music in Latin was permitted in colleges and universities and in the Chapel Royal. Sarum liturgies continued surreptitiously among recusants such as William Byrd and, until 1577, at the English College at Douai. Anglican scholars such as W.H. Frere and H.M. Bannister led the resurgence of interest in the Use of Sarum during the late nineteenth and early twentieth centuries.

BIBLIOGRAPHY

Baxter, Philip. *Sarum Use: The Development of a Medieval Code of Liturgy and Customs.* 1994.

Frere, Walter Howard. *Antiphonale Sarisburiense.* 1901.

———. *Graduale Sarisburiense.* 1901.

———. *The Use of Sarum.* 1898–1901.

Legg, John Wickham. *The Sarum Missal.* 1916.

Sandon, Nick. *The Use of Salisbury.* 3 vols. 2nd edition. 1990–1991.

R. Todd Ridder, S.M.

SEE ALSO

Anglicanism; Book of Common Prayer; Byrd, William; Cornysh, William; Cranmer, Thomas; Eton Choirbook; Fayrfax, Robert; Merbecke, John; Music, History of; Ordinal; Tallis, Thomas; Taverner, John; Tye, Christopher

Satire

Satire is a broadly comprehensive literary mode that may appear in virtually any genre, although the genre most often thought of as distinctly satiric is the "formal verse satire" modeled on the satires of the Roman poets Horace, Persius, and Juvenal. Satire has as its aims the *laus et vituperatio* ("praise and blame") of the demonstrative oration of classical rhetoric. As such, satire retains some of the

S

variousness suggested by its derivation from Latin *satura,* which as a noun means a "bowl of mixed fruit," and as an adjective means "full" or "saturated."

During the Tudor period, satirical writing in English often evinced more of its medieval than its classical heritage. Although not an original satirist himself, Alexander Barclay translated Sebastian Brant's *Narrenschiff* as *The Shyp of folys* into rime royal in 1509 and presented the portrayal of a ship in a harbor full of personifications of folly. Similarly reminiscent of the medieval tradition is the *Bowge of Court* (1510?), by John Skelton, which is in the form a dream-vision and in rime royal and narrates the interaction among various allegorical representations of vices associated with the court. Skelton wrote other verse satire in highly original, not to say peculiar forms, including *Speke, Parrot, Colin Clout,* and *Why Come Ye Nat to Court?*; the first in rime royal, the second and third in the short lines that came to be known as "Skeltonics"—metrically irregular lines of two or three stresses. While *Colin Clout* is in the generalized complaint tradition, *Speke, Parrot* and *Why Come Ye Nat to Court?* are highly topical and personal in their criticism of Cardinal Thomas Wolsey. Such specifically personal satire would not recur in a major way until the formal satire and epigrams of the late 1590s.

Satirical writing in the complaint tradition continued throughout the second half of the sixteenth century and tended to concentrate on social and economic conditions. It frequently drew inspiration from the first printed texts of Langland (and Langland apocrypha). Robert Crowley undertook such criticism himself in a prose tract in 1548, *An informacion and Peticion agaynst the oppressours of the pore Commons of this Realme,* and in a series of versified "lessons" in *The Voyce of the laste trumpet* (1550). A later instance of this tradition is George Gascoigne's *The Stele Glas* (1576). Gascoigne casts his satire in the new form of blank verse, and besides using the enduring figure of Langland's Piers exploits the standard trope of the *speculum* or mirror by which he holds the mirror up to all of early Elizabethan society and to a highly critical, pessimistic gaze. The medieval practice of regarding society as a group of "estates" and trades, and the self-conscious style of rough language and unadorned English, continue in *Prosopopia or Mother Hubberds Tale* (c. 1580; printed 1591), by Edmund Spenser. By the 1590s, satirical writing most often focused on London. In 1592, the pamphlet *A Qvip for An Vpstart Courtier: or, A quaint dispute between Veluet breeches and Clothbreeches. Wherein is plainely set downe the disorders in all Estates and Trades,* by

Robert Greene, singled out the principal causes for the dislocation of traditional social order as the influx of foreign capital and fashion.

While the native English tradition of satire continued throughout the century, a humanist tradition with its decidedly classical bent began to emerge. The earliest collection of epigrams in English appeared in 1550, Robert Cowley's *One and thyrte Epigrammes,* though they are more in the vein of medieval complaint than the Roman epigrammatist Martial. During the next several decades, John Heywood issued more than a dozen collections of epigrams, which were humorously satirical in the manner of the wisdom and proverbial apothegm. In 1577, Timothy Kendall published some of the earliest English translations of Martial as well as English translations of contemporary humanists anticipating Ben Jonson's translations a generation later: brief poems distinguished by wit and humor, typically concluding in a rhetorically figured point, and generally regarded as less than gravely serious in moral and aesthetic intention. This conception governs the epigrams written by Sir John Harrington, Sir John Davies, Edward Guilpin, and Thomas Bastard (c. 1565–1618).

The principal genre of classical satire was the formal verse satire: a quasi-dramatic poem of medium length in which the satirist/speaker responds critically to the world about him, often prompted by another speaker or *adversarius.* Formal satire appeared in England during the 1530s with the epistolary satires of Sir Thomas Wyatt, which were not printed until 1557. These were translations into *terza rima* of Italian imitations of Horace by Tomasso Alamanni. A more direct manifestation of the classical tradition is Thomas Drant's *Medicinable Morall* (1566), which contains the first English translation of Horace's satires, a translation of the Book of Lamentations (thought to be by the prophet Jeremiah), and several pages of complimentary epigrams, funeral elegies, and debate poems. Drant thus combines Roman satire, biblical complaint, and occasional celebratory verse in a variegated collection of praise and blame; it is in this way literally satirical. The volume also contains the first definition of satire in English and provides a comprehensive theoretical statement: "A Satyre is a tarte and carpyng kynd of verse. / An instrument to pynche the prankes of men" (sig. A3). Four etymologies of the word *satire* follow. Drant suggests that it comes from an Arabic word that means "glaive," a sword or sharp cutting device; from satyr, the rough woodland god, hence the Elizabethan spelling of *satire* as *satyr(e)*; from Saturn, the sullen, melancholy god; or, finally, from Latin *satura.*

Satire   623

S

While isolated formal verse satires appeared in the 1580s and 1590s—such as those by Thomas Lodge in 1584, 1589, and 1595—a flurry of such writing occurred in the late 1590s. The most notable formal satires were by John Donne, Joseph Hall, and John Marston. Although Donne wrote and circulated his five satires in manuscript between 1593 and 1598, they did not appear in print until 1631. Donne's first satire ridicules pretentious figures on the London streets by means of the fawning "motley humorist." The second deals with the excesses of contemporary love poetry. The third treats religion and satirizes the extremes of various sectarians. The fourth is an adaptation of Horace (*Satires* 1.9) and satirizes the bore, who is a would-be courtier and gossip. The fifth treats the law courts and the general inefficiency of the legal system. The satiric persona varies from being actively, almost dramatically involved, as in Satires 1, 2, and 4, to rather more detached and observant, as in 3 and 5. Joseph Hall's satires appeared in print in 1598 and 1602 as *Virgidemiarium Sixe Bookes* (the first three books in 1597).

Apparently taking up Hall's challenge for someone to become the second English satirist, John Marston published *Metamorphosis of Pigmalion's Image and Certaine Satyres* and *The Scourge of Villanie* in 1598. The first volume contains an Ovidian narrative based on the Pygmalion myth and five verse satires; the second volume contains three books of satires (eleven all told) in which Marston strives to achieve a Juvenalian authority in his censure of the world's iniquities. The topics are familiar: bad poets, arrogant critics, pretentious parvenus, Roman Catholics, and Puritans.

Marston is much more personal and specific in his satire than Hall, and in fact refers explicitly to Hall in Satire 10 (lines 47–57). Comparable personal attacks began to occur in other satirical verse and drama, such as Edward Guilpin's *Skialetheia or, A shadowe of Truth, in certaine Epigrams and Satyres* (1598), the Parnassus Plays (1598–1601), and Jonson's comical satires (1599–1601). Officials soon took steps to curb the literary disorder. In June 1599, the archbishops of Canterbury and London issued a prohibition of the printing of the satires of Hall, Marston, Guilpin, and Davies, and ordered that "noe Satyres or Epigrams be printed hereafter." A few days later there was a burning of books, though Hall's satires were spared. Unofficial response to the escalating quarrels of the satirists took the form of several efforts to quiet the growing furor. In 1599, John Weever published *Epigrammes in the Oldest Cut & Newest Fashion* in which he distanced himself explicitly from Hall and Marston and

refused to cast in "Enuies teeth defiance." In 1600, he brought out *Faunus and Melliflora, or the Original of our Englysh Satyres,* which includes translations of Horace, Juvenal, and Persius, and concludes with a condemnation by Venus of current satirists and mentions Hall and Marston by name (sig. F3). This was followed by the anonymous *Whipping of the Satyre* (1601), an attack on the vain satirist, epigrammatist, and humorist—probably Marston, Nicholas Breton, and Ben Jonson—proposing that excessive satirical criticism is unseemly and un-Christian. The same year, two further verse pamphlets appeared: Breton's *No Whippinge, nor tripping: but a kinde friendly Snipping* and the anonymous *The Whipper of the Satyre his pennance in a white Sheete. No Whippinge* agrees with *The Whipping* that satire is inappropriate and argues that poets should embrace religious themes; *The Whipper,* on the other hand, asserts that by exposing vice satire asserts truth and promotes virtue. Satire had clearly become problematic, in large part because of the topicality and the concern that it provoked. Not surprisingly, neither official nor unofficial disapproval stopped the writing of satire. Verse satire continued to be published; but satirical drama—both comic and tragic—became the chief forms of satire by the early seventeenth century.

BIBLIOGRAPHY

Donne, John. *The Satires, Epigrams, and Verse Letters.* Helen Gardner, ed. 1967.

Hall, Joseph. *The Poems.* Arnold Davenport, ed. 1969.

Hester, M. Thomas. *Kinde Pitty and Brave Scorn: John Donne's Satyres.* 1982.

Hudson, Hoyt H. *The Epigram in the English Renaissance.* 1947.

Kernan, Alvin. *The Cankered Muse: The Satire of the English Renaissance.* 1959.

Marston, John. *The Poems.* Arnold Davenport, ed. 1961.

Peter, John. *Complaint and Satire in Early English Literature.* 1956.

Smith, Hallett. *Elizabethan Poetry: A Study in Conventions, Meaning, and Expression.* 1952.

The Three Parnassus Plays. J.B. Leishman, ed. 1949.

Peter E. Medine

SEE ALSO

Brant, Sebastian; Crowley, Robert; Davies, John; Donne, John; Epigrams; Gascoigne, George; Greene, Robert; Guilpin, Everard; Hall, Joseph; Heywood, John; Jonson, Ben; Marston, John; Skelton, John

Saxton, Christopher (c. 1542–after 1610)

Creator of the first atlas of English and Welsh county maps and estate surveyor, Christopher Saxton was born in or near Dewsbury in Yorkshire but soon moved to his life-long home, the nearby hamlet of Dunningley. He is first recorded in 1570 as the servant of John Rudd (c. 1500–1579), the vicar of Dewsbury and a noted cartographer with contacts at the royal court. It was almost certainly from Rudd that Saxton received his training in surveying and mapmaking; Rudd's failed project to create "a more perfect and truer" map in the early 1560s may have been the predecessor to Saxton's atlas.

Saxton's immediate patron was Thomas Seckford (1515–1587), a leading judge and former fellow student of Elizabeth I's first minister, William Cecil, Lord Burghley. The crown, however, facilitated the undertaking through the grant of passes and of a printing privilege (1577), and probably by allowing Saxton access to the government records, containing regional mapping from the 1530s, and the libraries of the national leaders. Saxton was rewarded by repeated grants of lands and a grant of arms. It seems to have been the crown's administrative needs that dictated that Saxton's maps be county-based, while prepublication copies of the individual maps were passed to Burghley for his personal use.

Saxton began work, apparently in Norfolk, in the early 1570s. The atlas format was influenced by the appearance of Abraham Ortelius's *Theatrum Orbis Terrarum* in 1570. The survey of the Welsh counties completed the survey, and the atlas was published, prefaced by a map of England and Wales, in 1579.

The disappearance of his working papers means that one can only speculate over Saxton's methods. Contemporaries commented that he was "most skilled in geometry." It is likely that he created the framework for the maps through field surveys in the summer months, employing a form of triangulation based on the theories of Gemma Frisius. The detailed information would have been supplied from local knowledge, and in the winter months from books and existing maps.

In 1583, Saxton published a twenty-sheet wall map of England and Wales, derived from the county maps. Because of the differing scales, the absence of grids of latitude and longitude, and geographical inconsistencies between the individual county maps, its creation must have involved a high level of mathematical skill. The remainder of Saxton's career was spent creating large-scale local maps for private individuals, institutions, and the crown. More than twenty-five manuscript maps survive from the period 1587 to 1608, and more are being discovered. They are characterized by their clarity and simplicity, with an almost total lack of decoration that distinguishes them from the work of most of Saxton's contemporaries and perhaps hints at his personality. His surveying methods are not known.

There remained considerable gaps in detail, as well as inconsistencies in content and outline, between different maps showing the same areas; Saxton's successors, notably John Norden, William Smith, and John Speed, did much to remedy these weaknesses. Nevertheless, all of them acknowledged their debt to Saxton, and the counties were not to be surveyed afresh and his maps rendered obsolete until the late eighteenth century.

BIBLIOGRAPHY

Evans, Ifor, and Heather Lawrence. *Christopher Saxton, Elizabethan Map-maker.* 1979.

Marcombe, David. "Saxton's Apprenticeship: John Rudd, a Yorkshire Cartographer." *Yorkshire Archeological Journal,* vol. 50, pp. 171–175.

Ravenhill, William. "Christopher Saxton's Surveying: An Enigma." In *English Map-making, 1500–1650.* Sarah Tyacke, ed. pp. 2–119. 1983.

———. *Christopher Saxton's 16th Century Maps. The Counties of Wales and England.* 1992.

Skelton, R.A. *Saxton's Survey of England and Wales. With a facsimile of Saxton's Wall-map of 1583.* 1974.

———. *County Atlases of the British Isles, 1579–1850. A Bibliography, 1570–1703,* pp. 7–16. 1978.

Peter Barber

SEE ALSO
Cecil, William; Norden, John; Mapmaking

Scholasticism

See Aristotelianism; Humanism; Logic; Ramism; Rhetoric

Science, History of

Tudor contributions to the making of "modern" science may seem slight compared with the English contribution during the second half of the seventeenth century, for only William Gilbert is today deemed a "consequential" figure. The community of English men of science has been relegated a peripheral role in the flourishing of continental scientific culture. Scholars have instead tended to

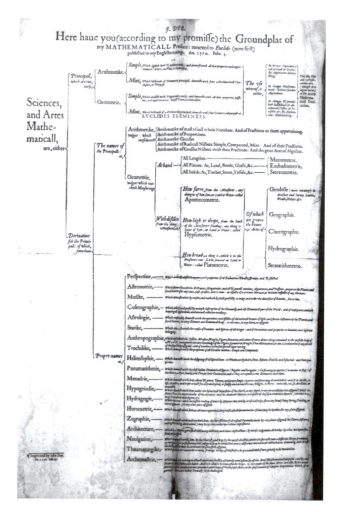

John Dee, from *Mathematicall Praeface to Euclide* (1570). Dee's celebrated Preface to the first English translation of Euclid was a major statement of the mathematical sciences in England, which lagged behind the continent in scientific development. The "Groundplat" outlines Dee's exhaustive invoentory of the "Sciences and Artes Mathematicall" and may have influenced similar outlines by writers such as Francis Bacon. Reproduced from the original by permission of the Henry E. Huntington Library and Art Gallery.

emphasize the presumed utilitarianism of English practitioners, the emergence of an empiricist and experimentalist tradition, and the alleged contribution of Puritanism to English science, thereby suggesting an absence of meaningful "theoretical" activity in natural philosophy and the mathematical sciences. Certainly, English men of science became involved in a range of practical ventures. Nevertheless, the image of them as practitioners largely consumed by utilitarian concerns is exaggerated, based on a misconception of the nature of their research as well as on an incomplete record of their activities. The fact that

they researched and taught topics such as magnetism and, later, logarithms represented the cutting edge in natural philosophy and the mathematical sciences, respectively, and research into them—no less than in astronomy—must be considered as theoretical. That such topics were immediately useful was simply an added benefit, but in itself, utility was not a primary motivation for research.

There had been a flurry of activity in the domain of the mathematical sciences from the early years of the sixteenth century, when earnest efforts to introduce high-level instruction were made at Cambridge and later at Oxford. As the century progressed a growing number of individuals, including John Dee, Richard Hakluyt, Thomas Hood, and Edward Wright, attempted to effect the endowment of lectureships in mathematics at both Oxbridge and London. Although such efforts failed, they indicated the maturation of a community of individuals who recognized the need for a strong institutional basis for the mathematical sciences, as well as the urgency of promoting a native tradition of instrument-making and involving a wider scientifically literate community. Initially, these activists were predominantly university-trained mathematicians who, in addition to their promotional efforts, instructed both students and London artisans and navigators. Consequently, there emerged in London by the early seventeenth century a community of nonuniversity teachers of mathematics and mathematically-skilled navigators, surveyors, and other like practitioners. Furthermore, owing largely to the ingenuity of these university-educated men a large number of scientific instruments for astronomy, surveying, and computation were designed (or improved), and such skills were inculcated among a growing number of instrument makers and other practitioners. The foundation of Gresham College at the closing years of the century provided a visible proof to the new vitality of the mathematical sciences in England. Endowed with the first two mathematical professorships in the country, Gresham served not only as an important research and teaching center, but as the meeting place for all those interested in the sciences for decades to come.

While laying the foundation for a flourishing and sophisticated mathematical community, and helping introduce mathematics to a host of professions, members of this burgeoning community also made modest, but hardly negligible, contributions to the new science. John Dee and Thomas Digges, for example, corroborated and expanded on Tycho Brahe's observations of the new star of 1572 and the comet of 1577, while Henry Savile participated in the continental discussion over Copernicanism and the technical details of observational astronomy. The three joined other practitioners in disseminating the new astronomy in England, as well as in bridging more broadly the domain of the mathematical sciences and natural philosophy, an example of which is the semicollaborative effort today known as William Gilbert's *De Magnete* (1600). Other practitioners, such as the navigators Robert Norman and William Borough, contributed the results of their own investigations into magnetism, and together with their better educated colleagues helped enshrine the ethos of experimentalism in England. Not that more speculative ideas did not exist. Bold conjectures into the realm of natural philosophy were made by the one-time fellow of St. John's College, Oxford, Nicholas Hill, whose *Philosophia Epicurea* was published in Paris in 1601, as well as by Thomas Hariot, Walter Warner, and Nathaniel Torporley, whose work on atomism, cosmology, and mechanics, however, remained unpublished.

Paradoxically, perhaps, what made it possible for the English to emerge in the forefront of scientific developments by the 1610s and 1620s was their one significant backwardness during the Tudor period: the absence of a Aristotelian tradition comparable to that in Italy, France, or Germany. Though conventional natural philosophy was taught at the universities, neither Oxford nor Cambridge had any philosophy professorship. Likewise, no distinguished philosophers practiced in England and no philosophical textbooks or other treatises were published there. Consequently, the English allegiance to Aristotle lacked serious commitment or depth and, consequently, we find nothing like the fierce debates that surrounded Aristotelians on the Continent. (The only exception, the debates over Ramism, were largely over discipline and Puritanism, not philosophy.) Equally significant, the strong humanist focus of Oxbridge teaching further lessened the centrality of Aristotlelian natural philosophy in the curriculum. Hence, no sooner were the ideas of Bacon, Galileo, Descartes, and Gassendi published than they were embraced by many tutors and students at Oxford and Cambridge—and elsewhere in England—with little resistance. And, in sharp contrast to what occurred on the Continent throughout the seventeenth century, none of the new philosophies were ever condemned in England.

BIBLIOGRAPHY

Cormack, Lesley B. *Charting an Empire: Geography at the English Universities, 1580–1620.* 1997.

Feingold, Mordechai. *The Mathematicians' Apprenticeship: Science, Universities, and Society in England, 1560–1640.* 1984.

McLean, Antonia. *Humanism and the Rise of Science in Tudor England.* 1972.

Nutton, Vivian. *John Caius and the Manuscripts of Galen.* 1987.

Schmitt, Charles. *John Case and Aristotelianism in Renaissance England.* 1983.

Taylor, E.G.R. *The Mathematical Practitioners of Tudor and Stuart England, 1485–1714.* 1954.

Thomas, Keith. *Religion and the Decline of Magic.* 1972.

Wear, Andrew, R.K. French, and I.M. Lonie, eds. *The Medical Renaissance of the Sixteenth Century.* 1985.

Mordechai Feingold

SEE ALSO

Aristotelianism; Astronomy; Bacon, Francis; Dee, John; Digges, Thomas; Education; Gilbert, William; Hakluyt, Richard; Hariot, Thomas; Medicine and Health; Ramism

Scot, Reginald (c. 1538–1599)

Author of the skeptical tract, *The Discoverie of Witchcraft* (1584), Reginald Scot was probably born on his father's estate in Kent in 1538. He studied briefly at Oxford, but left without a degree and settled at Smeeth, Kent, in 1568, where an inheritance allowed him to dedicate himself to study. His interest in agriculture led to the publication of *A Perfite platform of a Hoppe Garden* (1574); important enough to attract further editions in 1576 and 1578, this manual contributed to the eventual independence of Kentish hop growers from the continental monopoly on this important brewing crop. Scot began public service around 1578 with his appointment as justice of the peace. He later served as collector of subsidies for the crown in Kent during 1586–1587, and in 1588 he was elected Member of Parliament for New Romney. There is evidence that he also served that year as a captain of foot soldiers marshaled in defense of the Armada.

Scot's rigorous and skeptical appraisal of demonology and witchcraft trials in *The Discoverie* is grounded in his judicial experience and wide reading on the subject. Although the incidence of witch hunting in Kent was mild compared to the notorious trials in neighboring Essex, Scot's long book presents an exhaustive inventory of types of alleged witches, the common charges against them, and the quality of evidence used in their prosecution. Limiting

S

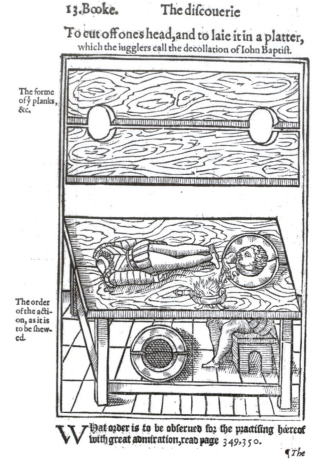

13.Booke.   The difcouerie

To cut off ones head, and to laie it in a platter,
which the iugglers call the decollation of Iohn Baptift.

The forme of ÿ planks, &c.

The order of the acti-on, as it is to be fhew-ed.

What order is to be obferued for the practifing hereof with great admiration, read page 349, 350.

¶ The

Reginald Scot, *To cut off ones head and to laie it in a platter.* From *The Discoverie of Witchcraft* (1584). Scot's skeptical book on witchcraft also included detailed explanations of "the knaverie of conjours" such as this trick "which the jugglers call the decollation of John Baptist." Reproduced from the original by permission of the Henry E. Huntington Library and Art Gallery.

sensational textbook on witch persecution, the *Malleus Maleficarum* (1498) by Heinrich Institoris and Jacob Sprenger, and Jean Bodin's influential *De la Demono-manie de Sorciers* (1580). Scot also treats—perhaps with less authority—astrology, alchemy, and "natural magic" such as the curative properites of the lodestone. His criti-cism of occult claims extends even to prestidigitation, the "art of juggling," always cautious that artful deceptions of the credulous not be attributed to divine power.

Scot was aggressively reformist and deeply supsicious of ritual practices within the church. Although he was careful to assert his faith in angels, the devil, and the Trinity, his scepticism of otherworldly intervention in human affairs left his orthodoxy vulnerable to his chief opponent, James VI of Scotland (later James I of England). James's *Dae-monologie* (1597) follows Bodin in retailing the horrors of witchcraft, and in his preface James calls Weyer a witch and Scot a Sadduccee for disavowing the reality of spirits. It is perhaps true that James ordered *The Discoverie* publicly burned sometime after Scot's death in 1599; in any case, subsequent English editions did not appear until after 1651. It is likely that Scot's debunking and James's response influ-enced Shakespeare's treatment of the occult in *Macbeth*.

BIBLIOGRAPHY

Haining, Peter, ed. *The Witchcraft Papers: Contemporary Records of the Witchcraft Hysteria in Essex, 1560–1700.* 1974.

James I. *Daemonologie in Forme of a Dialogue* (1597). G.B. Harrison, ed. Bodley Head Quartos, no. 9. 1924.

Scot, Reginald. *The Discoverie of Witchcraft.* Hugh Ross Williamson, ed. 1964.

West, Robert H. *Reginald Scot and Renaissance Writings on Witchcraft.* 1984.

David W. Swain

SEE ALSO

Agriculture; James VI and I; Magic; Skepticism; Witchcraft

his commentary to local cases only, Scot impugns the jus-tice available to accused witches and heaps scorn on the claims of special authority and occult power imputed to them. His tone is investigative and reportorial, and much of his material is derived from either his involvement in the trials, multiple eyewitnesses accounts, or interviews with participants. Throughout, Scot engages authorities for and against claims of witchcraft, ranging from classi-cal authors to contemporary continental sources. Among them Scot admiringly cites the skeptic Pietro Pompon-azzi and Johann Weyer, a student of Henricus Cornelius Agrippa, who had defended accused witches on the grounds of their ignorance and the implausibility of their pacts with demons. His strongest criticism targets the

Scotland, History of

The history of sixteenth-century Scotland appears to begin at a very low point. The undoubtedly successful reign of the charismatic and able James IV went down to disaster in the mud at the battle of Flodden Field in 1513. The attempt to fulfil his part of the "Auld Alliance" with France by attacking northern England in order to compli-cate the war-hungry Henry VIII's invasion of France led only to the catastrophic defeat of one of the biggest armies ever raised in Scotland by a second-string English army; the king himself and a large proportion of the ruling elite were killed. The realm now had a king who was an infant of seventeen months, son of James IV and Henry VIII's sister, Margaret, a woman whose marital exploits and irresponsible ambitions were only just bettered by her brother, but whose position made her an unavoidable force in Scottish politics; while that brother, ruler of Scotland's "auld inemie," bent on winning glory by emulating the mightiest of English medieval kings, might well take time off from playing Henry V in France to revive the ambitions of two other predecessors, Edward I and Edward III, and claim overlordship of an all too vulnerable Scotland.

Ninety years later, in 1603, it was a very different matter. A jubilant Scottish king, James VI, finally shattered the old English imperialist dream when he arrived in London as James I, king of England. Now it was Scottish morale that was high; English morale—thanks to Elizabeth's relentless determination to leave no heir of her body—was low. Yet both these images, the misery of 1513 and the joy of 1603, are something of a mirage. Paradoxically, it was the weakened Scotland of 1513 that was to recover its strengths as the pushy little northern kingdom that made its insistent mark on European affairs, the vibrant Scotland of 1603 that was to suffer the sad and inevitable decline into marginalization and neglect. For it was the independent kingdom of Scotland that defied all the normal rules of wealth and power that underpinned successful states and flourished, the Scotland that became one of the multiple kingdoms of the British Isles that lost its role and, with it, its self-conceived prestige.

Flodden Field was in fact a temporary setback in a period when, most unusually, an English king was jealous of his northern neighbor. The megalomaniac and bombastic Henry VIII, passionately anxious to be the model of the "Renaissance prince," found to his horror when he succeeded in 1509 that a distinguished court culture was to be found in Edinburgh rather than London. It was a Scottish poet, Gavin Douglas, who in c. 1513 produced the first translation within the British Isles of Vergil's *Aeneid*. James IV had the poet of towering talent, William Dunbar, Henry VIII only the old-fashioned and grumpy John Skelton; when Henry VIII in 1514 wanted a flyting for the entertainment of his court, copying the Scottish example, the best he could produce for his verse quarrel were Skelton and a gentleman usher not noted for his poetic output, Christopher Garnesch,

and the result wholly failed to match the brilliance of the flyting of Dunbar and Walter Kennedy of 1507. Small wonder that Skelton loathed the Scots, and turned his undoubted talent for invective against them in his three anti-Scottish poems of 1513 and a fourth in 1524; more important, it is a revealing fact that Henry, who had to wait for almost two decades before he had, in Thomas Wyatt, a poet who could rival Dunbar, found Skelton of use only in the art of Scot-bashing, and indeed put on his version of Scottish flyting a year after he had so decisively defeated the Scots in battle. And it was not only the Scottish court that inflamed Henry VIII. James IV was an enthusiastic builder of ships. His mightiest was the "Great Michael"—"the greattest scheip . . . that ewer saillit in Ingland or France"—completed in 1512. This time an envious English king did not wait; 1512 saw the construction of his "Henri Grace a Dieu," built almost to the same specifications.

In literary culture, in ships, so also in architecture did the Scottish monarchy aim high. James IV and James V never got near to rivalling the number of palaces built by Henry VIII—more than fifty. But what they did build, at Linlithgow, Edinburgh Castle, Holyrood, Stirling, and Falkland was elaborate and impressive, and showed a far more focused European awareness than the eclectic and rather more insular creations of Henry VIII. The main external influence, particularly in James V's buildings, was French. But one has to look as far east as the Wawel palace in Krakow to find a parallel, in scale and size, to the remarkable "Stirling Heads," huge carved oak medallions depicting real and mythical figures that decorated the ceiling of James's presence chamber at Stirling.

Such things are a far better clue to the nature of early sixteenth-century Scotland than the "once-off" disaster of Flodden. But it was not just grandiose image-making by the monarchy that gave Scotland its self-confidence. The immediate consequence of Flodden, the death of a successful adult king, and the accession of a young child, which meant a lengthy minority, introduces another element in that self-confidence, the pragmatic nature of Scottish politics and the ability to keep things going in adverse circumstances. The 1513 battle was not the first time that defeat by the English had removed the king; David II had languished in England from 1346 until 1357, and James I from 1406 to 1424. Moreover, the Scots were well used to minorities, which had ushered in every reign since 1406; the Stuarts were a remarkably able line of kings, but they were also an intermittent line, and that resulted in what by contemporary standards was an

S

unusually low level of royal interventionism and a high degree of local autonomy that produced a substratum of local control mitigating the problems of the absence of effective royal rule. Equally, they were well used to defeat by the English; only once, at Bannockburn in 1314—the one Anglo-Scottish battle that had actually been crucial, and far more decisive than the great English victories at Agincourt or against the Armada—had they won. If an infant king and a defeat on the scale of Flodden could not exactly be shrugged off, therefore, they were at least not as fatal to the stability of the kingdom as might at first sight appear, and much less demoralizing than, for example, the English loss of France in the mid-fifteenth century and of Calais in the mid-sixteenth.

In the first half of the century the realm was in fact remarkably stable, particularly during the strong and effective personal rule of James V, when the crown continued to behave as its predecessors had done, as a leading force in Europe. But James's death immediately after another English defeat of the Scots, at Solway Moss in 1542, once again left an infant to succeed, this time a week-old baby with the added misfortune of being a girl. Moreover, there were new and menacing factors. This time Henry VIII did make a bid for Scotland, first by his attempt to marry his son, Edward, to the infant queen Mary and, when that failed, by launching the sustained and bloody campaigns against Scotland in 1544–1545 known as the Rough Wooing, and followed up after his death by protector Somerset's victory at the battle of Pinkie in 1547 and a renewed effort to unite England and Scotland. This threatening situation was drastically complicated by the advent of Reformation. James V had strenuously maintained the Catholic Church throughout his life. His death opened the way for the Protestant advance so much sought by the English crown. But the scale of English aggression turned even Protestant Scots back to their old ally, France; and the religious position remained in stalemate throughout Mary's minority, until the deaths of Mary Tudor and the regent and mother of Mary Queen of Scots. Moreover, the support of Mary of Guise, and the much more gentle backing given by Elizabeth I to the Scottish Protestant lords compared to the heavy-handed and offensive presence of French troops in Scotland, opened the way for the Protestant victory achieved in the Reformation Parliament of 1560.

The Scottish reforming movement was intensely radical from the beginning. Because for the first twenty-five years of its existence there was no effective monarch on the throne, it was able to maintain an anti-erastian stance that contrasted sharply with the church in England. There was no comparable royal supremacy; and the kirk was not subject to the doctrinal swings of the monarchy. From the mid-1580s, the period of James VI's adult rule, a major battle was fought between the king and the great Presbyterian reformer Andrew Melville and his followers over the powers of church and state: Was the king head of the church on earth, or was he merely a member of Christ's congregation and subject to ecclesiastical stricture? In practice, the issue turned on bishops, essential in the king's view for his authority, anathema to the Melvillians, whose vision of a pure church was one governed by a hierarchy of courts, from General Assembly to kirk session, and therefore more closely following the desired Calvinist model. Neither side wholly won. By 1603, James was well on the way to trouncing the Melvillians, but the church over which he presided in the last years of his life was an extraordinary hybrid, a Presbyterian church with bishops. Surprisingly, it was a compromise that worked well under the flexible James; it was his foolish son Charles I who would destroy it.

More generally, the very existence of the church courts, from national to local, were an immense source of strength. It enabled the kirk to keep a very tight grip on its members; kirk sessions maintained stringent controls over the ordinary sinners of the individual parishes. Yet if an obsessive moral harshness became the order of the day, the very determination and vitality of the kirk, compared to its pre-Reformation predecessor, was impressive and effective. The Calvinist faith put down deep roots in Scottish society, so deep that when in the seventeenth century in other parts of Europe Calvinism lost its dynamic force, Scotland remained a passionately Calvinist country.

At the same time, secular society was changing fast. In an age of inflation, and a notoriously spendthrift king, the Scots for the first time found themselves paying regular taxation to an increasingly intrusive government. The new faith had its own impact on that government, as the kirk withdrew its ministers from state service, leaving a gap filled by laymen now pushing their way into law and administration. As in England, vagrancy became an issue; the Calvinist response was to treat vagrants as offenders against the twin virtues of thrift and hard work, reflected in the harsh poor laws of 1574 and 1579. In the 1590s, Satan's minions, the witches, began to stalk the land. The initial group aimed very high indeed, at the king himself; this was the first outbreak of a series of witch-hunts, which were to make Scotland one of the great persecuting societies of the seventeenth century.

But it was not all gloom. To Scotland's three medieval universities, St. Andrews, Glasgow, and Aberdeen, were added a further two, Edinburgh and a second college at Aberdeen; indeed, an enthusiastic Aberdeenshire laird tried to found a sixth, which failed. Nevertheless, this was an impressive commitment to education paralleled by the Reformers' drive for a school in every parish; Scotland, in attitude and achievement, had begun to outstrip England, and would continue to do so until the nineteenth century. At the end of the century as at the beginning, the king's court became a center of talent and distinguished culture, distinctively Scottish and also open to European and English influence. Bands of English players were invited north to Scotland by the future king of Britain. There was, therefore, much in which to take pride when the greatest morale boost of all occurred in 1603 and Scotland sent its king to England.

BIBLIOGRAPHY

Donaldson, G. *Scotland: James V–James VII.* 1965.

Lynch, M. *Scotland: A New History.* 1991.

Mason, R., ed. *Scotland and England.* 1987.

Smout, T.C. *A History of the Scottish People.* 1971.

Wormald, J. *Court, Kirk, and Community: Scotland 1470–1625.* 1981.

Jenny Wormald

SEE ALSO

Calvinism; Church of Scotland; Douglas, Gavin; Dunbar, William; Erastianism; Flodden Field; Henry VIII; James IV; James V; James VI and I; Margaret Tudor; Mary Queen of Scots; Melville, Andrew; Seymour, Edward; Skelton, John

Sculpture

In early Tudor England sculpture was almost entirely religious and included both the ornamentation of church furniture and the making of funeral monuments. Reformation iconoclasm ended the sculptural ornamentation of church buildings and furniture, but the market for funeral sculpture increased, and the building of the period's many great houses created a substantial new market for secular work.

Sculptural production before the Reformation was almost entirely governed by ritual practices. The output of carved woodwork, in the form of bench ends, stalls, misericords, and screens, was particularly significant, and at major regional centers like Ripon, production could be

Monument to the Duchess of Somerset (d. 1584). Westminster Abbey, London. By permission of the National Monuments Record.

organized on a large scale. Woodcarvers also provided the dominant images in church interiors: the carved and painted rood groups of the Virgin, St. John, and the crucified Christ. These formed an important focus of lay piety. The numerous saint-cults of the period fueled the demand for further statues. The alabaster workshops of Nottinghamshire and Derbyshire were important centers for the production of carved altarpieces and small mass-produced devotional images for private use. Little of this devotional sculpture survived the iconoclastic movements of the sixteenth and seventeenth centuries. More remains, however, of early Tudor sepulchral monuments. Many of these commemorated their subjects in engraved brass, but the wealthier landowners and high-ranking ecclesiastics often favored sculpted monuments, the most prestigious of which were carved from alabaster in the midlands workshops that also dominated the trade in high-quality tomb-making.

The typical early Tudor monument conformed to a long-established pattern consisting of recumbent life-sized effigies on top of a rectangular tomb chest. The chests are

S

frequently embellished with "weepers," figures echoing the mourners who accompanied the coffin at the funeral ritual, and with shields of arms, often supported by angels. The effigies are not portraits but generalized representations of the subject as in life, with careful attention given to the details of dress and armor that indicated the subjects' social rank. They invariably face east, eyes open and hands joined in prayer, in expectation of the Second Coming. The spiritual function of such images was to sustain the memory of the deceased in the prayers of the living, in the hope of gaining relief from the pains of Purgatory. Inscriptions on tombs directly address the spectators, reminding them of their own inevitable mortality and soliciting their intercession—an appeal addressed visually in a number of tombs that incorporate representations of the subject as a cadaver or skeleton. This memento mori motif is also found on brasses of the period. Because only the rich and powerful could command burial sites near the high altar or in private family chapels adjoining the chancel, however, such tombs were also emphatic reminders of the realities of temporal power.

In chantries like those of Prince Arthur in Worcester Cathedral (d. 1502, begun 1504) or Bishop Alcock in Ely Cathedral (d. 1500, begun 1488), the tomb is housed in a separate vaulted enclosure providing supports for additional sculptures, usually of the patron's favored saints. Henry VII's new chapel at Westminster Abbey, begun in 1503, was the most magnificent chantry project of the early Tudor period. Built to house the tombs of himself, his queen, and his mother in close proximity to the tombs of generations of English kings and queens, it was designed as a powerful assertion of the legitimacy of the Tudor succession. The ambitious sculptural program of the interior, the best surviving ensemble of late medieval figure sculpture in England, represents "all the holie companie of heven" to whose special mediations Henry entrusted his soul, but equally prominent are the Tudor emblems of portcullis and rose repeated over the interior and exterior surfaces of the chapel, underlining its role as dynastic mausoleum. These are further repeated, together with heraldic beasts and saints, in the bronze grille which surrounds the sumptuous double tomb of Henry and Elizabeth of York. The grille, and probably much of the figure sculpture, was the work of Flemish craftsmen, but the black touchstone and white marble tomb with its gilt bronze effigies was commissioned from the Florentine sculptor Pietro Torrigiano, who also worked on the tomb of Lady Margaret Beaufort. Torrigiano's tombs are notable for introducing Italian Renaissance detail and motifs into

English sculpture, principally on the tomb chests embellished with pilasters, naked putti, and circular garlands, and in the bronze child angels seated at the four corners of the King's monument. Nevertheless the overall design is orthodox, especially in the use of gilt bronze effigies, echoing those on many of the earlier royal tombs at Westminster. Torrigiano may also have made the extraordinarily vivid painted terracotta bust of Henry VII (Victoria and Albert Museum, London), one of only a very few examples of portrait sculpture in Tudor England. The face was probably modeled from a death mask, such as that incorporated into the (still partially surviving) wood and plaster effigy of the King used at his funeral ceremony.

By the 1520s and 1530s, Franco-Italian Renaissance motifs were being employed in a range of sculptural projects, most notably in the great screen at King's College, Cambridge, of the early 1530s, and, on a smaller scale, in the terra-cotta screens of the Bedingfield Chantry at Oxburgh (Norfolk) or on the de la Warr Chantry at Boxgrove Priory (Sussex), where gothic structural elements are overlaid with "anticke" details.

The effects of the Reformation laws against images left the sepulchral monument as the only legitimate occasion of figure sculpture in English, and for the remainder of the century tomb-making was the principal focus of sculptural activity. Elizabethan sculptors increasingly drew on the vocabulary of northern European renaissance design, known from engravings and pattern books, but this stylistic transformation of funeral sculpture was accompanied by an even more significant transformation in function and meaning. Protestant theorists developed a justification for monuments that stressed their didactic value as moral exemplars, permanent reminders of virtue and honor. In practice the monuments commissioned by Elizabethan nobility, and, more and more, by the gentry and professional classes, emphasized the dignity and status of family and lineage through displays of heraldry and through inscriptions recording marriage alliances, offices, and achievements.

Stripped of overtly religious imagery and of exhortations to intercessory prayer, the traditional architectural and iconographic formulas were reworked for a Protestant culture. The freestanding tomb chest with recumbent effigies retained its ancient authority, and continued to be commissioned throughout the period, although, in an adaptation characteristic of the new emphasis on lineage, figures representing the children of the deceased occupy the place of the angels and mourners of the pre-Reformation tomb. Typical of the later Elizabethan period are the large architectural wall tombs, sometimes reaching enormous heights, where the effigies are set within an arched recess framed by classical columns. These are particularly associated with the workshops of refugee Netherlandish sculptors who settled in Southwark in the 1560s and who quickly supplanted the Midlands alabasterers in the market for high-quality monuments. The monument to the duchess of Somerset (d. 1587) in Westminster Abbey is a characteristic example of Southwark work, with its tiers of coupled columns, strapwork cartouche, big top achievement, and prominent use of obelisks, a much-used device that symbolized eternity. The rich coloring of the monument, both in the contrasts of different colored stone and in the painting and gilding of effigy, crests, and shields, is also typical of the period.

Greater diversity in monument types is evident in the last decades of the sixteenth century, particularly in the more "active" interpretation of the effigy. Kneeling, reclining, and much more rarely, preaching figures can be found on a range of Elizabethan tombs; an early example of this last type is the small wall monument to Laurence Humphrey (d. 1590) in Magdalen College Chapel, Oxford. Sometimes, however, the effigy is dispensed with altogether and the family arms form the chief focus of the monument. The most successful of the new formulae employed kneeling figures of husband and wife facing each other across a prayer desk, often with kneeling children ranked behind their parents or set in relief panels in a lower register. The flexibility of this format, which could be scaled up or down, made it particularly adaptable to the needs of different social ranks, and monuments of this type proliferated all over Elizabethan England.

Secular uses for sculpture were, during most of the Tudor period, largely confined to architectural or interior decoration. In the earliest Tudor domestic work exterior sculpture was predominantly heraldic and was typically concentrated on the principal entrances and oriel windows of great houses. From the 1520s onwards the new "anticke" motifs imported from Italy and France were absorbed within these native traditions of hierarchical ornamentation. At Hengrave Hall (Suffolk, 1538) Italianate putti support shields of arms on the porch oriel, and at Wolsey's Hampton Court the gatehouses were embellished in 1521 with Giovanni da Maiano's terracotta roundels of Roman emperors' heads, evoking classical busts or medals. Variants on this bust motif are found later in the century at Longleat and at Wollaton Hall. Few Elizabethan houses were as exuberant in their exterior treatment as Wollaton, and ornamental sculpture was

more commonly focused on the interior, its chief vehicle being the large architectural chimneypiece with carved overmantel, the most elaborate incorporating caryatids and mythological figures as well as heraldic devices. These could be the work of the plasterer as much as the wood or stone carver, as for example, at Hardwick Hall (1590s), where some of the overmantels were modeled by the same craftsman who supplied the richly figured plaster friezes of the High Great Chamber. Garden statuary provided the only significant genre of freestanding sculpture. Fountains and statues of emblematic and mythical figures, such as those recorded at Nonesuch in the 1590s, were erected in a number of important Elizabethan gardens, but few of these now remain.

BIBLIOGRAPHY
Lindley, Philip. *Gothic to Renaissance: Essays on Sculpture in England.* 1995.
Llewellyn, Nigel. *The Art of Death: Visual Culture in the English Death Ritual c. 1500–c. 1800.* 1991.
Whinney, Margaret. *Sculpture in Britain, 1530–1830.* 1964; 2nd edition, John Physick, ed., 1988.

Louise Durning

SEE ALSO
Architecture; Beaufort, Margaret; Gardens; Hardwick, Elizabeth; Henry VII; Reformation, English; Royal Palaces; Wollaton Hall

Senecanism

An aspect of English (indeed European) Humanism, Senecanism is based on uses of the works of Lucius Anneas Seneca, the first-century Roman moralist (and tutor of the Emperor Nero). Senecanism matured in the closing decades of the Tudor period and, peaking under the early Stuarts, was intimately associated with the simultaneous emergence of Neostoicism, as well as being closely associated with Tacitism (a political outlook based on readings of the first-century Roman historian, Tacitus). To distinguish Senecanism as distinct from these and apart from the humanist endeavor is almost artificial, although certain strains deserving the adjective Senecan can be isolated. The starting point lies with the growing availability of Seneca's writings.

The moral essays and epistles had been known throughout the Middle Ages, but their impact on Tudor England came, in the first place, from the application to them of the "new learning" by Desiderius Erasmus, who

S

sought to expunge from the writings of antiquity the corruptions and emendations produced by medieval scholarship. Erasmus's first full edition of Seneca (1515) was prepared during his stay in England; it was followed in 1529 by a corrected edition, and later, in 1585, the French scholar in exile at Rome, Marc-Antoine Muret, produced another, superior, edition. This cycle of scholarship was not completed until 1605, when the Flemish scholar, Justus Lipsius, published the *Opera Omnia* that remained authoritative for almost two centuries and was the basis for the first complete English translation of Seneca's works by Thomas Lodge (which did not appear, however, until 1614). In the meantime, the moral treatise *De remediis fortuitorum* had been available in English since 1547 (trans. Robert Whyttington) and an English version of *De beneficiis* (trans. Arthur Golding) appeared in 1579.

From these philological endeavors, Senecanism first manifested itself in the area of rhetoric. Champions of Seneca pitted his pithy, clipped style against the copious, rounded prose of Cicero, which was the standard in the universities but in which, according to the famous criticism leveled by Francis Bacon, "words are valued more than matter." Ciceronian rhetorical flourish was attacked throughout the sixteenth century: Erasmus's *Ciceronianus* of 1528 saw the beginnings of a campaign that was continued by Muret in Rome, and by Lipsius in the Low Countries; in England the attack was taken up by the Cambridge scholar Gabriel Harvey (in his 1577 version of *Cicerionianus*). Senecan prose style, if properly understood in the context of Tudor England (and sixteenth-century Europe), is better called "Silver Latin," for other exemplars included Plutarch and Tacitus. But as a rhetorical method it was applied throughout learning and as a pedagogical tool.

Yet rhetoric was not just an academic discipline. In the humanist scheme, eloquence and wisdom went hand in hand, and the distinctiveness of Senecanism concerned the lessons to be extracted from Senecan utterances. Surviving commonplace books are filled with "sentences" (or axioms) on the qualities of an upright life, on the virtue of civic participation, on the role of friendship in an individual's life, on withstanding the vicissitudes of fortune, and so on, mostly derived from Seneca's original moral writings. The compatibility of Seneca's practical philosophy with Christianity had been a staple for centuries, but in the aftermath of the Reformation the Roman stoicism most explicitly set forth by Seneca was seen as offering real consolation and guidance to many facing the new ethical dilemmas provoked by the religious and political divisions of the day.

The outstanding exemplar here was Lipsius. In 1584, he published his Latin dialogue, *De constantia,* which applied Senecanism to the current context, and in the process introduced a new form of stoicism to Europe. It was a runaway best-seller and was immediately translated into most European vernaculars. The English translation (by John Stradling) did not appear until 1595, suggesting how well the Latin edition itself was received. Lipsius also composed a hugely popular advice book for princes, the *Politica* (1589), in which Senecan morality and Tacitist (indeed, Machiavellian) political realism were completely interwoven. Meanwhile, in France, Montaigne adopted the sententious, aphoristic style and through his *Essais* (1580) produced a vernacular version of Senecanism that was widely admired and emulated; Bacon adopted the same technique in English and in 1595 published his own collection of *Essayes,* borrowing his title from Montaigne but maintaining in the second and expanded edition (of 1612) that Seneca's Epistles themselves were nothing other than essays. As the Epistle, too, came into greater vogue, these literary forms became vehicles for questioning the merits of received traditions and dogmas, for discussing how best to conduct one's life, and whether, in the midst of pervasive political change and religious upheaval, to remain actively engaged in governance.

Rhetorical and philosophical Senecanism flowed, as well, through the streams of Tudor drama. Seneca's plays were translated between 1560 and 1581; and if Seneca's influence on Elizabethan drama is no longer as central as once believed, it still permeated it, parting ways, perhaps, because English dramatists of the period could not, in the end, be consciously pagan. In his own tragedies Seneca treated with pessimistic conclusions issues of human vice and betrayal, the capricious nature of fortune, and the vulnerablity of human virtue, themes that in the 1580s and 90s infused the "closet drama" written by Samuel Daniel, Fulke Greville, and others—so-called because such plays were supposedly not intended to be performed (Senecan drama, however, was written and performed in Latin, in the universities). Senecan language, forms, and outlook are to be particularly noted in the writings of members of Robert Devereux, the Earl of Essex's, circle. After the fiasco of Essex's rebellion, which resulted in his execution, the trend deepened, as Seneca, his classical counterparts, and their contemporary mediators were perceived by the survivors to offer the means by which to meditate on the changing nature of English politics. Sir William Cornwallis's *Essaies* of

1601 were written in this spirit, and in the same year he also published his *Discourse Upon Seneca the Tragedian,* which considered the relevance of Senecan phrases for the contemporary statesman.

Senecanism was not, however, whole-heartedly embraced by all. Seneca was no longer taken as the crypto-Christian portrayed by the medieval scholars as a number of them harangued against his (and his imitators') clipped, hopping language, others warned against his fundamentally pagan morality. These criticisms were taken seriously by Joseph Hall, who in 1603 was a young clergyman and aspiring moralist. He was soon to become recognized as the "English Seneca" for following Seneca as a philosopher but going beyond him as a Christian, as he put it in the preface to *Heaven Upon Earth* (1606). As the Tudor dynasty made way for the Stuarts, Senecanism was about to be rendered totally domestic and to become enfolded within an English, Protestant tradition in the making.

BIBLIOGRAPHY

Costa, C.D.N., ed. *Seneca.* 1974.

Croll, Morris. *"Attic" and Baroque Prose Style: The Anti-Ciceronian Movement.* J. Max Patrick and Robert O. Evans, eds. 1966.

McCrea, Adriana. *Constant Minds: Political Virtue and the Lipsian Paradigm in England, 1584–1650.* 1997.

Salmon, J.H.M. "Stoicism and Roman Example: Seneca and Tacitus in Jacobean England." *Journal of the History of Ideas,* vol. 50, pp. 199–225.

Todd, Margo. *Christian Stoicism and the Puritan Social Order.* 1987.

Adriana McCrea

SEE ALSO
Bacon, Francis; Cornwallis, William; Ciceronianism; Daniel, Samuel; Devereux, Robert; Drama, History of; Erasmus, Desiderius; Greville, Fulke; Hall, Joseph; Harvey, Gabriel; Humanism; Rhetoric

Sermons

The decades of the Tudor age saw dramatic transformations in the sermon as an oratorical form, an occasion of public gathering, a vehicle of religious teaching, and a site for theological and political controversy. An important part of religious observation in the late medieval period, the sermon assumed even greater significance during the English Reformation as reformers included both the form and content of medieval preaching and its infrequency of practice among their major charges against the medieval church and then with state direction sought to proclaim new doctrines through official homilies. The reformed English church saw the sermon take on political and cultural significance as a major form of social commentary and become an issue in the growing division between defenders of the establishment and supporters of greater reform. By the death of Elizabeth I, English pulpit oratory was entering into a golden age that would in turn provoke even more opposition.

The task of preaching is at heart the exposition of scriptural meaning and its application to the world of the auditor. Preaching is thus fundamentally an oratorical task, with the sermon experienced primarily as a work to be delivered and heard, although the increasing popularity of sermons, and of specific preachers known for their homiletic effectiveness, did lead by the end of Elizabeth's reign to a significant market for printed sermons, either in volumes devoted to a single sermon or to collections of sermons related to a specific topic or representative of the preaching style of a popular preacher. The purpose of preaching was thus variously justified in the Tudor period, with some supporters encouraging preaching for its appeal to the mind, as the most effective way to educate layfolk in the meaning and practice of the Christian life, or to inform them of the content of Christian doctrine. Others saw the role of the preacher more evangelistically, with the heart or the feelings as the focus of appeal, with the sermon intended to encourage rejection of false teaching, or to provoke repentance, or to arouse devotion.

Actual homiletic practice during the reigns of Henry VII and Henry VIII is often obscured by Reformation polemic, which characterized ordinary late medieval clergy as unlettered and incapable of preaching, and clergy who were learned enough to preach as deliberately obscurantist and fanciful in homiletic content because they used allegorical and symbolic methods of biblical exegesis. Nevertheless, for the more representative parish priest preaching was but one of several duties including saying Mass, hearing confession, and celebrating the other sacraments, as well as teaching the content of the faith. More learned clergy preached actively and traveled for the purpose; but people flocked to their sermons often as much because they sought an occasion for a social gathering as an opportunity for theological instruction.

The phenomenon of extraliturgical preaching, which was to persist throughout the Tudor age, was thus already entrenched in the reigns of Henry VII and his son. Clergy trained in the scholastic mode of exegesis did interpret

S

Scripture according to the traditional four-fold exegetical precepts for providing the literal, tropological, allegorical, and anagogical meanings of the text. In the early Tudor period, this approach was complemented by producers of preaching handbooks that offered short model homilies on specific points of church doctrine and the practice of personal piety. Erasmus, John Colet, George Stafford, and other advocates of the New Learning promoted the importance of preaching as both affective and informative.

This approach was affirmed by the first generation of English reformers who criticized the medieval church for its willingness to accept unlearned clergy and settle for a laity uninformed about the meaning of the rituals, which they observed the clergy performing or through which they shaped their own piety. A major theme of the English Reformation was education of laity, as well as of clergy left over from the former dispensation, and so basic documents of the Reformation included the Bible in English (1539), the Book of Common Prayer (1549), and the Book of Homilies (1547). This latter text contained twelve sermons that espouse reading the Bible, affirming justification by "a true and lively faith," performing good works of charity that reveal that one has the true and lively faith and form of Christian life that leads to salvation, avoiding the private devotional practices of the old religion, and rejecting sins against the commonwealth such as perjury, rebellion, adultery, and disobedience.

Support for or opposition to the reformation of religion divided clergy, leading to the practice of episcopal licensing of clergy to preach and prohibition of some clergy from preaching. Those supportive of the new religion were encouraged to promote it from the pulpit, and Hugh Latimer, John Hooper, and Thomas Lever, among others, developed reputations in the reign of Edward as effective preachers to learned and unlearned audiences alike. Like the official Homilies, their sermons adopted a plain style and straightforward structure and organization and often employed imagery drawn from rural or working-class life to make their points. Clergy deemed unable to preach sermons supporting the reformed faith, either because they were uneducated or illiterate or because they supported the old religion, were required to read these official Homilies, one each Sunday and Holy Day, in the order they appeared in the Book of Homilies.

Even though the Edwardian Book of Homilies was augmented by an additional twenty sermons in the Elizabethan Book of Homilies (1563), the discipline of a steady diet of official sermons must have become tiresome with time; Rosalind may reflect lay fatigue in her request

to Orlando that he tell her "what tedious homily of love have you wearied your parishioners withal, O most gentle pulpiter" (*AYLI*, III.ii. 155–157).

Nevertheless the Elizabethan period saw the sermon become a chief means through which the desire of the Geneva party for further reform came to clash with the efforts of the hierarchy to maintain the Church of England as a national church with room for a diversity of theological emphases and spiritual disciplines. Attempts to continue regional gatherings of clergy planned by Thomas Cranmer during Edward's reign for the purpose of continuing education so that clergy could become more effective preachers were squashed by Elizabeth in 1579 because she saw them as occasions for the spread of religious dissent. Archbishop Edmund Grindal protested; the queen suspended him from his duties.

The sermon also began to reflect cultural and social differences. Clergy supportive of the establishment drew on Ciceronian standards of eloquence and a range of learned references to support the emerging ideal of *Ecclesia Anglicana* as a *via media* between Geneva and Rome before audiences able to appreciate their learning and style. Clergy desiring further reform on the Genevan model employed a carefully planned simplicity of style and plainness of diction to appeal for popular support for their plans. Sometimes different approaches achieved their own kind of balance; Richard Hooker and Walter Travers performed their struggle for Mastership of the Temple in the same chapel, so that according to Thomas Fuller, "Here the pulpit spake pure Canterbury in the morning, and Geneva in the afternoon."

By the end of Elizabeth's reign, the sermon was well established as a major social phenomenon, such that specific preachers attained popular followings, and extraliturgical preaching events like the regular sermons at Paul's Cross became major public gatherings to which people flocked for news and for the particular entertainment of theological and political controversy. In addition, the idea that regular worship would include a sermon was firmly established; thus there were more occasions to preach and to listen. Clergy like Henry Smith had become well-known public figures as a result of their homiletic skills, a notoriety enhanced by the popularity of printed sermons, which numbered in the many hundreds in the late years of the sixteenth century. When Lancelot Andrewes began to preach at St. Giles's in Cripplegate in 1589, and was named Dean of Westminster Abbey in 1601, all was ready both for the eloquence of metaphysical preaching and for the violent reaction against it.

S

BIBLIOGRAPHY

Blench, J.W. *Preaching in England in the late Fifteenth and Sixteenth Centuries.* 1964.

Bond, Ronald, ed. *Certain Sermons or Homilies.* 1987.

Booty, John E., David Siegenthaler, and John N. Wall. *The Godly Kingdom of Tudor England: Great Books of the English Reformation.* 1981.

Davies, Horton. *Like Angels from a Cloud: the English Metaphysical Preachers, 1588–1645.* 1986.

———. *Worship and Theology in England, 1534–1603.* 1970.

Duffy, Eamon. *The Stripping of the Altars: Traditional Religion in England, 1400–1580.* 1992.

Herr, Alan *The Elizabethan Sermon: A Survey and a Bibliography.* 1940.

MacLure, Millar. *The Paul's Cross Sermons, 1534–1642.* 1958.

Shuger, Debora Kuller. *Habits of Thought in the English Renaissance: Religion, Politics, and the Dominant Culture.* 1990.

Thomas, Keith. *Religion and the Decline of Magic.* 1971.

John N. Wall

SEE ALSO

Andrewes, Lancelot; Bible Translations; Book of Common Prayer; Calvinism; Church of England; Cranmer, Thomas; Grindal, Edmund; Homilies, Books of; Hooker, Richard; Hooper, John; Latimer, Hugh; Paul's Cross Sermons; Reformation, English; Smith, Henry; Travers, Walter

Sexual Offenses

Before the Reformation sexual offenses fell largely under the jurisdiction of the church and were tried in ecclesiastical courts. Rape had always belonged to the secular courts, carrying the death penalty, and other serious offenses were made felonies by acts of Parliament in 1533 and 1563 (sodomy) and 1604 (bigamy). The secular courts also prosecuted prostitutes and bawds, and in 1576, justices of the peace were authorized to punish bastard-bearers and their partners. Incest, fornication, and adultery remained ecclesiastical offenses, and were punished by humiliating public penance, in which the offender, garbed in a white sheet, begged forgiveness before God and the community in the parish church.

While the Tudor machinery of sexual regulation was harsh, courts and local officials operated with considerable pragmatism and moderation. There were very few indictments for the more serious offenses, and skeptical juries frequently threw them out or acquitted those accused. Although convicted rapists were likely to be hanged, juries demanded conclusive evidence of guilt, and many rape victims undoubtedly chose not to press charges. Cases of sodomy and buggery very rarely reached the courts, which then often exercised discretion by imposing lesser penalties. Bigamy was relatively common in an age that offered no provision for divorce and remarriage, though a considerable number of offenders were people who had separated and believed or hoped that their first spouse was dead. Incest was more broadly defined than today, covering sexual relations or marriage between people within the prohibited degrees, and some offenses were committed in ignorance of their precise scope. Only sexual relations between parents and children or with siblings or in-laws aroused popular repugnance, and while incest featured prominently in Elizabethan and Jacobean tragedy, it was not an issue of widespread concern.

The true level of sexual offenses is impossible to ascertain. There was certainly a substantial "dark figure" of undetected or unreported offenses, especially in the case of fornication and adultery. Neighbors and churchwardens often preferred to settle matters informally, prosecuting only when offenders had ignored warnings and flouted public opinion, or when an unmarried woman became pregnant. Even those presented might escape punishment, if they denied the charges and could find respectable neighbors ("compurgators") to swear to their good character. But the court hearing served to give warning that they were under suspicion, and was often enough in itself to secure the primary goal of ending a suspicious liaison. Despite the "dark figure" it would be wrong to paint a picture of widespread sexual promiscuity. Parish registers suggest that in 1600, only about 3 percent of births were illegitimate, a very low figure given the late age of marriage and the lack of effective contraception. Sexual intercourse between couples intending to marry, also fornication in the church's eyes, was widely practiced and condoned among the population at large. As many as 20 percent of brides were pregnant at the time of their marriage.

Professional prostitution was largely confined to London and its suburbs. Before the Reformation there were some licensed brothels, but attitudes hardened, and in 1546, the public "stews" in Southwark were suppressed by royal proclamation. Although some brothels survived, bawdy houses were far more common, with a male or female bawd procuring women on an *ad hoc* basis for their clients, often using a tavern or victualing house as cover. The women

Sexual Offenses 637

S

might be maidservants out of service, or married to small tradesmen and laborers. The London Bridewell, established in 1553, waged a vigorous campaign against prostitution, but its efforts were doomed by the huge demand from apprentices and others, including hangers-on at court, and the plentiful supply of vulnerable young women flocking to London to seek work. Provincial prostitution, on a very much smaller scale, was generally casual and opportunistic.

Attitudes toward sexual transgressions varied over time and across the social spectrum. The most enduring element was the "double standard" of morality that regarded women's sexuality as the property of fathers or husbands, so that a sexual lapse by a woman was a crippling badge of shame while male lapses were often regarded as relatively minor. Similarly, a wife's infidelity provided grounds for the husband to turn her away, but not vice versa. Many noblemen and gentlemen felt little shame in fathering bastards, and some even mentioned them in their wills, though this became much less common later in the century. By 1600, concern over the growing burden of the poor, sometimes reinforced by Puritan religious zeal, was making many parish clergy and churchwardens more willing to present sexual offenders. Single mothers were now almost certain to be prosecuted before the church courts, and increasingly likely also to be sentenced to a whipping by the secular courts. Overall, however, popular pragmatism and common sense continued to modify the zeal of reformers and the harshness of the law.

BIBLIOGRAPHY

Bray, Alan. *Homosexuality in Renaissance England.* 1995.

Griffiths, Paul. "The structure of prostitution in Elizabethan London." *Continuity and Change,* vol. 8, pp. 39–63.

Ingram, Martin. *Church Courts, Sex, and Marriage in England, 1570–1640.* 1987.

Thomas, Keith. "The double standard." *Journal of the History of Ideas,* vol. 20, pp. 195–216.

Bernard S. Capp

SEE ALSO

Gender; Homosexuality; Justice of the Peace; Marriage and Marriage Law; Southwark

Seymour, Edward, Duke of Somerset (c. 1506–1552)

Edward Seymour, eldest surviving son of Sir John Seymour of Wolf Hall, Wiltshire, and Margery, daughter of Sir Henry Wentworth, is said to have received a university education at Oxford and Cambridge. He began a military career in 1523 with service in France and the following year became an esquire in the household of Henry VIII, but the marriage of his sister, Jane, to Henry VIII in 1536 led to a more rapid ascent. Seymour was created Viscount Beauchamp (1536) and subsequently earl of Hertford (1537). In 1536, he was admitted to the Privy Council. The death of Queen Jane did not impede his advancement at court, and he received extensive land grants and offices of responsibility through the king's favor. During the 1540s, military commands in Scotland, where his forces burned and pillaged Edinburgh, and in France made Seymour one of the most powerful nobility. In religious affairs he identified with the Reformers and benefited from their influence. The fall of Thomas Howard, duke of Norfolk, and disfavor of Stephen Gardiner, bishop of Winchester, at the end of the reign of Henry VIII paved the way for his appointment as lord protector when his nephew, Edward VI, succeeded to the throne in 1547.

At the beginning of the new reign Seymour became duke of Somerset, and as protector governed the country on behalf of the nine-year-old king. Family problems troubled his efforts to rule as conflict with his younger brother, Thomas, Lord Seymour of Sudeley, led to the latter's execution. Somerset pursued a vigorous program of political, social, and religious reform, but his foreign policy followed along the lines of Henry VIII. While victory over the Scots at Pinkie brought him fame, his attempt to conquer and garrison Scotland was costly and provoked intervention by France. Protestant reforms and an attack on enclosures contributed to the outbreak of widespread popular rebellions in 1549 that undermined his authority and led to his removal from the office of lord protector. Briefly imprisoned in the Tower of London, he was subsequently released and restored to the king's council in April 1550. Efforts to regain authority formerly exercised as protector culminated in a second fall in April 1551. He was tried by his peers for treason, but the charge was amended to felony under a statute forbidding anyone from assembling twelve or more persons for the purpose of killing or imprisoning any member of the king's council. Of the latter offense he was convicted and sentenced to death. While Londoners hoped that the king would pardon his uncle, Somerset was beheaded on January 22, 1552. Alternatively defamed as an inept and rapacious authoritarian and praised as the "good duke" for his liberalism and popularity with the common people, Somerset was in reality a man of his own times who was created and destroyed by political, social, and religious forces that he could not control.

BIBLIOGRAPHY
Bush, M.L. *The Government Policy of Protector Somerset.* 1975.
Jordan, W.K. *Edward VI: The Young King.* 1968.
Pollard, A.F. *England under Protector Somerset.* 1900.

Barrett L. Beer

SEE ALSO
Edward VI; Gardiner, Stephen; Henry VIII; Howard, Thomas; Scotland, History of; Seymour, Thomas

Seymour, Thomas, Lord of Sudeley (c. 1508–1549)

Thomas Seymour was the fourth son of Sir John Seymour of Wolf Hall, Wiltshire, and Margery, daughter of Sir Henry Wentworth. The marriage of his sister, Jane, to Henry VIII in 1536 led to his rapid advancement at court. His career survived Jane's death in 1537 following the birth of her son, Prince Edward. The recipient of numerous land grants from the king, Seymour served with embassies to France, Germany, and the Netherlands. He also held military commands beginning in 1543 and was appointed master of the ordnance for life the following year. As admiral of the fleet, he resupplied Boulogne and defended the coast against the French. He was knighted for his service and five days before the king's death in 1547 became a privy councilor.

At the beginning of the reign of Edward VI, he was elevated to the peerage as Lord Seymour of Sudeley. He sought the hand of Princess Elizabeth, and according to other rumors also made advances to Princess Mary and Anne of Cleves, but his secret marriage to Henry VIII's widow, Queen Catherine Parr, only a few months after the king's death, identified him as a man of reckless ambition. After Catherine's death, he came increasingly into conflict with his brother, Edward, duke of Somerset, who became lord protector and governor of their nephew, Edward VI. Seymour regarded his own political position as unsatisfactory and sought greater influence with the young king. On the authority of hostile testimony collected after his arrest for treason, it appears that he tried to build up military support in local communities, win favor among the nobility to defy his brother, and get control of King Edward. Seymour was arrested in January 1549, interrogated extensively, and attainted by Parliament but never

brought to trial. Executed on March 19, 1549, he is a controversial figure who may have harbored no ill intentions against the state, but he exhibited behavior indicative of paranoia.

BIBLIOGRAPHY
Bernard, G.W. "The Downfall of Sir Thomas Seymour." In *The Tudor Nobility.* G.W. Bernard, ed. Pp. 212–240. 1992.
Maclean, John. *The Life of Sir Thomas Seymour, Knight, Baron Seymour of Sudeley, Lord High Admiral of England, and Master of the Ordnance.* 1869.
Smith, Lacey Baldwin. *Treason in Tudor England.* 1986.

Barrett L. Beer

SEE ALSO
Edward VI; Henry VIII; Parr, Catherine; Seymour, Edward; Treason

Shakespeare, William (1564–1616)

Poet and dramatist, actor and man of the theater, William Shakespeare was baptized in Holy Trinity Church, Stratford-upon-Avon, Warwickshire, on April 26, 1564. The exact date of his birth is unknown, but it is traditionally commemorated on April 23, which is also the date of his death. He was the eldest son of John Shakespeare, a glover and dealer in other commodities, who seems also to have practiced moneylending. In William's childhood John played a prominent part in local affairs, becoming bailiff (town mayor) and justice of the peace in 1568; later, his fortunes declined. He had married Mary Arden, who came from a higher social background, around 1557, and they had eight children, of whom four sons and one daughter survived childhood.

We know virtually nothing of Shakespeare's boyhood. John Shakespeare's position would have qualified his son to attend the King's New School, a reputable grammar school; its records are lost, but it has been amply demonstrated that the education lying behind Shakespeare's works is such as he could have acquired at the school. He appears to have continued to live in Stratford for some years, at least, after leaving school, probably at the age of around fifteen. On November 28, 1582, when he was eighteen, a bond was issued permitting him to marry Anne Hathaway of Shottery, a village close to Stratford. She was his senior by eight years, and pregnant. A daughter, Susanna, was baptized in Stratford on May 26, 1583, and twins, Hamnet (a form of Hamlet) and Judith, on

S

February 2, 1585. By this time Shakespeare was almost twenty-one. We do not know how he was employed in early manhood, though various legends grew up during the seventeenth century. John Aubrey (1626–1697) states that "he had been in his yonger yeares a Schoolmaster in the Countrey"; this is not implausible, but if, as is usually assumed, it means that he taught away from Stratford—perhaps in Lancashire, as a number of scholars, most notably Ernst Honigmann, have postulated—it leaves unexplained the years between leaving school and completing his family. We have no writings that can be confidently ascribed to his early years, with the possible exception of the poetically undistinguished and formally irregular Sonnet 145 which, Andrew Gurr has suggested, puns on the name Hathaway in the couplet: "'I hate' from hate away she threw, / And saved my life, saying 'not you'."

Nor do we know how, or in what capacity, Shakespeare entered the theater. Schoenbaum speculates that he may have joined the Queen's Men when they visited Stratford in 1587 shortly after one of the company had died of manslaughter, but this is no more than an intriguing possibility. The first printed allusion comes in 1592 in the pamphlet *Greene's Groatsworth of Wit* composed ostensibly by Robert Greene but possibly written or edited by Henry Chettle, and is oblique. Mention of "an vpstart Crow" who "supposes he is as well able to bombast out a blanke verse as the best of you" and who "is in his owne conceit the onely Shake-scene in a countrey" implies rivalry, and parody of a line from one of the most powerful episodes of the then-unpublished play apparently known in its own time as *The Second Part of the Contention*, but later printed as *Henry the Sixth Part Three*, suggests that, even if Shakespeare were an "vpstart," he was already well enough known on the theatrical scene, which centered on London, for the allusion to be recognized. The earliest clear evidence of Shakespeare's affiliation with a particular theater company comes on March 15, 1595, when he is named as joint payee of the Chamberlain's Men, a company formed a few months earlier for performances given at court during the previous Christmas season. He was to remain with this company for the rest of his working life, and seems to have been the only playwright of his time to have enjoyed so stable a relationship with a single company.

A number of legal records demonstrate that Shakespeare based his professional life in London (though as the name was not particularly uncommon we cannot be absolutely sure that all references are to the dramatist). In

1596, for example, one William Wayte petitioned for sureties of the peace against "Willm Shakspere" and others; in November 1597, someone of the same name, of Bishopsgate Ward in London, was listed as not having paid taxes due in February; and on October 1, 1598, he was named as a tax defaulter in the same ward. During the 1590s, too, allusions in works published in London demonstrate his growing reputation as both poet and dramatist. He is mentioned as the author of *The Rape of Lucrece* in Henry Willobie's *Willobie his Avisa* in 1594, and as "Sweet Shakespeare," in William Covell's *Polimanteia* in 1595. In 1598, he is listed as one of the "principall Comedians" in Ben Jonson's *Every Man in his Humour;* in the same year, too, his name appears for the first time on the title pages of any of his plays—the second quartos of *Richard II* and *Richard III* and the first (surviving) quarto of *Love's Labour's Lost;* his narrative poems are praised by Richard Barnfield in his *Poems in Divers Humours.* On May 16, 1599, the newly built Globe theater is mentioned as being in the possession of William Shakespeare and others. On May 13, 1602, an Inns of Court man, John Massingham, recorded a mildly scurrilous anecdote about Shakespeare and Burbage, the leading actor of his company, and in 1603, Shakespeare is listed among "The principall Tragoedians" in Ben Jonson's *Sejanus* and, along with other poets, is called on—apparently in vain—to lament the death of Queen Elizabeth I in Henry Chettle's *A mourneful Dittie, entituled Elizabeth's Losse.*

Along with these and other references to Shakespeare in London go others relating to his family and to his home town. In August 1596, his only son died and was buried there; two months later, John Shakespeare was granted a coat-of-arms, which gave him (and subsequently his son) the status of gentleman, though it was not until 1599 that John was permitted to impale his arms with those of the Arden family. In 1597, Shakespeare bought a substantial property, New Place, said to have been the second largest house in Stratford-upon-Avon. The purchase indicates that he was already very prosperous. There can be no doubt that he regarded New Place as home for him and his family; although he himself is generally said to have based his working life in London, it would not be surprising if he retreated to New Place as often as he could to work in peace. A succession of legal records indicate Shakespeare's continuing involvement with the town and its people. On October 15, 1598, for instance, Richard Quiney wrote to him asking for a loan of the very considerable sum of £30; his is

S

the only surviving item of Shakespeare's correspondence. The letter was preserved among Quiney's, not Shakespeare's, papers, so we cannot be sure that it was ever delivered, let alone whether the request was granted. In 1602, he consolidated his Stratford estates with the purchase, for £320, of land in Old Stratford, as well as buying a cottage in Chapel Lane. Allusions to Shakespeare in Stratford records continue to appear in the reign of James 1; for instance, in 1605, he paid £440 for an interest in a lease of tithes, and in 1614, he was involved in disputes relating to enclosures in the area—the subject of the play *Bingo*, by Edward Bond.

The earliest of Shakespeare's works that can be dated with any confidence are the two Ovidian narrative poems, *Venus and Adonis* and *The Rape of Lucrece*, published successively in 1593 and 1594 and each bearing a dedication, followed by Shakespeare's name, to Henry Wriothesley, the third earl of Southampton, who on this evidence, as well as that of later legend, may be regarded as Shakespeare's patron—though for how long and to what effect we cannot know. He has often been supposed to be the principal subject of Shakespeare's 154 sonnets, most of which may well have been written around 1593–1596, though there is reason to suppose that they may have been revised and reordered around 1602. Versions of two of them appeared without authorization in *The Passionate Pilgrim*, a collection published by William Jaggard in 1599 and ascribed to William Shakespeare, though it includes a number of poems certainly written by others. The rest of Shakespeare's sonnets remained unpublished until 1609. Continuing investigation of Southampton's life remains one of the more promising possible sources of additional information about Shakespeare. The only other work by Shakespeare certainly written for the press is the enigmatic and beautiful poem "The Phoenix and Turtle," published in 1601 in a collection of poems by a variety of writers in Robert Chester's *Love's Martyr*.

The dating of Shakespeare's plays presents many problems, and is particularly acute in the earlier part of his career. Dates of printing are of little help as many plays never reached print, and others did so only many years after being first performed; around half of Shakespeare's plays were first printed in the Folio of 1623, seven years after he died. From the start he seems to have been determined to succeed in a wide range of dramatic kinds. The three plays on the reign of Henry VI, best known by their Folio titles of *Henry VI Parts One, Two,* and *Three,* and their sequel, *Richard III,* are more ambitious than anything that precedes them and, in some ways, than Shake-

speare himself later essayed. Versions of Parts Two and Three were printed as *The First Part of the Contention betwixt the Famous Houses of York and Lancaster* (1594) and *The True Tragedy of Richard, Duke of York* (1595). There is reason to believe that Part One was the last to be written. A version of *Richard III* appeared in 1595. These are among his earliest works, as are the comedy *The Two Gentlemen of Verona* and the neo-Senecan tragedy *Titus Andronicus* (printed in 1594). Other early comedies are *The Taming of the Shrew,* the neo-Plautine *The Comedy of Errors* (acted at Gray's Inn in 1594), and *Love's Labour's Lost* (printed in 1598). All these plays appear to have been written by 1595.

Particularly difficult to date is *King John; Richard II,* printed in 1597, is usually dated around 1595. Both plays are written entirely in verse. For some years after this Shakespeare concentrated on comedy, in *A Midsummer Night's Dream* (first printed in 1600) and *The Merchant of Venice* (entered on the Stationers' Register in 1598 and printed in 1600), *The Merry Wives of Windsor* (related to the later history plays, and first printed in a corrupt text in 1602), *Much Ado About Nothing* (printed in 1600), *As You Like It* and *Twelfth Night,* probably written in 1600 or soon afterward. *Romeo and Juliet* (ascribed to the mid-1590s) is a tragedy with strongly comic elements, and the tetralogy begun with *Richard II* is completed by three comical histories, *Henry IV Parts One* and *Two,* each printed a year or two after composition (Part One, 1598, Part Two, 1600), and *Henry V,* almost certainly written in 1599 and printed in a short and suspect text in 1600. In 1598, Francis Meres, a minor writer, published *Palladis Tamia: Wit's Treasury,* mentioning twelve of the plays so far listed (assuming that by "Henry the 4" he means both parts) along with another not now known:

> As Plautus and Seneca are accounted the best for Comedy and Tragedy among the Latines: so Shakespeare among ye English is the most excellent in both kinds for the stage; for Comedy, witness his G(entleme) of Verona, his Errors, his Loue labors lost, his Loue labours wonne, his Midsummers night dreame, & his Merchant of Venice; for Tragedy, his Richard the 2. Richard the 3. Henry the 4. King Iohn, Titus Andronicus and his Romeo and Juliet.

Some of the plays named here had already been published or alluded to by 1598, but for others Meres supplies a date by which they must have been written. Meres also refers to Shakespeare's "sugard Sonnets among his priuate friends," which suggests that some at least of the poems

S

printed in 1609 were already circulating in manuscript, and praises the narrative poems. "Loue labours wonne" does not survive, but the occurrence of the title in a bookseller's list of around 1603 suggests that it reached print; there is no reference to it in the 1623 Folio. It may be an alternative title for one of the surviving plays, though no known edition of any of them supports this hypothesis.

Late in the century Shakespeare turned again to tragedy. A Swiss traveler, Thomas Platter, saw *Julius Caesar* at the Globe in September 1599. Hamlet apparently dates from a year or two later; it was entered on the register of the Stationers' Company in July 1602; a short, apparently memorially reconstructed text appeared in 1602, and a good text, apparently printed from Shakespeare's manuscript, in 1604. A play that defies easy classification is *Troilus and Cressida,* probably written in 1602, but not printed until 1609. The comedy *Measure for Measure* (played at court in December 1604) and the tragedy *Othello,* played at court in the previous month, are probably of this period; *All's Well that Ends Well* may come a little later.

Soon after the accession of James 1 in 1603, the company of players with which Shakespeare was associated came under his patronage as the King's Men; he remained with them for the rest of his career, which saw the composition of *King Lear, Macbeth, Timon of Athens, Antony and Cleopatra, Pericles, Coriolanus, The Winter's Tale, Cymbeline, The Tempest,* and, in collaboration with John Fletcher, the play printed in the Folio as *Henry VIII* but known before then as *All Is True, The Two Noble Kinsmen,* and the lost *Cardenio.* He signed the draft of his will in Stratford in March 1616 and died in April. His widow died in 1623, the year in which the Folio collection of his plays appeared, and his last surviving descendant, Elizabeth Hall, who became Lady Bernard, in 1670.

BIBLIOGRAPHY

Allen, M.J.B., and Kenneth Muir, eds. *Shakespeare's Plays in Quarto.* 1981.

Bullough, G., ed. *Narrative and Dramatic Sources of Shakespeare.* 8 vols. 1957–1975.

Gurr, A.J. *The Shakespearian Playing Companies.* 1997.

Hinman, Charleton, ed. *The First Folio of Shakespeare: The Norton Facsimile.* 1968; repr. Peter W.M. Blayney, intro. 1996.

Schoenbaum, S. *Shakespeare: A Documentary Life.* 1975; compact edition, 1977.

Wells, S. *Shakespeare: A Life in Drama.* 1995; 2nd edition. 1997.

———, and Gary Taylor, with John Jowett and William Montgomery. *William Shakespeare: A Textual Companion.* 1987.

Vickers, Brian, ed. *Shakespeare: The Critical Heritage, 1623–1801.* 6 vols. 1974–1981.

The best fully annotated editions of separate plays are the Arden and Oxford series (both ongoing). Annotated editions of the complete works include *The Norton Shakespeare,* Stephen Greenblatt, ed. (1997), based on the Oxford (1986) text, and the *Riverside Shakespeare,* G. Blakemore Evans, ed. (2nd edition, 1997).

Stanley Wells

SEE ALSO

Actors; Burbage, Richard; Chester, Robert; Chettle, Henry; Drama, History of; Greene, Robert; Jonson, Ben; Kemp, William; Meres, Frances; Sonnet Sequences; Theater Companies, Adult; Theaters; Willobie, Henry; Wriothesley, Henry

Sheppard, John (c. 1515–c. 1560)

John Sheppard was appointed instructor of the choristers (*informator choristarum*) at Magdalen College, Oxford, in 1543. There are no records pertaining to his birthplace or the establishment where he was trained in music, although he was probably born around 1515. He stayed at Oxford for five years, moving to the Chapel Royal sometime between 1548 and 1552. In a petition of 1554 for the degree Doctor of Music from Oxford, he calls himself "studiosus Musices" for a period of twenty years and mentions the composition of numerous "cantiones." He was present at the coronation of Elizabeth I on January 17, 1559, and is presumed to have died between that date and September of 1560, when the Chapel Royal Cheque books' first lists of deaths and resignations were copied. Sheppard's name is not in these or any other, later records. He left fifteen English anthems, forty-one psalm tunes, and an appreciable quantity of Service music, including three services, two Creeds, and a setting of the Lord's Prayer, all of it evidently composed during the short reign of Edward VI.

Sheppard belongs to the first generation to compose for both the Sarum and Anglican liturgies. His music for the Sarum rite comprises five Masses, one of which is based on the *Western Wynde* tune employed by Taverner, two Magnificats, and sixty-six motets, all liturgical and the overwhelming majority (58) for the Offices. Sheppard preferred composing active counterpoint around a chant set in the tenor of his responsories and in the top voice of his hymns. Much of his music, unfortunately, is now incomplete, although missing tenor voices can be reconstructed from chant.

Sheppard was drawn to rich textures, frequently composing for a six-part choir of treble and mean (boys' voices), two countertenors, tenor, and bass, and then dividing parts for even greater sonority. *Sacris solemniis,* a hymn in eight parts for vespers at Corpus Christi; *Media vita in morte sumus,* the antiphon to the canticle at Compline for two weeks before Passion Sunday; and his *Second Service in f fa ut* are representative examples of his best writing. His harmonies are audacious at times, and his use of false relations striking.

BIBLIOGRAPHY

Chadd, David, ed. *John Sheppard: Responsorial Music.* Early English Church Music. Vol. 17. 1977.

Sandon, Nicholas, ed. *John Sheppard: Masses.* Early English Church Music. Vol. 18. 1976.

Thurlow, Alan John. "The Latin Church Music of John Sheppard (Edition and Commentary)." Dissertation, Cambridge University. 1979.

Wulstan, David, ed. *John Sheppard (ca. 1515–ca. 1560): Collected Works.* 1978.

Laura S. Youens

SEE ALSO

Sarum, Use of; Taverner, John

Sheriff

Dating from the eleventh century, the office of sheriff involved both administrative and judicial responsibilities within a county by a local gentleman on behalf of the crown. His appointment was for a year. Selection occurred in a ceremony in the fall when the monarch used a bodkin to prick a name from a list. Major towns also had sheriffs—usually two—but they were part of the *cursus honorum* of city offices and were not appointed directly by the crown. There were a few anomalies such as Westmorland in which the office was the inheritance of a private family and the County Palatine of Durham in which the bishop appointed. From their inception in the fourteenth century the Justices of the Peace had supplanted many of the functions of the county sheriff. It is usually assumed that this process accelerated during the sixteenth century as the J.P.s acquired yet more responsibilities and that the office of sheriff became residual.

However, it is more appropriate to see the nature of the office altering in response to both changes in local government and in the character of gentry society.

The sheriff continued to account with the Exchequer for the collection of many of the crown's revenues. This was burdensome and could last for years after the term of office. He also had a central role in the administration of justice—receiving writs, apprehending felons, and overseeing punishments. He presided over the County Court. Its residual function under the Tudors was to act as the forum for the election of M.P.s with the sheriff as returning officer. Much of this work was highly technical and in fact was carried out by his personal appointee: the under-sheriff. This post was sought after and could be remunerative for the incumbent. In contemporary parlance it is often the under-sheriff who is referred to as "sheriff" and the sheriff-proper is called "high sheriff." Other staff included clerks, bailiffs, stewards of Hundred courts, and jailers. The number of sheriffs increased after the Act of 1567 (8 Eliz. c.6), which severed many of the counties that hitherto had shared sheriffs.

Under the Tudors there was an elaboration of the ceremonial and social functions of the high sheriff. These focused especially on the biannual visitations of the Justices of Assize. The sheriff met them at the county border with followers in his livery, trumpeters, and javelin men. Entertainment at the "sheriff's table" was provided for the Justices for the duration of their stay, and for the local gentry. Originally the sheriff's chaplain had been responsible for the spiritual welfare of prisoners, especially at executions. He also began to deliver the assize sermon to the county's gathered dignitaries. With the emergence of religious differences this could be an opportunity for a particularly zealous sheriff to express his beliefs through his nominee.

All this enforced an emulatory competition before the appraising eyes of the county. Despite central admonitions and local agreements within counties, costs continued to rise. This may be one of the reasons why in this period those counties that had shared a sheriff were split and each given a separate appointee.

BIBLIOGRAPHY

Elton, G.R. *The Tudor Constitution.* 2nd edition. 1982.

Hartley, T.E . "The Sheriff and County Elections." In *The Parliaments of Elizabethan England.* D.M. Dean and N.L. Jones, eds. Pp. 163–190. 1990.

List of Sheriffs for England and Wales, from the Earliest Times to 1831 Compiled from Documents in the PRO.

S

Public Record Office Lists and Indexes, vol. 9. HMSO. 1898; repr. 1963.

Quintrell, B.W., ed. *Proceedings of the Lancashire Justices of the Peace at the Sheriff's Table during Assizes Week, 1578–1694.* The Record Society for Lancashire and Cheshire, vol. 121. 1981.

Smith, A. Hassell. *County and Court: Government and Politics in Norfolk, 1558–1603,* pp. 139–154. 1974.

———, Gillian M. Baker, R.W. Kenny, Jane Key, Victor Morgan, and Barry Taylor, eds. *The Papers of Nathaniel Bacon of Stiffkey 1556–.* 4 vols. to date; in progress. Norfolk Record Society and the Center of East Anglian Studies. 1979–.

Wilson, Jean S. "Sheriff's Rolls of the Sixteenth and Seventeenth Centuries." *English Historical Review,* vol. 47, pp. 31–45.

Victor Morgan

SEE ALSO

Exchequer; Government, Local; Justice of the Peace

Shipbuilding

Even though the shipwright can be found at work up and down Tudor England, building small boats in creeks and ocean-going vessels in the larger ports, the economics of the industry in Tudor times have been neglected by historians. Naval historians, on the other hand, have explained in great detail how the Tudors, employing native skills, built a navy of great strength, sophistication, and efficiency. Fortunately, their contribution to the knowledge of naval shipbuilding had considerable relevance to the commercial industry. Links between the two were close, and the growth of the one had substantial inputs for the other. In particular, the skills and experience gained in building and maintaining England's first permanent navy in the reign of Henry VIII were transferred to commercial shipyards. More than most forms of manufacturing, shipbuilding required a highly skilled workforce at all stages of construction. In the Tudor period the skills were put at a greater premium by radical changes in ship design and construction. The new technology of the carvel-built ship that began to appear in north European waters from the middle of the fifteenth century did not transform traditional craft skills, and the tools of the trade remained the same. Those skills, however, were no longer sufficient. Mathematical knowledge was required to design ships frame-first, rather than from the shell inward as in traditional clinker-construction, and managerial skills were needed to oversee and organize construction.

Significantly, the first English ship known to have been carvel-built was Henry VIII's *Mary Rose* (1509); and the first English shipwright to provide documentary proof of the reception of the new mathematical design was Matthew Baker (c. 1530–1613), a master shipwright who served under four monarchs. Under Mary and Elizabeth I he worked alongside Peter Pett (d. 1589), who left Harwich for the Thames, where he founded a dynasty of shipwrights and administrators that served the crown for almost two centuries. The Petts in particular exemplify the links between naval and merchant shipbuilding. Having acquired or honed their skills in the royal dockyards, they and other master shipwrights were free to practice them commercially and to pass them on to sons and apprentices. This they did in private yards in Deptford, close to the royal dockyard built by Henry VIII in 1514, and in Limehouse and other riverside suburbs.

The promotion of skills by the navy and their transfer to the commercial sector was of particular relevance for the Thames-side industry. In the early sixteenth century it appears to have been small in scale and resources, demand being limited by the narrow concentration of commerce on nearby markets. Ships using the port were small and many were foreign. By building and basing his fleet on the Thames and recruiting shipwrights from all over the country, Pett created the pool of skills that could be drawn upon when the reorientation of trade routes and markets in Elizabeth I's reign created a substantial market for commercial builders. Official registers of shipping using the port show that the volume roughly doubled to around 50,000 tons, with fewer foreign vessels and a substantial increase in the average size of local ships. Further evidence of growth is to be found in the record of subsidy payments on the building of ships of 100 tons and above. In the 1560s, when the subsidy was paid on close to 5,000 tons of new ships, none was described as being "of London." West-country ships were particularly prominent in the record. In the 1590s, 71 percent of the total of more than 35,000 tons of subsidized shipping was based on the Thames. Not all the ships were necessarily built there, but in all probability many were; and even more of the ships "of London" would be repaired locally—an important part of the shipwright's trade.

Shipbuilding also flourished in busy ports like Ipswich, and in more specialized locations: Harwich, Woodbridge, and Shoreham, where there was a long tradition of building ships for the London market as well as for local owners. Easy access to supplies of timber and other naval stores were important factors in the growth of the east coast industry, as was the increasing demand for transportation from the north-east coalfields. Ships continued to be built at Bristol and other west country ports, but the industry there seems to have experienced a decline in the sixteenth century, reflecting that in overseas trade. London undoubtedly benefited disproportionately in this area of economic growth, as it did in others.

As the industry grew, the technology changed, and skill levels rose; the production methods employed in shipbuilding became more advanced. Before the sixteenth century even the largest vessels, warships as well as merchantmen, were built or repaired on temporary sites and in primitive conditions. If a "dock" was needed to protect the ship it was essentially an artificial ditch, which was abandoned after the work was completed. By the end of the sixteenth century, shipyards on the Thames and perhaps elsewhere occupied sites, extending over several acres, where ships continued to be built and repaired until relatively recent times. And one reason for that degree of continuity was the Elizabethan "invention" of the graving dock, equipped with gates, which transformed the shipyard's character and production methods. The modern dock put shipbuilding in the rare category of manufactures that required purpose-built premises and expensive equipment, as well as high levels of skill on the part of the master shipwright, who occupied the yard, and his workforce of shipwrights, caulkers, and apprentices. The industry also provided employment for various auxiliary crafts and services—boatbuilders and mastmakers, anchorsmiths and blacksmiths, makers of rope, pulleys, pumps, blocks, and treenails—which extended its influence on the local port economy. The rising demand for timber and naval stores also had a considerable impact on foreign trade, particularly with the Baltic. In London certainly, if less assuredly elsewhere, it can be said that by the end of the Tudor period an obscure, ill-recorded craft had evolved into a substantial but still little-known industry.

BIBLIOGRAPHY
Abell, Sir W. *The Shipwright's Trade.* 1948.
Davis, Ralph. *The Rise of the English Shipping Industry.* 1962.
Dietz, B. "The royal bounty and English merchant shipping in the sixteenth and seventeenth centuries." *The Mariner's Mirror,* vol. 77, no. 1. 1991.
Loades, David. *The Tudor Navy.* 1992.

Brian Dietz

SEE ALSO
Industry and Manufacture; Trade, Overseas

Shipping
See Privateering; Shipbuilding; Trade, Overseas; Transportation

Shrewsbury, Earls of
See Hardwick, Elizabeth; Talbot Family

Sidney, Henry (1529–1586)
Lord deputy of Ireland and father of Sir Philip Sidney, Sir Henry Sidney was probably born at Baynard's Castle, London, in 1529. Henry early established his importance in the Tudor courts. He spent his childhood as constant companion and playfellow to Prince Edward; and when Edward VI succeeded to the crown, he appointed Henry one of the four principal gentlemen of his privy chamber. He was knighted in 1550, at the same time as William Cecil, and given a number of minor offices, including the position of chief cupbearer for life.

Sidney remained influential in Edward's court, which attracted the attention of Sir John Dudley, earl of Warwick, later duke of Northumberland. In 1551, Sidney married Dudley's oldest daughter, Mary, and consequently became involved in his father-in-law's scheme to place Lady Jane Grey and Guildford Dudley on the throne. He witnessed the will conferring the crown to Lady Jane, and was holding Edward in his arms when the king expired.

But Sidney quickly abandoned Dudley, and declared loyalty to Queen Mary. In 1554, he accompanied John Russell to Spain to obtain ratification of the marriage articles between Mary and Philip II, during which time he also enlisted the sympathy of Philip for the Dudleys. Later that year, his first son, Philip, was born, and the Spanish king traveled to Penshurst to stand as godfather.

In 1558, Sidney replaced Thomas Radcliffe as lord justice of Ireland, and in 1559 was appointed lord president of the marches of Wales by Elizabeth I, which allowed him more time in court. He supported Robert Dudley's aspiration for Elizabeth's hand, but was opposed by Sir William Cecil, and dispatched on diplomatic missions to France and Scotland. He had five more children after Philip, including Robert, later earl of Leicester, and Mary, later countess of Pembroke.

In October 1565, five months after Elizabeth invested him with the Order of the Garter, she commissioned Sidney as Lord Deputy of Ireland, in which capacity he put down the Irish leader Shane O'Neill in 1567. Except for a

S

Sir Henry Sidney in Ireland. From John Derricke, *The Image of Ireland* (1581). As the queen's representative in Ireland, Sidney is received in this ironic portrait with great ceremony by local landowners and dignitiaries. By permission of David Evett.

return to England between October 1567 and September 1568, he was away from home during much of Philip's adolescence. Sidney left charge of Ireland to Sir William Fitzwilliam in 1571 and returned to court and his duties as President of Wales; yet he was reappointed to Ireland in 1575, where Philip visited him in 1576.

Sir Henry Sidney is considered the ablest of the men that governed Ireland under Elizabeth, although he was little rewarded. He was also reputed for his humanitarianism and knowledge of history, genealogy, heraldry, and antiquities. He governed Ireland until 1578, when he returned to court and his residence at Ludlow Castle, where he died on May 5, 1586.

BIBLIOGRAPHY

Collins, Arthur, ed. *Letters and Memorials of State.* 1973.
Great Britain Historical Manuscripts Commission. *Report on the MSS of Lord De'L'Isle and Dudley Preserved at Penshurst Palace.*
Hay, Millicent. *The Life of Robert Sidney.* 1984.
Osborn, James. *Young Philip Sidney: 1572–1577.* 1972.
Wallace, Malcolm. *The Life of Sir Philip Sidney.* 1967.

Thomas A. Deans

SEE ALSO

Dudley, John; Dudley, Robert; Edward VI; Grey, Lady Jane; Ireland, History of; Mary I; Philip II; Radcliffe, Thomas; Sidney, Philip; Sidney, Mary

Sidney, Mary (1561–1621)

Mary Sidney was the first woman in England to earn a significant contemporary reputation as a literary figure. First known by her own self-designation as "the Sister of Sir Philip Sidney," she evidently began her public literary career in an effort to memorialize her brother by encouraging works praising him, composing original elegies for him, publishing his works, and completing his metric paraphrase of the Psalms. Because she has been so identified with her brother, and because she employed the familiar modesty topos, her own audacity as a writer may be overlooked. Speaking for her brother and through the words of God, she paradoxically found a personal voice. In an age when print was still déclasé, she circulated her *Psalmes* through scribal publication in the approved aristocratic fashion, but she also printed translations under her own name. Equally audacious is her self-presentation in the portrait engraved by Simon van de Passe: she proudly holds out to the viewer her metric paraphrases labeled *Davids Psalmes,* and she is depicted not only with the ermine robes and coronet that signify her rank, but also with the poet's laurel crown.

The daughter of Sir Henry Sidney and Lady Mary Dudley, Sidney was born into a family that experienced dramatic reversals in fortune. Her maternal grandfather John Dudley, duke of Northumberland, had virtually ruled England under young King Edward VI, but was eventually executed for his attempt to put Lady Jane Grey on the English throne. Her maternal uncles were among the most powerful lords at Elizabeth I's court: Robert Dudley, earl of Leicester; Ambrose Dudley, earl of Warwick; and Henry Hastings, earl of Huntingdon. Her father, who had been raised with the Dudleys and with young King Edward, later served Queen Elizabeth as lord president of the marches of Wales and lord deputy of Ireland. Among them, her male relatives administered more than half the land under Elizabeth's rule. Her mother was one of Elizabeth's closest friends during the early years of her reign and nursed the queen through smallpox. After she was scarred by the disease herself, Lady Sidney largely withdrew from court life, although her husband continued to rely on her political acumen.

Invited to court by Elizabeth when she was just fourteen, Mary Sidney was present for the great festivities at Kenilworth. In 1577, Leicester arranged her marriage to his wealthy ally, Henry Herbert, earl of Pembroke. Throughout the next decade her life was largely devoted to her family. Between 1580 and 1584 she bore four children: William, who became the third earl of Pembroke; Katherine, who died in early childhood; Anne, who died unmarried in her early twenties; and Philip, whom King James I created earl of Montgomery and who eventually succeeded his brother as fourth earl of Pembroke.

As mistress of the Pembroke estates, she encouraged writers among her friends and household, including Samuel Daniel, Abraham Fraunce, Thomas Moffet, her brothers Philip and Robert, and, in the next generation, her son William and her niece Mary, later Lady Wroth. Her own literary endeavors apparently began in the late 1580s, after her children were out of infancy, and while she was mourning a devastating series of family deaths: her young daughter Katherine, both her parents, and her brother Philip, who died fighting with English forces against Spanish occupation of the Netherlands. She encouraged praise of her brother, including works by Thomas Moffet, Abraham Fraunce, and Edmund Spenser.

"The Doleful Lay of Clorinda," apparently her first literary work, was published in 1595 with Spenser's "Astrophel" as part of a collection of elegies. She also praised her brother in a dedicatory poem, "To the Angell Spirit of the most excellent Sir Philip Sidney," and supervised the printing of his works, notably the *Arcadia* (1593) and his sonnet sequence *Astrophil and Stella,* included in the 1598 edition of the *Arcadia.*

In 1592, she published two translations from French, *A Discourse of Life and Death,* by the Huguenot Philippe de Mornay, a family friend, and *Antonius,* a Senecan drama by Robert Garnier. Among the first English dramas in blank verse, *Antonius* used historical drama to comment on contemporary politics, serving as a precursor to Shakespeare's Roman plays. Samuel Daniel wrote *Cleopatra* as a companion to *Antonius* at her request, and Shakespeare drew from it for his *Anthony and Cleopatra.* She also translated Petrarch's "The Triumph of Death," preserving the *terza rima* of the Italian. Like the *Discourse,* "The Triumph of Death" offers consolation to the bereaved; the poem also permitted the countess to interject through her portrayal of Laura a female voice into the Petrarchan tradition, anticipating the poems of her niece, Lady Wroth.

Two original poems praise Elizabeth. "A Dialogue between two shepheards in praise of Astrea" is a pastoral debate written for the queen's planned visit to Wilton; "Even now that care" dedicates the Sidneian *Psalmes* to the queen, appropriately comparing her to the psalmist King David. Her most important literary work is her metric paraphrases of Psalms 44–150, completing the work her brother had begun. Employing a dazzling array of rhymed and quantitative verse forms, her paraphrases drew on the best Protestant scholarship available to her in English, French, and Latin; she may also have had access to Hebrew. By expanding metaphors and descriptions present in the scriptures themselves or in commentaries, she used the Psalmic "I" to find an original voice, commenting on contemporary politics, on the obligations of the nobility, on her experiences of arranged marriage and childbirth, on her scientific interests, and on her own role as woman poet.

After her husband's death in 1601, Mary Sidney faded in importance at court as her son William, third earl of Pembroke, assumed her role as patron of writers. Yet she remained an inspiration to women writers, including her niece Lady Wroth, who shadows her in characters such as the learned Queen of Naples in her *Urania* (1621), and Aemilia Lanyer, who praises her *Psalmes in Salve Deus Rex Judaeorum* (1611). The Sidneian *Psalmes* also strongly influenced seventeenth-century religious verse by other

S

writers, including George Herbert and John Donne, who praises the Sidneys as Moses and Miriam, saying that they "Both told us what, and taught us how to do. . . . They tell us *why*, and teach us *how* to sing." In her final years Sidney continued exchanging manuscripts with friends. She died of smallpox in 1621 and was buried in Salisbury Cathedral "in a manner befitting her degree."

During her life and into the next century, the countess of Pembroke was celebrated as a poet by writers who praised her work or, more significantly, borrowed from it, including Barnabe Barnes, Samuel Daniel, John Davies, John Donne, Michael Drayton, Gabriel Harvey, George Herbert, Aemilia Lanyer, William Shakespeare, Edmund Spenser, and Mary Wroth. In the nineteenth and early twentieth century her work was nearly lost under the shadow of her brother, Philip, but today she is once again recognized as a significant religious writer and an innovative poet.

BIBLIOGRAPHY

Brennan, M.G. *Literary Patronage in the English Renaissance: The Pembroke Family.* 1988.

Hannay, M. *Philip's Phoenix: Mary Sidney, Countess of Pembroke.* 1990.

———. *Silent But for the Word: Tudor Women as Translators, Patrons, and Writers of Religious Works.* 1985.

Kay, D. *Melodious Tears: The English Funeral Elegy from Spenser to Milton.* 1990.

Krontiris, T. *Oppositional Voices: Women as Writers and Translator of Literature in the English Renaissance.* 1992.

Lamb, M.E. *Gender and Authorship in the Sidney Circle.* 1990.

Lewalski, B.K. *Protestant Poetics and the Seventeenth-Century Religious Lyric.* 1979.

May, S. *The Elizabethan Courtier Poets.* 1991.

Rathmell, J.C.A. "Introduction." *The Psalms of Sir Philip Sidney and the Countess of Pembroke.* 1963.

Roberts, J. "Recent Studies in Women Writers of Tudor England, Part II: Mary Sidney, Countess of Pembroke." In *Women in the Renaissance.* K. Farrell, E. Hageman, and A. F. Kinney, eds. 1988.

Waller, G. *Mary Sidney, Countess of Pembroke: A Critical Study of Her Writings and Literary Milieu.* 1979.

Margaret P. Hannay

SEE ALSO

Daniel, Samuel; Dudley, John; Dudley, Robert; Fraunce, Abraham; Hastings, Henry; Kenilworth; Moffet, Thomas; Sidney, Philip; Spenser, Edmund

Sidney, Philip (1554–1586)

Now best remembered as one of the Elizabethan age's premier literary talents, Sir Philip Sidney had by the time of his death at age thirty-one secured a reputation among contemporaries at home and abroad as a paradigm of English courtly demeanor. His premature demise from a wound received in battle against Spanish forces in the Netherlands served to fix Sidney's renown for prodigious learning, charismatic wit, and political promise into an almost iconic representation of national heroism and dedication to the Protestant cause. Yet the celebrated potential would largely go unrealized, at least in the arena of civic affairs to which Sidney most anxiously aspired. Public image veiled a life of continuous personal frustration at court, subtly though pervasively registered in his surviving correspondence and poetical works.

His father and maternal uncle served Philip as contrasting role models. Sir Henry Sidney's ample administrative gifts, displayed throughout a difficult tenure as lord deputy of Ireland from 1564 to 1578, garnered small reward from the queen, who appeared willing to credit the attacks of his most querulous detractors. The compensatory honor of a barony that she extended in 1572 had to be declined, since it stood beyond the family's already attenuated financial resources. By comparison, the respect afforded to Mary Sidney's notoriously impetuous brother, Robert Dudley, earl of Leicester, went practically undiminished even throughout the latter's most tumultuous dealings with Elizabeth I. A witness to the slights that his father's cautious sensibility had earned, Philip from early maturity found himself temperamentally drawn to his uncle and the militant Protestant faction over which he presided. "My chiefest honour is to be a Dudley," he wrote in a vehement 1584 defense of Leicester.

In 1564, Sidney entered Shrewsbury School, where his precociously bookish inclinations quickly became evident. Formal education continued at Christ Church, Oxford, followed possibly by another year at Cambridge. It was, however, his subsequent grand tour of the Continent from 1572 to 1575 that marked the most formative stage of his early development. He was in Paris on the eve of the bloody St. Bartholomew's Day Massacre; the horrifying spectacle of more than 3,000 French Protestants slaughtered at the command of the Catholic regime, as well as his own narrow escape from the carnage, predictably steeled Sidney's religious militancy. His charm won the admiration and suits of patronage from humanists and literary figures in his subsequent travels through

Germany, Switzerland, Hungary, and Italy. Even more significantly, these early contacts seem to have fixed Sidney in the minds of continental Protestants—particularly the Huguenot political theorist Hubert Languet, who maintained an intimate correspondence with Sidney—as a sympathetic and influential voice who might help secure English support for anti-Catholic projects.

Sidney returned to England prepared for governmental service. His embassy in 1577 to the Emperor Rudolph II at Prague, and the Counts Palatine, Ludwig, and Casimir, was designed covertly to gauge sentiment for the formalization of a Protestant alliance against the perceived Catholic threat. William of Orange, formidable leader of Protestant insurgency in the Netherlands, was sufficiently impressed with Sidney to offer him his daughter in marriage. Neither William's proposal, nor the larger mission itself, however, would produce any practical results.

The unspecified though incapacitating hostility that the queen evidently felt toward Sidney remains difficult to diagnose. Elizabeth may well have felt that the flattering honor Sidney had received from his continental associates, however nominal, elevated him above a station that she alone reserved the right to determine. Either she simply did not share the high opinion by so many contemporaries, or she discerned in him an ambition that she needed to keep in check. Her possible awareness of his meeting with the expatriate priest Edmund Campion during the Prague visit may have left Sidney open to suspicion of Catholic sympathies. More tangibly, Sidney would in 1579—likely on the prompting of the Leicester faction—write a warning to the queen against her marriage to the Catholic duke of Alençon, a presumption for which other subjects had been brutally censured. An ongoing quarrel with an antagonist of superior social standing, Edward de Vere, the earl of Oxford, may also have identified Sidney as an upstart. In any case, he was not hereafter to be rewarded with the kind of substantive office for which he deemed himself suited. Appeals for an assignment in the Low Countries went unheeded, and whatever hopes he may have entertained of filling his father's old office of lord deputy of Ireland were dashed with the appointment of Arthur, Lord Grey, to the post in 1580. Even the knighthood that he eventually secured in 1583 was granted on a technicality: his ceremonial appointment to stand proxy for Casimir's installation as a knight of the garter required his titled status—a dubious promotion at which Sidney no doubt chafed.

From an artistic standpoint, Sidney's political frustration proved a blessing. Deprived of any other outlet, his energies found expression in what he referred to as his "unelected vocation" of poetry. Likely the earliest surviving fruit of this "idle" period was his pastoral masque *The Lady of May,* performed before the queen at Leicester House in 1578. More significantly, his *Arcadia*—crafted from 1579 to 1581 allegedly at the request of Mary, countess of Pembroke, the sister with whom he sustained a lifelong intimacy—stands unrivaled as the period's finest work of prose fiction. The elegant romance narrative, divided into five books punctuated by lyric interludes or "eclogues," unfolds the tragicomic tale of Pyrocles and Musidorus, two young princes drawn fatefully into the Arcadian ruling household's dynastic crisis and threatened dissolution. The fictional predicament in which the characters find themselves reflects in curious ways the ongoing trauma of the Tudor monarchy, plagued as it was by uncertainties of succession and the follies of headstrong leadership. Sidney would return to the romance in 1583–1584, weaving further narrative and political complications into an expanded structure. After his death, Mary edited the original version and its fragmentary reworking into a composite text, published in 1593.

Sidney ranks as a literary innovator in poetic theory and practice as well. His ardent championing of imaginative literature against the specious moral protests of *misomousoi* or "poet-haters" renders his *Defence of Poetry* an exemplary document of English literary criticism. Balancing humanist idealism and deliberately self-deprecating caricature, Sidney advocates the "golden" world that poetry realizes over the knotty abstractions of philosophy and history's predetermined obligation to fact. In so doing, he manages to celebrate and encourage an indigenously English literary tradition. Sidney's own poetic efforts had already yielded the *Arcadia*'s richly various pastoral interludes and the accomplished lyrics compiled as *Certain Sonnets.* The poet's outstanding achievement would take shape in his *Astrophil and Stella* of 1582–1583. Potentially inspired by Sidney's supposed infatuation for Penelope Devereux after her marriage to Lord Rich in 1581, the collection of 108 sonnets and eleven songs is regarded by some as the greatest of all English sonnet sequences.

Whatever autobiographical obsessions may stand behind *Astrophil and Stella,* in 1583 Sidney married Frances Walsingham, daughter to Elizabeth's trusted minister. Although apparently a happy one, the marriage and the daughter it produced the following year also exacerbated a deteriorating financial situation. The birth of Leicester's son in 1581 had displaced Sidney as his uncle's

S

heir; and although the child did not survive, the event brought home to Sidney an awareness of his own precarious status. Still lacking a position that would adequately fund his familial responsibilities or his future at court, Sidney came to regard his prospects with increasing desperation. So thorough had the professional disillusionment become by early 1585 that his appointment as governor of Flushing that summer did little to restore morale.

Sidney's foreign office essentially placed him under Leicester's command as part of a force supporting anti-Spanish resistance in the Netherlands. The campaign, ill-managed and poorly maintained, rapidly became yet another source of annoyance for one who now more than ever longed to realize some significant military or political accomplishment. His ambitions abruptly came to an end on September 22, 1586, when he suffered a gunshot wound to the leg in a skirmish outside the fortified city of Zutphen. Within a month Sidney was dead, hailed immediately by his peers as a martyr to the Protestant cause. His body was returned to London where, after a funeral befitting a national hero, Sidney was at last interred at St. Paul's in February 1587.

Numerous poetic tributes fueled the mythology that rapidly collected around the fallen Sidney, Edmund Spenser's pastoral elegy *Astrophel* most noteworthy among them. The expansive prose dedication written by Sidney's lifelong friend, Fulke Greville, best illustrates the "hagiographic" approach to his image. Modern historians still affirm the fascinatingly representative quality of Sidney's character. Whether we now choose to see him as the victim of a royal prejudice disdainful of the impressive, threatening potential he embodied, or as a figure whose own arrogant precocity blinded him to the delicate protocol of aristocratic promotion, he remains a touchstone for our understanding of the Elizabethan court's inner workings. His restless civic humanism incontestably marks the time in which he lived, and his artistic legacy uncontroversially ensures him a place with William Shakespeare and Edmund Spenser.

BIBLIOGRAPHY

Allen, M.J.B., et al., eds. *Sir Philip Sidney's Achievements.* 1990.

Duncan-Jones, Katherine. *Sir Philip Sidney, Courtier Poet.* 1991.

Hamilton, A.C. *Sir Philip Sidney: A Study of His Life and Works.* 1977.

Kay, Dennis, ed. *Sir Philip Sidney: An Anthology of Modern Criticism.* 1987.

Kinney, Arthur F., ed. *Essential Articles for the Study of Sir Philip Sidney.* 1986.

Martin, Christopher. "Misdoubting His Estate: Dynastic Anxiety in Sidney's *Arcadia.*" *English Literary Renaissance,* vol. 18, pp. 369–388.

———. "Turning Others' Leaves: Astrophil's Untimely Defeat." *Spenser Studies,* vol. 10, pp. 197–212.

McCoy, Richard C. *Sir Philip Sidney: Rebellion in Arcadia.* 1979.

Osborn, John M. *Young Philip Sidney, 1572–1577.* 1972.

Pears, Stuart A. *The Correspondence of Sir Philip Sidney and Hubert Languet.* 1845.

Ratiere, Martin N. *Faire Bitts: Sir Philip Sidney and Renaissance Political Theory.* 1984.

Van Dorsten, J.A., et al., eds. *Sir Philip Sidney: 1586 and the Creation of a Legend.* 1986.

Christopher Martin

SEE ALSO

De Vere, Edward; Dudley, Robert; Elegy; Elizabeth I; Greville, Fulke; Huguenots; Literary Criticism; Pastoral; Sidney, Henry; Sidney, Mary; Romance; Spenser, Edmund

Simnel, Lambert (c. 1477–c. 1535)

Lambert Simnel was the young boy who impersonated Edward, earl of Warwick, in a Yorkist conspiracy to unseat Henry VII in 1487. His origins are obscure. A herald who wrote a chronicle of events for the early years of Henry VII names him simply as John; the surname may have been derived from "simnel cakes" in reference to the profession of his father, a baker. One tradition holds that Simnel was the son of an Oxford organ maker, but the acts of attainder against the conspirators identify him as the son of Thomas Simnel, an Oxford joiner. The name Lambert, uncommon in England, may indicate Walloon origins, for the cult of St. Lambert was popular among the French-speaking people of the Low Countries.

Simnel was the student of William Simonds, an Oxford priest who, perhaps as early as 1486, devised a scheme to pass off the ten-year-old boy as a Yorkist prince. Rumors about the escape of the earl of Warwick from imprisonment seemed to have inspired Simonds. John de la Pole, earl of Lincoln, nephew of the Yorkist kings and Richard III's designated heir, supported the scheme, as did Margaret of York, dowager duchess of Burgundy and Edward IV's sister. The Fitzgerald earls of Kildare and Desmond, angry over Henry VII's support of their Butler

S

rivals, also joined the plot. Maximilian I, the king of the Romans, fearing that Henry was a French puppet, gave encouragement and the use of 2,000 mercenaries under the command of Martin Swartz. Henry, learning about the conspiracy from his network of spies, convened a great council at Sheen on February 2, 1487. The earl of Lincoln, who had been shown favor by Henry, attended and then fled abroad to Flanders.

Simonds took Simnel over to Ireland, where he was crowned Edward VI at Dublin on the Feast of the Ascension, May 24. The Yorkist army landed with their puppet pretender at Furness, Lancashire, in early June. Henry VII marched north with his army, and on June 16, at the battle of Stoke, defeated the Yorkists after three hours of bloody fighting. Lincoln and Swartz were killed, and Simnel and Simonds were captured. Henry regarded Simnel as the pawn of the Yorkists. Some thought was given to making him a priest because he had been anointed; but Henry decided to employ him as a scullion in his kitchen. Simnel eventually became the king's falconer. After Henry's death, he joined the household of Sir Thomas Lovell, Henry's treasurer. Simnel attended Lovell's funeral in 1525, and appears to have been alive ten years later. Richard Simnel, canon of St. Osith's, Essex, may have been his son.

BIBLIOGRAPHY

Bennett, Michael. *Lambert Simnel and the Battle of Stoke.* 1987.

John M. Currin

SEE ALSO

Henry VII; Wars of the Roses

Skelton, John (c. 1463–1529)

No one knows where or exactly when John Skelton was born, although it seems likely that it was in 1463 in the north of England, in either Northumberland or Yorkshire. Musical references in his work suggest that he had a choir school education before going to the university that, as he tells us in his late *A Replycacion* (1528), was Cambridge, where he probably received his B.A. in 1480. If the poem on the death of Edward IV is indeed his (as it seems to be), then he was already a poet by 1483. In about 1488 or 1489, Oxford conferred on him the relatively new postgraduate degree in rhetoric of poet laureate, an honor of which he was inordinately proud. Cambridge ratified the Oxford degree in 1493,

mentioning that a foreign university (known to be Louvain) had also laureated him. These degrees indicate powerful, probably royal, backing. In fact, he seems to have been in royal service by 1488, and in early November that year he inaugurated the curious private calendar by which he dated his work. In 1489, he wrote his first undoubted and datable poem to survive, *Upon the Dolorus Dethe and Muche Lamentable Chaunce of the Mooste Honourable Erle of Northumberland.* Shortly afterward, William Caxton, in the preface to his *Eneydos,* praised him for his mastery of English, mentioning his translations of Cicero's letters (now lost) and Diodorus Siculus. The dream allegory, *The Bowge of Courte,* certainly in existence before 1495, was probably written in the 1480s, too. While still in his twenties, therefore, Skelton was well embarked on a literary career.

His chief patron at court seems to have been the Lady Margaret, Henry VII's mother, who had charge of the royal childrens' education. With her backing, sometime in the 1590s he became the future Henry VIII's schoolmaster, and he may have taught Prince Arthur as well. In 1498, however, his career took a surprising turn when he entered into holy orders and celebrated mass before Henry VII. In 1502/3, aged thirty-nine or forty, his employment at court ended, and he became the rector of of the parish church of St. Mary's, Diss, a town in Norfolk, where he lived until 1512. The benefice was in the gift of the crown.

Surviving records show that during this period of court employment Skelton kept in touch with university officials as well as with noble patrons outside London and the court. The Northumberland elegy, written with an insider's knowledge of the events it describes, and addressed to the dead earl's young heir, survives in a magnificent manuscript that belonged to him, and concludes with Latin verses addressed to William Ruckshaw, succentor of York Minster, a Cambridge-educated cleric in service to the Percy family. The implication is that Skelton himself had intimate knowledge of the Percy household. It is now known, too, that Skelton's long dream-allegory, *The Laurel* (retitled in the nineteenth century *The Garland of Laurel*), written at Sheriff Hutton castle in Yorkshire for Elizabeth, countess of Surrey, was composed c. 1495, nearly thirty years before its publication in 1523. Since the poem refers to other, earlier works written for the countess, and reveals that Skelton was a familiar presence in the household, it is apparent that his connection with the Howard family, long thought to have been a feature of his later years, must have extended over his entire career.

S

When Skelton went into Norfolk as rector of Diss, he kept up with friends in the Howard circle; Jane Scrope, for whom he wrote *Phyllyp Sparowe*, became the sister-in-law of Margaret Tylney, one of the countess of Surrey's waiting-women for whom he wrote a poem in *The Laurel*. He also sought company in nearby Cambridge. In 1504–1505, the university gave him permission to wear his royal robe there, a concession that would have had no point unless he was a fairly frequent visitor. *Ware the Hauke*, a macaronic satire on a parson Skelton found training his hawks in Diss church, and perhaps his first poem in Skeltonics, may well have been written to amuse an audience of academic friends at Cambridge.

Skelton is usually thought of as a poet of Henry VIII's time and court, yet one important consequence of the early dating of *The Laurel* is that with the exception of fourteen works mentioned in nine stanzas (nos. 133–141) that Skelton interpolated in the 1523 text of the poem, all the works mentioned in the poem's lengthy "bibliography"(many of them now lost), were written before 1495 when Skelton was about thirty. They include, besides lost plays, translations, poems, and prose works, *The Laurel* itself, *The Bowge of Courte*, and an early form of *Speke, Parrot* called *The Popagay*—striking evidence of the precocity and industry of the young Skelton. At Diss he seems to have written far less, although those years saw the invention of the Skeltonic and the writing of his most famous poem, *Phyllyp Sparowe*, an enormously extended lament for a pet sparrow, set in a framework provided by the vespers of the dead.

Skelton greeted the accession of his former pupil as Henry VIII on June 24, 1509, with a poem that survives in Skelton's own hand in one of the manuscripts of the treasury, *A Lawde and Prayse Made for Our Sovereigne Lord the Kyng*. Sometime between 1509 and 1512, he sent Henry, in the form of a handsomely copied collection of Latin writings, including one written for him as a schoolboy, *Speculum principis*, a plea for reinstatement at court. This and other importunities must have been successful, for by 1512 or 1513, aged about fifty, Skelton was calling himself "Orator regius," and writing pro-government work such as the anti-Scottish *A Ballade of the Scottysshe Kynge* and *Agaynst the Scottes*, celebrating the victory of his old patron, the earl of Surrey, over the Scots at Flodden Field. About 1514, apparently to amuse Henry VIII, he wrote the flyting *Agenst Garnesche*, which survives among John Stow's manuscript collections. *The Tunnyng of Elynour Rummyng* followed, probably in 1517. Most readers would agree that none of this later work approaches the quality of Skelton's best writing under Henry VII. One exception might be the remarkably original and effective political morality play *Magnyfycence*, sometimes dated 1516, and once thought to be written against Cardinal Thomas Wolsey. It now seems probable, however, that this too is an earlier work, though probably written after 1495, and for performance in a private household.

In 1519–1521, for reasons that are by no means clear, Skelton, by now living within the sanctuary of Westminster and so immune from reprisal, began to attack Cardinal Wolsey. His first anti-Wolsey poem was an extremely cryptic, reworked version of a much older work, *The Popagay* (now lost), under the title *Speke Parrot*. This poem survives in two versions, one printed for the first time in 1545 by Richard Lant in the collection called *Certayne Bokes*, the other written into a manuscript owned by a London grocer, John Colyns. Lant's text preserves the body of the poem; Colyns's text consists of Lant's first fifty-seven lines followed by a series of short poems or envoys, most of which comment on Wolsey's conduct of foreign affairs at the Calais Conference in late 1521. After *Speke Parrot* came *Collyn Clout* (1521–1522) and *Why Come Ye Nat to Courte?* (late 1522), both in Skeltonics, both plain-spoken; *Why Come Ye* is remarkably abusive. It seems very likely that Skelton was writing these poems on behalf of a powerful patron, and that when the campaign ended with Skelton's presentation of the thirty-year-old *Laurel* to the king and the cardinal with a warily written congratulatory envoy, it was because the principals had come to some agreement. Shortly after the publication of *The Laurel* in late 1523, Skelton wrote another work dedicated to Wolsey, *Howe the Douty Duke of Albany . . . ran away*, celebrating yet another discomfiture of the Scots in which his Howard patrons had a hand. In 1528, he wrote *A Replycacion Agaynst Certayne Yong Scolers*. This attack on two young Cambridge men who had been convicted of heretical opinions, Thomas Arthur and Thomas Bilney, was also dedicated to Wolsey, and was Skelton's last known work. He died June 21, 1529, probably aged sixty-six, and was buried before the high altar in St. Margaret's, Westminster.

Born into a period of great political, religious, scientific, technological, and linguistic change, Skelton was the first real English man of letters, prolific in verse and prose, original and translated; and although he would not qualify as a humanist by the standards of the generation after him, by the standards of his own generation he was an exceptionally learned writer who contributed immensely to the development of English as a versatile, flexible, literary language. In verse he continued the Chaucerian tradition and invented the Skeltonic, in his hands a subtle and eloquent medium; as we learn from his own list of his work, he pioneered such genres as the pastoral and the complaint, popular with the Elizabethans. Whatever his reputation with critics, the poets have always respected him, as William Wordsworth said, for he was a demon in point of genius.

BIBLIOGRAPHY

Brownlow, F.W, ed. *The Book of the Laurel.* 1990.

Carlson, David R., ed. *The Latin Writings of John Skelton. Studies in Philology,* vol. 88. 1991.

Kinney, Arthur F. *John Skelton: The Priest as Poet.* 1987.

Kinsman, Robert S., and Theodore Yonge. *John Skelton: Canon and Census.* Renaissance Society of America. 1967.

Nelson, William. *John Skelton, Laureate.* 1939.

Pollet, Maurice. *John Skelton (c. 1460–1529).* 1962; trans. John Warrington, 1971.

Scattergood, John, ed. *John Skelton: The Complete English Poems.* 1983.

F.W. Brownlow

SEE ALSO

Bilney, Thomas; Caxton, William; Flodden Field; Henry VIII; Pastoral; Satire; Stowe, John; Versification; Wolsey, Thomas

Skepticism

Historically, there were two distinct traditions of skeptical philosophy: academic skepticism and Pyrrhonian skepticism. Academic skepticism originated in the Platonic Academy of the third-century B.C., derived from the teachings of Arcesilas and Carneades. Academic skeptics denied that certain knowledge was possible. Theirs was an antidogmatic stance, according to which all knowledge claims are at best provisional since it is impossible to know anything with absolute certainty. Pyrrhonian skeptics, following Pyrrho of Elis, held that we should suspend judgement on all questions of knowledge since there is insufficient and inadequate evidence to determine or deny whether any knowledge is possible. Pyrrhonism is a more radical form of skepticism since it doubts even skeptical judgement. The chief sources for academic skepticism are Cicero's *Academica* and his *De natura deorum,* as well as the refutation of skepticism in St. Augustine's *Contra academicos.* The chief sources for Pyrrhonian skepticism are the compilation of Pyrrho's arguments in the writings of a minor figure, Sextus Empiricus, and the *Life of Pyrrho* in Diogenes Laertius's *Lives of the Philosophers.*

Until the publication of Sextus Empiricus's *Outlines of Pyrrhonism* in 1562, the form of skepticism best known in the Renaissance was academic skepticism. In the Ciceronian sources it figured as one among a number of ancient philosophies, including Platonism, Stoicism, and Epicureanism. These had been either partially or wholly unknown during the Middle Ages. Petrarch's recovery and recommendation of the *Academica* encouraged the interest of leading humanists (e.g., Salutati and Valla). Deriving from Clitomachus and Carneades, Ciceronian skepticism fed into, though should not be confused with, fideistic anti-intellectualism that characterizes one strand of western Christianity. Even so, in the sixteenth century the potential of skepticism was a polemical tool in the religious disputes of the Reformation and post-Reformation from Martin Luther and Desiderius Erasmus through Sextus's editor, Gentian Hervet. Skepticism was brought into the philosophical arena as a weapon against Aristotelian dogmatism in sixteenth-century Paris, especially through the edition of the *Academica* (1548) of Omer Talon, friend of Pierre de la Ramée (Ramus). In the resulting attacks by Pierre Galland (*Contra novum academiam Petri Rami oratio,* 1551) and Guy de Brus (*Dialogues contre les Nouveaux Academiciens,* 1557), the Ramists were branded as "new academicians." It is in this context that the references to skepticism appear in Rabelais's *Gargantua et Pantagruel (Le Quart Livre).* Rabelais also ridicules the skepticism of Henry Cornelius Agrippa's fideistic diatribe, *De incertitudine et vanitate scientiarum (Le Tiers Livre).* Academic skepticism was available to the Renaissance as widely as the works of Cicero were known. A general, if perhaps superficial, awareness of skepticism in Tudor England may be assumed on account of Reformation and Ramist debates. A diverse variety of theological and philosophical thinkers of the sixteenth century were aware of this more probabilistic, antidogmatic version of skepticism.

Among those with connections with Tudor England, references to skepticism are made by Reginald Pole, friend of the antiskeptic Jacopo Sadoleto, and Giordano Bruno (*La cena degli ceneri,* 1584), while Sebastian Castellio draws on Cicero in his *De haereticis* (1554) and his unpublished *De arte dubitandi* (1561). The greatest skeptic of Tudor times was Michel de Montaigne, whose *Essais* were an important source of skeptical thought, especially the Pyrrhonist strain. The example of Montaigne illustrates the fact that, after the printing of Latin translations

S

of the works of Sextus Empiricus in 1562 and 1569, academic skepticism lost ground to the radical doubt of Pyrrhonism.

BIBLIOGRAPHY

Allen, D.C. *Doubt's Boundless Sea. Skepticism and Faith in the Renaissance.* 1964.

Copenhaver, B.P., and C.B. Schmitt. *Renaissance Philosophy.* 1992.

Popkin, R.H. *The History of Scepticism from Erasmus to Descartes.* 1968.

Schmitt, C.B. *Cicero scepticus. A Study of the Influence of the Academica in the Renaissance.* 1972.

Sarah Hutton

SEE ALSO

Bruno, Giordano; Ciceronianism; Erasmus, Desiderius; Humanism; Platonism; Pole, Reginald; Pyrrhonism; Ramism

Slave Trade
See Hawkins, John

Smith, Henry (c. 1550–1591)

The moderate Puritan divine Henry Smith, Thomas Nashe's "silver-tongued Smith," was among the greatest of the Elizabethan preachers. Related to Lord Burleigh, he was born at Withcote, Leicestershire. He entered Queens' College, Cambridge, in 1573, but soon left without formally matriculating. He continued his studies with Richard Greenham, who instilled in him Puritan principles. In March 1575/1576, he matriculated at Lincoln College, Oxford, and, in spite of conscientious scruples against subscription, graduated B.A. in February 1578/1579. He then officiated in the church of Husbands Bosworth, although it is uncertain whether he obtained the rectory. In 1587, he was elected, with Burleigh's support, lecturer of St. Clement Danes, without Temple Bar, by the rector and congregation. Despite his great popularity, he was suspended from preaching in 1588 by John Aylmer, bishop of London, on grounds of not holding a license from his diocesan, not subscribing to the Articles, and having made derogatory remarks concerning the Book of Common Prayer. With strong congregational support, Burleigh intervened on his behalf, and Smith was restored to his ministry. Owing to ill health, he resigned his lectureship about the end of 1590, and retired to Husbands Bosworth. During his sickness he prepared his works for the press and revised his sermons, dying in July 1591 before they were published.

BIBLIOGRAPHY

Knappen, M.M. *Tudor Puritanism: A Chapter in the History of Idealism.* 1963.

Smith, Henry. *Collected Sermons.* 8 vols. 1592; repr. 1657 and 1675 with a brief *Life* by Thomas Fuller.

——. *Works.* 2 vols. 1866–1867.

Lee W. Gibbs

SEE ALSO

Articles of Religion; Aylmer, John; Book of Common Prayer; Greenham, Richard; Sermons

Smith, Thomas (1513–1577)

Early political economist and interpreter of the Tudor constitution, Thomas Smith, a farmer's son, was born in 1513 near Saffron Walden, Essex. He studied in Queens' College, Cambridge, and later abroad, becoming professor of civil law and Greek, vice-chancellor, and then provost of Eton. Ever a shrewd realist, he was intellectually indebted to Aristotle and Machiavelli. He was member of Parliament during the reigns of Edward VI, Mary, and Elizabeth I, and gained a reputation in financial matters. Friend and colleague of William Cecil, Lord Burghley, Smith was a principal secretary of state under Edward and Elizabeth, and served the latter as ambassador to France. He died in 1577.

Smith is known for two posthumously published books. A dialogue entitled *A Discourse of the Commonweal of This Realm of England* (published anonymously in 1581) went through eight editions. This work, originally written in 1549 and circulated in manuscript was, until recently, attributed to John Hales. Smith's second work, *De republica Anglorum* (1583), was written in the mid-1560s.

An important work of Tudor economic thought, the *Discourse* discusses the causes and remedies of the serious inflation plaguing England since the 1530s. The major cause, according to Smith, was the debasement of coinage beginning under Henry VIII; other causes were rackrenting (charging inflated rents) and the influx of gold and silver from overseas. Since the Tudor economy was predominantly agricultural, Smith focused on agrarian problems rather than on commerce and manufacture. Bleakly conceptualizing human nature as distinguished by human greed, Smith insists that men cannot be other than they are, avaricious profit-seekers. To avoid anarchy and to unify society, Smith proposes the maintenance of an artificial harmony aimed at the common interests of security and prosperity through skillful manipulation by prudent and informed government action. He also contends that the increasing economic interdependence of advanced nations promotes international peace and friendship.

The *Republica,* until recently the sole basis of Smith's reputation, has long been recognized as a classic commentary by a contemporary on the Tudor constitution. By depicting England as it is, not as it should be, Smith imagines he is following in the footsteps of Aristotle's lost treatises on ancient Greek constitutions. Half of the first of three parts is devoted to a theory of the state, and half to the political sociology of the realm. The remainder describes and assesses governmental and legal arrangements and powers. Smith defines "common wealth" or state as a collection of free individuals united by mutual interests. For Smith, English society is divided into gentlemen, citizens of towns, yeomen, and laborers. Defining yeomen as forty-shilling freeholders and "farmers to gentlemen" employing laborers on their holdings, Smith suggests (as he does in his *Discourse*) the triad of landlord, tenant farmer, and worker, living respectively on rents, profits, and wages. England is a mixed or parliamentary kingdom ruled by monarch, gentlemen, and yeomen. Yeomen, unlike laborers, possess the franchise, but cannot be elected to Parliament. Every Englishman is thus present in Parliament either in person or by proxy. Women have no direct political role in Smith's England.

Smith's writing is characterized by an individualistic, rationalistic, secular, and utilitarian spirit. Responding to and reflecting basic structural changes in Tudor England, not least the emergence of agrarian capitalism, he stresses government's fundamental economic function.

BIBLIOGRAPHY

Dewar, Mary. *Sir Thomas Smith: A Tudor Intellectual in Office.* 1964.

Ferguson, Arthur B. *The Articulate Citizen and the English Renaissance.* 1965.

Johnson, E.A.J. *Predecessors of Adam Smith: The Growth of British Economic Thought.* 1937.

Smith, Sir Thomas. *A Discourse of the Commonweal of This Realm of England.* Mary Dewar, ed. 1969.

———. *De Republica Anglorum.* Mary Dewar, ed. 1982.

Wood, Neal. *Foundations of Political Economy: Some Early Tudor Views on State and Society.* 1994.

———. "Avarice and Civil Unity: The Contribution of Sir Thomas Smith." *History of Political Thought,* vol. 18, pp. 24–42.

Neal Wood

SEE ALSO
Money, Inflation, and Moneylending; Political Thought

Social Classes and the Social Order

The classic sixteenth-century statement of concern with social order and hierarchy was that read to congregations in parish churches throughout the land from 1547–1548: the *Homily on Obedience.* In reciting the "duty and order" appointed to "every degree of people in their vocation, calling and office," the *Homily* unequivocally demonstrates that Tudor social theory was dominated by the inegalitarian assumption that a society consisting of divinely ordained "estates" and "degrees," of functionally interdependent but unequal social ranks, was not only inevitable but desirable. This concern with "most excellent and perfect order" recurred in contemporary treatises from Thomas Elyot's *The Boke Named the Gouvernour* (1540) to Robert Burton's *The Anatomy of Melancholy* (1621), and was characterized by three distinct hierarchies: those of estate or degree, of gender, and of age.

The most frequently discussed evidence for contemporary thinking about the hierarchy of estate and degree is to be found in formal and literary descriptions, especially in the social categories of Tudor sumptuary legislation, which defined dress codes, and in the treatises of William Harrison, Sir Thomas Smith, Sir Thomas Wilson, and Edward Chamberlayne. Taken together, this evidence amounts to a description of an entire social world, and it has three notable features. First, the commonplace medieval division of society into three functional orders (those who worked, those who fought, those who prayed) is entirely absent. Second, these writers lack any modern conception of "class" as a means of defining social groups. Third, the conventions employed seem to have been specific to the early modern period and involved a single hierarchy of status and occupational groups. For example, William Harrison's *Description of England* (1577) referred to four degrees of men: gentlemen, citizens and burgesses of the towns, yeomen, and the ruled, "who have neither voice no authority in the commonwealth." By the early seventeenth century, Robert Reyce was able to describe the social order of his native Suffolk by reference to seven degrees of people: peers, knights, gentlemen, yeomen, townspeople, hus-

S

bandmen, and the poor. Both these models employ a "classical" hierarchy of social ranks, although both amount to simplifications of the complexities of reality. There were, for example, formally recognized gradations within the peerage. The implication of these models is, however, clear: the social order was never rigidly defined, and the criteria for belonging to most social groups were never made explicit.

While it may have been self-evident that peers were those entitled to trial in the House of Lords, who enjoyed parliamentary status, and who possessed heritable lands, the boundaries of status groups below the level of the peerage were not legally defined. There were, for example, no patents for "gentle" status. The definition of "gentility" seems to have been particularly problematic. Harrison was especially vague; his suggestion that gentlemen were recognized as such by their "race and blood or at least their vertues" hinted that gentility might possibly be achieved as well as inherited. Similar difficulties arose with respect to yeomen. The law implied that yeomen must have a minimum annual income of forty shillings from freehold land, but less formal evidence suggests that they were large farmers, enjoying preeminence and social esteem on the basis of their ability to keep a good house. Contemporary writers were even more hesitant over the classification of those merchants and professionals whose earning power qualified them to purchase the material trappings of gentle status. The criteria of status were, therefore, complex. Membership of an estate arose from a compound of social and cultural qualities, a multiplicity of factors. Tudor social groups were neither legally constituted nor religiously cast, and should be regarded less as institutions than as byproducts of a series of other factors. Their boundaries, furthermore, were evidently semipermeable, as the frank if sometimes grudging recognition of the realities of individual social mobility suggests. Contemporaries were often pejorative of "arrivistes," and both Smith and Wilson were anxious to emphasize the relationship between gentility, lineage, and ancient riches. The adoption of a certain lifestyle on the basis of new money was insufficient to acquire the honor and reputation on which gentility depended. The distinctions contemporaries recognized, therefore, arose from the interplay of several variables; both status and status-consciousness were frequently the outcome of a largely informal process of social assessment.

It should be apparent that these conventional social descriptions present problems to the historian. How far, for instance, is it possible to reconcile the normative or prescriptive literature with the descriptive, and with the objective reality? Furthermore, in the absence of independent evidence, it is impossible to calculate with any degree of precision the relative proportions of the population falling into each status group, or to gain anything other than a view of social hierarchy from above. The formal conventional studies are based on the unrepresentative perceptions of elites and are therefore of limited usefulness. Confronted with these problems, historians have attempted a "social-distributional" approach in an attempt to verify contemporary distinctions statistically. Such studies have adopted various approaches to measure the wealth and influence of social groups, especially those elites for which most evidence survives. Thus, "gentlemen" appear to have constituted only 2 percent of the early seventeenth-century population of counties as diverse as Lancashire or Kent; yet they controlled the country's wealth, especially when measured in terms of land ownership. Estimates suggest that by 1640, 15 percent of the nation's land was owned by the titular peerage, and a further 50 percent by the gentry. Such wealth was reflected in the panoply of lifestyle of these elite social groups, that ostentatious "theater of the rich," comprising the diet, dress, hospitality, civility, and self-conscious provision for posterity of a distinctively "patrician culture." Such generalizations are made more complex by analysis of distinctions within the ranks of the gentry revealed in county studies, which conventionally divide the gentry into greater, middling, and lesser gentlemen. In late Tudor Yorkshire, for example, knights (usually with an annual income exceeding £1,000) constituted 11 percent of the gentry, and esquires (with annual incomes between £250 and £1,000) a further 36 percent. The bulk (some 53 percent) of Yorkshire gentry were "mere gentlemen" with incomes below £250 per annum. Distinctions of wealth seem, however, to have been less significant than those of honor and officeholding. The real test of status within the ranks of the gentry was selection for office, with high constables and surveyors of highways being drawn from the ranks of the mere gentry, justices of the peace from among the esquires, and deputy-lieutenants, members of Parliament, and senior or long-serving magistrates from the knights. The gentry were, therefore, a differentiated but united class.

The influence of the gentry in rural England was paralleled by that of leading merchants, lawyers, and physicians in the towns. These groups often had close family ties to the gentry, characteristically being younger sons who had entered apprenticeship or professional training.

Their sources of wealth were less secure than the real property of their rural cousins, although they frequently came to exercise authority in urban government. This was all the more remarkable since many were the sons of country yeomen, and therefore not of genteel origin. Trade and the professions were an avenue of social mobility through which claims to genteel status might eventually be staked.

The most significant transformation of the social order in Tudor England was the increasing stratification within the middling groups of rural communities. Yeomen, husbandmen, artisans, and cottagers had rather diverse experiences of the demographic and economic pressures of the late sixteenth century. Yeomen were usually in possession of a "substantial acreage" of property, whether freehold or leasehold, while husbandmen held small family farms of up to thirty acres. Cottagers, however, eked out a living on less than a dozen acres and a garden, often supplementing their meager incomes through the exploitation of common rights on fen and pasture, or through wage-earning in agricultural by-employments. The inventories and account books of the period demonstrate the differing fortunes of these groups. By 1613, for example, the Berkshire yeoman Robert Loder could record an annual profit of £185 on his 150 acres. A husbandman holding thirty acres might expect to make between £3 and £4 annual profit after the demands of subsistence, a living that was tolerable but by no means easy. Cottagers and artisans, meanwhile, were in serious danger of falling into want, vulnerable both to the harvest failure and price inflation that might stretch expenditure beyond income, and to the periodic dislocation of the by-employments and proto-industrial trades, usually (though not exclusively) in textiles, with which that income was supplemented. In the villages of Tudor England, therefore, the social order was dictated by wealth, usually measured by access to land, and landholding itself conferred greater status than any other wealth. In towns, however, the crucial status distinction was between freemen, those who had successfully completed indentured apprenticeship, and the rest.

The conventional social categories employed by contemporaries and the social-distributional analyses of historians therefore give a rough guide to the wealth, status, and life opportunities of social groups. They do, however, have certain limitations: they exaggerate the homogeneity of groups at the lower end of the social order, they fail to allow for regional and local variations, and they present a rather neat, idealized picture of the social order, one that underestimates the degree of overlap between status

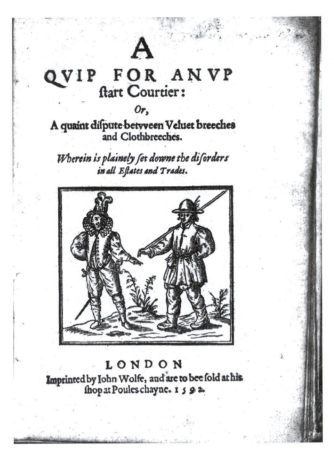

Title page of Robert Greenee's *A Quip for an Upstart Courtier I* (1592). Reproduced from the original by permission of the Henry E. Huntington Library and Art Gallery.

groups, especially in terms of wealth. Moreover, although wealth overlapped with status, it did not confer it.

Differences between social groups varied in significance and depth, and only analysis of the self-perception of particular social groups will clarify the extent to which the social order was rigidly graded. Analysis of marriage behavior, for example, indicates considerable willingness to marry outside status groups, suggesting that equal gradations of status were not rigidly reflected in contemporary practice. The relative looseness of social identity is further reflected in the informal language employed by the late sixteenth century to describe the social order. The private correspondence, petitions, and diary entries of the period demonstrate that contemporaries used simpler, cruder terms rather than the formalized language of classical social hierarchy to describe the social order. This "language of sorts" was both socially resonant and morally divisive. Distinctions between the "better" and the "meaner" "sort" of people were gradually overlaid with pejorative overtones, the poorest groups often being

S

described as the "common," "vulgar," or "worser" sort of people. Contemporaries therefore had two ways of looking at the social order of Tudor England: a finer, formal language of estates and a cruder, informal language of sorts.

Both these languages, however, were almost exclusively applied to adult males, and to discuss them in isolation is to ignore significant distinctions of gender and age. As individuals, women always took their social rank from their husbands and fathers, but collectively they were distinguished by the social construction of gender. Tudor women were expected, on the basis of scriptural authority, to be the "dutiful adjunct" to man, and their role was conditioned by powerful assumptions about their inferior strength, physical ability, and emotional stability. *The Homily of the State of Matrimony* referred to women as "weak creatures, not endowed with strength or constancy." Female behavior was conditioned by expectations of chastity, modesty, and obedience, and female friendships were accordingly expected to be based only on female acquaintances. These values appear to have been publicly challenged only rarely (and with painful consequences for both men and women), although the picture of gender relations conducted in private seems to have been very different. Women, for example, appear to have exerted considerable authority over household servants and, on occasion, their husbands.

Youth was regarded as a time of passion, rashness, and licentiousness, and accidents of inheritance were generally the only ways through which the young could exercise authority. Although the legal ages of discretion were fourteen for boys and twelve for girls, full adult membership of the community was achieved only through marriage. Conversely, extreme age does not appear to have been accorded respect, especially since old age was often a period of dependency. England appears to have been ruled by those in their forties and fifties. Most of the truly aged were women, often widows, who occupied a position of double or even triple marginality.

The social order of Tudor England was therefore constructed through hierarchies of status, gender, and age, and all these in turn were overlaid with a powerful and resonant, though often informal, language of social description.

BIBLIOGRAPHY

Amussen, Susan. *An Ordered Society: Gender and Class in Early Modern England.* 1988.

Campbell, Mildred. *The English Yeoman Under Elizabeth and the Early Stuarts.* 1942.

Cressy, David. "Describing the Social Order of Elizabethan and Stuart England." *Literature and History,* vol. 3, pp. 29–44.

Harte, N.B. "State Control of Dress and Social Change in Pre-Industrial England." In *Trade, Government, and Economy in Pre-Industrial England.* D.C. Coleman and A.H. John, eds. Pp. 132–165. 1976.

Heal, Felicity, and Clive Holmes. *The Gentry in England and Wales, 1500–1700.* 1994.

Stone, Lawrence. *The Crisis of the Aristocracy, 1558–1641.* 1965.

Thomas, Keith. "Age and Authority in Early Modern England." *Proceedings of The British Academy,* vol. 62, pp. 205–248.

Wrightson, Keith. "'Sorts of People' in Tudor and Stuart England." In *The Middling Sort of People: Culture, Society, and Politics in England, 1550–1800.* Jonathan Barry and Christopher Brooks, eds. Pp. 28–51. 1994.

———. "Estates, Degrees, and Sorts: Changing Perceptions of Society in Tudor and Stuart England." In *Language, History and Class.* Penelope J. Corfield, ed. Pp. 30–52. 1991.

———. "The Social Order of Early Modern England: Three Approaches." In *The World We Have Gained: Histories of Population and Social Structure.* Lloyd Bonfield, R.M. Smith, and K.E. Wrightson, eds. Pp. 177–202. 1986.

Steven Hindle

SEE ALSO

Agriculture; Economy; Elyot, Thomas; Gender; Harrison, William; *Homilies, Books of;* Knighthood; Marriage and Marriage Law; Population and Demography; Smith, Thomas; Sumptuary Laws; Towns; Wilson, Thomas

Society of Antiquaries
See Antiquarianism

Somerset, Duke of
See Seymour, Edward

Song

English song can be defined as a combination of secular verse and musical setting in which the poetic structure is enhanced by the presence of music. Most typically a song features a solo voice or several voices in homophonic or hymnlike style, presenting the verse in enhanced or heightened declamation. Frequently a song is a strophic composition with the same music repeated for more than one stanza of text. Finally, a song is a conscious, written creation and thus distinguished from folk or popular vocal music, even though a specific song may seem to imitate the folk or popular style and may undergo substantial alteration as it is disseminated by hand copying or from memory. Given this definition, English song emerged at the beginning of the Tudor period and flowered into the genre known as air or lute song that enjoys renown, along with the madrigal of roughly the same period, as one of the sublime achievements of the late Elizabethan years. Throughout the Tudor period, song is associated primarily with music-making at the court or in the homes of the nobility.

Early Tudor composers of vernacular songs include Richard Davy (active c. 1490–1506); Robert Fayrfax, namesake of the "Fayrfax MS," one of three principal sources of English secular vocal music before 1530, which is so named for its association with him; and William Cornysh, who is usually regarded as the most accomplished composer of his generation. In addition to the Fayrfax MS, however, early English songs are featured in "Henry VIII's MS," which includes no less than thirty-three compositions attributed to Henry himself, as well as others ascribed to Cornysh, Fayrfax, and other composers. As is typical of such sources, about one-third of the compositions are anonymous. A third important source of secular songs in English from the early period is known as "Ritson's MS" after its nineteenth-century owner.

In all of the early sixteenth-century sources, vernacular songs are largely in the style of the medieval carol with its characteristic refrain and frequently dance-like musical form. The English song for which the later part of the period is known developed in conjunction with the rise of humanism and with the Protestant Reformation, both of which brought a new emphasis on words and the importance of understanding a text in musical setting. Changes in poetic taste and style in England during the Tudor years also had a significant impact on the growth of secular song. While a fascination with musical influences from the Continent, particularly from Italy and France, and increasing prominence of music and dancing in courtly circles are important factors in the musical characteristics of English song as it emerged during the course of the sixteenth century, these philosophical and literary factors encouraged the conscious fusion of the musical and literary arts that is the hallmark of the mature genre.

The humanists, drawing inspiration from what they learned from ancient Greek writing about music, spoke of a need for the text to predominate in vocal music, insisting that "the fassion of the melodye dothe so represente the meaning of the thing, that it doth wonderfullye move, stire, pearce, and enflame the hearers myndes" (Sir Thomas More, in *Utopia*, 1516). In practice, two methods of linking music to verse appeared. In one, based largely on French models, the external or formal structure of a poetic text was strictly recreated in musical form so that the words were presented without repetition or interpretive nuance. In the other, more Italian, technique musical devices were used to enhance the meaning of the text so that the resulting song is more an interpretation of the poem than a heightened reading. Both methods, however, represented a conscious effort to make a single work of art from the two languages.

One of the first to essay the new style was Thomas Whythorne (1528–1596), who was both poet and composer. His *Songes, for three, fower, and five voyces*, which appeared in 1571, is notable chiefly as the first printed book of English secular music to survive and the only printed collection between the *XX Songes* printed in 1530 (of which very little is extant) and William Byrd's *Psalmes, Sonets, & songs* of 1588. During the 1540s, Whythorne worked for the poet John Heywood, learning the crafts of poetry and music and copying the poetry of such poets as Wyatt and Surrey for Heywood's use. Whythorne's songs are rudimentary compared to those of the better known composers, but they exemplify the mid-century experimentation with fairly strict musical rendering of poetic structure in four-square, homophonic settings.

Of later composers, Whythorne is most suggestive of Thomas Campion, who was also both the poet and the composer as a writer of songs. Although more skilled than Whythorne, producing especially some of the late Elizabethan period's most graceful lyrics, Campion nevertheless adhered closely to the premise that the poem was complete and needed music not to interpret but to present. Campion had spent time in France and was very likely influenced in his thinking about the musico-poetic liaison by the ideas of the French humanist group known as the Pléiade.

The second approach to musical representation of poetry, in which the music serves to express the meaning of the words, led most directly to the flowering of the English madrigal which, as a polyphonic composition, does not figure in the present discussion of song. The

S

technique, however, was useful to writers of songs as well and became the hallmark of the air (or ayre) made famous by John Dowland and others. Many of these songs use devices known as word-painting, such as an ascending scale to represent the word "mountain." Critics of the day (such as Thomas Morley) decried such literal representation, however, and the more skillful composers of ayres learned to use the expressive capabilities of musical setting in a manner closer to metaphor or metonymy to suggest the emotional affect suggested in the poetic text. Dowland and his contemporary John Danyel (c. 1565–1630) both excelled at representing the states of emotion appropriate to a text in the lute accompaniment in such a manner that the vocal declamation of the verse was still eminently clear and intelligible.

A special type of song, particularly prevalent from the 1570s through the end of the century, has come to be known as the "consort song." Like the air, the consort song is an accompanied melody. The text is usually carried by a single voice, most often the treble, but it is accompanied by a "consort" of stringed instruments that weaves polyphonically behind and below the voice. The presentation of the text is formal and unadorned by interpretive nuance, but the accompanying instruments are free to engage in a more interesting musical texture. William Byrd composed many songs in this style, although he then supplied text for the instrumental parts in some of them in order to conform to a taste for part-singing and thus, as he acknowledges, make his songbooks more salable. Songs in the consort style became a frequent vehicle for highly emotional laments in plays as well. Richard Edwardes, as playwright, poet, and composer, wrote a lament for his tragicomedy, *Damon and Pithias* (c. 1564), that is the best-known exemplar of this kind of Tudor song.

The extent to which a concept of song as a musico-poetic genre was accepted is evident in the many instances in which songs exist in a literary context with the fiction that they are being sung. Richard Tottel's *Miscellany,* which was originally published as *A Book of Songs and Sonnets* in 1557, established a vogue for anthologies that continued through the remainder of the century. Songs, in these collections, are loosely distinguished from other verse types by their formal structure, typically in stanzas, and by their simpler diction and less argumentative stance. While many do exist in musical setting, the style was identifiable in the absence of actual music. Almost every Elizabethan poet produced some sort of "songs and sonnets," many so

titled (the poet-composer Thomas Whythorne even wrote an autobiography in the 1570s that he entitled "A book of songs and sonetts") and some (such as Sir Philip Sidney's "Astrophil and Stella") demonstrating in practice the contrastive fictional styles of "sonnet" and "song."

BIBLIOGRAPHY

Brett, Philip. "The English Consort Song, 1570–1625." *Proceedings of the Royal Musical Association,* vol. 88, pp. 73–88.

Doughtie, Edward. *English Renaissance Song.* 1986.

Stevens, John. *Music and Poetry in the Early Tudor Court.* 1961; repr. 1979.

Turbet, Richard. *Tudor Music: A Research and Information Guide.* Music Research and Information Guides, no. 18. 1994.

Wulstan, David. *Tudor Music.* 1985.

Elise Bickford Jorgens

SEE ALSO

Air; Byrd, William; Campion, Thomas; Carol; Consort Music; Cornysh, William; Dowland, John; Edwardes, Richard; Fayrfax, Robert; Henry VIII as Composer; Heywood, John; Madrigal; Sonnet Sequences; Tottel, Richard

Sonnet Sequences

A collection of sonnets, usually the traditional fourteen-line Shakespearean form (three quatrains and a couplet) or the Italian (an octave and a sestet), were written in narrative sequences in the Tudor period depicting the tormenting and unavailing love of a young poet for a beautiful, blonde, young woman ("the cruel fair"). The idea of the sequence originated with Dante's *La vita nuova,* the story of his lifelong love for Beatrice. The form achieved its classic expression in the *Rime sparse,* or *Canzoniere,* of Petrarch, 317 sonnets interspersed with *canzoni, ballate, madrigali,* and *sestine,* telling of the love of Petrarch for Laura.

In England, the Petrarchan sonnet was introduced by Sir Thomas Wyatt and Henry Howard, earl of Surrey, in their works published as *Tottel's Miscellany* (1557) but written during the reign of Henry VIII. The first real sequence is Sir Philip Sidney's *Astrophil and Stella* (1591). Attempts to give primacy to Anne Locke, *A meditation of a Penitent Sinner* (1560), or Thomas Watson, *Hekatompathia, or passionate centurie of love* (1582), or even John

Soowthern, *Pandora* (1584), pale in comparison with Sidney's undoubted achievement. Many sequences followed the posthumous publication of Sidney's poems: Henry Constable's *Diana* (1592), Samuel Daniel's *Delia* (1592), Barnabe Barnes's *Parthenophil and Parthenophe* (1593), Giles Fletcher's *Licia* (1593), Thomas Lodge's *Phillis* (1593), Thomas Watson's *The Teares of fancie* (1593), the anonymous *Zepheria* (1594), Michael Drayton's *Ideas Mirrour* (1594), William Percy's *Sonnets to the fairest Coelia* (1594), E.C.'s *Emaricdulfe* (1595), I.C.'s *Alcilia* (1595), and Richard Barnfield's *Cynthia* (1595). Others include *Amoretti and Epithalamium* (1595), by Edmund Spenser; *Fidessa* (1596), by Bartholomew Griffin; *Diella* (1596), by Richard Lynche; *Chloris* (1596), by William Smith; and *Laura* (1597) and *Alba* (1598), by Robert Tofte. William Shakespeare's *Sonnets* did not appear until 1609, and Lady Mary Wroth's *Pamphilia to Amphilanthus* was first published in 1621.

Most of these sequences follow the example of using the allegorical name of the lady as the title of the sequence unlike the titles of Sidney, Barnes, and Sidney's niece, Lady Mary Wroth, with the notable exception of Shakespeare's generic title. Most follow the conventions of the unresponding lady and the lamenting poet, as in Sidney, but none resorts to the Italian expedient of having the lady die. Only Spenser's *Amoretti* concludes with a marriage hymn, *Epithalamion*. Shakespeare turns the conventions upside down by making the unresponsive loved one a Fair Young Man and by introducing that compliant Dark Lady, who sleeps with both the Fair Young Man and Will the poet, leaving all unsatisfied at the end. Barnes makes the most extreme and indecorous breach of the conventions by having his Parthenophil rape Parthenophe in the final poem of the sequence, the first triple-sestina in English.

The sonnet sequence was also used as a vehicle of religious devotion: Anne Locke, *A meditation of a Penitent Sinner* (1560); Henry Lok, *Sundry Christian Passions* (1593); Barnabe Barnes, *A divine centurie of spirituall sonnets* (1595); Henry Lok, *Ecclesiastes* (1597); and Nicholas Breton, *The Soules Harmony* (1602). Two religious sequences exist in manuscript: the forty-three sonnets of William Alabaster and the *Spirituall Sonnettes* of Henry Constable (1562–1613).

The sonnet sequence disappeared as a form in England after the middle of the seventeenth century and was only resuscitated in the late-eighteenth and nineteenth centuries. But these later sequences have little resemblance to their Renaissance predecessors.

BIBLIOGRAPHY

Greene, Roland. *Post-Petrarchism: Origins and Innovations of the Western Lyric Sequence.* 1991.

John, Lisle Cecil. *The Elizabethan Sonnet Sequence.* 1938.

Lever, J.W. *The Elizabethan Love Sonnet.* 1956.

Roche, Thomas P., Jr. *Petrarch and the English Sonnet Sequences.* 1989.

Smith, Hallett. *Elizabethan Poetry.* Chap. 3: "The Sonnet." 1952.

Wilkins, Ernest Hatch. *The Invention of the Sonnet and Other Studies in Italian Literature.* 1959.

Thomas P. Roche

SEE ALSO

Barnes, Barnabe; Breton, Nicholas; Daniel, Samuel; Drayton, Michael; Howard, Henry; Lodge, Thomas; Lok, Henry; Lyric; Petrarchanism; Shakespeare, William; Sidney, Philip; Spenser, Edmund; Versification

Southampton, Earls of

See Wriothesley, Henry; Wriothesley, Thomas

Southwark

Tudor Southwark was that area south of the river Thames consisting of five manors, known (in 1550) as Paris Garden, Clink, Guildable, Great Liberty, and King's. This area also comprised the parishes of St. George, St. Margaret's, St. Olave's, St. Thomas, and St. Mary Magdalen. These last two were united to form the parish of St. Saviour's in 1539. Southwark's administration was decentralized among these manorial and parochial bodies. For the first half of the period the city owned the Guildable manor, and ecclesiastical bodies owned the remainder. An attempt was made to incorporate the developed area of Southwark into the administration of London when the city acquired the King's and Great Liberty manor, and together with the Guildable manor formed Bridge Ward Without in 1550. Unfortunately, no ward structure was ever erected, and the two remaining western manors of the Clink and Paris Garden remained autonomous.

Other bodies also claimed authority in Southwark, notably the officers of its prisons—namely, the Marshalsea, the King's Bench prison, the bishop of Winchester's prison (the Clink), and the White Lyon (built in 1550s). Such administrative confusion meant that Southwark had a well-deserved reputation for sheltering

S

various criminal and undesirable elements, as well as proving a good place to locate trades and industries outside the jurisdiction of the city of London. Tudor Southwark was famous for its prostitutes: the "Stews" on the Bankside, located in the Clink manor (owned by the bishops of Winchester), was one of only two London districts where brothels were sanctioned officially. The Stews were closed by royal proclamation in 1546. Morally suspect services continued in Southwark, however. Bearbaiting began in the Bankside in the 1540s, and that same district saw the erection of public theaters, like the Globe (1598/1599).

Southwark's population appears to have begun growing in the late fifteenth century and may have been between 8,000–9,200 in 1548. By 1603, its population was around 19,000. In the second half of the Tudor period, this population expansion helped to alter the social topography of Southwark dramatically. Lay palaces, such as Suffolk Place, and other pre-Reformation monastic buildings were converted into overcrowded tenement dwellings. Tudor Southwark was one of the wealthiest urban districts in England, ranking twelfth in taxable wealth in the Lay subsidy of 1524–1527. Brewing and a large leather industry were well established by the Tudor period, and of particular importance was its service industry. Southwark was linked to London by the only bridge over the Thames, and the main roads from Kent and Surrey ran through its High Street, and it was famous for large public inns, notably the Tabard, that served this traffic. Southwark's location also favored maritime and waterborne trades; a large number of watermen worked in western Southwark. Southwark also had the "Doche," a large alien community, consisting largely of Flemings and located mostly in eastern Southwark. These immigrants followed typical Southwark trades but also dominated some highly skilled ones, such as glazing and printing. A new wave of such refugees settled in Southwark in the 1560s and 1570s. The Protestant Reformation found many converts in Southwark, a fact that became politically important when its inhabitants supported Wyatt's Rebellion against Mary in 1554.

BIBLIOGRAPHY

Carlin, M. *Medieval Southwark.* 1996.
Johnson, D.J. *Southwark and the City.* 1969.

Jeremy Boulton

SEE ALSO

Aliens; London; Sexual Offenses; Wyatt's Rebellion

Southwell, Robert (1561–1595)

Poet, prose writer, priest, and martyr, Robert Southwell was born in 1561 at Horsham St. Faith, Norfolk, to a wealthy, well-connected Catholic family. In 1576, aged fourteen, he was sent to school at Douai, where he studied at the Jesuit College. At seventeen he entered the Jesuit novitiate at Rome (1578), and in 1581 was transferred to the English College, where he became prefect of studies. He was ordained priest in 1584. In 1586, his superiors reluctantly gave permission for him to be sent on the mission to England, where he landed secretly, July 7, with Henry Garnet. Assisted by the countess of Arundel, whose chaplain he became, Southwell survived six years before being caught in a Catholic household near London, June 26, 1592, by priest-hunter and torturer Richard Topcliffe. He underwent forty hours of torture in Topcliffe's house, followed by further torture and interrogation in the Gatehouse Prison. Later, in response to a petition from his family, he was moved to solitary confinement in the Tower, his health broken. In February 1595, the government brought him to trial for treason under the statute of 1585 against being a priest in England. Found guilty and sentenced, the next day, February 21, he was hanged, drawn, and quartered at Tyburn.

Southwell began writing in Rome, taking as models the fashionable Counter Reformation literature of repentance and tears. Holograph drafts survive of rough translations from Tansillo's *Lagrime di San Pietro* and from a homily on Mary Magdalen, first efforts at the subjects of his later *Saint Peter's Complaint* and *Mary Magdalen's Funeral Tears,* both extremely successful books. Since Southwell's and Garnet's superiors sent them to England with instructions to write and publish books, it is likely that Southwell took some poetry and prose in manuscript with him on the mission, although most of his surviving work was written in England. He wrote nothing after capture.

Within months of landing, Southwell and Garnet acquired a printing press and published Southwell's first book, *An Epistle of Comfort* (1587), a work in the ancient genre of encouragement to martyrdom; it originated in letters written to Henry Fitzalan, the earl of Arundel, imprisoned for his Catholicism. *Mary Magdalen's Funeral Tears,* dedicated to Dorothy Arundell, was published by Gabriel Cawood in 1591. Other prose works circulated in manuscript: *An Epistle of a Religious Priest unto His Father* (1589, secretly published 1596–1597), written to reconcile his father to the church; a consolatory epistle to Arundel for the death of his half-sister, Lady Margaret Sackville (1591), published 1595 as *The Triumphs over Death* (not

ת

Southwell's title); *A Short rule of Good Life* (1591, secretly published 1596–1597); and *An Humble Supplication* (1591), arguably Southwell's prose masterpiece, a response to the government's anti-Catholic proclamation of late 1591. His poems, both *Saint Peter's Complaint* and a collection of lyrics, circulated in manuscript texts for which Southwell provided introductory matter. Posthumous editions appeared in 1595 (*Saint Peter's Complaint, With Other Poems; Mœoniæ*).

As a poet-missionary, Southwell wished to adapt secular styles and subjects to religious use, and to change current taste by challenging contemporaries to compete in writing on religious subject matter. The first led him into uninspired versifying in a Tottellian or "drab" Tudor style, but the second, enabling him to introduce into England the themes and styles of Counter Reformation writing, produced his most original work: in prose, *An Epistle of Comfort* and *Mary Magdalen's Funeral Tears;* in verse, *Saint Peter's Complaint,* his short poems on religious mysteries, and "A Vale of Tears."

BIBLIOGRAPHY

Brown, Nancy Pollard, and James H. McDonald, eds. *The Poems of Robert Southwell.* 1967.
Brownlow, F.W. *Robert Southwell.* 1996.
Cousins, A.D. *The Catholic Religious Poets from Southwell to Crashaw: A Critical Study.* 1991.
Devlin, Christopher. *The Life of Robert Southwell, Poet and Martyr.* 1957.
Martz, Louis. *The Poetry of Meditation.* 2nd edition. 1962.
Scallon, Joseph. *The Poetry of Robert Southwell.* 1975.

F.W. Brownlow

SEE ALSO

Counter Reformation; English College of Rome; Fitzalan, Henry; Jesuits; Treason

Spain, Relations with England
See Foreign Relations and Diplomacy

Spanish Armada
See Armada, Spanish

Spanish Literature, Influence of

The genuine affection for Spanish letters among Tudor diplomats, courtiers, and writers is often overshadowed by the larger literary contributions of Italy and France, and by the later impact of Cervantes and the Spanish theater during the seventeenth century. But Spain gave Tudor readers and writers more than popular sources of romance and manners. Cultural exchange was promoted by ambassadors and courtiers at the courts of Spain and England—particularly during the marriage alliances of Katherine of Aragon and Philip II—and Spanish letters became a wellspring of courtly advice literature. Spain's many works on exploration, navigation, and natural history were also a unique resource for Tudor merchants and promoters of colonial development. Last, the rivalries of the English and Spanish courts created a tradition of satire and imitation by English writers.

Beginning in 1483 with William Caxton's inclusion of thirteen fables by Pedro Alfonso in his *Aesop,* Spanish literature appeared in Tudor England most frequently in adaptation or translation. Many courtiers and humanists knew Spanish, and Henry VIII and Elizabeth I could read it, but French was better known until the 1590s, when Spanish grammars and readers became available, among them the *Bibliotheca Hispanica* (1599), compiled by John Minshieu. English translations of Spanish texts were often based on readily available French versions; in turn, a French version often exerted an influence on Tudor writers before an English version became available, as in the case of the huge collection of Spanish romances known as the *Amadís de Gaula.* Assembled in part by Garcí Ordóñez de Montalvo, the *Amadís* was not fully "Englished" until 1617 by Anthony Munday, but the French version of Nicholas de Herberay (Books 1–8, 1540–1548), Gabrielle Chapuys, and others influenced Philip Sidney, who praises the *Amadís* in his *Defence* and uses material (especially from Book 11) for both the *Arcadia* and *Astrophil and Stella* (especially in the eighth song). Edmund Spenser, on the other hand, likely knew the *Amadís,* but it is difficult to prove the influence of analogous scenes and motifs on *The Faerie Queene.*

A similar case for literary influence can be made for Jorge de Montemayor, whose pastoral romance, *Diana* (1559), drew heavily on the Italian of Sanazarro and was available in many continental versions. Traces of Montemayor in English appear first in the *Eclogues, Epitaphs, and Sonnets* (1563) of Barnabe Googe, who had spent several years in Spain. Both Spenser's *Shepherdes Calendar* and Sidney's *New Arcadia* rely on plots from Montemayor, as does Anthony Munday's *History of Felix and Philomela* (1585), which in turn provided plot elements for William Shakespeare's *Two Gentlemen of Verona.*

S

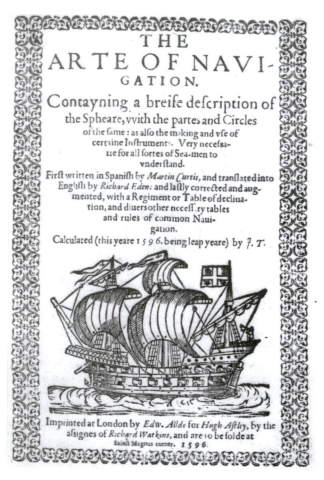

Martin Cortes, *The Arte of Navigation, translated by Richard Eden,* 1561 (1596). Eden's important translation of this major work of Spanish navigational science was one of the many such works translated for Elizabethan merchants and naval tacticians. Translations such as this may have played a role in the defeat of the Spanish Armada, but they certainly contributed to the rise of English naval power and the expansion of late-Tudor exploration. Reproduced from the original by permission of the Henry E. Huntington Library and Art Gallery.

Bartholomew Yong's complete translation of the *Diana* (1598, relying on the French version of Gabriel Chapuys, 1597) brought together Montemayor's text with versions by Alonso Perez and Gaspar Gil Polo (both 1564).

Because Spanish literature before Cervantes often domesticated Italian forms that were also to reach England independently, it is hard to estimate Spanish influence where Petrarchanism is concerned. Imitation of Petrarch was used by Garcilaso de la Vega to revive the Spanish lyric in the late 1520s, and Castiglione's *Il Cortegiano* was quickly translated by his friend and literary executor, Juan Boscán. But the fact that Thomas Wyatt knew Boscán while he was ambassador in Spain has provided no clear evidence that the Petrarchan revival in Spain, though prior, influenced the English revival begun by Wyatt and the earl of Surrey. Nevertheless, the achievement of Garcilaso and Boscán was such that an excerpt from an eclogue by Garcilaso is translated by Googe in *Eclogues, Epitaphs, and Sonnets,* and Abraham Fraunce quotes both poets generously (in Spanish) in *The Arcadian Rhetorike* (1588).

Several other Spanish literary texts enjoyed prominence in England. Fernando de Rojas's *La Celestina* (1499) was adapted, probably by John Rastell, around 1530, as *An Interlude of Calisto and Melibea.* A semidramatic piece featuring "the bewte and good propertes of women" and "theyr vycys and evyll condicyons," it appears influenced by the educational theories of the Spanish humanist, Juan Luis Vives, who had been teaching at Oxford in the 1520s. This adaptation was characteristically based on a French version, and became a popular source for anticlerical satire and moral aphorism. A vogue for didactic literature further developed in 1535 when John Bourchier, Lord Berners, translated (also from a French version) Antonio de Guevara's *Relox de príncipes o Libro aureo* (1529), *The Golden Booke of Marcus Aurelius.* Many editions followed, along with a competing translation by Sir Thomas North, *The Diall of Princes* (1557, 1568, 1582). Several other works by Guevara on court and country life were also frequently translated. His enormous popularity was perhaps matched only by the devotional writer, Father Luis de Granada, whose diverse works on sin and prayer were translated by Francis Meres, Thomas Lodge, and others. San Juan de la Cruz was also part of this vogue for Spanish mysticism, and he was well known by devotional poets, among them John Donne, but he remained untranslated during this period. The anonymous *Lazarillo de Tormes* (1554) became the prototype for an emerging rogue literature in England. First translated by David Rowland before 1576, with more editions in 1586 and 1596, Lazarillo may have been the model for Thomas Nashe's Jack Wilton in *The Unfortunate Traveler.* Finally, a unique work of early modern science and psychology by Juan Huarte de San Juan, *Examen de Ingenios Para las Sciencias* (1575), was translated by Richard Carew from the Italian version by M. Camillo Camilli (1582) as *The Examination of Men's Wits* (1594, with three later editions).

Spain was England's chief source of information about the New World; while Richard Hakluyt's *Principal Navigations* (1589) is the best-known anthology of literature promoting exploration, earlier translations established the preeminence of Spanish sources. Richard Eden's *Decades of the New Worlde* (1555), based on Peter Martyr Vermigli's collection of voyage chronicles, printed in Spain in 1516, also relied on material from the *Sumario de la Natural y General Historia de las Indias* (1526) by Gonzalo Fernández de Oviedo y Valdés, and the *Historia General de las Indias* (1552) by Francisco Lopez de Gómara. Gómara was more fully translated by the Merchant Adventurer Thomas Nicholas, whose *Pleasant History of the Conquest of the West Indies* (1578) was cited by many writers, among them Sir Walter Ralegh. An important work that further developed the "black legend" of Spanish cruelty in the Americas was the *Brevísima Relacion* (1552) of Bartolomé de las Casas, translated as *The Spanish Colonie* (1583) by one M.M.S. Finally, a major work of natural history by José de Acosta, *Historia Natural y Moral de las Indias* (1590), was translated in 1601 by Edward Grimstone, but not published until 1604.

Along with natural history of the New World, navigation itself became a practical genre for merchant translators, beginning in 1561 with Eden's *The Arte of Navigation,* translated from a 1551 treatise by Martin Cortés. Eden's version went into four more editions. There was great demand for the subject, for in 1578, Edward Hellowes translated the *Aguja de Marear* (1539) of Antonio de Guevara, followed by 1581 and 1595 editions of John Frampton's translation of *Arte de Navegar* (1545) by Pedro de Medina. It was Frampton who had also translated the major Spanish New World pharmacopia, Nicholas Monardes's *Historia Medicinal* (1569, 1571, 1574), as *Joyfull Newes of the new found World* (1577), enlarging on his account of a plant that was to be vital to English colonial interests: tobacco.

The preeminence of Spain during much of this period made it as much a subject as a source of literary material; a body of occasional literature built up around Spanish topics such as imperial events, battles, colonial affairs, and Catholic conspiracies against Elizabeth I. A ferocious pamphlet war was fought after the Spanish Armada among London courtiers, propagandists, and literary opportunists. The battle of Alcazar became a featured subject in George Whetstone's *English Myrror* (1586), drawing on plot material from Pedro Mexía's *Silva de varia lección;* George Peele also wrote a topical play, the *Battle of Alcazar.*

More generally, Spanish history (real and imaginary) was a favorite theme among Elizabethan dramatists. Most notable are the plays Thomas Kyd wrote in the late 1580s, *Ieronimo* and *Spanish Tragedy.* Capitalizing on a popular sensation, in 1596, Henslowe's company treated the Spanish career of the English adventurer, Thomas Stukeley, in *Stewtley.* Nevertheless, Elizabethan playwrights seemed unaware of a flourishing Spanish theater and the prolific Lope de Vega. Spaniards on the Elizabethan stage were generally fixed comic types, usually arrogant, cruel, or pompous in varying degrees; and often little more than a Spanish name was needed to establish a character such as Shakespeare's Don Armado. This reduction of Spanish culture and character to types had as much to do with anti-Catholic satire as with a real affection for Spanish culture.

BIBLIOGRAPHY

Harrison, T.P. "Googe's *Eglogs* and Montemayor's *Diana.*" Texas Studies in English, no. 5, pp. 68–78. 1925.

O'Connor, John J. *Amadis de Gaule and Its Influence on Elizabethan Literature.* 1970.

Oliveira e Silva, J. de. "Sir Philip Sidney and the Castilian Tongue." *Comparative Literature,* vol. 34, pp. 130–145.

Rudder, Robert S. *The Literature of Spain in English Translation: A Bibliography.* 1975.

Santoyo, Julio-César, and Isabel Verdaguer, eds. *De Clásicos y Traducciones: Clásicos Españoles en Versiones Inglesas.* 1987.

Selig, Karl Ludwig. "Garcilaso in Sixteenth-Century England." *Romanische Forschungen,* vol. 84, pp. 368–371.

Stubbings, Hilda U. *Renaissance Spain and Its Literary Relations with England and France: A Critical Biography.* 1969.

Underhill, John G. *Spanish Literature in the England of the Tudors.* 1899.

Ungerer, Gustav. *Anglo-Spanish Relations in Tudor England.* Swiss Studies in English. Vol. 38. 1956.

David W. Swain

SEE ALSO

Bourchier, John; Carew, Richard; Caxton, William; Discovery and Exploration; Fraunce, Abraham; Googe, Barnabe; Hakluyt, Richard; Katherine of Aragon; Nashe, Thomas; Pastoral; Peele, George; Petrarchanism; Philip II; Rastell, John; Romance; Sidney, Philip; Spenser, Edmund; Stukeley, Thomas; Vermigli, Peter Martyr; Vives, Juan Luis; Whetstone, George

Spenser, Edmund (c. 1552–1599)

Described on his funeral monument as "the Prince of Poets in his tyme," Edmund Spenser ranks today among a

S

handful of the greatest and most influential of English poets. Born in London, Spenser attended (1561–1569) the Merchant Taylors' School, whose headmaster, Richard Mulcaster, was to become a famous and influential humanist. While still at school, the sixteen- or seventeen-year-old Spenser contributed verse translations to an anti-Catholic volume, *A Theatre for voluptuous Worldlings* (1569), published by a religious refugee from the Low Countries, Jan van der Noodt. In 1569, Spenser also matriculated as a "sizar," that is, a poor but not necessarily impoverished student, at Pembroke Hall, Cambridge, and received his B.A. in 1573, his M.A. in 1576. By 1578, he became secretary to John Young, bishop of Rochester, who had been master of Pembroke during Spenser's time there. In 1579, Spenser married Macabyas Chylde at Westminster, entered the service of the Robert Dudley, the earl of Leicester, enjoyed some familiarity with Philip Sidney and his circle, and published *The Shepheardes Calender.*

In 1580, Spenser and his Cambridge friend, Gabriel Harvey, published five letters, two of which Spenser wrote. As those letters reveal, Spenser was then at work on his great romance-epic, *The Faerie Queene*. Also in 1580, Spenser was appointed secretary to the new lord deputy of Ireland, Arthur Lord Grey of Wilton, with whom he moved to Ireland. Until 1582, he worked in Dublin, as clerk of the Privy Council. From 1581–1588, he held the post of clerk in chancery for faculties, a sinecure. He leased the property of New Abbey, near Dublin in County Kildare, in 1582, was commissioner of musters for the county in 1583–1584, and in 1584, became deputy to Lodowick Bryskett, clerk of the Council of Munster. By 1588 or 1589, Spenser had clearly prospered from his work as an agent of English colonialism, for he then occupied Kilcolman, an estate of around 3,000 acres. This land, confiscated from Irish opponents, lay between Limerick and Cork, not far from the 42,000-acre estate of Spenser's patron, Sir Walter Ralegh.

His star continuing to rise, Spenser accompanied Ralegh to the court of Queen Elizabeth I in 1589. In 1590, the first three books of *The Faerie Queene* were published there, dedicated to Queen Elizabeth, "the most mightie and magnificent empresse." In the following year, the queen granted Spenser a lifetime pension of £50 per year—a stunning pecuniary acknowledgment from so parsimonious a monarch. Other publications followed these successes: *Daphnaida* and *Complaints* appeared in 1591; *Colin Clouts Come Home Againe, Amoretti* and *Epithalamion* in 1595; and *The Faerie Queene*, Books 1–6, *Fowre Hymnes*, and *Prothalamion* in 1596. As *Colin Clouts* indicates, Spenser

had returned to Ireland by 1591, where he married Elizabeth Boyle, probably in 1594, an event beautifully celebrated in *Epithalamion*. He visited England again in 1595–1596, perhaps to oversee his current publications, which included Books 4–6 of *The Faerie Queene.*

In 1598, Spenser's prose work *A Vewe of the present state of Irelande* (first published in 1633) was entered in the Stationer's Register. In that year, Spenser was named sheriff of the county of Cork, receiving in the process commendation "for his good and commendable parts, being a man endowed with good knowledge in learning and not unskillful or without experience in the service of the wars." But then a rebellion against the English hegemony and its agents resulted in the sack of Kilcolman. Having taken refuge in Cork, Spenser carried letters from Sir Thomas Norris, lord president of Munster, to the Privy Council in London, where he arrived on December 24, 1598. He died on January 13, 1599, and was buried in Westminster Abbey. Ten years later, *The Faerie Queene* was republished. This volume for the first time included a beautiful fragment titled the *Cantos of Mutabilitie.* Spenser was survived by a son (Sylvanus) and a daughter (Katherine), children of his first marriage, and by his widow, Elizabeth Boyle, and their son (Peregrine).

Although he is named only Immerito (the unworthy one) in the volume itself, *The Shepheardes Calender* gave Spenser an exceptionally well-advertised entrée into the literary world. The letters exchange between Spenser and Harvey had already listed an array of works (either fictional, or subsequently lost) the poet had completed or on which he was then at work. Next, the *Calender* appeared, its text set off by an elaborate scholarly apparatus—introductions, commentary, illustrations—of the kind heretofore afforded only to the most admired classical and modern authors. The commentary, supplied by an indefatigable but unidentifiable person, "E.K.," perhaps a Cambridge acquaintance, Edward Kirke, perhaps a fiction disguising Spenser and Harvey themselves, provides sometimes helpful, often eccentric glosses for archaic words and etymologies, comments on rhetorical tropes and schemes, keys to allegorical or symbolic meanings, and so on.

This imposing apparatus frames and (imperfectly) illuminates a sequence of twelve pastoral eclogues. The eclogue was originated by Theocritus (third century B.C.) and sophisticated by Vergil, Petrarch, Boccaccio, and Mantuan, among others. Spenser's eclogues yield immediate delight by means of their engaging poetry, which takes a stunning variety of metrical and stanzaic forms: alliterative verse, ballad stanza, quatrains, lay, ode, *rime couée* (or "tail rhyme"), roundelay, and even a sestina, the first in English. These features, together with the charm that subtle touches of characterization grant the shepherd singers, make the *Calender* a virtuoso performance that is at the same time remarkably beautiful.

The *Calender*'s abundant poetic charms render the more delightful and seductive its persistent thematic seriousness, a characteristic Spenser's predecessors from Vergil onward had given pastoral poetry. Spenser's versions of pastoral, in the *Calender* and in recurrent pastoral moments in *The Faerie Queene*, raise serious issues of politics, of ethics, of religion, and of love, treated in ways that bring love's spiritual implications to the fore. By treating these issues in a sequence linked to the succession of months and seasons, Spenser gives his pastorals a georgic modulation, placing them within the planetary and astronomical cycles through which God was thought to govern natural and human affairs.

This immanence of ultimate perspectives and the *Calender*'s thematic earnestness appear most plainly in the group of eclogues that E.K. labels "moral" (eclogues 2, 5, 7, 9, 10). Here, biblical and medieval precedents enable shepherds readily to represent clerics, foxes and wolves to represent corrupt ministers, and oaks and briars, old and new religious institutions. Comparable if less explicit substantiveness appears in the other sets, which E.K. terms the plaintive (1, 6, 11, 12) and recreative (3, 4, 8).

Spenser's greatest poem, *The Faerie Queene*, luxuriously and at enormous length develops the virtuosity of language, variety of genre and content, weightiness of substance, and seductive charm that the *Calender* comprises on a far smaller scale. The poetry of *The Faerie Queene* exfoliates in a form so distinctive that it has received the name "Spenserian stanza," nine-line stanzas rhyming ababbcbcc; the first eight lines are typically pentameter, the last, an hexameter or "Alexandrine." This final line serves to punctuate the stanza, providing a pause at which the reader feels invited to reflect.

Opportunities for reflection are appropriate because the poem's varied materials are, as Spenser explains in his "Letter to Ralegh," printed with the 1590 edition, his poem is "a continued Allegory, or dark conceit," which for that reason requires of readers the attentive pursuit of clues to meanings not altogether self-evident. This dark conceit aims to "fashion a gentleman or noble person in virtuous or gentle discipline" by depicting a comprehensively accomplished hero, Prince Arthur, who at crucial moments throughout *The Faerie Queene* arrives to rescue a fellow knight from moral or spiritual disaster. By depicting such a hero, the poet aims

also to fashion his readers, teaching them by means of delightful but instructive fictions, "so much more profitable and gratious is doctrine by ensample, then by rule."

Each book of *The Faerie Queene*'s six books focuses on what Spenser calls a "private moral virtue," championed by individual knights: Book 1 concerns holiness, Book 2 depicts temperance, Book 3 chastity, Book 4 friendship, Book 5 justice, Book 6 courtesy. Although the knights who act as patrons for each virtue sometimes personify the virtue they defend, Spenser's allegory remains richly fluid, demanding alert attention to shifting implications. The hero of Book 1, the knight "of holiness," usually named Red Cross Knight, for example, acts throughout most of his book as a focus for the author's and his readers' explorations of human striving for an extremely elusive virtue, a striving fully achieved, contemporary theology asserts and Spenser's poem suggests, only in the next life. As they move through landscapes of mysterious forests, gardens, and palaces populated by monsters, magicians, seductions, and images of their own defects, the knights of every book remain at once capable and imperfect, as does even the superior knight, Arthur himself.

A recurrent point of Spenser's teaching seems to be that human striving, even if aided by the divine, can attain only modest heights. This includes the sheer capacity to comprehend the world in which they live. Even the most impressive heroes find themselves repeatedly nonplused as the poem explores complex contentions of early modern Europe: the means to salvation, the status of the genders, the corruption and venality of court politics, religious warfare, England's aspirations to colonial expansion. All such pressing matters seem to elude the grasp of human intellect.

So sober a thesis remains itself seductive, not only because Spenser persistently manages extraordinary displays of poetic skill within the confines of his stanzaic form, but also because the materials of his fictions offer delightful variety. His narratives of "knights and ladies gentle deeds" are enriched by metaphors and inset narratives drawn from the heritage of classical culture, most obviously represented by allusions and figures from the myths of Greece and Rome as interpreted by late classical, medieval, and Renaissance allegorists. He draws extensively, too, on the Bible and from classical philosophy, which, infused with leading ideas of Christian (especially Reformed Protestant) theology and ethics, inform magnificent visionary settings that illuminate the narrative.

Famous among these places are the House of Holiness, where the Red Cross Knight receives instruction in holiness in Book 1; the Bower of Bliss, a garden of sensual seduction

S

that the knight of temperance, Guyon, destroys in Book 2; the Gardens of Adonis, which provide a richly philosophical treatment of love as represented in the adventures of Britomart, the lady knight who champions chastity in Book 3; the grand confluence of rivers in the marriage of Thames and Medway in Book 4, or friendship; the temple of Isis, which concerns equity and justice, and the court of Mercilla, which treats of the origins and interplay of justice and mercy in Book 5, the book of justice; and Mount Acidale, where the poet Colin Clout conjures up and Calidore, the knight of courtesy, experiences a momentary pastoral epiphany in Book 6. Fittingly, the *Cantos of Mutabilitie* offer Spenser's last such setting, one that concludes in a prayer for ultimate vision, "a Sabaoth's sight" beyond the vicissitudes of the world of striving, contention, and moral and spiritual compromise so convincingly depicted throughout *The Faerie Queene*'s immense length.

This otherworldly focus at the end of *The Faerie Queene* recapitulates an impulse visible in his career. Though published in 1591, *Complaints: Containing sundrie small Poemes of the Worlds Vanitie* presents some of Spenser's earliest works, some but recently completed. In all nine of these pieces, the stress on the vanity of human wishes finds little relief. In later works, *Amoretti and Epithalamion* (1595) and *Fowre Hymnes* (1596) (not to mention *The Faerie Queene*), one finds a more characteristically Spenserian emphasis. Here, the limitations of human capacity and the pain of frustrated desire are subsumed in larger patterns of fulfillment. The egocentric, aspiring Petrarchan lover of the sonnet sequence, *Amoretti,* seems to move toward greater maturity, and toward a marriage, celebrated in *Epithalamion.* This beautiful, extended *canzone* places individual marriage, including, explicitly, Spenser's own marriage to Elizabeth Boyle, in larger contexts of society, nature, and the divine. In Fowre Hymnes, the Christianized Neoplatonic philosophy conspicuous in *Amoretti and Epithalamion* receives direct and systematic elaboration.

That Spenser ended his publishing career with *A Vewe of the Present State of Ireland* (1598) and ended his life on a mission for English colonial powers in Ireland may suggest why his poetry so often aspires to place life's challenges in the broadest and most meaningful contexts. Both the most down-to-earth and the most spiritual elements of his work have powerfully affected subsequent readers and authors. His fame began early: more than 100 references to his work or imitations of it survive from his own lifetime. Augustan, romantic, and the Victorian critics and authors have construed him in their own ways

and for different purposes, as have a virtual industry of scholars in the twentieth century. The story of Spenser's fame, well told in recent scholarship, effectively justifies the boast with which he concluded *The Shepheardes Calender.* His works, the young poet there proclaims, "steele in strength, and time in durance shall outweare."

BIBLIOGRAPHY.

Anderson, Judith H., Donald Cheney, and David A. Richardson, eds. *Spenser's Life and the Subject of Biography.* 1997.

Berger, Harry. *Revisionary Play: Studies in the Spenserian Dynamics.* 1988.

Cavanagh, Sheila T. *Wanton Eyes and Chaste Desires: Female Sexuality in* The Faerie Queene. 1994.

Gless, Darryl J. *Interpretation and Theology in Spenser.* 1994.

Hadfield, Andrew. *Edmund Spenser's Irish Experience: Wilde Fruit and Salvage Soyl.* 1997.

Hamilton, A.C., Donald Cheney et al., eds. *The Spenser Encyclopedia.* 1990.

Oram, William A. *Edmund Spenser.* 1997.

Spenser, Edmund. *Edmund Spenser's Poetry.* Hugh Maclean and Anne Lake Prescott, eds. 3rd edition. 1993.

———. *The Faerie Queene.* A.C. Hamilton, ed. 1977.

———. *The Faerie Queene.* Thomas P. Roche, Jr., ed. 1981.

———. *The Yale Edition of the Shorter Poems of Edmund Spenser.* William A. Oram, Einar Bjorvand, Ronald Bond, Thomas H. Cain, Alexander Dunlop, and Richard Shell, eds. 1989.

Darryl Gless

SEE ALSO

Arthurian Legend; Bryskett, Lodowick; Colonial Development; Dudley, Robert; Harvey, Gabriel; Ireland, History of; Pastoral; Ralegh, Walter; Romance; Sonnet Sequences; Versification

Spies and Spying

See Espionage

St. Paul's Cathedral

In 1485, St. Paul's Cathedral was one of the largest buildings in Europe, and was already nearly 800 years old. The vast nave dated from the twelfth century, and the choir, twelve steps higher and closed off from the transepts by a high stone screen, was largely of thirteenth- and early fourteenth-century work. North of the church lay the bishop's palace, the Pardon Churchyard, and its cloister with a celebrated painting of the Dance of Death on the walls. South of the cathedral stood the octagonal chapter house in another small cloister, and further to the south were the houses of canons and officers of the cathedral. East of the cathedral lay St. Paul's School, founded in 1509 by Dean John Colet. At its foundation this was the largest school in England, providing free education for 153 children. This number was traditionally associated with the Gospel miracle of the draught of fishes—scholars wore a silver fish in their buttonholes. Famous pupils would include Thomas Lupset and Thomas Starkey, and, later, John Milton and Samuel Pepys.

Before the dissolution of the monasteries in 1532–1535, St. Paul's, though it was the cathedral, was only one of more than twenty religious precincts in and around the city. After the dissolution, it was the only intact large religious establishment to remain, and the bulk of the cathedral building, emphasized by its situation on the hilltop above the Thames, dominated the entire city. At the Reformation in 1549, however, the cathedral suffered in turn. The high altar was demolished and replaced by an ordinary table for the Sacrament of Holy Communion. The nave, now known as Paul's Walk, became a thoroughfare, a covered passage where servants could be hired and lawyers received clients.

Although Elizabeth I attended services in the cathedral several times and donated to its repair, the building gently declined. The spire, one of the tallest in Christendom, was hit by lightning in 1561, and caught fire; it was afterward demolished. The crashing of parts of the spire through the roof into the church damaged the tomb of Bishop Richard Fitz-James (d. 1521), which had a chapel of timber built over it. Nevertheless, the interior of the cathedral remained thronged with prominent tombs, especially of bishops, nobility, and mayors from the thirteenth to sixteenth centuries. Elaborate funerals accompanied the interments of Sir Philip Sidney in 1586 and Sir Christopher Hatton in 1591. A few fragments of effigies survive in the crypt of the present cathedral, saved from the debris of the Great Fire of 1666.

Northeast of the cathedral was Paul's Cross, where royal proclamations, victories in war, and papal bulls had been announced for many generations. Carlyle called Paul's Cross the "Times newspaper of the Middle Ages." The Cross, an octagonal pulpit with a lead roof, was used for open-air sermons and political speeches. Here, in

1527, Tyndale's translation of the Bible was publicly burned, as were the works of Martin Luther. Events around the Cross mirrored the religious turbulence of the age. In February 1538, a rood that had been venerated by pilgrims at Boxely in Kent, and that had moving eyes and lips, was brought to the Cross and publicly destroyed. In 1553, on the other hand, during the reign of Mary, Catholic preachers at the Cross had to be guarded by up to 200 soldiers, and one had a dagger hurled at him that struck the pulpit. Victories continued to be announced here, such as that over the Spanish Armada in 1588, when eleven ships' flags taken from the Spanish decorated the battlements of the cathedral.

Toward the end of the century the area around the Cross became a center for the selling of books, and many publishers had their workshops nearby. Stationers leased the vaults below the cathedral and kept their stock there. The churchyard was generally a central place for doing business and foreigners might try to trade here without the permission of the city livery companies.

Fragments of the Tudor cathedral survive in jumbled form in the walls of the crypt of Wren's cathedral (1675–1710). Carved stones from pillars, arches, and tombs of the pre-fire cathedral appear whenever the crypt walls are pierced in building work, since Wren reused much of the demolished fabric as rubble.

BIBLIOGRAPHY

Blayney, Peter. *The Bookshops in Paul's Cross Churchyard.* The Bibliographical Society Occasional Paper, no. 5. 1990.
Schofield, John. *The Building of London from the Conquest to the Great Fire.* 2nd edition. 1993.
Stow, John. *Survey of London.* 2 vols. C.L. Kingsford, ed. 1908; repr. 1971.

John Schofield

SEE ALSO

Architecture; Colet, John; Education; Printing, Publishing, and Bookselling; St. Paul's Cross Sermons

Stafford, Edward, Third Duke of Buckingham (1478–1521)

Edward was the eldest son of Henry Stafford, second duke of Buckingham, whose rebellion against Richard III had led to his attainder. This was reversed on the accession of Henry VII, and the young Edward placed in the wardship of the king's mother, Margaret, countess of Richmond. He saw military action against the Cornish rebels in 1497, and

S

performed a variety of ceremonial roles at court. Under Henry VIII he became increasingly frustrated at the king's refusal to recognize his superior status within the nobility. Buckingham's critical error was his inordinate pride in his ancestry, which could be traced back to Edward III. Henry refused to recognize his claim to exercise one of the four great offices of state, the constableship, by hereditary right, preferring to leave the office dormant. In 1519, the duke's servant, Sir William Bulmer, was prosecuted for wearing ducal livery in the king's presence, and Buckingham was subsequently heard muttering threats against councilors. There is no proof that Cardinal Thomas Wolsey sought his destruction, and indeed some evidence that the cardinal tried to avert the catastrophe that followed. In February 1521, Buckingham sought to visit his Welsh lordships with 400 retainers, and Henry VIII, ever sensitive to dynastic challenges, feared a mobilization against him. The duke was summoned to court and arrested, tried for treason, and convicted on the testimony of his own servants.

BIBLIOGRAPHY

Harris, Barbara. *Edward Stafford, Third Duke of Buckingham, 1478–1521.* 1986.

Rawcliffe, C. *The Staffords, Earls of Stafford and Dukes of Buckingham, 1394–1521.* 1978.

Ian W. Archer

SEE ALSO

Henry VIII; Treason

Stanley Family

In Tudor England, the Stanleys, especially as earls of Derby, were the dominant political authority under the crown in the northwest region of England, north Wales, and the Isle of Man. The senior branch of the family, the Stanleys of Storeton and Hooton, were influential in Lancashire, Yorkshire, and North Wales by the end of the fifteenth century. However, the more powerful earls of Derby sprang from the junior branch, the Stanleys of Knowsley and Lathom, which, through marriage and the favor of Lancastrian and Yorkist kings, had acquired high offices and vast estates in the Isle of Man and in Lancashire and Cheshire.

Thomas Stanley of Lathom (c. 1406–1458/9) became a baron in 1456. His son, Thomas the second Lord Stanley (c. 1435–1504), maintained and extended the family's lands and influence by shifted allegiances during the Wars of the Roses, as did his younger brother, Sir William Stanley of Holt (d. 1495). Both held important offices under Edward

IV and Richard III. Although married to Lady Margaret Beaufort, mother of Henry Tudor, Lord Stanley played a game of watchful waiting in the summer of 1485, in part because his heir, George, Lord Strange (d. 1503), was held hostage by Richard III. Sir William's belated intervention at the battle of Bosworth Field assured Henry's victory. When victory was in hand, Lord Thomas joined Henry and placed upon his head Richard's crown. Henry VII needed the support of the Stanleys. Thomas became the earl of Derby; Sir William was rewarded with additional offices in Wales and at court, including the post of chamberlain of the royal household, and Lord Strange was appointed warden of the marches toward Scotland. The Stanleys called out their large affinity to support Henry VII during the Simnel rebellion of 1487; but in 1495, Sir William became involved in the Warbeck conspiracy, perhaps because of residual loyalty to the Yorkists, or because of anger over Henry's refusal to make him earl of Chester. Earl Thomas did not support his brother's treason, and Henry, not wanting to alienate his powerful stepfather, allowed him and his son to dispose of Sir William's estates, some of which were given to Sir Edward Stanley (c. 1460–1523), the earl's youngest son.

Because George, Lord Strange, preceded his father to the grave, his son, Thomas (d. 1522), succeeded to the earldom of Derby in July 1504. He was a companion of Henry VIII, and served on diplomatic and military missions. In 1513, while campaigning with the king in France, his uncle, Sir Edward Stanley, and his cousin, John Stanley of Harford, won military glory at the battle of Flodden Field. In 1520, Earl Thomas attended the Field of the Cloth of Gold and the receptions for Emperor Charles V at Canterbury and Gravelines. The following year, shortly before his death, he was one of the peers who condemned the duke of Buckingham to death.

The third earl, Edward (1508–1572), a boy of eleven at the time of his father's death, was a royal ward reared in Cardinal Wolsey's household. The crown exploited the Derby estates, making it difficult for Earl Edward as an adult to repay the debt his father owed the king. Nevertheless, Edward settled the debt and restored the Derby estates and the Stanley's regional influence. Earl Edward skillfully maneuvered himself through the tumultuous religious changes of mid-Tudor England. Although partial to traditional Catholic piety, he supported Henry VIII's break with Rome in 1534. He helped suppress the Pilgrimage of Grace in 1536, and even acquired a few of the dissolved monastic estates. Earl Edward disliked the more radical reformation under Edward VI. His relations with protector Somerset and with the earl of Warwick (later duke of Northumberland) were similarly strained. He attended meetings of the Privy Council infrequently, but was one of the judges who condemned Somerset to death in 1551. Earl Edward was among the first to oppose openly Northumberland's scheme to divert the succession to Lady Jane Grey in 1553. After Mary I's accession, Edward again became a frequent member of the Privy Council. In 1554, he was among the nobles who welcomed Philip II to England; but, despising the Spanish, he withdrew to his estates in the north. In enforcing Mary's religious policy, Edward took part in proceeding against heretics, such as the burning of John Brandford. Edward welcomed the accession of Elizabeth I, and accompanied the queen on her entry into London in 1558. He found the vague generalities of the religious Elizabethan Settlement of 1559 acceptable to his conservative temperament. So as not to provoke the Catholics in Lancashire to rebellion, he tolerated continuing Catholic practices and resisted pressure to prosecute recusants vigorously. He did nothing to encourage or hinder the Northern Rebellion of 1570, although two of his sons, Sir Thomas and Sir Edward, took part in a plot to free Mary Queen of Scots.

Henry, the fourth earl, also exhibited the Stanleys' talent for political agility. Reared at the court of Edward VI, he kept on good terms with both Somerset and Northumberland and earned the trust of both Mary I and Elizabeth I. Earl Henry reflected the generational shift in religious attitudes, becoming a Protestant and a staunch defender of the Elizabethan Settlement against Roman Catholics and radical Puritans alike. In Lancashire during the 1580s and 1590s, he stepped up arrests of recusants and Catholic priests and tried to suppress Catholic practices, but the government thought his action not vigorous enough. Earl Henry was also employed on diplomatic missions to France and to the Low Countries. As lord high steward of the household, he presided over the trial of Philip Howard, earl of Arundel, in 1589. His cousin, Sir William Stanley of Hooton (1548–1603), the head of the senior branch of the family, remained a Catholic and faithfully served Elizabeth in Ireland and the Netherlands until 1587, when, after betraying the town of Deventer to the duke of Parma, he defected to Spain.

Ferdinando (c. 1559–1594), who succeeded as fifth earl of Derby in 1593, attended St. John's College, Oxford, taking the M.A. in 1589. He gained administrative experience in Lancashire during the 1580s while his father was away on the queen's business, and as the lord lieutenant. Like his father, Ferdinando was a committed Protestant and loyal servant of the queen, although he maintained friendships with some of the Catholic gentry. Richard Hesketh, a member of a prominent Lancashire Catholic family and agent of

Cardinal William Allen, offered Catholic support for Ferdinando's claim to the throne after Elizabeth in exchange for toleration. Ferdinando had Hesketh arrested, and the affair strained relations between him and the Hesketh family. Fernando fell ill and died in April 1594, reportedly poisoned by the pro-Catholic conspirators he had spurned. As he had no male heir, the entailed Derby estates passed to his brother, William (1561–1642), the sixth earl. William spent the next thirteen years in acrimonious litigation with Ferdinando's widow, Countess Alice, who was suing to get some of the Derby estates in Lancashire and the Isle of Man for herself and her two daughters.

The Stanley earls of Derby were also patrons of poets, playwrights, and actors, such as the Chester players, and the troupe of traveling performers known as "Strange's Men" (later "Derby's Men"). Earl Ferdinando was the most famous patron of the family. His death was greatly mourned by such poets as Edmund Spenser.

BIBLIOGRAPHY

Bagley, J.J. *The Earls of Derby, 1485–1985.* 1985.

Coward, Barry. *The Stanleys Lords Stanley and Earls of Derby, 1385–1672: The Origins, Wealth, and Power of a Landowning Family.* 1983.

Jones, Michael K. "Sir William Stanley of Holt: Politics and Family Allegiance in the Late Fifteenth Century." *Welsh History Review,* vol. 14, pp. 1–22.

John M. Currin

SEE ALSO

Bosworth, Battle of; Field of the Cloth of Gold; Flodden Field; Simnel, Lambert; Northern Rebellion; Warbeck, Perkin; Wars of the Roses

Stanyhurst, Richard (1547–1618)

Richard Stanyhurst was born into an Old English family, long resident in Dublin. His grandfather, once lord mayor of the city, had done well out of the Reformation; his father was recorder of Dublin and, as a supporter of the English government, three times speaker of the Irish House of Commons. Richard Stanyhurst was educated in Peter White's School in Kilkenny, then at University College, Oxford (B.A., 1568); he also studied law at Furnival's Inn and Lincoln's Inn. While at Oxford, he worked on a study of Porphyry, the Hellenistic Neoplatonist. The book, completed when Stanyhurst was nineteen and published when he was twenty-three, was dedicated to Sir Henry Sidney, Elizabeth I's lord deputy in Ireland and a friend of the family; it also won praise from the great Oxford scholar, Edmund Campion, another Sidney

S

client who was thus introduced to the Stanyhurst circle. When Stanyhurst returned to Ireland in 1570, Campion—then in the process of abandoning his early Protestantism—accompanied him, and was given refuge by the Stanyhursts and their friends, repaying them, and Sidney, by working on a history of Ireland. Young Stanyhurst, meanwhile, ran into difficulty finding suitable employment. Family connections were no longer sufficient for, during the 1570s, the Old English like the Stanyhursts were gradually being displaced by new arrivals from England. Richard Stanyhurst thus had to settle for the post of tutor to the children of the earl of Kildare, and it was in this capacity that he returned to London in 1575. While there, he became part of the group involved in the first edition of Raphael Holinshed's *Chronicles,* contributing a "Description of Ireland" and a revision of Campion's history.

The years between 1575 and 1581 brought the death of Stanyhurst's wife, father-in-law, pupil, and—most important—the horrible execution of his friend, Edmund Campion. Stanyhurst himself was interrogated and briefly imprisoned. Early in 1581, he left for the Netherlands and was granted a pension by the Spanish authorities. In these early years of self-exile, perhaps as a sort of reminder of the Sidney patronage, he prepared his translation of Vergil's *Aeneid* into quantitative verse. Thereafter, Stanyhurst produced an account of Ireland, *De rebus in Hibernis gestis* (Antwerp, 1584) and a Latin life of St. Patrick (Antwerp, 1587). Besides giving advice to the Spanish on Irish matters, he now turned to a new career as a physician, developing so great a reputation for his chemical cures that (in 1591) he was called to Spain and given a laboratory in the Escorial. He did not return to Flanders until 1595, nor did he cease his diplomatic activities until the disaster at Kinsale in 1601. Around 1605, after the death of his second wife, Stanyhurst was ordained a priest, and served as a chaplain to the archduke in Brussels, which remained his home for the remainder of his life. In these last years, he continued his correspondence with scholars of both religious persuasions, including Justus Lipsius, Richard Verstegan, and James Ussher (Stanyhurst's nephew, who became the Protestant archbishop of Armagh), while also becoming widely known for such devotional works as *Hebdomada Mariana* (Antwerp, 1609) and *Hebdomada Eucharistica* (Antwerp, 1614). Two of his sons became Jesuits.

Stanyhurst's writings about Ireland were those of an apologist for the Old English, the settlers of English stock who had been resident in the island for centuries, who distrusted in almost equal measure the Old Irish inhabitants and the new (and Protestant) English interlopers.

After his departure from Ireland, his books also emphasized the continuity of Irish Catholicism. However, of all his writings, *The first four books of Virgil's Æneis translated into English heroical verse* (1582) has attracted most recent attention. Stanyhurst's work here was influenced by Gabriel Harvey, but he went far beyond Harvey in the consistency with which he matched his translation to his own analysis of what Latin prosody had been. Like others of the group attempting to naturalize ancient metric systems in England, Stanyhurst did so in order to raise the status of poetry and of the poet: quantitative verse required great learning and hard work. The result, while vigorous and inventive, relied on onomatopoeic word-coinages and lacked a poetic decorum that would have rendered his intentions more successful.

BIBLIOGRAPHY
Attridge, Derek. *Well-weighed Syllables.* 1974.
Lennon, Colm. *The Life of Richard Stanihurst the Dubliner.* 1981.

F. J. Levy

SEE ALSO
Campion, Edmund; Classical Literature, English Translations; Harvey, Gabriel; Holinshed, Raphael; Ireland, History of; Sidney, Henry; Versification

Stapleton, Thomas (1535–1598)

Thomas Stapleton, a member of the Catholic literary circle at Louvain, was one of the most brilliant theologians and writers of his generation. Born in Henfield, Sussex, in 1535, the son of the steward of the bishop of Winchester, Stapleton received his formative education at Canterbury. In 1550, at the age of twelve, he became a scholar at Winchester, and three years later, was elected a fellow of New College, Oxford, receiving the B.A. after a further three years of study. In 1558, he was made prebend of Woodhorne in Chichester Cathedral.

Unable to accept the Elizabethan Settlement, Stapleton went abroad to study theology at Louvain and ancient languages at Paris. He obeyed his father's request to return to England in 1563, but refused to submit to his bishop and swear the Oath of Supremacy. Deprived of his prebendary, Stapleton returned to Louvain, taking with him members of his family, including his father. In 1569, he joined another Louvainist, William Allen, in founding the English College at Douai, becoming rector in 1574. Stapleton received the D.D. in 1571, the same time as Allen. He wanted to become a Jesuit in 1584, but illness forced him to quit the novitiate before taking his vows. Stapleton returned to teaching and writing. By 1590, his fame as a theologian and polemicist had spread throughout Europe. In 1590, King Philip II appointed him to the royal chair of Scripture at Louvain, as successor to Michel Baius, and the king conferred on him several lucrative benefices. Income from these benefices, together with the fees he earned as a tutor, enabled him to care for poorer English Catholic exiles. Pope Clement VIII, who had Stapleton's writings read aloud during meals, wanted to appoint him to positions in Rome, but Stapleton declined the offers. In 1597, however, he accepted the post of prothonotary apostolic. There followed speculation that he would be made a cardinal.

Stapleton's twenty-seven publications include translations and works of theology, polemics, and politics. He engaged in controversies with several noted Anglican divines, such as William Whitaker, William Rainolds, Bishop John Jewel, Bishop Robert Horne, and Bishop John Bridges. Stapleton published an important biography of Thomas More in his *Tres Thomae*, which set More's life alongside those of St. Thomas the Apostle and St. Thomas Becket. His famous translation of Bede's *Ecclesiastical History of the English People* was meant to remind Elizabeth I of England's ancient membership in the Roman Catholic Church. Stapleton also wrote in support of the Spanish king. In 1592, when Elizabeth's popularity in England was declining, he published *Apologia pro Rege Catholico Philippo II*, in which he denounced the queen as a vicious persecutor, whose bastardy and loose morals were bringing about the collapse of morality and religion in England. Stapleton died on October 12, 1598.

BIBLIOGRAPHY

Albion, Gordon. "An English Professor at Louvain: Thomas Stapelton, 1535–1598." In *Miscellanea Historica Alberti de Meyer*. 1946.

Guilday, Peter. *The English Catholic Refugees on the Continent, 1558–1795*. 1914.

Holmes, Peter. *Resistance and Compromise: The Political Thought of Elizabethan Catholics*. 1982.

O'Connell, Marvin R. *Thomas Stapleton and the Counter Reformation*. 1964.

Southern, A.C. *Elizabethan Recusant Prose*. 1950.

John M. Currin

SEE ALSO

Allen, William; Catholicism; Counter Reformation; Jewel, John; More, Thomas; Philip II; Supremacy, Act of

Star Chamber, Court of

Termed the High Court of Star Chamber by 1603, the court had its origins in the king's council as a group of councilors sitting to hear petitions and grievances concerned with law enforcement and its abuse. Some proceedings emanated from the reign of Henry VII, but the origins remain obscure. Certainly in his reign the council in Star Chamber heard cases between private parties, and was used on behalf of the monarch to suppress violence and handle overmighty subjects. Its history as a formal court, however, stems from Thomas Wolsey, who revived its authority and encouraged its use in the late 1520s. Like the Privy Council, it became a contraction of the old council in the early 1530s, and a separate institution with its own records in August 1540. From that moment, the court was composed of the chancellor (its presiding officer), together with the two chief justices and several peers of the Privy Council.

The court's procedure was civil law, with written pleadings. For private parties, there were hundreds of legal counsel who practiced before the court by the late sixteenth century, but a smaller group of forty to fifty were advocates for more than 40 percent of the cases. Cases involving the crown could be brought *pro Rege* by the attorney general, who would select one of the serjeants at law as associate counsel to give weight to the cause. The attorney general might also be involved in "cases of state," which often came by a referral from the monarch. While the court's practitioners were undistinguished, every court sitting had to have a barrister present to represent the attorney general for opinions on points of law. By the late Elizabethan period, there were a number of such eminent practitioners before the court who served as a "sub-bar."

The court was quite popular in the mid- and late-sixteenth century. While it met only during term time, its process was relatively speedy and efficient. Having jurisdiction of breaches of the monarch's peace by intimidation, conspiracy, assault, or riot, it was also the principal court for fraud, forgery, and perjury. Often artisans, husbandmen, and laborers would bind together for what might be called class action suits against an employer, landowner, or local official. It became so popular by the time of Sir Thomas Egerton that he had to issue orders to curb procedural abuses of court clerks, decrease the number of underclerks and their fees, and avoid frivolous, insufficient, and lengthy pleas. It became successful in this period because Egerton attained influence with privy councilors, judges, lawyers, and the queen.

S

Success, however, also bred the seeds of failure. Many of its suitors became plaintiffs or defendants in parallel litigation at common law or equity. Heavy fines eventually cost it support among the aristocracy. Further, sitting as a prerogative court dependent on the power of the crown, and including civilians among its officials, it had begun to attract the disapproval of common lawyers whose belief in the ancient, customary courts fed their gradual opposition. The misuse of the court by Charles I and William Laud led to its abolition by the Long Parliament in 1641.

BIBLIOGRAPHY

Barnes, Thomas G. "Due Process and slow process in the late Elizabethan–early Stuart Star Chamber." *American Journal of Legal History,* vol. 6, pp. 221–249, 315–346.

———. *List and Index to the Proceedings in Star Chamber for the Reign of James I.* 3 vols. 1975.

Elton, G.R. *Star Chamber Stories.* 1958; repr. 1974.

Guy, J.A. *The Cardinal's Court. The Impact of Thomas Wolsey in Star Chamber.* 1977.

———, ed. *The Court of Star Chamber and Its Records to the Reign of Elizabeth I.* 1985.

Louis A. Knafla

SEE ALSO

Egerton, Thomas; Henry VII; Law, Civil; Law, Common; Wolsey, Thomas

Starkey, Thomas (c. 1495–1538)

English humanist and political thinker, Thomas Starkey's *Dialogue between Pole and Lupset* is one of the best-known works of Henrician political thought, and his relationship with Reginald Pole contributed to one of the more dramatic moments in Henry VIII's reign. Starkey was educated in Oxford, proceeding M.A. of Magdalen College in 1521. Thereafter he went to Padua (probably 1521–1526). This training made Starkey a convinced Aristotelian and persuaded him of the superiority of Italian notions of the commonwealth, encapsulated in the model of Venice. His ideas about reforming England to that standard were summed up in the *Dialogue,* written mainly between 1529 and 1532. Initially meant to bring Pole to take his proper place at the head of a revived government by the nobility, Starkey later made the work a general plan for such a regime. Granting Starkey's wish, Thomas Cromwell brought him into royal service in 1534. Starkey chose as his showpiece "What is policy after

the sentence [opinion] of Aristotle." Cromwell put Starkey to work instead writing a sermon in defense of the royal supremacy (*An Exhortation to the People instructing them to Unity and Obedience,* published in 1536). The work had very little impact, in large part because its most important ideas were the common coin of the team directing Henrician policy. Nevertheless, it has been read as highly important in the evolution of the *via media.* Perhaps even more important to Cromwell, Starkey also collected news from Italy, and took the principal part in corresponding with his former patron Pole in 1535–1536 in an effort to induce him to endorse the supremacy and return to England. Starkey failed, but that did not lead to his disgrace in the long term, and near the end of his life he was appointed Lenten court preacher. He maintained his ties to Pole and his circle, however, and had not Starkey died when he did, he would have been indicted among the Exeter conspirators, who, in 1538–1539, were charged with having planned to overthrow Henry. He certainly passed a warning to Pole of the English moves to assassinate him. In his final work, a set of notes for a refutation of Albert Pighe's *Hierarchiae ecclesiasticae assertio* (1538), a massive defense of papal primacy, Starkey maintained most of his intellectual positions, above all his emphasis on conciliar government in both secular and ecclesiastical spheres. Starkey also underlines how unimportant the ideas of Marsilio of Padua are to him, despite the claim that his plan of conciliar government was almost entirely derived from the fourteenth-century Italian theorist of communal government.

BIBLIOGRAPHY

Elton, G.R. *Reform and Renewal: Thomas Cromwell and the Common Weal.* 1973.

Ferguson, Arthur B. *The Articulate Citizen and the English Renaissance.* 1965.

Mayer, T.F. *Thomas Starkey and the Commonweal: Humanist Politics and Religion in the Reign of Henry VIII.* 1989.

Starkey, Thomas. *An Exhortation to the People Instructing Them to Unity and Obedience.* 1536; *STC* 23236; repr. 1973.

———. *Dialogue Between Pole and Lupset.* T.F. Mayer, ed. Camden 4th series, vol. 37. 1989.

Zeeveld, W. Gordon. *Foundations of Tudor Policy.* 1948.

Thomas F. Mayer

SEE ALSO

Cromwell, Thomas; Henry VIII; Pole, Reginald; Political Thought

Stationer's Company

See Censorship Printing, Publishing, and Bookselling

Sternhold, Thomas (d. 1549)

We know little of the early life of Thomas Sternhold, who rendered the Psalms of David into metrical English verse. He was probably born at either Southampton or Awre on the Severn and educated at Christchurch, Oxford, but he did not earn a degree. Through Thomas Cromwell, perhaps, he was introduced to Henry VIII and became one of the grooms of the robes to the king. Sternhold was elected to represent Plymouth in the Parliament that met in 1545, but nothing is known of his politics. His fame rests solely on his versifying the Psalms. It was commonly believed, in Sternhold's time, that metrical versions of David's Psalms more accurately reproduced the structure of the Hebrew originals than available prose translations. There was a desire, in addition, to substitute the Psalms for the "obscene" ballads popular among the people. Sternhold used as his model the alternating iambic tetrameter/trimeter form of "Chevy Chase," that is, ballad meter. The choice has had a lasting impact—not only on subsequent metrical psalters but also on English hymns in general. ("Amazing Grace," for example, follows the pattern.) Collections of Sternhold's Psalms appeared in 1547, 1549, and 1562, and a full edition came out in 1562. Sternhold himself lived to see only the first book, dedicated to Edward VI, in print; he died on August 23, 1549.

BIBLIOGRAPHY

Holland, J. *The Psalmists of Great Britain.* Vol. 1, pp. 91–105. 1843.
Patrick, M. *Four Centuries of Scottish Psalmody*, pp. 27–30. 1949.

Mark Goldblatt

SEE ALSO

Hymns; Versification

Stow, John (1525–1605)

One of the most active members of the growing antiquarian community in late sixteenth-century England, John Stow made signal contributions as a collector of rare books and manuscripts, as an editor of literary and historical texts, as a chronicler, and as an urban chorographer.

Stow, who proudly styled himself "citizen of London," was born in the parish of St. Michael, Cornhill, the son and grandson of tallow-chandlers. Apprenticed to a tailor, he was admitted to the freedom of the Merchant Tailors' Company in 1547 and prospered sufficiently to begin amassing the collections on which his antiquarian work depended. His first publication was an edition of John Lydgate's *Serpent of Division* in 1559. *The Works of Chaucer* (1561), a first *Summary of English Chronicles* (1565), and the works of John Skelton (1568) quickly followed.

Not surprisingly, Stow's *Summary* aroused the enmity of Richard Grafton, who had brought out his own abridged chronicle just two years earlier. Hoping for political advantage, Grafton attacked Stow for "the defacing of prince's doings" and claimed that in Stow's work "the gates are rather opened for crooked subjects to enter into the field of rebellion, than the hedges or gaps of the same stopped." Suspicion of a related sort turned Stow's way in 1569. In January, he was brought before the lord mayor on a charge of spreading Spanish propaganda, and a month later his collections were searched by order of the Privy Council. "His books," concluded the ecclesiastical officer who conducted the search, "declare him to be a great favorer of papistry." But no disciplinary action followed. Indeed, at much the same time, Stow's antiquarian work was attracting the friendly notice of the scholarly archbishop of Canterbury, Matthew Parker. To Parker, whom he later credited for having "animated [him] in the course of these [historical] studies," Stow presented editions of the *Flores Historiarum* (1567), the chronicle of Matthew Paris (1571), and Walsingham's chronicle (1574)—all books of the sort that had caught the attention of the ecclesiastical investigator.

Whatever Stow's religious views—and they seem never to have strayed far from those of Elizabeth I—his many chronicles are clearly marked by his civic loyalties. When Thomas Nashe spoke slightingly of "lay chronographers, that write of nothing but of mayors and sheriffs, and the dear year, and the great frost," he may well have had Stow in mind, for Stow was always as careful to record the terms of mayors and sheriffs as of monarchs; and for him, as for his burgher readers, fluctuations in prices and extremities in weather were of no less importance than the political doings of nobles and kings. His dedications are accordingly divided between such figures of national significance as the earl of Leicester and the archbishop of Canterbury and representatives of the civic hierarchy, like the lord mayor and aldermen of London. This divided perspective—at once national and civic—characterizes all Stow's work as a chronicler: the *Summaries of English Chronicles* that appeared in successive editions from 1565 to 1590; the *Chronicle* of 1580; the *Annals* of 1592, 1600,

S

1601, and 1605; the many *Abridgements* of these longer works from 1566 to 1604; and the contributions he made to Holinshed's *Chronicles* in both the 1575 and 1587 editions. And though by the end of Stow's life, miscellaneous chronicles of the sort he had compiled were giving way to more sharply focused and gentrified forms of humanist historiography, his civic perspective persisted in new, updated editions of his own works and in such successor genres as almanacs, newsbooks, and city drama.

But no chronicle or chronicle spin-off did more to express an urban consciousness than Stow's own last major compilation, his *Survey of London* (1598; enlarged 1603). Here, too, the double perspective is much in evidence. Not only is Stow keenly aware of greater London's role as the seat of royal government and of the part kings and courtiers have played in the city's development, but he also inscribes his chorographic work in a broader project of national description. Twenty-two years earlier, William Lambarde, Stow's friend and fellow antiquary, had concluded his *Perambulation of Kent* with the hope "that someone in each shire would make the enterprise for his country [i.e., county] to the end that by joining our pens and conferring our labors . . . we might at the last by the union of many parts and papers compact one whole and perfect body and book of our English antiquities"—a word he later changed to "topography." Stow presents his *Survey* as London's answer to this call and relates it as well to what he calls that "singular work of the whole," William Camden's *Britannia*. In the 1580s, Camden had founded the Society of Antiquaries, of which Stow was an active member, as were several other leading chorographers, and the tensions that occasionally emerge between their land-based descriptive project and the dynastic claims of the royal government were inevitably shared by Stow's *Survey*. The proud citizen was not always easily subsumed in the obedient subject. But still more obvious in the *Survey* is the contrast between the remembered London of Stow's distant youth and the present London of the late 1590s. Like all chorographies, Stow's *Survey* is a book of memory, a book about change in place, about how one topographical spot has been home to many buildings, many people, many institutions, and many customs—and the change, Stow clearly feels, has often been for the worse. His antiquarian celebration of his native city is thus suffused with nostalgia.

In his own time and after, Stow's massive collections were much used by other antiquaries and historians. Significant parts of the collection can still be consulted at the British Library. But as his collections grew, Stow's fortunes declined. In his need, he petitioned the mayor and aldermen of London for a pension, received an annuity from the Merchant Tailors' Company, perhaps had another from Camden, and was granted the right to solicit gratuities by King James. This array of civic, trade, antiquarian, and royal sponsors nicely evokes the diverse and sometimes conflicting interests served by Stow's long historical labors.

BIBLIOGRAPHY

Archer, Ian. "The Nostalgia of John Stow." In *The Theatrical City*. David L. Smith, Richard Strier, and David Bevington, eds. 1995.

Fussner, F. Smith. *The Historical Revolution.* 1962.

Levy, F.J. *Tudor Historical Thought.* 1967.

Manley, Lawrence. "Of Sites and Rights." In *The Theatrical City.*

Patterson, Annabel. *Reading Holinshed's "Chronicles."* 1994.

Stow, John. *A Survey of London.* Charles Lethbridge Kingsford, ed. 1908.

Richard Helgerson

SEE ALSO

Antiquarianism; Camden, William; Grafton, Richard; History, Writing of; Raphael Holinshed; Lambarde, William; London

Stuart Family

See Darnley, Lord Henry Stuart; Hepburn, James; James IV, James V; James VI and I; Mary Queen of Scots; Stuart, Francis

Stuart, Francis, Fifth Earl of Bothwell (1563–1612)

Francis Stewart was the son of Lord John Stuart, an illegitimate son of James V of Scotland. Educated in Italy, he later went to Paris (1581) to study with Archbishop James Beaton, developing a love of poetry and the arts at an early stage of his life. He was named after Francis II, the first husband of Mary Queen of Scots, his godmother, and remained a passionate defender of Mary's interests throughout his life. Created commendator of Kelso when Mary married the fourth earl of Bothwell in 1567, he became earl of Bothwell himself in 1581. As nephew of the regent Moray he was seen by the Protestants as their natural figurehead, and he was involved in the "Ruthven Raid," the ultra-Protestant kidnapping of James VI in 1582. Nevertheless, he favored Scottish support of the Spanish Armada, in revenge for Elizabeth I's execution of Mary in 1587.

Defiantly aristocratic in thought and behavior, Bothwell is now best known for his spectacular infringements of the king's privacy and his attacks on John Maitland of Thirlestane, the professionally trained and politically much more astute chancellor. James's reactions to Bothwell's increasingly outrageous pranks (including trafficking with witches) mixed admiration for this cavalier relative with fear, and his attempts to curb Bothwell's endeavors to be the country's dominant political force were remarkably inconsequential. Bothwell, however, was equally incapable of either achieving his aim or giving it up. When he sought refuge in England in 1593 and 1594, Elizabeth both times forced him to return to Scotland. His overtures toward Catholic aristocrats finally caused the Presbyterians to excommunicate him in February 1595. Bothwell fled to France, then to Spain, eventually dying in poverty in Naples.

BIBLIOGRAPHY

Cowan, Edward J. "The Darker Vision of the Scottish Renaissance: The Devil and Francis Stewart." In *The Renaissance and Reformation in Scotland*. Ian B. Cowan and Duncan Shaw, eds. pp. 125–140. 1983.

Murray, M.A. "The 'Devil' of North Berwick." *Scottish Historical Review*, vol. 15 (1917–1918), pp. 310–321.

Roughead, William. *The Rebel Earl and Other Studies.* 1926.

Theo van Heijnsbergen

SEE ALSO

James VI and I; Maitland Family; Mary Queen of Scots

Stuart, Mary
See Mary Queen of Scots

Stubbes, Philip (c. 1555–c. 1610)

Little of the personal life of Philip Stubbes is recorded. Although as a pamphleteer he is much concerned with matters of faith, Philip Stubbes is best known for his sharply etched if sour critique of contemporary English society, *The Anatomy of Abuses*. The work appeared in five editions from 1583 to 1595, by which time the inkhorn terms were eliminated to create a more direct, exhortative text. While by no means an enemy of Anglicanism, his antitheatrical prejudice, his virulent dismissal of popular entertainments, and his wholesale condemnation of fashion's follies link Stubbes to the Puritans' increasingly frequent, increasingly vitriolic censure of England's secular and religious life.

But Stubbes's castigation of all forms of theatricality was, in fact, part of his larger critical project: an examination, not to say an anatomization, of the consequences of proto-capitalism and the selfish individualism it unleashed. He was outraged by the extent to which greed had become the motive engine of change in the transformation of English society, whether its signs were expressed in apparel, rapacity, or avaricious tricks of the trade practiced by butchers, drapers, and merchants who export goods wanted at home. He was particularly distressed by the sufferings of the poor attendant on the enclosure of common lands that would cause "the state of the whole Realme [to] mightily decay, a few shall be inriched, & many a thousand poore people, both men, women, and children, in citie and country, utterlie beggered."

But Stubbes's attitude toward all modes of entertainment was not unequivocally harsh. Although removed in the later editions, Stubbes in his initial "Preface to the Reader" asserted "that some kind of playes, tragedies, and enterludes, in their own nature are not onely of great ancientie, but also very honest and very commendable exercyses." More interesting than the excised prefatory matter were Stubbes's sanctions of certain forms of amusement by privatizing them. For him, both dance and music were acceptable when performed indoors in private spaces for gender-segregated audiences by gender-segregated performers. Although it has been relied on for its apparently typical representations of late-sixteenth-century antitheatricality, *The Anatomy of Abuses* provides a more complex examination of modes of public behavior and private conduct than has been recognized.

BIBLIOGRAPHY

Chambers, E.K. *The Elizabethan Stage.* Vol. 1. 1923; repr. 1974.

Kidnie, M.J. *A Critical Edition of Philip Stubbes's "Anatomy of Abuses."* Dissertation, The Shakespeare Institute, University of Birmingham. 1996; Renaissance English Text Society. Forthcoming.

Stubbes, Philip. *Anatomy of Abuses in England.* Frederick J. Furnivall, ed. The New Shakspere Society. 1877–1879.

Iska Alter

SEE ALSO

Drama, History of; Enclosures; Puritanism; Sumptuary Laws

S

Stubbs, John (1541–1590)

Despite his reputation as a barrister, Parliament member, Puritan, and translator, John Stubbs is notable for the political scandal surrounding his book, *The Discovery of a Gaping Gulf* (1579), for which he was arrested and punished. In 1561, Stubbs received his B.A. from Trinity College. Admitted to Lincoln's Inn (1562), he subsequently was called to the bar (1572) and appointed to be steward of the reader's dinner (1578), an honor awarded to men of great learning. At some time between 1572 and 1578, Stubbs married Anne, the daughter of Aubrey de Vere, and had two sons and one daughter. He aided in translating two books: Theodore Beza's *A Discourse Containing the Life and Death of Mr. John Calvin* (1564) and *The Life of the LXXth Archbishop of Canterbury Presently Sitting* (1574).

Many books were suppressed by the Tudors, but few achieved the notoriety of *The Gaping Gulf*. Published in August 1579, the book argued against Elizabeth I's intended marriage with Francis, duke of Alençon. Elizabeth issued a proclamation prohibiting, on pain of death, possession of the book, which she condemned as "lewd and seditious," objecting to its discussion of her personal life and to its attempt to incite in the people fears that she would restore Catholicism and make France an ally. The queen ordered the book's confiscation, commanded the archbishop of Canterbury to calm the clergy and the people, and arrested and tried Stubbs, Hugh Singleton, the printer, and William Page, a distributor of the book. All three had their right hand struck off as punishment. Afterward, still loyal, Stubbs reportedly took off his hat and said, "God save the Queen." He was imprisoned until 1581.

After his release, Stubbs translated Beza's *Christian Meditations upon Eight Psalms* (1582), and, commissioned by William Cecil, Lord Burghley, replied to Cardinal William Allen's attack on Burghley's *The Execution of Justice in England* (1587). He reentered public service as steward of Yarmouth (1585), acted as secretary to Lord Willoughby (1585–1587), was made an associate to the bench of Lincoln's Inn (1587), and elected to Parliament (1588). Until his death in 1590, Stubbs never publicly waivered in his loyalty to God or Elizabeth.

BIBLIOGRAPHY

Berry, Lloyd, ed. *John Stubbs's Gaping Gulf with Letters and Other Relevant Documents.* 1968.

Buckman, Ty F. "The Perils of Marriage Counselling: John Stubbs, Philip Sidney, and the Virgin Queen." *Renaissance Papers.* Pp. 125–141. 1995.

Howard, Jean E. "The Stage and the Struggle for Special Place in Early Modern England." In *Place and Displacement in the Renaissance,* pp. 1-24. 1995.

Melinda Emmons

SEE ALSO

Duke of Alençon and Anjou; Allen, William; Censorship; Elizabeth I

Stukeley, Thomas (c. 1520–1578)

Son of Sir Hugh Stukeley, sheriff of Devon in 1544, and Jane Pollard, Thomas Stukeley ranks as one of the most audacious, misleading, and mysterious figures of the Tudor age. Believed by some of his contemporaries to have been an illegitimate son of Henry VIII, Thomas Stukeley initiated his dubious military career as a retainer of Charles Brandon, duke of Suffolk, with whom he took part in the siege of Boulogne. Following his master's death in 1545, Stukeley then became a captain at Berwick Castle against the Scots; he did not last long in that post, for in 1550 he was involved in the conspiracy against the duke of Northumberland. After his release from prison, he marched through Europe as a mercenary captain, employed by the emperor against the French and by the French against the imperial cause. He campaigned in Picardy, Artois, and the Low Countries until 1554, when he was allowed by Queen Mary I to return to England. He subsequently married Anne Curtis, granddaughter and heiress of Alderman Sir Thomas Curtis. The squandering of his wife's fortune, a serious charge of counterfeiting, which led to his arrest, and his first buccaneering experiments fill the Marian years and explain in part his obscure role in an expedition to Florida in 1563, following Jean Ribault's visit to Britain and his publication of *The Whole and True Discovery of Terra Florida*. Whether he ever reached this French colony on American soil is still uncertain. Contemporary written evidence suggests the contrary, presenting a Stukeley deeply involved in piratical activities against vessels from different nationalities, including English ones, in the Gulf of Biscay. Banished from the Elizabethan court as a result of these activities, he retired to Ireland where he became seneschal of Wexford and established connections with the Catholic clans opposed to English rule.

In 1570, following his imprisonment in Dublin Castle for seventeen weeks and the loss of his possessions, he landed in Spain, where he was knighted by Philip II and given a pension of 6,000 ducats to maintain his motley retinue of almost thirty people. He presented himself as a loyal Catholic and an experienced soldier who could be entrusted with an army for the conquest of Ireland, two claims that did not fully convince the Spanish court. They were effective, however, in Rome, where with the help of Dr. Nicholas Sander, an English Jesuit, Gregory XIII presented him and James Fitzgerald Fitzmorris O'Desmond with a force of 1,000 men. This was the band that on its way to Ireland, by way of Lisbon, joined King Sebastian's army bound for northern Africa. Stukeley met his end at the battle of Alcazar on the August 4, 1578.

His life, a secular epic, was the subject of several ballads and two large popular plays, George Peele's *The Battle of Alcazar,* and the anonymous *The Famous Historye of the Life and Death of Captain Thomas Stukeley.* Also, a play, which Henslowe called "Stewtley," was performed by the Lord Admiral's Men ten times between the end of 1596 and the summer of 1597.

BIBLIOGRAPHY
Anonymous. *The Famous History of Captain Thomas Stukeley.* Judith C. Levinson, ed. The Malone Society Reprints. 1970; repr. 1975.
Braunmuller, A.R. *George Peele.* 1983.
Foss, Michael. *Undreamed Shores. England's Wasted Empire in America.* 1974.
Simpson, Richard. *The School of Shakspere.* 1878.

Juan E. Tazón

SEE ALSO
Brandon, Charles; Ireland, History of; Piracy; Jesuits

Submission of the Clergy, Act of

When Henry VIII began to encounter delays and opposition at Rome to his request for an annulment of his marriage to Katherine of Aragon, he decided to harness lay opposition to the power and privileges of the church. As early as 1529, Thomas Cromwell had prepared a list of grievances against the clergy, which was presented to the king in the form of a petition from the House of Commons in 1532. The Commons demanded that the king take control of the church in order to clean up the abuses of which the clergy were supposedly guilty.

The bishops could not remain indifferent to the charges of corruption made against them, and they immediately issued a detailed refutation of the petition. The "Reply of the Ordinaries," as this extraordinary document is called, is now recognized to contain a large measure of

truth, but at the time the clergy lacked the sympathy of the nation, and the bishops soon realized that they had little alternative but to submit to the king's will. On May 15, 1532, the clergy submitted to the king by agreeing that they would not attempt to legislate independently of Parliament or of the royal will. Two years later, this was given statutory confirmation by the Act for the Submission of the Clergy (25 Henry VIII c. 19), parts of which remain in effect to this day.

BIBLIOGRAPHY
Bray, G.L. *Documents of the English Reformation.* 1994.
Gerald Bray

SEE ALSO
Clergy; Cromwell, Thomas; Henry VIII

Sumptuary Laws

Sumptuary legislation was the generic term for statutes that prescribed what people might wear and eat and what sport they could play. Of these the most comprehensive and important were the Acts of Attire. Following precedent dating back to the mid-fourteenth century, Tudor Parliaments promulgated five such acts between 1510 and 1554, and considered numerous bills on the same subject in Elizabeth I's reign. There were, in addition, many lengthy proclamations reminding people of the law and occasionally modifying or extending it. Each statute was concerned with what people might or might not wear in terms of dress and ornamentation according to their rank or wealth, from the royal family and peerage down to laborers and servants. Velvet, for example, might be restricted to the aristocracy, silk to the gentry. Color and where colored fabrics might be worn were also restricted. Men were the particular target, in part because they dressed more brightly and expensively than women; in part also because in a patriarchal society it was assumed that wives and daughters would dress according to the status of the head of the household.

The significance of the legislation lay in its reflection of concepts of social groups—what these were and how they stood in relationship to each other—and the wish to preserve the hierarchy through emblems of dress and ornamentation. The laws might also serve specific economic purposes. The act in 1510 linked excess in attire with impoverishment and the temptation to robbery. There was usually, too, an element of protectionism in the restrictions on the wearing of expensive imported fabrics and

S

furs. Economic concerns were, however, secondary: there were more direct and effective forms of protectionism. Social distinctions and social cohesion were the dominant concerns in a time of rapid change and development. As the different stations in life became more numerous and the concordance between rank and wealth less close, it became necessary for legislators to modify schemes of social groupings and make them more comprehensive. Ranks in the peerage offered no problems of precedence, but below the degree of knight, the act of 1510 recognized the need to introduce income bands even though the next "estate," that of the gentry, was a crucial social distinction. The Act of 1533 recognized a further need to distinguish "estates and pre-eminences," while that of 1554 was designed to control the "meaner sort" more strictly. The lower orders were indeed a particular problem. In an extremely fashion-conscious age the dictates of fashion could be disturbing, whether on grounds of decency or taste or extravagance, at all levels. Double ruffs worn at the collar, excessively long cloaks, and extravagant styles of hosiery were examples of fashionable attire that offended the susceptibilities of Queen Elizabeth. But fashion was considered to be most problematic when followed by the lower orders. Dressing above one's station and aping one's betters was not merely excessive, it was socially subversive too.

Sumptuary legislation was overall unsuccessful. The best evidence of failure lies in the repeated complaints in the statutes and proclamations that earlier versions had not been observed. Particular difficulties were encountered in determining a person's wealth or income, and there seem to have been strikingly few prosecutions. More records of enforcement are to be found in London than elsewhere, but this probably reflects the scale of the problem rather than more conscientious and effective policing. Although the legislation undoubtedly mirrored the social concerns and assumptions of the age, the Tudors lacked the resources to enforce a law requiring so much attention to detail. When it was repealed in 1604 it was not replaced.

BIBLIOGRAPHY

Baldwin, F.E. *Social Legislation and Personal Regulation in England.* 1926.
Harte, N.B. "State control of dress and social change in pre-industrial England." In *Trade, Government, and Economy in Pre-Industrial England.* D.C. Coleman and A.H. John, eds. 1976.

Brian Dietz

SEE ALSO
Clothing and Costume; Social Classes

Supremacy, Acts of

"Acts of Supremacy" is the name commonly given to two statutes of Parliament. The first of these is very short, and was passed on November 3, 1534, sanctioning the dissolution of the ties that bound the Church of England to the papacy, and making the king Supreme Head on earth of the church. It gave the king power to teach doctrine, to order worship, and to reform the church, but not to preach, ordain, or administer the Sacraments. The claims to teach doctrine and to order worship were the most controversial aspects of the Supreme Headship, although they have never been abandoned and are now exercised by Parliament.

The 1534 act was rescinded by Mary I; but when Elizabeth I ascended the throne, she had a similar statute passed by Parliament, which took effect on May 8, 1559. The second Act of Supremacy revived most of the legislation passed under Henry VIII and Edward VI concerning the Reformation of the church, with the significant exception of the 1549 acts allowing the marriage of priests, of which Elizabeth disapproved. Elizabeth altered the title of Supreme Head to that of Supreme Governor, in deference to those who felt that only Christ was Head of the Church; but the substance of the earlier legislation remained in effect. Much of the 1559 statute has been repealed, but parts are still in effect today.

BIBLIOGRAPHY

Bray, Gerald L., ed. *Documents of the English Reformation.* 1994.
Elton, G.R. *The Tudor Constitution.* 2nd edition. 1982.

Gerald Bray

SEE ALSO
Church of England; Elizabeth I; Henry VIII; Reformation, English; Sacraments

Surveying

See Agas, Ralph; Mapmaking; Norden, John; Saxton, Christopher

T

Talbot Family

The Talbots, earls of Shrewsbury, were a leading north Midlands noble family whose title dated back to 1442. The main areas of their property holding were Shropshire, Derbyshire, and Hallamshire (the area centered on Sheffield, their principal seat). The family prided itself on its traditions of service to the prince. The loyalty of George, fourth earl (1468–1538), who had served Henry VII at the battle of Stoke in 1487, was recognized in offices of trust of which the most important was the lord stewardship of the royal household, which he obtained in 1502. His military service was also of importance to the crown. He campaigned in France in 1492 and 1513, and on the borders in 1522 and 1532. His loyalty to the crown in 1536 was critical in preventing the Pilgrimage of Grace from turning into a full-scale civil war: the earl had declared his intention to "live and die in defense of the crowne if it stood upon a stake." His son, Francis, the fifth earl (1500–1560), was a key element in the maintenance of northern security. He acted as lieutenant-general in the Scottish campaigns of 1544–1545, 1548, and 1557, and was appointed to the presidency of the Council of the North in 1549. His loyalty was strained in 1550–1551 by the duke of Northumberland's favor to his rivals and by his own sympathies for the position of the Lady Mary. But his threatened rebellion did not materialize, probably because of his calculation that his interest lay with the dynasty whose grants of land and office continued to underpin the prosperity of his family.

The income of the Talbots in the early sixteenth century was probably lower than in the mid-fifteenth century, but George, sixth earl (1528–1590), was the beneficiary of grants and purchases of former monastic estates by his predecessors and was probably the wealthiest member of the Elizabethan aristocracy. He was the largest demesne farmer of his day, an investor in maritime enterprise and a leading industrial entrepreneur with interests in lead, iron, and steel. It was of him that Francis Bacon wrote: "I knew a nobleman of England that had the greatest audits of any man in my time, a great glazier, a great sheep-master, a great timber-man, a great collier, a great corn-master, a great lead-man, and so of iron, and a number of like points of husbandry; so as the earth seemed a sea to him in respect of the perpetual importation."

It was the sixth earl's misfortune, however, to be the unwilling custodian of Mary Queen of Scots from 1568 until 1584. His allowance in no way compensated him for cost of maintaining the Scottish queen's household. He also was cut off from political influence, becoming a prey to the backstairs intrigues of his enemies. The custody of Mary put his marriage to Elizabeth St. Loe (Bess of Hardwick) under considerable strain, and relations were worsened by Bess's arrangement without his knowledge of the impolitic marriage of her daughter, Elizabeth, to Charles Stuart, brother of Mary Queen of Scots' ex-husband, Lord Darnley, in 1574. By 1583, relations between the Earl and his wife had irretrievably broken down, as Bess and her sons spread rumors that Shrewsbury was having an affair with his prisoner. The earl was humiliated by the Privy Council's ruling that he take his wife back and honor his financial arrangements with her and her sons. His enforced compliance did not lead to improved relations, and he took a mistress, Mrs. Eleanor Britton. Bess and her children by her previous marriage to William Cavendish were the winners in the long run, as she secured control of her own estates and a very handsome jointure on his death

T

in 1590. Her aspirations to greatness are amply represented by the splendid mansion at Hardwick she built for herself on George's death.

BIBLIOGRAPHY

Batho, G.R., ed. *Calendar of Talbot Papers in the College of Arms.* 1971.

Bernard, G.W. *The Power of the Early Tudor Nobility: A Study of the Fourth and Fifth Earls of Shrewsbury.* 1985.

Bill, E.G.W. *Calendar of Shrewsbury Papers in Lambeth Palace Library.* 1966.

Ian W. Archer

SEE ALSO

Dudley, John; Hardwick, Elizabeth; Mary Queen of Scots; Pilgrimage of Grace

Tallis, Thomas (d. 1585)

The first record we have of Thomas Tallis is that of his appointment as organist of the Benedictine Priory of Dover in 1532. Although there is no documentary confirmation of his birthdate and place, he was probably born in Kent in the early years of the sixteenth century. By 1537, he was employed by the London church of St. Mary-at-Hill. He moved to Waltham Abbey the following year. Following the dissolution of the monastery, he went to Canterbury Cathedral, where he was a lay clerk by 1541. In 1577, he claimed that he had served in the Chapel Royal for forty years, but he is not listed in any of its documents until 1545.

Tallis served as organist and composer under Henry VIII, Edward VI, Mary Tudor, and Elizabeth I. His lengthy tenure at court thus led to his composing sacred music for both Catholic and Anglican services. In 1575, Elizabeth granted Tallis and his pupil, William Byrd, an exclusive license to publish music; their only joint production was an anthology of thirty-four Latin motets (seventeen by each, probably for the seventeenth year of Elizabeth's reign) titled *Cantiones sacrae.* It is the only contemporary published source of his music. Tallis died November 23, 1585, in Greenwich, and was buried in the parish church of St. Alphege. In his epitaph, he was described as a "myld and quyet Sort," undoubtedly an ideal musician for such a differing succession of rulers. Byrd's musical lamentation for his teacher concludes, "Tallis is dead, and music dies" in one of the most heartfelt expressions of sorrow in Western music.

The larger part of Tallis's output consists of sacred vocal music. Among forty-seven Latin-texted compositions are two Magnificats, two sets of Lamentations for the matins *Tenebrae* service of Maundy Thursday in Holy Week (his most well-known works), and two masses, including the seven-voice *Missa Puer natus est nobis* from the time of Mary Tudor's reign. The Marian votive antiphons, such as *Gaude gloriosa Dei mater,* are considered to be earlier works. His most famous composition is the forty-voice *Spem in alium* ("I have not hoped in any but thee, O God," for eight five-voice choirs), on a respond at matins during the October readings from Judith. This massive motet was modeled after *Ecce beatam lucem,* also in forty voices, by Alessandro Striggio (1535–1592). Striggio had brought his motet to England in 1567, and Tallis apparently composed *Spem in alium* at the behest of Thomas Howard, the fourth duke of Norfolk. It was performed at Arundel House, the London home of the duke's father-in-law.

Most of the seventeen surviving keyboard pieces, probably no more than a minute portion of a practicing organist's output, are imitative settings to a chant and were copied in the Mulliner Book (British Library, Additional MS 30513). His Anglican music, among the earliest to be composed, comprises three Services (only the bass voices of two are extant), a Psalm sequence for Christmas, Benedictus, Te Deum, litany, two preces and responses, twenty-four anthems (fourteen of which are adaptations from motets), and nine four-part Psalms for Archbishop Matthew Parker's *The Whole Psalter* of 1567. Of the last-named, "God grant we grace" ("Tallis's canon") is the most well-known.

With some exceptions, Tallis's music is technically masterful, albeit unostentatious. At his best, as in the exquisite Christmas respond *Videte miraculum* ("Behold the miracle"), the lamentations, and *In jejunio et fletu* from the *Cantiones Sacrae,* he is unmatched.

BIBLIOGRAPHY

Doe, Paul. "Tallis's *Spem in alium* and the Elizabethan Respond-motet." *Music and Letters,* vol. 51, pp. 1–14.

Ellinwood, Leonard, ed. *Thomas Tallis: English Sacred Music.* Early English Church Music. Vols. 12–13. 1974.

———. "Tallis's Tunes and Tudor Psalmody." *Musica disciplina,* vol. 2, pp. 189–203.

Kerman, Joseph. "The Missa 'Puer natus est nobis' by Thomas Tallis." *Sundry Sorts of Music Books: Essays on the British Library Collections.* 1993.

———. "Byrd, Tallis, and the Art of Imitation." *Aspects of Medieval and Renaissance Music: A Birthday Offering to Gustave Reese.* 1966.

le Huray, Peter. *Music and the Reformation in England, 1549–1600.* 1967.

Milsom, John. "Tallis's First and Second Thoughts." *Journal of the Royal Musical Association,* vol. 113, pp. 203–222.

Stevens, Denis. "A Songe of Fortie Partes, Made by Mr. Tallys." *Early Music,* vol. 10, pp. 171–181.

———. "The Keyboard Music of Thomas Tallis." *Musical Times,* vol. 93, pp. 303–307.

———, ed. *The Mulliner Book.* Musica Britannica. Vol. 1. 1951.

———. *Thomas Tallis: Complete Keyboard Works.* 1953.

Laura S. Youens

SEE ALSO

Byrd, William; Howard, Thomas; Motet; Music, History of; Parker, Matthew

Tapestries

See Interior Decoration

Tarlton, Richard (d. 1588)

The leading comic actor of the early Elizabethan stage, Richard Tarlton's renown lasted well after his death. A few documented facts are known about his life and career, but there is a great deal of contemporary legend about him, which even at its most unlikely is at least testimony to his fame.

Tarlton first appears in written records as an author of a ballad in 1570, and other publications by him followed in the 1570s. He is first mentioned as an actor by Gabriel Harvey in 1579. It seems likely that the publications bore a direct relationship to Tarlton's appearances on the stage; he was best known as a performer of jigs and of extemporally improvised "themes," and after his death a number of ballads and jest books were published in imitation of his style. He may therefore have begun to act at around the same time as his name appeared in print. He was chosen as a founding member of the Queen's Men in 1583, and he performed with that company for the remaining five years of his life. He was acting at the Red Lion Inn in Norwich in June 1583 when a fatal fight began between the actors and some members of the audience; in London, contemporary accounts connect him with shows at various city inns and at the Curtain playhouse.

Gabriel Harvey also praised Tarlton as a playwright; *The Seven Deadly Sins,* written during Tarlton's career with the Queen's Men, survives today only in a later outline or "platt." But it was as a performer that Tarlton was most admired and enjoyed by his contemporaries. He specialized in the stage persona of a rustic simpleton, whose sharp replies belied his apparent idiocy. His antics as a clown were evidently supported by a strong and athletic physique, since Tarlton was a skilled fencer, and was admitted as a master of fence in the year before he died (an incidental indication that he was not very old at his death). Despite his skill with a sword, or perhaps because of it, he appears to have attempted to act as a peacemaker in the Norwich fray.

Tarlton was also celebrated in pictures, and his image evidently became a popular sign for taverns. Soon after his death his colleague, Robert Wilson, memorialized Tarlton in his play, *The Three Lords and Three Ladies of London,* in the scene when a ballad-seller holds up Tarlton's picture while he speaks in his praise. This stage property was probably a print that was for sale in the London streets of the day, very likely the same woodcut that decorates the earliest surviving edition of *Tarlton's Jests* (1613). This was copied by John Scottowe for the drawing frequently reproduced in modern histories of the stage, but which, as a decoration in an expensive manuscript book, was not the image widely known in the fifty years after Tarlton's death. Both pictures show Tarlton dressed in his simple costume as a clown, wearing a cap, and playing on a pipe and tabor while executing a dance step.

BIBLIOGRAPHY

Chambers, E.K. *The Elizabethan Stage.* 1923.

Joseph, Bertram. *Elizabethan Acting.* 1964.

Mann, David. *The Elizabethan Player.* 1991.

Nungezer, Edwin. *A Dictionary of Actors.* 1929.

John H. Astington

SEE ALSO

Actors; Ballad; Harvey, Gabriel; Jest Books; Theater Companies, Adult

Taverner, John (c. 1490–1545)

The first unequivocal archival reference to John Taverner, from 1524, lists him as a lay clerk of the collegiate church choir of Tattershall in Lincolnshire. He was probably born around the year 1490 in Lincolnshire. In 1526, he accepted the invitation to become first instructor of the

T

choristers (*Informator choristarum* of the choir of Cardinal College, Cardinal Thomas Wolsey's new foundation, now Christ Church). In 1530, after Wolsey's fall, Taverner left Cardinal College, and his whereabouts are not known until later in the 1530s. He might have returned directly to Lincolnshire, where he became lay clerk and instructor of the choristers of the Boston parish church of St. Botolph. The rich Guild of St. Mary subsidized a lavish music establishment there. Unfortunately, its sources of revenues dried up after 1535, and by 1537, Taverner became an agent for Thomas Cromwell. Surviving letters show that he surveyed and evaluated the holdings of the area friaries for Cromwell. Taverner died in Boston on October 18, 1545. Although two of the Cardinal College choristers recruited by him were accused of Lutheranism, and John Foxe wrote in 1563 that Taverner had repented of composing "popish ditties," there is no real evidence of Lutheran sympathies.

With the exception of four secular part-songs and two instrumental pieces, Taverner's music comprises vocal settings of Latin sacred texts, surviving in some thirty manuscripts. Of his eight masses, all of which lack a Kyrie and portions of the Credo, three, *Corona spinea, Gloria tibi Trinitas,* and *O Michael,* are elaborate works for six voices, although the vocal groupings for reduced numbers are quite varied. The *Missa Gloria tibi Trinitas,* based on a vespers antiphon for Trinity Sunday and scored for high and low boys' voices, two countertenors, tenor, and bass, is particularly celebrated, as the four-voice "in nomine Domini" section of the Sanctus was the basis of the rich instrumental *In nomine* tradition that lasted through the seventeenth century. His five other Masses are shorter and less ornate. Of the three five-voice Masses, *Mater Christi* and *Sancti Willelmi devotio* derive from antiphons. The *Mean Mass* is freely composed, as is the four-voice *Plainsong Mass.* Their titles, none Taverner's, refer in the first instance to the range of the top voice, and in the second to its chant-like idiom and predominantly chordal sound. The *M. Western Wynde,* a variation mass, is based on a secular tune heard nine times in each of its four movements in three of the four voices. Taverner also composed four Mass Ordinary movements (two of which survive only as fragments), six Mass Propers, three Magnificats, one Te Deum, and eleven votive antiphons. Unfortunately, eight of these lack one or more voices. Those works presumed to be later are marked by consistent use of imitation and a simplification of texture and line. With its closing reference to the Holy Trinity, the masterful *O splendor gloriae* may have been composed for Cardinal College, whose statues required the daily singing of an antiphon to the Trinity. Taverner was the last to compose exclusively to the Sarum liturgy.

BIBLIOGRAPHY

Benham, Hugh. "The Formal Design and Construction of Taverner's Works." *Musica Disciplina,* vol. 26, pp. 189–209.

———. "The music of John Taverner: a study and assessment." Dissertation, University of Southampton. 1969.

———. "The Music of Taverner: a Liturgical Study." *Music Review,* vol. 33, pp. 251–274.

Bowers, Roger. "The cultivation and promotion of music in the household and orbit of Thomas Wolsey." *Cardinal Wolsey: Church, State, and Art.* 1991.

Hand, Colin. *John Taverner: His Life and Music.* 1978.

John Taverner, c. 1495–1545. Tudor Church Music. Vols. 1 and 3. 1923–1924.

Josephson, David. *John Taverner: Tudor Composer.* 1979.

Laura S. Youens

SEE ALSO

Cromwell, Thomas; Lutheranism; Music, History of; Sarum, Use of

Taverns

See Inns, Taverns, and Alehouses

Taxation

During the Tudor period the financial resources of the monarchy were subject to many pressures that demanded increased spending, which in turn motivated innovations in raising money. Foremost were the escalating costs imposed by changing military technology. In particular, the more regular and sophisticated use of gunpowder weapons required the development of more elaborate defensive fortifications, while developments in shipping and naval battles required spending on coastal fortifications and on the navy. Part of the pressure for increased military costs was the need to assert the prestige of the crown, although this was not just a military matter. Court spending served the important political purposes of projecting the image of the crown both at home and abroad, and offering incentives to political loyalty. Court tastes were also changing in ways that demanded extra spending, as in the competitive pressure for increasingly elaborate display. As a result, the general pressure of inflation was probably felt most acutely by the government because its spending was potentially more rapid than the general rise in prices.

Tudor monarchs sought to meet these pressures for spending by resorting to a variety of financial resources: crown lands, prerogative rights, parliamentary taxation, or by requiring goods or services from localities that then imposed local rates in order to meet the cost. The crown lands provided not just a source of revenue, but a means of reward and assets that could be sold for cash in times of particularly urgent need. They were not managed, therefore, simply with a view to raising revenue. Regular income could also arise from the prerogative rights of the crown that could be turned to financial advantage, such as the right to take into wardship the estates of minors who inherited estates of particular kinds. The estates could then be run for the profit of the crown, or leased to someone else, until the minor came of age. These sources of revenue were of relatively fixed value, however, and slow to respond to inflation. More promising were means of raising money for particular purposes. Parliamentary taxation was raised intermittently and for special purposes: its use was extraordinary rather than part of the normal income of the crown. Finally, localities could be required to provide goods to the court (purveyance) or men or ships for military service. These services imposed considerable costs on the localities, and were financed by local rates, but they were not really taxes. "Taxation" in the modern sense was only one of a number of means by which the pressures for spending could be met.

The forms of "taxation" were limited, reflecting the administrative difficulties of locating and assessing taxable wealth in the absence of a bureaucracy. Land was the most visible form of wealth and the principal source of income, and so most forms of direct taxation (such as the subsidy and the fifteenth and tenth) fell primarily on the land. The assessment of landholdings was in local hands, however, and there was an increasing tendency toward undervaluation. Trade was taxed by means of the customs. The customs imposed rates on particular goods according to standardized estimates of their value contained in the Books of Rates, and these values did not always reflect current market prices. Thus, effective rates of taxation (the proportions of actual wealth or income taxed) for land and trade were low. Other kinds of wealth or income were even more lightly taxed. Customs, for instance, only affected international trade; the inland trade remained largely invisible to central government.

Forms of wealth other than land, and sources of income other than international trade, were difficult to tax, and the people engaged in these activities paid according to what they possessed rather than to what they earned. The same administrative pressures applied to the raising of local rates, too, while the impact of wardship depended on forms of tenure rather than on the value of lands. As a result of all this, although the general rates of taxation were low by modern standards, the impact of these financial obligations was very uneven.

Each of these rights and resources was associated with particular kinds of financial need, and was regulated appropriately. There was a generally accepted view that the crown should be self-supporting under normal circumstances or, as contemporaries put it, that the crown should "live of its own." This meant that under normal conditions the crown should not have to resort to parliamentary taxation. Instead, it should derive enough income from its lands and prerogative rights to meet the ordinary costs of government and only resort to other, "extraordinary" sources for particular purposes such as warfare. The ideal position, according to this view, was one in which the crown lived within the constraints of its ordinary revenue, thus accumulating a small surplus. This surplus would provide the means to meet extraordinary needs and would then be supplemented by resort to extraordinary sources of income. More particularly, specific rights could be used to meet particular financial needs. Thus, pressure for court spending was met in part by trying to increase the effectiveness of purveyance. The duty to supply goods was transformed, gradually, into a payment to the crown to buy the goods for itself, effectively turning purveyance into a local rate. Similarly, in response to the need to modernize defensive military capacities, the subject's duty of military service was gradually transformed into the obligation to pay rates to support the militia. Rather than supply ships in times of war, port towns made payments to support shipbuilding. But these rates—for purveyance, the militia, and ship-levy money—did not contribute to a general fund. They were particular solutions to particular parts of the financial problems of the crown.

Not all of the financial resources of the Tudor crown were equally open to increase, and particular sources of revenue were used only for particular kinds of expenditure. As a result, the financial pressures on the crown in this period caused not just financial but also political difficulties, as established rights were tested and extended. For example, parliamentary taxation was raised with

T

increasing frequency in the later sixteenth century. This may have represented a "new principle" of taxation for peacetime purposes, or a redefinition of wartime spending to include preparation for war, or the need to pay off debts arising from war. The monarch was also able to introduce what were, effectively, new customs duties (impositions) through prerogative powers to regulate trade. For example, fines imposed for breaches of new trade regulations may have been the real purpose behind them: they were a means of taxing trade rather than regulating it. One of the most contentious of such "taxes" was the use of the prerogative power to grant monopolies of the production or sale of particular commodities. This power was intended to reward and encourage invention, but like the impositions on foreign trade, the purpose of many of these grants was financial: the revenue arising from fines imposed for breaches of the regulations was, in some cases, the real motive for their introduction. Monopolies were thus a kind of indirect taxation, a very crude means of taxing forms of economic activity untouched by existing financial means.

Such extensions, or reinterpretations, of existing rights caused political friction. Another level of political difficulty arose from trying to secure accurate valuations. The most obvious example of this is the subsidy. It was a form of direct taxation imposing a standard rate of taxation on the wealth of taxpayers as it was recorded in the subsidy rolls. But these subsidy rolls were drawn up locally, and individuals could escape taxation as a result of undervaluation or by being left off the roll altogether. The problem of evasion became more and more serious as parliamentary taxation was raised more frequently. The more general problem of compliance and the general phenomenon of low rates of effective taxation was compounded by evasion and avoidance.

Throughout the Tudor period there were financial innovations that provoked political problems, either of contested principle or of local resistance to valuation. The attempt to collect an Amicable Grant in the 1520s led to open rebellion, and fears about financial innovation played a role in provoking the Pilgrimage of Grace. The financial windfall from the dissolution of the monasteries and stringency during the first half of Elizabeth I's reign meant that financial problems were a less significant problem. War with Spain and the effects of inflation on forms of revenue that were of relatively fixed values, however, meant that from the 1580s onward there were increased pressures for innovation. During the 1590s, the use of monopolies, ship money, and the burdens of local rates to support military activity resulted in a number of political disputes. At the same time, evasion and avoidance of the subsidy increased dramatically.

Such conflicts arose despite the generally limited impact of these exactions and the fact that effective rates of taxation were low by comparison with what came later. But the political rights on which these exactions were based were ambiguous, and their actual financial impact was uneven. Particular kinds of wealth, or areas of the country, felt disproportionate burdens. There were considerable limitations in this system of finance both in taxing particular kinds of wealth or income at all, and in securing accurate valuation of those forms of wealth and income that were taxed. Moreover, many exactions fell on the localities in the form of local rates, records of which were dispersed and now survive unevenly. As a result, the records extant from this system provide only rough guides to the distribution of wealth in this period, either by region or by social group.

BIBLIOGRAPHY

Braddick, M.J. *The Nerves of State: Taxation and the Financing of the English State, 1558–1714.* 1996.
Dietz, F.C. *English Public Finance, 1485–1641.* 2 vols; repr. 1964.
Williams, P. *The Tudor Regime.* 1979.

Michael J. Braddick

SEE ALSO

Government, Central Administration of; Monastic Orders; Money, Inflation, and Moneylending; Monopolies; Trade, Inland; Trade, Overseas; Wards, Court of

Technology and Production

The term "technology" is anachronistic for the Tudor period, where it is more appropriate to refer to manufactures, crafts, or the mechanical arts. Included are numerous artisan crafts such as pottery; leathermaking; metalwork in tin, lead, pewter, gold, and silver; carpentry; glasswork; baking and brewing; milling for a variety of purposes; industries including mining, textile manufacture, and the building trades; shipbuilding; and agriculture. Most crafts and industries were carried out using customary medieval materials and techniques. It would be misleading to distinguish sharply between medieval or late medieval artisanal and industrial production and Tudor practices, despite some important Tudor developments.

An expanding population during the sixteenth century provided the basis for increasing agricultural productivity. The benefits were reaped not by peasant farmers but by commercially oriented farmers who increased agricultural productivity in several ways: agricultural products were diverted from peasant to market consumption, open fields were enclosed, and areas of cultivation were extended and more intensely cultivated. Coastal marshes were drained, as were inland fens. Deer parks and hunting grounds were converted to cultivation. From the 1560s to the 1580s, many farmers adopted "convertible husbandry" or "up-and-down husbandry," a new system of land use in which cultivation was alternated with pasturage on the same field. Near the end of the sixteenth century the technique of "floating meadows" (flooding meadows for certain parts of the year) allowed farmers to protect them from frost, deposit silt, and provide adequate water in the summer, thereby increasing their productive capacity.

The most important manufacturing industry in Tudor England was the textile industry, including silk, cotton, and linen, but most importantly, wool. At the beginning of the period broadcloths dominated, but gradually they lost ground to cheaper and lighter cloths, called "new draperies." Spinning was most often executed by women and was usually put out to individuals working in their own cottages. Although spinners used the distaff and spindle to spin the finest thread, they increased their use of the spinning wheel during this period. They turned the wheel with one hand and drew off the yarn off with the other. The attachment called the U-flyer, allowing continuous spinning and winding, arrived around the late fifteenth or early sixteenth century. After 1555, a treadle-wheel called the Saxony wheel was used; it included flyers and bobbins for winding the yarn, and a pedal so that the spinster's hands were left free to handle the cloth, increasing speed and productivity. Dyeing, usually carried out by specialists, was accomplished in vats that were heated on furnaces or ranges with wood or charcoal. The most important dyestuffs were woad and madder, while alum was the most important fixative. For weaving, the standard loom was the horizontal frame loom or treadle-loom. Weavers carried out pattern-weaving by the use of the two-harness method, in which a figure harness formed the design and another harness dealt with detailed weaving. From the mid-sixteenth century, two new looms were introduced from Flanders—the velours loom and the drawloom, which was equipped with a "figure-harness" that allowed designs to be woven repeatedly into the fabric. Finishing usually involved scouring and fulling, drying on tenter-frames, raising and cropping. Fulling was carried out at mills operated by fullers who employed several workmen. Many completed cloths were pressed in a cold iron-screw packing press. Hot presses for this purpose were introduced into England in or before 1549. Finally, an important branch of the textile industry produced hosiery. Handknitting of hosiery was a widespread practice until the invention of the knitting frame at the end of the sixteenth century transformed the industry.

The second most important Tudor industry was leather manufacture. Leather work was divided between those who worked the raw material and those who made leather objects, including shoes, belts, buckets, saddles, and bellows for furnaces. Tanning involved the preparation of skins by soaking them in diverse mixtures, including water and oak bark, then drying and scraping them with a variety of tools.

The building trades expanded greatly in the Tudor period because commercial farmers and landowners habitually enlarged and improved their houses. Country farmhouses became more comfortable as they acquired second stories, staircases, glazed windows, and exterior chimneys. Numerous parish churches and other buildings also were constructed and renovated. Artisan manufactures that accompanied the growth of building trades flourished, including carpentry, brickwork, stonework and masonry, tilemaking, glassmaking for windows, and iron smithing for such items as nails and hinges.

Shipbuilding became increasingly important during the Tudor period as England responded to a growing need for overseas trade, exploration, and a standing navy. As the industry grew and technology changed, skill levels rose and production methods employed in shipbuilding became more advanced. Before the sixteenth century even the largest vessels were built or repaired in temporary "docks," artificial ditches that were abandoned after the work was completed. The Elizabethan "invention" of the graving dock, equipped with gates to retain water, transformed the shipyard's character and production methods. The modern dock put shipbuilding in the rare category of manufactures that required purpose-built premises and expensive equipment, as well as high levels of skill on the part of the master shipwright and his workforce of shipwrights, caulkers, and apprentices. The industry also provided employment for various auxiliary crafts and services: boatbuilders and mast-makers, anchorsmiths and blacksmiths, makers of rope, pulleys, pumps, blocks, and treenails.

Iron was one of the most common ores found in England. Traditionally, iron ore was processed at a bloomery. The ore was washed, roasted, and broken into small pieces.

T

It was then usually smelted in a bloomery furnace shaped like a bowl lined with baked clay. The furnaces were packed with layers of crushed ore and charcoal. Forced air was supplied through tuyeres that were attached to bellows. Slag went to the bottom while the iron, at this stage called the bloom, was removed with tongs and hammered at a forge. The use of waterpower for bellows driven by waterwheels, and for waterpowered hammers, allowed the construction of larger furnaces. Bloomery furnaces continued to be used throughout the Tudor period. In addition, in the late fifteenth century, the process of making cast-iron in a blast furnace began. The first known English blast furnace was built in 1496 at Newbridge (Sussex), where it was used to produce cannon shot and cannon. The furnace produced iron carbide that ran to the bottom and could then be cast into pigs. During the sixteenth century the productive capacity of blast furnaces increased greatly. Cast-iron production rose from 5,000 tons of pig iron a year in the 1550s to 15,000 tons a year by the 1580s. The greater supply allowed an increase in the use of iron in farm equipment, artisan tools, household goods such as cast-iron cooking vessels, and most importantly, iron guns and iron shot.

Miners also excavated lead, tin, and copper. Lead was used for low-grade pewter, for military supplies such as shot, in the building trades as a roofing material, and for guttering, pipes, and glazed windows. Although most of the expansion of lead mining occurred in the seventeenth century, deeper mines began to be dug late in the sixteenth century. Deep mines required extensive pumping and winding gear, as well as drainage measures. Cornish tin, mostly used for the manufacture of fine pewter wares, was primarily exported. Tin increasingly was mined from deep shafts in the Tudor period. Copper mining began in the 1560s as an enterprise in which foreign entrepreneurs teamed up with local merchants. German methods of wiredrawing and brassmaking were introduced.

Specialty and luxury crafts were established most often in London, frequently with the help of foreign experts. Printing, brought to London by William Caxton in 1477, expanded rapidly during the Tudor era. In the early 1560s, gunpowder manufacture was established with the help of German experts, as was papermaking in 1588. Crystal glass production was well established in London by the late sixteenth century. Crafts such as jewelry, clock and watchmaking, and instrument manufacture developed in London as well, particularly during the late Elizabethan period, driven by developments in astronomy and navigation.

While Tudor governments actively attempted to regulate manufacturing and craft production, regulations—which greatly multiplied in the sixteenth century—were intended to encourage native manufactures and to reduce imports. The Statute of Artificers, enacted in 1563, attempted to limit occupational mobility by increasing the time required for apprenticeships and by requiring minimum periods of employment, among other measures. In addition, patents of monopoly were awarded to both Englishmen and to foreigners who brought new skills and inventions, in order to encourage the development of new industries on English soil.

BIBLIOGRAPHY

Abell, Sir W. *The Shipwright's Trade.* 1948.

Blair, John, and Nigel Ramsay, eds. *English Medieval Industries: Craftsmen, Techniques, Products.* 1991.

Clay, C.G.A. *Economic Expansion and Social Change: England, 1500–1700.* 2 vols. 1984.

Kerridge, Eric. *Textile Manufactures in Early Modern England.* 1985.

Long, Pamela O. *Science and Technology in Medieval Society.* Annals of the New York Academy of Sciences. Vol. 441. 1985.

Palliser, D.M. *The Age of Elizabeth: England under the Later Tudors, 1547–1603.* 2nd edition. 1992.

Salzman, L.F. *Building in England Down to 1540: A Documentary History.* 1952.

Thirsk, Joan. *Economic Policy and Projects: The Development of a Consumer Society in Early Modern England.* 1978.

Pamela O. Long

SEE ALSO

Agriculture; Cloth Industry; Coal Industry; Goldsmith's Work; Industry and Manufacture; Metal Industries; Shipbuilding

Textile Industry
See Cloth Industry

Theater Companies, Adult
The adult theater companies in the Tudor era are too numerous to name, much less describe in terms of their histories, leaders, political connections, and repertories. Here are included the adult companies with some measurable influence on the political acceptance and commercial expansion of the theatrical industry. Such criteria narrow the discussion to companies with a politically con-

nected patron, regular access to a London-area playhouse, theatrically sensational plays, and/or entrepreneurially minded players.

Before the formation of the Queen's Men in 1583, three companies fit these criteria. Leicester's Men, under the patronage of Robert Dudley (earl of Leicester, 1564), were touring by 1559, and they performed at court in the early 1560s and from 1572 to 1583. Few titles and no texts from their repertory survive. The commercial importance of Leicester's Men is the presence of James Burbage, who built the Theater in 1576 and thus gave the company a London venue. A letter to the earl in 1572 in which his players ask to be certified as his household servants provides the names of company players: James Burbage, Thomas Clark, William Johnson, John Laneham, John Perkin, and Robert Wilson. In the mid-1580s the company toured in the Low Countries. A letter to Leicester in 1585 names the following players: George Bryan, William Kemp, Daniel Jonns, Thomas King, Robert Percy, Thomas Pope, and Thomas Stevens. But Leicester's Men folded with the death of their patron in 1588.

Sussex's Men, under the patronage of Thomas Radcliffe (earl of Sussex, 1557), were touring by 1569; when the earl became lord chamberlain in 1572, the company performed at court each year through 1582–1583. Few titles and no texts from their repertory survive. Sussex's Men are important because they established a prerogative through Radcliffe's chamberlainship to perform at court. Henry Radcliffe became the earl of Sussex in 1583, and his company played in the provinces, 1583–1593, and at court in 1591–1592. From December 27, 1593, to February 6, 1594, the company performed at Philip Henslowe's Rose playhouse. Henslowe's "diary" names twelve offerings, texts for four of which survive: *George a Greene, William the Conqueror* (if it is *Fair Em*), *The Jew of Malta*, and *Titus Andronicus*.

A company of Warwick's Men, under the patronage of Ambrose Dudley (earl of Warwick, 1561), were touring in the country by 1559; they performed at court in 1564–1565, and occasionally from 1575–1579. Few titles but no texts from their repertory survive. The company's commercial significance is in the entrepreneurial energies of Jerome Savage, a player who had a hand in the building of a playhouse at Newington Butts in 1576, coincident with the building of the Theater. The company included the brothers John and Lawrence Dutton, both gifted and flamboyant personalities. Warwick's Men performed at the Newington playhouse into 1580, at which time Savage retired and the Duttons left for Oxford's Men.

Oxford's Men, whose patron provided them not only livery and protection but also plays, are the best known of a group of companies associated with prominent noblemen during Queen Elizabeth's reign who toured regularly and gave the occasional performance at court, but had no sustained record of playing in a London playhouse. Other companies in this category are Essex's Men, Vaux's Men, Rich's Men, Abergavenny's Men, Arundel's Men, Hertford's Men, Lane's Men, and Lincoln's Men.

In March 1583, Sir Francis Walsingham authorized Edmund Tilney to "choose out a companie of players for her maiestie." Among those chosen were John Adams, John Bentley, Lionel Cooke, John Dutton, John Garland, William Johnson, John Laneham, Toby Mylles, John Singer, Richard Tarleton, John Towne, and Robert Wilson. Lawrence Dutton joined later. In the summer of 1583, the Queen's Men toured, creating a stir at the Red Lion in Norwich on June 15. They performed at court from 1583–1584 to 1591–1592, supplanting the prerogative of Sussex's Men. Theater historians generally agree that they also supplanted the prerogative of Leicester's Men at the Theater. Thus the Queen's Men seem to have had overwhelming advantage in their political connections, players, and access to a London playhouse. Yet they did not maintain this advantage much beyond 1588. Tarleton's death due to plague is one reason; another may be their repertory. Scott McMillin theorizes that the Queen's Men kept old-fashioned plays with the comedic sight gags of the interlude and the jigging meter of the fourteener (e.g., *Three Lords and Three Ladies of London*), while newly emerging companies acquired the likes of *Tamburlaine*, which introduced Christopher Marlowe's "mighty line." The company performed at the Rose in April 1594, for a week of performances jointly with Sussex's Men, and they may have opened Francis Langley's Swan playhouse in 1595. They toured the provinces, 1595–1603, after which time they became the Duke of Lennox's Men. Between 1591 and 1599, the following Queen's Men's plays were printed: the two-part *Troublesome Reign of King John*, *Friar Bacon and Friar Bungay*, *True Tragedy of Richard III*, *Selimus*, *The Old Wives Tale*, *Famous Victories of Henry V*, and *Clyomon and Clamydes*.

Derby's Men and Pembroke's Men merit attention between the plague years of 1588 and 1594. A company of Derby's Men toured during Henry VIII's reign and the early decades of Queen Elizabeth's reign, including court performances in 1579–1580 and 1581–1582. But their commercial impact occurred in 1592 when, as Lord Strange's Men (under the patronage of Ferdinando Stanley,

T

later the earl of Derby, 1593), they performed at the Rose playhouse from February 19 to June 22 and December 29 to February 6, 1593. Henslowe's *Diary* provides the titles of plays in their repertory, texts for a few of which survive. Best known among the offerings are William Shakespeare's *Henry VI*, Thomas Kyd's *The Spanish Tragedy* and its lost forepiece (*The Comedy of Don Horatio*), Marlowe's *Jew of Malta* and *Massacre at Paris*, and *A Knack to Know a Knave*. A plot for *The Seven Deadly Sins, Part 2* (putatively theirs) identifies by last name the following players: George Bryan, Richard Burbage, Richard Cowley, John Duke, Thomas Goodale, John Holland, Thomas Pope, Augustine Phillips, Robert Pallant, John Sincler, and William Sly. The company toured in 1593 with a license that names not only Pope, Phillips, and Bryan but also Kemp, John Heminges, and Edward Alleyn (who is designated a servant of the lord admiral). A company of Derby's Men were touring after 1594. In 1599, Derby's Men performed at the Boar's Head under the leadership of Robert Browne; the earl himself putatively wrote plays for them. Their best-known offering is the two-part *Edward IV*, which contributed to the number and quality of plays on the Wars of the Roses on London stages in the 1590s. They performed at court, 1599–1601. Browne's death from plague in 1603 coincided with the death of the company.

Pembroke's Men, under the patronage of Henry Herbert (earl of Pembroke, 1570), were commercially significant in 1592–1593, and again in 1597. In 1592–1593, they were on tour with a dynamite repertory: Shakespeare's *Richard III*, *2* and *3 Henry VI*; the non-Shakespearean *Taming of a Shrew* and *Hamlet*; *Arden of Faversham*, and Marlowe's *Edward II* and *Doctor Faustus*. Simon Jewell's will implies that the countess of Pembroke was for a time the company patron. Nonetheless, Pembroke's Men broke up in the summer of 1593. According to Philip Henslowe, they were forced to pawn their apparel to pay their bills. Company players are deduced from names in a plot of *Dead Man's Fortune* (Richard Burbage) and the accidental naming of players in company scripts (Gabriel Spencer, John Sincler, and Humphrey Jeffes). Spencer and Jeffes were members of the 1597 company of Pembroke's Men who turned up at the Swan playhouse in February. A subsequent law suit with Francis Langley reveals the names of additional players: William Bird, Thomas Downton, Richard Jones, and Robert Shaa. The critical event of Pembroke's 1597 run at the Swan was their playing of *The Isle of Dogs*, the political fallout from which sent its part-author Ben Jonson to

jail for a couple of months with Shaa and Spencer, and its part-author Thomas Nashe fleeing his London home for Yarmouth. Some company, perhaps designated Pembroke's Men, remained at the Swan, but the above-mentioned players joined the Admiral's Men at the Rose. A company of Pembroke's Men played briefly at the Rose in 1600.

In May 1594, a company of Admiral's Men under the patronage of Charles Howard (earl of Nottingham, 1596) began a run at the Rose that lasted into 1600 and continued thereafter at the Fortune. Alleyn was their lead player; his father-in-law, Henslowe, kept a record of their business, including a calendar of repertory offerings, 1594–1597, and expenses, 1597–1603. Members of this company putatively came from Worcester's Men in 1585; rumor has it that they were guilty in November 1587 of an accidental shooting during a performance in which one member of the audience was injured and two were killed. In an incident at the Theater in 1589, Alleyn's brother, John, who got in the middle of a quarrel between the Burbages and their opponents in a lawsuit, exchanged harsh words with the Burbages himself. At some time during 1587–1589, the Admiral's Men introduced *Tamburlaine*, with Alleyn in the title role. Marlowe's plays remained a staple of their repertory at the Rose and Fortune, joined by the latest work by George Chapman, Henry Chettle, John Day, Thomas Dekker, Michael Drayton, William Haughton, Ben Jonson (in 1597–1598), John Marston, Thomas Middleton, Anthony Munday, Henry Porter, Wentworth Smith, and John Webster. In 1597, the company absorbed members of the splintering Pembroke's Men. In 1603, the Admiral's Men became Prince Henry's Men.

By June 1594, the company of Chamberlain's Men that acquired the talents of Shakespeare as player, dramatist, and investor had been formed and was playing jointly with the Admiral's Men at the playhouse in Newington Butts. Their patron, Henry Carey (Baron Hunsdon, 1559), had had a company when he became lord chamberlain in 1585. In 1594, after a stint during the winter at the Cross Keys Inn, the new company moved into the Theater. The Chamberlain's players came largely from Strange's-Derby's Men in 1594 (Bryan, Heminges, Kemp, Phillips, Pope, and Sly) and Pembroke's Men (Burbage, Sincler). James Burbage bought the property in Blackfriars for the company's use in 1596, but Richard leased it instead to a boys' company in 1600. When the lease on the Theater expired, the Chamberlain's Men played for a year at the adjacent Curtain. Securing a site across the corner from the Rose in Maid Lane, they dismantled the Theater, and in late summer 1599 reconstructed it as the Globe. In the decade leading up to 1603, the Chamberlain's Men presented not only Shakespeare's plays but also Jonson's *Every Man in his Humour* and *Every Man out of his Humour* and Dekker's *Satiromastix*. Among the better known of their anonymous offerings are *Mucedorus, A Warning for Fair Women, An Alarum for London,* and *The Merry Devil of Edmonton.* In 1603, the company became the King's Men.

Worcester's Men, under the patronage of Edward Somerset (earl of Worcester, 1589), flourished at the end of the Tudor era. Edward Alleyn and James Tunstall had belonged to a version of the company in 1583–1585, but they moved to the Admiral's Men, and other players were assembled during the 1590s, primarily for touring. In 1599, Worcester's Men turned up at the Boar's Head playhouse, subletting the playhouse from Robert Browne and Derby's Men. Thomas Heywood wrote for Worcester's Men (e.g., *A Woman Killed with Kindness,* 1603); William Kemp, John Duke, and Christopher Beeston joined them from the Chamberlain's Men. The company played at the Rose, 1602–1603, where it acquired plays from the same group of dramatists who supplied the Admiral's Men. In 1604, the company became Queen Anne's Men.

BIBLIOGRAPHY

Baldwin, T.W. *The Organization and Personnel of the Shakespearean Company.* 1927.
Bentley, Gerald E. *The Jacobean and Caroline Stage.* 1941.
———. *The Profession of Player in Shakespeare's Time, 1590–1642.* 1984.
Berry, Herbert. *Shakespeare's Playhouses.* 1987.
Chambers, E.K. *The Elizabethan Stage.* 4 vols. 1923.
Evans, G. Blakemore. *Elizabethan-Jacobean Drama: The Theatre in Its Time.* 1988.
Greg, W.W. *Dramatic Documents from Elizabethan Playhouses.* 1931.
Gurr, Andrew. *The Shakespearean Stage: 1574–1642.* 1991.
———. *The Shakespearian Playing Companies.* 1996.
Hattaway, Michael. *Elizabethan Popular Theatre.* 1982.
McMillin, Scott. *The Queen's Men and Their Plays.* 1998.

Roslyn L. Knutson

SEE ALSO

Actors; Alleyn, Edward; Burbage, James; Henslowe, Philip; Jonson, Ben; Marlowe, Christopher; Tilney, Edmund; Shakespeare, William

Theater Companies, Boys

Two commercialized companies of boy actors flourished in London in the last years of Elizabeth's reign and for a few years into James's. They evolved out of theatrical productions by troupes of grammar school pupils and choirboys. Humanist pedagogues encouraged the acting of Latin and neo-Latin plays, and some choirmasters had their choirboys appear in theatrical productions before elite patrons. Because these choristers were skilled instrumentalists and singers, their plays usually included rich offerings of music and song.

As early as the reign of Henry VIII, schoolmasters and choirmasters were paid to have their charges take part in the elaborate entertainments at court. Henry and his guests saw Plautus done by the schoolboys of St. Paul's and watched the Children of the Chapel Royal participate in courtly revels under the direction of their *kappelmeister,* William Cornysh. Henry's successors followed suit. Mary ordered her Revels Office to assist productions by Nicholas Udall and his pupils from Westminster grammar school. Elizabeth, during the first half of her reign, favored boy companies over adults. The master of her own Chapel Royal, Richard Edwardes, often had his choirboys perform plays at court. The queen also patronized the grammar school students of the Merchant Taylors' school under the direction of Richard Mulcaster, and the choirboys of St. Paul's Cathedral under the direction of John Redford and later Sebastian Westcote (or Westcott).

Realizing the commercial advantages of royal patronage, Mulcaster and Westcote had their troupes "rehearse" or "revive" their court productions before paying audiences in indoor venues. In the 1570s and 1580s, Mulcaster's boys performed in the Merchant Taylor's guild hall. During Westcote's tenure as almoner and choirmaster at Paul's (1547–1582), his troupe used a hall somewhere within the cathedral precincts. In 1576, William Ferrant (or Farrant), choirmaster of the Windsor and court chapels, built a theater in Blackfriars, a former Dominican priory, which he ran until his death in 1580. Soon afterward, the troupe was taken over by a businessman named Henry Evans, whose partners were the earl of Oxford, under whose name the company sometimes performed, and Oxford's client, John Lyly, who provided the company with scripts. In the 1580s, this syndicate sponsored a combined troupe of choristers from both Paul's and the Chapel Royal. Eventually, the companies separated and by the early 1590s had ceased playing, probably shut down because of their involvement in the Marprelate affair, a satiric controversy over the Anglican episcopacy.

T

Around 1599, both the Children of Paul's and the Children of the Chapel Royal were revived. New masters, Edward Pierce at Paul's and Nathaniel Giles at the Chapel Royal, joined in partnership with speculators, Thomas Woodford and Henry Evans, respectively, and later with other investors. Apparently, the masters supplied and trained the boys and the businessmen furnished venture capital. Their interest was piqued not by the possibility of rewards for court appearance, which had stopped in the 1590s, but by potential proceeds from performances in small indoor upscale playhouses, or "private" theaters. The Paul's Boys continued to play somewhere on the cathedral grounds, although exactly where remains a mystery. The Chapel Children resumed playing at Blackfriars, but in a second and larger playhouse constructed in 1596.

The two revived children's troupes attracted spectators willing to pay higher admission than that charged by adult troupes at the larger open-roofed amphitheaters, or "public theaters." Having started as purveyors of courtly revels, they ended at the sophisticated end of a burgeoning urban entertainment industry. Shakespeare, who wrote only for adult troupes, had traveling players in *Hamlet* complain that competition from "little eyases" had forced them to tour. More than sixty plays performed by children's troupes plays are extant, a few morality plays, romances, and tragedies, and a host of later satiric comedies by such writers as Ben Jonson, George Chapman, John Marston, John Webster, Thomas Dekker, and Thomas Middleton. Their best plays sparkle with festive mockery directed at their audiences, at other plays, and at such stock comic butts as lawyers, middle-class citizens, figures of paternal authority, Scots knights, and even King James himself.

Arousing the displeasure of powerful victims seems to have weakened the links between the revived children's troupes and the choirs that allegedly sponsored them. Masters of the Chapel Royal had traditionally been authorized to "impress" or draft boys into their choirs, but that privilege was withdrawn from Giles. His troupe gradually passed into adolescence and early manhood and styled itself as the Children of the Queen's Revels, and subsequently as the Children of Blackfriars. By about 1609, the boy companies of Paul's and Blackfriars were both inactive, although a new "children's" troupe performed for about two years at Whitefriars. But in the decade or so after their resuscitation in 1599, the boy companies performed several dozen highly significant plays and helped establish the indoor hall playhouse as the emergent venue for the London theater.

BIBLIOGRAPHY
Gair, Reavely. *The Children of Paul's.* 1982.
Gurr, Andrew. *The Shakespearean Stage.* 3rd edition. Pp. 33, 49–55. 1992.
Shapiro, Michael. *Children of the Revels.* 1977.

Michael Shapiro

SEE ALSO
Cornysh, William; Drama, History of; Edwardes, Richard; Lyly, John; Marprelate Controversy; Merchant Taylors; Mulcaster, Richard; St. Paul's Cathedral; Udall, Nicholas

Theaters

By the latter half of the fifteenth century, the theatrical profession achieved a national standing in England. Established companies of actors traveled from place to place to make a living under patronage of persons of national importance; perhaps one early company bore the name of the king himself. But so far as public performances went, the profession was peripatetic and would remain so for another hundred years. Entrepreneurs did not think of investing in buildings to house plays because players did not appear very often in any given place, and when they did appear they did not stay long. The theaters of the time, therefore, were buildings and open places ordinarily used for other things, like parish or town halls or the yards of inns.

In the 1560s, men with money to invest concluded that they could make a great deal of money quickly by creating places in which players could regularly act plays in and around London. The first permanent structure meant from the start for the performance of plays was built there in 1567. Soon four inns were adapted so that they could house plays as well as remain inns, and two old buildings were adapted to house plays. Then in 1576–1577, three purpose-built theaters were erected. By the 1570s, companies of players were acting more or less permanently in and around London, and by 1603 no fewer than sixteen places had been built or adapted to house plays there. The investors in these playhouses were mostly small-scale capitalists—artisans, small traders, actors—but they included a large-scale financier or two. Most had the same goal (to make money quickly) and the same difficulty (not enough capital or patience to see their schemes through). A few made fortunes, such as William Shakespeare, for example, James and Richard Burbage, Philip Henslowe, and Edward Alleyn. But, when mutually antagonistic realities interfered with mutual aspirations, many of these people got into difficulties that led to losses and in some cases to ruin. The difficulties also led to lawsuits, the documents of which now provide much of what is known about Tudor playhouses.

These playhouses belonged to two clearly defined types, the public and private.

Public Playhouses. Most of the public playhouses were just outside the city of London, so that their owners and tenants could partly escape the jurisdiction of the mayor and aldermen, who were usually hostile to them. The players who played in them were men and boy apprentices. The essential features of these places were a central yard open to the weather in which spectators stood, galleries around the yard in which spectators stood or sat, and a stage jutting out into the yard so that spectators in the yard stood around it on three sides. The larger ones had three tiers of galleries, one above the other; others had fewer. The top gallery was roofed so that all seated spectators were relatively protected from the weather. The floor of the bottom gallery was usually not much above the level of the yard. Behind the stage was a façade through which actors passed to get on and off the stage, and behind the façade was a tiring house—one or more rooms that served for dressing and storage. At first the stage seems not to have been roofed, but by the mid-1590s it was, and in the roof was usually machinery for "flying" actors and properties onto and off the stage. Above the façade was a gallery for musicians and a few spectators who probably paid well to be seen as well as to see. Ordinary spectators first paid a small amount (a penny is mentioned several times) to get into the yard and then, if they wanted a better place, further small amounts to get into galleries.

Most of these playhouses seem to have been sufficiently polygonal that people saw them as round, but some were square or rectangular, and one more or less elliptical. The plays took place in the afternoon by natural light, but, especially in the winter when darkness came early, the last acts could be lighted by rope and pitch burning in cressets. Many, perhaps all, public playhouses had rooms or adjoining houses in which spectators could refresh and relieve themselves. These playhouses were open to the general public and, though their dimensions may seem modest now, they accommodated huge audiences, numbering 1,500 or more. There were thirteen public playhouses.

The Red Lion was in a farmyard at Mile End, a mile east of the city boundary, near fields where Londoners amused themselves and the London militia mustered. Built in 1567 by John Brayne, a grocer, it had scaffolds for spectators and a stage five feet high, forty feet across, and thirty feet deep, with a curious tower on it rising twenty-five feet above the stage. Brayne probably risked no more than about £15 in the venture, which was to be finished in July so that a play could take place there. Nothing subsequently was heard of the place.

Four inns were adapted so that they could house plays as well as their usual trade. The first was the Bel Savage on the north side of Ludgate Hill, which may have been offering plays as early as 1568 and certainly was by 1575. The Bull on the west side of Bishopsgate Street may have offered plays in 1573, and certainly did in 1578. The Bell and the Cross Keys, both in Gracechurch Street, were offering plays in 1577 and 1578. All were in the city of London, and all continued as playhouses until about 1596.

The Theater was in Shoreditch, on the present corner of Great Eastern Street and New Inn Yard, just north of the boundary of the city of London. James Burbage, a joiner and player set out to build it, but, lacking money, he took in his brother-in-law as partner. That was John Brayne, who had built the Red Lion. They built the Theater in 1576, spending some £700. It was probably the most important Tudor playhouse, and Burbage's son, Cuthbert, believed that it was the first. If cost, size, and influence are decisive, it was. It was a timber-framed building with three tiers of galleries around an open yard—the familar Tudor scheme of which it may have been the archetype. Because Burbage's lease had run out, his successors dismantled the place in the Christmas season of 1598–1599 and carried its timbers and other parts across the Thames to Southwark, where they used them to build the first Globe.

The Newington Butts was named for the high street of Newington on which it stood. Built in 1576 or so by Jerome Savage, a player, it was used until 1594 at least, and had ceased to exist perhaps by 1595, certainly by 1599. Nothing is known of its size or shape.

The Curtain was, and its site is, on the south side of Holywell Lane, north of the boundary of the city of London and a little south of the Theater. It was built in 1576 or early 1577, but it is not known by whom. One candidate is Henry Lanman, a yeoman of the queen's guard, since he was collecting its profits in 1585. It was still standing in 1660 and perhaps well after that, but it was not used for plays after the 1620s.

Philip Henslowe, a dyer, built the Rose in 1587 at the eastern corner of Maid Lane (now Park Street) and Rose Alley in Southwark; more than half its remains were unearthed in 1989. A timber-framed building of thirteen or fourteen irregular sides, it was probably smaller than the Theater: about seventy-two feet across, the lowest gallery about eleven feet six inches deep, and the yard about fifty feet across. It probably had three tiers of galleries, like the Theater and Curtain. The stage, which was on the northeast side of the yard, was thirty-seven feet nine inches across at the back, tapering to twenty-eight feet at the front, and was eighteen feet deep. Henslowe enlarged the place in 1592 by extending its northern half some six feet northwards, so that in ground plan the playhouse became rather elliptical and held more people. The Rose may have stood until the 1620s but was not used for plays after 1603.

The Swan was in Paris Garden. Like the Rose and Globe, it was near the south bank of the Thames but more than 500 yards west of them. The site is west of the present Hopton Street near the southern end of Blackfriars Bridge. Francis Langley, a goldsmith and financier, built it in 1595. It was a large timber-framed building whose interstices were filled with flints and cement rather than the usual lath and daub. It conformed to the familiar Tudor scheme, with three tiers of galleries around an open yard. The famous DeWitt drawing of 1596 shows what it looked liked on the inside. Plays ceased there in 1621 or so, but it was still in use for other things in 1634.

The Boar's Head was in the main yard of the Boar's Head Inn, on the eastern corner of Hog Lane (now Middlesex Street) and Whitechapel, a few feet east of the boundary of the city of London. Richard Samwell, a yeoman, and Oliver Woodliffe, a haberdasher, built a primitive playhouse there in 1598, then tore it down in 1599 and built a much more expensive one. The yard was, roughly, fifty-five feet square. A single gallery six feet deep, above the yard on posts, ran along the north and south sides. Spectators stood under it. On the east side were two galleries eight feet deep, one above the other, similarly on posts in the yard. On the west side was the stage, thirty-nine feet seven inches wide, and a gallery seven feet deep above it for spectators. The playhouse continued in use until 1616, but afterward it was converted into small holdings.

The first Globe was on the south side of Maid Lane (now Park Street), across the street and some yards east of the Rose. James Burbage's sons, Cuthbert and Richard, and a group of players in the Lord Chamberlain's company built it in 1599. Because its main members were the timbers of the Theater, it must have had much the same size and shape. It burned to the ground in 1613 and was replaced in 1614 on the same site by the second Globe. The modern Globe, which is about 300 yards west, is described as a replica of the first, but not much is known of the first apart from what appears in a drawing of the outside of the second. A small portion of the remains of the second Globe Theater were unearthed in 1989. The rest lie under a listed building, Anchor Terrace, which stands on the east side of Southwark Bridge Road.

The Fortune was about 100 yards north of the boundary of the city of London, between Golden Lane and Whitecross Street, where Fortune Street is now. Edward Alleyn, the player, and his father-in-law, Philip Henslowe, the dyer, built it in 1600 to replace the Rose. It was a square timber-framed building. Three tiers of galleries, measuring eighty feet on a side outside and fifty-eight feet inside, stood around the yard. The lowest gallery was twelve feet deep. The stage, extending from one side to the middle of the yard, was forty-three feet wide and twenty-seven feet deep. The Fortune was destroyed by fire in 1621.

Private Playhouses. The private playhouses were all in large rooms in buildings originally meant for other uses, and all were inside the walls of the city of London. The players in them were boy choristers who were supposed to be ready to perform plays for the monarch, but whose managers could allow people to attend rehearsals for a fee. These playhouses were private because, in theory, they were not open to the public (after the Tudor period, men replaced the children and the theory disappeared). They, like the public ones, had stages and tiring houses. Spectators sat comfortably out of the weather in galleries, boxes, and the pit, a place equivalent to the yard. How these things related to one another architecturally is not clear. The arrangement could have resembled that in public playhouses, but scholars usually prefer an arrangement suggesting that of the proscenium-arch theaters built in Britain after 1660. Plays took place by candlelight and usually involved music and dancing, especially between acts, rather than the rougher jigs that followed plays in the public playhouses. These playhouses, therefore, accommodated many fewer people than public playhouses, charged much higher prices, and attracted people of pretension.

Glittering as productions in private playhouses must have been, for the ordinary playgoer the great plays of

Elizabethan times belonged almost wholly to public play-houses. There were three private playhouses. St. Paul's was a small playhouse in a building belonging to and near St. Paul's Cathedral. It was in use in 1575 if not earlier, while Sebastian Westcott, a musician, was in charge. It continued until 1591, then resumed from 1599 to 1606. The building was presumably destroyed when the Great Fire of 1666 burned the cathedral.

The first Blackfriars was in the upper story of a building formerly belonging to the London convent of Dominican Friars. The southern part of Apothecaries Hall in Black Friars Lane now occupies the site. Richard Farrant, a musician, leased six rooms for the playhouse. He pulled down some partitions so as to have perhaps twenty-six feet by forty-six feet for the playhouse proper, but how he arranged that space is unknown. The playhouse was probably open by the end of 1576. It continued until 1584, when it was adapted to other uses.

The second Blackfriars was in a former convent building that adjoined the south side of the building that held the first. Some of the rooms of the first were part of the space of the second, and the external staircase that served the first also served the second. The site begins at the southern end of Apothecaries Hall and runs across Playhouse Yard and along the eastern side of Black Friars Lane. In 1596, James Burbage bought the Chamber and made it into a playhouse for the Lord Chamberlain's Men. Much grander and more commodious than the first playhouse, it measured sixty-six feet by forty-six feet. Boxes were adjacent to and level with the stage, which was at the southern end, along with one of the forty-six-foot sides. Because neighbors objected, however, the men could not use it, and Burbage's successors leased it in 1600 to a company of boys. Men moved into it in 1609 and continued there until 1642. The building probably stood until destroyed in the Great Fire of 1666.

BIBLIOGRAPHY

Berry, Herbert. *Shakespeare's Playhouses.* 1987.
———. *The Boar's Head Playhouse.* 1986.
———, ed. *The First Public Playhouses: the Theatre in Shoreditch, 1576–1599.* 1979.
Hodges, C. Walter. *The Globe Restored. A Study of the Elizabethan Theatre.* 2nd edition. 1968.
Ingram, William. *A London Life in the Brazen Age: Francis Langley, 1548–1602.* 1978.
Nelson, Alan H. *Early Cambridge Theatres: College, University, and Town Stages, 1464–1720.* 1994.

Herbert Berry

SEE ALSO
Actors; Alleyn, Richard; Burbage, James; Burbage, Richard; Drama, Staging, and Performance; Henslowe, Philip; London; Southwark; Theater Companies, Adult; Theater Companies, Boys

Throckmorton Plot

The Throckmorton Plot was one of the final conspiracies designed to depose Elizabeth I and place Mary Queen of Scots on the English throne. The discovery of the plot in 1583 caused considerable consternation among Protestants in England, and directly led to the Privy Council's issuing the Bond of Association.

Francis Throckmorton, the nephew of Sir Nicholas Throckmorton, after being educated at Oxford left England with his brother, Thomas, for a prolonged tour of the Continent in 1580. Raised by a Catholic father, the brothers soon came into contact with English Catholic exiles and learned of an enterprise being devised to restore Catholicism in England. Financed by the papacy and Philip II of Spain, the duke of Guise proposed to raise troops in the Low Countries for an invasion of England aimed at freeing Mary. Francis discussed the plans with Sir Francis Englefield in Madrid, and in Paris conferred with Thomas Morgan and Charles Paget, Queen Mary's agents. In 1583, Francis Throckmorton returned to London, took up residence at Paul's Wharf, and began to act as the means of communication between Mary, Morgan in Paris, and Bernardino de Mendoza, the Spanish ambassador to Elizabeth's court.

Not long afterward, Sir Francis Walsingham learned from a well-placed spy in the French embassy of Throckmorton's connection to the queen of Scots. Walsingham's spies followed Throckmorton for six months, taking note of his frequent trips to Mendoza's house and accumulating evidence against him. In November 1583, Throckmorton was arrested at his home where, although he made an attempt to destroy documents in his possession, lists of English Catholic supporters of the proposed invasion and possible landing sights were discovered.

Throckmorton at first denied any knowledge of the documents or the plot, but several trips to the rack weakened his resolve. He was tried, convicted, and condemned at Guildhall on May 21, 1584. He was executed at Tyburn on July 10. Shortly after his trial, the government published its account of the conspiracy entitled *A Discoverie of the Treasons Practiced and Attempted against the Queene's Majestie and the Realme by Francis Throckmorton.*

T

In the wake of Throckmorton's arrest many of the Catholic conspirators fled England, including Francis's brother, Thomas, who settled in Paris as an agent of the queen of Scots. Others, such as the earls of Northumberland and Arundel, were arrested and placed in the Tower. Although the Spanish ambassador enjoyed immunity, Mendoza's role in the plot could not be overlooked. He was summoned before the council, given his passport, and given a fortnight to leave England. Mendoza was the last resident Spanish ambassador during Elizabeth's reign.

The discovery of the Throckmorton plot added a great deal of anxiety to an already tense England. It occurred on the heels of John Somerville's arrest for planning to assassinate Elizabeth and William of Orange's murder, which occurred only a week before Throckmorton's execution. For many Englishmen, these events were evidence of a renewed Catholic offensive against Protestant nations and their leaders. In response to this threat, William Cecil, Lord Burghley, and Walsingham drafted the Bond of Association in October 1584, which pledged to defend the queen, and promised swift retribution, in the form of killing the queen of Scots, if Elizabeth's life was threatened.

BIBLIOGRAPHY

Guy, John. *Tudor England.* 1988.
Read, Conyers. *Mr. Secretary Walsingham.* Vol. 2. 1967.
Rowse, A.L. *Ralegh and the Throckmortons.* 1961.

Gregory P. Ripple

SEE ALSO

Espionage; Foreign Relations and Diplomacy; Mary Queen of Scots; de Mendoza, Bernardino; Philip II; Throckmorton, Nicholas; Walsingham, Francis

Throckmorton, Nicholas (1515–1571)

The courtier and diplomat Sir Nicholas Throckmorton was born in 1515. He began his career as a page to Henry VIII's illegitimate son, Henry Fitzroy, duke of Richmond, and by 1544 he was a member of the household of Queen Catherine Parr. It was probably there that he first became an ardent partisan of religious reform. Throckmorton's Protestant convictions helped him to thrive in Edward VI's reign, during which time he became a well-to-do landowner, a gentleman of the Privy Chamber, and a favorite attendant of the young king.

Under Mary I, Throckmorton's fortunes radically altered. Throckmorton opposed the queen's decision to

wed Philip II of Spain, and he discussed with Sir Thomas Wyatt and others the possibility of rebellion. Although Throckmorton never took arms against the queen, Mary considered him to be a party to Wyatt's failed uprising and demanded that he be tried for treason (April 1554). In one of the most famous trials of the Tudor era, Throckmorton brilliantly contested the crown's charges, arguing that under existing law discussions of rebellion alone could not be prosecuted as treason. He forcefully denounced his judges' attempts to "wrest and exceed" the words of the treason statute to help the queen's attorney, and he begged the jury to treat him with fairness. Against all expectations, he was acquitted, a decision that infuriated the queen, cheered Protestants, and resulted in the vindictive imprisonment of his jury.

In 1556, Throckmorton fled abroad after his name was linked with another planned uprising. Later, he made contact with Princess Elizabeth and, after Elizabeth I's accession, he became her ambassador to France in May 1559. Among his chief tasks in France were to protect continental Protestants and to reduce French influence in Scotland. Throckmorton pursued these two goals more vigorously than Queen Elizabeth liked, and he frequently expressed frustration over Elizabeth's cautious foreign policy. It was in France that Throckmorton became acquainted with Mary Queen of Scots, a woman whom he admired and, despite his strong Protestant leanings, supported in her desire to be named Elizabeth's heir.

Throckmorton ended his diplomatic career with two failed embassies to Scotland. Since he had long been known to have favored a marriage between Mary Queen of Scots and Thomas Howard, duke of Norfolk, the government arrested him after the collapse of the Northern Rebellion of 1569. He was released in 1570, but took no further part in politics. He died on February 12, 1571.

BIBLIOGRAPHY

Bindoff, S.T., ed. *The History of Parliament: The House of Commons, 1509–1558.* 1982.
MacCaffrey, Wallace. *The Shaping of the Elizabethan Regime.* 1968.
———, ed. *The Trial of Nicholas Throckmorton.* 1998.
Pollitt, Ronald. "The Defeat of the Northern Rebellion and the Shaping of Anglo-Scottish Relations." *The Scottish Historical Review*, vol. 64, pp. 1–21.
Rowse, A.L. *Ralegh and the Throckmortons.* 1962.
Williams, Neville. *Thomas Howard, Fourth Duke of Norfolk.* 1964.

Scott Lucas

SEE ALSO
Howard, Thomas; Mary Queen of Scots; Northern Rebellion; Philip II; Wyatt's Rebellion

Tichbourne, Chidiock (c. 1558–1586)

Chidiock Tichbourne is remembered largely for his part in the Catholic Babington Plot on Elizabeth I's life and for the poem, commonly referred to as his "Elegy" or "Lament," which he wrote in the Tower while awaiting execution. Born sometime near Elizabeth's accession into a family described in contemporary records as "obstinate Papists," Tichbourne had connections with enemies of Elizabeth on the Continent and as a young man traveled abroad several times without authorization.

In 1580, he met Anthony Babington in France, establishing a relationship to which he always referred in the ardent terms of chivalrous friendship. In London, he and Babington were said to have "lived together in most flourishing estate," enjoying the spirited life of young gentlemen—"walking, talking, feasting, sporting"—and although Tichbourne claimed that "matters of state" were far from their minds, both had apparently already joined a secret group of young men of good family sworn to aid the Jesuit cause in England. Twice in ensuing years, Tichbourne came under the suspicion of the government, first in 1583, when he was interrogated about certain "popish relics" in his possession, and again in 1586, when a servant informed on the family's "popish practices."

In 1586, he became involved in Babington's plan to assassinate the queen, helping his friend decipher a crucial letter from Mary Queen of Scots and eventually agreeing to be one of the men assigned to the actual murder. In spite of his papist loyalties, Tichbourne participated in the plot with some reluctance. He considered the murder of a sovereign "impious" and gave, in William Camden's phrase, "a kind of Consent" only after he was "with much ado perswaded" by his friend the Jesuit John Ballard that the action could be performed in good conscience. Out of "regard for my friend," Tichbourne claimed, "I was silent, and so consented." Later, after Ballard had been apprehended, Tichbourne advised Babington to abort the plan and flee, but to no avail. By August 15, all of the conspirators had been arrested, and Tichbourne was hanged, drawn, and quartered with Babington and the other main offenders on September 15, 1586. On the scaffold Tichbourne's dignified speech aroused pity in the crowd, and the poetical "Lament" he wrote while imprisoned captures in stirring antitheses his sense of canceled youth. It

has been called a "universally moving threnody on a life wasted almost before it began." Usually seen as a precursor to the poetry of Robert Southwell, the poem won instant popularity after Tichbourne's death and is frequently anthologized today.

BIBLIOGRAPHY
Camden, William. *The History of the Most Renowned and Victorious Princess Elizabeth.* Wallace T. MacCaffrey, ed. Pp. 226–237. 1970.
Hirsch, Richard S.M., ed. "The Works of Chidiock Tichborne." *English Literary Renaissance,* vol. 16, pp. 303–318.
Howell, T.B., ed. *A Complete Collection of State Trials.* Vol. 1, pp. 1127–1162. 1816.
Pollen, John Hungerford. *Mary Queen of Scots and the Babington Plot.* 1922.

Philip White

SEE ALSO
Babington Plot; Jesuits; Mary Queen of Scots

Tilney, Edmund (c. 1536–1610)

The only child of Philip Tilney and Malyn Chambre, Edmund Tilney was Elizabeth I's master of the revels. Tilney was the grandson of Sir Philip Tilney (d. 1534) of Shelley Hall, Suffolk, treasurer in the Scottish Wars in 1522 under Thomas Howard, earl of Surrey (later, third duke of Norfolk). Edmund's father, a younger son of Sir Philip, was usher of the Privy Chamber to Henry VIII. When he died in debt in 1541, his widow, Malyn, received a promise of help from Agnes Tilney, dowager duchess of Norfolk. Malyn, who became chamberwoman to queen Katherine Howard, was implicated in the scandal surrounding the Queen's adultery, and, along with Agnes, Lord William, and other members of the Howard household, she was convicted of misprision of treason on December 22, 1542, sentenced to life imprisonment and loss of goods, but pardoned shortly afterward.

Edmund was brought up in the household of lord William Howard, Lord chamberlain (1558–1572). He was roughly the same age as his cousin, Charles Howard, later lord admiral and earl of Nottingham. His name does not appear in the university registers, but his later writings and his mention as a possible envoy to Spain indicate a firm grounding in Latin and Spanish, and at least a reading knowledge of French and Italian, along with a broad acquaintance with history, law, economics, geography,

T

genealogy, chronology, mythology, and government. His only published work, *A brief and pleasant discourse of the duties in Marriage, called the Flower of Friendshippe,* was entered in the Stationers' Register in 1568 and went through at least five editions between 1568 and 1587. Tilney's principal source is Pedro de Lujan's *Coloquios matrimoniales,* and the work reveals an interest in humanist ideas and the literary and philosophical conventions of the continental *conversazione.* The book was dedicated to Elizabeth I in a bid for court recognition.

Patronage was not immediately forthcoming, and for the next decade Tilney remained close to the Howards in Surrey. In the election of 1572, Charles Howard was returned to the House of Commons, and Tilney accompanied him as a burgess for Gatton. Charles maintained a company of players in the mid-1570s, who appeared at court on three occasions between December 1576 and January 1578. Immediately afterward Tilney took over the duties of master of the revels. The appointment, which he owed to his cousin's influence, was confirmed by patent on July 24, 1579. All dramatic performances at court, as well as entertainments, and contributions to certain spectacles, such as the accession day tilts and other martial exhibitions, were under his direction. In 1583, Edmund married Mary Bray, daughter of Sir Thomas Cotton of Oxenheath, Kent, and fourth wife, now widow, of Sir Edward Bray. The couple, who had no children, purchased the largest house in Leatherhead, Surrey, where they entertained Elizabeth I on August 3, 1591. Mary died on February 20, 1604.

Tilney's appointment as master of the revels followed a protracted period of difficulties in the Revels Office, and the changes put in place within a few years of his appointment were oriented toward achieving economy, toward enhancing the queen's image in the revels, and toward making practical political use of the master. Tilney was issued a royal commission in 1581, the first part of which gave him extraordinary powers to effect economy in running his office, and the second part of which made him censor of plays. The Revels Office effected economy by assuming responsibility for a set number of entertainments at court each year, principally plays, which had always been far cheaper to produce than masques. Since Tilney answered directly to the queen's circle of close advisors, control of entertainments in court and oversight of the drama outside of court was concentrated close to Elizabeth. By virtue of his position Tilney became one of the most influential patrons of the drama of the period.

In the late 1590s, Tilney began to compile his confidential diplomatic manual on Europe, "Topographical Descriptions, Regiments, and Policies." He had initially planned to present this to Elizabeth I, and after her death he revised it again for presentation to James I. Never presented to either monarch, the manuscript was probably a bid for a higher post at court at a time when the reversion to the patent as master of the revels had become an issue. Sir George Buc, whose family was distantly related to the Tilneys by marriage, received a reversion and a renewal of the 1581 commission on June 23, 1603. Buc's family were also dependents of the Howards, and the lord admiral's influence prevailed again, disappointing the hopes of John Lyly, who expected the reversion, and Edward Glasscock, who had already received one in May of that year. However, Tilney did not get another post, and he continued to execute his duties as master until his death on August 20, 1610.

BIBLIOGRAPHY

Eccles, Mark. "Sir George Buc, Master of the Revels." In *Thomas Lodge and Other Elizabethans.* C.J. Sisson, ed. 1933.

Streitberger, W.R. "On Edmond Tyllney's Biography." *Review of English Studies,* n.s., vol. 29, pp. 11–35.

———. *Edmond Tyllney.* 1986.

———, ed. *Jacobean and Caroline Revels Accounts, 1603–1642.* Malone Society Collections. Vol. 13. 1986.

———, ed. *Edmond Tyllney, Topographical Descriptions, Regiments, and Policies.* 1991.

Tilney, Edmund. *The Flower of Friendship: A Renaissance Dialogue Contesting Marriage.* Valerie Wayne, ed. 1992.

W.R. Sreitberger

SEE ALSO

Buc, George; Censorship; Drama, History of; Howard, Catherine; Revels Office

Tin

See Metal Industries and Mining

Toleration, Religious

Religious toleration is the belief that individuals or groups of people should be permitted to worship in their own way, even if this is not conformable to the standards of religious practice established by the state. In this respect, toleration, which is essentially a permission granted for exceptions to the norm to exist without incurring legal penalties, is distinct from religious freedom, where all beliefs are treated equally.

In sixteenth-century Europe, religious freedom as we know it today did not exist, and *de iure* toleration was extremely rare. The only partial exception was France, where the Edict of Nantes (1598) granted a limited measure of toleration to Protestants. However, this did not last, and after decades of increasingly severe restrictions, the edict itself was revoked in 1685. Curiously enough, it was at nearly the same time that *de iure* toleration became a reality in England, with the passing of an Act of Toleration in 1689. This permitted Protestant dissenters, but not Roman Catholics, to organize their own religious communities, although certain disabilities remained until 1828.

However, when we turn from the legal position to examine *de facto* toleration, the situation becomes more complex. In Elizabethan England, for example, Puritan ministers received a good deal of unofficial tolerance, and this situation was so widely accepted that when church authorities tried to apply the letter of the law, they met with considerable opposition and were even accused of innovation. Roman Catholics, too, were often let alone, although the pope's excommunication of Elizabeth I in 1570 complicated matters considerably. Even so, persecution of religious dissent was usually connected with some pressing political necessity, such as the threat of foreign invasion, and was seldom practiced on a systematic basis. Indeed, it can be argued that when an attempt was made to enforce conformity in the 1630s, the end result was civil war and the abolition of almost all real restrictions on religious practice.

BIBLIOGRAPHY

Bray, G.L. *Documents of the English Reformation.* 1994.
McGrath, P. *Papists and Puritans Under Elizabeth I.* 1967.
Gerald Bray

SEE ALSO

Catholicism; Puritanism; *Regnans in Excelsis;* Recusancy

Torture

See Askew, Anne; Campion, Edmund; Clitherow, Margaret; Heresy; Marian Martyrs

Tottel, Richard (d. 1594)

Tottel's *Miscellany* can be viewed as the single text that originated the English literary Renaissance, or, in Ben Jonson's terms, "began Eloquence with us." The man behind this event in early June 1557 was a printer, perhaps not quite thirty, who had been in business for only a few years. Born in Exeter, Richard Tottel (or Tothill) had published on Fleet Street under the sign of the Hand and Star since 1553. In that year the young entrepreneur had secured his valuable patent to publish all the common law books of the kingdom, the staple of his printing press for the rest of his career; renewed in 1556, the patent was granted for life shortly after Elizabeth I's ascension. In the year he published his most famous text, the *Miscellany,* he was a charter member of the Stationers' Company of London, a crucial labor collective for the publishing and intellectual society of Renaissance England, to which he belonged until his death in 1594. Thus Richard Tottel remained far more of an arbiter in the construction and origination of texts in Tudor society than the idea of a common printer might imply.

The decision to print literary texts must have been Tottel's from the start. One of his earliest texts in 1553 was Sir Thomas More's *Dialogue of Comfort,* followed in the next years by John Lydgate's *Fall of Princes,* and Stephen Hawes's *Pastime of Pleasure.* The More text reveals the political cunning that would win Tottel both financial and social rewards for two reigns, the *Dialogue* written in prison by a Catholic martyr emphasizing the new restoration and freedom of Mary I. The same sense of business cunning and political maneuvering combined again in the first edition of his *Miscellany.* In this text Tottel made two editorial decisions that would make the nine editions of his *Miscellany* a continuing "goldmine," as C. S Lewis notes, and as William Shakespeare's Slender in the *Merry Wives of Windsor* proves when he "had rather than forty shillings I had my book of Songs and Sonnets here" (1.1.205–206).

The first strategy concentrated on the universal subjects of all lyrics, love poems and elegies, sex and death. For an audience weary of ideological battles and the collapsing political structures of the Marian regime, these subjects brought assurance of an enduring nature to their histories, both personal and collective. The second strategy related this text to the highest level of English nobility outside of the royal family and, once more, to recall to the English court another martyr, in this case, Henry Howard, the beheaded poet earl of Surrey, the last victim of Henry VIII and the father of the most powerful nobleman in the

T

kingdom in 1557, Thomas Howard, the young fourth duke of Norfolk. The title (the same in all nine editions) is almost forced in its determination to make the first edition of 271 poems Surrey's: *Songes And Sonnettes, written by the ryght honorable Lorde Henry Hawarde late Earle of Surrey, and other.* As though to underscore his connection, Tottel published in late June between the first and second editions of his *Miscellany* Surrey's new translations of the *Aeneid* with its invention of that most influential of all Renaissance forms, blank verse. This combination of the old and new (the new queen, Elizabeth I, was also a Howard, the second cousin of the martyred poet earl and a poet herself) paid off.

The book's popularity made Tottel's preface to his *Miscellany* all the more impressive. For the first time, a printer—a craftsman—could shape literary history: "That our tong is able" to imitate the lyric verse of "diuers Latines, Italians, and other" and so "praiseworthy" is due to the "honorable stile of the noble earle of Surrey, and the weightinesse of the depewitted sir Thomas Wyatt" and his whole book thus published "to the honor of the Englishe tong, and for profit . . . of Englishe eloquence."

Tottel's health failed in the late 1580s and his prolonged absences almost lost him his membership in the Stationer's Company. The company's register lists his son as his dealer in 1593; Tottel died the following year and his patent for law books passed to Charles Yetswiert, who also succeeded to his shop in Fleet Street.

BIBLIOGRAPHY

Greene, Roland. *Post-Petrarchism: Origins and Innovations of the Western Lyric Sequence.* 1991.

Lewis, C.S. *English Literature in the Sixteenth Century Excluding Drama.* 1954.

Roche, Thomas P., Jr. *Petrarch and the English Sonnet Sequences.* 1989.

Sessions, William A. *Henry Howard, Earl of Surrey.* Twayne English Authors. 1986.

Tottel's Miscellany (1557–1587). 2 vols. Hyder E. Rollins, ed. 1929–1930; 2nd edition. 1966.

————. Scolar Press Facsimiles. 1970; repr. 1973.

Roche, Thomas P., Jr. *Petrarch and the English Sonnet Sequences.* 1989.

W.A. Sessions

SEE ALSO

Hawes, Stephen; Howard, Henry; Petrarchanism; Printing, Publishing, and Bookselling; Verse Anthologies; Versification

Tournaments

See Accession Day; Knighthood

Towns

Viewed from the perspective of continental Europe, the urban structure of Tudor England was curious, for it contained only one major city, London; the provincial towns were notable for their small size and limited numbers. With a total population of about 200,000 in 1600, London was a major European city by any reckoning, but the largest provincial city, Norwich, contained at the same date no more than 12,000 people; and the other leading provincial towns, Bristol, York, and Newcastle, could hardly list 10,000 inhabitants each. This curious feature of English life reflected the unrivaled strength of the capital in centralizing around itself so many aspects of English life—political, administrative, financial, commercial, industrial, and social. The provincial cities found it impossible to compete with the colossus, a situation that would persist until the eighteenth century. England was, however, rich in small towns, with a network of important administrative, commercial, and shopping centers at the county level with populations of 1,500–3,000 and below them a basic pattern of several hundred market towns that met the needs of neighboring countryfolk with 500–1,500 inhabitants. The countryside and its concerns remained very close to all these Tudor townsmen: pigs roamed the streets, the fields were physically close, and on market days cattle and sheep crammed the marketplaces. Yet it would be unwise to conclude from all of this that townsmen did not have distinctively urban attitudes, even in the smallest of towns. For if the towns were small, villages were even smaller; and if agricultural concerns permeated even the largest towns, the primacy of commerce and industry still distinguished small towns from typical villages.

The largest regional centers lay in the south and east: Exeter and Plymouth in the southwest, Bristol and Salisbury in central southern England, Canterbury in the southeast (for London acted as regional center as well as capital for much of this area), Norwich, Yarmouth, Cambridge, Ipswich, and Colchester in East Anglia. Oxford, Worcester, Coventry, and Shrewsbury covered the Midlands, with the northern towns of Chester, York, and Newcastle supplying the only other towns in 1600 with populations more thatn 5,000 and commensurate regional roles. Below this level lay towns of importance within their counties, often the focus of local trading networks and the center of administration for the state or church: Hereford, Lincoln, and Derby are good examples. However, commerce was much more important than administration in endowing some towns with local prominence. Below this rank again were the market towns, serving the countryside within a four- or five-mile radius. There were more than 500 of these market towns in the sixteenth century, forming a network that was at its most dense in parts of lowland England, although some southern counties were short of them. The magnitude and prosperity of the rural population had a large influence on the numbers of market towns in any particular region, but of special significance was the nature of local farming: specialized farming for the market, organized within small localities and with some rural industry, gave rise to the greatest density of market towns.

This pattern of English towns was remarkable for its antiquity and its stability. By about 1300, the Tudor structure was established, and it was not disturbed on any radical scale until the Industrial Revolution. Of course there was change; in the later Middle Ages the growth of a rural cloth industry in counties such as Suffolk, Devon, and the West Riding of Yorkshire encouraged extensions of the urban network, and other towns lost important industrial and commercial roles in the early modern period. But such processes were much more likely to encourage losses or gains in size and wealth than to lead to the creation of new towns or the extinction of old ones.

Historians have argued for decades about the reality of an "urban decline" in the later Middle Ages and the sixteenth century. An influential school points to the great decline of the national population in the later Middle Ages that does not seem to have been reversed until about 1510, and the inevitable contraction in the size of most towns that accompanied this process. The archives of the central government are full of pleas of poverty and general distress from towns, and there does seem to have been a group of towns that undeniably fell into depression and contraction—Lincoln, York, Winchester, Boston, and Beverley, for instance. On the other hand, some historians stress the skill with which late medieval Englishmen responded to the rapid economic change consequent upon a falling population; they point to the vigor of the cloth industry, with its booming exports from prospering industrial towns such as Salisbury and Exeter. Every attempt to resolve this conflict has foundered on the ambiguity of the available evidence, such as taxation records, and the impossibility of coming to valid generalizations about a world inadequately documented, diverse, and changing very rapidly. All that can be done is to point

to the importance of regional change, in which areas such as the northeast suffered long-term contraction, while others, such as the south and southwest, seem to have inherited much of the migrating prosperity of once-favored districts.

During the course of the sixteenth century itself, the fortunes of towns seem to have pivoted around the year 1560. Before that point, late medieval conditions continued, and complaints of difficulty from some towns were still present. After that date, there seems to have been a general economic improvement based on an agricultural prosperity derived from the ever-expanding food needs of a growing population. Since the whole economy rested on agriculture, urban economies prospered on the trade in rural produce that passed through their marketplaces and on satisfying the consumer demands of country people with money to spend. Although the varying fortunes of the cloth industry and of overseas trade led to difficulties for some towns (Reading, Southampton) and prosperity for others (Worcester, Exeter), there seems to have been a general expansion in most English towns in the Elizabethan period that can be measured most reliably in their increasing populations.

Outside the economic sphere, the Reformation stands as a very clear watershed in the life of Tudor townspeople. The monasteries were very important urban institutions, and their destruction under Henry VIII had a major impact on the physical structure of towns as well as on their social and cultural life. The dissolution of the religious guilds and the general shift to Protestantism under Edward VI struck at that delicate web of institutions and practices that underlay much of the social life of townsmen, inextricably linked with traditional religion; the whole process affected economic prosperity (the pilgrimage trade, for instance), systems of local government and cultural and social life. The effects were not all destructive, however, for the disappearance of monastic and episcopal lords encouraged a great extension of municipal self-government that is one of the most positive aspects of Tudor towns. In many towns a group of leading citizens was able for the first time to acquire chartered rights from the crown that enabled them to set up an elaborate municipal administration. This was in any case a period of enterprise and self-confidence for the small oligarchies of wealthy men that controlled most Tudor towns. As central and local government developed elaborate systems for coping with the growing problem of periodic and chronic poverty, new administrative responsibilities fell on town governments at the same time as the provision of

T

schooling under municipal auspices expanded. Protestantism encouraged town worthies to concern themselves with the moral and religious lives of their fellow citizens, all in addition to the already multifarious responsibilities of these independently minded local rulers. The Tudor period represents a golden age for the traders who ran municipal governments, endowed with considerable power to control their communities before this independence was eroded in the seventeenth century by the irruption of national politics into these local worlds.

Thus the medieval urban community survived the shock of the Reformation and the other changes of the sixteenth century. Towns preserved their inherited sense of communal homogeneity; shared values continued to underpin urban society; and responsible local cliques governed with paternalistic yet widely accepted policies. There were, of course, stresses caused by religious and economic change, but the general impression given by the towns of Tudor England is of serious challenges successfully met.

BIBLIOGRAPHY

Barry, J., ed. *The Tudor and Stuart Town: A Reader in English Urban History.* 1990.

Clark, P., and P. Slack. *English Towns in Transition, 1500–1700.* 1976.

Dyer, A. *Decline and Growth in English Towns, 1400–1640.* 1991.

Girouard, M. *The English Town.* 1990.

MacCaffrey, M.T. *Exeter, 1540–1640: The Growth of an English Country Town.* 1958.

Palliser, D.M. *The Age of Elizabeth: England under the Later Tudors, 1547–1603.* 1992.

Sacks, D. *Trade, Society, and Politics in Bristol, 1500–1640.* 1985.

Tittler, R. "The End of the Middle Ages in the English Country Town." *Sixteenth Century Journal,* vol. 18, pp. 471–487.

Alan Dyer

SEE ALSO

Agriculture; Bristol; Cloth Trade; Economy; Fairs and Markets; Government, Local; London; Monastic Orders; Population and Demography; Reformation, English; Trade, Overseas

Trade, Inland

Much more is known of the structure, volumes, and mechanisms of trade overseas than of internal commerce, but greater knowledge does not denote higher importance. On the contrary, even in the absence of records of the transaction of goods and services internally comparable to those for overseas trade, there is no question that the bulk of incomes and employment throughout the Tudor period derived from home trades and services. Even woolen cloth exports were almost certainly exceeded by domestic sales; of the total agricultural and industrial production, merchants trading abroad handled only a small part. The great bulk was sold, wholesale and retail, in an extensive, complex network of domestic fairs and markets. Some 700 market towns served mainly local needs, most customers and traders traveling a short distance to attend the market. Urban craftsman-retailers provided a local service, working to order or speculatively, while in the larger towns and cities toward the end of the Tudor period there were many shopkeepers, some specialists, others stocking a miscellany of goods. Providing a service on the fringes of the marketing system were peddlers, unpopular with the authorities but ubiquitous and indispensable for customers, particularly in the countryside. Fairs widened the area in which goods were transacted, creating regional markets that attracted wholesale merchants over considerable distances. Many traveled from London to dispose of goods purchased abroad. Many imported wares were redistributed in this fashion in the provinces. The presence of metropolitan merchants at the provincial fairs was indicative of what was to be the key development in inland trade under the Tudors. The basic elements and locations of the home market were well established by the late fifteenth century.

Thereafter, with increasing momentum in the later Tudor period, the trend was toward the integration of markets, the metropolitan market subsuming regional markets, just as those had subsumed local ones. A list of goods, agricultural and industrial, traded in and out of the capital in the late sixteenth century would be far too long to enumerate, as would the regions that supplied them. Welsh and north country cattle were driven to London though the midland counties where they were fattened for the market. Corn was supplied from Kent, East Anglia, Berkshire, and Oxfordshire. Coal, in rapidly increasing quantities in Elizabeth I's reign, was shipped along the coast from Newcastle. There were areas, some close to the capital, that remained relatively detached from the metropolitan marketing system. But the progress toward the system itself, unique in Europe, was of the highest importance for long-term economic growth and development.

BIBLIOGRAPHY

Chartres, J.A. *Internal Trade in England, 1500–1700.* 1977.

Willan, T.S. *The Inland Trade.* 1976.

Brian Dietz

SEE ALSO

Coal Industry; Economy; Fairs and Markets; Pedlars; Towns; Transportation

Trade, Overseas

The Tudor regime coincided with a period of exceptional growth and development in European trade, beginning in the last quarter of the fifteenth century when there was a widespread recovery from a mid-century recession. The advance was occasionally checked, most severely in the middle and last decades of the sixteenth century, but the underlying trend was for markets to become more active, integrated, and, following the period of exploration and discovery, more extensive. When the recovery got underway, England was on the periphery of the system of international exchange. Though close to the main arteries of trade linking the Baltic with the Mediterranean, and western with central and eastern Europe, the nature of the commodity exchange and the role of foreign merchants defined the position as one of inferiority relative to the more advanced regions of Italy, France, the Low Countries, and southern Germany. Some progress had been made in the fifteenth century when woolen cloth supplanted wool as the staple of the export trade. But the benefits of substituting manufacture for raw material were reduced by the preponderance of cloth that was only partly manufactured, finishing and dyeing being completed abroad; and the gains made by adding the value of labor to exports were offset by the displacement of domestic by imported manufactures, adding to the already wide range of finished goods entering the country. Many did so through London, the main channel also of the export trade. The only English city to rank as a major center of European trade, London was nonetheless overshadowed by those in Italy, the Netherlands, and Germany. In addition, much of the business transacted in the capital was in the hands of merchants from abroad. Upwards of half of the goods leaving and entering the port were registered in the customs in the names of members of the German Hanseatic League, who enjoyed a specially privileged position in the city, and of Italian merchants whose position depended not on privileges but on their unrivaled experience and expertise in business.

In the early Tudor period the process of growth tended to consolidate or accelerate earlier trends. Wool shipments continued to fall sharply while those of woolen cloth rose. Between 1480 and 1550, when cloth accounted for 80 percent or more of the export trade, shipments doubled. At the same time the proportion leaving London had continued to rise. In the early years of the recovery the benefits were more widely shared. Bristol, the second port, Southampton, Ipswich, Hull, and other outports prospered, but by the end of Henry VIII's reign growth had become largely confined to London, where the short crossing to Antwerp, the great center or *entrepôt* of European commerce, linked the capital to the principal markets for cloth in the Netherlands, Germany, and central Europe. When exports achieved record highs in the late 1540s, close to 90 percent were shipped from the Thames. Bristol's cloth trade was in absolute decline from the 1490s, Southampton's from the 1520s when Italian merchants transferred their business to the capital. The recovery at Hull was also short-lived. Wool exports, the town's speciality, soon fell, and the decision of Hanseatic merchants, like the Italians, to move to London halted the recovery. Only Ipswich, with ready access to East Anglian cloths, and Antwerp, kept pace with London, though at a much lower level of sales. The course of the import trade, though more difficult to trace and measure, seems to have been similar to that of exports, with evidence of growth led by London. The effect was to confirm and perhaps increase the country's dependence on imported manufactures, many of which were channeled through Antwerp, where the range of goods offered, some produced locally, others from distant parts, was unique. The import of a miscellany of commonplace manufactures—inexpensive textiles, metalware, and glassware—as well as luxury fabrics and other upmarket wares, was indicative of the persistent backwardness of domestic industry. By way of exchange, Antwerp continued to insist on trading in unfinished cloths to the detriment of English clothworkers. And foreign merchants were almost as prominent in metropolitan trade in the 1540s as they had been a half-century or so earlier. Although the Merchant Adventurers, who had a monopoly of native trade with the Low Countries, had gained considerably in wealth, confidence, and experience under the early Tudors, their rivals from abroad were hard to dislodge.

The sustained growth of the early Tudor period, which was led by exports in the later stage, ended abruptly in

T

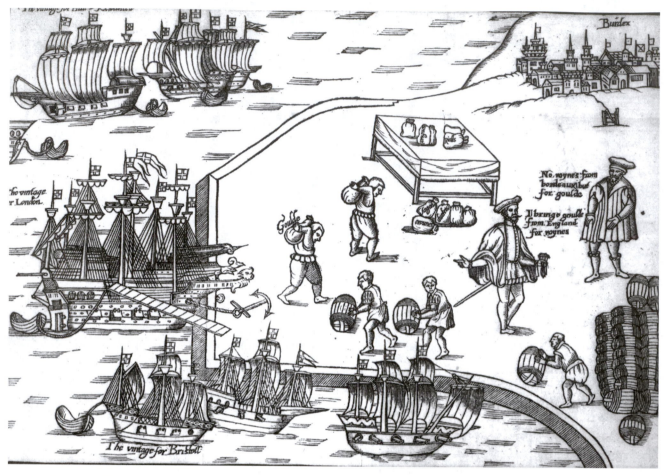

Robert Hitchcock, *The Balance of Payments between England and France,* from *A Pollitique platt for the honour of the prince, the profite of the state . . .* " (1580). Among the instances of imbalanced trade between England and the Continent was the importation of French wine; this illustration suggests a French demand for payment in bullion rather than exchange of goods. Reproduced from the original by permission of the Henry E. Huntington Library and Art Gallery.

1552 when the drastic fall in cloth exports in that year marked the beginning of a period of dislocation and recession in international trade that lasted for two decades. Out of the crisis emerged a markedly different pattern of overseas trade. An early response to the difficulties in established markets was a search for new ones. In the 1550s trade was established with Russia, Morocco, and the Guinea coast. In the same decade English merchants and ships returned to the Baltic after a long absence. In 1569, an embargo on trade with the Low Countries forced the Merchant Adventurers to transfer their staple to Hamburg. Ten years later the formation of the Eastland Company confirmed the growing importance of trade with the Baltic countries. English ships also found their way back to the Mediterranean in 1570, a half-century after direct links had been severed when

trade was rerouted overland from Italy to Antwerp. The vessels were first seen in Italian ports and the Ionian Islands before negotiations with the Turkish sultan allowed them to trade with Turkey, Syria, and Egypt. Spices, especially pepper, were a staple of the Levant trade, and when sales were threatened by Dutch imports from Asia via the Cape, members of the Levant Company were instrumental in forming the East India Company in 1599 to compete with the Dutch in the Indian Ocean. Meanwhile, the outbreak of war with Spain (1585) had closed another established market, one of some importance to merchants in London and the west country. For Londoners in particular, privateering was a valuable substitute for trade, the prospect of plunder drawing ships to the Caribbean and into the South Atlantic, while in Exeter, Plymouth, and other western ports investment

704   Trade, Overseas

was diverted into the North Atlantic where their ships had belatedly joined the Portuguese, Spanish, and French in the fishing grounds off Newfoundland in the 1570s. Salt was brought from southwest France to cure the cod that was marketed abroad as well as at home.

The breach of the London-Antwerp axis thus produced a substantially more diverse and extensive pattern of routes and markets. There was, however, continuity as well as change, most notably in the export trade. Woolen textiles remained dominant, and despite the introduction of the "new draperies," light, fashionable textiles that were eventually to find a ready market in southern Europe, the Merchant Adventurers continued to rely on sales of the traditional woolens in essentially the same markets in Germany and central Europe. Of the "new" trades, only the Baltic offered serious prospects of growth. Rising demand, in particular for cheaper woolens in Poland, revived overseas trade in Hull and, to a lesser extent, Newcastle. Hull's gain was London's loss, but only marginally so, metropolitan control of the cloth trade being almost as tight at the end of Elizabeth I's reign as it had been at the beginning. There was continuity also, or stability, in the volume and value of the cloth trade that conspicuously failed to expand in the new commercial structure. And in the light of this failure it is clear that underlying the changes was the search for alternative sources of imports, rather than new outlets for cloth. The merchant's problem was that while the facilities for finishing and marketing cloth in Hamburg and other German towns were adequate (more so than was once thought), no one port, whether in Germany or elsewhere, could substitute for Antwerp as *entrepôt* and emporium, offering such a vast range of commodities in the one place. The problem, and the need to find a solution, were particularly pressing for the Elizabethan merchant because increasingly his best chance of growth and profit, particularly in London, lay in supplying the domestic market rather than in exports. As the city's population grew, more than doubling in Elizabeth's reign, the capital developed as an *entrepôt,* relaying import goods to the provinces. The customs accounts confirm that growth was indeed transferred from exports to imports. While the cloth trade stagnated, the value of London's imports more than doubled.

The significance of import-led growth was twofold. Firstly, it was no less favorable to London than export-led growth by way of Antwerp had been earlier. Metropolitan merchants alone had the skills and capital needed to "go

around the world," in the words of a contemporary, in search of new markets; and through their control of the monopoly trading companies, which were a feature Elizabethan overseas trade, they were well placed to protect themselves against provincial competitors. Secondly, evidence that growth was transferred from exports to imports had obvious implications for the balance of trade. This had become an official concern during the mid-century crisis. Fears then expressed that the balance was unfavorable, draining specie out of the country, would not have been allayed by later developments, although the question was not raised again in government circles until the 1620s, when those fears seemed to have been confirmed. For the historian what evidence there is, beyond the bare record of imports and exports for London alone, is ambiguous and uncertain. There are, however, signs that the policy adopted in the 1560s of promoting domestic manufactures to substitute for imports had some effect. Significant also was the increase in supplies of imported timber and naval stores from the Baltic, Norway, and Russia for the shipbuilding and shipping industries that expanded rapidly to service the long-distance trades, the earnings from freight being set against any losses on the commodity exchange. Lastly, the role of foreign merchants, who were blamed for taking commercial profits out of the country, had been substantially reduced. Hanseatic merchants had been deprived of many of their privileges in the 1550s and 1560s and of much of their trade before they were expelled from London in 1598, while the Italians had left much earlier after the collapse of their base in Antwerp. By 1600, when alien exports were negligible, their share of imports had been halved.

The presence of English ships carrying native merchants' goods in the Indian Ocean and in the Atlantic at the end of Elizabeth's reign demonstrated how far the country had progressed since her grandfather's accession. England had moved from the near fringes to a more central position in the widening framework of European commerce. There were, however, limits to the progress that had been made, just as there was continuity as well as change in the overall pattern or structure of foreign trade. The first voyage of the East India Company, and the last of the reign, was a speculative undertaking, launched with much hesitancy and difficulty, and on a scale quite overshadowed by the Dutch, whose remarkable mercantile and maritime expansion in the 1590s threatened competitors in all the important branches of European trade. Westward expansion was likewise limited in ambition and

T

achievement. Plans to share in the wealth of the New World by colonizing North America had failed spectacularly, merchants showing little interest, while privateering was essentially a short-term expedient that had to be abandoned when the war ended in 1604. The only permanent Tudor achievement in the Atlantic region was the west coast Newfoundland fishing industry. Commerce thus remained overwhelmingly inter-European, while within Europe the continuity in the commodity exchange and the distribution of markets must again be emphasized. The most significant advances in Tudor commerce had been the "nationalization" of trade and transportation, the parallel growth in confidence, wealth, and entrepreneurial skills of the native merchant community, and the rise in the ranking of London as a commercial capital. While many contemporaries were critical of the way so many branches of international trade were concentrated on the capital, historians prefer to stress the long-term benefits of the development of an integrated metropolitan market that served as an increasingly powerful "engine of growth" for the economy of the country as a whole.

BIBLIOGRAPHY

Andrews, K.R. *Trade, Plunder and Settlement: Maritime Enterprise and the Genesis of the British Empire, 1480–1630*. 1984.

Brenner, Robert. *Merchants and Revolution. Commercial Change, Political Conflict, and London's Overseas Traders, 1550–1653*. 1993.

Clay, C.G.A. *Economic Expansion and Social Change in England, 1500–1700*. Vol. 2: *Industry, Trade, and Government*. 1984.

Davis, R. *English Overseas Trade, 1500–1700*. 1973.

Ramsay, G.D. *English Overseas Trade During the Centuries of Emergence*. 1957.

Willan, T.S. *Studies in Elizabethan Foreign Trade*. 1959.

Brian Dietz

SEE ALSO

Bristol; Cloth Trade; Discovery and Exploration; East India Company; Economy; Fish and Fishing; Industry and Manufacture; London; Merchant Adventurers; Privateering; Shipbuilding

Translations

See Classical Literature, English Translations; French Literature, Influence of; Italian Literature, Influence of; Spanish Literature, Influence of

Transportation

In an age when the costs of carriage by road could double the price of bulky commodities like coal over a ten-mile journey, England was fortunate in the natural endowment of seas and rivers that offered much cheaper means of transportation. Coastal and overseas trade was conducted at nearly a hundred ports, creeks, and inlets in the Tudor period, the most important linking with an extensive network of navigable rivers to provide efficient transportation over large areas of the country. Boats on the Thames carried goods almost to Oxford; those in the Bristol Channel and on the Severn served markets in South Wales, North Devon, and north as far as Shrewsbury, while the rivers Ouse and Trent and their tributaries carried traffic deep into the most populous eastern and midland counties. York, Norwich, Cambridge, Lincoln, and Peterborough all had direct access by water to the sea.

The condition and effectiveness of the roads and land transportation are more difficult to judge. Contemporary complaints, often quoted by historians, that everywhere roads were in a deplorable and worsening condition, are not borne out by evidence of the existence in the late Middle Ages of a sophisticated network of highways, radiating in all directions from London, with solid, stone-built bridges across all the major rivers and many of the lesser ones. Tudor roads undoubtedly left much to be desired, particularly in winter, but year-round, door-to-door traffic was possible in many parts of the country where the soil was light and permeable, and stone-surfaced causeways eased passage over more difficult ground. The network of roads was undoubtedly capable of a steady increase in traffic through the sixteenth century, with regularly scheduled services between London, Norwich, York, Chester, and other cities and towns by the end of the Tudor period.

The main freights southward were textiles, often carried by packhorse and from as far away as the border counties. Leather, leather goods, and hardware were other goods of high value to bulk that could bear the costs of carriage by road, particularly if it were by wheeled vehicles. Early in Elizabeth I's reign these were made more efficient by the introduction of the long four-wheeled wagon. By the end of the reign the wagon, with a much greater capacity, had generally replaced the two-wheeled cart. This was one of the few innovations and improvements in transportation undertaken by the Tudors. Responsibility for road maintenance was given to the parish in 1555, but it is unclear how effectively the law was enforced. No such initiatives were undertaken in promoting and improving inland water transportation; the country lagged behind its continental neighbors in developing river navigation, either by improving those stretches that were already navigable or by making unnavigable rivers navigable, and in the building of canals. Only two small pound locks, at Exeter and on the river Lea, were built in the sixteenth century. But even without significant and obvious improvement there is no doubt that the interlocking, interdependent system of roads, navigable rivers, and seaports was a key enabling factor in commercial and economic progress generally in the Tudor period.

Transportation was also an industry in its own right. Land carriage was an important by-employment for members of the farming community. Around 1500 they provided most of the carriers. The growth of longer-distance, regular, scheduled transportation, however, led to the development of a more urban-based, professional service. Boatmen and bargemen who navigated the inland waterways also became more numerous and professional, often, as at Worcester, trading on their own account as well as providing a service for others. As an industry shipping had long been relatively discrete and professional. By the end of the Tudor period the increased demand for seaborne transportation, especially for the domestic coal trade, had substantially enhanced the role and importance of the industry.

BIBLIOGRAPHY

Chartres, J.A. *Inland Trade in England 1500–1700.* 1977.

Harrison, D.F. "Bridges and Economic Development, 1300–1800." *Economic History Review,* vol. 45, part 2, pp. 240–261.

Willan, T.S. *River Navigation in England.* 1936.

Brian Dietz

SEE ALSO

Coal Industry; Industry and Manufacture; Shipbuilding; Trade, Inland; Trade, Overseas

Transubstantiation

See Eucharist; Sacraments

Travel Literature

Travel literature in the Tudor period is anything but homogeneous. Many kinds of writing, undertaken for different motives, intended for different readers, about journeys of different sorts, may come under this heading. What might be called pure travel literature—writing for profit about travel undertaken for the sheer pleasure and excitement of traveling—comes in only at the very end of the Tudor period, with Fynes Moryson, who traveled in Europe with an inexhaustible enthusiasm for strange sights and customs in the mid-1590s, although he did not publish his *Itinerary* until 1617. The wider literature of travel grew greatly in bulk in the later Elizabethan period, testifying to England's recognition of itself—or rather of Britain—as a nation growing in prosperity and power though oversea trade and settlement. The pleasure of reading this literature was not only the excitement of vicarious adventure and contact with the exotic but also confirmation of nationhood and pride in national achievement.

There was an increasing interest in the territory of England itself, its towns and its castles, its rivers and terrain, its history and antiquities. John Leland advertised his forthcoming description of England in his *Laborious Journey* in 1549, writing of being "inflamed with a love to see thoroughly" all parts of the kingdom, though his *Itinerary* was in fact not published until the eighteenth century. William Lambarde's *Perambulation of Kent* appeared in 1576, and John Stow's monumental *Survey of London* in 1598. Scotland and Wales were included in William Harrison's "Historical Description of Britain," printed with Holinshed's *Chronicles* in 1577. The most substantial survey of the country to be published in Tudor times was in Latin, William Camden's *Britannia* (1586; there was an English translation by Philemon Holland, entitled *Britain,* in 1610). This is a work of topography and history rather than of travel, but there are many personal touches about Camden's experiences in going about the kingdom and making his observations. For Ireland we have only hostile and scornful observers such as John Derricke, in *The Image of Ireland* (1581).

Probably the best accounts of land travel outside Britain are the reports sent by Anthony Jenkinson in mid-century to his employers, the Muscovy Company, about his eventful peregrinations in Russia and the land of the Tartars seeking markets for English cloth, and reconnoitering an overland route to Cathay. In comparison with Jenkinson, Giles Fletcher's ambassadorial account, *Of the Russe Commonwealth* (1591), appears pompous, staid, and prejudiced. Enforced land travels in another quarter of the globe were those of Job Hortop and Anthony Knivet, each of whom describes his adventures in the southern American continent after being set ashore, the first by Hawkins and the second by Cavendish.

T

The main substance of Tudor travel literature is, of course, the record of the voyages of discovery, mostly in the narratives assiduously collected by Richard Hakluyt. Although these voyages were the preliminary probings to establish what became the vast British Empire, they more often than not provide stories of failure, frustration, and disaster. There are, for example, the many records of the dogged and unavailing attempts to find first a northeast and then a northwest passage that would furnish the Englishman's special route to the riches of Cathay and the East. George Best described Martin Frobisher's three attempts amid the ice of northwestern waters in *A True Discourse* (1578). Much of the time that should have been spent on exploration went into loading onto the ships tons of ore wrongly thought to be gold-bearing. Best's account is notable for its story of Frobisher's blundering contacts with the inhabitants of Baffin Island, whom Best charitably calls "those ravenous, bloody, and man-eating people." A much more sympathetic and detailed account of the native peoples encountered on these northwestern voyages was given by Frobisher's successor, John Davis, who made three major voyages in 1585–1587.

A famous account of failure is Edward Hayes's story of Sir Humphrey Gilbert's attempt to found a colony in Newfoundland and the adjoining mainland in 1583, and his death at sea on the return voyage. What parades itself as a celebration of valor and endurance turns out to be an insidious undermining of Gilbert's qualifications for carrying out what Hayes, like Hakluyt, regarded as England's divine destiny, the colonization of North America. Sir Walter Ralegh's efforts to found the colony of Virginia did not succeed before the end of the Tudor dynasty. The narratives of his first attempts at an English foothold on the American continents range from the lyrical account by Arthur Barlowe of the earthly paradise he says he found in his 1584 reconnaissance, to the all-important account by Thomas Hariot, *A Briefe and True Report of the New Found Land of Virginia* (1588). Hariot is altogether free of the arrogance, insolence, and insensitivity that characterize most of the accounts of the meeting of the old and new worlds. He may have been naive to think that the Indians would enthusiastically adopt European culture, but at least he knew that the way to that end was not by the truculent severity of the majority of the colonists.

After the failure of his two Virginia colonies, Ralegh turned his attention to Guiana, recorded in his 1595 expedition as *The Discovery of the Large, Rich, and Beautiful Empire of Guiana* (1596). This is perhaps the grandest and best written of all Tudor travel writings. Its purpose was to make the country as alluring as possible, in order to convince Elizabeth I and potential investors of the worth of exploiting the country. Ralegh himself was quite convinced, and the prospect of a vast yield of gold drew him back for his fatal last expedition in 1618.

From the innumerable accounts of other voyages in Elizabethan times, one might select the final expedition of Thomas Cavendish in 1591–1593. Cavendish wanted to be the first man to sail round the world twice, and the substantial documentation of his voyage, including his own frenzied aplogia, penned immediately before he died (presumably by his own hand), dramatically illustrates the blend of dream and disaster to be found in many of these records. In this connection, the diary of Richard Madox, fellow of All Souls College, Oxford, recording with dry cynicism the unhappy voyage of Edward Fenton in 1582, has unique value.

It is a question how far fiction has a right to be included within "travel literature." An obvious contender would be Thomas Nashe's brilliant and scathing satire, *The Unfortunate Traveller* (1594). Thomas Deloney's novels contain fascinating glimpses of domestic travel in Elizabethan times. But are we also to include *The Faerie Queene,* whose characters are continuously traveling? The antitravel movement should certainly be noted. That travel is corrupting was a very ancient notion, and in *The Schoolmaster* (1570) Roger Ascham rephrased this concern in his attack on the Italianate Englishman, who suffers in morals, manners, and religion from his contact with foreign countries. Skepticism about the value of travel also informs the character of Jaques in *As You Like It;* he is said to "have nothing" from having "seen much" (4.1.21).

The value of travel literature does not lie in the quality of the writing, which is often clumsy, repetitive, pedestrian. It is the immediacy of lived experience that gives it its value, especially in the extremities so often the subject of the sea narratives. But there is no direct line from that experience to the reader. It is not only clumsiness and inarticulacy that put a screen between the reality and us. Travel literature, defined as writings about actual events and people, can be the most evasive of literature. The various motives for writing—financial, patriotic, exculpatory—generally demand that the story of "what really happened" be bathed in a light that never was on sea or land. Many travel narratives apologize for lack of eloquence, explaining that there is compensation in the truth of what is told. A good deal of the reader's interest rests in divining what is *not* told. The writing certainly does have the virtue of involving us in the reality of lived life, but only through the additional excitement of trying to detect that reality beneath the refracting haze of self-justifying narratives.

BIBLIOGRAPHY

Donno, E.S. *An Elizabethan in 1582: The Diary of Richard Madox.* 1976.

Edwards, Philip, ed. *Last Voyages: Cavendish, Hudson, Ralegh.* 1988.

Hakluyt, Richard. *Principal Navigations.* 1589.

Hortop, Job. *Travels of an Englishman.* 1591.

Markham, A.H. *The Voyages and Works of John Davis the Navigator.* 1880.

Quinn, D.B., and A.M. Quinn. *Virginia Voyages from "Hakluyt."* 1973.

Philip Edwards

SEE ALSO

Ascham, Roger; Camden, William; Davis, John; Deloney, Thomas; Discovery and Exploration; Frobisher, Martin; Gilbert, Humphrey; Hakluyt, Richard; Hariot, Thomas; Harrison, William; Holinshed, Raphael; Lambarde, William; Leland, John; Moryson, Fynes; Nashe, Thomas; Ralegh, Walter

Travers, Walter (c. 1548–1635)

The Puritan polemicist Walter Travers was born about 1548 in Nottingham and educated at Christ's College, Cambridge, where he graduated B.A. in 1565 and M.A. in 1569, the same year he was elected a senior fellow. He then moved to Geneva, befriending the Calvinist theologian Theodora Beza, whose views reinforced Travers's belief in the need for further reformation of the English Church. This became the subject of his Latin treatise, translated into English by his friend Thomas Cartwright as *A full and plaine declaration of Ecclesiasticall Discipline . . .* (1574). Thereafter, Travers returned to England. He earned his B.D. at Cambridge, then moved to Oxford for his D.D. in 1576. He would not subscribe to the Thirty-nine Articles, however, and was denied a license to preach. By 1578, he had moved abroad again, joining Cartwright in Antwerp; Cartwright immediately ordained him, and Travers finally began to preach. He returned to England again, about 1580, and was appointed domestic chaplain to William Cecil, Lord Burghley, through whose efforts Travers became afternoon lecturer at the Temple, quickly winning a wide reputation. He was the Puritans' chief advocate at the Lambeth Conference of 1584 and was recommended to become master of the Temple. Archbishop John Whitgift blocked the move, and the conformist Richard Hooker was awarded the position instead. Travers continued to preach, however, and he and Hooker became engaged in an oratorical duel in which Travers would refute, in his afternoon sermon, whatever Hooker had preached that very morning. Although the two preachers remained friends throughout, Whitgift took a dim view of the debate and, in the end, silenced Travers, who moved on to a divinity chair at St. Andrews University in 1591, then to the provostship of Trinity College in Dublin (1595), which he was compelled to resign three years later because of illness. Returning to London, he lived in obscurity until his death in January 1634.

BIBLIOGRAPHY

Bauckham, R. "Hooker, Travers, and the church of Rome in the 1580s." *Journal of Ecclesiastical History,* vol. 29, pp. 37–50.

Knox, S.J. *Walter Travers: Paragon of Elizabethan Puritanism.* 1962.

Lake, Peter. *Anglicans and Puritans? Presbyterian and English Conformist Thought from Whitgift to Hooker.* 1988.

Mark Goldblatt

SEE ALSO

Articles of Religion; Cartwright, Thomas; Hooker, Richard; Puritanism; Sermons; Whitgift, John

Treason

In early modern England, treason was widely perceived as one of the most heinous of crimes. Because it denied the monarch's divinely instituted authority, high treason was regarded as a threat to the entire social order. Tudor England witnessed a marked expansion of treason law, as its rulers altered the juridical understanding of treason to incorporate common-law precedents, to buttress royal authority, and to address problems stemming from England's break with Rome.

When Henry VIII became king in 1509, the crime of high treason was defined by an act of 1352. This act (25 Edw. III, st. 5, c. 2.) made it treason to compass the death of the king or to levy war against the king in his realm. The act was narrow in scope: to convict a person of political subversion, it demanded overt proof of treasonous activity. During the early years of his reign, Henry VIII left the law unaltered. But when he established himself as

T

the supreme governor of the English Church, he came to believe that it was deeply flawed, since its demand for overt proof left him unable to prosecute cases such as that of Elizabeth Barton (c. 1506–1534). Barton, also known as the Holy Maid of Kent, gained considerable public attention when in 1533 she was sent to the Tower for prophesying the death of Henry VIII if he married Anne Boleyn. Although they were beyond the jurisdiction of existing treason law, Barton and her promoters were nevertheless attainted for treason without trial at the common law and put to death in April 1534. To address such cases, Parliament passed a new treason law in 1534. This act (26 Henry VIII, c. 13.) expanded the juridical understanding of treason to include not merely actions but also words. The statute stipulated that it was treason to "maliciously wish, will, or desire, by words or writing . . . any bodily harm to the King's person." Under this act Thomas More (1477–1535), lord chancellor of England, was tried on charges of treason. During his trial, More disputed ever having spoken "maliciously" against the king's authority; his argument, however, was rejected; More was convicted on the evidence of a single witness and executed in 1535.

After Henry's death in 1547, Edward Seymour, lord protector Somerset, repealed these recent additions to treason law. Soon, however, Somerset was forced to add provisions specifying that denial of the royal supremacy in deed or writing was treason on the first offense. Mary Tudor began her reign by restoring the 1352 act, effectively denying that words alone could ever constitute treason. After her marriage to Philip II of Spain, however, she added provisions to the treason law to protect her husband. In 1555, Mary extended the law even further, making it treason to speak against the restoration of Catholicism in England.

During the reign of Elizabeth I, treason law reflects the advance of the Counter Reformation in England. In 1570, Pope Pius V published a bull, *Regnans in Excelsis*, which excommunicated Elizabeth I and absolved English Catholics of their allegiance to her sovereignty. In the context of the arrival of Mary Queen of Scots in England, the Northern Rebellion (1569), and the Ridolfi Plot (1570–1571), Elizabeth and her government considered the bull an act of aggression. They responded with a statute that made it treason to bring in, or publish, any documents from Rome (13 Eliz. I, c. 2). Even more alarming to the authorities, however, was the arrival of Jesuit missionaries on English soil in 1577. Trained by Cardinal William Allen at the Jesuit College at Douai in the Spanish Netherlands, these highly

trained "soldiers of God" arrived with one goal: to nourish and sustain the scattered adherents of the Catholic faith in England. Although the missionaries claimed that their activities were strictly religious, Elizabeth I and her government were convinced that their ultimate goal was political subversion. Under the existing treason law, however, the authorities could not convict the missionaries as traitors, since they could produce no evidence of treasonous activity, and the priests themselves steadfastly denied any desire to subvert Elizabeth's rule. To address the threat posed by the missionaries, Parliament passed a series of acts criminalizing their activities: a 1581 statute extended the existing treason law to include any person who sought to withdraw a subject's allegiance from either the queen or the Church of England (23 Eliz. 1, c.1); a 1585 act made it treason simply to be a Jesuit priest and banished the priests from England (27 Eliz. 1, c.2). It was under these laws that Robert Southwell and Edmund Campion were captured, convicted, and executed as traitors. By the end of Elizabeth's reign, more than 187 Jesuits had been executed as traitors under these laws; still more were imprisoned and tortured.

BIBLIOGRAPHY

Bellamy, John. *The Tudor Law of Treason.* 1979.
Elton, G.R. *The Tudor Constitution.* 2nd edition. 1982.
———. *Policy and Police: The Enforcement of Religion in the Age of Thomas Cromwell.* 1972.
Guy, John. *Tudor England. 1992.*

Paula McQuade

SEE ALSO

Barton, Elizabeth; Campion, Edmund; Catholicism; Counter Reformation; Elizabeth I; Howard, Thomas; Jesuits; Mary I; More, Thomas; Northern Rebellion; Reformation, English; *Regnans in Excelsis;* Ridolfi Plot; Southwell, Robert; Supremacy, Act of

Trent, Council of (1545–1563)

When the Council of Trent finally opened in 1545, one of the three legates was the Englishman, Cardinal Reginald Pole, who had been involved in planning for it since 1538. His role first in leading it and then in drawing up various ecclesiastical reforms that the Privy Council later took over is probably the most important English link to Trent. Pole's cousin, Henry VIII, had refused—after some hesitation lest he be the only prince to do so—to send representatives to Trent or any of its proposed predecessors, and his excommunication in 1538 firmly closed the door. In 1545, Henry was alleged to have hired Italian soldiers both to disrupt the council and to kill Pole. Although plans were made to send Pole as legate to England again after Henry's death, the translation to Bologna and then suspension of the council shortly thereafter meant that no approach was made to the English.

Between 1552 and 1561 the council did not meet. During that interval, after the accession of Mary I, Pole was legate to England. In that capacity, he held a synod in 1555–1556 which, among other things, created seminaries for education of the clergy, building on plans developed by his mentor, Gian Matteo Giberti, bishop of Verona. Very similar designs were later adopted at Trent. This strand of "Catholic reform" passed through an English phase before becoming the Counter Reformation.

When Pius IV (1560–1565) reconvened the council, he hoped to induce English participation. To that end, he sent one of Pole's close associates, Vincenzo Parpaglia, as nuncio in 1560, and Celso Martinengo in 1561, but neither was admitted to England. Queen Elizabeth I might have been willing to negotiate a private compromise on the score of English attendance, but her chief minister, William Cecil, who was engineering the first anti-Catholic moves just then (in part for domestic political reasons), would have nothing to do with any papal nuncio. At the close of the council, other of Pole's former allies, among them Thomas Goldwell, proposed to the council that Elizabeth be excommunicated. The plan was rejected. Despite the fact that the council's decrees made clear that a member of the church in England could not be a good Catholic, the English largely ignored Trent, perhaps because that decision was not officially circulated in England until later, and also because most Catholic clergy did not make much of the council's importance. While continental Protestants produced one attack on it after another, no such work appeared in England until Palo Sarpi's *Istoria del concilio di Trento [History of the Council of Trent]* was translated in 1619.

BIBLIOGRAPHY

Bayne, C.G. *Anglo-Roman Relations, 1558–1565.* 1913; repr. 1968.

Jedin, Hubert. *A History of the Council of Trent.* 2 vols. 1961.

Thomas F. Mayer

SEE ALSO

Church of England; Cecil, William; Counter Reformation; Pole, Reginald

Tunstall, Cuthbert (1474–1559)

The illegitimate first son of a prominent Lancashire nobleman, Cuthbert Tunstall was born in Yorkshire. About 1491, he went to Oxford, probably to Balliol College, and he later studied at Cambridge and at Padua, where he became expert in both civil and canon law. Ordained in 1509, his legal knowledge earned him the post of chancellor to Archbishop William Warham (1511). In 1515, he became archdeacon of Chester, and in the following year he was made master of the rolls. In 1519, he was sent to the emperor Charles V as Henry VIII's ambassador, and was thus in a position to observe the outbreak of Lutheranism in Germany. A strong opponent of Luther, Tunstall did all he could to ensure that Luther's teachings would not circulate in England.

In 1521, Tunstall was made dean of Salisbury, and a year later the pope appointed him bishop of London. In 1523, he became keeper of the privy seal, and in 1525, he returned to Germany as ambassador to Charles V. In 1527, he helped Cardinal Thomas Wolsey negotiate the Treaty of Cambrai. When Wolsey was forced to give up the bishopric of Durham in 1530, Tunstall was appointed to the see. He acquiesced in the break with Rome in 1534, and three years later was appointed the first president of the newly formed Council of the North.

Tunstall's friendship with Thomas Cranmer and with Edward Seymour, lord protector Somerset, allowed him to escape deprivation under Edward VI, but only for a time. In 1551, he was placed under house arrest in London, and in the following year he was finally ejected from his see, which was suppressed. When Mary I ascended the throne, Tunstall was released and restored to Durham. In 1558, he was told he would not be welcome at the court of Elizabeth I, and the following year he was deprived of his see once more (September 28, 1559). He died on November 18 of that year.

Tunstall was a traditionalist Catholic who did all he could to make the English Reformation as theologically conservative as possible. Because he was associated with the disastrous policies of Mary I, there is still no major study of his life and achievement.

BIBLIOGRAPHY

Loades, D.M. "The Last Years of Cuthbert Tunstall, 1547–1559." *Durham University Journal*, vol. 66, pp. 54–66.

———. *The Reign of Mary Tudor.* 1991.

Gerald Bray

Turberville, George (c. 1544–c. 1597)

Second son of George Turbervile and Jane Bampfield, nephew of the bishop of Exeter, James Turbervile, and brother of Nicholas Turbervile, the younger George Turbervile descended from a Dorsetshire family whose genealogy figured in Thomas Hardy's *Tess of the D'Urbervilles*. The incipient narrative in his poems on the "Lover" and "his Lady"—often identified by their sobriquets Tymetes and Pyndara, respectively—anticipates the vogue of sonnet sequences at century's end. Turberville also deserves credit for his epistolary travel writing, his translations from Latin, Italian, and French, and his experimental versification: though his fourteeners and poulter's measure made his poetry outmoded by 1590, he was the fifth practitioner of blank verse. Puttenham lists him with Philip Sidney, Walter Ralegh, and Fulke Greville, among a "crew of courtly makers Noble men and Gentlemen of her Majesties owne servauntes, who have written excellently well" (*The Arte of English Poesie* [1589], 1.31).

After attending Winchester and then New College, Oxford, where he did not take a degree, Turberville proceeded to one of the Inns of Court where his literary coterie included Arthur Brooke, Barnabe Googe, and George Gascoigne. While serving as secretary to Thomas Randolph, whom he accompanied on a diplomatic trading mission to Russia (1568–1569), he wrote poems about his experiences abroad; Richard Hakluyt printed three of these epistles in his *Voyages* (1589).

Turberville's *Epitaphes, Epigrams, Songs and Sonets, with a Discourse of the Friendly affections of Tymetes to Pyndara his Ladie* (1567), dedicated to Anne Russell, countess of Warwick, was a heterogeneous collection of epitaphs, epigrams, moralizing verse, addresses to friends, answer poems, and love poems. This collection shows the influence of the *Greek Anthology* or its Latin humanist imitations, Richard Tottel's *Miscellany*, Googe's *Eglogs, Epitaphes, and Sonettes* (1562), and the story of betrayal in Chaucer's *Troilus and Criseyde*. Turberville published a further group of occasional poems, *Epitaphes and Sonnettes,* along with *Tragicall Tales* (ca. 1574? 1576?—extant in 1587 edition), and "some other broken pamphlettes and Epistles, sent to certaine his frends in England, at his *being in Moscovia.* Anno 1569."

George Turberville, *Training of a Falcon,* from *The Book of Faulconrie* (1575). Turberville's was one of a number of manuals on the gentlemanly arts of hunting. Here a gentleman trains a hawk to perch on his gauntleted hand. A perch is fixed in the ground below. Hawks were used to hunt small game, such as rabbits. Reproduced from the original by permission of the Henry E. Huntington Library and Art Gallery.

From Latin, he translated as *The Heroycall Epistles* (1567) Ovid's twenty-one *Heroides* and three answering epistles attributed to Aulus Sabinus; the first nine of Mantuan's ten *Eclogues* as *The Eglogs of the Poet B. Mantuan Carmelitan, Turned into English Verse and set forth with the argument to every Eglog* (1567); and Dominicus Mancinus's didactic poem *De Quatuor Virtutibus* as *A plaine Path to perfect Vertue* (1568).

Turberville translated ten *Tragicall Tales* from Italian: seven verse narratives from Boccaccio's *Decameron* and three from Mambrino da Fabriana's *La Selva* (1556), itself a translation of Pedro Mexia's Spanish *Silva:* no. 2 derives from Plutarch's *Mulierum Virtutibus;* no.5 and no. 8 from Bandello's *Novelle.* Turberville's last translations offer interest for cultural studies: based on Italian and French sources, *The Booke of Faulconrie, or Hawking* (1575), a practical manual on the care of hawks, is often bound together with an anonymous translation from French, *The Noble Art of Venerie, or Hunting,* traditionally ascribed to him.

In 1573, Turberville escaped an attack on his life but succumbed to illness; married in the mid-1570s, he became a landholder at Shapwick; during his final years, he performed minor governmental services, and he may be Edmund Spenser's "good Harpalus" in *Colin Clouts Come Home Againe.*

Fittingly, the poet who expressed regret at abandoning his plan to translate Lucan's *Pharsalia* because he could not do justice to the Roman historian's "stately stile" and "worke of weightie pryce," himself earned Sir John Harington's praise, not only for his effort "To pollish Barbarisme with purer stile" but also for his success in remaining "Sincere and just."

BIBLIOGRAPHY

Hankins, John. *The Life and Works of George Turberville.* 1940.

Panofsky, Richard J., intro. *Epitaphes, Epigrams, Songs and Sonets (1567) and Epitaphes and Sonnettes (1576).* George Turberville. Scholars' Facsimiles and Reprints. 1977.

Sheidley, William E. "George Turbervile and the Problem of Passion." *Journal of English and Germanic Philology,* vol. 69, pp. 631–649.

———. "George Turbervile's Epigrams from the Greek Anthology: A Case-study of 'Englishing.'" *Studies in English Literature,* vol. 12, pp. 71–84.

Andrea Sununu

SEE ALSO

Brooke, Arthur; Classical Literature, English Translations; Epigrams; Gascoigne, George; Googe, Barnabe; Italian Literature, Influence of; Sonnet Sequences; Travel Writing

Turner, William (c. 1512–1568)

Botanist and religious controversialist, Turner was born in Morpeth, Northumberland. He entered Pembroke Hall, Cambridge, thanks to the support of Thomas, Lord Wentworth, and graduated B.A. in 1530. Two years later he was elected fellow and served as college treasurer. In addition to developing a passion for botany while at Cambridge—a subject little cultivated by his Cambridge contemporaries—Turner also became a zealous Protestant, thanks to the teachings of Nicholas Ridley and Hugh Latimer. Throughout his life his publications attest to the congruity of both interests in his mind. While at Cambridge he published translations of two short religious works, as well as his *Libellus de re herbaria novus* (1538; repr. 1965), in which he provided the Greek, Latin, and English names of plants. Turner's strong religious sentiments prompted him to leave Cambridge in 1540 and become an itinerant preacher. Preaching without a license, however, Turner was imprisoned, and after his release he opted to leave for the Continent, making his way to Italy by way of Holland and Germany. In Italy, he studied botany with Luca Ghini and also obtained an M.D. degree. He then traveled to Switzerland, where he not only continued to collect plants but also formed an intimate friendship with Conrad Gesner in Zurich and possibly met as well with Leonard Fuchs while in Basle. Proceeding to Germany and Holland, Turner continued his studies, publishing in 1544 his *Avium praecipuarum* (trans. 1903). Nor did he neglect his religious studies, publishing among other things *The Huntyng and Fyndyng out of the Romishe Fox* (1543), which initiated a protracted and vitriolic pamphlet war with Bishop Stephen Gardiner. Following the accession of Edward VI to the throne in 1547, Turner returned to England, representing Ludgershall in Edward's first Parliament, and became physician (and possibly chaplain as well) to Edward Seymour, duke of Somerset. Prosperity, however, did not follow, and Turner, complaining of many distractions and the encumberments of a large family, desperately sought some clerical preferment. After several disappointments and delays, he was finally appointed dean of Wales in 1550. The first volume of *A Newe Herball,* much of which was written while Turner was still on the Continent, appeared in 1551.

With Mary I's accession, Turner was removed from the deanery and subsequently left again for the Continent. His second exile hardly interrupted his botanical studies. During the next five years he stayed in various cities in Germany, and at least in two of these he established both a medical practice and his own garden. In 1555, he published *A New Booke of Spirituall Physick.* Turner returned to England in 1558 following Mary's death and was reinstalled by Elizabeth I as dean of Wales. Six years later, however, he was again removed from his position, this time in view of his uncompromising nonconformist position. He then moved to London where he remained until

T

his death. Between 1562–1568, the final two parts of the *Herball* appeared, establishing Turner's reputation as the founder of modern English botany.

BIBLIOGRAPHY

Carlson, Eric J. "The Marriage of William Turner." *The Bulletin of the Institute of Historical Research,* vol. 65, pp. 336–339.

Jones, Whitney R.D. *William Turner: Tudor Naturalist, Physician, and Divine.* 1988.

Pineas, Rainer. "William Turner's `Spirituall physik.'" *Sixteenth Century Journal,* vol. 14, pp. 387–398.

Wheeler, Alwyne, Peter S. Davis, and Elizabeth Lazenby. "William Turner's (c. 1508–1568) notes on fishes in his letter to Conrad Gessner." *Archives of Natural History,* vol. 13, pp. 291–305.

Mordechai Feingold

SEE ALSO

Gardiner, Stephen; Medicine and Health; Seymour, Edward

Tusser, Thomas (c. 1524–1590)

Fourth son of William Tusser and Isabella Smith, Thomas Tusser began a career in music before becoming a farmer and writing poetry about agriculture and life on the farm. His *A Hundredth Goode Pointes of Husbandrie,* printed by Richard Tottel (1557), was followed by *A Hundreth Good Pointes of Husbandry, lately maried unto a hundreth Good Poyntes of Huswifery* (1570). By 1573, the hundred points had grown to five hundred; an autobiographical poem, "The Author's Life," prefixed the new volume, *Five Hundreth Pointes of Good Husbandry united to as many of Good Huswifery.* Although awkward in meter, grammar, and syntax, Tusser's quaint, zestful verse offers the rewards of technical vocabulary, delight in language, and an encyclopedia of seasonal tasks, domestic chores, and proverbial lore.

A chorister at the chapel of Wallingford castle, Berkshire, and under organist John Redmon's direction, at St. Paul's School, London, Tusser then studied at Eton under Nicholas Udall and at Cambridge. Elected to King's College in 1543, he moved to Trinity Hall, where congenial company contrasted with his childhood experiences at Wallingford chapel. Forced by illness to leave the university, he joined the court, where he served for ten years as musician to William Paget, whom Tusser described as "good to his servants," and to whom he later dedicated the 1557 edition of his poetry. On moving to Cattiwade,

Suffolk, he wrote the *Hundredth Good Pointes of Husbandrie* and introduced the culture of barley. His wife's ill health led to a move inland to Ipswich; after her death, he married Amy Moon, who bore him three sons and one daughter. Five more moves followed: to West Dereham, Norfolk; in 1559, after his patron Sir Robert Southwell died, to Norwich, where John of Salisbury's influence secured him a living, probably as singer in the cathedral; to Fairsted, Essex, where he farmed unsuccessfully; to London; and with the onset of the plague in 1573–1574, to Cambridge, where he matriculated as a servant of Trinity Hall. He died in London on May 3, 1580, a prisoner for debt.

Sixteen reprintings of Tusser's work between 1577 and 1692 testify to its continuing popularity, as does the updated version, *Tusser Redivivus* (1710, 1744). Tusser's celebration of activities in field, garden, wood, and home conveys the challenges and joys of "husbandry" and "housewifery" along with a joyful love for the land.

BIBLIOGRAPHY

McRae, Andrew. "Husbandry Manuals and the Language of Agrarian Improvement." In *Culture and Cultivation in Early Modern England: Writing and the Land.* Michael Leslie and Timothy Raylor, eds. Pp. 35–62. 1992.

Tusser, Thomas. *The Five Hundred Points of Good Husbandry.* Geoffrey Grigson, ed. 1984.

Andrea Sununu

SEE ALSO

Agriculture; Gardens; Paget, William; Udall, Nicholas

Twyne, John (c. 1507–81)

Born at Rullington, Hampshire, Twyne was educated at Oxford. No details of his matriculation and college affiliation survive, but Anthony Á Wood claims he was a member of New Inn Hall. Twyne certainly frequented Juan Luis Vives' public lectures at Corpus Christi College. In 1525, Twyne graduated and moved to Canterbury where he married and became master of the town's free school. Although he appears to have remained Catholic throughout his life, we hear an accusation in 1534 from a local monk that Archbishop Thomas Cranmer sent Twyne twice weekly to Sandwich "to read a lecture of heresy." During the 1530s, Twyne also began his literary career. In all likelihood he was the anonymous translator of Henry of Caumpeden's *History of Kyng Boccus and Sydracke,* and two years later he produced an edition of Chaucer. Twyne's reputation as an educator was very high and the influx of students to his school made him wealthy. He also became active in local politics, serving as sheriff of Canterbury in 1544–1545, and in the following decade as alderman and mayor in 1553 and 1554, respectively. While serving as mayor, he played a not inconsiderable role in raising troops to suppress Wyatt's Rebellion. During 1553–1554, he also represented Canterbury in Parliament. In 1560 and in 1562, at the instigation of Archbishop Matthew Parker, Twyne was charged with riotousness and drunkenness—accusations that, in a Protestant context, usually denoted clinging to Catholicism—and such harassment apparently prompted Twyne to resign his headmastership and retire to Preston-by-Wingham, Kent, where he devoted himself to his historical studies. His only publication, apart from his two early editions, was *De rebus Albionicis, Britannicis atque Anglicis, commentariorum libri duo,* published by his son in 1590. The book is significant for its abandonment of traditional accounts of the origins of Britain, suggesting instead that before it became an island Britain was first settled by Albion, son of Neptune, and not by the Trojans, and later was invaded by the Phoenicians. None of his other works appears to have survived.

BIBLIOGRAPHY

Emden, A.B. *A Biographical Register of the University of Oxford A.D. 1501 to 1540,* pp. 582–583. 1974.
Ferguson, Arthur B. "John Twyne: A Tudor Humanist and the Problem of a Legend." *Journal of British Studies,* vol. 9, pp. 24–44.

Mordechai Feingold

SEE ALSO

History, Writing of; Parker, Matthew; Vives, Juan Luis; Wyatt's Rebellion

Tye, Christopher (c.1505–c.1572)

Christopher Tye belongs to the transition generation between Catholicism and Anglicanism at court. He was named master of the choristers at Ely Cathedral in 1543 and earned a doctorate at Cambridge in 1545. His career was apparently aided by his mentor, Richard Cox, a church reformer who was archdeacon of Ely and later chancellor of Oxford. Like Tye, he studied at King's College; as tutor to Prince Edward, he is the likely candidate to have introduced Tye to court. Tye's name does not appear in the extant court records of Edward's reign, but he probably served in some sort of unofficial capacity. Ely Cathedral records seem to suggest that he was reappointed there after a decade's absence. In 1560, he was ordained a priest, and in 1561 he resigned his post at Ely in favor of his son-in-law, Robert White, and was appointed to several parishes in the area. It is not known when he died, but a successor to his Doddington parish was appointed in 1573.

Tye composed in the various church styles popular at the time, including vocal music with Latin and with English texts and music for instrumental consorts. Only about half of Tye's Latin church music is extant. Dating from the reign of Henry VIII are the earliest motet, *Ave caput Christi,* and two of his three masses, a five-voice mass now lacking its tenor voice and the *Missa Western Wynde* (contrapuntal variations on a secular tune that was also made into masses by John Taverner and John Sheppard). The editor of *M. Euge bone* has suggested a connection between that work and the motet *Quaesumus omnipotens* that would make the good and faithful servant of the title a collective reference to Edward's court, true to both God and the new king. His instrumental music consists of consort arrangements of vocal works and five-voice *In nomine* settings with enigmatic titles such as *Howld fast* and *Rachells weepinge.*

In the play *When you see me you know me,* Samuel Rowley (who may have been Tye's grandson) suggests that Henry VIII said that England ". . . one Doctor hath / For musick's art, and that is Doctor Tye, / Admired for skill in musick's harmony." Tye may well have been a religious opportunist, but his compositional adaptibility, particularly in a forward-looking imitative style, is evident in his surviving music.

BIBLIOGRAPHY

Benham, Hugh. "Latin Church Music under Edward VI." *Musical Times,* vol. 116, pp. 477–480.
Davison, Nigel, ed. *Christopher Tye III: Ritual Music and Motets.* Early English Church Music. Vol. 33. 1987.
———. "The Western Wind Masses." *The Musical Quarterly,* vol. 57, pp. 427–443.
Doe, Paul, ed. *Christopher Tye II: Masses.* Early English Church Music. Vol. 24. 1980.
Morehen, John, ed. *Christopher Tye I: English Sacred Music.* Early English Church Music. Vol. 19. 1977.
Satterfield, John R. "A Catalogue of Tye's Latin Music." *Studies in Musicology: Essays in the History, Style, and Bibliography of Music in Memory of Glen Haydon.* 1969.

T

Weidner, Rorbert W. "The Instrumental Music of Christopher Tye." *Journal of the American Musicological Society,* vol. 17, pp. 363–370.

Karen M. Bryan

SEE ALSO

Anglicanism; Catholicism; Cox, Richard; Music, History of; Shepperd, John; Taverner, John

Tyndale, William (c. 1494–1536)

Reformer and biblical translator, William Tyndale was born of yeoman stock in Gloucestershire around 1494. A resident at Magdalen Hall, Oxford, he earned his B.A. in 1512 and M.A. in 1515. He then probably studied at Cambridge, where Desiderius Erasmus had taught Greek from 1511–1514. Inspired by Erasmus's Latin-Greek New Testament (1516) and Luther's German version (1522), he resolved to translate the Bible into English. When the bishop of London, Cuthbert Tunstall, failed to authorize this project, Tyndale left England permanently in 1524.

Before the authorities intervened, Tyndale printed his New Testament as far as Matthew 22:12 in Cologne (1525). Fleeing to Worms, he was able to publish the first complete New Testament translated into English from Greek (1526). Tyndale published his remaining works in Antwerp. His translations of the Pentateuch (1530) and Jonah (1531) were the first English versions made from Hebrew. He brought out revised New Testaments in 1534 and 1535.

These biblical translations occasioned independent works. *Parable of the Wicked Mammon* (May 1528) denied merit for good works. *Obedience of a Christian Man* (October 1528) was Tyndale's most influential book outside the Bible because it prescribed absolute obedience to secular rulers except for ungodly commands. *Practice of Prelates* (1530) asserted the validity of Henry VIII's marriage to Katherine of Aragon. Thomas More's relaxed *Dialogue Concerning Heresies* (1529) evoked Tyndale's incisive *Answer to More* (1531), but Tyndale ignored More's labored *Confutation against Tyndale* (1532–1533). *Exposition of 1 John* (1531) and *Exposition of Matthew* (1533) praised authentic faith and gave pastoral counsel. Other writings include a pamphlet on the Eucharist as memorial only and two letters to John Frith in the Tower (c. 1533). On October 6, 1536, Tyndale was executed near Brussels for rejecting human merit and papal authority. He was strangled and his corpse burned.

Tyndale's New Testament and Pentateuch were included in Coverdale's Bible (Zurich, 1535), commissioned by Thomas Cromwell. His Joshua through 2 Chronicles were first published in Matthew's Bible (Antwerp, 1537), licensed by Henry VIII. These translations were substantially included in a direct line of descent to the Great Bible (1539), the Bishops' Bible (1568), and in the collateral Geneva Bible (1560), all culminating in the Authorized Version (1611). The King James Bible removed Tyndale's radical ecclesiology—such as changing "congregation" to "church"—but rejected a Latinate style for his clear and forceful English.

BIBLIOGRAPHY

Daniell, David. *William Tyndale: A Biography.* 1994.

Day, John T., Eric Lund, and Anne M. O'Donnell, eds. *Word, Church, and State: Tyndale Quincentenary Essays.* 1998.

Independent Works of William Tyndale. Anne M. O'Donnell, SND, ed. 4 vols. 1998.

Works of William Tyndale. Henry Walter, ed. Parker Society. Vols. 42–44. 1848–1850.

Anne O'Donnell

SEE ALSO

Bible Translations; Cromwell, Thomas; Erasmus, Desiderius; Frith, John; Lutheranism; More, Thomas; Tunstall, Cuthbert

Tyrell, James (c. 1445–1502)

James Tyrell is most famous—and most infamous—for carrying out Richard III's desire for the elimination of Edward IV's male heirs, who were being held prisoner in the Tower. Tyrell's account of their death in William Shakespeare's *Richard III* is stunningly poignant. Shakespeare's primary source was Sir Thomas More's *The History of King Richard the Third,* probably as filtered through the later chroniclers Hall and Holinshed.

Tyrell was born of gentry in Gipping, Suffolk. Knighted for Yorkist service at Tewkesbury, he rose through a series of offices (including M.P.) as a favorite first of Richard (history thus gives the lie to More's and Shakespeare's portrayal of him as unknown to Richard before the assassination), then of Henry VII. He was Richard's chamberlain of the Exchequer, but he awaited the outcome of Bosworth Field as keeper of Guisnes Castle at Calais. Thereafter he served Henry in various capacities until he was tricked into surrendering Guisnes. For this treason he was exiled to the Tower and was executed May 6, 1502. More maintains that in the Tower Tyrell confessed to murdering the princes, but that confession has never been found, and modern scholars dispute whether Tyrell had anything to do with it.

BIBLIOGRAPHY

Busch, Wilhelm. *England under the Tudors.* 1895.

Churchill, George B. *Richard the Third up to Shakespeare.* 1900; repr. 1976.

Gairdner, James. *History of the Life and Reign of Richard the Third.* Revised edition. 1898.

More, Thomas. *The Complete Works of St. Thomas More. Vol. 2: The History of King Richard the Third.* Richard Sylvester, ed. 1963.

Rowse, A.L. "Yorkists: Richard III and the Murder of the Princes." *The Tower of London in the History of England,* pp. 19–32. 1972.

Wedgwood, Josiah C. *History of Parliament.* 1936.

J. Douglas Canfield

SEE ALSO

Bosworth Field; Henry VII; More, Thomas; Wars of the Roses

U

Udall, John (c. 1560–1592)

Born to a gentry family usually known as Uvedale, John Udall entered Christ's College, Cambridge, in 1578. Soon afterward he transferred to Trinity College, where he became noted as a Puritan theologian and Hebraist. From about this time he was a close associate of John Penry. In 1584, he became curate of Kingston-on-Thames, and two years later he was cited before the High Commission for nonconformity. He was closely associated with the Marprelate Tracts (1588–1589), and his own writings bear many similarities to them, but it was never proved that he actually wrote any of them himself. He was summoned to London for investigation on December 29, 1589, and after his trial (July 24, 1590) he was sentenced to death for sedition. Many people supported him, however, and there was a campaign for his release. At first the authorities would not relent, but at least Udall was not executed. In June 1592, he was finally pardoned, but his health had given way and he died on June 15, only a few days after his release from prison.

BIBLIOGRAPHY

Collinson, P. *The Elizabethan Puritan Movement.* 1967.

Gerald Bray

SEE ALSO

High Commission, Court of; Marprelate Controversy; Penry, John

Udall, Nicholas (1505–1556)

Born in Hampshire in 1505, Nicholas Udall's career is emblematic of the humanist scholars of his generation. A graduate of Winchester College and Corpus Christi, Cambridge, Udall became a fellow of Corpus Christi in 1524, but his reputation for Lutheran leanings prevented him from taking the M.A. until 1534. By that time, Udall had written an influential textbook, *Floures for Latine spekynge selected and gathered oute of Terence,* which was frequently reprinted. In 1534 he became headmaster of Eton, a position he held for eight years and in which he gained a reputation for overzealous flogging. As headmaster, Udall would have directed the annual playing of Latin comedies for the feast of St. Andrew; his most enduring work, *Ralph Roister Doister,* was once thought to be written for such an occasion. Accused in 1541 of sodomy and of complicity in the theft of silver (he pleaded guilty to the first charge), Udall was dismissed from Eton and briefly imprisoned in Marshalsea, though his reputation seemed to suffer no permanent harm. By 1544, he had resigned his vicarage of Braintree (held since 1537) in order to pursue scholarly interests. The 1540s were a period of great productivity: he translated the third and fourth book of Desiderius Erasmus's *Apothegmes* (1542) and Erasmus's *Paraphrases on Luke* (1545), and worked on the translation of Erasmus's *Paraphrases of the New Testament,* all under the patronage of Catherine Parr. At Edward VI's behest, he wrote a reply to Catholic rebels in the western provinces in 1549. His translation of Peter Martyr's tract on the Eucharist earned from Edward the privilege of printing of volumes of the Bible, a privilege Udall apparently never exercised. Under Mary Tudor's reign Udall apparently adapted to the shifting theological winds, for in 1553 he sought to extract a recantation from Protestant Thomas Mountain and, under royal warrant in 1554, was engaged to write

U

"dialogues and interludes" for the royal household, one of which may have been *Respublica*. He was appointed headmaster of Westminster School in 1554, a token of his lasting esteem as a scholar and servant of the court. He died two years later.

Although Udall made significant contributions to humanist pedagogy, translation, and theological controversy, he is now remembered primarily as a playwright. Though some scholars have argued for his authorship of *Thersites, Jack Juggler,* and *Respublica,* the only surviving drama securely attributable to Udall is *Ralph Roister Doister,* widely regarded as the first "regular" comedy in English. Internal evidence suggests that it was written no earlier than 1545, perhaps as a Christmas entertainment at a boy's school or at court. The play deftly transplants motifs from Latin comedy to distinctively English turf and thus anticipates the manner of William Shakespeare's and Ben Jonson's early comedies. The braggart soldier Ralph Roister Doister initiated a long line of comic blusterers in Elizabethan theater that was to include Jonson's Bobadill and Shakespeare's Falstaff. Although not printed in its entirety until 1566, passages from the play—such as Ralph's mispunctuated letter to Dame Custance—appear in Thomas Wilson's *Rule of Reason* (1553) as examples of "ambiguitie." It is likely that these were the model for the comic prologue in the final act of Shakespeare's *A Midsummer Night's Dream.* The 1566 edition now exists in a single copy in the Eton College library. Except for verses for Anne Boleyn's coronation, which Udall contributed along with his lifelong friend, John Leland, none of Udall's other known plays—including a translation of Bernard Occhin's *Tragoedia de Papatu* and the Biblical tragedy *Ezekias*—has survived.

BIBLIOGRAPHY

Baldwin, T.W. "Schoolmaster Udall Writes the First Regular English Comedy." In *Shakespeare's Five-Act Structure.* 1947.

Bevington, David. *Tudor Drama and Politics.* 1968. Pp. 109–126.

Edgerton, William L. *Nicholas Udall.* 1965.

Nicholas Udall's Roister Doister. G. Scheurweghs, ed. 1939.

Pittenger, Elizabeth. "'To Serve the Queere': Nicholas Udall, Master of Revels." In *Queering the Renaissance.* Jonathan Goldberg, ed. 1994.

Reed, A.W. "Nicholas Udall and Thomas Wilson." *Review of English Studies,* vol. 1, pp. 275–283.

Douglas Lanier

SEE ALSO

Erasmus, Desiderius; Drama, History of; Homosexuality; Leland, John; Parr, Catherine; Vermigli, Peter Martyr; Wilson, Thomas

Uniformity, Acts of

The Acts of Uniformity is the name popularly given to four statutes of Parliament whose main intention was to standardize and regulate the conduct of public worship in the Church of England. The rationale for this was set out by Archbishop Thomas Cranmer in his preface to the 1549 Book of Common Prayer (reprinted in the 1662 book), entitled *Concerning the Service of the Church.* Cranmer believed that the great diversity of usage that existed in pre-Reformation times was harmful to the preaching of the Gospel and destructive of the English Church's unity. He therefore proposed a single, simple liturgy in English that would reflect the teaching of the Bible and of the fathers of the early church as closely as possible.

The first Act of Uniformity was passed by Parliament in 1549, and came into effect on June 9 (Whitsunday). It enjoined the use of the new Book of Common Prayer in every parish, with penalties for noncompliance. In spite of some opposition, the 1549 book was generally accepted in most places. The second Act of Uniformity was made necessary by the substantial revisions to the Prayer Book that Cranmer made in 1552. The act came into force on November 1, 1552, and is noteworthy because it compelled weekly church attendance for the first time. Both of these acts were repealed by Mary I on December 20, 1553.

The third Act of Uniformity was enacted by the first Parliament of Elizabeth I, and came into effect on June 24, 1559. It enjoined the use of a new Prayer Book, which was only a slight revision of the 1552 version; its language repeats that of the earlier acts almost verbatim. Compulsory church attendance was retained, and the penalties for noncompliance were generally doubled. This act, along with the Act of Supremacy, which Parliament passed at the same time, formed the legal basis for the Elizabethan Settlement of the church. One of its main purposes was to include as many theological viewpoints as possible, and, initially at least, it was successful. Many people of Catholic persuasion continued to attend their parish churches, although they refused to receive Holy Communion. For this they were called recusants (Latin: *refusers*).

At the other end of the spectrum were the more radical Protestants, who saw the act as the first stage of further reform. Many Protestant clergy accepted it in principle, but tested its limits by refusing to wear the prescribed vestments, by praying aloud in their own words, and by preaching at times and in places not prescribed in the Prayer Book. This was nonconformity, a term still used to refer to non-Anglican Protestantism in England. Elizabeth I spent much of her reign trying to suppress this nascent Puritanism, but with limited success.

The Acts of Uniformity were historically important because they gave Parliament a claim to decide the worship and doctrine of the English Church. The Tudor monarchs regarded this as a matter of expediency, rather than as a right, but when their Stuart successors chose to ignore Parliament and govern the English Church independently of it, they provoked strong opposition, which was a major factor leading to the outbreak of civil war in the 1640s.

BIBLIOGRAPHY
Bray, Gerald L., ed. *Documents of the English Reformation.* 1994.
Elton, G.R. *The Tudor Constitution.* 2nd edition. 1982.
Gerald L. Bray

SEE ALSO
Book of Common Prayer; Church of England; Cranmer, Thomas; Supremacy, Act of

Universities

The Tudor age was a period of growth and adaptation for Oxford and Cambridge, although their path was far from smooth. Indeed, when Henry VIII dissolved all the religious houses between 1536 and 1540, the universities lost half a dozen monastic colleges and several large friaries, causing student numbers to plummet. In addition, priceless collections of books and manuscripts vanished forever during the transformation. Because of their staunch Protestant views, several college heads lost their positions when Mary I ascended the throne in 1553, and five years later a drastic purge of Mary's Catholic appointees occurred shortly after Elizabeth I's accession. During the 1560s and early 1570s, the Puritans mounted a serious challenge to doctrine and authority at Cambridge. That challenge was effectively countered by John Whitgift, the master of Trinity College and regius professor of divinity, who had strong support from Queen Elizabeth and William Cecil, Lord Burghley, the university's chancellor. In 1580, Oxford closed its doors to Catholic students

because of the arrival of scores of missionary priests from Douai, a special seminary established in 1568 by William Allen, who had been a prominent figure at Oxford during Mary's reign. During those same years undergraduate enrollments increased again and greatly exceeded those of the pre-1536 period by the time of the Spanish Armada. But during the general depression of the 1590s there was a second contraction in the universities' size, which was not overcome until 1610.

Despite their many problems the universities were stronger institutions by the end of the Tudor period than they had been at the beginning. Between 1485 and 1603, they received a steady stream of gifts and bequests from donors large and small. During the years 1485–1535, those donors included wealthy bishops such as John Alcock of Worcester, who established Jesus College, Cambridge, in 1496; Richard Fox of Winchester, who founded Corpus Christi College, Oxford, in 1517; and Thomas, Cardinal Wolsey, whose main educational work was the establishment of Cardinal College, Oxford, in 1525, later refounded by Henry VIII and renamed Christ Church. After Henry VIII's break from Rome and the beginning of the partial disendowment of the English Church, which led to a substantial decline of episcopal income by 1603, the bishops were unable to found new colleges as they had done before the Reformation. However, the three Elizabethan archbishops of Canterbury, Matthew Parker, Edmund Grindal, and John Whitgift, all gave important collections of books and manuscripts to Oxford or Cambridge colleges, as did two bishops of Durham, James Pilkington and Richard Barnes, and a learned bishop of Chester, William Chaderton.

If episcopal support of the universities waned as the sixteenth century wore on, that of the royal family remained strong. As early as 1497, Lady Margaret Beaufort, the mother of Henry VII, established endowed professorships in divinity at the universities; and eight years later she gave massive aid to Godshouse, a struggling society at Cambridge, which she greatly enlarged and renamed Christ's College. In her will of 1509, Lady Margaret bequeathed all her books to that college, as well as additional lands worth approximately £320 a year. But she earmarked most of her estates for the establishment of yet another Cambridge college, St. John's, which opened its door seven years later. Because of its distinguished faculty, which included Robert Wakefield, one of England's earliest Hebrew and Arabic scholars, St. John's was the leading college at Cambridge until the 1540s, when Lady Margaret's grandson, Henry VIII, founded Trinity College.

U

Arguably England's greatest educational patron, Henry VIII established Trinity College in 1546 by combining two older societies, The King's Hall and Michaelhouse, and endowing them with lands intended to produce £1,640 a year. Although those lands seem to have yielded about £300 less, Trinity was easily the richest college at Cambridge and has been described as an "academic palace." It soon acquired an outstanding faculty, and by 1567 it included 306 members out of 1,267 enrolled in the university as a whole. During the last years before his death in 1547, Henry VIII established five endowed professorships at either university: the regius professorships of Greek, Hebrew, medicine, divinity, and law. Attached to Christ Church and Trinity, those professorships carried stipends of £40 a year, or twice the yearly salaries of the Lady Margaret professorships of divinity.

Henry VIII's educational work was continued by his three children. Under Edward VI, royal commissioners carried out a visitation of the universities in 1549, and, on the basis of their recommendations, the Privy Council made sweeping changes regarding curricular matters. Because a mastery of Latin grammar was now considered a prerequisite for admission, that subject was abolished altogether and its place in the undergraduate program was assigned to mathematics. In accordance with humanistic precepts, a much greater emphasis was given to rhetoric, although logic and dialectic were not banished altogether. Finally, for students seeking bachelor's degrees in medicine, they now had to observe at least two human dissections, while students seeking doctor's degrees were required to observe at least two more. Unfortunately, those changes decreed by the Privy Council seem to have been ignored by the universities, largely because of the dearth of suitable textbooks and the continuing preoccupation of most students and scholars with religion.

Between 1553 and her death in 1558, Mary I assisted the universities in several small ways. In 1554, she granted Trinity College estates worth almost £380 a year; and two years later she began the construction of the Old Library and a large new chapel at Trinity, which took nine years to complete. At Oxford she gave financial support to Christ Church, Magdalen College, and New College. In 1554, she granted the university itself lands worth almost £135 a year.

Elizabeth I also assisted the founding of Jesus College, Oxford, in the 1570s, donated thirty loads of timber from the royal estates to assist with the rebuilding of the chapel at Corpus Christi College, Cambridge, and in the 1580s, established scholarships of five marks each for the support of six poor students at Brasenose College, Oxford, and five others at Emmanuel College, Cambridge.

Partly because of the continuing interest of the Tudor monarchs in education, the aristocracy sent its sons to study at the universities in greater numbers. During the fifteenth century only a handful of boys from upper-class families had studied at Oxford or Cambridge, largely because most aristocrats did not yet value advanced studies; they regarded the universities primarily as seminaries for the clergy, and preferred to send their older sons to the Inns of Court, the fashionable but expensive law schools in the capital. However, during the reigns of Henry VII and Henry VIII the aristocratic disdain for university training declined, and during the last decade of Henry VIII's reign swarms of boys from the upper class entered the universities for the first time. By the accession of Edward VI, important figures like Hugh Latimer and Roger Ascham were complaining bitterly about the influx of rich men's sons, who were crowding out the sons of the lower class.

Although the social composition of the universities rose from the 1530s, the universities never became an exclusive preserve of the aristocracy. Hundreds of scholarships for poor boys were established after 1540, including eight through a bequest of Mrs. Joan Trapps of London (d. 1563), six established in 1572 by Alexander Nowell at Brasenose College, Oxford, and six more by Lord Keeper Nicholas Bacon for Corpus Christi College, Cambridge, in 1579. In addition, three new colleges were established by rich laymen: Trinity College, Oxford, by Sir Thomas Pope (1555); St. John's College, Oxford, by Sir Thomas White (1557); and Gonville and Caius College, Cambridge, by the famous physician Dr. John Caius (1559). The last two colleges founded during the Tudor period were both at Cambridge. In 1584, Sir Walter Mildmay, Queen Elizabeth's long-time chancellor of the exchequer, established Emmanuel College; and five years later, Frances Radcliffe, countess of Sussex, left an educational bequest of £5,000, which her nephew, Sir John Harington, augmented before founding Sidney Sussex College in 1596.

By the 1580s and 1590s, mathematical and scientific studies had finally put down roots at the universities, just as the framers of the abortive curriculum reform of 1549 had hoped. Students at Oxford included the accomplished mathematician Lawrence Kemyss, Nicholas Torporley, a respected astronomer and mathematician by the time he completed his M.A. degree in 1591, and Henry Wotton, who delivered three lectures on the physiology of the human eye in 1588. Thomas Allen, who studied geography and mathematics, influenced such famous scientists and geographers of the next generation as Richard Hakluyt, Thomas Hariot, Robert Hues, and Walter Warner. Although science seems to have attracted fewer adherents at Cambridge, the university graduated William Bedwell, who attained such a mastery of astronomy by the late 1590s that a contemporary writer compared him to the great Danish astronomer Tycho Brahe.

The establishment of mathematical and scientific studies at the universities by the 1580s was partly owing to the gift of thousands of books to the college libraries during earlier decades. In 1573, a campaign to reestablish the Cambridge University Library was organized by Dr. Andrew Perne, the energetic master of Peterhouse. The Cambridge University Library had declined from almost 600 books in the l480s to only about 175 by the early 1570s, and Dr. Perne and other scholars hoped to reverse what had happened. Within a short time they secured important donations from Archbishop Parker and Bishop Pilkington of Durham; while in 1575 or 1576, Lord Keeper Bacon presented seventy-three books, mostly on mathematics, geography, and music. On his death in 1589, Dr. Perne enlarged the growing library with 120 of his own books, many of them scientific treatises; and two years later, the regius professor of medicine, Thomas Lorkin, bequeathed his collection of 140 medical books. After the receipt of eighty-nine folios from Lord Lumley in 1598, the Cambridge University Library could boast almost 950 books in all.

At Oxford, where the medieval university library had completely disappeared by 1556, a similar campaign was organized in 1598 by Sir Thomas Bodley, a former diplomat who had retired from public life two years before. By 1600, that campaign was well advanced: A handsome library room had been fitted up; more than 600 books had been received from a dozen contributors. The Bodleian Library was the most important educational foundation at either university during the Tudor age. When it opened its doors to the academic community in November of 1602, its collection numbered approximately 2,500 books and manuscripts. By 1605, the collection included almost 6,000 titles, and by 1620, approximately 16,000. After negotiating an agreement with the Stationer's Company in 1610, the Bodleian automatically received copies of all the books printed each year by its dozens of members. By the 1640s, the Bodleian had the largest holdings of any library in Europe, with the exception of the Vatican Library in Rome.

BIBLIOGRAPHY

Curtis, Mark H. *Oxford and Cambridge in Transition, 1558–1642.* 1959.

Kearney, Hugh F. *Scholars and Gentlemen: Universities and Society in Pre-Industrial Britain, 1500–1700.* 1970.

Stone, Lawrence, ed. *The University in Society.* Vol. I: *Oxford and Cambridge from the 14th to the Early 19th Century.* 1974.

McConica, James, ed. *The Collegiate University.* 1986.

Porter, Harry C. *Reformation and Reaction in Tudor Cambridge.* 1958.

Dent, C.M. *Protestant Reformers in Elizabethan Oxford.* 1983.

Feingold, Mordechai. *The Mathematicians' Apprenticeship.* 1984.

Michael V.C. Alexander

SEE ALSO

Allen, William; Bacon, Nicholas; Beaufort, Margaret; Bodley, Thomas; Book Ownership; Education; English College of Rome; Grindal, Edmund; Hariot, Thomas; Henry VIII; Medicine and Health; Mildmay, Walter; Parker, Matthew; Science, History of; Social Classes; Whitgift, John; Wolsey, Thomas

Uprisings and Rebellions

See Agrarian Uprisings; Kett's Rebellion; Northern Rebellion; Pilgrimage of Grace; Wyatt's Rebellion

Urbanization

See Bristol; London; Southwark; Towns

Utopia

Utopia is a neologism that Thomas More invented in 1516 by combining the Greek adverb *ou,* not, and the noun *topos,* place, to arrive at the name Noplace (or Place-that-is-not) for the imaginary island (called Nusquama, Nowhere, before publication) that is described in detail in the second book of his *Libellus vere aureus nec minus salutaris quam festivus de optimo reip[ublicae] statu, deque noua Insula Vtopia* (Louvain, 1516), known as *Utopia.* But More was also playing a second Greek adverb, *eu,* meaning happily; utopia also suggests a Good Place or Happy Place and is an inherently ambiguous and paradoxical term.

Although it originally referred to one place and one text, utopia has come to be used for any self-enclosed

U

community that is (or purports to be) better than an existing society, for any text that describes such a society, and, more broadly, for a way of thinking—the possibility of social and human transformation and the desire for a new social order. Taken positively, utopia refers to a better or a desirable vision of social reality; pejoratively, to an impracticable or absurd scheme for human improvement and/or perfection. A later development, the dystopia, presents a society that extrapolates what is seen as worst in an existing society; vision or dream becomes nightmare, as in George Orwell's *1984*.

While more complicated, ironic, and ambiguous than its descendents, More's *Utopia* is the classic instance of utopia as literary genre. Besides the prefatory letter and other preliminary matter, there are two books, the first a dialogue criticizing contemporary societies, the second a detailed description of an imaginary society by a narrator who insists that Utopia exists and that it is far better than the societies of western Europe. Unlike England or continental Europe, places that are portrayed as acquisitive, wasteful, self-aggrandizing, devoted to war, and fundamentally unjust, Utopia meets the needs (but only what are considered the true needs) of every citizen; all goods are shared, and no one lacks housing, food, medical care, education, employment, or leisure. For Utopia's "discoverer," a Portuguese traveler called Raphael Hythlodaeus (the first name is angelic, the last means speaker of witty nonsense), Utopia is the best, indeed the only true, commonwealth. But More's persona, "More," who claims merely to write out what Hythlodaeus reports, is skeptical, and the work is open-ended, engaging in a dialogue with its readers.

As early as 1533, two small communities patterned after More's Utopia were founded in Mexico by Vasco de Quiroga, and utopia and utopian were used both affirmatively and pejoratively in Tudor England. But utopian texts are most characteristic of the Renaissance, and many other utopias—including Tommaso Campanella's *City of the Sun* ,and Francis Bacon's *New Atlantis*—followed. A poetics was only articulated later, and critics continue to disagree as to how and where to draw the boundaries of the genre. Should constitutions, for instance, be considered utopias?

The literary utopia remains a popular genre; recent instances include Ernest Callenbach's *Ecotopia* and Ursula Le Guin's science-fiction utopias. Generally, only the formal elements of More's second book appear, however: a traveler or guide describes in detail an imaginary place, isolated in time or space, where institutions and relationships are organized on a more perfect basis than in the author's society. But an analysis and critique of the sort that emerges through the dialogue in Book 1 of More's *Utopia* is implicit in subsequent utopias. This means that utopia is an exercise in extrapolation, presenting an alternative to a radically imperfect society. At once satiric and visionary, speculative and interrogatory, utopia tries to negate negations, visualize possibilities, and promote thought about the nature of human institutions, customs, values, and social and political relationships.

BIBLIOGRAPHY

Elliott, Robert C. *The Shape of Utopia: Studies in a Literary Genre.* 1970.

Levitas, Ruth. *The Concept of Utopia.* 1990.

Manuel, Frank E., ed. *Utopias and Utopian Thought.* 1967.

More, Thomas. *Utopia: Latin Text and English Translation.* George M. Logan, Robert M. Adams, and Clarence H. Miller, eds. 1995.

Ruppert, Peter. *Reader in a Strange Land: The Activity of Reading Literary Utopias.* 1986.

Sargent, Lyman Tower. *British and American Utopian Literature, 1516–1985: An Annotated, Chronological Bibliography.* 1988.

Elizabeth McCutcheon

SEE ALSO

Humanism; More, Thomas; Neo-Latin Literature

V

Vagrants

The vagrancy problem in Tudor England was the consequence of a long-term deterioration in the living standards of the laboring poor. Population increase, price inflation, enclosure, and harvest failure drove large numbers of individuals out of the ranks of settled society and onto the open road. Many parishes acquired areas in which squatters and immigrants struggled to support themselves. These cottagers were irregularly employed, if they could find work at all, and were particularly vulnerable to periodic economic depressions and rising food prices. They were among the most mobile sections of the population, migrating in search of subsistence as economic circumstances deteriorated. Although socio-historical analysis of the origins and nature of this population of "masterless men" has sophisticated our understanding of the problem, contemporary perceptions of population mobility and its implications are the necessary starting point for any understanding of the significance of this issue.

Late Tudor estimates of the numbers of vagrants ranged from 10,000 to 100,000, and virtually all commentators were convinced that the migrant poor traveled in organized criminal gangs. The literary stereotype, which finds its best expression in Thomas Harman's *Caveat for Common Cursetors* (1567), was of a social group that rejected all the values of respectable society, leading lives of idleness, immorality, theft, and sexual promiscuity. At its most hysterical, in the royal proclamations in the wake of the Northern Rebellion (1569), and in the jury charges of the 1590s, this view represented vagrants as a coherent threat to national security. Given the emphasis on the household as the fundamental unit of socialization in early modern England, those who lived on the road were considered masterless and therefore, by definition, undisciplined. Vagrants were the idle able-bodied poor, the sturdy beggars against whom moralists had fulminated for generations. These perceptions help explain the severity of legislation against vagrancy. In 1547, the government attempted to impose slavery as a punishment for the refusal to work. An escaped slave was to be branded; for a second escape he was to be executed. Subsequent legislation was slightly more restrained, although the Elizabethan poor laws codified in 1597 and 1601 empowered constables to whip vagrants back to their parish of origin and to incarcerate them in houses of correction where they were to be disciplined with hard labor.

The reality of vagrancy was, however, very different from its image. The typical vagrant was a young adult, usually aged between twenty and forty; most were single, and men predominated. In a sample of 3,000 early seventeenth-century vagrants, more than half (51.4 percent) were unmarried males, the rest consisting of single or separated women (24.9 percent), married couples (12.9 percent), and children under the age of fifteen (10.8 percent). They were most frequently apprehended singly or in pairs, or occasionally in family groups, rather than in the organized bands of literary fantasy, and in almost half the cases had traveled less than forty miles from their parish of origin at the time of arrest. These people were isolated though troublesome individuals struggling to put together an expedient existence on the road, often in search of work, occasionally resorting to trespass or opportunistic theft in order to survive. Many, it seems, had broken the terms of apprenticeship or had failed to find a secure economic niche at the end of a period of service. Although this was very different from the fraternity

V

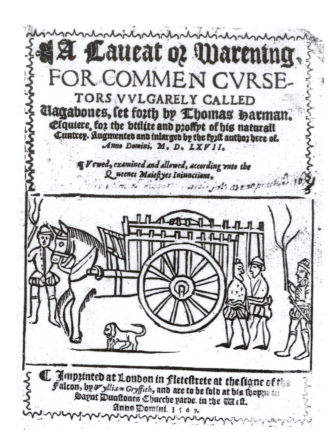

Thomas Harman, *Rounding up of Vagabonds,* from *A Caveat for Common Cursetors Vulgarely Called Vagabones* (1567). Harman's work is the best known of many tracts against transients, immigrants, and the homeless, all of whom were perceived to be criminal threats to citizens and a burden on local economies. This naively drawn title page illustrates vagabonds being rounded up in a wagon under threat of whipping. Reprinted by permission of The Folger Shakespeare

of vagabonds fantasized by Harman, it was nonetheless a makeshift, mobile subculture that was, by definition, difficult for the gentry of Tudor parishes to control.

The close association in the late Tudor public mind between vagrancy and theft may well explain the peak in prosecutions for property crime that appear in the judicial records of several counties. In Hertfordshire, in particular, the large number of vagrants tramping the roads to London in search of work were particularly threatening to the settled population. The most dramatic peaks in prosecution occurred in parishes near or adjacent to the two main roads from the north. The clear convergence of the main migration routes and the heaviest concentrations of indicted offenses suggest a strong relationship between migration and prosecutions for theft. Given the prevailing suspicion of vagrants and outsiders, it is probable that this

relationship can in part be attributed to a special willingness to prosecute migrants.

The governors and property owners of Tudor society, therefore, lived in terror of the tramp. Vagabonds posed new and perplexing problems to early modern governors, and pushed the regime into the creation of carceral institutions that might serve as prisons for the poor. Although the negligence of the parish constables responsible for policing the vagrancy problem has been exaggerated in accordance with the literary stereotype of William Shakespeare's "Dogberry," the bridewells and whipping posts of Tudor England were probably of symbolic rather than instrumental significance. Most vagabonds received summary trials and punishment at parish level, their cases finding their way into judicial archives only when they were recalcitrant or notorious offenders. The vagrants of Tudor England therefore loomed far larger in the imagination of Elizabethan governors than they do in the surviving records of the criminal courts.

BIBLIOGRAPHY

Beier, A.L. "Vagrants and the Social Order in Elizabethan England." *Past and Present,* vol. 64, pp. 3–29.

———. *Masterless Men: The Vagrancy Problem in England, 1560–1640.* 1985.

Kent, Joan. "Population Mobility and Alms: Poor Migrants in the Midlands During the Early Seventeenth Century." *Local Population Studies,* vol. 27, pp. 35–51.

———. *The English Village Constable: A Social and Administrative Study, 1580–1642.* 1986.

Kinney, Arthur F. *Rogues, Vagabonds, and Sturdy Beggars.* Revised edition. 1990.

Lawson, P.G. "Property Crime and Hard Times in England, 1559–1624." *Law and History Review,* vol. 4, pp. 95–127.

Salgado, Gamini. *The Elizabethan Underworld.* 1977.

Slack, Paul. "Vagrants and Vagrancy in England, 1598–1664." *Economic History Review,* 2nd series, vol. 27, pp. 360–379.

Steven Hindle

SEE ALSO

Agrarian Uprisings; Apprenticeship; Crime; Government, Local; Northern Rebellion; Pedlars; Poor Laws; Population and Demography; Price Revolution; Social Classes

Valois, Hercule-François de

See Alençon and Anjou, Duke of

Valor Ecclesiasticus

The name given to a census that was undertaken in 1535, *Valor Ecclesiasticus* evaluated the property of the English Church. The census was made necessary by an act of Parliament that transferred the "annates" or "first-fruits" of clergy benefices from the papacy to the crown. It had been the practice since the crusades for the new incumbent of a benefice to surrender his first year's revenue to the pope, and Henry VIII wanted to maintain the practice as a form of taxation. However, there had not been a church census since 1291, and the records were seriously out of date.

The *Valor Ecclesiasticus* was an immense undertaking, comparable in scope and importance to the Domesday Book of 1086. Despite some errors and omissions, including the loss of the records for a few dioceses, its standard of accuracy is extremely high, and it may be still be cited today as evidence in disputes over church property. Modern historians have noticed that where comparisons with other evidence are possible, the *Valor* can be shown to have underestimated the worth of church property, thus reducing the burden of taxation.

The *Valor* was in regular use for at least a century. It was mentioned in the Canons of 1584, where bishops were advised to use it as a guide to the value of parishes in their dioceses.

BIBLIOGRAPHY

Caley, J., and J. Hunter, eds. *The Valor Ecclesiasticus*. 6 vols. 1810–1834.

Gerald Bray

SEE ALSO

Annates; Clergy; Taxation

Vergil, Polydore (1470–1555)

Italian-born papal official and humanist historian, Polydore Vergil was born in Urbino and arrived in England in 1502, remaining there (save two short diplomatic visits to Italy in 1514 and 1516–1517) until 1553, when he returned to Urbino, dying there two years later. Vergil served successively the duke of Urbino and Pope Alexander VI before becoming the client of Adriano Castello of Corneto, an Italian who was preferred to the see of Hereford and later to Bath and Wells, and who was also the collector of Peter's Pence. Vergil served as Castello's deputy in the collectorship from 1502–1515, was given a variety of preferments in the church (including, from 1508–1554, the archdeaconry of Wells), and undertook a series of diplomatic missions on behalf of the English court. He survived the disgrace of his patron in 1517 after having endured a brief imprisonment in 1515 at the hands of Cardinal Thomas Wolsey. On his return to England from Italy in 1517 he withdrew from participation in public life and concentrated on scholarly interests.

Vergil, part of the steady stream of Italian humanists who flocked to England under Henry VII and Henry VIII, wrote a number of books including the *Adagia,* the *De Prodigiis* (a work on prodigies), the *Commentariolum in Dominicam Precem* (a commentary on the Lord's Prayer), and an edition of the medieval English historian Gildas, which he dedicated to Cuthbert Tunstall. He is, however, best known for two works. The first, and more widely read in his day, was the *De inventoribus rerum* ("Concerning the Inventors of Things"). This was first published in 1499, three years before Vergil came to England, and was expanded to five books in 1521. It was immensely popular and by the time of his death had reached more than thirty editions in several languages. An immensely erudite digest of classical and modern learning, it provided readers with a learned guide to antiquities and customs in many countries, and was marked by precise scholarly reference to Vergil's sources. The second, more widely read since his time, is Vergil's *Anglica Historia,* the only full-length Latin humanist history of England to be written under the early Tudors. In this work, Vergil brought his considerable scholarly talents to a retelling of English history from authentic sources, including an account of the fifteenth century, the Tudor accession, and the reign of Henry VIII. First published at Basle in 1534, it was reissued there in 1546 and again in 1555; a partial translation into English of Books 1 through 8, up to the Norman Conquest, was published only in the nineteenth century. Some significant variations exist in all these versions.

As an historian, Vergil was influenced both by his humanist inclinations and by the chronicles from which he drew much of his information. He was an historiographical innovator in at least two ways, literary and methodological. First, he modeled his history not on the annalistic arrangement of the chronicles but rather on the newer humanist histories of his native Italy (for instance, the *Florentine History* of the fifteenth-century chancellor Leonardo Bruni) and of the French court, such as the writings of Robert Gaguin and the Italian expatriate Paolo Emili. He began, like Pliny, with a general description of the land, thereafter proceeding chronologically up to 1066. From that point, he adopted a biographical pattern from Suetonius and the medieval chronicler William of Malmesbury, each book

V

being devoted to the reign of a king. This set the pattern for the later, regnal histories of the late Tudor and early Stuart period that would ultimately displace the chronicle as the standard form of historical literature; the book's providential scheme, the first to discern a pattern beginning with Richard II's deposition and leading by stages through the calamitous fifteenth century to the triumphant Tudor accession, became a commonplace of later Tudor accounts of recent history. Vergil's second, methodological, innovation consisted in assuming a foreigner's critical attitude to much of the received knowledge about the more remote, pre-Roman, British past. For centuries chroniclers had, with few exceptions, assumed the veracity of the *Historia Regum Britanniae* by the twelfth-century writer Geoffrey of Monmouth; in particular, they had taken as beyond dispute the existence of Brutus (the mythical Trojan "founder" of Britain) and of King Arthur, historically a war leader against the Saxon invaders but now turned, through the influence of romance, into the more famous figure of chivalry and knight-errantry. Vergil challenged the accounts of both Brutus and Arthur (and by implication most of Geoffrey's genealogy of British kings) because they were supported neither by contemporary reference nor by external documentary evidence; he also cast doubt on particular details in Geoffrey, such as the latter's spurious etymologies for the names of towns. Although his conclusions were hotly contested by English writers such as John Leland and John Bale, who dismissed him as both a foreigner and a Catholic, by the end of the century most historical scholars were expressing some doubts about the early legends, even if they cautiously refused to throw them over altogether.

BIBLIOGRAPHY

Gransden, Antonia. *Historical Writing in England.* Vol. 2: *c. 1307 to the Early Sixteenth Century.* 1982.

Hay, Denys. *Polydore Vergil: Renaissance Historian and Man of Letters.* 1952.

Levy, F.J. *Tudor Historical Thought.* 1967.

D.R. Woolf

SEE ALSO

Antiquarianism; Arthurian Legend; Bale, John; History, Writing of; Humanism; Leland, John

Vermigli, Peter Martyr (1500–1562)

Peter Martyr Vermigli was born at Florence on September 8, 1500; his father had been a supporter of Savonarola, but the loss of his children in infancy caused him to vow that if another son were born, he would name him after the thirteenth-century Italian St. Peter Martyr, who ironically was the patron saint of inquisitors. Vermigli was educated at Fiesole and became an Augustinian Friar. In 1530, he was made abbot of the monastery at Spoleto, and three years later transferred to Naples. There he began to study the Bible and to read the works of Martin Bucer and Huldrych Zwingli. He was soon accused of heresy; but the charges were dismissed, thanks in part to the intercession of Reginald Pole.

Vermigli soon had to flee Italy, and after a brief sojourn in Switzerland, he was made professor of theology at Strasbourg (1542), where Bucer was the leading influence. In 1547, he was invited to England, and in the following year was made regius professor of divinity at Oxford. He was arrested on the accession of Mary I in 1553; but because he was a foreigner, he was allowed to leave the country. He went to Strasbourg, where he recovered his professorial chair, but his views on the Eucharist proved to be unacceptable. In 1556, he migrated to Zurich, where he became professor of Hebrew. He subsequently engaged in a voluminous correspondence with a number of leading English divines and was influential in shaping the pattern of the Elizabethan Settlement of 1559. He died at Zurich on November 12, 1562.

BIBLIOGRAPHY

Robinson, H., ed. *Zurich Letters.* Parker Society. 4 volumes. 1842–1845.

McNair, P. *Peter Martyr in Italy. The Anatomy of Apostasy.* 1967.

Gerald Bray

SEE ALSO

Bucer, Martin; Eucharist; Heresy; Pole, Reginald

Verse Anthologies

The earliest extant printed anthology of Tudor verse, *The Court of Venus,* is known from two fragmentary editions dated c. 1538 and 1563. Its contents included love lyrics, some by Sir Thomas Wyatt, and the pseudo-Chaucerian "Pilgrim's Tale," an anti-Catholic satire. *A Boke of Ballets* (c. 1549) printed some of the same lyrics found in *The Court,* although the two remaining leaves of the only surviving copy provide insufficient evidence for determining the relationship between these two collections. In 1557, Richard Tottel brought out the most popular Tudor verse anthology, the *Songes and Sonettes,* which saw eleven editions by 1587. Tottel's "Miscellany," as it is often termed, is essentially a three-man anthology that attributes ninety-six poems to Sir Thomas Wyatt and forty poems apiece to Henry Howard, earl of Surrey, and Nicholas Grimald, while including another ninety-four poems by such poets as John Harington the Elder, John Heywood, and Thomas, Lord Vaux.

Tottel's aristocratic authors contrast with the common balladeers represented in Clement Robinson's *A Handfull of Pleasant Delites;* a unique copy of the 1584 edition preserves the full collection of thirty-two ballads in this volume. Although Robinson's anthology was probably issued as early as 1566, only fragments from editions of c. 1575 and c. 1595 also survive. A more popular collection was *The Paradise of Dainty Devices,* which saw at least ten editions between 1576 and 1606. This volume was apparently based on a manuscript anthology compiled by Richard Edwardes, the royal musician and playwright to whom thirteen of the *Paradise* lyrics are attributed in every edition. Many of its remaining hundred-odd lyrics, however, are by poets who wrote after Edwardes's death in 1566, among them Edward de Vere, earl of Oxford, William Hunnis, Lodowick Lloyd, and George Whetstone. Unlike the earlier anthologies that are dominated by love lyrics, the *Paradise* was more somber in tone, its lyrics largely devoted to penitence, friendship, and moral instruction. Thomas Proctor's *Gorgeous Gallery of Gallant Inventions* (1578) attempted to cash in on the popularity of the *Paradise,* although it saw only one edition. It borrowed poems from Tottel's *Songes and Sonnettes,* the *Handful,* and the *Paradise* as well. Proctor included at least ten of his own works, with others by poets such as Thomas Churchyard, Thomas Howell, and Jasper Heywood. From *The Court of Venus* through the *Gallery,* these printed collections are dominated by verse in what C.S. Lewis termed the "drab" style of mid-sixteenth century poetry. Long-line forms such as fourteener couplets and poulter's measure are characteristic of this style; its rhetoric favors copious examples and frequent allusions to classical mythology.

Verse in the "drab" style remained common in the later Elizabethan anthologies, but during the 1590s, it was increasingly replaced by the "golden" style initiated by Sir Philip Sidney and his circle, and perfected by such poets as Michael Drayton, Samuel Daniel, and William Shakespeare. In 1591, there appeared two anthologies connected with Sir Philip Sidney, who had died in 1586. *Syr P.S. His Astrophel and Stella,* the unauthorized first edition of Sidney's sonnet sequence, is actually a poetic anthology. Appended to the incomplete text of *Astrophil and Stella* is a collection of verse by Samuel Daniel, Thomas Campion, and Fulke Greville. *Brittons Bowre of Delights,* also published in 1591, opens with Nicholas Breton's "Amoris Lachrimae," the first of three elegies for Sidney in the volume. Among its fifty-six poems are lyrics by Arthur Gorges, Geoffrey Fenton, the earl of Oxford, and Ferdinando Stanley, Lord Strange. While Breton (the "Britton" of the book's title) probably wrote most of the *Bowre's* lyrics, he attacked its printer, Richard Jones, in the preface to his *Pilgrimage to Paradise* (1592), claiming that only a few of the poems were his, and all were printed without his permission. Undaunted, Jones published, in 1594, *The Arbor of Amorous Devices . . . By N.B.,* including in it numerous verse excerpts from Breton's *Pilgrimage.* The *Arbor* reprinted as well ten poems from the *Bowre* and two from Tottel's *Songes and Sonnettes.*

Another anthology influenced by Sidney's death, *The Phoenix Nest* (1593), opens with a verse elegy for Sidney's uncle, Robert Dudley, earl of Leicester, followed by three elegies for Sidney. Its compiler, the unidentified "R.S. of the Inner Temple Gentleman," included the works of such courtier poets as Sir Walter Ralegh, Sir Arthur Gorges, and Sir Edward Dyer, yet the elite origins of *The Phoenix Nest's* texts have been somewhat exaggerated. Its principal contributors, Breton, Thomas Lodge, and George Peele, were commercial rather than courtly writers. This anthology preserves nevertheless a high-quality cross-sampling of "golden" Elizabethan poetry.

Sidney's posthumous fame affected one other Elizabethan collection in an unexpectedly anonymous fashion. The 1592 edition of Henry Constable's sonnet sequence, *Diana,* was followed by two greatly expanded editions, c. 1594 and 1595, which are, in fact, poetic anthologies. To Constable's works were added eight poems by Sidney, none of which is attributed. The book also included one poem by Richard Smith and forty-six lyrics by unidentified poets.

Englands Helicon (1600, 1614) was compiled entirely from previously published sources and organized around a pastoral theme often maintained by editorial insertions of shepherds and flocks into nonpastoral lyrics. The 150 poems in the first edition include lyrics by Sidney, Michael Drayton, Thomas Lodge, Robert Greene, Bartholomew Young, and Anthony Munday. The *Helicon* vies with Francis Davison's *Poetical Rhapsody* in offering readers the highest quality of anthologized verse printed during Elizabeth's reign, with a greater variety of technical

V

forms and genres than any of the earlier collections. The *Rhapsody* first appeared in 1602 and saw three more editions by 1621. While more than 100 of the first edition's 176 poems were composed by Francis and Walter Davison, this collection preserves as well a dramatic verse entertainment by the Mary Sidney, countess of Pembroke, an ode from the earl of Cumberland's May Day show before Elizabeth I, and lyrics by such poets as Sidney, Henry Constable, Sir John Davies, Thomas Campion, Robert Greene, and Thomas Spelman.

The traditionally accepted printed anthologies of Tudor verse are available in sound, modern editions, yet the genre lacks any consistent definition. Excluded from the list are the age's most popular anthologies of lyric verse, the metrical psalters, which appeared in scores of editions that combined psalm translations with other devotional verse by a variety of poets. The printed songbooks of such composers as William Byrd, John Dowland, and Thomas Morley are likewise poetic anthologies that set to music many of the lyrics printed in the recognized anthologies. Two collections of verse published in 1600, Robert Allot's *Englands Parnassus* and John Bodenham's *Belvedere or the Garden of the Muses*, anthologize thousands of verse excerpts under commonplace headings, yet the disjointed effect of so many snippets from longer poems has apparently kept these books from being accepted as literary anthologies. These examples represent the kinds of anthologies that are customarily but rather arbitrarily excluded from accounts of Tudor poetic miscellanies.

BIBLIOGRAPHY

Cheney, Donald, intro. *Diana. Or, The excellent conceitful Sonnets of H. C. Augmented with diuers Quatorzains of honorable and lerned personages.* Facsimile edition. 1973.

Davison, Francis. *A Poetical Rhapsody, 1602–1621.* Hyder E. Rollins, ed. 2 vols. 1931.

Edwardes, Richard. *The Paradise of Dainty Devices.* Hyder E. Rollins, ed. 1927.

Fraser, Russell A. ed., *The Court of Venus.* 1955.

Proctor, Thomas. *A Gorgeous Gallery of Gallant Inventions.* Hyder E. Rollins, ed. 1926.

Robinson, Clement. *A Handful of Pleasant Delights (1584).* Hyder E. Rollins, ed. 1924.

Rollins, Hyder E., ed. *Brittons Bowre of Delights.* 1933.

———, ed. *England's Helicon.* 2 vols. 1935.

———, ed. *The Arbor of Amorous Devices.* 1936.

———. *The Phoenix Nest.* 1931.

———, ed. *Tottel's Miscellany (1557–1587).* 2 vols. Revised edition. 1966.

Sidney, Philip. *Syr P.S. His Astrophel and Stella.* Facsimile edition. 1970.

Steven May

Versification

Tudor verse survived and recovered from fifteenth-century metrical incoherence, which was marked by the disappearance of competent four-stress alliterative verse and the deterioration of an aurally intelligible Chaucerian decasyllabic line into an array of line-types formed by combining regular, headless, catalectic, or hypermetrical half-lines. From this metrical confusion, Tudor poets had to reconstruct their craft, to find and form verse lines that were metrically intelligible and would combine readily into larger units of verse. It fell to John Skelton, Thomas Wyatt, and Henry Howard, earl of Surrey, to begin this work of reconstruction.

Skelton's most original poems are invectives that owe something to the Scottish fifteenth-century *flyting* and are cast in a lively, sharply inflected, free-standing half-line, following the lead of Middle English lyrics like "I sing of a maiden / That is makeles . . . ," but Skelton uses a larger range of playful variations and a mischievous multiplication of rhymes. Some of Wyatt's inventions are almost as eccentric, but they hold more promise of being widely imitable. He wrote skillful shorter-line stanzas of complaint (often meant for musical setting); he invented the jaunty poulter's measure; but he also crafted a new kind of decasyllabic line that augments the fifteenth-century's varied line types, with a range of expressive options and a syllabic opportunism derived from the Italian hendecasyllable, and he used it not only for sonnets (which he and Surrey were the first to import from the Continent) and other love poems but also for three conversational "Epistolary Satires" (in *terza rima*) and for expressive translations of the Penitential Psalms (in *terza rima* and *ottava rima*). Along with blank verse, Surrey's invention for his translation of parts of Virgil's *Aeneid,* these innovations, first published in *Tottel's Miscellany* (1557), helped poets achieve the rich verse of the later sixteenth century: songs; sonnets; narrative, satiric, elegiac, and moralizing poetry; and dramatic verse, both rhymed and blank.

One key to developing this impressive English poetry was the ease with which lines combined with others to form larger units of verse—either strophes and stanzas or stichic sequences of rhymed or unrhymed lines. Songs or short-lined poems generally lodge relatively brief, uncomplicated phrases ("Love me little, love me long, / Is the burden of my song") in lines shorter than the decasyllable but in rhyming strophes. Whether or not they are set to music, their beat is usually palpable, their musical design is augmented with euphonious sound patterns, sometimes with refrains, and their amorous or moral argument often uses patterned rhetorical figures. Elizabethan poets devised hundreds of such new and nonce short-line lyrics.

They also produced, but with far less success, rhymed long-line couplets (or sometimes quatrains), either the "tumbling verse" (roughly anapestic and often with four clear beats to a line) of much popular poetry and drama, or the six- or seven-beat line of hexameter, heptameter ("fourteeners"), or poulter's measure (six iambic feet in one line, seven in the next). These latter forms, used widely for poems of love or prayer and in plays till late in the century, read like uneasy joinings of shorter lines, and it is possible to suspect that in English verse of the time *all* lines are really short except the pentameter or decasyllabic. (A genuine exception to this rule, however, because heard as an authentic long line, is the hexameter, or occasionally heptameter, line that appears now and then in pentameter poems, such as the last line in a Spenserian stanza.)

But much of the strength of Tudor verse lay in its gradual discovery of the force, flexibility, and resilience of what has come to be called the iambic pentameter line. Wyatt and Surrey had used it with some subtlety, but for most of the next forty years listeners to it preferred a highly regular beat and a phrasal break that came, as it had in the fifteenth-century decasyllabic line, almost always after the fourth (or sometimes the sixth) syllable. Many of them naively thought that English poetry needed a standard line as various and as expressive as they took the classical hexameter to be, and they believed that the accentual nature of English, by insisting on a fixed number of syllables in each measure, worked against the subtlety available to the classical poet, whose menu of

long and short syllables allowed more options. In this belief, Edmund Spenser, Sir Philip Sidney, Richard Stanyhurst, Thomas Campion, and others experimented with various kinds of quantitative English verse, built either on the same rules that governed the ancients (a vowel was long either by nature or if it was followed by more than one consonant) or on a relaxed system for determining what in English constituted length. The closer these experiments stayed to ancient practice, the surer their failure to produce any memorable English verse.

By the 1580s, poets came to understand that, for better or worse, the pentameter was going to have to serve as the heroic English line, and they soon were enchanted by its adaptability as well as by its complex internal dynamics. Christopher Marlowe could fashion elegant pentameter couplets for the narrative of "Hero and Leander." John Donne could write racier, more eccentrically metrical couplets for his incisive but quirky satires, elegies, and epistles. The heroic line, like its shorter counterpart, could combine into impressively structured stanzas: heroic quatrains, forceful and grave (*abab*); the Venus and Adonis stanza (*ababcc*); sonnets in either the Petrarchan (Italian) mode (*abbaabba cdecde*) or the English (Shakespearean) kind (*ababcdcdefefgg*); or the old Chaucerian rhyme royal (*ababbcc*), which appeared in work as different as the highly moralistic *Mirror for Magistrates* (1559), Sir John Davies' elegant *Orchestra* (1596), and William Shakespeare's courtly tragic poem, *The Rape of Lucrece* (1594). Donne showed later poets how to combine the pentameter line with lines of other lengths to form witty, compelling stanzas; and Edmund Spenser not only devised for *The Faerie Queene* the deliberate, processional stanza named for him, with its interlocking rhyme scheme (*ababbcbc₅c₆*), but also developed casually grand and complex long stanza forms for his two marriage odes, "Prothalamion" and "Epithalamion." These poems' inclusion of shorter lines in their wandering, seemingly wayward, yet carefully controlled design was surely in John Milton's mind when he composed "Lycidas."

All these forms depended on a five-foot line whose strengths the poets—after two generations of marching, as it were, in place—explored with zest in the last two decades of the sixteenth century. Specifically, their practice showed that the line had at least as much variability as the classical hexameter, but its variations were of different kinds, as was to be expected of verse written in an accentual language. They found that listeners could easily retain their sense of an iambic decasyllabic line even if its key stressed syllables (2, 4, 6, 8, 10) were not stressed

V

equally strongly, if the intervals between them were not uniform, and if, in certain patterns that the ear permitted, stress was sometime displaced from an even- to an odd-numbered syllable. A line need not follow the regular five-beat boom—*I may, I must, I can, I will, I do* (Sidney, *Astrophel and Stella*, 47: 0); instead, poets could craft lines of varying stress-design, all of which would fulfill the essential rhythmical obligations of the pattern: "Now at the last gaspe, of loves latest breath" (Drayton, *Idea*, 31:9); "Feare, sicknesse, age, losse, labour, sorrow, strife" (Spenser, *Faerie Queene*, 1.9.44.6); "Shall I compare thee to a summer's day?" (Shakespeare, Sonnet 18).

As poets worked out the variations that an ear attuned to this meter could enjoy as falling within the normal range, they heard the advantages, too, of varying the position of the usual midline phrasal break. The five-foot line could not divide into equal metrical or phrasal halves, and its inherent imbalance could be exploited as a source of constant pleasurable tension and interest. The midline break, then, need not come after the fourth or sixth syllable, as earlier poets from John Lydgate to George Gascoigne had almost always contrived it; it might come earlier, later, more than once, or not at all; and if it came late, the phrase that ended the line might carry over into the next. Lines might "run on" instead of being "endstopped," and if they did, they usually worked better—that is, sounded more natural—if they dispensed with rhyme. If, in the years when blank verse began to dominate the English stage, "Marlowe's mighty line" was its model, with its powerful, regular, endstopped, five-beat thump, by the end of the Tudor period Shakespeare's dramatic blank verse commonly began and ended sentences in midline, often framing interior full lines: "But long it could not be / Till that her garments, heavy with their drink, / Pull'd the poor wretch from her melodious lay / To muddy death" (*Hamlet*, 4.7.180–183).

Although rhyme still has ceremonious and end-of-scene signaling uses for the theater, this enjambed blank verse, making frequent use of short, clipped phrases to begin and end speeches of a certain length and gravity, provides a fluent and tonally plausible language for people talking with each other on the stage, and it engages the line and the sentence more tensely than verse that more simply limits each thought, or part of a thought, to a ten-syllable line. It permits the verse utterance of lengthy, complex, coherently and interestingly segmented sentences; and it also suggests that the line and the sentence work *through* each other: when one is finished, the other is still going on, as in life our different concerns are never, until death, all finished at once.

BIBLIOGRAPHY

Attridge, Derek. *Well-Weighed Syllables: Elizabethan Verse in Classical Metres.* 1974.

Brogan, T.V.F. *English Versification, 1570–1980.* 1981. (See also his and other authors' articles in *The New Princeton Encyclopedia of Poetry and Poetics.* 1993.)

Hardison, O.B., Jr. *Prosody and Purpose in the English Renaissance.* 1989.

Hollander, John. *Vision and Resonance: Two Senses of Poetic Form.* 1975.

Ing, Catherine. *Elizabethan Lyrics: A Study in the Development of English Metres and Their Relation to Poetic Effect.* 1951.

Peterson, Douglas. *The English Lyric from Wyatt to Donne: A History of the Plain and Eloquent Styles.* 2nd edition. 1990.

Thompson, John. *The Founding of English Metre.* 1961.

Woods, Susanne. *Natural Emphasis: English Versification from Chaucer to Dryden.* 1985.

Wright, George T. *Shakespeare's Metrical Art.* 1988.

George T. Wright

SEE ALSO

Ballad; Campion, Thomas; Davies, John; Donne, John; Elegy; Howard, Henry; Marlowe, Christopher; Shakespeare, William; Sidney, Philip; Skelton, John; Song; Sonnet Sequences; Spenser, Edmund; Tottel, Richard; Verse Anthologies

Vestiarian Controversy

The Vestiarian Controversy was a dispute in 1563 over the wearing of clerical vestments. At the time of the Reformation, little attention had been paid to clerical dress, most of which was retained unaltered. This was part of Thomas Cranmer's policy of introducing Protestant theology without causing unnecessary disruption to the existing order of things. However, as early as 1550, Bishop John Hooper of Gloucester objected to the wearing of garments that he regarded as indicative of a non-reformed sacramental theology, and his views gradually gained a wider currency.

At the time of the Elizabethan Settlement in 1559, a certain limited toleration of vestments was accepted, although the precise nature of this toleration has long been disputed. Those who shared Hooper's views did not immediately protest, because the Act of Uniformity made provision for future changes, which they naturally assumed would favor them. When it became clear that no changes were forthcoming, a number of Puritan ministers protested, focusing their objections on the wearing of the surplice. Various attempts were made by Archbishop Matthew Parker to reach some form of compromise but these did not work, and after 1565, coercion was applied to dissenting clergy. Parker himself composed a series of regulations on the subject, which formed a major part of the so-called *Advertisements* that he published in 1566.

The Vestiarian Controversy was the first round in a battle between Puritans and conformists that did not finally end until the former were ejected from the Church of England in 1662. Even now, however, clerical dress is a controversial matter that arouses passions within the Church of England that in many ways parallel the issues raised in the 1560s.

BIBLIOGRAPHY

Collinson, Patrick. *The Elizabethan Puritan Movement.* 1967.

Gerald Bray

SEE ALSO

Advertisements, Book of; Cranmer, Thomas; Hooper, John; Parker, Matthew; Puritanism; Reformation, English; Uniformity, Act of

Vice, The

The term "The Vice" had theatrical currency from the time of John Heywood to that of Ben Jonson. At its height, c. 1550–1580, this character was practically indispensable to writers of interludes such as Ulpian Fulwell in *Like Will to Like* (1568). He was played by the leading player in small, often itinerant, acting companies; the strength and prestige of the role are shown by its not often being doubled with other parts.

As the interlude was broadened to take in an increasingly wide range of subjects, it retained from the morality play a preoccupation with moral discourse, much of which was concentrated in the Vice. It was often he who took the lead in plotting the downfall of the hero, but he also had a primary function to represent and embody evil forces. Doubling schemes enabled him to be accompanied by evil companions, but he retained his centrality, encountering both good and bad characters.

Apart from this moral function, however, his main attraction for dramatists was his usefulness as a theatrical lead. There were many conventional features in his versatile performance, such as crocodile tears and mocking

laughter, and he was equipped with a wooden sword or dagger. The role was rich in verbal features particularly "Freudian" slips of the tongue, proverbs, puns, and sometimes an extensive nonsense patter related to his miscellaneous travels. He often sang songs, and there are many hints of physical agility, including fisticuffs. Although he showed emotion, he was not a human character likely to excite sympathy. This feature is particularly concentrated in his final predicaments: sometimes he is punished, even executed, for his evil deeds, but he can also escape to further adventures.

He is less specific and less monolithic than such abstractions as the Seven Deadly Sins, and although he sometimes has family links with the devil, he is distinct from him and often mocks him. The commonest name for him is Iniquity, a name remembered by William Shakespeare and Ben Jonson, who both made dramatic capital out of his now faded reputation. The names given to him often suggested cunning, as in Ambidexter and Subtle Shift.

Some of his peculiar effectiveness may be associated with folk-play characters, although this is difficult to prove. He shares some characteristics with Fools, with characters in the *Commedia dell'Arte*, with the Dutch Sinnekens, and with Till Eulenspiegel. The work of John Heywood and John Bale played an important part in the evolution of the mischief and folly inherent in his role. Some importance must also be attached to publication of plays, since it becomes clear that those interested in selling copies thought that to put a Vice on the title page was advantageous.

BIBLIOGRAPHY

Cushman, Lysander W. *The Devil and the Vice in the English Dramatic Literature before Shakespeare.* Studien zur Englischen Philologie. Vol. 6. 1900; repr. 1973.

Dessen, Alan C. *Shakespeare and the Late Moral Plays.* 1986.

Happé, Peter. "Sedition in *Kyng Johan:* Bale's Development of a Vice." *Medieval English Theatre*, vol. 3, pp. 3–6.

———. *Two Moral Interludes.* Malone Society Reprints. 1991.

Spivack, Bernard. *Shakespeare and the Allegory of Evil.* 1958.

Peter Happé

SEE ALSO

Bale, John; Drama, History of; Fulwell, Ulpian; Heywood, John; Jonson, Ben; Shakespeare, William

V

Virginia Colony

See Colonial Development; Discovery and Exploration; Hariot, Thomas; Ralegh, Walter

Vives, Juan Luis (1492–1540)

Vives was born in Valencia to Jewish parents who had just been converted to Catholicism. At fourteen he enrolled in the local *Estudio General,* where he distinguished himself, among other ways, by delivering an impassioned oration against the new grammatical theories of Antonio de Nebrija at the behest of his teacher Jeronimo Amiguet—an accomplishment Vives later regretted. Between 1509–1512 Vives studied logic at the University of Paris, but found the course of studies arid and the professors uninspiring—both of which he later ridiculed in his *Adversus Pseudodialecticos* (1520). In 1512, Vives left for Bruges, where he accepted a position of tutor to the children of an exiled Spanish Jewish merchant, returning briefly to Paris in 1514 to publish an edition of Hyginus and two devotional works. In 1516, Vives made the acquaintance of Desiderius Erasmus, who became instrumental in his appointment as tutor and companion to Guillaume de Croy, the young archbishop-elect of Toledo. Vives remained with de Croy in Louvain for more than three years, and in 1520 obtained permission from the university authorities to teach publicly, even though he held no degree. At the same time he also embarked, at Erasmus's request, on a commentary to Augustine's *De Civitate Dei.* The exchange between the two over that contribution foreshadowed the complex relations that developed between the two humanists, and Erasmus's rather ambivalent attitude toward the ingenious young Spaniard.

Following the accidental death of de Croy in early 1521, Vives was forced to become a private teacher again. Seeking more secure patronage, Vives wrote Thomas More, who had been enthusiastic about the *Adversus Pseudodialecticos,* to intercede on his behalf with Henry VIII and, in September of that year, Vives met More, as well as Cardinal Thomas Wolsey, in Bruges. In all likelihood it was More who suggested that Vives dedicate the commentary on Augustine to Henry VIII. Nothing further transpired in the matter until 1523, when Vives resolved to accept Wolsey's invitation to visit London en route to Spain, where he had been offered Nebrija's chair of philology in Alcalá. Once in London, however, Vives was offered by Cardinal Wolsey the position of Greek lecturer in the newly founded Cardinal College in Oxford. Since the building had not been completed, Vives took up residence in Corpus Christi College, and began delivering there his lectures during Michaelmas term of 1523. From Oxford Vives also dedicated to his benefactress, Queen Katherine of Aragon, his *De ratione studii puerilis*—earlier that year he had also dedicated to her his famous manifesto advocating the education of women, *De institutione feminae Christianae*—and both works were intended to be used in educating Princess Mary. In May 1524, at the end of the academic year, Vives returned to Bruges, where he married his distant relative Margareta Valdaura and saw through the press his *Introductio ad sapientiam.* Although he returned to England for the next academic year, he was prevented from lecturing on account of the plague, so he returned to Bruges, resuming his teachings only in January 1525. By then, Cardinal Wolsey's attitude toward Vives had cooled considerably in view of the changing political situation that now saw an alliance between England and the French against Emperor Charles V. Vives lost favor both on account of his explicit pacifist views and because of his intimacy with the queen. Despite Wolsey's manifest displeasure, which included the termination of Vives's lectureship, the king himself appears to have remained supportive. Vives's pension was continued and the scholar was requested by the king to contribute to the group effort to rebut Martin Luther's critique of the English monarch. At the insistence of Katherine, in October 1527, Vives was even appointed tutor to Princess Mary. Yet his increasingly close ties with the queen heightened Wolsey's suspicion, and Vives suffered the ignominy of house arrest for nearly six weeks during the winter of 1528. At Katherine's advice, he left England, only to return in November as a member of Cardinal Campeggio's papal delegation to inquire into the matter of the divorce. Vives provoked Katherine's anger by counseling her not to take part in the trial, so that he left immediately thereafter, never to set foot in England again.

Vives returned to Bruges, where, save for short trips, he remained until his death. With the discontinuation of the English pension, he was forced to seek other sources of income. By 1532, he became the beneficiary of an imperial pension and later that of Doña Mencía de Mendoza, whose preceptor he became in 1537–1538. The last decade of his life proved his most productive. In 1531, Vives published both *De concordia et discordia in humano genere,* dedicated to Charles V, and the monumental collection of his educational works, *De disciplinis.* These were followed by his penetrating treatise on human nature, *De anima et vita* (1538), and his religious masterpiece, *De veritate fidei Christianae,* which remained unfinished at the time of his death and was published in 1543 by Francis Craneveld.

BIBLIOGRAPHY

Bonilla y San Martin, Adolfo. *Luis Vives y la Filosofía del Renacimiento.* 1903.

Emden, A.B. *A Biographical Register of the University of Oxford, A.D.1501 to 1540,* pp. 594–596. 1974.

Guerlac, Rita, ed. *Juan Luis Vives against the Pseudodialecticians.* 1979.

Noreña, Carlos G. *Juan Luis Vives.* 1970.

Vives, Juan Luis. Vives: On Education. Foster Watson, trans. Repr. 1971.

———. *Declamationes Sullanae.* Edward V. George, trans. 1988.

Mordechai Feingold

SEE ALSO

Education; Erasmus, Desiderius; Humanism; Katherine of Aragon; More, Thomas

Vowell, John

See Hooker, John, alias Vowell

Wales, History of

On his accession to the throne, Henry Tudor was enthusiastically supported by the Welsh people because of his family connections with North Wales. Subsequent to the Owain Glyndwr Revolt (1400–1415), and the imposition of penal laws (1402), which restricted the rights and privileges of the Welsh people, an intense feeling of national consciousness emerged and, following his victory at Bosworth Field, Henry VII was regarded as the "son of prophecy," the national leader come to liberate the nation from alien rule. The chief exponents of this myth, which had origins well rooted in the medieval past, were the professional bards who addressed him as the nation's "deliverer." His rule in Wales, however, was to be far less spectacular. He revived the Council in the Marches, and attempted some reform in the Marches and granted Charters of Enfranchisement (1505–1508) to some northern marcher lordships and the principality of North Wales. They enabled their inhabitants to enjoy equality of status with the English and prepared the way for more fundamental changes in the 1530s and 1540s.

The fifteenth and sixteenth centuries saw the rise of powerful landowning families whose owners asserted regional authority based on privileged status derived from ancient royal or clan antecedents. They were the ambitious gentry, known in Welsh sources as *uchelwyr* (highborn freemen), and urban settlers who arose out of decaying social and economic conditions in native Welsh and marcher regions.

In 1536, Thomas Cromwell, Henry VIII's chief secretary, assimilated Wales with England as part of the momentous changes that created the national sovereign state. The policies adopted in 1534–1535 by his henchman, Rowland Lee, president of the Council in the Marches, were based on fear and repression, for he attacked the symptoms rather than the root causes of disorder in the Marches. The Acts of Union (1536–1543) dissolved the Marcher lordships, created five new shires, introduced quarter and great sessions courts, strengthened the Council in the Marches, imposed English inheritance laws, and gave Wales a measure of parliamentary representation. In law and administration, English was imposed as the official language, thus preventing monoglot Welshmen from holding office under the crown.

Cromwell's policy was not revolutionary, since changes had previously occurred that gave Welsh gentry opportunities to hold office and develop their landed power. Although the Acts of Union established uniformity in government, the statutory powers given the Council in the Marches and great sessions gave Wales some legal and administrative autonomy. The settlement strengthened the landed gentry, who were responsible for maintaining law and order, and identified their interests with those of the Tudor monarchy. The Tudor settlement also forged a close relationship between Henry VIII and Wales since it was conceived as a means whereby the extended principality might be presented to his heir, Edward, as Prince of Wales. That, however, was not to be, but the constitutional link between Wales and the crown remained a principal feature of the settlement.

The 1530s brought Reformation changes into England and Wales. The Welsh Church felt their impact through the imposition of the Act of Supremacy, the dissolution of the monasteries, the abolition of shrines and pilgrimages, and the doctrinal changes introduced in the reign of Edward VI. In Wales, radical changes were accepted without resistance. While some local gentry houses clung tenaciously to it and led local resistance, particularly in Elizabeth I's reign, the majority of the gentry supported the crown.

In an age of Protestant fervor, when emphasis was placed increasingly on the need for the Scriptures in vernacular languages, efforts were made by Protestant scholars, principally Sir John Price and William Salesbury, the chief exponent of Protestant humanism in Wales, to translate parts of the Scriptures. In 1546, the Creed, the Lord's Prayer, and the Ten Commandments appeared in the first Welsh printed book, *Yny lhyvyr hwnn* (In this book . . .), and in 1551, *Kynniver llith a ban* (As many lessons and chapters . . .), the Gospels and epistles contained in the Book of Common Prayer.

Although Mary Tudor attempted to restore the old faith, time was too short, and the accession of Elizabeth I and the religious settlement strengthened the allegiance of the majority of the Welsh gentry to the crown and Protestantism. Since the English Bible and Book of Common Prayer were unintelligible to the Welsh peasantry, an act in 1563 provided for the translation of the Scriptures into Welsh. This provision advanced the Protestant faith and preserved the literary standards of the language. The New Testament and Book of Common Prayer appeared in 1567, translated by Salesbury, Richard Davies, bishop of St. David's, and Thomas Huet, but it was not until 1588 that the complete Bible was translated by William Morgan, vicar of Llanrhaeadr-ym-Mochnant. This fine achievement guaranteed the survival of the native language, the progress of Protestantism, and the strengthening of Welsh national consciousness. In an age when the new church was led by a band of dedicated Welsh-speaking bishops, the Bible became the lasting gift of the Tudors to the Welsh nation. It combined Protestant aspirations with the desire to elevate the language as a vehicle of the Renaissance.

Roman Catholic scholars fled to the Continent in 1558 and settled at centers such as Douai, Rome, and Milan. Among the most important were Morus Clynnog, who became master of the English College of Rome and who published *Athravaeth Cristnogavl* (Christian Doctrine) in 1568, and Gruffydd Robert, a distinguished scholar who moved to Milan where he became confessor to Archbishop Carlo Borromeo and published a Welsh grammar in 1567. The first Welsh printed book, *Y Drych Cristianogawl (The Christian Mirror)*, a work of Catholic theology, produced in a cave near Llandudno, appeared in 1587. Catholic resistance was led by some powerful gentry families and a few Jesuit priests but, owing to social disabilities and state opposition to it, the old faith never recovered, although pilgrimages to shrines remained popular.

In the reign of Elizabeth I, Welsh landowners advanced rapidly in office, politics, social life, and court connections. Membership of Parliament gave the most prominent an opportunity to pursue their political ambitions, which often led to faction and bitter hostility between rival houses. Their prosperity was based largely on acquiring crown lands, arranging propitious marriage alliances, education, and developing economic resources to advance their social position. Although adverse economic conditions seriously affected them, they continued to maintain their domination as masters of their communities and servants of the Tudor state. They retained their Welsh character, but gradually their role as cultural leaders declined with devastating effects on the professional bardic order. The years following the accession of James I broadened their ambitions and enabled them to cultivate a common citizenship with English gentry.

BIBLIOGRAPHY

Herbert, Trevor, and Gareth E. Jones, eds. *Tudor Wales.* 1988.

Jones, J. Gwynfor. *Early Modern Wales, c. 1526–1640.* 1994.

Thomas, Hugh. *A History of Wales, 1485–1660.* 1972.

Thomas, W.S.K. *Tudor Wales.* 1983.

Williams, Glanmor. *Renewal and Reformation: Wales c. 1415–1642.* 1993.

———. *Wales and the Reformation.* 1997.

J. Gwynfor Jones

SEE ALSO

Book of Common Prayer; Cromwell, Thomas; English College of Rome; Henry VII; Reformation, English

Walsingham, Francis (c. 1530–1590)

Francis Walsingham was probably born in either London or Kent; his father, William, held important local offices in both places and purchased Footscray manor in Kent. The exact date of Walsingham's birth is unknown. His mother, Joyce, was sister to Sir Antony Denny, privy councilor and friend to Henry VIII. The Walsinghams and Dennys were both new gentry families recently risen to prominence. Walsingham matriculated from King's College, Cambridge, in 1548 and stayed until 1550, apparently without taking a degree; in 1552, he became a student at Gray's Inn. When the Catholic Mary I came to the throne the following year, Walsingham left for the Continent where he stayed until the end of the reign in 1558. His sojourn abroad attests to the strong Protestant beliefs that marked his entire career; family contacts with leaders of both Northumberland's and Wyatt's actions against Mary's accession may have provided a directly political reason for his voluntary exile as well. Walsingham registered at the universities of Basle and Padua, and it is likely that he established some of the European contacts that supported his precocious career in foreign affairs on his return to Elizabeth's England.

Walsingham served as member of Parliament for Banbury in 1559 and for Lyme Regis from 1563 until 1567. After 1573, he sat for Surrey in successive Parliaments. He married Anne Carleil in 1562 and, a few years after her death, Ursula Worseley in 1567 (she died in 1602). Both women were widows of some wealth; Anne was childless by Walsingham, but the marriage to Ursula produced a daughter, Frances. Patronized by William Cecil, later Lord Burghley, Walsingham quickly became involved in soliciting and coordinating espionage. In 1568, he investigated a scheme to marry Norfolk to the recently imprisoned Mary Queen of Scots and helped Cecil expose the Ridolfi Plot for a Spanish invasion on her behalf. He was sent as an envoy to Paris and then made resident ambassador there from 1570 to 1573, achieving an alliance with France through the Treaty of Blois. After an abortive proposal to marry Elizabeth I to Henri, duc D'Anjou, the future Henri III, Walsingham managed the first round of marriage negotiations with his younger brother, Francis, duc d'Alençon, under Elizabeth's direct instructions and the watchful eye of Catherine de Medicis. Commissioned as well to argue on behalf of the Huguenots, Walsingham began to press for English aid to Dutch Protestants against the Spanish occupation of the Netherlands. He seems to have become Robert Dudley, earl of Leicester's, client about this time. The St. Bartholomew Day's massacre of August 1572 put an end to these matters, but it cemented Walsingham's association with Sir Philip Sidney, who stayed with him during the violence and who married his daughter, Frances Walsingham, in 1583.

Recalled at his own request in 1573, Walsingham was appointed principal secretary to the Privy Council by the queen in December, a place he would hold until the end of his life. Although he shared the office with Sir Thomas Smith and others, Walsingham made it his own. He presented issues to the council on behalf of the queen, oversaw matters in Ireland and the Marches, and handled foreign affairs. All diplomatic correspondence passed through his hands, and he personally undertook several difficult diplomatic missions. The systematic use of spies and informers abroad and at home became an increasingly important part of Walsingham's task: he was not the only councilor or courtier to employ spies, but his purview in foreign policy and its links to domestic conspiracy, coupled with his access to the queen as principal secretary, eventually made him the chief conduit for intelligence at court.

Walsingham continued to press for intervention in the Netherlands and in Scotland during the later 1570s. In 1578, Elizabeth sent him to the Low Countries to reconcile Spain and the Estates General and determine the role that Alençon might play there. The mission failed, and on his return Walsingham found himself enmeshed in the second round of marriage negotiations between Elizabeth and her French suitor. He tried to undermine the courtship, which finally came to an end when Alençon turned on the Dutch at Antwerp in 1583. Later that year Walsingham reluctantly traveled to Edinburgh with a view to persuading James VI against further negotiation with France and Spain on behalf of his imprisoned mother, Mary Stuart. The results were inconclusive. Successes followed on both the Netherlandish and Scottish fronts between 1585 and 1586: Walsingham first brokered the compromise between Elizabeth and the Estates General that led to Leicester's campaign against Spain, and then uncovered (or partially manufactured, as some maintain) the Babington Plot to free Mary and assassinate Elizabeth. Walsingham's spies produced correspondence implicating Mary in the latter charge; she was convicted in October of 1586 and executed the following February. The prospect of the English succession, skillfully dangled by Walsingham, dissuaded James from retaliation.

News of Spain's planned armada against England came to Walsingham's attention as early as 1586, from merchants and travelers, rather than spies. He drew up an elaborate plan for Spanish intelligence and apparently carried it out by 1588, as the accurate reports of the size and timing of the Armada he obtained attest. With one eye still on Spain, Walsingham turned his attention to France, urging covert support of Henri of Navarre and moving quickly moving to support the latter's succession after Henri III's assassination in 1589. Walsingham complained that his rewards for such services were few, but he was compensated by queen Elizabeth I in various ways. Knighted in 1577, he was chancellor of the order of the garter, 1578–1587. In 1579, he purchased Barn Elms in

Surrey after selling Footscray. Walsingham held several posts in Hampshire, Lancaster, and Essex, and was granted a lease of customs and other economic privileges. He appears to have died in debt, however, a result of covering the costs of Sidney's state funeral and part of Sidney's debt. Having suffered from ill health throughout the latter part of his life, Walsingham died in London on April 6, 1590.

BIBLIOGRAPHY

Read, Conyers. *Mr. Secretary Walsingham and the Policy of Queen Elizabeth*. 3 vols. 1925.

Wernham, R.B. *Before the Armada: The Growth of English Foreign Policy, 1485–1588*. 1966.

John Michael Archer

SEE ALSO

Alençon and Anjou, Duke of; Armada, Spanish; Babington Plot; Cecil, William; Elizabeth I; Espionage; Foreign Relations and Diplomacy; Howard, Thomas; Marian Exiles; Mary I; Mary Queen of Scots; Ridolfi Plot; Sidney, Philip

Warbeck, Perkin (c. 1474–1499)

An impostor and pretender to the throne of Henry VII, Perkin Warbeck was born Pierrechon Werbecque (or Osbeck) in Tournai around 1474, was educated there, and placed in merchant service in Antwerp and Middelburg. His travels eventually took him to Ireland in 1491 where—by his own account—he was mistaken in Cork for a member of the House of York. Warbeck was coached into assuming the identity of Richard, duke of York, the younger son of the Edward IV, imprisoned during the reign of Richard III and presumed dead. Like Lambert Simnel, the pretender whose brief career ended at the battle of Stoke in 1487, Warbeck received initial support from the Fitzgerald earls of Kildare and Desmond, probably in retaliation for Henry's support of the rival Butler family. Similarly, Warbeck also received the patronage of Edward IV's sister, Margaret of York, dowager duchess of Burgundy, who claimed him as her nephew. Archduke Philip, who protected Margaret, refused to dissociate himself from Warbeck despite Henry's formal protest. Yet Warbeck sought even higher support; in 1491, Warbeck was backed by Charles VIII of France, who used him to destabilize Henry's alliance with Emperor Maximilian against France. But after Henry's failure to invade France led to a separate peace treaty at Etaples in November 1492, Charles VIII expelled Warbeck, who then visited Vienna in 1493 and received recognition from Emperor Maximilian; he in turn become an instrument of Maximilian's displeasure over Henry's rupture of the old alliance with Burgundy.

The strength of Warbeck's support abroad encouraged plotting among Henry's courtiers, foremost among them Sir Robert Clifford, who first recognized Warbeck's claim as true but then accepted Henry's pardon in exchange for exposing the other plotters. Many were hanged, but one plotter, Sir William Stanley, was a prominent noble to whom Henry was indebted at Bosworth for his crown. At this time, Warbeck had consolidated his support on the Continent and in exchange signed a will on January 24, 1495 granting Maximilian, and then his son, Philip, all rights to his presumptive kingdoms if he did not have a male heir. Warbeck had also signed documents granting Margaret—on his accession—repayment of losses incurred after the death of Edward IV and in promoting his claim. On May 8, 1495, Margaret appealed to the pope on Warbeck's behalf. Then in early July of 1495, with Maximilian's support, Warbeck launched an expedition against England that failed utterly to further his cause. Warbeck was careful not to land, but most of his men who did were immediately captured. The pretender sailed away, but within three weeks Warbeck had gathered another fleet in Ireland and laid seige to Waterford with the support of the earl of Desmond. After eleven days the unsuccessful seige was lifted, and Warbeck soon left Ireland to seek support in Scotland.

James IV greeted Warbeck in Sterling on November 27, 1495, during a time when relations with England were uneasy, and other courts watched to see if James would exploit Warbeck's presence to provoke Henry. However, Henry had spies within James's court, and a plan for a Scottish invasion in September of 1496 was foreseen. The raid itself failed to gather momentum against Henry and was not opposed, but Henry capitalized on the threat by raising levies and taking loans in defense against Scotland and Warbeck. James, on the other hand, had Warbeck's assurances of reward on his accession, and had secured his loyalty by marrying his kinswoman, Katherine Gordon, to Warbeck. However, Warbeck had political value in that he became a negotiable commodity with which the courts of Scotland, Spain, and France established relations with Henry. Charles VIII of France sent Henry certification that Warbeck was an impostor. Ferdinand and Isabella attempted to moderate James's position but were eager to demonstrate Warbeck's imposture as they sought Henry's alliance against the French in Italy.

Ultimately, Warbeck became a liability for James, and the pretender was sent away to Cornwall, but not before Warbeck again failed to marshal support in Ireland. Arriving at Land's End, Warbeck soon attracted the popular support of three or four thousand men and laid seige to Exeter on September 17, 1497; repulsed repeatedly, he abandoned his men and fled after four days. Henry's forces cut off all escape, and on advice from royal servants, Warbeck submitted to the king and made a confession. Brought to London and put under house arrest, Warbeck escaped the following June but was soon recaptured, exhibited on scaffolds in Westminster and Cheapside, and put in the Tower. He was not tried until November 16, 1499, and then with the earl of Warwick, who had posed another threat to Henry. After another confession, Warbeck was hanged at Tyburn along with his friend, John Walters, the mayor of Cork, on November 23, 1499.

BIBLIOGRAPHY

Arthurson, Ian. *The Perkin Warbeck Conspiracy, 1491–1499.* 1994.

Dunlop, David. "The 'Masked Comedian': Perkin Warbeck's Adventures in Scotland and England from 1495 to 1497." *Scottish Historical Review,* vol. 70, no. 190, pp. 97–128.

Gairdner, James. *History of the Life and Reign of Richard III, to Which is Added the Story of Perkin Warbeck, from Original Documents.* 3rd edition. 1898.

Weightman, C. *Margaret of York, Duchess of Burgundy, 1446–1503.* 1989.

David W. Swain

SEE ALSO

Henry VII; Margaret of York; Simnel, Lambert; Wars of the Roses

Wards and Liveries, Court of

Wardship was a right and duty that gave a lord responsibility for the upbringing and education of an heir who was a minor on the death of the owner of a landed estate. If any part of the estate was held directly by the crown, by prerogative wardship, became responsible for the whole. Since the right gave the lord or king all the revenues from the land and the marriage of the heir, it was a valuable resource that could be allocated as a reward by the monarch to favored friends or servants, or, more commonly, sold. An early master, Sir John Hussey, was bound by recognizance to sell the king's wards "without favour, mede or parcialitie" and without taking any rewards.

Grants of wardship were recorded in the Exchequer, but under Henry VII and in Henry VIII's early years, wards were managed by officials called the masters of the wards. Under Henry VIII, a separate Court of Record was set up to manage all aspects of jurisdiction arising from wardship that had previously been scattered around a number of revenue courts. The receiver general for the court paid most of the revenue to the treasurer of the chamber and fixed amounts to the cofferer and others. While the amount raised varied from year to year, it averaged £4,500 at the end of Henry VII's reign, rose to £15,000–£20,000 by 1559, and then fell until the early seventeenth century.

Financial gain was only one use of wardship, and the reduction of income under William Cecil's mastership may reflect other objectives. Wardship of recusants could be used to convert a family to the established church. Wardship was thus a duty easily abused and much resented by those subject to it. The Court of Wards disappeared only when all feudal rights were abolished by the Long Parliament of 1640.

BIBLIOGRAPHY

Bell, H.E. *Introduction to the History and Records of the Court of Wards & Liveries.* 1953

Hurstfield, J. *Queen's Wards; Wardship and Marriage under Elizabeth I.* 1958.

Public Records Office. Records E36/246–248.

Sybil M. Jack

SEE ALSO

Cecil, William; Exchequer; Government, Central Administration of; Henry VII; Henry VIII; Taxation

Warfare

See Archery; Armada, Spanish; Bosworth, Battle of; Flodden Field, Battle of; Military History; Ordnance

Warham, William (c. 1450–1532)

Civil lawyer, diplomat, archbishop of Canterbury, lord chancellor of England, and patron of Desiderius Erasmus, William Warham was a man moderate in temperament, although jealously protective of his legal prerogatives, whose skills as a politician ultimately proved incommensurate with his abilities as a lawyer. Born in Malshanger,

Hampshire, and educated at Winchester College, Warham was scholar and fellow at New College, Oxford, between 1473 and 1475, but left in 1488, after taking the degree of LL.D., to become an advocate in the Court of Arches and principal of the school of civil law at Oxford. In 1490, he was proctor at the Roman Curia for John Alcock, bishop of Ely, and for the priory of Christ Church, Canterbury. Henry VII appointed him in April 1491 a commissioner to the Anglo-Hanseatic diet at Antwerp. Two years later he joined Sir Edward Poynings on an embassy to protest the support given to Perkin Warbeck by Archduke Philip and by Margaret of York. Between 1496 and 1501, Warham traveled abroad on several other embassies, negotiating commercial and political treaties with the Habsburgs and with Riga. He also participated in treaty negotiations for the marriage between Prince Arthur and Katherine of Aragon in 1496 and for the truce between England and Scotland in 1497.

Diplomatic service earned Warham advancement in both church and state. First ordained subdeacon of Litchfield in 1493, he soon became precentor of Wells; archdeacon of Huntington; prebend of Timsbury, Hampshire; rector of Barley, Hertfordshire; and rector of Cottenham, Cambridgeshire. Consecrated bishop of London in 1501, Warham was translated to the archiepiscopal see of Canterbury in 1503. He was appointed master of the rolls in 1494, keeper of the great seal in 1502, and, on becoming archbishop, lord chancellor of England in 1504. He became chancellor of Oxford University in 1506. As archbishop and chancellor, Warham continued his involvement in the king's diplomacy, negotiating the proposed marriage of Henry VII to Margaret of Savoy in 1506, and receiving the Habsburg envoys who came to conclude the marriage between Mary Tudor and Archduke Charles (the future Emperor Charles V) in 1508.

Warham crowned Henry VIII in 1509, but under the new king his political influence waned. Thomas Wolsey's cardinal's hat and legatine commission reduced Warham's status and authority in the English Church. Although Warham resigned the chancellorship to Wolsey in 1515, he continued to participate in diplomatic affairs, such as meetings with Charles V and Francis I in 1520 and 1521. He continued to act as the king's representative in Kent, which made him the butt of local discontent over the "Amicable Grant" of 1525 that Wolsey had imposed without parliamentary approval.

Warham, more interested in the judicial than in the pastoral, often placed his archiepiscopal duties second to his responsibilities at court, and thus it was eight years before he was able to make a personal visitation of his own diocese. His involvement in the affairs of his suffragans provoked bitter complaints about encroachments on their jurisdictions, even though Warham maintained the authority of local bishops over the clergy of their dioceses regardless of his disagreements with them. Thus, while blocking Bishop Ralph Fitzjames's prosecution of John Colet for heresy, Warham upheld his order temporarily suspending Colet from preaching, an action that Colet's friends, including Erasmus, sharply criticized. Warham seemed little worried about the influx of Lutheran ideas into England. While he was present for the burning of Lutheran books at St. Paul's in May 1521, he refused to undertake a zealous purge at Oxford, believing that Lutheranism was limited to only a few individuals and thus posed little danger.

In the political maelstrom of Henry VIII's divorce from Katherine of Aragon, Warham sought to avoid conflict between his fealty to the king and his loyalty to the pope and to the prerogatives of the English Church. This attitude rendered him ineffectual as Katherine's chief counsel because he feared angering Henry. In the summer of 1530, Warham signed the letter of the peers of England urging Pope Clement VII to grant Henry's divorce. After the matter of the divorce turned into an attack on the prerogatives of the clergy, Warham, hoping that moderation and compromise could resolve the growing political crisis, got the province of Canterbury to accept Henry VIII's claim as protector and supreme head of the English Church with the qualification "in so far as it is allowed by the laws of Christ." Thomas Cromwell, with the king's support, continued to move anticlerical legislation through Parliament. This finally compelled Warham in early 1532 to declare his opposition boldly to all recent acts of Parliament derogatory to the authority of the pope and contrary to the prerogatives of the province of Canterbury. Thus facing a charge of *praemunire*, Warham drafted a speech defending himself. He may not have delivered it, for, exhausted and in failing health, he died on August 22, 1532.

BIBLIOGRAPHY

Hook, Walter Farquhar. *Lives of the Archbishops of Canterbury.* Vol. 6. 155–421. 1868.

Kentish Visitations of Archbishop William Warham and His Deputies, 1511–1512. Kathleen L. Wood-Legh, ed. Kent Archaeological Society Record Series. Vol. 24. 1984.

Thomson, John A.F. *The Early Tudor Church and Society, 1485–1529.* 1993.

John M. Currin

SEE ALSO
Arthur Tudor; Colet, John; Cromwell, Thomas; Erasmus, Desiderius; Foreign Relations and Diplomacy; Henry VIII; Katherine of Aragon; Lutheranism; Margaret of York; Poynings, Edward; *Praemunire;* Warbeck, Perkin; Wolsey, Thomas

Warner, William (c. 1558–1609)

William Warner is best remembered for his *Albions England* (1586), a verse history of Britain, covering in its final edition events from Noah to the reign of James I. He also wrote *Pan his Syrinx* (1584), a collection of prose tales. A translation of Plautus's *Menaechmi* (1595) is often attributed to Warner, but the attribution is questionable.

Little is known of Warner's biography. Born about 1558—probably in London—Warner worked as an attorney of the Court of Common Pleas in the same city, where he developed his reputation as an author and most likely associated with other men of letters. Michael Drayton, in his poem "To my most dearly-loved friend Henery Reynolds Esquire, of Poets and Poesie," refers to Warner as "my old friend." Warner's patrons included Henry Carey, first Lord Hunsdon, lord chamberlain, to whom Warner dedicated *Albions England.* Carey's son George, second Lord Hunsdon, to whom Warner had dedicated *Pan his Syrinx,* probably did not continue his father's patronage. Warner died in 1609; his burial is recorded in the parish register of Great Amwell, Hertfordshire. Several traditional features of Warner's biography—that he was born in Warwickshire, attended Magdalen Hall, Oxford, left without taking a degree, and knew Christopher Marlowe in London—cannot be documented.

Pan his Syrinx, Warner's earliest known work, consists of seven moralistic tales. The narratives contain many classical allusions but seem to be largely of Warner's invention. The work's style is strongly influenced by John Lyly, its structure by Heliodorus. *Pan his Syrinx* was first entered in the *Stationers' Register* on September 22, 1584; a second edition was published in 1597. It went through only these two editions and has gone largely unnoticed by critics, although Thomas Warton mentions it briefly.

The episodic history, *Albions England,* written in fourteen-syllable lines, incorporates much fictional and mythical material; its structure is influenced by Ovid. This popular work went through several editions during Warner's lifetime, each adding material to the narrative. The first, consisting of four books, was published in 1586 and relates events through the Norman Conquest. The second (1589), consisting of six books, covers events to the accession of Henry VII. The third edition (1592) added Books 7–9, bringing the chronicle to the accession of Elizabeth I; a fourth (1596) added Books 10–12 and expanded Book 9. The fifth edition (1602) extended Book 13, and in 1606, Books 14–16 were published separately. The final edition (1612), consisting of sixteen books, covers events through the reign of James I.

Warner enjoyed a strong reputation during his lifetime, due mostly to the success of *Albions England.* Thomas Nashe, Gabriel Harvey, and Francis Meres all praised Warner, Meres stating in his *Palladis Tamia* (1598) that "I have heard him termd of the best wits of both our Universities, our English *Homer.*" Robert Allott's *England's Parnassus* (1600), a collection of quotations from contemporary works, quotes only Edmund Spenser and Michael Drayton more than Warner. But Warner's modern reputation has suffered. C.S. Lewis said of *Albions England,* "It was a spirited attempt to avoid the formlessness of the mere metrical chronicle, but Warner failed in the execution."

BIBLIOGRAPHY
Lewis, C.S. *English Literature in the Sixteenth Century.* 1954.
Warner, William. *Pan his Syrinx, or, Pipe, Compact of Seven Reedes.* Wallace A. Bacon, ed. 1950; repr. 1970.

Barclay Green

SEE ALSO
Classical Literature, Influence of; Drayton, Michael; History, Writing of; Lyly, John; Meres, Francis

Wars of the Roses

The Wars of the Roses traditionally refers to the period in English history, mostly between 1450–1487, when two rival branches of the Plantagenet dynasty, the House of Lancaster and the House of York, supported by magnates made overmighty by the corruption of "bastard feudalism," fought for possession of the crown, with the Lancastrians taking the red rose as their emblem, and the Yorkist the white rose. This symbol is misleading, for neither side made frequent use of rose emblems. Recent research has rendered too simplistic the notion that the conflict was merely dynastic, and has made the concept of bastard feudalism almost meaningless. There were few bloody pitched battles, and apart from the landed families of England and their retainers, the wars little affected the lives of ordinary people.

The wars grew out of a deepening political crisis during the 1450s brought on by Henry VI's incompetence and subsequent insanity. This crisis was intensified by humiliation over the loss of lands in France, except for Calais, and by a European-wide economic recession that further weakened the crown's finances, which had been depleted already by corruption and by the cost of the war in France. Contributing to the crisis was the breakdown of effective "good lordship," which held baronial affinities together, helped maintain order in local communities, and tether localities to the court. Henry VI's unwillingness and inability to exercise his regal "good lordship" left dangerous rivalries unchecked as noble cliques vied for control of the wealth and patronage of the crown for their own enrichment and for the benefit of their families and retainers. The dissolution of the Beauchamp affinity in Warwickshire and of the de la Pole affinity in East Anglia resulted in increased instability in those regions.

First Phase. The first phase of the Wars of the Roses, lasting from 1455 to 1471, became a dynastic struggle between York and Lancaster. Since 1447, Edmund Beaufort, second duke of Somerset and illegitimate descendant of John of Gaunt, dominated the council of Henry VI with John de la Pole, duke of Suffolk, excluding from power Richard, duke of York, the heir presumptive to the throne. In 1450, discontent was rife, especially among the gentry and yeomanry, with fiscal mismanagement; corruption and mishandling of the war in France culminated in Jack Cade's Rebellion in Kent and in Suffolk's impeachment and murder. Richard of York, leaving his post as lieutenant of Ireland, returned to England, claiming that he had come to restore good government. But Somerset, who had the king's favor, kept his lock on power. York, frustrated, suffered humiliation in 1452 after he failed to field an army against Somerset. Circumstances changed in August 1453. King Henry collapsed into a catatonic stupor, and York was appointed protector of the realm. Margaret of Anjou, anxious to protect the rights of her newborn son, Edward of Lancaster, allied herself with Somerset and the opposition to York, and helped nurse Henry back to lucidity by Christmas 1454. With Somerset restored to power, York faced charges of treason when Parliament met at Leicester in 1455. York and his Neville supporters, Richard, earl of Salisbury, and his son, Richard, earl of Warwick, hoped to forestall this event by forcibly seizing the king.

The ensuing affray, called the first battle of St. Albans (May 22, 1455), marks the start of the first phase of the wars. Somerset and many Lancastrian lords were slaughtered, and the king was wounded. York, ensconced again as protector, purged his enemies from the government. But the first battle of St. Albans sparked a blood feud among the aristocracy. By the autumn of 1456, Queen Margaret, moving the court and king to Coventry, had revived the Lancastrian faction. Among her supporters were the sons of the lords who fell at St Albans, including Henry Beaufort, third duke of Somerset. York and the Nevilles were isolated. York returned to Ireland; Salisbury withdrew to his estates in the north; but Warwick held on to his strategic office as captain of Calais.

The years 1459–1464 were one of the most violent periods of the conflict. The Yorkist lords gathered their armies in England, intending to strike first. In September 1459, Salisbury, bringing his force south from Yorkshire to join York, Warwick, and other Yorkist lords at Ludlow, defeated a superior Lancastrian army at the battle of Blore Heath (September 23). The Yorkists positioned their combined armies at Ludford Bridge to check the Lancastrian advance on Ludlow, but the desertion of many of their soldiers to the other side forced the Yorkist lords to flee. York escaped to Ireland with his second son, Edmund, earl of Rutland, while Salisbury, Warwick, and York's eldest son, Edward, earl of March, took refuge at Calais. The following June, the three earls at Calais invaded England, where they were supported by the Kentishmen and welcomed into London. Defeating the Lancastrians at the battle of Northampton (July 10, 1460), they captured the king; but Margaret escaped with her son and the prominent Lancastrian lords. York returned from Ireland in October, and before Parliament, astounding even his own adherents, he asserted his claim to the throne. At this point the war turned into a dynastic conflict. A compromise whereby York would succeed Henry VI was rejected by Margaret, who refused to allow the disinheriting of her son. The army she assembled in the north surprised and defeated York and Salisbury at the battle of Wakefield (December 30, 1460). York died in the fighting; his son, Rutland, was cut down while fleeing; and Salisbury was executed after the battle. Margaret's army advanced south, defeating Warwick at the second battle of St. Albans (February 17, 1461) and recapturing the king. London lay before Margaret, vulnerable and frightened; but instead of taking the city, Margaret withdrew to the north. Meanwhile, Edward, earl of March, was defeated at Mortimer's Cross (February 2, 1461). The Lancastrian army was assembled in Wales by Jasper Tudor, earl of Pembroke, Henry's VI's half-brother. Edward joined Warwick, "The Kingmaker," entered London, and was proclaimed King Edward IV. Edward then routed the Lancastrians at Towton on Palm Sunday (March 29, 1461). This battle, fought in a blizzard, was the biggest and bloodiest of the wars. Margaret, Henry VI, and Prince Edward fled to Scotland with several lords. Warwick's brother, John, Lord Montague, gradually wore down Lancastrian resistance in the north, achieving final victory at Hexham (May 15, 1464). He was rewarded with the earldom of Northumberland, confiscated from Henry Percy. William, Lord Herbert's, long campaign against the Lancastrians in Wales ended with the capture of Harlech in 1468. Jasper Tudor eluded capture and escaped to France, but his nephew and ward, Henry Tudor, earl of Richmond, became Lord Herbert's prize, as did Jasper's confiscated earldom of Pembroke. The Yorkists recaptured Henry VI in 1465, and Margaret fled to France with her son and vanquished Lancastrian lords.

Edward IV's first reign (1461–1470) was precarious. Edward built up an affinity around powerful men of his own creation, such as William, Lord Hastings; William Herbert, the new earl of Pembroke; Humphrey Stafford, earl of Devon; Thomas, Lord Stanley; and Sir William Stanley of Holt. He married secretly the widow of a minor Lancastrian knight, Elizabeth Wydeville-Gray. Members of the Wydeville family quickly advanced themselves. The queen's brother, Richard, was created Earl Rivers, and several of her kin obtained lucrative marriages with members of the nobility. Warwick and his followers were the most aggrieved by the Wydevilles' growing political influence and crass social climbing. Edward's brothers, George, duke of Clarence, and Richard, duke of Gloucester, were also offended. Edward and Warwick differed over foreign policy as well. Warwick, continuing the lines of Lancastrian policy, wanted to conclude a peace and marriage alliance with France, while Edward, adhering to the anti-French policy of his father and abetted by the Wydevilles, sought an alliance with Burgundy, intending a renewal of the war against France. The Anglo-Burgundian alliance of 1468, cemented by the marriage of Margaret of York to Charles the Bold, embarrassed Warwick, who was in the midst of negotiation with Louis XI of France, Charles the Bold's archenemy.

By 1469, Warwick was openly in opposition, claiming that his quarrel was with the base-born persons about the king, namely, the Wydevilles. Instead of driving his rivals from court, Warwick was forced to flee to Calais. However, he won over Clarence, marrying him to his daughter, Isabel. The disgruntled earl took advantage of resurgent Lancastrian opposition and the increasing unpopularity of the king. A series of rebellions broke out in 1469; one was led by Warwick's retainer, Sir John Conyers, who styled himself "The Robin of Redesdale." Edward summoned Pembroke from Wales, and sent out a Yorkist army to deal with Redesdale. Warwick and Clarence, returning from Calais, joined forces with Redesdale and defeated the Yorkist army under Pembroke and Devon at Edgecote (July 26, 1469). Pembroke, Devon, Earl Rivers, and Sir John Wydeville were put to death, and King Edward, who was not at the battle, was imprisoned in Warwick Castle. Unable to govern without the king, Warwick freed Edward in mid-September. The following spring, Warwick and Clarence aided an insurrection in Lincolnshire, but this time Edward moved swiftly, forcing Warwick and Clarence again to seek refuge abroad. This time, Warwick was denied admittance to Calais and went to the court of Louis XI.

King Louis wanted to see the Anglo-Burgundian alliance against France replaced by an Anglo-French alliance against Burgundy, which would only happen under a Lancastrian king. Louis helped reconcile Warwick with Margaret of Anjou, and in mid-September 1470, while Edward was in the north, Warwick and Clarence returned to England, adherents of the house of Lancaster. Lord Montague, angry that Edward had restored the earldom of Northumberland to Henry Percy, now turned against the king, forcing Edward, Gloucester, Hastings, Anthony, and the second Earl Rivers into exile at the Burgundian court. The witless Henry VI was brought out of the Tower of London for a brief "Re-adeption" as king. Warwick then repaid his debt to the French king, joining him in a war on Burgundy. In response, Duke Charles outfitted a small expedition to return Edward to England.

Edward landed at Ravenspur in the North in March 1471. Lancastrian disorganization allowed Edward to march unimpeded through the Midlands and into London. Clarence defected from Warwick, and rejoined his brother. Edward and Warwick clashed for the final time at the battle of Barnet, which was fought in the fog on Easter Sunday (April 14, 1471). Warwick and his brother, Montague, died in the fighting. Edward then marched west and smashed the Lancastrian army of Margaret of Anjou at Tewkesbury (May 4, 1471). Many Lancastrians, including Prince Edward, were slaughtered while fleeing the battle. Others who had taken refuge in the nearby abbey were hauled out and executed. Lancastrian resistance fizzled with the failure of Thomas Neville, the bastard of Fauconberg's siege of London. On May 21, Edward extinguished the House of Lancaster for good, ordering the murder of Henry VI, and so ended the first phase of the wars. Hopes for a Lancastian revival lay with Margaret Beaufort's fourteen-year-old son, Henry Tudor, who escaped to Brittany with his uncle, Jasper.

Second Phase. The second phase of the Wars of the Roses, a dynastic conflict between the House of York and Tudor, began as the result of factionalism within the wider Yorkist affinity. Edward ruled securely, and even severely, during his second reign (1471–1483). Under him, Lord Hastings mastered his large affinity, and Richard, duke of Gloucester, built a powerful affinity in the north from the remnants of the Neville affinity. Humphrey Stafford, second duke of Buckingham, the wealthiest peer of the realm, came of age during these years. The Wydevilles maintained their prominence as well. But Clarence's continuing intrigues against his brother led to his trial and condemnation to death for treason in 1478. He was quietly murdered instead of publically executed. King Edward's premature death on April 9, 1483, brought the rivalries into the open. Gloucester may have been designated protector for the minor King Edward V, but the boy was residing at Ludlow Castle with Earl Rivers. Fearing that the Wydevilles would bring the young king to London for a hasty coronation, Gloucester, aided by the duke of Buckingham, intercepted Rivers at Stony Stratford and took possession of the king. Gloucester had Rivers and two of his companions imprisoned in Yorkshire and later executed. The queen, hearing news of Rivers's arrest, took refuge in Westminster Abbey with her daughters and her second son, Richard, duke of York. She later allowed York to join his brother in the Tower. Gloucester was emboldened by his success to take the throne away from his nephew. In June, he charged Lord Hastings with conspiring with the queen against him, and ordered him summarily executed. He then arranged for his nephews to be declared bastards and himself acclaimed King Richard III. Buckingham backed Richard's ambitions, as did John, Lord Howard, who was rewarded with the dukedom of Norfolk. However, most of the wider Yorkist affinity refused to accept his usurpation, and suspicion that Richard had murdered his nephews rent further the Yorkist affinity, leaving support for Richard centered on his own northern affinity.

Yorkist and Lancastrian opposition to Richard coalesced around the exiled Henry Tudor, earl of Richmond. Margaret Beaufort and Elizabeth Wydeville forged a family alliance, agreeing to the marriage of Henry with Elizabeth of York, Edward IV's eldest daughter. Although Buckingham had been rewarded by Richard with increased power in Wales and western England, he turned against the king, putting himself at the head of an insurrection. Buckingham's rebellion of October 1483 was hampered by disorganization and torrential rains. The duke was captured and executed. Henry Tudor sailed from Brittany to join the rebellion, but, discovering its collapse, returned to his exile. Richard's triumph did not enhance his security. In 1484, his only son, Edward of Middleham, and his queen, Anne, died. His scheme to marry his niece, Elizabeth, shocked even his most loyal adherents. However, Richard's attempts to get hold of Henry Tudor received a boost when Pierre Landois, the treasurer of Brittany, agreed to hand Henry over to Richard in exchange for an Anglo-Breton alliance against France and a contingent of English archers. Henry, warned of these developments, escaped to France. The government of Anne de Beaujeu, fearful of English intervention in a French civil war, outfitted a small force for Henry, intending that he would distract Richard. Henry landed in Wales in early August 1485. He advanced slowly into England, gathering followers gradually, while Richard marched south from Nottingham. Most nobles and gentlemen held aloof, including Lord Stanley, whose son, Lord Strange, was held hostage by Richard. The two armies clashed at the battle of Bosworth (August 22, 1485). Richard died fighting, and Norfolk was slain as well. Henry Tudor, crowned on the field of battle King Henry VII, married Elizabeth of York in Early 1486.

The founder of the Tudor dynasty made certain that the surviving male Yorkist, Clarence's son, Edward, earl of Warwick, was locked away in the Tower. King Richard's nephew and designated heir, John de la Pole, earl of Lincoln, joined a Yorkist conspiracy, backed by Margaret of York and rebel Irish lords, to have Lambert Simnel impersonate the imprisoned Warwick. A Yorkist army, commanded by Lincoln, invaded from Ireland in June 1487, and was defeated in the hard-fought battle of Stoke (June 16, 1487). After Stoke, the Wars of the Roses was fought in the arena of intrigue. From 1491–1497, Yorkist sympathizers and Henry's foreign enemies promoted the claim of Perkin Warbeck, who impersonated Edward IV's younger son, Richard, duke of York. Defeated and captured in 1497, Warbeck was executed with Warwick in 1499. Yorkist pretenders Edmund de la Pole, earl of Suffolk, and his brother, Richard, fled abroad in 1501, but failed to win international support for their cause. In 1506, Archduke Philip of Austria turned Suffolk over to Henry VII. He was executed in 1513 by Henry VIII. Richard de la Pole remained abroad, styling himself "the White Rose of York." His death in 1525, fighting for Francis I at Pavia, ended the Yorkist threat to the Tudor dynasty.

BIBLIOGRAPHY

Carpenter, Christine. *The Wars of the Roses: Politics and the Constitution in England. c. 1437–1509.* 1997.

Gillingham, John. *The Wars of the Roses: Peace and Conflict in Fifteenth-Century England.* 1981.

Goodman, Anthony. *The Wars of the Roses: Military Activity and English Society, 1452–1497.* 1981.

Pollard, A.J., ed. *The Wars of the Roses.* 1995.

John M. Currin

SEE ALSO

Bastard Feudalism; Beaufort, Margaret; Bosworth, Battle of; Margaret of York; de la Pole, Edmund; Simnel, Lambert; Stanley Family; Warbeck, Perkin

Weelkes, Thomas (c. 1575–1623)

The most original and daring of the English madrigal composers, Thomas Weelkes was organist of Winchester College when he composed the sixty-eight madrigals issued in three volumes between 1597 and 1600, and one madrigal, *As Vesta was from Latmos hill,* for *The Triumphs of Oriana* of 1601. We know next to nothing about his origins, childhood, or musical training: according to the preface of his first print, he was born in the middle to later 1570s. If he was the son of John Weeke, rector of Elsted, he was baptized October 25, 1576.

He then moved to Chichester Cathedral, where his only remaining secular collection, the *Ayres, or fantastic spirits for three voices,* was printed in 1608. At first successful, earning the bachelor of music degree at Oxford (for which he may have written the six-voice *Laboravi in gemitu meo,* his one Latin work) and marrying the daughter of a wealthy merchant, Weelkes was reprimanded for drunkenness and neglect of his duties. He was dismissed in 1617, and although he was reinstated as organist (although not as instructor of the choirboys) in 1622, complaints about him continued, although it is possible that the documents have been misinterpreted. Weelkes died in London in 1623, the immense promise of his early works unfulfilled.

Because Weelkes always worked for a church establishment, it is not possible to date any of his church music. There are twenty-seven anthems that are considered to be both complete and authentic. Because of Chichester's limited musical resources, Weelkes favored the verse anthem. His best include *Give ear, O Lord* and *Give the king thy judgements, O God.* Of his ten services, the "Service for Trebles," musically related to the six-voice full anthem, *Alleluia, I heard a voice,* is outstanding.

With the first madrigal collection of 1597 is found an example of what was to become a mannerism on Weelkes's part: *Our country swains* is divided into two large sections, one moving in rapid quarter- and eighth-note figures, and the other in half and whole notes replete with suspensions. An even stronger signal of a radical new voice is found in the astonishing chromaticism and intense emotion of *Cease sorrowes now.*

A year later, in 1598, Weelkes issued the *Balletts and Madrigals to Five Voyces,* probably in response to Thomas Morley's collection of 1595. Because the ballett form is strophic, and expressive madrigalisms are usually out of place, Weelkes temporarily abandoned the chromatic experiments of the previous set. However, *Harke all ye lovely saints above,* one of the (deservedly) best-known English balletts, while exhibiting the usual bipartite structure and "fa la la" refrain, contrasts syllabic style and triple meter in the first strain with duple meter, longer note values, and chromatic harmonies in the second. This collection ends with an elegy, *Cease now delight* for Lord Borough, in which Weelkes makes a mannerism out of simultaneous use of the major and minor third of a chord, particularly at cadential points.

His most outstanding collection, *Madrigals of 5. and 6. Parts* of 1608, comprises ten madrigals for five voices and ten madrigals for six voices and includes *O Care, thou wilt despatch me,* the culmination of Weelkes's experiments with the expressive use of both chromaticism and conventions of the ballett (notice the mournful and predominantly minor "fa la" refrain). He excelled at word painting: there is no better demonstration of the delights of this technique than *As Vesta was from Latmos hill descending.* One of his six-voice madrigals, *Thule the period of cosmography,* is a monument to the Elizabethan voyages of discovery, musically describing marvelous geographical curiosities.

To his last collection, *Ayres or Phantasticke Spirites for Three Voices* of 1608, Weelkes appended a six-voice elegy for Thomas Morley, *Death have deprived me of my dearest friend.* Some of his most frequently performed works, *Strike it up Tabor, Come sirrah Jack hoe, Fowre armes two neckes, Tan ta ra ran tan tant cryes Mars* come from this print.

Weelkes, aided by his vivid musical imagination and mastery of contrapuntal technique, reconciled the English polyphonic style with the expressivity of the Italian madrigal.

BIBLIOGRAPHY

Arnold, Denis. "Thomas Weelkes and the Madrigal." *Music and Letters,* vol. 31, pp. 1–12.

Brown, David. "The Anthems of Thomas Weelkes." *Proceedings of the Royal Musical Association,* vol. 91, pp. 61–72.

———. *Thomas Weelkes: A Biographical and Critical Study.* 1969.

Brown, David, Walter Collins, and Peter le Huray, eds. *Thomas Weelkes Collected Anthems.* Musica Britannica. Vol. 23. 1966.

Dart, Thurston. "Music and Musicians at Chichester Cathedral, 1545–1642." *Music and Letters,* vol. 42, pp. 221–226.

Fellowes, Edmund Horace. *The English Madrigal School.* Vols. 9–13. 1916–1921; 2nd edition. *The English madrigalists.* Vols. 9–13. 1956.

Ford, Wyn. "Chichester Cathedral and Thomas Weelkes." *Sussex Archaeological Collections,* vol. 100, pp. 156–172.

Kerman, Joseph. *The Elizabethan Madrigal: A Comparative Study.* 1962.

Monson, Craig. "Thomas Weelkes: A New Fa-la." *Musical Times,* vol. 113, pp. 133–135, with musical supplement.

Shepherd, John. "Thomas Weelkes: A Biographical Caution." *The Musical Quarterly,* vol. 66, pp. 505–521.

Laura S. Youens

SEE ALSO

Anglican Church Music; Anthem; Madrigal; Morley, Thomas

Wentworth, Paul (1534–1594)

A strong Puritan and anti-Catholic, Paul Wentworth was a Buckinghamshire gentleman best known for his strong views in Parliament on the issue of the succession. He was born in 1534, his father's estate lying technically in Oxfordshire, but in a part of the county nestled in Buckinghamshire. Accordingly, when Paul Wentworth first sat in the House of Commons in 1559, he did so for the Buckinghamshire borough of Chipping Wycombe. He consolidated his local standing through an advantageous marriage to Helen Agmondesham, widow of William Tildesley, a groom of the chamber. Through her, Wentworth obtained Burnham manor, and he added to the property in later years. Wentworth has left no record of his activities either in the 1559 Parliament or in the first session of the next, held in 1563, when he sat for the larger borough of Buckingham. It was in this Parliament's second session, in 1566, that he made his most important contribution to Elizabeth I's Parliaments.

On November 9, 1566, Elizabeth ordered the House of Commons to end its discussions on the desirability of her marriage and a settlement of the question of succession. The house acquiesced, turning to other business. On the next working day, however, Wentworth demanded to know of his fellow members whether the queen's command "was not against the liberties" of the Commons. He put a number of specific questions to them. Was the commandment not a breach of free speech? Did the privy councilors who delivered her command have the authority to enforce the order or even to insist that the Commons acknowledge that the order should be obeyed? If the answers to these questions was yes, then what offense was committed by those who thought otherwise and declared their opposition publicly in the House? His questions provoked a lengthy debate, but the matter was left unresolved. The subject would be taken up again by his brother, Peter, in later Parliaments. Wentworth's actions did not noticeably affect his career, although he never achieved a position on the justices bench for which he was qualified.

In 1569, Wentworth was called on to play a role in the crisis provoked by the treason of England's leading nobleman, Thomas Howard, fourth duke of Norfolk. It was at Wentworth's manor at Burnham that Norfolk was kept in close confinement before his transfer to the Tower. Elected to the 1572 Parliament, although this time for a Cornish borough and probably with the help of Francis Russell, second earl of Bedford, Wentworth participated in the debates on Norfolk and Mary Queen of Scots. In one speech, he put the matter of the Scottish queen succinctly, and with simple brutality: "whether we should call for an axe or an act." In 1581, he called for the Commons to order a public fast and daily preaching, the latter to take place at seven in the morning before the members assembled. Again the queen was forced to intervene to end discussion on the proposal.

Wentworth did not sit again in Parliament, his time presumably being spent with his large family (four sons and four daughters) and on local affairs. He is certainly known to have been involved in campaigns against recusancy, corresponding over Catholic undergraduates in Oxford and discovering instructions for a mass in a Buckinghamshire house. The queen renewed the lease of his manor at Burnham in 1589, acknowledging his "loyal care, trouble and charge" during the duke of Norfolk's imprisonment. He died in 1594, and was buried in Burnham church, leaving a will with a determinably Protestant preamble.

BIBLIOGRAPHY

Hartley, T.E., ed. *Proceedings in the Parliaments of Elizabeth I, Vol. 1: 1558–1581.* 1981.

Hasler, P.W., ed. *The History of Parliament: The House of Commons, 1558–1603.* 1981.

Neale, J.E. *Elizabeth I and Her Parliaments, 1559–1581.* 1953; repr. 1971.

David Dean

SEE ALSO

Howard, Thomas; Mary Queen of Scots; Parliamentary History; Recusancy

Wentworth, Peter (1524–1597)

The eldest son born to an Oxfordshire gentleman in 1524, Peter Wentworth, like his younger brother, Paul, was known for his enthusiasm for settling the succession issue and defending the liberties of the House of Commons. His second marriage was to Elizabeth, sister of Elizabeth I's secretary, Sir Francis Walsingham. Since another of Walsingham's sisters married the chancellor of the Exchequer, Sir Walter Mildmay, Wentworth was thus related to two of Elizabeth's leading councilors, both determinedly Protestant like himself.

Wentworth served as a justice of the peace in Oxfordshire between 1559 and 1562; his removal was probably due to the fact that his estate was situated in a small outpost of the county in Buckinghamshire. In 1571, he represented Barnstaple in Devon and in the three sessions of the 1572 Parliament he represented the Cornish borough of Tregony. The likely source of patronage here was Francis Russell, second earl of Bedford. He secured a more local seat at Northampton for whom he sat in 1586, 1589, and 1593.

Wentworth was an active M.P. in 1571. It was during this assembly that the division between the radical and moderate Protestants became clear, with a number of acrimonious debates leading to the temporary imprisonment of several vocal Puritans. Wentworth, although he quarreled with Archbishop Matthew Parker over the episcopal drive to enforce the Articles of Religion and the Book of Common Prayer, was much more agitated over criticisms of Robert Bell, who had spoken out against royal licenses. Along with his brother, Paul, Wentworth was active in the parliamentary proceedings against Thomas Howard, fourth duke of Norfolk, and Mary Queen of Scots in 1572. Relentless in his determination, his several speeches urged the House to act quickly in securing their execu-

tion. Once Norfolk was executed and it became clear that Mary would live, Wentworth seems to have lost interest in Parliament, with one of his only two speeches being, characteristically, on the subject of "tale tellers" threatening freedom of speech in the House.

It was in the second session of this Parliament, held in 1576, that Wentworth offered further thoughts on this issue. On the first day he lay out the rights of M.P.s to speak freely according to their consciences, without fear of being seen as disloyal. Frank speech, he argued, was essential for the well-being of the monarch and the state; flattery served the devil, while true speech served the Lord. M.P.s, he claimed, were being constrained by reports that the queen supported a particular matter and would be offended by anyone objecting to it, or that she opposed a matter and anyone promoting it would suffer her displeasure. Such rumors hindered M.P.s' duties to their monarch, themselves, and those they represented. Wentworth also objected to the monarch's ability to affect proceedings by sending messages to the House, such as those prohibiting discussion on religious matters. This last point was a clear attack on the bishops and the royal prerogative, and Wentworth was subsequently silenced. Had the remainder of his surviving speech been delivered, M.P.s would have heard direct criticism of Elizabeth I for her failure to accept their urging Mary Stuart's execution in 1572.

Rather than support their outspoken colleague, the Commons forced Wentworth to defend his words before a committee and then sent him to the Tower, where he remained for all but the final two days of the session. Relatively inactive in his next Parliament, 1581, he did not sit in 1584–1585. In that of 1586–1587, Wentworth tried again to speak on the freedom of M.P.s to speak without constraint after Sir Anthony Cope's bill promoting a radical Prayer Book was halted by the speaker. Wentworth found himself temporarily in prison once again.

Thereafter Wentworth occupied himself with writing a tract on the succession. Its promotion led to more months in prison. Shortly before the 1593 Parliament, again agitating over the succession, Wentworth was sent to the Tower again and not released. His wife, Elizabeth, joined him in confinement; she died in 1596, and Wentworth himself a year later. His *Pithie Exhortation to her Majestie for establishing her successor to the crowne* was published posthumously.

BIBLIOGRAPHY

Elton, G.R. *The Parliament of England, 1559–1581.* 1986.

Hartley, T.E., ed. *Proceedings in the Parliaments of Elizabeth I.* Vol. 1: *1558–1581.* Vol. 2: *1584–1589.* Vol. 3: *1593–1601.* 1981, 1995.

———. *Elizabeth's Parliaments. Queen, Lords, and Commons, 1559–1601.* 1992.

Hasler, P.W., ed. *The History of Parliament: The House of Commons, 1558–1603.* 1981.

Neale, J.E. *Elizabeth I and Her Parliaments, 1559–1581.* 1953; repr. 1971.

———. *Elizabeth I and Her Parliaments, 1584–1601.* 1957; repr. 1971.

David Dean

SEE ALSO

Articles of Religion; Book of Common Prayer; Elizabeth I; Howard, Thomas; Mary Queen of Scots; Mildmay, Walter; Parker, Matthew; Parliamentary History; Walsingham, Francis

Westminster Palace
See Royal Palaces

Whetstone, George (1550–1587)

Remembered most widely for his play *Promos and Cassandra,* George Whetstone was also an elegist, moralist, poet, and soldier. He was born in 1550, the third of Robert Whetstone's (d. 1557) five sons by two wives. His father was a Westcheap haberdasher who resided in St. Vedast parish and owned considerable London property, along with country estates in several counties. Despite his wealth, Robert Whetstone spent most of 1554 imprisoned in the Tower for having been the foreman of the jury that refused to find Sir Nicholas Throckmorton guilty of treason for his role in Wyatt's Rebellion. From his father, George inherited three houses in Cheapside and five smaller ones in St. Vedast parish, receiving tenant income from all of them. George's mother was Margaret Barnard, daughter and coheiress of Philip Barnard of Suffolk. When George was seven his father died and his mother remarried Robert Browne, on whose estate, Walcot Hall in Northamptonshire, George is likely to have spent some, perhaps much, of his youth—next door to the William Cecil's Burghley House, and only four miles from Stamford, where George Gascoigne died in 1577 with Whetstone present.

Whetstone's earliest literary productions are connected with Gascoigne and their circle of friends during the 1570s, likely including Thomas Churchyard, Nicholas Bowyer, and John Bodenham. In 1575, Whetstone contributed prefatory verse to Gascoigne's *Posies* and later wrote an elegy and metrical life of Gascoigne (1577). The elegy form suited Whetstone, and he went on to elegize Nicholas Bacon (1579), James Dyer (1582), Thomas Radcliffe, earl of Sussex (1583), Francis Russell, earl of Bedford (1585), and in 1587, Sir Philip Sidney, alongside whom Whetstone's brother, Barnard (b. 1547), fought at Zutphen.

Throughout his career, Whetstone wrote with an eye toward patronage, dedicating works to Sir Christopher Hatton, Sir Edward Osborne, and Sir William Cecil (Lord Burghley), among others. Whetstone's first book, *The Rocke of Regard* (1576) was a compilation of verse and prose pieces, where he fashioned himself, in the popular practice of the time, an English gentleman of Italian tastes. The book opens with "The Disordered Life of Bianca Maria, Countesse of Celaunt," derived from William Painter's *Palace of Pleasure,* also used later by John Marston for the plot of *The Insatiate Countess* (1613). *The Rocke of Regard* comprises mostly poems of love, both requited and not, but the fourth and longest section (dedicated to Thomas Cecil) ends with a long, semiautobiographical piece in alternating verse and prose, describing, in part, Whetstone's misfortunes as a young man in London, as well as his studies at Furnivall's Inn. Since little of his life is documented elsewhere, many biographical details about Whetstone derive from this piece, and the difficulty in separating the narrative persona from the man makes Whetstone's biography at times problematic.

In 1578, Whetstone published the two-part, ten-act play *The Right Excellent and famous Historye, of Promos and Cassandra,* derived from a novella in Giraldi Cinthio's *Hecatommithi* (1565). *Promos and Cassandra* was never acted and evidently not seen through the press by Whetstone. William Shakespeare later derived the plot of *Measure for Measure* from *Promos and Cassandra,* and may have also used Cinthio's own reworking of the story into the play *Epitia* (1583). Whetstone retold the story himself in *An Heptameron of Civill Discourses* (1582). Although the interconnection of all these works is still debated today, critics often find little merit in *Promos and Cassandra* beyond its link to *Measure for Measure.*

If the autobiographical sections of *The Honorable Reputation of a Soldier* (1585) are to be believed, Whetstone set out to sea after completing his play. He joined Sir Humphrey Gilbert's attempts to reach Newfoundland and the Continent in 1578–1579, though they were repeatedly driven back by rough seas. After traveling through Italy in 1580, Whetstone turned his literary energies to the advice and moral correction of his fellow soldiers, courtiers, and countrymen-at-large. His subjects included marriage and male-female relations in An *Heptameron of Civill Discourses* (1582), and then government, soldiering, gambling, vice, and even the theater in other works of the mid-1580s: *A Mirour for Magestrates of Cyties* and *A Touchstone for the Time* (published together in 1584), followed by *The Honorable Reputation of a Souldier*—all precursors to *The English Myrror* (1586).

In January of 1587, a first edition was published of Whetstone's treatise on the Babington Plot (and other conspiracies), *The Censure of a Loyall Subject;* but the beheading of Mary Stuart barely a month later made necessary a quickly amended, second edition. Whetstone's last publication was the Sidney elegy; and whether he was present or not with his brother when Sidney was killed at Zutphen, he most certainly was in the Netherlands in 1587, at the request of Burghley, when he was killed in September fighting a duel outside Bergen-op-Zoom.

BIBLIOGRAPHY

Alsop, J.D. "George Whetstone and the Sidney Circle." *Notes and Queries,* vol. 37, no. 235, p. 165.

Eccles, Mark. "George Whetstone in Star Chamber." *Review of English Studies,* n.s., vol. 33, pp. 385–395.

Izard, Thomas. *George Whetstone: Mid-Elizabethan Gentleman of Letters.* 1942.

Prouty, Charles T. "George Whetstone and the Sources of *Measure for Measure.*" *Shakespeare Quarterly,* vol. 15, pp. 131–145.

Scanlon, Paul A. "Whetstone's *Rinaldo and Giletta:* The First Elizabethan Prose Romance." *Cahiers Elizabethains,* vol. 14, pp. 3–8.

W.T. Chmielewski

SEE ALSO

Babington Plot; Churchyard, Thomas; Elegy; Gascoigne, George; Gilbert, Humphrey; Italian Literature, Influence of; Painter, William; Shakespeare, William; Sidney, Philip; Throckmorton, Nicholas; Wyatt's Rebellion

Whitaker, William (1548–1595)

The Puritan divine William Whitaker was a dominant theological force in late Elizabethan England. Born at Holme in the parish of Burnley, Lancashire, and educated at St. Paul's School, London, he matriculated in 1564 at Trinity College, Cambridge, where he commenced B.A. in 1568 and M.A. in 1571. He was installed canon of Norwich Cathedral in 1578, the same year he received his B.D., and was incorporated at Oxford. In 1580, he was appointed by the crown to the Regius Professorship of Divinity, to which Elizabeth I added the chancellorship of St. Paul's, London. From this time he emerged as the champion of the teaching of the Church of England interpreted in its highest Calvinist sense. He was as resolute in his opposition to Lutheranism as to Roman doctrine and ritual. In 1586, he was appointed to the mastership of St. John's College, Cambridge. The following year he received his D.D., and in 1595, was installed canon of Canterbury. The furor created at Cambridge concerning the teachings of the Dutch Arminius prompted Whitgift to invite his collaboration in drawing up the Lambeth Articles; in the final draft Whitgift moderated some of the more extreme Calvinist doctrines initially advocated by Whitaker. Disappointed, Whitaker returned to Cambridge, where he fell ill and died on December 4.

BIBLIOGRAPHY

Cannon, Charles K. "William Whitaker's *Disputatio de Sacra Scriptura:* A Sixteenth-Century Theory of Allegory." *Huntington Library Quarterly,* vol. 25, pp. 129–138.

Oxford Dictionary of the Christian Church. P. 1454. 1958.

Porter, H.C. *Reformation and Reaction in Tudor Cambridge.* 1958.

Whitaker, William. *Opera Theologica.* 2 vols. 1610; with a *Life* by A. Assheton, vol. 1, pp. 698–704.

Lee W. Gibbs

SEE ALSO

Arminianism; Calvinism; Church of England; Lambeth Articles; Whitgift, John

Whitchurch, Edward (d. 1561)

Under the patronage of Thomas Cromwell, Edward Whitchurch collaborated with Richard Grafton in publishing the Matthew Bible (1537) and Great Bible (1539), both of which were printed largely at overseas presses. Close in time to his patron's fall, he began a career as a London printer, initially in collaboration with Grafton at shared premises in Greyfriars. By 1545, he operated an independent printing establishment at the sign of the Sun on Fleet Street. Under the terms of patents royal issued under Edward VI, Whitchurch collaborated with Grafton, the king's printer, in operating what were *de facto* government presses at separate locations. In addition to their monopoly on the *Book of Homilies* and Book of Common Prayer, they issued Desiderius Erasmus's *Paraphrases on the New Testament* under government orders that permitted them to commandeer the workers and equipment of other printers. He joined Grafton in printing Protestant propaganda on behalf of the crown. When Mary I excluded Whitchurch from pardon at her accession to the throne, he joined other militant Protestants in fleeing into exile on the Continent. His printing career reached an effective end at that time, with the exception of a single extant book printed under Elizabeth I.

BIBLIOGRAPHY

Duff, E. Gordon. *A Century of the English Book Trade.* 1905.

King, John N. *English Reformation Literature: The Tudor Origins of the Protestant Tradition.* 1982.

John N. King

SEE ALSO

Bible Translations; Cromwell, Thomas; Erasmus, Desiderius; Grafton, Richard; Marian Exiles; Printing, Publishing, and Bookselling

Whitehall Palace
See Royal Palaces

Whitgift, John (1530/1533–1604)

Archbishop of Canterbury and scourge of nonconformists within the English Church, John Whitgift was born sometime between 1530 and 1533 in the port town of Great Grimsby, Lincolnshire. He spent the turbulent reign of Mary I at Cambridge, a hotbed of Calvinism at a time when Roman Catholicism was being reintroduced into the Church of England, graduating B.A. in 1554 and M.A. three years later. But he waited to take holy orders until after the accession of the Protestant Elizabeth I. His reputation as a preacher soon flourished, and he became chaplain to Richard Cox, bishop of Ely. After he earned his B.D. in 1563, Whitgift was appointed Lady Margaret professor of divinity at Cambridge. Within three years, he was licensed as one of the university preachers and, in 1567, was elected master of Pembroke Hall—the same year he was created D.D. Advancements followed in rapid succes-

sion as he became master of Trinity College, then regius professor of divinity. It was at Trinity that he first evinced his autocratic side, passing statutes that ensured conformity in religious as well an academic matters. Such effort gained the notice of the queen; he preached before her in 1569, and Elizabeth invited him to become one of her royal chaplains. Two years later, Whitgift was elected dean of Lincoln, an office he held concurrently with several other ecclesiastical preferents. In 1572, he took it upon himself to respond to a seditious Puritan tract entitled "An Admonition to Parliment" and became embroiled in an acrimonious literary exchange with Thomas Cartwright, an old foe whom Whitgift had expelled from Trinity College. Whitgift eventually discontinued the exchange, perhaps because it had become too undignified, but out of it emerged the foundation on which Whitgift's protégé, Richard Hooker, would build his epic defense of the Church of England as established, *Of the Laws of Ecclesiastical Polity.*

At the suggestion of Archbishop Matthew Parker, Whitgift was created bishop of Worcester in 1577. He brought to his new position the same zeal for conformity that marked his years at Trinity, and, in 1583, he was nominated to succeed Grindal, who had succeeded Parker, as archbishop of Canterbury. Whitgift set out to ensure uniformity of practice within the church; he drew up a set of articles that enforced the Act of Uniformity and use of the Book of Common Prayer, employing the oath *ex officio* to interrogate clergy suspected of illicit activities. The resemblance to the Inquisition was not lost on Whitgift's Puritan opponents, and even the House of Commons questioned the practice. He was undaunted, however, and in 1586 passed the Star Chamber decree, which prohibited public criticism of church polity. Out of this were born the Marprelate Tracts— venomous pamphlets deriding the church in general and Whitgift in particular. He personally directed the search for the responsible parties and, in the case of John Penry, oversaw his execution. In 1593, Whitgift persuaded Elizabeth to put forward legislation banishing anyone who refused to attend church or who attended unauthorized religious meetings. Yet two years later, he drew up nine articles at Lambeth that adopted Calvinist views on predestination and election. Whitgift's doctrinal leanings were always with the Puritans; it was in ecclesiastical practice that he and they parted company. He was at the queen's bedside when she died in 1603 and acted as the chief mourner at Elizabeth's funeral. He himself died the following year.

BIBLIOGRAPHY

Dawley, P.M. *John Whitgift and the English Reformation.* 1954.

Goldblatt, Mark. "John Whitgift." *Dictionary of Literary Biography.* Vol. 132, pp. 333–339. 1993.

Lake, Peter. *Anglicans and Puritans? Presbyterianism and English Conformist Thought from Whitgift to Hooker.* 1988.

Strype, John. *The Life and Acts of John Whitgift, D.D.* 1718.

Mark Goldblatt

SEE ALSO

Book of Common Prayer; Calvinism; Cartwright, Thomas; Church Polity; Cox, Richard; Hooker, Richard; Lambeth Articles; Marprelate Controversy; Parker, Matthew; Penry, John; Puritanism; Recusancy; Uniformity, Act of

Whittingham, William (c. 1524–1579)

Born in Lancashire about 1524, William Whittingham went up to Brasenose College, Oxford, in 1540. In 1545, he became a fellow of All Souls, and three years later was made the senior student of Christ Church. In 1550, he went on study leave to France, where he remained until 1553. He returned to England in that year, but was soon forced to depart again because of his Protestant views. He made his way to Frankfurt-am-Main in 1554, and became the leader of the English exiles there. He was a close friend and colleague of John Knox, and because of this supported replacing the 1552 Prayer Book with a more clearly Calvinist liturgy.

This project divided the Frankfurt Church, and in 1555, Whittingham followed Knox to Geneva, where they were made more welcome. During this time Whittingham was engaged in the translation of the Geneva Bible, which remains his chief monument. In 1559, he became senior minister of the English Church at Geneva, but after the Bible was published in the following year, he returned to England. In 1563, he was made dean of Durham, where he remained until his death.

Whittingham was a Puritan sympathizer, and in 1566, he was attacked for abandoning clerical vestments. His tenure at Durham was marked by strong opposition from more conservative clerical circles, who in 1578 managed to establish a commission to investigate complaints of irregularity against him. The proceedings were delayed by powerful supporters of Whittingham, and still had not advanced very far when he died on June 10, 1579.

BIBLIOGRAPHY

Pollard, A.F. "William Whittingham." *Dictionary of National Biography.* Vol. 21, pp. 150–153. 1909.

Gerald Bray

SEE ALSO

Bible Translations; Calvinism; Knox, John; Marian Exiles; Vestiarian Controversy

Wilbye, John (1574–1638)

Wilbye was already an established madrigal composer in 1601, when *The Lady Oriana* was printed in *The Triumphs of Oriana.* He was born in Diss in 1574 and entered musical service for the Kytson family of Hengrave Hall by 1598. He published two collections of madrigals, the first, *The First Set of Madrigals to 3.4.5. and 6. Voices* in 1598, followed in 1609 by *The Second Set of Madrigales.* Although he lived until 1638, his last ten years spent with Lady Rivers, Lady Kytson's youngest daughter, he composed very little after 1609. It has been suggested that the management of a sheep farm occupied him in his later years.

His output totals fourteen madrigals for three voices, fourteen for four voices, twenty for five voices, and sixteen for six voices. Despite his evident preference for larger-voiced works, his vocal scoring is usually transparent, his melodic lines are marked by sequences, with subtle, always telling major-minor changes of mode. He was influenced by the Italian madrigalists, as shown by his aristocratic appropriation of the Italianate canzonet idiom and use of Italian texts translated into English (*Lady, your words doe spight mee* being one example), and by Thomas Morley, to whom all of the English madrigal composers owed a debt.

Among the most popular of Wilbye's madrigals are *Adew sweet Amaryllis, Oft have I vowde, Stay Coridon thou swaine, Lady when I beehold, Flora gave mee fairest flowers,* and the two-part *Sweet hony sucking Bees.* The melancholy *Draw on sweet night* from his second book, restrained, tightly integrated in structure, yet intensely emotional, is often singled out as the supreme masterpiece of the English madrigal school.

BIBLIOGRAPHY

Brown, David. *John Wilbye.* 1974.

Collet, Robert. "John Wilbye: Some Aspects of his Music." *Score,* vol. 4, pp. 57–64.

Fellowes, Edmund Horace. *John Wilbye: First Set of Madrigals* (1598) and *Second Set of Madrigals* (1609).

The English Madrigal School. 2nd edition. Vols. 6 and 7. 1966.

Kerman, Joseph. *The Elizabethan Madrigal: A Comparative Study.* 1962.

Teo, Kian-Seng. "John Wilbye's Second Set of Madrigals (1609) and the Influence of Marenzio and Monteverdi." *Studies in Music,* vol. 20, pp. 1–11.

Wilson, Christopher. "Some Musico-Poetic Aspects of Campion's Masques." In *The Well Enchanting Skill: Music, Poetry, and Drama in the Culture of the Renaissance: Essays in Honour of F.W. Sternfield,* pp. 91–105. 1990.

Laura S. Youens

SEE ALSO
Madrigal; Morley, Thomas

Willobie, Henry (c. 1574–c. 1596)

Descended from an illegitimate line of the famous Willoughby family, Henry Willobie was second son of Henry and Jane Willoughby. He had an elder brother named William and a younger one, Thomas. He might be the same Willobie who attended Oxford University in 1591 and graduated in 1594–1595 with a B.A.

He was supposed to be the writer of *Willobie his Avisa,* which was first published in 1594 and subsequently underwent six editions. In the preface, one Hadrian Dorrell explains that he publishes it without the notice of the author, who is then abroad in service to the queen. The book consists of seventy-four cantos describing Avisa's firm rejections to the courting of five suitors. Subtitled *The true picture of a modest Maid, and of a chaste and constant wife,* its focus is the praise of Avisa's constancy, whose name means "Amans vxor inuiolata semper amada" ("A louing wife, that neuer violated her faith, is alwaies to be beloued"). She turns down one suitor before marriage and four after. The first suitor is an Italian nobleman; the second is a Spaniard named Caveleiro; the third, a Frenchman initialed D.B. The fourth is D.H., a German and Englishman. The last one is an Italian and Spaniard, Henrico Willobego, who takes the rejection harder than the others and lingers for thirty-one cantos. Attached to his courtship is a long preface explaining how his familiar friend W.S., coveting "to see whether it would sort to a happier end for this new actor, then it did for the old player," gives him ill advice.

Although Dorrell warns us against reading this story as "politike fiction," and in the second edition plainly assures us that neither Avisa nor the suitors refer to real persons, topical readings are always the scholars' main interest about this poem. Acheson thinks W.S. refers to William Shakespeare and that both Avisa and the Dark Lady in Shakespeare's sonnets refer to Ann Davenant, John Davenant's wife. Harrison treats the poem as an answer from the Ralegh group to the attacks from the camp of the earl of Southampton, Henry Wriothesley, to whom Shakespeare dedicated *Venus and Adonis* and *The Rape of Lucrece.* Deluna interprets the story as an artful presentation of the constancy of Elizabeth I under the attacks of her suitors. The riddle remains unresolved.

BIBLIOGRAPHY

Acheson, Arthur. *Shakespeare's Sonnet Story: 1592–1598.* 1933.

Brooke, Tucker. "Willobie's Avisa." *Essays on Shakespeare and Other Elizabethans,* pp. 167–178. 1948.

Deluna, B.N. *The Queene Declined: An Interpretation of Willobie his Avisa with the Text of the Original Edition.* 1970.

Harrison, G.B., ed. *Willobie his Avisa: With an Essay on Willobie his Avisa.* The Bodley Head Quartos. 1966.

Roe, John. "*Willobie his Avisa* and *The Passion Pilgrim:* Precedence, Parody, and Development." *Yearbook of English Studies.* Vol. 23. Pp. 111–125.

Lin, Chih-Hsin

SEE ALSO
Shakespeare, William; Wriothesley, Henry

Wilson, Thomas (c. 1523–1581)

Humanist and statesman, Thomas Wilson was a member of the important group of mid-Tudor Cambridge humanists that included John Cheke, Thomas Smith, and Roger Ascham. Like theirs, his career led him from academic distinction to service to the crown. While still at Cambridge, Wilson became tutor to Charles Brandon, the younger son of the dowager duchess of Suffolk. When Charles and his brother died in 1551, Wilson took the major role in compiling *Vita et obitus duorum fratrum Suffoiciensium,* a volume of Latin prose and Latin and Greek verse; among Wilson's own contributions was a biography of the brothers. Also in 1551, Wilson published *The Rule of Reason,* the first comprehensive text on logic printed in English. This was followed in 1553 by *The Arte of Rhetorique.* Early in Mary's reign Wilson went abroad, spending time first at Padua where he studied civil law. At Rome in 1558, Wilson was imprisoned by the Inquisition, but he was set free in riots following the death of Pope Paul IV, and returned to England by 1560.

Wilson then embarked on the practice of civil law, as an advocate in the Court of Arches and a master of the Court of Requests. He sat in every Parliament from 1563 until his death, and was a royal emissary to Portugal in 1567 and to the Netherlands in 1574 and 1576. He was an investigator of conspiracies surrounding Mary Queen of Scots, and a supporter of English aid to William of Orange. Two further substantial publications were closely related to Wilson's political career. In 1570, he published the first English translation of Demosthenes, *The three Orations of Demosthenes . . . in favour of the Olynthians . . . with those his fower . . . against King Philip;* the elaborate scholarly apparatus with which Wilson surrounded this text included parallels between Philip of Macedon's threat to ancient Athens and Philip II of Spain's threat to contemporary England. *A discourse uppon usurye, by way of Dialogue and oracions,* printed in 1572, strongly opposed renewed legalization of lending at interest, an issue then before Parliament. Through the 1560s and 1570s, Wilson accumulated considerable wealth and lands. In 1577 he became a secretary of state. He died four years later.

The Rule of Reason and *The Arte of Rhetorique* were highly influential texts in their time, going through seven and eight editions, respectively. *The Rule* covers much of the basic content of Scholastic logic, while reflecting to some extent the humanistically oriented logical reforms of Rudolph Agricola. It insistently illustrates its points through references to crucial items of Protestant doctrine. The *Arte* is a comprehensive treatment of all five of the "great arts"— invention, disposition, elocution (style), memory, and pronunciation (delivery)—of which rhetoric was composed in the full Ciceronian conception. Probably the *Arte's* most famous passage is Wilson's critique of "inkhorn terms," words "borrowed" from Latin and other foreign languages, as involving a misguided reaching for eloquence at the expense of intelligibility. At the same time, Wilson advocated "amplification," the heaping up of arguments, sententiae, analogies, and examples, in support of overwhelming rhetorical effectiveness. *A discourse uppon usurye* carries forward the tradition of the humanist dialogue, and displays the knowledge of financial complexities that Wilson gained through his legal and diplomatic work.

In general, Wilson is very representative of the patterns of life and thought of mid-Tudor university-trained intellectuals and crown servants. The works of logic and rhetoric communicate with special vividness the central ambitions and ideals of Wilson and his times, in particular the image of the trained, energetic, and effective orator.

BIBLIOGRAPHY

Howell, Wilbur S. *Logic and Rhetoric in England, 1500–1700.* 1956.

Medine, Peter E. *Thomas Wilson.* 1986.

Mueller, Janel. *The Native Tongue and the Word.* 1984.

Wilson, Thomas. *The Arte of Rhetorique.* Thomas J. Derrick, ed. The Renaissance Imagination. Vol. 1. 1982.

———. *The Art of Rhetoric* (1560). Peter E. Medine, ed. 1994.

———. *A Discourse upon Usury.* R.H. Tawney, intro. 1925.

———. *The Rule of Reason.* Facsimile edition. The English Experience. Vol. 261. 1970.

———, trans. *The three Orations of Demosthenes . . . in favour of the Olynthians . . . with those his fower . . . against King Philip.* Facsimile edition. The English Experience. Vol. 54. 1968.

John F. McDiarmid

SEE ALSO

Ascham, Roger; Brandon, Charles; Cheke, John; Humanism; Logic; Rhetoric

Windsor Palace

See Royal Palaces

Wishart, George (c. 1513–1546)

The facts of the Scottish Reformer George Wishart's early life and education are obscure. Son of an Angus laird and educated at the University of Aberdeen, he taught his pupils in Montrose to read the New Testament in Greek. Threatened with a charge of heresy in 1538 by the bishop of Brechin, he fled to Bristol, England, where a similar accusation was brought against him by John Kerne, dean of Worcester. He was sent to the archbishop of Canterbury, by whom he was convicted and condemned. Wishart recanted, but chose in 1539 or 1540 to leave England for Strasburg, Basle, and Zürich. Here he came into contact with the Swiss Reformers, whose confession, known as *The First Helvetic,* Wishart adopted. Back in England in 1542, he was made a tutor in Corpus Christi College, Cambridge. While there he translated the *Helvetic Confession* from Latin into English. In 1543–1544, he returned to Scotland, where he began, with the assistance of John Knox, to speak out actively to large audiences in support of Reformed doctrines and against current abuses. Wishart was arrested in January 1546, and soon after transferred to Edinburgh Castle. He was burned at the stake by Cardinal Archbishop David Beaton at St. Andrews on March 1, 1546.

BIBLIOGRAPHY

Burleigh, J.H.S. *A Church History of Scotland.* 1960.
Donaldson, Gordon. *The Scottish Reformation.* 1960.
Oxford Dictionary of the Christian Church. P. 1474. 1958.
Lee W. Gibbs

SEE ALSO

Beaton, David; Church of Scotland; Knox, John

Witchcraft

Although belief in witchcraft, sorcery, and magic was embedded in all levels of society by the end of the Middle Ages, the sixteenth century witnessed the development and intensification of those beliefs. The spread of Neoplatonic ideas during the Renaissance encouraged a strong sense of the connection between the physical and spiritual worlds, and among certain sections of the educated elite stimulated investigation of the occult. Conjuration of spirits, alchemy, and astrology were all engaged in as forms of serious scientific inquiry, most famously by John Dee, but increasingly pushed against what was considered lawful. To the majority of the population the magical and spiritual world was no less real, but generally manifested itself in different ways. The insecurity of daily lives meant that ordinary people depended on a range of magical practices, often mixing orthodox church liturgy with folk wisdom, in order to protect themselves from adversity. Cunning folk were often on hand to provide specialist services—for example, healing humans and livestock, finding lost or stolen goods, fortune-telling, or reversing the effects of harmful witchcraft (known as *maleficium*). Both maleficent witches and cunning folk were prosecuted by church and state in the fourteenth and fifteenth centuries, but it was the middle decades of the sixteenth century that ushered in the period of prosecution commonly associated with the so-called European "witch craze."

Political and religious changes in the sixteenth century help to explain the rise of witchcraft prosecutions. Precise origins are unclear, but the frequent occurrence at court of plots involving witchcraft, combined with the insecurity of Tudor monarchs, seem likely causes. The Protestant Reformation from the 1530s, and the associated godly crusades launched in the 1560s, were profoundly significant, as well. Traditional magical practices, frequently tolerated by the medieval church, became outlawed either as superstitious backsliding or a corruption of the new religion. Prayer and faith, it was argued, afforded the only proper protection against misfortune and evil. In addition, via the demonological concerns of educated clergymen, Protestantism encouraged a more widespread popular belief in the direct agency of the devil in daily life—a logical counterbalance to the pervasive and persistent influence of divine Providence. Perhaps most important of all was the move toward political centralization that took place under the Tudors, of which the Reformation and the consequent merging of church and state were the most manifest expressions. Given that centralized unitary authority was first enshrined in law during the reign of Henry VIII, it was perhaps to be expected that a witchcraft act should also have appeared on the statute books at this time. Moreover, the active development of a popular legal culture from the mid-sixteenth century onward formed an essential element of the strengthening of the Tudor state in the peripheries, and it is in this context that the rise of witchcraft prosecutions should be seen.

Not much is known about the legislative procedures by which the "act against conjurations, witchcrafts, sorcery and enchantments" of 1542 came about, but it would seem likely that it was little used; it was repealed in 1547. During the period of the Edwardian Reformation and Marian Counter Reformation no witchcraft act was in force, although prosecutions in the church courts in the 1550s (especially those specifying *maleficium*) do perhaps indicate that official and popular concern with witchcraft was on the increase. Under Elizabeth I an act against witchcraft was finally formulated in 1563. To be convicted of causing death by witchcraft was punished with hanging for a first offense; to harm persons or livestock by a year's imprisonment for a first offense, and death for a second offense. This act was slightly more lenient than its predecessor, but then its application in the courts was much more widespread, and in any case was replaced by another more severe statute in 1604, which lasted until its repeal in 1736. The ecclesiastical authorities continued to try people accused of sorcery and magic after 1563, although prosecutions seem to have been in decline by the end of the 1580s. More common in the church courts after this date were cases of defamation where plaintiffs sought to restore their good name after being being called witches publicly by their neighbors.

The rise in prosecutions cannot simply be explained by changes imposed from above. English justice, as opposed to inquistorial procedure on the Continent, relied on villagers to prosecute suspected criminals, and to provide witnesses to prove a case before a jury. Witchcraft trials and the conflicts that precipitated them, therefore, accurately reflect social tensions in England from the mid-sixteenth century onward: population increase resulting in land hunger, rural unemployment, social dislocation, and price inflation. The scale of poverty, widening economic divides between neighbors, and the institutionalization of poor relief all contributed to circumstances where charity was more likely both to be requested and refused. Denial, harsh words, guilt, and subsequent misfortune could set an accusation in motion, especially if the suspect had a preexisting reputation for using magical arts. Any conflict between neighbors, however, could lead to accusation, given that witchcraft was simply a form of power either imagined by one party, or consicously attempted by the other, as a means of triumphing in a dispute. Most of the accused (80–90 percent) were women, because women were believed to be more susceptible to diabolical temptation than men, and because women's power was commonly held to be more verbal than physical. Explanations of the witch craze that look to a male conspiracy launched against women are unhelpful, especially since it was common for women to accuse other women over conflicts occurring within exclusively female spheres of activity, and for men also to be accused and convicted of *maleficium*.

How important witch-beliefs and witchcraft prosecutions were for the lives of sixteenth-century people has been partly obscured by the disproportionate historical interest in the subject. One gauge is the number of people who were actually executed, in all likelihood less than 500 for the whole of the early modern period. For the Tudor period specifically, the best records survive for the counties of the southeast, where about 250 people were indicted between 1558 and 1597, of whom fewer than a quarter were hanged. Many suspicions and accusations that did reach the courts were never recorded, but even so the scale of the witch craze could never have been that imagined in the more sensationally lurid or politically inspired historical accounts. A statistical profile of the whole early modern period reveals that witchcraft prosecutions were actually in decline from the 1590s, and only saw a brief resurgence (albeit an exceptionally bitter one) in the 1640s. Skeptical voices, such as those of the Kentish gentleman Reginald Scot in the 1580s, were by no

The Witches' Sabbath, from Dr. Fian, *Newes from Scotland* (1592?). This woodcut represents several events in the story narrating how a coven of witches laid a spell on a man who had offended them, causing him to go mad for an hour every day. Reproduced from the original by permission of the Henry E. Huntington Library and Art Gallery.

means common, but it is clear that after 1600, judges and juries were increasingly more reluctant than their predecessors to convict on the sort of evidence offered by victims and witnesses. Witch-beliefs at the village level, however, did not disappear and were still commonplace throughout the seventeenth and eighteenth centuries.

BIBLIOGRAPHY

Briggs, Robin. *Witches and Neighbours: The Social and Cultural Context of European Witchcraft.* 1996.
Sharpe, James. *Instruments of Darkness: Witchcraft in England, 1550–1750.* 1996.
Thomas, Keith. *Religion and the Decline of Magic: Studies in Popular Beliefs in Sixteenth- and Seventeenth-Century England.* 1971.

Malcolm Gaskill

SEE ALSO

Dee, John; Gender; Population and Demographics; Scot, Reginald

Wolfe, John (c. 1547–1601)

The prolific Elizabethan printer John Wolfe was apprenticed on March 25, 1562, to John Day for ten years; he served, according to his own report, only seven. He was also a member of the Fishmonger's Company. Some scholars place his birth as early as 1547 (later dates have been proposed); his family origins are unknown, but suggestions range from a London origin to a family recently emigrated from the Continent. The latter would account for his predilection for publishing Italian and French texts in their original languages, by and for continental Europeans and emigres.

That Wolfe lived for a time in Italy is attested to by two 1576 colophons of Italian religious poems printed in Florence (*La Historia e Oratione di Santo Stefano*, and *Historia et Vita di Santo Bernardino*). In 1579, he published two titles in London, and was probably a partner of the established stationer Henry Kirkham at the Black Boy, opposite the middle door of St. Paul's Cathedral. Wolfe set up his own shop in 1582 on Distaff Lane, near the sign of the Castle. At this time he printed illegally the copyrights of other members of the Stationers' Company and operated secret presses at various places in London. A famous dispute ensued with the Stationers' Company on the right to print. During this period Wolfe was jailed and his printing shop raided by the Stationers' Company. Wolfe transferred from the Fishmongers' to the Stationers' Company (June 11, 1583), and made his peace with them in the following year. He served as substitute beadle and then beadle (1587–1598), during which period he helped persecute the Puritan writer "Martin Marprelate." At this time, he kept an office in Stationers' Hall as well as, after 1591, places of business over against the "Great South Door" of St. Paul's and on St. Paul's Chain.

Wolfe's annual production ranges from under two (1579, 1580) to as many as fifty-four (1590). He effectively stopped printing his own titles in 1591, when his trade materials passed to Robert Bourne, the real printer of titles in 1591–1593 usually credited to Wolfe. He was printer to the city of London (1593–1601). In 1593, his printing materials were dispersed to Adam Islip and John Windet; the latter printed his publications after that date. Windet was appointed the executor of Wolfe's estate (April 22, 1601).

John Wolfe was responsible for the publication of a startling collection of texts in Italian. Many of these were surreptitious, with fictitious places of publication indicated on the title pages; these he sold both in London and on the Continent, notably at the Frankfurt book fairs.

The selecting, editing, proofreading, translating, and introducing of these texts were a collaborative effort, unique at the period, involving Wolfe and a variety of men, many of whom were Italian emigrés living in London. Wolfe's Italian texts included Machiavelli's *I discorsi, Il principe*, 1584, *Historie fiorentine, L'Arte della guerra*, 1587, and *Lasino d'oro*, 1588. He also printed serious essays on religious toleration (*J. Acontius, Essortatione al Timor di Dio*, 1579; F. Betti, *Lettera* [originally 1559], 1587; G. B. Aurelio, *Esamine di varii giudici*, 1587; and Erastus, *Explicatio utrum excommunicatio*, 1589). Other important Italian texts include works on international law by A. Gentili. In addition, Wolfe published Italian and English translations of accounts of foreign travel and exploration (such as Juan Gonzalez de Mendoza, *L'Historia . . . della China*, 1587, 1588; and Giovanni Tommaso Minadoi, *History of the Warres between the Turkes and the Persians*, 1595).

Wolfe published French texts on contemporary news events in France; his works account for about 25 percent of all news from France before 1600. Again, he published French essays involving reasoned assessment of the contemporary religious disputes and espousing a moderate, or "politique" position in support of the claim to the French throne of Henri of Navarre (M. Hurault, *Discourse upon the Present Estate of France*, 1588; *The Excellent Discourse . . . [the Second Discourse]*, 1592; and *Antisixtus*, 1590).

In the area of British literary history, Wolfe had a long professional association with Gabriel Harvey, who probably worked for him as editor and proofreader. He published Harvey's side in the Harvey-Nashe quarrel (1592–1596), and also authors Harvey praised: Edmund Spenser's *Fairie Queene* 1–3 (1590), Barnabe Barnes's *Parthenophil and Parthenophe* (1593), Thomas Churchyard's *Churchyard's Challenge* (1593), Anthony Chute's *Beawtie Dishonoured* (1593), and Robert Southwell's *St. Peter's Complaint* (1595). A prolific and important printer, Wolfe died in 1601.

BIBLIOGRAPHY

Huffman, Clifford C. *Elizabethan Impressions: John Wolfe and His Press.* 1988.

Loewenstein, Joseph. "For a History of Literary Property: Wolfe's Reformation." *English Literary Renaissance*, vol. 18, pp. 389–412.

Parmelee, Lisa Ferraro. *Good Newes from Fraunce: French Anti-League Propaganda in Late Elizabethan England.* 1996.

Clifford C. Huffman

Wollaton Hall

Attributed to Robert Smythson, the master mason and architect responsible for both Longleat House in Wiltshire (1570s) and Hardwick Hall in Derbyshire (1590s), Wollaton Hall is one of a handful of Tudor structures that contributed to the evolution of a distinctive English building type, the "country house," which, though physically located in the country, drew its inspiration and cultural life from the sophisticated art world of London and the court. Like a number of great houses built from the mid-eighteenth century on, Wollaton incorporated classical motifs and sculpture inspired by Italian, Dutch, and Flemish models. Unlike earlier examples, however, it also drew on continental planning devices, notably the ordered, geometrical villa designs of Andrea Palladio, known to both architects and patrons from his *Quattro libri dell'architectura*. The fresh influences ensured that Wollaton Hall represents a significant departure from tradition and a watershed in English architecture.

The house was built between 1580 and 1588 for Sir Francis Willoughby, a wealthy landowner whose estates and coal mines throughout the Midlands supported his extensive patronage of the arts and architecture. It combines a medieval-looking castellated silhouette and corner tourelles with an orderly sequence of classical columns and pilasters that frame the bays and establish clear divisions between the floors. This mixture of styles reflects Willoughby's ambivalent values as a patron: anxious to establish his claim to hereditary status and patriarchal privilege both on his estates and within his family, he favored an architecture that recalled English history and military power, but he was equally concerned with displaying the fruits of his humanist education and his familiarity with Italianate classicism.

At Wollaton, the use of symmetry and axial planning was limited to the upper floor of the house (containing a long gallery and two great chambers with associated suites of smaller chambers and rooms) and to the garden; the ground floor preserved the traditional, symmetrical English sequence of spaces and a complex circulation pattern, frequently found in castles and manor houses, which forced the visitor to execute a series of right-angle turns and to traverse a darkened screens passage before passing through the screen and arriving in the double-height great hall. Nevertheless, by introducing Italianate planning elements into the design of an English country house, Smythson and Willoughby signaled the increasing importance of continental fashions and court culture among English architects and patrons, and thus the erosion of the traditional way of life in the countryside.

BIBLIOGRAPHY

Friedman, Alice T. *House and Household in Elizabethan England: Wollaton Hall and the Willoughby Family.* 1989.

Girouard, Mark. *Robert Smythson and the Elizabethan Country House.* 1983.

Alice T. Friedman

SEE ALSO

Architecture

Wolsey, Thomas (c. 1474–1530)

Born the son of an Ipswich butcher, Thomas Wolsey rose from his humble station to become the most powerful figure in the English state and church for a decade and a half. Traditionally seen as vain, pompous, avaricious, and ambitious, it is now recognized that Wolsey was not primarily driven by private aspirations and the desire to become pope but by his ambition to serve Henry VIII. But he saw himself as the king's junior partner in government, not as a mere crown servant, and his diplomacy left England isolated, his plans for reforming the administration of justice, the economy of England, the finances of the crown, and the affairs of the church being, at best, imperfectly implemented.

Intelligent and hard-working, Wolsey earned a B.A. from Magdalen College, Oxford, in 1488, at age fifteen. He was elected fellow of the college in 1497 and ordained a priest in March 1498. After graduating with the M.A., he became master of the Magdalen College school, where he taught the sons of Thomas Grey, the first marquis of Dorset. He served as junior and senior bursar of Magdalen from 1498–1500, and financed the construction of the college tower. Through Dorset, Wolsey received a rectory in Somerset. He soon acquired two other benefices, and a papal dispensation to hold all three *in commendam*. Following Dorset's death in 1501, Wolsey became chaplain to Henry Deane, archbishop of Canterbury, and then chaplain to Sir Richard Nanfan, deputy of Calais, who in turn recommended him to Henry VII. In 1508, Wolsey went on diplomatic missions to Scotland and to the Low Countries. Two months before his death, Henry VII rewarded him with the deanery of Lincoln.

Wolsey's close ties with Richard Fox, bishop of Winchester, and Sir Thomas Lovell, two of the late king's closest advisors, were an advantage; yet Wolsey's meteoric rise came about because of his effective management of supply and logistics for the king's army and navy during the Anglo-French War of 1512–1513. As reward for negotiating the Anglo-French alliance of 1514, Wolsey received the bishoprics of Lincoln and Tournai; he was appointed archbishop of York on the death of Cardinal Christopher Bainbridge in July 1514; and the following year, at the insistence of Henry VIII, Pope Leo X made him a cardinal. That same year, Wolsey succeeded William Warham as lord chancellor of England.

Wolsey directed all aspects of royal government from the council in Star Chamber; and its rise as an equity court began under Wolsey, who wanted to check corruption and ensure efficient and fair justice, especially to the humble. From Star Chamber, Wolsey regulated prices and carried out a vigorous campaign for the enforcement of statutes against enclosures and the conversion of arable land to pasture. In 1519 and 1525–1526, Wolsey proposed reforms of the royal court and household and of the crown's finances. But his endeavors to make the crown financially self-sufficient were undermined by Henry VIII's personal extravagance and by the exorbitant cost of war and diplomacy. Wolsey succeeded in increasing tax revenues by developing the subsidy, but he was never able to erase the crown's fiscal deficit.

Wolsey centralized his control over the English Church, but by undermining the authority of his fellow bishops he helped clear the way for establishment of the royal supremacy. While Archbishop of York, Wolsey held the dioceses of Bath and Wells (1518–1523), Durham (1523–1529), and Winchester (1529–1530); and he ran the sees of Salisbury, Worcester, and Llandaff for their nonresident Italian bishops. He held in plurality several other benefices, including abbot of St. Albans, one of the wealthiest abbeys in England. In 1518, Pope Leo X reluctantly appointed him legate *a latere*, which gave him precedence and power over all other ecclesiastical authorities in England, including the archbishop of Canterbury. In 1524, under the guise of reforming the English Church, he persuaded Pope Clement VII to grant him this office for life.

Although intricate details of foreign policy occupied much of Wolsey's time, it is now acknowledged that no coherent plan guided this policy, and that he was directed by the whim and will of Henry VIII, seeking the most expedient means to satisfy the king's pleasure and magnify his honor and influence among European princes. For years Wolsey worked assiduously in the treacherous world of continental diplomacy to place Henry at the center of European politics and to allow him to play arbiter of Europe. But the ever-shifting tides of Habsburg-Valois-Papal politics and wars overwhelmed his efforts both to aggrandize his king and country and, later, to enlist support for Henry's divorce from Katherine of Aragon. Both Henry and England were left isolated.

In 1529, following an indictment for *praemunire*, Wolsey was forced to surrender the great seal and withdraw to York. In the spring and summer of 1530, Wolsey engaged in secret correspondence with Francis I, Charles V, and Clement VII. Perhaps he wanted to show Henry his usefulness as a diplomat; instead he exposed himself to charges of treason. Wolsey was placed under arrest, but died a broken man on November 24 while en route to London.

BIBLIOGRAPHY

Bernard, G.W. *War, Taxation, and Rebellion in Tudor England: Henry VIII, Wolsey, and the Amicable Grant of 1525.* 1986.

Gunn, S.J., and P.G. Lindley, eds. *Cardinal Wolsey: Church, State, and Art.* 1991.

Guy, J.A. *The Cardinal's Court: The Impact of Wolsey in Star Chamber.* 1977.

Gwyn, Peter. *The King's Cardinal: The Rise and Fall of Thomas Wolsey.* 1990.

Ridley, Jasper. *The Statesman and the Fanatic: Thomas Wolsey and Thomas More.* 1982.

Scarisbrick, J.J. *Henry VIII.* 1968.

John M. Currin

SEE ALSO

Bainbridge, Christopher; Enclosures; Foreign Relations and Diplomacy; Fox, Richard; Henry VIII; *Praemunire*; Royal Household; Star Chamber, Court of; Taxation; Universities; Warham, William

Wray, Christopher (c. 1521–1592)

Speaker of the House of Commons and lord chief justice of the Court of Queen's Bench, Sir Christopher Wray was born of an unremarkable Yorkshire family. He began his education at Cambridge but did not take a degree. Wray entered Lincoln's Inn and soon after married a young Lincolnshire widow, Anne Girlington. He and his family seem to have been Catholic sympathizers. During Mary's reign he represented Boroughbridge in each meeting of Parliament. His religious beliefs were probably not strong, however; they certainly did not hurt his career either at Lincoln's Inn or in governmental service. He rose under Elizabeth I to become Lent reader in 1563 and 1567, and treasurer in 1565. In 1567, he entered the service of the crown as a serjeant-at-law and within a few years had become a justice of Lancaster. The crown's confidence in him was demonstrated by his selection as speaker of the House of Commons for the 1571 session. Wray did not distinguish himself, however, as he was unable to exert firm leadership in the face of strong criticism from members concerning the issue of free speech. Instead of regulating debate on a number of bills seeking to make changes in the religious settlement of 1559, he gave many members interested in reform the opportunity to express their views. William Cecil, Lord Burghley, had to admonish him to regain the initiative in the House. He did not sit for Parliament again. Instead, he was appointed a justice of Queen's Bench in 1572 and chief justice two years later. In these offices he advised the House of Lords in time of Parliament. As chief justice he presided over the trials of John Stubbe, William Parry, Edmund Campion, and Sir John Perrot, to name a few.

BIBLIOGRAPHY

Elton, G.R. *The Parliament of England, 1559–1581.* 1986.
Hasler, P.W. *The House of Commons, 1558–1601.* 1981.
Neale, J.E. *Elizabeth I and Her Parliaments, 1559–1581.* 1958.

Robert J. Mueller

SEE ALSO

Campion, Edmund; Cecil, William; King's or Queen's Bench, Court of; Parliamentary History

Wriothesley, Henry, Third Earl of Southampton (1573–1624)

Best known as a soldier and literary patron of William Shakespeare and others, and while prominent in his own time, Henry Wriothesley never reached the political heights anticipated for him. Born into a Catholic family, his grandfather, the first earl, was Henry VIII's lord chancellor. Southampton's father, the second earl, died before his son's eighth birthday, at which time (his older brother having died) he both succeeded to the earldom and became a royal ward; his guardian was William Cecil, Lord Burghley, in whose household he was introduced to humanistic education. Southampton went up to St. John's College, Cambridge, in 1585; before he took his degree four years later, his name was entered on the books of Gray's Inn.

Presented at court around 1590, he attracted favorable notice from Elizabeth I and others and became the friend and protege of the earl of Essex. At about this time, he paid a substantial fine out of his estate for refusing to marry Cecil's granddaughter, Lady Elizabeth Vere. Southampton quickly became known as a literary patron; Barnabe Barnes, Thomas Nashe, and John Florio all dedicated works to him, as did Shakespeare—*Venus and Adonis* in 1593 and *The Rape of Lucrece* in 1594. He won recognition for bravery on Essex's largely unsuccessful expedition to the Azores in 1597. Shortly thereafter, Southampton was involved for the first time (though not for the last) in a scuffle at court. He further antagonized Elizabeth by marrying without her permission a maid of honor, Elizabeth Vernon, Essex's first cousin, when she became pregnant; the queen briefly committed them both to the Fleet.

Southampton then embarked on a path that nearly cost him his life. When Essex equipped an army to fight in Ireland, he wanted Southampton as general of his horse; but the queen blocked the nomination. Arriving in Ireland, Essex defied the queen and made the appointment himself. She dismissed Southampton and rebuked Essex. Planning for Essex's insurrection took place at Southampton's London residence; the conspirators negotiated with the Lord Chamberlain's Men a revival of Shakespeare's *King Richard II,* which took place on February 7, 1600/1, the day before the rebellion. Southampton, Essex, and others were condemned for treason. Essex was executed; Southampton, spared following Robert Cecil's intervention, remained in jail until Elizabeth's death two years later. Painted many times, in one portrait he is in a room of the Tower, accompanied by his cat.

Even before traveling to England to be crowned, James I freed Southampton. His lands and title were restored, and James conferred on him a number of minor appointments without extending full trust. Southampton helped finance colonial exploration as a shareholder; he was a member of the Virginia Company (of which he became treasurer in 1620), the East India Company, and the North-West Passage Company. The king appointed him a privy councilor in 1619. As a member of Parliament, Southampton opposed the king's favorite, Buckingham, and encouraged a pro-Protestant foreign policy, having converted to the faith at an earlier (unknown) date. Accompanied by his elder son, he made his last military expedition as a volunteer to fight in the Low Countries against Spain. Both fell ill of a fever; the son predeceased his father by five days.

Many scholars have identified Southampton with the male friend of Shakespeare's sonnets, though certainty on the matter is impossible. The young man is portrayed as the literary patron of the speaker and others; Southampton is the only known patron of Shakespeare, whose second dedication sheds the stiff formality of the first. The earlier sonnets of the sequence, presumably written not long after the later dedication, are consistent with the known facts of Southampton's life at the time. A contemporary describes Southampton's daily attendance at plays, and he knew leading members of Shakespeare's acting company. In 1709, Nicholas Rowe reports on the (possibly dubious) authority of William D'Avenant that Shakespeare was given £1,000 by Southampton to "go through with a purchase which he heard he had a mind to."

BIBLIOGRAPHY

Akrigg, George Philip V. *Shakespeare and the Earl of Southampton.* 1968.

Green, Martin. *Wriothesley's Roses in Shakespeare's Sonnets, Poems, and Plays.* 1993.

Rowse, A.L. *Shakespeare's Southampton, Patron of Virginia.* 1965.

Stropes, Charlotte Carmichael. *The Life of Henry, Third Earl of Southampton.* 1922.

Richard A. Levin

SEE ALSO

Barnes, Barnabe; Cecil, William; Devereux, Robert; East India Company; Florio, John; Nashe, Thomas; Shakespeare, William

Wriothesley, Thomas, First Earl of Southampton (1505–1550)

Born into a line of heralds, Thomas Wriothesley owed his ascent to his cultivation of the law. He studied civil law at Trinity Hall, Cambridge, under the tutelage of Stephen Gardiner, and in 1534 he was admitted to Gray's Inn. Wriothesley was employed as a clerk of the signet from 1530, at which time he was resident in Gardiner's house;

but he had early attached himself to Thomas Cromwell, who used Wriothesley as his representative in the office of the privy seal. An embassy to the Netherlands was followed in 1539 by Wriothesley's election to Parliament, Cromwell being his nominator. In 1540, he joined the Privy Council and became joint principal secretary with Ralph Sadler. Created a baron in 1544, Wriothesley also became lord chancellor on the death of Thomas Audley in that year. His financial expertise and assiduous attention to business earned him praise from Henry VIII and the earldom of Southampton on the king's death.

Wriothesley's religious opinions are complex. Gardiner had disliked his plans to use ex-monastic revenue to fund public works and a standing army, and their distance was increased by Wriothesley's destruction of St. Swithin's shrine in Winchester in 1538. He invested heavily in monastic land, and vilified the papacy on his election as chancellor. Yet Wriothesley is notorious for having personally racked Anne Askew, and may have been viewed by Edward Seymour, duke of Somerset, as a religious conservative; this would explain his loss of the chancellorship in March 1547. The official grounds, stating that Wriothesley had exceeded his authority in delegating his Chancery duties, are highly implausible. The earl had clashed with Seymour in the 1540s and was suspicious of Somerset's political character. He was thus a prime mover in the coup against Somerset of October 1549, which may have been planned at his London house.

Hans Holbein's drawing of Wriothesley survives.

BIBLIOGRAPHY

Jordan, W.K. *Edward VI: The Young King.* 1968.

Slavin, Arthur J. *Tudor Men and Institutions.* 1972.

———. "The Fall of Lord Chancellor Wriothesley: A Study in the Politics of Conspiracy." *Albion,* vol. 7. 1975.

J.P.D. Cooper

SEE ALSO

Askew, Anne; Audley, Thomas; Cromwell, Thomas; Gardiner, Stephen; Sadler, Ralph; Seymour, Edward

Wyatt's Rebellion

Named for the Kentish gentleman Sir Thomas Wyatt the Younger, a member of Henry VIII's council in France during the campaigns of the 1540s, and one of the initial ringleaders of this rising, Wyatt's Rebellion arose after the failure of parliamentary petition of November 1553, asking that the newly crowned Mary Tudor marry an Englishman. Fearful of the foreign match with Philip of Spain, which then proceeded to unfold, the plotters probably hoped to have Princess Elizabeth marry an English aristocrat, Sir Edward Courtenay, and supersede Mary as queen.

The leading conspirators included Sir Peter Carew, Sir James Croft, and Henry Grey, the duke of Suffolk, as well as Wyatt. They planned for a coordinated series of risings to erupt simultaneously in mid-March 1554, in Herefordshire, Kent, Devon, and Leicestershire, along with French naval support in the Channel. Word of the plot leaked out, causing the leaders to act sooner then they had planned and in some cases to abandon their hopes at an early stage. Only Wyatt, gathering a substantial force dominated by his own numerous tenants in late January, managed to proceed as planned. From such Medway valley centers as Maidstone, Rochester, Tonbridge, and Sevenoaks, Wyatt's forces managed to sweep royalist opposition from their path. They then marched on Gravesend, where the aged third duke of Norfolk had been sent to stop him with some 500 Londoners. When most of this force deserted and joined the rebels, Norfolk retreated hastily to London.

But Wyatt himself was slow to catch up with the vanguard of his forces, allowing time for Londoners to prepare their defences. This they did with the encouragement of Queen Mary, who rallied them with a stirring speech at the Guildhall. Though Wyatt took Southwark, he found no sympathy among the Londoners themselves. A desperate march west along the south bank of the Thames to Kingston, then across the bridge and back east to attack the city on February 6, failed by a hairsbreadth as the queen's defenders stood their ground at Ludgate.

Wyatt's surrender, along with several hundred followers, marked the end of the most nearly successful of all Tudor rebellions, and proved a victory of strategy and command for the novice queen. Having rallied her subjects to her side, Mary sustained her political triumph by treating most of Wyatt's forces with leniency, though Wyatt himself and some forty of his chief followers were executed. Some controversy remains as to whether the episode should be seen as an anti-Catholic rising, as Mary's supporters interpreted it, or merely an anti-Spanish protest, as Wyatt insisted. The former interpretation allowed the government to cast Protestants in a treasonous light; the latter allowed them to appear loyal subjects fearful of Spanish influence. Both considerations still seem significant, as do a variety of economic and political tensions among Wyatt's followers in Kent.

BIBLIOGRAPHY

Clark, Peter. *English Provincial Society from the Reformation to the Revolution: Religion, Politics, and Society in Kent, 1500–1640.* 1977.

Loades, D.M. *Two Tudor Conspiracies.* 1965.

Thorp, Malcolm. "Religion and the Wyatt Rebellion of 1554." *Church History,* vol. 47. 1978.

Robert Tittler

SEE ALSO
Mary I; Philip II; Treason

Wyatt, Thomas
See Sonnet Sequences; Tottell, Richard; Versification; Verse Anthologies

Wyatt, Thomas, the Younger
See Wyatt's Rebellion

Y

Yelverton, Christopher (c. 1535–1612)

Judge, parliamentarian, and amateur dramatist, Christopher Yelverton was educated at Gray's Inn in the 1550s. While a student, Yelverton wrote an epilogue to the blank verse tragedy *Jocasta* (c. 1566), written by his colleague George Gascoigne. The play was subsequently performed at the Inn, and it might have been this event that encouraged Yelverton to take an active part in other masques and celebrations there. (Yelverton was treasurer of the society in 1579 and 1585.)

His political and legal careers were substantial. In the Parliament of 1562–1563, he represented Brackley, Northamptonshire; in 1572, he was returned to Parliament; and the same year he was appointed recorder of Northampton. Yelverton performed other parliamentary services in 1592–1593 and 1597. During this last period he was chosen speaker. He is reputed to have written a devotional poem that he read to the house every morning.

Yelverton was appointed queen's serjeant in 1589, and justice of the Court of King's Bench on February 2, 1602. James I renewed this patent and made him a knight of the Bath the next year. He married Margaret, daughter of Thomas Catesby, and had two sons and four daughters. His eldest son, Henry, followed in his father's footsteps as a judge and parliamentarian for Northampton.

BIBLIOGRAPHY

Stagg, Louis Charles. *The Figurative Language of the Tragedies of Shakespeare's Chief Sixteenth-Century Contemporaries.* 1984.

Yelverton, Christopher. *The Farewell Address of Sir Christopher Yelverton to the Hon. Society of Gray's Inn on becoming Queen's Serjeant . . . in 1589.* 1882.

S.P. Cerasano

SEE ALSO

Gascoigne, George; Inns of Court; King's or Queen's Bench, Court of; Parliamentary History

Yeomen

See Social Classes

Secondary Materials for Tudor Visual Arts

There is no comprehensive treatment of the visual arts in Tudor England. The closest approximation is Eric Mercer, *English Art, 1553–1625* (Oxford, 1953), which does give some coverage to things produced prior to the accession of Elizabeth, but treats them much less fully than Elizabethan and Jacobean work. James Lees-Milne, *Tudor Renaissance* (London, 1951), sets the visual arts in relation to English culture in general with regard to this major development in style and stance. *Albion's Classicism: the Visual Arts in Britain, 1550–1660,* eds. Lucy Gent and Nigel Llewellyn (New Haven and London, 1995), is a lively collection of essays by several contributors that brings various postmodern perspectives to bear on work in many forms; it is more useful for suggesting ways to think about early modern art than as an introduction to the art forms themselves. As might be expected, painting (especially portraits), architecture, and sculpture dominate the bibliography, but Mercer has instructive pages on interior decoration and furniture, and there are excellent recent treatments of silver and jewelry.

Important general studies of Tudor painting include Ellis Waterhouse, *Painting in Britain, 1530 to 1790* (New Haven and London, 1994 and many earlier editions); David Piper's chapter on "Tudor and Stuart Painting" in *The Genius of British Painting* (New York, 1975); and Roy Strong, *The Elizabethan Image* (London, 1969). Strong has produced many books and articles on Tudor portraits; see especially *The English Icon* (London and New Haven, 1969), and *Tudor and Jacobean Portraits* (2 vols., London, 1969). His book on *The English Renaissance Miniature* (London and New York, 1983) is a good place to start an investigation of this appealing body of work; see also Erna Auerbach, *Tudor Artists* (London, 1954), which is very

useful for the earlier painters, and Mary Edmonds, *Hilliard and Oliver* (London, 1980), which also offers a look at the immigrant artistic community in London, whose members produced much of the art in England toward the end of the period.

The standard introduction to Tudor architecture is John Summerson, *Architecture in Britain, 1530 to 1830* (Harmondsworth and New York, 1991 and many earlier editions). Malcolm Airs, *Tudor and Jacobean: a Guide and Gazetteer* (London, 1982), and Marcus Whinney, *An Introduction to Elizabethan and Jacobean Architecture* (London, 1952), both supply useful overviews. For royal palaces, the best current study is Simon Thurley, *The Royal Palaces of England* (London, 1993). Maurice Howard, *The Early Tudor Country House: Architecture and Politics, 1490–1550* (London, 1987), counters the Elizabethan and stylistic bias of earlier treatments. The many works of Mark Girouard investigate the lifestyle as well as the visual style of the Tudor country house. Both Girouard, in *Robert Smythson and the Elizabethan Country House* (New Haven, 1983), and Alice T. Friedman, in *House and Household in Elizabethan England: Wollaton Hall and the Willoughby Family* (Chicago, 1989), discuss the work of the builder-architect who designed some of the period's most distinctive buildings. Malcolm Airs, *The Tudor and Jacobean Country House* (Phoenix Mill, 1995 and earlier editors) pays special attention to building as a craft. These books concentrate on the great houses built by rulers and magnates, but Eric Mercer, *English Vernacular Houses* (London, 1975), gives much information on the dwellings of ordinary people.

The major survey of Tudor sculpture is John Physick's revision of Margaret Whinney, *Sculpture in Britain, 1530 to 1830* (London and New York, 1988). Arthur M. Hind,

Engraving in England in the Sixteenth and Seventeenth Centuries (3 vols., Cambridge, England, 1952–1964), has long been the gateway to study of Tudor woodcuts and engravings, and the *Guide to English Illustrated Books, 1536–1607,* by Ruth Luborsky and Elizabeth Morley Ingram (Tempe, 1999), greatly facilitates access to this richest and most various element of the Tudor visual legacy. See also Sidney Colvin, *Early Engraving and Engravers in England (1545–1695)* (London, 1905). Diana Scarisbrick has filled a long-standing gap with her account of *Tudor and Jacobean Jewellery* (1995), and Philippa Glanville supplies a comprehensive view of the art form that was also the most important form of portable wealth in the period, *Silver in Tudor and Early Stuart England: A Social History and Catalogue of the National Collection, 1460–1660* (London, 1990). Although specialized, Santina M. Levey's *An Elizabethan Inheritance: The Hardwick Hall Textiles* (1998) is a richly illustrated introduction to woven interior decoration at one of the great Tudor houses.

Tudor visual art is scattered through dozens of museums and hundreds of houses; many of the finest items are part of the British royal collections and rarely, if ever, available for general viewing. However, most of the great Tudor houses are open to the public and have splendid Tudor objects on display: Hampton Court Palace, Knole Park, Hatfield House, and Hardwick Hall are particularly rich. The largest and widest assortment of items in all media—including the primary collection of Tudor miniatures—will be found in the Victoria and Albert Museum in London. The Fitzwilliam Museum in Cambridge also has fine holdings of ceramics, textiles, and silver. Many of the best Tudor portraits are assembled in the National Portrait Gallery, just off Trafalgar Square in London. The National Gallery around the corner also has important works.

David Evett

Materials for Tudor Education and Science

Broad surveys of English education during the Tudor period include Kenneth Charlton, *Education in Renaissance England* (London, 1965); Joan Simon, *Education and Society in Tudor England* (Cambridge, England, 1967); Michael V.C. Alexander, *The Growth of English Education, 1348–1648* (University Park, Pa., 1990); and Rosemary O'Day, *Education and Society, 1500–1800* (London, 1982). For the Grammar schools—in addition to the above—see T.W. Baldwin, *William Shakspere's Small Latine and Lesse Greeke* (Urbana, 1944), Jo Ann H. Moran, *The Growth of English Schooling, 1348–1548* (Princeton, 1985), David Cressy, *Literacy and the Social Order: Reading and Writing in Tudor and Stuart England* (Cambridge, England, 1980), and Rebecca W. Bushnell, *A Culture of Teaching* (Ithaca, N.Y., 1996). For the universities, see James McConica, ed., *The Collegiate University* (Oxford, 1986); Mark H. Curtis, *Oxford and Cambridge in Transition, 1558–1642* (Oxford, 1959); and W.T. Costello, *The Scholastic Curriculum at Early Seventeenth-Century Cambridge* (Cambridge, Mass., 1958). The changing role of intellectuals within political culture has been discussed by Fritz Caspari, *Humanism and Social Order in Tudor England* (Chicago, 1954); James K. McConica, *English Humanists and Reformation Politics Under Henry VIII and Edward VI* (Oxford, 1965); Arthur B. Ferguson, *The Articulate Citizen and the English Renaissance* (Durham, N.C., 1965); and Alistair Fox and John Guy, eds., *Reassessing the Henrician Age* (Oxford, 1986).

An excellent broad survey of classical learning in early modern England is J.W. Binns, *The Intellectual Culture in Elizabethan and Jacobean England: The Latin Writings of the Age* (Leeds, 1990). For the role of print, reading practices, and publication see Elizabeth L. Eisenstein, *The Printing Press as an Agent of Change* (Cambridge, England, 1979); William H. Sherman, *John Dee: The Politics of Reading and Writing in the English Renaissance* (Amherst: University of Massachusetts Press, 1995); Eugene Kintgen, *Reading in Tudor England* (Pittsburgh, 1997); Arthur F. Marotti, *Manuscript, Print, and the English Renaissance Lyric* (Ithaca, N.Y., 1995); and H.R. Woudhuysen, *Sir Philip Sidney and the Circulation of Manuscripts* (Oxford, 1996). Historical studies and antiquarianism is the subject of studies by F.J. Levy, *Tudor Historical Thought* (San Marino, Calif., 1967); Arthur B. Ferguson, *Clio Unbound* (Durham, N.C., 1979); and Stan A.E. Mendyk, *"Speculum Britanniae": Regional Study, Antiquarianism, and Science in Britain to 1700* (Toronto, 1989).

The introduction of scientific studies into England is covered in Antonia McLean, *Humanism and the Rise of Science in Tudor England* (New York, 1972); Francis R. Johnson, *Astronomical Thought in Renaissance England* (rpt. New York, 1968); Mordechai Feingold, *The Mathematicians' Apprenticeship: Science, Universities, and Society in England, 1560–1640* (Cambridge, England, 1984); E.G.R. Taylor, *The Mathematical Practitioners of Tudor and Stuart England, 1485–1714* (Cambridge, England, 1954); and David W. Waters, *The Art of Navigation in England in Elizabethan and Early Stuart Times,* 2nd edition (Greenwich, England, 1978). For the role of geographical knowledge in English culture, see P.D.A. Harvey, *Maps in Tudor England* (London, 1993); *Monarchs, Ministers, and Maps: The Emergence of Cartography as a Tool of Government in Early Modern Europe,* ed. David Buisseret (Chicago, 1992); and Lesley B. Cormack,

Charting an Empire: Geography at the English Universities, 1580–1620 (Chicago, 1997).

For astrology, see Don Cameron Allen, *The Star-Crossed Renaissance: The Quarrel about Astrology and Its Influence in England* (repr. New York, 1966); Bernard Capp, *Astrology and the Popular Press: English Almanacs, 1500–1800* (London, 1979); and J.C. Eade, *The Forgotten Sky: A Guide to Astrology in English Literature* (Oxford, 1984). Allen Debus's *The English Paracelsians* (London, 1965) provides a good introduction to the alchemical literature of the Tudor age. See also Stanton J. Linden, *Darke Hierogliphicks: Alchemy in English Literature from Chaucer to the Restoration* (Lexington, Ky., 1996). For botany, see R.T. Gunther, *Early British Botanists and Their Gardens* (Oxford, 1922), and Charles E. Raven, *English Naturalists from Neckam to Ray* (Cambridge, England, 1947).

Attitudes toward secular learning in Protestant England are discussed by Howard Schulz, *Milton and the Forbidden Knowledge* (New York, 1955), and John Morgan, *Godly Learning: Puritan Attitudes Towards, Reason, Learning, and Education, 1560–1640* (Cambridge, England, 1986). For the relationship between science and religion, see Paul Ho. Kocher, *Science and Religion in Elizabethan England* (repr. New York, 1969). For discussion of secularization and rationalization, see Keith Thomas, *Religion and the Decline of Magic* (London, 1972), and C. John Sommerville, *The Secularization of Early Modern England* (Oxford, 1992).

Mordechai Feingold

Primary Materials for Tudor Literature

Tudor literature is fortunate in being the earliest to bene-fit in its preservation and transmission by the invention of the printing press and moveable type. Words have often changed meaning, but the historically based *Oxford English Dictionary* in thirteen volumes with three supplementary volumes (1933–1982), now available online, gives the earlier meanings, often citing Tudor authors. R.B. McKerrow's *Dictionary of Printers and Booksellers* (London, 1910) is an index to early publishing, and his *Introduction to Bibliography for Literary Students* (Oxford, 1927; repr. 1967) tells how books were made. The *Register of the Company of Stationers of London, 1554–1640,* ed. Edward Arber (5 vols.; London, 1875–1894), lists all the books licensed for publication; and the (revised) *Shorttitle Catalogue,* ed. Katharine F. Pantzer (London, 1976–1991), lists all books extant, as well as the location of early copies in America and elsewhere. *Dramatic Documents from Elizabethan Playhouses* have been collected by W.W. Greg (Oxford, 1931), and since 1979 the ongoing *Records of Early English Drama* reproduces all early documents by county (Toronto). Alexandra Halasz, *The Marketplace of Print* (Cambridge, England, 1997), discusses sales; for the language, consult Paula Blank, *Broken English* (Pittsburgh, 1996).

Nearly all the early printed works have been reproduced on microfilm by University Microfilms, and many literary works have been reproduced in facsimile as *The English Experience* by Theatrum Orbis Terrarum Ltd. (Amsterdam) and DeCapro Press (New York). A number of reliable facsimiles are also available from Scolar Press (Menston), and plays and dramatic documents from the Malone Society publications (Oxford). The Renaissance English Text Society annually publishes facsimiles or accurate transcriptions of manuscripts or rare texts of prose and poetry, such as the poetry of Sir Walter Ralegh and Lady Mary Roth's *Urania*. Editions of rare texts by early modern women are being issued in the series Women Writers in English, 1350–1850, based on the Women's Writers Project at Brown University (www.wwp.brown.edu). Scolar Press is issuing *The Early Modern Englishwoman: A Facsimile Library of Essential Works (Part One: The Essential Writings, 1500–1640),* with two more series projected: *Essential Works for the Study of Early Modern Women,* and *Manuscript Writing.* Facsimile editions of the New and Old Testaments of William Tyndale, ed. David Daniell (New Haven, 1989, 1992), of the Coverdale Bible (London, 1838), and of the Geneva Bible, ed. Lloyd Berry (Madison, Wis., 1969), are also useful.

Anthologies of Tudor poetry have been edited by Richard S. Sylvester (New York; repr. 1984), and Emry Jones (Oxford, 1991), of fiction by Paul Salzman (Oxford, 1987), of prose by Edmund Creeth (Garden City, N.Y., 1969), of criticism by G. Gregory Smith in three volumes (Oxford, 1904; repr. 1964), and of non-Shakespearean drama by Arthur F. Kinney (Oxford, 1999). The most reliable texts of the individual plays are those published in the Revels Plays (Manchester, England) and the New Mermaids (London). Popular rogue literature is most recently edited by Arthur F. Kinney (Amherst, Mass., 1990). Poetry by women is collected in *Women Poets of the Renaissance,* ed. Marion Wynne-Davies (New York, 1999).

Arthur F. Kinney and William B. Long

Secondary Materials for Tudor Literature

Secondary scholarship in Tudor literature, principally poetry and drama, has set high standards that have served as models for work in other periods. The most important surveys are C.S. Lewis, *English Literature in the sixteenth Century, Excluding Drama* (Oxford, 1959; under revision by Jonathan Bate); *Elizabethan Poetry* by Hallet Smith (Cambridge, Mass., 1952); *Humanist Poetics* (for fiction) by Arthur F. Kinney (Amherst, Mass., 1986); *The English Drama, 1485–1585* by F.P. Wilson and G.K. Hunter (Oxford, 1963); *English Drama, 1585–1642,* by Hunter (1998); and *A New History of English Drama,* eds. John D. Cox and David Scott Kastan (New York, 1997). Other important surveys include W.S. Howell, *Logic and Rhetoric in England, 1500–1700* (1961); Thomas M. Greene, *The Light in Troy: Imitation and Discovery in Renaissance Poetry* (New Haven, 1984); Barbara K. Lewalski, *Protestant Poetics and the Sixteenth-Century Religious Lyric* (Princeton, 1979); and Douglas L. Peterson, *The English Lyric from Wyatt to Donne* (Princeton, 1967) for poetry; Walter R. Davis, *Idea and Act in Elizabethan Fiction* (Princeton, 1969) for fiction; and for drama, *Elizabethan-Jacobean Drama,* ed. G. Blakemore Evans (London, 1987), Gerald Eades Bentley, *The Professions of Dramatist and Player in Shakespeare's Time, 1590–1642* (Princeton, as one volume, 1986), Alan Dessen, *Elizabethan Stage Convention and Modern Interpretation* (Cambridge, England 1984), and *Recovering Shakespeare's Theatrical Vocabulary* (Cambridge, England, 1995); and the works of Andrew Gurr, especially *Playgoing in Shakespeare's London* (Cambridge, England, 1987), *The Shakespearean Stage, 1547–1642* (3rd edition, Cambridge, 1992), and *The Shakespearean Playing Companies* (Oxford, 1996). Finally, recent studies in drama include Scott McMillin and Sally-Beth MacLean, *The Queen's Men and Their Plays* (Cambridge, 1998), and Greg Walker, *The Politics of Performance in Early Renaissance Drama* (Cambridge, 1998).

Important studies on writing by women include Elaine V. Beilin, *Redeeming Eve* (Princeton, 1987), *Women and the English Renaissance,* by Linda Woodbridge (Urbana, Ill., 1984), and *Silent But for the Word,* ed. Margaret P. Hannay (Kent, Ohio, 1985), which discusses women as patrons, translators, and religious writers.

The Tudor period has been studied more than most other periods of English literature, and there are countless studies that are important to students and scholars alike. Some of these are Judith Anderson, *Biographical Truth* (New Haven, 1984); Joel B. Altman, *The Tudor Play of Mind* (Berkeley, 1978); Paul Alpers, *What is Pastoral?* (Chicago, 1996); M.C. Bradbrook, *The Rise of the Common Player* (London, 1964); Curtis C. Breight, *Surveillance, Militarism and Drama in the Elizabethan Era* (London, 1996); Julia Briggs, *This Stage-Play World* (Oxford, 1983); Sandra Clark, *The Elizabethan Pamphleteers* (Madison, N.J., 1983); Madeleine Doran, *Endeavors of Art* (Madison, Wis., 1954); Heather Dubrow, *Echoes of Desire* (Ithaca, N.Y., 1995); Richard Dutton, *Mastering the Revels* (London, 1991); Stephen Greenblatt, *Renaissance Self-Fashioning* (Chicago, 1980); Richard Helgerson, *Forms of Nationhood* (Chicago, 1992); Christopher Highley, *Shakespeare, Spenser, and the Crisis in Ireland* (Cambridge, England, 1997); Daniel Javitch, *Poetry and Courtliness in Renaissance England* (Princeton, 1978); David Kastan and Peter Stallybrass, eds., *Staging the Renaissance* (London, 1991); Ritchie D. Kendall, *The Drama of Dissent* (Chapel Hill, N.C., 1986); Alvin

Kernan, *The Cankered Muse* (New Haven, 1959); John N. King, *English Reformation Literature* (Princeton, 1982); Richard A. Lanham, *The Motives of Eloquence* (New Haven, 1976); Lawrence Manley, *Convention, 1500–1700* (Cambridge, Mass., 1980); H.A. Mason, *Humanism and Poetry in the Early Tudor Period* (London, 1959); Steven W. May, *The Elizabethan Courtier Poets* (Columbia, Mo., 1991); Louis A. Montrose, *The Purpose of Playing* (Chicago, 1997); Janel M. Mueller, *The Native Tongue and the Word* (Chicago, 1984); Steven Mullaney, *The Place of the Stage* (Chicago, 1988); David Norbrook, *Poetry and Politics in the English Renaissance* (London, 1984); Annabel Patterson, *Censorship and Interpretation* (Madison, Wis., 1984); Debora Kuller Shuger, *The Renaissance Bible* (Berkeley, Calif., 1994); Bruce R. Smith, *Ancient Scripts and Modern Experience on the English Stage (1500–1700)*, and *Sexual Desire in Shakespeare's England* (Chicago, 1991); John Stevens, *Music and Poetry in the Early Tudor Court* (London, 1961); Edward W. Tayler, *Nature and Art in Renaissance Literature* (New York, 1964); E.M.W. Tillyard, *The English Epic and Its Background* (London, 1954); Greg Walker, *Plays of Persuasion* (Cambridge, England, 1991); Tessa Watt, *Cheap Print and Popular Piety, 1550–1640* (Cambridge, England, 1991); and Susanne Woods, *Natural Emphasis* (San Marino, Calif., 1984).

The Spenser Encyclopedia, eds. A.C. Hamilton, Donald Cheney et al. (Toronto, 1990), is a compilation of essays that stretch far beyond Spenser, who has also enjoyed a recent chronology by Willy Maley (Basingstoke, 1994). G.K. Hall (New York) has published reference guides to Thomas Dekker by Doris Ray Adler (1983); Sir Thomas Elyot and Roger Ascham by Jerome S. Dees (1981); Robert Greene by James S. Dean (1984); Christopher Marlowe by Lois Mai Chan (1978); John Skelton by Robert S. Kinsman (1979); Sir Philip Sidney by Donald V. Stump, Jerome S. Dees, and C. Stuart Hunter (1994); and Sir Thomas Wyatt and Henry Howard, earl of Surrey, by Clyde W. Jentoft (1980). There are also concordeances to

the works of Marlowe by Robert J. Fehrenbach, Lea Ann Boone, and Mario DiCesare (Ithaca, N.Y., 1982), Sidney by Herbert S. Donow (Ithaca, N.Y., 1975), and Skelton by Alastair Fox and Gregory Waite (Ithaca, N.Y., 1987).

There are several useful biographies of individual authors including Marlowe by John M. Bakeless (Cambridge, England, 1942); Thomas More by Richard Marius (New York, 1984) and Peter Akroyd (London, 1998); Sidney by Katherine Duncan-Jones (London, 1991); Shakespeare, most recently by Jonathan Bate (New York, 1998) and Park Honan (Oxford, 1998); Surrey by William Sessions (Oxford, 1999); and Tyndale by David Daniell (New Haven, 1994).

Finally, Shakespeare is always a special case and merits separate attention. Helpful overall introductions include *A Companion to Shakespeare,* ed. David Scott Kastan (Oxford, 1999), and the *Bedford Companion to Shakespeare* by Russ McDonald (Boston, 1996). Other background books to consult are Bernard Beckerman, *Shakespeare at the Globe, 1599–1609* (New York, 1962), Herbert Berry, *Shakespeare's Theaters* (New York, 1987), Roslyn Lander Knutson, *The Repertory of Shakespeare's Company, 1594–1613* (Fayetteville, Ark., 1991), and W.B. Worthen, *Shakespeare and the Authority of Performance* (Cambridge, England, 1997). The proposition that Shakespeare may have revised or rewritten his plays is raised in *The Division of the Kingdoms: Shakespeare's Two Versions of King Lear,* eds. Gary Taylor and Michael Warren (Oxford, 1983). The reception of Shakespeare (and the utilization of his plays) from his time until the present day is reviewed by Taylor in *Reinventing Shakespeare* (New York, 1989).

Three journals on Shakespeare publish the latest appraisals—*Shakespeare Quarterly, Shakespeare Survey,* and *Shakespeare Studies;* other journals in the field are *ELH, English Literary Renaissance, Journal of Early Modern Literature, Medieval and Renaissance Drama in England, Sidney Journal, The Sixteenth Century Journal, Spenser Studies,* and *Studies in English Literature, 1500–1900.*

Arthur F. Kinney and William B. Long

Primary and Secondary Materials for Tudor Music

There is never any substitute for looking at the music. A large number of the editions cited in the entries on Tudor music and musicians are part of the national monuments series *Musica Britannica,* published since 1951 by the Royal Musical Association. The series *Early English Church Music,* published since 1963 by the British Academy, includes editions organized both by composer (William Mundy, Robert Ramsey, Thomas Tomkins, vols. 2, 5 and 8, and 7, respectively, among others) and by genre (Masses, Magnificats, fifteenth-century liturgical music, vols. 1, 4, and 9, respectively). Its "Supplementary Volumes" comprise various research tools for scholars, such as May Hofman's and John Morehen's *Latin Music in British Sources c.1485–c.1610* (no. 2). David Wulstan's *Voces musicales* series includes the complete works of John Sheppard, as well as individual works by Tye, Tallis, Byrd, White, and Weelkes; the complete works of Fayrfax were edited by Edwin Warren for the series *Corpus mensurabilis musicae.* Edmund H. Fellowes's series *The English Madrigal School,* for all original volumes of which he was the sole editor, is indispensable. Completed in 1924, it was revised by Thurston Dart and retitled *The English Madrigalists.* Fellowes's other editorial feat, *The English school of lutenist song writers,* was published in two series of sixteen volumes each. In 1959, Dart began revising and adding to the series, which is now titled *The English Lute Songs.* Alison Hall has published an index to both the madrigal and lute ayre editions in the *MLA Index and Bibliography Series* (no. 23). Available in inexpensive editions from Dover Publications are editions of the Fitzwilliams Virginal Book and the Elizabeth Rogers Virginal Book. *The Byrd Edition,*

whose general editor is Philip Brett, provides a model of scholarly procedure for future generations of music editors.

Sarum chant, England's unique chant dialect, was first studied by W.H. Frere at the beginning of the twentieth century. Since 1990, Philip Baxton and Nick Sandon have updated this knowledge and provided modern editions of this repertory. The research of Francis James Child and Bernard Bronson constitutes the bedrock of ballad scholarship, just as that of Richard Leighton Greene is necessary to carol scholarship.

Modern musicology emphasizes scrupulous documentation and the consultation of writings from the period. Thomas Morley's treatise *A Plain and Easy Introduction to Practical Music* has long been available in an inexpensive paperback edition. Only just completed is Andrew Ashbee's nine-volume *Records of English Court Music.* Covering the period from 1485 to 1714, it compiles the musical materials from English court archives in an accessible format; it will be an essential tool for generations of future specialists in English Renaissance and baroque music. Accompanying it will be *A Biographical Dictionary of English Court Musicians, 1485–1714,* the joint work of Andrew Ashbee, David Lasocki, and Peter Holman.

Scholars are always grateful for annotated bibliographies. Garland Publishing has printed two by Richard Turbet, *William Byrd: A Guide to Research* and *Tudor Music: A Research and Information Guide,* that are bibliographically much more complete on Tudor musical topics than any of the entries in the present volume can pretend to be. They are indispensable to any Tudor music scholar. The latter volume, published in 1994, concludes with an appendix updating the guide to Byrd.

Scholarship marches on after bibliographies are printed; scholars and music lovers alike can check RILM, *Répertoire International de Littérature Musicale* [International Repertory of Music Literature], now available online, for the most recent dissertations, articles, and monographs. One often finds the newest scholarship in journals and yearbooks; the May 1997 issue of Oxford University Press's *Early Music,* for example, is entirely devoted to "Music in and around Tudor London." Garland's series *Outstanding Dissertations in Music from British Universities,* edited by John Caldwell, makes English doctoral dissertations on a variety of topics, not just Tudor music, more readily available to scholars.

Festschriften should never be overlooked, since the scholarly essays contributed by the designee's friends and colleagues often represent the latest in specialized research. Not to be missed for its six essays on Tudor topics is *Sundry Sorts of Music Books* (1993), for O.W. Neighbour, former music librarian of the British Library.

Among the outstanding monographs available on Tudor music are Joseph Kerman's on the English madrigal, Diana Poulton's on John Dowland, Christopher Wilson's on Campion, David Josephson's on John Taverner, Joseph Kerman's and Oliver Neighbour's on John Byrd, John Stevens's on Tudor court poetry and music, Peter Le Huray's and Peter Phillips's on English sacred music, and Peter Holman's on the violin in England. Examples of the recent resurgence of research on instruments and their makers are the two-volume *British Harpsichord Music* edited by John Harley, and David Lasocki's and Roger Prior's study of the Bassano family of wind players and instrument makers. Robert Cavanaugh and Denis Stevens both have contributed to our knowledge of Thomas Tomkins and his music. One of this generation's most protean scholars is David Fallows, whose studies on fifteenth-century music from England and the Continent have recently appeared in the Variorum Collected Studies Series under the title *Songs and Musicians in the Fifteenth Century.* David Wulstan's *Tudor Music* is organized less as a monograph than as thirteen chapter-essays on such topics as vocal performance, Latin music under Mary and Elizabeth I, street and minstrel music, music of the court and household, and keyboard music.

Happily, music can be approached from a variety of different angles, and musicology has recently been energized by an infusion of new ideas from other disciplines. In the future, scholars studying patronage, local traditions and repertories, performance practice, sources and source criticism, reception, and archival records, among others, will continue add to our knowledge of music in Tudor England.

Laura S. Youens

Primary Sources for Tudor Politics and Government

The essential foundation sources for political history are the state papers. Little survives for the reign of Henry VII, but see J. Gairdner (ed.), *Memorials of the Reign of Henry VII* (Rolls Series, London, 1858). For Henry VIII, J.S. Brewer, J. Gairdner, and R.H. Brodie, *Letters and Papers, Foreign and Domestic of the Reign of Henry VIII, 1509–1547* (twenty-one vols., London, 1862–1910; addenda, one vol. in three parts, London, 1929–1932) is indispensable. Thereafter, *Calendar of State Papers, Domestic, Edward VI, Mary, Elizabeth I* (twelve vols., London, 1856–1872): the early volumes lack detail, and a more scholarly edition is in progress, edited by C.S. Knighton, of which several volumes have appeared. *Calendar of State Papers Foreign: Edward VI, Mary, Elizabeth I* (London, 1861–, in progress); *Calendar of State Papers, Spanish* (thirteen vols., and two supplements, London, 1862–1954); *Calendar of State Papers, Venetian* (nine vols., London, 1864–1898); *Calendar of State Papers Relating to Ireland of the Reign of Elizabeth I* (eleven vols., 1860–1912); *Calendar of the Carew Manuscripts at Lambeth, 1515–1624* (six vols., London, 1867–1873) facilitate the study of foreign affairs and of England's relations with the rest of the British Isles. At a time when there was no central governmental responsibility for the preservation of the nation's records, the correspondence of many ministers passed into family archives. Among the most important are *Calendar of the MSS of Lord De L'Isle and Dudley Preserved at Penshurst Place* (three vols., 1925–1936); *Calendar of the MSS of the Marquess of Salisbury at Hatfield House* (twenty-four vols., London, 1883–1976); *Calendar of the of the MSS of the Marquess of Bath at Longleat* (five vols., London, 1904–1980); T. Birch, *Memoirs of the Reign of Queen Elizabeth; From the Original Papers of Anthony Bacon* (two vols., London, 1754). The preoccupations of an aristocratic family are brought to life in M. St. Clare Byrne (ed.), *The Lisle Letters* (six vols., Chicago, 1981). Chronicles often provide lively perspectives on politics from outside immediate government circles. Among the more useful are A.H. Thomas and I.D. Thornley (eds.); *The Great Chronicle of London* (London, 1938); E. Hall, *The Union of the Two Noble and Illustre Famelies of York and Lancaster* (standard edition by H. Ellis, London, 1809); W.D. Hamilton (ed.), *A Chronicle of England During the Reigns of the Tudors* (two vols., London, 1875–1877); and D. MacCulloch (ed.), *Vita Mariae Angliae Reginae* (Camden Miscellany, London, 1984). W.K. Jordan, *The Chronicle and Political Papers of Edward VI* (London, 1966), provides a unique insight into the politics of the young King's reign. Also useful can be the correspondence of figures on the fringe of the court who provide invaluable political gossip: among the most entertaining are N.E. McCLure (ed.), *The Letters of John Chamberlain* (two vols., Philadelphia, 1939). Useful guides to the members of the political elite can be found in the volumes published by the History of Parliament Trust: S.T. Bindoff, *The House of Commons, 1509–1558* (three vols., London, 1982), and P.W. Hasler (ed.), *The House of Commons, 1558–1603* (three vols., London, 1981). For an introduction to the terms in which contemporaries conceptualized politics, see Thomas Starkey, *A Dialogue Between Pole and Lupset*, ed. T.F. Mayer (London, 1989), and Sir Thomas Smith, *De Republica Anglorum*, ed. M. Dewar (Cambridge, England, 1982).

The best starting point for the student of the institutional workings of government is G.R. Elton, *The Tudor Constitution* (second edition, Cambridge, England, 1982). J.R. Dasent (ed.), *Acts of the Privy Council of England* (thirty-two vols., London, 1890–1907), and P.L.

Hughes and J.F. Larkin (eds.), *Tudor Royal Proclamations* (three vols., London, 1964–1969), together demonstrate the executive priorities of the regime. T.E. Hartley (ed.), *Proceedings in the Parliaments of Elizabeth I* (three vols., Leicester, 1981–1995) is an invaluable collection of materials for the content of Parliamentary debates, while A. Luders et al. (eds.), *The Statutes of the Realm* (London, 1810–1828), provides the record of legislation. The best introduction to the reform of the common law is J.H. Baker (ed.) *The Reports of Sir John Spelman* (two vols., London, 1976–1977).

The implementation of government policy can be pursued through a plethora of local record society publications. A selection indicating the main spheres of government activity is offered here. R.W. Hoyle (ed.), *Early Tudor Craven, 1510–1547: Subsidies and Assessments* (Leeds, 1985), is a useful introduction to the workings of the fiscal machinery of the state, while J. Goring and J. Wake (eds.), *Northamptonshire Lieutenancy Papers and other Documents, 1580–1974* (Gateshead, England, 1975), demonstrates the ways in which military resources were mobilized. Social welfare in a pioneering corporation is explored in J.F.

Pound (ed.), *The Norwich Census of the Poor, 1570* (Norwich, England, 1971). Urban communities are particularly well documented. Among many publications, see A. Raine and D. Sutton (eds.), *York Civic Records* (nine vols., Leeds, 1939–1976), and W.H. Stevenson et al. (eds.), *Records of the Borough of Nottingham* (nine vols., London, 1882–1956). For government at a county level, A.H. Smith et al. (eds.), *The Papers of Nathaniel Bacon of Stiffkey* (three vols., Norwich, England, 1979–1990), are very useful. For administration at quarter sessions, see S.A.H. Burne (ed.), *Staffordshire Quarter Sessions Rolls* (five vols., Kendal, 1931–1940), and for the operation of the assizes, J.S. Cockburn (ed.), *Calendar of Assize Records* (six vols. for home circuit counties under Elizabeth I, with introductory volume, London, 1975–1985). At the very base of the apparatus of local government, there are numerous editions of churchwardens' accounts: see, for examples, A. Hanham (ed.), *Churchwardens' Accounts of Ashburton, 1479–1580* (Torquay, 1970), and C.J. Litzenberger (ed.), *Tewkesbury Churchwardens' Accounts, 1563–1624* (Stroud, 1994).

Ian Archer

Secondary Sources for Tudor Politics and Government

The basic narratives are now J. Guy, *Tudor England* (Oxford, 1988), and P. Williams, *The Later Tudors: England 1547–1603* (Oxford, 1995). The best biographies of the respective monarchs are S.B. Chrimes, *Henry VII* (1972), J.J. Scarisbrick, *Henry VIII* (1968), J. Loach, *Edward VI* (forthcoming), and D. Loades, *Mary Tudor: A Life* (1989). In spite of numerous attempts, Elizabeth has been poorly served by biographers, and the political history of the reign is probably best served by Wallace MacCaffrey's trilogy, *The Shaping of the Elizabethan Regime: Elizabethan Politics, 1558–1572* (London, 1969), *Queen Elizabeth and the Making of Policy, 1572–1588* (Princeton, 1981), and *Elizabeth I: War and Politics, 1588–1603* (Princeton, 1992). More thematic introductions to government and politics are available in S.J. Gunn and P. Lindley (eds.), *Cardinal Wolsey: Church, State, and Art* (Cambridge, England, 1991); D. MacCulloch (ed.), *The Reign of Henry VIII* (London, 1995); J. Loach and R. Tittler (eds.), *The Mid-Tudor Polity, c. 1540–1560* (London, 1980); C. Haigh (ed.), *The Reign of Elizabeth I* (London, 1984); and J. Guy (ed.), *The Reign of Elizabeth I: Court and Culture in the Last Decade* (Cambridge, England, 1995). For noble power, see contrasting views offered by M. James, *Society, Politics and Culture: Studies in Early Modern England* (Cambridge, England, 1986), and G.W. Bernard (ed.), *The Tudor Nobility* (Manchester, England, 1992). The debate over the nature of court politics has become particularly intense in recent years. The best starting point is D. Starkey (ed.), *The English Court from the Wars of the Roses to the Civil War* (London, 1987), although the factional interpretations of that collection have not gone uncontested. For other perspectives, see S.J. Gunn, "The Structures of Politics in the Reign of Henry VIII," *Transactions of the Royal Historical Society*, sixth series, vol. 5 (1995). There have been several recent attempts to reinsert ideology into the political narratives: see P. Collinson on the Elizabethan "exclusion crisis" in his *Elizabethan Essays* (London, 1994); S. Alford, *The Early Elizabethan Polity: William Cecil and the British Succession Crisis, 1558–1569* (Cambridge, England, 1998); and B. Worden, *The Sound of Virtue: Sidney's Arcadia and Elizabethan Politics* (1996). Foreign policy remains poorly served, but see the contrasting works of R.B. Wernham, *Before the Armada: The Emergence of the English Nation, 1485–1588* (London, 1966), and *After the Armada: Elizabethan England and the Struggle for Western Europe, 1588–1595* (Oxford, 1984). The Armada quatercentenary produced some good work, among which C. Martin and G. Parker, *The Spanish Armada* (London, 1988), is the most accessible introduction.

The historiography of Tudor government must begin with the prodigious output of Sir Geoffrey Elton. Perhaps the best way into his work is through the collections of his essays: *Studies in Tudor and Stuart Politics and Government* (four vols., Cambridge, England, 1974–92). For a reassessment of his work, see the essays "The Eltonian Legacy," in *Transactions of the Royal Historical Society*, sixth series, vol. 7 (1997). For less Westminster-oriented views of the workings of Tudor government, P. Williams, *The Tudor Regime* (Oxford, 1979) is indispensable, while S.J. Gunn, *Early Tudor Government, 1485–1558* (London, 1995), provides a state-of-the-art reinterpretation. The best of the local studies are M. James, *Family, Lineage, and Civil Society: A Study of Politics, Society, and Mentalities in the Durham Region* (Oxford, 1974); A.H. Smith, *County and Court:*

Government and Politics in Norfolk, 1558–1603 (Oxford, 1974); D. MacCulloch, *Suffolk and the Tudors: Politics and Religion in an English County 1500–1600* (Oxford, 1986); D.M. Palliser, *Tudor York* (Oxford, 1979); and W. MacCaffrey, *Exeter, 1540–1640: The Growth of an English County Town* (Cambridge, Mass., 1958). For Ireland, Wales, and Tudor interests, introductions are provided by S.J. Ellis, *Tudor Ireland: Crown, Community and the Conflict of Cultures, 1470–1603* (London, 1985); G. Williams, *Renewal and Reformation: Wales c. 1415–1642* (Oxford, 1987); and B. Bradshaw and J.S. Morrill (eds.), *The British Problem, c. 1534–1707: State Formation in the Atlantic Archipelago* (London, 1996).

Ian Archer

Primary Materials for Tudor Religious History

The primary materials for Tudor religious history can be divided into two types: documents of various Parliaments, convocations, and other church or state authorities, on the one hand, and the writings of prominent theologians and church leaders on the other. For the first, the best collections currently available are G.L. Bray, *Documents of the English Reformation* (Minneapolis, 1994), and *The Anglican Canons 1529–1947* (Rochester, N.Y., 1998), both of which contain major sources in full. The latter also has a full critical apparatus for all the canons of the Church of England that were issued in the Tudor period. Edward Cardwell edited a number of documents in the nineteenth century, which may be found in his *Documentary Annals of the English Church* (Oxford, 1838) and *Synodalia* (Oxford, 1842). He also edited the *Reformation of the Eclesiastical Laws* (Oxford, 1850), though this is about to be replaced by G.L. Bray, *The "Reformatio Legum Ecclesiasticarum"* (Rochester, forthcoming), which will also contain the first critical edition of the Henrician canons of 1535. Also still of interest are the many works of John Strype, originally written in the first part of the eighteenth century but subsequently republished at Oxford in the years 1821–1840. Aside from biographies of John Aylmer, Thomas Cranmer, Edmund Grindal, Matthew Parker, and John Whitgift, all of which contain numerous source documents, there are the important *Annals of the Reformation* (4 vols.) and *Ecclesiastical Memorials* (three vols.). Also indispensable as a general source for official church documents is David Wilkins's *Concilia Magnae Britanniae et Hiberniae* (London, 1737), in four volumes, of which the last two cover the Tudor period. Finally, those interested in church discipline and administration must consult *Visitation Articles and Injunctions of the Period of the Reformation,* edited in three volumes by W.H. Frere and W.P. Kennedy (Oxford, 1910).

The so-called King's Book has been republished in the twentieth century (London, 1932), as has the important 1534 translation of William Lyndwood's *Provinciale* (London, 1929), which contains the English canon law as it was known and applied in Tudor times. The first and second Prayer Books of Edward VI were reprinted by the Parker Society (see below) in 1844 and have appeared in various editions since, of which the most important is in the Everyman Series (London, 1910, and many reprints). The 1559 Prayer Book has also been edited and published by John Booty (Charlottesville, Va., 1976). There is no modern edition of the *Homilies,* though the one produced at Oxford in 1833 was reprinted in 1986. There is likewise no edition of the Bishops' Book of 1537, nor of the many primers which were circulating after 1535. Modern editions of Tudor Bibles are also rare, although the Geneva Bible of 1560 is occasionally reprinted in facsimile editions, the most recent being one from Cambridge University Press (1998), and David Daniell has produced excellent editions both of William Tyndale's New Testament (New Haven, 1989) and the portions of the Old Testament that he translated (New Haven, 1992).

For the writings of major theologians of the period, the best single source is the series of works published by the Parker Society at Cambridge from 1833 onward. These concentrate on mainstream Anglican reformers, and contain the complete extant works of John Bale, Thomas Becon, John Bradford, Miles Coverdale, Thomas Cranmer, Edmund Grindal, John Hooper, Roger Hutchinson, John Jewel, Hugh Latimer, Matthew Parker, John Philpot, William Tyndale, and John Whitgift. The series also contains the two liturgies produced in the reign of Edward VI and a large collection of original letters. John Foxe's *Acts and Monuments* has recently been reedited by a team working under David Loades (Oxford, 1997), and this seems set to replace the hitherto standard edition of S.R. Cattley's, which was produced in eight volumes (London, 1836–1841).

For other writers of the period, Stephen Gardiner's letters have been edited (New York, 1933), as have those of John Greenwood (London, 1962, 1970) and Henry Barrow (London, 1970). The Marprelate Tracts are also available in a modern edition edited by W. Pierce (London, 1911). Richard Hooker's writings have been carefully edited, with an excellent critical apparatus in seven volumes (Cambridge, Mass., 1977–1982, and Tempe, Ariz., 1993–1998), as have those of Thomas More in ten volumes (New Haven, 1963–1986). John Knox's works are available in a six-volume nineteenth-century edition (Edinburgh, 1846–1864). Unfortunately, however, most of the writings of the Catholic reformers who were active under Mary Tudor and later are not available in modern editions, and must be consulted in the original sixteenth-century versions, all of which are listed in the *Revised Short-Title Catalog* and are available on microfilm.

Gerald Bray

Secondary Materials for Tudor Religious History

The range of secondary literature for religion in Tudor England is enormous and constantly growing. The basic introduction remains A.G. Dickens, *The English Reformation,* now available in a second edition (London, 1989), which takes account of scholarly controversies up to that date and defends the view that Protestantism had already penetrated many layers of English society by 1553, and that Mary Tudor merely helped it to secure a firm hold by her untimely persecutions. Along similar lines but with a broader perspective is G.R. Elton's *Reform and Reformation* (London, 1977). The opposite view is most famously expressed by Eamon Duffy in *The Stripping of the Altars* (New Haven, 1992). Duffy argues that Protestantism did not make real headway among the people until after 1580, and that before that time it was resisted at the grassroots level by a wide spectrum of both clergy and laity. A more moderate version of the same thesis can be found in Christopher Haigh, *English Reformations* (Oxford, 1993). Duffy's views have been countered by Diarmaid MacCulloch in his Birkbeck Lectures (1998). MacCulloch is also the author of a standard biography of Thomas Cranmer (New Haven, 1996), in which he portrays the archbishop as a genuine Protestant concerned to implant Evangelical beliefs on English soil. It is a rehabilitation that will undoubtedly shape future work in the field, and which has made earlier studies of the man and his times virtually redundant, although P.N. Brooks, *Cranmer in Context* (Cambridge, 1989), is still a useful guide to his liturgical theology. Other important biographies are those of William Tyndale by David Daniell (New Haven, 1994) and Thomas More by Peter Ackroyd (London, 1998), which may replace the earlier biography by Richard Marius (New York, 1984).

Of enduring value are R. G.Usher's classic works, *The Reconstruction of the English Church* (New York, 1910), which is still the best account of the work of Archbishop Whitgift, and his *The Rise and Fall of High Commission,* which was reedited with a new introduction by David Tracy (Oxford, 1968). Also still important is C.C. Butterworth, *The English Primers (1529–1545)* (Philadelphia, 1953), which is one of the best accounts of popular devotion in the mid-sixteenth century. Susan Brigden's *London and the Reformation* (Oxford, 1989) has become the classic account of how Protestantism penetrated the capital, and will be the basis of all future work on the subject. For the rise of Puritanism, Patrick Collinson's *The Elizabethan Puritan Movement* (London, 1967) remains the foundational modern study, which may be supplemented by his subsequent writings, notably *The Religion of Protestants* (Oxford, 1982) and Peter Lake's *Anglicans and Puritans?* (London, 1988). Also still of some value is P. McGrath, *Papists and Puritans under Elizabeth I* (London, 1967), not least because it brings out by a comparative study of the main dissidents how Elizabeth established and maintained her *via media.* For a good short introduction that covers the whole subject and gives a good outline of the different scholarly opinions that are currently being advanced, see William Lamont, *Puritanism and Historical Controversy* (London, 1996).

On the reign of Mary Tudor, David Loades's *The Oxford Martyrs* (London, 1970) remains a classic, which has recently been supplemented by E.A. Macek, *The Loyal Opposition. Tudor Traditionalist Polemics, 1535–1558* (New York, 1996), which gives a good survey of the "Catholic" side during the same period. For the influence of Lutheranism, N.S. Tjaernagel, *Henry VIII* and the Lutherans (St. Louis, 1965), remains the central source, and Carl Trueman's *Luther's Legacy: Salvation and the English Reformers, 1525–1556* (Oxford, 1994) completes the picture by looking at Lutheran ideas in the leading divines of the period.

More specialized treatments are those of William Haugaard, *Elizabeth and the English Reformation,* and Ralph Houlbrooke, *Church Courts and the People during the English Reformation, 1520–1570.* The former concentrates on the Elizabethan Settlement of 1559 and reproduces a number of documents from the time, and the latter is the standard work on its subject. For the later period, M. Ingram, *Church Courts, Sex and Marriage in England, 1570–1640* (Cambridge, England, 1987), is an important survey, though one that is more narrowly focused than Houlbrooke's. The subject of marriage and the church is also dealt with by E.J. Carlson, *Marriage and the Reformation* (Oxford, 1994), who gives full attention to the theological and disciplinary aspects of the matter. Also of great value is Stanford Lehmberg, *The Reformation Parliament, 1529–1536* (Cambridge, 1970), which deals with the legal aspects of the Henrician reformation in considerable detail, and A.G. Dickens, *Lollards and Protestants in the Diocese of York* (London, 2nd edition, 1982), which remains the model of regional studies on the subject. Finally, mention may still be made of H.C. Porter, *Reform and Reaction in Tudor Cambridge* (Cambridge, England, 1958), which deals with the nerve center of the academic Reformation, though it needs considerable updating now, and N. Sykes, *Old Priest and New Presbyter* (Cambridge, Endland, 1956), which covers an important theological controversy that divided the sixteenth-century church.

Gerald Bray

Primary Materials for Tudor Social History

The starting point for many students of Tudor social history is the account provided by the Essex minister William Harrison in his *Description of England,* the most accessible edition of which was edited by G. Edelen (Washington, D.C., 1968). The classic R.H. Tawney and E. Power (eds.), *Tudor Economic Documents* (three vols., London, 1924), contains much of value for the social historian. Much of the innovative work of the last quarter-century has utilized the splendid series of judicial records contained in the public record office and the county record offices of England. The assize records have been comprehensively calendared for the home circuit by J.S. Cockburn, *Calendars of the Assize Records for Essex, Herts., Kent, Surrey, and Sussex, Elizabeth I* (London, 1975–1980). A sample of church court material is available in E.R.C. Brinkworth, *Shakespeare and the Bawdy Court of Stratford* (London and Chichester, 1972), and J. Raine (ed.), *Depositions and Other Ecclesiastical Proceedings from the Courts of Durham, Extending from 1311 to the Reign of Elizabeth* (Surtees Society, 1845). Some of the materials for the study of witchcraft were assembled by C. L'Estrange Ewen, *Witchcraft and Demonianism: A Concise Account Derived from Sworn Depositions and Confessions Obtained in the Courts of England and Wales* (London, 1933). Urban communities have often generated dense archives, some of which are in print. For a selection, see M.D. Harris, *The Coventry Leet Book or Mayor's Register* (four vols., Coventry, 1907–1913); M.E. Bateson (ed.), *Records of the Borough of Leicester, 1509–1603* (Cambridge, England, 1905); W.H. Stevenson (ed.), *Records of the Borough of Nottingham* (six vols., Nottingham, 1882–1914); and T. Kemp (ed.), *The Black Book

of John Fisher, 1580–88* (n.d.), the latter of which is particularly interesting on petty crime. The urban poor are enumerated in fascinating detail in J.F. Pounds (ed.), *The Norwich Census of the Poor 1570* (Norwich, 1971), and contemporary anxieties about them may be realized through the texts assembled by A.V. Judges, *The Elizabethan Underworld* (London, 1930). Churchwardens' accounts have been used to shed light on many aspects of communal life; for a listing see R. Hutton, *The Rise and Fall of Merry England: The Ritual Year 1400–1700* (Oxford, 1994), and for an example (in addition to those listed there), see C.J. Litzenberger, *Tewkesbury Churchwardens' Accounts, 1563–1624* (Stroud, 1994). The domestic life of the elite is best illustrated through diaries and correspondence. For examples, see D.M. Meads (ed.), *The Diary of Lady Margaret Hoby* (London, 1930), and *Historical Manuscripts Commission Middleton* (London, 1911). For those lower down the social scale, one is dependent on court materials, but other information may be gleaned from wills and inventories, collections of which have been published in profusion. See, for example, *Essex Wills,* edited by F.G. Emmison and others (twelve vols., in progress, Chelmsford, 1982–), and L.M. Munby (ed.), *Life and Death in King's Langley: Wills and Inventories 1498–1659* (King's Langley, 1981). An introduction to ballads is H.L. Collman (ed.), *Ballads and Broadsides Chiefly of the Elizabethan Period* (Oxford, 1912), and a fascinating insight into how they might illuminate literary texts can be found in Frances Dolan's edition of *The Taming of the Shrew* (London and New York, 1996).

Ian Archer

Secondary Materials for Tudor Social History

Although its starting date lies toward the end of the period, the best survey on social history is contained in Keith Wrightson's *English Society 1580–1680* (London, 1982), but useful orientations might also be found in D.M. Palliser, *The Age of Elizabeth: England Under the Later Tudors* (London, 1983), and J. Youings, *Sixteenth-Century England* (London, 1984). There is a wealth of literature on the fortunes of different social groups, but for a cross section, see L. Stone, *The Crisis of the Aristocracy 1558–1641* (Oxford, 1965); F. Heal and C. Holmes, *The Gentry in England and Wales, 1500–1700* (London, 1994); M. Spufford, *Contrasting Communities: English Villagers in the Sixteenth and Seventeenth Centuries* (Cambridge, England, 1974); D. Woodward, *Men at Work: Labourers and Building Craftsmen in the Towns of Northern England 1450–1750* (Cambridge, England, 1994); or A.L. Beier, *Masterless Men: The Vagrancy Problem in England 1560–1640* (London, 1985). For urban life, there are numerous local studies, but a useful point of entry is P. Clark (ed.), *The Cambridge Urban History of Britain, vol. II, 1540–1800* (Cambridge, England, 1999). For the treatment of the social problems generated by economic change, see P. Slack, *Poverty and Policy in Tudor and Stuart England* (London, 1988). Social regulation has generated considerable interest, and a useful introduction to the literature may be found in Jim Sharpe, *Crime in Early Modern England, 1550–1750* (London, 1984), but also important because it breaks the barrier separating late medievalists from early modernists is M. McIntosh, *Controlling Misbehavior in England, 1370–1600* (Cambridge, 1998). For disorder, A. Fletcher, *Tudor Rebellions* (London, 1968), provides a useful introduction, but see also the essays gathered in P.

Slack (ed.), *Rebellion, Popular Protest and the Social Order in Early Modern England* (Cambridge, England, 1984). Keith Thomas's *Religion and The Decline of Magic: Studies in Popular Belief in Sixteenth and Seventeenth Century England* (London, 1971) remains seminal, but many of his conclusions on witchcraft have been revised by subsequent scholarship, of which Jim Sharpe, *Instruments of Darkness: Witchcraft in England 1550–1750* (London, 1996) provides a useful synthesis. For many years historians directed their energies to revising Lawrence Stone's *Family, Sex and Marriage in England 1500–1800* (London, 1977), and the fruits of their labors are summarized accessibly in R. Houlbrooke, *The English Family, 1450–1700* (London, 1984). More recently, scholars have turned their attention to gender relations. A. Fletcher, *Gender, Sex and Subordination in England 1500–1800* (London, 1995), and A. Laurence, *Women in England, 1500–1760: A Social History* (London, 1994), represent contrasting approaches. If gender was a principle of order in Tudor England, so too was age, on which P. Griffiths, *Youth and Authority: Formative Experiences in England 1560–1640* (Oxford, 1996), and I. Ben-Amos, *Adolescence and Youth in Early Modern England* (London, 1994), offer very different accounts. For the rituals of the life cycle, see D. Cressy, *Birth, Marriage, and Death: Ritual, Religion, and the Life-Cycle in Tudor and Stuart England* (Oxford, 1997). Among the dynamics of cultural change, literacy commands attention. D. Cressy, *Literacy and the Social Order* (Cambridge, England, 1980), adopts a rigorously statistical approach to the subject, while J. Simon, *Education and Society in Tudor England* (Cambridge, England, 1966), provides a useful introduction to education. The cultural importance of popular print is splendidly recounted in T. Watt's *Cheap Print and Popular Piety, 1550–1640* (Cambridge, England, 1991). For popular culture, see also R. Hutton, *The Rise and Fall of Merry England: The Ritual Year in England 1400–1700* (Oxford, 1994), and the essays in P. Griffiths, A. Fox, and S. Hindle (eds.), *The Experience of Authority in Early Modern England* (London, 1996).

Ian Archer

Secondary Materials for Tudor Economic History

Until the publication of Peter Ramsey's *Tudor Economic Problems* (London, 1963), there had not been a useful textbook relating to economic development in the Tudor period since World War II; although somewhat dated, it can still provide a firm foundation for students. It was followed by a series of useful volumes, most of which cover a longer period referred to either as "the early modern period" or "the pre-industrial period." L.A. Clarkson achieved a substantial breakthrough with his book *The Pre-Industrial Economy in England* (London, 1971), which looked at the early modern economy through the eyes of a development economist; this was followed by valuable surveys by D.C. Coleman and B.A. Holderness, whose books were, respectively, *The Economy of England, 1450–1750* (Oxford, 1977) and *Pre-Industrial England: Economy and Society from 1500–1750* (London, 1976). The most recent offering covering the longer period is the fine two-volume work by C.G.A. Clay, *Economic Expansion and Social Change in England, 1500–1700* (London, 1984). Both of the volumes in the Longman series covering the sixteenth century have substantial sections dealing with the development of the economy: they are W.G. Hoskins, *The Age of Plunder: The England of Henry VIII, 1500–1547* (London, 1976), and D.M. Palliser, *The Age of Elizabeth: England under the Later Tudors* (London, 1983 and 1992). The volume by Hoskins is rather opinionated in places and needs handling carefully. The magnificent three-volume *Tudor Economic Documents* (London, 1924), edited by R.H. Tawney and E. Power, published more than seventy years ago, remains far and away the best collection of documents relating to the society and economy of Tudor England.

Donald Woodward

Index

Agrippa, Henricus Cornelius, 36, 526, 579, 628
Ainsworth, Harrison, 311
Ainsworth, Henry, 72
Air (Ayre), **9–10**
Alabaster, William, **10,** 511, 661
Alae seu scalae mathematicae (Digges), 194
Alaham (Greville), 309
Alamanni, Luigi, 389
Alamanni, Tomasso, 623
An Alarum Against Usurers (Lodge), 438
Albions England (Warner), 743
Alchemist, The (Jonson), 92
Alchemy, **10–11,** 454
Alciati, Andrea, 142, 190, 228
Alcock, John, 742
Alehouses, **381–382**
Alençon, Marguerite d', 78
Alençon and Anjou, Duke of, **12**
Alexander, William, 223
Alexander III, Pope, 467
Alexander of Aphrodisias, 193
Alexander VI, Pope, 727
Alexius, Alexander, **12–13**
Aliens, **13**
    See also Immigration
Allde, Edward, 278, 504
Allde, John, 278, 504
Alleluia, I heard a voice (Weelkes), 747
Allemande, 175–176
Allen, Don Cameron, 159–160
Allen, Thomas, 47, 179, 723
Allen, William, **14–15,** 37, 58, 107, 116, 120, 161, 162, 231,
        394, 395, 533, 672, 678, 710, 721
Alleyn, Constance, 15
Alleyn, Edward, 1, 2, **15–16,** 207, 341, 342, 365, 690, 691,
        692, 694
Alleyn, Giles, 98
Alleyn, Joan, 15
Alleyn, John, 15, 690
Allot, Robert, 730, 743
All Ovids Elegies, 465
All Saints, 102
Allyn, Robert, 223
Alman, 176
Almanacs, 559
Alock, John, 721
Alphonsus, King of Aragon (Greene), 306
Althamer, Andreas, 71
Amadas, Francis, 197
Amadis de Gaula (Sidney), 608, 663
Ambien Hill, 83
Amicable Grant, 267, 338, 686
Amiguet, Jeronimo, 734
Aminta (Tasso), 274
Amoretti and Epithalamion (Spenser), 448, 668
Amyot, Jacques, 275, 514
Anabaptists, **16–17,** 49, 254
    Articles of Religion and, 42–43
Analytics (Aristotle), 439
An Apologie of the Schoole of Abuse (Gosson), 294
Anatomie of Absurditie, The (Nashe), 509
Anatomy of Abuses (Stubbes), 397, 509, 677
Anatomy of Melancholy, The (Burton), 655

André, Bernard, 40
Andrewes, Lancelot, 15–16, **17–18,** 39, 81, 281, 418, 636
Ane Admonitioun Direct to the Trew Lordis (Buchanan), 97
Ane Detecioun of the duings of Marie Quene of Scottes (Buchanan),
        343
Anerio, Felice, 453, 499
Ane Satyre of the Thrie Estaitis (Lindsay), 70
Anglica Historia (Vergil), 319, 349, 429, 727
Anglicana Ecclesia, 593
Anglicanism, **20–22,** 462
    Antichrist and, 24, 60
    and *The Book of Advertisements,* 4–5, 527, 575
    hymns and, 374–375
    John Jewel and, 396
    music in, **18–20,** 23, 481, 501–502, 747–748
    ordination rites of, 518
    recusancy and, 590–591
    Regnans in Excelsis in, 595
    Richard Field and, 257
    See also Church of England
Anglo-French War (1512–1513), 760
Anglorum Feriae, Englandes Hollydayes (Peele), 540
Anglo-Spanish war (1585), 154
Anjou matrimonial scheme (1578–1581), 581
Ankwyll, John, 303
Annales of England (Stow), 261, 350, 531
Anna of Austria, 546
Annates, **22**
Anne of Cleves (1515–1557), 22, **22,** 50, 166, 227, 337–338,
        364, 489, 639
Anne of Denmark, 490
Annulment, 22, 78, 96, 167–168, 364
Answer to the Supplication, An (Hooker), 359
Anthem, **22–23**
Anthologies, verse, 728–730
Anthony, Francis, 11
Antibossicon (Lily), 431
Antichrist, **24,** 60
Anti-enclosure riots (Attleborough), 407
Antiquarianism, **24–25,** 67–68, 359, 429–430
    Henry Fitzalan and, 259
    John Stow and, 675–676
    Richard Carew and, 110
    See also Libraries
Antwerp money market, 308, 610
Aphthonius, 581, 600
Apologie for Poetrie, An (Sidney), 375, 421, 435, 447
Apology for Actors, An (Kyd), 414
Apology for Raymond Sebond (Montaigne), 579
Apology for the Church of England, An (Jewel), 159, 396
Apology (Melanchthon), 444
Apology to Certain Imputations Concerning the Earl of Essex
        (Bacon), 55
Apostles' Creed, 42, 113
Appellants, 395
Apprenticeship, **25–27,** 118
Apuleius, Lucius, 3
Aquinas, Thomas, 440, 554
Arbeau, Thoinot, 175
Arbella, 323
Arber, Edward, 241
Arcadia, **27**
Arcadian Rhetorike, The (Fraunce), 274

Burbage, Cuthbert, 98, 694
Burbage, James (c. 1531–1597), **98,** 206, 689, 690, 692, 693,
    694, 695
Burbage, Richard (c. 1568–1619), 2, **98–99,** 207, 690, 692, 694
Burden, 111
Burdet, Nicholas, 356
Burdet, Thomas, 355
Burghley House (Cambridgeshire), 32
Burleigh, Lord. *See* Cecil, William (Lord Burghley)
Burlesque almanacs, 559
Burley, Walter, 440
Burnet, Gilbert, 311
Burroughes, Jeremiah, 136
Burton, Henry, 223, 282
Burton, Robert, 262, 506, 655
Busnois, Antoine, 505
Bussy D'Ambois, 125
Butler, Charles, 505, 601
Butts, Newington, 206
Buver, Martin (1491–1551), **96**
Byrd, William (1543–1623), 19, 20, 23, **99–100,** 111, 158, 175,
    332, 408, 499, 502, 506, 622, 659, 660, 682, 730
Byrne, Muriel St. Clare, 459

C

cabala of the pegasean horse and the heroic frenzy, The (Bruno), 94
Cabeo, Niccolo, 291
Cabot, John (c. 1450–1498), **101,** 154, 195, 215
Cabot, Sebastian (c. 1482–1557), **101–102,** 195–196, 196
Cade, Jack, Rebellion, 744
Cadiz expedition (1587), 202
Caelica (Greville), 309, 310
Caelius, Lodovicus, 190
Caesar, Julius, 342
Caesar, Sir Julius, 15
Caesarius, Johannes, 193
Caius, John, 30, 217–218, 260, 328, 478, 479, 503, 722
Caius College Book, 505
Cajetan, Enrico, 32, 33, 231
Cajetan (Cardinal), 33
Calais Conference (1521), 338, 488
Calcar, Hans Stephan van, 233
Calendar
    church, 102–103, 263–264, 356–357
    Julian, 103
    secular, 1, 103, 263–264, 282
Calepino, Ambrosio, 189
Calisto and Melebea (Rastell), 586, 587
Callenbach, Ernest, 724
Callice, John, 548, 549
Callimachus, 374
Calvin, John (1509–1564), 72, 73, 96, 103, 135, 221, 275, 368,
    594, 604
Calvinism, 2, 43, 97, **103–105,** 368, 520, 630
    Articles of Religion and, 42–43
    hymns and, 374
    John Jewel and, 161, 396
    Lambeth articles and, 418
    Marian Exiles and, 462
    Marprelate controversy and, 466–467
    Peter Baro and, 66
    Ramism and, 586
    Richard Bancroft and, 62–63

Calvinism (*continued*)
    theory behind, 135–136
    Thomas Becon and, 69–70
    William Whitaker and, 751
Cambrai, Treaty of, 711
Cambridge University, 700, 721
    Library of, 81, 723
    See also Universities
Camden, William (1551–1623), 24–25, 47, 81, **105–106,**
    110, 209, 351, 402, 417, 607, 676, 697, 707
Camerarius, Joachim, 190, 490
Camilli, M. Camillo, 664
Campanella, Tommaso, 724
Campaspe (Lyly), 446
Campeggio, Lorenzo (Cardinal), 405
Campion, Edmund (1540–1581), **107–108,** 394, 471, 504,
    532, 649, 671–672, 710, 761
Campion, Thomas (1567–1620), 9, **108,** 160, 176, 222, 435,
    448, 506, 659, 729, 730, 731
Candida Casa, 133
Canon law, 86, **424–425**
    Reformatio Legum Ecclesiasticarum in, 591–592
Canons of 1604, 42
Canterbury, Convocation of, 158
Canterbury Cathedral, 22, 24, 682
Canterbury Tales, The (Chaucer), 332
Canticles or Ballards of Solomon in English Meters, The
    (Langston), 59
Cantiones sacrae (Byrd), 99, 502, 682
Cantus Circaeus (Bruno), 93
Canzonets, or Little Short Songs to Three Voyces (Morley), 498, 499
Canzoniere, 543
Capital punishment, **109–110**
Capito, Wolfgang, 71
Caput apri defero, 111
Carbone, 393
Cardano's Comforte (Bedingfield), 186
Cardinal College (Oxford), 30, 505, 684, 721
Carew, George, 517
Carew, Peter, 340, 358, 359, 388, 763
Carew, Richard (1555–1620), 105, **110,** 150, 209, 351, 422, 664
Carew, Thomas, 223
Carey, Catherine, 365, 412
Carey, Elizabeth, 510
Carey, Henry, 164, 365, 690, 743
Carey, Katherine, 411
Carey, Robert, 164
Carey, William, 411
Carisbrooke Castle, 486
Carleil, Anne, 739
Carlos, Don, 546
Carlos I (King), 545
"Carmen de moribus" (Lily), 431
Carneades, 653
Carolina, 171
Caroline Book of Orders, 557
Carols, **110–111,** 160–161
Caroso, Fabritio, 175
Carpe diem poem, 535
Carthusian London Charterhouse, 492
Carthusians, 491
Cartier, Jacques, 262
Cartigny, Jean de, 275

Edward (Lord Grey of Powis), 85
Edward (Lord Herbert of Cherbury), 178
Edwards, Thomas, 235
Edward V, 226, 319
Edward VI (1537–1553), 611
   accession of, 210–211
   archery and, 27
   birth of, 223, 337
   chantries and, 125
   correspondence from Bullinger and, 97
   Cranmer as regent for, 168, 219–220
   death of, 462, 651
   Edmund Grindal and, 312
   education and, 166, 303, 722
   finance and, 538
   foreign relations and diplomacy under, 120
   guilds and, 313
   health care and, 478
   heresy and, 345
   King's Book and, 409
   knighthood and, 411
   laws under, 172
   libraries and, 81
   military and, 487
   Nicholas Heath and, 334
   Nicholas Ridley and, 604
   Parliament and, 528
   printing and, 302
   Privy Chamber and, 570
   Reformation and, 594
   reign of, 12, 65, 69, 115, 127, 272, 338, 473, 638, 639
   religion and, 20–21, 42, 78, 85, 130, 132, 291, 422, 444, 520, 521, 604
   Royal Injunctions and, 380
   sodomy as crime under, 357
   succession of, 530, 638
   Thomas Seymour and, 639
Edward VI Grammar Schools, 29
Effect of certain Sermons concerning the Full Redemption of Mankind by the Death and Blood of Christ Jesus (Bilson), 75
Egerton, Thomas (1540–1617), 124, 198, **220–221,** 673
Eirenarcha: Or of the Office of the Justices of Peace (Lambarde), 417–418
Elder, John, 177, 460
Elegy, **221–223**
Elegy (Chaloner), 311
Elias, Norbert, 164
Eliot, George, 107–108
Eliot, John, 235, 262, 276
Eliot, T. S., 125, 199
Elizabethan College of Antiquaries, 351
Elizabethan Grub Street, 559
Elizabethan patronage, 52
Elizabethan poor law, 556
Elizabethan Settlement (1559), 4–5, 21, 75, 145–146, 240, 292, 345, 360, 396, 516, 576, 594–595, 672, 720, 728, 732
Elizabethan Society of Antiquaries, 259
Elizabeth I (1533–1603)
   accession day and, 1
   Acts of Supremacy and, 680
   Acts of Uniformity and, 720
   architecture under, 30, 31
   Babington Plot and, 51, 52–53, 697

Elizabeth I (*continued*)
   birth of, 337
   Book of Advertisements and, 4–5
   capital punishment and, 109
   censorship and, 122–123
   characterization of Winchelsea, 139
   Counter Reformation and, 161–162
   court and patronage under, 54–55, 152, 163–164, 187–188, 211–212, **223–226,** 246, 346, 367–368, 406, 411–412, 486, 536, 582–585, 738–740, 761
   creation of Court of High Commission and, 164–165
   death of, 334
   Edmund Guest and, 313
   education and, 292, 304, 721, 722
   espionage and, 240
   excommunication of, 161–162, 356, 595–596, 605, 699, 710
   exploration and colonialization under, 154–155, 289, 307, 570
   financial affairs and, 308, 486, 538
   first parliament of, 503
   foreign relations and diplomacy under, 37–38, 97, 119–121, 187–188, 266, 268–269, 330–331, 531–532, 606–607, 617–619, 738
   gardening and, 284
   horsebreeding and, 8
   humanism and, 606
   immigration under, 377
   Inns of Court and, 381
   interest in Paul's Cross, 537
   justices of the peace and, 403–404
   knighthood and, 411
   Lambeth articles and, 418
   laws under, 172
   masques and, 473
   military and, 487, 488
   music and, 407
   Northern Rebellion and, 541
   Parliament and, 528, 575
   portraits during reign of, 490
   printing and, 302
   Privy Chamber under, 570
   Privy Council under, 180
   property ownership and, 504
   proposals of marriage to, 12
   recusancy and, 590–591
   Reformation and, 594–595
   reforms under, 165
   regulated companies and, 596–597
   reign of, 699
   religion and, 14, 16–17, 21, 42, 65, 70, 73, 78, 80, 132, 244, 272, 312, 359, 374, 445, 492, 540, 548, 575–577, 621, 622, 713–714, 748–749, 752
   Ridolfi Plot and, 367, 368, 430, 595, 604–605, 710, 739
   Royal progresses and, 572
   shipbuilding and, 644
   sodomy as crime under, 357
   St. Paul's Cathedral and, 669
   succession and, 611
   theater and, 463
   Throckmorton Plot and, 695–696
   treason and, 710
   witchcraft and, 756

Hatton, Christopher (1540–1591), 62, 90, 187, 192, 224, 282, **330–332**, 451, 541, 750
  Holdenby garden of, 283
  interment of, in 1591, 669
Hatton, Elizabeth, 152
Haughton, William, 181, 183, 690
Have with You to Saffron Walden (Nashe), 46, 65, 330, 510
Hawes, Stephen (d. 1523?), 275, **332**, 699
Hawkins, John (1532–1594), 38, 120, 201, 202, 333, **333**, 420
Hawkins, Richard (c. 1562–1622), 215, 317, **333–334**
Hawkins, William, 569
Hay any Work for Cooper? (Marpriest), 466, 467
Haydocke, Richard, 525
Hayes, Edward, 289, 708
Hayward, John (c. 1564–1627), 122, **334**, 350
Hayward, Ralph, 310
Hazlett, W. Carew, 563
Health. *See* Medicine and health
Healths Improvement (Moffet), 490
Hearne, Thomas, 429
Heath, Nicholas (c. 1501–1578), **334–335**
Heaven upon Earth (Hall), 320
Hegendorf, 599
Heinsius, Daniel, 143
Hekatompathia (Watson), 453
Heliodorus, 143, 608
Helvetic Confession (Wishart), 755
Hemings, John, 2, 690
Hemmingsen, Niels, 600
Henderson, Andrew, 301
Heneage, Thomas, 504
Hengrave Hall, 633
Heninger, S. K., 242
Henri III of France (duc d'Anjou), 12, 93, 739
  assassination of, 369, 739
  reconversion to Catholicism, 513
Henrician injunctions, 380
Henrician Reformation, 145, 339, 396, 553
Henrician Visitation Commission, 343
Henri IV of France (Henri of Navarre), 739
  reconversion to Catholicism, 513
Henry, Earl, 269, 671
Henry II, death of, 268
Henry IV, 33, 202, 541
  and heresy, 345
Henry (Prince of Wales), 490, 611
  marriage treaty with Katherine or Aragon and, 40
Henry Tudor, 564, 745
Henry V, and heresy, 345
Henry VI, 226, 335
Henry VII (1457–1509), 226, **335–337**, 472, 564, 611
  accession of, 84, 156
  architecture and, 28
  bastard feudalism and, 67
  Catholicism and, 114
  common law and, 427
  court and patronage under, 536, 553, 570, 673–674
  death of, 40
  espionage and, 239–240
  foreign policy and diplomacy under, 40, 229–230, 266–267, 295, 296, 564
  funeral of, 259
  Lambert Simnel and, 650–651

Henry VII (*continued*)
  merchant-taylor and, 482
  naming of first son by, 40
  Parliament and, 528
  Perkin Warbeck and, 740–741
  religion and, 436, 552, 716
  succession and, 405
  warfare and, 83–84
  War of the Roses and, 83–84
Henry VIII (1491–1547), 30, **337–341**
  Accession Day of, 1
  accession of, 237, 652
  Act of Submission of the Clergy and, 679
  Acts of Supremacy and, 680
  Anglicanism and, 20
  archery and, 27
  architecture and, 28, 139
  art and, 353
  Articles of Religion and, 42–43
  astrology and, 46
  Book of Common Prayer (1559) and, 78
  capital punishment and, 109
  chantries and, 125
  civil law and, 425
  common law and, 426
  as composer, 340–341, 407, 505–506, 659
  Convocation and, 158–159
  court and patronage under, 43, 50, 283, 411, 432, 536, 537, 570, 669–670
  as Defender of the Faith, 182, 243
  dissolution of monasteries by, 68
  education under, 217, 303, 722
  English Reformation and, 592–594
  espionage and, 240
  Field of the Cloth of Gold and, 256–257
  finance and, 494, 538
  foreign policy and diplomacy under, 120, 498, 628–629
  funeral of, 285
  gardening and, 283–284
  government of, 295, 296, 297, 444
  health care and, 478
  heresy and, 345
  horsemanship and, 8, 361
  King's Book and, 409
  laws under, 171–172
  libraries under, 81
  liturgy under, 436
  love of jewelry by, 397
  mapmaking and, 459
  marriages of, 22, 67, 77–78, 96, 114, 116, 166, 168, 292, 346, 364, 405, 424, 498, 528, 530–531, 541, 593, 611, 716, 742
  military and, 486, 487, 488
  Oath of Succession and, 259
  painting under, 523
  Parliament and, 528
  Pilgrimage of Grace and, 44, 547
  political thought and, 674
  portrait of, 489
  praemunire and, 564
  privateering and, 569
  Reformation Parliament and, 172–173
  reforms under, 165

James VI and I (*continued*)
  Ruthven Raid and, 676–677
  shipbuilding and, 629
  Sir Walter Ralegh and, 584
  succession of, 63
  writings of, 251
Jane (Viscountess Rochford), 364
Jasper Tudor, 744, 745
Jay, Thomas, 107
Jeffes, Humphrey, 690
Jegon, John, 456
Jenkinson, Anthony, 196, 460, 707
Jeremiah (Broughton), 92
Jest books, **393–394,** 559, 683
  pornography in, 562–563
Jesuits, 161, 394, **394–396,** 532–533, 662
  Archpriest controversy and, 32–34
  Edmund Campion and, 107–108
  English College of Rome and, 14, **231,** 294, 395, 504, 533,
    738
  English College of Rome and, 231
  See also Catholicism
Jesus College, 721, 722
Jewel, John (1522–1571), 21, 159, 244, 271, 313, 356, 359,
  396–397, 673
Jewel House of Art and Nature (Plat), 284
Jewell, Simon, 690
Jewelry, **397–398**
Jew of Malta, The (Marlowe), 451–452, 464
Jews, **398–399**
Job (Broughton), 92
Jocasta (Gascoigne), 285, 286
Johan Johan (Heywood), 347
John III (Duke), 22
John of Gaunt, 335
John of Salisbury, 556
Johnson, Daniel, 61
Johnson, Francis, 17, 307
Johnson, Robert, 29, 242
Johnson, Thomas, 288
Johnson, William, 689
John XXII, Pope, 622
Joint Stock Companies, **399–401,** 596–597
  East India Company as, 180, 213, **213,** 333, 400, 704, 705, 761
Jones, Inigo, 344, 473
Jones, Richard, 690, 729
Jones, Robert (fl. 1597–1615), 9, **401,** 454, 506
Jonns, Daniel, 689
Jonson, Ben (1572–1637), 92, 103, 125, 128, 143, 144, 177, 178,
  181, 183, 191, 203, 204, 207, 208, 221, 236, 251, 262,
  324, 342, 344, **401–403,** 446, 449, 452, 464, 469–470,
  473, 623, 624, 640, 690, 691, 692, 699, 720, 733
Jonson Folio, 406
Jovius, Paulus, 176–177
Jubilee of 1575, 475
Juby, Edward, 2
Judicial Committee of the Privy Council, 184
Julian, 374
Julian calendar, 103
Julio, Henry, 200
Julius II, Pope, 58, 261
Julius III, Pope, 132, 552
Julius Excluded, 237

Junius, Hadrianus, 367
Justice of the Peace, **403–404**
*Justificacion of Queene Elizabeth in Relacion to the Affaire of Mary
  Queene of Scottes, A* (Puttenham), 577–578
Justification, doctrine of, 74
Juvenal, 534

K

Katherine of Aragon (1485–1536), 67, 77, 96, 114, 116, 126,
  131, 167, 223, 225, 260, 266, 267, 335, 337, 346, **405,**
  473, 498, 528, 541, 593, 611, 679, 716, 734, 742
  annulment of marriage to Henry VIII, 22, 96, 166–167
  battle of Flodden Field, 261–262
  divorce of, 227, 338
  Fisher's defense of, 259
  food and diet and, 265
  marriage of, 22, 39–40
  music and, 407
Kebel, Alice, 76
Kellyk, Hugh, 243
Kemp, William (d. 1603–1609?), 2, 38, 116, **406,** 509, 689, 691
Kempe's Nine Daies Wonder (Kemp), 406
Kempis, Thomas á, 69
Kemyss, Lawrence, 722
Kendall, Timothy, 260, 623
Kenilworth, 284, **406–407**
Kennedy, Walter, 629
Kenninghall, 31
Kepler, Johannes, 47, 48–49, 291, 327
Kermode, Frank, 125
Kerne, John, 755
Ketel, Cornelius, 332
Kett, Robert, 211, 407
Kett's Rebellion, 6, 211, **407**
Keyboard music, 61–62, 175, **407–409**
Killigrew, William, 52
Kind Hart's Dream (Chettle), 128
King, Henry, 510
King, Thomas, 689
Kingham, Philip, 401
King James Bible, 71–72, 74, 92, 527, 716
King John (Bale), 60
King Lear (Shakespeare), 356
King's Bench, Court of, **409–410,** 425, 426, 428
King's Book, The (1537), 42, 168, 173, **409**
King's Chamber, 296
King's College (Cambridge), 303, 505
King's Hall, 722
King's Men, *See* Acting companies
Kingsmill, Andrew, 469
Kingston-on-Thames, 719
Kinsale, battle at (1602), 518
Kinwelmershe, Francis, 140, 286
Kirbye, George, 454
Kirby Hall (Northamptonshire), 31
Kirke, Edward, 666
Kirkham, Henry, 758
Knighthood, **410–411**
  heraldry and, 343–344
Knight of the Garter, 397
Kniver, Anthony, 707
Knollys, Francis (c. 1514–1596), 164, 411, **411–412,** 412
Knollys, Lettice (Countess of Leicester) (c. 1540–1634), 189, **412**

Knox, John (c. 1513–1572), 16, 42, 50, 69, 75, 103, 133, 239, 396, **412–413,** 430, 437, 462, 554, 555, 575, 753, 756
Knoxians, 166
Knyvet, Henry, 123
Kokeritz, Helge, 206
Kratzer, Nicholas, 46, 48, 271, 459
Kyd, Anna, 414
Kyd, Francis, 414
Kyd, Thomas (1558–1594), 144, 204, 207, 275, **414–415,** 452, 465, 509, 665, 690
Kyme, Master, 45

L

Laborious Journey (Leland), 60, 707
La Celestina (Rastell), 587
Ladies Hall, 303
Ladye Nevells Booke, My (Byrd), 100
Lady Margaret Foundation, 581
Lady of May, The (Sidney), 572
Lady Oriana, The (Wilbye), 753
Laertius, Diogenes, 579
Laetus, Pomponius, 430
Lamb, William, 260–261
Lambarde, William (1536–1601), 24, 25, 81, 209, 351, **417–418,** 460, 529, 676, 707
Lambe, Walter, 243
Lambert, François, 71
Lambeth Articles (1595), 66, 103, **418,** 520, 621, 751, 752
Lambeth Choirbook, 255, 505
Lambeth Conference (1584), 709
Lamb of God, The (Harvey), 330
Lamentable tragedy mixedful of pleasant mirth, conteyning the life of Cambises king of Percia, A (Preston), 565
Lamentations of Amyntas, The (Faunce), 274
Lancaster, James, 399
Land and landscape, **419–420**
    Arcadian, 27
Land carriage, 707
Landino, Cristoforo, 142
Lando, Ortensio, 526
Landois, Pierre, 746
Lane, John, 222
Lane, Ralph (c. 1530–1603), 326, **420–421**
Laneham, John, 206, 689
Laneham, Robert, 406, 473
Lane's Men, 689
Langley, Francis, 689, 690, 694
Langton, Christopher, 59
Language, history of, **421–422**
Languet, Hubert, 275, 607, 649
Lanman, Henry, 693
Lanquet, Thomas, 159, 350
Lant, Richard, 652
Lanyer, Aemilia, 647, 648
Large, Robert, 118
Lassus, Orlande de, 502
Latimer, Hugh (c. 1485–1555), 69, 74, 85, 88, 173, 273, 327, 345, 393, **422–424,** 462–463, 604, 636, 713
lattre examination, The (1547, Askew), 45
Laud, William, 39, 345, 674
Lawiers Logike, The (Fraunce), 274, 440
Laws
    Canon, 424, **424–425**

Laws (*continued*)
    civil, **425**
    common, **425–427**
    criminal, 109–110, 171–172
    sumptuary, 397, 679–680
Lawyers, **427–429**
Layer Marney (Essex), 31
Lead industry, 378, 485, 688
Leather manufacture, 687
Le Chevalier délibéré (de la Marche), 68
Ledrede, Richard de, 111
Lee, Edward, 238
Lee, Henry, 1, 540
Lee, Richard, 459
Lee, Rowland, 737
Lee, Sidney, 260
Lee, Thomas, 525
Lefevre, Raoul, 567
Legatine Constitutions of Cardinals Otho (1237) and Othobon (1268), 592
Le Guin, Ursula, 724
Le Havre, 488
Leicester, Earl of. See Dudley, Robert (Earl of Leicester) (1532/33–1588)
Leicester's Commonwealth (Parsons), 212, 533
Leicester's Men, 598, 689
Leigh, Joan, 123
Leland, John (c. 1503–1551), 24, 25, 60, 77, 221, 328, 351, **429–430,** 431, 460, 707, 728
Le Morte D'Arthur (Malory), 40, 118, 608
Lenten Stuffe (Nashe), 510
Lentino, Giacomo da, 543
Leo XIII, Pope, 108, 475
Leo X, Pope (1513–1521), 182, 243, 593, 760
LeRoy, Guillaume, 140
Le Roy, Pierre, 276
Leslie, John (1527–1596), 69, 77, **430**
Lessons for Consort of 1609 (Rosseter), 157
Letter to Raleigh, 608
Levant Company, 213, 596, 704
    See also Joint stock companies; Regulated companies
Lever, Thomas, 636
Lewis, Anne, 401
Lewis, C. S., 699
Lewis, Owen, 231
Lewkenor, Lewis, 276
Lex Mercatoria (Malynes), 566
Leyden, Lucas van, 348
Lhuyd, Humphrey, 460
Libellus de re herbaria novus (Turner), 713
Libellus sophistarum ad usum Oxoniensem and ad usum Cantabrigiensen, 440
Liber ruralium commodorum (de' Crescenzi), 283
Liber sextus (Pope Boniface VIII), 424
Liberties. See Government, local; London
Libraries
    Bodleian (Oxford University), 76, 81, 82, 270
    book ownership and, 81–82
    Cambridge University, 81, 82, 723
    Gabriel Harvey's, 329
    of Henry VIII, 429
    John Dee's, 82
    Lumley, 81

New Inn Yard, 693
New Letter of Notable Contents, A (Harvey), 330
Newman, John Henry, 17
Newman, Mary, 202
Newman, Thomas, 509
Newport, Christopher, 570
News Quartos, **512–513**
Newton, Thomas, 141, 429
New Way of making Fowre Parts in Counter-point, by a most Familiar, and Infallible Rule, A (Campion), 108
New World. *See* Colonial development; Discovery and exploration; Travel literature
Nicene Creed, The, 42
Nicholas, Thomas, 665
Nicholas IV, Pope, 22
Nichols, T., 140
Niclaes, Hendrik, 254
Night's Conjuring (Dekker), 129
Nine Days Queen (Luke), 311
Nine Years' War, 517–518
Nizoli, Mario, 35
Nobilis (Moffet), 490
Noble Art of Venerie, or Hunting, The (Turberville), 713
Nodt, Jan van der, 233
Nonsuch Palace, 284, 613, 614
Noodt, Jan van der, 666
Norden, John (c. 1547–1625), 5, 209, 233, 460, **513–514**, 625
Norfolk, Duke of. *See* Howard, Thomas
Norman, Robert, 291, 460, 627
Norman Conquest, 130
Norris, Henry, 337, 606
Norris, John, 488
Norris, Richard, 525
Norris, Thomas, 666
Norris, William, 78
North, Council of, 146, 581, 681, 711
North, Thomas (c. 1535–c. 1601), 140, 488, **514**, 664
Northern passage, discovery of, 289
Northern Rebellion (1569), 188–189, 225, 331, 365, 367, 368, **515**, 541, 581, 605, 696, 710, 725
Northumberland, Duke of. *See* Dudley, John
Northumberland, Earls of. *See* Percy Family
Northumbria, 419
Northwest Passage, 101, 102, 179, 277
North-West Passage Company, 761
Norton, Thomas (1532–1584), 144, 204, 207, **515–516**, 618
Norwich, 419, 700
Nosce Teipsum (Davies), 178, 179
Notable Discovery of Coosnage, A (Greene), 305
Noue, François de la, 275
Nova Albion, 197
Nova scientia (Tartaglia), 194, 519
Noves, Laura de, 543
Novum Organum (Bacon), 55, 56
Nowell, Alexander (c. 1507–1602), **516**, 722
Nowell, Laurence, 186, 417, 460

O

Oath of Allegiance, 498
Oath of Succession, 259
Oath of Supremacy (1559), 334, 532, 672
Obedience of a Christian Man (Tyndale), 716
Obel, Matthias de L', 288

Oberon, the Fairy Prince (Jonson), 251
Observations in the Art of English Poesie (Campion), 108, 176, 435
Occult sciences. *See* Alchemy; Astrology; Magic; Witchcraft
Ockeghem, Johannes, 505
Octavia!, 451
O'Desmond, James Fitzgerald Fitzmorris, 679
O'Donnell, Hugh Roe (Lord of Connell) (1571?–1602), **517**
Oecolampadius, Joannes, 469
Of Gentylnes and Nobylyte (Rastell), 586, 587
"Of Resolution" (Cornwallis), 159
Of the cause, principle and one (Bruno), 94
Of the Church Five Bookes, by Richard Field, Doctor Divinity (Field), 257
Of the Disciplines (Vives), 36
Of the infinite universe and worlds (Bruno), 94
Of the Lawes of Ecclesiastical Polity (Hooker), 63, 359, 437, 555, 595, 752
Of the Office of Seruauntes, a Boke Made in Latine by one Glybertus Cognatus, 124
Of the Origin of Sects (Vives), 36
Of the Russe Commonwealth (Fletcher), 707
Of the Vanitie and Uncertainty of the Artes (Agrippa), 36
Of Tribute, Or Giving What is Due (Bacon), 56
Oldcastle, John, 273
Oldenbarnevelt, 39
Old Wives Tale, The (Peele), 539
Oliver, Isaac, 489–490
Olney, Henry, 159
Oman, Charles, 486
O Maria Deo (Fayrfax), 255
O Michael, 684
O'Neill, Hugh (Second Earl of Tyrone) (c. 1550–1616), 188, 256, 388, 486–487, 517, **517–518**
O'Neill, Shane, 386, 388, 645–646
On the Interpretations of Nature, 56
Opinion Diefied (Riche), 602
Orchestra (Davies), 49, 178, 191
Order and Usage of the Keeping of a Parliament in England (Hooker), 358–359
Order for Conflagration, 469
Order of Householde, The (Fenner), 364
Order of the Garter, 233, 397
Ordinal, **518**, 620
Ordnance, **518–520**
Ordóñez de Montalvo, Garcí, 663
Organon, 585
Origin of the English Drama, The (Kyd), 414
Orlando Furioso, 306, 608
Ornaments Rubric, **520**
Ornatus and Artesia (Forde), 573
Orphic Hymns, 374
Orrell, John, 205
Ortelius, Abraham, 105, 351, 607, 625
Osborne, Edward, 750
Osorius, Hieronymous, 138
O splendor gloriae, 684
Ostler, William, 178
Otho (1237–1241), 22
Othobon (1265–1268), 22
Oughtred, William, 217
Outlines of Pyrrhonism (Sextus), 579
"Outworking," 147

Ralegh, Walter (1554–1618), 40, 117, 152, 154, 163, 179–180, 187, 188, 197, 215, 222, 225, 234, 262, 289, 307, 317, 325, 326, 327, 399, 420, 453, 465, 535, 558, 579, **582–585,** 665, 666, 708, 712, 729
Ralph Roister Doister (Udall), 719, 720
Rameé, Pierre de la, 329, 585
Ramism, 192, 274, 330, **585–586,** 627
Ramsey, John, 301
Ramus, Peter, 35, 138, 274, 479, 585, 600, 601, 607
Ramusio, G. B., 318
Randolph, Thomas, 712
Rape, 637
Raphael, Marco, 399
Rastell, Joan, 586
Rastell, John (c. 1475–1536), 154, 196, 203, 277, 346, 393, 586, **586–587**
Rastell, William (1508–1565), 346, 586, **587–588**
Rastell, Winifred, 588
Rathlin Island, 189
Ravenscroft, Thomas, 62, 158
Reading, 503
Reading Abbey, 303
Reading practices, 432–434, **588–589,** 701
Rebellions
    Essex (1601), 177, 179, 203, 226, 412, 456
    Kett's, 6, 211, 407
    Lincolnshire, 44
    Northern (1569), 188–189, 225, 331, 365, 367, 368, 515, 541, 581, 605, 696, 710, 725
    Western (1497), 335
    Wyatt's, 193, 311, 452, 556, 662, 696, 715, 750, **762–763**
Receptionism, 619
Recorde, Robert (c. 1512–1558), 47, **589–590**
Recusancy, 75, **590–591**
Recuyell of the Historyes of Troys (Caxton), 422
Red Book of Ossory (de Ledrede), 111
Redford, John, 408, 506, 691
Red Lion, 693
Redmon, John, 714
Reeve, Ralph, 401
Reformatio Legum Ecclesiasticarum, 132, 424, **591–592**
Reformation
    adiaphora and, 3
    Articles of Religion and, 42–43
    Henrician, 145, 339, 396, 553
    Irish, 92, 387–388
    Scottish, 133, 412–413, 430, 755–756
    sculptural production before, 631
    See also English Reformation
Reformation iconoclasm, 631
Reformation of the Ecclesiastical Laws, 575
Reformation Parliament (1529–1536), 173, 528
Regiment of Helthe (Paynell), 364
Regiment of Life, The (Phaer), 545
Regnans in Excelsis, 116, 161, 368, 590, **595–596,** 605, 710
Regulated companies, **596–597**
Religion (Greville), 310
Religious toleration, **698–699**
Religo Medici, 242
Remains of a greater work concerning Britain (Camden), 106
Renaissance antiquarianism, 24
Renaissance humanism, 71, 137
Renart, Jean, 111

Reneger, Robert, 569
Repentance, 620
Replycacion, A (Skelton), 651
Reply of the Most Illustrious Cardinall of Perron, The (Cary), 112
Reply of the Ordinaries (Gardiner), 285, 679
Reports (Coke), 152
Rerum in Ecclesia Gestarum (Foxe), 273
Rerum Scoticarum Historia (Buchanan), 97
Responsio ad Lutherum (More), 498
Responsio and Edictum Elizabethae (Parsons), 533
Restoration, 308
Restraint of Annates, Act in, 339
Restraint of Appeals, Act in, 339
Retramnus, 243
Return from Parnassus, The (Lok), 441
Reuchlin, Johannes, 600
Revels, 473
Revels Office, **597–598,** 612, 697–698
Revenge for a Father, A (Chettle), 129
Revenge (ship), 307
Revitalized Exchequer, 296
Reyce, Robert, 655
Reynolds, Richard, 492
Rheims New Testament, 74
Rhetor (Harvey), 329
Rhetoric, 585, **598–602**
Rhetorica ad Herennium (Traversagni), 35, 599
Ribault, Jean, 678
Riccio, David, 342
Rich, Barnabe, 221, 385
Rich, Lord Richard (c. 1496–1567), 45, 601, **601**
Rich, Penelope, 541
Richafort, Jean, 341
Richard (duke of York), 335
Richard (earl of Kent), 64
Richard II (England), 334
    and heresy, 345
    reign of, 473
Richard II (Shakespeare), 411
Richard III (England), 40, 69, 226, 335, 500
    death of, 83
    Parliament and, 528
    reign of, 740
Richard III (Shakespeare), 452, 716
Richard IV, 552
Richard of Gloucester, 118
Riche, Barnabe (1542–1617), 332, 487–488, 573, **602–604**
Rich His Farewell to Military Profession (Riche), 573
Richmond Palace, 613, 615
Rich's Men, 689
Ridley, Mark, 291
Ridley, Nicholas (c. 1500–1555), 85, 243, 273, 311, 312, 327, 345, 396, 422, 462–463, **604,** 713
Ridolfi, Roberti di, 604
Ridolfi, Roberto, 368
Ridolfi Plot (1570–1571), 367, 368, 430, 595, **604–605,** 710, 739
Ritson Manuscript, 111
Ritwise, John, 431
Rivales (Gager), 281
Rivers, Anthony Earl, 118
Rivers, Earl, 118, 567, 745
Rizzio, David (c. 1533–1566), 177, 199, 472, **605–606**

Valla, Lorenzo, 35, 237, 370
Valois, Hercule-François de. *See* Alençon and Anjou, Duke of
Valor Ecclesiasticus, 22, **727**
Van Dyck, 353, 541
Vatican Library, 723
Vaughan, Anne, 441
Vaughan, Henry, 535
Vaughan, Rowland, 8
Vaughan, William, 364
Vautrollier, Thomas, 585
Vaux's Men, 689
Vavasour, Anne, 186
Vega, Garcilaso de la, 664
Vega, Lope de, 665
Vegius, Mapheus, 234
Veldener, Johannes, 118
Vendeville, Jean, 14
Venerable Bede, 71, 263, 328, 350–351
Venice Company, 596
Venus and Adonis (Shakespeare), 438, 535
Verderdort, Abraham, 525
Vere, Elizabeth, 761
Vergil, Polydore (1470–1555), 27, 142, 200, 319, 328, 349,
    429, 534, **727–728**
Vermigli, Peter Martyr (1500–1562), 166, 396, 515, 665,
    719, **728**
Vernon, Elizabeth, 761
Verona, Guarino da, 369
Verse anthems, 23
Verse anthologies, 186, **728–730**
    of Alabaster, 10
    Breton and, 86–87
    De Vere and, 186
Verse jests, 393
Versification, 675, **730–732**
Verstegan, Richard, 121, 672
Very Fruitful Exposition of the Commandments, A (Babington),
    52
Vesalius, Andreus, 233, 478
Vesey, Judith, 514
Vesta was from Latmos hill descending, As (Weelkes), 747
Vestiarian Controversy, 278, 555, 575, **732–733**, 753
Vewe of the Present State of Ireland, A (Spenser), 668
Vice, The, **733**
Victoria (Fraunce), 274
Vida, Marco Girolamo, 235, 374
Videte miraculum, 682
View of the Present State of Ireland (Spenser), 389
Virgidemiarum (Hall), 320, 562
Virginals, 408
Virginia colony, 117, 420
Virginia Company, 344, 761
Vision of Delight, The, 506
Vision of Piers Plowman, The (Crowley), 173
Vision of the Twelve Goddesses, The (Daniel), 176
Visitations, 164
Vitae Episcoporum Aberdonesium et Murthlacensium (Boece), 77
Vittels, Christopher, 254
Vives, Juan Luis (1492–1540), 35, 36, 76, 271, 551, 600, 611,
    664, 714, **734–735**
Volpone (Jonson), 452
Vowell, John. *See* Hooker, John (alias John Vowell) (c. 1527–1601)

Vulcanius, Peter (Bruges), 76
Vulgate, 14

W

Wabeck, Perkin, 40
Wager of law, 156
Wakefield, Robert, 721
Waldegrave, Robert, 466
Wales, 419
    history of, **737–738**
Wales, Council of, 309
Walpole, Henry, 395
Walpole, Richard, 395
Walsingham, Francis (c. 1530–1590), 51, 52, 58, 93, 120, 136,
    180, 206, 224, 225, 240, 294, 295, 309, 317, 332, 368,
    479, 481, 606, 649, 689, 695–696, **738–740**, 749
Walsingham, Joyce, 738
Walsingham, William, 738
Walters, John, 741
Walton, Isaac, 87, 198
Wanamaker, Sam, 205
Wanley Partbooks, 19, 23
Warbeck, Perkin (c. 1474–1499), 266, 335, 391, 455, 461, 564,
    740–741, 742, 746
Ward, John, 453
Wards and Liveries, Court of, **741**
Warfare
    archery and, 27–28
    artillery and ballistics and, 518–520
    See also Bosworth, Battle of (1485); Flodden Field, Battle of
        (1513); Military history; Spanish Armada
Warham, William (c. 1450–1532), 67, 153, 167, 237, 711,
    741–743, 760
Warner, John, 478
Warner, Walter, 326–327, 627, 723
Warner, William (c. 1558–1609), 483, **743**
War of the Theatres, 183
Wars (Greville), 310
Wars of the Roses, **83–84**, 226, 319, 349, 410, 411, 500,
    740–741, **743–747**
Warwickshire, 419
Warwick's Men, 186, 689
Watkins, Richard, 544
Watson, C., 141
Watson, Thomas, 143, 274, 390, 445, 453, 615, 660, 661
Watts, John, 570
Wayland, John, 59
Waynflete, William, 303
Wayte, William, 640
Weakest Goeth to the Wall, The (Chettle), 129
Weald, 419
Webbe, William, 141, 186, 222, 545
Webster, John, 144, 183, 223, 452, 522, 690, 692
Wechel press, 585
Weelkes, Thomas (c. 1575–1623), 20, 23, 453, 506, **747–748**
Weever, John, 235, 624
Weir, Alison, 311
Welsh Church, reform of, 540
welspring of wittie conceites, The (Fiston), 599
Wemyss, James, 301
Wentworth, Elizabeth, 749
Wentworth, Henry, 638

Wonderful News of the Death of Paul the Third, 59
Wonderful Year, The (Dekker), 183
Wood, Anthony Á, 61, 544, 714
Woodcuts, 231–234, 288, 513
Woodford, Thomas, 692
Woodland, 419
Woodliffe, Oliver, 694
Woodville-Grey, Elizabeth, 226
Woodward, Henry, 341
Woolens, 147
Worcester, 701
Worcester's Men, 186, 406, 690, 691
Worde, Wynken de, 64, 119, 231–232, 568
Wordsworth, William, 653
Works (Becon), 364
Worlde of Wordes (Florio), 262
World's Hydrographical Description (Davis), 179
Worseley, Ursula, 739
Worshipful Company of Scriveners, 457
Worsteds, 147
Wotton, Henry, 53, 198, 722–723
Wounds of Civill War, The (Lodge), 439
Wrays, Christopher (c. 1521–1592), **760–761**
Wright, Benjamin, 233
Wright, Edward, 47, 217, 291, 626
Wright, Leonard, 600
Wriothesley, Henry (Third Earl of Southampton) (1573–1624), 45, 81, 262, 456, 510, 641, 754, **761–762**
Wriothesley, Thomas (First Earl of Southampton) (1505–1550), 338, 521, 620, **762**
Writing Schoolemaster, The (Bales), 61
Wroth, Mary, 178, 648, 661
Wyatt, Thomas, 78, 143, 163, 221, 222, 224, 311, 366, 389, 429, 447, 448, 459, 526, 623, 660, 664, 696, 728, 729, 730, 731, 762
Wyatt's Rebellion, 193, 311, 452, 556, 662, 696, 715, 750, **762–763**
Wyckes, Elizabeth, 172
Wycliffe, John, 71, 444, 593

Wydeville, Elizabeth, 746
Wydeville, John, 745
Wydeville-Gray, Elizabeth, 745
Wylkynson, Robert, 242, 243

X
Xenophobia, 13
Xenophon, 364

Y
Yarmouth, 700
Yellow Ford, Battle of (1598), 488, 518
Yelverton, Christopher (c. 1535–1612), **765**
Yelverton, Henry, 765
Yelverton, Margaret, 765
Yeomen. *See* Social classes
Yeomen of the Guard, 612
Yet Another Twelve Wonders of the World (Davies), 179
Yetswiert, Charles, 700
Yetswiert, Nicasius, 606
Yetswiert, Susan, 607
Yong, Bartholomew, 664
Yonge, Nicholas, 499
York, 700, 701
    Convocation of, 158
York cycle, 122
Yorkists, 500
Yorkshire, 701
Yorkshire insurrection, 44
Young, Bartholomew, 139, 729
Young, John, 666

Z
Zodiacal Man, 46
Zodiac of Life (Palingenius), 260
Zodiake of Life, The (Googe), 293
Zurich, 593, 594
Zwinger, Theodore, 490
Zwingli, Huldyrch, 96, 97, 104, 243, 360, 619, 728